Lecture Notes in Computer Science 856

Edited by G. Goos, J. Hartmanis and J. van Leeuwen

Dimitris Karagiannis (Ed.)

Database and Expert Systems Applications

5th International Conference, DEXA '94
Athens, Greece, September 7-9, 1994
Proceedings

Springer-Verlag
Berlin Heidelberg New York
London Paris Tokyo
Hong Kong Barcelona
Budapest

Series Editors

Gerhard Goos
Universität Karlsruhe
Postfach 69 80, Vincenz-Priessnitz-Straße 1, D-76131 Karlsruhe, Germany

Juris Hartmanis
Department of Computer Science, Cornell University
4130 Upson Hall, Ithaka, NY 14853, USA

Jan van Leeuwen
Department of Computer Science, Utrecht University
Padualaan 14, 3584 CH Utrecht, The Netherlands

Volume Editor

Dimitris Karagiannis
Institut für Angewandte Informatik und Informationssysteme, Universität Wien
Brünner Straße 72, A-1210 Wien, Austria

CR Subject Classification (1991): H.2, H.4, H.5.2, I.2.1, I.2.4-5

ISBN 3-540-58435-8 Springer-Verlag Berlin Heidelberg New York

CIP data applied for

Printed in Germany

Typesetting: Camera-ready by author
SPIN: 10478970 45/3140-543210 - Printed on acid-free paper

Preface

The Database and Expert Systems Applications - DEXA - conferences are dedicated to providing an international forum for the presentation of applications in the database and expert systems field, for the exchange of ideas and experiences, and for defining requirements for the future systems in these fields.

DEXA '94 in Athens is the 5th conference in the series after Vienna (1990), Berlin (1991), Valencia (1992) and Prague (1993) and has some new features. This year there was a total of more than 300 submitted papers from over 30 different countries in all continents. Only 78 papers could be accepted.

The collection of papers in these proceedings offers a cross-section of the issues facing the area of databases and expert systems, i.e. topics of basic research interest on one hand and questions occurring when developing applications on the other.

Major credit for the success of the conference goes to all of our colleagues who submitted papers for consideration and to those who have organized and chaired the panel sessions.

Many persons contributed numerous hours to organize this conference. The names of most of them will appear on the following pages. In particular we wish to thank the Organizing Committee Chairman Roland Wagner and the Local Organization at Athens. Special thanks also go to Gabriele Kaiser (University of Vienna) and Gabriela Wagner (FAW Linz), as well as Sofia Tachmintzoglou (TEE Athens), the Tutorial Chairs and Panel Chairs and the Greek Chamber. Finally, many thanks to Robert Strobl (University of Vienna), who supported the reviewing process and managed the publication work.

Dimitris Karagiannis
Programm Committee Chairman

Vienna, July 1994

Conference Committee

Programm Committee

Chairman:

D. Karagiannis, University of Vienna, Austria

Panel Chairs:

F. Golshani, Arizona State University, USA
G. Grigoropoulos, NTU Athens
A.M. Tjoa, University of Vienna, Austria

Tutorial Chairs:

P. Constantopoulos, University of Crete, Greece
T. Sellis, NTU Athens, Greece

Programm Committee Members:

H. Afsarmanesh, University of Amsterdam, The Netherlands
H.J. Appelrath, University of Oldenbourg
K. Bauknecht, University of Zürich, Switzerland
T. Bench-Capon, University of Liverpool, Great Britain
J. Bing, NRCCL Oslo, Norway
I. Bratko, University of Ljubljana, Slovenia
S. Christodoulakis, University of Crete, Greece
B. Croft, University of Massachusetts, USA
W.S. Cellary, Technical University of Poznan
J. Debenham, University of Technology, Sydney, Australia
P. Drazan, RIKS Maastricht, The Netherlands
J. Eder, University of Klagenfurt, Austria
A.L. Furtado, University of Rio de Janeiro, Brazil
F. Galindo, University of Zaragoza, Spain
G. Gardarin, INRIA, France
G. Gottlob, Technical University of Vienna, Austria
A. Hameurlain, Toulouse, France
I. Hawryskiewycz, University of Technology, Syndney, Australia
P. Henderson, University of Southampton, GB
K. Hirota, Hosei University, Japan
J.K. Hong, IBM Tokyo, Japan
D. Hsiao, Naval Postgraduate School, USA
M. Jarke, University of Aachen, Germany
M. Kamel, Naval Postgraduate School, USA
Y. Kambayashi, IMEEL, Japan
G. Kappel, University of Linz, Austria
M.A. Ketabchi, Santa Clara University, USA

P. Kroha,	Technical University of Chemnitz/Zwickau , Germany
J. Lazansky,	Czech Technical University, Czech Republic
T.W. Ling,	University of Singapore, Singapore
F. Lochovsky,	HKUST, Hong Kong
V. Lum,	Chinese University of Hong Kong, Hong Kong
V. Marik,	Czech Technical University, Czech Republic
G. Müller,	University of Freiburg, Germany
M.-A. Neimat,	HP Laboratories, USA
E. Neuhold,	GMD-IPSI, Germany
A. Olive,	Universitat Politecnica de Catalunya, Spain
G. Ozsoyoglu,	University Case Western Research, USA
G. Pagalos,	University of Thessaloniki, Greece
M. Papazoglou,	National University, Australia
G. Quirchmayr,	University of Vienna, Austria
I. Ramos,	Technical University of Valencia, Spain
C. Rolland,	University Paris I, France
C.-R. Rollinger,	University of Osnabrück, Germany
N. Roussopoulos,	University of Maryland, USA
F. Saltor,	Facultat d'Informatica, Portugal
A. Sernadas,	University of Lisbon, Portugal
J.C. Smith,	University of British Columbia, Canada
D. Specht,	Technical University of Cottbus , Germany
P. Spirakis,	University of Patras, Greece
R. Studer,	University of Karlsruhe, Germany
M. Takizawa,	Tokyo Denki University, Japan
K. Tanaka,	Kobe University, Japan
C. Thanos,	IEI-CNR, Italy
C.H. Thoma,	Ciba-geigy, Switzerland
C. Van Dorsser,	ORIGIN, The Netherlands
J. Vassiliou,	University of Athens, Greece
K. Vidyasankar,	Memorial Univ. of Newfoundland, Canada
R.R. Wagner,	FAW, University of Linz, Austria
T. Yokoi,	EDR, Tokyo, Japan

Organizing Committee

Chairman:

R.R. Wagner — FAW, University of Linz, Austria

Local Organization(TEE Greece):

D. Pavlopoulos,	C. Sinanis
D. Georgarakis,	A. Kalofolias
D. Korobilis,	N. Mekras
V. Triantafilou	

List of Referees

Each paper was carefully reviewed mostly by the Programm Committe. However, invaluable help was provided by the referees listed below.

K. Aberer
J. Angela
H. Amano
M. Arikawa
T. Barothy
H. Behrends
W. Benn
L. Boumedjout
C. Breiteneder
R. Busse
C. Caleiro
M. Castellanos
K-U. Carstensen
C. Cauvet
W. Chen
D. Chinlu
M. Dobrovnik
K-H. Eder
T. Eiter
D. Fensel
D. Fischer
G. Fischer
H. Frank
A.W. Fu
T. Furukawa
M. Garcia-Solaco
J. Geiger
B. Geurts
G. Grosz
N. Guenet
H. Gust
M. Heidenfeld
K. Hemm
J. Herbst
K. Hinkelmann
R. Holbein
G. Huck
A. Hutchison
W. Hütker
H. Jasper
St. Junginger
A. Karduck
I. King
T. Koszlajda
Z. Kouba
Z. Krolikowski
I. Kumishima
D. Landes
P. Lasala
J. Lee
M.L. Lee
S.H. Lee
W. Liebhart
Q. Li
S. Lifschitz
D. Luchin
P. Ludewig
L. Marinos
D. Meddahi
N. Mekras
P. Meseguer
T. Morzy
T. Mühlherr
P. Muro-Medrano
N. Nakatsu
S. Neubert
K. Neuhold
M. Nomoto
N. Okboshi
J. Paredis
Z. Peng
R. Peratello
M. Peterhans
V. Plihon
N. Poos
B. Pröll
F. Puntigam
S. Rausch-Schott
P. Resende
W. Retschitzberger
H. Rodriguez
M. Ryan
J. Rykowski
C. Sauter
P. Scheidegger
D. Schoder
A. Schutzelaars
K. Schwarz
F. Semmak
C. Sernadas
S. Si-Said
V. Stalder
C. Stary
R. Strobl
M. Stumptner
T. Tesch
R. Telesko
P.K. Teo
S. Teufel
U. Thiel
T. Tschernko
M. Vazquez
J. Wäsch
W. Weitz
W. Wieczerzycki
M. Wiedijk
W. Winiwarter
K-F. Wong
K. Yokota
O. Zukunft

Table of Contents

Keynote Speech

Object-Oriented Databases

Data Management (I)

Cooperative Office Applications

Object-Oriented Modelling

Data Management (II)

Industrial Applications

Temporal Databases

Conceptual Modelling

Legal Systyems

Keynote Speech

Active Databases

Evolving Environments

Geographical Databases

Keynote Speech

Keynote Speech

Knowledge Engineering

Hypermedia Databases

Information Retrieval

Advanced Databases and Expert Systems Concepts

Advanced Querying Concepts

Medical Systems

Integration of Databases and Expert Systems

Distributed Databases

Computer Integrated Manufacturing

Keynote Speech

Research as a Catalyst for Industrial Innovation

D. Tsichritzis
GMD National Research Centre for Information Technology, Germany
&
University of Geneva, Switzerland

There are three kinds of Research: Research for the advancement of Science, Research for educating people and Research for Industrial Innovation. Only the third kind brings a direct economic advantage. To promote Industrial Innovation Research has to be concentrated, applications oriented and in cooperation with Industry. A number of examples will be given in different areas of Information Technology especially in Communications and Multimedia.

In all these projects GMD plays a role of catalyst between applications companies and technology companies. To achieve this role GMD had to be rationalized, restructured and move to a new scientific direction to follow market trends.

Peplom^d: an Object Oriented Database Programming Language Extended with Deductive Capabilities

Pascal Dechamboux
Claudia Roncancio

Bull Research Centre – Grenoble (France)
Laboratoire de Genie Informatique – IMAG
e-mail: {P.Dechamboux, C.Roncancio}@frgu.bull.fr

We present Peplom^d, an object oriented database programming language extended with deductive capabilities[(2)]. The central aspects addressed here are the clean integration of a deductive query language within a procedural language and the support of derived data. The language, offers at the same time an imperative part, for structuring and writing the bulk of applications and a declarative part, for writing expressions and queries necessaries when handling large amount of persistent data[(3)].

1 Introduction

Most of the recent developments in the database research area are related to two kinds of systems [15][8]: object–oriented (OO) database systems and deductive database systems. On the one hand, OO systems merge features from object–oriented languages and database technologies in order to improve the expressiveness and power of both data modelling and programming for database applications. On the other hand, deductive systems provide logic based declarative languages which greatly improve query expressions as well as the support for derived data.

Among the wide variety of applications needing database technology, a large part of them would certainly take advantage of facilities offered by both the object–oriented and the deductive approach. In our opinion, combining the best aspects of these approaches in a single deductive and object–oriented (DOOD) system is a promising

(2) Peplom^d stands for "PErsistent Programming Language for Object Manipulation" extended to Derived Data and Deductive capabilities.

(3) This research is partially supported by the EEC in the framework of Esprit Project 6333, IDEA ("Intelligent Database Environment for Advanced Applications"

solution as seems to show the intensive activity in this area. Building such a system is the goal of the IDEA project, the framework of our investigations.

There is currently no proposal for an OO database system which integrates completely a deductive query language while avoiding the impedance mismatch problem. Several proposals describe SQL like query languages using an object–oriented data model like EXCESS, OQL, Reloop, O2SQL or XSQL. Languages such as Col or IQL present a theoretical framework for such an integration but do not consider technical aspects of merging two computation models (a logic one and a procedural object–oriented one).

We aim at integrating a declarative deductive language with a procedural object–oriented one, resulting in the database programming language (DBPL) of the IDEA system[6]. In this way, the programmer will have the possibility to use the deductive capabilities to define data and operations within an object–oriented framework. We argue that a smooth combination of declarative and procedural constructions for writing applications can ease the task of the programmer: this one will be able to use a powerful object–oriented procedural language for dealing with complex programs and, at the same time, to use a declarative deductive language for set–oriented queries. Thus, the use of deductive capabilities is restricted to querying whereas updates are performed with imperative code only.

We propose a DBPL, called Peplom, which issues many features like persistence, OO concepts and set–oriented constructors and manipulations in a similar way as PS–Algol, Galileo or DBPL. We have taken care of concepts orthogonality as we consider it as a major improvement for language users. Futhermore, it tightly integrates the main features of deductive languages in an OO persistent programming language. Although two programming paradigms coexist, all impedance mismatch problems have been solved in a clean and clear way, giving a consistent and coherent result. Moreover, our implementation strengthens this integration.

The first objective of the paper is to show the usefulness of such an integration and then to describe how it is done in Peplom^d. The paper is composed of six sections. Sect.2 introduces the general notions of the procedural OO part of the language. Sect. 3 discusses the distinction between stored and derived data, describing how we have extended Peplom^d for supporting derived data in a natural way. Section 4 is devoted to the deductive part of the language and its use within the procedural part. Section 5 discusses some related works which aim at offering deductive capabilities along with a database programming language. Our conclusion and some short hints about the implementation status are given in section 6.

2 The Peplom Language: Rationale and Model

Peplom^d is a general database programming language allowing to express computations of unbound complexity on data,independently from any host language.

It is composed of an imperative part (corresponding to the original Peplom) having the flavour of C++ and a declarative part which is based on Datalog . Peplom^d can directly interact with C for performing functions such as I/O.

Section 2.1 introduces the concepts of the data model which are necessary in the sequel of the paper. Sections 2.2 and 2.3 introduce classes and modules which are the two Peplom^d concepts available for structuring applications. Classes are object generators with runtime semantics whereas modules are mainly compile time entities allowing to gather together global names (global variables, functions or procedures) that are related to each other. A Peplom schema is organized as shown below.

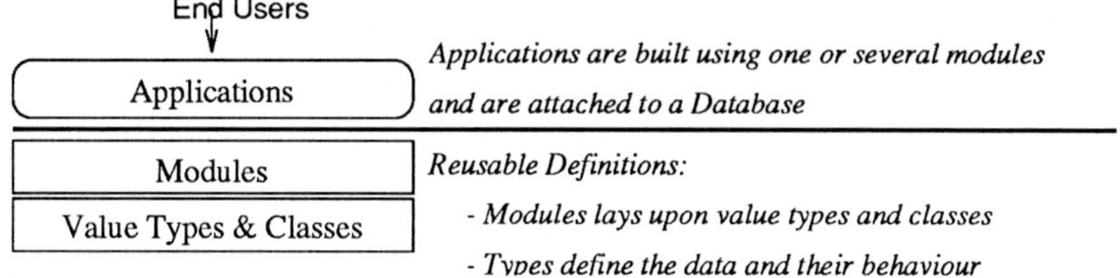

2.1 The Data Model

The data model associated with Peplom^d supports values and objects. Values are instances of types, being non–shared and non–mutable entities. Objects are instances of classes, being mutable and sharable. They have a state, comprising attribute values, and an object identifier (OID).

Values can be either atomic or structured. Atomic values are of basic types like character, integer, boolean, real or string. Structured ones are instances of structured types defined using type constructors such as tuple, union, array and collections (set, bag or list). *Objects* are always handled through their OID. They are created using the **new** and **pnew** operators which yield the OID of the created object. They can be deleted only explicitly, using the **delete** operator. An OID is a value in the data model, whose type is implicitly defined by the class of the object it refers. The operators supported for OIDs are the assignment, the equality operators for testing object identity, and the dot operator for accessing object attributes and methods.

The language is strongly typed: the compiler is able to statically detect most type errors. Type conformity, supporting ad–hoc polymorphism, defines the substitution semantics for data, i.e., one can substitute an instance of T instead of an instance of T' iff T conforms to T' ($T \leq T'$). Type conformity is compliant to the rules defined by Cardelly but is restricted to structural equivalence for values for efficiency reasons.

The imperative part of Peplom^d supports the same instruction set as C. One of the main differences is that Peplom^d expressions do not have side effects, e.g., the assignment is an instruction in Peplom^d whereas it is an expression in C. Peplom^d also allows to handle complex terms such as sets or tuples and pointers are not available.

2.2 Classes

As in usual object–oriented programming languages, a class in Peplom[d] defines object attributes and methods. These elements define the state and the behaviour of the objects of the class. Definition elements can be either public or private. Private elements can be used only within the class itself, whereas public ones can be also used in other classes or modules. A multiple inheritance relationship between classes is supported, as illustrated in the following example:

```
class Employee: Person, Taxpayer {
attributes { Company Comp;
             float   Salary;
             Service Service;
             Person  derived Friends{}; }
functions { float Tax(); }
procedures { IncreaseSalary(float rate); } };
```

ATTRIBUTES Attributes are variables local to objects. They can be stored or derived. Values of stored attributes compose stored state of an object while those of derived ones are computed each time they are used. The stored state of an object also contains the values of the inherited attributes. Futhermore, as the stored state is a whole, stored attributes are either all persistent or all transient.

Derived attributes are defined by an expression or by deductive rules. Using rules for this purpose is an important aspect as the programmer can take advantage of declarativity as developed in section 4.3.

Inherited attributes cannot be redefined. On the other hand it is possible to define an attribute having the same name as an inherited attribute. In such a case, two distinct attributes are present in the object state. A discriminating method based on class name prefixing is used to distinguish one attribute from the other. The same method can be used for solving potential name conflicts due to multiple inheritance.

Private attributes are completely encapsulated by methods whereas public ones can be readed directly. In any case, updates must be done through methods.

METHODS Methods are partitioned into functions and procedures. Functions do not have any side effect whereas procedures are the only means to modify an object state. Side effects in procedures consist either in modifications of visible stored variables, or in object updates, creations or deletions, or in calls to other procedures or to external C functions. The only modifications that can appear in a function are those performed on its local variables. Methods are usually written using the imperative language but can be also defined by using deductive rules as presented in section 4.3.

Unlike attributes, methods can be overloaded in sub–classes at two levels: the signature definition and the code implementing the method (method overriding). In this respect, the system supports a late binding mechanism at runtime. Arguments are always passed by value in Peplom[d]. Thus, the signature overloading policy for parameters is contro–variance, following Cardelli's rules. This enables type checking to be static with respect to this purpose.

2.3 Modules

Peplom^d modules aim at structuring global names and operations, for "programming in the large". Like classes with attributes and methods, modules define stored and derived variables as well as operations (functions and procedures). These elements can be private or public. Deductive rules can be used for defining derived variables and function bodies. At this level, rules play an important role because they are an excellent way for supporting views.

The module is the basic entity for constructing a Peplom^d application. Modules are organized into a graph by an import relationship (authorizing cycles). This relation gives access to the public part of the modules imported by a given one. An application has a root module defining a special operation acting as a "main" function. Thus, such an application is composed of all the modules directly or indirectly imported by the root one and of the classes they use. Here after the signature of a module:

```
module HumanResourceManagement {
variables { Company persist TheCompany; }
procedures { HireEmployee(); }     };
```

Modules provide a simple way for reusing code as they can be used in different applications that even use different databases. Indeed, modules as well as classes are dynamically loaded at runtime in a lazy way. Bindings to some persistent entities are then done at load time (e.g., `TheCompany`).

3 Stored and Derived Data

All the data managed by the language are accessible through names which can be either variables or functions. Names always denote values that can be object identifiers. Like in usual languages such as C, all data lifetime in Peplom^d depend on their associated name, except for objects that roughly behave like C heap data. Two main categories of data are distinguished: stored and derived data. Stored data have a concrete existence in memory while derived data have only a virtual one because they are materialized only when used in an expression being evaluated. The ability of using data in the same way independently of their category (persistent or transient, derived or stored) is an important issue for integration. This section describes how this transparency is achieved.

3.1 Stored Data

By default a variable corresponds to a stored value. Three different lifetimes (storage classes) are possible for stored variables: local,global transient and global persistent

Local variables are either function or procedure parameters, or variables defined within a block of code. They have the lifetime of the function or block execution (stack data).

Global variables are defined within modules. Transient ones have the lifetime of the application execution (similar to usual global C variables). Persistent ones (e.g. `TheCompany` in section 2.3) have the lifetime of the database. They are similar to E's persistent variables and can also be compared to names in O2. Such variables are organized and encapsulated by Peplom^d modules.

While stored variables define the storage class for values (including object references), objects have their own storage behaviour which is not related to any kind of name. Objects can be either transient, having the lifetime of the execution of the application which creates them, or persistent, having the lifetime of the database. Object attributes have the storage class of the object itself. An object can be made persistent explicitly at creation time, by using **pnew** or by using the **`persist`** instruction. It can also become persistent implicitly if it is referred to by a name which propagates its persistent status (this is the default case). In order to avoid persistence propagation, the **`nprop`** keyword can be specified at name definition. Thus, Peplom^d supports a persistence semantics based on reachability like PS–Algol or O2, as well as a simpler semantics like in C++ based OO systems, both semantics being interesting.

All objects are accessible through the extensions of their class. Class extensions are maintained by the system containing all objects of a class as well as those of its subclasses. Two generic meta–functions give access to the extensions: **`pext`**`(C)` and **`npext`**`(C)` yielding respectively the set of persistent and non persistent objects (OIDs) of the class `C`. Thus, an object is always reachable even if no name refers to it.

3.2 Derived Data

The support for derived data is one of the major contributions of the Peplom^d language. Derived data are defined either by a function or a derived variable. In the former case, derived data are computed either by a block of imperative instructions or by a set of deductive rules.

The content of a derived variable is defined by an expression of the language. Let us give an example, which defines the derived variable YNbFullMoonDays and uses the stored variable ThisYear denoting the current year:

```
int YNbFullMoonDays as card(FullMoonDays(ThisYear));
```

This variable allows to retrieve the number of full moon days of the current year. Its content is specified by an expression that computes the cardinality (generic function **`card`**) of the set produced by the function `FullMoonDays` (defined elsewhere) applied to `ThisYear`. It is essential to realize that expressions defining a derived variable can be as complex as necessary and involve other derived or stored data. They can also involve powerful deductive queries (see next section) and functions. Procedures cannot be used within expreesions and therefore inside rules.

It is important to distinguish the two ways for computing derived data: functions and derived variables. Indeed, derived variables are similar to views in relational DBS: the expression defining their value is expanded wherever they appear. This expression can then be globally optimized together with the construction containing it, thus leading to a wider range of opportunities for optimization. This is not the case for functions which has to be optimized in isolation without taking into account the calling context.

4 Deductive Capabilities

This section presents the deductive capabilities introduced within the imperative part of Peplom^{d}, putting emphasis on their integration. These capabilities are expressed through a logic–based declarative query language which is in the style of [3]. We do not attempt to innovate in deductive query languages but we propose a way for integrating such a language in an imperative one.

The notion of rule is the key concept of the deductive language. The definition of such a rule is preceded by its signature as illustrated hereafter:

```
Project BigProjects{} as
BigProjects(X)<- pext(Project)(X) & X.Budget > 3000;
```

In this example, the variable `X` ranges over the persistent extension of the class `Project`. The `Budget` attribute is tested for each project in order to select the set of "big" one. Notice that the signature of the rule is similar to a variable definition.

While restricting deductive capabilities to query contexts improves the expressiveness of the query language, it disallows to perform query optimization strategies also in update operations on database. Again, we think that encapsulation can be violated for read access to object attributes but not for modification purpose as encapsulation allows, in this last case, to enclose object semantics in classes.

Section 4.1 presents the declarative query language. A key issue in this language is that every set is considered as a predicate. Futhermore, aggregate operators are introduced as generic functions that naturally fit in the language, where expressions are essentially functional. Conversely, every declarative query is considered as a set–valued expression within the imperative part of the language as shown in section 4.2. Thus, querying becomes completely orthogonal in the programming language, enhancing undoubtedly the integration.

4.1 The Declarative Query Language

Two main syntax categories are used to build rules and queries: *terms* and *formulas. Terms* denote values while *formulas* express propositions about the entities of the model. In this context every stored or derived set is considered as a predicate.

TERMS They can be atomic or complex, including constants, variables and functions. Functional terms are defined by an n–ary function symbol whose arguments are also terms. For example, if `t1`, `t2`, ..., `tk` are terms then `{t1, t2, ..., tk}` is a set term and **`struct`**`{t1,t2,...,tk}` is a tuple term. There are also other functional terms that are related to usual expressions such as `FullMoonDays(1993) - {1}` and aggregates operators (like group and avg) wich are a special kind of terms. See [7] for some details about aggregates.

As rules are always defined within a context like a block of instructions, a class or a module, variables of this context can be used in rules. It is well worth noting that this greatly improves the integration of deductive rules within the rest of the language.

FORMULAS As usual in logic languages [2], *formulas* are either atomic (literals) or complex. The former are composed of a predicate symbol and a list of parameter terms. Positive atomic formulas can belong to the following categories (let us assume that `X`, `Y`, ..., `Z` are terms):

– Stored predicates corresponding to stored collections: if `C` denotes a stored collection `C(X)` is a membership formula. Moreover, if `C` is a collection of tuples, `C(X,Y,...,Z)` is a licit membership formula, `X`, `Y`,...,`Z` represent the attributes.

– Derived predicates corresponding to derived collections, are defined either by rules or functions like `BigProjects(X)` or **`pext`**`(Project)(X)`. They can also be n–ary predicates if the derived collection contains tuples.

– Boolean expressions including formulas like `X < Y` or `X == Y`.

– Quantified formulas built using the quantifiers **`all`** and **`some`**, which are defined as boolean generic functions [7].

If `F` is a positive atomic formula, `!F` denotes the negation of this formula and is a negative atomic formula. Complex formulas are conjunctions (expressed by `&`) of positive and negative atomic formulas. In order to avoid infinite answers to queries, only range–restricted formulas are valid in the language [7].

RULES A predicate can be defined by a set of rules. A rule is of the form `R(x1, ..., xm) <- F` where `R` is the name of the predicate, `F` is a formula and `xi` is a local variable of the rule. Rules can be recursives. Let us suppose that there is an attribute `Members` giving all the employees working in a project. The projects where all the members earn more than 10000 are computed by the following rule :

```
RichProject(X) <- pext(Project)(X) &
                  all(X.Members(Y),Y.Salary > 10000)
```

A set of rules must be safe. A rule is safe if every variable in its left hand side (the head) occurs in at least one positive atomic formula of its right hand side (the body). In addition, the rule body is expected to be range–restricted. Negation and sets are supported only for stratified programs. This intuitively means that for a set of rules recursively referring to each other, there is no recursive cycles that involves negation and sets. This point will not be further developed in this paper as it is out of its scope.

A set of rules defining a single predicate can be written using the following notation: A <- F1 | ... | Fn. Each Fj correspond to an independent alternative formula defining the predicate. Safety requirements must hold for each couple A<–Fj.

The type of variables local to a rule is inferred using terms having a known type (the basic ones are terms that do not use any local variable). Variables appearing in the head of the rule are constrained to a type conforming to the type specified in the signature of the rule.

4.2 Predicates as Set Expressions

The previous section has shown that any collection can be considered as a predicate. Declarative queries are integrated within the imperative OO language as set expressions. They can be used anywhere within the imperative code and can use variables available in the context. Thus, querying becomes completely orthogonal in the programming language, enhancing the integration.

As a formula can also define new local variables, such a formula must begin with the list of these variables in order to be able to distinguish them from variables of the including context. For example, [y1,...,yp]Fj defines the yk as local variables of Fj where the type of these variables is inferred from Fj. The local variables defined in the head do not have to appear in this list as the head acts as their declaration (their type being also inferred). These local variables can be compared to those of a function (parameters + local variables). Being able to distinguish such variables allows to involve a complete name resolution and type checking for rules, wherever they are defined. The integration of queries as set–valued expression is achieve by using the special rule operator **query**. Let us give an example:

```
float high_sal{}, rate_sal = 9000;
...
high_sal   =   query(S)   <-   [E]   pext(Employee)(E)   &
                                E.Salary == S & S > rate_sal;
```

The **query** operator, which behaves as a rule head, always yields a set. The type of the selected elements is inferred from the body of the rule. This type can be of any kind if **query** is unary as before or a tuple if it is n–ary (e.g., `query(X, Y, Z) <- ...`). Note that attributes (and arguments) are identified by their position in tuples (and predicates) and not by their name. In the previous example, the same result could have been obtained differently:

```
high_sal(S) <- [E] pext(Employee)(E) &
                                E.Salary == S & S > rate_sal;
```

Indeed, it is equivalent to populate a set by using the usual imperative assignment operator (=) to assign the result of a query, or to define this set as a stored predicate which is populated by a rule. Anyway, the **query** operator is necessary in other situations like, for example, passing a query result as a function argument (using an intermediate variable would imply two copies of the resulting set). It is interesting here to notice that querying and storage are orthogonal. As a matter of fact, as every set is a predicate, it can be defined by a rule, being it derived or stored.

4.3 Derived Data in Classes and Modules

This section emphasizes the relationship of derived data with classes and modules. We present attributes and methods of classes, considering problems related to inheritance. Module derived global variables and functions can be defined using declarative statements. The use of derived global variables for supporting views is illustrated in the last part of the section. Functions defined within modules are not discussed as they are similar to functions in classes.

ATTRIBUTES Derived attributes are a means for supporting attributes whose value must be calculated or for supporting a kind of "view" of the object. The value of these attributes must be defined with expressions. This allows the use of any kind of expression, in particular the use of deductive rules for set valued attributes. The definition context of such expressions is composed of the attributes and functions of the object (accessible using **`this`**) and the extensions of classes. The following example shows the definition of the derived attribute `Friends` of the class `Employee` introduced in section 2.2.

```
Person  Employee::Friends{}  as
Friends(X)  <-  this.Person::Friends(X) |
        this.Comp.Employees(X)  &  X.Service  =  this.Service;
```

The friends of an employee are defined as his personnal friends plus his colleagues at work (!). It is interesting to notice that the `Friends` attribute is also defined in the super–class `Person` as a stored one. Consequently, two attributes `Friends` exist in the class `Employee` as there is no attribute redefinition. One important reason for forbidding attribute redefinition is performance: this choice allows to perform global optimizations using rewriting techniques like for relationnal views.

METHODS Methods that are functions can also be implemented using a rule.The function defined below computes the project partners of an input country c.

```
Organization  Project::CountryPartners{}  (string c)  as
CountryPartners(X)<-  this.Partners(X)  &  X.Country  ==  C
```

The interesting point here is that late binding can be performed on derived data defined by rules. Anyway, enabling the usage of late binding for rule–based derived data has a drawback: only optimizations local to the function rule can be performed. The reason is that, since methods can be overridden in subclasses, the rule being used in an instruction that uses the function can only be known at runtime.

GLOBAL VARIABLES Finally, we illustrate the use of rules for defining a derived global variable. We use the variable `WorksFor` for maintaining a view giving the couples of employees working the one for the other:

```
    struct{ Employee   empl, boss;}   WorksFor{} as
    WorksFor(X,Y)  <-  pext(Employee)(X)  &
                              X.department.responsible  ==  Y;
```

The `WorksFor` variable can be used as a simply variable for obtaining the entire view, (as in (1) hereafter) or can be used for obtaining a part of the view by giving a value for some of the selected elements. In the example hereafter, we assume that `TheBigBoss` is a variable referencing to an employee. (2), selects people depending directly on him. Notice, the use of the **`free`** keyword for indicating that no value is given for the first argument.v1 is supposed to be a variable of the appropriate type.

```
{  ...  v1  =  WorksFor;                        (1)
        v1  =  WorksFor(free,  TheBigBoss);     (2)  ...}
```

5 Related Work

Several efforts to integrate declarative querying in object–oriented database systems have been made. Our purpose here is rather to compare our work with deductive systems that try to offer a complete DBPL environment. Systems like LDL, Glue–Nail or Aditi aim at doing this in the logic programming framework. Peplom^d follows the DOOD approach like Coral and Noodle while providing a language that integrates deductive and OO programming paradigms in a tighter way than those two systems.

The goal of LDL [10] is to provide a unique declarative language for doing both deductive queries and updates. The LDL language extends Datalog with sets, negation (for stratified programs) and updates. Updates are supported through special rules having a body composed of a querying part, which selects data to be updated, and a procedural part which performs updates. Peplom^d differs from LDL by forbidding updates in declarative statements. Updates can only be performen using imperative statements of Peplom$^{d.}$.

In this respect, it ressembles the Glue–Nail [11] DD system which proposes two complementary languages: the Glue procedural language and the Nail declarative one. The programming paradigms of both languages are very similar, i.e., logic programming, whereas Peplom^d introduces deductive capabilities in an OODBPL. The type system of Glue–Nail consists basically of relations allowing attributes to refer to sets. A set is always denoted by a name and cannot be extensionally included in an attribute (the set is referred to by this name). Glue–Nail allows to organize code by using modules which are pure compile time entities and may contain Glue procedures and Nail rules as well. Modules in Peplom^d also contain declarative and imperative code and offer an import/export capability as Glue–Nail does.

The Aditi project [13] aims at offering an efficient DD system that offers a query language, called Aditi–Prolog, which is a pure declarative variant of Prolog augmented with *declarations*. These declarations allow to ask for a special evaluation strategy or to tell the compiler which arguments of a predicate will be known at call time. Aditi–Prolog supports aggregate operators and negation which is not limited to stratified programs. Aditi includes an interface to the NU–Prolog language: NU–prolog can call Aditi–Prolog and conversely. The comparison cannot be deeper with respect to integration purpose as we lack of information.

Coral [12][14] is a DD system whose deductive language is similar to LDL although it does not support updates. The Coral declarative language can be used in C++ code using the embedded approach that yields to usual impedance mismatch problems. The Coral++ extension allows to support C++ objects in database facts and to use a restricted set of C++ expressions in queries, thus improving integration with OO capabilities. As truth semantics of C++ expressions is different from the one of Coral (no boolean type in C++), such expressions cannot be used in rule bodies whereas Peplom^d allows it as it offers a uniform truth semantics for expressions in declarative and imperative code. Imperative rules of Coral++ can invoke arbitrary methods and can be used within the C++ code but, the orthogonality of this integration is not clear so far.

Coral modules, containing only declarative statements (unlike Glue–Nail and Peplom^{d}), are compilation units within which one can specify the evaluation strategies to be used. No type checking or inferencing is performed at compile time in Coral whereas the objective of Peplom^{d} is to do as much as possible at compile time, thus saving execution time overhead.

Noodle [9] is a rule based declarative query language for an OOD system. It is being integrated within a procedural language (O++ of the ODE database system). Unfortunately, we have very little information on the subject. An important functionality of Noodle is the ability to query the schema, like in Hilog [4], in the same way as data e.g., variables can range over class names and attribute names. Unlike Peplom^{d}, attributes are referenced by name rather than position in predicates. Finally, Noodle allows methods to be defined declaratively as in Peplom^{d}.

6 Conclusion

We have propose in this paper Peplom^{d}, a language resulting from a clean integration of deductive capabilities (expressed with a declarative query language) within a procedural OO persistent programming language. Considering that the OO and deductive approaches both improve database technology in complementary ways, we think that the combination of both paradigms in a single DBPL will ease the task of the programmer. Declarativity of deductive languages is added to the programming power and application structuring capabilities supplied by OODBPL.

Most important aspects discussed in this paper correspond the support of derived data and the use of deductive rules in the OO language. Deductive rules are specially useful for querying data just as easily for atomic and structured values than for objects. The solution to achieve a good integration of the query language is three–fold: (1) it allows to use deductive rules for the definition of classes and modules, (2) it allows to use general expressions (including context variables) of the imperative part of the language in the definition of terms in rules, and (3) it allows to use such queries as set expressions in the imperative part. Notice that the query language can perfectly be used apart from the rest of the language as a simply query language.

A first prototype has been developed within the framework of [5]. It essentially covers the compilation of the imperative part of the language including the object–oriented features, plus some basic manipulations on collections. Some choices made in the data model, e.g., conformity rules and the language were guided by execution efficiency objectives. The compiler performs incremental compilation based on a powerful schema manager which serves several application development tools [1], all together playing an important role in mastering the complexity of today's applications. A new prototype, including the deductive extensions as well as other features like distribution and parallelism, is currently being developed within the framework of the IDEA project. Several experiments with real applications are planned for the near future and a large application on software test management is presently under development as well as another one concerning genetics.

Acknowledgements: we would like to thank M.Adiba, C.Collet and M.Santana for their remarks and corrections as well as M.Lopez and M.Riveill for their comments.

References

1. M. Adiba, C. Collet, P. Dechamboux and B. Defude, Integrated Tools for Object–Oriented Persistent Application Development, *Proc. DEXA 92*, Sept. 1992.
2. S. Ceri, G. Gottlob and L.Tanca, *Logic Programming and Databases*, Springer Verlag, 1990.
3. S.Ceri and R.Manthey, *First Specification of Chimera*, (IDEA.DD.2P.004.02), Politecnico di Milano, Italy, May 1993.
4. W. Chen, M. Kifer and D.S. Warren, Hilog: A Foundation for Higher Order Logic Programming, *Journal of Logic Programming*, 1992.
5. P. Dechamboux, *Gestion d'objets persistants : du language de programmation au système*, PhD Thesis, Université Joseph Fourier (Grenoble), February 1993.
6. P. Dechamboux and C. Roncancio, *Peplom: The IDEA EDBPL*, (IDEA.DD.1B.001.2), Bull, Grenoble – France, November 1993.
7. P. Dechamboux and C.Roncancio, Integrating Deductive capabilities an Object Oriented DBPL, *10th Journe'es Bases de Done'es Avancées*, Sept. 1994.
8. P.C. Lockmann, Object–Oriented Databases and Deductive Databases: Systems without Market? Market without Systems?, *Proc. DEXA 92*, September 1992.
9. I.S. Mumick and K.A. Ross, Noodle: a Language for Declarative Querying in an Object–Oriented Database, *Proc. DOOD 93*, pp. 360–378, December 1993.
10. S. Naqvi and S. Tsur, A Logical Language for Data and Knowledge Bases, *Computer Science Press*, New York, 1989.
11. G. Phipps, M.A. Derr and K.A. Ross, Glue–Nail: a Deductive Database System, *Proc. ACM SIGMOD Conference*, pp. 308–317, May 1991.
12. R. Ramakrishnan, D. Srivastava, S.Sudarshan and P. Seshadri, Implementation of the CORAL Deductive Database System, *Proc. ACM SIGMOD*, May 1993.
13. K. Ramamohanarao, An Implementation Overview of the Aditi Deductive Database System, *Proc. DOOD*, Springer Verlag, Phoenix, Dec. 1993.
14. D. Srivastava, R. Ramakrishnan, P. Seshadri and S.Sudarshan, Coral++: Adding Object–Orientation to a Logic Database Language, Dublin, Aug. 1993.
15. J.D. Ullman, A Comparison between Deductive and Object–Oriented Database Systems, *Proc. DOOD 91 Conference*, pp. 263–277, December 1991.

Object-Oriented Database Systems: How Much SQL Do They Understand?

Uwe Hohenstein, Regina Lauffer, Petra Weikert

Siemens AG, ZFE BT SE 44, Otto-Hahn-Ring 6, D-81730 München, Germany

Abstract. This paper gives a comprehensive overview of the associative query facilities of commercial object-oriented database systems. We introduce general concepts of query languages, and analyse the query facilities of the systems. The analysis leads to a classification of query languages, precisely differentiating the capabilities. Further aspects concern the embedding and the style of query formulation. The comparison is based upon empirical evaluations.

1 Introduction

The field of object-oriented database management systems (OODBMS) has rapidly evolved. Non-standard application areas like Computer Aided Design and Software Engineering Environments benefit considerably from the use of object-oriented database systems. Besides navigational access, advanced application areas require associative query facilities more and more [AWSL92, FKSD+91]. Research prototypes already took this demand into account, defining high-level query languages. Two examples are EXCESS of EXODUS [CDV88] and OSQL of the IRIS system [Bee88]. In addition, much work has been spent on theoretic foundations, algebras [Bee90] and calculi [BNPS92] for object-oriented query languages.

Nowadays, a number of commercial OODBMS products have established themselves on the market. Most of the currently available OODBMS encorporate associative query facilities – at some degree. Relying on rather dissimilar approaches, notations, and paradigms, it is very difficult to differentiate the query languages and to assess the functionality of individual systems. Recent papers do compare the functionality (e.g. [Sol92, AWSL92, Ern93]) and the performance (e.g. [CDN93]) of commercial object-oriented database systems, but neglect querying. In this paper, we concentrate on this aspect, and give a comprehensive overview of the associative query facilities of several commercial OODBMS. Our comparison results from empirical evaluations in an industrial environment. We chose six of the best known OODBMS based on C++, which we will treat anonymously. The comparison deals with current system versions of the year 1993. Additionally, we had a closer look at the standardization proposal OMDG93 [Cat93] as a future OODBMS standard.

As the title suggests, SQL has affected the syntax and functionality of even object-oriented query languages. We take the term '(Object) SQL' as a synonym for associative query capabilities, but we don't suggest taking SQL as a model for object-oriented queries.

Our main emphasis is put on what *functionality* is obtained by individual languages, independent of their syntax. Particularly it is important, how object-oriented concepts are reflected in query languages. Another interesting aspect concerns the embedding of queries in an object-oriented programming language, i.e. how query results are represented in the host language C++. The comparison is completed by examining the style of query formulation.

The rest of the paper is organized as follows. Section 2 discusses requirements object-oriented query languages should meet. Section 3 compares in detail the query facilities of six commercially available OODBMS, and presents a classification of object-oriented query languages. Section 4 gives a short summary.

The following schema serves as a basis for the query examples in the next sections.

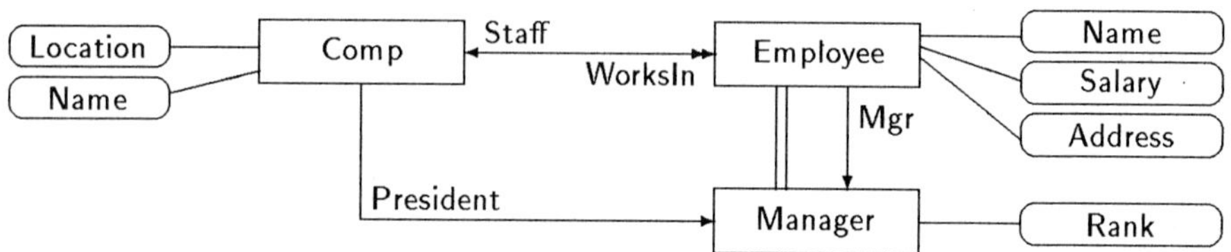

The schema is modelled in a unified, kernel object-oriented model with *object types* (rectangles), *attributes* (ovals), *subtypes with inheritance* (double line) and *references*. We distinguish between *single-* (→) and *multi-valued* (↠), *unidirectional* and *bidirectional* references (↞↠). We exclude multiple inheritance.

2 Concepts of Object-Oriented Query Languages

Object-oriented database systems rely on a more complex data model than the relational one. Consequently, object-oriented query languages should reflect these advanced object-oriented modelling concepts by corresponding constructs. We summarize the most important functional demands on object-oriented query languages given in the literature (e.g., [Bee88, CDV88, Bee90, Kim91, BNPS92]), and the effects they impose on querying.

In OODBMS, each object possesses a unique *object identifier* [ABD+89]. Two objects are *identical*, if and only if they have the same object identifier. *Equality* means that objects possess same attribute values and references. [KhC86] tells apart *shallow* and *deep* equality. Corresponding predicates should be available [BNPS92] to compare objects with regard to identity, shallow, and deep equality.

Collections require special predicates like membership test (`IN`) and additional functions like selecting the i-th element in a list [HoE92].

References are the object-oriented concept to model relationships between objects. Query languages should thus be able to relate objects by references. Quite often, *paths* are suggested as an adequate concept [Bee88], concatenating references by a dot notation, e.g., `e.WorksIn` makes use of the reference `WorksIn` to join the types `Employee` and `Company`. Normally, multi-valued references must not occur within paths, except the tail of a path. Such paths represent a collection: `e IN c.Staff` claims that an employee `e` is in the staff of company `c`. [BNPS92] allows multi-valued references within paths, but requires explicit quantifiers: `c.∃Staff.Salary >3000`. Please note that the direction of references determines the direction of access. For instance, `Mgr` is a unidirectional reference between `Employee` and `Manager`. In general, it is not possible to navigate opposite to that direction, i.e., to compute the employees who work for a given manager. However, special concepts can allow such queries.

Inheritance of properties from supertype to subtypes should also be reflected adequately. Hence, it should be possible to access for each **Manager** the **Name** attribute, inherited from **Employee**. Another point concerns selection of elements or instances: *Elements* of a type are all objects of the type itself and all its subtypes (in the following, we denote the set of elements of an object type as its *extent*). In contrast, *instances* are only the objects of the type. Corresponding constructs should enable one to choose between selecting instances or elements. For instance, [Kim91] suggests special ranges: **Employee** contains all the elements, while **Employee*** is the set of instances.

Specifying *methods* suggests itself using methods in queries. If there is a method **GetName** defined for **Employee**, it should be possible to use this method in the same way as the attribute **Name**. Arguments of methods might either be terms of the query language or C++ expressions.

Relational SQL incorporates some concepts that might be useful in the context of object-oriented query languages. *Aggregate functions* like computing the **SUM**, possibly combined with grouping (**GROUP-BY-HAVING**), may be included in object-oriented query languages, too. As in SQL, joins can be used to perform ad-hoc *value-based join* conditions. Closely related to joins are complex formulas using $\exists$ and $\forall$ quantifiers (**EXISTS(SFW)**) as well as nested queries (**IN(SFW)**).

3 Comparison of Object-Oriented Query Languages

In this section, we discuss the query languages of commercial OODBMS in detail. We are mainly interested in the *functionality* achieved by syntactic constructs. In order to make a rough distinction, we first consider the *kind of results*, i.e., what the result is made of:

- Objects of exactly one type, e.g., querying "all employees (in type **Employee**) who earn between 3000 and 5000",
- objects of several types, however, yielding a flat result ("employees and the company they work in"), and
- arbitrarily structured results, like "for each company the *set* of all employees".

The structure of this section is subject to this classification. The differences in functionality between the systems are detected by means of examples. The examples are chosen to stress the relevant differences, and embody the concepts discussed in the previous section.

Additional comparison aspects are taken into account. The first point concerns *embedding* of queries in the host language, i.e., how the result is represented in C++, and how the result can be accessed. The systems also differ in the *style* of formulating queries. Roughly speaking, we can distinguish between C++-like notation and SQL-like syntax (following relational SQL). All these aspects, functionality, embedding, and style are not independent of each other. For instance, the structure of the result affects the last two points: If only objects of one type can be selected, there is no chance to join types. Otherwise, embedding becomes much easier (the result consists of whole objects of that type), and an SQL-like style seems to be unreasonable.

Before discussing the query languages of commercial systems, we summarize their common grounds. All languages allow comparisons `attribute` θ `value` with usual predicates θ like >, <=, etc. Conditions can generally be composed of logical connectives like **AND** and **OR** as well as brackets. The predicate '==' is always understood as identity of objects. There is no system supporting shallow and deep equality. Inheritance of attributes, i.e., using attributes of the supertype for building formulas, is instead a common feature. Equality and inheritance are thus disregarded in the discussion.

Please note that our main concern is the functionality of query languages. Hence to homogenize the presentation, we portray the query syntax in simplified terms and refrain from system-specific syntactic peculiarities. For instance, we use neutral names like `int` for data types instead of `ooint` or `osint`. The same holds for method names.

3.1 Objects of One Type Can Be Selected

Selecting objects of one type simplifies embedding queries into C++, as the result of queries is always a set of elements of this object type. However, the power of querying is fairly restricted: Only whole objects can be selected, projections on attributes are not possible and thus must be performed in the programming language.

The systems in this category generally do not support general aggregate functions like average (**AVG**), value-based joins, and selection of instances. The direction of a reference has relevance for access, navigation in the opposite direction is excluded. The systems within this category differ in whether conditions can utilize properties of objects that are related by single- and multi-valued references. Sometimes a simple **CNT** function is provided.

System 1

The system that possesses the simplest query language uses an iterator approach, i.e., a predefined iterator provides functions to traverse the result:

Example 1. Employees who earn between 3000 and 5000

```
Itr<Employee> EmpItr;
EmpItr.Select("Salary>3000 AND Salary<5000");
while (EmpItr.Next())
      { Employee *emp = EmpItr; ... emp->Name ... };
```

`EmpItr` is an iterator defined for `Employee`, the query result is consequently related to the object type `Employee`. Each iterator possesses a generic function `Select` [1], the parameter of which is a string of type `char*` representing the query. Dynamic queries are possible, since the query string can be assembled at run-time. Traversing the result can be done by applying a `Next` function to the iterator, which will return the next object. The iterator itself can be used as an object of `Employee`, i.e., in general a C++ pointer `*emp`.

As the result is not explicitly represented as a set, e.g., `Set<Employee>`, it cannot be manipulated by inserting or deleting objects.

The syntax of queries has a simple structure combining comparisons like `Salary>3000` by applying logical connectives and brackets. Attributes must belong to the type to be selected or to its supertype. There is no chance to put conditions on object types that are related by references. Methods, even simple `GetAttr` access methods for attributes, are generally excluded.

[1] Please call to mind that function names have been unified due to standardization.

System 2

The next system in this category enhances the features of System 1 by relating objects via references. Selection conditions can thus refer to properties of related objects. The peculiarity of System 2 is that querying is absolutely compatible with C++ syntax, specifying queries by means of methods. Each object type possesses a class `Query`, e.g., `Employee_Query`, which must be used to specify queries over this type. An instance `EmpQ` of this class has to be created, and query specification is then done by calling methods successively.

Example 2. Companies that employ an employee earning between 3000 and 5000

```
Set<Company>* CompSet;     // result variable
Extent<Company> CompExt; // extent of Company
Employee_Query EmpQ;         // Queries on Employee and Company
EmpQ.Salary(3000,GT); EmpQ.BoolOp(AND); EmpQ.Salary(5000,LT);
Company_Query CompQ; CompQ.Staff(1,GE,EmpQ);
CompExt.Select(CompQ,CompSet);          // Execution
for (ok=CompSet->First(); ok==0; ok=CompSet->Next())
    { Company* comp; CompSet->Get(comp); ... comp->Name ... }
```

The `Query` classes possess for each attribute a corresponding method that allows for comparing attributes with values given as parameters. Specifying the condition `Salary>3000 AND Salary<5000` is done stepwise by calling predefined functions `Salary` (representing the attribute `Salary`) and `BoolOp` (applying the connective `AND`). Bracketing is possible by means of special methods.

Queries specified in this manner are passed to a function `Select` which is related to a special predefined class `Extent`. The extent exists for any object type and is maintained automatically. The function `Select` expects two parameters, a "`Query`-Instance" `CompQ` representing the query, and a variable `CompSet` of type `Set<Company>` obtaining the result. Since the structure of a query is fix at compile-time, dynamic queries are possible only in a limited way. More precisely, all the parameters are dynamic, i.e., the comparison predicates, the logical connectives, and values. The representation of the result is done by parameterized `Sets` (in the sense of C++ templates). A `for`-loop, `First` and `Next` methods allow traversing the set successively.

In the above example, a first query `EmpQ` selects the employees who earn between 3000 and 5000. `EmpQ` is a query of its own, hovewer, is here used in a subsequent query `CompQ` constraining `Company`. Navigation across references can be done by using methods like `staff` that are related to references. There must be at least (`GE`) one (the first parameter is 1) instance in `Employee` that is related by `Staff` and that satisfies the `EmpQ` query.

Due to the direct embedding in C++, this system enables one to use C++ variables in queries. For example, we could define a variable `Employee *emp`, assign a concrete employee to it, and pass the variable to `CompQ.Staff` instead of `EmpQ`. A simple way of defining parameterized queries is achieved.

The function `Staff` can furthermore be used to specify simple counting conditions, e.g., `CompQ.Staff(3,EQ,EmpQ)`. However, the mechanism is not sufficient to specify any kind of `CNT`s known from SQL.

Please note that value-based joins cannot be formulated. Furthermore, the direction of a reference is *significant* for the access. It is not possible to search for employees who have a certain manager.

System 3

This system has the same functionality as System 2, however, relying on quite a different kind of embedding and style of query specification.

As in System 1, queries are passed as strings to a `Select` method. Dynamic queries can be built at run-time. This system is characterized by the fact that the `Select` function is associated with *arbitrary* collections, not just only extents. The following piece of code can use either an extent variable `companies` (representing the set of all companies stored in the database) or an arbitrary variable defined for class `Set<Company>`.

Example 3. Companies that employ an employee who earns more than 3000 and is subordinated to manager 'Smith'

```
Set<Company> cSet = companies->Select("Staff[Salary>3000 AND
                                       Mgr->Name=='Smith']");
for (Company *c=cSet->First(); cSet->More(); c=cSet->Next())
      { ... c->Name ... };
```

Collections are represented by `Set` templates, which provide methods to insert, delete, and traverse elements. Accessing the elements of the result is done by applying predefined methods like `First` and `Next`. It is important to mention that associative access takes into account both persistent *and* transient objects.

Object types are not collections automatically by default. If an access to all instances of a type is desired, then an extent *must* be defined and maintained manually by inserting and deleting objects in the extent, too.

Navigation along multi-valued references takes place by using square brackets. Hence, a company is only selected if there exists at least one member in the set of referenced `staff` objects that satisfies the inner condition `[Salary>3000 AND Mgr->Name=='Smith']`. Brackets can be nested in order to compose more complex queries. Single-valued references do not require any special concepts, they can be used like `Mgr->Name`.

Methods that return an integer value can be used in comparisons instead of values. Parameters of those methods must be C++ objects or values. For instance, `CONTAINS` (membership test) and `CARD` (cardinality of a collection) are special methods predefined for collections, which can be applied to multi-valued references directly, e.g., `Staff.CARD==3`. `CARD` is useful for simple counting, but only a rudimentary substitute of the aggregate function `CNT`, because its use is restricted to multi-valued references in queries. Again no value-based joins and no navigation inverse to a reference can be formulated.

3.2 Objects of Several Types Can Be Selected

First representatives of ObjectSQL's are found in this group. As in the first category, navigating along single- and multi-valued references is possible, in one case however only in a limited form. In contrast to the previous category, new features are partly supported: Telling apart elements and instances when selecting objects, following references in inverse direction, and value-based joins. The ability to yield objects of several types requires special mechanisms to embed the query language into C++.

The two subsequent ObjectSQL's orientate themselves syntactically towards the `SELECT-FROM-WHERE` (`SFW`) block of relational SQL. The functionality of both query languages is only slightly different. But they differ in the kind of embedding and syntactic notation.

System 4

The first system of this category demands results to consist of possibly several, but whole objects. Projections on particular attributes are forbidden.

In contrast to most other systems, the syntax of C++ is here extended: SQL-like queries are directly written as program code. On the one hand, only static queries (no strings are passed!) can be executed, on the other hand this approach requires a precompiler.

Example 4. Pairs of employees and companies that have the same location

```
SQL* result = SELECT FROM Employee e, Company c
              WHERE e.Address == c.Location;

for (i=0; i < result->Size(); i++)
     { Company* comp = (*result)[i][Company];
       Employee* emp = (*result)[i][Employee]; }
```

Embedding is done by a predefined class `SQL` that will receive the query result. It can be understood as an n*m array. Here, n represents the tuples of the result, and m corresponds to the object types in the `FROM` clause. Access to the objects occurs by C++ field indexing, e.g., `(*result)[i][Company]` to address the component `Company` of the i-th tuple. Instead of using the object type for indexing, index numbers can be specified. A special function `Size()` yields the number of result tuples. The number of components is fix and known at compile-time.

Joining object types, along references or value-based, can be specified, since several object types may occur in the `FROM` clause. These object types are then automatically part of the result. The example given in query 4 specifies a join between `Employee` and `Company` comparing their locations.

Results of queries are valid ranges for subsequent queries. A special form of `FROM x IN result` allows binding variables to previous query results providing type compatibility. Particularly, further constraining of results can easily be done in this way.

Unfortunately, it is difficult to relate objects by means of references, the intended form of expressing relationships in object-orientation. References cannot be used by default, there is a need for additional *user-defined* methods that must be specified in the sense of access paths. This remedial action is only applicable, because methods can be part of queries.

Example 5. Companies that employ an employee who earns more than 3000 and is subordinated to manager 'Smith'

```
SELECT FROM Company* c
WHERE  EXISTS (SELECT FROM Employee *e
               WHERE  c->inStaff(e) AND e->Salary>3000
               AND    e->giveMgr().Name=='Smith');
```

One would expect a formula `e IN c->Staff` or `e->WorksIn==c`, resp., by applying references `Staff` or `WorksIn`. But neither of them is syntactically correct. Instead, we had to implement a boolean method `inStaff(Employee*)` for class `Company` that determines whether the employee `e` works in `c`. Similarly, the method `giveMgr` defined for `Employee` returns the manager of a given employee. Summarizing up, navigation can be performed along single-valued references, providing corresponding methods.

In return, the query language provides means to inverse the direction of references, a new feature occuring in our discussion for the first time. The form `EXISTS(SFW)` facilitates specification:

Example 6. Managers who have a direct subordinate named 'Smith'

```
SELECT FROM Manager *m
WHERE EXISTS (SELECT FROM Employee *e
              WHERE  e->Name=='Smith' AND e->giveMgr()==m)
```

Let us finally spend some remarks on the syntax of this ObjectSQL. There are no aggregate functions (at least in the C++ embedding of the system). Furthermore, there is no `UNION` operator. Object types and intermediate results (a special declaration form `x IN result`) are the only ranges for variables. Nested queries `IN(SFW)` are not possible.

System 5

In contrast to system 4, which allows for querying objects of several types, system 5 goes one step beyond. The query result can here consist of objects *and* elementary values, providing the result is flat. Hence, we are able to specify arbitrary joins between object types and can compute projections on attributes.

Embedding is done by predefined iterator classes `Iterator` and `RowIterator`. They define specific functionality for iterating over all result tuples and all values in a tuple, resp.

Example 7. Companies that employ an employee who earns more than 3000 and is subordinated to manager 'Smith'

```
Iterator It = new Iterator
                  ("SELECT c.Name,e FROM Company c, Employee e
                    WHERE  e IN c.Staff AND e.Salary>3000
                    AND    e.Mgr.Name=='Smith'             ");
while (It->More())                      // for each tuple do:
      { RowIterator rowIt = It->RowIterator();
        while (rowIt->More())           // for each component do:
              { Company *comp = (Company*)(Entity*)(*rowIt)();
                ... comp->Name ... }; };
```

An instance `It` of the predefined iterator class `Iterator` is created, specifying the query as a string. The iterator has a method `More` checking for end of result. The "tuples" of the result are then fetched one by one. To access an item of the result, an inner `RowIterator` can be defined. The row iterator must be converted ("casted") to class `Entity`, which is the superclass of all data values and all persistent object classes. An additional casting is necessary to make the `Entity` instance an object of type `Company`. The type of the items in the result can be determined only at run-time due to dynamic queries. Consequently, there are special methods that return the type specifications at run-time.

The query language provides concepts to perform arbitrary joins between object types, no matter whether value-based or using single- or multi-valued references. Example 7 reformulates query 3 and demonstrates, how relationships given by references are employed for selections.

Value-based joins do not make any problems, and can be formulated analogously to example 4, however, without the need of user-defined methods. Following references in the opposite direction can be done similar to example 6. But a join must be specified here instead of `EXISTS(SFW)`, because this system does not support either `EXISTS(SFW)` or `IN(SFW)`. Using a join is in fact a substitute, having a slightly different effect than intended: Due to computing the cross product, the result may contain duplicates.

Among the systems discussed so far this is the first to provide means to distinguish between instances and elements. An extension of the predicate `IN` provides the solution. For example, the condition `NOT(Manager IN Employee)` restricts the `Employee` elements to those being not elements of `Manager`.

The `SELECT` list of this ObjectSQL can contain several object and data-valued terms. Such target terms can be composed by applying single-valued attributes and single-valued references. Methods are also applicable, if they do not return collections. Hence projections like `c.Name` and `c.President.Name` can be specified, but in contrast `c.Staff` is forbidden. Paths using references and methods can not only be used as target terms of queries, but also in the `WHERE` part building formulas. Here, multi-valued paths are possible, particularly within `IN` predicates (`e IN c.Staff` in query 7). Ranges of variables are object types, sets of constants, and paths yielding collections. Declaring several variables in a `FROM` clause enables one to specify value-based joins in direct analogy to SQL.

Concerning the form and functionality of queries, this query language does not allow for nested queries of the form `IN(SFW)` in contrast to SQL. On the other hand a special form `IN path` for multi-valued paths exists. Furthermore, no aggregate functions, even no primitive cardinality check, and no `UNION` are available.

3.3 System 6: Arbitrarily Structured Results

The query language of the last commercial system comprises the most extensive ObjectSQL from a functional point of view. Objects, data values and collections over them can be combined in a result. Above all, nestings known from the NF^2 proposals [PiD89] are possible. Embedding the query language in the programming language takes place by a global function `Select`.

Example 8. *Compute for each company the average salary of its employees, provided the company employs more than 3 employees and a manager named 'Smith'*

```
Select(result,
   "SELECT tuple(c.Name, salaries: AVG(SELECT e.Salary
                                       FROM   e IN c.Staff) )
    FROM   c In companies
    WHERE  EXISTS e IN c.Staff: (e.Mgr.Name=='Smith')
    AND    CNT(c.Staff) > 3                              ");
```

The variable `result`, declared for class `Set<Result>`, takes the result and provides methods for iteration. `Result` in turn must correspond to the structure of the query result. In contrast to the other approaches, the structure of the query result can be arbitrarily specified by applying constructors `array`, `set`, `bag`, `list`, and `tuple`. The parameter string represents the ObjectSQL query.

Please note that again explicit extents (`companies` in the example) must be defined in the schema as entry points for querying and have to be managed manually.

This variant of an ObjectSQL is characterized by its absolute orthogonality: Multi-valued paths and `SFW` blocks represent collections, which can be used at any place a collection is expected: As a value range for variables, and as an argument for aggregate functions like in `CNT(c.Staff)`. Collections possess usual operations like `UNION` and predicates like test for element (`IN`). Special functions are defined for lists and arrays, e.g., selecting the i-th element in a list. Aggregate functions applied to collections are terms that are valid in several contexts. They can be used as target terms (behind `SELECT`), inside formulas, and as an argument for arithmetic functions. `EXISTS` (and a corresponding `FORALL`, too) provide means to nest queries. The form is different to relational SQL owing to more orthogonality.

Value-based joins can be formulated similar to query 4, and furthermore, all the other queries are also possible. Finally, it is worth mentioning that methods can be invoked in queries. Assuming `f` to be a method, $\texttt{x.f(t}_1\texttt{,...,t}_n\texttt{)}$ is a term of the query language. In contrast to the other languages allowing for methods, the parameters are conventional terms $\texttt{t}_i$ of the query language.

3.4 OMDG93 Standard

Future development of object-oriented database systems will be strongly shaped by the proposal OMDG93 of the Object Database Management Group (ODMG). The ODMG is associated with the Object Management Group (OMG), and aims at standardizing object-oriented database systems. The group was founded in 1991 by the leading vendors of OODBMS. Voting members are representatives of Ontos Inc., Object Design Inc., Objectivity Inc., O_2 Technologies, Servio Corp. and Versant Object Technology. Consulting members come from Hewlett Packard Company, Poet Software GmbH, Itasca Systems Inc., MICRAM GmbH, Intellitic International, Digital Equipment Corp., and Texas Instruments. The voting member companies and most of the reviewer member companies are committed to support this standard by 1995.

The first version of the ODMG standard [Cat93] defines an object model, an Object Definition Language (ODL), and an Object Query Language (OQL), which all are independent of concrete programming languages, as well as specific C++ and Smalltalk bindings. The OQL is based upon relational SQL and is quite similar to the query language discussed in section 3.3. Embedding the OQL in C++ can be done in several ways.

The first possibility provides each collection class with a member function `query (Ref<Collection<T>> result, char* predicate)`. The parameter `predicate` is a string following the syntax of the `where` clause of the OQL. This approach works on a principle similar to the category discussed in subsection 3.1. The second variant caters for a free overloaded function `oql(result,query)`. The parameter `result` is a variable that receives the result. The type of this variable can be either an object type, an elementary data type, or a (structured) collection. `query` contains the query in OQL syntax. The functionality is equivalent to the one of the query language of subsection 3.3. In both cases, the C++ binding requires that extents must be explicitly defined in the schema and maintained manually.

4 Conclusions

In this paper we discussed general concepts of object-oriented query languages and examined the functionality of six commercially available OODBMS. The *functionality* of a system is essentially shaped by the kind of query results. Thus, the systems can be divided into three categories: selecting objects of one type, selecting objects of several types and arbitrarily structured results. Within the three categories there are some more functional differences betweeen the systems. The systems may differ, e.g., in the use of single- and multi-valued references or in offering aggregate functions. The following table briefly summarizes the functional aspects of the systems.

	One Type			Several Types		Arbitrary Structure
	System 1	System 2	System 3	System 4	System 5	System 6
Equality/Identity	identity	identity	identity	identity	identity	identity
Inheritance	Yes	Yes	Yes	Yes	Yes	Yes
References (single/multi)	No	Yes	Yes	Yes [2]	Yes	Yes
Inverse References	No	No	No	Yes	Yes	Yes
Aggregate Functions	No	`CNT` [3]	`CNT` [3]	No	No	All
Methods	No	No	Yes [4]	Yes	Yes	Yes
Value-based Joins	No	No	No	Yes	Yes	Yes
Instances/Elements	No	No	No	No	Yes	Yes

Further functional concepts have not been investigated in detail, since these are peculiarities of only a few systems. For instance, system 4 extends the benefits of associative queries to other operations like `DELETE` and `UPDATE`. Other systems support arithmetic operations. Encapsulation is not respected by some of the systems so that private properties of an object type can be accessed. An important concept, which is supported only by system 1, is to select objects in *several* databases by a single query.

Comparing the systems we were also interested in the *embedding* of queries in the host language and in the *style* of query formulation. Embedding means how the result of a query is represented in the programming language C++. Query formulation can be done in two different styles: Specifying a query in C++-like notation or using a syntax similar to that of SQL.

How an object-oriented query language should look like is a very controversial question at a moment. A number of database researchers tend to adopt the concepts of SQL for object-oriented querying. [Sto90] characterizes SQL as 'intergalactic data speak', [Sel93] speaks of SQL as 'esperanto'. Others criticize an SQL-ish style of object-oriented query languages [Odb92]. They argue that those languages provide only for nested and aggregate objects, but will not reflect the real concepts of object-orientation. The standardization proposal OMDG93 in its current form [Cat93] prefers an SQL-like notation. But the standard is not settled yet, and further discussions might also influence the query language of the standard. So it remains an open question, which direction commercial systems will take with respect to query languages.

[2] Navigation along references requires special user-defined methods.

[3] The cardinality of referenced collections can be computed and used in comparisons.

[4] Only methods that return an integer can be used.

References

[ABD+89] M. Atkinson, F. Bancilhon, D. DeWitt, K. Dittrich, D. Maier, St. Zdonik: *The Object-Oriented Database System Manifesto.* In [DOOD89]

[AWSL92] S. Ahmed, A. Wong, D. Sriram, R. Logcher: *Object-Oriented Database Management Systems for Engineering: A Comparison.* Journal of Object-Oriented Programming 5(3), June 1992

[Bee88] D. Beech: *A Foundation for Evolutions from Relational to Object Databases.* In J.W. Schmidt, S. Ceri, M. Missikoff: Advances in Database Technology – EDBT '88, Venice 1988

[Bee90] C. Beeri: *Formal Models for Object-Oriented Databases.* In [DOOD89]

[BNPS92] E. Bertino, M. Negri, G. Pelagatti, L. Sbattella: *Object-Oriented Query Languages: The Notion and the Issues.* IEEE Trans. on Knowledge and Data Engineering 4 (3), 1992

[Cat93] R. Cattell (ed.): *The OMDG-93 Standard for Object Databases.* Morgan-Kaufmann Publishers, San Mateo (CA) 1993

[CDN93] M.J. Carey, D. DeWitt, J.F. Naughton: *The OO7 Benchmark.* ACM SIGMOD 1993 22(2)

[CDV88] M.J. Carey, D. DeWitt, S.L. Vandenberg: *A Data Model and Query Language for EXODUS.* Proc. of the ACM SIGMOD Int. Conf. on Management of Data, Chicago 1988

[DGJ92] S. Dar, N.H. Garhani, H.V. Jagadish: *A SQL for Ode Object-Oriented DBMS.* In: Advances in Database Technology – International Conference on Extending Database Technology (EDBT'92), Vienna, March 1992

[DOOD89] W. Kim, J.-M. Nicolas, S. Nishio (eds.): Proc. 1st Int. Conf. on Deductive and Object-Oriented Databases 1989 (DOOD'89), Kyoto 1989

[Ern93] K. Erni: *Integrating Object-Oriented Databases into Applications – A Comparison.* Int. Conf. on Database and Expert Systems (DEXA'92), Valencia 1992 (446–449)

[FKSD+91] M. Fuller, A. Kent, R. Sacks-Davis, J. Thom, R. Wilkinson, J. Zobel: *Querying in a Large Hyperbase.* In: Int. Conf. on Database and Expert Systems Applications (DEXA'91), Berlin 1991 (455 – 458)

[HoE92] U. Hohenstein, G. Engels: *SQL/EER: Syntax and Semantics of an Entity-Relationship Based Query Language.* Information Systems 1992, 17(3)

[KhC86] S. Khoshafian, G. Copeland: *Object Identity.* In: Proc. of the 1st Int. Conf. on Object-Oriented Programming Systems, Languages, and Applications (OOPSLA'86) 1986

[Kim91] W. Kim: *Introduction to Object-Oriented Databases.* Series Computer Science, The MIT Press (Cambridge, Mass.), 2nd printing 1991

[Odb92] E. Odberg: *What "What" is and isn't: On Query Languages for Object-Oriented Databases. Or: Closing the Gap – Again.* In: Proc. of the 8th Int. Conf. on TOOLS 1992.

[PiD89] P. Pistor, P. Dadam: *The Advanced Information Management Prototype.* In S. Abiteboul, P.C. Fischer, H.-J. Schek (eds.): *Nested Relations and Complex Objects in Databases.* Springer Verlag, 1989. Lecture Notes in Computer Science No. 361 (3 – 26)

[Sel93] P. Selinger: *Predictions and Challenges for Database Systems in the Year 2000.* In: Proc. of the 19th Int. Conf. on Very Large Databases (VLDB'93), Dublin 1993

[Sol92] V. Soloviev: *An Overview of Three Commcercial Object-Oriented Database Management Systems: ONTOS, ObjectStore, and O_2.* ACM SIGMOD 21(1), 1993

[Sto90] M.Stonebraker (The Committee for Advanced DBMS Function): *Third-Generation Database System Manifesto.* SIGMOD RECORD, 19(3), 1990.

An Object-Centered Application Development System

M. A. Ketabchi, S. Dasananda, R.Mikkilineni, X. Li, F. Xu, M. Yan
Object Technology Laboratory
School of Engineering
Santa Clara University
Santa Clara, CA 95053

Abstract. Recent advances in object technology have given rise to a set of powerful tools that are referred to as application builders. Application builders attempt to raise the level of abstractions in application development process from programming to composition of predefined components. To achieve this, application builders provide a set of components and facilities to compose these components. However, the composition facilities of the current application builders are primitive and the set of predefined components they provide can only be extended by programmers. Application builders that allow developers to build applications using domain specific components, semantics and primitives are needed. This article presents an Object-Centered Application Development System which provides a set of flexible high-level modeling and composition constructs and supports domain specific application development.

1 Introduction

In organizations where software application systems constitute an important element of many aspects of the operations, from telephone switching and billing to manufacturing and maintenance, the ability to build reliable, robust and user-friendly software applications rapidly is essential.

Traditional application development process takes too much time and effort because it is performed at a very low level of abstraction, and involves multiple loosely related tools and techniques. It requires human intensive communication among individuals and groups with different areas of expertise such as programming and user interface and database design.

A breakthrough in application development technology is going to happen when application development systems which allow application developers to build their applications using domain specific components, semantics, and primitives become available. Domain experts will develop application domain models and application developers will build applications by composing the components in these models.

In order to support domain specific application development, an executable model of the domain of the application needs to be developed first. For advanced domains such as communication, health care, and computer integrated manufacturing, existing semantic modeling tools are too restrictive and existing object-oriented programming languages are too primitive. A flexible, expressive, and easy to use meta model that provides expressive high-level modeling constructs and powerful composition abstractions is needed. Such a meta model can serve as the underlying formalism of a domain modeling tool for building application domains and an application building tool for synthesizing applications.

Object-oriented paradigm is a promising meta-model and has led to the development of a set of powerful application builders to address this problem. Current application builders generally provide:

(i) A set of predefined objects with generic base functionality.
(ii) Facilities to compose these functionalities to realize application logic or to define new objects.
(iii) Facilities for developing user interfaces for the application logics so composed.
(iv) Tools to execute, test, and debug the applications.

The current application builders generally provide technology domain objects such as graphic user interface and database management systems interface objects, and generic objects such as tables and dictionaries. They do not provide high-level modeling facilities for domain experts to define application domains. Defining new objects and making them available to application developers require programming expertise rather than application domain knowledge only. Moreover, the composition facilities in current application builders are very limited.

This article presents a model-based Object-Centered Application Development System (OCADS) which provides a set of flexible high-level modeling and composition constructs. The modeling constructs are the underlying formalism of a domain modeling tool. The composition constructs are the underlying formalism of an interactive direct manipulation domain specific application builder. These constructs have been integrated into an Object Specification Language (OSL) which is the host language of OCADS.

Section 2 gives an overview of a selected set of application builders. Section 3 describes the approach of OCADS. An overview of OSL, a Domain Modeling Tool (DMT), and an Application Building Tool (ABT) based on OSL are also presented in section 3. Section 4 offers concluding remarks.

2 An Overview of Selected Current Application Builders

NeXTstep [1] is an interactive application development environment. The application development process in NeXTstep starts with implementing the application interface by the NeXTstep Interface Builder. Interface Builder allows developers and potential users to test the interface before the application is built.

For objects in the application to send and receive messages, they need connections to one another. Interface Builder provides a graphical way of connecting objects. The source of the connection is the message sender and the destination is the receiver of the message. NeXTstep support a delegation mechanism [2] which makes it easier to reuse a class. An object may designate another object, its delegate, to handle certain tasks on its behalf. Delegates can eliminate the need to define a subclass of a complex class. After the interface is designed and the connections are defined, the custom classes are implemented in Objective-C. The Interface Builder generates skeletal source code files which include custom class declarations. The application developer writes Objective-C code for the methods, declares and implements any other variables and methods needed to implement the functionality of the class.

Message passing which is the only way to specify the application flow control occurs along the explicitly specified connections. Explicit message passing is not powerful enough in some applications because making the point to point message connection manually among objects can be very tedious. Moreover, NeXTstep requires intimate knowledge of the class implementations and programming. The predefined objects in NeXTstep constitute a form of domain model where only the concepts of class and explicit message passing are supported.

ObjectVision (OV) [3] is an application development tool for data-intensive applications. It supports graphical data definitions and manipulations. User interface objects such as forms and fields get their values from user inputs, calculations using the notion of Value Tree, and external links to database tables. A value tree consists of three elements: fields, conditions and conclusions. Fig. 1 shows an example of a simple value tree which represents the calculation: IF RoomOccupied = False THEN RoomWorkingTemp = DesiredTemp - 5. Value trees can be combined together to represent more complex calculations.

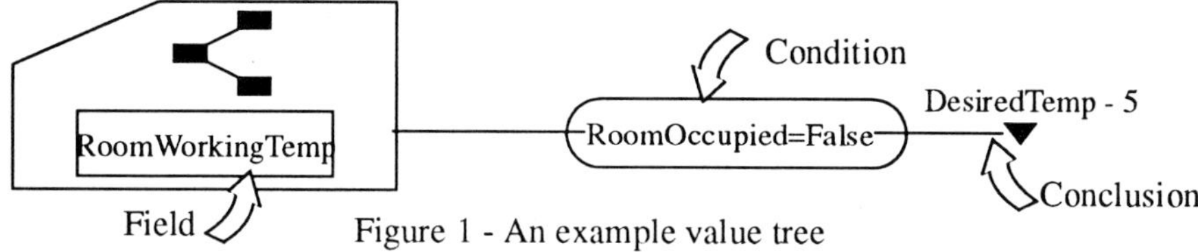

Figure 1 - An example value tree

OV supports a notion of Event Tree for specifying control flow. An event tree has three parts: window object, event, and conclusion. Fig. 2 illustrates an example event tree which states that If the ClearLivingPattern button is clicked, the event function CLEAR(LivingPattern) will be performed.

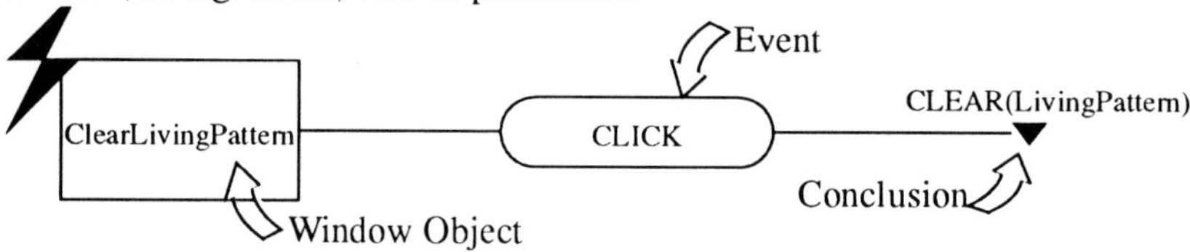

Figure 2 - An example Event Tree

IntelligentPad (IP) [4] represents each object as a pad. A pad has state and behavior defined as its model (M), appearance defined as its view (V), and interactions defined as its controller (C). These three MVC [5] components are all objects. Message-passing paths are provided from C to V and from V to M. Each pad also has an update propagation path from M to V so that a state change of M automatically updates V.

Each pad maintains a list of slots which are the only part of the pad that can be accessed through its view. Each slot may be either a value or an attached procedure. When accessed, it either accesses its value or executes its procedure. Three different messages set, get, and update define standard interfaces between pads.

A new pad can be defined either by combining existing pads through paste operations or by writing C++ classes that follow a set of conventions. A pad can be pasted onto another pad for the layout design and the functional composition of a new pad. This composition can be nested at any level, i.e., the new pad can be further pasted on another pad. Thus each pad may have a hierarchical structure.

IP provides the simple and intuitive pad metaphor. There are standard message paths between a subpad and its master pad. Additionally, IP provides a special horizontal connection between two pads. In IP message passing occurs between slave pads and master pads. There is no direct message passing between two arbitrary pads. If two arbitrary pads need to interact they should have a common master pad. The master pad propagates messages among its subpads. IP is a flexible easy to use end-user oriented application builder.

An application built with ObjectBuilder (OB) [6] can be thought of as consisting of three parts: the application's graphical front end, the application back end, and the bridge to translate user events (such as button presses) into calls to the application back end. The application developer writes the code for the back end which realizes the logic of the application. The User Interface Builder allows the application developer to assemble and customize the graphical user interface. A user interface object is bound with other user interface objects by the parent/children or sibling relationship. An object is parented to another object by drag and drop. The bridge between the application's front end and back end is the callback stubs. The application developer fills in callback functions which binds the user events to the application back end.

Although the graphic front end of applications is built through direct manipulations of user interface objects, the application back end and binding between application front end and back end are established through the programming.

3 Object-Centered Application Development System (OCADS)

OCADS is a layered model-based application development system. The kernel of OCADS is a collection of classes which encapsulate technology domains such as user interface systems and software tools. Domain experts use OCADS host language OSL to develop application domain model on top of OCADS kernel. The end-users of OCADS develop applications on top of the application domain model by utilizing domain specific semantics and objects.

An important component of OCADS is its host language OSL. OSL is a declarative object-oriented language for modeling application domains and composing objects. OCADS DMT is a graphic user interface environment for OSL. Domain experts use DMT to develop application domain models. The composition facilities of OCADS are available through OCADS ABT. The next three subsections give an overview of OSL, DMT, and ABT.

3.1 Object Specification Language OSL

OSL is an object-oriented non-procedural language for modeling advanced application domains such as network management. OSL is different from common object-oriented programming languages such as C++ in that it provides extensive modeling facilities. It is different from data definition and semantic modeling languages such as SQL, OSQL (Object SQL) [7], and ER (Entity Relationships) because it provides facilities for modeling interactions among objects and activities of domains [8]. Different specification languages such as SDL [10], Z [10], Oasis[11] and Spec [12] have been developed for different objectives. Some specification languages have been designed to facilitate validation while some others have been designed to facilitate high-level system description. Several of these specification languages are being enhanced with object-oriented concepts [13,14]. OSL has been designed to facilitate the modeling of application domains by allowing the specification of not only the structure and behavior of application domain objects, but also the interactions and activities among them.

OSL has a single powerful logical model which integrates recent advances in modeling and programming language technologies into a declarative language. OSL objects are not limited to classes and their instances. Relationship, event, rule, trigger, task, and process and their instances are first class objects in OSL. OSL class construct is similar to class constructs in C++ and SmallTalk. The following subsections give an overview of OSL relationship, event, rule, and trigger. The detailed discussion of these and other OSL facility are given in OSL Users' Guild [15].

3.1.1 Relationship

A relationship represents an association among objects. Relationship is very natural concept for users and has been used in one form or another in a variety of systems successfully. OSL Relationships are organized into a relationship-subrelationship hierarchy. An instance of a relationship can not exist on its own, it's existence depends on the existence of its participant objects. An OSL Relationship has structure and behavior paragraphs. There are three sections in the structure paragraph of a relationship: the Participant section, the RelationshipAttribute section, and the InstanceAttributes section.

The Participant section contains two or more participant specifications. The relationship attributes section is similar to the class attributes of the class construct in each OSL instance. The instance attributes section specifies the attributes associated with the relationship. They generally model intersection data of relationships. The behavior paragraph consists of the relationship operations section and the instance operations section. These sections are similar to the class operations section and the instance operations section in the class construct respectively. Every OSL relationship has a set of translator generated operations not available in any class. These operations are used for creating and deleting relationships and associative access to participants.

Figure 3 gives an example relationship Supply. The cardinality constraints specify that each Supplier object may participate in at least 0 and at most 1 Supply relationships, each Part object may participate in at least 0 and at most n (unlimited) Supply relationships, and each Project object may participate in at least 0 and at most 2 Supply relationships. The multiplicity constrains indicate that each supply relationship will have one supplier, none or many parts and between 2 and 10 projects.

```
BeginRelationshipSpec
RelationshipName Supply;
SuperRelationshipName Relationship;
Structure
        Participants
            s: Supplier Multiplicity(1..1) Cardinality(0..1);
            p: Part Multiplicity(0..n) Cardinality(0..n);
            j: Project Multiplicity(2..10) Cardinality(0..2);
        InstanceAttributes
            quantity: Integer;
EndRelationshipSpec
```

Figure 3 - OSL relationship example

3.1.2 Event

An OSL event construct is a mechanism to specify a pattern of communication among objects. The communication pattern includes an object expressing interest in certain changes in the state of other objects, and wanting to be notified, or specifying actions that must take place when the changes happen. An event is any change of interest in the object state. The manner of handling an event can be specified at the time of registering interest in the event. The same event may elicit different responses in different objects.

All OSL events are refinements of the system-defined OSL Event construct. An OSL event has Context, Raise, When and Operation sections. The Context section provides necessary information for binding references in other sections of the event by specifying the class or classes of objects. The Raise section specifies an operation after which the condition specified in the when section should be checked. In case no operation is specified, a meaning of "always" is implied. The When section specifies the state which resulted because of the changes the object has undergone. The condition is described using logical expressions. The Operations section provides system-defined methods, register(), notify(), and check() for the construct. Figure 4 shows an example of event which is defined over Employee class and is raised when an employee is promoted.

```
BeginEventSpec
EventName       Promotion;
SuperEvent      OSL event;
Context         e : Employee;
RaiseAfter      promote();
When            e.title > e.oldTitle;
EndEventSpec
```

Figure 4 - OSL event example

3.1.3 Trigger

An OSL trigger has Context, When, OnRequest and Perform sections. All OSL triggers are refinements of OSL system-defined Trigger. The Context section provides information for binding references in other sections of the trigger. The When section specifies a state or a condition. OnRequest section specifies a method of an object or a task. It is under the condition or in the state specified in When section and after the invocation of the method or task specified in OnRequest section that the trigger becomes relevant. In this case the actions specified under Perform section, are performed. The OnRequest and Perform sections can further be qualified by conditions.

If the When section is not specified the meaning of always is implied. Figure 5 shows an example of OSL trigger. This trigger specifies that after a student adds a course, the class count for that course should be updated.

```
BeginTriggerSpec
TriggerName         updateClassCount;
Context             c:Class;
                    st:Student;
OnRequest           st.addCourse();
Perform             c.updateClassCount();
EndTriggerSpec
```

Figure 5 - OSL trigger example

In addition to class, relationship, event, rule, and trigger constructs, OSL provides selector, iterator, repeater, process, task, and signal constructs [15]. The selector construct allows a subset of objects that satisfy a given condition to be selected from a larger set of objects. The iterator construct separates the selection of object in a set from their processing. Everytime the iterator defined in a set is invoked, it returns one element in the set based on a selection criteria defined as part of the iterator until there is no more element. The repeater construct takes a set of objects and an operation and applies the operation to each element of the set. OSL tasks are meaningful units of work that are either executed completely or are not executed at all. The same way that states provide isolation from the attributes of objects, tasks provide isolation from the methods of objects. The invocation of the methods of objects are hidden in the tasks. An OSL process is an independently executable unit that has its own states and memory. Processes communicate with each other via signals. The functionality provided by the application are defined as OSL processes.

The prototype implementation of OSL is available. Figure 6 shows the block diagram of OSL implementation. OSL-IF is the OSL internal form that provides the in-memory representation for the OSL translator and encapsulator. OSL translator generates C++ code for OSL specifications. OSL encapsulator parses a collection of C++ classes and generate the equivalent OSL classes. Once a library class has been encapsulated, OSL users can define other OSL constructs, such as events and triggers on the class and enhance its functionality by adding semantics through those OSL constructs.

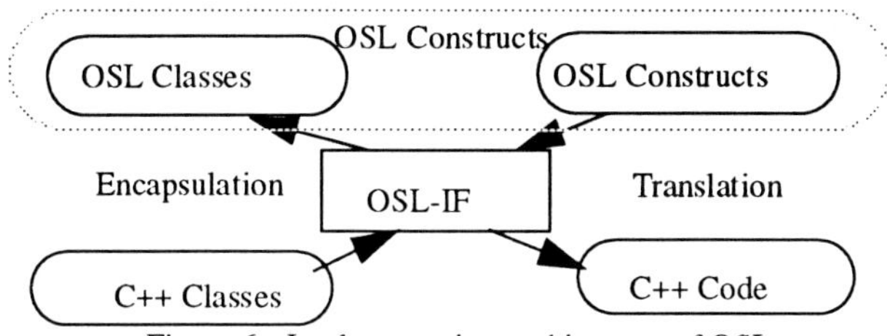

Figure 6 - Implementation architecture of OSL

3.2 OCADS Domain Modeling Tool

DMT [16] is a graphic user interface to OSL. It supports the creation of application domain models through the graphic manipulation of OSL modeling constructs. Through the simple "point-and-click" action of the mouse, iconic forms of the OSL constructs are created and their various properties such as name, inheritance relationships, context, participants and compositions are defined. This is similar to sketching the model on a paper. The modeler can then select each construct in the sketch and specify its details using forms that are presented by the system and are partially filled by the information already available through the sketch. The specifications of the details and sketching maybe interleaved and in general is an iterative process.

The models developed using DMT can be saved and edited at a later point in time for extensions and modifications. DMT models may be defined using the OSL textual representation and then browsed and edited through the DMT. DMT provides a default automatic layout that can be modified and saved. The OSL models defined graphically can be translated to C++ or to OSL textual representation. The OSL Encapsulator encapsulates C++ classes in OSL classes. DMT provides transformations from any representation of the model (graphics, OSL text, C++) to any other representations.

In addition to providing a convenient way for defining models using OSL, on line help and error checking, DMT provides extensive browsing, filtering, and abstraction facilities to simplify the construction and use of large domain models. Any construct in the model can be searched for by name, any types of constructs that are not of interest at the time of browsing the model can be filtered out, and any types of constructs that are the focus of attention can be expanded for more detailed representation. The DMT has been implemented using GuidePower [17] and C++. The current version of DMT uses file system to provide model persistency. This makes sharing a model by multiple simultaneous users as well as the incremental extensions of large models difficult. The next version of DMT will use ODBII [18] as a persistent model repository.

Application domain experts using DMT can define icons, representations, and interactions for each construct in the model. This is similar to MVC (Model, View, and Controller) model. The icon and the representation are like the view component. The interactions are like the controller components. The DMT domain models are presented to ABT by their views and controllers rather that by their generic icons and forms. The next section gives an overview of OCADS ABT.

3.3 OCADS Application Building Tool

Once the domain model is available, application developers will use domain specific objects in the model to build applications using the ABT [19] of OCADS. ABT uses the OSL constructs Relationship, Rule, Trigger, Event, Selector, Repeater and Iterator for composing domain objects to realize application logics.

In every application, in addition to the application domain, there are other domains such as the graphic user interface domain that the application developer will need to understand and utilize. The graphic user interface domain is of special importance because all sophisticated applications require high-level graphic user interfaces. In many user interface intensive applications the development of the user interface accounts for a major portion of the application development cost. In OCADS building the graphic user interface will follow the same paradigm as building the application itself. In the same way that applications are built using the application domain objects and the composition schemes provided by OCADS, user interfaces are built using the user interface domain model and the set of composition schemes provided by OCADS.

ABT consists of six functional components, namely the ABT Main Window, the ABT Object Window, the ABT Interface Window, ABT Data Link editor, ABT Control Link Editor, and the ABT Debugging and Testing Environment. The process of application development using ABT may be divided into four steps:

1. Invoke the ABT Main Window to create a new application or to modify an existing application.
2. Compose the application objects using the ABT Object Window.
3. Assemble the application user interface with the interface domain objects using the ABT Interface Window.
4. Build, debug, test and refine the application.

ABT allows the application interface to evolve independently of the application logic. The application back end is built from a set of the application objects belonging to the application domain created in the domain modeling phase. The application front end is built from a set of user interface objects such as buttons and forms in a predefined OCADS user interface domain. Building an application user interface is in fact building an application on top of the OCADS public user interface domain. Fig. 7 shows the ABT object.

The Object Window allows graphical instantiation of domain classes and their compositions through relationships, activation of rules, and registration of objects on events. Instantiation of classes and relationships is achieved by selecting an object from the object palette and dragging it onto the working canvas. Each object or relationship icon is associated with an instantiation form. Registering the interest of an object on an event is done as follows:

1. Select the object that may raise the event from the working canvas.
2. Select the interested object, and then click on event register on the link menu.
3. Fill out the Event Registration Form shown in Figure 8.

Assume, the instance hs of Heating System is interested in the event StopHeat raised by bedroom1 (see figure 7). After selecting hs, the bedroom1 and the event registration

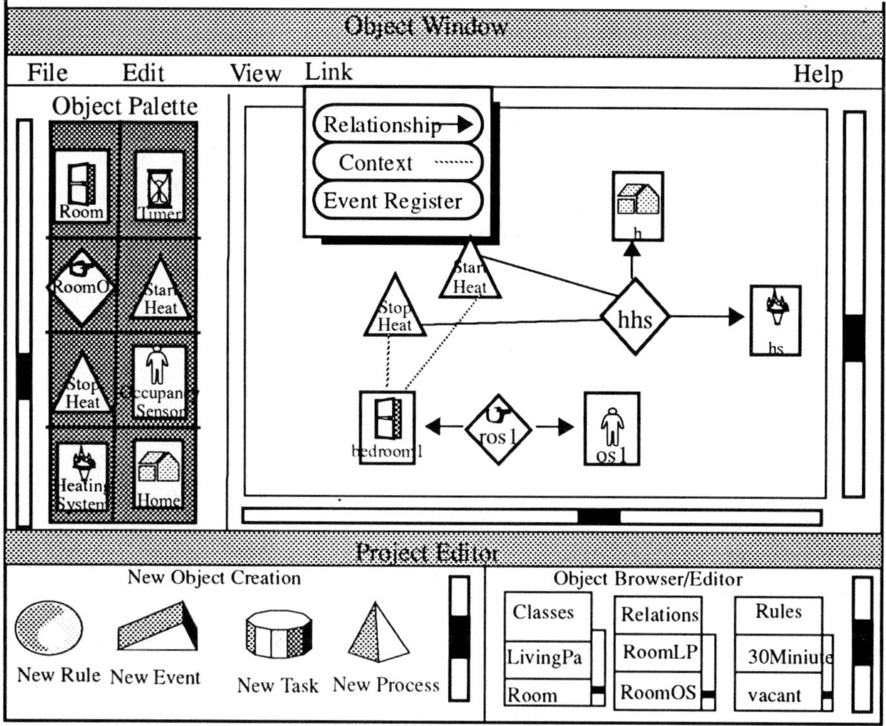

Figure 7 - ABT Main Window

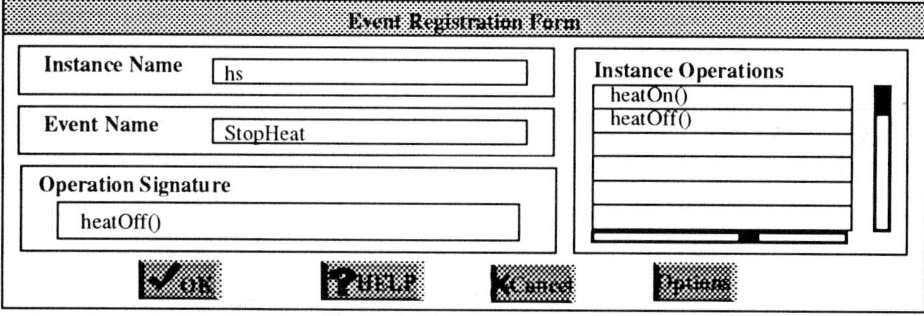

Figure 8 - Event registration

entry in the menu, the event registration form in figure 8 is presented to user. User can then select any operations from the Instance Operations defined on the object hs as the event handler. If the handler field is not filled then when the event is raised, instead of executing an event handler, hs will get notified.

4 Concluding Remarks

The implementation of the first version of OSL and DMT has been completed at the Object Technology Research Laboratory. This prototype includes an OSL to C++ code generator and an encapsulator. DMT provides a high level graphic and form based interface for OSL users who develop application domain models. OSL encapsulator takes C++ class libraries and encapsulates them as OSL classes. Once C++ classes are encapsulated, the OSL rules, triggers, events, tasks, signals, and processes that span multiple C++ and OSL classes can be specified. The design of ABT and prototype experimental implementation of certain aspects of it are underway. IP is closely investigated as the basis of ABT implementation after necessary enhancement and extensions.

Acknowledgment

The work on OSL design and development project has been funded by Fujitsu, Japan, Fujitsu Network Transmission Systems, USA, U S West Advanced Technologies, USA, and Santa Clara University, USA.

References

[1] Simon Karfinkel and Michael Mahoney, "NeXTstep Programming Step One: object-Oriented Application", Springer-Verlag, 1993.

[2] Lynn Andrea, "Delegation Is Inheritance", OOPSLA'87.

[3] "ObjectVision 2 Reference Guide", Borland International Inc., copy right 1991.

[4] Yuzuru Tanaka, "Intelligent Pad", Japan Computer Quarterly, 1993, No. 92.

[5] Sam S. Adams, "Meta Methods: The MVC Paradigm", HOOPLA, July 1988.

[6] "ObjectBuilder C++ User Interface Builder User Guide Release 1.0," ParcPlace Systems, Inc.

[7] D. Fishman, et. al., "IRIS: An object-oriented database management system," ACM Transaction on Office Information Systems, 5, 1, PP. 48-69, Jan. 1987

[8] M. A. Ketabchi, N. Sehgal, S. Dasananda, R. Mikkilineni, X. Li, "Modeling Activities of Application Domains," International Conference on Applications of Databases, June 1994, Sweden.

[9] F. Belina and D. Hogrege, "the CCITT - Specification and Description Language SDL," Computer Network and ISDN System 16, North-Holland, Amsterdam, the Netherlands, 1988-89, pp. 311-341.

[10] J. B. Wordsworth, "Software Development with Z: A Practical Approach to Formal Methods in Software Engineering", Addison-Wesley, 1992

[11] Oscar P. Lopez, Fiona Hayes, Stephen Bear, "Oasis: An Object-Oriented Specification Language", Proceedings of the CAiSE, 1992, Valencia

[12] Valdis Berzins, Luqi, "Software Engineering with Abstractions", Addison-Wesley, 1990.

[13] Moller-Pederson et al., "Rationale and Tutorial on OSDL: An Object-Oriented Extension od SDL", Computer Networks, Vol. 13, No. 2, 1987.

[14] David Duke, Roger Duke. "Towards a Semantics for Object-Z," Lecture Notes in Computer Science no. 428, Springer-Verlag, 1990.

[15] M. A. Ketabchi, S. Dasananda, R. Mikkilineni, X. Li, "OSL User Guide," Technical Report, TR#OTL-1994-8, Object Technology Lab, Santa Clara University, 1994.

[16] A. Antablian, Z. Li, M. Ketabchi, "DMT User Guide," Technical Report, TR#OTL-1994-9, Object Technology Lab, Santa Clara University, 1994.

[17] "GuidePower User Manual", Fujitsu, Japan, Inc.

[18] "ODBII User's Guide," Fujitsu, Japan, Inc.

[19] H. Xu, M. A. Ketabchi, "OCADS ABT," Technical Report, TR#OTL-1994-10, Object Technology Lab, Santa Clara University, 1994

Flora: A Functional-Style Language for Object and Relational Algebra *

Michael Novak, Georges Gardarin, and Patrick Valduriez

INRIA-Rocquencourt, Projet Rodin,
B.P. 105, 78153 Le Chesnay Cedex, France
email: novak@madonna.inria.fr, [Georges.Gardarin, Patrick.Valduriez] @inria.fr

Abstract. Flora is a low-level language for implementing object-oriented databases. It is not intended as a user language, but rather as an intermediate language capable of supporting a variety of higher-level languages and applications. Flora has a very general data model with complex values and objects, constructs for specifying data storage, and a functional-style action language that incorporates set processing operations and a user-defined function capability. Flora provides the low-level building blocks that allow the calling language to appropriately model higher-level constructs such as classes and inheritance, and to build complex queries in a manner that readily supports various optimization schemes.

1 Introduction

Relational databases have succeeded in traditional business data processing for one major reason: the availability of a high-level query language (relational calculus) which increases user productivity and enables automatic optimization. The basis for such optimization is the mapping of relational calculus into relational algebra, which is an *intermediate* language suitable for direct implementation.

To address a larger class of applications, with new requirements in terms of computing power (e.g., recursion, complex updates) and modeling (e.g., complex objects), *object-oriented databases* (OODB) are emerging. We believe the objective should be to provide a more powerful model and language while retaining the primary advantage of relational databases (i.e., high-level, optimizable language). The basis for a OODB language can be a rule-based language, such as Datalog, with an object-oriented model supporting concepts like object identity, classes, methods, and type inheritance. IQL [1] and Logres [4] are examples of powerful OODB languages which differ in their type systems and query language primitives. A OODB language can also be made upward compatible with relational databases by extending SQL in a language like ESQL [9] or XSQL [12], viewed as a syntactic variation of a more formal Datalog-based language.

Although many high-level OODB languages have been proposed, this is not the case for intermediate OODB languages. One reason may be the position that a simple extension of relational algebra to deal with nested relations [15]

* This work was partially funded by the Esprit project IDEA.

is sufficient. However, if the full power of an object model, in particular, object identity, and constructs like recursion, are to be supported, then the problem of coming up with a language which is both a good target language and a good vehicle for optimization and efficient implementation remains.

There have been a few efforts in designing and implementing intermediate languages, e.g., Fad [8], Pil [11] and Reloop [6]. Reloop is mostly focused on extending relational algebra to deal with complex objects. Fad is a general database programming language with constructs for manipulating complex objects within the parallel DBMS Bubba [3]. But, its general purpose nature was a major source of difficulties for compilation into efficient code. Pil is lower-level, adopts a RISC (Reduced Instruction Set Computer) design approach, and provides a value-based model with a set of optimizable and parallelizable language features. However, it does not directly support object concepts.

Flora is an intermediate language for compiling a language such as Logres or ESQL for execution on DBS3 [2], a parallel database system developed within the Esprit project IDEA. The main design objective is that it be a simple, algebraic language incorporating support for an object-oriented data model and advanced computational capabilities. It is not intended as a general database programming language, but rather as a convenient target language for compiling a variety of high-level languages. Therefore, Flora supports complex values and complex objects with object identity, while excluding high-level concepts such as class inheritance. It combines the modeling power of the object-oriented paradigm with a manipulation language designed specifically as a good vehicle for optimization and parallelization.

2 Data Model

In order to support high-level data models, Flora must be capable of modeling complex objects. Also, since Flora must be compatible with a variety of high-level models, the data model must be general enough for a variety of models to map easily into it. To this end, Flora provides direct modeling of complex data (both values and objects), along with the associated definition and manipulation capabilities, but no direct support for high-level concepts such as classes. Like O2 [Lecluse88] and Exodus [Carey88], Flora differentiates between values and objects (both may be arbitrarily complex). However, unlike most high-level models, only the minimal capabilities needed to deal with complex objects are supplied. Thus, high-level concepts such as a class mechanisms are not supported. Instead, they can (and should) be provided by higher-level tools in the client environments. Thus, Flora avoids the generally hopeless task of mapping one complex class inheritance mechanism into another, while also providing the ability to support multiple class-based systems.

2.1 Data Types

Flora types can be broken into two categories, atomic and structured. The Flora atomic types include **bool**, **int**, **float**, **string**, and **extern** [16]. Structured types are user-defined types built with the atomic types. Structured type constructors in Flora are *tuple* and *collection*. A tuple is a record of attributes, each attribute having a name and a value (can be atomic or structured). We use square brackets to represent the tuple type constructor.

A collection is composed of a number of data elements. By adding specific constraints (e.g., key uniqueness) or access methods (e.g., indices), different implementations and access methods can be obtained. Currently, Flora supports two general collection constructors: *multiset* and *list*, and a host of built-in functions for manipulating them (described in the next section). We use the term *set* instead of multiset in the rest of this paper, except where it may be ambiguous.

Objects and values are distinguished between in Flora. Each object has a unique identity (a logical address created automatically by the system) that uniquely identifies the object and allows object sharing and an updatable state which stores the data elements of an object. The state may consist of values or other objects. An object is accessed implicitly via its identity. Even though an object's type may change via object migration, it's identity will remain unchanged. A value has no unique identity and is thus not sharable.

All Flora data has a default value upon creation. For objects, it is **null** (an unknown or nonexistent object with no valid state). For values, it is a valid value of the correct type (e.g., zero for integers and empty set for sets).

Although there is only one equality operator in Flora (=), there are actually two kinds of equality, identity and simple. Identity equality compares two object references to see if they reference the same object, and simple equality compares values. Thus, object references are tested for identity equality and values, which have not notion of identity equality, are tested for simple equality. A value may be compared with the state of an object, but comparing a value with an object reference results in a type error.

2.2 Low-Level Support

Since we wish to support a variety of high-level data models, Flora provides low-level support that enables data to be modeled as flexibly as possible. The design choice generally made is to sacrifice features in favor of increased flexibility. Thus, the compiler responsible for producing Flora code must specify rules for Flora to follow when handling persistency, data deletion, etc.

Type Compatability. Type compatability in Flora is based on name, not structure, due to ease of implementation. A simple name-based subtyping mechanism was also introduced into Flora primarily so that subclasses in the higher level would not have to be "artificially" mimiced in Flora, and to allow for function overloading. Since the Flora data model is quite simple (e.g., we don't have classes), we have chosen a very simple subtyping mechanism. A subtype will be compatible where a parent type is specified, however, Flora will not do any checking for structural compatability. It will be up to the higher-level to guarantee "safe" usage. A sample type and subtype definition is:

```
type obj([name:string]) person;
type obj([name:string, ID:int]) student subtype of person;
```

Data Persistence. Persistence of objects in a Flora program is defined explicitly at the object level. Thus, persistence is orthogonal to type (the property of persistence is attached to the object, not its type). The same types can uniformly describe transient or persistent objects. That is, specific objects (values cannot be persistent except when encapsulated in an object), not specific types, are made persistent. Transient objects become persistent if referenced by a persistent object. This gives Flora maximum flexibility for persistence modeling.

Object Migration. Most current object-oriented data models do not support object migration, but there are several that do. Although the way object migration is handled differs in [Cacace90], [Kim90], and [Ghelli90], they all support only migration from a class to one of its subclasses. In [Danforth92a], objects may migrate to any class with a common ancestor using *up* and *down* operations. Object migration in Flora is less restrictive than in these models. Flora allows an object to migrate from a type into any other type desired. Thus, Flora is capable of supporting these other views of object migration. The price paid is that the higher level must provide the mechanism for insuring that a migration does not cause type inconsistencies.

In general, there are three main steps to object migration: 1) deleting any object references that may become mistyped, 2) doing the migration (changing the type and updating the state), and 3) rebuilding the necessary object references. Flora provides direct support only for step two. To change the type of object **x** to **newtype** and its state to **newstate** (this argument is optional and default values are used if it is not given), the following built-in is invoked:

```
migrate(x, newtype, newstate);
```

3 Action Language

The Flora action language is made up of definitions and expressions. Data is defined and created using the action language, while types are not. Definitions include variable definitions and function definitions. Expressions also include two kinds, those that return data (*data expressions*), and those that do not (*action expressions*). Data expressions include variables, function calls, etc. Action expressions include control actions (**if** and **else**), and special actions, such as assignment, object deletion, etc. The main reason for this division is to provide sound semantics, especially for optimization. Thus, in some cases we may allow only a data expression as an argument in order to isolate or minimize side effects.

3.1 Data Expressions

Data expressions may be simple data (constant, data variable, or constructed data) or functions that return data. The functions include operators, as well as built-in, user-defined, and external functions, Although not a general purpose language, Flora also provides some general purpose constructs, such as arithmetic, logical, and string manipulation operators, and assignment.

Built-in functions include generic functions applicable to all types and specialized functions for dealing with specific types (such as tuples or collections). Collections, in particular, have a large set of built-ins associated with them: **count**, **empty**, **exists_in**, **extent**, **reduce**, **remove**, and **select**. Those applicable only to sets are **choice**, **difference**, **insert**, **intersection**, and **union**. **Concat**, **insert_at**, **nth**, **remove_at**, and **replace_at** are applicable only to lists.

Of particular interest are **extent**, **reduce**, and **select**. **Extent** returns a collection of all objects of a given type. **Reduce** takes a binary function and a collection as arguments, then reduces the collection to one element by applying the function pairwise to each element of the collection. Thus, **reduce(+, x in {1,2,3})** returns **6**.

Select was designed with two main goals in mind: to provide a powerful, general purpose way of constructing Flora queries, and as a basis for optimization. It is primarily for the second reason that we have the restriction that select expressions should not be nested if it is possible to write the same query in a non-nested manner. This restriction will not diminish the expressive power of a Flora program, but may slightly diminish the ease of writing certain queries. Since Flora is meant to be an intermediate language, this is not particularly significant. The syntax, with the third argument being optional, is:

```
<select> ::= select(<data expr>, <range expr>, <formula>)
```

The following query returns set of all people live in the same city as all their children. Note that **x.children** is an implicit form of **x.state.children**.

```
type obj([name:string, residents:set(Person)] City;
type obj([name:string, city:City, children:set(Person)]) Person;
select(x, x in extent(Person),
          forall y in x.children (x.city = y.city));
```

3.2 Action Expressions

Action expressions may be *control actions* or *special actions*. Neither return data. Control actions (**if** and **while**), which are used to control the sequencing of actions have a syntax very similar to that of C (shown in a later example). The special actions include compound expressions, **delete**, **make_persist**, and **return**. To help predict and isolate side effects for the purpose of optimization, **assignment** is also classified under the action expressions.

4 A Database Example

How Flora can be used to implement a high-level application can best be seen through an example. Figure 1 shows a very simple schema for a computer network, where **computer**, **micro**, **multiuser**, **mainframe**, and **workstation**

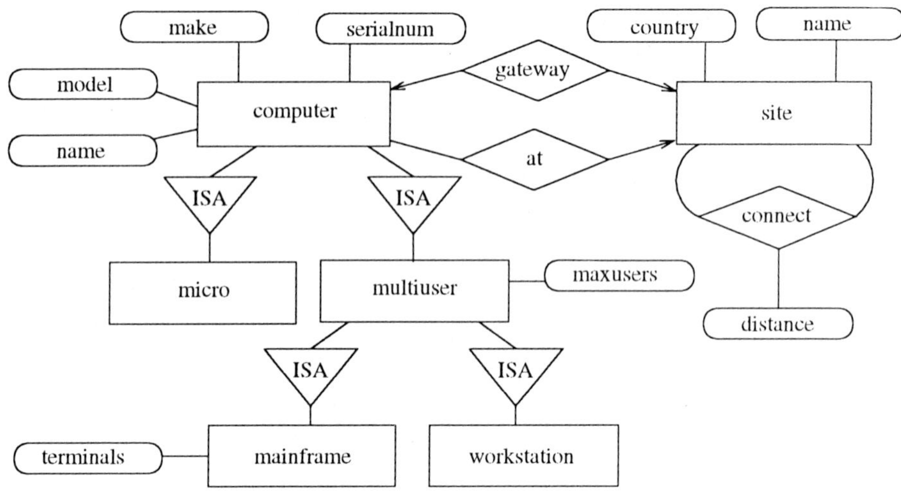

Fig. 1. Computer Network Schema

represent a class hierarchy and sites have the following three relationships; 1) with other sites they are directly connected to (many-to-many), 2) with the computer that is the gateway for the site (one-to-one), and 3) the other computers at that site (one-to-many).

4.1 Modeling Data

The schema model shown in Figure 1 has several possible interpretations. We assume that a subclass inherits all attributes and all methods of a superclass. Thus, any method applicable to a class, must be supported by all its subclasses. This is a fairly common interpretation, however, it is not the only possible one (also not the only one that Flora can support). Given this interpretation, there are still several ways that Flora can model this schema.

Separating the Class Hierarchy and Relationships. One obvious way of modeling the class hierarchy is to simulate a class hierarchy in Flora, and to represent non-ISA relationships as tuples containing the related objects, as follows:

```
type obj([name:string, country:string]) site;
type obj([make:string, model:string, name:string,
                                    serialnum:int]) computer;
type obj([make:string, model:string, name:string,
        serialnum:int]) micro subtype of computer;
type obj([make:string, model:string, name:string, serialnum:
           int, maxusers: int]) multiuser subtype of computer;
```

```
type obj([make:string, model:string, name:string, serialnum:
         int, maxusers:int]) workstation subtype of multiuser;
type obj([make:string, model:string, name:string, serialnum:
         int, maxusers:int, terminals:int]) mainframe subtype
                                                of multiuser;
type obj([st:site, cmps:set(computer)]) at;
type obj(set(st1:site, st2:site, dst:distance]) connect;
type obj([st:site, cmp:computer]) gateway;
```

One-to-one relationships (**gateway**) are modeled as simple tuple objects, one-to-many (**at**) as tuple objects consisting of a simple attribute and a collection, and many-to-many (**connect**) as collection objects consisting of tuples.

Combining the Class Hierarchy and Relationships. The data can also be modeled by building the relationships into one of the two related types. In this approach, the types **at**, **connect**, and **gateway** do not exist.

```
type obj([name:string, country:string, gateway:computer
                  connect:set([st:site, dst:distance])]) site;
type obj([make:string, model:string, name:string,
                           serialnum:int, at:site]) computer;
type obj([make:string, model:string, name:string,
            serialnum:int, at:site]) micro subtype of computer;
type obj([make:string, model:string, name:string, serialnum:int,
         at:site, maxusers:int]) multiuser subtype of computer;
type obj([make:string, model:string, name:string, serialnum:int,
      at:site, maxusers: int]) workstation subtype of multiuser;
type obj([make:string, model:string, name:string,
               serialnum:int, at:site, maxusers:int,
               terminals:int]) mainframe subtype of multiuser;
```

4.2 Data Manipulation

To support a variety of high-level languages and applications, Flora must support many data manipulation techniques, including complex updates, aggregation, recursion, data migration, etc. The following examples (based on one of the above schemas) show how these techniques are implemented using Flora.

Calculating a Shortest Path. Of primary importance is supporting the kind of recursion necessary for compiling constructs such as Datalog rules into a low-level language. This can be supported using the **while** construct. For example, finding the shortest path between nodes can be done using a semi-naive computation of all paths originating at **from**, finding the subset that end at **to**, then chosing the shortest. We assume the shortest path contains the least nodes, not the shortest total distance. We start with an empty set (**allpaths**), then use

while to return the set of all paths that begin at **from**. Then, **reduce** uses the output of **select** (which finds the subset of paths between **from** and **to**) and the binary function **short** to find the single shortest path. Sites and connections are modeled using the second data model above.

```
type list(site) path;
type set(paths) pathset;
type list(p:path, s:site) tmptype;

path short(p1:path, p2:path) {           // returns shorter path
  if count(p2) < count(p1) then return(p2); else return(p1);
}

path shortest (from:site, to:site) {     // returns shortest path
  pathset : allpaths;  // set of all paths beginning at from
  pathset : delta;     // set of new paths
  tmptype : tmp;

  insert(delta,set(from));
  while not(empty(delta)) do {             // until no new paths
     allpaths := union(allpaths,delta);
     tmp := select([p:x,s:z], x in allpaths and y in
       x[count(x)].connect and z in y.site, not(exists_in(x,z));
     select (insert_at(t.p,count(t.p) + 1, t.s), t in tmp);
     delta := select(t.p, t in tmp);
  };
  return(reduce(short, select(x,
          x in allpaths, x[1] = from and x[count(x)] = to)));
}
```

While finds all paths of length one, then all of length two, and so on. Another stop condition for the loop could be the existence, within **delta**, of a path ending in the **to** site. This would stop the loop much sooner, but would result in searching the delta each time through the loop.

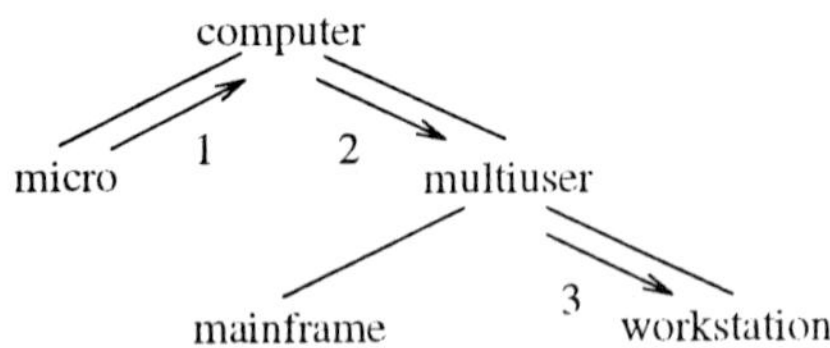

Fig. 2. Object Migration

Object Migration. Now, suppose we wish to upgrade one of the micro computers at a site into a workstation. The standard migration path is shown in

Figure 2. Using the first data model above and assuming the micro **x** has state **[model:"Generic", name:"myhost", serialnum:0001]**, the Flora code for upgrading it to a workstation with 4 users maximum, looks as follows:

```
migrate(x, mainframe, [make:string, model:x.model, name:x.name,
                       serialnum:x.serialnum, maxusers:4]);
```

The references to this object within objects of the types **at** and **gateway** do not need to be changed, since all these types reference an object of type **computer**, which is a parent type of both **micro** and **multiuser**.

5 Conclusions

In this paper, we have presented the design of Flora, an intermediate language for supporting database languages on parallel systems. Flora is a simple, algebraic language with type and language constructs suitable for mapping high-level language features such as class inheritance and recursive rules.

Flora's data model is quite general and yet simple. It supports values and objects, which can be arbitrarily nested within tuples and collections. Explicit values are of primary importance for exchanging transient data between nodes in a parallel system. Data persistence is orthogonal to type, therefore allowing support for reachability-based persistence at a higher-level. Finally, Flora provides simple, consistent semantics for default values, thus easing error control.

The Flora action language provides a full set of data manipulation and algebraic query capabilites combined with a syntax that provides for ease of optimization. To this end the language provides built-ins (e.g., to perform a computation on data elements), control actions for execution sequencing, and a generalized select built-in for doing algebraic queries on complex data.

We have used a computer network application to illustrate Flora. We have shown that Flora could support different implementations of the same class hierarchy, depending on the higher-level requirements. Data manipulation was illustrated by examples of associative searches on complex objects with path expressions and recursive query (shortest path) support through iteration (using the while construct).

A prototype version of the Flora system, including the optimizer, currently runs on top of the O2 database system. Concurrently, important components of the parallel database system such as the optimizer, the parallelizer and the run-time support are being significantly extended to support Flora.

Acknowledgements

The authors wish to thank all the participants of the IDEA project for their support, and particularly S. Bressan, S. Ceri, P. Dechamboux and E. Simon for important suggestions during the design of Flora.

References

1. S. Abiteboul, P. C. Kanellakis: Object Identity as a Query Language Primitive, *ACM SIGMOD Conference Proceedings*, Portland, 1989, pp. 159-173.
2. B. Bergsten, M. Couprie, P. Valduriez: Prototyping DBS3, a Shared Memory Parallel Database System, *Proceedings of the International Conference on Parallel and Distributed Information Systems*, Miami, December 1991.
3. H. Boral, W. Alexander, L. Clay, G. Copeland, S. Danforth, M. Franklin, B. Hart, M. Smith and P. Valduriez, Prototyping Bubba, a Highly Parallel Database System, *IEEE Transactions on Knowledge and Data Engineering*, Vol. 2, No. 1, March 1990.
4. F. Cacace, S. Ceri, S. Crespi-Reghizzi, L. Tanca, R. Zicari: The Logres Project: Integrating Object-Oriented Data Modeling with a Rule-Based Programming Paradigm, *ACM SIGMOD Conference Proceedings*, Atlantic City, 1990, pp. 225-236.
5. M. Carey, D. DeWitt, S. Vandenberg: A Data Model and Query Language for EXODUS, *ACM SIGMOD Conference Proceedings*, Chicago, 1988.
6. S. Cluet, C. Delobel, C. Lecluse, P. Richard: RELOOP: An Algebra Based Query Language for an Object-Oriented Database System, *Proceedings of the First International Conference on Object-Oriented and Deductive Databases*, Kyoto, December 1989.
7. S. Danforth, E. Simon: A Data and Operation Model for Advanced Database Systems, in *The Next Generation of Information Systems - from Data to Knowledge*, Springer Verlag, 1992.
8. S. Danforth, P. Valduriez: A FAD for Data-Intensive Applications, *IEEE Transactions on Data and Knowledge Engineering*, Vol. 4, No. 1, February 1992.
9. G. Gardarin, P. Valduriez: ESQL2, an Extended SQL2 with F-logic Semantics, *Proceedings of the IEEE International Conference on Data Engineering*, Phoenix, Arizona, February 1992, pp. 320-327.
10. G. Ghelli: A Class Abstraction for a Hierarchical Type System, *Proceedings of the Third International Conference on Database Theory*, Springer Verlag LNCS No. 470, 1990.
11. W. Hasan, R. Krishnamurthy: PIL: An Optimizable Functional Language for Data Intensive Applications *Proceedings of the Fifth International Workshop on Persistent Object Systems: Design Implementation, and Use*, San Miniato, Italy, 1992.
12. M. Kifer, W. Kim, Y. Sagiv: Querying Object-Oriented Databases, *ACM SIGMOD Conference Proceedings*, San Diego, 1992, pp. 393-402.
13. W. Kim, N. Ballou, J. Garza, D. Woelk: Architecture of the Orion Next-Generation Database System, *IEEE Transactions on Knowledge and Data Engineering*, Vol. 2, No. 1, March 1990.
14. C. Lecluse, P. Richard, F. Velez: O2, an Object-Oriented Data Model, *ACM SIGMOD Conference Proceedings*, Chicago, 1988.
15. H. Schek, Nested Relations, a Step Forward or Backward, *IEEE Data Engineering Bulletin*, Vol. 11, No. 3, September 1988.
16. P. Wilms, P. Schwarz, H. Schek, L. Haas: Incorporating Data Types in an Extensible Database Architecture, *Proceedings of the Third International Conference on Data and Knowledge Bases*, Jerusalem, Israel, June 1988.

On the Optimal Top-down Evaluation of Recursive Queries

Yangjun Chen Theo Härder

Department of Computer Science, University of Kaiserslautern
P. O. Box 3049, 67653 Kaiserslautern, Germany

Abstract. In this paper, we present a top-down but set-oriented method for handling recursive queries. Based on the RQA/FQI's mechanism for recording "path information" [14], we try to eliminate many of the expansion operations that have to be done by any other top-down strategy. Further, we speed up the evaluation for cyclic data by generating most answers to a query directly from the intermediate results and the relevant path information instead of evaluating them by performing algebraic operations. In this way, high efficiency can be achieved. On one hand, the search space becomes smaller in our method. On the other hand, the cost of generating an answer is much less than that of evaluating an answer by algebraic operations or by other standard methods.

1. Introduction

One area in the field of logical programming, known as deductive databases, is concerned with developing logic-based programming systems which manipulate large quantities of data efficiently. An important matter of research in such systems is the evaluation of recursive queries expressed as sets of Horn Clauses over a database. A number of strategies for the problem have been developed: interpreted and compiled approaches, optimization and evaluation strategies, top down and bottom up, recursive and iterative [2, 3, 5, 10, 11, 16]. In this paper, we present an optimal top-down method for handling recursive queries, based on the RQA/FQI (*Recursive Query Answering / Frozen Query Iteration*) algorithm. RQA/FQI has been introduced for handling recursive axioms in deductive databases by Nejdl [14]. It is a variant of the QSQR method [17] and proves to be complete over all kinds of linear recursion defined by means of function free Horn Clauses [14]. The algorithm consists of two steps. In the first step of it, the search tree is expanded top down, storing not only the answers already found but also incomplete branches. In the second step, all incomplete branches of the search tree are processed by completing the repeated subqueries iteratively. We show that an optimal method can be developed based on the "two-step" fashion and the mechanism, available in RQA/FQI, for recording "path information". First, we try to reduce the search space generated during the expansion step, by removing redundant expansion operations. Then, we further separate the second step into two phases. In the first phase, we compute only some answers for the first incomplete branch of the search tree. In the second phase we generate the remaining answers for the other incomplete branches directly from the answers already found and the corresponding path information. Because the search space is smaller than that of RQA/FQI and the cost of generating an answer is much less than that of evaluating an answer by performing algebraic operations, the refined algorithm improves the efficiency of RQA/FQI significantly.

As with the other top-down strategies, a preprocessor is implemented to reorder the body predicates such that the predicates with some of their variables bound to constants (in terms of the query submitted to the system) are before the predicates whose variables have no bindings. In addition, a further step is required. If any two correlated non-recursive predicates are separated by a recursive predicate, we change the position of that one after the recursive predicate such that both of them are before the recursive predicate. (We say that two predicates are correlated if they have at least one shared variable.) This requirement is not only for optimization, but also for the application of the technique for generating answers directly (see below). An example of a reordered rule is the non-linear version of the same-generation program:

$sg(x, y)$:- $flat(x, y)$
$sg(x, y)$:- $up(x, z_1), sg(z_1, z_2), flat(z_2, z_3), sg(z_3, z_4), down(z_4, y)$.

In the remainder of the paper, we assume that all rules are reordered in this way. In the next section, we briefly outline the RQA/FQI algorithm and the necessary terminology from [14]. In Section 3, we describe the optimal algorithm for linear recursion. In Section 4, we compare the computational complexity of the refined algorithm with other strategies. Section 5 is a short conclusion.

2. RQA/FQI and Relevant Definitions

In this section, we briefly describe the RQA/FQI algorithm and some relevant concepts which are necessary for clarifying the main idea of our refined algorithm. For further details, please refer to the description in [14].

RQA/FQI is a top-down, but set-oriented method. That is, although bindings for arguments are propagated in a tuple-oriented manner, queries over database predicates or database views (database equivalent predicates - described by non-recursive predicates) are processed set-oriented. The newly produced answers are stored in the Prolog database and retrieving these tuples from the Prolog database is done tuple-oriented again. In order to avoid infinite derivations, RQA/FQI distinguishes between two classes of repeatedly appearing subgoals and treats them differently.

Definition 2.1 A *repeated incomplete query* (RIQ) is a query which is subsumed by a previous query which has not yet been answered completely (i.e., subsumed by a query which has appeared earlier on the same derivation path as the RIQ). We say that a query q is subsumed by another query q' if q appears after q' and at the same time has the same bound arguments as q'. For instance, query s(c, u) appearing in the search tree of Example 3.2 (see below) is subsumed by s(c, y).

The RIQ's are the only nodes which cannot be expanded during an expansion process (in order to avoid cycles). However, cutting the execution path in the search tree at an RIQ may affect the completeness of any goal relying on this subgoal. If an RIQ is encountered, only the answers already produced can be used in the further expansion of the search tree. (in RQA/FQI, such expansions are postponed to the second step and done iteratively.)

Definition 2.2 A *repeated complete query* (RCQ) is a query which is subsumed by a previous query which has already been answered completely (i.e., subsumed by a query which has appeared but not on the same derivation path as the RCQ).

If an RCQ is encountered, all its answers can be taken from the answers already produced. In order to guarantee the completeness, RQA/FQI introduces an artificial subgoal added in front of each recursive subgoal to record the bindings evaluated so far. After the expansion process, we can then compute the remaining answers in terms of the instantiations for these subgoals in some way. This consideration leads to the following three definitions.

Definition 2.3 A *propagation subgoal* (PSG) is a special artificial subgoal added in front of each recursive subgoal in a clause. This can be done manually or by a preprocessor. For example, the rules defining ancestor can be transformed by a preprocessor into:

ancestor(*x*, *y*) :- *parent*(*x*, *y*)
ancestor(*x*, *y*) :- *parent*(*x*, *z*), PSG(id, *x*, *y*, *z*), *ancestor*(*z*, *y*).

The purpose of adding PSG's in a clause is to record and propagate the arguments instantiated so far. Therefore, a PSG for a recursive predicate contains the arguments occurring in the predicate of the head of the clause and the predicates of the body occurring before the recursive subgoal in the original clause (assumed that we proceed from left to right).

Definition 2.4 A *frozen query* (FQ) is a query defined by a newly constructed clause (when an RIQ is encountered during the expansion process) which contains an RIQ as a subquery in its body.

For example, if *Q* :- *E, P, S* is a clause and *P* is an RIQ, then *Q* is a frozen query. It will be stored in the form FQ (*Q* :- PSG, *P*, *S*), where PSG is a propagation subgoal. Together with a set of different instantiations of the propagation subgoal a frozen query stores the current step of the evaluation for a clause which cannot be evaluated completely in an expansion process.

Definition 2.5 A *critical path* (CP) is a path of the search tree which can not be completely evaluated in the expansion of the search tree (i.e. a path from an RIQ to its subsuming query). Each critical path is represented by a frozen query and a set of different instantiations of the associated PSG and can be used to evaluate the remaining answers in an iteration process (see below).

Based on the above description, RQA/FQI can be summarized as follows:

In the first step of the algorithm, a recursive processing strategy like that of PROLOG is used, expanding the search tree top-down. Answers to recursive queries are stored to be re-used later. The expansion stops whenever RIQ's are encountered, or after subqueries are answered completely using basic facts and nonrecursive predicates. The second step uses a different approach. There are still branches (critical paths) in the search tree which are incomplete because of a subsumed query (RIQ), and therefore have been stored as *frozen clauses* (frozen queries and the set of instantiations for propagation subgoals). These are processed using an efficient variant of Least Fixpoint iteration over these frozen clauses, working bottom-up both from database facts and facts which have already been found as answers to recursive queries. This step is necessary in order to propagate all answers of the evaluated subsuming goal to its corresponding frozen counterparts (subsumed goal). It corresponds to plugging new answers into subsumed queries and using these answers to expand the search tree further. If new recursive subgoals are found during the iteration step, they are expanded by means of calling the top-down evaluation strategy recursively.

3. Refined Algorithm

Now we present our refined algorithm. First, we discuss the possibilities of the refinement by using path information. Then, we summarize the key ideas of the new method in subsection 3.2..

3.1 Main Ideas of Refinement

In this subsection, we clarify the main ideas of the improvement by tracing the steps of RQA/FQI for two examples, with each being used to show what the search space reduction means and how some answers can be directly generated, respectively. As the first example, consider the following program:

Example 3.1 axioms: (1) $s(x, y)$:- $r(x, y)$
(2) $s(x, y)$:- $p(x, z)$, $s(z, w)$, $q(w, y)$.

facts: $p(a_1, a_2)$, $p(a_1, a_3)$, $p(a_2, a_3)$, $r(a_3, b_3)$, $q(b_3, b_2)$, $q(b_2, b_1)$.

The corresponding version of RQA/FQI is:

(1) $s(x, y)$:- $r(x, y)$
(2) $s(x, y)$:- $p(x, z)$, $PSG(id, x, y, z)$, $s(z, w)$, $q(w, y)$.

Given the query ?-$s(a_1, y)$, the search tree depicted in Figure 1 will be generated by RQA/FQI.

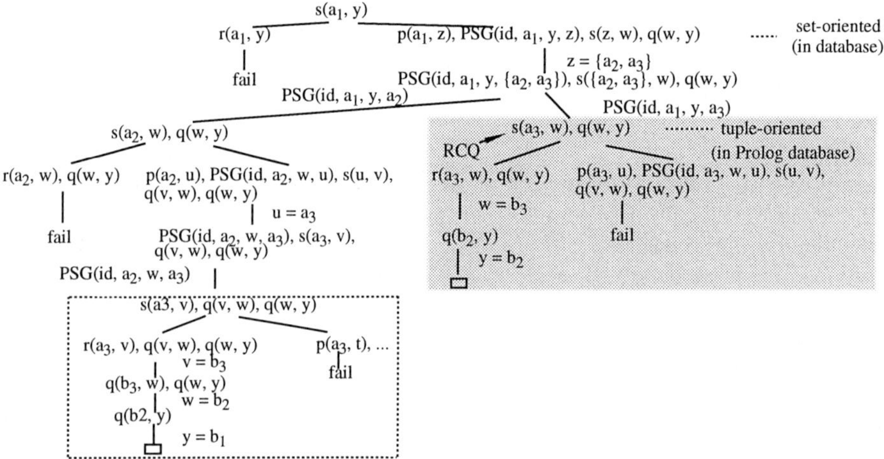

Figure 1. Search tree for Example 3.1

This is a normal behaviour of the top-down strategy except that the path information is explicitly recorded as a set of instances of the propagation subgoal (When a propagation subgoal is encountered, we only store it and do nothing else.) Since no cyclic path exists (no RIQ's are encountered during the expansion), the second step does not need to be executed.

Note that the path information is very useful for optimizing the expansion step. For example, during the above process, two paths shown in Figure 2 have been recorded. (For exposition, we assume that the propagation subgoal for the initial query ?-$s(a_1, y)$ is $PSG(id, \_, \_, a_1)$)..

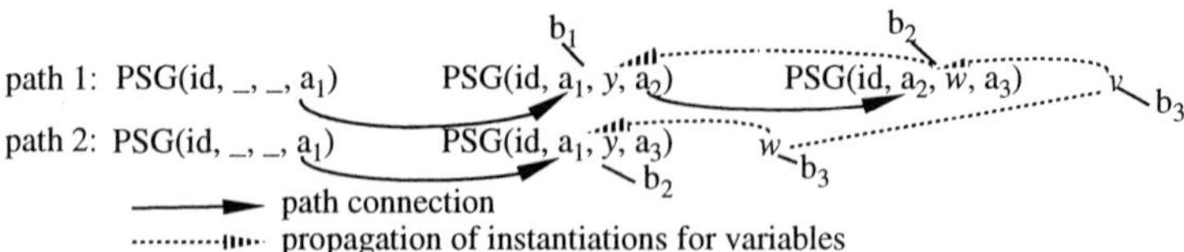

Figure 2. Paths recorded as sets of instances of PSG's

After the subtree rooted at "$s(a_3, v)$, $q(v, w)$, $q(w, y)$" (enclosed by a dotted rectangle in Figure 1) is expanded, variables v, w and y appearing on the first path are instantiated to b_3, b_2 and b_1, respectively. From this and the fact that the fourth argument of PSG(id, a_2, w, a_3) (on the first path) has the same value (a_3) as the fourth argument of PSG(id, a_1, y, a_3) (on the second path), we can directly instantiate the variables appearing on the second path instead of expanding the corresponding subtree. That is, we instantiate variables w and y on the second path to b_3 and b_2 respectively, without searching the subtree rooted at "s(a_3, w), q(w, y)" (marked with a grey rectangle in Figure 1). The reason for this is that since the fourth argument of PSG(id, a_2, w, a_3) on the first path is instantiated to the same value as the fourth argument of PSG(id, a_1, y, a_3) on the second path (in other words, "s(a_3, w), q(w, y)" is subsumed by "s(a_3, v), q(v, w), q(w, y)"), variable w on the second path will have the same value as variable v on the first path. Further, in terms of the program property described in the introduction, variable y on the second path will be instantiated to the same value as variable w on the first path, and so on. Figure 2 helps to clarify this claim. (If the first path is shorter than the second, only some of the answers for the second path can be generated and the remaining answers must be evaluated by the standard methods.)

In this way, any subtree rooted at some RCQ can be cut off, since in this case, we can feasibly find the relevant answers in terms of the path information available. Therefore, much time will be saved.

Next, we show another possibility of optimization in the case of cyclic data. In this case, several critical paths will be stored during the first step and will be processed iteratively in the second step. Consider the following example.

Example 3.2

axioms: (1) s(x, y) :- r(x, y)
(2) s(x, y) :- p(x, z), s(z, w), q(w, y)

facts: p(c, d), p(c, b), p(b, c), p(b, f), p(f, c)
r(d, e)
q(e, a), q(a, i), q(i, o), q(o, g).

Given the query ?-s(c, y), RQA/FQI first generate a search tree as shown in Figure 3.

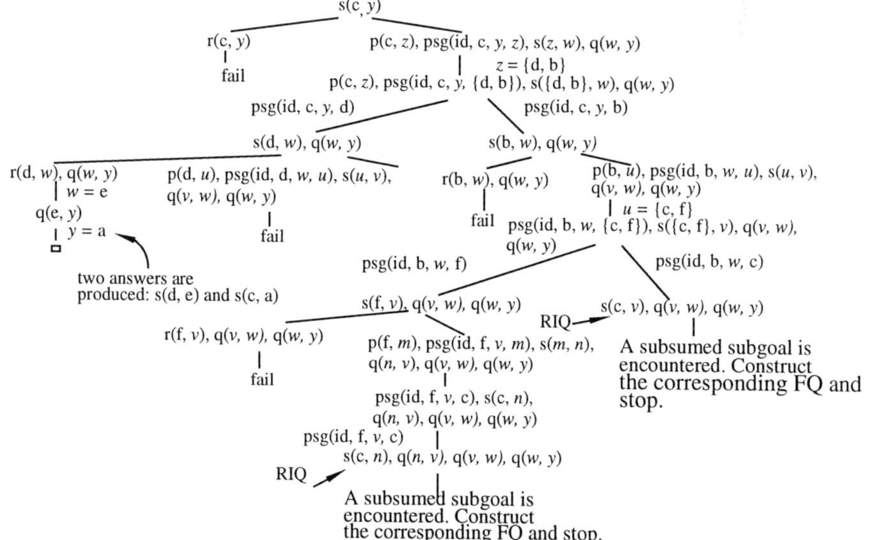

Figure 3. Search tree for Example 3.2

During the expansion step, two answers: s(d, e) and s(c, a) are produced. In addition, a set of propagation facts:

psg(id, c, *y*, d), psg(id, c, *y*, b), psg(id, b, *w*, f), psg(id, b, *w*, c), and psg(id, f, *v*, c),

is generated and a frozen query: FQ(s(*x*, *y*) :- PSG(id, *x*, *y*, *z*), s(*z*, *w*), q(*w*, *y*)) is constructed. By running the frozen query against the propagation facts and the answers already found (in a bottom-up manner), the following answers will be found:

s(b, i), s(c, o), s(b, g)
s(f, i), s(b, o), s(c, g), s(f, g).

Observe that the set of propagation facts corresponds to two critical paths (cyclic p aths):

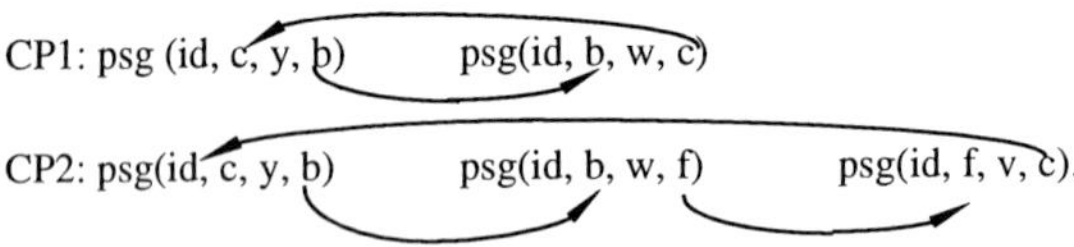

In this case, we can further optimize RQA/FQI by elaborating the second step as follows. First, we only evaluate some answers for the first critical path. Then, we generate the answers for the second path directly from the associative PSG's and the answers already found. For example, the answers for the first path are s(b, i), s(c, o) and s(b, g), and so we can directly generate s(f, i) from s(b, i) and the third PSG (psg(id, f, *v*, c)) on the second critical path instead of evaluating it by performing algebraic operations. Similarly, we can directly generate s(b, o) from s(c, o) and the second PSG (psg(id, b, *w*, f)) on the second critical path, and so on. The following figure illustrates this feature.

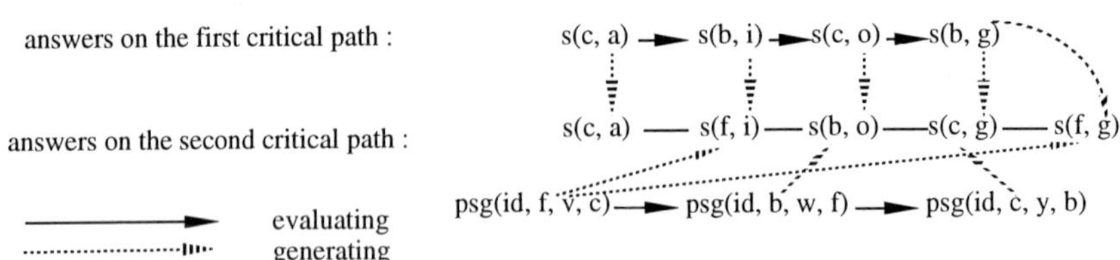

Figure 4. Answers on two critical paths associated with

FQ(s(*x*, *y*) :- psg(id_1, *x*, *y*, *z*), s(*z*, *w*), q(*w*, *y*))

In general, the new answers generated for one critical path can further be used to generate new answers for the other critical paths again. For the above example, we can imagine two circles (C_1 and C_2) with each corresponding to a cyclic path. We run respectively along C_1 and C_2 in the same direction and generate some answers for C_2 from C_1 at each step. We do this continually until no new answers for C_2 can be generated. Then we generate new answers for C_1 from C_2 in the same way. This process is repeated until no more new answers can be generated. We describe the process formally as follows. Let C_1 be the first cycle $psg_1 \leftarrow psg_2 \leftarrow \cdots \leftarrow psg_n \leftarrow psg_1$ and $A_1 = \{a_1, ..., a_n, a_{n+1}, ..., a_{2n}, ..., a_{in}, ..., a_{in+j}\}$ the answer set evaluated along C_1, where *i*, *j* are integers and $0 \le j \le n$. (It should be noticed that each a_l ($1 \le l \le in + j$) is a subset which is evaluated by running the frozen query with PSG subgoal being instantiated to psg_l.) Let C_2 be the second cycle $psg_1' \leftarrow psg_2' \leftarrow \cdots \leftarrow psg_m' \leftarrow psg_1'$. In addition, we define

$$A_2 = \{a_{n+1}, ..., a_{2n}, ..., a_{in}, ..., a_{in+j}\},$$
$$A_3 = \{a_{2n+1}, ..., a_{in}, ..., a_{in+j}\},$$
$$\dots\dots$$
$$A_i = \{a_{in}, ..., a_{in+j}\}.$$

Then, in terms of A_k $(1 \le k \le i)$ and C_2, we can generate the first part of answers for C_2 as follows. (Note that we do not necessarily compute all A_k $(1 \le k \le i)$. In practice, each time an A_k needs to be used in the computation, we shrink A_{k-1} by leaving out certain sets (some a_i's))

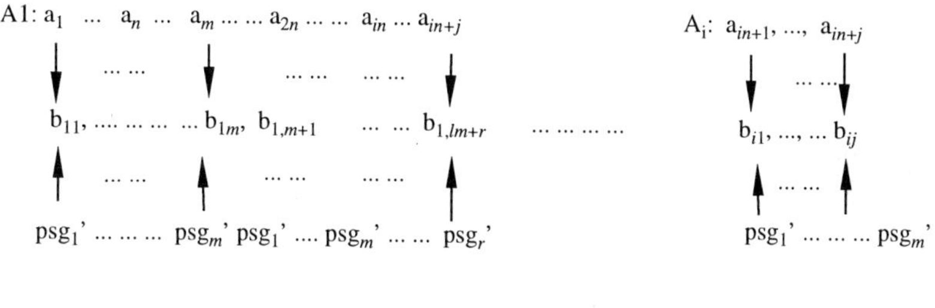

Figure. 5 Illustration of answer generation

If $n = m$, no more new answers can be generated after this step. Otherwise, in terms of C_1 and the newly generated answers for C_2, we can further generate some new answers for C_1 in the same way. To this end, we first merge the newly generated answers.

$$b_1 = b_{11} \cup b_{21} \cup ... \cup b_{i1},$$
$$\dots\dots$$
$$b_{lm+r} = b_{1,lm+r} \cup \dots\dots .$$

(This process is called a *merging operation.*) Then, we construct B_k $(1 \le k \le l - 1)$.

$$B_1 = \{b_1, ..., b_{lm+r}\},$$
$$B_2 = \{b_{m+1}, ..., b_{lm+r}\},$$
$$B_3 = \{b_{2m+1}, ..., b_{lm+r}\},$$
$$\dots\dots$$
$$B_l = \{b_{lm+1}, ..., b_{lm+r}\}.$$

(This process is called a *separating operation.*)

In terms of C_1 and B_k $(2 \le k \le l)$, some new answers for C_1 can be generated as described above. Note that B_1 will not be used in this step. It is because no new answers can be generated in terms of it, i.e., using it, only the same answer set as A_1 can be generated. In the next step, some new answers for C_2 can be generated in terms of C_2 and the newly generated answers for C_1.

Because evaluating answers by performing algebraic operations requires access to the external storage or search of large relations but the "generating" operation happens always in the main memory and requires only access to small data sets (i.e. the answers already evaluated or generated on the other critical path), the generation of answers is much more efficient than the evaluation of answers. Thus, the algorithm is optimal in time complexity in comparison with RQA/FQI.

3.2 Description of the Refined Algorithm

Based on the analysis above, the new algorithm (for linear recursion) should be composed of four processes:

(1) expansion process which acts like that of Prolog, but with "search space reduction" being integrated.
(2) generation process for RCQ's, by which all answers for repeated complete queries (RCQ's) are generated directly in terms of the associated path information and its subsuming query.
(3) iteration process, by which some answers for the first critical path are evaluated in a bottom-up fashion.
(4) generation process for RIQ's, by which all answers for the other critical paths are generated directly from the associated PSG's and the answers already found.

Due to space limitations, we can not describe the algorithm in detail. The reader can find a formal description of the algorithm together with a more detailed discussion in [8].

4. Comparison with other Strategies

In order to compare the time complexity of the refined algorithm with RQA/FQI, we consider the following linear recursive program:

s(x, y) :- r(x, y)
s(x, y) :- p(x, z), s(z, w), q(w, y).

Assume that the graph representing the relation for "r" contains n_r nodes and e_r edges, the graph for "p" contains n_p nodes and e_p edges, and the graph for "q" contains n_q nodes and e_q edges. At an abstract level, the expansion phase of RQA/FQI can be viewed as two processes: a constant propagation process and a variable instantiation process. The former corresponds to the traversal of the graph for "p". The latter corresponds to the traversal of the graphs for "r" and "q". If the indegree and outdegree of each node i in the graph are denoted as *indegree*(i) and *outdegree*(i), respectively, then the cost of the expansion phase of RQA/FQI is:

$$O(e_p) + O(e_r) + O\Big(\sum_{(i,j)\in A} indegree(i) \times outdegree(j)\Big),$$

where A denotes the set of answer tuples. O(e_p) is the cost for the traversal of the graph for "p". O(e_r) is the cost for the traversal of the graph for "r". The cost for the traversal of the graph for "q" is $O\Big(\sum_{(i,j)\in A} indegree(i) \times outdegree(j)\Big) = O(e_p \cdot e_q)$. The graph shown in Fig.6(a) helps to clarify the result.

From this graph, we see that crossing the edge (i, j), each edge incident to j will be visited indegree(i) times.

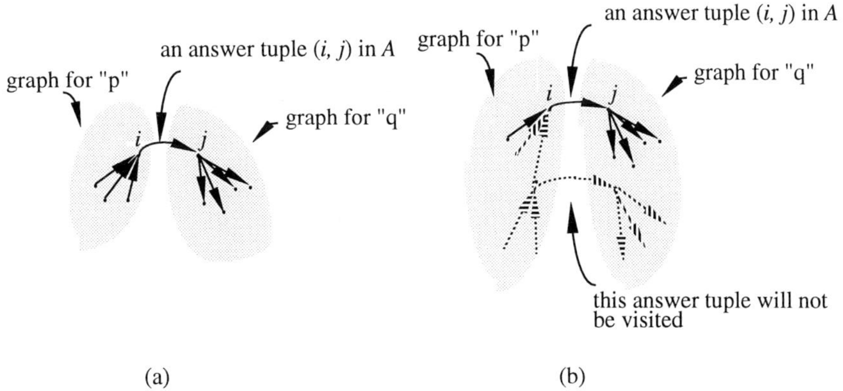

Fig. 6 Illustration of graph traversal

Similarly, the expansion phase of the refined algorithm can be viewed as two processes. However, due to the answer generation for RCQ's, the cost is reduced to

$$O(e_p) + O(e_r) + O(\sum_{some\ (i,j)\ \in\ A} outdegree\ (j)\ ).$$

See Fig.6(b) for illustration. On one hand, due to the "answer generation", each edge incident to j can be visited at most once. On the other hand, some answer tuples may not be traversed for the same reason. Therefore, its time complexity is smaller than $O(n_p \cdot e_q)$.

In the above analysis, we do not take the cost for "generating answers" into account. In fact, in comparison with the cost of evaluating an answer (by algebraic operations: *join, selection, projection, ...*), the cost of generating an answer is very little such that we don't need to consider it. (In practise, the time complexity of a computation mainly depends on the number of accesses to the external storage which in turn depends on the number of the relations participating in the computation and their cardinalities). In addition, in the case of cyclic data, the refined algorithm can further improve the efficiency of RQA/FQI by a factor consisting of the number of the critical paths if we do not take into account the cost of generating an answer.

Many other strategies have been proposed to handle this problem, among which the magic set method receives much attention. For the above simple program, the magic set method works in a two-phase manner. In the first phase, the magic set is produced by executing magic rules [13]. In the second phase, modified rules are executed using the magic set to restrict the bottom-up computation. Essentially, these two phases correspond to the constant propagation process and the variable instantiation process of a top-down evaluation, respectively. Therefore, the cost of the magic set method is $O(e_p \cdot e_q)$ (see [13] for details). The counting method is an indexed version of the magic set method. It improves the magic set method by a constant factor. In fact, its time complexity is $O(n_p \cdot e_q)$. In addition, a lot of experiments have been done [6] and it shows that QSQR, an another top-down strategy [17], has the same time complexity as the magic set method. Therefore, our method is also better than QSQR.

5. Conclusion

In this paper, a top-down but set-oriented algorithm for the evaluation of recursive queries has been presented which is much more efficient than RQA/FQI. The key idea of the improvements is to distinguish between RCQ's and RIQ's and to use the path information associated with them elaborately. We may reduce the search space by cutting off any subtree rooted at a RCQ because we can feasibly find the relevant answers in terms of the path information available. Then we minimize the time complexity by separating the second step of RQA/FQI into two phases and generating most answers for each critical path directly from the intermediate results and the associated PSG's after some of answers for the first critical path are evaluated, without performing algebraic operations. In practice, since performing algebraic operations requires access to the external storage or search of large relations but the "generating" operation happens always in the main memory and requires only access to small data sets, the cost of generating an answer is much less than that of evaluating an answer. Thus, the refined algorithm achieves high efficiency.

References

1. Aly, H. and Ozsoyoglu, Z. M., Synchronized Counting Method, Proc. of the 5th International Conf. on Data Engineering, Los Angeles, 1989.
2. I. Balbin, G. S. Port, K. Ramamohanarao and K. Meenakshi, *Efficient Bottom-up Computation of Queries on Stratified Databases,* J. Logic Programming, November 1991, 295-344
3. F. Bancilhon, D. Maier, Y. Sagiv and J. D. Ullman, Magic Sets and Other Strange Ways to Implement Logic Programs, *Proc. 5th ACM Symp. Principles of Database Systems,* Cambridge, MA, March 1986, 1-15.
4. F. Bancilhon, Naive Evaluation of Recursively Defined Relations, in: *On Knowledge Base Management Systems-Integrating Database and AI Systems,* Springer-Verlag, 1985.
5. F. Bancihon and R. Ramakrishnan, An Amateur's Introduction to Recursive Query Processing Strategies, *Proc. 1986 ACM-SIGMOD Conf. Management of Data,* Washington, DC, May 1986, 16-52.
6. S. Ceri, G. Gottlob and L. Tanca, Logic Programming and Databases, Springer-Verlag, Berlin,1990
7. C. Chang, On the Evaluation of Queries Containing Derived Relations in Relational Database, in: *Advances in Data Base Theory,* Vol. 1, Plenum, 1981.
8. Y. Chen and T. Härder, An Optimal Top-down Evaluation Algorithm for Recursive Queries, ZRI-Report, University of Kaiserslautern, Germany, 1994.
9. R. W. Haddad and J. F. Naughton, Counting Method for Cyclic Relations, in: *Proceedings of the 7th ACM SIGMOD-SIGACT Symposium on Principles of Database Systems,* 1986, pp. 16-23.
10. J. Han, Chain-Based Evaluation - A Bridge Linking Recursive and Nonrecursive Query Evaluation, *Proc. 2th Int. Workshop on Research Issues on Data Engineering: Transaction and Query Processing,* Los Alamitos, CA, February 1992,132-139.
11. L. J. Henschen and S. Naqvi, On Compiling Queries in Recursive First-Order database, *J. ACM,* **31**(1), 1984, 47-85.
12. M. Kifer and Lozinskii E.L., Filtering Data Flow in Deductive Database, *Proc. 1st International Conf. on Database Theory*, Roma, September 1986.
13. A. Marchetti-Spaccamela, A. Pelaggi, and D. Sacca, Comparison of Methods for Logic-query Implementation, *J. Logic Programming*, 1991:10:333-360.
14. W. Nejdl, Recursive Strategies for Answering Recursive Queries - The RQA/FQI Strategy, *Proc. 13th VLDB Conf.* Brighton 1987, 43-50.
15. S. Shapiro and D. Mckay, Inference with Recursive Rules, in: *Proceedings of the 1th Annual National Conference on Artificial Intelligence,* 1980.
16. J. D. Ullman, *Principles of Database and Knowledge-Base Systems, Vol. 2,* Computer Science Press, Rockville, MD, 1989.
17. L. Vieille, Recursive Axioms in Deductive Databases: the Query-Subquery Approach, *Proc. First Int. Conf. on Expert Database System,* L.Kerschberg ed., Charleston, 1986.

A Study of Spatial Clustering Techniques

Akhil Kumar

College of Business
University of Colorado, Boulder, CO 80309.

Abstract. This paper proposes a new interleaving-based method for spatial clustering developed by combining gray codes with a new ordering technique called *nu-ordering*. This method is compared with two existing interleaving-based techniques and another technique called hilbert-ordering. The performance comparison is done by means of a simulation study. The results show that the choice of the technique affects the clustering performance dramatically. Among the four techniques considered, both nu-ordering and hilbert method outperformed the other two methods by more than 35%; however, with minor exceptions, the hilbert technique was the best among the four techniques evaluated.

1 Introduction

The need for indexing spatial data arises in any application where objects lie in multi-dimensional space. Consider the following queries:

- Find all gas stations in a one-mile square area around the Boulder campus on a map showing all gas stations in Colorado state.
- Find all employees who are less than 30 years old and make a salary greater than $100K.

In both cases, the objects under consideration (gas stations, and employees) lie in multi-dimensional space. Indexing techniques, like B-trees, which work well on linear data, do not perform as well when the data is in multidimensional space, and, therefore, new techniques have been devised.

Two of the earliest methods for organizing multidimensional data are Quad trees and K-D trees. Assuming two-dimensional data, Quad trees [6] successively divide the data space into four smaller quadrants at each stage by examining the X and Y coordinate values. On the other hand, K-D trees [1] divide the space into two parts at each stage by examining alternating coordinates, one coordinate at a time. Both these structures are primarily main memory resident and are not very suitable for secondary storage. These trees can also get unbalanced easily.

A common approach for organizing such data on secondary storage is to divide a k-dimensional space or region into smaller k-dimensional partitions or subregions, and store one or more partitions in a single disk block or a *bucket*. To answer a query, the relevant buckets are brought into main memory from disk and searched. In *Grid files* [8, 10], a directory is maintained to track the correspondence between partitions and disk buckets. In *KDB trees* [13], the regions are organized into a tree similar to a B-tree. The leaf pages of this tree correspond to disk buckets, while higher level pages encompass successively larger *non-overlapping* regions, which are navigated in order to locate the appropriate leaf page. R-trees [7] are somewhat similar; however, they permit non-overlapping regions. Both KDB-trees and R-trees can be maintained on secondary storage. Examples of other structures are BD trees [2, 3], and zkdb trees [11, 12]. (See [14] for an excellent discussion of these methods.)

Since the disk space is a continuum of buckets, it is logically one-dimensional. Therefore, a mapping is required from the multidimensional data space into the one-dimensional disk space. A very desirable property for this mapping to have is that it should be *distance preserving*, i.e. points that are close in the multidimensional space should also be close in the one dimensional space.

A naive technique for mapping is to number the buckets sequentially along one dimension (row-wise or column-wise) and then change one dimension at a time. But this does not work very well. A better technique for performing a distance-preserving mapping is called z-order. The basic idea behind z-order [11, 12] is that the partition number values along each dimension (in binary code) are interleaved together to form a single value that would correspond to a bucket number.[1] It was shown in [4] that even better clustering can be achieved by using *Gray codes* instead of binary codes for numbering each axis. *Gray codes* are also based on two values (0 and 1); but, they have the additional property that only one bit changes between any two successive numbers. Yet another method called hilbert-ordering was investigated at length in [5], This method is based on reflection and rotation of a basic pattern, and cannot be produced by bit interleaving. However, it was shown to be far superior to the above interleaving based methods.

In this paper, we propose a new ordering method also based on interleaving called *nu-ordering*, and compare it with the other interleaving based methods and the hilbert-ordering method. The rest of this paper is organized as follows. Section 2 describes the three clustering schemes in detail. Section 3 describes the results of various simulation tests comparing the clustering performance of the four methods. Section 4 gives a brief discussion of other work directly related to ours, and Section 5 concludes the paper.

2 Clustering Schemes

We first describe three existing clustering schemes, called BZ, GZ and H clustering, The first two are based on z-ordering with binary and gray codes, while the third one is based on hilbert ordering. Then, we turn to discuss a new proposal called GN clustering, based on nu-ordering with gray codes. For ease of exposition, we assume that the data space is two-dimensional, and that the data is distributed into square buckets of equal size. In general, the buckets need not all be of equal size so long as the data space is divided into a rectangular

[1] Both naive ordering and z-ordering are explained at more length in Section 2.

grid, and an index is maintained to map individual grid elements into disk buckets. By mapping more than one neigboring grid elements into the same bucket, the bucket utilization can be improved. The clustering principles described here would still be applicable.

2.1 Binary codes with z-ordering (BZ Clustering)

BZ clustering (see [11, 12]) is based on z-ordering with binary codes. First, label each axis in binary code. Then, combine the X and Y coordinate for any bucket by interleaving them one bit at a time from left to right. This produces the pattern shown in Figure 1. Notice that in this figure, the X coordinate was interleaved before the Y coordinate to produce the zig-zag result called z-ordering. If the Y coordinate was interleaved first, then again the resulting pattern would be similar but rotated by 90 degrees.

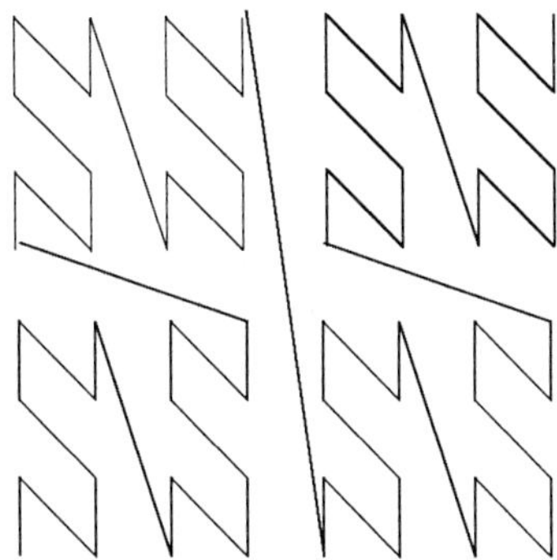

Fig. 1. Binary z-order (BZ) clustering

2.2 Gray Codes with z-ordering (GZ Clustering)

This section will, first, briefly review gray codes, and, then, describe how they are used in conjuction with z-ordering for designing a clustering scheme called GZ clustering.

Overview of Gray Codes Gray codes have the property that any two successive codewords differ in only one bit position [4]. The most common type of gray codes are called *binary reflected gray codes* and we shall refer to them simply as *gray codes.* We now briefly describe a simple recursive algorithm for generating a `m-bit` gray code. A 1-bit gray code consists of just two words, 0 and 1. A 2-bit code word is obtained by generating two branches from each 1-bit word as shown in Figure 2. The two branches are numbered 0 and 1 according to the following rule: if the number of 1's on the path so far is *even*, then branch "0" appears above branch "1"; else branch "1" appears above branch "0". To generate a m-bit gray code, simply extend the tree for a `m-1`-bit gray code, by producing two new branches from each leaf node, and numbering them appropriately according to the above rule. Now, the leaves of this tree are in order from top to bottom, and the gray code associated with a certain leaf node is simply determined by following the path from the root to that node and stringing together the bits along the path from left to right. Figure 2 shows how a 4-bit gray code is generated by this algorithm. By starting at the root and following the upper branch at each node, the top-most leaf node is reached, which corresponds to 0000 in gray code or decimal 0. On the other hand, if the lower branch is followed at each step from the root, then the bottom-most leaf node is reached which corresponds to 1000 in gray code or decimal 15. The complete set of gray codes for m=4 generated by this tree along with their binary and decimal equivalents are shown in Table 1.

The decimal value of a word in gray code is computed as follows. Assume there is a b-bit long number in Gray Code, $(G_b, G_{b-1}, \ldots, G_1)$, where G_b is the most significant bit. A corresponding parity vector $(P_b, P_{b-1}, \ldots, P_1)$ is constructed from G as follows: P_b `= 0;` P_j `= XOR(`$P_b, \ldots, P_j + 1$`), for` $j = 1, \ldots b-1$. Therefore, in the parity vector, bit P_b is always 0, while the values of other bits j are determined by taking the **`exclusive-or`** of bits b thru bit $j+1$ in G. Now the decimal value of gray code G is: $\sum_{i=1}^{i=b}(\overline{P_i}G_i + P_i\overline{G_i})2^{i-1}$.

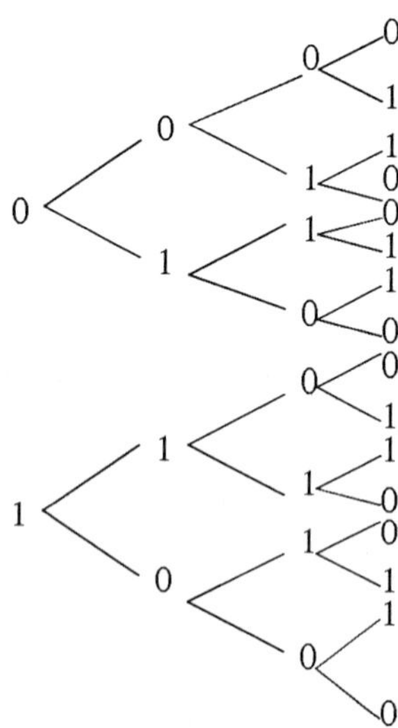

Fig. 2. Generating gray codes

decimal value	binary value	gray code
0	0000	0000
1	0001	0001
2	0010	0011
3	0011	0010
4	0100	0110
5	0101	0111
6	0110	0101
7	0111	0100
8	1000	1100
9	1001	1101
10	1010	1111
11	1011	1110
12	1100	1010
13	1101	1011
14	1110	1001
15	1111	1000

Table 1. Decimal, binary and gray code values

GZ Clustering To map an object from 2-dimensional space into one dimension, the `m-bit`-long X and Y coordinates (in gray code) are interleaved together producing a `2m-bit`-long string. This is called GZ clustering because it combines *Gray* codes with *z*-ordering. Figure 3 (a) gives an example of GZ clustering for `m=2`. This figure is different from Figure 1 in that the two axes are ordered in gray code sequence. However, as in the case of binary z-order, the X and Y coordinates for any square are again interleaved together to produce the 4-bit-long string. The gray code strings produced by the interleaving and their corresponding decimal values are shown inside each square. In the next section, we introduce a new ordering scheme called *nu-ordering*.

2.3 Gray Codes with nu-ordering (GN Clustering)

Now, we turn to describe a new ordering scheme for mapping two dimensional Gray codes into one dimension. Assuming each coordinate X and Y is m bits long, and x_i (y_i) is the ith bit from the left of the X(Y) coordinate ($i = 1, \ldots, m$), then *nu-ordering* [2] is performed as follows:

`If` m `is` *even*,
`f(X,Y) = concatenate(`$\overline{x_1}, \overline{y_1}, \overline{x_2}, \overline{y_2}, \ldots, \overline{x_m}, \overline{y_m}$`)`
`If` m `is` *odd*,
`f(X,Y) = concatenate(`$x_1, y_1, \overline{x_2}, \overline{y_2}, \ldots, \overline{x_m}, \overline{y_m}$`)`

[2] The name *nu-ordering* is given to this ordering scheme because the pattern it creates is a recursive pattern of alternating, lower-case n's and u's.

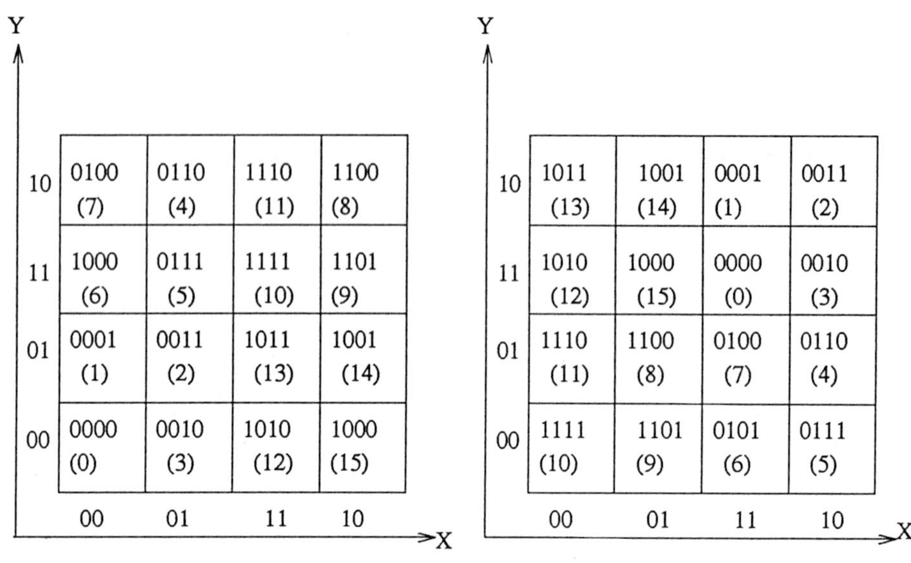

(a) Gray codes with z-ordering (GZ) (b) Gray codes with nu-ordering (GN)

Fig. 3. Examples of GZ and GN clustering schemes

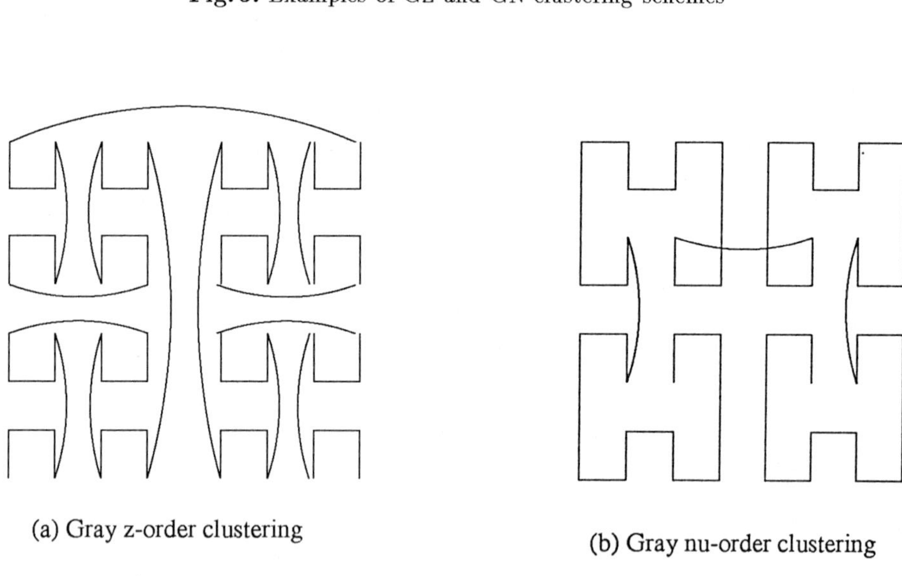

(a) Gray z-order clustering (b) Gray nu-order clustering

Fig. 4. Patterns made by GZ and GN clustering schemes

The function f(X,Y) above specifies how the individual bits of the X and Y coordinates are *concatenated* in order to map an object from 2-dimensional space into one dimension.[3] This scheme can also be generalized into k dimensions. In general, if m is *even*, the mapping function interleaves the inverse of each bit in the k coordinates; and, when m is *odd*, the mapping function interleaves the first bit of each coordinate unchanged, and the remaining bits are first inverted and then interleaved. Figure 3 (b) gives an example of nu-ordering with gray codes for $m = 2$. As in Figure 3 (a), the axes are again numbered in gray code sequence. The strings inside each square are obtained by combining the X and Y coordinates according to the above expressions that describe nu-ordering. The decimal equivalents of the strings (interpreted in gray code) are shown in parentheses. This clustering scheme developed by combining gray codes with nu-ordering is called GN clustering. Figure 4 shows the patterns created by the GZ and GN clustering schemes in a 8×8 space.

2.4 Hilbert Codes (H Clustering)

Hilbert ordering is produced by taking an initial pattern and rotating and reflecting it to produce a new pattern that spans a larger region. This idea is illustrated in Figure 5. The first pattern H_1 corresponds to the case where the X and Y coordinates are represented by one bit. In the next two patterns, H_2 and H_3, each coordinate is represented by 2 and 3 bits respectively. Given the first pattern, any subsequent pattern can be visually constructed in an inductive manner by the following instructions: Make a copy of the previous pattern and rotate the copy by 90 degrees clockwise. Place the rotated copy directly under the pattern. Connect the top left corner of the copy with the bottom left corner of the pattern. Make a vertically reflected mirror-image copy of this new pattern on the right. Join the two images. Basically, as shown in Figure 5, each successive pattern is four times the size of the previous pattern. Therefore, assuming there are four quadrants, the previous pattern is placed in the top-left quadrant; its rotated image is placed in the bottom-left quadrant and connected to it. Finally, a mirror image of the two left quadrants is placed in the two right quadrants, and connected.

An algorithm for determining the hilbert code for a given coordinate position in a $2^n \times 2^n$ grid is [5]:

Algorithm H1

1. Read in the n-bit binary representation of the x and y coordinates.
2. Interleave bits of the two binary numbers into one string.
3. Divide the string from left to right into two-bit strings, s_i, for $i = 1, \ldots, n$.
4. Give a decimal value, d_i, for each two bit string as follows: ''00" equals 0; ''01" equals 1; ''10" equals 3; ''11" equals 2.

[3] $\overline{x_i}(\overline{y_i})$ are the inverse values of $x_i(y_i)$, respectively, i.e., $x_i = 1 - x_i$.

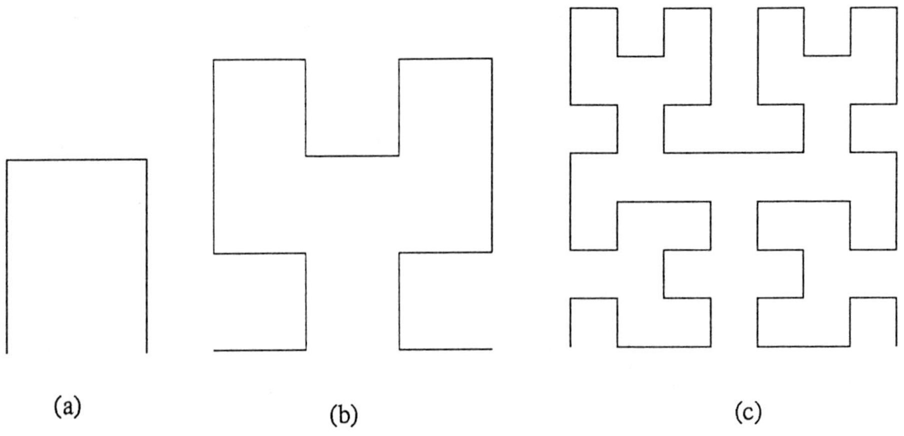

Fig. 5. Hilbert ordering (H_1, H_2, H_3)

5. For each number i in the array, if ...

   i=0 then switch every following occurrence of 1 in the array to 3 and every following occurrence of 3 in the array to 1;

   i=3 then switch every following occurrence of 0 in the array to 2 and every following occurrence of 2 in the array to 0;

6. Convert each number in the array to its binary representation (two-bit strings), concatenate all the strings in order from left to right, and calculate the decimal value.

2.5 Summary

In this section, we described three existing and one new scheme for clustering objects that lie in multiple dimensions. The BZ, GZ and GN codes are computed by examining the bits of each coordinate one at a time and interleaving them (or their inverse as in GN), while the H code is computed by an algorithm that involves some additional computational steps. In all the methods, the steps of clustering algorithm can be reversed to separate the individual coordinates if the clustered code value is known. We did not consider nu-ordering with binary codes because, when m is even, it would be exactly like z-ordering, while, when m is odd, it produces an even more unfavorable clustering than BZ clustering.

3 Measuring Performance by Simulation Experiments

3.1 Introduction and Overview of Tests

This section describes the results of experimental tests by means of simulation to evaluate the performance of the four different schemes discussed above. These results give insights into how the various methods fare relative to one another in a variety of situations.

Our simulation criterion is *the average number of clusters* of buckets that must be accessed to answer a query. For instance, say, the 9 buckets that must be accessed to answer a query are: 10, 12–13, 16–20, and 25. In this case there are 4 clusters; on the other hand, if the buckets to be accessed are numbered 10–14, and 22–25, this corresponds to only 2 clusters. From a clustering point of view, the second arrangement is 50% better than the first one. The simulation algorithm and a brief overview are given next, and the results of the experiments follow afterwards.

The BZ, GZ, GN and H clustering schemes were tested by simulation experiments using the above criterion. We considered a two-dimensional bucket space, and randomly generated (by simulation) the boundaries of rectangular query regions of various sizes within it as follows. The X and Y coordinates of the bottom-left corner of the query rectangle were generated randomly, and a query rectangle of certain given dimensions was placed there. Then, the number of clusters into which the buckets lying within the query region would fall was determined.

The steps of the simulation algorithm are listed in Figure 6. This experiment is repeated 1000 times and the average values are reported. The basic principle of the algorithm is identical for all the schemes; however, implementation details will vary according to the method of computing each code value for the various codes. The specific details of those computations are omitted here because they were covered in Section 2. The algorithm must randomly place a query region of a fixed size inside the data space, and determine the appropriate code value (BZ, GZ, GN or H) for each bucket that lies in the query region. For each bucket, the coordinates of its *successor* bucket, i.e. the bucket which follows next in the code sequence, must also be computed. Any time the successor of a bucket lies outside the query region, the variable `clusters` is incremented by 1. After this loop is executed 1000 times the average number of clusters is computed.

3.2 Vary total region size, query region fixed

In the first set of experiments, the size of the bucket space was varied, between 32×32 and 512×512, while the query region was a constant square of size 8×8 buckets. A bucket is identified by randomly generating its X and Y coordinates. Then, an 8×8 query region is placed there, and the number of clusters required to access all the buckets in the query region is computed. This experiment was repeated 1000 times by running the simulation algorithm of Figure 6, and the average values are reported in Table 2 for BZ, GZ and GN clustering.

```
Algorithm Simulation
clusters = 0;
repeat(1000 times)
begin
Generate a random query region of given size;
For each bucket inside the region {
 1. Calculate the {BZ, GZ, GN, H} code.
 2. Calculate the coordinates of {BZ, GZ, GN, H}-successor.
 3. If (successor is outside query region)
          clusters++;
                                  }
end
average = clusters/1000;
```

Fig. 6. Simulation algorithm

In Table 2, the percentages in parentheses show how these schemes fare in relative comparison with BZ clustering. The results show that GZ clustering is better than BZ clustering, but by a very small margin (usually less than 1%); however, GN clustering is better than both BZ and GZ clustering by approximately 35%. Finally, H clustering is the best among all four, with a 44% advantage over BZ. A second observation to be made from this table is that, for all three methods, the size of the total bucket space does not affect the average number of clusters or the relative performance of the various methods. The average number of clusters lies within a narrow 2% range even though the size of the bucket space varies widely.

total area	BZ	GZ	GN	H
32×32	16.02(0%)	15.89(0.9%)	10.48(35%)	8.87(44%)
64×64	16.17(0%)	16.06(0.7%)	10.58(35%)	8.99(44%)
128×128	16.11(0%)	16.01(0.6%)	10.56(34%)	9.01(44%)
256×256	16.10(0%)	16.01(0.6%)	10.49(35%)	9.00(44%)
512×512	16.25(0%)	16.17(0.5%)	10.64(35%)	9.07(44%)

Table 2. Vary total area, size of query region fixed at 8×8 buckets

3.3 Vary query region size, total bucket space fixed

In this section the bucket space was kept fixed at 512×512 buckets, while the size of the query region was varied from 4×4 buckets to 64×64 buckets. The purpose of this set of experiments was to see what impact the size of the query region would have on the relative performance of the various methods. Again, the simulation was repeated, and the results are shown in Table 3. The

total area	BZ	GZ	GN	H
4 × 4	8.28(0%)	8.15(1.6%)	5.80(30%)	5.04(39%)
8 × 8	16.25(0%)	16.17(0.5%)	10.64(35%)	9.07(44%)
16 × 16	32.34(0%)	32.29(0.2%)	20.26(37%)	17.16(47%)
32 × 32	64.50(0%)	64.47(0%)	39.60(39%)	33.25(48%)
64 × 64	128.53(0%)	128.51(0%)	78.11(39%)	65.18(49%)
128 × 128	256.55(0%)	256.54(0%)	154.97(40%)	129.24(50%)

Table 3. Vary size of query region (total space = 512 × 512 buckets)

total area	BZ	GZ	GN	H
4 × 8	10.94(0%)	10.87(0.6%)	7.41(32%)	7.08(35%)
4 × 16	15.97(0%)	15.59(2.4%)	10.56(34%)	11.11(30%)
4 × 32	25.84(0%)	24.58(1%)	16.82(35%)	19.22(26%)
4 × 64	45.31(0%)	42.14(7%)	29.18(36%)	35.27(22%)
8 × 16	21.63(0%)	21.59(0.2%)	13.87(36%)	13.11(39%)
8 × 32	31.99(0%)	31.53(1.4%)	20.26(37%)	21.16(34%)
8 × 64	52.27(0%)	50.72(3%)	32.89(37%)	37.11(29%)

Table 4. Vary rectangular query regions (X dimension is *shorter* than Y)

percentages in parentheses represent the relative improvement of a scheme over BZ.

This table shows that, again, GZ and BZ clustering perform about the same, with the improvement of GZ over BZ only between 0% and 1.6%. On the other hand, GN clustering is superior to BZ by 30% to 40%; while H clustering is still better than GN by another 9%. In fact, the relative superiority of GN increases from 30% to 40% as the size of the query region grows from 4×4 to 128×128. The relative superiority of H increases from 39% to 50% over the same range. Again, GN and H perform considerably better than BZ and GZ, with H even outperforming GN consistently.

On the other hand, the advantage of GZ over BZ, though minor through out, decreases from 1.6% to 0% while the size of the query region increases from 4 × 4 to 128 × 128.

total area	BZ	GZ	GN	H
8 × 4	13.24(0%)	12.75(3.7%)	8.94(32%)	7.04(39%)
16 × 4	22.98(0%)	21.55(6.2%)	15.14(34%)	11.05(52%)
32 × 4	42.35(0%)	38.86(8.2%)	27.54(35%)	19.11(55%)
64 × 4	80.88(0%)	73.28(9.4%)	52.22(35%)	35.11(57%)
16 × 8	26.53(0%)	26.02(1.9%)	16.94(36%)	13.12(51%)
32 × 8	46.86(0%)	45.24(3.5%)	29.57(37%)	21.24(55%)
64 × 8	87.30(0%)	83.25(4.6%)	54.80(37%)	37.35(57%)

Table 5. Vary rectangular query regions (X dimension is *longer* than Y)

3.4 Rectangular query regions

In the experiments above, only square query regions were considered. In the next set of experiments, we consider rectangular query regions in order to see whether making one dimension of the query region longer than the other would affect the relative performance of the clustering schemes. We also wanted to study how the orientation of the rectangle affected relative performance, i.e., if the longer side of the rectangle was along the X- or Y-axis. Consequently, in a 512 $\times$ 512 bucket space, we considered all combinations of rectangular query regions where one dimension was 4 and 8, and the other was 8, 16, 32 and 64. This set of rectangular regions was used for evaluating the three clustering techniques. Table 4 gives the results for regions in which the X dimension is shorter than the Y, while the opposite is the case for all the regions in Table 5.

These tables show that the absolute values of the results are indeed sensitive to the orientation of the query rectangle for all four schemes. A comparison across Tables 4 and 5 shows that the three interleaving based schemes are asymmetric, i.e., clustering is better when the side of the rectangle along the X axis is shorter than the side along the Y axis. However, the H scheme is almost perfectly symmetric. Moreover, in the interleaving based schemes, the relative advantage of one orientation of a rectangle over the other increases as the rectangle becomes larger. For instance, the 4×8 (see Table 4) query region clusters 17% better than the 8×4 region (see Table 5) using the BZ clustering scheme; however, the 4×64 query region clusters 44% better than the 64×4 region.

Tables 4 and 5 also show that the trend in relative performance across the three interleaving based schemes is quite similar to what was observed in the previous sets of experiments. For both orientations it can be seen that GN clustering is better than BZ by between 32% and 37%; thus, the orientation of the rectangle does not affect this relative performance gap. On the other hand, these tables also show that: (a) in general, the relative gap between GZ and BZ is larger for rectangular regions in comparison with the corresponding gap for square regions; (b) this gap increases as the dimensions of the rectangle increase; and, (c) the gap is even greater for the orientation in which the longer dimension is along the X axis. However, in all cases, in Tables 4 and 5, the gap between GZ and BZ never exceeds 10%.

Between GN and H, since the former is asymmetric and the latter is symmetric, GN does better than H for the orientation in which the Y dimension of the query region is larger, i.e. the preferred orientation for GN. On the other hand, H does better than GN, when the X dimension of the query region is larger, corresponding to the less preferred orientation of GN. In relative terms, the advantage of the H over GN in the second scenario is greater than the advantage of GN over H in the first, and therefore, overall H is superior.

3.5 Further Discussion of Results

The results show that among the interleaving based methods GN clustering is better than both BZ and GZ clustering in all cases, typically by 35%; however, the H method is the best among all four. It was also found that the relative superiority of GN and H clustering increases for larger query regions. Moreover, the margin of difference between BZ and GZ is very small.

An intuitive understanding for these relative results can be obtained by re-examining Figures 1, 4 and 5. These figures show the patterns that result from connecting consecutive buckets in the four schemes in a 8×8 bucket space. One simple way of evaluating a scheme with respect to its clustering properties is to consider the number of times a move other than a one-unit horizontal or vertical move takes place in the connectivity pattern. If the number of such "jumps" is small, and their length is short, it would be one indication of better clustering. H clustering does best because there are no such jumps in its pattern. On the other hand, among the other three schemes, it is evident that the fewest such "jumps" occur in GN clustering, and the maximum number of such moves occur in BZ. Moreover, the length of such jumps is also smaller for GN.

Another nice property of the hilbert method is that it is symmetric, i.e. its clustering performance is not affected by the orientation of the query rectangle. The interleaving based schemes are asymmetric, and the large difference in the absolute values for the two orientations of the rectangles can be explained by examining the ordering method more closely. Recall that in all the methods the X coordinate is interleaved before the Y coordinate. Therefore, the orientation in which the smaller side of the rectangle is along the X dimension leads to better clustering and fewer clusters. This behavior is consistent across all three schemes. If the Y coordinate was interleaved before the X coordinate, then the opposite results would be found.

The relative performance of GZ with respect to BZ is better in both orientations of the rectangular query region. However, the magnitude of the gap is very small when the smaller side is along the X-axis, and slightly larger when the longer side is along the X axis. This can be explained by noting that the basic "U" (or inverted "U") pattern created in GZ clustering has two vertical neighbors and one horizontal neighbor, while the "N" pattern of BZ clustering has only two vertical neighbors and no horizontal neighbors. This affects the BZ pattern more adversely when the query region is longer in the horizontal (along the X axis) direction.

4 Discussion of Related Work

BZ clustering is the most common method and it was described in [11, 12] as a means of organizing k-dimensional data and processing spatial queries. The GZ clustering method described in [4] is more recent. Finally, the hilbert ordering was investigated at length in [5].

In [5], these three techniques were compared and it was shown that the hilbert ordering considerably outperforms the other two schemes. The comparison was done for bucket spaces with dimensions of upto 16×16, and all possible query ranges were considered. For the 16×16 space, the Hilbert clustering outperformed BZ clustering by nearly 40%. Our study corroborates the results of this study, but also includes the new GN clustering method. Moreover, we were able to consider much larger bucket spaces since we used simulation. Finally, we give the results separately for query regions of different sizes in order to see the effect of varying the size of the query region.

Another study which compares the same three methods as in [5] along with the naive clustering method is reported in [9]. In this study, the queries are restricted to a 2×2 size query regions. The analysis for 2×2 regions shows that the hilbert code does better than BZ by approximately 24%, while the GZ clustering does better than BZ by approximately 20%. Our results described above sugest that the analysis for 2×2 regions cannot be generalized to larger query regions. We found that when query regions are larger, the relative difference between the various schemes grows even more.

In [4], Faloutsos presented gray codes (instead of binary codes) as a technique for improving the performance of partial match and range queries. Faloutsos noticed that gray codes have the nice property that only one bit changes at a time between two consecutive numbers, and that this property could be exploited for improving the performance of partial match and range queries. In a partial match query the values of some fields are *exactly* specified, while others are left unspecified. Therefore, a partial match query is a n-bit long string containing k bits which are explicitly specified and the remaining bits can take any legitimate values. It was shown that gray codes provided better clustering than binary codes for partial match queries by more than 50%.

5 Conclusions

Several data structures for organizing multidimensional data on disk partition the data into regions, and write a region into one disk block or bucket. Therefore, the partitions or regions must be mapped into one dimension before being written to disk. This mapping should have the distance-preserving property, i.e., regions that are close in the multidimensional space must also be close in one dimension. This would lead to better clustering of buckets on disk, and improve response time for various range queries on this data.

A new clustering scheme for multidimensional data called *nu-ordering* was proposed in this paper and described in detail. The performance of this scheme was compared against three existing schemes, binary z-ordering, gray z-ordering, and hilbert-ordering by simulation. All four methods in this study have the common feature that they are based on recursively partitioning the data space. The BZ, GZ and GN codes can be computed by interleaving, while the hilbert code requires a few more computational steps. We simulated various range queries and measured the number of clusters of disk buckets that would have to be accessed in order to answer the query in each case. Both square and rectangular query regions were considered in the performance evaluation.

It was shown that the clustering performance for range queries is affected significantly by the choice of the clustering scheme. The gap between the best and the worst was typically 40% and, in some cases, nearly 60%. The gap was found to increase for larger query regions and rectangular (as opposed to square) query regions.

References

1. Bently, J., "Multidimensional Binary Search Trees used for Associative Searching," Communications of ACM, 18, 9, September 1975, pp 509-517.
2. Dandamundi, S., and Sorenson, P. "An Empirical Performance Comparison of Some Variations of the k-d Tree and BD tree," International Journal of Computer and Information Sciences, 14, 3, June 1985, 135-159.
3. Dandamundi, S., and Sorenson, P. "Algorithms for BD-Trees," Software Practice and Experience, 16, 12 (December 1986), 1077-1096.
4. Faloutsos, C., "Gray Codes for Partial Match and Range Queries," IEEE Transactions on Software Engineering, Vol. 14, No. 10, October 1988.
5. Faloutsos, C. and S. Roseman, "Fractals for Secondary Key Retrieval," Proc. of the ACM Conference on Principles of Database Systems, March 1989, pp. 247-252.
6. Finkel, R., and J.Bently, "Quad Trees: A Data Structure for Retrieval on Multiple Keys," Acta Informatica, 4,1, (1974) pp 1-9.
7. Guttman, A., "R-trees: a Dynamic Index Structure for Spatial Searching," Proceedings of the ACM SIGMOD Conference, Boston, June 1984, pp 47-57.
8. Hinrichs, K., "Implementation of the Grid File: Design Concepts and Experience," BIT 25, 4 (1985), 569-592.
9. Jagadish, H.V., "Linear Clustering of Objects with Multiple Attributes," Proc. ACM SIGMOD Conference, May 1990, Atlantic City, NJ, pp. 332-341.
10. Nievergelt, J., Hinterberger, H. and Sevcik, K., "The Grid File: An Adaptable, Symmetric Multikey File Structure," ACM Transactions on Database Systems, 9, 1, March 1984, 38-71.
11. Orenstein, J., and Merrett, T., "A Class of Data Structures for Associative Searching," Proc. Third ACM SIGACT-SIGMOD Symposium on Principles of Database Systems, Waterloo, April 1984, 181-190.
12. Orenstein, J., "Spatial Query Processing in an Object-Oriented Database System," Proceedings of the ACM SIGMOD Conference, Washington, D.C., May 1986, 326-336.
13. Robinson, J. T., "The KDB Tree: A Search Structure for Large Multidimensional Dynamic Indexes," Proceedings of the ACM SIGMOD Conference, Ann Arbor, MI, April 1981, 10-18.
14. Samet, H., The design and analysis of spatial data structures, Addison Wesley, 1991.

Efficient Management of 2-d Interval Relations

Nikos Lorentzos and Yannis Manolopoulos

Informatics Laboratory, Agricultural University of Athens, 118 55 Athens, Greece.
Department of Informatics, Aristotle University, 54006 Thessaloniki, Greece.

Abstract. We identify a number of problems concerning the management of interval data and propose efficient algorithms in the case of 2-dimensional *interval* relations. The approach is of practical importance and has many applications, one of which is spatiotemporal databases.

1 Introduction

The term *interval* is quite generic. *Time intervals* mark the duration of events (the lifespan of a person). *Alphabetic intervals* have many applications (family names in the range A-C). Given the wide use of intervals, their handling is of major importance. However, there is a number of problems which relate to their management. Such of them were initially identified in research in *temporal databases*. In particular, the necessity to support temporal data led to the formalisation of many distinct temporal extensions to the relational model [1]. In spite however of the major differences between the various modelling approaches, one characteristic, common to almost all of them, is that the ordinary *projection*, *set-union* and *set-difference* operations are adapted appropriately, in all of them, so as to apply appropriately to data incorporating time intervals. Next, it was identified that the same problems arise in the management of certain types of *spatial data* [2, 3], and this gave recently rise in research in *spatiotemporal databases* [4].

The *Interval-Extended Relational Model* (IXRM) was defined to handle them in a uniform way. In this paper we investigate the properties of the IXRM operations and propose efficient algorithms for the above operations. Our work restricts to relations with two *pure* interval attributes. The algorithms have been based on the geometric interpretation of the contents of pure interval attributes and improve substantially the time and space requirements. The remainder of this work is as follows: In section 2 we identify certain problems concerning the management of interval data. In section 3 we present briefly the IXRM and investigate the properties of its operations. In section 4 we make use of these properties and provide efficient algorithms. Conclusions are drawn in the last section.

2 Motivation

In this section we demonstrate the problems concerning the projection, insertion and deletion of interval data. Commercial DBMSs do not support them directly.

Projection: In relation ASSIGNMENT (figure 1) we record the history of employee assignments to projects. The query "list the time intervals during which each employee was assigned to some project" requires to project out the second attribute of ASSIGNMENT. If the standard *projection* operation is used to this end, A1 (figure 1) will be obtained. In contrast, the user would rather obtain A2 (figure 1). We say that A2 is a *normalised* relation, to denote that it does not contain adjacent or overlapping intervals, which data duplication. For example, the fact that John was assigned to some project for each of the dates in [d20,d50), is implicit in A1, from both its first and third tuple.

Assignment

Name	Proj	Time
John	P1	[d10,d50)
John	P1	[d80,d120)
John	P2	[d20,d80)
John	P3	[d80,d100)
Alex	P1	[d30,d50)
Alex	P2	[d70,d150)

A1

Name	Time
John	[d10,d50)
John	[d80,d120)
John	[d20,d80)
John	[d80,d100)
Alex	[d30,d50)
Alex	[d70,d150)

A2

Name	Time
John	[d10,d120)
Alex	[d30,d50)
Alex	[d70,d150)

Fig. 1. Relations with interval data.

LAND

Pno	Depth	Time	pH	
1	[0,20)	[d0,d80)	8.0	r1
1	[0,100)	[d120,d200)	8.0	r2
1	[30,120)	[d0,d80)	8.0	r3
1	[0,30)	[d80,d120)	8.2	
2	[0,60)	[d10,d50)	8.3	
2	[60,100)	[d30,d90)	8.3	

L

Pno	Depth	Time	pH	
1	[70,140)	[d40,d160)	8.0	r2
2	[60,120)	[d10,d40)	8.3	

Fig. 2. Relations with two pure interval atributes.

Similar problems also arise in relations with more than one pure interval attribute. For example, LAND (figure 2) has two such *attributes*, Depth, Time, of an *integer, time interval* type, respectively. A non-trivial projection of LAND on a set of attributes which include either Depth or Time will yield a non-normalised relation. Therefore, the projection of a relation with pure interval attributes has to be replaced by some *normalisation* operation, before the result relation is presented to the user.

Data Insertion: Assume that we want to insert into LAND the contents of L (figure 2). Using the standard insertion operation, this will result in relation LAND1 (figure 3). LAND1 is *non*-normalised (for example the soil pH at depth 70 on date d40, is recorded in both r2 and r4). In fact, we would like to obtain LAND2 (figure 3), which is normalised.

Data Deletion: If we use the *standard* deletion operation, to delete from LAND the contents of L, nothing will actually be deleted, whereas we would like to obtain LAND3 (figure 3).

3 The Interval Extended Relational Model

In this section we describe shortly the IXRM, which overcomes the problems identified in the previous section. Its formalisation can be found in [5].

LAND1

Pno	Depth	Time	pH	
1	[0,20)	[d0,d80)	8.0	r1
1	[70,140)	[d40,d160)	8.0	r2
1	[0,100)	[d120,d200)	8.0	r3
1	[30,120)	[d0,d80)	8.0	r4
1	[0,30)	[d80,d120)	8.2	
2	[0,60)	[d10,d50)	8.3	
2	[60,100)	[d30,d90)	8.3	
2	[60,120)	[d10,d40)	8.3	

L

Pno	Depth	Time	pH	
1	[0,20)	[d0,d80)	8.0	t1
1	[30,70)	[d0,d80)	8.0	t2
1	[100,120)	[d0,d160)	8.0	t3
1	[70,100)	[d0,d200)	8.0	t4
1	[120,140)	[d40,d160)	8.0	t5
1	[0,70)	[d120,d200)	8.0	t6
1	[0,30)	[d80,d120)	8.2	
2	[100,120)	[d10,d40)	8.3	
2	[0,60)	[d10,d50)	8.3	
2	[60,100)	[d10,d90)	8.3	

L

Pno	Depth	Time	pH
1	[70,120)	[d0,d40)	8.0
1	[0,20)	[d0,d80)	8.0
1	[30,70)	[d0,d80)	8.0
1	[0,70)	[d120,d200)	8.0
1	[70,100)	[d160,d200)	8.0
1	[0,30)	[d80,d120)	8.2
2	[0,60)	[d10,d50)	8.3
2	[60,100)	[d40,d90)	8.3

A3

Name	Time
John	d10
...	...
John	d119
Alex	d30
...	...
Alex	d49
Alex	d70
...	...
Alex	d149

Fig. 3. Insertion and deletion of interval data. Result of operation unfold.

A *1-dimensional* (1-d) space is a non-empty, finite, totally ordered set D of *points*: $D = d_1, d_2, ..., d_n$. (Without loss of generality, we occasionally start numbering from d_0.) A (1-d) interval over D is defined as

$$[d_m, d_n) = \{d_k | d_m \leq d_k < d_n, d_m, d_n \in D\}.$$

The points d_m, d_n are the boundaries of $[d_m, d_n)$, denoted by *start*$([d_m, d_n))$, *stop*$([d_m, d_n))$, respectively. An interval $[d_i, d_{i+1})$, with exactly one point, is called *elementary*. The set of all intervals over D is denoted by I(D). Thus, if DATES=$d_0, d_1, ..., d_{200}$ is a set of consecutive dates then $[d_{10}, d_{21})$ is an interval in I(DATES). If $[d_m, d_n)$ and $[d_p, d_q)$ are two intervals, we define a predicate, *merges*, as

$$[d_m, d_n) \textit{ merges } [d_p, d_q) \text{ if and only if } (d_n \geq d_p \text{ and } d_q \geq d_m)$$

If $D_1, ..., D_n$ are spaces then every subset R of the Cartesian product $I(D_1)$ x ... x $I(D_n)$ is an *n-d interval relation*. Each tuple (element) of R represents an *n-d interval.* An n-d interval $([d_{i1}, d_{i1+1}), [d_{i2}, d_{i2+1}), ..., [d_{in}, d_{in+1}))$ with exactly one *n-d point* $(d_{i1}, ..., d_{in})$, is called *n-d elementary interval.* We further notice that a point d_i can be seen as an interval $[d_i, d_{i+1})$. Therefore, if we use the notation X(D) to denote exclusively either I(D) or D, then every subset of $X(D_1)$ x ... x

$X(D_n)$ is, up to an isomorphism, an interval relation. Hence, all the relations in figures 1-3 are interval relations.

Two operations have been formalised in the IXRM: If R(A,B=I(D)) is a relation then for each tuple $(a,[d_m, d_{n+1}))$ in R, S=*unfold*[B](R) consists of the set of tuples: (a, d_m), (a, d_{m+1}), (a, d_{m+2}), ..., (a, d_n). Conversely, if S consists of the above tuples, but it does not contain any of (a,d_{m-1}) and (a,d_{n+1}), then *fold*[B](S) produces from them the single tuple $(a,[d_m,d_{n+1}))$. More generally, *fold coalesces* two or more overlapping or adjacent intervals into one. Examples of these operations, based on the relations in figures 1-3, are

A3=*unfold*[Time](A1), A3=*unfold*[Time](A2), A2=*fold*[Time](A3), A2=*fold*[Time](A1)

If $[B_1, ..., B_m]$ is any list of the attributes of a relation $R(A_1, ..., A_n)$, the definitions of *unfold* and *fold* are now extended as follows:

$$unfold[B_1, B_2, ..., B_m](R) = unfold[B_m](... (unfold[B_2](unfold[B_1](R))))$$
$$fold[B_1, B_2, ..., B_m](R) = fold[B_m](... (fold[B_2](fold[B_1](R))))$$

Another operation, *normalise*, can also be defined in terms of *unfold* and *fold*:

$$normalise[B_1, B_2, ..., B_m](R) = fold[B_1, B_2, ..., B_m](unfold[B_1, B_2, ..., B_m](R))$$

By the definition of *normalise*, *unfold* initially eliminates duplicate tuples. Next *fold* yields a relation which does not contain adjacent or overlapping intervals.

Finally, if R and S be two union-compatible relations, operations *unique points set-union (punion)* and *unique points set-difference (pdiff)* are defined as

$$punion[B_1, ..., B_m](R, S) = fold[B_1, ..., B_m](unfold[B_1, ..., B_m](R) \cup unfold[B_1, ..., B_m](S))$$
$$pdiff[B_1, ..., B_m](R,S) = fold[B_1, ..., B_m](unfold[B_1, ..., B_m](R) - unfold[B_1, ..., B_m](S))$$

By their definition, these operations return a normalised relation. It is easy to show that

$$punion[B_1, .., B_m](R,S) = fold[B_1, .., B_m](unfold[B_1, .., B_m](R \cup S)).$$

Using the above operations, the problems identified in the previous section are faced as follows:

Normalisation: A2 = *normalise*[Time](A1),
LAND2 = *normalise*[Time,Depth](LAND1)
Insertion of Interval Data: LAND2 = *punion*[Time,Depth](LAND, L)
Deletion of Interval Data: LAND3 = *pdiff*[Time,Depth](LAND,L)

The above three operations can be used to handle relations with arbitrarily many pure interval attributes. However, their definition in terms of *unfold*, makes them prohibitively costly. In the sequel we investigate the properties of *unfold* and *fold* and provide efficient algorithms in the next section.

An interval $[d_m, d_n)$ can geometrically be seen as a line segment which is closed to the left and open to the right. Hence, every tuple of an n-ary relation can be seen as an n-d cuboid. Thus, the single tuple of relation R (figure 4(a)) is represented by the orthogonal rectangle WXYZ (figure 4(b)). The 2-d points on sides XY and YZ are not points of the interval. In contrast, the 2-d points in the rectangle and also those on sides WX and WZ (excluding X and Z) are points of it. If R1=*unfold*[B](R) is now issued, then R1 will consist of four tuples, ([1, 4), i), $i = 1, 2, 3, 4$. Since point i is isomorphic with the interval $[i, i+1)$, each of these tuples can geometrically be interpreted by one of the four adjacent rectangles in figure 4(c). This figure shows that *unfold*[B](R) *splits* each tuple (interval) of a relation R into intervals whose values for attribute B are elementary intervals. Similarly, if we issue next R2=*unfold*[A](R1) we obtain a relation consisting of 2-d elementary points whose geometric interpretation is shown in figure 4(d).

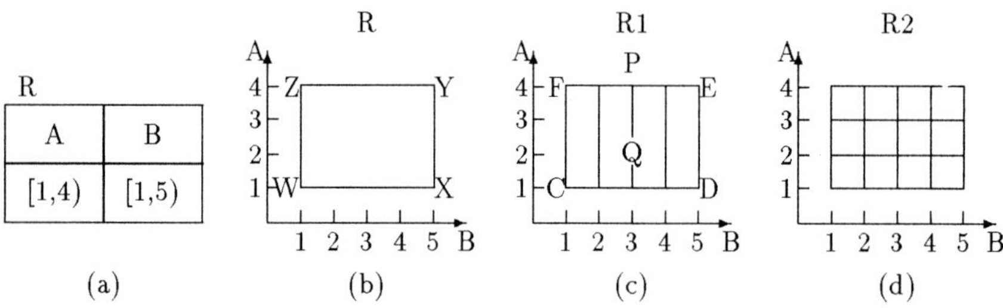

Fig. 4. Geometric interpretation of a 2-d interval and of operations unfold and fold.

It can easily be seen that the relations, whose representation is given in figure 4, satisfy R1=*fold*[A](R2), R=*fold*[B](R1) and, therefore, R=*fold*[A,B](R2). The following properties can be deduced from the definition of *fold* (the reader can found their formal proofs in [6]).

Property 1: *unfold*[B,A](R) = *unfold*[A,B](R).

Property 2: If a relation R(A,B) is sorted with respect to A and B then *fold*[B](R) can be accomplished in one pass, by scanning sequentially the tuples of R.

Property 3: If $R_1, R_2, ..., R_k$ is a partition of R(A,B) such that all the tuples in the same R_i have identical A values whereas tuples in distinct R_i and R_j have different A values, then

$$fold[B](R) = fold[B](R_1) \cup fold[B](R_2) \cup ... \cup fold[B](R_k).$$

Property 4: Let R(A,B=I(D)) be a relation and BP a subset of points in D. If S is the relation obtained from R if all the tuples of R are split with respect to the points in BP, then

$$fold[B](R) = fold[B](S).$$

Property 5: *fold*[B](R) = *fold*[B](*unfold*[B](R)).

Property 6: Let R(A,B=I(D)) be a relation and BP be a subset of points in D. If S is the relation obtained from R if all the tuples of R are split with respect to the points in BP, then

$$fold[B](unfold[B](R)) = fold[B](S).$$

Property 7: For any relation R,

$$fold[A,B](unfold[A,B](R)) = fold[A,B](unfold[B](R)).$$

Because of the above properties *normalise* and *punion* are equivalent to

$$normalise[B_1, B_2, ..., B_m](R) = fold[B_1, B_2, ..., B_m](unfold[B_2, B_3, ..., B_m](R))$$

$$punion[B_1, ..., B_m](R,S) = fold[B_1, ..., B_m](unfold[B_2, B_3, ..., B_m](R \cup S)).$$

4 Efficient Algorithms

Using the properties of the previous section, we now provide efficient algorithms for normalise, *punion* and *pdiff*.

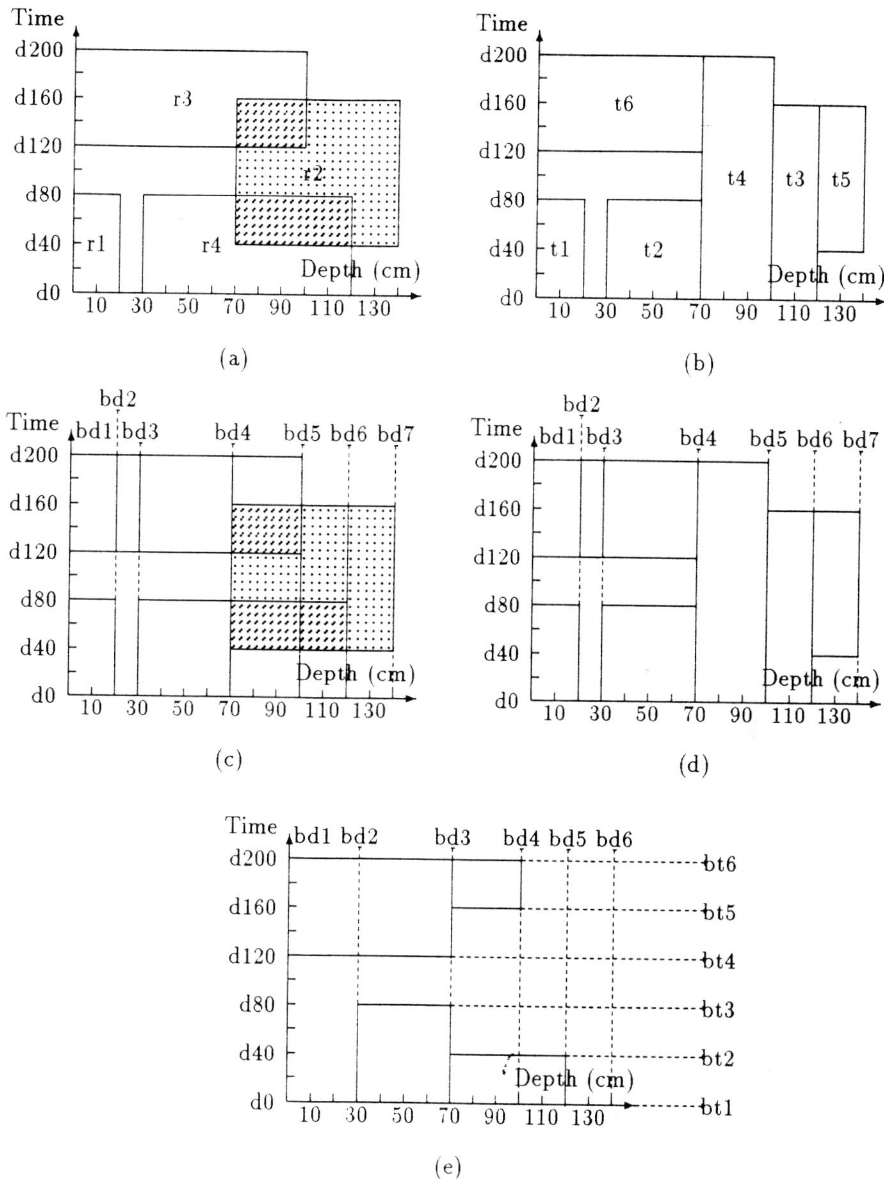

Fig. 5. Geometric interpretation of efficient operations.

4.1 Efficient Normalization of 2-d Interval data

LAND1 (figure 3) is non-normalised, therefore *normalise/fold* has to be applied. From property 3 it suffices to normalise each distinct set in the partition of LAND1. Indeed, LAND1 is already sorted with respect to Pno and pH and the partition is {P,Q,R}, where P consists of the first four tuples, Q consists of the fifth and R contains consists of the last three tuples. The interpretation of P is shown in figure 5(a). Tuple r2, in particular, is dark. The rectangles in r2 which are darker, including their bottom and left sides, denote duplicate points.

If we now issue *normalise*[Time,Depth](P), we shall obtain the first six tuples of LAND2 (figure 3). The interpretation of these tuples is shown in figure 5(b). By using property 7, the number of attributes on which LAND1 has to be unfolded may by reducing by one, that is
normalise[Time,Depth](LAND1) = *fold*[Time,Depth](*unfold*[Depth](LAND1)).
If we issue *unfold*[Depth](LAND1), each of the rectangles in figure 5(a) will be *split* into a large number of rectangles with Depth components of exactly one point each. The same result can be obtained if the rectangles in figure 5(a) are *split* only into sub-rectangles with respect to the boundary points of their Depth values. This *split* is shown in figure 5(c). The set of these boundary points with respect to which the *split* will take place, is *DepthBoundaries*={bd1,...,bd7}. Hence, rather than using *unfold*, we can use this *split*, to finally achieve an equivalent result. Thus, if P1 is the relation having as tuples the rectangles in figure 5(c), then the interpretation of P2=*fold*[Time](P1) is shown in figure 5(d). Finally, P3=*fold*[Depth](P2) shown in figure 5(b), is the interpretation of the normalised relation LAND2. The above procedure has to be repeated for each set in the partition {P,Q,R} of LAND1.

```
Input : Relation R(NI, A, B), Index(NI) of relation R.
Output: Relation S=normalise[A,B](R).
begin
    for each distinct ni value stored in Index(NI) do
    begin
        retrieve the subset Ri of R with Ri[NI]=ni
        for each tuple r(ni,a,b) of Ri do
        begin
            store the boundaries of b in BBoundaries(B)
            store (a,b) in Temp(A,B)
        end
        sort BBoundaries(B) and eliminate any duplicate rows
        split each tuple in Temp(A,B) wrt the points in BBoundaries(B)
        fold(Temp)
        for each tuple r(a,b) in Temp(A,B), write S(ni,a,b)
    end
end
```

Table 1: Algorithm for *Efficient-normalise* on two attributes.

Let NI be a set of zero or more attribute and let R(NI,A=I(D1),B=I(D2)) be a relation. We assume that two temporary files, BBoundaries(B=D2) and

Temp(A=I(D1),B=I(D2)) can fit in main memory. For simplicity, we assume also that the result of a *split* or *fold* in a main memory structure, is stored in this same structure. The algorithm *normalise*, shown in table 1, calls algorithm *fold*, given in table 2.

Input : Relation Temp(A,B).
Output: Relation *fold*[A,B](Temp).
begin
    sort Temp(A,B) on B, A
    fold Temp(A,B) on A
    sort Temp(A,B) on A, B
    fold Temp(A,B) on B
end

Table 2: Algorithm to fold on two attributes.

4.2 Efficient Insertion of 2-d Interval Data

Consider LAND (figure 2), indexed on NI=[Pno, pH] and assume that we want to insert into L (figure 2). By using property 3, we initially partition L with respect to its distinct NI values and for each set in this partition we consider only the respective partition in LAND. More precisely, L can be partitioned into two sets, of one tuple each. The Pno and pH values of the tuples in the first set (tuple r2) are 1 and 8.0, respectively. For this set, it suffices to consider from LAND only those tuples with the same respective values. However, tuple r1 (figure 5(a)) can in fact be excluded because neither its Time nor its Depth component merges with the respective component of r2. In contrast, tuples r3 and r4 of LAND have to be involved in *punion* because: (i) Their Pno and pH values are identical with the respective values of r2 (also satisfied by r1) and (ii) both their Depth and Time values merge with the respective values of r2 (not satisfied by r1).

Input : Relations R(NI,A,B), Index(NI) of relation R, T(NI,A,B)
(* R is normalised with respect to A, B *)
Output: Relation R=*punion*[A,B](R,T)
begin
    sort T on NI
    for each subset Ti(NI,A,B) of T with identical NI values **do**
    begin
        for each tuple r(ni,a2,b2) of Ti **do**
        begin
            store the boundaries of b2 in BBoundaries(B)
            store (a2,b2) in Temp(A,B)
            for each tuple r(ni,a1,b1) in R such that
                (a1 *merges* a2) and (b1 *merges* b2) **do**
            begin
                store the boundaries of b1 in BBoundaries(B)
                store (a1,b1) in Temp(A, B)

```
            delete r from R
          end
        end
        sort BBoundaries(B) and eliminate any duplicate rows
        split each tuple in Temp(A,B) wrt the points in BBoundaries(B)
        fold(Temp)
        for each tuple r(a,b) in Temp(A,B), write R(ni,a,b)
    end
end
```

Table 3: Algorithm for efficient punion on two attributes.

It is now clear from sub-section 4.1, that if *punion*[Time,Depth](LAND,L) is issued, the resulting relation will contain the tuples t2-t6 (figure 5(b)), in place of tuples r3 and r4 (figure 5(a)). This means that tuples r3 and r4 have to be deleted from LAND and tuples t2-t6 will next have to be inserted into LAND. Furthermore, since only the tuples r2-r4 need be split, the set of the Depth boundary points with respect to which the split will take place, is *DepthBoundaries* = {bd1,bd3,...,bd7} (figure 5(c)).

Finally, the tuples derived by this split have to be folded on Time and Depth and be inserted into LAND. The same procedure has to be repeated with each set into which L is partitioned. The above imply the algorithm for *punion* which is given in table 3.

4.3 Efficient Deletion of 2-d Interval Data

Now assume that we want to delete from LAND the contents of L (figure 2). Since *pdiff* involves *fold*, similarly to *punion*, L has to be partitioned with respect to the values of its tuples on attributes NI. Then *pdiff*[Time,Depth](LAND,L) can be implemented by considering separately each distinct set in this partition, with the respective partition in LAND. The first set in the partition of L consists of tuple r2, only. The respective set of LAND consists again of the tuples r1, r3, r4 from which only r3 and r4 have again to be considered because (i) their Pno and pH values match with the respective values of r2 and (ii) both their Depth and Time values merge with the respective values of r2. As can be seen in figure 5(a), only the portion in dark of tuples r3 and r4 has to be eliminated. Figure 5(e) shows the tuples which LAND will contain in place of r3 and r4, after the execution of *pdiff*. This implies that (i) once r3 and r4 have been identified, they have to be deleted from LAND and (ii) once the tuples in figure 5(e) have been computed, they have to be inserted into LAND. The tuples in figure 5(e) can be computed as follows:

Input : Relations R(NI,A,B), Index(NI) of relation R, T(NI,A,B)
(* R is normalised with respect to A, B *).
Output: Relation R=*pdiff*[A,B](R,T).
begin
  sort T on NI
  for each subset Ti(NI,A,B) of T with identical NI values **do**

```
begin
    for each tuple r(ni,a2,b2) of Ti do
    begin
        store the boundaries of a2 in ABoundaries(A)
        store the boundaries of b2 in BBoundaries(B)
        store (a2,b2) in Temp2(A,B)
        for each tuple r(ni,a1,b1) in R such that
            (a1 merges a2) and (b1 merges b2) do
        begin
            store the boundaries of a1 in ABoundaries(A)
            store the boundaries of b1 in BBoundaries(B)
            store (a1,b1) in Temp1(A,B)
            delete r from R
        end
    end
    sort ABoundaries(A) and eliminate any duplicate rows
    sort BBoundaries(B) and eliminate any duplicate rows
    split each tuple in Temp1(A,B) wrt the points in ABoundaries(A)
    split each tuple in Temp1(A,B) wrt the points in BBoundaries(B)
    split each tuple in Temp2(A,B) wrt the points in ABoundaries(A)
    split each tuple in Temp2(A,B) wrt the points in BBoundaries(B)
    delete from Temp1(A,B) the tuples in Temp2(A,B)
    fold(Temp1)
    for each tuple r(a,b) in Temp1(A,B), write R(ni,a,b)
 end
end
```

Table 4: Algorithm for efficient pdiff on two attributes.

Firstly, by comparing figures 5(a) and 5(e), it is clear that, initially, tuples r2-r4 have to be split twice: The first split will be with respect to their Depth boundary points, *DepthBoundaries*={bd1,...,bd6}. The tuples obtained this way, will next have to be split with respect to their Time boundary points, *TimeBoundaries*={bt1,...,bt6}. Thus, two distinct main storage structures have now to be maintained, *DepthBoundaries* and *TimeBoundaries*. The result obtained after the split of r3 and r4 is maintained in a main storage structure, Temp1(A,B). Similarly, the result obtained by the split of r2 is maintained in a main storage structure Temp2(A,B).

Secondly, in order that the dark rectangles of figure 5(c) are eliminated, we have to issue

$$\text{Temp1(A,B)} = \text{Temp1(A,B)} - \text{Temp2(A,B)}.$$

Finally, the result of *fold*[Time,Depth](Temp1), shown in figure 5(e), has to be inserted into LAND. Hence, the algorithm for an efficient *pdiff*[A,B] is the one given in table 4.

5 Conclusions

We considered relations with two interval attributes and examined the problems arising when certain operations are applied to them. At the logical level, it was shown how the relational algebra should be extended to overcome these problems, by using two additional operations, *fold* and *unfold*. We investigated the properties of these operations and presented efficient algorithms for the management of 2-d interval data. Work concerning their implementation can be found in [6]. In our approach we considered indices on non-interval attributes but spatiotemporal indexing approaches have also been proposed (see for example [7, 8, 9] for surveys). However, the indexing of interval data is still an open research problem. Thus, for the problems examined in this work, even more efficient algorithms have to be investigated.

Acknowledgment

This work has been funded by the ESPRIT III Project ORES, 7224.

References

1. L.E. McKenzie and R.T. Snodgrass: *Evaluation of Relational Algebras Incorporating the Time Dimension in Databases*, ACM Computing Surveys 23(4), 501-543, 1991.
2. C.S. Jensen and R.T. Snodgrass: *Extending Normal Forms to Temporal Relations*, TR 92-17, Computer Science Dept., University of Arizona, 1992.
3. S.K. Gadia: *Parametric Databases: Seamless Integration of Spatial, Temporal, Belief and Ordinary Data*, ACM SIGMOD RECORD 22(1) 15-20, 1993.
4. K.K. Al-Taha, R.T. Snodgrass and M.D. Soo: *Bibliography on Spatiotemporal Databases*, ACM SIGMOD Record 22(1), 59-67, 1993.
5. N.A. Lorentzos: *The Interval Extended Relational Model and its Application to Valid Time Databasesr*, in *Theory, Design and Implementation* (ed. A. Tansel et.al.), Benjamin/Cummings, 67-91, 1993.
6. N.A. Lorentzos, A. Poulovassilis and C. Small: *Implementation of Update Operations for Interval Relations*, The Computer Journal, 37(3), 164-176, 1994.
7. Y. Manolopoulos and G. Kapetanakis: *Overlapping B+trees for Temporal Data*, Proc. 5th JCIT Conference, 491-498, 1990.
8. H. Samet: *The Design and Analysis of Spatial Data Structures*, Addison-Wesley, Reading MA, 1990.
9. C. Kolovson: *Indexing for Historical Databases*, in *Theory, Design and Implementation* (ed. A. Tansel et.al.), Benjamin/Cummings, 418-432, 1993.

Managing Structured Documents in Distributed Publishing Environments

Franz Burger[1], Gerald Quirchmayr[1,2], Siegfried Reich[1], A Min Tjoa[1,2]

[1] FAW - Research Institute for Applied Knowledge Processing, A-4232 Hagenberg - Austria. E-Mail:{franz, sre}@faw.uni-linz.ac.at

[2] University of Vienna Institute for Applied Computer Science & Information Systems, Information Engineering Group, A-1010 Vienna - Austria. E-Mail: {tjoa,jerry}@ifs.univie.ac.at

Abstract. Advanced developments in the area of broadband communications, as well as database and groupware technology propose to enable more efficient cooperation in workgroups. A scenario sketching the cooperative production of innovative electronic reference works is used to derive requirements for data management. Based on these requirements an integrated architecture, consisting of workflow- and document management components, is proposed. The focus of this paper is on document management in distributed environments. Additionally, we show implementation aspects of an abstract interface for flexible handling of structured documents.

1 Introduction

Electronic versions of highly complex publications, such as professional reference works, do increase the demand on publishing environments. Traditionally used systems having the focus on layouting do not provide any support for semantically structured documents, an approach which does backfire with the growing amount of data involved in the production of large scale reference works. As the process of producing such publications additionally is highly distributed, tools for efficiently supporting the cooperative work of different experts are needed.

The work described in this paper has been carried out as part of the European RACE [3] project R2042 EUROPUBLISHING [4].

The Application Pilot *Dictionary of Art (DoA)*, being part of the above mentioned project, is a comprehensive reference work to be published (on paper with more than 30.000 pages) in 1995 by the British Publisher Macmillan. It represents one of the largest publishing projects currently in production anywhere and is clearly a product from which derivative publications - whether conventional or new media - will be prepared.

The systems used for the publication of reference works in general - and the *DoA* in particular - are conventional, isolated publishing tools. Yet the prepara-

[3] Research and Development in Advanced Communication Technologies in Europe

[4] This work has been sponsored by the Austrian Federal Research Foundation (FFF) under grant no. 2/289.

tion of such a reference work is a large-scale collaborative venture among specialist authors, editors, indexers, and advisors, as well as designers and production managers. Typically, these people are distributed widely but intermittently consult and collaborate closely. The requirements of such an undertaking clearly include document management of compound structured documents, tracking of contributions and versions thereof, quality and design, layout, presentation, indexing and hypertext composition tools.

In order to enable access to and use of shared information and to integrate the different facilities required in a publishing environment, an Integrated Document and Workflow Management System is currently being developed at our institute. This system is seen as a tool for providing consistent management of compound structured documents.

2 Structured Documents - SGML

In publishing, cooperation is mainly based on the exchange of documents, but on the other hand most publishing tools rely on different data formats and so the problem of document exchange is hard to solve. Information provided by external sources has to be moved into the publisher's editorial system. To make document exchange possible during the publishing process, a system- and device-independent data representation format for hypermedia-documents is required.

Besides the aspect of device independent storage it is important that the information being handled is of high quality as is required by the end-users of professional reference works [5]. High quality thereby is meant in terms of query, markup and structuring, etc.

Another aspect of hypermedia publications concerns the multi-mediality of information, i.e. the documents representing the information are compound documents with their content containing, besides normal text, additional types of media, such as graphics, images, video, or sound.

With respect to the above mentioned issues of the publishing process an international standard has been defined. SGML (Standard Generalized Markup Language) [7] is an international standard for structured documents. It allows the system independent specification and handling of a document's content and its structure. SGML standardises the syntax for tagging documents. Thus it can be used to represent arbitrary document types, e.g. a biography on an artist, a spreadsheet with references to other documents, or a multimedia presentation.

The figure below shows portions of an SGML document representing a biography on Picasso[6].

A Document-Type-Definition (DTD) describes the structure of a set of documents, and therefore can be seen as equivalent to a class, the documents themselves being instances of this class. A DTD, in general, describes documents in a tree-like structure. Additionally, cross-references between elements within a document can be specified. Further details on SGML can be found in [2] [4] [5].

[5] Potential users are e.g. art historians.

```
<!DOCTYPE BIOGRAPH SYSTEM "biography.dtd.nov6" [ ]>
<BIOGRAPH><HEAD>
<NAME TYPE="LAST">Picasso</NAME>
<FRSTNAME>Pablo</FRSTNAME><MIDNAME>Ruiz</MIDNAME>
<BIOGDATA><BIRTH><PLACE>Malaga</PLACE>
<DATE><DAY>25</DAY>
<MONTH>Oct</MONTH><YEAR>1881</YEAR></DATE></BIRTH>
<DEATH><PLACE>Mougins, France,</PLACE>
<DATE><DAY>10</DAY>
<MONTH>April</MONTH><YEAR>1973</YEAR></DATE></DEATH> </BIOGDATA>
<LABEL><NATIONAL>Spanish</NATIONAL><ROLE>painter, sculptor, draughtsman,
print- maker, decorative artist and writer</ROLE>, active in
<ACTIVE>France </ACTIVE></LABEL>
<SHORTDES> He dominated 20th-century ...
```

Fig. 1. Biography on Picasso

3 Requirements

The objective of efficiently handling structured documents in a distributed environment leads to a number of requirements for data management. Generally speaking, all these requirements result from the basic goals of data management which could be summed up as follows:

1. flexibility during the process of producing innovative publications
2. enhanced control of the publication process and
3. support of cooperation between several different roles of users

Basic requirements to be met are persistent storage, efficiency in general (both concerning design aspects and technical aspects, e.g. a client-server architecture and the use of compression), the possibility of managing high volume data, communication, use of standards in order to guarantee exchangeability and reusability.

Besides these general prerequisites, domain specific requirements have to be dealt with:

Compound Structured Documents (R1) Structured in this context means SGML- and HyTime-based [6], compound stands for addressing the aspect of multimedia (i.e. images, video, audio, and text, can be incorporated within one document). Not only different types of data, but also different formats (e.g. for images) have to be considered. Due to the high volume of data being typical of the application, this aspect is extremely challenging. Depending on the role, in which a user is acting, different representations of the documents content and different task-specific views on documents and parts of documents have to be provided.

[6] HyTime (Hypermedia Time based Structuring Language, [8]) is an application of SGML, developed for the handling of hypermedia documents.

Distribution (R2) As publishing is an inherently distributed activity, the co-operation of a wide variety of experts, each of them focusing on one or more tasks, has to be supported. Therefore the distribution of documents is one of the crucial requirements for efficient data management. As access to consistently stored data at different locations has to be guaranteed, issues such as global naming of data objects and concurrency control have to be considered.

Versioning (R3) The publishing process being a design activity requires the management of final and interim data that arises incrementally. Both, state- and task-oriented versioning are needed due to the publishing process being highly iterative[14].

Query, Navigation, Browsing (R4) Access to documents in general, and SGML documents especially, as well as parts or attributes of structured documents demands query and navigation tools as typically provided by structured document management systems. In addition to that the system has to support mechanisms for browsing and structuring (e.g. filtering and sorting by name, date, kind, status, etc.).

Authorization (R5) A basic authorization control mechanism has to check the rights of users (write, read, create new instance or version respectively) in different roles (editor, writer, proof-reader).

Recording of History / Changes of Documents (R6) To be able to scroll through the life-cycle of a document and to locate and correct errors having occurred in previous tasks, a protocol mechanism is needed for recording the changes and the history of documents.

4 Overall Functional Architecture

The set of requirements has led to the development of an overall architecture on an abstract level. The functional architecture providing the requested management services is based on a modular approach by separating the whole system in components as shown in Fig. 2. The area enclosed by dashed lines shows the parts of the system this paper mainly focuses on.

An administration tool is used to generate the system configuration information. It allows the administrator to specify the workflow components (e.g. job, task, user, role) and document-related information, such as the structure of documents, their location, and access rights. System information is stored in the respective databases (workflow database, document base).

The workflow control component is aimed at coordinating and activating (triggering) tasks as well as handling exceptions (e.g. errors and delays). That is why access to the workflow database and to the document management component is needed. Furthermore, applications can be launched directly (shown by

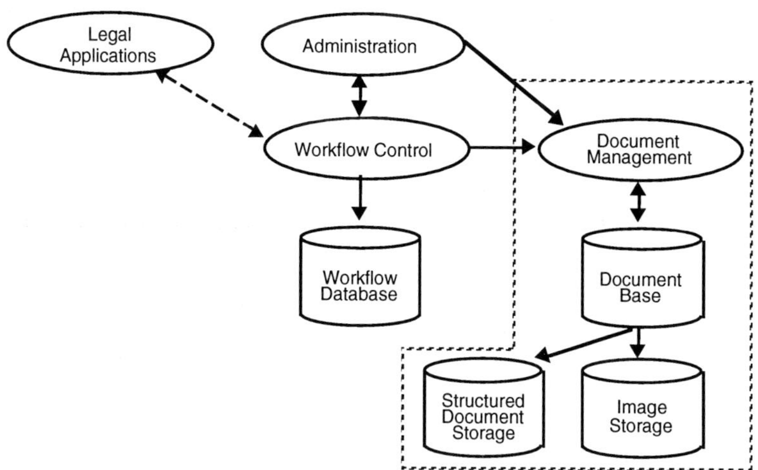

Fig. 2. Functional Architecture

the dashed arrow). The underlying workflow database does contain an object-oriented model of the task concept, application-specific task templates and information about currently existing instances of application-specific tasks.

The document management has to provide services dealing with creation and maintenance of meta-information on documents, as well as access to document instances and to their physical components via the document base. In order to enable access to documents and parts of them, location information has to be provided and references contained in task specifications have to be interpreted. Access control is done via the specification of access rights on group-level, the status of tasks, and the document status. Check-in and check-out functionality provided by the system therefore is a major feature allowing the transfer and exchange of document components.

5 Architecture for Distributed Document Management

In order to deal with R2 *Distribution*, a system architecture for distributed document management has been developed. The architecture has to fit into the overall functional architecture and is based on the principles of the client-server concept. A similar approach has been chosen for a prototype image server involving interactive selection of images from a remote image database, and the subsequent transfer of selected images via ISDN [7] to a customer site [9]. Fig. 3 gives an overview of the architecture.

Besides others, requirement R1 *Support of Compound Structured Documents* has led to partitioning the document management system into separate modules. This approach allows the system to be flexible for changes and future extensions. The kernel of the architecture is a document server which contains

[7] Integrated Services Digital Network

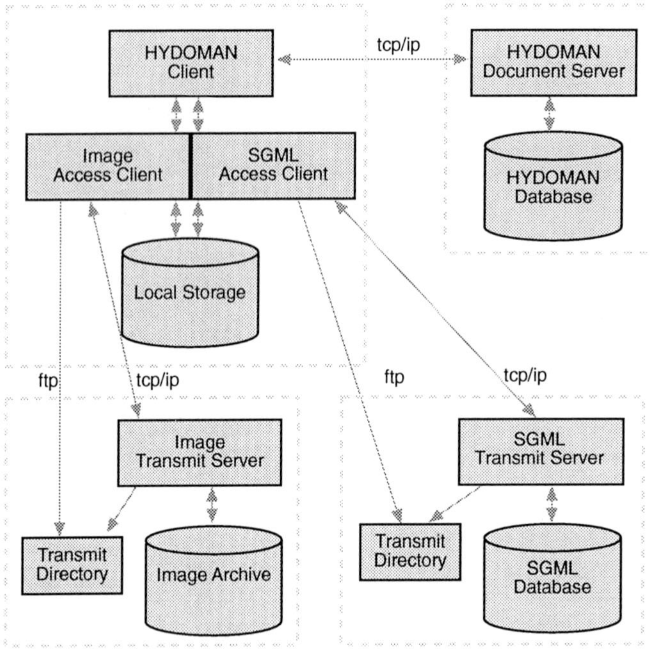

Fig. 3. Distributed Document Management

meta-information and actual instances of documents handled in the publishing environment, as well as pertinent configuration and system information. The usage of a database allows to make use of system services like access control and transaction handling. The only way to access document information is via the document server and therefore should guarantee consistency and correctness.

For controlling authorization of users R5 *Authorization* role-based authorization control will be used. An appropriate concept of role-based security in combination with concepts of object-oriented databases has been proposed in [13]. The role-based concept will be extended towards a specification of those activities which are allowed to be performed on data objects.

Users performing tasks in the publication process have access to a client which interacts with a document server. It has to be stated that, depending on the organisation of the publishing process, one or more document servers may be established. Subsequently users have the choice to select one of the document servers they want to connect to. The communication between client and server is realised on top of the TCP/IP network protocol.

Both, the document server and the client together, offer the functionality needed for organising and managing document information. What is still missing is functionality providing access to the actual information units (e.g. being physical files or objects stored in a database) representing the contents of a publication. This functionality is encapsulated in the second part of the distributed architecture.

When accessing an actual information unit, e.g. for editing or layouting, the user selects the corresponding component from the document and requests its check-out. The document server provides the local client with a reference to the physical data object. This reference represents a unique identifier and can be passed to a responsible access server available at the client site. It may depend on the type of the data object or on the type of external data storage (e.g. file system or database) which access server is invoked. By providing several access servers and not performing the access directly from within the client itself, it is possible to incorporate additional types of external storage services without major modification of the existing environment.

An access server communicates with its corresponding transmit server located at the remote site. The access server sends a check-in or check-out request for a specified object. The transmit server responds with a message indicating whether the object can be accessed or otherwise returns an error message. If the object is available for check-out the transmit server stores a copy of the object into a transmit directory and the object is locked until the object is checked-in again or a release of the lock is enforced otherwise. In case of concurrent access other users are notified that the actual object is currently locked. By allowing users to create a new version of a locked object a higher degree of concurrency is achieved, but different versions have to be merged manually.

The actual transfer of an object from the remote to the local site is performed by file transfer (FTP). A designated directory at the client's workstation may be used for storing the transferred objects. This local directory is used by the access server and may improve performance by allowing the caching of data objects.

Due to the modular design of components the document management system can easily be configured according to the requirements of distributed publishing environments. A further advantage is the openness of the architecture for integrating other tools and applications.

The separation of access functionality does not only allow to make use of already existing internal data sources but also to incorporate the services offered by external providers (e.g. multimedia design, image provider).

The usage of well established network communication protocols and services such as TCP/IP (Transmission Control Protocol/Internet Protocol) and FTP available on all major platforms allow the usage of heterogeneous network services (e.g. X.25, ISDN) and migration to future developments.

The object-oriented programming environment VisualWorks\Smalltalk is used for the implementation of system components and ensures that the system can easily be ported to other platforms.

6 An Abstract SGML Interface

As already stated in the previous sections the usage of SGML as a standard for encoding the handled information (R1 *Compound Structured Documents*) is a must. This and additional requirements (R2 *Distribution* and R4 *Query, Navigation, Browsing*) are dealt with by the development of an abstract SGML database interface. This abstract interface is the main building block for the realisation of a transmit server for SGML documents and thus provides a rather low-level functionality within the whole system. The interface has been realised using the Objectworks\Smalltalk development environment. The main objectives and benefits of this interface are to

1. be independent from the underlying SGML-Engine [8]
2. provide functionality for different applications (not restricted to workflow or document management)
3. build a basis for a future HyTime Engine [9]
4. make use of Smalltalk's modelling and programming features (abstract classes, etc.)
5. build a 'portable' interface (by using Smalltalk), i.e. not only can the underlying SGML-machine be changed but also can the interface be ported on different systems

The figure below gives a graphical representation of the idea of the abstract interface.

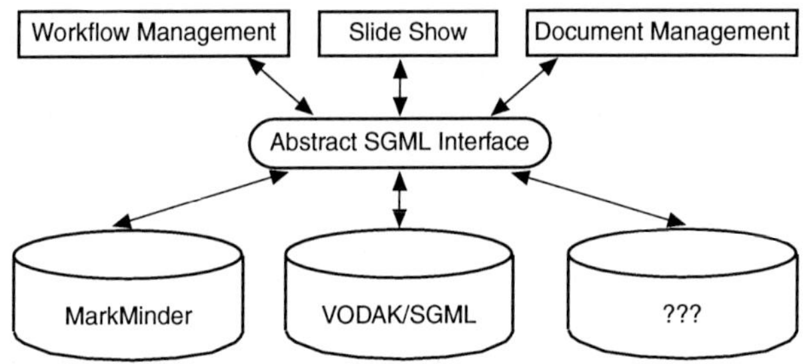

Fig. 4. Abstract SGML Interface

The top layer is being built by SGML-aware applications, such as the document management system presented in this paper. The application makes use of the SGML functionality by invoking method calls being provided by the abstract interface. For each underlying SGML-Engine concrete subclasses with their corresponding methods have to be instantiated. These subclasses hide the actual implementation of the SGML-machine, be it a C++ library as is with MarkMinder [11], or VML methods as is for VODAK [10] [10]. The abstract interface also

[8] The term 'SGML-Engine' is used following the term 'HyTime-Engine' (see below).

[9] A 'HyTime Engine' is 'a program (or portion of a program or a combination of programs) that recognizes HyTime constructs in documents and performs application-independant processing of them.' [8], p.5

[10] VODAK = Verteiltes Objektorientiertes Datenbanksystem, an object-oriented database system developed at GMD-IPSI, Darmstadt.

allows future SGML machines to be integrated into existing environments. The implementation of a specific SGML-Engine into Smalltalk can of course be hard work, as is for instance the case with integrating a C++ library via Smalltalk's C-interface.

The applications which make use of the SGML functionality do not have to care about the SGML-machine actually providing the required functionality. It is possible to change the underlying SGML machine without changing the application. This can even be done at run-time.

Some portions of the actual Smalltalk code shall demonstrate the use of the concept more clearly. The application (e.g. the document management system) requires a new document from a global SGML-Manager. The corresponding Smalltalk code would be the following:

```
myDocument := GSGMLManager newDocument: aUniqueDocumentName.
```

Depending on the SGMLManager's type, different actual implementations of this method newDocument are invoked. The MarkMinder C++ implementation might for instance look like the following:

```
newDocument: aDocumentNameAsString
"call of an external C++ library function which returns
a document pointer"
^ExternalCInterface new newDocument: aDocumentNameAsString
```

The actual call of the C++ library function is encapsulated in Smalltalk's C-interface. For testing purposes and to demonstrate the flexibility of the concept we have also implemented a so called 'Main-Memory-SGML-Engine' which handles SGML-documents and elements in main memory. The relevant portions of Smalltalk-code are the following:

```
myDocument := GSGMLManager newDocument: aUniqueDocumentName.
```

and for the SGML-Manager:

```
newDocument: aDocumentNameAsString
"simply return a new instance of document and remember it"
tmp := SGMLDocument new: aDocumentNameAsString.
documents add: tmp.
^tmp
```

This second example shows that for the application nothing changes. Only the actual implementation of the SGML-Engine differs.

7 Summary

The introduction to this paper describes the unsatisfying situation with regard to tool integration and information exchange in existing publishing environments. The requirements for distributed management of structured documents have been derived on the basis of a distributed publishing scenario.

In order to go one step further towards advanced publishing environments a general functional architecture for a distributed document management system has been developed. The modular design of major components allows the system to be configured flexibly according to the identified requirements. The usage of well established network communication protocols and services as well as the separation of access functionality are the basics for integrating existing and future systems and data sources.

Furthermore, parts of a prototypical implementation clearly showing the benefits of the object-oriented paradigm such as polymorphism, inheritance and abstraction, have been demonstrated.

References

1. BROWN Heather: Standards for Structured Documents; In: The Computer Journal, Vol. 32, No. 6, (1989).
2. BRYAN Martin: An Author's Guide to the Standard Generalized Markup Language. Addison-Wesley Publishing Company. Reading (1988).
3. GOLDBERG, A., ROBSON D.: Smalltalk-80 The Language. Addison-Wesley (1989).
4. GOLDFARB Charles F.: The SGML Handbook. Clarendon Press Oxford. New York (1990).
5. HERWIJNEN Eric van: Practical SGML. Kluwer Academic Publishers. Dordrecht/ Boston/London. (1990).
6. HÜSER Christoph, et. al.: AP1: Requirements, Publishing Process and Environment. Deliverable No. 8 (R2042/GMD/IPSI/DS/R/008/b1), Europublishing Project - RACE programme, March (1993).
7. Information Processing - Text and Office Systems - Standard Generalized Markup Language (SGML), ISO 8879, International Organization for Standardization (1986).
8. Information technology - Hypermedia/Time-based Structuring Language (HyTime), ISO/IEC 10744, International Organization for Standardization (1992).
9. LEASE Karen: A Prototype Image Server. In: Deliverable No. 12 (R2042/SOG/COM/DS/012/b1), Europublishing Project - RACE programme, August (1993).
10. KLAS et al.: VODAK Design Specification Document. VML - VODAK Model Language. Version 3.1. GMD-IPSI. Darmstadt, September (1993).
11. MarkMinder 0.9.4 System User Guide. TechnoTeacher, Inc.,Tallahassee, Florida, (1993).
12. NEWCOMB Steven R., KIPP N. A., NEWCOMB Victoria T.: The "HyTime" Hypermedia/Time-based Document Structuring Language. In: Communications of the ACM, Vol. 34, No. 11/92. New York, November (1991).
13. NYANCHAMA Matunda, OSBORN Sylvia: Role-Based Security, Object-Oriented Databases & Separation of Duty. University of Western Ontario. Submitted to SIGMOD RECORD, June (1993).
14. WEBER Anja: Publishing Tools Need Both: State-Oriented and Task-Oriented Version Support. Proc. of the 15th Annual International Computer Software and Applications Conference, pages 633-639. Tokyo, Japan, September (1991).

A Generalized Semantic Model for CSCW Systems

Igor Hawryszkiewycz

School of Computing Sciences
University of Technology, Sydney, Australia.

Abstract. The paper describes a method for modeling CSCW systems. The method is general in the sense that it caters for the entire spectrum of CSCW work and is based on both theoretical foundations as well as empiric principles. A three level model is proposed, a high level interaction model, a detailed elaboration of model constructs and behaviour based on state transitions.

1. Introduction

CSCW (Computer Supported Cooperative Work) (Schmidt, 1992) is characterized by its open nature, adaptability to changing requirements, and support for flexible coordination between users. CSCW systems can be viewed in the following dimensions:

- the collaboration process, which defines the interaction between the cooperating team members,

- the collaboration technology used to support collaboration and on artifact management, and

- the computer interface that defines the presentation of both the artifact and the interaction with other users while supporting a natural mental model of this process.

- the organizational context within which collaboration takes place with emphasis on maintaining awareness of collaborators. Knowledge of the organizational context should be eventually structured to provide intelligent assistance for the organization's users.

A well designed system will thus be a match of technical and social processes that support coordination that is socially conducive to effective cooperation. Few guidelines exist on how to design such CSCW systems and the many variables that exist in collaboration have so far prevented the construction of a widely accepted methodology for CSCW design.

One of the impediments to design methodologies has been the lack of a model, which integrates these aspects to describe a collaboration process using natural terms. Such a specification would usually be made visually with direct conversion to an implementation. This paper defines such a model and concentrates on the model representation methods, suggesting three levels of elaboration. The model includes a structure as well as behaviour that support modeling abstract concepts such as awareness. It supports both the collaboration semantics as well as artifact semantics and integrates them in a unified way.

2. A Model for Knowledge about Cooperation

The generic concepts in our model (Hawryszkiewycz, 1993b) have drawn from both theoretical and empirical work. The model uses ideas from activity theory proposed by Kuutti (1992) as well as those drawn from ontology (Wand and Weber, 1993). As shown in Figure 1, activity theory views cooperative activities as a group of active subjects working on a joint object supported by information technology. The important words here are active subjects and joint object. The word active implies that the subjects themselves can determine the course of action as well as changing the structure. In contrast passive subjects merely react to a request in a prespecified manner. The word joint rather than shared is used to imply common ownership. Thus the whole group is interested in the state of the whole object and may jointly decide on the future evolution of the object rather than simply using parts of that object for their own needs. A whole organization may be made up of a number of such groups and these groups may also be connected. Thus coordination exists both within groups and between groups.

The concepts of tool, subject and object are sufficient to describe the simple concept of work. The model in Figure 1 extends these basic concepts to place them into the context of wider organization. The first extension is to define a community within which the work proceeds. Thus all of the subjects will come from the community, and the community as a whole can show interest in the object. The idea of rules is to specify the behaviour of subjects in the community. Thus the community can set the rules by which subjects must conform. These rules will define the interactions between subjects in any collaborative work. The division of labor is again defined by the community and assigns work on objects to community members.

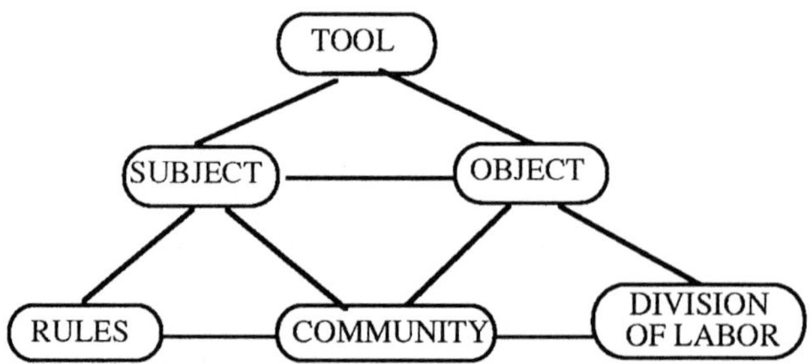

Figure 1 - Activity Theory as applied to CSCW

Using the structure described in Figure 2 as a guideline we propose the following set of CSCW semantic concepts:

Artifacts - Artifacts represent the organization's information base. These can include files as well as artifacts such as reports, designs and so on. The artifact can include data values as well as methods to operate on these values, constraints and rules about the values, and policy rules used in the decision making process or in selecting appropriate roles to perform tasks.

Roles and Actors - Roles are abstract entities that represent system decisions. For example, purchasing a part requires a purchase requisition to be made and approved. The requisition and approval decisions are modeled as two separate roles. An actor is assigned to each role to make the decision. Actors are often positions that can be derived using organizational rules. Roles are not permanently associated with positions but are dynamically assigned using organizational rules. Responsibility changes can thus be made by only changing an organizational rule and not the system structure. A person can have thus many roles and there is nothing to prevent a person from transferring knowledge (informally) between roles as often happens in organizations.

Tasks - Task objects carry out some well-defined function in a problem domain and are generally of shorter duration than environments. They can be parts of complex transaction or simple work tasks such as editing a document.

Environments - Environments model the support structures for groups. Environments can be of prolonged duration and support a variety of processes (known as activities) each composed of tasks and roles. Environments can include other environments, as well as tasks, roles or data. They also define the social context for collaboration.

Activities - Each activity is within an environment and includes a process to model interactions between a subset of objects in the environment. The processes can be defined by standard conversations.

Ports - Ports model connections between objects. They can be of a number of levels of complexity (Hawryszkiewycz, 1993a) ranging from basic ports to speech act ports (Searle, 1969) and to conversation ports, where speech acts are composed of basic ports and then conversations are synthesized from speech acts. Thus roles or groups can be empowered with ports, which give them certain coordination capabilities.

2.1. Framework for Data Semantics

Figure 2 illustrates the idea behind artifact semantics. It sees the structure of an artifact to be made up of a number of parts. Each part goes through a number of states, each state can have a number of versions at a particular point in time. We use three states in the model described here - working, pending and released - but the generality of the model allows alternate sets of states. At the same time, customizations can be kept for each the artifact in each state to allow a return to a previous state or to generate a customized document.

A particular system may include any number of artifacts some of which may be related, or indeed an artifact may be subdivided into a number of parts. Thus a joint report can be divided into say the introduction, a proposal and an evaluation. Each such part can be assigned to a different role or workgroup. The development of the whole report must then be coordinated so that individual groups can work independently although they must be aware of what other groups are doing. The system must then integrate the parts into a report.

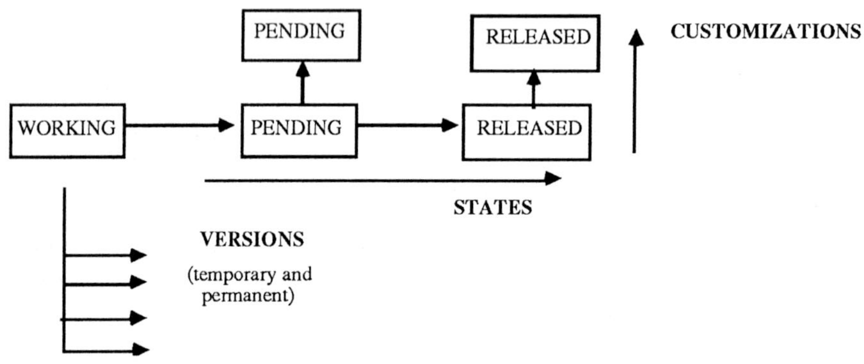

Figure 2 - Artifact Semantics

Thus generalized artifact semantics must include assignment of responsibilities for particular parts, states and versions to workgroups or roles and coordinated their work. Figure 3 shows one model for such distribution. Here authors work on a documents, whereas an editor finally checks a document and accepts it or returns it for further work. The complete model defines the process followed here.

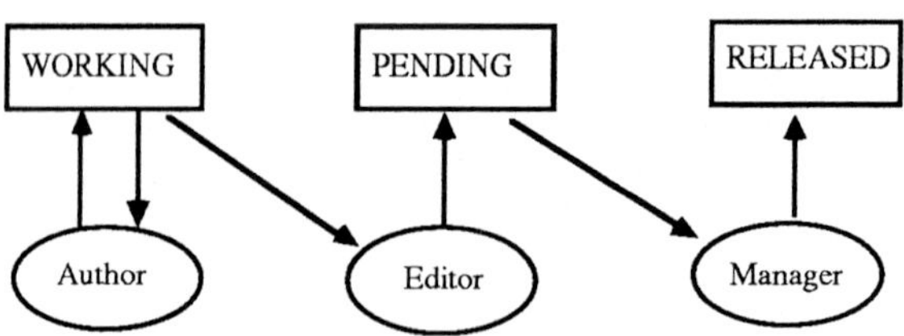

Figure 3 - Linking Roles to Artifacts

2.2 Explanation of Choice

Our choice of objects can be related to activity theory as well as ontological theory. In the ontological context, our choice is one where the data objects predominantly correspond to the physical ontological elements while behaviour is modeled using state transitions between objects.

The proposed concepts are also consistent with the argument put forward by Kuutti (1992) that defines cooperation as "A set of multiple active subjects sharing a common object, supported by information technology". In our case the active subjects are the roles, the objects are the artifacts and tasks provide the tools.

The concept, environment, is an extension of Kuuti's model as it gives us the ability to group and manage definitions of interactions. In Kutti's model all the interactions between subjects are described as one whole. The idea of splitting Kutti's activity into environment and activity in our model gives us an opportunity to 'modularize' the interactions. We thus see the environment as corresponding to Kutti's activity, and then use our activities to group interactions into semantically meaningful groups. Environments are flexible and can be expanded to create other environments that include their own roles, tasks, artifacts and activities, thus further improving modularity and providing the ability to model larger systems.

Another specific choice made in the model is to distinguish between role and actor. A role identifies a logical focus of responsibility, whereas the actor is the physical agent that carries out this responsibility. A number of other modeling methods simply use the term agent to mean an active subject, but do not make a distinction between the logical responsibility and physical agent that carries in out. We make the distinction for two reasons. One is to model the real life situation where one people can be an agents in more than one application. Another reason is to allow the physical actor to dynamically change as happens in practice. We can then use a knowledge base to assign actors to roles. This is similar to rules between subject and community in activity theory - in this case the subject is the role whereas the rule selects a particular actor for the role.

Our concepts can be related to other prototypes. The concept environment also appears in ConversationBuilder (Kaplan, 1992) and is to some extent similar to an OVAL (Malone, 1992) view. We also make a clearer distinction between environment and activity to allow us to model a variety of cooperating processes within the same environment. Many other systems, as for example, ConversationBuilder also use the term activity in the same way as we do. However, we make a further clear distinction between activity and coordination. Activity describes the collection of environment objects that work together to achieve some goal whereas coordination defines the processes used in the activity. The separation of coordination and activity also increases independence by allowing generic coordination patterns to be defined independently of activities.

In our prototype implementation (Huang, 1992) each object is represented by a workspace, which becomes a window on the screen. The object window contains the objects in its context as well as the properties, rules and methods applicable to the object. The object contents can be selected using the window menus. We describe how such objects can be combined to realize semantics commonly found in work environments.

Coordination needs some further explanation as it is central to modeling system dynamics. Dynamics are modeled through object states. The general semantic here is that a trigger state value initiates an object method. The completion of a method becomes an event which serves as a trigger to another object. An activity can include any number of objects and events. Rules that specify such coordinations are stored in an activity. Alternatively a generic set of rules can be stored in *coordination objects*, which can be included in activities. Our model thus differs from some other models in the way that dynamics are modeled because the emphasis is on states rather than messages. This enables the definition of generic coordination objects, which define coordination by state transitions. One goal is to also identify generic coordination objects that can be reused in applications. The structure of such generic coordination objects is discussed later.

Generic coordination objects do not appear in most systems. OVAL, for example, uses an approach where agents operate on folders that receive messages. An agent can be triggered by the arrival of a message. Following agent action, the agent may move a message into another folder, thus triggering a further agent. Coordination is thus distributed between agents and no facilities for generic coordination are described. ConversationBuilder treats activity and coordination synonymously, referring to the coordination process as a protocol but not indicating whether generic protocols are supported.

3. A Representation Method

We suggest a three level representation for CSCW systems. We use a graphical representation to describe high level interactions. The second level is a formal specification outlining the structure of the high level objects. The third level describes the interactions in detail.

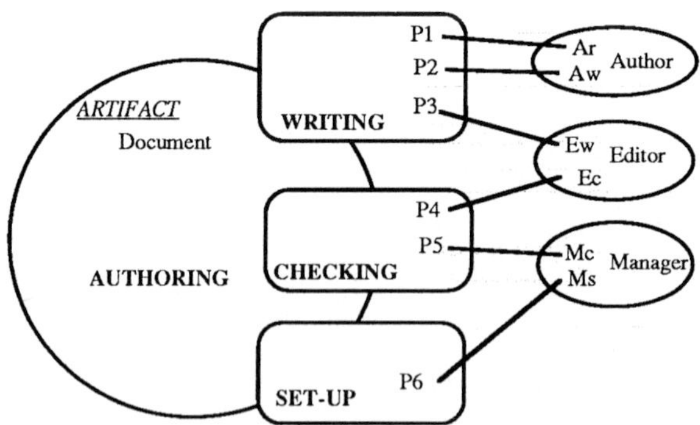

Figure 4 - An interaction diagram for authoring

3.1 Level 1 - High Level Interactions

Figure 4 is an example of a high level interaction diagram that defines the major activities in an environment for developing a document. It includes activity ports and objects connected to the ports. The three major activities shown in Figure 4 are to set up the document, write it and check it. The diagram also shows the ports between objects.

3.2 Level 2 - Describing Structure

This level describes the structure of the objects in Figure 4 and defines the ports in more detail. It takes the following form.

```
ENVIRONMENT  AUTHORING

   ROLES
         Author, Editor, Manager;

   ARTIFACTS
         Document;

   PORTS
         P1  links to Author uses Document; {request for document};
         P2 links to Author uses Document; {receives an amended document
             from author};
         P3 links to Editor uses Document; {sends document for checking};
         P4 links to Editor uses Document; {accepts edited document};
         P5 links to Manager uses Document; {request for approval};
         P6 links to Manager uses Document, Document-Structure;

   ACTIVITIES
         WRITING
             PORTS P1, P2, P3;
             {process to construct an edited document};
         CHECKING
             PORTS P4, P5;
             {process to accept a document};
         SET-UP
             PORTS P6;
             {process to initiate document};

   PROPERTIES
         {Environment Status - useful  for  awareness}
         DOCUMENT-STRUCTURE;
         DOCUMENT-USAGE;
```

```
RULES
        {monitoring rules};
        {activity relationships};
        if state = 'begin' then = 'begin-set-up;
        end-set-up : record-progress --> begin-write;
        end-write : record-progress --> start-accept;

METHODS
        get-version;
        place-version;
        return-a-document;
        edit-document;
        record-progress;
```

3.3 Defining Interactions

The next level of modeling is to define the details of activity coordination. This is done by defining the interaction between components and relating each interaction to a port state. Figure 5 shows the transitions in the interactions for one activity, WRITING. In our behaviour model objects indicate their requirement through a port which sets an environment state. This state is used by the activity rules to activate some other object. Thus for example, when port P1 has a request, then state is set toe s1. This indicates to the activity that the author requires a document version. The activity starts a method 'get-version', which sets the state to s2. This state eventually activates port P3 thus sending the version back to the author.

The interactions shown in the transition can then be included in the script as follows:

```
ACTIVITY
    WRITING
        states
           {s1 : author needs document;
            s2 : document ready for author;
            s3 : author has returned a version;
            s4 : version ready for editing;
            s5 : evaluation requests more work;
            s6 : evaluation completed;}
        rules
           begin-write --> P2('more');
           P1('request') --> s1;
           s2 --> P1('ready');
           P2('done') --> s3;
           s4 --> P3('ready');
           P3('OK') --> s6;
           P3('more') --> s5;
           s1 : get-document --> s2;
           s3 : place-document --> s4;
           s5 --> P2('more');
           s6 --> end-write;
```

Here port P2 informs the author if there is work to be done. The author when ready gets work through port P1 and returns the document through port P2. The writing process is completed when state s6 is reached. The state is then set to 'end-write' which records the completion of writing and begins acceptance.

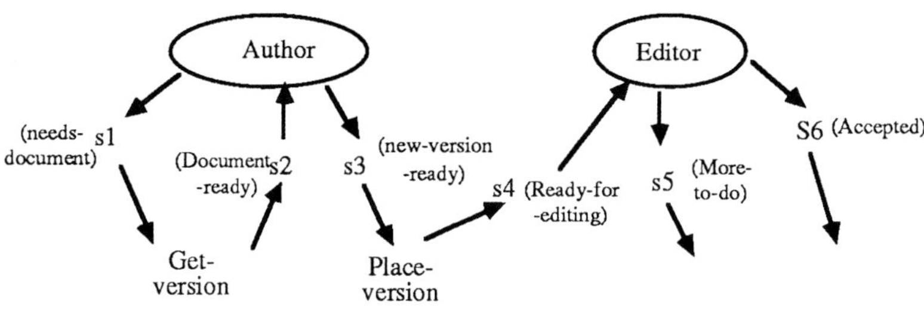

Figure 5 - Transition Diagram

4. Summary

The paper described the need for a model to be used in CSCW design. It then proposed a model together with a three level representation. The first level showed the major interactions, the next described the structures of the objects and the third described behaviour using state transitions.

5. References

Hawryszkiewycz, I.T. (1993a): "Coordination Support for CSCW Systems" Proceeding of the International Symposium on Autonomous Distributed Systems (ISADS), Kawasaki, March 1983, pp. 225-231.

Hawryszkiewycz, I.T. (1993b): "A CSCW Design Tool based on Generic Concepts" 12th. International Conference of the Design of Computer Supported Cooperative Work and Groupware Systems" Schaerding, Austria, June, 1993, to be published in book form by North-Holland.

Huang, Y. (1992): "SPOOCS: An Object Oriented Open Systems Prototype" Key Center for Advanced Computing Sciences, University of Technology, Report. No. 92.6.

Kaplan, S.M., Tolone, W.J., Bogia, D.P., Bignoli, c. (1992): "Flexible, Active Support for Collaborative Work with ConversationBuilder" Proceedings CSCW92, Toronto, 1992. pp. 378-385.

Kuutti, K., Arvonen, T. (1992): "Identifying Potential CSCW Applications by Means of the Activity Theory Concepts: A Case Example" Proceedings CSCW92 Conference, Toronto, 1992, pp., 233-240.

Malone, T.W., Kum-Yew, L., Fry, C. "Experiments with OVAL: A Radically Tailorable Tool for Cooperative Work" Proceedings CSCW92, Toronto, 1992. pp. 289-297.

Schank, R.C., Abelson, R.P. (1977): "Scripts, Plans, Goals and Understanding" Lawrence Erlaum Associates, Hillsdale, New Jersey, 1977.

Schmidt, K., Bannon, L. (1002): "Taking CSCW Seriously" Computer Supported Cooperative Work, An International Journal, Vol.1., No.1, 1992.

Searle, J.R. (1969): Speech Acts, Cambridge University Press, Cambridge, 1969.

Wand, Y., Weber, R. (1990): "Towards a Theory of Deep Structure of Information Systems" Proceeding of the 11th International Conference on Information Systems, Copenhagen, 199, pp.61-72..

C-TORI:
An Interface for Cooperative Database Retrieval

H. Ulrich Hoppe & Jian Zhao
GMD-IPSI, 64293 Darmstadt (FRG)
e-mail: {hoppe,zhao}@darmstadt.gmd.de

Abstract. C-TORI (Cooperative TORI), a cooperative version of TORI (Task-Oriented Database Retrieval Interface), is presented in this paper. It extends interactive query formulation and result browsing by supporting cooperation between multiple users. In the cooperative environment, three basic additional operations are provided: *copying*, *merging* and *coupling* for three types of TORI objects (query forms, result forms, and query history windows). Cooperation with query forms allows end users to jointly formulate queries; cooperation with result forms supports users in jointly browsing through results and in sharing retrieved data without re-accessing the database; cooperative use of query histories yields a specific mechanism to share "memory" between users. The implementation is based on the concept of shared UI objects as an application-independent cooperation and communication model.

Keywords: Information Retrieval, Groupware, CSCW, Database Interfaces

1 Introduction

An important direction of research on end user support in information retrieval (IR) over the last ten years has been focused on "intelligent interfaces", including the understanding of natural language formulations of information needs as well as the generation and evaluation of formal queries [c.f. e.g. Belkin & Vickery, 1985; Brooks, 1987; Smith et al., 1989]. Given the current experience with intelligently supported interactive IR by end users, the quality of these systems as compared to traditional practice or to approaches based on a batch-oriented automatic translation of natural language descriptions of information needs may be arguable. But intelligent retrieval interfaces have certainly not yielded the expected practical effects in terms of giving large groups of new "naive" users access to public databases. We still have more or less trained end users accessing databases via "command languages", and we have indirect access supported by retrieval specialists. So, in practice IR, still involves human-human interaction. In the following, we want to elaborate on the potential of supporting this and also new types of IR-related human-human interaction by *computer-mediated communication*. Indeed, it is somewhat unnatural that database access which per se heavily relies on networks and distributed computing should only be considered as an individual activity from the user's perspective.

From a more general point of view, supporting human-human communication and cooperation in complex task environments is consistent with a current trend that stresses the role of social interaction in achieving high-level cognitive tasks [e.g. Winograd & Flores, 1987]. There is a tendency to propagate this view of systems design and use as an exclusive alternative to intelligent assistance. We do not share this attitude, but we believe that there is a great potential in combining intelligent assistance and computer-mediated human-human interaction. Currently, there is a deficit particularly in defining task-specific communication and cooperation mechanisms. In this paper, we focus on this latter aspect for the retrieval task.

Recent studies indicate that certain forms of information-sharing can indeed improve retrieval quality: Belkin et al. [1993a] report that combining boolean queries formulated by expert searchers almost unconditionally improved performance: "The basic message of our results is that combining different, independently generated boolean query formulations has, in general, a positive effect upon retrieval performance; and that in general, the more such formulations are used, the better the performance." In a following study [Belkin et al., 1993b], this finding was confirmed by more data. Also, positive effects were found, not only for combining queries, but also for merging data ("data fusion") from different ranked lists of query results.

These studies directly corroborate the usefulness of sharing two types of information in the retrieval situation: (a) query formulations and (b) result sets. In the studies, information sharing is the result of a formal operation applied to the given queries and not the result of an interactive cooperative process involving the experts. However, it is intuitively plausible that cooperative information sharing should yield similar effects on performance, and, on the other hand, it could be much more flexibly employed. In principle, users may work in parallel on similar tasks and compare and evaluate their results later, or they may define complementary tasks from the beginning. Also the assignment of different (or equal) roles in the group situation is relevant. In our setting, we assume that there is a moderator or coordinator who manages the communication links. However, this person is not necessarily a retrieval expert. A special application is the training of retrieval skills, in which would indeed assume that the moderator is a retrieval expert guiding the trainees. In more open group retrieval sessions, the role of the moderator may just be assigned to one participants acting as "primus inter pares".

Another important factor is the type of database. IR is traditionally focused on bibliographic databases. Here, the semantic structure (or the database schema) is rather simple and homogeneous, and the problem lies in extracting information from full text components. Certain types of factual databases have a much richer semantic and syntactic structure. This is an additional challenge since the user may not only be ignorant about information instances but also about the structure of the semantic space [cf. Hoppe et al., 1990; Hoppe, 1990]. With our model of communication and cooperation we concentrate on the needs of complexly structured databases. This implies that we focus on cooperative access to these structures, but also that we currently do not deal with problems specific to text retrieval, such as e.g. terminological knowledge bases, thesauri etc..

The solution presented in this paper is called *C-TORI*. It is a cooperative version of our previous prototype TORI (Task-Oriented database Retrieval Interface). To serve as an intelligent intermediary between user and database, TORI focuses on the *operative support* in a twofold sense: (a) how to map the information request onto the system, and (b) how to support certain higher-level plans or procedures that are introduced by the logic of some external task [Hoppe & Schiele, 1992]. The communication and cooperation mechanisms of C-TORI have been implemented using an application-independent communication and collaboration model [Zhao & Hoppe, 1994].

The next section will briefly describe the TORI system. Section 3 presents the cooperation model of C-TORI. In Section 4, we concentrate on the discussion of cooperatively formulating queries among users. Section 5 discusses the C-TORI's implementation on the communication aspect. Finally, some conclusion and perspectives for future work are outlined.

2 The TORI retrieval interface

In general, the basic task of database retrieval interfaces is to "mediate" between the user and the DBMS. It is widely acknowledged that various support strategies should be available in more intelligent and user-friendly database retrieval interfaces [cf. Parsaye et al., 1989, chapter 6]. To provide this kind of user support, particularly including the task perspective, we developed TORI (a Task-Oriented database Retrieval Interface).

The TORI architecture consists of a *forms-DBMS interface* and a set of *support modules*. The *forms-DBMS interface* translates form-based query specifications into the database retrieval language and converts the retrieval results into a form-based presentation. The user interface of TORI uses enhanced forms for the specification of queries, thereby hiding the DBMS data manipulation language from the user. The *support modules* provide task-oriented mechanisms for the retrieval process. Currently, we have developed four support modules. Since we do not concentrate on their functionalities in this paper, they are not discussed here.

TORI definition language

Deriving interfaces to databases from a database description or from an external specification is attractive, since it allows for easily adapting the database interface system to many different databases. In TORI, we use a specification language to express more than the usual database description. This language is processed by an interpreter that maps the specifications onto interaction objects such as query forms and result browsers. TORI forms can be defined to cover more than one relation or view, in which case the query will be will be translated using join operations. Thus, details of the database schema are hidden from the user. Various interaction techniques can be specified in query forms by providing specific *user interface templates* for the presentation of database attributes (e.g. selection menus). Templates can be created interactively with a user interface builder (TOE: Toolbox Object Editor) [Zhao et al., 1993].

In addition to the mapping of attributes, database relations, views, and joins onto interactive forms of the user interface, the TORI language also allows for defining the semantic equivalence between attributes in different forms. This equivalence information is used to (1) re-use previous query specifications and result sets to partially instantiate different forms, and (2) perform cooperation operations in C-TORI, e.g. to match attributes that can be coupled, copied or merged in two different query forms.

TORI query language

TORI can be customized to interface with many relational DBMSs[1] which support different query languages which differ in both expressiveness and syntax. To bridge this gap, TORI defines a common *forms-based query language*. It covers a common subset of most query languages.

Although form-oriented querying is attractive to novice users, it restricts the query expressiveness [Tuori, 1988]. For example, the flexible specification of logical connectors between different attribute fields in a form may considerably complicate the ease-of-use. Moreover, it is difficult to specify complex constraints for database attributes. In order to keep the advantages of form-oriented queries, but loosen their restrictions, TORI provides a pop-up menu for each attribute, from which users can choose among different *modes* of the entries they put into the text fields.

- *equal* interprets an entry as an attribute value for exact matching;
- *like* interprets an entry as a substring;
- *one of* or *like one of* (*all of* or *like all of*) interpret a list of terms entered in an attribute as a disjunction (conjunction) with either full or truncated matching;
- *less than* or *more than* are interpreted numerically;
- *SQL* mode provides a means for specifying attribute values with standard SQL (the name of the database attribute is omitted in the attribute value).

Another means to loosen the restrictions imposed by the forms interface in TORI is a mechanism to combine previous queries by different logical connectors. This mechanism is called *query by combination* [Zhao et al., 1993]. (Currently C-TORI supports cooperation only for the standard *query forms*, i.e. *query by attribute*.)

Although TORI systems can support arbitrary relational databases, we have one special test case, a relational version of the CORDIS database of European research which contains information on projects (over 10.000), programmes, organizations, responsible persons, and publications (about 28.000). The examples used in this paper are taken from this information environment.

3 Cooperation model

Information search in databases should be a highly interactive process in which the steps of *target recognition* (i.e. result browsing) and *query reformulation* are iterated to approximate an optimal result. Intelligent support and human-human cooperation between end users are complementary means to support this process. To support human-human cooperation, we have to consider synchronous and asynchronous communication channels. In this respect, we assume certain means of asynchronous transfer of information to be given, e.g. a mail system and a multi-user file system. In our model, we concentrate on synchronous communication and cooperation in the task environment.

1. Currently, Ingres and Sybase have been defined in TORI. Ingres® and Sybase® are the relational database management systems of Ingres Corp. and Sybase Inc. respectively.

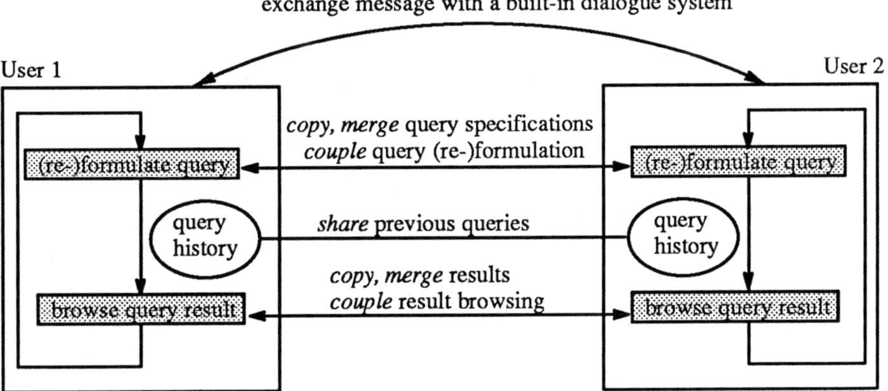

Figure 3. Cooperative querying & browsing cycle

As shown in Figure 3, communication in the cooperation model of C-TORI takes is supported by three general operations (*copy, merge, couple/decouple*) in each step of the iterative cycle of database retrieval. The *copy* and *merge* operations cause a one-step information transfer, whereas *coupling* initiates a period of sharing information in certain objects (query forms or attribute fields).

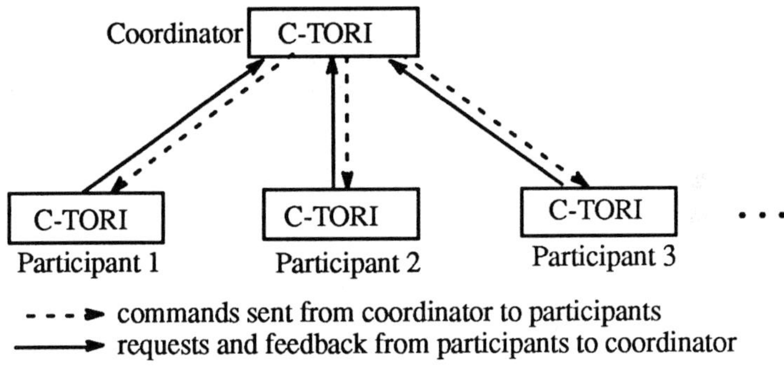

Figure 4. Centralized cooperation control in C-TORI

C-TORI employs a centralized cooperation control shown in Figure 4. A *coordinator* distributes retrieval tasks to a group of information searchers who may work remotely. Each searcher uses his or her knowledge and tools to perform the assigned tasks individually. Once a task has been finished, the coordinator is requested to collect and integrate the results, by opening multiple query (and result) forms to which the participant's query specification or query result is copied, or with which the participant's query (result) window is coupled. During his or her individual work, each participant is free to communicate with the coordinator for suggestions and discussions, or to ask the coordinator for establishing direct couple links with other participants. Currently, cooperation operations (i.e. *couple*, *copy*, *merge*) can only be initiated by the coordinator.

Cooperatively formulating queries

Even in the formulation of single queries, users may cooperate, e.g. exploiting their different knowledge of the domain vocabulary or of the semantics of the database. C-TORI supports a group of users in jointly specifying a query at the same time. In the next section, *cooperatively formulating query* will be discussed in detail. In tightly-coupled mode, each action (e.g. entering a query specification, evaluating a query, or display of results) issued by one user is displayed and re-executed in the other user's environment. This WYSIWIS-like ("What You See Is What I See" [Stefik et al., 1987]) behavior can e.g. be used to train novice users.

Sharing query histories

Interaction histories are a valuable source of empirical knowledge to support users in user-centered interactive systems. In our case, a *query history* consists of an ordered set of previous queries. Each *previous query* contains the query specification and potentially a selective subset of results obtained from the execution of the specification. The original TORI system supports several operations for the reuse of previous queries, e.g. take a previous query as a new query specification, or display the selectively stored results of a previous query.

C-TORI provides a runtime *shared history mechanism.* All of the three cooperation operations (i.e. *copy, merge*, and *couple*) are provided for sharing previous queries between users. Whenever the query histories of a group of users are coupled, each query issued by one member of a coupled session is inserted into each other member's query history. Of course, history entries are also shared after evaluating coupled query forms. The difference between coupling the query history and coupling query forms is that in the first case queries are not re-executed in the other users' environments (but only recorded) for coupled histories, but they are for coupled forms.

Cooperatively browsing results

Query results in TORI are displayed either instance by instance in a result form which is similar to query form, or – to provide an overview – as a result table. Cooperative query formulation allows a group of users to express their search goals jointly. Result browsers that are invoked from coupled query forms are also coupled by default. However, this involves multiple execution of the joint query. We also allow for *cooperative result browsing* by only coupling browsers without coupling the respective query forms. This is attractive for the following reasons: (1) it reduces retrieval costs; and (2) it allows a user to browse through result sets retrieved from other databases and by other users.

4 Cooperatively formulating queries

Centralized control

C-TORI employs a centralized control model for cooperation, i.e. the cooperation operations can only be initiated by a moderator or coordinator. Figure 5 shows the window used by the coordinator to issue cooperation operations for the cooperative formulation of queries.

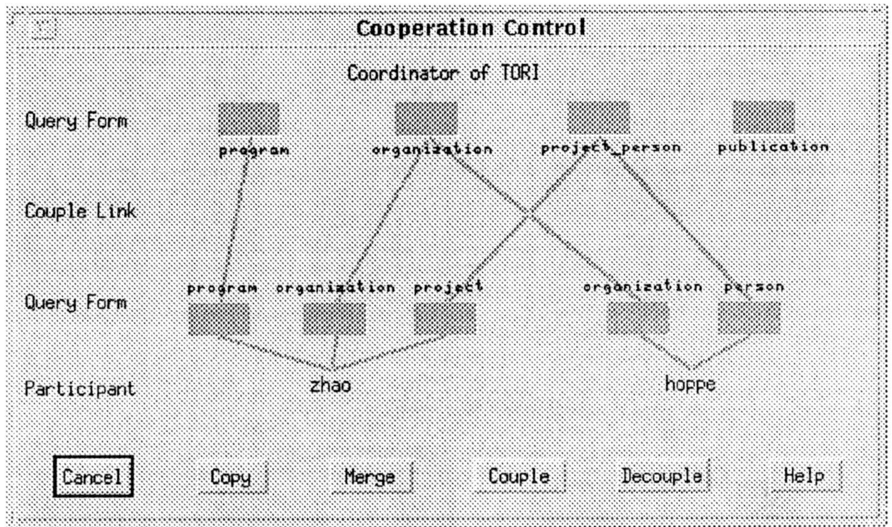

Figure 5. Controlling cooperative query formulation

When a user (either the coordinator or a participant) creates a query form, it is displayed on this control window as an icon labelled with the name of the form. By choosing two icons the coordinator can invoke one of the cooperation operations (i.e. *copy*, *merge*, and *coupling*) on the selected forms.

All cooperation operations are *directed*: the first selected icon is the dominating query form, and the second selected icon is the dominated form. For the *copy* operation, the content of the dominated form is overwritten with the content of the dominating form. For the *merge* operation, the constructively merged query specification derived from the the contents of the two original forms replaces the content of each form (see below). After coupling two query forms, users work in partial WYSIWIS mode [Stefik et al., 1987]. After decoupling, the data from the joint session are kept in each environment. Moreover, coupling implies an initial synchronization by applying either a *copy* or a *merge* operation. The couple link is *transitive*, e.g. in Figure 5, Zhao's *organization* form has been coupled with Hoppe's *organization* form because each of them has been coupled with coordinator's *organization* form.

Cooperatively formulating queries in identical query forms

By coupling identical query forms between users, they can (1) specify query constrains on different attributes of coupled query forms, or even (2) enter query terms on a coupled attribute at the same time. C-TORI employs an automatic locking mechanism to avoid conflicts when multiple users try to make input at the same time in the same place.

In the first case, each user is assumed to work on his or her specific attributes of the joint query form. For example, in a coupled *project* query form, a group of users searches for a ESPRIT project on 'multimedia user interfaces'. One of the users may work on the *title* and *objectives* descriptions of projects, and others on formal criteria such as *start date* etc.. The locking unit in this case is an attribute field, i.e. a field in which one user's editing cursor is located is uneditable by other participants that share the same form. In the second case, locking units are elements of the surface structure of the attribute-specific subquery, e.g. single terms or enumerations.

Cooperatively formulating queries in different query forms

Not only identical but also different query forms can be coupled. Furthermore, a query form can be coupled with more than one query forms of different users. When two different query forms are copied, merged, or coupled, their *equivalent* attributes (cf. section 2) are matched. For example, the coordinator's *project_person* can be coupled with participant P_1's *project* form and P_2's *person* form at the same time. In the coordinator's *project_person* query form, some attributes are coupled with the corresponding attributes in both the *project* form of P_1 and the *person* form of P_2.

Merging query specifications

C-TORI supports two ways of initially synchronizing query specifications among query forms of different users before these forms can be tightly coupled: *copy* and *merge*. As a general application-independent approach for initial synchronization, our communication model provides primitives to copy the contents and even structures of complex user interface objects from one application instance to another. The content of UI objects is determined by their attributes, and a complex object is a hierarchically structured collection of primitive UI objects. To copy between two complex UI objects with different structures in two application instances, we have proposed *destructive merging* and *flexible matching* [Zhao & Hoppe, 1994].

However, *content-oriented merging* typically depends on the semantics of the objects involved, i.e. it is application-specific. In joint document editing, this leads to complex requirements for versioning [Haake & Haake, 1993]. For query specifications, there are simpler ways to avoid information loss by destructive copying. In C-TORI, we support a constructive *merge* operation applied to *form-oriented* query specifications.

Each query form f is characterized by a set of conjunctively combined attributes *attr(f)*. In a concrete instance, i.e. in a filled query form, we can distinguish three subsets of these attributes: *specified attributes* (the attributes on which the user enters query conditions), *requested attributes* (the attributes selected to instantiated and displayed in the result), and *other attributes* that are neither specified nor requested. We denote these subsets as *spec(f)*, *req(f)*, and *other(f)* respectively. The *query specification* of each specified attribute $a \in spec(f)$ is composed of a mode operator *mode(a)* (cf. section 2) and the query content *content(a)* (i.e. an enumeration of query terms or a boolean SQL expression). Assume f_1, f_2 are two instances of potentially different query forms. As mentioned above, the semantic equivalence of attributes between different forms is explicitly declared and thus available. Under the constructive merge operation, the two forms f_1, f_2 are transformed, giving two variants f_1', f_2'. This transformation is governed by the following set of rules (since this operation is symmetric in f_1 and f_2, only f_1' is specified):

For any attribute $a_1 \in attr(f_1)$ not equivalent to an attribute $a_2 \in attr(f_2)$, the query specification of a_1 is unchanged.

For any attribute $a_1 \in spec(f_1)$ equivalent to some $a_2 \in req(f_2) \cup other(f_2)$, the query specification of a_1 is unchanged.

For any attribute $a_1 \in req(f_1) \cup other(f_1)$ equivalent to some $a_2 \in spec(f_2)$, $mode(a_1') \leftarrow mode(a_2)$ and $content(a_1') \leftarrow content(a_2)$.

For any attribute $a_1 \in spec(f_1)$ equivalent to some $a_2 \in spec(f_2)$,
/* the following rules are only incomplete set of examples! */

if $mode(a_1) = mode(a_2)$ and the mode operator is *'equal'*
    /* the *'equal'* mode implies content is only a query term */
    let $content(a_1)$ be $'t_1'$ and $content(a_2)$ be $'t_2'$
then $mode(a_1') \leftarrow$ *'one of'* and $content(a_1') \leftarrow 't_1, t_2'$;

if $mode(a_1) = mode(a_2)$ and mode operator is *'like'* or *'like one of'*
    /* *'like one of'* mode implies that the attribute content is an enumeration of terms separated by a comma */
    let $content(a_1)$ be $'t_{11}, t_{12}, \ldots, t_{1n}'$
        where n is the number of the query terms entered in a_1, and
    let $content(a_2)$ be $'t_{21}, t_{22}, \ldots, t_{2m}'$
        where m is the number of the query terms entered in a_2
then $mode(a_1') \leftarrow$ *'like one of'* and
    $content(a_1') \leftarrow 't_{11}, t_{12}, \ldots, t_{1n}, t_{21}, t_{22}, \ldots, t_{2m}'$;

.....

The above rules merge the contents of query forms *disjunctively.* This is specifically evident in the last case in which the component specifications of the two original queries are combined disjunctively. *Conjunctive merging* can be defined accordingly, though it leads to a higher selectivity that easily gives empty results. Therefore it may make less sense in real situations than disjunctive merging.

5 Implementation

The communication mechanism used in C-TORI is based on the principle of *shared user interface objects* [Zhao & Hoppe, 1994]. During coupling, selective user events on each coupled object are broadcasted to other objects in a coupled object group. Thus the behavior of coupled objects is fully synchronized. This *shared UI object* communication model has been implemented as a fully replicated server-client architecture. The central controller or server broadcasts user actions and coordinates communication and access control.

Closely related to our communication model are e.g. the *Rendezvous* system [Patterson et. al, 1990] and the *Suite* system [Dewan et al., 1991]. In the *Suite* coupling model, a set of coupling parameters is defined to indicate *what kinds of couple links* are established between interaction entities. This gives a high flexibility in coupling interaction entities, e.g. by synchronizing the visibility or by coupling semantic actions. The major difference with our communication model is that *Suite* is based on a UI-replicated architecture, i.e. a single application is linked to multiple user interfaces through which users communicate with each other. Furthermore, our communication model is directly based on UI objects (particularly, an extension of the OSF/Motif widget set). Thus it allows us to build arbitrary user interfaces for a wider range of applications.

Since our communication mechanism is located on the level of the user interface which is constructed from a set of standardized UI objects, it possible to convert single user into multi-user application almost without additional effort. Of course, only those data can be accessed and shared that are explicitly represented as UI objects or object attributes in the user interface. Thus a major part of C-TORI was directly recompiled with only few changes to the original TORI (only several lines of source code). Major additions for C-TORI were in the synchronization of semantic data (i.e. internal application data structures, e.g. query histories), and the cooperation control component (cf. Figure 5).

Since most internal TORI objects are associated with surface UI objects (e.g. *query form*), most application data in TORI can be synchronized automatically by sharing UI data. For the internal data structures that do not directly correspond to UI data, C-TORI provides a specific mapping function. This function copies or merges application data between different C-TORI instances, and furthermore updates the user interface according to the synchronized application data.

6 Conclusion

C-TORI supports cooperative IR between end users as a highly interactive joint activity. It provides *query formulation* and *result browsing* as group operations. The specific features demonstrated in C-TORI are:

- By tightly coupling forms-based query specifications, multiple users can cooperatively formulate queries. This is also the key function for using C-TORI for training purposes.
- By tightly coupling result forms (or tables), users can cooperatively browse through results to evaluate and reformulate queries. Thus, the evolution of queries does not only depend on the individual achievements.
- By sharing query histories, accumulated query formulations and results can be reused by all users in a group without explicit coupling of query forms or browsers (minimal interference).

We plan to make cooperation control more flexible, allowing not only the coordinator but also each participant to initiate cooperation operations. As a consequence, we will have access permissions explicitly controlled by the system.

Our work is only an initial step towards designing and implementing *cooperative information retrieval systems*. We plan to integrate the cooperative model with intelligent components or agents inside the system. Thus, cooperative retrieval and information use may be an example of *cooperative problem solving* in which several users interact through and with a locally intelligent system. It appears as natural to integrate TORI's *task support* components (task parser and planner) with the cooperative environment. Then, the joint execution of tasks could be supported in a way similar to the individual task by monitoring and extrapolating plans. The cooperative situation offers the interesting possibility to initiate consultation between users if the system is e.g. not able to suggest a meaningful next action as an extrapolation of the previous actions.

Acknowledgements We want to thank Franz Schiele for reading a draft of this paper, and also the other members of the TOSS group at GMD-IPSI for their contributions to developing TORI.

References

Belkin, N.J.; *Cool*, C.; *Croft*, W.B.; *Calla*, J.P. (1993a). The effect of multiple query representations on information system performance. In: Proceedings of ACM SIGIR '93 (Pittsburgh, PA, June/July 1993). pp. 339-346.

Belkin, N.J.; *Kantor*, P.; *Cool*, C.; *Quatrain*, R. (1993b). Combining evidence for information retrieval. In: Proceedings of the TREC-2 Conference (preprint).

Belkin, N.J. and *Vickery*, A. (1985). Interaction in information systems. (Library & Information Research Report 35). London: The British Library, 1985.

Brooks, H.M. (1987). Expert systems and intelligent information retrieval. Information Processing and Management, 23 (4). pp. 367-382.

Dewan, P. and *Choudhary*, R. (1991). Flexible user interface coupling in a collaborative system. In: Proceedings of ACM Conference on Human Factors in Computing Systems CHI '91 (New Orleans, April 28-May 2, 1991). pp. 41-48.

Haake, A. and *Haake*, J.M. (1993). Take CoVer: Exploiting version support in cooperative systems. In: Proceedings of the InterCHI' 93 (Amsterdam, Netherlands, April 26-29, 1993). ACM Press, 1993. pp. 406-413.

Hoppe, H.U.; *Ammersbach*, K.; *Lutes-Schaab*, B.; *Zinssmeister*, G. (1990). EXPRESS – an experimental interface for factual information retrieval. In: Proceedings of ACM SIGIR '90 (Brussels, Belgium, September 1990). pp. 63-81.

Hoppe, H.U. (1990). Intelligent access to public data banks. In: Proceedings of the International AI Symposium (IAIS '90, Nagoya, Japan, November 1990).

Hoppe, H.U. and *Schiele*, F. (1992). Towards task models for embedded Information Retrieval. In: Proceedings of ACM CHI '92 (Monterey, Calif., USA, May 3-7, 1992).

Parsaye, K.; *Chignell*, M.; *Khoshafian*, S.; *Wong*, H. (1989). Intelligent Databases, Object-Oriented, Deductive Hypermedia Technologies. New York et al.: John Wiley & Sons, 1989. pp. 293-433.

Patterson, J.F.; *Hill*, R.D.; *Rohall*, R.S.; Meeks, W.S. (1990). Rendezvous: An architecture for synchronous multi-user applications. In: Proceedings of the Conference on Computer-Supported Cooperative Work (Los Angels, USA, 1990).

Smith, P.J.; *Steven*, J.S.; *Galdes*, D.; *Chignell*, M.H. (1989). Knowledge-based search tactics for an intelligent intermediary system. ACM Transactions on Information Systems, 7(3). pp. 246-270.

Stefik, M.; *Foster*, G.; *Bobrow*, D.G.; *Kahn*, K.; *Lanning*, S.; *Suchman*, L. (1987). Beyond the chalkboard: Computer support for collaboration and problem solving in meetings. Communications of the ACM, 30(1). pp. 32-47.

Sybase Inc. (1989). Sybase Commands Reference Manual. Emeryville, CA: Sybase Inc. Release 4.0, May 1989.

Tuori, M.I. (1988). A Framework for Browsing in the Relational Data Model (PhD thesis, 1987). Toronto: University of Toronto, January 1988 (Technical Report CSRI-202).

Winograd, T. and *Flores*, F. (1987). Understanding Computers and Cognition. Reading, MA: Addison-Wesley.

Zhao, J. and *Hoppe*, H.U. (1994). Supporting flexible communication in heterogeneous multi-user environments. To appear in: Proceedings of the 14th International Conference on Distributed Computing Systems (Poznan, Poland, June 21-24, 1994).

Zhao, J.; *Kostka*, B.; *Müller*, A. (1993). An integrated approach to task-oriented database retrieval interfaces. In: R. Cooper (ed.). Interfaces to Database Systems. London et al.: Springer-Verlag, 1993. pp. 56-73.

Organization Models for Cooperative Office Applications

Walter Rupietta
Siemens Nixdorf Informationssysteme AG
D-33094 Paderborn

Abstract: Regulated communication and cooperation between members of an enterprise relies on organization structures of the enterprise. This is explained in the introduction implying that an organization model is necessary for realizing application systems to support this type of cooperative work. The main part of this paper describes the Organization and Resources Management system ORM which makes it possible to build organization models and use them in application systems. As an example, the use of ORM in a workflow management system is described. ORM stores its models in a relational database with an SQL interface and implements a set of automatic inheritance rules for authority assignments to organizational entities. These rules follow common organizational practice. Problems of implementing these features with a relational database are discussed. Finally, directions for future developments and exploration areas are suggested.

Keywords: Organization model, workflow management, organization-directed access control, synchronization of heterogeneous databases

1 Introduction

Every enterprise or public authority is organized in one way or another. Organization[1] determines when and how tasks are processed and by whom. It is an important topic in the context of office work but usually less important in the world of factory work. Organization covers static structure as well as dynamics of business processes (workflow) taking place in the context of the static structures. Organization structure divides enterprises into organizational units and defines relationships between them, assigns tasks and authorities to organizational units and sets the framework for business workflow.

Organization also determines which business procedures are automated and in which way. Each software system, being an automated part of a business process, must conform to the underlying organization structure. According to Dzida's (1983) description of the IFIP model for user interfaces, the *organization interface* is characterized by rules determining how the tasks of one user are connected to other users' tasks. Organization determines division of labor, official channels and cooperation.

Employees of an enterprise, organizational positions, functions, or units, tasks, resources, authorities, procedures, activities, rules ... are objects of organization This list is of course incomplete but should give an idea of the complexity of organization and name some of the most important concepts. Some of these concepts are also used in office systems or applications. User databases register those persons that are entitled to use the application system or parts of the system. Information from the user database is used for identifying system users in order to control access to system resources or to address users within a network. Users may also be assigned functional roles (like network administrator) implying certain access rights and responsibilities.

1 In this paper, the term organization refers to the result, not to the process of organizing.

Different components of an office system, e.g. a document filing system or a database system, use different user databases which differ from each other and from the underlying operating system's user database.

For an office system the collection of all its user databases represents the system's user organization. Most user databases are implemented to meet technical and not organizational requirements. This means that the adaptation of an office system to the needs of the organization requires a mapping between organizational concepts and technical concepts. To best match office systems to their organizational environment, it is necessary to apply the organization principles of the environment to the office system to achieve the best possible congruence between the two organizations. However, while user databases of an office system can express only limited organizational concepts (individual users and their access rights for some system resources) enterprise organization is a rather complex field.

With the advent of CSCW-applications (see Winograd, 1988) organization concepts have become even more important for office systems. Especially the support of *regulated communication and cooperation* between members of an enterprise (which is common, for example, in banks, insurance companies or public authorities) in workflow management systems requires that organizational rules be closely followed. Workflow management systems allow the description of business procedures, i.e. the dynamic aspects of organization. Dynamic business organization relies on an underlying static organization structure which is generally more complex than simple user databases can express.

Software applications in general automate portions of office procedures or business processes. Consequently, application systems need information on the enterprise organization in order to fulfill their tasks according to the underlying organization structure. Organization models are a special aspect of *enterprise modeling* which is an attempt to cover all aspects of an enterprise (see, for example, Scheer, 1990). Their structure is more complex than usual application user databases, so more powerful representation mechanisms than flat files or tables are necessary for implementing an organization model.

Related work can be found in the area of office systems. Ellis (1983) models dynamic aspects of office work, static structure is only present in goal and resource structure and in roles or job titles needed to perform certain activities. The office model described in Ishii and Kubota (1988) is a knowledge base prototype representing office procedures, organization structure and resources. Recently, organization models are explored in CSCW systems, especially workflow management applications. An overview of requirements for organization knowledge bases for supporting cooperative processes is given in Schmalz (1991). Workflow management systems often contain organization descriptions (see, for example, Karbe, 1993), that are accessible only by the workflow management system itself, not by other applications. The *Organization and Resources Management System* (ORM) described in this paper is used in the WorkParty® workflow management system to model organization structure in a relational database. However, it is an independent platform with interfaces for implementing applications relying on organization structure. An early prototype of ORM was described in Rupietta (1990). In the research prototype system

TOSCA (see Prinz 1993) an object-oriented database is used for storing an organization model which also comprises an interface for use by other applications.

2 The Organization and Resources Management System ORM

The *Organization and Resources Management* system (ORM) was developed to provide application systems with information on the underlying enterprise organization in a standardized form. A single database with a model of the organization structure is available to different application systems. Thus a consistent image of the organization structure is guaranteed for all application systems.

2.1 The Conceptional Model of ORM

The ORM conceptional model emerged as an object-oriented design consisting in a set of related *object classes* representing concepts from business organization theory. The object classes were mapped onto database relations to be stored in a relational database with an SQL interface. Relational databases were favored over object-oriented approaches because of their general and widespread availability. The implementation of the model would have been more natural using an object-oriented database. The ORM model comprises the object classes (concepts) listed in Table 1.

Employees	The people working in the enterprise. Employees are integrated in the organization by assignments to positions.
Organizational units	Organizational units are sets of positions with common or related tasks grouped together to form a larger operational unit. Organizational units can be subordinate to other organizational units and can themselves have subordinate organizational units, i.e. they can form hierarchies.
Positions	A position represents the workplace of an employee and thus is a kind of "abstract employee". Positions are the basic elements that constitute an organization.
Functions	Organizational functions like department manager, accounting clerk, secretary are assigned to positions.
Authorities	Authority is a combination of authorizations and responsibilities. Authorizations are expressed by resource assignments and responsibilities by task assignments.
Tasks	A task is a goal set for the activity of employees.
Resources	Working materials, work objects and tools used in the office system context. Resources can be subordinate (e.g. as constituents) of another resource and can have subordinate resources.

Table 1: Objects managed by ORM

Relationships between objects of these classes are shown in Figure 1 which is derived from an entity-relationship diagram of the ORM data model. Organizational Units and Resources can be hierarchically ordered, positions are assigned to organizational units and employees as well as roles can be assigned to positions. Authorities can be assigned to either employees, positions, roles, or organizational units. Tasks and resources can be assigned to authorities which then serve for bundling tasks and required resources. One of an organizational unit's positions can be marked as lead position. One of an employee's position is marked as regular position, other employees can be assigned as proxies for a position.

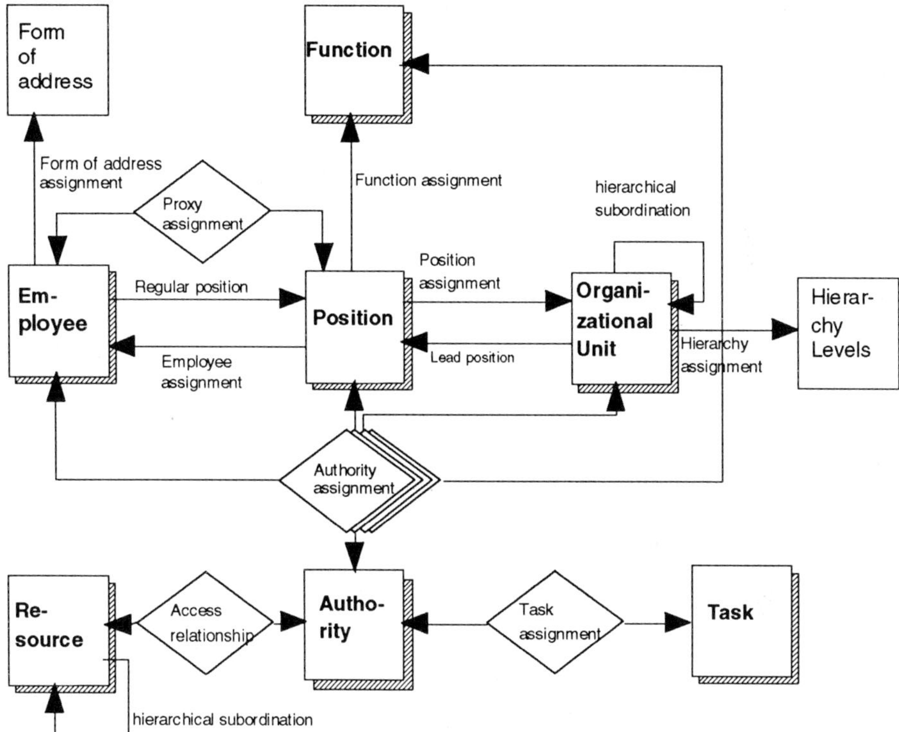

Figure 1: ORM model

The ORM model possesses sufficient expressive power to describe real enterprise organization structures using concepts from organization theory. At the same time it is flexible enough to model small workgroup organizations as well as large hierarchically structured organizations, although it is best suited for modeling enterprises with well-defined organization structures of moderate size.

As an example, the ORM model makes it possible to express statements like "Jones is the manager of the accounting department. He is authorized to sign payment orders up to 5000 ECU. The accounting department is part of the internal administrations section. If Jones is absent, either Smith or Henley may act as proxies." This statement can be modeled by defining an employee object named Jones, which is assigned to a position object in the organizational unit object Accounting with the hierarchy level Department. His position can be marked as lead position of the organizational unit. An authority object representing the authorization for signing payment orders can be defined and assigned to Jones' position. Employee objects named Smith and Henley are assigned as proxies for Jones' position.

2.2 Implementation Aspects

ORM's database implementation is rather straightforward: object classes (concepts) are mapped onto database tables. Each object (i.e. each instance of an object class) is implemented by a row in the corresponding table and identified by a short name unique in its class. Internally an *object handle* is used for identifying objects, for example in foreign key references. While the short name of an object may change, its handle remains unchanged through the lifetime of an object. Other attributes are particular to each object class. A position, for instance, is characterized by short name, long name, organizational unit reference, position holder reference, function reference, address and comment. Relationships represented by a rhombus in Figure 1 are called *relationship classes* and are also mapped onto database tables while all the other relationships are represented by foreign key attributes of the respective tables. Each object class (and each relationship class) can be supplemented by user-defined attribute sets called *subclasses*[2]. Subclasses are also implemented as separate database tables. Thus information attached to an object in the ORM model can be tailored to the user's needs. Each application system using ORM data can register itself by attaching its own subclasses to store additional information.

Expert systems aspects within ORM are based on the proposition that authorities of an employee in an enterprise are primarily based on his or her placement within the enterprise's organization structure and do not depend on the individual employee. Consequently a set of *inheritance rules for authority assignments* was defined to reflect rules explicitly and more often implicitly used in enterprise organizations. Employees inherit authority assignments from their positions. Positions inherit from their functions and - depending on the inheritance policy for the specific authority - from their organizational units. Organizational units may inherit authority assignments from their superior units. The inheritance of authority assignments is automatically recalculated when relevant updates occur.

This inheritance mechanism is a problematic part of the ORM database implementation. No relational database can provide integrity constraints that automatically keep the ORM model consistent with respect to authority inheritance. The (re-) calculation of authority inheritance is thus implemented in the ORM API as a database transaction to preserve consistency of the ORM model. However, this recalculation can be time consuming, if, for example, subtrees of an organization hierarchy are restructured, resulting in rather long transactions.

An alternative approach would be not to precalculate authority inheritance at the time when an authority assignment is made or changed, but to traverse the organization hierarchy for authority assignments, when they are retrieved. In the latter case, updates would be faster but retrieval would be much slower. Our current implemen-

2 Use of the term subclass is different from the concepts of object-oriented programming.

tation favors execution speed for retrieval operations because they occur more frequently than organization restructuring operations.

Complex retrieval operations as, for example, *"Find all employees holding a position with a specific function in a given organizational unit who are assigned a given set of authorities"* are not directly supported by the SQL interface, but require a combination of multiple database retrieval operations. Other retrieval functions of comparable complexity are required for implementing workflow applications. For large, complex organization models such operations are very time-consuming.

2.3 ORM Architecture and Interfaces

ORM was developed using remote database access within a local area network. The database may reside on a SINIX® server system, while the database client and the ORM software are located on a PC running Microsoft® Windows™ and connected to the server system. To be independent from a specific database management system, a database access layer was implemented as part of ORM's low level access interface.

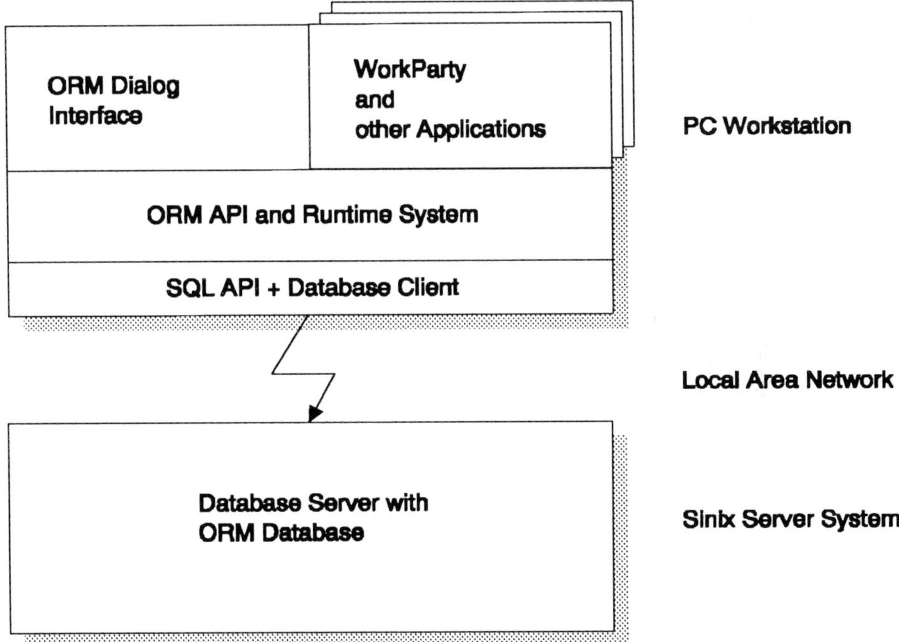

Figure 2: ORM architecture

ORM can be accessed and administered via its *dialog interface*. Each object class is presented in its own dialog window where relationships can be tracked by double-clicking on the appropriate reference item (comparable to hypertext systems): the referenced item will then come up. The main innovation of ORM compared to other attempts at modeling organization structure is its *API* allowing other application systems to access organization structures modeled in ORM. The API is implemented as a dynamic link library (DLL) and serves as a *runtime system* for ORM (see Figure 2).

In addition there is also an import/export interface for exchanging complete or partial models in a format that can be processed by other applications.

The API comprises functions for creating, retrieving, updating and deleting objects and related subclass objects, subclasses and subclass attributes as well as functions for administrative purposes. The API is session-oriented and therefore has functions for logging on and off. In addition there are functions for starting, committing, or rolling back API transactions. All API functions maintain *model consistency* using database transactions where necessary. API transactions are implemented as database transactions requiring that commit operations used within API functions are deferred until the API transaction is committed.

We envisage that office systems will always be heterogeneous systems comprising a collection of tools and applications from different manufacturers. Thus, in addition to the ORM API as a means for writing applications that directly use ORM, different techniques were developed for linking application systems to the organization model in ORM, depending on the type of application:

- *ORM-compliant* systems directly use information from ORM via its programming interfaces.
- *ORM-aware* systems replicate some information contained in the ORM model in their own proprietary format and thus need to be notified of relevant changes. A *notification mechanism* will be provided in a future version.
- *ORM-unaware* systems are completely independent of ORM but maintain user (or other) data also present within the ORM model. These may be automatically adapted by a specific *software agent* that implements replication mechanics as in the former case, provided the ORM-unaware system is equipped with an appropriate programming interface. The ORM change log can be evaluated to check for relevant updates.

An example of the second category is SNI's X.500-based address management system that is being combined with ORM.

2.4 Application Examples

ORM is currently used within SNI's workflow management system WorkParty. While ORM represents the static organizational structure WorkParty models dynamic aspects of organization in form of workflow procedures. Workflow procedures in WorkParty are represented graphically. For each activity (i.e. each unit of work carried out on a single workplace) the authorized user is specified by a *user profile.* A user profile consists of the names of (optionally) an employee, a function, a position, an organizational unit and one or more authorities and selects a set of employees from the ORM model who match all of the given entities.

A workflow procedure in WorkParty is graphically defined, the programs implementing activities and their interfaces are specified via dialog boxes. During the definition process ORM is consulted to fill in the user profiles of procedure initiator, procedure administrator and authorized user for each activity. When the definition is finished, a procedure is released to the *template folder archive* (see Figure 3). When

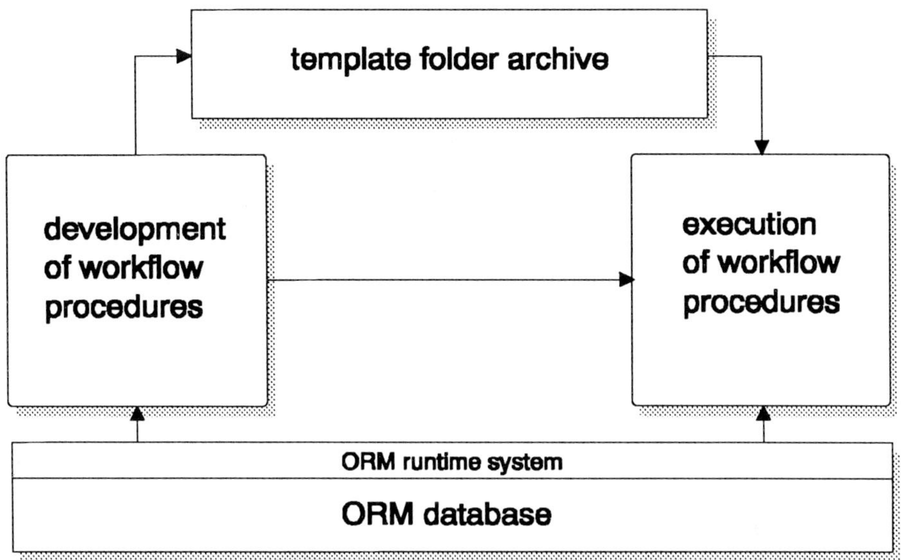

Figure 3: Use of ORM in workflow management

a workflow procedure is being initiated from the template folder archive ORM is again consulted to match the user profile of the initiator against the actual system user and his position within the organization model. When the procedure is executed the matching of user profiles is carried out for each activity to find the set of authorized users. Thus WorkParty ensures that a workflow procedure is routed through the organization according to the structure that is valid at the moment of procedure execution, not of procedure definition. In this way static structures and dynamic workflows are combined and synchronized to resemble real life business procedures.

Another application prototype has demonstrated how the administration of different ORM-unaware services in a local area network can be unified using ORM as a central administration database. Services (e.g. a database or a file server in a local area network) and their resources (e.g. database tables, shared file systems, printers) were modeled as resources in ORM. Access rights were defined by assigning resources to appropriate authorities and these authorities in turn to organizational entities (employees, positions, organizational units or functions), thereby exploiting the inheritance rules for authority assignments. A mapping of these relationships to entries in the target services' user databases was specified. A background agent scanned ORM's change log and automatically propagated relevant updates to the target systems. This synchronization procedure could be carried out periodically or at specific request.

3 Conclusion and Ideas for Future Development

Contrasted to the selective view represented by collections of independent user databases in current application environments, each defining a limited view of the organizational environment, the organization model gives a more *holistic view* and certainly reflects more closely the organizational environment of an information system. SNI's intention is for ORM to become a single access point for all organization-related information requirements from applications and services in the office system environment. This is a long term prospect because the employment of an organization model requires its acknowledgment by most applications and services in the system.

The organization model affects all areas where application systems' user databases are used. Each of them can be replaced by an appropriate view on an organization model. The availability of such a model makes it possible to replace currently used concepts by other, more appropriate concepts. For example, using authorities instead of user IDs in access control lists of application systems automatically leads to an *organization-directed access control scheme* (employing the authorities inheritance mechanism). In addition, application systems can make use of organizational relationships such as the assignment of authorities, functions, tasks etc. to reflect these relationships in their behavior.

All applications supporting regulated communication and communication among members of an organization are naturally affected by an organization model. As an example a workflow management system was described in the previous chapter. Of course, only formal relationships and dependencies are captured in an organization model. Informal structures are intentionally left out because it is doubtful whether they can and should be explicitly represented in a computer system.

Further development of the ORM as described in the previous chapter is guided by requirements from existing office applications and from applications being developed. We are currently exploring the following directions:

- Enrichment of organization structure: multi-function and multi-employee positions, relationships between different functions (e.g. mutual exclusion), hierarchies of functions and authorities
- Extended features for application-specific subclasses, namely support of binary large objects as subclass attributes (to attach, for example, an image of an employee or a document describing requirements for a position)
- Organization-directed security and access control policies (using the inheritance mechanism for authority assignments).
- Techniques for distribution of databases across networks: distributed databases vs. application-specific distribution concepts (e.g. distribution according to organization structure).
- The use of object-oriented databases instead of relational databases. Which object-oriented databases are commercially available? Do they support large databases and complex retrieval operations?
- Further development of techniques to integrate information from different data sources: autonomous agents acting in the background for synchronizing independent and mutually unaware databases.

The latter point seems to be especially important considering *heterogeneous environments*. In such environments independent databases with redundant information exist. Examples are the user databases of a database management system or the underlying operating system (e.g. the /etc./passwd of a SINIX system), the registration database of a Microsoft Windows system, or an X.500-compliant directory service. In many cases, it is not necessary to wholly integrate such a federation of databases (see, for example, Hsiao, Kamel, Wu, 1990), but only to synchronize selected subsets of data. With the aid of autonomous software agents synchronization of data can be achieved without user interaction (see, for example, Haugeneder, Steiner, 1991). An organization model can serve as a master dataset for synchronization.

A different vision for future developments is the employment of an organization model as a unique information base integrated into a computer system's (or network) operating system replacing current collections of user databases with a single unified organization database. This means incorporating database management functions into the operating system to enable it to maintain complex organization models. Object-oriented operating system concepts as in Microsoft Windows NT™, for example, would allow this rather easily: adding database objects and a database driver to the system, possibly as a replacement for file objects and a file system driver. Each application or service could *register* itself in the organization model as a new resource class and supplement its own organization related information. The integration of a richly structured, extensible organization and resources model in the operating system would free designers of application systems of the need to invent their proprietary user database models.

4 Literature

Custer, H.: Inside Windows NT. Microsoft Press, Redmond, WA, 1993.

Dzida, W.: Das IFIP-Modell für Benutzerschnittstellen. Office Management, 31. Jahrgang, Sonderheft 1983, p. 6-8.

Ellis, C.A.: Formal and Informal Models of Office Activity. In: Mason, R.E.A. (ed.): Information Processing 83, Elsevier Science Publishers (North Holland), 1983, p. 11-22.

Esswein, W.: Das Rollenmodell der Organisation: Die Berücksichtigung aufbauorganisatorischer Regelungen in Unternehmensmodellen. Wirtschaftsinformatik 35 (1993) 6, p. 551-561.

Haugeneder, H.; Steiner, D.: Cooperation Structures in Multi-Agent Systems. In: Brauer, W.; Hernandez, D. (eds.): Wissensbasierte Systeme - Verteilte künstliche Intelligenz. Springer Verlag, Berlin, Heidelberg, New York, 1991, p. 160-171.

Hsiao, D.K.; Kamel, M.W.; Wu, C.T.: The Federated Databases and System: A new Generation of Advanced Database Systems. In: Tjoa, A.M.; Wagner, R. (eds.): Database and Expert Systems Applications. Springer Verlag, Wien, 1990, p. 186-190.

Ishii, H.; Kubota, K.: Office Procedure Knowledge Base for Organization Office Work Support. In: Office Information Systems: The Design Process. Working Conference, IFIP WG 8.4, August 15-17, 1988, Linz, Austria, p. 40-57.

Karbe, B.: Flexible Vorgangssteuerung mit ProMinanD. In: Hasenkamp, U.; Kirn, S.; Syring, M. (Eds.): CSCW - Computer Supported Cooperative Work. Addison-Wesley, , Bonn, 1994, p. 117-133.

Microsoft Corporation: Microsoft Windows Kompendium. 1992.

Pagé, P.: Architekturen für Anwendungslösungen: Offen nach allen Seiten. Business Computing 1/94, p. 60-63.

Prinz, W.: TOSCA - Organisationswissen für CSCW-Anwendungen. In: Hasenkamp, U.; Kirn, S.; Syring, M. (Eds.): CSCW - Computer Supported Cooperative Work. Addison-Wesley, Bonn, 1994, 161-177.

Rupietta, W.: An Organization & Resources Model for Adapting Office Systems to Organization Structures. In: Tjoa, A.M.; Wagner, R. (eds.): Database and Expert Systems Applications. Springer Verlag, Wien, 1990, p. 346-350.

Rupietta, W.: Organisationsmodellierung zur Unterstützung kooperativer Vorgangsbearbeitung. Wirtschaftsinformatik 34 (1992) 1, p. 26-37.

Rupietta, W.; Wernke, G.: Umsetzung organisatorischer Regelungen in der Vorgangsbearbeitung mit WorkParty und ORM. In: Hasenkamp, U.; Kirn, S.; Syring, M. (Eds.): CSCW - Computer Supported Cooperative Work. Addison-Wesley, Bonn, 1994, p. 135-154.

Scheer, A.-W.: Modellierung betriebswirtschaftlicher Informationssysteme. Wirtschaftsinformatik 32 (1990) 5, p 403-421.

Schmalz, H.: Anforderungen an Organisationswissensbasen als Grundlage von Systemen zur Unterstützung arbeitsteiliger Prozesse. Diploma Thesis, University of Marburg, 1991.

Weikum, G.: Transaktionen in Datenbanksystemen. Fehlertolerante Steuerung paralleler Abläufe. Addison-Wesley, Bonn, Reading, MA, 1988.

Winograd, T.: Where the Action is. Byte, December 1988, p. 256A-258.

Semantically Enriching Relational Databases into an Object Oriented Semantic Model

Malú Castellanos, Félix Saltor, Manuel García-Solaco
Dept. Llenguatges i Sistemes Informàtics
Universitat Politècnica de Catalunya
{castellanos, saltor, mgarcia}@lsi.upc.es

Abstract

A method to convert relational schemas to an object oriented semantic model is presented. It makes explicit knowledge about the semantic of the database that was implicit in the schemas or in the extension, through a knowledge acquisition phase. The method is general, semiautomatic, and has a number of applications.

Key words: Semantic enrichment, knowledge acquisition, semantic level, reverse engineering, object oriented models, semantic models.

1. Introduction

The semantic level of relational schemas is usually rather poor, while a number of usages of the databases require a deep understanding of them, as will be seen in section 4. Therefore, there is a need to upgrade the semantic level of the schemas, and a semantic model is required for this enrichment.

The subject of mapping a DB schema from one model to another has been studied by many authors. Most of the work refers to mappings from a more semantic model to a less semantic one, particularly from a conceptual schema in the Entity-Relationship (ER) model or some extensions of it, to a DBMS schema expressed in the relational model. However, the subject of mapping from a less semantic model to a more semantic one has been less studied. In fact, it is more than just a mapping, since knowledge must be acquired in some way in order to upgrade the schema to a higher semantic level (*semantic enrichment*). As far as we know, all papers on this topic deal with conversion from the relational model to the ER model or some extension of it (see [CasAma83], [NavAwo87], [DavAro87], [JohKal89], [MarMak90], [ChiBarSto93]). Furthermore, many of them make many assumptions and simplifications, such as considering only well designed schemas, or just primary keys, or only key-based inclusion dependencies, or relying entirely on the DBA

In contrast, our approach is quite general. It covers both well and badly designed schemas. We consider every single candidate key as well as every single inclusion dependency, either key or non key based; exclusion and complementariness dependencies are taken into account, too. Moreover, we include a knowledge acquisition phase to discover additional semantics by analysing not only the schema but also the extension of the database. The whole enrichment process in mostly automatic, requiring minimal user intervention when ambiguities arise and for confirmation of results. The work presented in this paper also differs from other work in that we do not use an extended ER model as the target one, but a semantic extension of an object oriented model. Finally, our method is more global and general and the resulting schemas are richer than in other approaches.

This paper is organised as follows: Section 2 presents our target model. Semantic enrichment is covered in Section 3. Section 4 presents some applications. We conclude in Section 5.

2. The BLOOM Data Model

The *expressiveness* of a data model is the degree to which the model can directly represent (express in a natural way) a conceptualization, no matter how complex this conceptualization might be, and which concepts compose it. For our work on semantic enrichment we wanted to upgrade the semantic level of the schemas as much as possible, so that we had to choose as the target model some model with a high degree of expressiveness. *BLOOM* (BarceLona Object Oriented Model [CasSalGar91]) is a semantic extension of object oriented models. It was designed specifically to satisfy all desirable characteristics found in our analysis [SalCasGar91], both in expressiveness and in semantic relativism.

The main constituents are objects and classes. Classes describe the structure and behaviour of their object members, including relationships to other objects. Modelling with BLOOM allows to capture a rich set of semantic relationships, along each one of the three dimensions of the modelling space:

- *Classification/Instantiation* dimension: 4 levels: objects, classes, metaclasses and the metametaclass. *Metaclasses* are fundamental in BLOOM. They do not only specify the behaviour of their class instances, but also that of the instances of their instances.

- *Generalization/Specialization* dimension: Classes are specialised into sets of subclasses according to an specialization criteria. Four kinds of specialization are supported, expressed as 4 metaclasses:
  -*Disjoint specialization:* each object of the superclass belongs *at most* to one subclass.
  -*Complementary specialization:* each object of the superclass belongs *at least to* one subclass.
  -*Alternative specialization:* each object belongs to *one and only one* subclass.
  -*General specialization:* this one has no restrictions.
  A unique characteristic of BLOOM specialization is the automatic generation of specialization semilattices as explained in [Sal+94].

- *Aggregation/Decomposition* dimension: Three kinds of Aggregation, expressed as 3 metaclasses:
  -*Simple aggregation:* this is the simplest type of aggregation and is employed to express that the attributes involved in it are just properties of the object being described and nothing else. Each attribute takes as domain either a *primitive* class such as integer, or a user defined class such as department (*derived*). The construct for this abstraction is *s_aggr_of*, and its inverse *s_partic_in*.
  -*Collection aggregation* (or just *collection):* the collection of some objects of a given class gives rise to a new complex object. This abstraction permits to treat each collection of objects -such as a convoy of ships- as a single one. The construct for it is *collection_of* and its inverse *collected_in*.
  -*Composition aggregation* (or just *composition):* the aggregate object is formed by aggregating objects from different classes. The component objects are not simply properties of the aggregate but it is their aggregation what gives rise to it. The construct is *composed_by* and its inverse *component_of*. The aggregate object, in turn, has its own properties specified by the simple aggregation.

Each one of the previous abstractions has an inherent behaviour, given by the insert, delete and update constraints, corresponding to the ***inherent existence dependencies***. This behaviour constitutes the behavioural interpretation of the semantics of the model. It is defined in the *metaclasses* corresponding to the different abstractions [CasSalGar91].

3. Semantic Enrichment

As mentioned in the introduction, our approach converts relational schema into BLOOM schemas. Our methodology of semantic enrichment comprises two phases: *knowledge acquisition* and *schema conversion*, explained next. A complete description along with algorithms is given in [Cas93].

3.1. Knowledge Acquisition

Since the purpose of the enrichment process is to obtain rich descriptions of the objects, and the semantics of an object is given to a big extent by its semantic relationships to the other ones, the focus of our approach is on discovering the exact nature of these relationships. The restrictions imposed to the database in the form of keys and dependencies embody this kind of semantic information. The goal of the knowledge acquisition phase is precisely to *discover* them. This is done by analyzing not only the schemas, but also the extensions of the databases, where implicit semantics is hidden. Emphasis is put on minimizing the cost given mainly by the number of disk accesses required to analyze the extension. The different steps of this phase are shown in the figure, and are discussed next.

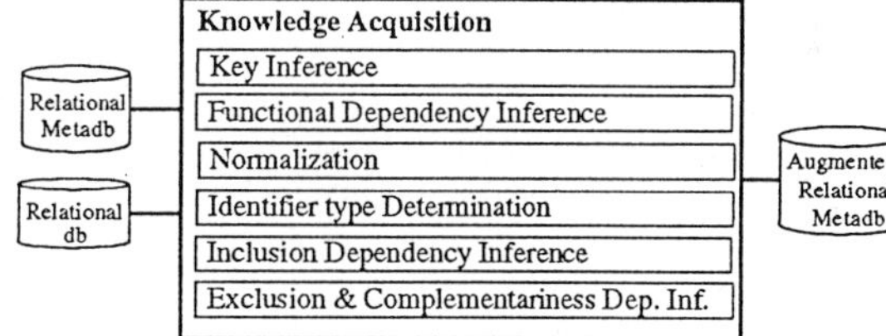

Step 1: Key Inference: in this step we obtain all the keys (simple and composite) of each relation. It is not necessary to obtain their type, primary or secondary, because design anomalies (see step 4) covered in our methodology make irrelevant this distinction. To infer keys (those not found in the schema), different combinations of attributes are checked for the uniqueness property by comparing its cardinality with the one of the relation. Redundant work is avoided by imposing an order on the attribute combinations to be tested that guarantees that only minimal keys are obtained. Since the cardinalities of potential composite keys are not found in the catalogue, computing them would be rather costly, so these keys are derived later from the FDs obtained in the next step.

Step 2: Functional Dependency Inference: our algorithm [CasSal93] to discover functional dependencies (FDs) *lhs* $\rightarrow$ *rhs* (left hand side functionally determines right hand side) from the extension of the DB, establishes an order in the sequence of left hand sides to be analyzed. The analysis of a lhs involves first identifying its possible rhs's and then testing that the restriction imposed by each candidate FD holds in the extension of the relation. Since we must test that tuples with the same value for 'lhs' also agree in the value for 'rhs', we sort the relation by using 'lhs' as the sort key. Furthermore, the number of sorts is reduced by grouping the candidate lhs's by 'maximal sort keys' (for example, a sort by ABCD is used to test the candidate lhs's A, AB, ABC, and ABCD). For every pair of (consecutive) tuples that are compared, all the candidate FDs on the lhs's which use the same sort key are tested together. The idea is that once two tuples have been retrieved, we test on them all that we can. Also, once a FD is discovered, we apply transitivity to obtain derived dependencies and for every FD to be proposed as candidate, we first check if it is not redundant by augmentation. The emphasis of this algorithm is on minimizing the number of disk accesses.

Step 3: Normalization: having relations that describe unique concepts is important for the conversion phase. 3NF is the minimum requirement to be satisfied without losing the semantics of FDs. Any standard algorithm for normalization can be used.

Step 4: Determination of the Type of the Identifiers: design anomalies like choosing as primary key a candidate key that does not correspond to the intention of the relation are considered in our methodology. Moreover, from the set of candidate keys some of them really identify the relation: *proper identifiers* (P_id), while others only satisfy the uniqueness property but do not result adequate identifiers from a semantic point of view: *extraneous identifiers* (E_id). For every key, its type is disambiguated with the aid of the user.

Step 5: Inclusion Dependency Inference: since INDs in all generality are considered in the conversion phase, all the INDs that hold in the database are found in this step. In our algorithms ([CasSal93]), heuristics are used to reduce on one side the set of possible INDs, and on the other, the number of sorts and comparisons for the remaining possible INDs. The main idea is to sort all attributes with same domain by their cardinality and compare them in such an order that we can guarantee that *only direct* INDs are obtained by analyzing the extension, while *all transitive* dependencies are derived by simply applying the transitivity rule.

Step 6: Exclusion and Complementariness Dependencies: these two types of dependencies are used in the next phase of the methodology to determine the kind of specialization (alternative, complementary, disjoint or general) when there is such a relationship. Since a specialization relationship exists when there is an IND between the key attributes of two relations, only those key attributes that appear in INDs with common right hand side (rhs) have to be compared with each other to test disjointness and complementariness.

3.2. Schema Conversion

Inclusion dependencies (IND's) constitute the core of the conversion phase because they can be interpreted in terms of the general abstraction principles of semantic data models, in particular, of the BLOOM model. Semantic structural relationships conform a network of connections among the classes and it is the nature of these connections what must be precisely defined (through the abstractions of the model) in a class description to express all the semantics that they embody. Since we do not assume that schemas have been well designed, an attribute can reference any kind of attribute in another table. Thus INDs in its whole generality are considered as shown in the next table:

S.b / R.a	Simple Key SK	Comp. Key CK	Simple Part CK (s.p.CK)	Composite Part CK (c.p.CK)	Non Key (s.NK)	Non Key (c.NK)
Simple Key (SKI)	S - S	——	S - s.p.C	S - c.p.C	S - s.N	S -c N
Composite Key (CK)	——	C - C	——	C - c.p.C	C -s.N	C -c N
Each Part CK (e.p.CK)	e.p.C - S	e.p.C - C	e.p.C - s.p.C	e.p.C - c.p.C	e.p.C-s.N	e.p.C-c.N
Only Part CK (o.p.CK)	o.p.C - S	o.p.C - C	o.p.C - s.p.C	o.p.C - c.p.C	o.p.C-s.N	o.p.C-c.N
Non Key (NK)	N - S	N - C	N - s.p.C	N - c.p.C	N -s.N	N -c.N

Table 1. Case Analysis of an IND R.a $\subset$ S.b.

Each case of the table has in turn several subcases treated through the steps of the conversion phase shown in the figure:

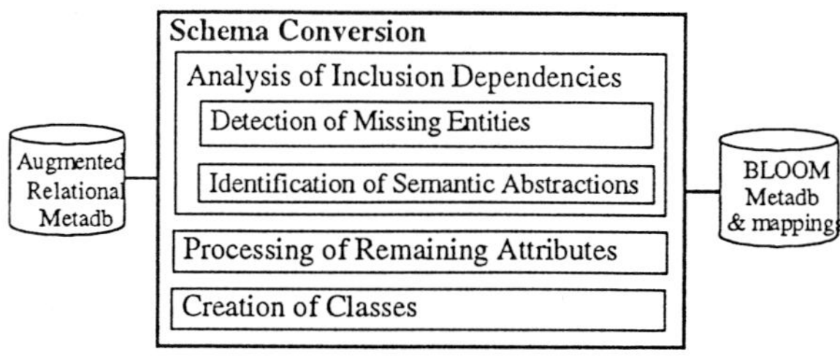

Space limitations prevent us from giving a description of each one of these steps, so we only give an idea of the first two which are the main ones. A complete description of each one of these steps along with the algorithms is presented in [Cas93].

Step 1: Detection of Missing Entities: in this step all cases of INDs from which missing entities can be detected are analyzed through the following substeps:

Substep 1.1: all INDs on part of key or non key are analyzed here.
Substep 1.2: all INDs that involve extraneous identifiers are considered.
Substep 1.3: every component of a composite key not involved in any IND is analyzed.

A *missing entity* is one that conceptually exists but has not been made explicit as a relation in the relational schema. The solution adopted to overcome this anomaly is to create a *virtual relation* for the missing entity which later will be made explicit in the BLOOM schema as a class. The creation of a virtual relation has the effect of creating a pair of new INDs and transferring all the INDs on the attribute where the entity was implicit, to the key of the virtual relation. This is illustrated in the example given in step 2.

The detection of missing entities is very important not only to make them explicit in the enriched representation, but also for the correct modelling of other classes to which they are connected. If these entities are not detected, then, their relationships with other entities will not be detected either. This leads not only to an incomplete description of a class, but even to an incorrect modelling of the nature of the relationships because a missing IND may lead to classifying another IND into a case that doesn't correspond to the real semantics, for example, as o.p.CK $\subset$ X instead of e.p.CK $\subset$ X.

Step 2: Identification of Semantic Abstractions: in this step all inclusion dependencies on a key, i.e. first and second columns of table I, are treated. According to the type of the identifiers (P_id or E_id) of the keys, different subcases are distinguished and analyzed. Moreover, different semantic situations correspond to each subcase depending on whether the inverse IND exists or not. Space limitations prevent us from describing each subcase, consequently only some examples are presented here to give an idea of the conversion process. Partial descriptions of the classes are given with the purpose of illustrating the effect of the IND corresponding to the subcase being analyzed.

Example 1: illustrates first the detection of missing entities described in step 1, and then the following subcases of Simple Key $\subset$ Simple Key, which is the first case analysed in step 2:

P_id $\subset$ P_id without inverse IND,
E_id $\subset$ P_id without inverse IND,
E_id $\subset$ P_id with inverse IND and
E_id $\subset$ E_id without inverse IND.

Relational schema: Department (d#[1] , dname, manager)
Project (p#, pname, responsible)
Project.responsible ⊂ Department.manager

Since this is an IND on an extraneous identifier, in substep 1.2.A where missing entities for E_id's on the right hand side of INDs are detected, this dependency is analysed giving rise to:

- virtual relation: Manager (m_name)
- new INDs: Department.manager ⊂ Manager.m_name {⊂ P_id}......................(1)
  Manager.m_name ⊂ Department.manager {inverse: ⊂ E_id}.......(2)
- transference of INDs on/of Department.manager to Manager.m_name:
  Project.responsible ⊂ Manager.m_name {E_id ⊂ P_id}...........(3)

Then, in step 1.2.B that detects missing entities for E_id's on the left hand side of INDs, dependency (3) is considered and the user is inquired about the adequacy of creating a new class for the E_id, that is, for project.responsible. Two possible situations can arise depending on the answer of the user:

A) If the user answers 'no' then, dependency (3) is treated in substep 2.1 (simple key ⊂ simple key), subcase E_id ⊂ P_id where it is converted to:

class project
  s_aggreg_of
    manager [as responsible]
end_class

class manager
  s_particip_in
    project [*as* responsible]
end_class

and then IND (1) is treated in substep 2.1, subcase E_id ⊂ P_id along with its inverse (2) giving rise to:

class department
  s_aggreg_of
    manager
end_class

class manager
  s_particip_in
    project
    department *[obligatory]*
end_class

B) However, if the user answers 'yes', then there is a missing entity for the E_id and this gives rise to:

- virtual relation: Responsible (r_name)
- new INDs: Project.responsible ⊂ Responsible.r_name {⊂ P_id}.................... (4)
  Responsible.r_name ⊂ Project.responsible {inverse: ⊂ E_id}....... (5)
- transference of INDs on/of Project.responsible to Responsible.r_name:
  Responsible.r_name ⊂ Manager.m_name {P_id ⊂ P_id}............ (6)
  {notice that the original IND has been transferred first to (3) and then to (6)}

then IND (6) is treated in substep 2.1 (simple key ⊂ simple key) subcase P_id ⊂ P_id resulting in:

class manager
  generaliz_of responsible
  s_aggreg_of m_name
end_class

class responsible
  specializ_of
    manager
end_class

[1] P_id's are double underlined, while E_id's are single underlined.

and finally IND (4) is analyzed in substep 2.1, subcase E_id ⊂ P_id along with its inverse (5), as well as, IND (1) and its inverse (2). The result of converting INDs (1) and (2) is the same as in A) while (4) and (5) are converted to:

```
class project
  s_aggreg_of
        responsible
end_class

class responsible
  specializ_of
        manager
  s_particip_in
        project [obligatory]
end_class
```

Example 2: illustrates a possible semantic situation for INDs of type non key ⊂ simple key.

club (c_name, d_founded, site)
person (p_id, name, club); (in this example a person can be member of only one club)
person.club ⊂ club.c_name

The corresponding abstraction for this IND is the collection aggregation:

```
class club
   collection_of person
end_class

class person
   collected_in club
end_class
```

3.3. A complete example

Finally we present a complete example (only the input and output of the semantic enrichment) where the semantic upgrading of a relational schema can be appreciated.

Relational Schema:

person (ss_num, car_num, name, phone, club)
employee (ss_num, salary, hired, job, dept)
project_assignment (emp, project, hours, delivery)
department (name, manager, budget)
children (emp, name, birth, gender)
club (name, meet_place, founded)
car (plate, model, owner)

BLOOM Schema:

```
class person
  compl_generaliz_of
        employee, student
  collected_in  club
  s_particip_in car [as owner]
  s_aggreg_of
        name: char[15]
        phone: char[8]
        id ss_num: char[10]
end_class

class employee
  compl_specializ_of person
  generaliz_of manager
  has_int_deps children
  s_set_particip_in department
  component_of proj_assignment
  s_aggreg_of
        salary: float
        hired: date
        job: char[8]
end_class

class department
  s_aggreg_of
    set_of employee
    manager
    budget: float
    id name: char[10]
end_class
```

class children
  id name *int_dep_on* employee
  s_aggreg_of
    birth: date
    gender: char[3]
end_class

class project
  component_of
    proj_assignment
  s_aggreg_of
    p_name: char[8]
end_class

class proj_assignment
  composed_by
    employee
    project
  s_aggreg_of
    hours: float
    delivery: date
end_class

class car
  s_aggreg_of
    person [*as* owner]
    plate: char[7]
    model: char[8]
end_class

class manager
  specializ_of employee
  s_particip_in department
end_class

class club
  collection_of person
  s_aggreg_of
    meet_place: char[15]
    founded: date
    name: char[12]
end_class

4. Applications

From the examples given in section 3, we can appreciate the big difference in semantic expressiveness between the relational schemas and their BLOOM counterparts. This upgrading in semantic level is very useful for many applications, like the following ones:

A. Database Design
Database design is traditionally based on relationships between entities, that give rise to constraints that the stored data must satisfy. Such constraints are abstract entities, and it is easy for the database designer to overlook some constraints that should hold. Generating examples to help the designer in getting a better intuitive idea about the consequences of the constraints has been reported in [ManRai86]. The role of the examples is more profound than just being an illustration of a prospective design. It is important for the designer to be provided with examples that satisfy exactly the set of constraints specified by him (*Armstrong relations*), because these examples are good in revealing missing constraints. By using examples, the designer can easily point out and correct any fact that cannot hold in the real world, even if he doesn't realize that this is due to a missing constraint. Thus, it is equally important to provide him with the possibility of modifying the generated examples so that there is no violation of the missing constraints. Then, the system infers these constraints from the modified example. The techniques for inferring dependencies from the extensions of relations, developed for the knowledge acquisition phase of my enrichment methodology, are useful to make full use of this duality.

B. Migration to another DBMS
Databases are implemented in a DBMS that responds to the requirements of the applications for which they are designed. These requirements are not only of information, but also of structuring and performance. The DBMS chosen from those commercially available ones is the one that best fits their requirements. The need for more powerful modelling capabilities has originated the emergence of new models that provide the structures and characteristics required for non traditional new applications. DBMSs based on these new data models have begun to appear in the market, providing better functionalities for these applications (OODBMSs, Extended Relational DBMSs, etc.). The benefits provided by these new technologies have motivated a growing trend to migrate existing databases supported by old

DBMSs to the new ones. The first action to be taken for this migration is to transform the database schemas to the new model of the DBMS to be used. Since new data models provide enough constructs to cover most of the structural aspects of new applications, and traditional data models do not provide them, there is a need to extract the semantics that the constructs of the new models are able to capture. Therefore here again, an enrichment process is required.

C. Documentation of the meaning of existing databases
During the life cycle of a database, its conceptual schema is subject to modifications and reorganizations. As time passes, there often arrives a moment when nobody really understands well what is the contents of the database. Even if the structure of the database has not been subject to such dynamics, but there is a lack of documentation of its meaning, the exact understanding of the data is lost over the years ("semantic degradation"). In order to perform an eventual redesign of the database, or simply to make effective utilization of the data by developing new applications that use its contents, there is a need to derive from them new schemas expressed in semantic models that can be used as a documentation aid. Therefore, the missing semantics must be extracted and captured through an enrichment process. In fact, this process is an example of *Reverse Engineering*.

D. Integrated Access to Interoperable Databases
Interoperable databases which cooperate sharing their data while maintaining their autonomy as much as possible present semantic heterogeneities (different representations for a same or related concepts) between them. Integrated access to interoperable databases means that through a single query it is possible to simultaneously access data in the different component databases and receive a single consolidated answer. Several approaches exist for achieving integrated access, they differ in the degree of integration. However, in any approach it is necessary to solve the semantic heterogeneities which in turn requires first to detect them. Detection is a very difficult task because a deep understanding of the meaning of the databases is necessary. Since the schemas are expressed in traditional data models whose expressive power is so limited, they do not help to acquire this semantics being semantically very poor. An upgrading of the schemas through a semantic enrichment process can be very helpful for the detection task. Moreover, if appropriate semantics is elicited in this process, detection can be semi-automatized as in [GarCasSal93].

E. Knowledge Based Interfaces: Natural Language
Users do not necessarily have a good understanding of which data are stored in a DB, and of their meaning; this is specially true for end users. In particular, natural language interfaces require an accurate description of the meaning of the databases. Such interfaces often require more information about the meaning of the data than what is contained in the database schema. This extra information which cannot be represented in the schema is extracted from some source and given in an enriched representation. Techniques reported in this paper are applicable for this purpose.

5. Conclusions

Semantic enrichment has a wide range of applications. This is why it is so important to count on complete methodologies, that deal with the problem in all its magnitude and that are able to deal with any kind of schema (not only with well designed ones). Here we have presented one such methodology that upgrades the semantic level of relational schemas. It comprises not only the conversion of these schemas to richer ones expressed in an adequate model, but also the knowledge acquisition process that analyses the schemas as well as the extension of the database to discover implicit semantics. Emphasis has been put on one side, on the efficiency aspect because analysing extensions has a high cost given by the required accesses to disk, and on the other side, in minimizing the user intervention so that the methodology can be the basis of a tool that automates the whole enrichment process as much as possible. We plan to extend the enrichment with additional information extracted from other sources, mainly behavioural knowledge discovered in the applications and made explicit as class methods.

Acknowledgements

This work has been partially supported by the Spanish PRONTIC programme, under projects TIC89/0303 and TIC93-0436.

References.

[Cas93] M.Castellanos: *Semiautomatic Semantic Enrichment for the Integrated Access to Interoperable Databases*. PhD dissertation, Dept. LSI, UPC, June 1993.

[CasAma83] M.Casanova & J.Amarel: "Designing ER Schemas from Conventional Information Systems". *Proceedings, third International ER Conf*, 1983.

[CasSal93] M.Castellanos & F.Saltor: "Extraction of Data Dependencies". In: *Proceedings, The 3rd European-Japanese Seminar on Information Modelling and Knowledge Bases*, Budapest, 1993.

[CasSalGar91] M.Castellanos, F.Saltor & M.García-Solaco: "The Development of Semantic Concepts in the BLOOM Model using an Object Metamodel". Report LSI-91-22. U.P.C., Barcelona.

[ChiBarSto93] R.Chiang, T.Barron & V.Storey: "Performance Evaluation of Reverse Engineering Relational Databases into Extended Entity-Relationship Models". *Proc. 12th Int. Conf. on Entity-Relationship Approach*, Arlington, TX, 1993.

[DavAro87] Davis & Arora: "Converting a Relational Database Model into an ER Model". In [Mar88].

[GarCasSal93] M.García-Solaco, M.Castellanos & F.Saltor: "Discovering Interdatabase Resemblance of Classes for Interoperable Databases". In: H. Schek, A. Sheth & B. Czejdo (eds.): *Proceedings 2nd Int. Workshop on Interoperability in Multidatabase Systems* (RIDE IMS-93). IEEE-CS Press. Vienna. Apr. 1993.

[JohKal89] Johannesson & Kalman: "A Method for Translating Relational Schemas into Conceptual Schemas". *Proc. 8th Int. ER Conference*, Toronto, 1989.

[ManRai86] H.Mannila & K-J.Räihä: *Algorithms for Inferring Functional Dependencies*. Dept. of Computer Science, Univ. of Helsinki, Report C-1991-41.

[Mar88] S.March (ed.): *Proceedings of the 6th International Conference on the Entity-Relationship Approach*. NewYork, 1987.

[MarMak90] Markowitz & Makowsky: "Identifying Extended ER object Structures in Relational Schemas". *IEEE Trans. on Software Engineering, Vol.16*, No.8. 1990.

[NavAwo87] Navathe & Awong: "Abstracting Relational and Hierarchical Data with a Semantic Data Model". In [Mar88].

[Sal+94] F.Saltor, M.Castellanos, M.García & T.Kudrass: "Modelling Specialization as BLOOM Semilattices". To appear in *Proceedings of the 4th. Euro-Japanese Seminar on Information Modelling and Knowledge Bases*. Stockholm. 1994.

[SalCasGar91] F.Saltor, M.Castellanos & M.García-Solaco: "Suitability of Data Models as Canonical Models for Federated Databases". *ACM SIGMOD Record, Vol.20*, No.4 (Dec. 1991)

Consistency Checking of Evolving Methods

X. Li[1] Z. Tari[2]

[1] Queensland University of Technology, School of Computer Science, Brisbane
[2] Queensland University of Technology, School of Information Systems, Brisbane

Abstract. In this paper we present a framework of method evolution handling for object-oriented databases. Behavioural consistency is also addressed. Two levels of granularity for method evolution are described. The first level relates to the evolution of methods in the context of a class inheritance hierarchy, and concerns the semantics of the polymorphism of methods. The second level is the behavioural evolution in which the chain of calling relationships between methods is considered. A graph based approach is used for the behavioural consistency checking in order to prevent the following problems: run-time type errors, side-effects, redundant methods, and unexpected behaviours.

1 Introduction

The problem of object-oriented schema evolution concerns the ability to alter a schema. A schema may be altered at different aspects. An alteration may be done either at the structural aspect or at the behavioural aspect.

- Schema evolution is widely addressed in the literature [7, 10, 11, 12]. Structural modifications may be performed at different levels of granularity within a schema: class level, relationship level, instance level. Many of the researches address these levels [3, 8, 9]. For each level a set of alteration operations and semantic rules to ensure consistency, are provided. Some of these approaches propagate the changes at the instance level [3, 9] by providing converter operators (e.g. convert) and with different mechanisms of propagation (e.g., deferred and immediate). A detailed study of schema evolution in such systems can be found in [9].
- The second aspect of the update concerns the evolution of the behaviour of objects. The operations relate to the possibility to modify both the signature and the code of the methods, and to ensure the correctness of these operations. To our knowledge no system really supports behavioural changes. Some structural changes, such as updating relationships between objects, may induce changes of method behaviours.

Method evolution is weakly addressed due, principally, to the absence of a formal definition of the semantics of methods. Although there is much literature about the modelling of behaviours [1, 6], the problem here is about the change of behaviours. Since the behaviours are packed into objects as methods, the change of the behaviours requires the change of methods. Thus the problem is that the changed methods may not reflect the change of the behaviours or may not be consistent with the parts of the schema [5, 13].

This paper proposes our contribution in the area of method evolution and behavioural consistency. Method evolution refers to the updates of the methods including the operations of deletion, insertion, and modification. Behaviour inconsistency relates to the situations which involve (1) run-time type errors, (2) side-effects, (3) unchanged methods made redundant or meaningless, (4) unexpected results given by methods.

In order to provide the solution for the situations (1)-(4), the semantics of methods has to be represented declaratively. This is done by using graphs, a graph for representing inheritance relationships between methods and a graph for describing calling relationships. Because the information about method behaviours are represented in graphs, the behavioural inconsistency problems can be checked out by search the states represented in graphs. Briefly, our approach has three aspects: a method representation framework, the method evolution operations, and the checking algorithms. The framework for representing the semantics of methods is declaratively given as:

- the two parts of a method: definition (signature) and implementation (pre-post conditions, local attributes to be used as actual parameters, and the methods to be called),
- the relationship amongst methods described by a class inheritance hierarchy,
- the relationship amongst methods described by a method-calling structure.

Based on this framework, the checking on the inconsistent behaviours is performed on states of the graphs. When a method is modified the both graphs mentioned above are modified too. Since a node of these graphs representing the information about a method, and an edge of the graphs representing a relationship between two methods, the consistency checking algorithms actually take these modified graphs as the input and output the validation of the graphs.

The rest of the paper is organised as follows. Next section presents a formalisation of the semantics of methods. In section 3, the method update operations are described. Section 4 presents the strategies for behaviour consistency checking. We finally conclude about the future work in section 5.

2 Semantics of Methods

This section briefly outlines the notations which will be used in the framework for method evolution. The semantics of method will be presented. The semantics of method behaviours is captured in the method intensions. They involve properties of methods and the relationships between them. Two kinds of graphs are used to represent these relationships: *method definition graph* and *method dependency graph*.

In the following, the reader is assumed to be familiar with the object oriented paradigm and terminology [2]. The class inheritance hierarchy of an object-oriented schema is a directed acyclic graph <C,E>, where C is the set of classes and E is set of isa relationships between classes. By polymorphism, a same method may be redefined in the subclasses. Given a class c and a method m, we identify the method m in c by c.m which is called a method identifier.

A method schema describes all information related to methods of an object-oriented schema. It represents the behaviour part and is represented as a tuple <C,M,ID,I> in which

- C is the set of all class names of the schema.
- M is the set of all method names of the classes.
- ID is the set of all method identifiers.
- I is the class inheritance hierarchy.

Given two classes c and c', we denote by

- $c \uparrow c'$: c is a subclass of c'.
- $c.m \downarrow c'.m'$: the method m of the class c calls the method m' of the class c'.
- $c.m \longrightarrow c'.m$: the method m in the class c is redefined from the class c', where $c \uparrow c'$ and $\nexists c$" such that m is defined in c", $c.m \longrightarrow c".m$ and $c' \uparrow c"$.

A method consists of two parts: the *definition part* and the *implementation part*. The former is in the form of $c.m : S \longrightarrow t$ where c is a class name; m is a method of the class c; S is a set of input attributes used by the method; and t is the output attribute of the method. The function St is the signature of the method. The implementation part is the body of the method and this is represented in the form of c.m(P,Q,R,U), where

- P is a set of attributes local to m in c.
- Q is a set of constraints on the method input attributes. They are predicates specifying the preconditions before the method is executed. The variables of the predicates are taken from the signature S.
- R is a set of predicates specifying the post conditions after the method is executed.
- U is a set of methods directly called by c.m. Elements of U can be expressed by method identifiers with the signatures which are substituted by the attributes from P or S.

Every method is involved in two orthogonal hierarchical structures: the method definition directed acyclic graph and the method dependency graph. The former is a graph which model the inheritance relationships between methods, and the latter models the calling relationships. These graphs are defined as following.

Definition 1 *(Method Definition DAG) Given a method schema $< C, M, ID, I >$ and a method m of M, the method definition directed acyclic graph of m is a graph DAG(m)= $< C', E' >$, where*

- $C' = \{c' | c' \in C$, *and m is declared in c'*$\}$
- $E' = \{e' | e' : c'.m \longrightarrow c".m$ *where* $c' \in C', c" \in C', m \in M, c'.m \in ID, c".m \in ID\}$.

Definition 2 *(Method Dependency Graph) Given a method schema* $< C, M, ID, I >$*, a class c of c and a method m of M, the method dependency graph of c.m method represents the methods of M which are linked to c.m by the calling relationship. This graph is in the form of MDG(c.m)=* $< ID', E' >$*, where*

- *ID'* = {*c'.m'*|*c'.m'*∈*ID, and c.m*↓*c'.m' or* ∃ *c".m"*∈*ID' such that c".m"*↓*c'.m'*}
- *E'* = {*e*|*e: c'.m'*↓*c".m", c'*∈*C, c"*∈*C, c'.m'*∈*ID', c".m"*∈*ID'*}.

With all the concepts introduced in this section we may model the semantics of a method. This is called the method intension, and involves the identifier of the method, the signature, the implementation, and the corresponding method definition and method dependency graphs.

Definition 3 *(Method Intension) Given a method m of a class c, the semantics of c.m is defined by the tuple* $INT(c.m) =< c.m : S \longrightarrow t, c.m(P, Q, R, U)$, $DAG(m), MDG(c.m) >$ *where: c.m is the method identifier,* $S \longrightarrow t$ *is the signature of c.m,* $c.m(P, Q, R, U)$ *is the method implementation of c.m, DAG(m) is the method definition DAG defined over c.m, and MDG(c.m) is the method dependency graph of c.m.*

3 Method Updates

The evolution of a method may be done by method-changing operations which are: the deletion of a method, the insertion of a method, and the modification of a method. Our approach considers the only two basic method-changing operations of deletion and insertion. Other operations such as moving operation is regarded as a composition of deletion and insertion operations. A method-changing operation should be coded as a transaction to avoid dangling situations. For instance, the modification of a method is described as a transaction of deletion followed by an insertion. The consistency checking is done after the transaction. Within a transaction, a virtually deleted method can still be accessed. This section discusses the syntax of the method-changing operations and emphasises what can be changed rather than how to be changed.

Bearing the fact in mind that a method can be changed by designing a transaction consisting of only two basic method-changing operations, a method can be changed by following operations:

Deletion: deletion of a class (then, all its methods are implicitly deleted), and deletion of a method.

Insertion: insertion of a method with a new class, and insertion of a method within a class.

Modification: modification of the name or the signature of a method, modification of the implementation of a method, and modification of both the definition and the implementation of a method.

The set of the proposed operations may be reduced to a minimal set. For instance, a method can be deleted explicitly from a class or deleted implicitly due to the deletion of a class. The implicit deletion is sequenced within a transaction into two distinct operations: the deletion of all methods defined within the class, and the deletion of the class. Similarly, the insertion of a method may be done with two distinct operations: the insertion of a new class followed with the insertion of the method. Since the structural evolution of a schema is not addressed in this paper, the insertion and the deletion of a class will not be discussed. Consequently, the set of method-changing operations is reduced to the situations 2., 4., 5. and 6. The syntax of the method evolution language is the following.

```
method_changing_operation   ::=   <deletion>|<insertion>|<modification>
deletion                    ::=   delete_method (<method_identifier>
method_identifier           ::=   <c>.<m>
c                           ::=   <class name where m is defined>
m                           ::=   <name of the method>
insertion                   ::=   insert_method (<method_definition>,
                                  <method_implementation>)
method_definition           ::=   <method_identifier> [:<method_signature>]
method_signature            ::=   <input_type> -> <output_type>
method_implementation       ::=   <method_identifier> <method_body>
method_body                 ::=   ([<P>,<Q>,<R>,<U>])
P                           ::=   {<local_variables>}
Q                           ::=   {<pre-conditions>}
R                           ::=   {<post_conditions>}
U                           ::=   {<method_identifiers>}
modification                ::=   <modify_definition>|
                                  <modify_implementation>|<modify_method>
<modify_definition>         ::=   modify_def ([<method_definition>],
                                  <method_definition>)
<modify_implementation>     ::=   modify_imp ([<method_implementation>],
                                  <method_implementation>)
<modify_method>             ::=   modify_mtd ([<method>],<method>)
<method>                    ::=   (<method_definition>[,<method_body>])
```

4 Behavioural Consistency

In this section we show how to handle method-changing operations as well the consistency checking. For that we introduce the concept of method scope which is defined as a set of integrated graphs and a set of method intensions. We will show how the method scope is built, and propose strategies for consistency checking using the method scope.

4.1 Semantics of Method Changing

The dynamics of a schema is regarded as the whole activities of methods that retrieve and manipulate objects in a database. Method behaviours are the consequences of these activities. The consistency of method behaviours can be seen as the possibility to call a method and then to get expected results. Inconsistent situations are described as (1)-(4) in section 1.

Definition 4 *(Behavioural Consistency) An object-oriented schema is behaviourally consistent if and only it satisfies the following conditions:*

1. *The behaviours of a method m in a class c is prescribed by c.m:S⟶t and c.m(P,Q,R,U).*
2. *The relationships among methods are described in method definition DAGs and MDGs.*
3. *There are no such consequences caused directly by method-changing: run-time errors, side-effects, redundant methods*[3]*, and unexpected behaviours.*

For a given method schema $H =< C, M, ID, I >$, a method c.m∈ID, with c.m:S⟶t and c.m(P,Q,R,U) as the definition and the implementation parts, can be updated using the proposed method-changing operations. The principles of behavioural consistency checking are the followings:

- Any arbitrary method changing is allowed.
- The consistency checking is a decidable problem if the set of method intensions {INT(c.m)|c.m∈ID} is given.
- When a method c.m is changed. INT(c.m) becomes INT'(c.m') which may be empty if c.m is deleted.
- The checking criteria are used to check the following situations:
  - the signature of c.m is type-consistent within MDG(c.m).
  - The signature of c.m is consistent with regards to the redefined methods within DAG(m).
  - There are no two methods c'.m' and c".m" such that they have identical signatures and pre- and post conditions.
  - There is no such a method intension INT(c".m") such that the pre- and the post condition P" and Q" of are false in any case of calls within the graphs.
  - All the c.m(P,Q,R,U) in INT(c.m) are checked using MDG(c.m). The principle of checking is to satisfy the matches between the formal and actual parameters, i.e the substitution of signatures by the input or local attributes for the called methods.
  - If c.m is deleted, then INT(c.m) should be deleted too. For any other INT"(c".m"), where c.m appears either in DAG(m") or in MDG(c".m"), c.m should be deleted from the DAG(m") and the MDG(c".m"). Then, the consequent deletions are checked in terms of the abovementioned criteria.

The checking procedure may refer to many different method intensions for deciding about the consistencies amongst methods. Indeed, a global view on methods is needed to optimise the checking strategies. For that we introduce

[3] *Methods with the same signature and the same implementation*

the concept of method scope as the integration of all method intensions. Since there may exist several method intensions such that they all share the same DAG, DAGs are integrated as a global DAG(M) in the method scope. On the other hand, MDGs are integrated as MDG(ID) because that an MDG may be a subgraph of some others.

Definition 5 *(Method Scope) The method scope of a method schema $< C, M, ID, I >$ is a tuple which consists of integrated graphs and method intensions. It is defined as $SCOPE =< C, M, ID, DAG(M), MDG(ID), INT >$ where,*

- *DAG(M) is a union of DAG(m), m∈M.*
- *MDG(ID) is a union of graphs given by MDG(c.m), c.m∈ID. This graph contains all call relationships of methods.*
- *INT = {INT(c.m)|c.m∈ID, c∈C, m∈M }.*

4.2 Building Method Scope

We may treat the SCOPE as a generic class. Its instances are built up gradually with the development of a method schema. Initially, the SCOPE is empty. Then, when a method is added to schema, an INT(c.m) is created in the SCOPE for c.m. When a method is deleted, the INT(c.m) will be deleted from the INT and the SCOPE is modified accordingly. The operations on the SCOPE should be in transactions and be coupled with the consistency checking. When a checking is failed, the transaction should roll back. Particularly, when

- m is added in c, since every method is also associated with an MDG, MDG(c.m) DAG(m) found, then a new DAG(m) is created. Otherwise, the c.m will be added into a DAG(m) according to the position of *c* in its inheritance hierarchy. Consequently, DAG(M) is also modified.
- m is added in c, since every method is also associated with an MDG, MDG(c.m) will be created and MDG(ID) is consequently updated. This process of building MDG(ID) follows a bottom-up pattern, which means that every method must be inexistence before it can be called.
- c.m is dropped from a schema, the corresponding INT(c.m) including DAG(m) should also be modified or deleted.

4.3 Semantic Consistency Checking

Unexpected behaviours of methods are the activities performed by methods which are not specified by the method declarations. The update of one method may cause the changes of the behaviours of other methods. It is crucial to the consistency checking that each method is guarded by its signature and its pre-post conditions. Therefore, we can say that a method-changing handling mechanism works on the principle that a user must specify not only what the change is but also what the change is/is not meant to be. Otherwise, there would not be any "unexpected" behaviours. Whether a user specifying "is meant to be"or "is not meant to be", the pre- and post conditions of methods are the only vehicle to take this meaning into the system. In other words, if there are unexpected behaviours, then some pre- or post conditions will become false. Then, there must have some inconsistent pre- and post conditions in the method calling chain. Thus, the checking of unexpected behaviours is actually the checking of the inconsistencies in the method scope left by the method-changing operations.

To ensure the behavioural consistency, a two-level checking strategy is proposed. The first level checking concerns the prevention of run-time errors and side effects. This is done mainly on DAGs. The second level checking relates to the unexpected and redundant behaviours of methods. This is done mainly on MDGs. These levels are complete in the sense that they involve all possible situations of the consistency. Here we describe these two levels in terms of the method-changing operations.

Method Insertion. When a method m is inserted in a class c, for the first level checking, INT(c.m) is created and used to check the consistency of the names and signatures of m. The following conditions need to be checked:

1. There is no name conflict, i.e. m has not been defined in c before.
2. There is no c'.m⟶c.m exists in DAG(m) such that c'↑c∈I. This is to ensure that there is no method redefined from c.m before c.m is inserted. It can be seen that the acyclicity of DAG(m) is also ensured by this condition.
3. c.m:S⟶t is compatible with those methods in DAG(m). The compatibility of the common part of signatures is to be checked. This checking is composed of (i) the covariance subtype rule [5] and (ii) the contravariance subtype rule [4] (for more details, see section 2). The violation of either the covariance subtype rule or the contravariance subtype rule in the non-common part of the signatures is not regarded as a problem until the method is to be called (i.e., the non-common part is checked later within MDG). The bottom line is to support the overloading and later binding semantics.
4. There is no redundant method in SCOPE.

For the second level checking, the implementation part of the method INT(c.m) is checked. The following conditions should be satisfied:

- For every c'.m' involved in MDG(c.m), INT(c'.m') is defined.
- For any c".m"↓c'.m' in MDG(c.m), with the method intension INT(c".m") and INT(c'm') respectively, ensure that S'∪t'⊆P"∪S"∪{t"} and check if R"⊇Q'.

Deletion of a Method. When the deletion of a method m from class c is requested, as for the insertion of a method the two-level checking is carried out. At the first level of checking, c.m should be deleted from DAG(m). The rest of nodes in the graph should be reconnected or dropped. In particular, all the successors of c.m may need to be reconnected with the predecessor(s) of c.m, and the compatibility of signatures between the reconnected nodes are checked.

At the second level, the MDG is modified according to the methods which call c.m or are called by c.m.

Since MDG(c.m) is gone with the deletion of INT(c.m), MDG(ID) needs to be modified. The second level of checking ensures that all references to c.m in MDG(ID) should be modified. This is done in two steps: the modification of the caller methods of c.m, and the modification of the called methods of c.m.

Modification of the Callers

The modification on the caller methods of c.m regards the set of $\{INT(c'.m')|c'.m' \downarrow c.m, c.m \in ID, c'.m' \in ID\}$. There are two cases on modifying caller methods. In the first case, the c.m may be replaced by a method in the DAG(m). If this is not possible, then the alternative is to try the MDG(c.m) to determine a method to replace c.m.

Modification of the Called

In this case, c.m is a root node or has successors in the MDG(ID). The modification on the called method of c.m regards the set of $\{INT(c'.m')|c.m \downarrow c'.m', c.m \in ID, c'.m' \in ID\}$. There are three ways to maintain the method scope: *cascade*, *nullified*, and *restricted*. This strategy can be compared with the strategy of maintaining the data referential integrity in a relational database.

Modification of a method. Method modification is a transaction of deleting and inserting operations. Thus the checking of the behaviour consistency can be different from that of insertion or deletion only operations.

Within a transaction, a method is virtually deleted and then inserted with changed parts. The consistency checking is therefore made in two steps. In the first step, the checking is made on deletion: the reaction of the checking will be suppressed. In the second step, the checking on insertion is made and the reaction of the checking is also suppressed. When the transaction is completed, all suppressed checking reactions then will be synthesised.

5 Conclusion

In this paper we have discussed the semantics of method evolution. We have defined the behavioural consistency for method-changing operations. One of the advantages of the proposed approach is that two kinds of graphs are defined to hold the structural information of methods. By using method definition DAGs, all method definitions are properly grouped in terms of their class structures. By using method dependency graphs, the pre- and post conditions of methods are chained together with the signatures to validate the method behaviours. Not only the run-time errors and side-effects can be detected but also the behaviour inconsistency problems such as redundancy and unexpected behaviours can be refrained. The scope of methods is treated as an umbrella of method behaviours. Whenever method definitions are changed, an evolution handling mechanism is able to know what is changed and what the change is meant to be according to the information held in the method scope.

We are considering an experimental implementation of the proposed ideas. Rather than using an existing language (e.g. ONTOS or C++) to define methods for an object-oriented database schema, a design of a stand-alone system to especially deal with the behavioural inconsistency problems is preferred. This would allow the simplification of implementation details of method-changing operations (i.e., a method recompilation mechanism). After a prototype is tested, the practical implementation with both structural and behavioural consistency will be considered.

References

1. Abiteboul, S., Kanellakis, P., and Waller, E., "Method Schemas", Proc. 9th ACM SIGACT-SIGMOD-SIGART Symposium on Principles of Database Systems, Nashville, Tennessee, April 1990.
2. Atkinson M., Bancilhon F., et al, "The Object-Oriented Database System Manifesto", Proc First Int. Conf. on Deductive and Object-Oriented Databases, Kyoto, Japan, December, 1989.
3. Banerjee J.W., Kim W., Kim H-J. and Korth H.F., "Semantics and Implementation of Schema Evolution in Object-Oriented Databases," Proc. SIGMOD Int. Conf. on Management of Data, pp311-322, San Francisco, 1987.
4. Cardelli, L., "A Semantics of Multiple Inheritance", Information and Computation Vol. 76, Academic Press, pp138-164, 1988.
5. Coen-Porisini, A., Lavazza, L. and Zicari, R. "The ESSE Project: An Overview", Proc 2nd Far East Workshop on Future Database Systems, Kyoto, Vol. 3, pp28-37, 1992.
6. Lingat, J.Y., Nobecourt, P., and Rolland, C., "Behaviour Management in Database Applications", Proc. 13th VLDB, pp185-196, 1987.
7. McLeod D., "A Learning-Based Approach to Meta-Data Evolution in an Object-Oriented Database," Advances in Object-Oriented Database Systems, Lecture Notes in Computer Science, No. 334, Springer-Verlag, pp219-224, 1988.
8. Monk, S. and Sommerville, I, "Schema Evolution in OODBs Using Class Versioning", SIGMOD Record, Vol. 22, No. 3, pp16-22, September 1993.
9. Nguyen G.T. and Rieu D., "Schema Evolution in Object-Oriented Database Systems", Data and Knowledge Engineering, Vol 4, pp43-67, 1989.
10. Osborn S.L., "The Role of Polymorphism in Schema Evolution in an Object-Oriented Database," IEEE Transactions on Knowledge and Data Engineering, pp310-317, Vol. 1, No. 3, 1989.
11. Panel on Schema Evolution and Version Management, "Report on the Object-Oriented Database Workshop", SIGMOD Record Vol. 18., No. 3, pp78-101, 1989.
12. Skarra A.H. and Zdonik S.B., "Type Evolution in an Object-Oriented Database", in Research Directions in Object-Oriented Programming, B. Shriver and P. Wegner (eds), MIT Press, 1987.
13. Waller E., "Schema Updates and Consistency", Proc. Deductive and Object-Oriented Databases, 1991.

Designing and Integrating Human Genome Databases with Object-Oriented Technology

Norihiro Sakamoto and Kazuo Ushijima

Department of Computer Science and Communication Engineering
Kyushu University, Hakozaki, Higashi-ku, Fukuoka 812, JAPAN
e-mail: {nori, ushijima}@csce.kyushu-u.ac.jp

Abstract. The lack of a well-designed class hierarchy holds back the development of an object-oriented database (OODB) for genome information. This paper describes the design of a standard class hierarchy for genome information with object-oriented technology and the integration of genome information stored in different database files into an OODB. First, we define the rules for finding objects and creating classes for genome information, which can be put to use building new classes in other fields of biological sciences. Second, we implement more than 80 classes for genome information. Finally, we demonstrate the importance of well-designed classes in the development of an OODB and that of the good graphical user interface.

1 Introduction

Object-oriented technology is a new programming paradigm. It helps a user think abstractly about a problem based on real world entities and concepts. It also enables a user to simulate them on computers. Through the use of composite objects, class hierarchies and other structures, object-oriented technology can effectively represent increasingly complex information. Genome information has to be one of the most complex problems in the real world today, that object-oriented technology must grapple with.

A genome is a complete set of instructions for making a living organism. A genome contains the master blueprint for all cellular structures and activities for the lifetime of a cell or an organism. Found in every nucleus of a human being's 1.0×10^{12} cells, the human genome is composed of tightly coiled threads of deoxyribonucleic acids (DNA) and associated protein molecules, organized into structures called chromosomes (Fig.1). Consequently, genome information includes many different types of objects.

Four different bases or nucleotides are present in a DNA molecule - adenine (A), thymine (T), cytosine (C), and guanine (G). The particular order of these bases is called a DNA sequence. Since DNA sequences can be handled as strings, molecular biologists initially collected and stored them in text files. However, as the data stored in text files grew large, the maintenance of the data and the related application programs became laborious. Database management systems (DBMS) are known to have the advantage of reducing the labor involved

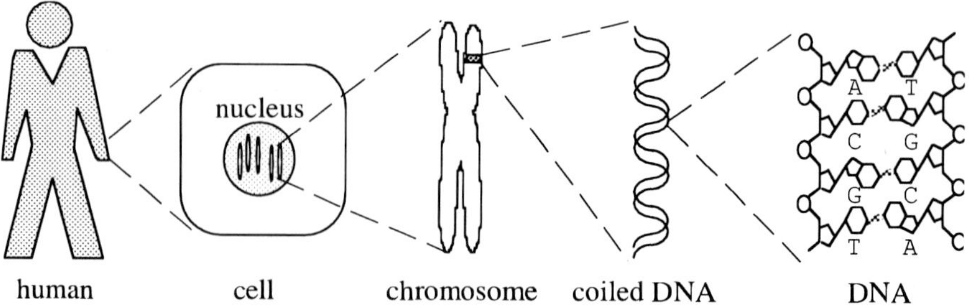

Fig. 1. Schematic relationship of a human being, a cell, a chromosme, and a DNA

with huge data. For several years, molecular biologists have employed relational database management systems (RDBMS) to manage the DNA sequence data.

Most of the current databases for genome information, such as GenBank [BL1], GDB [CF1], and PIR [BG1], are based on relational database technology. RDBMS is now the most popular and relational data models are easy to understand thanks to their simple data structure or tabular form. However, techniques on molecular biology have been marvelously improved and they have produced a large variety of data and knowledge on genomes. Nowadays, in addition to DNA sequences, molecular biologists are interested in the location of a given gene on a chromosome, that is, chromosome mapping data, the three dimensional formation of a DNA molecule that calls for a graphical presentation, and so on and so forth [Ka1]. RDBMS seems to have little ability to meet the above requirements of molecular biologists. In contrast to it, the object-oriented database management system (OODBMS) has been proven to fulfil the similar requirements in CAD and other fields. Nevertheless, there have been only a few reports on the application of OODBMS for managing genome information [CC1].

The success of an application of object-oriented technology to a new field depends on the development of standard and reusable classes [Kr1]. These classes will be the fundamental building blocks in similar fields. However, a design of standard and reusable classes requires a designer with much expertise in the target field.

In general, object-oriented languages and database management systems provide a comprehensive library of good and reusable classes. For instance, Smalltalk's built-in classes handle almost all routine operations on the computer. The supplied classes are so general that a user can fit the needs of almost any application. Unfortunately, they do not cover the classes necessary for genome information. This lack of well-designed classes has resulted in the slow development of an object-oriented database for genome information.

2 Class Design

The fundamental rule in designing classes for genome information is specialization. Class creation by specialization is a direct use of the "is-a" relationship.

Yet, how to apply the rule to genome information is often unclear. Hence, we must define another rule useful in the class design for genome information.

We devide the classes for representing genome information into the following two groups:

- *Material Classes*
  Material classes describe only substantial things or physical existences in the real world. In material classes, values of attributes should also be real scientific existences. For example, biological molecules, such as DNA and proteins, can be instances of material classes.
- *Conceptual Classes*
  Conceptual classes are used to represent unreal objects or logical existences. Objects which are conceived for some purpose should be instances of conceptual classes. For example, a DNA which has been given an identification number belongs to a conceptual class, whereas DNA, alone, is an instance of a material class.

Generally, the properties of substantial things or real scientific existences hardly ever change. Hence, we rarely need to alter material classes. On the other hand, we are supposed to modify conceptual classes more often because we define conceptual classes for objects whose characteristics depend on observers.

An additional rule for class design is *material class priority*. First, we design a material class. Then, we create conceptual classes relevant to the material class. In other words, a conceptual class should have at least one material class among the superclasses and should not have any material class as a subclass. This rule lessens the risk of changing or inverting the class hierarchy because superclasses consisting of material classes are seldom put in a claim for alteration. If new scientific findings demand the modification of an existing material class, we can accommodate the demand by creating a new subclass with new attributes, which is also a material class. When a new concept is introduced into an existing material or conceptual class, a new conceptual class is made. As a matter of convenience, we look upon database objects, such as records and entries, as instances of material classes.

To illustrate an application of this rule, we show the example of a class design of a nucleotide sequence. A nucleotide sequence is a chain of nucleotides that are actually chemical substances. Therefore, we build a class named **NucleotideSequence** as a material class. Because a nucleotide sequence is a completely new object in an OODB, the **NucleotideSequence** class has no superclass except the **GenomeObject** class that is the root class for most genome information. The **NucleotideSequence** class has at least one attribute, the *sequence* for an array of nucleotides "A", "C", "G", and "T". After the discovery of DNA, molecular biologists turned up another type of nucleotide, precisely, ribonucleotides. Ribonucleic Acid (RNA) is not a subtype of DNA although RNA is usually transcribed from DNA. As a consequence, we make a couple of new material classes, the **DNASequence** class and the **RNASequence** class as subclasses of the **NucleotideSequence** class which is left in preparation for other new findings. When numbers of DNA sequences were determined, molecular biologists had to name each of them to manage them efficiently. This led to the need for a new attribute representing a name. However, DNA's name is not its natural character but artificial one. For this reason, we choose to create a new conceptual subclass rather than to adjust the **DNASequence** class by the addition of an attribute.

Based on this strategy, we constructed a standard class hierarchy for genome information. A part of the major classes and their relationships are shown in Fig.2.

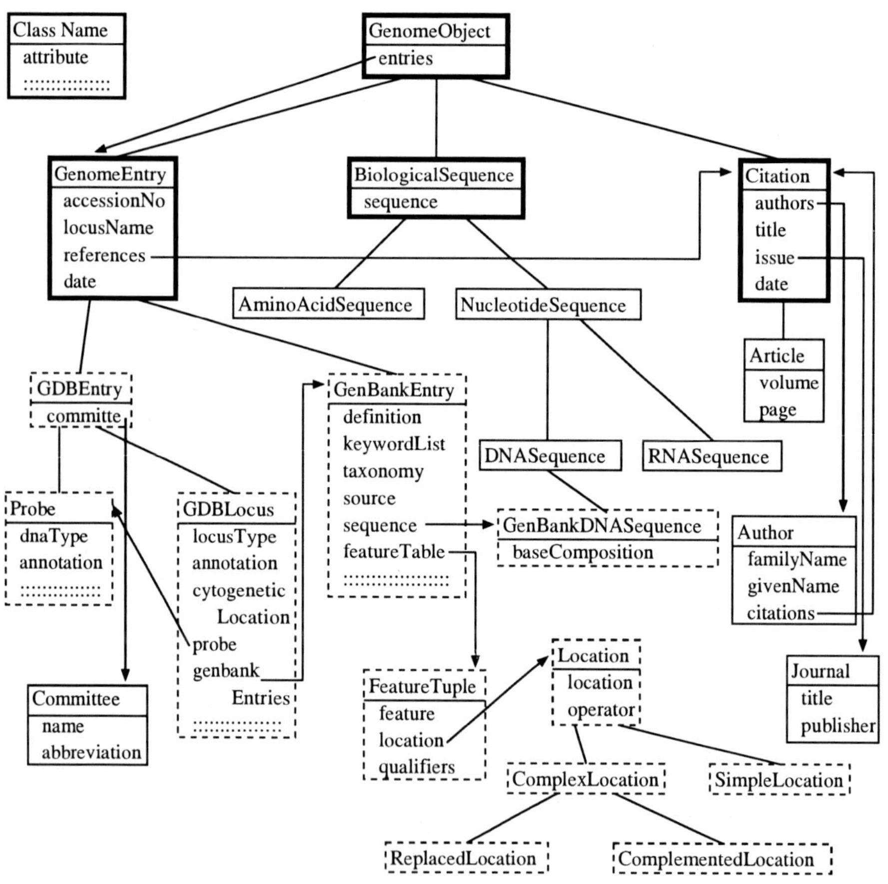

Fig. 2. A part of the class design for genome information. Boxes drawn with thick, thin and dotted lines indicate abstract, material and conceptual classes, respectively.

3 System

An OODBMS used for the integration of genome information is GemStone version 3.2.0, commercially available from Servio Corporation. GemStone supports C, C++, and Smalltalk as its programming language. We used Objectworks\Smalltalk version 4.1 (ParcPlace Systems, Inc.) among them because Smalltalk is completely object-oriented and suitable for rapid prototyping. Although Smalltalk runs comparatively slow, the speed of accessing hard disks is usually slower in database management.

All original data on the human genome were obtained from both the Genetic Sequence Data Bank (GenBank) sequence data release 80.0 (December 1993) in a text file format and the Genome Data Base (GDB) human genome map data version 5.1 (September 1993). GenBank collects nucleotide sequence data of many species of organisms. We utilized the data concerning Homo sapiens which contain 45,980 entries and 329,21,954 nucleotides in an 89 MByte file. GDB offers human chromosome mapping data and pertinent data in a tab separating format. We made use of 21,661 loci and 33,338 sources, *etc.*, in approximately 45 MBytes of files.

4 Implementation

The implementation was incremental and divided into the two steps.

4.1 Implementation for GenBank

First, we converted GenBank data into the OODB. We created 55 new classes. The **GenomeObject** class is a direct subclass of the **Object** class and the top class of most classes for genome information. Against the material class priority rule, the **GenomeObject** class seems to be a conceptual class because there is no genome object in the real world. However, the **GenomeObject** class is not a conceptual class but an abstract superclass. An abstract class is used to create subclasses, for which there are no direct instances. The **GenomeObject** class has just one attribute, *entries*. The attribute *entries* holds pointers to instances of the **GenomeEntry** class. This attribute makes the navigation from one object to a related object possible.

Every class designed for genome information possesses a special class variable named '*SetOf* + (its class name) + *s*'. The *Ourselves* class variable is a general term for this special class variable. The *Ourselves* class variable keeps all the direct instances of the class by adding each of them to the *Ourselves* class variable upon creation. Every class responds to the message *yourselves* and returns a value of the *Ourselves* class variable. For example, an instance of the **GenBankEntry** class is a counterpart of an entry or a record in GenBank data. The **GenBankEntry** class has an *Ourselves* class variable *SetOfGenBankEntries* keeping a set of all instances of the **GenBankEntry** class. Instead of combing the whole GenBank text file, we scour the content of *SetOfGenBankEntries*. On keyword searches, we exploit *SetOfKeywords* of the **Keywords** class.

The most complicated classes for genome information are the **Location** class and its related classes. They are counterparts of location descriptions in the Feature Table in GenBank data. The location descriptions in the GenBank text file vary and sometimes refer to other GenBank entries. In the beginning of implementation, since it was difficult to completely comprehend the format and contents of location descriptions at a glance, we regard the data just as text. After we store all the GenBank data into the OODB, we analyze it in detail and create the **Location** class and its related classes. An OODB allows the user such stepwise development while an RDB requests the user to determine all the data types in the beginning of a development and doesn't give permission to modify them after having created relational tables [ST1].

4.2 Integration of GDB

GDB collects mainly human chromosome mapping data. In the existent databases including GenBank and GDB, the DNA sequence data and the chromosome mapping data are separately and independently managed. Nonetheless, references between the GDB loci and the GenBank entries are frequently requisite. GDB keeps pointers for external references from the GDB loci to the GenBank entries in a relational table *object_genbank_eref*. When a user wants to get the DNA sequence connected with a GDB locus, he first searches the *locus* table and gets the *locus_id*, second, he searches the *objet_locus_iref* table using the *locus_id* and gets the *object_id*, then, he searches the *object_genbank_eref* table using the *object_id* and gets the *genbank_ref* which is equivalent to the GenBank accession number. Finally, he moves to the GenBank database and searches for an entry by the accession number. Because these steps in the searching procedure are too laborious and put a heavy burden on the user, the integration of the GenBank and GDB data is of great significance to molecular biologists.

For implementation of chromosome mapping data and related data in GDB to the OODB, we created 24 new classes. Twenty-two classes created for the GenBank data were reused. For example, **Journal**, **Article**, and **Author** classes have been reused for GDB data even though they were originally created for the GenBank data. Besides this, they will also be reused for other biological databases. This reusability reduces the time needed for implementation of GDB data on the OODB to about 40 % of that for the first implementation of GenBank data.

The whole conversion of both GenBank and GDB data of text file format into the OODB took about 30 hours on a SUN SPARC station 2 with 64 MByte memory. The OODB repository is 220 MBytes while the original files total about 135 MBytes. The OODB file is approximately 1.6 times larger than the original text files.

4.3 User Interface

We provide a good graphical user interface for retrieving genome information (Fig.3). The graphical user interface comprises more than 12 browsers and enables the user to navigate from one set of data to another relevant data set just by clicking a mouse. There are only a few cases in which the user must type keywords and accession numbers, as in the case of a search. The **GenBank Entry Browser** and the **GDB Chromosome Browser** are the main browsing tools for retrieving GenBank data and GDB data, respectively. Because browsers are vital until the user explicitly close them, retrieved results may be compared on the browsers whenever needed.

5 Discussion

We created more than 80 classes for GenBank and GDB data by using object-oriented technology. These classes can be used as standard classes for other biological information because they are created as universally as possible, according to the material class priority rule. When a new biological database is developed, these classes work as templates. In fact, on the integration of GDB data, nearly half the classes built for GenBank data were reusable. Moreover, because the class design is independent of OODBMS, another database for genome information can easily be developed on a different OODBMS, such as Versant or ONTOS.

We also provide such a powerful graphical user interface, that the user can browse all genome information painlessly. However, a query language, equivalent to SQL for RDBMS, is not available in the OODB. We are now extending the OODB and developing a deductive engine and a deductive query language for OODBMS.

6 Acknowledgments

We would like to thank Prof. T. Takagi and Dr. S. Goto at Human Genome Center, Institute of Medical Science, the University of Tokyo for numerous discussions about DBMS. This work was supported in part by a Grant-in-Aid (04261101) for Scientific Research on Priority Areas from the Ministry of Education, Science and Culture in Japan.

References

[BG1] Baker, W.C., George, D.G., Mewes, H.-W., Pfeiffer, F., Tsugita, A.: The PIR-International databases. Nucleic Acid Res. **21** (1993) 3083–3092

[BL1] Benson, D., Lipman, D.J., Ostell, J.: GenBank. Nucleic Acid Res. **21** (1993) 2963–2965

[CC1] Carhart, R.E., Cash, H.D., Moere, M.A. StrateGene: object-oriented programming in molecular biology. Computer Applications in the Biosciences **4** (1988) 3–9

[CF1] Cuticchia, A.J., Fasman, K.H., Kingsbury, D.T., Robbins, R.J., Pearson, P.L.: The GDB human genome data base anno 1993. Nucleic Acid Res. **21** (1993) 3003–3006

[Ka1] Kamel, N.N.: A profile for molecular biology databases and information resources. Computer Applications in the Biosciences **8** (1992) 311–321

[Kr1] Kroha, P.: Objects and Databases. The McGRAW-HILL International Series in Software Engineering, The McGraw-Hill, London (1993)

[ST1] Sakamoto, N., Takagi, T., Sakaki, Y. Development of the Overlapping Oligonucleotide Database and its application to signal sequence search of the human genome. Computer Applications in the Biosciences **9** (1993) 427–434

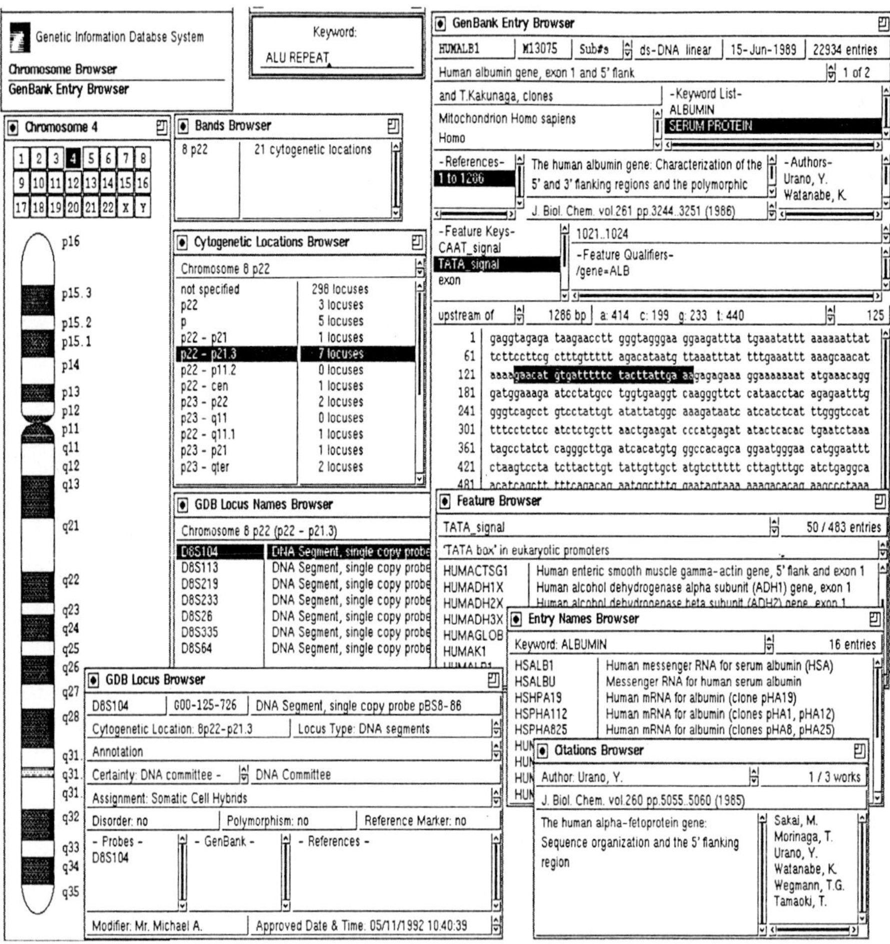

Fig. 3. A snapshot of browsing tools for genome information

On Evidential Feature Salience

George Spanoudakis and Panos Constantopoulos

Department of Computer Science, University of Crete and,
Institute of Computer Science
Foundation of Research and Technology, Hellas

Abstract. This paper describes a method for estimating the salience of features comprising conceptual descriptions of software artifacts. Salience estimates are used in a model analyzing the similarity between such descriptions so as to promote the analogical reuse of the artifacts described by them. Salience is conceived as belief on the dominance of a feature, which is defined on the basis of three general properties that a feature may have in a conceptual model, namely the abstractness, the characteristicity and the causality. This belief is measured according to evidence inherent in conceptual schemas organizing software repositories.

1. Introduction

In this paper, we define a method for evaluating the salience of features comprising conceptual descriptions of software artifacts(i.e code, designs or specifications). The method has been implemented by a system estimating similarities between such descriptions of software artifacts so as to promote their analogical reuse[18].

The analysis of similarity (whose details can be found in [17,18]) results into measures of conceptual resemblance and identifies analogies between software artifacts. Such measures and analogies are used for retrieving artifacts, stored in a Software Information Base[2] and identifying subcomponents of them with prospects for reuse.

The problem of distinguishing between features of different salience arises, while estimating the similarity and detecting analogies between the attributes of two artifact descriptions. Distinctions of salience are critical for analogical reasoning [5,6,7]. Salient features enable the retrieval of source analogs that may lead to consistent and pragmatically usefull conjectures about a target analog, unlike the non salient ones[8,13].

Thus, computational models of analogical reasoning need to estimate the salience of features in the descriptions they operate on. Such estimates are derived either from relevant assertions about features, as in PROTOS[14] and EBL+CBR systems[3], or from assessments of the results of reasoning sessions, provided by external observers(e.g CBL4 algorithms[1]).

As opposed to such estimates, whose derivation is knowledge acquisition intensive, we estimate salience from the conceptual descriptions of artifacts, themselves. The whole approach is based on the concept of *feature dominance*, a compound property derived from three other primitive properties. These are the *characteristicity*, the *abstractness* and the *causality*. All these properties are defined by logical conditions related to the modeling of features over conceptual models, organizing artifact descriptions. Salience is then introduced as belief to the truth value of the dominance of a feature and thus it provides a graded alternative to the logical strictness of it.

The rest of the paper is organized as follows. In the second section, we review the Telos language, which is used for expressing conceptual descriptions of artifacts. In the third section, we discuss and define dominance. In the fourth section, we define the concept of salience and in the fifth section we give an example of estimating salience. Finally, in the sixth section, we summarize the whole approach and review its basic open issues.

2. Telos: A Conceptual Modeling Language for Salience Estimation

Our approach to the estimation of salience is discussed and defined on the basis of the Telos language[12]. Telos offers three modeling abstractions (i.e *multiple and meta classification, multiple generalization* and *typed attribution*) which constitute a structurally object oriented data model, expressive enough, to describe software artifacts[2,4,9].

Telos objects are partitioned into *entities* and *attributes* and into *tokens* and *classes*. All objects are described through instantiation relations, have attributes and are uniquelly identified by system identifiers. Class objects are further described through generalization (i.e Isa) relations.

Each Telos class i has an intension INT[i](i.e a set including the identifiers of the attributes it introduces, inherits or refines) and an extension EXT[i](i.e a set including the identifiers of all its instances). Furthermore, for each attribute class i we distinguish its *scope* $S[i]$(i.e the set of all the classes to which it applies), its *refining classes* $R[i]$ (i.e the set of all the classes introducing or refining it) and its *possible ranges* $AR[i]$(i.e all the classes/ranges of the attribute, in the classes of its scope). These sets are used for the definition of dominance.

3. Factors of Attribute Dominance

We introduce the concept of dominance to express the importance that an attribute may have in: (i) the construction of conceptual schemas adequately classifying an underlying population of objects with respect to the needs of an application (ii) the existence and the behavior of the objects which are instantiated under the classes to which it applies and, (iii) determining the values of other attributes in its scope. These kinds of importance are realized as the properties of the characteristicity, the abstractness and the causality, respectively.

The Charactericity of Attributes. We define as characteristic (CH_i) any attribute i, which has distinct range classes, for all the classes in its scope, that is $|S[i]| = |AR[i]|$.

Our definition is motivated by the way of forming Isa hierarchies in conceptual modeling. Such hierarchies , consist of classes, which are specialized when particular subsets of their instances have one or more special properties. These properties may be an additional attribute or the restriction of the possible values of an existing attribute. In such cases, the original class may be specialized into a new subclass, which introduces the new attribute or refines the existing one. Refinement is the specialization of the class/range of the attribute by the subclass inheriting it. Introduced and refined attributes are characteristic of the new subclass. Furthermore, to the extent that they are refined in other classes they become characteristic of entire Isa hierarchies and conceptual schemas.

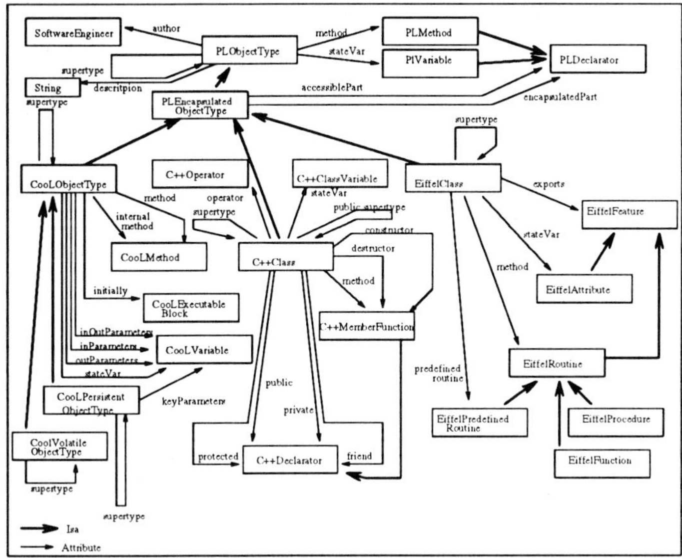

Fig. 1. A Conceptual Model for Object Types of OO Languages

Figure 1 presents characteristic and non characteristic attributes of object types programming languages modeled according to[19]. The attribute *method,* which expresses the methods supported by an object type is characteristic, since it has distinct range classes in all the classes of its scope. Unlike it, the attribute *author* is not characteristic. The way it has been modeled, implies that nothing differentiates the software engineers, who implement Eiffel, CooL and C++ object classes, worth of being abstracted into the conceptual schema.

The Abstractness of Attributes. We also distinguish attributes into abstract and non abstract ones, according to the class which introduces them, in a conceptual schema. In the object oriented data modeling literature, classes are divided into *abstract* and *concrete*, according to whether or not they have any instances of their own [10,11,15]. Abstract classes tend to have attributes, which are essential for the existence and the behavior of the instances of their subclasses.

Consider for example the significance of let's say the attribute *hasSteeringSystem* of a vehicle and the attribute *laggageCarryingCapacity* of a car. The former is essential for driving any sort of vehicle(e.g airplanes, trains, cars), while the latter neither applies to all vehicles(e.g fighting airplanes) nor relates to the functionality of the special kind of vehicles owning it (i.e the cars).

Hence, we define an attribute i to be abstract(i.e ABS_i), if and only if the class which introduces it in a conceptual schema(i.e its *original class*) is abstract. A class j is defined to be abstract (i.e AB_j) if and only if $EXT[j]=EXT_s[j]$ where $EXT[j]$ is the extension of j and $EXT_s[j]$ is the *shared extension* of j (i.e the set of its instances, which also belong to one or more of its subclasses).

The Causality of Attributes. We consider as *causal*, attributes whose values, determine the values of other attributes and as such they lead to conjectures about these latter values. For example, the model of a car could dictate the place where it has been produced, if the relevant manufacturer produces its different models, in different countries. This notion of causality has also been realized in the area of explanation based learning, where predefined types of dependency relations are offered in languages for specifying explanations [14]. In order to avoid the cost of acquiring such relations, we restrict our interest in dependencies between attributes that have the same domain and in a special case of them, the *total equivalences*. Both these dependencies have the special property that the conceptual schema may imply their impossibility.

Formally, if two attributes x and y are defined as associations of the following form $x{:}D_x \rightarrow I_x \quad y{:}D_y \rightarrow I_y$ where I_x and I_y denote the images(i.e the sets of their actual values) of the attributes x and y, we will say that the attribute y depends on the attribute x if and only if they have identical domains(i.e $D_x \equiv D_y$). A dependency can be defined as a mapping $M_{xy}{:}I_x \rightarrow I_y$. Total equivalences between x and y, hold in cases where M is a total and onto isomorphism.

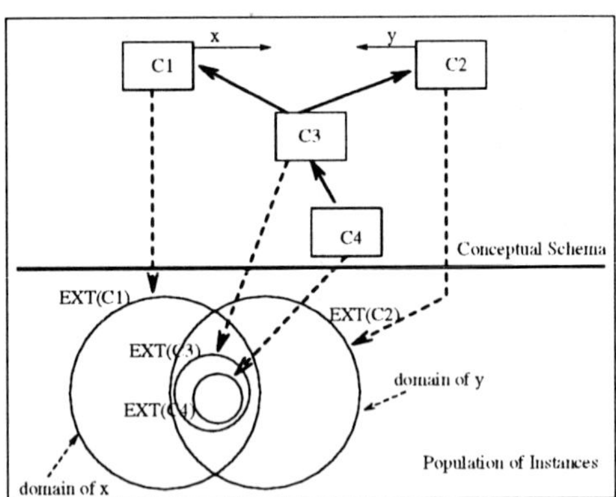

Fig. 2. Non Common Classes of Attributes

The domain equality condition of dependencies is derived from the identity of the scopes of the involved attributes(i.e $S[i] = S[j]$). As it can be observed in figure 2, non common classes in the scopes of two attributes indicate non identical domains(i.e objects in EXT[C1]-EXT[C2] and EXT[C2]-EXT[C1]), unless we assume that all the instances of the class C1 must be also instances of the class C2. However, the presence of two distinct classes in the conceptual schema indicates that their extensions are not identical in general. Otherwise, there would be no need for retaining both classes in the schema (it would be sufficient to have only one class aggregating the attributes of both of them). According to this observation, we will a dependency between the attributes x and y(M_{xy} or $M_{y,x}$) won't be definable whenever $(cnd1)\ :\ S[x] \neq S[y]$.

Futhermore, the definability of total equivalences depends on an additional condition. Given two attributes x and y, a total equivalence mapping between their images cannot be defined if their refining classes do not coincide(i.e $(cnd2)\ :\ R[x] \neq R[y]$).

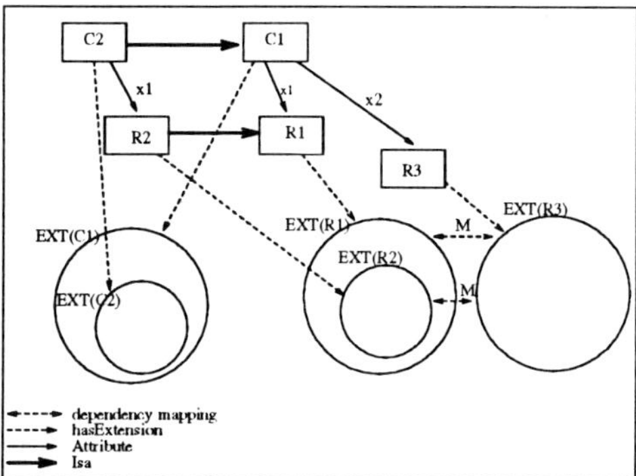

Fig. 3. A Case of Non Common Refinement over the Conceptual Schema

Figure 3, presents a case violating this condition. The the attribute x1 is refined by class C2, unlike the attribute x2. If an equivalence mapping between these two attributes was definable it would be necessary for their images with respect to objects in C1 and to objects in C2, to have equal numbers of elements(i.e $|EXT(R1)| = |EXT(R3)|$ and $|EXT(R2)| = |EXT(R3)|$). Since, the attribute x1 is refined in C2, its image with respect to the objects in C2 will have less elements than its image with respect to objects in C1 (i.e $|EXT(R2)| < |EXT(R1)|$), which contradicts, the previous constraints.

On the basis, of interattribute dependencies, we define an attribute i to be causal (i.e CSL_i) if there can be defined a dependency mapping M_{ij} between its image and the image of any other attribute j, owned by one or more of the classes in its scope.

The Dominance of Attributes. The abstractness, the characteristicity and the causality of attributes determine their dominance. An attribute i, which is characteristic and abstract or causal is defined to be dominant(i.e $DOM_i \equiv (ABS_i \text{ and } CH_i) \text{ or } CSL_i$).

The conjunction between the abstractness and the characteristicity trades off between cases satisfying only one of these properties, as extreme ones. In fact, attributes may be introduced in abstract classes only because of their broad applicability. For instance, the attribute *description* of the class *PLObjectType* in figure 1, serves only as a textual annotation of object types with no essential role for the existence or the behavior of object types. Notice also, that attributes introduced in leaf classes of Isa hierarchies, although satisfying our definition of characteristicity, do not have a general classification significance for the entire conceptual schema. These extreme cases can be simultaneously precluded by the logical conjunction between the abstractness and the characteristicity.

In the next section, we present an evidential approximation of dominance, called attribute salience, which relaxes its logical strictness.

4. Salience of Attributes: Belief on their Dominance

We believe that the logical definition of dominance may be proven very strict in cases of incomplete and/or immature conceptual models. It may also be impractical in cases where finner than the two-fold distinctions between dominant and non dominant attributes are required.

Thus, we introduce attribute salience as a measure of belief that an attribute is dominant or not. This belief is estimated from partial beliefs about the three properties defining the concept of dominance. Partial beliefs are measured by functions defined over the conceptual schema, and relax the relevant logical definitions.

Our analysis is based on beliefs as they are conceived in the context of the Dempster-Shafer theory[16].

We define salience as a function S such that:

$S: A \rightarrow [0,...,1]$ and $\forall \ i:(i \,\varepsilon\, A) \rightarrow S(i) \,\varepsilon\, [Bel(DOM_i),...,P^*(DOM_i)]$

where A is the set of Telos attribute classes, $Bel(DOM_i)$ is the belief on the dominance of attribute i and, $P^*(DOM_i)$ is the upper probability(or plausibility) of the dominance of attribute i [Sha75].

In the following, we present four distinct belief functions, whose combination estimates these boundaries.

Judging Belief about Charactericity. Successive specializations of classes in a conceptual schema are not always introduced due to refinements of the same attribute. For instance, the class *PLEncapsulatedObjectType* is not introduced due a refinment of the attribute *method*, in figure 1. This observation led us, in a plausible relaxation of the logical definition of characteristicity (i.e $|S[i]| = |AR[i]|$), into a belief measure about this property defined as:

$$m_i^{ch}(P) = \begin{cases} c_i & \text{if } P = CH_i \\ 1-c_i & \text{if } P = \overline{CH_i} \end{cases} \quad \text{where } c_i = \frac{|AR[i]|}{|S[i]|}.$$

This function results to 1, whenever the defining condition of characteristicity is satisfied.

Judging Belief about Abstractness. Since abstract are only those attributes, which are introduced by abstract classes, the belief to the abstractness of an attribute i is derived from the belief to the abstractness of its original class j. We obtain this latter belief from the function:

$$m_i^{a}(P) = \begin{cases} e_j & \text{if } P = ABS_i \\ 1-e_j & \text{if } P = \overline{ABS_i} \end{cases} \quad \text{where } e_j = \frac{|EXT_s[j]|}{|EXT[j]|}.$$

This belief function relaxes the definition of abstract classes and gives a belief of 1 whenever this definition is satisfied. Furthermore, it is not as sensitive as that definition to cases where objects are instantiated under abstract classes in a conceptual schema, due to a temporal inability to instantiate them, under some concrete subclass of them.

Judging Belief about Non Causality. Belief about the non causality of an attribute can be measured as an approximate assessment of the conditions *cnd1* and *cnd2* in section 3.

We define the belief to the non existence of a dependency mapping between two attributes i and j, due to their non common classes as:

$$m_{ij}^{ncs}(P)=\begin{cases} d_{ij} & \text{if } P=\overline{M_{ij}} \\ 1-d_{ij} & \text{if } P=\Theta \end{cases} \quad \text{where } d_{ij}=\frac{(|S[i]-S[j]|+|S[j]-S[i]|)}{(|S[i]\cup S[j]|)}$$

According to $m_{ij}^{ncs}(P)$, the more the non common classes in the scopes of two attributes the less possible the definability of a dependency mapping between them. However, the absence of non common classes does not favour the existence of a dependency mapping, as it is evident by the assignment of the belief $(1-d_{ij})$ to the disjunction M_{ij} *or* $\overline{M_{ij}}$ (i.e Θ).

Also, the belief to the non existence of a total equivalence between two attributes i and j, due to their non common refinements over the schema, is defined as:

$$m_{ij}^{ncr}(P)=\begin{cases} r_{ij} & \text{if } P=\overline{M_{ij}} \\ 1-r_{ij} & \text{if } P=\Theta \end{cases}$$

$$\text{where } r_{ij}=\frac{|(S[i]-R[i])\cap R[j]|+|(S[j]-R[j])\cap R[i]|}{|R[i]\cup R[j]|}$$

According to m_{ij}^{ncr}, the more the non common refinements of two attributes over the schema, the less possible the definability of a total equivalence mapping between them. As with the m_{ij}^{ncs} function, the absence of non common refinements does not imply the existence of an equivalence mapping between the involved attributes.

Both the m_{ij}^{ncs} and the $m_{ij}^{ncr}(P)$ result into 0, whenever the negations of the conditions *cnd1* and *cnd2* are satisfied. Thus, they completely disfavour the non existence of dependency or total equivalence mappings between values of attributes.

Total Beliefs about Dominance. The defined partial beliefs can be combined, according to the rule of the orthogonal sum [Sha75] into the following total beliefs:

1. total belief on the dominance of an attribute i(u is the original class of i): $(F1): Bel(DOM_i)=e_u c$

2. total belief on the non causality and upper probability of the causality of an attribute i: $(F2): Bel(\overline{CSL_i})=\prod_{j=1}^{n} d_{ij}$ and $(F3): Bel(\overline{CSL_i})=\prod_{j=1}^{n}(1-(1-d_{ij})(1-r_{ij}))$

F2 and F3 apply when all possible dependencies or only total equivalences between attributes are taken into account, respectively.

3. upper probability of the dominance of an attribute i: $(F4): P^*(DOM_i)=(1-(1-c_i e_u)\prod_{j=1}^{n} d_{ij})$ and

$(F5): P^*(DOM_i)=1-(1-c_i e_u)(\prod_{j=1}^{n}(1-(1-d_{ij})(1-r_{ij})))$

F4 and F5 apply when all possible dependencies or only total equivalences between attributes are taken into account, respectively.

5. An Example

In this section, we give an example of salience estimates, which are computed from the conceptual schema of figure 4. This schema represents, the different types of employees of some research institute. The bold boxes in the figure denote the classes of the taxonomy of employees, and the numbers in their lower right corners are the numbers of the instances of these classes.

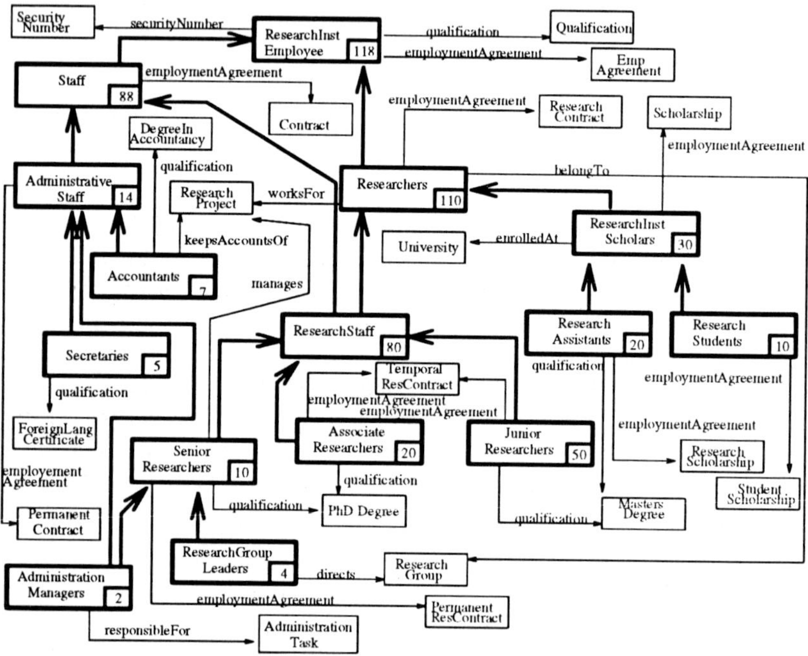

Fig. 4. An Example for Estimating Salience of Atrributes

Every employee has a social security number(i.e the attribute *securityNumber*) and a legal document determining its employment (i.e the attribute *employmentAgreement*). Also, (s)he needs some typical qualifications(i.e the attribute *qualification*) for occupying a certain position in the institute. Special types of employees may have additional attributes. On the basis of this conceptual schema, the boundaries of the salience of the attributes have been measured and presented in table 1.

The column $Bel(DOM_i)$ gives the lower bound of the total belief on an attribute's dominance. This lower bound may be used as a pessimistic estimate of salience, since it has been estimated without any source of evidence favouring the causality of the attribute in hand(see formula F1). According to it, most salient is the attribute *employmentAgreement*, which expresses the legal determination of the employment for any employee. On the other end of the spectrum, the attribute *keepsAccountsOf* is not essential for the employment, since it applies only to certain types of employees.

Table 1: Lower and Upper Boundaries of Salience

Attribute	$B(CH_i)$	$B(ABS_i)$	$B_1(CSL_{\bar{i}})$	$B_2(CSL_{\bar{i}})$	$B(DOM_i)$	$P{*}_1(DOM_i)$	$P{*}_2(DOM_i)$
employmentAgreement	.53	1	0	.17	.53	1	.92
qualification	.4	1	0	.15	.4	1	.91
enrolledAt	.33	1	.25	.47	.33	.83	.68
manages	.33	.6	.1	.28	.198	.92	.77
worksFor	.1	1	0	0	.1	1	1
belongsTo	.1	1	0	0	.1	1	1
securityNumber	.06	1	0	0	.06	1	1
responsibleFor	1	0	.44	.64	0	.56	.36
directs	1	0	.44	.64	0	.56	.36
keepsAccountsOf	1	0	.81	.77	0	.19	.23

The columns $P_1{*}(DOM_i)$ and and $P_2{*}(DOM_i)$ give the upper bounds of the beliefs on dominance. These estimates, obtained from the formulas F4 and F5, could be used as optimistic measures of salience. They only express the degree to which we fail to doubt about the dominance of attributes, according to the interpretation of plausibility by Shafer[Sha75]. According to them, the dominance of the attributes *worksFor* and *belongsTo*, expressing the project and the groups, which a researcher may belong to, could be certain. Both these attributes are not refined separately over the schema and they do not have non common classes. Thus, the existence of a total equivalence mapping between them, cannot be a priori precluded. In fact, it can be intuitively assumed that the participation of a researcher in some research group, determines the project in which (s)he is involved.

6. Concluding Remarks

In this paper, we presented a method for estimating the salience of features comprising descriptions of software artifacts. Salience estimates improve the analysis of similarity between such artifacts[18] which promotes their analogical reuse[17]. Our method only exploits knowledge inherent to conceptual schemas, organizing descriptions of artifacts in repositories. Thus, it is expected to be more practical than other knowledge acquisition intensive solutions to the salience estimation problem, which are incorporated in computational models of analogical reasoning. The described method could be applied to various organizational schemas for repositories, provided that they are expressible through classification, generalization and attribution relations, which are assumed in our framework.

Further research will concentrate on the evaluation of the method in software repositories organized according to diverse conceptual schemas and will investigate into the completeness of the properties used for defining dominance.

7. References

[1] Aha D., Case-Based Learning Algorithms, Proceedings of the DARPA Case-Based Reasoning Workshop, 1991

[2] Constantopoulos P., Doerr M., Vassiliou Y., Repositories for Software Reuse: The Software Information Base, In Proceedings of the IFIP Conference in the Software Development Process, Como,Italy, 1993

[3] Cain T., et al., Using Domain Knowledge to Influence Similarity Judgements, Proceedings of the DARPA Case-Based Reasoning Workshop, 1991

[4] Devanbu P. et al., LaSSIE: A Knowledge Based Software Information System, CACM 34(5), 1991

[5] Falkenhainer B., et al., The Structure Mapping Engine: Algorithm and Examples, Artificial Intelligence, 41, 1989

[6] Gentner D., Finding the Needle: Accessing and Reasoning From Prior Cases, Proceedings of the DARPRA Workshop on Case-Based Reasoning, 1988

[7] Hall R., Computational Approaches to Analogical Reasoning: A Comparative Analysis, Artificial Intelligence 39, 1989

[8] Holyoak K., Koh K., Surface and Structural Similarity in Analogical Transfer, Memory and Cognition 15(4), 1987

[9] Johnson L., et al., Representation and Presentation of Requirements Knowledge, IEEE Transactions on Software Engineering 18(10), 1992

[10] Johnson R., Designing Reusable Classes, Journal of Object Oriented Programming, June/July 1988

[11] Meyer B., Object Oriented Software Construction, C.A.R Hoare, Series Editor, 1989

[12] Mylopoulos J., et. al., Telos: Representing Knowledge About Information Systems, ACM Transactions on Information Systems, 8(4), 1990

[13] Novick L., Analogical Transfer: Processes and Individual Differences, Analogical Reasoning, Kluwer Academic Publishers, 1988

[14] Porter W.B., et al., Concept Learning and Heuristic Classification in Weak-Theory Domains, Artificial Intelligence, 45, 1990

[15] Sciore E., Object Specialization, ACM Transactions on Office Information Systems, 7(2), 1989

[16] Shafer G., A Mathematical Theory of Evidence, Princeton University Press, 1975

[17] Spanoudakis G., Constantopoulos P., Similarity for Analogical Software Reuse: A Conceptual Modeling Approach, Proceedings of the 5th Conference on Advanced Information Systems Engineering(CAiSE '93), 1993

[18] Spanoudakis G., Constantopoulos P.,Measuring Similarity Between Software Artifacts, Proceedings of the 6th International Conference on Software Engineering and Knowledge Engineering(SEKE '94, 1993

[19] Weber M., Implementation Models for the SIB, ITHACA.SNI.92.E2.#2, September 1992

The R-Link Tree: A Recoverable Index* Structure for Spatial Data

Vincent Ng and Tiko Kameda

School of Computing Science, Simon Fraser University, Burnaby, British Columbia, Canada. V5A 1S6

Abstract. So far, R-trees have been investigated for use in the single-user environment. We use the link technique proposed by Kung and Lehman to support concurrent operations (search, insert, and delete) on an R-tree. We present algorithms for implementing these operations, and also discuss recovery issues in case of failure.

1 Introduction

The R-tree was proposed by Guttman [1] as an extension to the B-tree, to be used as an index structure for spatial data in applications such as GIS, CAD, etc. The leaf nodes of an R-tree contain pointers to the actual geometric objects in the database, and each object in the database is pointed to by exactly one leaf node. For the purpose of indexing, each object is represented by its *minimum bounding rectangle* (*MBR*) that encloses it. Associated with each internal node in the tree is the MBR that encloses the MBR's associated with all its child nodes. Thus, for an object O pointed to by a leaf node L, the MBR of O is enclosed by the MBR's associated with all the nodes on the path from L to the root of the tree. An example of an R-tree with the corresponding MBR's is shown in Figure 1, where the entries of each node are labeled by their MBR's.

In [2], we presented three different extensions to the R-tree to allow concurrent operations. However, recovery of an R-tree from system failures has not been addressed. In this paper, we apply the *link technique* proposed by Kung and Lehman[3] to modify the R-tree to support recovery after system failures, as well as allowing concurrent operations. We call the new index structure the *R-link tree.* Our goal is to maintain a consistent tree across system crashes. We achieve this by using link pointers and decomposing the user operations into smaller atomic actions (cf. [4]).

We study three user operations in this paper. The *search* operation carries out the popular window query, which finds the objects whose MBR's overlap the search window. The *insert* operation inserts a new object into an R-tree, and the third operation, *delete*, removes an object from an R-tree. We reorganize the R-tree periodically using two system operations: *condense* and *reorganize*. The

* This work was supported in part by the Canadian Networks of Centres of Excellence and in part by the National Sciences and Engineering Research Coucil of Canada.

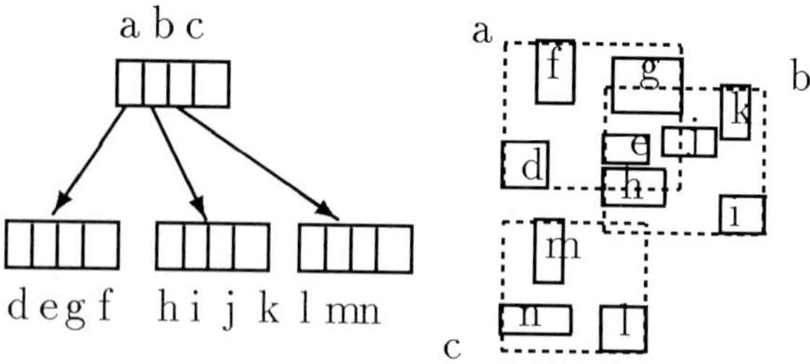

Fig. 1. An R-tree.

condense operation removes the under-utilized nodes in the tree, while the *reorganize* operation restructures the tree to improve search performance. Because of the space limit on the paper, they are not discussed here.

To simplify our discussions that follow, we now introduce a few short-hand notations.

$MBR(P)$ The MBR of node or object P.
$PARENT(P)$ Node identifier or pointer referencing the parent of P.
$FULL(P)$ Predicate indicating if node P is full.
$OVERFL(P)$ Predicate indicating if node P has overflowed.
$UNDERFL(P)$ Predicate indicating if node P has underflowed.
$DELETED(P)$ Predicate indicating if node P is marked as deleted.
$APPEND(Q, P)$ Appends the reference to P to queue Q
$NEXT(Q)$ The next item in queue Q or the link pointer of a node Q.
$NULL$ Null referencing pointer.

2 The Link Technique

The link technique was adapted by Lehman and Yao to B-trees [3]. They modified the B-tree to the *B-link tree* by adding a link pointer to each node. Each node of a B-link tree thus has two types of pointers: its *child pointers* point to the child nodes, while its *link pointer* points to its right neighbor at the same level of the tree. Therefore, link pointers provide an alternate path from a node to each of its child nodes via the leftmost child node. We take advantage of this redundancy for concurrency and recovery.

2.1 R-link Tree

Like the B-link tree, each node of an R-link tree contains a number of entries, one for each child node, and a link pointer. In addition, each node contains a list of *pending updates*, which is the distinguishing feature of the R-link tree (see Figure 2). The pending updates are maintained for the lazy updating of MBR's as a result of *insert*'s. As discussed below in more detail, our implementation of *insert* does not immediately modify the MBR's on the "insertion path" from the root to the leaf where a new object is inserted. Instead, the required update is recorded at each node on the path. When subsequent user operations visit these nodes, the recorded updates are incorporated into the tree level by level, starting at the leaf level. When a user requests an operation, we assign a sequence number, to the operation. This number will identify the operation and all its sub-operations. Each pending update has three fields: the *pending MBR*, the *sequence number* (of the insert operation that caused the change in the MBR), and the identity of the entry referencing the child node on the insertion path. The pending MBR field can be either a MBR or the value *DONE*, the latter indicating the fact that the node's MBR has already been updated and the need to update the parent's MBR. If the identity field has the value of 0, the node is a leaf node.

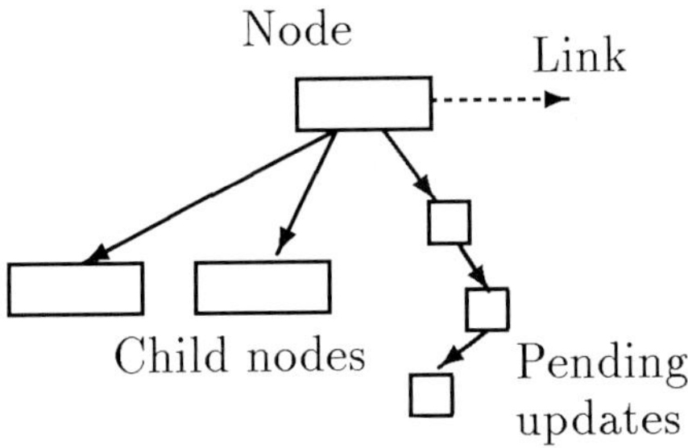

Fig. 2. A node of an R-link tree.

The search operation traverses the tree with the help of the MBR's and pending updates at each visited node. The *insert* operation may *cause* the following changes to the tree: (a) splitting nodes and adding new entries to their parents, and (b) adding and removing pending updates. These two changes may modify the size of the MBR's associated with some nodes. The *delete* operation removes an object and its corresponding entry in a leaf node. It may also cause a node to become empty, flagging the node as "deleted." Besides their main functions, the three user operations also assist in lazy updating, carrying out unfinished structural changes to the R-link tree which are necessitated by earlier *insert*'s and *delete*'s.

The system operation, *condense*, works on at most two levels of nodes in the tree, while the other system operation, *reorganize*, may lock a sub-tree in order to rearrange the nodes in it. In Figure 3, we summarize the changes caused by different operations. In order to facilitate the *condense* and the *reorganize* operations, at each level of the R-link tree, we introduce a head pointer pointing to the leftmost node.

	Changes	Levels affected
Insert	Update MBR's	2
	Split a node	1
	Add an entry	2
Delete	Update MBR's	2
	Remove a node	2
Condense	Update MBR's	2
	Remove a node	2
Reorganize	Rearrange nodes	≥ 2

Fig. 3. Structural changes resulting from an operation

2.2 Concurrency Control

To allow an orderly access to an R-link tree by user and system operations introduced in Section 2.1, we use two types of locks on the nodes. A ρ lock is a read/share lock that can be shared with other read operations[2] accessing the node. Unlike a ρ lock, an ϵ lock is exclusive, being incompatible with any other ϵ or ρ lock. A ρ lock (ϵ lock) on a data item I is denoted by $\rho(I)$ ($\epsilon(I)$). We require that all operations request locks in a top-down, left-to-right (among the children of a node) fashion. This order of lock request/acquisition guarantees deadlock freedom.

During a *search*, other operations such as *insert* and/or *delete* may be in progress. After a *search* read a child pointer, a concurrent *insert* may have split the child, or a concurrent *condense* may have removed the child. In such a case, link pointers provide an alternate path to reach a node or provide information that the child no longer exists. Unlike in a B-tree, however, the nodes at the same level are not linearly ordered according to some key scalar values. A *search* needs to move to the right neighbor, if the current node has been split since the child pointer in the parent was consulted. To check for this condition, we use a pointer pointing to its parent; if there has been a split which has not been reflected in the parent node, then this pointer is set to $NULL$.

2.3 Recovery

A recovery scheme for a tree allows the tree to restructure itself into a consistent state after a system failure.

Let us call a state of a B-link tree or an R-link tree *complete* if every node, except its root and the leftmost node at each level, can be accessed both via

[2] A user operation, such as *insert*, may carry out read operations while visiting a node.

a child pointer *and* link pointers; otherwise the tree is in an *incomplete* state. As a system failure can occur at any time, a structural change to the tree may be aborted in the middle, leaving the tree in an incomplete state. Shasha and Goodman [5] introduced the concept of the *well-formed* order for a B-tree, which assures that future operations will continue to perform correctly. With the use of the link pointers, Lomet and Salzberg [4] showed that even in an incomplete state, the B-link tree is well-formed. They describe a method whereby, after a system failure, they reconstruct the B-link tree gradually with the atomic actions invoked by normal operations (e.g., *search*).

Similarly, we want to maintain enough information in the R-link tree, so that it can always carry out future operations correctly. When the system crashes, the R-link tree may be left in an incomplete state. There can be a number of structural changes which were under way at the time of the failure. Some operations may have been in the middle of (1) splitting, (2) adding an entry to a node, (3) deleting a node, or (4) updating MBR's. In the second situation, the tree is in an incomplete state, while in all other three situations, the updating of the tree has not been finished.

Each structural change to the tree can be viewed as a sequence of steps and a step can give rise to one of the four situations above. We implement each step as an atomic action, which has the all-or-nothing property. Each action is considered as a database transaction in order to guarantee serializability as well as atomicity. We adopt *write-ahead* logging for all the actions [6]. Each action is first logged in stable storage before it is allowed to modify the tree. After its successful completion, we write the commit record in the log. With the log, the atomic actions can be restarted and all aborted actions can be rolled back completely. Locks may be held by some transactions when the system fails. We first release all the locks and restart all non-completed operations.

3 Atomic Actions

While executing any user operation, we perform four different tests on each node visited. We first check if the current node is a *DELETED* node (the *deletion test*), and if so, invoke *UpDeleteAction* given below. We then check whether the node is *FULL* (the *node-full test*), and if so, invoke *SplitAction* given below. We also test if the MBR's are up-to-date (the *MBR test*), and if not, invoke *UpMBRAction* given below. In this test, we make use of the lists of pending updates of P and $PARENT(P)$. If there is a pair of pending updates, U for P and U' for $PARENT(P)$, such that they have the same sequence number and U has the value *DONE* in its *MBR* field, this implies that the MBR of $PARENT(P)$ has not yet been updated. Finally, we test if there is a new entry representing a new node to be added (the *child split test*), and if so, we invoke *IndexAction* given below. (A node is new if its parent pointer field has the *NULL* value.) In order to achieve a higher level of concurrency for the *search* operation, updating actions which do not affect the results of *search* are not included. Only the *child split test* is included in each step of a search operation.

Starting with the root, at each node which a user operation visits, we perform the above four tests and the corresponding actions depending on the type of operation. Note that there are two structural changes involved in splitting P: the first is to split the node into two nodes, P and P', and the second is to add a new entry to their parent. We carry out these two changes by two different atomic actions, *SplitAction* and *IndexAction*, respectively (see below). This reduces the rollback effort if the system crashes.

Let P denote the node being visited.

- *UpDeleteAction*: This action finds the parent of P and updates the corresponding entry. If the parent's MBR changes as a result, it may necessitate the change of the grandparent's MBR, and so forth, which is carried out by *UpMBRAction* given below.
- *UpMBRAction*: The action updates the MBR of $PARENT(P)$, sets the MBR field of U' to $DONE$ and remove U from P. (See above for the definition of U'.) The MBR updates propagate upwards level by level and it may require several invocations of this action to complete them.
- *SplitAction*: This action performs only the first half of the structural changes, caused by a split. After creating a new node P', it moves about half of the entries of P to it. Initially, P' has no parent, which is indicated by its parent pointer, *ParentPtr*, being set to $NULL$. The link pointer of P is changed to point to P'.
- *IndexAction*: It performs the second structural change after a split. It adds a new entry in P's parent and adjust the parent's MBR accordingly.

Atomic actions are non-blocking, i.e., when an action is invoked, the invoking procedure initiates it and continues execution without waiting for the action to complete. When an action is aborted due to system failure, it will be rolled back and restarted. There are other atomic actions that are specific to individual user operations, which we describe in later sections.

4 Search

Like all other user operations, a *search* starts at the root of the R-link tree and descends down to the leaf level. At each visited node (e.g., A in Figure 4), a ρ lock on it must be acquired. After it has decided which child nodes to visit next, the ρ lock can be released. Let W be the search window. Several sub-search operations may be started when there is more than one entry in the current node, whose MBR overlaps W. If a child node (C in Figure 4) is a newly created node by a recent split, it is possible that no entry representing C has been placed in node A. As shown in Figure 4, the link pointer at B provides an alternate way to access node C even though A does not yet point to C. In our implementation, when a *search* visits C, it will test the value of the field *ParentPtr* in C. If the field is $NULL$, we start a new sub-search operation to search the subtree rooted at C. If the field is not $NULL$ and $MBR(C)$ overlaps with W, a sub-search would have been initiated at A already.

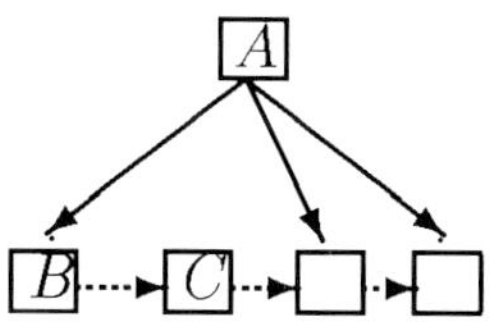

Fig. 4. Using the link pointer to search.

While executing a *search* operation, we perform the *child split test* as stated previously on each visited node. It is because the next node to be visited may have been split. The search operation would need to include the new areas. As the other three tests do not reveal a change in the MBR of the visited node, they are not included in the *search*. To give a flavor of our algorithms, we describe *search* in detail below. We carry out *search* by calling *Rl.Search(W, P,SeqNo)*, where W is the search window, P is the root of a sub-tree, and *SeqNo* is the sequence number assigned by the system to this instance of *search*. Initially, we set P to the root R of the tree.

Rl.Search$(W, P, SeqNo)$

1. Acquire $\rho(P)$.
2. **if** P is a non-leaf node **then**
   - Let $\{E_i = (MBR(P_i), P_i) \mid i = 1, \ldots, k\}$ be the entries in P such that $(MBR(P_i) \cup U_i) \cap W \neq \phi$, where U_i is the union of the MBR's of the pending updates which point to E_i.
   - **if** $(k > 0)$ **then**
     - For all entries E_i found above, continue the search in parallel, invoking *Rl.Search*$((MBR(P_i) \cup U_i) \cap W, P_i, SeqNo)$.

   else For all objects whose MBR's overlap with W return their object ids.
3. **if** $(NEXT(P) \neq NULL)$ **then**
   - $P' = NEXT(P)$.
   - Acquire $\rho(P')$.
   - **if** $(PARENT(P') = NULL)$ **then**
     - *Rl.Search*$(W, P', SeqNo)$.
     - $IndexAction(P, P')$.
   - Release $\rho(P')$.
4. Release $\rho(P)$.

5 Insert

Given an R-link tree with the root R and an object O to be inserted, the *insert* operation adds O to an appropriate leaf in the tree. If the leaf overflows, then it is split, and the *insert* propagates up the tree. The first phase is to select a leaf node to which to add O and insert it. The second phase is to propagate the required updates (i.e., splitting and/or enlarged MBR) upward along the insertion path.

The MBR's of some nodes on the insertion path will change if the object to be inserted covers additional area. If the MBR's of those nodes are updated immediately in the first phase, they may be changed again by a subsequent *condense* or *reorganize* operation, oblivious of the imminent insertion of O. This will cause a subsequent *search* to miss O. We solve this problem by delaying the update, recording the expanded MBR in the list of pending updates, which will be later (in the second phase) used to enlarge the node's MBR. This recording is carried out during the first phase as the *insert* traverses the tree downward along the insertion path. In the mean time, before an expanded MBR replaces the node's MBR, subsequent operations examine both the MBR of the node and the MBR's of its pending updates.

We use the action, *Rl.UpdateAction*,[3] to perform the reorganization of the tree as need. To simplify its work and to avoid multiple actions working on the same part of the tree, when this action is aborted, it will not be restarted. If the system fails during the updating action, the remaining part is cooperatively carried out by subsequent user operations. An *insert* itself pitches in to incorporate the exiting pending MBR's at some nodes on its insertion path as the nodes' new MBR's. To this end, during the first phase, an *insert* performs the four tests (as described in Section 3) at each visited node. Depending on the test outcomes, the appropriate atomic actions will be executed to complete tree updates. There is one atomic action to be invoked at the end of phase one: *Rl.InsertObject*, is used only by *insert* to add an object to a leaf node.

6 Delete

We use two phases to implement the *delete* operation. The first phase is for locating the leaf node L which points to the object O to be deleted. As in the *search* operation, at each visited node, a *delete* operation may branch off into multiple descending paths before reaching the leaf node, which contains the object to be removed. While descending the tree, we perform the four tests we described earlier on each visited node. Atomic actions will be executed to complete tree updates, including those necessitated by other *delete*'s. The atomic action, *Rl.DeleteAction*, is used to delete the unwanted object and to flag the leaf node as necessary. In the second phase, we need to perform the required updates, avoiding interference with the concurrent *insert*'s and the changing parent pointers and MBR's.

We use the "mark-and-remove" approach. If a node becomes empty as a result of deleting O form L, then it is flagged as "deleted." In the first phase, we do not remove the node immediately, because there can be other concurrent operations working on it. "Deleted" nodes are later garbage-collected periodically. If a node

[3] This, as well as *Rl.InsertObject* and *Rl.DeleteAction* which we will refer to later, is fully described in [7].

underflows after a deletion, we append it to a queue, which is used to record the underflowed nodes. If its size reaches a certain threshold, the *condense* operation is invoked to perform the delayed updates.

7 Serializability and Multiple Searches

Consider a scenario where there are two concurrent *search* operations, S_1 and S_2, having the same search window W. Suppose that at node A of the tree there are two entries whose MBR's intersect W. Thus S_1 is divided into S_{11} and S_{12}, which will take two different paths down the tree to look for objects. Similarly, S_2 is divided into S_{21} and S_{22}. As S_1 and S_2 have the same search window, they will follow the same search paths to reach the leaf nodes.

If overtaking is allowed for search operations, S_{21} may overtake S_{11} and S_{12} may finish before S_{22}. Let L and L' be the leaf nodes where S_{11} and S_{12} finish, respectively. If there is no *insert* inserting objects at L or L', then the results of S_1 and S_2 will be the same. Even if there is only one object inserted in either L and L', no inconsistency will result. However, if an *insert* operation I_1 inserts object O at L and I_2 inserts object O' at L', there can be inconsistency between S_1 and S_2. S_{21} may finish before I_1 and S_{11}, and S_{12} may finish before I_2 and S_{22}. If this happens, S_1, S_2, I_1 and I_2 cannot be serialized.

We solve the problem by validating an operation after it has finished but before it commits. However, if we abort an *insert*, a lot of recovery work would be required. Therefore, we abort only *search*'s to achieve consistency in the results. We maintain a table, which, for each *search* operation S, records its starting time (S^s), ending time (S^e), and the set of leaf nodes visited (V). For each inserted object, we also maintain a timestamp as to when it was inserted. The timestamp can be viewed as the finishing time of an *insert* operation. Old entries in the tables for *search* operations are purged periodically.

If there are two *search* operations, S_1 and S_2, and the following conditions are all satisfied, then either S_1 or S_2 should be aborted and restarted (see Figure 5).

1. Operational times T_1 of S_1 and T_2 of S_2 overlap.
2. S_1 and S_2 have common leaf nodes visited, i.e., $V_1 \cap V_2 \neq \phi$ where V_1 and V_2 are the set of leaf nodes visited by S_1 and S_2, respectively.
3. There is at least one object in V_1 and one object in V_2 and the timestamps of the objects are within the overlap of T_1 and T_2.

No major changes are needed to the algorithms presented in the previous sections. Before a *search* commits and returns its result, it will need to check the above conditions. The check can be done in the order as shown. If the test fails, then no further test will be needed. If all three conditions are satisfied, then the *search* operation is restarted.

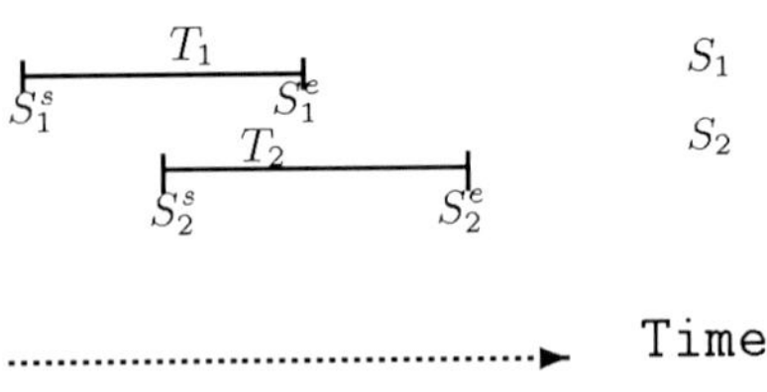

Fig. 5. Overlapping search times.

8 Conclusion

To allow concurrent accesses and failure recovery, we have adapted the link technique to the R-tree, introducing a new type of index structure, called the R-link tree. We discussed atomic actions to implement the three common operations, (*search*, *insert*, and *delete*). Finally, we presented the serializability conditions for the search and insert operations.

References

1. A. Guttman. R-Trees: A dynamic index structure for spatial searching, *SIGMOD Record*, Vol. 14, No. 2, June 1984, pp. 47-57.
2. V. Ng and T. Kameda. Concurrent accesses to R-trees, *Proc. Third International Symp. on Spatial Databases*, Singapore, June 1993, pp. 142-161.
3. P.L. Lehman and S.B. Yao. Efficient locking for concurrent operations on B-Trees, *ACM Trans. on Database Systems*, Vol. 6, No. 4, December 1981, pp. 650-670.
4. D. Lomet and B. Salzberg. Concurrency and recovery for index trees, *Technical Report CRL 91/8*, Digital Equipment Corporation, Cambridge Research Laboratory, August 1991.
5. D. Shasha and N. Goodman. Concurrent search structure algorithms, *ACM Trans. on Database Systems*, Vol. 13, No.1, March 1988, pp. 53-90.
6. J. Gray and A. Reuter. *Transaction Processing: Concepts and Techniques*, Morgan Kaufmann, San Mateo, CA (1992).
7. V. Ng and T. Kameda. The R-Link tree. *CSS/LCCR TR94-08*, August 1994, School of Computing Science, Simon Fraser University, Burnaby, Canada.

The Retrieval of Direction Relations using R-trees

Dimitris Papadias[1,2], Yannis Theodoridis[1], Timos Sellis[1]

[1]Dept. of Electrical and Computer Engineering, National Technical University of Athens, Zographou 15773, Athens, Greece. e-mail: {dp,theodor,timos}@theseas.ntua.gr

[2]Dept. of Geoinformation, Technical University of Vienna, Gusshausstrasse 27-29, Austria A-1040. e-mail: dpapadia@fbgeol.tuwien.ac.at

Abstract: R-trees and related structures, like R^+-trees and R^*-trees, have been used to answer queries involving topological information about objects represented by their minimum bounding rectangles (MBRs). This paper describes how the R-tree method can be used for the storage and retrieval of direction relations. Direction relations deal with order in space, as for instance, left, above, north, southeast etc. In this paper we define direction relations between points and extend the definitions to relations between objects. Then we present our tests regarding the retrieval of direction relations between objects using R-trees and discuss the representational properties of MBR approximations with respect to directions in 2D space.

1. Introduction

Conventional Database Management Systems are designed to store one-dimensional data, such as integers, real numbers, strings and records. As a result, the underlying structures, data models and query languages are not powerful enough to efficiently handle multi-dimensional data such as boxes, lines, polygons etc. On the other hand, the need to store, retrieve and present multi-dimensional data in applications, such as Cartography, Computer-Aided Design, and Computer Vision has led to the development of alternative *spatial access methods*.

The method proposed in (Guttman, 1984) divides the plane into appropriate sub-regions and stores these sub-regions in hierarchical data structures, called R-trees. R-trees have been used to answer queries involving topological information about objects represented by their minimum bounding rectangles (MBRs). According to the MBR approximation each object is abstracted as the minimum rectangle (with its sides parallel to the co-ordinate axes) which fully covers the object.

The R-tree data structure is a height-balanced tree which consists of intermediate and leaf nodes. The descriptions of data objects are stored in leaf nodes and intermediate nodes are built by grouping rectangles at the lower level. Data objects can be overlapping, covering each other, or completely disjoint. The MBRs of the actual data objects are assumed to be stored in the leaves of the tree. Each intermediate node is associated with some rectangle which encloses all rectangles that correspond to lower level nodes. Figure 1 shows an example set of data rectangles and the corresponding R-tree built on these rectangles (assuming a branching factor of 4).

This research is supported by the Esprit II Basic Research Program EP 6881 (*Amusing*) and by a research grant from the General Secretariat of Research and Technology of Greece (PENED 91).

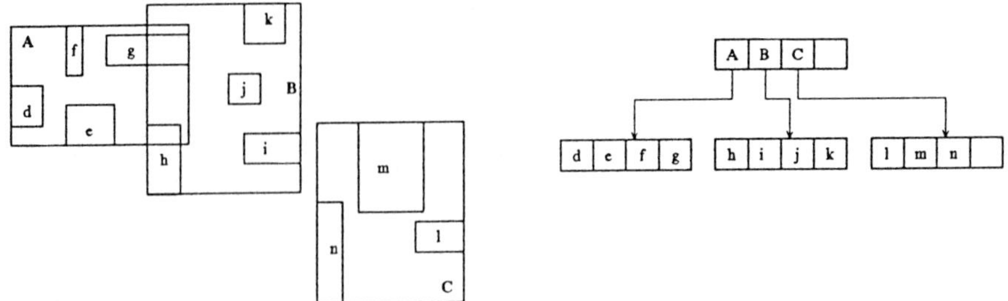

Fig. 1 Some rectangles and the corresponding R-tree

The fact that R-trees permit overlap among node entries sometimes leads to unsuccessful hits on the tree structure (for example, for a search window located in the common area of nodes A and B, both sub-trees rooted at nodes A and B must be searched). The R^+-tree (Sellis et al., 1987) and the R^*-tree (Beckmann et al., 1990) methods have been proposed to address the problem of performance degradation caused by the overlapping regions or excessive dead-space respectively. To avoid this problem, R^+-tree achieves zero overlap among intermediate node entries by allowing partitions to split rectangles. On the other hand, the R^*-tree permits overlap but tries to minimise it by organising rectangles into nodes using a more complex algorithm than the one of the original R-tree.

When the MBRs of two objects are disjoint then we can conclude that the objects that they represent are also disjoint. If the MBRs however share common points, no conclusion can be drawn about the topological relation between the objects. For this reason, spatial queries involve the following two step strategy:

- *Filter step*: The R-tree is used to rapidly eliminate objects that could not possibly satisfy the query. The result of this step is a set of candidates which includes all the results and possibly some false hits.
- *Refinement step*: Each candidate is examined (by using computational geometry techniques). False hits are detected and eliminated.

While the previous strategy refers to the retrieval of topological relations (i.e., disjoint, overlap), in this paper we will describe how the R-tree method can be used for the retrieval of direction relations. Direction relations deal with order in space (e.g., *left*, *above*, *north*, *southeast* etc.); depending on their definitions, direction relations may sometimes yield topological information. Section 2 defines two sets of direction relations between points that correspond to different levels of resolution. Section 3 extends the definitions to relations between objects and describes the direction relations that we use in our tests. Section 4 discusses the retrieval of direction relations using R-trees and presents our tests. Section 5 concludes the paper with a discussion and suggestions for further research.

2. Direction Relations between Points

The approach that is usually taken for the definition of direction relations is that each object is represented by one or more *representative points*, and the plane is divided into partitions using these points. The direction relation between two objects is then determined by the partition that the *primary*[1] representative points are in, with

---

[1] The term *primary point* denotes the point to be located and the term *reference point* denotes the point in relation to which the primary point is located.

respect to the *reference* representative points. There are several alternative ways to divide the plane into partitions. For instance, Hernandez (1993) used one point per object and defined the direction relations using angular directions between the observer's position (reference point) and a destination point (primary point). Dutta (1989) followed a similar approach, but in addition, he used fuzzy sets to denote membership in a relation. On the other hand, the definitions that we assume in the paper partition the plane using lines (projections) vertical to the co-ordinate axes (Frank, 1992), (Papadias Sellis, 1993). A similar approach was taken by (Chang et al., 1989), in their *symbolic projection method.*

Let p_i be a point of object p, q_j be a point of object q, and *X* and *Y* be functions that return the *x* and y co-ordinate of a point. Next we describe two sets of direction relations, namely d_1 and d_2, on which we will concentrate for the rest of the paper. The set d_1 contains the *primitive direction relations* which correspond to the highest resolution that we can achieve when reasoning in terms of points. When one point is used for the representation of the reference object the plane is divided into nine partitions which correspond to the primitive relations of d_1. Figure 2 illustrates the primitive relations depending on the position of a primary point with respect to a reference point denoted by *.

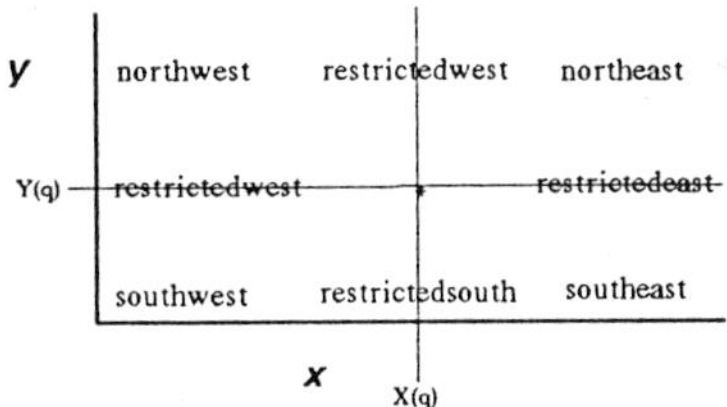

Fig. 2 Plane partitions using one point per object

The second set d_2 contains more general relations (i.e., lower resolution) that can generated from disjunctions of relations of d_1. Disjunctions of relations is a common way of representing uncertain spatial knowledge; they have been used, for instance, for topological relations (Randell et al., 1992). The relations of d_2 are:

north(p_i, q_j) ≡ northwest(p_i, q_j) ∨ restrictednorth(p_i, q_j) ∨ northeast(p_i, q_j)
east(p_i, q_j) ≡ northeast(p_i, q_j) ∨ restrictedeast(p_i, q_j) ∨ southeast(p_i, q_j)
south(p_i, q_j) ≡ southwest(p_i, q_j) ∨ restrictedsouth(p_i, q_j) ∨ southeast(p_i, q_j)
west(p_i, q_j) ≡ northwest(p_i, q_j) ∨ restrictedwest(p_i, q_j) ∨ southwest(p_i, q_j)
samelevel(p_i,q_j)≡restrictedwest(p_i, q_j)∨sameposition(p_i, q_j)∨restrictedeast(p_i, q_j)
samewidth(p_i,q_j)≡restrictednorth(p_i,q_j)∨sameposition(p_i,q_j)∨restrictedsouth(p_i,q_j)

The distinction between the relations of d_1 and d_2 is necessary because, as it will be shown later, the MBR approximations are always adequate for the representation of relations of d_2 between actual objects while the relations of d_1 may require a refinement step. The previous direction relations refer to points in two-dimensional space. In the next section we will extend the definitions to describe relations between contiguous objects. Furthermore we will show how MBR approximations and spatial data structures can be used to facilitate efficiency in the retrieval of direction relations.

3. Direction Relations between Objects

The MBR approximation, commonly used in spatial data structures, represents each object q as an ordered pair (q'_f, q'_s) of points that correspond to the lower left and the upper right point of the MBR q' that covers q (q'_f stands for the first and q'_s for the second point of the MBR). When we use two points for the representation of the reference (region) object, the plane is divided into 25 partitions which are illustrated in Figure 3. Thus, there are 25 possible ways to put a primary point in the plane, and therefore 25 primitive direction relations between a region and a point object. In general, the relation between two objects can be defined using the partitions that the primary points are located with respect to the reference points.

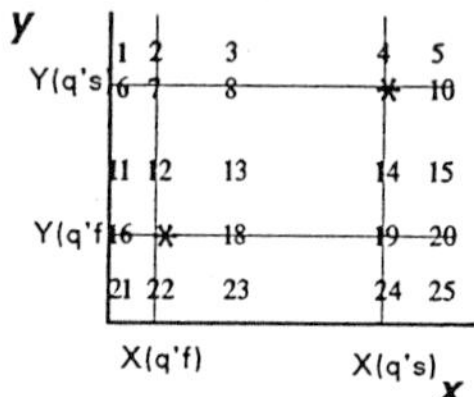

Fig. 3 Plane partitions using two points per object

Unlike the case of topological relations, where no conclusion can be drawn about the relation between the actual objects when the MBRs overlap, the MBR approximations have several attractive properties with respect to direction relations. Depending on the relative positions of the representative points of the MBRs, several conclusions can be drawn about the direction relationships between the actual objects, as for instance: *north*(p'_f, q'_f) $\Rightarrow \forall p_i \ \exists q_j$ *north*(p_i, q_j), *north*(p'_f, q'_s) $\Rightarrow \forall p_i \ \forall q_j$ *north*(p_i, q_j), *north*(p'_s, q'_f) $\Rightarrow \exists p_i \ \exists q_j$ *north*(p_i, q_j) and *north*(p'_s, q'_s) $\Rightarrow \exists p_i \ \forall q_j$ *north*(p_i, q_j).

For example, north(p'_f, q'_s) implies that all points of object p are north of all points of object q. This relation between p and q is called *strong_north* and can be defined as *strong_north(p,q)* $\equiv \forall p_i \ \forall q_j$ *north*(p_i, q_j). Figure 4a illustrates a configuration that corresponds to the relation strong_north. The objects that satisfy the query "find the objects strong_north of q" are all the objects whose MBRs satisfy the relation north(p'_f, q'_s). As in the case of strong_north, all the following queries regarding relations between objects will be reduced to queries involving relations between points.

Fig. 4 Strong_north and Weak_north relations

The relation weak_north between objects can be defined as: weak_north(p,q) $\equiv \exists p_i \ \forall q_j$ north(p_i, q_j) $\wedge \forall p_i \ \exists q_j$ north(p_i, q_j) $\wedge \exists p_i \ \exists q_j$ south(p_i, q_j). That is, p is weak_north of q if:

exist some points of p which are north of all points of q AND

for each point p_i exist points q_j such that north(p_i, q_j) AND
exist some points of p which are south of some points of q.

Although the definition of weak_north is more complicated than the strong_north definition, the relation can be easily understood using the illustration of Figure 4b. Object p is weaknorth of object q if its southmost point is in one of the partitions 11-15 and the northmost is in the partitions 1-5 with respect to q'. The result of the query "find all objects weak_north of q" consists of all MBRs such that north(p'_s, q'_s) $\wedge$ north(p'_f, q'_f) $\wedge$ south(p'_f, q'_s).

The relation strong_bounded_north is defined as: strong_bounded_north(p,q) $\equiv \forall p_i \forall q_j$ north(p_i, q_j) $\wedge \forall p_i \exists q_j$ northeast(p_i, q_j) $\wedge \forall p_i \exists q_j$ northwest(p_i, q_l). That is, we say that p is strong_bounded_north of q if:

all points of p are north of all points of q AND
all points of p are northeast of some points of q AND
all points of p are northwest of some points of q.

As Figure 5a illustrates, according to strong_bounded_north, all points of p must be in partition 3 with respect to q'. The result of the query "find the objects strong_bounded_north of q" contains all objects p whose MBRs satisfy the following conditions with respect to q': north(p'_f, q'_s) $\wedge$ northeast(p'_f, q'_f) $\wedge$ northwest(p'_s, q'_s). Unlike the strong_north and weak_north relations, where points p'_f and p'_s could belong to a number of possible partitions, strong_bounded_north is primitive because it constrains each point to exactly one partition; both p'_f and p'_s must be in partition 3 with respect to q'.

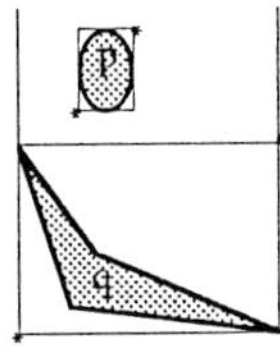

a

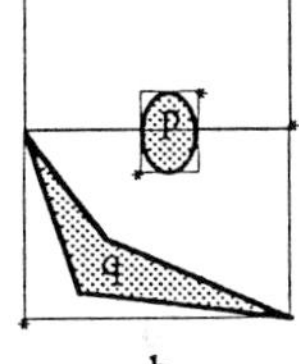

b

Fig. 5 Strong_bounded_north and Weak_bounded_north relations

In a similar manner we can define weak_bounded_north as, weak_bounded_north(p,q) $\equiv \exists p_i \forall q_j$ north(p_i, q_j) $\wedge \exists p_i \exists q_j$ south(p_i, q_j) $\wedge \forall p_i \exists q_j$ northeast(p_i, q_j) $\wedge \forall p_i \exists q_j$ northwest(p_i, q_j). According to this relation, all points of p must be in partitions 3, 8 and 13 with respect to q' (Figure 5b). The result of the query "find all objects weak_bounded_north of q" contains objects p whose MBRs satisfy the following conditions with respect to q': north(p'_s, q'_s) $\wedge$ south(p'_f, q'_s) $\wedge$ northeast(p'_f, q'_f) $\wedge$ northwest(p'_s, q'_s), i.e., all MBRs such that p'_f is in partition 8 and p'_s is in partition 3 (primitive relation). Unlike the previous queries, this one needs a refinement step since the MBRs are not adequate to express the relation between the actual objects. Figure 6 illustrates a configuration of objects whose MBRs satisfy the conditions expressed by the query, but the objects themselves do not satisfy the relation weak_bounded_north because it is not the case that $\forall p_i \exists q_j$ northeast(p_i, q_j). The refinement step is needed because we have overlapping MBRs and relations of d_1 are used in the definition of weak_bounded_north. In general, we can say that the relations of d_2 between objects are always preserved by their MBR approximations, while for relations of d_1 we may need a refinement step when the MBRs overlap.

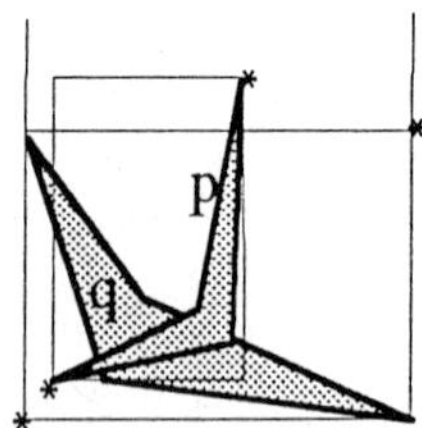

Fig. 6 Refinement step for Weak_bounded_north relation

Strong_northeast is a primitive variation of the strong_north relation which can be defined as strong_northeast(p,q) ≡ $\forall p_i\ \forall q_j$ northeast(p_i, q_j), i.e., all points of p must be in partition 5 with respect to q'. The objects that satisfy the query "find the objects strong_northeast of q" are the ones whose MBRs satisfy the relation northeast(p'_f, q'_s). Similarly we can define the weak_northeast relation as weak_ northeast(p,q) ≡ $\exists p_i\ \forall q_j$ northeast(p_i, q_j) ∧ $\exists p_i\ \exists q_j$ south(p_i, q_j) ∧ $\forall p_i\ \exists q_j$ northeast(p_i, q_j). The result of the query "find all objects weak_northeast of q" contains MBRs p' such that northeast(p'_s, q'_s) ∧ northeast(p'_f, q'_f) ∧ south(p'_f, q'_s), i.e., all MBRs whose second point is in the partition 5, and the first point is in partitions 13, 14, or 15. As in the case of weak_bounded_north, a refinement step is needed for the MBRs whose first point is in partition 13. The rest of the MBRs do not need a refinement step, i.e., all retrieved MBRs correspond to objects that satisfy the query. Figure 7 illustrates the strong_northeast and weak_northeast relations.

Fig. 7 Strong_northeast and Weak_northeast relations

We can also define variations of the same_level relation, as for instance, same_level(p,q) ≡ $\forall p_i\ \exists q_j$ samelevel(p_i, q_j). According to this relation, all points of p are in partitions 6-20 with respect to q'. The MBRs that satisfy the query "find the objects same_level with q" are the ones that satisfy the relation (samelevel(p'_f, q'_f) ∨ north(p'_f, q'_f)) ∧ (samelevel(p'_s, q'_s) ∨ south(p'_s, q'_s)). Same_level is not symmetric, i.e., same_level(p,q) does not necessarily imply same_level(q,p). We can define a symmetric version of same_level as strong_same_level(p,q) ≡ $\forall p_i\ \forall q_j$ samelevel(p_i, q_j). The objects that are strong_same_level with q are these for which samelevel(p'_f, q'_f) ∧ samelevel(p'_s, q'_s). Figure 8a illustrates a configuration that corresponds to the same_level relation, and Figure 8b a configuration that corresponds to the strong_same_level relation.

Fig. 8 Same_level and Strong_same_level relations

In Section 3 we have defined a set of direction relations between objects. Most of these are variations of the north relation; other directions can be formed in a similar manner. Numerous additional relations between region, line and point data can be defined and used in queries depending on the application needs. A discussion about the possible relations between MBRs can be found in Section 5.

4. Performance Issues Regarding Direction Relations

In this section we will show how direction relations can be retrieved using tree structures, and in particular, using a variant of the R-tree method, called R*-trees (Beckmann et al., 1990). The main idea of the R-tree-based methods is the grouping of MBRs by dividing the global area into partitions with minimal or zero overlap. According to this strategy, adjacent boxes are stored within adjacent partitions and objects that satisfy certain topological relations are quickly selected during the filter step. The same strategy can be applied for the retrieval of objects that satisfy certain direction relations since in this case also minimum overlap is required in order to avoid the refinement phase for relations of d_1.

To retrieve direction relations using R-trees one needs to define more general relations that will be used for propagation in the intermediate nodes of the tree structure. For instance, to find all the objects p that are strong_northeast of object q we need to retrieve all the MBRs p' within the leaf nodes that satisfy the constraint $northeast(p'_f, q'_s)$. However, the intermediate nodes P that could contain such MBRs should satisfy the more general constraint $north(P_s, q'_s) \wedge east(P_s, q'_s)$. Following this strategy, the search space is pruned by excluding the intermediate nodes P that do not satisfy the previous constraint. As an example, consider the R-tree of Figure 1 and the query: "Find the objects strong_northeast of object d". The intermediate node C is directly excluded because it does not satisfy the property $north(C_s, d'_s) \wedge east(C_s, d'_s)$ while nodes A and B are selected for propagation. The entries p' of the nodes A and B (leaf nodes) that are selected are the ones that satisfy the property $northeast(p'_f, d'_s)$, that is f', g', k'. Since a refinement step is not needed, all MBRs selected correspond to objects that satisfy the query. Table 1 presents the direction relations that have been implemented together with the constraints for the intermediate nodes to be searched.

Relation	Illustration	Intermediate Nodes P to be Searched	Leaf Nodes p' to be Retrieved
strong_north(p,q)	p q	north(P_s, q'_s)	north(p'_f, q'_s)
weak_north(p,q)	p q	north(P_s, q'_s)$\wedge$ south(P_f, q'_s)	north(p'_s, q'_s) $\wedge$ north(p'_f, q'_f) $\wedge$ south(p'_f, q'_s)

strong_bounded_ north(p,q)	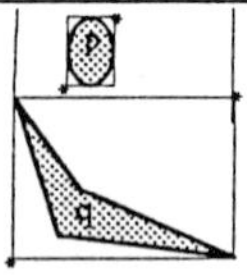	north(P_s, q'_s) ∧ west(P_f, q'_s) ∧ east(P_s, q'_f)	north(p'_f, q'_s) ∧ northeast(p'_f, q'_f) ∧ northwest(p'_s, q'_s)
weak_bounded_ north(p,q) refinement step needed	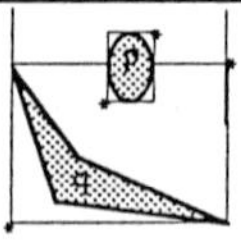	north(P_s, q'_s) ∧ south(P_f, q'_s) ∧ west(P_f, q'_s) ∧ east(P_s, q'_f)	north(p'_s, q'_s) ∧ south(p'_f, q'_s) ∧ northeast(p'_f, q'_f) ∧ northwest(p'_s, q'_s)
strong_northeast (p,q)	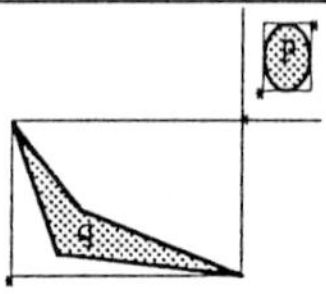	north(P_s, q'_s) ∧ east(P_s, q'_s)	northeast(p'_f, q'_s)
weak_northeast (p,q) refinement step needed	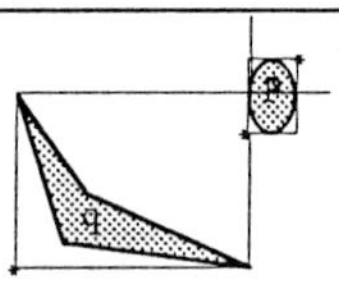	north(P_s, q'_s) ∧ south(P_f, q'_s) ∧ east(P_s, q'_s)	northeast(p'_s, q'_s) ∧ northeast(p'_f, q'_f) ∧ south(p'_f, q'_s)
same_level(p,q)	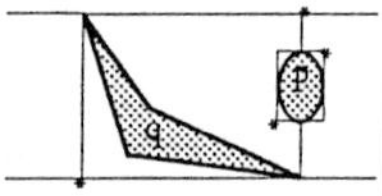	(north(P_s, q'_f) ∨ samelevel(P_s,q'_f)) ∧ (south(P_f, q'_s) ∨ samelevel(P_f, q'_s))	(samelevel(p'_f, q'_f) ∨ north(p'_f, q'_f)) ∧ (samelevel(p'_s, q'_s) ∨ south(p'_s, q'_s))
strong_same_ level(p,q)	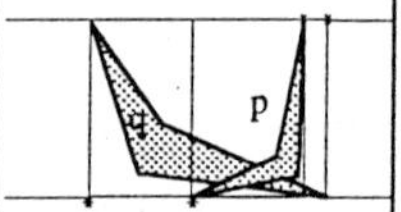	(north(P_s, q'_f) ∨ samelevel(P_s, q'_f)) ∧ (south(P_f, q'_s) ∨ samelevel(P_f, q'_s))	samelevel(p'_f, q'_f) ∧ samelevel(p'_s,q'_s)

Table 1 Direction relations implemented

After this short description of the implementation procedure, we present the results of our tests. To build the tree structure we used a data file containing 10000 rectangles, randomly generated, with the size of each rectangle along each axis to be at most 1% of the global size of the axis. The search procedure used a search file containing 100 rectangles, also randomly generated, with similar size properties like the data rectangles. Table 2 illustrates the results of our tests. For each relation implemented, the following parameters are represented:

- the number of hits per search which represents the selectivity of the relation,
- the number of disk accesses per search using R-trees and
- the number of disk accesses per search using serial retrieval[2] .

Direction relations	**avg hits per search**	**disk accesses per search (R-trees)**	**disk accesses per search (serial)**
strong_north	4863,64	145,9	200
weak_north	22,60	18,5	200

[2] The number of disk accesses per search using serial retrieval is equal to 200 for all relations because the size of the data file is equal to 10000 entries and the page capacity is equal to 50 entries.

strong_bounded_north	5,22	13,7	200
weak_bounded_north	0,04	3,1	200
strong_northeast	2431,32	97,3	200
weak_northeast	10,56	12,1	200
same_level	22,16	22,8	200
strong_same_level	2,06	22,8	200

Table 2 Table of results

As a conclusion, we can argue that the retrieval of direction relations using R-trees is much faster than the serial retrieval. With the exception of the least selective strong_north and strong_northeast relations, the improvement of the retrieval is about an order of magnitude, a fact that renders R-trees an appropriate data structure not only for topological, but for direction relations as well. Furthermore, most of the direction relations implemented, with the exception of the weak_bounded_north and the weak_northeast relations, need no refinement step (a time consuming procedure), while most topological relations can not avoid it.

5. Concluding Remarks

This paper discusses the retrieval of direction relations in 2D space using R-trees. Although R-trees so far have been used only for the extraction of topological relations between objects represented by minimum bounding rectangles, we believe that they are suitable for the retrieval of direction relations as well. In the paper we have defined two sets of direction relations between points that correspond to different levels of qualitative resolution and we have shown how relations between objects can be defined using relations between points. We have also implemented and tested a number of direction relations between objects showing that the number of disk accesses per search is improved up to one order of magnitude compared to the serial search. It is also important that only some of the direction relations need a refinement step, while the rest can be answered using the MBR approximations only.

The direction relations that we implemented for our tests are only few of the possible direction relations between objects represented by MBRs. The number of possible direction relations between objects in space is much larger. In case of 1D space, when two points are used for the representation of the reference object, the axis is partitioned in two points and three open line segments. If the primary object p is also represented by two points p'_f and p'_s ordered on axis x (i.e., $X(p'_f) < X(p'_s)$) then the number of primitive relations between the two objects in 1D space is 13; these relations correspond to the relations between time intervals introduced in (Allen, 1983) and extended for 1D space in (Freksa, 1991). In general, if k is the number of points used to represent the reference object, the number of axis partitions is $2k+1$; k of the partitions are points and $k+1$ are open line segments. In case of 2D space and k points, the plane is divided into $(2k+1)^2$ partitions; k^2 of the partitions are points, $2k(k+1)$ are open line segments and $(k+1)^2$ are open regions (Papadias Sellis, 1994)[3]. When we use two points for the representation of the reference (region) object, for instance, the plane is divided into 25 partitions; thus there are 25

[3] The numbers refer to the case that none of the k points has a common co-ordinate with some other point.

possible ways to place a primary point in the plane, and therefore there exist 25 primitive relations between a region object and a point object.

When the primary object is also a region, the constraint for the first and the second points of the MBR is: $X(p'_f) < X(p'_s) \wedge Y(p'_f) < Y(p'_s)$ and the number of possible primitive relations is 169 (13^2). The previous numbers refer to primitive relations. Relations of lower resolution (e.g., strong_north, same_level) can be defined by allowing points to be in more than partitions, i.e., using disjunctions of primitive relations. Out of the large number of possible direction relations between MBRs only few may be needed for an application domain. For example, it is improbable that a geographic extension of SQL would include 169 different expressions for primitive directions between region objects. Although we have implemented only a few of these relations for our tests, a number of additional relations, primitive or not, are a subject of future research.

References

- Allen, J.F. (1983) Maintaining Knowledge About Temporal Intervals. CACM 26 (11), 832-843.
- Beckmann, N., Kriegel, H.P. Schneider, V., Seeger, B. (1990) The R*-tree: an Efficient and Robust Access Method for Points and Rectangles. In the Proceedings of ACM-SIGMOD Conference.
- Chang, S.K, Jungert, E., Li, Y. (1989) The Design of Pictorial Database upon the Theory of Symbolic Projections. In the Proceedings of the First Symposium on the Design and Implementation of Large Spatial Databases (SSD). Springer-Verlag.
- Dutta, S. (1989) Qualitative Spatial Reasoning: A Semi-Qualitative Approach using Fuzzy Logic. In the Proceedings of the First Symposium on the Design and Implementation of Large Spatial Databases (SSD). Springer-Verlag.
- Egenhofer, M., Herring, J. (1990) A Mathematical Framework for the Definitions of Topological Relationships. In the Proceedings of the 4th International Symposium on Spatial Data Handling (SDH).
- Frank, A. U., (1992) Qualitative Spatial Reasoning about Distances and Directions in Geographic Space. Journal of Visual Languages and Computing, 3, pp 343-371.
- Freksa, C. (1991) Qualitative Spatial Reasoning. In Mark, D.M. and Frank, A.U (eds.) Cognitive and Linguistic Aspects of Geographic Space. Kluwer, Dordrecht.
- Guttman, A. (1984) R-trees: a Dynamic Index Structure for Spatial Searching. In the Proceedings of ACM-SIGMOD Conference.
- Hernandez, D. (1993) Maintaining Qualitative Spatial Knowledge. In Frank, A.U., Campari, I. (eds.) Proceedings of the European Conference on Spatial Information Theory (COSIT). Springer-Verlag.
- Papadias, D., Sellis, T. (1993) The Semantics of Relations in 2D Space Using Representative Points: Spatial Indexes. In Frank, A.U., Campari, I. (eds.) Proceedings of the European Conference on Spatial Information Theory (COSIT). Springer-Verlag.
- Papadias, D., Sellis, T. (1994) On the Qualitative Representation of Spatial Knowledge in Two-Dimensional Space. To appear in the Very Large Data Bases Journal, Special Issue on Spatial Databases.
- Randell, D. A., Cui, Z., Cohn., A., (1992) A Spatial Logic Based on Regions and Connection. In the Proceedings of the 3rd International Conferrence on Principles of Knowledge Representation and Reasoning (KR). Morgan Kaufman.
- Sellis, T., Roussopoulos, N., Faloutsos, C. (1987) The R^+-tree: A Dynamic Index for Multi-Dimensional Objects. In the Proceedings of the 13th VLDB conference.

A Unified Framework for Indexing in Database Systems

Odysseas G. Tsatalos* and Yannis E. Ioannidis**

Computer Sciences Department
University of Wisconsin
Madison, WI 53706

Abstract. Several types of data organizations have been proposed in the literature for object-oriented and relational databases. In studying these organizations, there appears to be no underlying common basis on which they can be compared. Many of these organizations impose restrictions on their applicability that seem unnecessary or ad-hoc. We present a unified framework for physical database storage. We show that most existing data organizations follow naturally as special cases of this framework. Furthermore, this framework permits the specification of new types of data organization that have not been proposed or that cannot be described in existing systems, yet appear to be useful.

1 Introduction

One of the most prominent characteristics attributed to modern database systems (DBMSs) is *physical data independence*. In an effort to increase the physical data independence in object-oriented and relational DBMSs, researchers have proposed numerous types of data organizations in the past few years. However, studying these data organizations reveals no underlying common basis on which they can be compared and many restrictions on their applicability seem unnecessary and rather ad-hoc. We have devised a mechanism that disassociates completely a logical schema from its physical representation, thus achieving genuine physical data independence [12]. In this paper, we briefly present the salient features of this mechanism and then use it as a conceptual framework to study various physical data models of DBMSs. We show that the vast majority of existing data organization types follow naturally as special cases of this framework, when restrictions are applied on the framework's properties. This helps in understanding the differences of these organizations better. More importantly, the developed framework permits the specification of new data organization types that cannot be described in existing systems, yet appear to be useful.

* Partially supported by the Advanced Research Project Agency, ARPA order number 018 (formerly 8230), monitored by the U.S. Army Research Laboratory under contract DAAB07-91-C-Q518

** Partially supported by grants from NSF (IRI-9113736, IRI-9224741, and IRI-9157368 (PYI Award)), DEC, IBM, HP, AT&T, and Informix.

2 The Gmap Mechanism for Physical Data Independence

In current DBMSs, the process of designing the physical schema is not clearly distinguished from the logical schema design. For example, each logical construct definition implies the creation of a corresponding physical data structure. In contrast, we propose using a completely separate physical data definition language (DDL) for the physical schema design. This language allows the definition of each physical data structure as a function of, possibly many, logical constructs. The function is a restricted query expression over the logical schema. User queries are expressed in terms of the logical schema and are not aware of the physical one. We have devised an efficient algorithm for translating such queries into access plans on the physical data structures. A prototype system [12] that incorporates the major aspects of this approach including update propagation and integration with the query optimizer is currently operational.

2.1 Logical Data Definition Language

We use a simple object-oriented data model in which schemas are displayed as graphs. Throughout this paper we illustrate our approach with an example schema describing a university with departments (`D`), faculty (`F`), students (`S`), courses (`C`) and teaching assistants (`TA`) (see Figure 1). Nodes in this graph

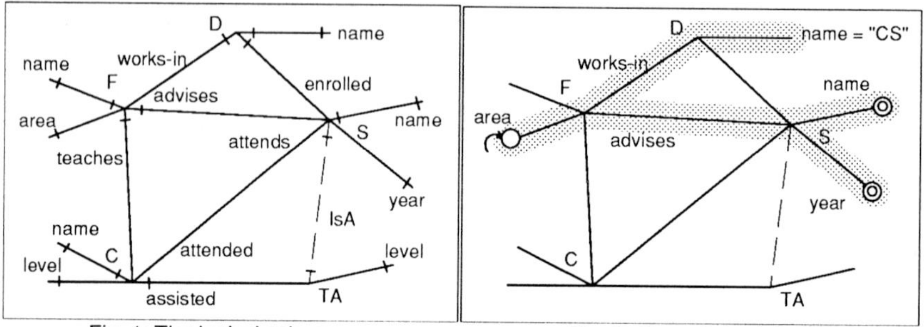

Fig. 1: The logical schema

Fig. 2: Query "simple"

represent domains (classes) and solid edges represent associations between them. Classes are divided into *primitive classes*, e.g., integers or character strings, and *entity classes*, whose members are identity surrogates (oids). There are two *kinds* of associations: relationships and inheritance associations. Associations have a *type* and a *cardinality ratio*. The type of relationships captures the intention of the user to view one of the two classes as an attribute of the other. The cardinality ratio of the relationship determines how many instances of one class may be related to an instance of the other class. When the cardinality of the relationship is "to-one" a mark is added in that direction of the edge. Finally, an inheritance association between two entity classes, classifies one class as a subclass of the other. Additional details can be found elsewhere [12].

2.2 Logical Data Manipulation Language

The query language serves the dual role of a simple language to be used in our examples and the language used by the physical DDL to define data structures.

As an example, the query that retrieves the name and year of all students advised by faculty working in the computer sciences department in a given area is

```
def_query simple by
  given Faculty.area select Student.name, Student.year
  where Faculty advises Student and
        Faculty works_in Dept and Dept.name = "CS".
```

The classes following the `given` and `select` keywords are called *input* and *output* classes, respectively. Input classes play the role of query parameters, i.e., they correspond to variables that can be bound to objects from those classes when the query is issued. Output classes indicate the types of objects included in the query result. The remaining parts of the query should be self-explanatory.

Each query can also be expressed graphically as a subgraph of the schema graph called *query graph*. Figure 2 shows the query graph of the example query. Shaded edges correspond to associations explicitly mentioned in the `where` clause or implicitly mentioned as part of primitive class names. Input classes are indicated by small arrows, and output classes are indicated by double circles.

2.3 Physical Data Definition Language

In our system, each physical storage structure is defined as a *gmap* (Generalized Multilevel Access Path). A gmap consists of a set of records (*gmap data*), a query that indicates the semantic relationships among their fields (*gmap query*), and a description of the data structure used to store the records (*gmap structure*). Issuing the gmap query on a database always produces the gmap data as a result.

For example, suppose we want to cluster together information about each student. Given the object identifier of a `Student` object, we should be able to retrieve the student name, the student year and the department the student is enrolled in. A gmap that meets these specifications may be defined as

```
def_gmap students_file as heap by
  given Student select Student.name, Student.year, Dept
  where Student enrolled Dept.
```

The statement defines the equivalent of a relation file, i.e., a heap structure directly accessible by the Student oid and containing all student attributes.

3 A Unifying Framework

We identify four aspects of the graph representation of a gmap query. Specifically, such graphs are characterized by their shape, the flavor of their input and output nodes, and their having any selection constraints. Figure 3 shows the possible restrictions that may be placed on each one of them. It then identifies the most important combinations of them (roughly from most to least restrictive), and for each one names the resulting indexing scheme category, which is discussed in a separate section below. For that part of the table, an empty entry implies that no restriction is placed on the corresponding graph characteristic.

A gmap query (without cycles) imposes a directionality on the edges it includes, from its input to its output nodes, essentially capturing how the edges are conceptually traversed when querying. We use the term *arc* to refer to an

Graph Characteristics Restrictions				
Graph characteristic	**Shape**	**Flavor of output nodes**	**Flavor of input nodes**	**Selection constraints**
Possible restrictions	*single arc* *linear path*	*endnodes*	*one endnode* *one node*	*disallowed*
Data Organization Categories				
single edge	single arc	endnodes	one endnode	disallowed
linear path	linear path	endnodes	one endnode	disallowed
multi-output	linear path		one endnode	disallowed
graph			one node	disallowed
multi-input				disallowed
partial				

Figure 3. Gmap categorization based on graph characteristics

edge coupled with such a direction. In many of the categories of Figure 3, existing types of data organizations impose additional restrictions on some characteristics of the arcs that may be part of a gmap query graph. These are the arcs' *kind*, *type*, and *cardinality ratio*, defined in Section 2.1. We use *IsA* and *rel* as abbreviations of inheritance associations and relationships, respectively. For inheritance associations, the arc type may be from class to subclass ($C \to Sub$) or from subclass to class ($Sub \to C$), while the cardinality ratio is always $1 \to 1$. For relationships, the arc type may be from class to attribute ($C \to A$) or from attribute to class ($A \to C$) and the cardinality ratio may take any value.

4 Single Arc Indexing

Every edge on the schema graph connects a pair of related classes. It is conceivable that for every such edge there exist a query that requires traversing it. Thus, it is desirable to be able to provide efficient traversal of every edge of the logical schema in both directions, independently of its kind, type, or cardinality ratio. Providing the needed efficiency is straightforward via gmap definitions.

4.1 Previous Techniques

• *Secondary indices in relational databases.* This category includes the conventional, single-key indices of relational databases. The arc properties of these secondary indices are [kind = *rel*, type = $A \to C$, card = $1 \to 1$ or $1 \to N$].
• *Secondary indices on set attributes.* In contrast to relational systems, object-oriented and nested relational systems allow multivalued attributes. This category includes all indices on such attributes. Examples of systems that allow the definition of such indices are ObjectStore [7] and Orion [3]. The arc properties of these indices are [kind = *rel*, type = $A \to C$].
• *Join indices* [13]. They have been proposed to enhance the performance of joins over many-to-many relationships. The related pairs are stored in two indices, each one ordered according to the two classes participating in the relationship. The two indices offer two different clusterings of the relationship data as well as associative access from both classes. The technique applies to any arc with properties [kind = *rel*] that connects entity classes. An example follows:

```
def_gmap join_index_part1  as btree by
  given Student select Course where Student attends Course
def_gmap join_index_part2  as btree by
  given Course select Student where Student attends Course.
```

• *Multi-indices.* These also use multiple single arc indices. Since their introduction [3, 8], multi-indices have been implemented in at least one commercial product [7]. They allow efficient traversal of a path on the schema graph, by adding indices along the arcs of the path. The important property that these indices should have is that the output of one should be usable as input of the next. This property allows chaining of indices, essentially piping the output of one to the next without accessing any other storage structure. Gmaps have this property, since they use a common object id representation for both output and input objects. For example, the following two gmap definitions create a multi-index that returns the oids of faculty members that work in a department specified by a given name:

```
def_gmap multiindex_part1 as btree by
  given Dept.name select Dept
def_gmap multiindex_part2 as btree by
  given Dept select Faculty where Faculty works Dept.
```

Both multi-index proposals [3, 9] impose the following restrictions on the index arc properties: [kind = *rel*, type = $A \rightarrow C$]. In addition, the proposal by Maier and Stein enforces the restriction [card = $1 \rightarrow 1$ or $1 \rightarrow N$].

4.2 New Applications

• *Class to attribute indices.* Indices that return the value of an attribute given an object id have never been considered, mainly because most systems do include efficient structures to access an object given its id. However, it may be the case that an object is very large, and therefore, the values of an attribute for many objects may span a very large space. For such cases, single arc indices of type $C \rightarrow A$ provide a better clustering. For example, for a query that requests the departments oids of several students, the gmap

```
def_gmap DeptStudent as btree by
  given Student select Dept where Student enrolled Dept
```

includes the needed data in fewer pages and potentially in a more convenient order than the gmap in Section 2.3.

• *Indices on inheritance associations. IsA* arcs do not capture relationships between distinct objects, but essentially between two different manifestations of the same object. For example, the information about a `TA` may be stored in two distinct objects, one for the attributes of the `TA` and the other for the generic `Student` attributes. In that case, an index may be valuable to find the oid of one of the objects given the oid of the other.

• *Extended multi-indices.* Any chain of gmaps such that the output nodes of one are the input nodes of the other forms an extended multi-index. For example, the following multi-index

```
def_gmap multiindex_part1 as btree by given Student.year select Student
def_gmap multiindex_part2 as btree by
  given Student select TA where  TA IsA Student
```

```
def_gmap multiindex_part3 as btree by given TA select TA.level
```

includes in its path both relationships and inheritance associations, both $C \rightarrow A$ and $A \rightarrow C$ arcs, and arcs of many cardinality ratios.

5 Linear Path Indexing

In the previous section, the input and the output classes of gmaps were connected with a single edge. We generalize this structure by allowing the input and output classes to be connected via an arbitrarily long chain of edges.

5.1 Previous Techniques

• *Nested indices.* Consider a linear path with all classes, starting from the input class, being attributes of the next class in the chain. Then, the input class is called a *nested attribute* of the output class. An index that maps objects of the nested attribute class to objects of the nesting class is called a *nested index* [3, 8]. The following statement defines a nested index over the same path we used to define a multi-index in Section 4.1 (Figure 4).

```
def_gmap nested_index as btree by
  given Dept.name select Faculty where Faculty works_in Dept.
```

Clearly, the chain of indices is replaced by a single index that performs the end-to-end mapping. This results in increased performance since a single index traversal is needed, but also implies reduced index usability and more expensive updates [2]. Originally, nested indices were proposed with the same restrictions on the arc properties as the multi-indices, i.e., [kind = *rel*, type = $A \rightarrow C$] [3] or [kind = *rel*, type = $A \rightarrow C$, card = $1 \rightarrow 1$ or $1 \rightarrow N$] [8].

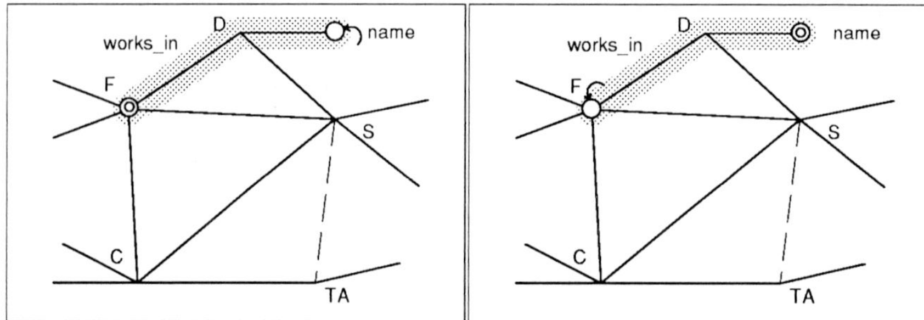

Fig. 4: Gmap "nested_index"

Fig. 5: Gmap "field_replication

• *Field replication.* Consider the exactly opposite case from above, where all classes starting from the output class are attributes of the next class in the chain. Then, it is the output class that is a nested attribute of the input class. Mapping objects of the nesting class to objects of the nested attribute is called *field replication* [4, 11]. By changing the role of the input and output attributes in the previous example, we derive an example of field replication (Figure 5):

```
def_gmap field_replication as heap by
  given Faculty select Dept.name where Faculty works_in Dept.
```

As in the case of class-to-attribute indices in Section 4.2, field replication allows an alternative clustering of the data, which can be important for many applications. Originally, field replication was proposed with the following restrictions on the arc properties: [kind = *rel*, type = $C \rightarrow A$, card = $1 \rightarrow 1$ or $N \rightarrow 1$].

5.2 New Applications

• *Extended nested indices.* We can generalize both previous techniques by removing all restrictions on the type and kind of the arcs. Note that by chaining nested indices together we obtain a generalization of the hybrid scheme originally proposed for chaining ordinary nested indices [3].

6 Multi-Output Indexing

While arbitrary chains of arcs can be described using the previous types of organizations, the output classes are always endnodes of a path. In this section, we study the opportunities that arise by relaxing this restriction.

6.1 Previous Techniques

• *Path indices.* When the whole path is included in the index output, the resulting data organization is called a *path index* [3]. As an example, consider the path that connects department names with courses taken by students enrolled in the department. The following gmap defines a path index on that path :

```
def_gmap path_index as btree by
  given Dept.name select Dept, Student, Course
  where Student enrolled Dept and Course attended Student.
```

By recording the whole path, the index is useful to more queries than the corresponding nested index, and often allows more efficient updates. Originally, path indices were proposed with the same restrictions on the arc properties as nested indices, i.e., [kind = *rel*, type = $A \rightarrow C$].

• *Access Support Relations (ASRs)* [5, 6]. These are also full materializations of chains of edges. ASRs are more flexible than path indices: they allow each arc to be either $C \rightarrow A$ or $A \rightarrow C$, but the type must be the same for all the arcs.

6.2 New Applications

• *Extended path indices.* Gmaps do not need the restrictions on arc properties originally imposed on path indices and ASRs. Furthermore, there is no reason to require that every single node of the path be included in the output. For some applications, it may be convenient to include in the gmap data only some of the classes in the path. For example, in the last example (Section 6.1), we may not be interested in `Dept` and `Student` oids but only in `Course` oid and `Course name`. A path index that stores exactly what is needed follows:

```
def_gmap extended_path_index as btree by
  given Dept.name select Course, Course.name
  where Student enrolled Dept and Course attended Student.
```

By eliminating path nodes from the output, the size of the gmap data may decrease significantly. Thus, the resulting gmap offers the needed data in a more compact form, which implies better performance.

7 Graph Indexing

In this section, we relax the restriction that one can only index along linear paths. In general, the gmap graph can be a tree or even have cycles. Although such shapes may not look familiar in the context of indexing, many of the most commonly used storage organizations belong in this category.

7.1 Previous Techniques

• *Relations.* As mentioned earlier (Section 2.3), relations can easily be described as gmaps. As a result, gmaps can be used to achieve a relational physical representation for any given logical schema. Gmaps that correspond to relation files imply the restrictions [kind = rel, type = $C \to A$, card = $1 \to 1$or $N \to 1$].
• *Class Extents and Nested Relations.* Class extents are similar to relations. One difference is that they may imply a different heap implementation to support a logical oid access. Another is that they may include multi-valued attributes. Thus, the only implied restrictions on arc properties are [kind = rel, type = $C \to A$]. Some systems allow storing in a class extent members of its subclasses [1]. Describing such organizations requires gmap queries with the union operator; hence, these variants cannot be represented within our framework.
• *Hierarchical Join Indices* [14]. These are a generalization of join indices that also requires a nonlinear query graph for its description. An HJI captures the structure of a complex object by recording the surrogates of the nested objects included in each complex object. Since complex objects have in general a hierarchical structure, the query graph for the index is a tree. For example, the HJI for the `Faculty` complex object can be defined as

```
def_gmap hierarchical_join_index as btree by
  given Faculty select Dept, Student, Course, TA
  where Faculty works_in Dept and Faculty advises Student and
      Faculty teaches Course and Course assisted TA.
```

8 Multi-Input Indexing

8.1 Previous Techniques

• *Indices with composite keys.* A relational index with a composite key, i.e., a key consisting of the concatenation of multiple relation fields, is the most common example of an organization whose query graph includes multiple inputs.

8.2 New Applications

• *Indices with composite key-paths.* Nested indices allow the input class to be many edges away from the output class; conventional indices with composite keys allow multiple input classes that are one edge away from the output class. By combining these, we have an organization with a composite key, such that every component of the key may potentially belong in a separate path. An example is shown in Figure 6. The index maps area/course-level pairs to faculty in that area who teach such courses:

```
def_gmap extended_composite as btree by
  given Faculty.area, Course.level select Faculty
  where Faculty teaches Course.
```

The order of the input classes is important and is captured as part of the gmap definition, although for simplicity it is not shown in the graphical representation.

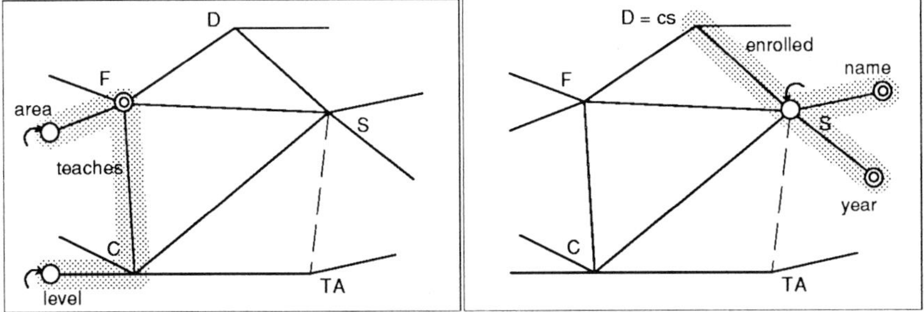

Fig. 6: Gmap "extended_composite"   Fig. 7: Gmap "cs_collection"

9 Partial Indexing

9.1 Previous Techniques

• *Collections of Objects.* Until now we assumed an extent-based system: queries were expressed in terms of classes. However, many objects-oriented DBMSs maintain only user-defined object collections, which include only a subset of the class members. The following gmap uses a restriction to define a collection containing only computer science students (Figure 7):

```
def_gmap cs_collection as heap by
  given Student select Student.name, Student.year
  where Student enrolled Dept and Dept = cs_oid.
```

In the above, `cs_oid` is the oid of the computer science department.

• *Indices on Collections of Objects.* Systems that store instances in explicit collections rather than class extents also allow the creation of indices on top of these collections [8, 10]. These indices provide a fast access path only to the class members that are included in the collection. For example, an index on student `year` for students in the computer science department can be defined as

```
def_gmap cs_collection_index as btree by
   given Student.year select Student
   where Student enrolled Dept and Dept = cs_oid.
```

9.2 New Applications

• *Intentionally defined collections.* In many cases, an alternative way to describe the contents of a set is through its intention, i.e., by using a query that defines the characteristics of the object in the set. Our approach permits the creation of such intentionally defined collections using arbitrary selection conditions in gmap queries, thus allowing arbitrary horizontal decompositions of the database.

10 Conclusions

Exploration of the space of alternative physical data organization types has been the focus of this paper. We have taken a mechanism that achieves genuine physical data independence and have used it as a conceptual, unifying, framework for describing such organizations. Most types of data organizations proposed earlier in the context of relational or object-oriented systems follow naturally as special cases of this framework. Also, the framework has permitted the specification of new useful data organizations that have not been proposed earlier. Given that the entire space of these alternatives is realizable within the existing implementation of gmaps by using different gmap queries [12], one may immediately apply our work to physical design problems.

References

1. R. Agrawal and N. H. Gehani. ODE : The Language and the Data Model. In *Proc. of the ACM SIGMOD Conf.*, pages 36–45, 1989.
2. E. Bertino. Optimization of Queries using Nested Indices. In *Proc. Int. Conf. on Extending Database Technology*, pages 44–59. Springer-Verlag, Mar. 1990.
3. E. Bertino and W. Kim. Indexing Techniques for Queries on Nested Objects. *IEEE Transactions on Knowledge and Data Engineering*, 1(2):196–214, June 1989.
4. K. Kato and T. Masuda. Persistent Caching. *IEEE Transactions on Software Engineering*, 18(7):631–645, July 1992.
5. A. Kemper and G. Moerkotte. Access Support in Object Bases. In *Proc. of the ACM SIGMOD Conf.*, pages 290–301, 1990.
6. A. Kemper and G. Moerkotte. Advanced Query Processing in Object Bases Using Access Support Relations. In *Proc. of the Int. VLDB Conf.*, pages 290–301, 1990.
7. C. Lamb, G. Landis, J. Orenstein, and D. Weinreb. The ObjectStore database system. *Communications of the ACM*, 34(10), Oct. 1991.
8. D. Maier and J. Stein. Indexing in an Object-Oriented DBMS. In *2nd Int. Workshop on Object-Oriented Database Systems*, pages 171–182, Sept. 1986.
9. D. Maier, J. Stein, A. Otis, and A. Purdy. Development of an Object Oriented DBMS. In *Proc. the Int. Conf. on Object-Oriented Programming Systems, Languages, and Applications*, pages 472–482, Portland, Oregon, Sept. 1986.
10. J. Orenstein, S. Haradhvala, B. Marguiles, and D. Sakahara. Query Processing in the ObjectStore Database System. In *Proc. of the ACM SIGMOD Conf.*, 1992.
11. E. Shekita and M. Carey. Performance Enhancement Through Replication in an Object-Oriented DBMS. In *Proc. of the ACM SIGMOD Conf.*, 1989.
12. O. Tsatalos, M. Solomon, and Y. Ioannidis. The GMAP: A Versatile Tool for Physical Data Independence. In *Proc. of the Int. VLDB Conf.*, Sept. 1994.
13. P. Valduriez. Join Indices. *ACM Transactions on Database Systems*, 12(2):218–246, June 1987.
14. P. Valduriez, S. Khoshafian, and G. Copeland. Implementation Techniques of Complex Objects. In *Proc. of the Int. VLDB Conf.*, pages 101–109, 1986.

AN INTELLIGENT SYSTEM TO IDENTIFY THE APPROPRIATE ORGANIZATION FOR A FACTORY

Julio Macedo
Institut de Stratégies Industrielles,
229 Forest, Pincourt, P.Q., J7V8E8, Canada

Rafael Ruiz Usano
School of Industrial Engineering, University of
Sevilla, Av. Reina Mercedes, 41012 Sevilla, Spain

Abstract. Most of the factories implement hybrid organizations that include one or more elements of the well known integrated organizations (craft production, mass production, just-in-time). This paper presents a new intelligent system that helps to conceive the appropriate hybrid organization for a factory. The suggested system is a knowledge base connected to a set of system dynamics models with neural network structure, named intelligent reference models. The knowledge base verifies if the logics of the current factory organization matches a reference model. If yes, a simulation by optimization of the reference model allows to conceive the appropriate organization for the factory.

Keywords: System Dynamics, Neural Networks, Expert Systems, Manufacturing Systems, Total Quality Management.

1. Introduction

The conception of a factory organization consists of specifying, at a conceptual level, the interactions of the productive resources (men, machines, materials) so that the product satisfies a target market. Sometimes, the target market are customers that buy large quantities of an standard low priced product; other times, the target market are customers that buy low quantities of many models of the same product.

In practice, most of the factories implement hybrid organizations that include one or more elements of the well known integrated organizations, craft production, mass production and just-in-time (Piper, 1990; Voss, 1990). As a result, only some factories, the ones that have organizations well focused on the target market, have large sales. These factories are the leaders of the industry.

This paper presents a new intelligent system named expert neural reference model system (ENREMOS) that helps to conceive the appropriate hybrid organization for a factory; "appropriate organization" means an organization well focused on the target market. The originality of ENREMOS with respect to the current intelligent systems (Macedo and Ruiz Usano, 1993b) is its hierarchical structure: high level expert system-low level neural network. This kind of structure requires less production rules than a pure expert system.

In the second part of this paper, the foundations and the structure of ENREMOS are presented. In the third part, it is demonstrated that ENREMOS helps to conceive the appropriate organization for the set-up operations of a manufacturer of washing machine doors.

2. The Expert Neural Reference Model System

The heart of ENREMOS is a system dynamics model with neural network structure named intelligent reference model (Macedo, 1993a; Macedo and Ruiz Usano, 1993b). The solution of a reference model using known values of its control variables, generates the right patterns of its state variables. However, in practice, the desired patterns of the state variables are known and the problem is to identify the values of the corresponding control variables. In order to solve this problem, ENREMOS uses a simulation by optimization procedure on the trained reference model. This procedure, an adaptation of a more general procedure named reference approach (Macedo, 1990), is presented in the following paragraphs.

2.1 Construction of the Intelligent Reference Model

A reference model is a system of differential equations that represent the dynamics of a set of state variables between their initial and final equilibriums (figure 1). A reference model has the property of being intelligent: it remembers the final values of its state variables when it receives the corresponding values of its control variables.

In order to understand why a reference model is intelligent, a close examination of figure 1 is necessary. As indicated, a state variable is moved from its initial equilibrium $x_i(0)$ to a new equilibrium $x_i(T)$ at a rate of variation $dx_i(t)/dt$. This latter

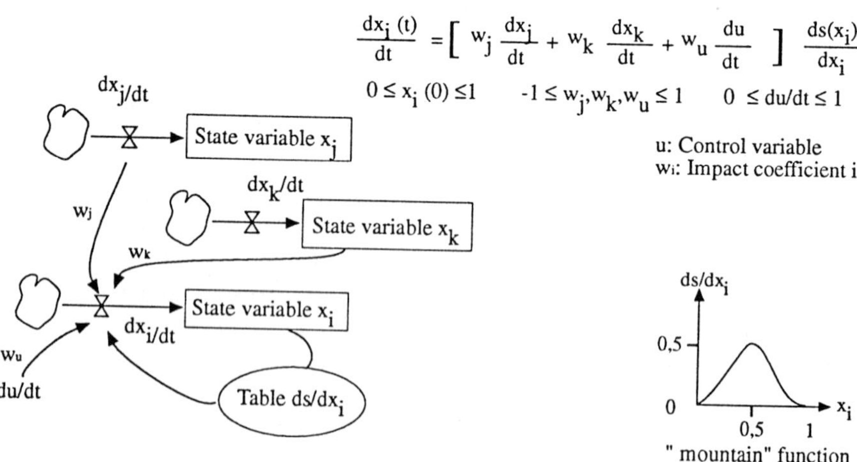

Fig. 1. Structure of a reference model equation.

results from the positive and negative influences that xi(t) receives from the rates of variation of the other state and control variables. These influences are weighted by impact coefficients. Hence, when these impact coefficients remain constant, xi(T) can reach any existent equilibrium, depending on the values of the control variables. The existent equilibriums are sets of zeroes and ones because the "mountain" function, which is the derivative of a logistic function (figure 1), limits the resultant values of the state variables to the range zero-one.

As indicated in figure 2, the construction of an intelligent reference model consists

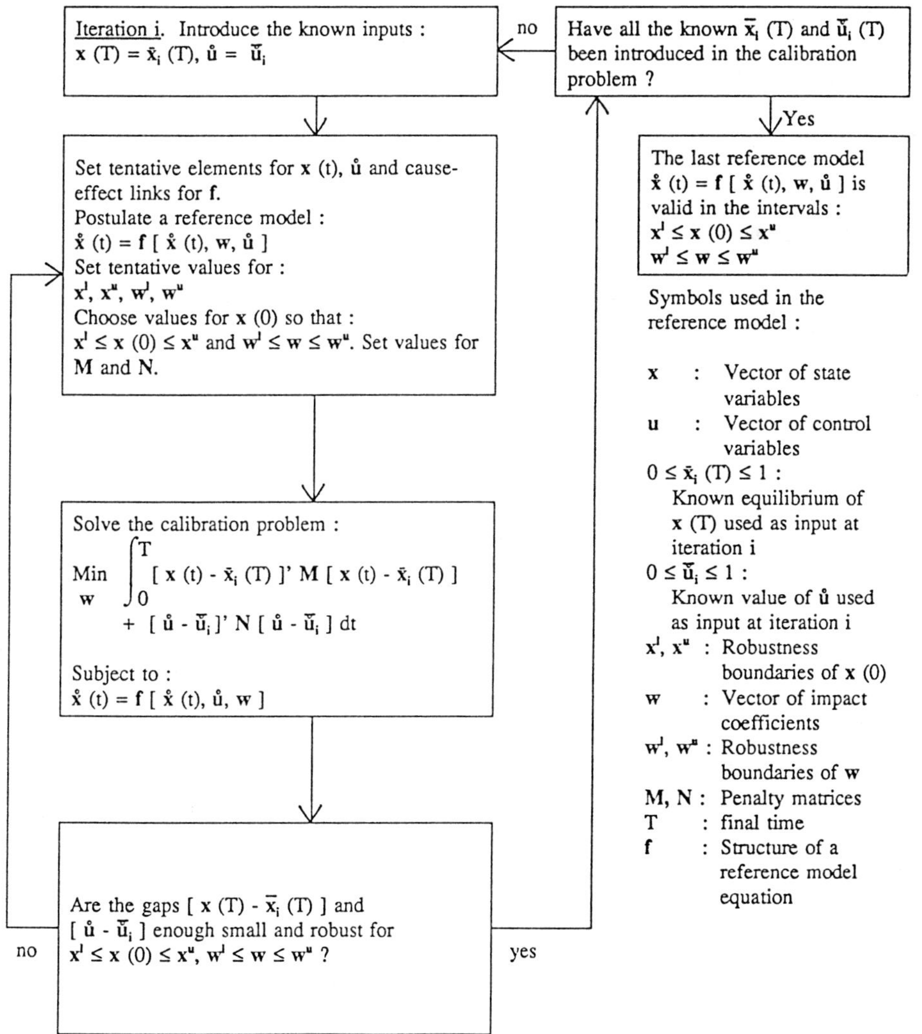

Fig. 2. Construction of a reference model.

of progressively identifying the differential equations that, activated by some known control variable values, produce final values of the state variables that correspond to some known equilibriums. In addition, the final values of the state variables must be robust to small variations of the impact coefficients. At this point it is interesting to note that the construction of an intelligent reference model is equivalent to the ordinary training process of a neural network as demonstrated elsewhere (Macedo, 1992).

2.2 The Expert Neural Reference Model System

As indicated in figure 3, ENREMOS has a hierarchical structure: high level knowledge base and low level reference model. The knowledge base, using production rules, stores the cause-effect relationships of the reference model and the intervals of validity of its impact coefficients. This information allows ENREMOS inference engine to verify if the cause-effect relationships of a particular factory

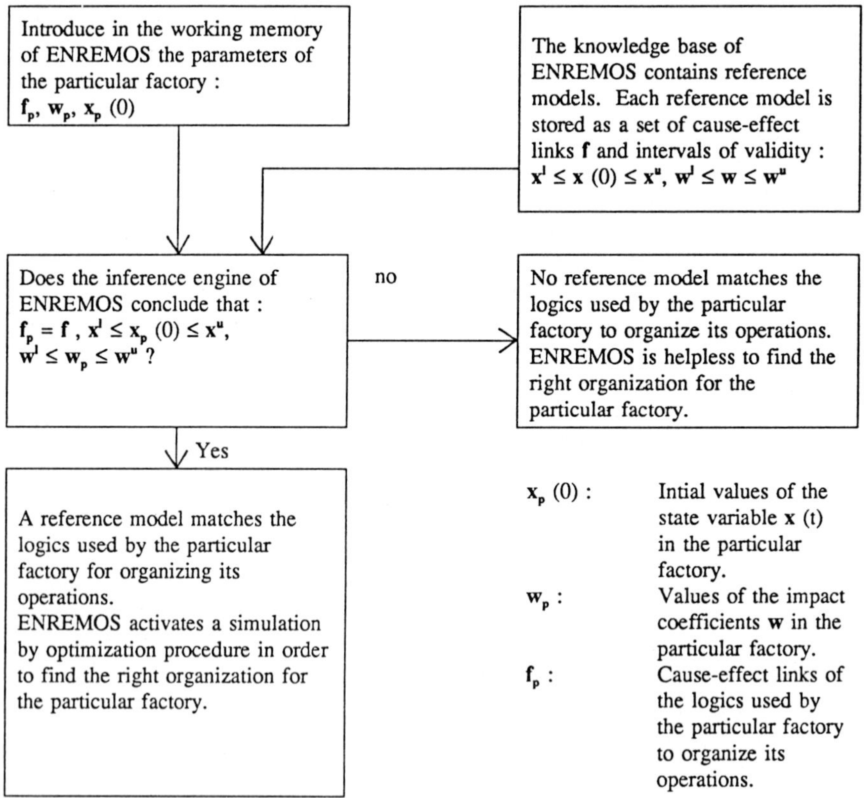

Fig. 3. The expert neural reference model system (ENREMOS) for identifying the right organization of a particular factory.

match the ones of an stored reference model; and, to verify if the impact coefficients of this factory are in the intervals allowed by the reference model. When these verifications have positive answers, ENREMOS orders the simulation by optimization of the matched reference model; however, when the answers are negative, ENREMOS cannot help to conceive an organization for the factory analyzed.

The simulation by optimization of a reference model is showed in figure 4. As indicated, the procedure consists of modifying an objective function until the reference model optimization generates the desired final values for the state variables. At this point, the values of the control variables represent the reference strategy. This latter is also the organization suggested for the factory analyzed because any reference strategy is always robust to variations of the impact coefficients in some allowed intervals.

At this point it is interesting to note that a reference strategy is superior to any strategy represented by the values of the control variables used as inputs during the construction of the reference model (figure 2). This is the result of two facts. First, the methodology used to construct the reference model (figure 2) that allows to incorporate in this latter the "union" of the control variables included in the different known inputs. Second, the simulation by optimization procedure (figure 4) that synthesizes the reference strategy from the "large" control variable space of the reference model.

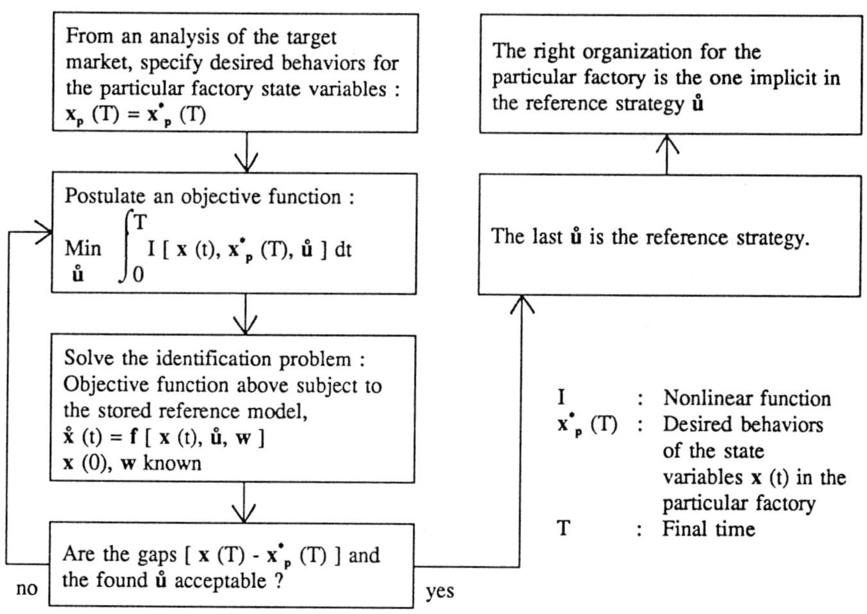

Fig. 4. Interactive simulation by optimization that allows to identify the right organization for a particular factory.

3. Validation of the Expert Neural Reference Model System

As mentionned in the Introduction, the "appropriate organization" of a factory is the one that is well focused on the target market. In the following paragraphs it is demonstrated that ENREMOS helps to conceive the appropriate organization for a factory.

3.1 Construction of the Intelligent Reference Model

Three leader firms whose target markets require products with no defects and quick delivery, were selected; then, the set-up operations of three of their machines (a paper cutting machine, a rubber injection machine and a metal sheet press) were observed. In addition, the set-up operations of an aluminium furnace and of a sugar refiner were observed; these machines belong to two firms whose target markets require low priced products.

The methodology used to construct the reference model was the following. From the current behaviors of the target state variables (percentage of defective products, production cost and production delay of the products made by the observed machine) the workers were asked Why? until the sources (control variables) of these behaviors were identified. This brainstorming exercise produced cause-effect relationships that were transformed to a reference model using the structure in figure 1. Finally, the reference model was optimized and its equations modified until the current patterns of the state and control variables of the factories were reproduced. The resultant intelligent reference model is in figure 5.

The dynamics of the reference model can be explained in the following form. When the handtools distant from the working area, the untraceable tools, the broken tools and the machine settling time to reach operating conditions decrease (increase); and, in addition, the machine structure easiness to install the tool, the repetition of the operations to fix the tool and the use of parallel installation operations increase (decrease), the machine set-up time decreases (increases). Hence, the production lot size is reduced (increased) and the number of production runs increased (decreased). As a result, the stock of products in process, the defective products and the production delay fall (rise), reducing (augmenting) the production cost. When this cost reduction (augmentation) is higher (lower) than the cost augmentation (reduction) due to the increase (decrease) of the production runs, the final production cost falls.

At this point it is interesting to note that seven control variables are included in the reference model; such large number of control variables would have never been identified by analyzing only one factory. In addition, the current degrees of activation of these control variables differ from one factory to another. For instance, the vector of control variables [dDIST/dt, dUNT/dt, dBROK/dt; dASS/dt, dREP/dt, dPAR/dt, dOPER/dt] has the value [0,1,0,1,0,1,1] for the paper cutting machine; [0,0,0,1,0,0,0] for the rubber injection machine; and [0,1,1,1,0,0,1] for the metal sheet press. Furthermore, these three vectors have control variable values which are far from the well focused strategies named "lean producer strategy" and "mass producer strategy" in figure 5. The conception of these two strategies is explained in the next section.

3.2 Conception of the Appropriate Organization for the Factory

The obtained reference model was stored in the knowledge base of ENREMOS using production rules, as showed in table 1. Then, the impact coefficients of the set-up operations of a press of washing machine doors (table 2) were introduced in the knowledge base of ENREMOS; this exercise was done by answering questions like the ones in table 1. Finally, ENREMOS ordered the simulation by optimization of the reference model in figure 5. At this time, two experiments were done in order to demonstrate that ENREMOS can help to conceive the right organization for the factory of washing machine doors.

```
Rule 1
IF DIST-INFL-OBT=Yes
AND OBT(0)≥0.5
AND OBT(0)≤0.7
AND W1≥0.2
AND W1≤0.4
AND UNT-INFL-OBT=Yes
AND W2≥0.2
AND W2≤0.4
AND BROK-INFL-OBT=Yes
AND W3≥0.2
AND W3≤0.4
THEN LINK1=DIST-UNT-BROK-
CAUSE-OBT
ELSE DEST=EXT-PROG
DISPLAY "USE EXTERNAL PROGRAM";

Rule 2
IF ASS-INFL-INST=Yes
AND INST(0)≥0.5
AND INST(0)≤0.7
AND W4≥-0.6
AND W4≤-0.4
AND REP-INFL-INST=Yes
AND W5≥-0.4
AND W5≤-0.2
AND PAR-INFL-INST=Yes
AND W6≥-0.2
AND W6≤0
THEN LINK2=ASS-REP-PAR-
CAUSE-INST
ELSE DEST=EXT-PROG
DISPLAY "USE EXTERNAL PROGRAM";

Rule 3
IF LINK1=DIST-UNT-BROK-CAUSE-
OBT
AND LINK2=ASS-REP-PAR-CAUSE-
INST
AND DOWN(0)≥0.3
AND DOWN(0)≤0.5
AND INST-INFL-DOWN=Yes
AND W7≥0.7
AND W7≤0.9
AND OBT-INFL-DOWN=Yes
AND W8≥0.7
AND W8≤0.9
THEN LINK3=OBT-INST-CAUSE-
DOWN
ELSE DEST=EXT-PROG
DISPLAY "USE EXTERNAL PROGRAM";

Rule (last)
IF...
THEN ACTIVATE SIMULATION BY
OPTIMIZATION
-----------------------------------------------------
Ask DIST-INL-OBT : Does the rate of
variation of DIST influence the rate of
variation of OBT ?;
CHOICES DIST-INFL-OBT : Yes, no;
Ask OBT(0) : What is the current value of
OBT ?;
CHOICES : 0.5, 0.6, 0.7;
Ask W1 : What is the influence of the rate
of variation of DIST on the rate of variation
of OBT ?;
CHOICES : 0.2, 0.3, 0.4;
```

Table 1. Part of the knowledge base of the expert neural reference model system (ENREMOS). The statements above the dashed line represent the structure of the reference model. The questions below the dashed line allow to introduce the parameters of a particular factory into ENREMOS.

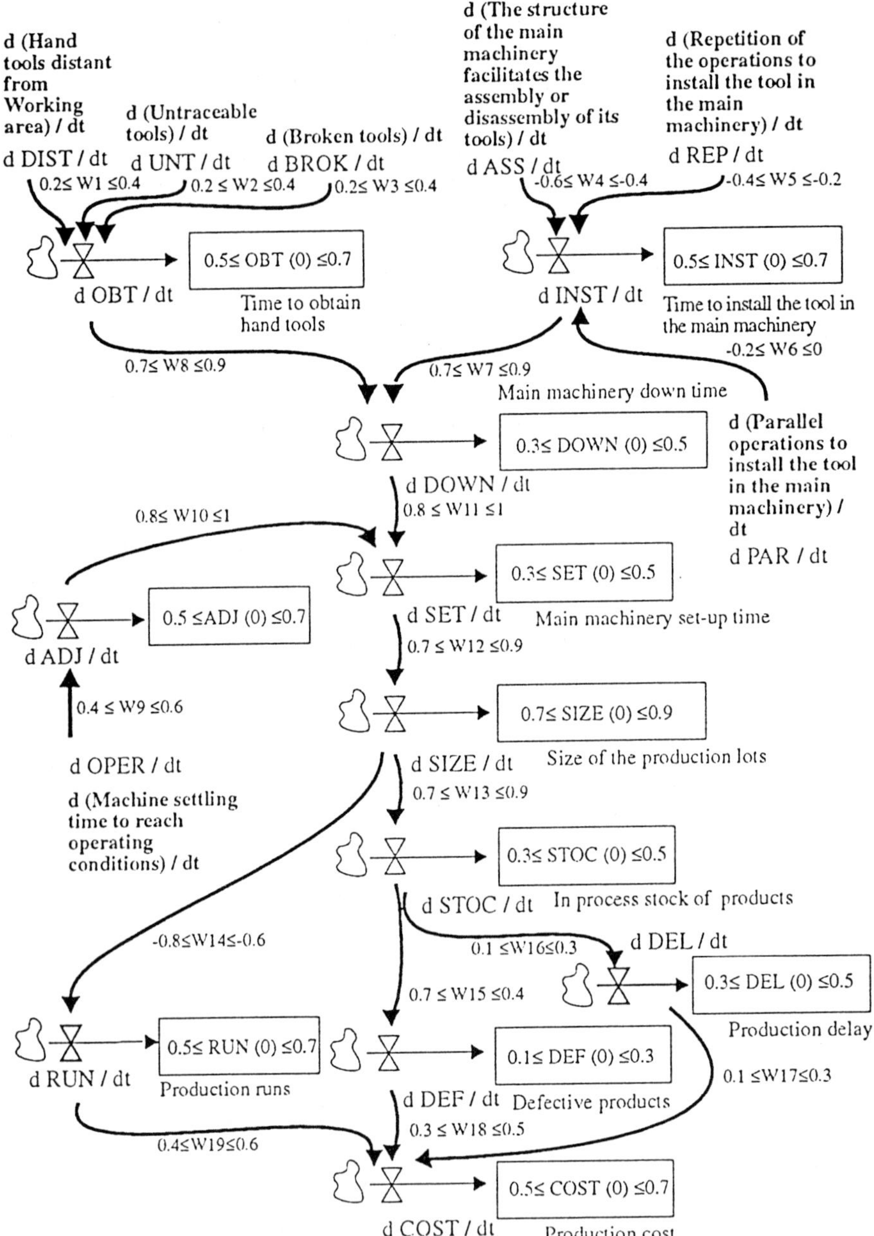

(d DIST / dt, d UNT / dt, d BROK / dt, d ASS / dt, d REP / dt, d PAR / dt, d OPER / dt)= (0, 0, 0, 1, 1, 1, 0) Lean producer strategy; = (1, 1, 1, 0, 0, 0, 1) Mass producer strategy.

Fig. 5. Reference model for the set-up operations of a machine. Note that the "mountain" function is not represented in order to alleviate the figure. The control variables are indicated in bold.

$x_p(0)$ =	[OBT(0) = 0.6 ; INST(0) = 0.6 ; DOWN(0) = 0.4 ; SET(0) = 0.4 ; ADJ(0) = 0.6 ; SIZE(0) = 0.8 ; STOC(0) = 0.4 ; RUN(0) = 0.6 ; DEF(0) = 0.2 ; DEL (0) = 0.4 ; COST(0) = 0.6]
w =	[W1 = 0.3 ; W2 = 0.3 ; W3 = 0.3 ; W4 = -0.5 ; W5 = -0.3 ; W6 = -0.1 ; W7 = 0.8 ; W8 = 0.8 ; W9 = 0.5 ; W10 = 0.9 ; W11 = 0.9 ; W12 = 0.8 ; W13 = 0.8 ; W14 = -0.7 ; W15 = 0.7 ; W16 = 0.2 ; W17 = 0.2 ; W18 = 0.4 ; W19 = 0.3]
$\mathring{u}$ =	[$\mathring{DIST}$ = 0.7 ; $\mathring{UNT}$ = 0.7 ; $\mathring{BROK}$ = 0.5 ; $\mathring{ASS}$ = 0.1 ; $\mathring{REP}$ = 0.2 ; $\mathring{PAR}$ = 0.1 ; $\mathring{OPER}$ = 0.4]
$x_p(40)$	[DEL (40) = 0 ; DEF (40) = 0 ; COST (40) = 0]

Table 2. Parameters of the set-up operations of a press in a factory that produces washing machine doors.

First, a target market that requires products with no defects, quick delivery and low cost was postulated by fixing the desired behaviors of the state variables DEL, DEF and COST (figure 5) to zero. Then, the objective function in figure 4 was modified until it was equal to the integral of [0.2 $DEL^2(t)$+0.8$DEF^2(t)$+$COST^2(t)$] for $0 \le t \le 40$.

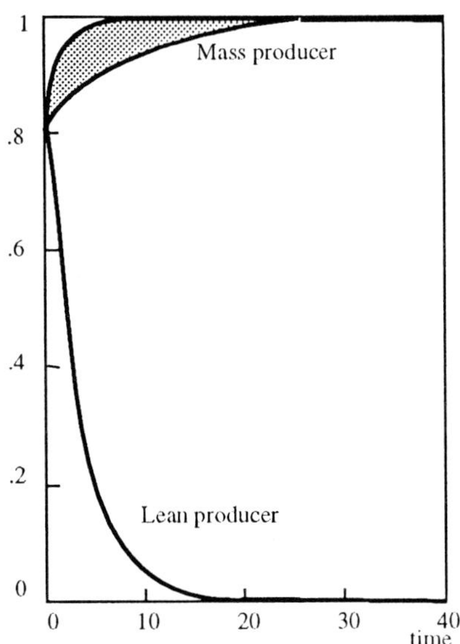

Fig. 6. Patterns of "size of production lots" obtained by simulating the reference model when the impact coefficients vary in the allowed intervals.

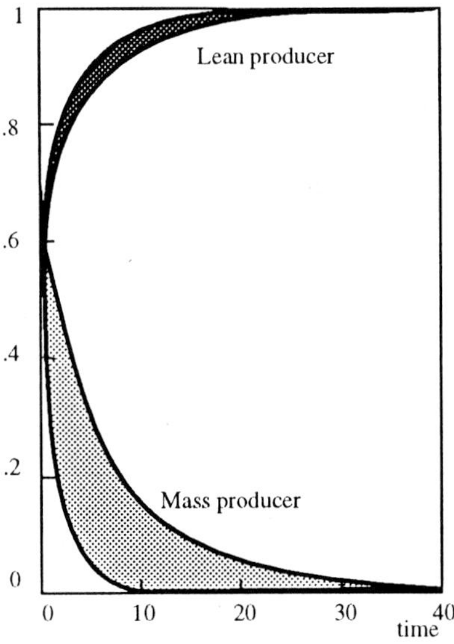

Fig. 7. Patterns of "production runs" obtained by simulating the reference model when the impact coefficients vary in the allowed intervals.

This objective function generated the reference strategy named "lean producer" in figure 5. This strategy implies small production lots and a large number of production runs, but reduces the number of defective products and the delivery delay, as desired (figures 6 to 9). Furthermore, as indicated by the shaded areas in figures 6 to 9, the found reference strategy is robust to variations of the impact coefficients in the intervals specified in figure 5. Hence, the "lean producer" strategy must be used to organize the set-up operations of the press when the target market requires doors with no defects, quick delivery and low cost.

In the second experiment, a target market that requires low priced washing machine doors was assumed; this was done by fixing the desired values of the state variable COST (figure 5) to zero. Then, the objective function in figure 4 was modified until it was equal to the integral of $COST^2(t)$ for $0 \leq t \leq 40$. This objective function generated the reference strategy named "mass producer" in figure 5. This strategy implies large production lots and few production runs so that the production cost tends to zero, as desired (figures 6 to 9). This "mass producer" strategy can be used by the washing machine door factory when its target market requires low priced products.

The two preceding experiments demonstrate that ENREMOS is an intelligent system. This new system can help to conceive factories well focused on their target markets.

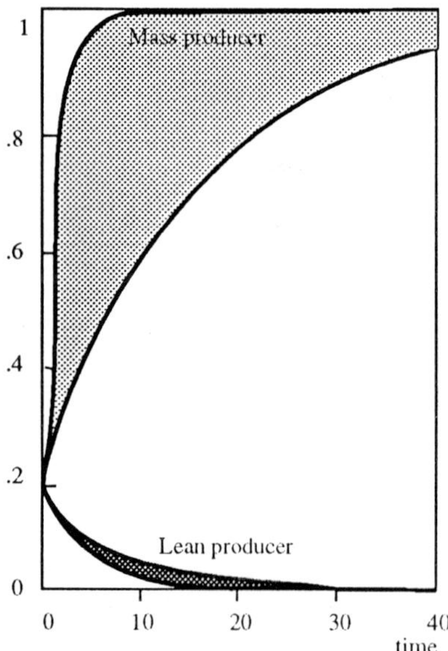

Fig. 8. Patterns of "defective products" obtained by simulating the reference model when the impact coefficients vary in the allowed intervals.

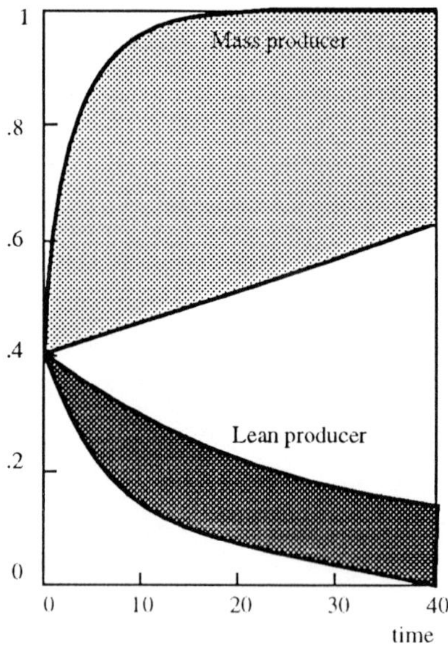

Fig. 9. Patterns of "production delay" obtained by simulating the reference model when the impact coefficients vary in the allowed intervals.

References

Macedo J. (1993a), An intelligent system for conceiving total quality manufacturing strategies. In International Conference on Industrial Engineering and Production Management Proceedings, A. Artiba (ed.), p. 899-908. Mons, Belgium: Computer Science Dept. of the Catholic Faculties of Mons.

Macedo J. and R. Ruiz Usano (1993b), A competitive intelligence system for total quality manufacturing strategies. In System Dynamics 93, p. 288-297. Cambridge, MA: System Dynamics Society.

Macedo J. (1992), An intelligent reference approach for redesigning the organization of a manufacturing system. In International Conference on Economics, Management and Information Technology Proceedings, T. Matsuda (ed.), p. 483-486. Tokyo: The Japan Society for Management Information.

Macedo J. (1990), Designing a manufacturing function as a competitive function using the reference approach. In System Dynamics 90, D. F. Andersen, G. P. Richardson, J. D. Sterman (ed.), p. 686-700. Cambridge, MA: System Dynamics Society.

Piper Ch. and R. Mc Lachlin (1990), Just-in-time production: Eleven achievable dimensions, Operations Management Review, Vol. 7, p. 1-8.

Voss Ch. and L. Okazaki-Ward (1990), The transfer and adaptation of JIT manufacturing practices by Japanese companies in the UK, Operations Management Review, Vol. 7, p. 24-29.

Object-Oriented Design of Manufacturing Database Helps Simplify Production Management in Small Firms

I.P. Tatsiopoulos

National Technical University of Athens, Dept. Mechanical Eng.
Section of Industrial Management & O.R.
15 780 Zografos, Athens, Greece

Abstract. This paper proposes design rules in order to simplify current MRP II software systems and make them suitable for the small manufacturing firm. Simplification rules apply to production data management by reducing database complexity. This has consequences to medium-term requirements planning which is moved toward the realization of simultaneous material and capacity plannning. The simplification procedure is completed by applying aggregate decision models to shop floor control which allow the introduction of a minimimal transaction processing system. Object-oriented analysis concepts are used for the design of the primary production data model, which has a consistent effect on transaction data and decisional procedures throughout the whole production management software system.

1 Introduction

The dominant research and development effort in manufacturing software, mainly of the MRP II type (Manufacturing Resources Planning), has been towards enhancing the functionality of systems to cope with the needs of large scale manufacturing enterprises. Little has been written about the suitability and acceptance of MRP II as an appropriate approach for the very small firm (Browne et al, 1988). However, small firm owners have good reasons to consider the implementation of MRP II software as a high risk investment.

Small firms are often reluctant to pay the cost for the creation and maintenance of detailed and accurate production management data-at-rest, like bills of materials, routings and machine capacities. As far as data-in-motion are concerned, the organizational defficiencies do not allow to have them accurate, error-free and on-time. However, all these quality data are quite necessary prerequisites for the successful implementation of a typical MRP II software package. In addition to these problems, the small size of the firms does not allow the hiring of MRP II and database specialists as employees for the implementation and maintenance of such complicated systems.

The central theme in these problems is the overwhelming complexity of information systems in the field of production. However, having in mind that the complexity of information systems is closely connected to the complexity of the organization it is argued that small firms with loose organizational structure need far less complicated production planning and control (PPC) systems.

The issue of simplified production management systems came into light since the appearence of JIT (Just-In-Time), see Schonberger (1982). The history of production management shows a climbing up from very simple systems like the reorder point and stock base systems (McGee and Boodman, 1968) to extremely complicated like MRP II, and then back to simplified systems like JIT. The MRP paradigm, particularly in the development towards MRP II, has sought sophistication but achieved complexity instead (Browne et al, 1988).

MRP II system technicians spend disproportionate time on issues related to computer operating and application software. These technicians need to comprehend the need for startling new objectives in the systems on which they are working. Examples are (Harmon, 1990): 80% reduction of computer code lines, 75% reduction in the number of input and output formats, 90% reduction of the number of transactions processed, 50% reduction of the data elements stored in the system, 50% reduction in the user work.

Apart from JIT, other approaches to the simplification of production management systems are based on Group Technology organization concepts, like Pels and Wortmann (1990), who push forward these concepts to the production database domain, arguing that the complexity of information systems is closely connected to the complexity of the organization. Therefore, a condition for the simplification of PMS is a simplification of the organizational structure by a way of defunctionalization and the forming of autonomous units with local database modules.

Period Batch Control (PBC) developed by Burbidge (1989) fills the bill for a production control system suitable for use with Group Technology. PBC is a single cycle ordering system where there is a regular series of order dates and due dates; any orders are issued at the beginning of a period for completion by the end of that period, all orders are issued in balanced product sets in quantities sufficient to cover the requirements for a specific quantity of products to be made in a specific assembly period.

All the above approaches to the problem of simplifying the production management system have as a basic prerequisite the extensive reengineering of the factory setting in order either to reduce setups, as in the case of JIT, or to apply the group technology principles as in the cases of PBC and Pels/Wortmann. Both methods are suitable for large factories.

This paper draws attention on simplifying the production management software system as such using object-oriented data modelling techniques and aggregation of decision models rather than reengineering the factory. Small firms have investment problems in applying JIT principles and their layout as a whole comes close to a group technology cell. Therefore, the simplification efforts should be directed to the information and decisional level rather than the technical level, trying to turn the flexibility and organizational looseness of small firms in their favour.

The proposed simplified CAPM system shows the following characteristics: (a) Minimum database complexity, (b) Maximum flexibility and tolerance concerning integrity, correctness and up-to-date status of shop-floor information and production database, (c) Aggregation of decision-making to conform with the accuracy of shop-floor data available.

The process of simplifying CAPM systems for small manufacturing firms proposed in this study can be applied to the following three subject areas: *production data management*, *mid-term requirements planning*, *shop floor control*.

Object-oriented analysis concepts (Coat and Yourdon, 1990) have been used for the design of the proposed system.

2 Manufacturing Database

The effort towards simplifying the production management database is done having in mind that the complexity of a database schema or subschema is a measure of the effort required to understand its structure and to design applications for it. This means according to Pels and Wortmann (1990) that the complexity is equal to the total number of specifications (entity classes, relationships, attributes, constraints or validation rules) in the database schema under consideration.

The classical conceptual database schema for the basic data-at-rest of production management systems (Scheer, 1978) includes numerous data entities with complex relations in order to define parts and their structures (bills of material), processing (routings, operations), capacities (work centers, machines, personnel) and suppliers.

The proposed simplification of this schema includes a reduction of entity classes through the introduction of a "Resources" entity which unifies bills of materials and routings and a "Sources" entity which unifies work centers and suppliers. These unifications give also the chance for a reduction of attributes through an object-oriented approach to the design of the production database.

2.1 The Resources and Sources Object Classes

Both materials and work center capacities may be considered as "Resources" needed in manufacturing goods. The reasons for their traditional separation in two different groups of data entities, those of bills of materials and routings, are mainly three: (a) To avoid an inflation of part numbers, (b) The existence of scheduling stages with intermediate stores, (c) The need for holding different attributes to the entities "materials" and "operations".

The obstacle (a) of creating inflationary part numbers (Sartori, 1988) and the need for separating scheduling stages (b) can be overriden in the case of small manufacturing firms. They usually produce either simple products for local or specific markets or single components for the assembly operations of larger manufacturing firms. In either case, the existence of simple bills of materials and a restricted number of manufacturing operations are the norm.

In this context a significant simplification to the database design can take place by unifying bills of materials and routings in the form of the so-called "Product Networks", an idea which is also implemented in the OPT system (Goldratt, 1988). Those networks have the general form of bills of materials, however they include manufacturing operations as well. They are composed of nodes representing stages in the "journey" of materials from the time they are purchased, through the processing and assemply, until they are finally sent to fulfill customer orders.

From a conceptual database design viewpoint, as implemented in the present study, we can have a single "Resources" object class. This "Resources" entity in relation to the parent-son "Structures" entity form the previously mentioned product networks.

The unification of BOMs and routings may or may not be made visible to the enduser depending on his traditional working parctices. This can be done by making
a proper use of the "create view" capabilities of relational DBMSs. However, there is practical evidence that users in small manufacturing firms prefer the unified view of the product network which they find easier to understand, handle and maintain, instead of the separate BOMs and routings views.

Another step towards simplification and integration at the same time can be taken by replacing the separate "work centres" and "suppliers" entities by a single "sources" entity. From the point of view of the production planner, the work centres and the suppliers are nothing else but sources providing either manufactured parts or raw materials.

The design of our simplified production database follows the object-oriented analysis approach (Coat and Yourdon, 1990) in order to achieve a reduction of entities and attributes through the explicit representation of commonality. This is done by defining a classification structure of the "Resources" and "Sources" objects. Classification structure portrays class-member organization, reflecting generalization-specialization and providing a basis for subsequent inheritance, giving explicit representation of attributes commonality within such a structure.

Classification structure also provides a "levelling" of information about a problem domain putting attributes that are common at a higher level, and then extending the attributes to a lower level. Within a classification structure, inheritance makes it possible to share attributes.

In this respect, the attributes that pertain to all "resources" or to all "sources" are defined higher in the classification structure, and are extended by the specializations (stocks and operations, machines and suppliers).

The proposed simplified production database conceptual schema can be seen in Fig.1.

2.2 Reduction of Database Attributes

A careful design of the generalized *RESOURCE* and *SOURCE* object classes would permit a minimization of the total number of attributes by assigning common meaning to as many as possible. In this way there would be left a relatively small amount of attributes to the specialized subclasses *MATERIAL*, *OPERATION* and *WORK CENTER*, *SUPPLIER* respectively (Fig. 1).

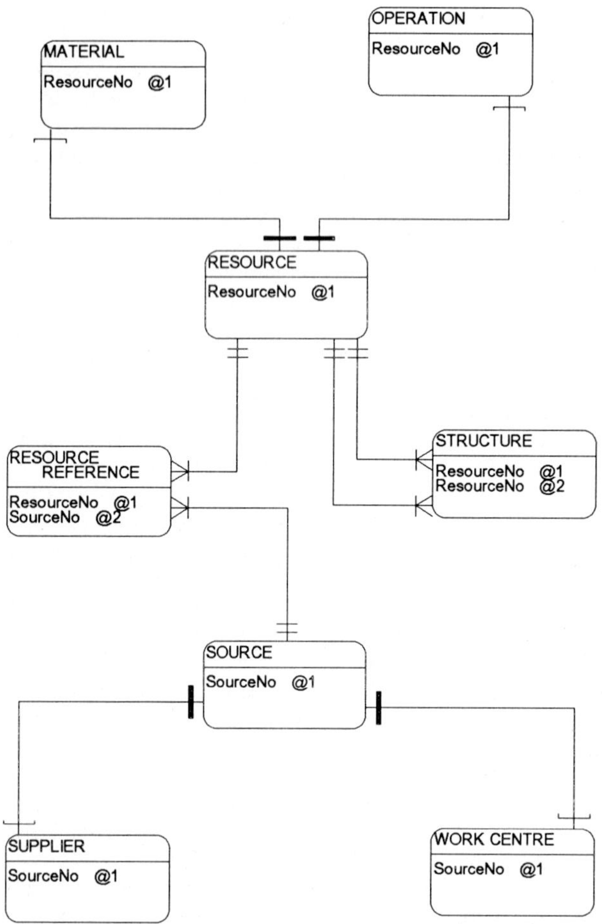

Fig. 1. Simplified and object-oriented production data management model

The simplification of structure and the reduction of attributes is achieved through a significant increase of code numbers for the resources (parts and operations) as well an increase of the structure records. However, this does not play a significant role in the small manufacturing firm due to the reduced sortiment of products and their simple structure.

3 Consequences for Mid-term Production Planning

A major critisism to the MRP II approach concerns the concept of successive material and capacity requirements planning. The results of the material requirements planning stage (MRP) are the input to the following capacity requirements planning stage (CRP) and feedback can be achieved only with difficulty. A further very strong drawback has its origin on the issue of planned lead times used in MRP calculations. The notion of MRP scheduling based on known average lead times makes MRP essentially capacity insensitive. It involves the major assumption that the actual shop floor loading at the time of planning conforms to these planned values, which is almost never the truth. What is needed is an integrated approach of simultaneous materials and capacity management (Scheer, 1989).

The most known effort to deal with the above problem is the OPT (Optimized Production Technology) system (Goldratt, 1988). OPT as well unifies bills of material and routings forming product networks. However, OPT represents a rather complicated finite scheduling approach which is very difficult to be explained to the manufacturing personnel of small firms and does not serve in any way our purpose of simplifying the MRP II system.

The approach presented here is based on the Input/Output Control (IOC) methodology (Plossl and Wight 1973, Kingsman/Tatsiopoulos/Hendry 1989, Wiendahl 1987, Bertrand 1981). IOC is similar to the graphical-tableau approach or aggregate production planning if one replaces physical inventories with work backlogs. The concept of IOC was originally advanced in connection with individual work centres at the shop orders release decision level and this is how it has been incorporated in some standard MRP II software packages (e.g. the module SOLAR of the COPICS package by IBM, 1983). In this paper we discuss how the method can be extended to include the medium-term production planning level forming a hierarchical input/output control system.

An idea of Fisk and Seagle (1973) is to use resource requirements planning in order to determine the capacity requirements of every work centre induced by the sales plan. Then an aggregate planning model is used in order to determine production rates for every particular work centre. The decision takes into account the projected work-in-process inventories expressed in production hours which are given by the difference of cumulative output (capacity requirements) and cumulative input (production rate) at the end of each planning period.

Against the attractiveness of the approach, Fisk and Seagle caution the user that it does not necessarily yield a feasible production plan. Dependencies between work centres can make it impossible to achieve the indicated production rates. For example, to inventory 100 hours in work centre 5 may require release of an order some weeks earlier to an already overloaded work centre 3.

In order to resolve the above difficulty a net-change MRP-like approach could be used. In stage-by-stage MRP the Net Requirements of the parent item become Gross Requirements for its components. In the same way, when in our case we take the decision to change the production rate of a particular work centre, this change induces changes in the capacity requirements of the work centre' s dependent previous work centre(s). What we need is a flow network showing the relations between the work centres in the shop stored in the computer memory exactly the same way that the bills of material of the products are stored.

This need is covered by using the unifying bills of material and manufacturing operations schema of Fig. 1. The calculations of the changes of capacity requirements back to the first work centre in the manufacturing sequence follow the gross-net requirements calculation principle of MRP. The role of inventories is played by the work backlogs in order to define the required changes of production rate (net requirements) of a dependent work centre caused by the changes in its capacity requirements (gross requirements). The backlog of the work centre may absorb the fluctuation and leave no need for change in production rate.

The implications concerning the extensions of the database schema to cover the material and capacity requirements planning are presented in Fig. 2 (simplified approach of this study for simultaneous material and capacity planning). During implementation it became apparent that this type of database modelling resulted in many benefits in terms of data handling, computer memory requirements and a very large increase in processing speed.

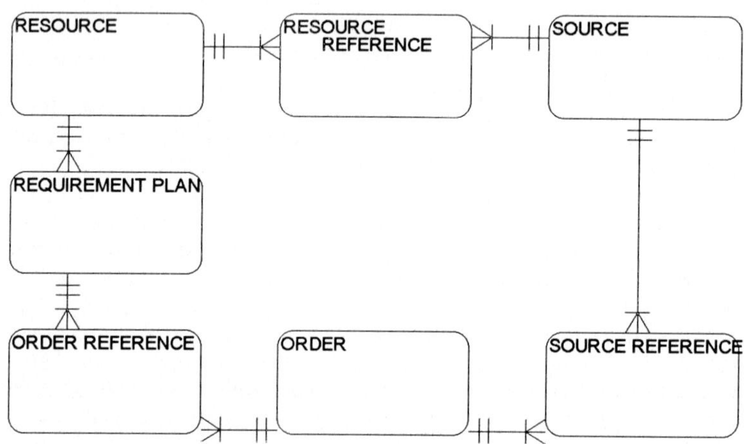

Fig. 2. Extension of simplified data model for requirements planning

4 Shop floor transaction processing

A manufacturing firm can be thought of as comprising two "factories". One makes products and the other (the hidden factory) processes transactions on papers and computer systems. Over time, the former factory has been decreasing in relative cost, compared with the latter, so that the consistently rising overhead costs tends to be the number one concern of manufacturing managers (Vollman et al, 1988). This is of particular concern to small firms who normally have very low overhead costs and they face the dilemma to significantly increase those costs in order to implement a computer-based production management system.

A major driver for these costs is transactions including the ordering, execution and confirmation of materials moving from one location to another. Included are the costs of personnel in receiving, shipping, expediting, data entry, data processing, accounting, and error follow up. The goal of the approach presented here is to eliminate transaction and associated costs as far as possible.

In the very small firm there are seldom closed stockrooms. The only transactions that take place using a manual system is receiving of raw materials and a daily production report coming out from every work center. No issues of materials and no move and operation start tickets.

Having in mind that operation assignment (input) transactions are missing for all downstream work centres, this need can only be covered by the *backflushing* method which serves the purpose of doing away with raw material requisitioning transactions.

Backflushing is a method by which material, labor and overhead are consumed automatically by the system when production is reported at a user-defined paypoint. Backflushing can drastically reduce the number of system transactions required to report production and maintain inventory control.

Backflushing can be performed on a single-level or multi-level basis as defined by the user at the component level of each bill of material. This allows inventory management to maintain tight control over designated components through direct issue while other components are issued automatically trough backflushing. Mult-level backflushing allows the user to process automatic transactions for as many levels of the bill of material as is desirable.

Backflush transactions are processed whenever production is reported at a paypoint in a product' s routing. Backflush transactions will also be processed for all routing steps between the paypoint reported and the previous paypoint defined on the routing.

Originally backflushing has been implemented as a key element of repetitive manufacturing management systems as is the JIT paradigm. However, small firms are often not suited for the application of JIT principles due to the lack of stable master schedule, engineering investments for cutting- down machine set-ups and implementing quality control standards in order to avoid deffected parts and reworking. In addition they are not in a position to apply pressure on their suppliers to make them deliver on a JIT basis. Therefore we propose here a MRP II based system which applies the backflushing principle for specific purposes within the shop-floor transaction system.

Problems arise if the flow of production is not fast enough so that serious deviations may happen between actual and updated inventory records. This problem may be solved by choosing as "phantom" operations for backflushing those that move fast, as well as by frequently doing physical inventory counting. This is feasible in the small firm due to the restricted number of materials and the easy-to- overview and easy-to-grasp ('eye management') characteristics of the environment.

5 Conclusions

The above presented analysis shows that the development of CAPM systems for the small manufacturing firms must take into consideration the difficulty to obtain and maintain complicated and accurate production databases both at the data-at-rest and the data-in-motion level. Suitable CAPM systems necessitate simplified data models, aggregated data and simplified decision models can be used to avoid this drawback. The latest information technology of object-oriented analysis as well as new "soft" production management technologies facilitate this task.

Implementation of CAPM systems based on the above concepts has been undertaken in an industry case that concerns a repetitive manufacturer of light metal sheet products (door locks). The proposed simplified system has been successfully installed on a PC network with emphasis on the simplified sources/resources data model, the simultaneous material and capacity requirements planning and the backflushing principle.

The simplified approach to the design of CAPM software has addmitedly some drawbacks which are discussed. However, these drawbacks do not have a severe impact on small firms due to the restricted sortiment of products and their simple structure. On the other hand, the simplifying approach can serve in a very satisfactory way the purpose of having a whole integrated and understandable system installed in the minimum of time.

References

1. Bertrand, J., 1981, The Effect of Workload Control on Order Flow Times, Proceedings of the IXth IFORS Conference on Operations Research (North Holland, Amsterdam).
2. Brown, J., Harhen J. and Shinvan,J., 1988, Production Management Systems (Addison Wesley, Reading MA).
3. Burbidge, J.L., Production Flow Analysis for Planning Group Technology, 1989 (London: Oxford Science Publications).
4. Burbidge, J.L., Plant Layout for GT and PBC, APMS 90 Conference, IFIP WG 5.7, Helsinki, 1990 (North Holland).
5. Coat, P. and Yourdon,E., 1990, Object-Oriented Analysis (Yourdon Press, New Jersey).
6. Fisk, J.C. and Seagle, J.P., 1978, The integration of aggregate planning with resource requirements planning, *Production & Inventory Management*, 3rd Quarter, 81-89.
7. Goldratt, E.M., Computerized Shop Floor Scheduling, 1988, *Int.J.Prod.Res.*, Vol.26, No3, 443-455.
8. Harmon, R., 1990, Breakthroughs in Manufacturing Today, *APMS 90*, IFIP WG 5.7, Espoo, Finland.
9. IBM, 1983, COPICS, Ein Informationssystem fuer Unternehmen der Fertigungs- und Grundstoffindustrie, Form W12-0056-1 (Muenchen: IBM Deutschland).
10. Kingsman, B., Tatsiopoulos, I.P. and Hendry, L.C., 1989, A structural methodology for managing manufacturing lead times in make-to-order companies, *EJOR*, 40, 196-209.
11. MaGee, J.F. and Boodman, D.M., 1967, *Production Planning and Inventory Control* (New York: McGraw-Hill).
12. Pappas, I.A., 1983, Problems in formalizing production planning in a threshold country, in Wilson,B. (Ed.), *Efficiency of Manufacturing Systems*, Plenum, New York, pp. 305-311.
13. Pels, H.J. and Wortmann, J.C., 1990, Modular Design of Integrated Databases in Production Management Systems, *Production Planning & Control*, Vol 1.,No.3, 132-146.
14. Plossl, G. and Wight, O., 1973, Capacity planning and control, *Production and Inventory Management*, 3rd Qtr., 31-67.
15. Rohloff, M., Design of a Decentralized production management System Based on an Object Oriented Approach, in: Pappas, I. and I. Tatsiopoulos (Eds), *Advances in Production Management Systems*, pp. 585-597, IFIP-North Holland, 1993.
16. Sartori, L.G., 1988, *Manufacturing Information Systems* (Addison-Wesley, UK).
17. Scheer, A., 1983, Production control and information systems, Proceedings of CIM 1983 Conference, Karlsruhe, September, Springer Verlag.
18. Scheer, A., 1987, CIM - Computer Steered Industry, Springer Verlag.

19. Schonberger, R.J., 1982, Japanese Manufacturing Techniques (The FreePress-McMillan, NY).
20. Sepehri, P.E. and N. Raffish, 1986, Developing and implementing control systems for repetitive manufacturing, Industrial Engineering, June, pp.34-46.
21. Vollmann, Th., Berry, W and Whybark, D.C., 1988, Manufacturing Planning and Control Systems (Illinois: Irwin).
22. Wiendahl, H.P., 1987, Belastungsorientierte Fertigungssteuerung (Muenchen: Carl Hanser Verlag).

A Solution Procedure for Solving the Nonrectangular Cutting Stock Problem of the Clothing Industry Using Expert Knowledge within an Intelligent CAD Environment

D.A Xerokostas(1) and K.G. Aravossis(2)

Department of Production Management & Operations Research, NTU Athens

ABSTRACT. A certain type of the cutting stock problem arises in the clothing industry. It is of the general non-rectangular two-dimensional type, but involves special considerations and restrictions. The solution procedure usually followed in the clothing industry is based on the experience of technicians, who use their skills to determine satisfactory cutting patters on the cutting table. In this paper a solution procedure for solving this problem-type is presented, which on a CAD environment combines O.R techniques and heuristics with expert knowledge for cutting-pattern generation. It produces a final cutting solution, which fully satisfies the orders for various garment-types. In the final stage of the solution-procedure the non-rectangular cutting stock problem is transformed into a rectangular one, that can be solved by means of heuristic methods. Numer ical examples taken from the clothing industry demonstrate the efficiency of this procedure.

1. Introduction

Cutting stock problems arise in a wide range of industries in one- two- and three-dimensional forms. The common feature of almost all problems is that some form of stock material is to be cut to produce smaller pieces of material in quantities matching orders received. One objective of most solution techniques is to minimise wasted material. The aim of this paper is to examine the problem as it occurs in the clothing industry and to propose a solution technique. Although this problem could be characterised as a two-dimensional, non-rectangular problem-type due to its characteristics, and restrictions it involves more difficulties, that have to be considered in the solution approach.

In the literature one can find various approaches for solvingt he general two-dimensional rectangular problem in which all the pieces to be cut are of the rectangular form. We only mention the papers by Gilmore and Gomory (1966) Christofides and Whitlok(1977), Hertz (1972), Beasley (1985), Wang (1983) and F. Oliveira and J. Ferreira (1990). They propose optimal solutions and heuristics that under special conditions satisfactorily deal with this problem-type. In the clothing industry however, the arising problem involves cutting of pieces of an irregular shape. It is not possible to present optimal solutions for the irregular problem-type, but one can find a few approaches in the literature presenting special heuristics. Adamowicj and Albano (1972,1976 b) and Haims and Freeman(1970) present solutions where one or more pieces are combined into rectangular modules, which are then allocated in a second stage. Haims and Freeman (1970) use a dynamic programming algorithm to allocate these rectanguler modules on rectangular sheets. Albano (1977) and Jorn Oian et al (1976) use an interactive nesting approach in order to allocate irregular pieces. C. Dagli and V. Tatoglu (1987) use a "building up" technique, where each new piece is allocated (by using special allocation-criteria) on the previously determined best pieces' assignment. Albano and Sapuppo (1980) propose a tree search of an interactive manner. There is however no known solution-proposal in the literature for solving the irregular cutting stock problem as it is found in the clothing industry. This paper presents a solution-procedure to solve this kind of problem with all the restrictions and characteristics we find in the clothing industry.

2. The Clothing Industry

The cutting stock problem of the clothing industry is one of a special nature, with certain restrictions and characteristics, so that it should be considered independantly of other similar problems. These characteristics can be summarised as follows :

(i) Cutting is performed on cutting-tables with lengths of often over 20m. The raw materials from which pieces are cut are rolls of fabric, which are practically not constrained in what their length is concerned, but that do have standard widths.

(ii) The pieces to be cut are irregular; however rectangles can be found too. Pieces represent the consisting parts of pieces of garments.

(iii) There is ususally a demand for a great number of different pieces to be cut with a relatively low demand for each.

(iv) The raw materials fabrics are usually anisotrop;i.e.there are special restrictions that do not permit a rotation of the pieces that have to be cut. Rotation is therefore only possible by 180 degrees.

(v) More layers of textile are usually cut together, so that cutting of one piece produces more indentical ones (as many as the layers are).

(vi) Not more than two to three pieces can usually be cut alongside the width of the roll.

The current practice, when an order for a certain garment -type is given, is to determine the demand for each individual piece that has to be cut in order to procuce all needed pieces. Then an experienced cutter moves cardboard-replicates of the pieces on a white paper-sheet with the dimensions of the cutting table in order to determine an allocation with the least trim -loss. In this process the techician uses rules of thumb deriving from his experience. When the allocation of the cardboard-replicates is completed, their edges are drawn on the paper-sheet, this is positioned on the textiles and then the equivalent pieces are cut out of the textile roll. It is obvious, that when following the above procedure, the cutting results depend greatly on the experience and skills of the workers and so do the material costs of each order (no standard wastes). This procedure is repeated for all the different grament-types and colours of the order.

3. The Proposed Methodology

In order to optimise and automate the above manual cutting process of the clothing industry, a methodology has been developed consisting of five stages. This can be analysed as follows.

3.1 Stage I: Automatic Analysis of the Order into its Consisting Pieces.

Orders in the clothing industry contain different garment- types, whereas for each a demand for various sizes has to be satisfied. Each garment-type consists of individual parts. A computer algorithm has been developed, that processes the orders and produces as an output a demand table with the actual demand for each individual part of each garment size. The algorithm performs all necessary calculations to determine the demand table by multiplying the garment demands of the order with the corresponding numbers of the individual parts. Table 1 shows an example of a demand-table for an order for two different garment-types (codes: TR and BA) arising in seven sizes (38-50).

Table 1. Order for two garnment types and corresponding demand table for the individual pieces

ΕΙΔΟΣ ΕΝΔΥΜΑΤΟΣ	ΜΕΓΕΘΟΣ						
	38	40	42	44	46	48	50
TRACTUM	6	7	7	8	8	7	7
BALI	8	8	9	9	8	7	6

ΟΝΟΜΑ ΤΕΜΑΧΙΟΥ	ΜΕΓΕΘΗ						
	38	40	42	44	46	48	50
TR-1	12	14	14	16	16	14	14
TR-2	12	14	14	16	16	14	14
TR-3	12	14	14	16	16	14	14
TR-4	24	28	28	32	32	28	28
TR-5	12	14	14	16	16	14	14
TR-6	12	14	14	16	16	14	14
TR-7	6	7	7	8	8	7	7
TR-8	6	7	7	8	8	7	7
TR-9	12	14	14	16	16	14	14
BA-1	16	16	18	18	16	14	12
BA-2	16	16	18	18	16	14	12
BA-3	16	16	18	18	16	14	12
BA-4	32	32	36	36	32	28	24
BA-5	16	16	18	18	16	14	12
BA-6	8	8	9	9	8	7	6
BA-7	16	16	18	18	16	14	12

3.2 Stage II: Grouping of Pieces and Creation of Rectangular Patterns consisting of one, two or more Pieces by using Expert-rules

During this stage the pieces are allocated into certain groups, according to their shape. An exhaustive survey of actual clothing-industry parts has been undertaken and it has been observed that the individual shapes of the pieces in the clothing industry follow certain characteristics that enable the creation of groups, where all members have common shape - forms. The observation of experienced cutters on their work has enabled the determination of the following groups. (experienced cutters use similar groupings of pieces in their manual cutting practices.) :

1. group of pieces, that have rectangular or almost rectangular shapes (rectangles with cut or rounded edges) (figure 1).
2. group of pieces, that have characteristical edges that permit them to create almost perfect rectangular patterns, if matched together in pairs (figure 2).
3. group of pieces with shapes that enable placing similar pieces next to them, rotated by 180 degrees in order to form almost rectangular patterns (figure 3).

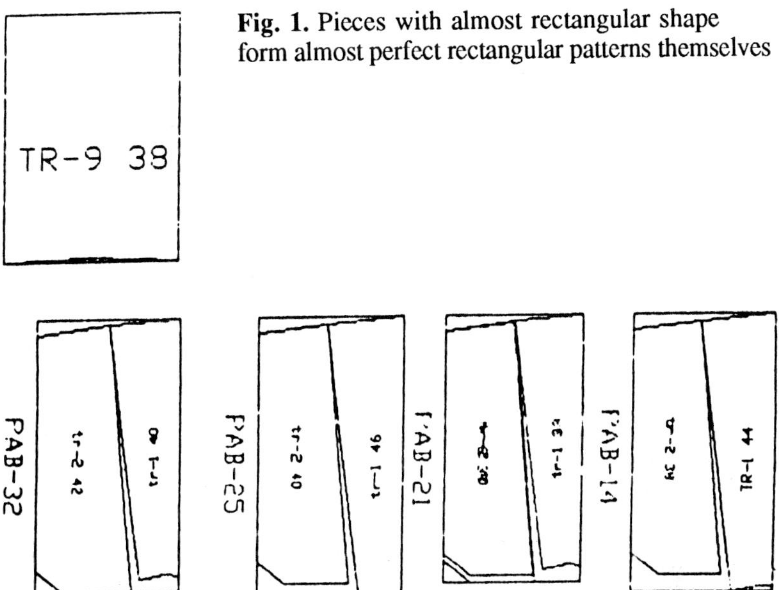

Fig. 1. Pieces with almost rectangular shape form almost perfect rectangular patterns themselves

Fig. 2. Pairing of pieces in almost rectangular patterns

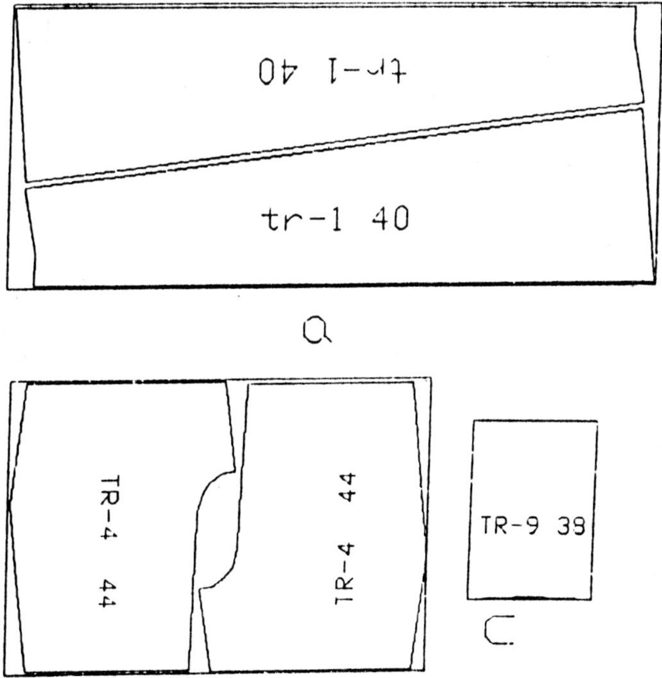

Fig. 3. Pieces that form almost perfect rectangular patterns with an identical piece rotated by 180

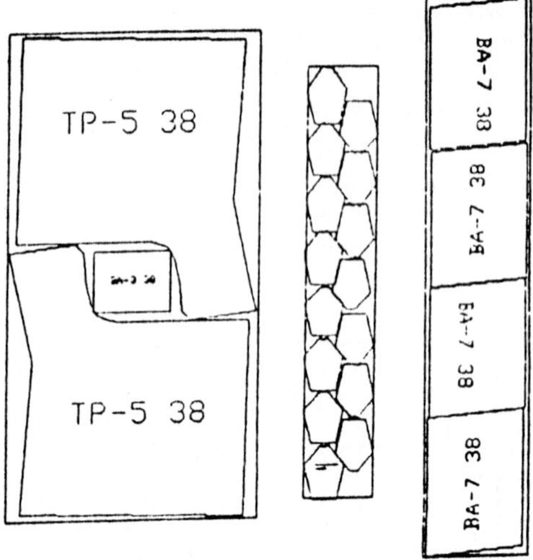

Fig. 4. Grouping of pieces in rectangular patterns

4. group of pieces with irregular shapes, that can be combined by repeated standard allocation schemes in order to create rectangular patterns of restricted dimensions (fig. 4). All different sizes of the pieces follow a basic shape. So when a near-rectangular pattern with pieces of certain sizes is established, similar ones for all the other sizes can also be made.

From the above general grouping observations it can be concluded, that it is possible to create a number of rectangular patterns, that will contain one or more of the individual pieces determined in the previous methodology stage (demand table) and then try to satisfy the demands for the individual pieces by allocating the appropriate number of rectangular patterns by solving a corresponding rectangular cutting stock problem. A CAD package (AUTOCAD) has been used to create an appropriate base on which the individual consisting pieces of the garments can be entered by means of a scanner or a digitiser. Special algorithms have been developed, that can be applied on the pieces of each group (the pieces are allocated interactively to the groups) and automate the creation-process of a rectangular pattern consisting of one or more pieces. The alorithms were written in AUTOLISP, a specialised LISP version, that can operate within the CAD environment. For each group of pieces a specialised algorithm is assigned, operating as follows

(i) It takes the first piece of the first size of each groupand determines a rectangular pattern according to the specific criteria of the group.

(ii) Each pattern is accurately defined by the coordinates of the opposite points of the rectangular enclosure of the pieces.

(iii) The internal waste (unused area percentage) of the pattern is calculated.

(iv) A similar rectangular pattern is automatically created for all the other respective sizes I.e : if there are seven sizes(38-50), six corresponding patterns are created for all the other sizes. Figure 5 shows an example of all rectangular patterns created by a piece (code-name : BA) paired with itshelf for all sizes.

3.3 Stage III: Determination of the best Rectangular Patterns, that satisfy the Initial Demand for the Pieces

During the previous stages of the procedure, rectangular patterns have been determined enclosing one, two or more pieces appropriately combined together in

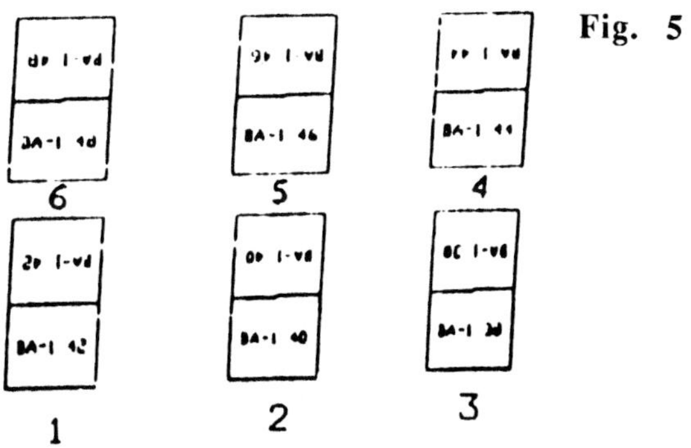

Fig. 5

their different sizes. It is possible however, that a piece appears in different groups and therefore in more rectangular patterns. Also a piece can appear in more rectangular patterns of the same group. It is therefore important to determine, which of the rectangular patterns are needed to satisfy the initial demands as well as the new demands for each of them. To do that an Integer Programming Model of the following form can be used :

minimise $Z=\Sigma W_j X_j$ Subject to $\Sigma a_{ij} X_j = b_i$ $i=1,.....m$ (m=number of pieces)
$j=1......n$ (n=number of rectangular patterns)
$X_j > 0$ for all $j=1,....n$ X_j integer

a_{ij} stands for the number of pieces of each type that are included in each pattern j and w_j is the internal scrap (i.e : the unused area-percentage) of each rectangular pattern. X_j determines the number of patterns of each type, that should be included in the final corresponding rectangular cutting-problem in order to satisfy the minimisation objective of the internal wastes.

3.4 Stage IV: Determination of the Optimal Number of Layers of Textile

As already mentioned in the cutting process of the clothing industry more layers of textile can be put together on the cutting table, so that more indentical pieces can be similtanously produced. In this stage a heuristic algorithm has been developed, that determines the optimal number of layers that should be used in order to satisfy the demand for the rectangular patters in the most efficient way. The goal is to minimise the times (stages) new layers of cloth are put on the cutting-table until the demand is fully satisfied. The algorithm uses following criterion to determine the number of layers (LA) for each stage:

$LAi=\min(Dki)$, where Dki= Demand for each pattern k of the stage i.

The number of cutting patterns, that will be cut at each stage with LAi layers of textile are determined by the following:

$Dk=\text{INTEGER}(Dki/LAi)$.

During this phase of the solution procudure the original problem is finally transformed into more rectangular cutting stock problems, where rectangular patterns consisting of individual pieces of garments are cut with LAi layers of textile.

Table 2 shows an example of the input data of the algorithm at this stage and table 3 shows the corresponding output data.

Table 2. Input to the algorithm of stage IV of the solution approach for optimal determination of textile layers

```
PATTERNS TO BE ALLOCATED:
        6

LENGTH AND WIDTH OF THE CUTTING TABLE:
    10000.0000000      1000.0000000

X- COORDINATES OF THE PATTERNS:
        743.0000000       123.0000000        120.0000000        120.0000000
        234.0000000       234.0000000

Y- COORDINATES OF THE PATTERNS:
        213.0000000       340.0000000        520.0000000        120.0000000
        350.0000000       230.0000000

DEMAND OF THE PATTERNS:
        6            7          12          14          16     9

TRIM-LOSS OF THE PATTERNS:
        6.0000000        12.0000000          5.0000000          9.0000000
        3.0000000         5.2000000
```

3.5 Stage V: Solution of the Coresponding Rectangular Cutting Stock Problems

At this stage the problem has been transformed into a special type of the rectangular cutting stock problem, where rectangular patterns of more different dimensions have to be cut out of a rectangular sheet with a concrete width, but practically unrestricted length.

In the literature one can find various solution proposals for this problem by means of optimal or heuristics algorithms. Wang (1983), Vasko (1989) and Hadjiconstantinou and Christofides (1991) present solutions, which cannot be effectively used for large scale problems like the present.. However for this case of the clothing industry, where a great number of different rectangular patterns are cut with smaller demands for each, a houristic solution-approach has been developed by K. Aravossis and D. Xerokostas (1993). By this approach we get very satisfactory results in a limited computation time. Thus in this stage the irregular cutting stock problem of the clothing industry can finally be solved by solving the corre- sponding rectangular problems for which known methods exist (fig.6).

4. Computational Results

On table 4 we can see the results of cutting problems taken from the clothing industry, that are solved by using the five-stage solution procedure presented here. For all cases we have as a result a combined scrap that consists of the internal scrap of all rectangular patterns determined on stage III of the methodology and of the external srap that derives from solving the rectangular cutting stock problems at stage V by means of a houristics algorithm. These results, if compared with the actual results produced by conventional manual procedures of the clothing industry (usually rules of thumb processes) are very satisfactory. Moreover, if rectangular

Table 3. Output of the algorithm of stage IV of the solution approach determining the optimal number of layers

```
THE   6 DIFFERENT PATTERNS REPRESENT  64 RECT/GL.

THE INNER TRIM OF ALL PATTERNS IS          6.2625000 %


THE  1 LAYOUT CONSISTS OF   6 LAYERS OF CLOTH
THE INNER TRIM OF THIS LAYOUT IS          6.3555560 %


THE  1 LAYOUT WILL USE THE FOLLOWING PARTS:
PATTERN : DEMAND :        INNER TRIM :       X- COORD :          Y- COORD
      1 :        1 :        6.0000000 :       743.0000000 :        213.0000000
      2 :        1 :       12.0000000 :       123.0000000 :        340.0000000
      3 :        2 :        5.0000000 :       120.0000000 :        520.0000000
      4 :        2 :        9.0000000 :       120.0000000 :        120.0000000
      5 :        2 :        3.0000000 :       234.0000000 :        350.0000000
      6 :        1 :        5.2000000 :       234.0000000 :        230.0000000
THE  1 LAYOUT CONSISTS OF MIN.          1.00 STEPS

THE  2 LAYOUT CONSISTS OF   1 LAYERS OF CLOTH
THE INNER TRIM OF THIS LAYOUT IS          5.7600000 %


THE  2 LAYOUT WILL USE THE FOLLOWING PARTS:
PATTERN : DEMAND :        INNER TRIM :       X- COORD :          Y- COORD
      1 :        0 :        6.0000000 :       743.0000000 :        213.0000000
      2 :        1 :       12.0000000 :       123.0000000 :        340.0000000
      3 :        0 :        5.0000000 :       120.0000000 :        520.0000000
      4 :        2 :        9.0000000 :       120.0000000 :        120.0000000
      5 :        4 :        3.0000000 :       234.0000000 :        350.0000000
      6 :        3 :        5.2000000 :       234.0000000 :        230.0000000
THE  2 LAYOUT CONSISTS OF MIN.          1.00 STEPS
```

patterns enclosing pieces of certain garment-types are determined once, then they can be used for all subsequent orders. A crucial advantage of the here presented procedure, if compared with conventional procedures, is that here one gets consistant satisfactory results independant of the presence of experienced cutters, since all their experience is already included in stage II and stage V of the solution process.

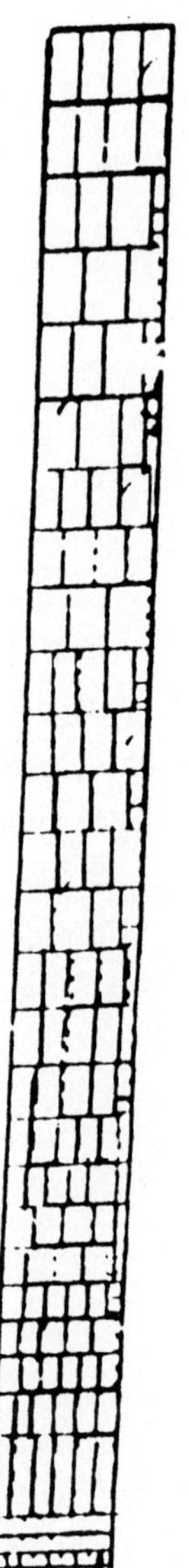

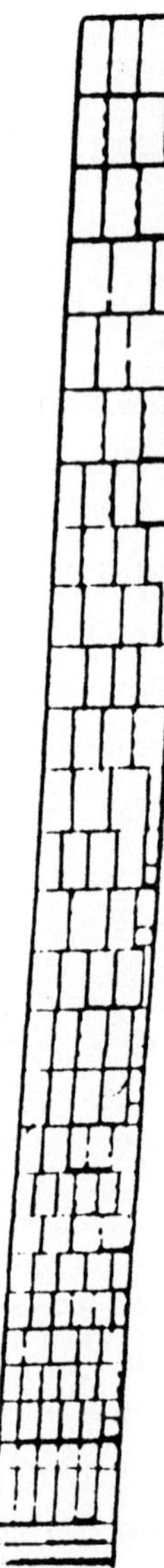

Fig. 6. Allocation of the rectangular patterns on the cutting table

Table 4

ORDER TYPE	TROUSER	TROUSER	SHIRT	COMBINATION OF TWO TROUSERS' TYPES
ORDER SIZE	50	55	24	105
NO. OF PIECES/GARMENT	9	7	3	9/7
NUMBER OF SIZES	7	7	4	7
NUMBER OF SELECTED PATTERN TYPES	63	47	13	112
INTERNAL WASTE (%)	6.68	6.18	19.1	6.52
EXTERNAL WASTE (%)	7.60	6.56	4.41	6.10
TOTAL WASTE (%)	14.28	12.74	23.51	12.67

5. Conclusion

A solution procedure to solve a type of the irregular cutting stock problem of the clothing industry has been destribed. This procedure renders very satisfactory results and provides an effective tool for solving this special problems indepedant of the presence of experienced cutters.

6. References

1) Adamowicz M., Albano A. (1972), "A two-stage solution of the Cutting Stock Problem", Information Processing, No.71, pp. 1086-1091.

2) Adamowicz M., Albano A. (1976b), "A solution of the rectangular cutting stock problem", IEEE Transactions on Systems, Man and Cybernetics, Vol. SMC-6, pp. 302-310.

3) Albano A. (1977), "A method to improve two-dimensional layout, CAD, Vol.9, 1977, No.1, pp.48-52.

4) Albano A., Sapuppo G (1980), "Optimal allocation of two dimensioanl irregular shapes using heuristic search methods:, IIEE Transactions, SMC-10, 5th May, pp.242-248.

5) Aravossis K., Xerokostas D. (1993). "A heuristic solution approach to a special type of the rectangular cutting stock Problem". 2nd Balkan Conference on O.R, 18-21 October 1993, Thessaloniki, Greece.

6) Beasley J.E (1985a), "Algorithm for Unconstrained Two-Dimensional Guillotine Cutting", Journal of the O.R. Society, Vol. 36, pp. 297-306.

7) Christofides N., Whitlock C. (1977), "An algorithm for two dimensional Cutting Problems, O.R., Vol.25, No.1, pp. 31-44.

8) Dagli C.H., TATOGLUM.Y. (1987), "An approach to two-dimensional cutting stock Problmes", Int.J.Prod.Res., Vol.25, No.2, pp.175-190.

9) Gilmore P.C. and Gomory R.E. (1965), "Multistage Cutting Stock Problems of two and more dimensions", O.R., Vol.11, pp.863-888.

10) Gilmore P.C. and Gomory R.E. (1966), "The Theory and Computation of knapsack Functions", O.R., Vol.13, pp.1045-1074.

11) Haims M.J, Freeman H. (1970), "A multistage solution of the template-layout problem", IEEE Transactions on Systems Science and Cybernetics, Vol. 55c-6, No.2, pp.145-151.

12) Hertz J. (1972), "Recursive computational procedure for two-dimensional stock cutting", IBM Journal of Research and Development, Vol.16, pp.462-469.

13) Jorn OIAN et al (1976), "An Interactive Computer Graphics approach to the problem of nesting plane parts on a raw steel format", CAD, Proceedings, pp. 166-170.

14) Oliveira J.F., Ferreira J.S. (1990), "An improved version of Wang's algorithm for two-dimensional cutting problems, European Journal of O.R., Vol.44, No.2, pp.256-266.

15) Wang P.Y. (1983), "Two algorithms for constrained two-dimensional cutting stock problems", O.R., Vol.31, No.3, pp.573-586.

An Object-Oriented Approach to a Temporal Query Language[1]

Nina Edelweiss*, **José Palazzo M. de Oliveira***, **Barbara Pernici**+

* Universidade Federal do Rio Grande do Sul – Porto Alegre – RS – Brazil
e-mail: [nina | palazzo]@inf.ufrgs.br

+ Politecnico di Milano - Milano - Italy
e-mail: pernici@ipmel2.elet.polimi.it

ABSTRACT

Time constraints and the temporal dimension are an essential aspect in many real world systems, like cooperative work and industrial production systems. Traditional database systems support these features only through application programs. The recent tendency consists of representing the temporal aspects in the database schema and in the corresponding query language and supporting them directly in the DBMS. In this paper the different aspects of adding the temporal dimension in an object-oriented data model are analyzed and a classification scheme is proposed for the types of possible queries. Based on this classification, a query language for the object-oriented TF-ORM data model is presented and discussed in detail. In TF-ORM, both transaction and valid times are associated to data, and the query language is used to retrieve information about the database current valid information, about past valid values, and about past histories.

KEYWORDS: Temporal Databases, Conceptual Modeling, Object-Oriented Data Model.

1. Introduction

Information about temporal values, temporal restrictions and evolutionary characteristics, is present in many real world problems. The complete representation of an application requires that all the applications aspects – the static and the dynamic – may be represented. A temporal data model is needed to represent all the application's characteristics.

For a richer semantic expressiveness in complex problems, one of the best alternatives is to use an object-oriented model. Object-oriented data models have received huge attention in recent database researches. Several of the existing object-oriented data models represent also temporal aspects [1, 3, 4, 12, 15, 16, 21, 26, 27]. However, temporal modeling in object-oriented databases is usually done in a limited way . Some important aspects are (from [18]): (i) dynamic objects - database objects can be dynamic as well static, in the sense that they can exhibit behaviour and aquire different roles over time; (ii) inheritance - classes share attributes and operations based on a hierarchical relationship; and (iii) complex objects - the state of an object may refer to another object.

---

[1] This work was partially supported by the Italian National Research Council, project "Temporal data and knowledge bases", and by the Brazilian Conselho Nacional de Desenvolvimento Científico e Tecnológico - CNPq.

Information manipulation and retrieval is an important aspect to be considered in object-oriented databases. We focus here only on the *query language*. Temporal queries are a special kind of queries. They can refer to temporal properties, retrieve information corresponding to a defined temporal instant or interval, and retrieve values based on temporal constraints. Some object-oriented query languages have been proposed [2, 3, 6, 8, 14, 19, 25, 26]. Most of them are based on SQL [5], like the Rose and Segev's TOOSQL, Dayal and Wuu's query language for the OODAPLEX functional data model, Cheng and Gadia's OOTempSQL and Käfer's MQL for the T-MAD data model. Stonebraker's Quel [24] and Snodgrass' TQuel [23] also influenced the development of temporal object-oriented query languages, like Carey's EXCESS query language for the EXTRA data model.

The main concern of this work is to define a taxonomy for a temporal object-oriented query language and to define a query language for the object-oriented temporal data model TF-ORM [9], a temporal extension of the F-ORM object-oriented model [7]. This language can be used to answer temporal and non-temporal queries. Special attention is given in this paper to temporal queries. The TF-ORM query language presents the general form of SQL, being also influenced by TQuel.

This paper is organized as follows. In Section 2 a brief case study is presented, to be used in the next sections examples. Section 3 analyzes the queries that can be made in the different database types and Section 4 verifies the relationship between query components and histories in a bitemporal database. A short explanation of the TF-ORM data model is presented in Section 5. The TF-ORM query language is detailed in Section 6 and some examples are presented in Section 7.

2. The Case Study

A simple case is described to be used in the examples of this paper. The example is based on the one developed in a document that had the central goal to provide the temporal community with a comprehensive consensus benchmark for temporal query languages [13].

Consider a company composed of departments and a set of employees. Each *employee* is characterized by a *name*, a *salary*, a *gender* and a *date of birth*. An employee works in a *department* and an employee can present one or more *skills* for which he is qualified. While the salary and department of an employee vary over time, both the gender and the date of birth are time-invariant. The name of the employee can also be occasionally modified (marriage or divorce). The skills of an employee may also vary over time - during an object evolution skills can be added and deleted from the defined skills set.

Departments are characterized by a *department name*. Each department has one *manager*, who must be one of the employees. The department's name may change over time, and so can also the manager.

3. Temporal Queries, Database Types and Histories

Temporal queries depend on the used temporal model and on the type of information to be retrieved. According to temporal representation, databases are classified as: snapshots, transaction-time, valid-time and bitemporal [22]. Depending on the *database type*, different temporal queries can be executed on temporal databases. *Snapshot databases* do not provide explicit support to temporal queries because only the last defined values are accessible, and only user defined times and external applications can be used to manage time aspects.

The *transaction-time representation* is oriented to the database manipulation, each update being an addition to the stored data. For this type of databases, in addition to the present property values queries, a new category of queries is defined: the queries referencing a past timeslice in the historical data representation. A query may specify any condition on past stored values of a property.

The *valid-time representation* is closer to the modeled reality in contrast with the transaction-time representation that is implementation-oriented. This type of representation allows queries about the *present perception* of a property's history. All the queries return values obtained from the properties present history representing the present valid values and their history in the past as it is known at the present timeslice.

Bitemporal databases combine the valid-time and transaction-time representations. Queries on any present or past state of the database can be executed. A query can retrieve (i) current values, (ii) values that were valid at past times according to the present state, and (iii) values that were supposed to be valid at a past state. The previous database types can be viewed as contained in this more general type, and so can also the queries. All the queries that can retrieve values of the previous database types can also be made in a bitemporal database.

A bitemporal database's present history is defined by all the values that are valid at the present moment, at past moments and are defined to be valid at future moments. This history corresponds to the present knowledge about the database present, past and future property values. During the database evolution, different data histories are defined as the result of knowledge modification. At a past moment – identified by the corresponding transaction time – there were values valid at that time and a set of past or future valid values – all these values define the history of valid values or the database knowledge at that transaction time.

Five different *database histories* can be identified, representing different interpretations of the storage structure implemented by the database:

- *present instant data*, represented by all the presently valid information;
- *past instant data*, representing a snapshot in the past according to the actual database history;
- *past history instant data*, considering all the information that was believed to be valid at a past transaction time, without considering the information defined in the following transactions;
- *historical data*, including all the stored information (past, present and future), according to the present valid history; and
- *past historical data*, analogous to the former but considering the history defined at a previous transaction time.

Figure 1 shows these histories representing the potential retrieved information of each one of them along a temporal axis. The first three represent all the data at the marked time points; the first two consider the actual database history and the third, the history believed on the marked time point. The last two lines represent all the data stored along the temporal axis as known on the marked time point.

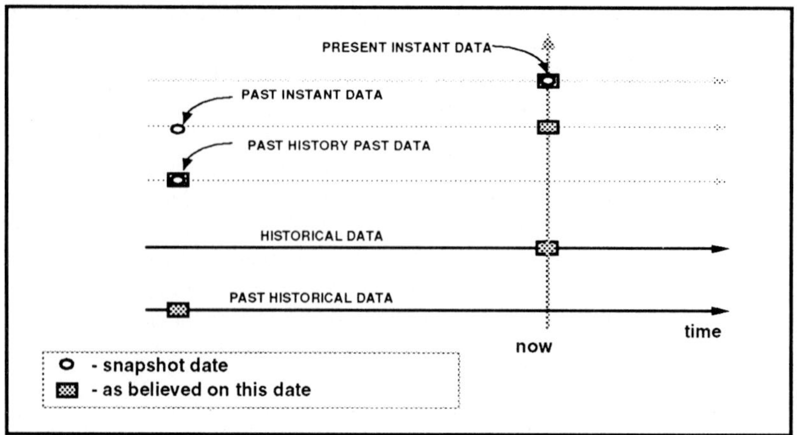

Fig. 1. Database Histories Information

4. Queries and Database Histories

Queries usually present two orthogonal components: an output (projection) component and a selection component. Considering bitemporal databases, a query can retrieve information from different database histories, depending on the stored data's seletion. In this section an analysis is done of the relationship between the query components and the database histories.

4.1. Selection and Output

The *selection* component of a query is represented by a logical condition. Conditions for temporal queries can be stated on: (i) data values; and (ii) temporal information associated to data (time stamps) representing transaction and valid time.

Depending on the *selection* of a query, the queries can be classified in: *data selection queries*, *time selection queries* and *mixed output queries*.

A query is classified as a *data selection query* when the conditions are stated only on data values, as in the example "select the objects which are instances of the departments class referring to the employee named John". Note that when user-defined temporal data types are available, like dates or hours, the use of these in the selection condition represents also a data selection query. An example is the query "select the name of the employees that have date of birth Jan/1/1950". *Time selection queries* are those is which only the temporal information is analyzed as in the example: "select the enterprise's employees from January/1/82 to May/1/82". In the *mixed selection queries* both forms are used in the conditions, like in the query "select all the names of the employees of the Book department that where qualified to drive from January/1/82 to May/1/82".

Analyzing the queries output, different types of retrieved values can be identified: an objects (identified by his object identifier), complex objects, object's properties values, temporal information, and output sets composed of both times and values. Depending on the *output* of a query, we can classify queries in three main groups: *data output queries*, *time output queries* and *mixed output queries*.

The *data output query* is a query in which the selected information corresponds to stored data values. An example of a temporal data query is: "select all the employees of the Book department that where qualified to drive in the period from January/1/82 to May/1/82"; the result will be a set of employees. In *time output queries* temporal values are retrieved. They are abstracted from the time stamped information associated to the data (usually transaction and valid time). These queries can retrieve time points, intervals or durations. An example of a temporal data query is: "select all the periods in which any employee of the Book department was qualified to drive"; the result will be a set of intervals. *Mixed output queries* retrieve both values and times, like sets of values with their associated transaction or valid times. An example of this query type is the following query: "select the salary values and validity times for the employee named John between Jan/01/82 and May/01/82".

Analyzing the combination of these two components we note that a query with time selection and time output is the only one not possible - some data must be involved in the query. Depending on the pair selection/output, the possible queries are:

- *data selection, data output*
- *data selection, time output*
- *data selection, mixed output*
- *time selection, data output*
- *time selection, mixed output*
- *mixed selection, data output*
- *mixed selection, time output*
- *mixed selection, mixed output*

4.2. Relationship Between Query Components and Database Histories

The mapping of the feasible combinations of selection and output components of a query to the different types of database histories is presented in the table of Figure 2. This figure shows the combination of components which may be used to retrieve data from each one of these histories.

	Actual Instant Data	Past Instant Data	Past History Instant Data	Historical Data	Past Historical Data
Data Selection Data Output	A1	A2	A3	A4	A5
Data Selection Time Output	B1	B2	B3	B4	B5
Data Selection Mixed Output	C1	C2	C3	C4	C5
Time Selection Data Output	D1	D2	D3	D4	D5
Time Selection Mixed Output	E1	E2	E3	E4	E5
Mixed Selection Data Output	F1	F2	F3	F4	F5
Mixed Selection Time Output	G1	G2	G3	G4	G5
Mixed Selection Mixed Output	H1	H2	H3	H4	H5

Fig. 2. Query Components and Database Histories

Only the white cells represent possible queries. The only acceptable query to retrieve information from the *present instant data* is represented in cell A1 (assuming current time as the default time), and does not correspond to a temporal query. Cells D2 and F2 show the possible query component combinations for *past instant data* - a time selection is necessary to define the past moment and only data output can be retrieved. D2 can be used for a recovery of a past state - all the valid information of that past instant are retrieved. A similar combination is present for *past history instant data*, represented in the cells D3 and F3. For *historical data* all the query component combinations are possible. For *past historical data* again a time selection is needed to define the past moment; time output is possible since historical data is considered.

Using the case study of Section 2, examples of queries for the valid cells are:

A1: select the actual department of an employee earning more than $500 and named John;
A4: select all the departments in which the employee named John has been (or will be) employed while earning more than $500;
B4: select all the periods in which the employee named John was qualified to drive;
C4: select all the salaries and their correspondent validity times for the employee named John;
D2: select the names of all the employees on Jan/1/90;
D3: select the names of all the employees on Jan/1/90 as believed on Jan/1/90;
D4: select the name of all employees from Jan/1/82 to May/1/82;
D5: select the names of all employees from Jan/1/82 to May/1/82 as believed on Jan/1/93, using the valid values on Jan/1/93;
E4: select the salaries and their correspondent validity times of all the employees from Jan/1/90 to Jan/1/92;
E5: select the salaries and their correspondent validity times of all the employees from Jan/1/90 to Jan/1/92, as believed on Jan/1/92;
F2: select the department of employee named John on Dec/1/90;
F3: select the department of employee named John on Dec/1/90 as believed on Jan/1/91;
F4: select all the departments in which the employee named John has been employed from Jan/1/82 to Dec/1/90;
F5: select all the departments in which the employee named John has been employed as believed on Jan/1/93;
G4: select all the periods in which the employee named John was qualified to drive, during the period of Jan/1/82 through Jan/1/90;
G5: select all the periods in which the employee named John was qualified to drive, during the period of Jan/1/82 through Jan/1/90, as believed on Jan/1/93;
H4: select the salaries and their correspondent validity times for the employee named John from Jan/1/90 to Jan/1/92;
H5: select the salaries and their correspondent validity times for the employee named John from Jan/1/90 to Jan/1/92, as believed on Jan/1/92.

5. TF-ORM – A Temporal Object-Oriented Data Model

TF-ORM (Temporal Functionality in Objects with Roles Model) [9] is a temporal object-oriented data model. Objects behavior is represented in TF-ORM through the concept of role. An occurrence of an object can play different roles during its life time. As an example consider a person in an university. The person may be an employee for some years, then attend a course playing the role of a student and keeping during this period the role of employee. In this case the TF-ORM object class *person* will have defined two roles: *student* and *employee*. More than one role can be played simultaneously and object can have more than one instance of the same role at the same time.

A class is defined by a name and a set of roles. A role is defined by a name, a set of properties, a set of abstract states the role can assume while playing this role, a set of messages the role can receive or send, and a set of rules (state transition rules and integrity rules). Logic formulas can be associated to the state transition rules, acting as conditions that constrain the state transitions.

Each class presents a special role, the *base-role*, where the global properties inherited by all other roles and the initial characteristics of the other roles are described. Properties may be static (having the same value during all the instance lifetime) or dynamic (properties that may assume different values with time). Dynamic properties have two different time points associated with each value: the *transaction time*, corresponding to the moment when the information is introduced in the database, and the *valid time*, the time when that information starts to be valid in the real world. When defining a property, a domain is assigned to the properties values. Possible domains are: an object, a set of objects or a list of objects. TF-ORM presents a set of pre-defined classes to be used as domains in properties definition, called *data types*. Besides usual numeric data types (*real*, *integer*), a number of temporal data types are defined (like *date*, *hour*, *instant*, *semester*). Time is modeled as varying in a discrete form.

6. Temporal Queries in TF-ORM

In this section a query language for the TF-ORM data model is presented. The TF-ORM data model associates to each property the transaction and the valid time, corresponding to a bitemporal database. Therefore each database data is represented by a triple (*data value x transaction time instant x valid time instant*). The transaction time is defined by the system; the valid time is given by the user. When the valid time is not defined, the system uses the same time as the transaction time. The valid time can be the same as the transaction time, previous or after this one.

The TF-ORM query language has the general form of a SQL query. Most of the SQL temporal extensions keep the basic SQL structure {SELECT, FROM, WHERE}, adding temporal conditions to the *SearchClause* [6, 11, 14, 20]. In [17] a TSQL is defined, adding a new clause for conditional expressions evaluating temporal predicates, a WHEN clause. Rose and Segev [19] also add this temporal clause to their TOOSQL; Cheng and Gadia [3] use a WHILE in place of the WHEN clause.

In the TF-ORM query language the two clauses (WHERE and WHEN) are used in an independent way, as in TQuel. The chosen option defines the retrieval universe. Using the WHERE clause, the information is searched in the database snapshot of the considered instant; this class of query corresponds to a normal, non historical, SQL query. The WHEN clause enlarges this universe to all the defined information of this considered history, including the past and the future defined data.

The following two structures are defined in the TF-ORM query language for snapshots and for historical queries:

SELECT *TargetClause*
FROM *ObjectIdentificationClause*
WHERE *SearchClause*
[**AS ON** *TemporalInstantClause*]

SELECT *TargetClause*
FROM *ObjectIdentificationClause*
WHEN *SearchClause*
[**AS ON** *TemporalInstantClause*]

The basic difference between the two structures is the choice between the WHERE and the WHEN clauses. When only the three clauses {SELECT, FROM, WHERE} are used, the present valid information is retrieved – present valid information about the current database valid history. The form {SELECT, FROM, WHEN} retrieves all the defined information of the current history - the present, the past and the future information. The *TemporalInstantClause* of the AS ON clause fixes the date where the history is to be retrieved.

The *TargetClause* defines the query's output component, identifying which parts of the object shall be shown by the query, or which temporal date or period shall be retrieved. When property values are required, it can be represented by a property name, a list of property names (output component of the query), or the symbol "*" representing that all the properties of the retrieved object are required. Properties whose domains are class names can not be used. The retrieved temporal information can be: (i) one or more dates, when using DATE after the SELECT; or (ii) one or more temporal periods (intervals), when using PERIOD.

The selection component is defined by the *ObjectIdentificationClause* and the *SearchClause*, where conditions that must be satisfied by the retrieved values are stated. The *ObjectIdentificationClause* specifies the domain of values to be analyzed, identifying the class and the corresponding role considered in the query. Several instances of a given class (objects) can be defined. Each object can present several instances of each of its roles. It may be necessary to identify which one of the class intances and role instances may be considered in the query, otherwise all the instances will be considered. When a query is to be executed only on one role of a class, this role's name shall be qualified by the corresponding class name because different classes may present equal role names. The role name can be used by default if all the role names of all the classes involved in the query are different.

The *SearchClause* specifies which instances of objects qualify for the query and the temporal constraints that identify dates or periods of past information to be considered in the retrieval. It is expressed by a first order temporal logic language formula [10]. The symbols to be used in the logic language formulas are: (i) classical (non-temporal) query clauses and operators, like property names, arithmetic values, character strings values, arithmetical operators, logical operators, predicates and functions; and (ii) temporal components. The defined temporal components are (i) temporal values, like time instants values, temporal interval values, temporal span values and temporal predicates and functions; (ii) the two temporal selection indicators "PERIOD in [<date>, <date>]", defining the period of historical data to be analyzed, and "DATE = <date>", defining a date to be used as selection; and (iii) a set of temporal operators, including "sometime past", "immediately past", "always past", "sometime future", "immediately future", "always future", "since", "until", "before" and "after".

The *TemporalInstantClause* fixes the date where the history is to be retrieved. This date can be defined explicitly, as in the previous examples, or through a temporal predicate.

7. TF-ORM Query Language Examples

In this section we ilustrate how the TF-ORM query language can be used to express some of the example queries presented in Sect. 4.3. Let us first consider query A1 (select the current department of an employee earning more than $500 and named John):

```
SELECT dept
FROM Person.Employee
WHERE name = "John" and salary > 500
```

The query will consider all the instances of the class *person* and, for each one of these, all the instances of role *employee*. Consider now the same query, just changing to the WHEN clause:

```
SELECT dept
FROM Person.Employee
WHEN ( name = "John" or sometime past name = "John") and salary > 500
```

In this query (A4) not only the present values are analyzed, but also all the past and future defined values. The query will retrieve all the names of departments in which the employee named John worked (or will work) with a salary bigger than US$ 500. The evolution of the database shall also be considered in the query. Dynamic properties can change their values as time passes. So, for example, the query "select the departments of the employee named John" shall consider the possibility that this name changed; it shall be expressed as "select the department of the employee that now has the name of John or that in some time in the past had the name of John".

The query example considering historical data with mixed selection and time output (G4 - "select all the periods in which the employee named John was qualified to drive, during the period of Jan/1/82 through Jan/1/90") may be expressed as follows:

```
SELECT PERIOD
FROM Person.Employee
WHEN (name = "John" or sometime past name = "John")
        and skill contains "drive" and PERIOD in [01/01/82, 12/01/90]
```

The AS ON clause is used when the query retrieves values from past historical data. As an example consider the following query (G5 - "select all the periods in which the employee named John was qualified to drive, during the period of Jan/1/82 through Jan/1/90, as believed on Jan/1/93"):

```
SELECT PERIOD
FROM Person.Employee
WHEN (name = "John" or sometime past name = "John")
        and skill contains "drive" and PERIOD in [01/01/82, 12/01/90]
AS ON 01/01/93
```

8. Conclusions

TF-ORM is a temporal object-oriented data model. This data model considers both the transaction and the valid time for the information time stamps. The implementation of applications specified using this data model requires the existence of a bitemporal database. This paper defines a query language for TF-ORM, based on SQL. Special attention is given to the temporal queries. Information belonging to different data histories can be retrieved. Much of the power of this model is due to the dynamic representation allowed by the roles.

Future work will concentrate on some of the aspects concerning the retrieval of temporal information about the evolution of objects. For instance, information about the sequences of activation of roles, and, if objects are allowed to migrate from one class to another, information about temporal evolution of an object as an instance of different classes. The retrieval of temporal information of several related objects will also be investigated, to answer queries such as "which are the employees who ever earned more than their current manager". Answering such queries requires the ability of dealing in the query language with different objects at the same time. Until now, it is only possible to deal with information related to only one set of objects and the objects they refer through navigation through attributes.

References

[1] ARAPIS, C. Specifying object life-cycles. D.TSICHRITZIS (ed.) *Object Management*. Genève: Universitè de Genève, 1990. p.197-225.

[2] CAREY, M.J.; DEWITT, D.J.; VANDENBERG, S.L. A Data Model and Query Language for EXODUS. *ACM SIGMOD Record*, v.17, n.3, p.413-23, Sept. 1988.

[3] CHENG, T.S.; GADIA, Shashi K. An Object-oriented model for temporal databases. *Proceedings* of the International Workshop on an Infrastructure for Temporal Databases, Arlington, Texas, June 14-16, 1993. p.N-1-N-19.

[4] CLIFFORD, J.; CROKER, A. Objects in time. *Data Engineering*, v.11, n.4, p.11-18, Dec. 1988.

[5] DATE, C. *Introduction to standard SQL*. Paris: InterEditions, 1987. 239p.

[6] DAYAL, U.; WUU, G.T.J. Extending existing DBMSs to manage temporal data: an object-oriented approach. *Proceedings* of the International Workshop on an Infrastructure for Temporal Databases, Arlington, Texas, June 14-16, 1993. p.J-1-J-8.

[7] De ANTONELLIS, V.; PERNICI, B.; SAMARATI, P. F-ORM Method: a F-ORM Methodology for reusing specifications. In: F.V. Assche; B. Moulin; C. Rolland (eds.) *Object Oriented Approach in Information Systems*. Amsterdam: North-Holland, 1991. p.117-35.

[8] DEUX, 0. et al. The O2 System. *Communications of the ACM*, New York, v.34, n.10, p.34-48, Oct.1991

[9] EDELWEISS, N.; OLIVEIRA, J.P.M. de; PERNICI, B. An Object-Oriented Temporal Model. *Proceedings* of the 5th International Conference on Advanced Information Systems Engineering (CAISE'93), Paris, 8-11 June, 1993. p.397-415. (Lecture Notes in Computer Science, n.685).

[10] EDELWEISS, N.; OLIVEIRA, J.P.M.de; CASTILHO, J.M.V.de. A Temporal Logic Language for Temporal Conditions Definition. *Proceedings* of the 13th. International Conference of the Chilean Computer Science Society, La Serena, Chile, Oct. 14-16, 1993. p.163-178.

[11] GABBAY, D.; McBRIEN, P. Temporal logic and historical databases. *Proceedings* of the 17th. International Conference on Very Large Databases, Barcelona, Sept. 1991. p.423-430.

[12] GREENSPAN, S.J.; BORGIDA, A.; MYLOPOULOS, J. A Requirements modeling language and its logic. In: M.L.BRODIE; J.MYLOPOULOS (eds.) *On Knowledge Base Systems*. New York: Springer-Verlag, 1986. p.471-502.

[13] JENSEN, C.S. et al. (eds.) The TSQL Benchmark. *Proceedings* of the International Workshop on an Infrastructure for Temporal Databases, Arlington, Texas, June 14-16, 1993. p.QQ-1-QQ-18.

[14] KÄFER, W.; SCHÖNING, H. Realizing a temporal complex-object data model. *Proceedings* of the ACM SIGMOD International Conference on Management of Data, San Diego, June 2-5, 1992. p.266-275.

[15] LOUCOPOULOS, P.; THEODOULIDIS, B.; PANTAZIS, D. Business rules modelling: conceptual modelling and object-oriented specifications. In: F.V.ASSCHE; B.MOULIN; C.ROLLAND (eds.) *Object Oriented Approach in Information Systems*. Amsterdam: North-Holland, 1991. p.323-342.

[16] MYLOPOULOS, J. et al. Telos: representing knowledge about Information Systems. *ACM Transactions on Information Systems*, v.8, n.4, p.325-62, Oct. 1990.

[17] NAVATHE, S.B.; AHMED, R. TSQL: A Language interface for history databases. In: C.ROLLAND; F.BODART; M.LEONARD (eds.) *Temporal Aspects in Information Systems*. Amsterdam: North-Holland, 1988. p.109-122.

[18] PISSINOU, N.; MAKKI, K.; YESHA, Y. Research perspectives on time in object databases. *Proceedings* of the International Workshop on an Infrastructure for Temporal Databases, Arlington, Texas, June 14-16, 1993. p.Y-1-Y-9.

[19] ROSE, E.; SEGEV, A. *TOOSQL - A Temporal object-oriented query language*. Berkeley: The University of California and Information and Computing Science Division, Mar. 1993. (Tech. Rep. LBL-33855).

[20] SARDA, N.L. Extensions to SQL for historical databases. *IEEE Transaction on Knowledge and Data Engineering*, v.2, n.2, p. 220-230, June 1990.

[21] SERNADAS, C. et al. In-the-large object-oriented design of information systems. In: F.V.ASSCHE; B.MOULIN; C.ROLLAND (eds.) *Object Oriented Approach in Information Systems*. Amsterdam: North-Holland, 1991. p.209-232.

[22] SNODGRASS, R.; AHN, I. A Taxonomy of time in databases. *Proceedings* of the ACM SIGMOD International Conference on Management of Data, Texas, May 28-31, 1985. p.236-46.

[23] SNODGRASS, R. The Temporal query language TQuel. *ACM Transactions on Database Systems*, v.12, n.2, p.247-298, June 1987.

[24] STONEBRAKER, M. et al. The Design and implementation of INGRES. *Transactions on Database Systems*, v.1, n.3, p.189-222, Sept. 1976.

[25] STONEBRAKER, M.; ROWE, L.A. The Design of POSTGRES. *ACM SIGMOD*, 1986. p.340-55.

[26] SU, S.Y.W.; CHEN, H.-H.M. Modeling and management of temporal data in object-oriented knowledge bases. *Proceedings* of the International Workshop on an Infrastructure for Temporal Databases, Arlington, Texas, June 14-16, 1993. p.HH-1-HH-18.

[27] WUDA, G.; DAYAL, U. A Uniform model for temporal object-oriented databases. *Proceedings* of the 8th. IEEE Data Engineering Conference, 1992.

A Framework for Developing Temporal Databases

S. Kokkotos and C.D. Spyropoulos
N.C.S.R. "Demokritos"
153 10 Aghia Paraskevi,Greece

TEL: + 30 1 6510310
FAX: + 30 1 6532175
e-mail: stavros@iit.nrcps.ariadne-t.gr
costass@iit.nrcps.ariadne-t.gr

ABSTRACT

Computerised information systems tend to become more sophisticated and complicated. In many application domains, information systems must manage data that change over time, or data that reflect the use of temporal attributes. For these reasons the domain of temporal databases is an active research field. In this paper we present TGDB, a framework for developing temporal database systems that manage both valid and transaction time as well as any kind of user defined time. TGDB offers to the user a relational-like view of the tables and fields, but it is not based on the relational model. Instead it is based on the TGS graph system for time management. TGS combines a very good performance with temporal data management independent from application or domain. The query language of TGDB is an extension of SQL.

KEY WORDS:

Temporal Databases, Time Graph, Temporal Data, Valid Time, Transaction Time

1 Introduction

Time is one of the most important but overlooked attributes of the real world events. Every activity deals directly or indirectly with time. Even if humans tend to forget the importance of time because it is inherent to any activity, computerised systems must explicitly manage the temporal aspect of information. Lately, information systems have become more complicated and sophisticated. Many of these systems deal with domains with inherent need for time management, such as banking, medical, accounting and reservation systems. The trend today is to use a relational SQL-supporting large DBMS. The existing Relational DBMSs can store and retrieve time as another field type, but this method time is very far from the ideal situation, because the management of the time-related information is application dependent. We need a DBMS that manages the temporal attributes not as another type of data fields but as the basis for the organisation of the stored information.

Snodgrass and Ahn in [19] present a categorisation of databases based on the use of time. The existing relational DBMSs, which support only user-defined time, are what Snodgrass and Ahn call snapshot databases. Except from user-defined time a DBMS may use time in two other ways: As transaction time, meaning the recording time of the information in the database, and as valid time, meaning the time that the information becomes valid in the real world. For example, in a ticket reservation system, a flight ticket is stamped with valid time 20 March 1994 10:00, transaction time 10 March 1994 12:23, and user defined time 20 June 1994, meaning that the ticked was issued at 10 March, the associated flight is scheduled for 10:00 of 20 March, while the customer may cancel this flight and use the ticket in a similar flight until 20 June 1994. Temporal databases must support all these time types.

During the last decade a plethora of ideas and implementations for temporal databases have appeared [5,13,16,21]. Most of these attempts are theoretical, aiming at the description of a new model for temporal databases [4,12,14,15,17,18]. Excellent presentations and evaluations of the most well known temporal algebras are presented in [16]. Most of the theoretical models have not been implemented or the implementations are inefficient prototypes. Some exceptions exist such as the TQuel extension of QUEL by Snodgrass [20], the implementation of temporal database by Ahn and Snodgrass[1,2] and the indexing method by Gunadhi and Segev [6].

In this paper we present a framework for the development of a temporal database system, supporting valid, transaction as well as any type of user defined time. The management of time is independent from the application that uses the database. The proposed framework eliminates the duplication of data and time values, without compromising the performance. It supports rules that calculate the values of specific fields. These rules differ from the triggers or procedures found in existing DBMSs, because they permit direct or indirect recursion with an unlimited call depth. An earlier version of this framework has been proposed for solving the arrears calculation payroll problems of the Greek public sector [7]. We call the proposed framework Time Graph DataBase (TGDB), because it is based on the Time Graph System kernel (TGS) for time management [9,11]. TGDB is not an extension of the relational model, but instead uses the underlying graph-based structure of TGS. The whole system has been implemented as a prototype in Prolog. The query language of TGDB is an extension of SQL.

In chapter 2 we briefly present the TGS system. In chapter 3 we present the TGDB structure while in chapter 4 we briefly describe the TGDB query language. Finally in chapter 5 we propose further improvements and discussion topics.

2 The Time Graph System Kernel

The TGS Kernel is an application independent, graph-based system for time management. We call temporal data the data that contain time attributes. The main idea behind TGS is to store and manage only the time attributes of temporal data, and to connect the time attributes with the data with arcs. TGS stores the recorded time attributes into a graph structure called the Time Graph. Figure 1 displays an example of a Time Graph instance.

TGS handles both absolute and relative temporal data. The time attributes of the absolute temporal data are defined using absolute time units, e.g. "5 March 1994, 10:00". The time attributes of relative temporal data are defined as temporal distances from other temporal data, e.g. "14 hours after event 'E'". TGS represents and manages both certain and uncertain temporal data. For the certain temporal data we know the exact time moment the data are stamped with, while for the uncertain we know an uncertainty time interval, during which the stamp of the data must lie. Another important feature of TGS is that it categorises the temporal attributes into independent categories, called time lines. The application defines and interprets the semantics of each time line.

The time attributes are stored into time nodes. The time nodes record the certain or uncertain time stamps of the temporal data. For this reason there exist two types of time nodes: certain and uncertain. If two or more pieces of temporal data are stamped by the same time attributes, then TGS stores these attributes into the same time node, and connects the time node to all the related data. In figure 1 there exist 4 certain time nodes (1, 3, 4, 7) and 3 uncertain time nodes (2, 5, 6). We have omitted the time stamps in order to make the figure more readable. The reader can assume that each certain time node contains a time point, while each uncertain contains a time interval. For example time node 1 may contain the time point {5 April 1994, 12:35}, while time node 2 may contain the interval {6 April 1994,10:00-6 April 1994,15:00}. Reference arcs connect the temporal data with the time nodes. In figure 1 the reference arcs are labelled as rn(m), where n is the identification of the arc while m is the time line to which it belongs. Time node 1 has 3 connected reference arcs labelled r1(1), r2(1), r3(2). More than one reference arcs may lead to the same piece of temporal data. The application must interpret the semantics of these multiple links.

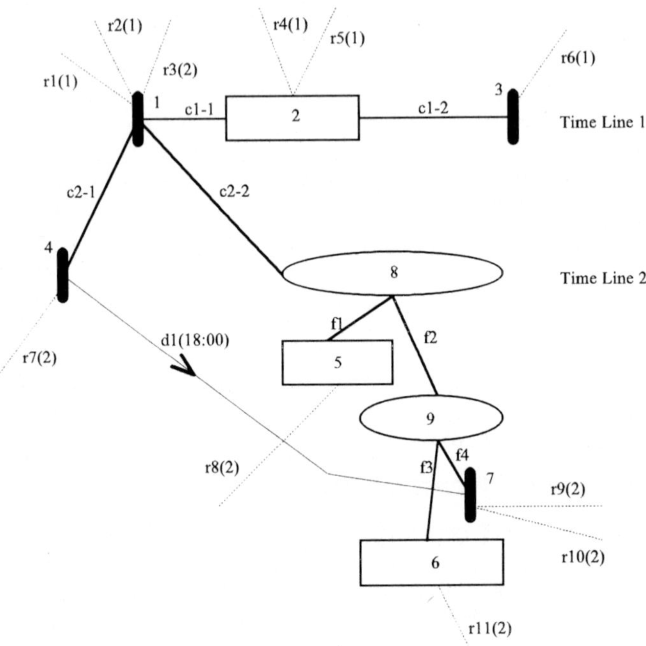

Fig. 1. A Time Graph Instance

TGS organises the time nodes into time lines, using the chain arcs. Each time line represents a time category. The interpretation of the time line semantics must be defined by the application that uses TGDB. In figure 1 there exist 2 time lines. As an example we can assume that line 1 records valid and line 2 transaction time. The chain arcs are labelled cn-m, where n is the time line label and m the identification of the arc within the time line. A time node may belong to more than one time lines. In figure 1 the time node 1 belongs to both time lines 1 and 2. The reference arcs r1(1) and r2(1) belong to time line 1, while the arc r3(2) belongs to time line 2.

The uncertain time nodes cause some irregularities to the ordering of the time nodes, because they may overlap with other nodes. For this reason TGS organises each set of overlapping time nodes into parent-left-right ordered binary trees. Family arcs connect the nodes in a tree. Time node 8 in figure 1 is the root of such a tree. We call this time node an artificial time node because it does not correspond to any temporal data, but exists simply to serve as the root of the tree. Another artificial time node is the one labelled 9, which serves as root of a subtree of the previous tree. The family arcs of the tree of figure 1 are labelled fn, where n is the identification of the arc. Therefore, only non-overlapping time nodes are chained in a time line. The overlapping time nodes belong to trees. This structure helps the indexing method of TGS to achieve a very good performance during retrieval.

TGS automatically converts the relative temporal data to absolute but it also stores the relative information. This simultaneous recording enables TGS to retrieve its data using absolute time attributes, while it retains the relative information. Dependency arcs store the relative information. In figure 1 the arc labelled d1 is a dependency arc. The arrow and the (18:00) after the label mean that the time node 7 is 18 hours after time node 4.

We consider the data structures that the TGS arcs create as independent from one another. In figure 1 we consider the tree, with root the time node 8, to be a binary tree. The arc d1 does not belong to this tree but to another structure, the dependency chain.

TGS uses an indexing scheme that enables it to access the time nodes and the temporal data with performance almost independent from the size of the Time Graph and the number of temporal data connected to it [9,10,11]. This indexing scheme uses an easily maintained structure of index nodes and index arcs. It is beyond the scope of the present paper to describe the indexing method. For the same reason we have not drawn the index nodes and index arcs in figure 1. The TGS indexing scheme is not necessary if TGS is to be implemented over a DBMS. In this case TGS can use the indexing methodology of the DBMS.

TGS has been implemented as a prototype in Prolog. It has already been used for the implementation of a resource management system and a scheduling system [10,22].

3 Description of the Time Graph DataBase

In this chapter we describe the structure of the TGDB. We define four logical modules in the database: the data definition module, the domain module, the data management module and the rule module. We will describe every module in the following sections. The examples in the following sections refer to figure 2. In figure 2 we display one table with one tuple. TGDB is linked to TGS with arcs. These arcs, viewed from TGDB, define the transaction, valid and user-defined times of the TGDB data. From the TGS point of view the connecting arcs are simple reference arcs.

3.1 The Data Definition Module

The data definition module consists from a number of nodes called table nodes. Each of these nodes contains the definition of a table. In figure 2 the set of 5 rectangles, at the top-left corner, is the table node of the relation "Customers". The topmost rectangle contains the name of the table. The other four rectangles contain information about the fields of the table such as name, the primary key, secondary keys, default values, etc. In figure 2 the field "Name" is defined as primary key, while there are no secondary keys.

From each table node, arcs lead to the TGS time lines "Data Definition Transaction Time Line" and "Data Definition Valid Time Line". TGDB automatically inserts the transaction time, which defines the table creation and deletion date and time. The valid time line defines the validity period of the table, i.e. the period during which the table fields have meaning. In figure 2 the dotted arcs lead to valid time lines, while the dashed arcs lead to transaction time lines. The fields of the table "Customers" have meaning between 1/1/85 and today, but the table actually exists in the system from 1/2/85 (retroactive insertion).

Upon deletion of a table definition TGDB adds another arc that connects the table node with the valid time line and defines the end of the validity period of the table. TGDB considers all time intervals, defined by pairs of arcs, as [closed,open). If two arcs connect a table node with the valid time line, then the table is valid only during the time interval between the two arcs. If two arcs connect a table node with the transaction time line, then the table definition has been "deleted" from the database (i.e. it can be reached only for queries that deal with the past). Deletion in a temporal database means that the deleted item is marked as non existent, while it still exists physically in the database. The modification of a table definition means the "deletion" of the old definition and the insertion of a new one, with start of validity period the end of the validity period of the old (deleted) table node.

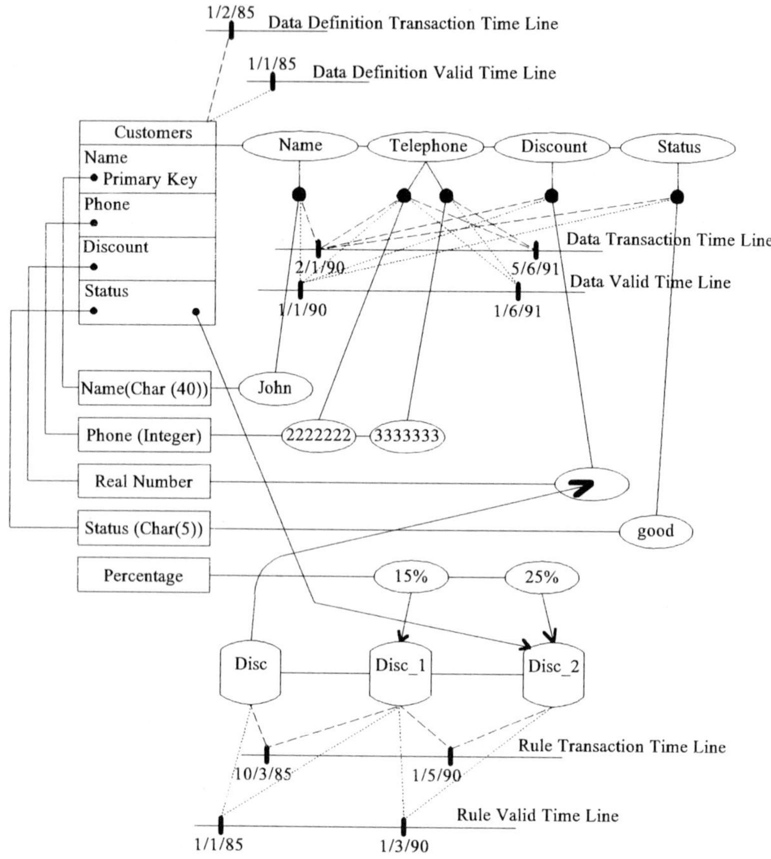

Fig. 2. Instance of a temporal database with one table and one tuple.

Apart from the valid and transaction time lines, the table nodes may connect to any number of user-defined time lines. In figure 2, we could connect the table node "Customers" to another time line, specifying the due time for a customer evaluation.

3.2 The Domain Module

The domain module consists of domain and value nodes. The value nodes are grouped into value chains. In figure 2, the domain nodes are in the middle-left of the picture (5 separate rectangles), while the value nodes are in the centre of the picture.

Arcs connect the table nodes with the domain nodes, defining the data types of the table fields. In figure 2 the four arcs, which connect the fields of the table node "Customers" with the domain nodes, define that the field "Name" is of type char(40), the field "Telephone" is an integer, the field "Discount" is a real number, while the field "Status" is Char(5).

Each of the domain nodes is connected to its value nodes. Arcs connect the value nodes creating a domain chain, which is sorted according to the user's requirements. In figure 2 we display alphanumerically sorted domain chains. When the user inserts a value in a field, TGDB checks the relevant domain and inserts a new value node in the appropriate position, if this value does not exist. In figure 2 the domain "Name" has only one value node for the value "John", while the domain "Telephone" has two values "2222222" and "3333333". The domain "Real Number" contains a value node without a value. This value is computed by a rule. We will describe the rules in section 3.4.

The domain and value nodes do not need to connect to the Time Graph, because the values are inserted or deleted independently from time.

3.3 The Data Management Module

The data management module consists of field nodes and data nodes. The field nodes are grouped in tuple chains. For each tuple, in the database, TGDB creates a tuple chain. A tuple chain consists of as many nodes as fields exist in the table. In figure 2 there exists one tuple chain for the table "Customers". This tuple chain consists of four field nodes, one for each field of the table. The field nodes are the ellipses at the top-right of the picture.

For each field node there exist one or more data nodes. For each field value change, TGDB creates a new data node, and connects it to the field node. In figure 2 the field "Telephone" has two data nodes. The value of this field changed from "2222222" to "3333333" at 5/6/91. An arc leads from each data node to a value node of the appropriate domain, defining the value assigned to the field. For example in figure 2 the data node of the field "Name" is connected to the value node "John", giving this value to its field.

Since the data nodes record actual changes in field values it is necessary to connect them with time. Each data node connects with one or two arcs to each of the two TGS time lines named "Data Transaction Time Line" and "Data Valid Time Line". These arcs define the existence and the validity period of the field value. If only one arc leads to the transaction time line then the value exists till now into the database. If only one arc leads to the valid time line then the value has still meaning.

In figure 2, the two data nodes of the "Telephone" field have existence periods [2/1/90-5/6/91) and [5/6/91-now] respectively. Their validity periods are [1/1/90-1/6/91) and [1/6/91-now]. This situation can be described as: "The customer's telephone was 2222222 from 1/1/90 till 1/6/91 when it changed to 3333333. The first telephone value was recorded at 2/1/90. The change of the telephone was recorded at 5/6/91 (retroactive updates)".

From the above discussion it is obvious that nothing is ever deleted from the database. Every value continues to exist but the database considers it as non-existent or non-valid, referring to the appropriate time line.

The data nodes may connect to any number of user defined time lines with any number of arcs. The application must interpret the meaning of these arcs. In figure 2 we could have another time line called "Review Time Line" and connect to it the "Name" data arc. Each connection could mean that a review of the customer's transactions is due at this time.

3.4 The Rule Module

The rule module consists of rule and subrule nodes. These nodes are at the bottom of figure 2. The rule and subrule nodes are organised into rule chains. A rule chain starts with the rule node and continues with all the subrules of this rule. In figure 2 we have one rule chain for the rule "Disc" This rule has 2 subrules labelled "Disc_1" and "Disc_2". The rule nodes record general information about the rule, such as author, scope, etc. The subrule nodes record the actual rule definition statements. When a rule is first inserted into the database it has only one subrule. TGDB creates a subrule node each time the rule changes.

Each rule or subrule node connects with one or two arcs to each of the two TGS time lines, called "Rule Transaction Time Line" and "Rule Valid Time Line". These time lines define the existence and validity period of the rule or subrule. In figure 2, the two subrules of the "Disc" rule have existence periods [10/3/85-1/5/90) and [1/5/90-now] respectively. Their validity periods are [1/1/85-1/3/90) and [1/3/90-now] respectively. This situation can be described as: "Rule 'Disc' has the definition 'Disc_1' from 1/1/85 till 1/3/90 when it changed to the definition 'Disc_2'. Ssubrule 'Disc_1' was recorded at 10/3/85. The definition change was recorded at 1/5/90 (retroactive update)".

Rule and subrule nodes can connect to any number of user defined time lines with any number of arcs. The application must interpret the meaning of these connections.

Some subrules have arguments. These arguments may be values of fields of a table. The arguments are indicated by arcs that start from the table node and lead to the subrule node. In figure 2 an arc connects the "Status" field of the table node "Customers" with the subrule node "Disc_2", defining the "Status" field of the current tuple as an argument of the subrule. Other arguments may be defined by arcs that connect value nodes and subrule nodes. The two subrules of rule "Disc" have as arguments two different values of the domain "Percentage".

Starting from the rule nodes, arcs lead to value nodes. These arcs define that the indicated value nodes take their value from the rule. In figure 2 the value node of the domain "Real Number" takes its value from rule "Disc". TGDB computes the value of the field "Discount", which is connected with the domain "Real Number", by firing the rule "Disc".

The body of the subrules is defined in a C-like language. An example of this language for subrules "Disc_1" and "Disc_2" is as follows:

```
Disc_1(X)
    { return(X) }
```

```
Disc_2(X,Customers.Status)
    { if(Customers.Status == "good") return(X)
      else return(X / 2) }
```

The definition of Disc_1 assigns 15% as discount percentage. The definition for Disc_2 assigns 25% as discount percentage if the customer is good else it assigns 12.5%.

The tuple displayed in figure 2, in relational form is represented as:

Name	*Telephone*	*Discount*	*Status*	*Valid Time*	*Transaction Time*
John	2222222	Disc_1(15%)	good	1/1/90-1/3/90	2/1/90-1/5/90
John	2222222	Disc_2(25%,Status)	good	1/3/90-1/6/91	1/5/90-5/6/91
John	3333333	Disc_2(25%,Status)	good	1/6/91-	5/6/91-

The actual valid and transaction intervals of the tuple are a combination of the respective intervals of the tuple and the rule. TGDB offers the possibility to assign time attributes to each field, while most temporal databases time-stamp the whole tuple. TGS handles the time-related data retrieval, offering a very good performance. Furthermore TGDB records every value only once.

3.5 Indexing Scheme

TGDB uses two indexing schemes: for the time attributes it uses the inherent indexing method of TGS, which offers a retrieval performance independent from the number of stored data. Using this indexing scheme we can retrieve the values of any field, at any validity or existence interval. For the non-temporal attributes TGDB uses a B+Tree indexing method on the value nodes.

4 The TGDB Query Language

Even if TGDB is not based on the relational model the user views his data as relational tables. The TGDB query language is an SQL extension. In order to use the time attributes we introduce 3 field attributes: VALID, TRANSACTION and USERTIME. Each of these attributes owns 3 methods: INTERVAL, START and END. Furthermore we introduce the 13 interval operators defined by Allen [3]: E (equals), B (before), A (after), O (overlaps), OD (overlapped by), M (meets), MD (met by), S (starts), SD (started by), F (finishes), FD (finished by), I (includes) and ID (included by).

The statement "CREATE TIME LINE x" creates the new user defined time line "x".

The field attributes, methods and operators are used in the *SELECT* SQL statement:

```
SELECT Name FROM Customers
    WHERE  Discount > 18%
       AND  Name.VALID.INTERVAL ID (1/5/90,15/7/92)
       AND  Name.TRANSACTION.START B 31/12/91
       AND  Status.USERTIME(Review).END A 1/1/92;
```

This statement will retrieve the names of the customers that have a discount of more than 18%, their validity interval lies inside the interval 1/5/90-15/7/92, they were inserted into the database before 31/12/91 and they have a review after 1/1/92.

An example of an INSERT statement is:

```
INSERT INTO Customers
      VALUES("George", 5556789, RULE.Disc, "good", VALID.START(1/5/92),
                    USERTIME(Review).START(1/1/93));
```

This statement inserts into the database the customer George with telephone number 5556789 and good status. The discount is hooked to the rule Disc. TGDB inserts automatically the transaction time. The customer's validity starts from 1/5/92. He has a connection with the Review time line at 1/1/93.

Changes to the database, either by use of the INSERT command or by the DELETE or UPDATE commands, do not actually delete data from the database, but merely change their valid and transaction times.

The following statement inserts a new rule in the database:

```
CREATE RULE xxx DATA (information) SUBRULE (description)
      VALID.START(valid);
```

The rule xxx is created, if it does not exist, with general information (author, etc.) described by "information" and validity starting from "valid". The subrule has definition "description". If the rule xxx exists, then the new subrule is added to its chain. For example the statement for inserting the "Disc_2" subrule into figure 2 is:

```
CREATE RULE Disc SUBRULE(Disc_2(X,Customers.Status)
                        { if(Customers.Status == "good") return(X) else return(X / 2) })
     VALID.START(1/3/90);
```

TGDB automatically inserts the end of the validity period of the subrule "Disc_1".

5 Conclusions

We presented TGDB, a framework for the implementation of a temporal database system, which is not directly based on the relational model. The proposed framework supports valid, transaction and user defined time. It manages the temporal attributes differently from the other data. The major differences from existing relational temporal databases are:

- TGDB stores every value only once, with multiple arcs to the fields that have this value. The conventional databases duplicate the values of fields with the same value.
- TGDB supports rules with unlimited call and recursion depth. Furthermore these rules may be valid or exist in the database for specific periods of time. According to our knowledge there exists no other database framework that supports this kind of rules.
- TGDB supports table definitions that have a user defined validity or existence period, so that it extends the time attributes to the data definition as well.

The advantage of using a graph-based methodology is that it can be implemented almost anywhere, using various tools and programming languages. TGDB may even be implemented over a relational DBMS, taking advantage of all the facilities offered by a DBMS.

The user of TGDB views the data as if the database was a relative one. The query language is an extension of SQL that allows the user to retrieve data according to their valid or transaction time, or according to any type of user defined time.

TGDB has been implemented as a prototype in Prolog. Currently an implementation over a relational DBMS is examined [8]. For this implementation we examine various implementation issues, such as concurrency control, transaction management, consistency, optimisation etc. When the system is completed we will evaluate its performance against other existing temporal database systems. Furthermore the issues of time-dependent table definitions are re-examined in depth.

The idea of a deductive temporal database is considered as a natural continuation of TGDB. Towards this we plan to extend the rule idea to support inheritance and deduction. Another extension under consideration is the adaptation of TGDB to support spatial as well as temporal data. This adaptation requires the existence of time lines that record spatial co-ordinates. A temporal-spatial database will be very useful in the GIS domain.

References

1. Ahn I. "Towards an Implementation of Database Management Systems with Temporal Support", Proceedings of the 2nd International Conference on Data Engineering, IEEE, pp.374-381, 1986.

2. Ahn I., Snodgrass R. "Partitioned Storage for Temporal Databases", Information Systems, Vol.13, No.4, pp.369-391, 1988.
3. Allen J.F. "Maintaining Knowledge about Temporal Intervals", Communications of the ACM, Vol.26, No.11, pp.832-843, 1983.
4. Ariav G. "A Temporally Oriented Data Model", ACM Transactions on Database Systems, Vol.11, No.4, pp.499-527, 1986.
5. Ariav G. "Design Requirements for Temporally Oriented Information Systems", Proceedings of the IFIP Working Conference on Temporal Aspects in Information Systems, France, pp.3-16, May 1987.
6. Gunadhi H., Segev A. "Efficient Indexing Methods for Temporal Relations", IEEE Trans. on Knowledge and Data Engineering, Vol.5, No.2, pp.496-509, June 1993.
7. Ioannidis E.V., Kokkotos S., Spyropoulos C.D. "A Temporal Framework for Managing Retroactive and Delayed Updates: An Application to the Payroll Information System of the Greek Public Sector", European Journal of Information Systems, Vol.2, No.2, pp.149-154, Apr. 1993.
8. Ioannidis E.V., Spyropoulos C.D., Panayiotopoulos T., Skordalakis E. "TIMERx, a Kernel for Managing Temporal References on a RDBMS", Working Paper, N.C.S.R. "Demokritos".
9. Kokkotos S., Spyropoulos C.D. "TGS: A Kernel Graph System for Time Management", Technical Report DEMO 90/6, N.C.S.R. "Demokritos", June 1990.
10. Kokkotos S., Spyropoulos C.D. "RASS: A ReActive Scheduling System Based on the TGS Kernel", Proceedings of the AIENG-90 Conference, Boston, MA, pp.523-533, July 1990.
11. Kokkotos S. "Independent Temporal Data Management for Information Systems", Ph.D. Thesis, Dept. of Electrical Engineering and Computer Engineering, National Technical Univ. of Athens, 1992, (in greek).
12. Lorentzos N., Johnson R.G. "Extending Relational Algebra to Manipulate Temporal Data", Information Systems,Vol.13, No.3, pp.289-296, 1988.
13. McKenzie E. "Bibliography: Temporal Databases", ACM SIGMOD RECORD, Vol.15, No.4, pp.40-52, 1986.
14. McKenzie E., Snodgrass R, "Extending the Relational Algebra to Support Transaction Time", Proceedings of the ACM SIGMOD International Conference on Management of Data, San Fransisco CA, pp.467-479, May 1987.
15. McKenzie E., Snodgrass R. "Supporting Valid Time in a Historical Relational Algebra: Proofs and Extensions, Technical Report TR 91-15, Dept. of Computer Science, Univ. of Arizona, 1991.
16. McKenzie E., Snodgrass R. "Evaluation of Relational Algebras Incorporating the Time Dimension in Databases", ACM Computing Surveys, Vol.23, No.4, pp.501-543, Dec. 1991.
17. Navathe S.B., Ahmed R. "A Temporal Relational Model and a Query Language", Information Science, Vol.49, pp.147-175, 1989.
18. Ola A., Ozsoyoglu G. "Incomplete Relational Database Models Based on Intervals", IEEE Trans. on Knowledge and Data Engineering, Vol.5, No.2, pp.293-308, Apr. 1993.
19. Snodgrass R., Ahn I., "Temporal Databases", IEEE Computer, Vol.19, No.9, pp.35-42, 1986.
20. Snodgrass R. "The Temporal Query Language TQuel", ACM Transactions on Database Systems, Vol.12, No.2, pp.247-298, 1987.
21. Soo M.D. "Bibliography on Temporal Databases", ACM SIGMOD RECORD, Vol.20, No.1, pp.14-23, Mar. 1991.
22. Spyropoulos C.D., Kokkotos S. "Interactive Fuzzy Scheduling Using the Time Graph System TGS", Proceedings of the AAAI SIGMAN Workshop on Manufacturing Scheduling, IJCAI-89 Conference, Detroit IL, Aug. 1989.

Efficient Storage Structures for Temporal Object-Oriented Databases

Chih-kuang Li and Shiwei Wang

Department of Computer Science and Information Engineering
National Chiao Tung University
Hsinchu, Taiwan, Republic of China

Abstract

Automatically managing the evolutionary histories of both schema and data is an attractive feature for temporal object-oriented database management systems (OODBMS). It can make the temporal OODBMSs more suitable for many new applications such as CAD, CAM, GIS, etc. However, this feature complicates the implementation of temporal OODBMSs. In this paper, we examined the problems raised by handling the schema evolution and the related issues about the storage structure in temporal OODBMSs. Then, we proposed a storage structure and its accessing algorithms for temporal OODBMSs which can handle both schema evolution and data history simultaneously. We also simulated several possible implementations of the storage structure for temporal data maintenance and compared their performances extensively. This work can be used as the basis of implementations of temporal OODBMSs.

Keywords: temporal databases, object-oriented databases, schema evolution, time index, storage structure.

1 INTRODUCTION

OODBMSs, because of their flexibility and expressing power, are believed to be more suited for the non-conventional applications such as CAD/CAM, GIS, etc. Furthermore, the constant decrease in price for secondary storages makes the inclusion of temporal information in databases an attractive feature. We believe that, to extend the potential usefulness of OODBMSs, we must also support features of the temporal data in OODBMSs. The temporal data representing the past states of databases are never deleted and will grow along the evolution of the databases. Thus, the storage structure of temporal OODBMSs should be designed carefully in order to increase the storage utilization and reduce the response time of temporal queries.

For the reason of simplicity, most of research works concerned with temporal OODBMSs have a simple assumption that the schema is not allowed to change during the life-span of the database. This assumption is very unrealistic because the schema may need to be updated to conform to new application requirements or changes of environments. Therefore, the temporal OODBMSs have to maintain the evolutionary histories of both schema and data simultaneously.

So far, most of existing work on temporal OODBMSs focused on data models and query languages of temporal OODBMSs [1, 2, 3]; only a few exceptions concerned with the storage structure of temporal OODBMSs [4, 5]. In [4], Blanken proposed a storage structure of complex objects versions and the processing algorithms for two types of queries, ASOF queries (which query the database for a fixed point in time) and WALK-THROUGH-TIME queries (which query the database for a whole time interval). However, the database schema are assumed to remain constant during the life-span of the database. As for the issues of schema evolutions, Ariav examined the problems caused by allowing the relational database schema to evolve over time [6]. In [7], a model of schema versions was proposed and the issues in implementing the model were explored.

The main contribution of this paper is an efficient storage structure that we proposed for temporal OODBMSs. In temporal OODBMSs, the storage units are complex object versions which represent the evolutionary histories of complex objects in databases. Using auxiliary pointers, this storage structure can allow the efficient retrieval of complex object versions. In addition, this storage structure also maintains both data and schema evolution histories and the corresponding relationship between data and schema.

The rest of this paper are organized as follows : In section 2, we explain some basic concepts of temporal DBMSs, OODBMSs, and temporal OODBMSs. In section 3, we present the storage structure and the algorithms for accessing evolutionary records of complex objects and schema in databases. In section 4, the conclusion and discussion are given.

2 Temporal Object-Oriented DBMSs

2.1 Basic Terminology

In order to describe the temporal DBMSs formally, we define the important concepts in the temporal DBMSs as follows.

Definition 1 (version) : A **version** of an object is a tuple $(v_1, v_2, \ldots, v_n)$ associated with a time interval (start_time, end_time), where $v_1, v_2, \ldots, v_n$ are respectively values of attributes, $(a_1, a_2, \ldots, a_n)$, of the object and (start_time, end_time) represents the **life-span** of this version during which this version is considered effective.

Definition 2 (current and historical versions) : The **current version** of an object is one version of the object whose life-span is (start_time, current_time). It means that the current version is the latest state of the object. Except the current version, other versions of the object are called **historical versions**.

Definition 3 (historical chain) : The **historical chain** of an object consists of all versions of the object which are linked according to their life-spans such that the version, v_1, is a immediate successor of another version, v_2, and v_2 is the immediate predecessor of v_1 if the value of start_time of v_1 is the same as that of end_time of v_2.

In temporal OODBMSs, historical versions of complex objects, which are called **time slices** in [2], represent the past states of the complex objects. For any point on the time axis, the complex object version for that point consists of the corresponding versions of all its component objects at that point. The formal definition of complex object versions is given below.

Definition 4 (complex object version) : A complex object version consists of corresponding versions of its component objects, and the intersection of their life-spans is the life-span of the complex object version. The life-span of the complex object is not allowed to be empty.

These definitons will be used in the rest of this paper.

2.2 Schema Evolution

From the prospective of the effects on databases, the schema changes of OODBMSs can be classified into two types : **soft changes** and **hard changes** [8]. **Soft changes** are the schema changes which do not require existing instances of some class to become instanes of other classes; the **hard changes**, on the other hand, are the schema changes which force some existing instances to associate some other class. In [8], the only two **hard changes** are the partitioning and combining of classes. These hard changes demand immediate updates to the database. The reason is that if the database is not updated immediately, the original instances of the partitioned or combined classes may leave the existing instances with no corresponding classes. However, in temporal DBMSs, the original classes are preserved and the information about the partition or combination is record there. Therefore, the immediate database updates can be avoided.

In temporal OODBMSs, the **soft changes** and the **hard changes** are reminicent of the **temporally shallow restructuring** and the **temporally deep restructuring** in temporal realtional DBMSs respectively [6]. The problems caused by the hard changes are identical to those caused by the temporally deep restructuring in the temporal relational DBMSs. However, these problems can be more readily solved in temporal OODBMSs. The main source of support to our conviction comes from the fact that the system generates the object identification (OID) attribute for every object in databases. The OID attribute of every object functions as a primary key to uniquely identify an object. Furthermore, the OID attribute is not allowed to be updated by users' queries in any circumstances. Therefore, object identity preserving problem will never occur.

2.3 Temporal Query Types

The query types of the temporal OODBMSs can be classified according to the following criteria :

1. as-of queries versus time interval queries :

   As-of queries are the queries which needs retrieve the states of objects at a certain point of time; time interval queries are the queries which retrieve the states of objects during a time interval.

2. simple object versus complex object manipulation query :

   Simple object queries need to retrieve only the states of an object; complex object queries need to traverse from one object to another object in complex objects in order to retrieve the necessary information.

According to the combination of these two criterias mentioned above, there are four kinds of queries : **as-of simple object look up query, time interval simple object manipulation query, as-of complex object manipulation** and **time interval complex object manipulation queries**.

3 Storage Structures for Temporal OODBMSs

As far as we know the storage structure proposed by Blanken for maintaining complex object versions is the only one that can be directly used in the temporal OODBMSs. The major disadvantage of this storage structure is that retreiving any of historical versions of an object needs to traverse from the beginning of the historical chain of the object. In order to remedy this disadvantage, we made some modifications to Blanken's original storage structure.

In the following subsections, we will describe Blanken's storage structure and the modifications we made for remedying its disadvantages. The protocol for maintaining the correspondence between data and schema versions is also presented here.

3.1 Blanken's Storage Structure

In [4], Blanken proposed a storage structure for the complex object versions and algorithms for processing two types of temporal queries : as-of query and work-through-time query. In this storage structure, the current data and historical data are stored in separated areas for efficient accession of current data. The basic storage units include data tuples and control tuples. The pointers (or OID) attributes and atomic-value attributes of an object are stored at the control tuple and the data tuple respectively. Therefore, the performance of traversing among complex objects can be improved.

Basically, the component objects in complex objects evolve independently and the historical versions of them are stored into their individual historical chains. When one object is modified, the content of the current version is directly updated to reflect this modification and a historical version is generated and added at the head of the historical chain.

An example of Blanken's storage structure is shown in the figure 1. In this example, the complex object consists of two objects : O_1 and O_2. Every object has an individual historical chain. Every version in the historical chain is a partial version except the current version. Using this storage structure, the system needs to traverse the historical chain from the beginning to reconstruct the wanted version.

3.2 Full-Image Versions

In order to avoid traversing the historical chain from the beginning, we create a full-image version for every fixed number of partial versions in the historical chain. The function of the full-image versions is to allow the system to traverse the historical chains from these full-image versions instead of the beginning. The definitions about full-image versions are given as follows.

Definition 5 (full-image and partial version) : A **full-image version** is a historical version which physically records all infomation about the version; a **partial version** records only difference between this version and its immediate ancestor. The current version of an object must be a full-image version.

Definition 6 (appropriate full-image version) : An **appropriate** full-image version for a wanted version is defined as the oldest full-image version which is young than the wanted version. In other word, there is no other full-image version between this **appropriate** full-image version and the wanted version in the historical chain.

Definition 7 (spacing between two successive full-image versions) : The spacing between two successive full-image versions is defined as the number of the partial versions between these two full-image versions in the historical chain.

The spacing between two successive full-image versions, defined by a parameter depending on the tradeoff between the storage space requirement and the system performance, is set statically for the historical chain. We can get the following lemma intuitively.

Lemma 1: Traversing the historical chain from the appropriate full-image version of a wanted version, the disk I/O cost for reconstructing the wanted historical version is bounded by the chosen spacing between two full-image versions.

3.3 Time Indexes

The second modification we made is that each object in databases has its own time index. The main function of the time indexes is to help the system to locate the appropriate full-image versions directly. The definitions about the time indexes are given as below.

Definition 8 (life-span of full-image version) : The life-span of a full-image version is defined as (start_time, end_time), where end_time is the time when this full-image version is created and the start_time is the time when the last full-image version was created or the object was created if it is the first full-image version in the historical chain.

Definition 9 (time index) : The **time index** for an object is a B^+ tree built on all the full-image versions of this object using the end_time of their life-spans as keys. The life-span of a leaf node is the life-spans of the full-image version pointed by the leaf node. The life-span of a interior node is the union of the life-spans of all its children nodes in the time index.

Basically, the time index of an object is used when the system directly looks up the versions of the object instead of traversing from another object using their auxiliary pointers. The concepts of auxiliary pointers will be described at the following subsection.

3.4 Auxiliary Pointers

In order to facilitate traversing among complex object versions, we append an auxiliary pointer to each referencing attribute of objects. The definitions about auxiliary pointers are given as below.

Definition 10 (auxiliary pointer) : Every referencing attribute of an object is associated with an **auxiliary pointer** which points to a full-image version or a time index node of the referenced object. The life-span of an auxiliary pointer is defined by the time the auxiliary pointer is set (start_time) and the time it is physically updated (end_time).

Definition 11 (correct and obsolete auxiliary poniter) : An auxiliary pointer is **correct** if it points to a node in the time index, a B^+ tree, or a full-image version of the referenced object whose life-span minimally subsumes that of the auxiliary pointer. Otherwise, the auxiliary pointer is called **obsolete**.

According to the definition of **correct** auxiliary pointers, we can derive the following lemma.

Lemma 2: If the auxiliary pointer is correct and points to a full-image version of the referenced object, then the referenced full-image version is an appropriate full-image version for those versions of the referencing object.

When the system traverses among complex object versions, it can use the auxiliary pointers of referencing objects to accelerate the traversing. From lemma 1, we know that if the auxiliary pointers effective at every historical version of referencing objects can point to the appropriate full-image versions of the referenced object, the number of disk I/Os needed for locating the corresponding version of the referenced object from the referencing object can be bounded by spacing between two full-image versions. In other word, the cost traveling among complex object versions will not be affected by the length of the historical chains of objects. Therefore, we have the following lemma.

Lemma 3: If the auxiliary pointers at every historical version of the referencing objects in database can point to the appropriate full-image versions of referenced objects, the disk I/O cost for traversing along a path at complex object is bounded by the product of the number of traversed objects and the spacing between two successive full-image versions.

In fact, the three features, full-image versions, time indexes and auxiliary pointers, are integrated tightly. The main function of full-image versions is to serve as vintage starting points for traversals through the historical chains. Traversing among complex object versions, the system can locate the appropriate full-image versions in the historical chains using auxiliary pointers of the referencing objects. However, when the system accesses versions of the roots of complex objects or looks up a set of objects directly, the time indexes will be used to locate full-image versions. The common goal of these features is to facilitate the traversal in the complex object versions.

3.5 Auxiliary Pointer Adjustments

The correct auxiliary pointers may become obsolete due to evolution of objects pointed by them. We use the example at figure 2 to explain this scenario. In this example, there is a simple complex object consisting of two objects : O_1 and O_2, and O_1 references O_2 in the database. Both O_1 and O_2 were created at time 0. O_1 was updated at time 1, 2, 3, and 4; O_2 was updated at time 4, 5, 6, and 7. The spacing between two full-image versions is chosen to be 2. Therefore, the third versions v3 of both O_1 and O_2 are full-image versions.

Now, we suppose that the current time is time 8 and the obsolete auxiliary pointers at versions of O_1 are not yet adjusted. The auxiliary pointers at both the third version v3 and current version of O_1 are obsolete because they still point to the current version of O_2 whose life-span, (6, 8), cannot subsumes their life-spans, (0, 3) and (3, 8). In fact, these auxiliary pointers of O_1 has become obsolete since the full-image version v3 of O_2 was created at time 3. Therefore, in order to maintain correct auxiliary pointers, the system must inform all referencing objects to adjust their obsolete auxiliary pointers as a new full-image version of the referenced object is generated.

Propagation vs. Non-propagation Adjustment

According to whether new versions are generated, there are two approaches to dealing with the adjustment of the auxiliary pointers : **propagation adjustment** and **non-propagation adjustment**.

The **propagation adjustment** approach is that when a referencing object is informed to adjust its obsolete auxiliary pointer, the system will do the following two things :

1. generating a **propagated** version for the object at the head of its historical chain to record an auxilairy pointer
2. adjusting the obsolete auxiliary pointers at full-image versions which still point to the current version of the referenced object causing this adjustment.

Both the auxiliary pointer at the propagated version and the obsolete auxiliary pointers at full-image versions of the referencing object will be adjusted to the newly generated full-image version of the referenced object which caused this adjustment. Furthermore, the auxiliary pointers of referencing objects' current versions still point to the current versions of the referenced objects. Therefore, accesses of the historical versions can be improved while accesses of current data remain unaffected. According to the definition of the propagation adjustment approach, we can get the following lemma.

Lemma 4: If the propagation adjustment approach is adopted, the auxiliary pointers at all the versions are guaranteed to point to the appropriate full-image versions of the referenced objects.

An example of the propagation adjustment is given at figure 3. This example is the same as the one in figure 2 except for the auxiliary pointers. Because we are using the propagation adjustment approach here, a propagated version v5 of O_1 is generated and the auxiliary pointers at version v3 and version v5 of O_1 are adjusted to the full-image version v3 of O_2. Now the life spans of the auxiliary pointers at both version v3 and v5 of O_1, (0, 3) and (3, 6), are subsumed by the life-span of version v3 of O_2, (0, 6). Therefore, the life-span of the auxiliary pointer at the current version of O_1 becomes (6, 8) and can be subsumed by the life-span of the current version of O_2. Therefore, the auxiliary pointers at the versions of O_1 become correct.

The **non-propagation adjustment** approach does not require the system to generate a version for the correction of the obsolete auxiliary pointer. Instead, the auxiliary pointers are physically recorded at only the full-image historical versions and the current versions of objects. The system will directly update the obsolete auxiliary pointers at the current version of the referencing object and adjusts them to the interior time index nodes of the referenced objects whose time intervals are minimal and can subsume that of the current version completely.

An example of the **non-propagation adjustment** is given in figure 4. This example is almost the same as the one in figure 3 except for the addition of propagated versions. The auxiliary pointers at the version v3 and the current version of O_1 are adjusted to the root of the time index of O_2 whose life-span, (0, 8), can subsume their life-spans.

Obviously, the data access performance of the **propagation adjustment** will be better than that of the **non-propagation adjustment**. However, the former needs more storage space than the latter. The tradeoff between these two approaches will be studied at next section.

Immediate vs. Deferred Adjustments

Depending on whether the system immediately adjusts obsolete auxiliary pointers at the referencing objects or not, the implementation of the auxiliary pointer adjustment can be divided into two categories : **immediate adjustment** and **deferred adjustment**.

The **immediate adjustment** scheme refers to the policy which requires the referencing object to update its obsolete auxiliary pointers upon receiving a notification message from the referenced object. If the immediate propagation approach is adopted, the disk I/O cost for traversing among a complex object will be bounded. The following theorem describes the fact.

Theorem 1: If the immdeiate propagation adjustment is adopted, the number of disk I/Os for traversing among a temporal complex object is bounded by the product of the number of traversed objects and the spacing between two successive full-image versions.

One of disadvantages of the immediate adjustment is that the system needs to maintain, at every referenced object, a list of reverse pointers to the objects referencing the object. When an object is referenced by a lot of objects, it needs to maintain a long list of reverse pointers and inform all of these referecing objects at once. This operation will cause a bursty workload.

In order to improve this disadvantage, the **deferred adjustment** scheme does not use the reverse pointers. The adjustment of the auxiliary pointers is delayed until the objects are accessed. Thus, every time an object accesses other object via the auxiliary pointer of the referencing attribute, this auxiliary pointer will be checked to see if they are still up-to-date. This procedure can be satisfied by checking if the time interval of the version of the referencing object is subsumed by the time interval of the referenced full-image version. If the auxiliary pointer is found to be obsolete, the auxiliary pointers are consequently updated. Of course, this update may cause the referencing object to generate new historical versions if the **propagation adjustment** scheme is adopted.

The main reason to defer the adjustment of auxiliary pointers is that, often, those seldom accessed objects will have lower probability to be accessed in the future. Updating the auxiliary pointers of those objects which are rarely accessed is a waste. Another reason is that the deferred updates of auxiliary pointers distribute the workload over the access operations. Although the access operations are delayed by the adjustment of auxiliary pointers at first access, subsequent accessing will be done without further delay.

3.6 Storage for Schema Evolution History

In temporal OODBMSs, the schema should be allowed to change and the histories of schema evolutions are automatically managed by the system. Every time the temporal OODBMS wants to access a version of a complex object, the system at first needs to access the corresponding version of the database schema for interpreting the data version. Therefore, efficient storages for schema evolution histories can improve the total performance of the temporal DBMSs. In fact, the database schema can be stored just like complex objects. The major difference is that the component objects in the "schema" complex object are the classes in DBMSs and the contents for these component objects are the definition of the attributes of these classes instead of the values. However, the storage contents should not affect the design of the storage structure. We think that the storage structure for managing complex object versions in last subsection can be also applied to the storage structure of the schema evolution history.

However, there are some important differences between schema and data which need to be taken into account in designing storage structure for schema evolution history. One is that the size of the database schema is much smaller than that of data stored in the database. Also, the schema are expected to be more frequently accessed than the data. Therefore, for efficient access and update, schema and its evolutionary history (i.e. schema versions) should reside in the main memory while the DBMS is running.

3.7 Correspondence between Schema and Data

DBMSs use the schema to interpret data because the schema contains the infomation about the relative positions and domain types of attributes of relations (or classes) in databases. In non-temporal (snapshot) DBMSs, only current versions of databases and the impacts of schema changes reflect on the databases directly.

In temporal OODBMSs, the schema changes will cause the system to generate both schema versions and data versions in order to record the original schema and existing data respectively. Therefore, the system also needs to maintain the correspondence between data versions and their schema versions. When the system retrieves some data version, it has to first fetch the version whose life-span can subsume that of the data version. The system then can properly interpret historical data versions beause only this schema version contains the proper definition for the data version.

Immediate vs. Deferred updates

As for physical implementions, temporal OODBMSs have two basic approaches in dealing with the impacts of schema changes on existing data : the **immediate update** and the **deferred update**. The **immediate update** approach requires the effect of the schema update operation to be immediately reflected on all existing instances involved in the operation. Thus, the schema change operation will cause a bursty system workload, especially when the number of affected instances is large.

When the **deferred update** approach is adopted, the schema changes are not reflected on the instances until they are acturally accessed. This approach distributes the workload of schema changes over the consequent data accessing operations. Every time the system want to access an data version, it will fetch its corresponding schema version and compare their **start_time** attributes to check if this instance version is out of date. If the **start_time** of the instance version is older than that of its corresponding schema version, it means that the schema has been modified since the time specified at the **start_time** of the instance version. Because of the deferred update, the effects of this modification has not yet been reflected upon the instance. Therefore, the cumulated impact of the schema evolution is applied in one shot to create a serial of new data versions and the wanted instance version can be found correctly.

Hard Schema Changes

As for **hard schema changes**, the temporal OODBMSs need to record the following infomation at the historical schema versions. For the combination of classes, the necessary information includes the time of the combination, the original classes involved in the combination, and the newly generated classes. For the partition of classes, the system will record the time of the partition, the newly-generated classes, the original classes, and the predicate about which original instances are dispatched to which new classes. Therefore, the system can have proper information for deferred reclassification of instances after hard schema changes. Then, the deferred effects can be applied to the instances and the desired historical instance can be retrieved.

4 Conclusions

In this paper, we mainly investigated the storage structures and their accessing algorithms for temporal OODBMSs which support the complex object features and manage the evolutionary histories of data and schema in databases. The two main issues about temporal OODBMSs we are interested in are the maintenance of the histories of schema evolutions and the performance of traversing among the temporal complex objects.

As for the maintenance of the histories of schema evolutions in temporal OODBMSs, we proposed an algorithm for correlating the object versions with their corresponding schema. This algorithm allows the effects on instances caused by schema changes to be deferred. We also describe why the hard changes do not need to force the databases to update immediately in temporal OODBMSs.

As for the performance of traversing among the temporal complex objects, we modified the Blanken's storage structure by adding full-image versions, auxiliary pointers and time indexes for the temporal objects and proposed the algorithms for adjusting the auxiliary pointers : the propagation adjustment and the non-propagation adjustment. In order to investigate the performance of these storage structures, we simulated the five storage structures, Blanken's, immediate propagation, immediate non-propagation, deferred non-propagation approaches and the accession list proposed by Ahn and Snodgrass, and compare their performance, and compared their performance. We found that although the performance of immediate propagation approach is the best, it needs tremendous storage space and the operation of immediate propagation for adjusting the auxiliary pointers. The performance of the non-propagation approaches is not as good as that of the immediate propagation approach, but the non-propagation approaches need much less storage space than the propagation approaches. Furthermore, the non-propagation adjustmet of auxiliary pointers does not affect other queries seriously. Therefore, depending on the tradeoff between the performance and the storage requirement, a storage structure appropriate for the applications can be chosen.

References

[1] Chu, W.W., Ieong, I.T., Taira, R.K. and Breant, C.M., "A Temporal Evolutionary Object-Oriented Data Model and Its Query Language for Medical Image Management," in *Proceedings of the 18th VLDB Confernece*, 1992, pp. 53-64.

[2] Käfer, W. and Schöning H., "Realizing a Temporal Complex-Object Data Model," in *ACM SIGMOD International Conference on Management of Data*, 1992, pp. 266-275.

[3] Wuu, G.T.J. and Dayal, U., "A Uniform Model for Temporal Object-Oriented Databases," in *IEEE Proceedings 7th International Conference on Data Engineering*, 1992, pp. 584-593.

[4] Blanken, H., "Implementing version support for complex objects," *Data & Knowledge Engineering* 6, 1991, pp. 1-25.

[5] Tsotras, V.J. and Salzberg, B., "Optimal Versioning of Objects," in *IEEE Proceedings 7th International Conference on Data Engineering*, 1992, pp. 358-365.

[6] Ariav, G., "Temporal oriented data definitions: Managing schema evolution in temporally oriented databases," *Data & Knowledge Engineering*, 6, 1991, 451-467.

[7] Kim, W. and Chou, H.T., "Versions of schema for object-oriented databases," in *Proceedings of the 14th VLDB Conference*, 1988, pp. 148-159.

[8] Kim, W., *Introduction to Object-Oriented Databases*, MIT Press, 1990.

[9] Cattell, R.G.G., "Object Operations Benchmark," *ACM Trans. on Databases Systems*, Vol. 17, No.1, 1992, pp. 1-31.

[10] Ahn, I. and Snodgrass, R., "Partitioned Storage for Temporal Databases," *Imformation Systems*, Vol.13, No.4, 1988, pp. 369-391.

[11] Bertino, E., "Indexing Techniques for Queries on Nested Objects," *IEEE Trans. on Knowledge and Data Engineering*, vol. 1, No. 2, 1989, pp. 196-214.

[12] Bertino, E., "An Indexing Technique for Object-Oriented Databases," in *IEEE Data Engineering Conf.*, 1991, pp. 160-170.

[13] Biliris, A., "Database Support for Evolving Design Objects," in *26th ACM/IEEE Design Automation Conference*, 1989, pp.258-263.

[14] Kemper, A. and Moerkotte, G., "Access Support in Object Bases," in *ACM SIGMOD Conf. on Management of Data*, 1990, pp. 364-374.

[15] Leung, T.Y.C. and Muntz, R.R. "Generalized Data Stream Indexing and Temporal Query Processing," in *IEEE Proceedings 7th International Conference on Data Engineering*, 1992, pp. 124-131.

[16] Lomet, D. and Salzberg B., "Access Methods for Multiversion Data," in *ACM SIGMOD Conf. on Management of Data*, 1989, pp. 315-324.

[17] Snodgrass, R., "A Taxonomy of Time in Databases," in *ACM SIGMOD Conf. on Management of Data*, 1985, pp. 236-246.

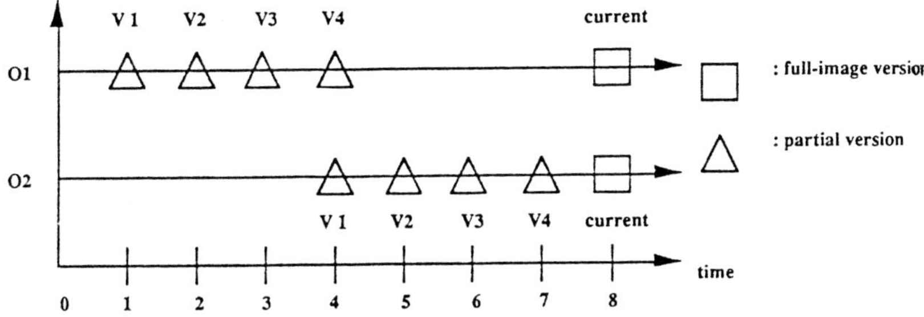

Figure 1: Blanken's storage structure

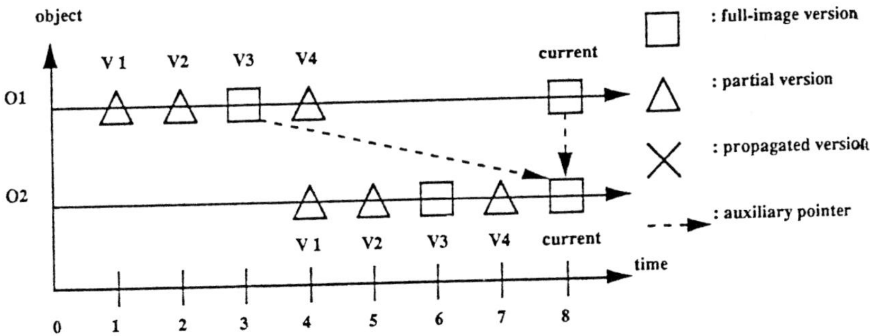

Figure 2: Storage structure with auxiliary pointers for complex object versions

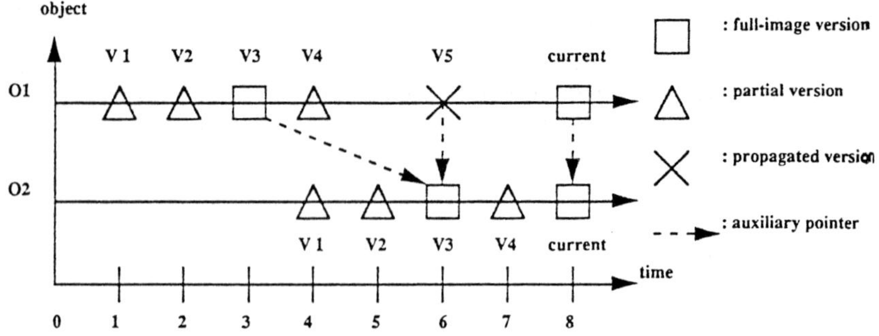

Figure 3: Storage structure with propagation adjustment of auxiliary pointers

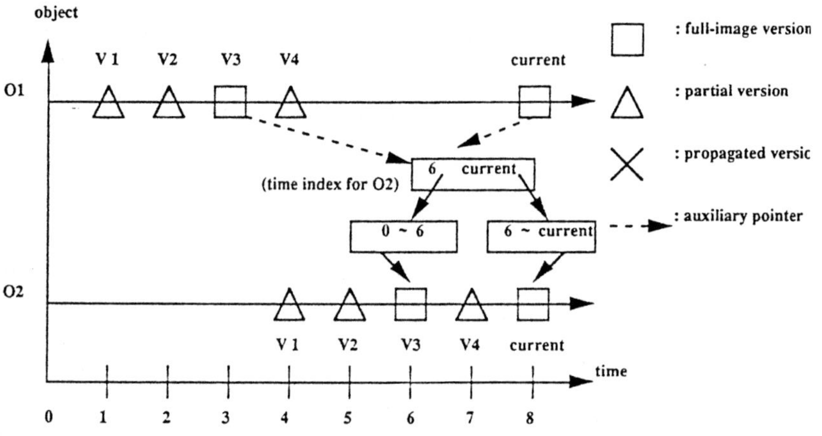

Figure 4: Storage structure with non-propagation adjustment of auxiliary pointers

TFDL: A Temporal Functional Language for the Management of Historical Databases

S. Soukeras and P.J.H. King

Department of Computer Science, Birkbeck College,
University of London, Malet Street, London WC1E 7HX
E-mail : ubacr17@uk.ac.bbk.dcs

Abstract. This paper introduces a Temporal Functional Database Language (TFDL), which realizes an event oriented approach to historical database modeling. According to this approach, the events that occur in an evolving system is the fundamental information which should be recorded. The time series of the system states is secondary information in the sense that it can be derived from the occurred events.

Keywords : Events, Functional Languages, Histories, Temporal Databases.

1.Introduction

Conventional database systems, *i.e.* those that offer no explicit facilities for temporal support, provide for the maintenance of a view of the current state of a real world system. We term this view the *current database state.* As changes in the real world system occur, this current database state is updated to reflect the new situation. Previous states can be recovered by use of the log tape to back out transactions.

Most previous research into the explicit representation of the temporal dimension within database systems has concentrated on extending the relational model. Typically, temporal information is included by providing for the timestamping of tuples [1, 2, 7, 12, 14], or for incorporating the temporal dimension in the attribute domain [5, 16], or both [3]. Effectively, such systems provide for the representation of a series of states of the database, each timestamped with the period during which it was valid.

In our view, a database state whether the current or a previous one, though vitally important from the point of view of database querying and transaction processing, is essentially secondary information in the sense that it is derivative from a series of events or change transactions, which constitute the primary information. In a conventional database system the lack of explicit temporal facilities implies that the database itself cannot include knowledge of how an event affects a state. Therefore, the interpretation and calculation of the consequences of event occurrences on the current database state is done outside the database system, with the resulting modifications being applied to the current state to produce a new current state.

It is our view that a temporal database system should offer facilities for capturing the events that occur in the real world, and for describing how they affect a database state. Using these descriptions, it then computes database states and the periods of their validity, as required. This approach is different from previous approaches to the explicit incorporation of temporal information.

Our view is that a record of the events which occur, which we term the *event database*, is the fundamental information which should persist. From this information the conventional database view, the *state database*, can always in principle be derived (figure 1). We believe that the approach to temporal databases of maintaining a history of timestamped database states is restrictive and troublesome. Whilst on occasions it may be expedient to compute the database state at a particular point in time from an earlier state and the intervening events, this is a matter of efficiency only and should not be allowed to confuse the basic semantic theory. It is the event database that is fundamental. We believe that our approach is better in offering the capability and flexibility necessary for modeling a world evolving in time [15].

This approach is realized in TFDL a Temporal Functional Database Language an extension and adaptation of FDL [6, 11], a database language which exploits the natural correspondence between the functional data model [13] and functional programming [18] to achieve computational completeness. An FDL database consists of a set of function definitions, which model both data and computation.

In section 2, an overview of TFDL with emphasis on its temporal features is given. An example of TFDL's use for modeling the local Government election system in Britain is presented in section 3. In section 4, the semantics of TFDL's temporal operators are defined, and a proof of TFDL's temporal completeness is given in section 5. Section 6 contains our conclusions.

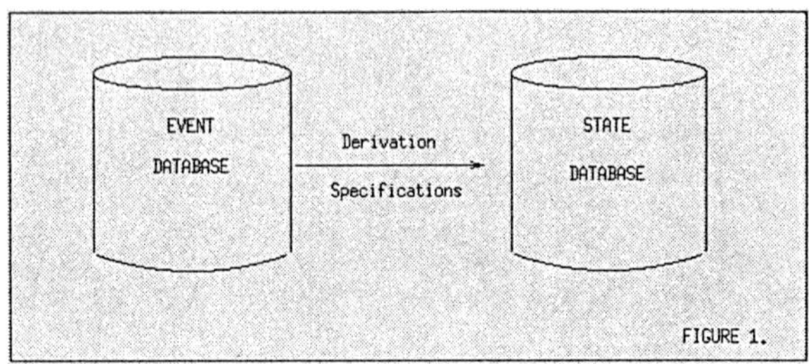

FIGURE 1.

2. TFDL

TFDL is a true superset of FDL extended to include *events*, *time elements*, *histories*, and features for their manipulation. Our description of TFDL will be brief for those aspects of the language that are common with FDL, and go into more detail for the novel features.

2.1. Data Types

The primitive data types of TFDL are string, integer, boolean and time. In addition, the user can declare extensible data types corresponding to abstract entities - called entity types, and to events - called event types. Entity types are modeling abstract entities, that is those without printable value *e.g.* a person. Entity instances are added and removed from the extent of an entity type via creation and deletion commands. The values of entities are hidden by displaying a transient global variable of the form \$x, where x is an alphanumeric identifier. For any entity type τ, a zero-argument generator function All_τ returns the current extent of τ in the form of a list. *e.g.*

```
person :: entity;
create person $p;     /* Create an instant of entity type person*/
All_person;           /* The function All_person returns the extension
 [$p]                    of the person type */
```

Event types are examined in detail in section 2.4. Another category of types corresponding to histories is available, and the types belonging to it are called history types. Their role in the representation of historical information is considered in section 2.5.

Also supported are arbitrarily nested lists, sums and products. *e.g. [1,4,5,10]* belongs to the type list(integer). Sum types represent unions of types and their components are tagged by upper-case identifiers termed constructor functions, which can be thought as functions without reduction rules.

```
tree :: sum;
LEAF : integer -> tree;  NODE : integer tree tree -> tree;
```

The tree sum type contains binary trees of integers which are constructed from the union of their leaves and nodes. Sum types can also be used to define types which are equivalent to enumerated types in C.

```
state :: sum;
ON : -> state; OFF : -> state;
```

Product types represent the Cartesian product of types. Values of product types can be thought as records. The product constructor '**' is used to declare product types. For example, the product of integer type and string type called tup may be declared thus :

```
tup :: integer**string; /*The value {3, "Paul"} is a value of tup*/
```

2.2. Functions

Functions model facts or computation as well as information of a hybrid nature. The type of a function must be declared before it is defined. The following declarations, declare name to be a function whose argument is a person and whose result is a string, and factorial to be a function which takes an integer argument and returns an integer result.

```
name : person -> string;  factorial : integer -> integer;
```

The definition of functions is incremental with the insertion and deletion of equations. The left hand side (LHS) of each equation consists of the function name followed by a number of patterns which may contain variables, constants, or constructors. Thus, in the following definitions $p, 0 and x are all patterns. x is a variable, $p and 0 are constants.

```
name $p <= "Jim";
factorial 0 <= 1;  factorial x <= x * factorial (x-1);
```

Functions are evaluated by pattern matching. When the function is applied to an argument, or arguments, the evaluator determines which equations have patterns that match those arguments. A pattern consisting of a constant will only match an argument which is equal to that constant, whilst a variable matches any argument. If more than one equations match the arguments of a function then the evaluator will use a Left to Right Best Fit (LRBF) algorithm, which is described by Poulovassilis [10], to choose one. Thus,

```
factorial 0; /* best match by the first equation of the definition */
 1
```

The LHS of equations must be unique, so if an equation is specified with the same LHS as an existing one, the existing right hand side (RHS) of the equation is replaced with the new RHS. For any function *f*, which has only entities or events for arguments, its inverse function is a list valued function and defined by the system with the name inv_*f*.

Finally, lambda calculus anonymous functions can be directly expressed in TFDL. For example the identity function :

```
lambda x. (x);
```

2.3. Time Type

Time elements are used for modeling the time when events take place in the real world. It is usually termed *valid* or *real time*, as opposed to *system* or *rollback time* which models the recording of the events in the database .Values of type time have the form Tx, where x is an integer. Our model of time is discrete, point based and totally ordered.

The built-in functions *timeoforder* and its inverse *orderoftime* define an isomorphism between the times and the integers.

```
timeoforder : integer -> time;  orderoftime : time -> integer;
```

The functions *before*, *after* and *at* define redundantly the total order in the set of time points.

```
before : time time -> bool;
before Tx Ty  <=  (orderoftime Tx < orderoftime Ty);

after : time time -> bool;
after T x Ty  <=  (orderoftime Tx > orderoftime Ty);

at   : time time -> bool;
at Tx Ty  <=  (orderoftime Tx = orderoftime Ty);
```

The constants Tmin and Tmax represent the earliest and latest times in the system.

Whilst the model of time is adequate for demonstrating our ideas for representing and manipulating historical information, it is perhaps too simple for many practical purposes, its restriction to one granularity of time being unrealistic. Our future target is a time model, flexible enough to satisfy most of the users views of how time requires to be represented and, additionally, one that offers enough support for easily constructing such user views. It should include the ability to refer to different time granularities and operate between them, and to define calendar systems. An approach to DBMS support for time can be found in [8].

2.4. Event types

Events represent instantaneous happenings, *i.e.* those occurring at a specific time point and having no duration. They are the means of representing the dynamic part of the system the database models because they are the only objects in the language that have a time reference associated with them, and therefore provide for entering information in the database, which is explicitly qualified by time. Events are central to our manipulation of the historical dimension, which is presented in section 2.5 below.

Event types are very similar to entity types. As with entity types, elements are added and removed from the extent of an event type via creation and deletion commands. The values of events are also hidden by assigning them transient global variables of the form $x, where x is an alphanumeric identifier. Finally, for any event type ε, a zero-argument generator function All_ε returns the current extent of ε in the form of a list. Additional to the entity types characteristics, the system declared but user defined function *tof* returns the time of occurrence for each instance of an event type. Other information about an event is modeled using functions.
As an example, a room has lamps and their switchings are events:

```
lamp :: entity;  switch :: event;
switched : switch -> lamp;
/* Switched returns the lamp that is switched in a switch event*/
```

The switching of a lamp at time T10 would be recorded as :

```
create lamp $lamp;
create switch $sw;  tof $sw <= T10;  switched $sw <= $lamp;
```

2.5 History Types

History types model historical information *i.e.* time variant relationships in a system. A *history of* τ or τ *history*, where is a type, is a total function from time to τ. It can be visualized as a sequence of the successive values an object takes across time, or as a set of pairs {...,(T0,τ_0), (T1,τ_1),...}, or as a time series. If the pair (Tn,τ_n) belongs to a history, then τ_n is the value of this history at time point Tn. The type constructor *history* when applied to any type τ, constructs the *history type of* τ, written history(τ), which consists of all possible τ histories. τ is the *value type* of history(τ). Thus, if temp is a type representing temperatures then history(temp) is the set of all possible time to temp functions (temperature time series). A particular history might be the one modeling the body temperature of a particular person.

2.5.1 History Constructors

A history type is realized in TFDL as a sum type, and thus consists of a number of constructor functions applied to zero or more arguments. The argument types of such a constructor function are called the *owner types* of the histories it constructs. Thus, these history constructing functions define disjoint partitions within a history type. For example, to model the states in time of any device with two modes of operation (on, off), we would construct the type history(state) by applying the type constructor *history* to the type state defined earlier. The elements of this type are all the state histories (time series of on and off values). By using a constructor function, *e.g.* LSTATE, that takes a lamp as argument and returns a history(state), a partition is defined in history(state) for modeling the state histories of lamps in particular.

```
LSTATE : lamp -> history(state);
```

LSTATE $lamp is a particular state history modeling the states of lamp $lamp in time. A partition for modeling the states of television sets in time could be constructed by another constructor function, *e.g.* TVSTATE :

```
TVSTATE : tv -> history(state);
```

The above mechanism of history representation provides for the treatment of temporal values as first class objects in the language. Therefore, TFDL has *temporal value integrity* as defined in [16].

2.5.2 History Specification Functions

TFDL is a realization of the event-oriented approach to historical information modeling, described in [14]. According to this approach historical information is always derived from facts about events through descriptions of i) which events modify (change the value of) a history; ii) when and how events modify a history; and iii) how a history persists when it is not affected by events.

TFDL provides three families of specification functions for the description of the semantics of histories:

i) *events*_ε, takes a history as argument and returns a list of ε type events that might modify it. Thus, the following equation in the definition of events_switch specification function describes which switch events might affect the state history of a lamp :

```
events_switch (LSTATE x) <= inv_switched x;
/* A lamp's state history is affected by the switchings of this lamp */
```

ii) *impact*_ε, takes a history of type history(τ) and an ε type event as arguments, and returns a list of tuples, whose first element is a time that the event affects the history and the second is its impact. The event's impact on the history is defined as a function (τ -> τ), that is a function from the value that the history would have at the time of the event's impact if the event had not taken place to its value due to the occurrence of the event. The following equation of the specification function impact_switch describes the time and nature of the impact that switching events have on the state histories of lamps :

```
impact_switch (LSTATE l) s <= [{tof s, reverse}];
/*A switch event affects a lamp's state history at the time of its occur-
  rence and it reverses its state; reverse is a function (state -> state)
  which returns OFF if the argument is ON and vice versa*/
```

Note, that it is possible for an event to affect a history at more than one times in a different way at each of them.

iii) *persists*, takes a history as an argument and returns its persistency. The persistency of a history describes how the value of a history persists when it is not affected by events, and it is modeled in TFDL with a sum type called *persistency*. All elements of persistency are constructed by applying the constructor function PERSIST to a function from time to the value type of the history, whose persistency is defined. This function argument of PERSIST models the evolution of the history's value at the time between changes caused by events. In the case of a lamp's state history, its persistency should specify that its value remains constant until it is changed by the impact of an event:

```
persists (LSTATE x) <= PERSIST lambda t. (value (LSTATE x) last t);
```

Value, is one of the temporal operators (see next section) offered by the system for the manipulation of histories and it returns the value of a history at a time point. Histories with the same kind of persistency as LSTATE histories are called stepwise constant histories. Due to their overwhelming majority in real life, the 0-argument constructor function STEPWISE_CONST is added to the persistency sum type, abstracting the stepwise constant persistency semantics.

```
STEPWISE_CONST :-> persistency;
persists (LSTATE x) <= STEPWISE_CONST;
```

2.5.3 Temporal Operators

TFDL provides a set of operators for extracting historical information from histories in accordance to their semantics as defined via the history specification functions. In the core of this set are two operators, *value* and *timelist*, which are not TFDL expressible and therefore their definition is built in the system. Their semantics are defined in section 4.

i) `value : history(alpha) time -> alpha;`
Value, is a polymorphic function (alpha is a type variable), which takes a history and a time for arguments and returns its value at this time. *e.g.* value (LSTATE $lamp) T10;

ii) `timelist : history(alpha) -> (list time);`
Timelist is a polymorphic function that takes a history as arguments and returns a list of times, at which events modify the history. *e.g.* timelist (LSTATE $lamp);

This small core of operators combined with the computational power of our functional language it would appear at least as powerful as any other historical query language. In section 5 we show that TFDL is at least as powerful as US logic, which is used in [16] as one of the basis for temporal completeness.

Nevertheless, we believe that despite the computational completeness of TFDL, built-in efficient historical operators are important for the success of a historical database system due to the massiveness of the expected data. Therefore, finding useful operators to be included in the language is a matter of great interest. Two extra operators, when and extent, are provided by the language although they are TFDL expressible. Their declaration and description follows :

iii) `when : history(alpha) (alpha -> bool) -> list(time ** time);`
when, takes as arguments a history and a function from the history's value type to bool (a condition on the value of the history) and returns a list of tuples. The first element of each tuple is a time point from the timelist of the history, such that the history's value at that point satisfies the condition but the value at the previous time in the timelist does not. The second element, is the next time in the timelist that the history's value does not satisfy the condition. Therefore, if the persistency semantics of the history is stepwise constant, the function returns the time intervals during which the condition is satisfied. *e.g.* when (LSTATE $lamp) (is_on); is_on is a function (state -> bool), that returns true if its argument is ON and false if it is OFF. For other persistency semantics further interpolation will be needed.

iv) `extent : history(alpha) -> list(alpha ** (time ** time));`
extent, takes a history as argument and returns its whole extent, that is all its values accompanied with their time interval, assuming that the history's persistency is stepwise constant. *e.g.* extent (LSTATE $lamp);

Additionally, the identification of useful operators for comparisons between histories is still a matter of on going research.

3. Example : Local Government Election (LGE) Database

The local Government election database models the local Government election system in London. The city is divided into 32 Boroughs each of which is divided into wards. Each ward has one or more council seats depending on its population. Every four years, these are filled by the winners of the full elections. When a council seat is vacated due to death, illness or the councillor's decision to resign, and the next full election is more than six months away, a by-election takes place to elect a new councillor in that person's place. We consider a database for the results relating to a particular Borough, Greenwich.
The entities of the LGE database are :

```
ward   :: entity;   w_res   :: entity; /* Ward result */
person :: entity;   c_res   :: entity; /* Candidate result */
party  :: entity;   counc_s :: entity; /* Council seat */
```

The events that take place in the system are the full elections, by-elections, and the vacating of seats.

```
fullel :: event; /* Full election */      byel :: event; /* By election */
csvac:: event;   /* Council seat vacancy */
```

The rest of the information about the system is recorded in the form of the following functions :

```
br : byel -> w_res;             /* By election Result */
fr : fullel -> (list w_res);    /* Full election Results */
fc : csvac -> counc_s;          /* council seat vacancy event For Council seat*/
rs : csvac -> string;           /* ReaSon of vacancy */
ww : c_res -> (w_res);          /* Candidate result Within a Ward result */
fw : w_res -> ward;             /* ward result For Ward */
rp : c_res -> party;            /* Representing Party of Candidate result*/
vt : c_res -> integer;          /* VoTes of Candidate result*/
cd : c_res -> person;           /* CanDidate of candidate result*/
pn : party -> string;           /* Party Name */
np : person -> string;          /* Name of Person */
sf : ward -> (list counc_s);    /* list of council Seats For the ward*/
wn : ward -> string;            /* Ward Name */
wc : ward -> string;            /* Ward Constituency */
```

The schema of the event LGE database is given graphically in Figure 2. A council seat occupancy is a history of person and it is a historical information that we would like to derive from the event database.

```
OC : counc_s -> (history pn);
events_csvac (OC x) <= inv_fc x;
/*The occupancy of a council seat is affecte by the csvac events of this seat */
impact_csvac (OC x) y <= [{tof y, undef}];
/*undef is a constant functions that returns the  '@' value, one of  TFDL's null
values, in this case representing a vacant council seat*/
events_byel (OC x) <= [ y || y <- All_byel & (member x (sf fw br y))];
```

Here, use is made of *list abstraction*, a construct found in many functional languages and analogous to the mathematical set abstraction {x such that x ε S and C(x) is true}. The symbol '||' is read as 'such that' and the symbol '<-' is a *generator* which instantiates the variable on its left by iterating through the list on its right. If the list abstraction is enclosed by parenthesis instead of square brackets then only the first element of the resulting list is returned. Hence, the list abstraction above returns the by_el events that had taken place in the ward that the seat belongs to.

```
impact_byel (OC x) y <= [{tof y, lambda p.(if (@ != p) p (pn || {cs, pn}<-
     by_winners y & (cs = x))}];
/*If the occupancy of a seat would have been undefined in the absence of a byel
  event (i.e. it had been  vacated) then it will be filled by the winner of the
  by election given by the function by_winners defined in the appendix,  other-
  wise it will remain as it was.*/

events_fullel (OC x) <= All_fullel;
impact_fullel (OC x) y <= [{tof y, lambda p. (pn || {cs, pn}<-
     full_winners y (head inv_sf x) & (cs = x))}];
/*All seat occupancies are affected by  full election events and are filled by
  the winners as given by the function  full_winners defined in the  appendix;
  head returns the first element of a list*/

persists (OC x) <= STEPWISE_CONST; /*The  occupancy of a council seat  remains
                             the same till it is changed by an event*/
```

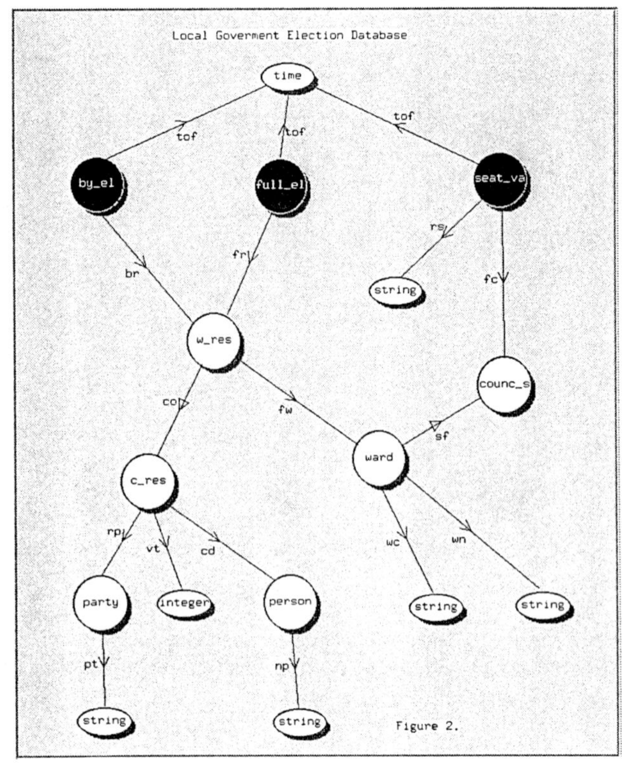

Figure 2.

The current event database extension covers all the full and by-elections in Greenwich from 1978 to 1990. In this database, the following query would return the names of the councillors for the Trafalgar ward on the 1/1/88 :

```
[np value (OC x) (map_calendar_time (1988,1,1)) | x <-sf head inv_wn "Trafalgar"];
 ["Birtles A J", "Farmer E J"]
```

4. Semantics of Temporal Operators

The semantics of the temporal operators value and timelist, will be given using a functional language with the same syntax as TFDL, but with events being represented by integers.

The overloaded function called *events* takes a string (the name of an event type) and a history as arguments and returns a list of events belonging to the argument event type, and it is defined to contain the information in the family of event_ε functions. Thus, the definition of the function events consists of a set of equations one for each event type ε :

```
events "ε" x <= events_ε x;
```

Similarly, the overloaded function *impact* takes a history, a string (the name of an event type) and an event that belongs to the previous event type as arguments, and is defined to return the information represented by the family of functions impact_ε.

```
impact x "ε" y <= impact_ε x y;
```

The 0-argument metalevel function Event_types returns the list of the names of all declared event types.

```
Event_types :-> (list string);
```

In this variation of TFDL we can define the temporal operator value :

```
value hst tm <= compose
      [impct || e_type <- Event_types &
        ev <- events hst e_type & (t,impct) <- impact hst etype ev & (t = tm)]
      let PERS f == persists h in (f tm);
/*compose returns the composition of a list of functions (alpha->alpha)*/
```

Thus, the value of a history at a time point is computed by collecting the events that are affecting the history at this time point, and then applying the composition of their impacts to the value that the history would have had in the absence of any event, as it is defined by the persists function. Note, that in the case of more than one event affecting the history at the same time, their impacts are composed in an undeterministic order.

Similarly, the timelist operator semantics are defined as :

```
timelist : history(alpha) -> (list time);
timelist hist <= remove_duplicates
      [tm || e_type <- Event_types &
        ev <- events hst e_type & (tm, impct) <- impact hst e_type ev];
```

The above two functions are the core operators for the manipulation of histories. Other temporal operators like when and extent, are computable from these core operators in TFDL.

5. Temporal Completeness

It has been shown [4] that US logic is fully expressive for a historical data model in the same sense that first-order logic is for a non-temporal data model. US logic is comprised of first-order classical logic with the addition of the modal operators *until* and *since*. Several different definitions of until and since have appeared in the literature, and we will use one that assumes a bounded discrete time model :

A until B is true at time Tn, if B holds at some time point Tq after Tn and A holds at all times in the interval (Tn, Tq]. At the end of the times is false.

A since B is true at time Tn, if B held at time Tq before Tn and A have held at all times in the interval [Tq, Tn). At the beginning of time is false.

It has also been shown that lambda calculus is as expressive as first order logic. Therefore, if we can express the two modal operators of US logic in TFDL we have proven that TFDL is at least as expressive as US logic.

The expressions A and B in the definition of since and until could be modeled in TFDL as histories of type history(bool). The operators since and until could also be modeled by the same type. Thus,

```
SINCE : history(bool) history(bool) -> history(bool);
UNTIL : history(bool) history(bool) -> history(bool);
```

The SINCE and UNTIL histories are not affected by any events therefore their semantics are defined solely via the persists function :

```
persists UNTIL x y <=
     PERSIST until_funct (lambda t1.(value x t1)) (lambda t2.(value y t2));
persists SINCE x y <=
     PERSIST since_funct (lambda t1.(value x t1)) (lambda t2.(value y t2));
```

The functions until_funct and since_funct both take two functions (time -> bool) and a time as arguments and return a bool. Thus, their partial application in the above definitions return functions (time -> bool). Their definition (see appendix) provide the histories constructed by the SINCE and UNTIL constructors with the same semantics with the operators of US logic. Thus, in the LGE example, if IN_COUNCIL is a history constructor which when applied to a person returns a history of bool, history(bool), modeling whether a person is a councillor or not in time, then the expression,

```
value (SINCE (IN_COUNCIL $p1) (IN_COUNCIL $p2)) T100;
```

would return true if person $p2 was councillor at a time Tn before T100, and person $p1 was councillor at all times in the interval [Tn, T100).

6. Conclusions

A Temporal Functional Database Language (TFDL) was introduced as the realization of the event oriented approach to temporal database modeling. It is an extension of the Functional Database language (FDL). Its new features have been examined in depth and the semantics of its temporal operators defined. Its use was demonstrated through a real world example. Finally, its temporal completeness was proven.

References

[1] J. Ben-Zvi. *The Time Relational Model.* PhD. thesis, computer Science department, UCLA, 1982.

[2] J. Clifford and D.S. Warren. *Formal semantics for time in databases.* ACM Transactions on Database Systems, 8(2):214-254, June 1983.

[3] J. Clifford and A. Croker. *The historical relational model (HRDM) and algebra based on lifespans.* In Proceedings of the Third International Conference on data Engineering, 528-537, Los Angeles, CA, February 1987.

[4] D. Gabbay. *The Declarative Past and Imperative Future, Temporal Logic in Specification.* Altrincham Workshop 1987, LNCS 398:409-448, Springer-Verlag, 1989.

[5] S.K. Gadia. *A homogeneous relational model and query languages for temporal databases.* ACM Transactions on Database Systems, 13(4):418-448, December 1988.

[6] P.J.H. King and A. Poulovassilis. *FDL: A language which integrates database and functional programming.* Actes du Congres INFORSID 88, La Rochelle (1988), pp 167-181

[7] N.A. Lorentzos and R.G. Johnson. *Extending relational algebra to manipulate temporal data*. Information Systems ,13(3):289-296, 1988.

[8] N.A. Lorentzos. *DBMS support for time and totally ordered compound data types*. Information Systems, Voll 7, No 5, pp. 347-358.

[9] S.B. Navathe and R. Ahmed. *A temporal relational model and a query language*. Information Sciences, 49(2):147-175, 1989.

[10] A. Poulovassilis. *A pattern-matching algorithm for functional databases*. The Computer Journal, 36(2):195-199.

[11] A. Poulovassilis and P.J.H. King. *Extending the functional data model to computational completeness*. Advances in Database Technology (EDBT 90), Lecture Notes in Computer science, No 416, Springer-Verlag, 1990.

[12] N.L Sarda. *Extensions to SQL for historical databases*. IEEE Transactions on knowledge and data Engineering, 2(2):220-230, July 1990.

[13] D.W. Shipman. *The functional data model and the data language DAPLEX*. ACM Trans. on Database Systems, 6:140-173, March 1981.

[14] R. Snodgrass. *The temporal query language TQuel*. ACM Transactions on database systems, 12(2):247-298, July 1987.

[15] S. Soukeras and P.J.H. King. *Temporal Databases : An Event Oriented Approach*. To appear in the proceedings of BNCOD12, Guildford, July 1994.

[16] A.U. Tansel. *A historical query language*. Information Sciences, 53:101-133, 1991.

[17] A.U. Tansel, J. Clifford, S. Gadia, S. Jajodia, A. Segev and R. Snodgrass. *Temporal Databases theory, design, and implementation*. Chapter 20: 496-533, Benjamin/Cummings.

[18] D.A Turner. *Miranda: A non-strict functional language with polymorphic types*. Lecture Notes in Computer Science, Vol 201, Springer-Verlag 1985.

Appendix

Auxiliary functions:

```
last : time -> time; last x <= timeoforder ((orderoftime x) - 1);

next : time -> time; next x <= timeoforder ((orderoftime x) + 1);

by_winners : be -> (list (cs ** pn));
by_winners x <= pair
      [y || y <- sf fw br x & (= @ value_oc (OC y) last tof x)]
      [a2 || {a1,a2} <- sort [{vt z, cd z} || z <- co br x]];
/* sort performs a quicksort on the number of votes*/

pair : (list alpha1) (list alpha2) -> (list (alpha1**alpha2));
pair [h1|t1] [h2|t2] <= CONS {h1,h2} pair t1 t2;  pair [] l2 <= [];

fu_winners : fe wd -> (list (cs ** pn));
fu_winners x w <= pair [y || y <- sf w]
      [a2 || {a1,a2} <- sort [{vt z, cd z} || z <- co head
      [r || r <- fr x & (= fw r w)]]];

times_between : time time -> (list time);
times_between x y <= if ((at x y) | (next x = y) | (last x = y)) [] /* |=OR */
                if (before x y) [next x| times_between (next next x) y]
                           [last x | times_between (last last x) y];

since_funct : (time -> bool)  (time -> bool) time -> (bool);
since_funct f1 f2 Tmin <= false;
since_funct f1 f2 t <= since_aux f1 f2 times_between Tmin t;

since_aux : (time -> bool) (time -> bool) (list time) -> bool;
since_aux f1 f2 [] <= false;
since_aux f1 f2 [t1|t] <= if ((f2 t1) and (f1 t1)) true
                  if (not f1 t1) false (since_aux f1 f2 t);
/* until_funct is similarly defined */
```

The ORES Temporal DBMS and the ERT-SQL Query Language

Babis Theodoulidis, Aziz Ait-Braham and George Karvelis

UMIST
Department of Computation , P.O. Box 88,
Manchester M60 1QD, United Kingdom

Tel: +44 61 200 3309, Fax: +44 61 200 3324
email: {babis,aab,karvelis}@sna.co.umist.ac.uk

Abstract: Up to date there exists no commercially available Temporal Database Management System (TDBMS). Current information server technology addresses *'time'* only to a limited extent, in the form of special purpose application programs. The ORES TDBMS, an ESPRIT project currently under development, is a system in which the success and adequacy of management of time related information is paramount. A major step towards achieving such an objective is the provision of a query language powerful enough to express queries, no matter how complex, and yet easy to use. ERT-SQL is such a language.
This paper, which is mainly devoted to this language, first presents an overview of the ORES project, followed by a brief description of the conceptual data model aspects. Then, the capabilities of the query language ERT-SQL are illustrated with a number of examples. There follows a summary and concluding remarks.

Keywords: Temporal (Historical) Databases, Temporal DBMS, Database Design, Design Tools, ORES, Conceptual Modelling, Entity-Relationship Time (ERT) Model, ERT-SQL .

1. Introduction

Nowadays, it is widely accepted within the database community that the incorporation of temporal capabilities into information systems is a highly desirable feature. There is no doubt, though, that the bulk of the research in the field of temporal databases has been done in the context of the relational data model. However, a number of proposals based on models commonly known as semantic data models, such as the entity-relationship, infological and object data models, have been put forward and the number grew dramatically in recent years. The motivation behind all of these approaches is that the relational data model is not considered to be expressive enough for complex database applications such as multimedia, executive information systems, computer-aided design (CAD), computer integrated manufacturing (CIM), and geographical information systems (GIS). These applications have strong requirements to model the temporal or spatio-temporal relationships between objects. Therefore, "temporality" is an important (even if not integral) part of the next generation of database systems [1]. Inevitably, these semantic data models are accompanied by query languages necessary to operate on data modelled in this fashion. Over the past decade or so, several researchers including [2,3,4,5,6] have proposed incorporating time into non-relational data models and their accompanying query languages. A comprehensive bibliography on temporal databases, mainly relational, can be found in [7].

ORES is a two year ESPRIT III project whose aim is to develop a demonstrator Temporal Database Management System (TDBMS). The ORES TDBMS will support the efficient and user friendly representation and manipulation of temporal knowledge and it will be developed as an extension of the relational database management system INGRES. The ORES project will result in a general purpose TDBMS [8], the development of which is based on a practical and yet theoretically sound approach. The fact that much investment has been committed to the relational database technology and the commercial reality of a large user base that understands and works with it, warrants an effort in endowing a relational DBMS with temporal extensions.

The paper is organised as follows. In Section 2, we present the overall idea and workings of the ORES project. In Section 3, we briefly describe the main concepts of the developed data model. In Section 4, the capabilities of the query language ERT-SQL are illustrated with a number of simple and complex queries. Finally, Section 5 consists of the conclusions.

2. ORES Overview

The ORES TDBMS architecture is illustrated in figure 1. As shown in this figure, ORES consists of two components, namely the valid-time component and the conceptual component. Within the ORES relational component, two categories of languages for reasoning and querying have been developed: a procedural language, *Valid-Time Relational Algebra (VT-RA)* [14], and a non-procedural language, *Valid-Time SQL (VT-SQL)* [15,16]. The objective is to provide languages which fit the architecture of relational databases, i.e. languages requiring minimum alteration to the existing technology [17]. The design and implementation of VT-SQL is done through VT-RA. VT-RA is itself an extension of the relational algebra.

The ORES conceptual component consists of a *data definition tool* for specifying graphically and textually the application domain, a *data manipulation tool* for manipulating application knowledge, a *data validation tool* for validating the application specification and a *database design tool* for transforming conceptual specifications to valid-time specifications.

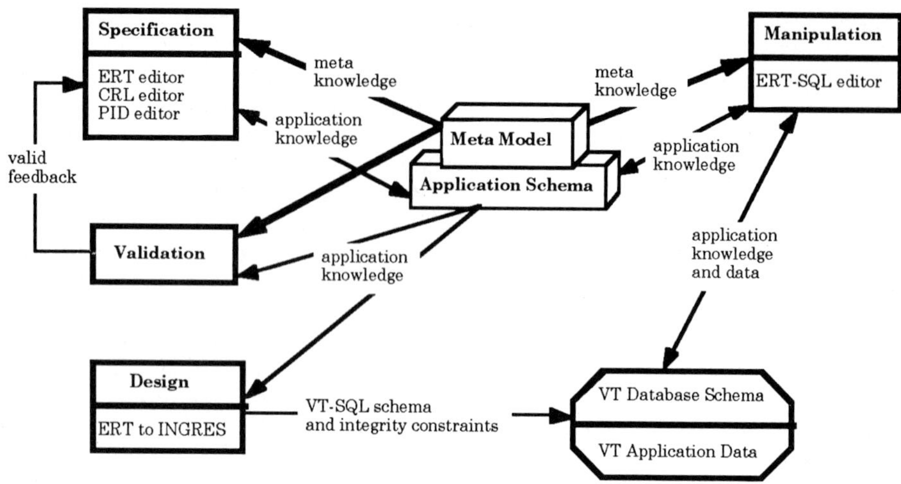

Figure 1: The ORES Prototype Architecture

Data definition and manipulation is based on the ORES Conceptual Design Formalism [18] which consist of the Entity-Relationship Time (ERT) model, the Conceptual Rule Language (CRL), the Process Interaction Diagram (PID) and the ERT-SQL query language, which will be the main subject of this paper. The ERT model provides constructs for describing the structural parts of an application, e.g. the classification of the objects and their associations. The CRL language provides constructs for describing rules of the application, e.g. derivation and constraints rules as well as the dynamics of the application. The PID model provides constructs for describing the processes of the application. The information about the application is held in a metamodel, an information repository [19]. Finally, ERT-SQL is a temporal query language operating on the ERT model.

Before the conceptual schema is handed out to the system analysts to serve as the basis for the implementation, the schema should be correct in some sense. The activity of ensuring the correctness of the schema is called *validation*. Validation in ORES [21] consists of a five-step process. First, the conceptual schema (CS) should be syntactically correct (*syntactic correctness*). CS consists of a structural part (described by ERT) as well as the associated rules (described by CRL) and processes (described by PID). Second, CS state the non-logical axioms of a theory over the reality of the information system, and in that the axioms should be true assertions about the reality (*soundness*). Third, CS should not leave out any assertion accidentally (*completeness*). Fourth, a CS should not contain contradictions (*consistency*). Fifth, the CS must make sense (*semantic correctness*).

3. ERT Model

Before we proceed with ERT-SQL, we will briefly present its underlying model, the ERT data model. The modelling constructs in ERT are *entity*, *value*, and *relationship* classes. The objects of the universe of discourse are classified into classes. The objects of an entity class are supposed to have an independent existence of other object, while objects in a value class are supposed to exist only if they are used to describe properties of entities. Entity classes may be *complex*, which define an abstraction called *is_part_of* relation. A relationship class is a set of associations and defined between two entity classes or between a value and an entity class. As a consequence, all relationship classes, except a special relationship class called ISA, are symmetric and binary. However, instead of regarding both (a,b) and (b,a) as belonging to the same relationship class, the directed subclasses of relationships are distinguished by *role names*. The description of the time model is also included in the ERT schema.

An entity class as well as a relationship class may be *derived*. Cardinality constraints for both roles of a relationship are expressed as a pair (*min* : *max*). ISA relationships are classified into one of the following categories: *total disjoint* (TD), *total overlapping* (TO), *partial disjoint* (PD) and *partial overlapping* (PO). An entity class as well as a relationship class may be *timestamped* or not. For an entity class, a timestamp specifies that the existence periods of the entities of the class is kept, while a timestamp on a relationship class indicates that the history of the relationships, i.e. pairs of objects, will be kept. (For more detail, the reader is referred to [18] and [20] where the concepts and semantics of ERT are discussed at length.)

4. ERT-SQL

This section introduces ERT-SQL, a new temporal query language. ERT-SQL is based on the standard SQL2 and on the VT-SQL. The language accommodates the use of time interval timestamps. ERT-SQL supports three different types of timestamps: *time points* (TP), *nondecomposable time intervals* (TI) and *decomposable time intervals* (TPI). Each of the above timestamp types can have a user-specified granularity. The provided granularity types are: second, minute, hour, day, month and year. Obviously, if the user specifies a granularity type for a timestamped ERT object, this granularity type supports all the supertypes of it. For example, if the day granularity type is specified, the actual timestamp values will have a year, a month and a day reference.

The aim of this section is to familiarise the reader with the ERT-SQL query language, through a number of examples.

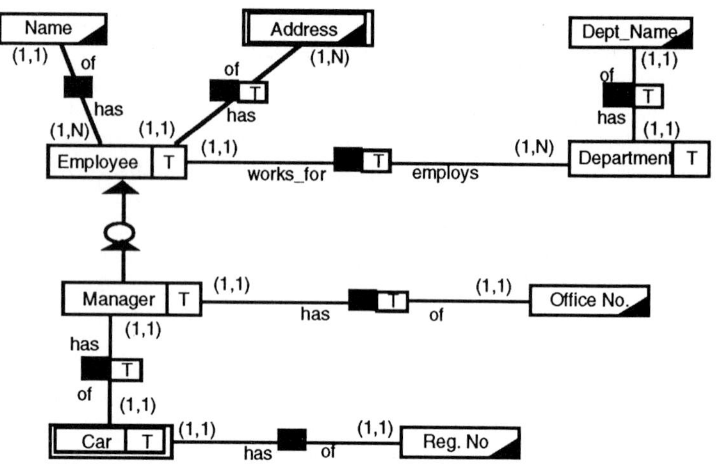

Figure 2: An example ERT schema

The ERT-SQL statements are divided into three language groups: Data Definition Language (DDL), Data Manipulation Language (DML) and Schema Manipulation Language (SML).

4.1. Data Definition Statements

The ERT-SQL recognises the following DDL statements: `CREATE ENTITY`, `CREATE COMPLEX ENTITY`, `CREATE DERIVED ENTITY`, `CREATE RELATIONSHIP`, `CREATE ISA RELATIONSHIP`, `CREATE DERIVED RELATIONSHIP` and `CREATE COMPLEX VALUE`.

The CREATE ENTITY statement expects an entity class name and the declaration of the value classes related to this entity. If this entity is timestamped, then we have to specify the type and the granularity of the timestamp. The value class definition part expects a keyword, which can be either VALUE or COMPLEX VALUE, the name for this value class and the information about the relationship with the entity class to which it is related.

The CREATE RELATIONSHIP statement requires the two entity class names, that this relationship is going to connect, as well as the role names, the cardinalities and, if it is a timestamped relationship, the timestamp structure definition . In the case of an ISA relationship creation, the names of both the entity superclass ("parent") and the entity subclasses ("children") are mandatory. Also, in the case of the derived relationship we have to specify the derivation rule for this relationship.

The CREATE COMPLEX ENTITY statement is used in order to define a complex entity class. This definition refers to all the values related with this class. Also, the definition of all the contained classes of this complex class is mandatory. For a complex class we have to define one "layer", i.e. one level of hierarchy, at a time.

The CREATE COMPLEX VALUE statement is used in order to define the components of a complex value class which we have already defined as a 'property' of an entity class.

In the CREATE DERIVED ENTITY statement we have to specify the name for this entity and the derivation rule which, actually, defines this entity.

Let us now show how the entity classes `Employee` and `Department` and the relationship between the two in the ERT schema shown in Figure 2 have been defined using DDL statements.

```
CREATE ENTITY Employee  (TI , YEAR )
  (VALUE, Name, CHAR(20), has, 1, N, of, 1, 1)
  (COMPLEX VALUE, Address,has,1,1, of,1,N (TPI, YEAR))

CREATE ENTITY Department (TPI, YEAR )
  (VALUE,Dept_Name,CHAR(20),has,1,1,of,1,1(TPI, YEAR))


CREATE RELATIONSHIP
  (Employee,Department,works_for,1,1,employs,1,N(TI,YEAR))
```

The components of the complex value class `Address` are shown in Figure 3.

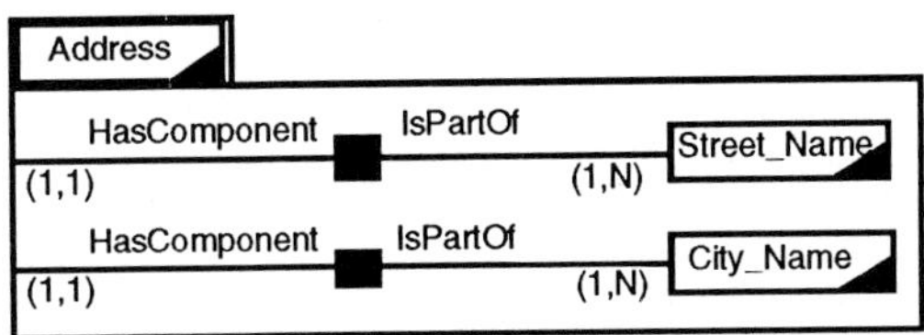

Figure 3 : The complex value class `Address`

4.2. Data Manipulation Statements

The DML statements supported in the ERT-SQL language are: `SELECT, INSERT, DELETE and UPDATE.`

4.2.1. SELECT

The SELECT statement has the structure and facilities similar to that of the standard SQL, but furthermore it is able to express and describe the temporal semantics of the ERT model.

Examples:
Applied to the schema in Figure 2, the following statement retrieves employees who live in Manchester.

```
SELECT Name
FROM Employee
WHERE Address.City_Name = 'Manchester'
```

"Get the periods during which a manager was in possession of a car."

```
SELECT [Manager, Car, has, of].TIMESTAMP
FROM Manager
```

"Get names of employees and departments. Eliminate duplicates."

```
SELECT Name
FROM Employee
UNION
SELECT Dept_Name
FROM Department
```

Note that when UNION is used the following conditions apply:

- the number of value expressions in each select list must be the same;
- the data types of the value expressions to which the UNION applies must be the same;
- use of UNION without ALL option causes redundant duplicate instances to be deleted . By adding ALL these duplicates are kept.

4.2.2. INSERT

The INSERT statement is used to add instances both to entity and to relationship classes.

Examples :
"Insert the 'Toys' department with existence period, 1/1/1993 to the end of the next year."

```
INSERT INTO Department
VALUES Dept_Name = 'Toys'
       TIMESTAMP = '[1/1/1993 , END_OF_NEXT_YEAR)'
```

"Insert a new employee 'Jones' and his related information."

```
INSERT INTO Employee
VALUES Name = 'Jones'
       TIMESTAMP = [NOW,)
       Street_Name = 'Oxford Rd.'
       City_Name = 'Manchester'
```

4.2.3. DELETE

The DELETE statement is used to delete unwanted instances from an entity class or from a relationship class.

Examples :
"Delete the employee with name 'Jones'."

```
DELETE FROM Employee
WHERE ( Name = 'Jones' )
```

"Delete the instances of the employee with name 'Jones' for the time period '[1/1/1990,31/3/1990)'."

```
DELETE FROM Employee
WHERE  (Name = 'Jones') AND
       (TIMESTAMP CP '[1/1/1990,31/3/1990)')
```

4.2.4. UPDATE

The UPDATE statement is used to alter the contents of an instance either of an entity class or of a relationship class.

Examples :
"Employee 'Jones' did not exist for the period '[1/3/1991,1/7/1992)'. Enter the correct period '[1/2/1991,1/5/1992)'."

```
UPDATE Employee
SET    TIMESTAMP = [1/2/1991,1/5/1992)
WHERE  (NAME = 'Jones') AND (TIMESTAMP = [1/3/1991,1/7/1992) )
```

"Enter the additional information that the employee 'Jones' had been working for the 'Toys' department for the period '[1/1/1970,1/1/1987)' and for the period '[1/1/1990, 1/1/1992)'."

```
UPDATE RELATIONSHIP (Employee,Department,works_for,employs)
ADD
      TIMESTAMP = '[1/1/1970,1/1/1987)','[1/1/1990, 1/1/1992)'
WHERE  (Dept_Name = 'Toys')
```

4.3. Schema Manipulation Statements

In the ERT-SQL language, DROP and ALTER serve as schema manipulation statements. The DROP statement is used to remove entity classes or relationship classes from an ERT schema. The ALTER statement is used to add and remove value classes related to an entity class or to add a new component to a complex object. Also, by using the ALTER statement, we can add or remove the constraints related to an entity class. When the DROP statement is used to remove an entity class, all the relationships and the value classes related to this entity class are removed as well. Furthermore, if the removed class is a complex one, then all its components are removed too.

Examples:
"Remove the Department entity class."

```
DROP ENTITY Department
```

"Add to the Employee entity, a value class with name 'Salary'."

```
ALTER ENTITY Employee
ADD (VALUE, Salary, INTEGER, has, 1, 1, of, 1, N)
```

"Remove the `Salary` value class from the Employee entity class."

```
ALTER ENTITY Employee
DROP Salary
```

5. Conclusions

In this paper, we described the overall architecture of the ORES TDBMS and discussed briefly its different components. The main objective and result of such a system is the support for efficient and user friendly representation, manipulation of and reasoning about temporal knowledge.

We also presented a new temporal query language, ERT-SQL which is an extension of SQL2 and VT-SQL languages. ERT-SQL is powerful enough to express all the possible temporal queries on an ERT schema. This language accommodates the use of time interval timestamps. We showed, through a number of examples, that the language, although rich and expressive, is easy to use.

Finally, the implementation of ERT-SQL will be achieved through VT-SQL, which itself is implemented through VT-RA. In other words, we will have to find some kind of correspondence between ERT-SQL constructs and VT-SQL constructs in the same fashion as we did between ERT objects and relational objects.

Acknowledgements

ORES is a collaborative ESPRIT project. The partners of the ORES consortium are: 01-Pliroforiki (Greece), Clinica Puerta de Hierro (Spain), Information Dynamics (Greece), Royal Institute of Technology (Sweden), UMIST (UK), Agricultural University of Athens (Greece) and University of Athens (Greece).
The conceptual component is developed jointly by UMIST and RIT whereas the valid-time component is developed jointly by 01-Pliroforiki, University of Athens, Agricultural University of Athens and Information Dynamics. We acknowledge the contribution to this work of all the other participants in the ORES project.

References

[1] Pissinou, N., Snodgrass, R.T., Elmasri, R., Mumick, I.S., Ozsu, M.T., Pernici, B. , Segev, A. and Theodoulidis, B.: "Towards an Infrastructure for Temporal Databases: Report of an Invitational ARPA/NSF Workshop", *TR*

94-01, Department of Computer Science, University of Arizona, January,1994.

[2] Klopprogge, M.R. and Lockmann, A.C.: “Modelling Information Preserving Databases: Consequences of the Concept of Time”, in *Proceedings of the 9th International Conference on VLDB*, Florence, Italy, pp. 399-416, 1983.

[3] Elmasri, R., Wuu, G. and Kouramajian, V.: “A Temporal Model and Query Language for EER Databases”, *Chapter 9, Temporal Databases: Theory, Design and Implementation*, Benjamin/Cummings, pp. 212-229, 1993.

[4] Rose, E. and Segev, A.: “TOODM - A Temporal Object-Oriented Data Model with Temporal Constraints”, in *Proceedings of the 10th International Conference on the Entity-Relationship Approach*, San Mateo, California, pp. 205-229, 1991.

[5] Rose, E. and Segev, A.: “TOOSQL: A Temporal Object-Oriented Query Language”, in *Proceedings of the 12th International Conference on the Entity-Relationship Approach*, Dallas, Texas, 1993.

[6] Cheng, T.S. and Gadia, S.K.: “An Object-Oriented Model for Temporal Databases”, in *Proceedings of the International Workshop on an Infrastructure for Temporal Databases*, Arlington, Texas, 1993.

[7] Kline, N.: “Bibliography on Temporal Databases”, *SIGMOD Record*, Vol..22, No.4, 1993.

[8] 01-Pliroforiki: “Specification of System Requirements”, *ORES Deliverable C2*, Athens, Greece, 1993.

[9] van der Lans, R. F. : “The SQL Standard. A Complete Reference”, Prentice Hall, 1988.

[10] van der Lans, R. F.: “Introduction to SQL”, Addison-Wesley, 1988.

[11] Date, C. J. : “A Guide to the SQL Standard”, 2nd Edition, Addison-Wesley,1982.

[12] Relational Technology Inc.: “INGRES/SQL Reference Manual”, Release 6.4, 1991.

[13] CPH: “User Requirements”, *ORES Deliverable B2*, Madrid, Spain, 1993.

[14] 01-Pliroforiki: “Implementation of Valid Time Relational Algebra”, *ORES Deliverable C4*, Athens, Greece, 1993.

[15] 01-Pliroforiki: “Specification of Valid Time SQL”, *ORES Deliverable D2*, Athens, Greece, 1993.

[16] 01-Pliroforiki: “Design of Valid Time SQL”, *ORES Deliverable D3*, Athens, Greece, 1993.

[17] 01-Pliroforiki: “Specification of Valid Time Formalism”, *ORES Deliverable C3*, Athens, Greece, 1993.

[18] RIT: “Conceptual Design Formalisms of ORES”, *Technical Report no. P7224/ORES/RIT/WPE/T5/R2/v1*, Stockholm, Sweden, 1993.

[19] UMIST: “The ORES Metamodel”, *Technical Report no. P7224/ORES/UMIST/WPE/3/v3*, Manchester, UK, 1993.

[28] Theodoulidis, C. et al: "A Conceptual Modelling Formalism for Temporal Database Applications", *Information Systems*, Vol. 16, No 4, pp 401-41 1991.

[21] RIT: “Specification of Validation Tool of ORES”. T Stockholm, Sweden, 1993.

[22] UMIST: “The Design Document”, *Techn P7224/ORES/UMIST/WPE/5/v2*, Manchester, UK, 1993.

Object-Oriented Constraint Analysis in Complex Applications

Flavio Bonfatti*, Paola Daniela Monari*, Paolo Paganelli**
* Faculty of Engineering, University of Modena
** Democenter scrl

Abstract: *It is the aim of this paper to propose an approach to constraint analysis and representation that makes conceptual modelling of real world applications more complete and effective. The need for this effort arises from the strong incidence that dynamics and constraints have within the knowledge captured while observing the application domain, expecially in the cases of complex applications. Constraint analysis is based on an object-oriented conceptual model that adopts the primitives of complex object and law to express, respectively, relationships among objects and interdipendencies of the relative states.*

Keywords: *conceptual modelling, object-oriented analysis, constraint representation.*

Introduction

In this paper we propose an approach to constraint analysis and representation that is aimed at improving conceptual modelling of real world entities and relationships. In the field of databases (as well as in that of expert systems, even though with a different form) great importance is attributed to this preliminary activity of the observer, whose objective is collecting the knowledge required for effective design of data structures and processing algorithms. Most of this knowledge concerns interdependencies among entities: conditions under which entities may interact with each other and mutual effects of interactions on the states of the involved entities.

Changes of state are the means the observer has available to perceive entity dynamics; they are the consequences of events occurring in the real world. An event is characterized by the coordinates of its occurrence (place, time, etc.), the involved entities and the effects it induces on them. Effects often present regularities that are recognized by the observer and can be expressed in form of constraints on the objects that model the entities. In order to keep the database contents correct and consistent, so as to constitute a faithful representation of the application domain, constraints must be satisfied by every operation. We consider complex an application where a large variety of events must be modelled, each entity participates in many events under different conditions, and events are related with each other by the entities they share.

Capability and form of constraint representation are strictly related to the characteristics of the model that is adopted. Database conceptual modelling usually employs either Entity/Relationship approach [10] or Object-Oriented Analysis [9,

12] depending on whether a relational or an object-oriented management system is available. Both methodologies are heavily lacking in constraint representation, since no primitive is provided to express them formally. Thus, most of the knowledge that is derived from observing the real world escapes any kind of control.

The approach we propose is based on a model, named Multidata, that has been studied within a project of the National Research Council (CNR) of Italy [2]. It adopts the complex object and law primitives; the former is introduced to model explicitly the relationship established among a number of entities because of their participation in an event, while the latter expresses formally the invariant relation that constraints states and state transformations of such entities. As we shall see, these new primitives constitute the basis for the definition of a disciplined methodology of constraint analysis.

Our approach presents some points of contact with other models that make use of invariant relations, such as the Z notation [13] and the Eiffel language [11]. However, with these models the knowledge is partitioned into a static component and a dynamic component; the former includes the invariant relation that defines the space of legal states, while aspects related to state transformations are coded in the latter in terms of operations characterized by pre- and post-conditions. Even though it may occur that some operations mirror events of the real world, they are indeed conceived as abstract representations of routines that should be developed to build up the application.

On the contrary, our approach adopts an ontological viewpoint [3, 6, 14], in that it is aimed at capturing the truth about the application domain, as it is perceived by the observer, independently of any implementation problem. Laws are associated to the schema objects on the basis of a clear semantic interpretation, and not for operational purposes. This results in criteria to drive definition of the objects that better represent real world entities and events and, in particular, to classify constraints on the basis of their meanings.

The paper is subdivided into eight sections. In the first section, some significant complex applications are briefly presented; they constitute the current test bed of this approach and provide examples for the following sections. The second section introduces the basic modelling primitives of the Multidata model. Sections 3 to 8 present the different types of constraints that can be recognized during the conceptual modelling phase; their distinction is useful to achieve a more expressive and controlled representation of the application domain dynamics.

1 Complex Applications

The modelling approach proposed in this paper is presently applied to some relevant and complex applications. Particularly interesting is an application in the area of computer integrated manufacturing and engineering, dealing with product and production process representation as support to design and planning activities. This problem constitutes the core of project 8224 of the ESPRIT programme, named RUMS (a Rule-based Manufacturing Modelling System), whose goal is providing small and medium enterprises with an advanced computer based tool that minimizes the amount of data to be managed, utilizes a declarative language, copes with the intrinsic complexity of entities and relationships in the engineering and manufacturing fields. Basic problems arising in this application are:

a) Product representation. It is required to describe the composition structure of product families, with all their versions, as well as the schemas of operations to be performed for obtaining each version from the elementary components [8]. The relationships between the composition structure of the single product in the family and its performances and external features must also be established.

b) Resource representation. The resources that participate in the production process (persons, machines, tools, energy, etc.) are modelled at different levels of detail, from single units to work centers, and the resulting representations are related to each other. Among the most challenging modelling problems we can cite sharing of auxiliary resources by the main resources as well as description of the operations they can perform in terms of input and output products, operation times, costs.

c) Production flow representation. Production flows express the ways how machines or work centers are linked in order to realize the whole production process. Each unit presents an input queue, with parts coming from previous units, and an output queue, with parts available to successive units; flow representation means queue sizing and management.

Another interesting application comes from the area of software engineering; in particular, our approach is presently under study as the means for specifying software requirements for programmable logic controllers. The objective is expressing in a high level (controllable and validable) formalism the structural and behavioural aspects of the system to automatize, since we hypothesize that this is a useful basis for the following phases of the software life cycle. Major benefits are expected in the phases of software design and software test, particularly in the cases of cooperative development and software modules reuse. This activity is carried out within project 10542 of the ESSI initiative, named EASIER (Enhancing Application Software Implementation for programmable logic controllERs).

Finally, our approach is under evaluation with respect to the design of geographical information systems [4, 5, 7]. The complexity of this application derives from the wide variety of aspects to be considered and put in relation, such as the following: descriptive and geometric features of geographic entities; relationships based on their topological properties; physical laws that describe natural phenomena; human laws to limit and govern the use of territory. The possibility of representing territory structure and dynamics by a unified approach is a fundamental condition for the design of effective decision support systems in the fields of environmental impact assessment and land use planning.

2 Complex Objects and Laws

The Multidata model adopts the basic principles of the object-oriented paradigm, but it introduces new primitives in order to overcome limitations in expressiveness concerning, specifically, the representation of constraints. Details on the modelling primitives will be given in the following sections by means of examples; the complete model sintax is reported in a forthcoming paper; here we only present the basic concepts of complex object and law.

The complex object primitive is introduced to represent relationships among entities. A relationship exists among some entities if changes in the state of one or more of them depend on the states of the others. This is the most common way the observer identifies relationships in the real world: whenever the behavior of an entity is determined by the combined states of other n-1 entities, the existence of an n-ary relationship is recognized. We model an n-ary relationship as a complex object having the participating objects as components. The complex object structure is described by a type declaration:

```
object ObjectName
A1 : domain1
A2 : domain2
...    ...    ...
C1 : ObjectName1
C2 : ObjectName2
...    ...    ...
```

where Ai is the name of the attribute and domain-i specifies the set of values the attribute can take; similarly, components are given by pairs (Ci,ObjectName-i), where Ci represents the role of the component in the relationship and ObjectName-i denotes the type of object that can hold that role.

Entities are modelled according to the same syntax; they produce simple objects, that is, objects characterized only by attributes.

Thus, a type declaration expresses static properties that are common to a class of objects, independently of whether they are entities or relationships. Laws are introduced, in their turn, to constraint the behaviour of the objects to which they are applied. Conceptual representation of dynamics implies that the space of states of an object type is partitioned into the space of legal states and the space of illegal states. The space of legal states is a subset of all possible combinations of values that can be assumed by the attributes of that type of object (and by the attributes of its components); this partition is given by a predicate that we express in form of laws. Moreover, it may occurr that a state transformation is considered illegal even if it maps from a legal state to another legal state: other laws are required to delimit the space of legal trasformations. If taken in conjunction, all the laws defined for an object type constitute the invariant that models its dynamics.Laws are written as expressions of the predicate calculus applied to the current and previous states of the object and its components [1], according to the following syntax:

```
laws on ObjectName
LawName1 : <expression1>
LawName2 : <expression2>
...    ...    ...
```

Then, the invariant establishes a bridge between the state of the object and the states of its components. In order to clearly separate these laws from those associated to the components, we assume that a law cannot refer directly to the states of components of the object components. The implications of this assumpions will be examined in the next sections. In the following we also assume that each law corresponds to a single boolean factor of the invarian relation, that is, an elementary condition whose false value makes false the whole invariant relation.

3 Constraints on Simple Objects

A first cathegory of constraints corresponds to those that define the space of legal states of an object type that models simple entities, so that it presents only attributes. Consider, for instance, the following definition of product batch:

```
object Batch
ProdType: string
Pieces: integer
UnitCost,TotalCost: real
Status: (inStock,moving,inUse,used)
Available,Assigned,Discarded: boolean;
laws on Batch
L1:    Pieces gt 0
L2:    TotalCost eq Pieces*UnitCost
L3:    Status in (inUse,used) <=> Assigned
L4:    Available <=> not Assigned and not Discarded
L5:    old Status eq inUse => not Status in (moving,inStock)
L6:    old Status eq used => Status eq used;
```

where different kinds of constraints are listed. Law L1 introduces a restriction of the definition domain of attribute Pieces; we consider this kind of restrictions as part of the invariant. Law L2 establishes a functional dependency between the cost of a single piece, the number of pieces and the total batch value; then, the three attributes must change in accordance with this law in order to keep the batch state in the legal space. Laws L3 and L4 express, by means of mutual implications, equivalences between predicates and boolean attributes; this is useful whenever we wish to sinthesize a significant combination of attribute values by a simple boolean value. Laws L5 and L6 define, in their turn, the space of legal state transformations; to this purpose, the current (modified) states are compared with the previous (old) states. In particular, the former says that it is not allowed a change of the Status attribute from inUse to moving or inStock, while the latter says that once a batch has been used its Status cannot change further. Observe that, with this approach, all laws can be viewed as post-conditions, that is, conditions that apply to the effects of events to check whether they satisfy the invariant.

Another example of simple object can be useful to show how constraints on state transformations are able to represent a behaviour that results in a sort of finite state automaton:

```
object Conveyor
HomeLoc,TargetLoc: Location
Status: (waiting,moving);
laws on Conveyor
L1:    not (Status eq waiting and HomeLoc ne TargetLoc)
L2:    not (Status eq moving and HomeLoc eq TargetLoc)
L3:    old Status eq waiting and HomeLoc ne TargetLoc
              => Status eq moving
L4:    old Status eq moving and HomeLoc eq TargetLoc
              => Status eq waiting;
```

Laws L1 and L2 delimit the space of legal states by excluding the cases that do not belong to the conveyor behaviour; laws L3 and L4 delimit the space of legal transformations by asserting that, having changed HomeLoc or TargetLoc (or both), the Status attribute must change as well. It should be noted that objects behaving like automata are rather frequent in dynamic applications; this kind of analysis is useful for identifying services in the data-driven object-oriented approach [9, 12].

4 Constraints on Complex Objects

A complex object presents components that correspond to entities linked by a relationship modelled by the object itself. In general, the invariant relates the spaces of legal states and transformations of the object to those of its components. A first example of complex object can be derived by the previous definition of product batch, provided the product type is introduced as an object in its own:

```
object Product
Name: string
UnitCost: real
Material: (steel,aluminium);

object Batch
Prod: Product
Pieces: integer
TotalCost: real
...     ...     ...
L2:     TotalCost eq Pieces*Prod.UnitCost
```

A more interesting example shows constraints based on presence or absence of components (absence being represented with the *nil* component instance):

```
object Tool
Name: string
Use: (steel,aluminium)
Installed: boolean;

object Machine
MTool: Tool
Status: (waitTool,ready)
ToolOn,ToolOff: boolean;
laws on Machine
L1:     ToolOn <=> old MTool eq nil and MTool ne nil
L2:     ToolOff <=> old MTool ne nil and MTool eq nil
L3:     Status eq waitTool <=> MTool eq nil
L4:     old Status eq waitTool and ToolOn
              => Status eq ready and MTool.Installed
L5:     old Status eq ready and ToolOff
              => Status eq waitTool and not MTool.Installed;
```

Laws L1 and L2 express by boolean attributes the state transformations that correspond to tool setting and removal, respectively. Law L3 establishes a dependency between the tool absence and a particular machine status. Finally, laws L4 and L5 relate the tool status to the machine status. It should be noted that this machine representation is very simplified; in practice its structure is more complex and the number of operations wider.

Whenever it is required to define constraints between the state of an object X and that of a sub-component A1 (that is, a component of the component A of X) we must remember the assumption that prevents from writing laws directly involving such two states. The solution consists in splitting the law into two parts: the one, associated to A, that introduces (imports) A attributes that mirror the A1 attributes of interest; the other, associated to X, that expresses the constraints with respect to the imported attributes. For instance, consider a queue of batches, waiting for processing on a given machine, and suppose that a general rule must be set that assures compatibility between product material and working tool:

```
object Machine                      object Batch
MUse: (steel,aluminium)             MatB: (steel,aluminium)
... ... ...                         ... ... ...
L6:  MUse eq MTool.Use              L7:  MatB eq Prod.Material
```

```
object Queue
Batches: list of Batch
Resource: Machine
laws on Queue
L1:    forall B in Batches itis B.MatB eq Resource.MUse
```

Then, with this approach, every object in the schema is characterized by two kinds of laws: internal (context-free) laws, that represent its intrinsic constraints possibly related to the component states, and external (context-dependent) laws, associated to the complex objects where it participates as component, that express its behaviours in the corresponding contexts. This realizes a neat separation between laws, since some of them can be changed without affecting those belonging to other contexts, thus obtaining a sort of additional bedded encapsulation.

On the other hand, context-free and context-dependent laws must be consistent, in that the latter should result more restrictive than the former. The logical form that has been adopted for laws makes consistency controls easier and creates the conditions for coherent and reliable schemas of the application domain.

5 Specialization Constraints

Concerning context-dependent constraints, it can be noted that they can be distinguished into two types depending on whether they refer to a single component or to a group of components. Constraints of the former type usually express conditions under which the component can participate in a complex object. With reference to the product batch definition, the following law could be added:

```
L4:    Prod.UnitCost lt 100
```

to say that only cheap products are grouped into batches. This can be interpreted as an implicit definition of a subtype of Product:

```
object CheapProduct isa Product
MinBatchSize: integer;
laws on CheapProduct
L1:    UnitCost lt 100
L2:    MinBatchSize gt 10;
```

```
object Batch
Prod: CheapProduct
... ... ...
L8:    Pieces mod Prod.MinBatchSize eq 0
```

where the restriction predicate is given by law L1; obviously, the specialization mechanism can be applied also to define subtypes of complex objects.

6 Context-dependent Constraints on Groups of Components

Other context-dependent constraints are those involving two ore more components of the complex object to which the laws are associated; usually, these constraints express the conditions the components must meet jointly in order to ensure that their participation in the complex object is legal. A first example has already been presented in Section 4 by law L1 on object Queue:

```
L1:    forall B in Batches itis B.MatB eq Resource.MUse
```

that relates the type of material a machine is able to work with that of the product batches to be worked. A further example introduces the definition of Operation, intended as manufacturing step that transforms input parts into an output part, and of Activity, intended as the assignment of a work to a machine:

```
object Operation
Name: string
Input: list of Product
Output: Product
AvgDurat: duration;
laws on Operation
L1:    not empty(Input)
L2:    Output ne nil
L3:    not Output in Input;
```

```
object Activity
Work: Operation
Resource: Machine
Start,End: time;
```

If we suppose that Machine presents a further attribute `Works: set of string` to identify the operations that it can perform, a compatibility law on Activity says:

```
L1:    Work.Name in Resource.Works
```

Observe that laws L1 and L2 express basic conditions for the Operation to be completely defined; even though Input and Output components are cited, we have not a specialization case because such laws do not involve Input and Output states. For the same reason, law L3 is not a context-dependent constraint on components.

7 Context-free Constraints on Groups of Components

If two or more objects participate together in different relationships, the corresponding complex objects have associated context-dependents constraints on their behaviour and mutual influence. It may occur that these laws share a common part: if existing, it represents the constraints that such objects must satisfy in any context, that is, their context-free constraints. These rules can be removed from the single relationships and associated to a virtual object, introduced to this purpose, where these objects play the role of main components. As an example, we introduce the general constraints concerning a pair of operations in sequence:

```
object SeqOper as Op1,Op2: Operation
TotDurat: duration;
laws on SeqOper
L1: Op1.Output in Op2.Input
L2: TotDurat eq Op1.AvgDurat+Op2.AvgDurat;
```

The auxiliary attribute TotDurat has been introduced to express a property of the pair of subsequent operations; if necessary, auxiliary components can also be used.

As virtual objects express general rules on their main components, say A and B, they can be used in defining laws in any other context where such components interact; in other words, the virtual object plays the role of virtual component in all the complex objects including type A and B components. For instance, we show a sort of generalized production routing, that is, the tree structure of operations that realize the manufacturing process of a given product:

```
object Routing
Root:Product
Tree: list of Operation;
laws on Routing
L1:    forall X in (Tree-first(Tree)) itis    exists unique Y
              in Routing suchthat SeqOper(Op1=X,Op2=Y)
L2:    first(Tree).Output eq Root
L3:    forall X,Y in Tree itis
              SeqOper(Op1=X,Op2=Y) => ord(X) gt ord(Y);
```

Law L1 gives the connection constraints of the tree; the condition `SeqOper(Op1=X,Op2=Y)` means that operations X and Y are subsequent. Laws L2 and L3 establish a partial ordering on operations such that each operation follows, in the list, all the operations that are executed later: this is an acyclicity constraint.

8 Constraints on Class Objects

So far we have dealt with constraints that are applied to single instances of simple or complex objects, but sometimes constraints relating the state of an istance to the states of the other instances of the same class are required. These typically involve conditions on class cardinality or synthesis (average, maximum, sum) values. From the modelling point of view, a class is represented as any other object with the addition of an implicit component (*Instances*) constituted by the set of all the instances. As an example we propose the class of the manufacturing activities introduced in Section 6.

```
object Activities = class of Activity
AvgDurat: Duration;
laws on Activities
L1:    AvgDurat eq sum(A.End-A.Start)/card(Instances)
              for A in Instances
L2:    forall A1,A2 in Instances itis
              A1.Resource eq A2.Resource =>
              A1.Start ge A2.End or A2.Start ge A1.End;
```

where law L1 defines the average duration of all the activities, while law L2 prevents from activities overlapping on the same production resource.

Final Remarks

The research is still in progress to go deeper into some open questions. In the first place, the model has been used so far to represent independent events: we are now investigating the implications of modelling concurrent events, with the relative time synchronization problems. Secondly, laws play an outstanding role since they express an amount of behavioural knowledge which is usually neglected by other conceptual models; however, laws are formulated without taking into account how to keep them satisfied: each of them is simply a piece of truth relative to the behaviour of an object. When mapping laws into software, they become either constraints against illegal state transformations or actions to undertake for moving the system from illegal to legal states; restoration actions are presently under study.

A computer-aided support, based on the approach proposed in this paper, is under development to help the observer in realizing a rich and reliable conceptual schema of the application domain. The observer enters definitions of objects and laws and the system provides a number of correctness and consistency controls. The resulting schema can be inquired by different keyes in order to verify and validate depth and quality of the representation, or it can be used as a sound basis for the design of database structures and the relative application software.

References

[1] Bertino E. et al.: Object-oriented query languages: the notion and the issues, IEEE Trans. on Knowledge and Data Engineering, 4, 3, 1992.

[2] Bonfatti F. (ed): Conceptual modeling of multimedia applications, Technical Report 5/13 of the National SI&CP Project, 1990.

[3] Bonfatti F., Pazzi L.: Modeling object complexity and behaviour: towards an ontological paradigm, COMPEURO 91 International Conf., Bologna, 1991.

[4] Bonfatti F.: Intensional design of geographical information systems, EGIS 93 International Conf., Genova, 1993.

[5] Bonfatti F. et al.: Object-oriented support to the design of geographical information systems, EGIS 93 Int. Conf., Genova, 1993.

[6] Bonfatti F., Pazzi L.: An ontology-driven approach to knowledge representation, Int. workshop on Formal Ontology in Conceptual Analysis and Knowledge Representation, Padova, 1993.

[7] Bonfatti F., Monari P. D.: Spatio-temporal representation of complex geographic structures, CSEIA 93 IFIP WG5.11 Conference, Como 1993.

[8] Bonfatti F., Monari P. D., Paganelli P.: Towards a rule-based unified product modelling, DKSME 94 Int. Conf., Hong Kong, 1994.

[9] Coad P., Yourdon E.: Object Oriented Analysis, Yourdon Press, 1990.

[10] Chen P. P. S.: The entity-relationship model - toward a unified view of data, ACM Trans. on Database System, 1, 1, 1976.

[11] Meyer B.: Eiffel, The Language, Prentice Hall Object-Oriented Series, 1992.

[12] Rumbaugh J. et al.: Object-Oriented Modeling and Design, Prentice Hall 1991.

[13] Spivey J. M.: The Z-notation, Prentice Hall 1989.

[14] Wand Y.: A proposal for a formal model of objects, in Object-Oriented Concepts, Databases and Applications, W. Kim F. Lochowsky eds., Addison Wesley, 1989.

A Conceptual DataBase Approach for Modelling 3D Objects of Irregular Geometry*

Krotopoulou A., Spirakis P., Terpou D., Tsakalidis A.
Department of Computer Engineering and Informatics,
University of Patras, 26500 Patras, Greece
Computer Technology Institute, Patras University,
PO Box 1122, 26110 Patras Greece
E-mail:{spirakis,terpou,tsak}@cti.gr,

Abstract: In this study we show how to suitably extend the power of the IFO semantic data model in order to capture topological relationships of 3D network structures of irregular geometry. We demonstrate our approach by modelling the layout and nerve structure of the human brain as an example.

1. Introduction.

This paper reports on research, currently in progress, on the development of a formal semantic database model - the 3D-IFO data model - which can serve the efficient conceptual design of spatial databases dealing with network structures of 3D objects. 3D network structures usually consist of objects of irregular geometry and interconnections among them. The interconnections are also non-uniform, usually of varying length, diameter or shape. A prime example of such networks is the layout of the human brain ([TT88]), in which our research was initially focused. Other examples include water-supply networks, other utility networks, blood circulation networks of the human body e.t.c.

Conceptual data models have been recently proposed to capture the characteristics of composite data (e.g. geographic information in GIS systems). A promising such model is the IFO model ([AH87]). Our work here shows how to extend IFO to model 3D network structures of objects of irregular geometry. We define new data types, constructors and operators and demonstrate their power via expressing some typical integrity constraints and complicated queries of the example of the human brain database. An adequate conceptual design can form the proper basis for the logical design of the database and also for the efficient implementation at the physical level.

2. The Topology of 3D Objects.

In this chapter we present the topological features of spatial objects, using human brain objects as a prototype. A brief description of the most essential and representative brain information is first presented, in order to extract conclusions about the topology of more complicate objects.

To begin, we mention that the human brain can be partitioned by many ways. For example, by a certain division, the brain consists of the white and the grey matter. Grey matter consists of the cerebral cortex and the nuclei, while the cortex is divided

* This research was partially supported by the ESPRIT Special Action project DELTA - CIME, the AIM project MAGNOBRAIN and CTI.

into forty seven Brodman areas. Furthermore, the surface of the human brain is full of convolutions and sulci ([TT88]). Additionally, the great cerebral functions are localised in certain principal cortical regions and nuclei. It is self-evident that this anatomic allocation of the certain major functions to different areas of the cerebral cortex is incomplete, approximate and slightly ambiguous.

As it can be easily seen from above, the human brain consists of brain areas with a certain characteristic (e.g. a brain area with a known anatomical name, a brain area in which a certain cerebral function is localised e.t.c.). All these brain areas have the topology of a *Region.*

Another important issue refers to the communication among brain areas, which is conducted by bundles of nerve fibres. These 3D objects have the topology of a *Bundle.*

Based on the above observations, we can say that brain objects can have a topology either of a Region or of a Bundle, Having this in mind, one can consider the human brain as a 3D network structure, which contains regions and bundles where every bundle connects regions traversing through other intermediate regions.

The agreement on a sufficient geometrical view of the human brain objects is of utmost importance. Medical people have considered that the human brain should be divided into cubes of side of 1mm - called *Basic Cubes* - whose edges are parallel to the reference lines of a certain reference system, the tree dimensional proportional grid system ([TT88]). After this consideration, any brain object (region or bundle) can geometrically be viewed as *the set* of the basic cubes that it includes ([AKSTT93]). In most cases, the number of those cubes is significantly large.

On the other hand, some of those cubes can be grouped into orthogonal parallepipeds with larger dimensions. In this way, the concept of *Flexible Box* is introduced ([AKSTT93]). Generally, given a connected (not necessarily convex) area of the brain represented as a set S of basic cubes, the set F(S) of flexible boxes that equivalently represents it, is defined to be the smallest possible number of orthogonal parallepipeds (parallel to axes) of varying dimensions that covers the area.

All the above considerations can be applied in other spatial network applications which deal with 3D irregular objects (e.g. human body blood circulation networks, telephone networks, water supply networks and other utility-pipe based networks).

3. 3D-IFO: An Extension of the IFO Data Model.

The conceptual data model 3D-IFO is an extension of the IFO data model, and has been defined in order to sufficiently model 3D objects of irregular geometry. Taking into account the peculiar characteristics of those objects, the following definitions are proposed:

A. Four new printable types.

Spatial information handling applications, as it can be seen from the previous chapter, deals with 3D objects which have a certain topology (Basic Cube, Flexible Box, Region or Bundle). After this observation, the first task that has to be considered is to ensure that there will be an atomic object - using IFO data model terminology - which will reflect the object's topology. Let us call this atomic object "Topology".

In a second step the domains of that object must be specified. Their implementation can be performed by adding new printable types to the classic ones (real, integer, string, date e.t.c). These new types are called *spatial* and are introduced in order to be able to operate efficiently on geometric objects. There are four such data types: *Basic Cube*, *Flexible Box*, *Region* and *Bundle*.

The domain, now, of the object "Topology" depends on the printable type:

1. If the object is of type "Basic Cube", the domain is defined to be the set of all the basic cubes. While each basic cube can be defined by the coordinates of its centre (which is a 3D point), $\Re^3$ forms the domain. It is remarkable, that the concept of "3D point", has no meaning in such applications. On the other hand, the basic cube has exactly that role, being the topological basis in our approach.

2. If the object is of type "Flexible Box", the domain is defined to be the set of all the flexible boxes. Every flexible box is defined by the coordinates of two 3D points (its centre and one of its vertexes). Consequently, $\Re^3 \times \Re^3$ forms the domain.

3. If the object is of type "Region", the domain is defined to be the set of all the regions. Every region is geometrically viewed as a set of flexible boxes. Consequently the powerset of $\Re^3 \times \Re^3$ ($\wp(\Re^3 \times \Re^3)$), forms the domain.

4. If the object is of type "Bundle", the domain is defined to be the set of all the bundles. Since every bundle can be geometrically viewed as a set of flexible boxes, the set $\wp(\Re^3 \times \Re^3)$ forms the domain.

We must mention, here, that in most cases, the actual domain is a subset of the ones defined above, defined according to the needs and limitations of the application .

B. A new constructor.

Various topological relationships among 3D objects have to be sufficiently modelled. Such a topological relationship referring to the human brain, is the one that indicates that a certain brain object lies on a specific position with respect to another one. For example, we consider that the two following topological relationships stand:

- Brodman area X lies north south of Convolution Y.
- Convolution X traverses Brodman areas A, B and C.

By observing the above expressions one can note that except of their relationship, ("lies north south", "traverses") the ordering of the areas which are involved in the upper relationship must clearly be defined. For example, the expression "Convolution Y lies north south of Brodman area X" gives a different information from the first example. Another issue to be considered here, arising from the second example, is related to the fact that the relationship can be many to many, while there is an ordering among the correlated objects. The order Brodman area A, Brodman area B and Brodman area C, indicates the order in which Convolution X traverses them.

In order to model such topological relationships, we introduce the constructor *"ordering"*.

Definition: The constructor *"ordering"* defines a finite set of ordered subsets of objects which are of the same or different type. In any subset, the order of the objects and the number of objects of every type, is predefined. Furthermore, the object type(s) which indicate the exact relationship of the correlated objects - in each subset - could be defined. Ordering is represented by a node (◯) which contains the symbol (↑) and is connected with simple lines with the object types that it correlates. Every line is augmented with parameters which indicate the ordering among the objects (x_1, .., x_z, y_1 ,...., y_w in Figure 1) and the number of objects of each type in every subset ((z), (w) in Figure 1). The object type which indicates the relationship of the correlated objects is presented in Figure 1 by a dashed orthogonal parallelogram, since it may or may not exist. For IFO symbols see ([AH87]).

The corresponding 3D-IFO schema of the first example is illustrated in Figure 2.

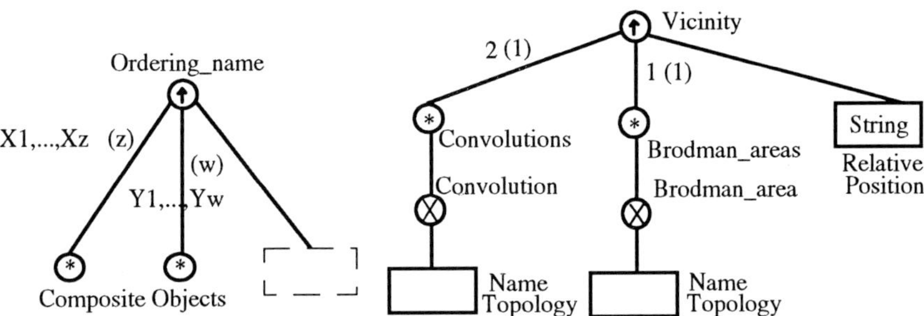

Fig1: Formal symbolism of ordering. **Fig 2:** Use of the constructor ordering.

C. A new type of attribute.

The task of keeping track of the changes that occur in an object, is confronted in a database system, via the concept of "versions". In the IFO data model, each version of the object is a distinct object, with a time based listing among the versions (objects).

While the concept of listing is already modelled in IFO model via the constructor 'listing', a way to model the criterion of the listing has now to be defined. In order to succeed in this, we introduce a new type of attribute: *based-on* (Figure 3).

Taking into account the above notion of versions, one can extend the use of this type of attribute in order to express the criterion according to which a certain "listing" or "ordering" stands. To make it more clear we illustrate two examples, which arise from the study of the human brain.

1. An essential information which may help to the localisation of epileptic foci, is that the latter appears in each brain area with different possibilities. In other words, brain areas are "ordered" according to this possibility (Figure 4).

The issue that arises here, is that the existing printable types can not express the type of the atomic object "possibility". This is because the possibility may be expressed not only as a number, but with more complicated expressions according to the case (use of integrals). To overlap this representation limitation, we introduce the printable type *'Distribution'*. The domain of this type is the set of function symbols (i.e. predefined character names).

2. The example presented in Figure 2 could be augmented by the concept of criterion according to which the particular ordering holds.

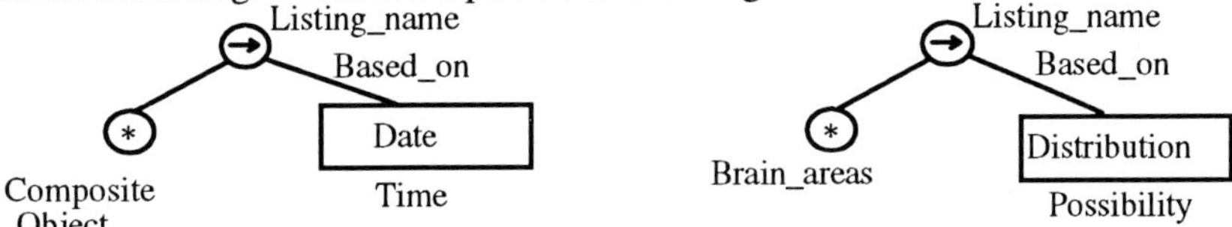

Fig3: Expressing the concept of version. **Fig 4:** Listing based on possibility.

4. Definition of New Operators.

For the manipulation of the new types of objects, a set of new operations which are performed via the use of new operators, is defined. Those operators have been categorised into four types: *Measurement, Geometric, Topological* and *Sorting*.

In the following definitions, Basic Cube, Flexible Box, Region and Bundle are defined to be the sets of all the objects that are of type "Basic Cube", "Flexible box", "Region" or "Bundle", respectively. Furthermore, the symbol P(Basic Cube) indicates the set of all the finite subsets of Basic Cube. The sets P(Flexible Box), P(Region) and P(Bundle) are defined in a similar way. Additionally, C, FL, RG, B are variables ranging over geometric objects whose type is "Basic Cube", "Flexible Box", "Region" or "Bundle", respectively. C_1, C_2, FL_1, FL_2, e.t.c are used analogously. Furthermore, the symbol RGB indicates an object whose type is "Region" or "Bundle".

A. Geometric operators.

1. *Projection* takes an object of type "Basic Cube" or "Flexible Box" and returns its projection to the planes defined by the three axes of the reference system. More precisely, it returns the ordered set (Xmin, Xmax, Ymin, Ymax, Zmin, Zmax). We define as Xmin (Xmax) the minimum (maximum) algebraic value of the vector which is formed by the projection of the object in the X reference line. Ymin, Ymax, Zmin, Zmax are defined analogously.

$$\text{Projection: (Basic Cube} \cup \text{Flexible Box)} \rightarrow \Re^6$$

2. *ConsistFlex* takes an object of type "Flexible Box" and returns the finite set of the basic cubes it includes.

$$\text{ConsistFlex: Flexible Box} \rightarrow \text{P(Basic Cube)}$$

Similarly, the operator *Consist* takes an object of type "Region" or "Bundle" and returns the finite set of the flexible boxes it includes. Since the object taken is one stored in the database, the resultant set consists of the already defined non-overlapped flexible boxes.

$$\text{Consist: (Region} \cup \text{Bundle)} \rightarrow \text{P(Flexible Box)}$$

3. *Union* takes a finite set of objects and returns an object which is the union of the areas of the given ones, and whose type can be "Flexible Box", "Region" or "Bundle" depending on the types and the topological relationship of the given objects. For example, the union of two basic cubes may be a flexible box or a region. We also note that if the derived object is of type "Region", the region can be simply connected 3D set or not, depending on whether the given objects have or not a common point.

$$\text{Union: P(Basic Cube} \cup \text{Flexible Box} \cup \text{Region} \cup \text{Bundle)} \rightarrow \text{(Flexible Box} \cup \text{Region} \cup \text{Bundle)}$$

4. *Setdifference*. It is defined in a same way as the operator union, and has the known meaning of set difference.

5. *Intersection* takes an object of type "Flexible Box" and an object of type "Region" or "Bundle" and returns the finite set of flexible boxes which are derived from the intersection of the given flexible box with the flexible boxes of which the given region or bundle consists.

$$\text{Intersection: Flexible Box} \times \text{(Region} \cup \text{Bundle)} \rightarrow \text{P(Flexible Box)}$$

Let FL and RGB be the given objects of type "Flexible" and "Region$\cup$Bundle" respectively and I be the resulting set of flexible boxes. The formal definition of this operator is:

Intersection(FL, RGB) = I

The set I can be computed as follows:

$I = I_1 \cup I_2 \cup I_3$ where

I_1 = {all the flexible boxes that compose RGB and totally enclose FL}

I_2 = {all the flexible boxes, that compose RGB and have at least one corner in FL}

I_3 = {all the flexible boxes, that compose RGB and enclose FL in one dimension while at least one of their sides is included in FL in the other dimension}

The above subsets can be computed in satisfactory time by applying geometric techniques presented in ([KP93]). For any of the above three cases we have defined the following operators:

enclose(FL, RGB) = I_1, cornerin(FL, RGB) = I_2, pureinter(FL, RGB) = I_3

enclose, cornerin, pureinter: Flexible Box $\times$ (Region$\cup$Bundle) $\rightarrow$ P(Flexible Box)

Based on the above definitions, the operator intersection is defined as follows:

intersection(FL,RGB)=enclose(FL,RGB)$\cup$cornerin(FL,RGB)$\cup$pureinter(FL,RGB)

6. *FlexibleCons* takes a finite set of objects whose type is "Basic Cube" and returns the finite set of the smallest possible number of flexible boxes that equivalently represents the given set.

FlexibleCons: P(Basic Cube) $\rightarrow$ P(Flexible Box)

The algorithm which is used for the implementation of this operator has been presented in ([MP93]).

7. *RegionCons* takes a finite set of objects whose type is "Flexible Box" and returns the region that they define.

RegionCons: P(Flexible Box) $\rightarrow$ Region

8. *BundleCons* takes a finite set of objects whose type is "Flexible Box" and returns the bundle that they define.

BundleCons: P(Flexible Box) $\rightarrow$ Bundle

B. Measurement operators.

1. *Distance* takes two objects and returns their minimum distance.

Distance: (Basic Cube$\cup$Flexible Box$\cup$Region$\cup$Bundle) $\times$ (Basic Cube$\cup$Flexible Box$\cup$Region$\cup$Bundle) $\rightarrow \Re_+ \cup \{0\}$

The formal definition of the operator "Distance" is described below:

Distance(K,L) = x where $x \in \Re_+ \cup \{0\}$. The formal definition of x depends on the type of the objects K and L.

a) if K, L $\in$ (Basic Cube$\cup$Flexible Box).

First of all, we assume that:

$X_1=X_{min}(K)$, $X_2=X_{max}(K)$, $X_3=X_{min}(L)$, $X_4=X_{max}(L)$

$Y_1=Y_{min}(K)$, $Y_2=Y_{max}(k)$, $Y_3=Y_{min}(L)$, $Y_4=Y_{max}(L)$

$Z_1=Z_{min}(K)$, $Z_2=Z_{max}(K)$, $Z_3=Z_{min}(L)$, $Z_4=Z_{max}(L)$.

In a next step, we construct the ordered sets : $[X_1,X_2]$, $[X_3,X_4]$, $[Y_1,Y_2]$, $[Y_3,Y_4]$, $[Z_1,Z_2]$ and $[Z_3,Z_4]$.

In order now to estimate the distance between the objects K and L we examine the three following intersections: $[X_1,X_2] \cap [X_3,X_4]$, $[Y_1,Y_2] \cap [Y_3, Y_4]$ and $[Z_1,Z_2] \cap [Z_3,Z_4]$.

i) If all the intersections have a value equal to the empty set ($\varnothing$):

$$x = \mathrm{Sqrt}\Big(\sum_{k=1}^{3} (\max\{W_1^k, W_3^k\} - \min\{W_2^k, W_4^k\})^2\Big) \text{ where } W_i^1 = X_i,\ W_i^2 = Y_i$$

$$\text{and } W_i^3 = Z_i,\ i \in N_4.$$

ii) If one of the intersections results a value not equal to the empty set ($\varnothing$):
In the case that $[X_1,X_2] \cap [X_3,X_4] \neq \varnothing$ then:

$$x = \mathrm{Sqrt}\Big(\sum_{k=1}^{2} (\max\{W_1^k, W_3^k\} - \min\{W_2^k, W_4^k\})^2 \text{ where}$$

$$W_i^1 = Y_i\ ,\ W_i^2 = Z_i,\ i \in N_4.$$

The value of x is defined analogously in the rest cases.

iii) If only one intersection results a value equal to the empty set ($\varnothing$):
In the case that $[X_1,X_2] \cap [X_3,X_4] = \varnothing$ then:

$$x = \max\{X_1,X_3\} - \min\{X_2,X_4\}$$

iv) If all the intersections result a value not equal to the empty set ($\varnothing$):

$$x=0.$$

b) if $K\in$ (Basic Cube$\cup$Flexible Box$\cup$Region$\cup$Bundle) and $L\in$ (Region$\cup$Bundle):

x = min{Distance(A,B) / (A=K if $K\in$ (Basic Cube$\cup$Flexible Box) $\vee$
$A\in$ Consist(K) if $K\in$ (Region$\cup$Bundle) $\wedge$ $B\in$ Consist(L))}.

2. *Diameter* takes an object of type "Basic Cube", "Flexible Box" or "Region" and returns its diameter.

Diameter: (Basic Cube$\cup$Flexible Box$\cup$Region) $\rightarrow \Re_+$

It's formal definition is:

a) if the object is of type "Basic Cube" or "Flexible Box" then

Diameter(K)=x where $K\in$ (Basic Cube$\cup$Flexible Box) and $x\in \Re_+$ and
$x=\mathrm{sqrt}((X_{max}(K)-X_{min}(L))^2+(Y_{max}(K)-Y_{min}(L))^2+(Z_{max}(K)-Z_{min}(L))^2)$

b) if the object is of type "Region" then the diameter is defined to be the maximum distance among two 3D points of the object, expressing the maximum width of the object.

3. *Length* takes an object of type "Bundle" and returns its average length.

Length: Bundle $\rightarrow \Re_+$

In order to define the length, the equidistant set of points (isothetic curve) is estimated, by the help of the Voronoi diagram ([PS86]), and its length is the demanded one.

4. *Position* takes an object of type "Basic Cube" or "Flexible Box" and returns its position. More precisely, it specifies the sphere in which the centre of the object lies and its exact position on this sphere. With this operator one can specify the relative position of two objects.

$$\text{Position: (Basic Cube} \cup \text{Flexible Box)} \rightarrow \Re^3$$

Its formal definition is:

Position(K)=(x,f,w) where K$\in$(Basic Cube$\cup$Flexible Box) and x,f,w$\in \Re_+$ and

$$x = \mathrm{Sqrt}(X_c^2 + Y_c^2 + Z_c^2) \text{ and } f=\tan^{-1}(Y_c/X_c) \text{ and } w=\tan^{-1}(Z_c/Y_c)$$

X_c,Y_c and Z_c are the coordinates of the centre of the given object, in each dimension.

C. Topological operators

Based on the operators defined above we can express the following basic topological operators.

1. *Cross(RG_1,RG_2)*. It specifies whether two objects of type "Region" (RG_1, RG_2) are intersected, or not.

$$\text{Cross}(RG_1,RG_2)=\text{true if } (\exists\, FL \in \text{Consist}(RG_1): \text{Intersection}(FL,RG_2) \neq \emptyset)$$

2. *Includes(RG_1,RG_2)*. It specifies whether the object RG_1 of type "Region" totally encloses the object RG_2 of type "Region", or not.

$$\text{Includes}(RG_1,RG_2)=\text{true if } (\forall FL_i \in \text{Consist}(RG_2): \text{Intersection}(FL_i,RG_1)=K_i \neq \emptyset \text{ where } i \in N_m,\ \text{RegionCons}(K_1,K_2,\ldots,K_m)=RG_2)$$

3. *Traverse(RG_1,B_1)*. It specifies whether the object B_1 of type "Bundle" traverses the object RG_1 of type "Region", or not.

$$\text{Traverse}(RG_1,B_1)=\text{true if } (\forall FL_i \in \text{Consist}(B_1): \text{Intersection}(FL_i,RG_1)=K_i \neq \emptyset \text{ where } i \in N_m,\ \text{RegionCons}(K_1,K_2,\ldots,K_m) \subseteq B_1)$$

4. *Connects(RG_1,RG_2,B_1)*. It specifies whether the object B_1 of type "Bundle", connects the objects RG_1, RG_2 of type "Region", or not.

$$\text{Connects}(RG_1,RG_2,B_1)=\text{true if } ((\exists FL_i \in \text{Consist}(B_1) : \text{Intersection}(FL_i,RG_1) \neq \emptyset) \wedge (\exists FL_j \in \text{Consist}(B_1) : \text{Intersection}(FL_j,RG_2) \neq \emptyset)).$$

5. *Equivalentclasses(RG_1B_1,RG_2B_2,$Class_1$)*. It specifies whether two objects of type "Region" or "Bundle" belong to the same class. An example of a class is the one which consists of the objects of the same conductivity. The variable "$Class_1$" defines the feature that classifies the class.

D. Sorting operators

The following operators are defined in order to sufficiently manipulate listings and orderings which are based on a certain object.

a. *Previous(object,sorting_name,x,z)* that returns :

i) if z=0 : the object which is the x_{th} one before "object", in the listing or ordering named "sorting_name".

ii) if z=1 : all the objects which intervene between "object" and the x_{th} object before it, in the listing or ordering named "sorting_name".

b. *Next(object,sorting_name,x,z)* which is defined in an analogous manner.

c. *Basis_of(object_type)* returns the object type(s) which is(are) the criterion (criteria) of the ordering(s) or listing(s) that the given "object_type" belongs to.

The following two operators, can mainly be used for those listings which indicate versions. Thus, we borrow the concept of "version" to express them in a more representative manner.

d. *According_to(object,sorting_name)* returns the version that "object" belongs, in the listing "sorting_name". For example, in the case illustrated in Figure 3, a possible expression may be: according_to(x,time)=1979.

e. *Same_according(sorting_name,* $object_1, object_2, ..., object_N$*)* returns a true or false value indicating if the defined objects ("$object_1$", "$object_2$",..."$object_N$") are of the same version or not, in the listing "sorting_name".

5. Representative Examples and Usage.

The reason behind the extension of the IFO data model (3D-IFO) and the introduction of new operators is that they can be used to define object classes and to express topological integrity constraints and database queries. In order to express the latter, we use the operators defined above, and a predicate calculus approach. The predicates that will be used are the following ones:

$\in, \exists, \forall$, M (M$x \in A$ means "for most x in A"), $\wedge, \vee$.

In the rest of this chapter, we shall illustrate some representative examples of such expressions, showing the power of the model proposed. In order to have a clear view of them, we make the following remarks.

Let E be the set that denotes the human brain and E_i the set of all the brain objects that have the same anatomical features (e.g. $E_{Brodman}$ is the set of all the Brodman areas). Every E_i is a composite object type. Every object that belongs to an E_i has at least an anatomical name and a topology .

a. Representative integrity constraints

1. Two brain objects which belong to the same E_i and are of type "Region" must not be intersected.

$\forall$x,y: x,y$\in E_i$ $\wedge$Topology(x)=Region $\wedge$ Topology(y)=Region, Cross(x,y)=false

2. The union of all the brain objects which belong to the same E_i must not override the set E.

$$Union_{x \in Ei} X \subseteq E$$

3. A bundle must connect two brain areas traversing some others.

$\forall$x: x$\in E_{bundle}$, ($\exists$y,z: y$\in E_i \wedge$z$\in E_j \wedge$Topology(y)=Region$\wedge$Topology(z)=Region $\wedge$Connect(y,z,x)=true) $\wedge$ ($\exists$w: w$\in E_k \wedge$Topology(w)=Region $\wedge$Traverse(w,x)=true)

b. Representative queries

1. Find the Brodman areas which are involved in the cerebral function 'CF1'.

Retrieve name(x) where (x$\in E_{Brodman}$ $\wedge$ ($\exists$y: y$\in E_{function}$ $\wedge$ name(y)='CF1' $\wedge$ Cross(x,y)=true))

A special case of this query is: "Find all the Brodman areas which are involved in function 'CF1', in their full extent. In this case instead of the operator "Cross", the operator "Include" should be used.

2. Find the bundles that connect the areas 'Brodman area A' and 'Brodman area B'.

Retrieve name(x) where (x$\in E_{bundle}$ $\wedge$ ($\exists$y,z: y,z$\in E_{Brodman}$ $\wedge$ name(y)='Brodman area A' $\wedge$ name(z)='Brodman area B' $\wedge$ Connect(y,z,x) = true)).

3. The existence of different approaches (estimations) concerning certain types of information, results in the need of the definition of queries which handle the information by this scope. An example is given below:

Find the Brodman areas which are involved in the cerebral function 'CF1', according to most considerations (or estimations).

Retrieve name(x) where ($x \in E_{Brodman}$ $\wedge$ ($\exists$B: Basis_of($E_{function}$)=B $\wedge$ ($Mv \in B$, $\exists$ y:$y \in E_{function}$ $\wedge$ name(y)='CF1' $\wedge$ according_to(y,B)=v $\wedge$ Cross(x,y)=true)))

6. Conclusion.

The theory which has been developed in the area of spatial database design is rather incomplete in comparison with database design for traditional business data processing. The characteristics of spatial data - their size complexity and irregular geometry, the fact that they are multi-dimensional, the existence of topological relationships and the subdivision of data in versions - lead to the necessity of specifying suitable design tools.

The spatial data model proposed for the conceptual database schema is an extension of the well known IFO data model. In the course of developing the extended IFO data model (3D-IFO), new types of objects have been defined (five new printable types, a new constructor and a new type of attribute). Furthermore, new operators (geometric, measurement, topological and sorting) were introduced, in order to manipulate the new types of objects.

By applying the 3D-IFO model to the human brain, (which is one of the most complex domains dealing with network structure of 3D objects), we have shown its practicality. More precisely, by providing examples (from the above area) of how some basic and representative topological integrity constraints and database queries can be expressed, we demonstrated the power of the model proposed.

References.

[AH87] Abiteboul S. and Hull R., "IFO : A Formal Semantic Database Model", ACM Transactions on Database Systems, 12.4 March 1987.

[AKSTT92] Anogianakis G., Krotopoulou A., Spirakis P., Terpou D., Tsakalidis A., "The logical design of the Brain Data Base", Technical Report MB1.2, AIM-Project, Magnobrain no A2020, September 1992.

[AKSTT93] Anogianakis G, Krotopoulou A,Spirakis P,Terpou D,Tsakalidis A, "Brain Data Base(BDB)",in Database and Expert Systems Applications(DEXA), 1993.

[HT92]: Hadzilacos T. and Tryfona N., "A model for expressing topological integrity constraints in geographic databases", GIS: From space to territory. Theories and Methods of SpatioTemporal Reasoning", Pisa, Italy, 1992.

[KP93] Kapelios V., Papamichail G., "Intersection of orthocanonic regions and computational geometry algorithms", Diploma Thesis, Department of Computer Engineering, University of Patras, Greece.

[MP93] Margioulas V. and Pikrakis A., "Algorithms for compression of files with geometric data", Diploma Thesis, Department of Computer Engineering, University of Patras, Greece.

[PS86] Preparata F. and Shamos M., "Computational Geometry. An introduction", Springer - Verlag 1986.

[TT88] Talairach J., Tournoux P.,"Co-Planar stereotaxic atlas of the brain",Georg Thieme Verlay Stuttgart,New York,Thieme medical publishers, Inc. New York, 1988.

An Algebraic Language for Event-Driven Modelling

Maguelonne Teisseire[2] and Rosine Cicchetti[1,2]

[1] IUT Aix-en-Provence
[2] LIM - URA CNRS 1787 - Université d'Aix-Marseille II
Faculté des Sciences de Luminy, Case 901
163 Avenue de Luminy, 13288 Marseille Cedex 9 FRANCE
E-mail: teisseir@lim.univ-mrs.fr

Abstract. This paper is devoted to the dynamic aspect of the IFO_2 conceptual model, an extension of the semantic IFO model defined by S. Abiteboul and R. Hull. It focuses on a specification language used to express particularly precise condition on event triggering. The original aspects of IFO_2 are a "whole-event" approach, the use of constructors to express combinations of events and the modularity of specifications in order to optimize the designer's work. Furthermore, it offers an overall vision of the represented behaviour.

1 Introduction

Conceptual approaches [2, 5, 8, 9, 11, 14, 15, 16] strive to propose models for representing a real world as faithfully as possible, taking into account its different aspects, both static (i.e. structural) and dynamic (i.e. behavioural). Some of these approaches can be criticized because they neglect one of these two aspects. In fact, for a long time, conceptual models (particularly semantic models) gave pride of place to data representation [7]. With the emergence of OODB models, the trend was reversed and several approaches [13] attached a dynamic component to them. From a strictly dynamic viewpoint, conceptual models deal with problems which are nearly similar to those of concurrent system design and software engineering [8].
In proposing the IFO_2 conceptual model [10, 17, 18], we intend to integrate both structural and behavioural representation of applications. It is based on the IFO model of S. Abiteboul and R. Hull [1]. Its structural part combines the advantages of both semantic and object-oriented approaches [10]. This paper is devoted to the dynamic aspect of IFO_2 and focuses on the specification language used to express particularly precise constraints on event triggering. The behavioural modelling part of IFO_2 is described in Section 2. We present the various concepts in an informal way (their definitions are given in [17]) and highlight their interest and originality. We also present the more interesting elements of the specification language used to define complex conditions of event occurrences (section 3).

2 IFO_2 behavioural part: an overview

An event is the representation of a fact that participates in the reactions of the modelled system. It occurs instantaneously, i.e. it is of zero duration. As in [4], we make the following assumption: no more than one event can occur at any given instant, and thus event occurrences are ordered according to the total order relation $<_{Time}$. The structural part of IFO_2 is defined with respect to the "whole-object" philosophy. We extend its scope to the behavioural part and refer to a *"whole-event"* representation. In fact, event modelling in IFO_2 complies with a dual precept: typing and identification. As regards the latter point, we use the instant of occurrence of an event as its identifier.

The IFO_2 behavioural part proposes two basic types. The *simple event type* (TES) represents the events that trigger an operation (i.e. a method) included in the IFO_2 structural description. The *abstract event type* (TEA) is used to specify external and temporal events or generators of other events. The associated graphic formalism is given in figure 1.

To illustrate this paper, the modelled system is a set of lifts. A simple event type involved in the description of the system behaviour is "Up", which triggers the ascending motion of a lift cage. It maps with an operation of the structural schema. The TEA "Satis-Request" describes events generated when the cage reaches the requested floor and the TEA "Floor-Request" represents external events occurring when users request a floor. To model a system behaviour, it is necessary to express

Fig. 1. Example of Basic Event Types

different variants of event conjunction and disjunction. To answer this need, we have chosen to represent complex events by using *constructors*. With this approach, we provide not only the required expressive power but also the uniformity with respect to the IFO_2 structural modelling. When representing both static and dynamic parts of an application, the designer handles concepts having the same philosophy. The four constructors composition, sequence, grouping and union (shown in Fig. 2) proposed in the IFO_2 model specify logical conditions on events. The event *composition* constructor reflects the conjunction of events belonging to different types. The *sequence* constructor is defined as the previous one but with a chronological constraint on the occurrences of the component events. Event collections, i.e. conjunctions of events belonging to the same type, are expressed by the *grouping* constructor. Finally, *union* expresses a disjunction of events of different types. In respect to our "whole-event" framework, each event may only take part in a single construction since it occurs only once. In figure 2, the union type "Up-Down" is an alternative between the two simple types "Up" and "Down" describing the descending or ascending lift motion.

In a general way, an event type is built up from simple, abstract and represented (described below) types and constructors which may be recursively applied. Apart from the identifier, IFO_2 events are defined by using the concept of event domain which determines the operations and events (only for complex events) which are triggered and the concept of parameter domain which gives the structural elements on which the events operate. An event is then defined as a triplet.

The event types are interconnected by functions through the *event fragment* concept, focused on a principal type called *heart*. Its role is to describe a subset of the modelled behaviour that can then be re-used and manipulated as a whole by means of the *represented event type* (TER), graphically denoted by a circle. More precisely, the fragment hearts are related to TERs with IS_A ecent links. These concepts offer a real modularity and re-usability of specifications: the designer can defer a type description or entrust it to somebody else, while using a represented type which symbolizes it.

Through IS_A links, TERs inherit from other type(s). This particular inheritance may be multiple when TERs have several sources. The TERs represent then a combination of the inherited "subbehaviours". Finally, overloading may be used to refine an inherited behaviour: the underlying represented type is specified as a new fragment heart and related through functions to other types.

The fragment functions express various constraints on the event chain. They combine the following features: simple or complex (multivalued); partial or total (necessary) and immediate or deferred. In addition, we differentiate between *triggering* and *precedence functions*. They roughly express the fact that an event triggers the occurrence of other ones or that it is preceded by the occurrence of other ones. In order to emphasize this, let us consider an external or temporal event. By its very nature, it cannot be triggered by another modelled event, therefore it is sometimes necessary to express that its occurrence is necessarily preceded by other events. Contrary to triggering functions, a precedence function, if it exists, is unique in a fragment since the representation of a combination of precedent events has to be modelled with the mentioned constructors. This makes it possible by adopting a specific observation point (the fragment heart) to have an overview of the behaviour in question, i.e. including not only generating events (preceding events) but also generated events (triggered events). The fragment can thus be really considered as a *unit of description* of the system behaviour. Combined with function features, this semantic refinement is a strong point of IFO_2 since it increases its expressive power. To highlight the precedence functions, we use a specific graphic notation (see the function from "Stop" to "Satis-Request" in Figure 3).

Figure 2 illustrates a fragment whose heart is an external event type "Floor-Request". In this fragment, there is no precedence function. This fragment describes the system's reactions when a user requests a floor (inside or outside the cage). The fragment heart is linked with a partial and deferred function to the simple type "Closure". The associated method in the structural schema closes the lift doors. The function is partial because, in some cases, an event of "Floor-Request" would not trigger a door closure, for instance if the user wants to go to the floor where he is currently located. The function is deferred to take into account the case where the user requests the lift while the cage is already engaged.

The TEA is also related to the composite type "Up-Down" which specifies an alternative between the two TESs "Down" and "Up". The triggering function between the heart and the union type is partial, deferred and complex. It is partial because in some cases a request do not trigger any motion for instance if the requested floor is served when satisfying other users. The deferred feature of the function takes into consideration the possible delay between the user request and the resulting lift motion. In fact the methods corresponding to the TESs "Up" and "Down" perform a single floor ascent or descent for the cage. This is why the triggering function is complex. The union type "Up-Down" is heart of a subfragment. The triggering function which relates it to the represented type "Arrival-Floor" (whose consequences are described in another fragment) is total and immediate. This means that any event of the types "Up" and "Down" generates an event of "Arrival-Floor". In order to

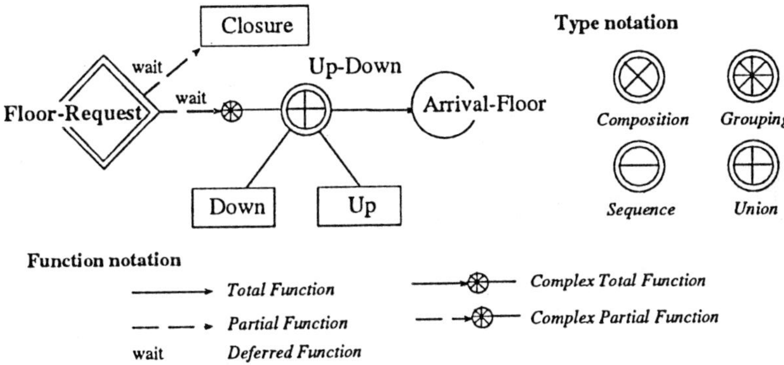

Fig. 2. The "Floor-Request" Event Fragment

model the general behaviour of the application, the partial views provided by the fragments are combined (via IS_A links) within an *event schema*.
Figure 3 shows the IFO_2 event schema "Lifts", involving three fragments, each one dedicated to a particular aspect of the lift reactions. "Floor-Request" describes the system's behaviour when a user request occurs. "Cage-Arrival" is a particular fragment since it is reduced to its heart which is a TES re-used in other fragments. The corresponding method in the structural schema returns the floor reached by the cage. Finally "Satis-Request" is dedicated to the lift behaviour when the cage arrives at the requested floor. These fragments are related by IS_A links through the represented types "Go-Floor", "Arrival-Floor" and "Arrival". The application behaviour is represented by the event schema. It may be simulated by navigation through the graph, from the root to the leaves, from left to right. An outline of this behaviour consists in a propagation of event triggering. It stops when all the actions reflecting the goal sought by the system are achieved. These actions are described in the schema, within one or more fragments called satisfaction fragments. In our example, there is one satisfaction fragment: "Satis-Request", which specifies that each user who requests a floor has to reach it, in the end.

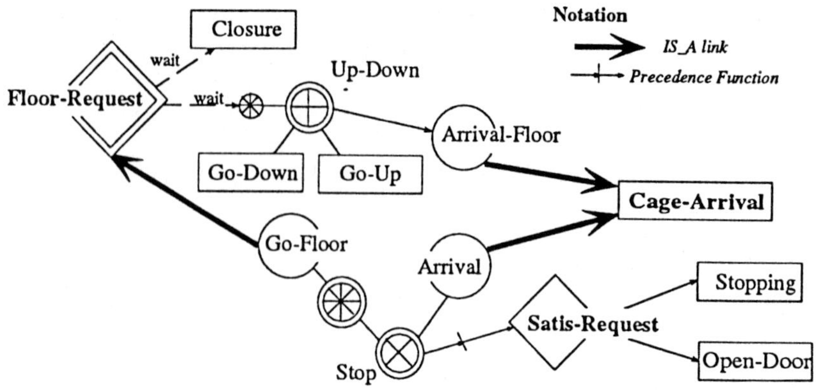

Fig. 3. The "Lift" Event Schema

3 Elements of the function specification language

An IFO$_2$ schema gives a general description of the behaviour of a system. Nevertheless, event triggering may be constrained by particularly precise conditions. Typical examples are conditions on values of structural objects or constraints on the past activity of the system. These conditions are expressed in the specification of fragment functions. The underlying language is not entirely described here, due to space limitation, but we give its more essential elements: the *cause* function, the trace concept and operators which are applied to traces.

3.1 Event Causality

With the same philosophy as in [3, 12], we formally introduce the *Cause* function, which determines the generator event for each event. A particular case - a complex type without generator type - has to be underscored because its occurrence stems from the occurrence of its component events. In other terms, an event of such a complex type is generated by events of its children. To simplify, we would say that this composite event is caused by itself[3] or, more exactly, by its event domain value, i.e. its components.

Definition 1 Let G_{S_e} be an event schema encompassing p event fragments ($p > 0$) and let $I_{G_{S_e}}$ be an instance of G_{S_e}. For each fragment F_e of G_{S_e} with heart T_{e0} whose root is r_{e0}, let I_{F_e} be the instance of F_e, let $a_1 = (r_{e0}, r_{e1})$, $a_2 = (r_{e0}, r_{e2})$, ... $a_n = (r_{e0}, r_{en})$ be the edges whose source is r_{e0}, let $a_b = (r_b, r_{e0})$ be the possible edge of target r_{e0} and let f_{a_b} be the function associated with the a_b edge. For each $i \in [1..n]$, let f_{a_i} be the function represented by the a_i edge and let Z_{ei} be the subfragment obtained from the maximal subtree with root r_{ei}.
The restriction of the function Cause to the root types of F_e, denoted by $Cause_{F_e}$, is defined by:

[3] This hypothesis may easily be modified without altering the definitions below.

1. $\forall e \in Evt(r_{ei}) \cap Tr_{F_e}$[4], $\exists\, e_j \in J_{T_{e0}}$ such that $e = f_{a_i}(e_j)$ then: $Cause_{F_e}(e) = e_j$.
2. $\forall e \in Evt(r_b) \cap Tr_{F_e}$, $\exists\, e_j \in J_{T_{e0}}$ such that $e_j = f_{a_b}(e)$ then:
   $Cause_{F_e}(e_j) = e$ and if r_b is not a TER then $Cause_{F_e}(e) = e$.

The schema function *Cause*, denoted by $Cause_{G_{Se}}$, is thus defined by:

$\forall e \in Tr_{G_{Se}}$ if $\nexists\, k \in [1..p]$ such that $Cause^k_{F_e}(e) \neq \emptyset$ then $Cause_{G_{Se}}(e) = e$
else $Cause_{G_{Se}}(e) = Cause^k_{F_e}(e)$.

The cause of events whose type is not root in a complex fragment is achieved by applying the previous definition to the concerned subfragment. Obviously, an event is not necessarily generated by another event in to the same fragment. To illustrate this case, let us consider represented types or types which are hearts of fragment and sources of IS_A specialization link. Their cause may be defined in another fragment: the fragment including the represented type, target of the specialization link. This is why all the schema fragments have to be examined.
In the general case, the cause is determined according to cause of the associated root event. If the considered event is generated, events that are involved in its construction have the same cause. For a given generator event, the origin of each of its component events is itself. Represented types are an exception to this rule since their cause is described in another fragment. At this stage, the cause of certain root type events can always be unknown. This is true for a complex type - whose occurrence depends on its component event occurrences - or for external events, which are themselves their cause.

Definition 2 Let F_e be an event fragment encompassing q types T_{ei} whose root is r_{ei} and let I_{F_e} be an instance of F_e. For each vertex s non-root of fragment, the restriction of the function Cause to s, denoted by $Cause_s$, is defined by using I_{F_e}:
$\forall e \in Evt\_att_s(I_{F_e})$:
If s is in the type with root r_{ei}, $\exists\, e_{r_{ei}} \in J_{T_{ei}} \cap Tr_{F_e}$ such that e builds $e_{r_{ei}}$ then:
if $Cause_{G_{Se}}(e_{r_{ei}}) = e_{r_{ei}}$ then if s is not a TER, $Cause_s(e) = e$
else $Cause_s(e) = Cause_{G_{Se}}(e_{r_{ei}})$.

In our example, events of the composite type "Stop", source of a precedence function, are considered as being their own cause, since they are generated from the occurrence of their component events. A "Cage-Arrival" event has the same cause than an "Arrival-Floor" event, i.e. an event of either "Down" or "Up".

3.2 Trace Concept

The concept of schema trace reflects the whole activity of the modelled system since its birth. It is defined as the ordered sequence, according to the $<_{Time}$ relation, of its instance events.

Definition 3 Let G_{Se} be an event schema and let $I_{G_{Se}}$ be its instance. The *trace* of G_{Se}, denoted by $Tr_{G_{Se}}$, is equal to: $Tr_{G_{Se}} =< e_1, e_2, ...e_j, ..., e_M >$ with $e_j \in I_{G_{Se}}$ and $\forall j \in [1..M-1]$, $Id(e_j) <_{Time} Id(e_{j+1})$.

[4] Tr_{F_e} is the fragment trace concept defined in the same way as in Definition 3.

3.3 Satisfied Event

A boolean function, *Satis*, is defined in order to know whether events are satisfied or not according to a satisfaction fragment. Depending on the context application, this function could be refined to express more specific conditions (as illustrated with our example in Section 3.5).

Definition 4 Let G_{Se} be an event schema, let F_{Sat} be a satisfaction fragment of G_{Se} and let $I_{F_{Sat}}$ be its instance. The boolean *Satis* function for F_{Sat}, denoted by $Satis_{F_{Sat}}$, is defined by: $\forall e \in Tr_{G_{Se}}$, $Satis_{F_{Sat}}(e)$ is true if and only if $e \in I_{F_{Sat}}$.

3.4 Operators on Traces

In order to constrain the system's "history", we define a set of operators which manipulate traces with the same philosophy as in [6, 12, 15]. Here we limit ourselves to the formal presentation of a primitive subset. In fact we are only interested in the operators involved in the expression of our example functions. The other ones are just intuitively described.

Restriction: When applied on a trace x, this operator, denoted by $x\lceil Te$, returns a new trace whose events are of type Te. Its recurrent definition is the following:

Definition 5 *Restriction*
$\forall (x \cdot e) \subseteq Tr_{G_{Se}}, \forall Te \in S_{Se}$:

1. $<> \lceil Te = <>$
2. $(x \cdot e)\lceil Te = \begin{cases} x\lceil Te & \text{If } e \notin Evt(Te) \\ (x\lceil Te) \cdot e & \text{Otherwise.} \end{cases}$

where $<>$ stands for the empty trace, $\cdot$ symbolizes the concatenation operator described below and $Evt(Te)$ represents the infinite set of possible events of type Te.

Last: This operator provides a trace reduced to the last event of a given type in the operand trace.

Definition 6 *Last*
$\forall x \subseteq Tr_{G_{Se}}$, $\forall Te \in \mathcal{TE}$,

$$Last(x, Te) = \begin{cases} e & \text{If } e \in x\lceil Te \text{ and } \nexists e' \in x\lceil Te \text{ such that } Id(e) <_{Time} Id(e') \\ <> & \text{Otherwise.} \end{cases}$$

where Id is the function which returns the event identifier.

After: This binary operator compares two traces x and y and achieves a new one encompassing the events of x, which occurred after the last event of y.

Definition 7 *After*
$\forall x, y \subseteq Tr_{G_{Se}}$,

1. $After(x, <>) = <>$ and $After(<>, y) = y$
2. $After(x, y) = \begin{cases} z \subseteq Tr_{G_{Se}} & \text{If } \exists x', y' \subset Tr_{G_{Se}} \mid x' \cdot x = y' \cdot y \cdot z \\ <> & \text{Otherwise.} \end{cases}$

Same-Parameter: This operator, Same-Parameter(x, e, To), creates a trace whose events belong to the trace x and have, within their parameters, a structural object being the parameter of type To of the event e.

Definition 8 ***Same-Parameter***
$\forall x \subseteq Tr_{G_{Se}}, \forall e \in Evt(Te), \forall To \in Dpara(Te)$[5],

$$Same\text{-}Parameter(x, e, To) = \begin{cases} z \subseteq Tr_{G_{Se}} & \text{If } \forall e' \in z : e' \in x,\ e' \neq e \\ & \text{and } Para(e, To) = Para(e', To) \\ <> & \text{Otherwise.} \end{cases}$$

where *Para* is the function wich gives the object parameter of the event for the specified type.
Other operators: The other algebraic operators are the following:

- **Element** which returns the ith event of a trace and **First**, being a particular case of the previous operator, that gives the first event of a given type in a trace.
- **Concatenation** which achieves from two traces a new one by gathering their events, only if the last event of one of them occurred before the first event of the other.
- **Union, Intersect** and **Minus** with a similar semantics as the corresponding set operators but which preserve the event order.
- **Before** which plays a reverse role in relation to After, i.e. it returns the events of a trace that occurred before the first event of another trace.
- **Between** which operates on two traces and achieves a new one whose events, belonging to the trace of either the schema or a given fragment, occurred after the last event of one operand and before the first event of the other.

3.5 Illustration

To illustrate the function specification language, we express the precedence function of the satisfaction fragment in our schema example and the functions having at least one of the following features: partial, deferred and complex.
As previously mentioned, the Satis function has to be refined in order to take into account the following particular case: the user wants to go to the floor where he is. Such a request is obviously satisfied, without any event triggering.
$\forall e_{F\text{-}R} \in Tr_{Lift}$, $Satis_{F_{Satis\text{-}Request}}(e_{F\text{-}R})$ is true if and only if
$e_{F\text{-}R} \in I_{F_{Satis\text{-}Request}}$ or $Para(e_{F\text{-}R}, Floor) = Lift\text{-}Cage(Position)$[6].

Let f_1 be the partial and deferred function from the "Floor-Request" to "Closure" types. When an event of the former type occurs, f_1 triggers an event of the latter type if the following condition holds: there has not been a door closure since the last door opening and (i) the floor requested by the user is different from the present floor where the cage is stopped or (ii) the cage has stopped to satisfy this floor request while it was already engaged.

[5] *Dpara* represents the type parameter domain.
[6] *Lift-Cage(Position)* denotes the position property of the lift cage in the structural schema.

$\forall e_{F\text{-}R} \in Evt(Floor\text{-}Request) \cap Tr_{Lift}$:

$$f_1(e_{F\text{-}R}) = \begin{cases} e_{Closure} & \text{If } After(Last(Tr_{Lift}, Open\text{-}Door), Tr_{Lift})[Closure = <> \\ & \text{and } (Para(e_{F\text{-}R}, Floor) \neq Lift\text{-}Cage(Position) \\ & \text{or } notSatis(Cause(Last(Arrival\text{-}Floor))). \\ \emptyset & \text{Otherwise.} \end{cases}$$

Let f_2 be the partial, deferred and complex function relating "Floor-Request" to "Up-Down". For any "Floor-Request" event, it would not generate a motion order (either an ascent or descent) until all the previous requests have been satisfied (deferred feature). Furthermore, such a triggering is performed only if the event has not been satisfied while answering previous current requests and if the user is not at the floor where he wants to go (partial feature). The function is triggered as many time as necessary to satisfy the user request (complex feature).

$\forall e_{F\text{-}R} \in Evt(Floor\text{-}Request) \cap Tr_{Lift}$,
if $Satis(Cause(Last(Tr_{Lift}, Up\text{-}Down)))$ and not $Satis_{Satis\text{-}Request}(e_{F\text{-}R})$:

$$f_2(e_{F\text{-}R}) = \begin{cases} e_{Ud} \in Evt(Down) & \text{If } Para(e_{F\text{-}R}, Floor) < Lift\text{-}Cage(Status). \\ e_{Ud} \in Evt(Up) & \text{If } Para(e_{F\text{-}R}, Floor) > Lift\text{-}Cage(Status). \end{cases}$$

Let f_3 be the precedence function of the satisfaction fragment. It has a dual goal: expressing the condition of a "Satis-Request" event occurrence and specifying which "Floor-Request" events are satisfied. The first aspect is translated by comparing the floor reached by the cage at the last "Cage-Arrival" event and the floors requested by all the users who are still waiting. When they are equal, the concerned requests are then satisfied by the occurrence of a "Satis-Request" event.

$\forall e_{Stop} = (id, [\{e^i_{F\text{-}R}\}, e_A], o_{Floor}) \in Evt(Stop) \cap Tr_{Lift},\ i \in [1..n]$,

$$f_3(e_{Stop}) = \begin{cases} e_{Satis\text{-}Request} & \text{If } e_A = Last(Tr_{Lift}, Cage\text{-}Arrival) \\ & \text{and } \forall e^i_{F\text{-}R} \in Evt(Floor\text{-}Request) \cap Tr_{Lift}, \\ & e^i_{F\text{-}R} \in Same\text{-}Parameter(Tr_{Lift}, e_A, Floor) \\ & \text{and not } Satis(e^i_{F\text{-}R}). \\ \emptyset & \text{Otherwise.} \end{cases}$$

4 Conclusion

In this paper, we have presented the behavioural part of the IFO_2 conceptual model. Its originalities are a "whole-event" approach, the use of constructors to express complex combination of events and the re-usability and modularity of specifications in order to optimize the designer's work. The IFO_2 model proposes a twofold specification, structural and behavioural, for application modelling. The advantage of this choice is the uniformity of the resulting approach. We think that such a feature is particularly important on a conceptual level. In the two frameworks, structural and behavioural, the designer uses the same fundamental concepts, such as re-usability, modularity, identification, etc. To complement the general description offered by IFO_2 event schemas, an algebraic language is provided. It includes operators to manipulate the past activity of the modelled system represented through the trace concept. When using this language, the designer can express particularly precise and complex conditions on event triggering. If a conceptual model is to be really used, it must be possible to implement it automatically, if possible. To demonstrate the feasibility of translation, we opt for E-C-A rules of the HiPAC model as the derivation target for IFO_2 [18].

References

1. S. Abiteboul and R. Hull. IFO: A formal semantic database model. *ACM Transactions on Database Systems*, 12(4):525–565, December 1987.
2. M. Bouzeghoub and E. Métais. Semantic modelling of object-oriented databases. In *Proc. VLDB'91*, pp. 3–14, Barcelona, Spain, 1991.
3. J. Carmo and A. Sernadas. A temporal logic framework for a layered approach to systems specification and verification. In *Proc. of the Temporal Aspects in Information Systems Conference (IFIP 88)*, pp. 31–46, 1988.
4. S. Chakravarthy. Rule management and evaluation: An active DBMS perspective. *Sigmod Record*, 18(3):20–28, September 1989.
5. J. Fiadeiro and A. Sernadas. Specification and verification of database dynamics. *Acta Informatica*, 25:625–661, 1988.
6. C. Hoare. *Communicating Sequential Processes*. Prentice Hall, 1985.
7. R. Hull and R. King. Semantic database modelling: Survey, applications and research issues. *ACM Computer Surveys*, 19(3):201–260, September 1987.
8. P. Loucopoulos and R. Zicari. *Conceptual Modeling, Databases and CASE: An Integrated View of Information Systems Development*. Wiley Professional Computing, 1992.
9. B. Pernici. Objects with roles. In *Proc. of the Conference on Office Information Systems*, pp. 205–215, Cambridge, 1990.
10. P. Poncelet, M. Teisseire, R. Cicchetti, and L. Lakhal. Towards a formal approach for object-oriented database design. In *Proc. VLDB'93*, pp. 278–289, Dublin, Ireland, 1993.
11. C. Quer and A. Olivé. Object interaction in object-oriented deductive conceptual models. In *Proc. CAiSE'93*, volume 685 of *LNCS*, pp. 374–396, Paris, France, 1993.
12. G. Reggio. Event logic for specifying abstract dynamic data types. In *Proc. of 8th Workshop on Specification of Abstract Data Types*, volume 655 of *LNCS*, pp. 292–309, Dourdan, France, 1991.
13. C. Rolland and C. Cauvet. *Trends and Perspectives in Conceptual Modeling.* in [8].
14. G. Saake. Descriptive specification of database object behaviour. *Data & Knowledge Engineering*, 6:47–73, 1991.
15. A. Sernadas, C. Sernadas, and H. D. Ehrich. Object-oriented specification of databases: An algebraic approach. In *Proc. VLDB'87*, pp. 107–116, Brighton,UK, 1987.
16. C. Sernadas and J. Fiadeiro. Towards object-oriented conceptual modeling. *Data & Knowledge Engineering*, 6:479–508, 1991.
17. M. Teisseire, P. Poncelet, and R. Cicchetti. Dynamic modelling with events. In *Proc. CAiSE'94*, volume 811 of *LNCS*, pp. 186–199, Utrecht, The Netherlands, 1994.
18. M. Teisseire, P. Poncelet, and R. Cicchetti. Towards event-driven modelling for database design. In *Proc. VLDB'94*, Santiago, Chile, 1994. To appear.

Prototyping Object Oriented Specifications in an Algebraic Environment[1]

A. Toval(*), I.Ramos(**), O.Pastor(**)

(*)Dept. de Informática y Sistemas. Facultad de Informática. Universidad de Murcia.C/Sto. Cristo, 1 (30001) Murcia (Spain); Fax. + 34-68-835418; e-mail atoval@dif.um.es

(**) Dept. de Sistemes Informatics i Computació (DSIC). Universitat Politecnica de Valencia. Camí de Vera, s/n. E-46071 Valencia (Spain). e-mail {iramos,plo}@dsic.upv.es

Abstract.- This paper presents an algebraic environment aimed to achieve operational prototypes [3] from an object-oriented description of the Universe of Discourse (UoD). Based on the OASIS object-oriented specification language [15] and the works initiated in [16], two algebraic specifications are provided: the first formalizes the OASIS language; the second is a formalization of the lives of the objects in the UoD. From an OASIS description of the conceptual scheme, the object-oriented algebraic prototyper (OOAP) automatically generates a validated ground term of the term algebra of the OASIS specification. After a consistency analysis OOAP generates an OBJ3 prototype for that specification which is internally executed as a rewriting system. It is then ready to be used by developers and users in order to validate and verify functional requirements of the information system. An implementation of the OOAP has been carried out using the functional language OBJ3.

Keywords.- algebraic specifications, conceptual modelling, object-oriented prototyping, object-oriented specification.

1 Introduction

The objective of our work is to design and implement a prototyping environment called OOAP (Algebraic Prototyper) based on a formal framework to achieve object-oriented functional prototypes [3]. This environment makes possible the simulation of the operational characteristics of the system being developed, starting from an OASIS description based on the object-oriented (shortly OO) paradigm; OASIS [15] is a language for open and active information Systems specification. In previous works we investigated these issues starting from Structured Analysis models [14], but we have found formal descriptions much more promising than structured models [20] [19], as we stated in [16] which initiated the present work.

The approach used for our work evolved from mainly integrating two formal specification techniques: firstly the well-known algebraic specifications theory [5], for the formalization of both the OASIS object-oriented specification language, and the Information Base, that is to say the lives of the objects in the UoD. The OASIS algebraic specification allows the formal representation of any conceptual scheme as a ground term of the corresponding ground terms set; the Information Base formalization allows us to represent the life cycles of the objects and provides operations for

[1] The research reported in this paper has been partially supported by the Spanish Ministries of Education and Industry, CICYT project PROTESIS TIC 91-0425 (1991/1993)

observing the system; secondly, we adopt the formalization of the object-oriented paradigm, trying to put into the practice the ideas in the literature, in particular those proposed by Sernadas and Ehrich [17] [4] [10] [11].

Section 2 describes the formal object-oriented model that we adopt for our work, together with the most significant features of OASIS. Section 3 briefly introduces OBJ and sections 4 and 5 describe in more detail the kernel and information base formalization. A Library example illustrates the ideas presented.

2 A Proposal for an Object-Oriented Formal Model

Currently, most approaches to object-oriented conceptual modeling are rather informal [2] [13], although new formal approaches are emerging, including those for FOOPS [7], CMSL [23] or the above quoted references from Sernadas and Ehrich. In this section we review the notions of object, class and life-cycles that we adopt.

2.1 Basic OO Formal Concepts

Object.- Objects are members of classes; the class has a template of its members, specifying their common structure. Summing up, an object consists of an oid (object identifier) and the template ob = (X,A,T,α), where X is a set of events, A is a set of attributes, $T \subseteq X^{\sigma}$ is a set of life cycles ($X^{\sigma} = X^{*} \cup X^{w}$ denotes the set of finite and infinite streams over X). Finite sequences are called traces over X. A valuation mapping , $\alpha : X^{*} \rightarrow obs(A)$, maps each trace in X into a valuation of the attributes in A . For each attribute a in A we assume a data type, type(a), determining the values a can have. We define an observation over A as a set of attribute-value pairs, $y \subseteq \{(a1{:}d1),\ldots(a_n{:}d_n)\}$, where a_i is in A and d_i is in type(a_i) for i=1...n. obs(A) denotes the set of observations over A.

Object communication and behavior.- Object interaction in this model corresponds to event sharing (message passing) and triggering relations. The history of any object is reflected in its life cycle which is a sequence of permissible events. Other approaches consider only one sequence representing all the object lives cycles interleaved, but we prefer to separate life cycles for each object. This separation will facilitate concurrence considerations and modelling. The use of preconditions ensure that only permitted events will ocurr to a particular object, depending on its structure and current trace. Section 5 shows an example of life cycles for the Library example.

Class Hierarchies.- Classes can be related to each other in the form of hierarchies. OOAP allows that collections of objects be arranged using the well-known class operators generalization/ specialization, aggregation/ projection and classification/ instantiation. In addition, OOAP incorporates parallel composition of objects as well as the appropriate mechanisms to make easy the introduction of new, user-defined, class operators (extensible operators) by reusing built-in class operators and primitive operations of the underlying algebraic specifications.

2.2 The OASIS Specification Language

OASIS [15] is a language for open and active information systems specification into an object-oriented paradigm, developed in the DSIC. We omit from this paper a detailed description of OASIS, but we shall introduce it here rather informally, illustrating how the formal concepts previously defined are considered in OASIS. The concept of template of a class consists of a set of (constant and variable) attributes, variable attributes depend on the ocurrence of events; a set of (private and shared) events, private events have an effect only on objects of the class, while shared events involve objects of two or more classes; process aspects are modelled by the use of preconditions and the notion of agent is described by triggering relations. These concepts are considered in the next straightforward example, for a class named "Borrower" in a library information system, which also contains classes "Book" and "Loan", not detailed here:

```
conceptual scheme Library
                                /* Primitive classes
      domains: nat, bool, string, time
                                /* Elementary classes
      elementary class Borrower
            attributes
            constant
                   key id-number:nat
                       name: string
                       age: nat
                   static constraints  16 < age < 100
            variable T: Time, L: Book, B: Borrower
            books-on-loan (Borrower,Time) : nat
            formulae
            books-on-loan(B,T)=books-on-loan(B,T-1)+1 if borrow(L,B,T)
            books-on-loan(B,T)=books-on-loan(B,T-1)-1 if return(L,B,T)
            books-on-loan(B,T) = 0  if  join(B,T)
            events T: Time, L: Book, B: Borrower
                  private new      join (B,T)
                          destroy  remove(B,T)
                                   notify(B,T)
                  shared           borrow(L,B,T)
                                   return(L,B,T)
           preconditions T: Time, L: Book, B: Borrower
                  remove(B,T) if books-on-loan (B,T) = 0
                  borrow(L,B,T) if books-on-loan (B,T) < 5
                  return(L,B,T) if books-on-loan (B,T) > 0
            triggering T: Time, B: Borrower
                  self:: notify(B,T) if books-on-loan(B,T) = 4
      end elementary class

      elementary class Book    ............end elementary class
                                  /* Complex classes
      complex class  Loan aggregation of Borrower, Book
          ...................end complex class

end conceptual schema
```

3 Algebraic Specifications and OBJ3

We assume the theory of order-sorted equational specification [6] [8] which extends the many sorted-case [5].

Algebraic specifications can be animated by means of a rewriting system, using an appropriate algebraic specification language. Besides the criterion of availability, we found in the last release of OBJ3 [9] a number of advantages that encouraged us to use it as the support for developing our system: OBJ3 is based upon order-sorted equational logic supporting exception handling, overloading, multiple inheritance (not in the sense of object-orientation, but in the sense of subsorting), parameterised programming, module expressions,etc. The release used has an acceptable speed for reductions and the environment, although not yet very friendly, is sufficiently accessible. In designing some of the components of OOAP, in particular the user interface, we have also taken advantage of the OBJ3 facility for encapsulating Lisp code, augmenting the system with new capabilities in connection with the formal theory. Details of the OBJ3 language are given in [9].

4 OOAP Kernel: The OASIS Algebraic Specification

OOAP provides a manageable formalization of classical object-oriented concepts such as inheritance, classification, precondition, the notion of event,etc... using an algebraic framework. This is realized by the kernel of OOAP: an algebraic specification, named AS-OASIS=(S,OP,E), (being S a set of sorts, OP a set of operation and constant symbols and E a set of equations describing the semantics for the signature (S,OP)). The formal definition of the system, the prototype and the life cycles of the objects belong to the same algebraic framework, so ensuring maintenance of the good formal properties. By convention, in OBJ3, module identifiers are all upper case. A full description of all the OBJ3 modules used in this paper can be found in [21]; in particular AS-OASIS should contain, among other, the following elements:

```
obj  AS-OASIS is sorts Cs DomDef .
      protecting CC-LIST .

*** HEAD (constructors)
      op conceptual schema : ClassId* DomDef EcList CcList → Cs .
      op domains : TermList →DomDef .
***   some non-constructor
      op cclassid- : ClassId Cs → Class .
            *** Error Handling
      op Error. _ is not a class : ClassId → Ec .
      .......
*** some non-constructor (queries)
      op ckey : Class Cs → CAttribList .
      op cnokey : Class Cs → CAttribList .
      op cevents : Class Cs → EventList .
      ........ axioms ......
endo
```

The sort Cs names all the possible conceptual schemata, ClassId* is the sort of names for conceptual schemata while ClassId is used for the rest of classes, DomDef is the sort of the primitive classes (ADT´s) and EcList, CcList respectively denote collections of elementary and complex classes. We also introduce sorts Ec and Cc describing elementary and complex classes which are built in a similar way as Cs. While Ec has only one possible constructor (named "elementary class"), Cc has a variety of them: one for each kind of class composition operation (specialization, aggregation,...) and also the one named "defined class" for user-defined operators.

"Protecting" is a module importation mode of OBJ3. CC-LIST is an instantiation of a parameterised module defining a collection of complex classes which is built as follows:

```
make CC-LIST is LIST[COMPLEX-CLASS]*(sort List to CcList) endm
```

Where COMPLEX-CLASS is the OBJ-module describing the OASIS complex classes. Analogously,

```
make EC-LIST is LIST[ELEMENTARY-CLASS]*(sort List to EcList) endm
```

ELEMENTARY-CLASS is the OBJ-module employed to define the signature and related equations describing the structure and behavior of the OASIS elementary classes. It contains, among other:

```
obj ELEMENTARY-CLASS is sort Ec .
      protecting EVENT-LIST .
      dfn CAttribList is ATTRIBCDEF-LIST .
      dfn VAttribList is ATTRIBVDEF-LIST .
      protecting CONSTRAINTS .
      protecting PRECOND-LIST .
      protecting TRIGGER-LIST .

sorts  Pc Class Attrib CAttrib  VAttrib Constraints Varsdecl Events
        Private Shared Preconditions Triggering .
subsorts    Pc Ec < Class .
*** CLASS HEAD
      op elementary class : ClassId Attrib Events → Ec .
*** ATTRIBUTES OPERATION SYMBOLS
      op attributes : CAttrib Constraints VAttrib → Attrib .
                  *** CONSTANT
      op constants : CAttribList CAttribList → CAttrib .
      ................
                  *** VARIABLE
      op variables : VAttribList → VAttrib .
      op vars : VardeclList → Varsdecl .
*** EVENTS, PRECONDITIONS AND TRIGGERING
      op preconditions : VardeclList PrecondList → Preconditions .
      op Error : → PrecondList .
      op events : Private Shared Preconditions Triggering → Events .
      op private _ ; new _ destroy _ ; _ : Varsdecl Event Event
           EventList → Private .
      op shared _ ; _ : Varsdecl EventList → Shared .
      op triggering : VardeclList TriggerList → Triggering .
      op Error : → TriggerList .           ..........
*** some non-constructor (also valid for complex class)
      op cclassid : Class → ClassId . *** returns class identifier
      op ceventid : Event → EventId .
      op ckey : Class → CAttribList .
      op cnokey : Class → CAttribList .
      op cnew : Class → Event .
           ........ axioms ......
endo
```

Components of classes are similarly formalized in this constructive way: we have algebraic specifications formalizing constant (ATTRIBCDEF, ATTRIBCDEF-LIST) and variable (ATTRIBVDEF, ATTRIBVDEF-LIST) attributes, static constraints (CONSTRAINTS) private and shared events (EVENT, EVENT-LIST), preconditions (PRECOND, PRECOND-LIST) and triggering relations (TRIGGER, TRIGGER-LIST). Error messages are included, as constants of different sorts, in most of the modules for handling exceptions and errors. In addition, a variety of non-constructor operations are included to consult different properties of objects and classes (Looking at term *cs* = *library* below will help to understand these specifications). Thus, we can formally specify any conceptual schema as a ground term *cs*, $cs \in T_{OP,Cs} \subseteq T_{OP}$, where T_{OP} is the ground terms set and $T_{OP,Cs}$ is the ground term set of sort Cs. *cs* is the unique (up to congruence) canonical term representing the conceptual scheme described by an OASIS specification. The fact of representing the conceptual schema as a ground term (without variables) will allow efficient reduction using the OBJ3 operational semantics (conditional rewriting). The concrete ground term *cs* formally describes the structure and dynamic properties of the object system. For instance, the internal term *cs* corresponding to our example is, now changed to "library":

```
let  library=  conceptual  schema('Library,domains('nat    'bool  'string
'time), Borrower Book,Loan)
```

with `Borrower,Book` $\in T_{OP,Ec} \subseteq T_{OP}$; `Loan`$\in T_{OP,Cc} \subseteq T_{OP}$

(we detail only subterm Borrower; Book and Loan would be similar subterms)

```
let Borrower = elementary class('Borrower,
      attributes(constants(key(cdef('id-number,'nat)),
                           nokey(cdef('name,'string) cdef('age,'nat))),
                           constraints('age < 100  ,  'age > 16),
            variables(vattrib('books-on-loan['Borrower,'time] is 'nat,
            equations((('L is 'Book )   ('B is 'Borrower) ('T is 'time)),
      < 'books-on-loan['B,'T] + 1,ev('borrow,key('L),key('B),'T) >
      < 'books-on-loan['B,'T] - 1,ev('return,key('L),key('B),'T) >
      < 0,ev('join,key('B),'T) >)))),
      events(private vars(('B is 'Borrower) ('T is 'time));
      new ev('join,key('B), 'T)
      destroy ev('remove,key('B),'T) ; ev('notify,key('B), 'T) ; nil,
            shared vars(('B is 'Borrower) ('L is 'Book) ('T is 'time)) ;
                  ev('borrow,key('L),key('B),'T)
                  ev('return,key('L),key('B),'T),
      preconditions(('B is 'Borrower) ('L is 'Book) ('T is 'time)),
      < ev('remove,key('B),'T),'books-on-loan['B,'T] = 0 >
      < ev('borrow,key('L),key('B),'T),'books-on-loan['B,'T] < 5 >
      < ev('return,key('L),key('B),'T),'books-on-loan['B,'T] > 0 >),
      triggering( vars (('B is 'Borrower) ('T is 'time)),
       self  < ev('notify,key('B),'T),'books-on-loan['B,'T] = 4 >) .
```

Note that each well-formed term *cs* represents a different conceptual schema for a particular object system, thus having a general tool of description of information Systems (Fortunately, *cs* terms are not visible to users¡).

4.1 Built-in Modules and Order-Sorting

An advantage provided by the use of OBJ3 was the possibility of using built-in OBJ3 modules (INT,NAT,BOOL,STRING,...) as primitive classes, in addition to those defined by ourselves. By subsorting on the related sorts we had the possibility of connecting them with the underlying arithmetic of Lisp so making the environment, not only formal and theoretical, but also operative for practical use.

4.2 Extensible Operators

A characteristic of our kernel is the facility given to the specification of defining new operators between classes that encourages reusability of primitive components: OASIS thus becomes an extensible language [1]. The objective is to allow developers to build new complex classes through the use of operators defined by themselves, starting from the standards operators provided by OASIS (generalization/ specialization, aggregation/ projection and classification/ instantiation) and offering the possibility of using the primitive operation symbols defined in AS-OASIS with its related stated semantics. Developers will give the syntactic definition for the operator together with its semantics using an equational theory.

For each new extensible operator defined it is required to add to AS-OASIS:

- The operation symbol (constructor) in mixfix form:

  op defined class _ <operation-name> __..._ : S1 S2...Sn → Cc .

where "defined class" is the keyword for extensible operators and "operation-name" is the name assigned by the developer to the new operator.

- A declaration of the variables to be used in the equations describing the semantics of the extensible operator.
- A set of equations describing the semantics of the extensible operator, which will be converted to rewriting rules by the OBJ3 rules generation system.
- A set of equations describing Error management, exception handling and trivial cases for that operator, which will also be converted to rewriting rules.

5 Formalization of the Information Base

The algebraic theory INFORMATION-BASE enriches AS-OASIS with new modules and operations for managing the information base:

```
obj INFORMATION-BASE is
      protecting  AS-OASIS .
      dfn ParallelTrace is PARALLELTRACE .
      dfn InfBase is INFBASE .

      .......new sorts, vars and operation symbols......

      .......axioms.......
endo

obj TRACE is
      sort Trace .
      protecting CLASSID .
```

```
      protecting EVENT .
      op nilTrace : -> Trace .
      op *ev : EventId ConsValList Trace -> Trace .
*** Error Handling in prototyping
      op Error. Bad input keys for _ : ClassId -> Trace .
      op Error : -> Trace .
endo

make PARALLELTRACE is ||[TERM-LIST,TRACE] * (sort Array to
                                              ParallelTrace) endm
make INFBASE is ||[CLASSID,PARALLELTRACE] endm
```

"||[INDEX VALUE :: TRIV]" is a parameterized module handling pairs of structures and TRIV is the trivial theory which only requires existence of at least one sort. Operation symbols (*acall, *av) are provided to implement the observability function α.

This specification allows the formal description of the information base states as a ground term, *ib*, of its ground term algebra, $ib \in T_{OP,InfBase} \subseteq T_{OP}$. This term is the unique (up to congruence) canonical term representing the state of the information base as the parallel composition of the state of each one of the objects living (or destroyed) in the system. Persistence of the information base is ensured by keeping term *ib* updated. Objects life-cycles tracing is done by reductions of the corresponding operations and terms with the underlying rewriting system:

```
*** INFORMATION BASE
*** Borrower individual traces (should be read from right to left)
..............
let ptrace1 = *ev('return, key(2),key(1),*ev('borrow, key(2),key(1),
*ev('borrow, key(3),key(1), *ev('return, key(1),key(1),*ev('borrow,
key(1),key(1), *ev('join, key(1),nokey('Maria 34), nilTrace)))))) .
```

"key(n)" refers to the book with oid n. The number following the name in "join" represents the age, e.g.: 'Maria 34.

Each occurrence of an event has associated a time instant (which does not appear in the text for the sake of clarity). For shared event ocurrences this time instant will be exactly the same.

```
*** All Borrower traces together:

let Borrowertrace = //(1, ptrace1, //(2, ptrace2, //(3,ptrace3,nilArr)))

*** // is an associative and commutative operation standing for
"parallel composition" of traces; ptrace2, ptrace3 describe the traces
respectively for persons "2" and "3" in a similar way as ptrace1 does.
```

If we similarly use the terms Booktrace and Loantrace for all the object traces from classes Book and Loan, respectively, the term ib (now renamed infbase) for our example is:

```
let infbase= //('Loan,Loantrace, //('Book, Booktrace, //('Borrower,
Borrowertrace, nilArr)))
```

Together with the kernel described above, we have designed an integrated set of computer-aid software tools to support prototyping of complex software system from an object-oriented perspective (OOAP environment) which consists of an User Interface , the Algebraic Theory described here and the Execution Support System (the OBJ3 rewriting system).

6 Conclusions

The kind of algebraic formalization shown in this article may have practical consequences e.g. in the requirements engineering phase, construction of CASE tools to assist in transformations of specifications, as a basis for OO code generation in an adequate OOP or OODB, or simply as a unification of the OO model concepts presented here. A related work for unifying Structured models (JSD, Structured Analysis, Structured Design) has been investigated in [22] using algebraic categorial theory. Finally, the algebraic formalization procedure described here (which is different from the one used in CMSL [23] or in FOOPS [7]) is easily carried to other languages similar to OASIS, such as TROLL [12] or OBLOG [17] [18].

Acknowledgments

The authors wish to thank Dr. Jose Meseguer, from SRI, for his support and the facilities offered with OBJ3 and related theoretical issues.

References

[1] M. Atkinson; F. Bancilhon; D. DeWitt; K. Dittrich; D. Maier and S. Zdonik. "The object-oriented database system manifesto". In Proc. of the First Int. Conf. on Deductive and Object-Oriented Databases, Kyoto, Japan, December 1989

[2] G.Booch. "Object Oriented Design with applications". The Benjamin/Cummings Publishing Company Inc. (1991)

[3] A.M. Davis. "Operational prototyping: a new development approach". IEEE Software. September 1992, vol. 9, n.5

[4] H.-D.Ehrich;A.Sernadas; C.Sernadas. "Objects,Object Types and Object Identification" in Categorical Methods in Computer Science, H.Ehrig (ed.). Springer-Verlag 1988

[5] H.Ehrig;B.Mahr. "Fundamentals of Algebraic Specification 1". Springer-Verlag. 1985

[6] J.A.Goguen; J.J Jouannaud and J.Meseguer. "Operational Semantics of order-sorted algebra", in W.Brauer (ed.) Proc. 1985 Int. Conf. on Automata, Languages and Programming, Springer 1985, LNCS n° 194

[7] J.A.Goguen; J.Meseguer. "Unifying Functional, Object-Oriented and Relational Programming with Logical Semantics". in Research Directions in Object-Oriented Programming, B.Shriver and P.Wegner (eds.). MIT Press (1987) pp.417-477

[8] J.Goguen; J.Meseguer, "Order-Sorted Algebra I", Technical Report, SRI International, Standford University, 1988

[9] J.A.Goguen; T.Winkler;J.Meseguer;K.Futatsugi and J.P.Jouannaud, "Introducing OBJ3" SRI-CSL Report (Draft of January 1992)

[10] IS-CORE: Information Systems - Correctness and Reusability Esprit-2 BRA WG 3023, Second Year Report, September 1991

[11] Udo W. Lipeck, G. Koschorreck (eds.). Proc. of the Int. Workshop on : Information Systems - Correctness and Reusability IS-CORE'93, Institut für Informatik, Hannover, September 1993

[12] R.Jungclaus, T.Hartmann, G.Saake, C.Sernadas, "Introduction to TROLL- A Language for Object-Oriented Specification of Information Systems" in . [10]

[13] B.Meyer, "Object-Oriented Software Construction". Prentice-Hall 1988

[14] Jesus G. Molina; Ambrosio Toval; Manuel González. "Sape: a structured analysis prototyping environment" stream: software development and maintenance (Poster Sessions). 12TH World Computer Congress. IFIP CONGRESS 92 Madrid (Spain). September 7-11,1992

[15] O.Pastor; Hayes,F.; S.Bear. "OASIS: An Object-Oriented Specification Language" in Proceedings of the CAISE-92 Conference, Spriger-Verlag (1992)

[16] I. Ramos; O. Pastor and J.H.Canós "On the use of algebras as a semantic domain for Objects Societies", Proc. of the Deductive Approach to Information Systems and Databases, Costa Brava (Catalonia, Spain), Sept. 92

[17] A.Sernadas; J.Fiadeiro; C.Sernadas; H.-D.Ehrich. "The Basic Building Blocks of information Systems" Proc. IFIP 8.1 Working Conference, Falkenberg, E.,Lindegreen,P. (eds.), North Holland, Amsterdam, 1989, pp.225-246

[18] Sernadas, A. ; Sernadas, C. Gouveia, P. ; Resende, P. "OBLOG: An Informal Introduction" Research Report INESC 1991.

[19] A. Toval. "EMTR-01: First Technical Report on the Euromethod Progress". Internal Report. E.U. Informática. Universidad de Murcia (Spain). October 1990.

[20] A. Toval. "EEC: EUROMETHOD IN PROGRESS". Short Note, IEEE Computer Society/TCSE Newsletter, April 1992

[21] A. Toval. "Formalización Algebraica de un Entorno de Producción Automática de Prototipos Orientados a Objetos". PH.D. dissertation. Departamento de Sistemas Informaticos y Computación. Universidad Politécnica de Valencia (Spain). Mayo 1994

[22] T.H.Tse. "A Unifying Framework for Structured Analysis and Design Models: an approach using initial algebra semantics and category theory". Cambridge University Press (1991)

[23] R.J.Wieringa. "Algebraic Foundations for Dynamic Conceptual Models". PhD Thesis, Vrije Universiteit, Amsterdam, 1990

IDENTIFYING PRECEDENTS UNDER UNCERTAINTY

A. de Korvin

University of Houston-Downtown
One Main Street, Houston, Texas 77002, USA
Internet: deKorvin@dt.uh.edu

G. Quirchmayr

Universität Wien, Institut f. Angewandte Informatik und Informationssysteme
Liebiggasse 4, A-1010 Wien, Austria
Internet: Quirchmayr@ifs.univie.ac.at

S. Hashemi

University of Houston-Downtown
One Main Street, Houston, Texas 77002, USA
Internet: Hashemi@dt.uh.edu

Abstract

Information about the case to be decided rarely is complete and precise. So dealing with imprecise information definitely is one of the major issues of legal decision making. In order to be able to identify a non-empty set of precedents most similar to our case, we introduce the Dempster-Shafer rule for combining information from independent sources and use the resulting mass functions to determine the importance of each precedent in our knowledge system. Additionally, the method is illustrated by an example.

Keywords:

Legal Decision Making, Information Retrieval in Law, Accessing Precedents, Fuzzy Logic and Legal Decision Making.

1. Introduction

Traditional legal expert systems try to represent the process of legal decision making with rule-based approaches. The problem with this approach however is that legal reasoning is mainly based on interpreting statutes and on identifying relevant precedents, a process which is not documented too well and does to a large extent depend on the personal experience of the individual lawyer. Additionally, the information that a lawyer usually is provided with is incomplete, and partly inconsistent, if not completely contradictory (e.g. eye witnesses). Therefore the results of Richard Susskind's 1987 analysis of expert systems in this domain [Susskind 1987], the main conclusion of which is that existing legal expert systems have not made it into practice in substantial numbers and are hardly accepted by lawyers, still hold true. Object-oriented extensions of rule-based legal expert systems [Gordon and Quirchmayr 1987] have helped to solve some of the problems by offering a possibility to deal with general rules with exceptions [Reiter 1978], but as they are mainly based on classical logic, they do not focus on coping with such typical legal problems as open texture and ambiguity.

To provide a sound theoretical basis for designing expert systems which can overcome these shortages we introduce fuzzy sets for representing precedents [de Korvin et al. 1993]. Decisions are modeled by fuzzy logic, considering fuzzy sets of precedents and their masses. The formal model described in this paper therefore is aimed at providing a framework which will give the user the opportunity to identify the precedent with the highest mass, i.e. selecting the precedent which is closest to the case to be solved.

2. Dealing with Uncertainty in a Legal Environment

Dealing with the problem of uncertainty in a legal environment means that we cannot limit ourselves to classical logic anymore. The standard tool used to handle likelihood is statistics, which does perform very well in standard situations, but does fail to produce accurate results whenever it is required to estimate probabilities, sometimes without even the benefit of relative frequencies. The Dempster-Shafer theory of evidence gives useful measures for the evaluation of subjective certainty and has recently gained in popularity. Fuzzy set theory is another tool used to deal with uncertainty where ambiguous terms are present. Other methods include rough sets, the theory of endorsements, and non monotomic logic [de Korvin et al. 1992] .

The formal theory of possibility proposed by R. Giles [Giles 1982] probably is the best-known approach. Jaffray [Jaffray 1990] shows that consequences of a decision can be viewed as belief functions and that a certain type of preference relation on the belief functions is characterized (up to a fine transformation) by a utility transformation generalizing the Von Neumann-Morgenstein utility function. Smetz points out that the belief function reflects the cradle belief, whereas probabilities reflect the pignistic belief (i.e., betting-belief) and shows how a belief function may generate a pignistic belief (i.e., a probability distribution for betting) [Smetz 1990]. A method for removing ambiguity in decision making when belief functions are used is given in [Strat 1990]. Focusing on the idea of calculating fuzzy pay-offs in [de Korvin et al. 1993], we combined the approaches of Zebda [Zebda 1984], Yager [Yager 1986] and de Korvin [de Korvin et al. 1992]. This paper describes an extended approach using the Dempster-Shafer rule for combining information from independent sources and use the resulting mass functions to determine the importance of each precedent in our knowledge system.

3. A Formal Model of Precedent Identification Under Uncertainty

Before constructing a formal model of precedent identification, we have to discuss some basic ideas and concepts which are going to be used later on.

Let X denote a finite set, and let mass function $m(\cdot)$ be defined over 2^X such that

$$m(\emptyset) = 0;\ m(A) \geq 0 \ \textit{for all}\ A \in 2^X$$

$$\sum_{A \subset X} m(A) = 1.$$

What we are interested in are the focal elements of mass function *m (•)*, that is sets for which m *(A) ≠ 0*.

For the Dempster-Shafer composition rule to work we must have independent features. This means that the report for one value of a feature must not use results for values of other features. It does not require statistical independence but the independence of sources of evidence. If, for example, we have two masses m_1 and m_2, we can compute the resulting mass m by the formula

$$m(C) = \sum_{A \cap B = C} m_1(A) m_2(B) / [1 - K]$$

$$K = \sum_{A \cap B = \emptyset} m_1(A) m_2(B) \quad (K \ldots conflict; \; 0 \leq K \leq 1)$$

Masses are combined according to the rule

$$m_1 \oplus m_2(A) = \sum_{B \cap C = A} m_1(B) m_2(C) / \sum_{B \cap C \neq \emptyset} m_1(B) m_2(C)$$

$$where \; A, B, C \in 2^X$$

This rule, called the Dempster-Shafer rule of composition, can be extended to any finite number of masses by induction as

$$m(\bullet) = \oplus_{i=1}^{n} m_i(\bullet)$$

where the composition of mass functions is performed pair-wise. For n=3 this would result in

$$m(\bullet) = (m_1(\bullet) \oplus m_2(\bullet)) \oplus m_3(\bullet) \cdot$$

4. Example

4.1 Retrieving the Closest Precedent - A Typical Legal Problem

A typical situation of legal decision making is one where only an approximate solution can be given due to uncertain or even contradicting information. This however is a general problem of modeling human reasoning and not limited to law. The theoretical model coming closest to human reasoning in such an environment is an analysis of precedents based on Fuzzy Logic.

A well-known problem in all legal systems is that of deciding whether a person's behavior has been adequate in a given situation [Marsh and Soulsby 1987], e.g. whether a driver has been waiting long enough after causing a road accident. It has been shown that rule-based systems, even those based on natural language analysis are inadequate in such a situation, because the only reliable source of information at hand is usually a collection of precedents. The key issue therefore is to identify a non-empty set of similar precedents.

4.2 The Formal Representation of the Problem

Assuming that injury and damage are the most important factors for deciding whether the behavior of a driver causing a road accident is correct, we can construct a computational model for identifying the environment with the highest mass and most similar to the actual case. Considering a situation in which we have access to a knowledge base containing representative precedents a table of precedents and factors can be constructed. For our example we use 5 precedents (x_1, ..., x_5) and two factors (injury and damage), and show the fuzzy reports in the following table:

PRECEDENT & FACTOR	INJURY	DAMAGE
x_1	.8/none+.2/light+.2/severe	.6/low+.2/high
x_2	.7/none+.6/light	.5/low+.5/high
x_3	.1/none+.2/light+.9/severe	.2/low+.7/high
x_4	.2/none+.2/light+.8/severe	.2/low+.8/high
x_5	.6/none+.3/light+.4/severe	.7/low+.3/high

The values for injury and damage can now be represented as fuzzy sets:

FUZZY SET / PRECEDENT	x1	x2	x3	x4	x5
Injury (none)	.8	.7	.1	.2	.6
Injury (light)	.2	.6	.2	.2	.3
Injury (severe)	.3	0	.9	.8	.4
Damage (low)	.6	.5	.2	.2	.7
Damage (high)	.2	.5	.7	.8	.3

An incoming new case x* could now be represented as Damage: .6/low+.4/high and Injury: .7/none+.2/light+.1/severe. {the sums have to add up to 1 !!}

The masses on the individual injury and damage values are given directly by the reports of the knowledge sources: m_1(Injury.none)=.7, m_1(Injury.light)=.2, m_1(Injury.high)=.1, m_2(Damage.light)=.6, and m_2(Damage.high)=.4.

The focal elements of the feature specific mass functions are obviously Injury.none, Injury.light, and Injury.severe for m_1 and Damage.low and Damage.high for m_2.

Employing the rule $\bigwedge_{i=1}^{n} F_i^{k_i}$ we can now compute the focal elements for the combined mass function:

FOCAL ELEMENT	CONSTRUCTED AS	x1	x2	x3	x4	x5
A_1	*Injury.none* ∧ *Damage.low*	.6	.5	.1	.2	.6
A_2	*Injury.none* ∧ *Damage.high*	.2	.5	.1	.2	.3
A_3	*Injury.light* ∧ *Damage.low* *Injury.light* ∧ *Damage.high*	.2	.5	.2	.2	.3
A_4	*Injury.severe* ∧ *Damage.low*	.3	0	.2	.2	.4
A_5	*Injury.severe* ∧ *Damage.high*	.2	0	.7	.8	.3

As none of the intersections is empty, there is no conflict, which means that K=0 and can therefore be ignored. Thus, the importance of each focal element assigned by the mass function *m (•)* is:

FOCAL ELEMENT	MASS (FOCAL ELEMENT)	CONSTRUCTION	COMPUTATION	RESULT
A_1	m (A_1)	m_1(Injury.none) * m_2(Damage.low)	.7 * .6	.42
A_2	m (A_2)	m_1(Injury.none) * m_2(Damage.high)	.7 * .4	.28
A_3	m (A_3)	m_1(Injury.light) * m_2(Damage.low) + m_1(Injury.light) * m_2(Damage.high)	.2 * .6 + .2 * .4	.20
A_4	m (A_4)	m_1(Injury.severe) * m_2(Damage.low)	.1 * .6	.06
A_5	m (A_5)	m_1(Injury.severe) * m_2(Damage.high)	.1 * .4	.04

The masses (listed in the column "result" of the above table) do of course have to sum up to 1.

When it comes to choosing the closest precedent, there is of course a wide number of strategies [Kleyle and de Korvin 1994], the easiest of which is to select the one with the highest mass, in our example A_1. Thus A_1 is the environment that best fits our case. Within that environment cases x_1 and x_5 are tied for the highest membership. In case additional formal techniques are needed for narrowing the solution set, they can be found in [de Korvin et al. 1992].

4.3 Evaluation of the Results

The results follow common sense analysis. As can be seen in environment A_1, precedents x_1 and x_5 are the ones most similar to x*. Whereas, precedent x_3 is very different in injury factor, and x_4 is very different in both injury and damage factors. Therefore they are ruled out. Finally, x_2 belongs strongly to A_2 as well as A_3 which are the second and third best environments. However, x_2 does not belong to environment A_1 as strongly as x_1 and x_5, because it does not give any valuable information on damage (.5 low and .5 high).

5. Conclusion

In our paper we have shown how a formal approach based on calculating the masses on fuzzy sets can contribute to the support of legal decision making by helping to identify the precedent or precedents which come closest to the actual case. Masses however have to be defined by the domain expert directly. For identifying the precedents coming closest to the actual case, several strategies are at hand, the easiest of which, selecting the highest mass, is described in this paper. Further strategies are currently under investigation and will be the subject of future publications.

References

[de Korvin et al. 1992] A. de Korvin, R. Kleyle, R. Lea, The object recognition problem when features fail to be homogeneous, International Journal of Approximate Reasoning 1993; 8:141-162.

[de Korvin 1993 et al.] A. de Korvin, G. Quirchmayr, S. Hashemi, Legal decision making under uncertainty, in Proceedings of Expersys-93 (H.S. Nwana, T. Martelli, Eds.), i.i.t.t, 1993: 50-67.

[Kleyle and de Korvin 1994] R. Kleyle and A. de Korvin, Two methods for object identification with imprecise information. To be published in 1994.

[Giles 1982] R. Giles, Foundations for a theory of possibility, in Fuzzy Information and Decision Processes (M. M. Gupta and E. Sanchez, Eds.), North Holland Publishing Co., 193-195, 1982.

[Gordon and Quirchmayr 1987] T. F. Gordon and G. Quirchmayr, Der Einsatz der Modellierungssprache OBLOG zum Entwurf von Juristischen Expertensystemen im Wege des Prototyping am Besipiel eines Modells des Verfahrens der Eidesstattlichen Versicherung, Springer IFB 143, 137-154, Berlin 1987.

[Jaffray 1990] J.-Y. Jaffray, Application of Linear utility theory to belief functions, in Uncertainty in Artificial Intelligence, Vol. 5, (Max Henrion, Ed.), New York, Elsevier Publishing Co., New York, 1-8, 1990.

[Marsh and Soulsby 1987] S. B. Marsh and J. Soulsby, Outlines of English Law, McGraw-Hill, London, 124 ff., 1987.

[Reiter 1978] R. Reiter, On Reasoning by Default, Proceedings of the 2nd Symposium on Theoretical Issues in Natural Language Processing, Urbana, Illinois.

[Smetz 1990] P. Smetz, Belief functions versus probability functions, in Uncertainty in Artificial Intelligence, Vol. 5, (Max Henrion, Ed.), New York, Elsevier Publishing Co., New York, 1-8, 1990.

[Strat 1990] T. M. Strat, Decision analysis using belief functions, Intern. J. Approximate Reasoning 4, 391-417, 1990.

[Susskind 1987] R. Susskind, Expert Systems in Law, Oxford University Press 1987.

[Zebda 1984] A. Zebda, The Investigation of Cost Variances: A Fuzzy Set Theory Approach, Vol. 15, 1984, 359-388. Decision sciences.

[Yager 1986] R. Yager, A general approach to decision making with evidential knowledge. Uncertainty in Artificial Intelligence (L. N. Kanal and J. F. Lemmer, Eds.), North Holland, Amsterdam, 317-327, 1986.

CONCAT - Connotation Analysis of Thesauri Based on the Interpretation of Context Meaning

Dieter Merkl[*], Erich Schweighofer[**], Werner Winiwarter[*]

[*]Department of Information Engineering, University of Vienna,
Liebiggasse 4/3, A-1010 Vienna, Austria
email: {dieter, ww}@ifs.univie.ac.at

[**]Institute of Public International Law, University of Vienna
Universitätsstraße 2, A-1090 Vienna, Austria
email: erich.schweighofer@univie.ac.at

Abstract–Knowledge acquisition constitutes the bottleneck for the creation of legal expert systems. Legal language must be formalised to such a degree that it can be processed automatically. We deal with this problem by supporting the process of creating a selective thesaurus for a legal information system which can be seen as prerequisite for further knowledge processing. This selectivity is obtained by means of connotation analysis of the individual descriptors which makes it possible to detect hidden word meanings and to distinguish between precise legal terms and words with fuzzy meaning. Within the prototype system CONCAT we applied both a statistical and a connectionist approach to connotation analysis and performed a comparative evaluation of the achieved results.

1 Introduction

Advanced use of information technology in the legal field requires formalisation of the legal data (e.g. statutes, treaties, court decisions or literature). Two main approaches are concerned with this situation. On the one hand, laws are rewritten as logic programs, a harsh simplification of the complexity of legal systems leading to severe limitations (e.g. open texture problem, appropriate deontic logic). On the other hand, the focus is put on the linguistic structure of legal language. Due to the arduous nature of linguistics, so far only partial analysis can be performed efficiently.

Our aim is the automatic representation of the expert knowledge about legal language. As the central subject of the lawyer's work a special vocabulary has been developed by jurisprudence which is clear, simple and pithy. Lawyers have formed definite concepts of human beings, objects, and processes by use of methods of abstraction and logic thinking.

The main hypothesis in the design of the prototype CONCAT is the assumption that legal thesauri can be used as tool for knowledge acquisition if the applied descriptors are selective. Intellectually created thesauri cannot be matched against document descriptors by means of Boolean retrieval logic because of their missing selectivity. Therefore, our attempt to overcome this deficit is to analyse automatically each descriptor with regard to its connotations. By that we can capture all distinct dimensions of word meanings as well as determine the feasibility to a certain domain.

The connotation analysis is based on the interpretation of the contexts of the individual legal terms which are represented as vectors. To calculate the similarity between descriptor occurrences we applied statistical techniques as well as neural networks. Both methods were evaluated on the basis of a small test database leading to a comparative analysis of the quality of results.

2 Related work

The traditional approach to legal knowledge representation was the use of intellectually produced thesauri or classifications providing a simple form of conceptual search. Due to cost reasons it has been often substituted by Boolean information retrieval. However, the formulation of Boolean queries in order to cover the underlying concepts turned out to be a tedious task [4].
An important improvement is represented by conceptual information retrieval systems. They make use of knowledge representation techniques in order to encode the semantics of legal concepts [5], [3]. The legal domain is mapped to a knowledge scheme. A great variety of representation techniques has been applied: semantic networks [16], conceptual graphs [6], concept frames [7], diagnostic expert systems [12] or object-oriented programming [14]. Although the obtained results were superior to Boolean logic, with respect to the high development costs only small systems have been built which are not applicable for commercial use within the legal field.
Neural networks seem to be an interesting tool for legal knowledge representation but their application has been restricted so far to conceptual information retrieval [1] and open texture [2], [15].
The approaches mentioned above suffer from the same shortcoming, the lack of automatic knowledge acquisition which is indispensable for the conceptual representation of the existent huge databases in the legal domain. A promising direction to overcome this deficiency was the application of statistical analysis. Most work within this area is based on the vector space paradigm which represents similarities as distances between vectors [20]. The similarity values are the basis for subsequent clustering resulting in improved precision and recall with regard to the retrieval results. Interesting adaptions of the standard model are the Generalized Vector Space Model (GVSM) [23] and Extended Boolean Logic [19]. Statistical methods for the representation of legal concepts have been introduced by Schweighofer and Winiwarter [21].

3 Generation of descriptor vectors

As basis for the computation we first transform the document texts to sequential word lists and remove all occurring stop words. By making use of a lemmatising module these sequential lists are then converted to a word index. The lemmatising module was designed to take care of important morphological phenomena, namely *spelling errors vowel-gradation*, *inflexions*, and *suffixes*.
In the same way, the documents are indexed by use of the thesaurus entries which results in an index containing the postings for the individual descriptor occurrences. The user is not restricted to the use of simple descriptors but can also apply synonyms and compound descriptors to the representation of the domain knowledge.
By merging the word and the descriptor index, the contexts of the descriptor occurrences are extracted and represented by vectors D_i according to the vector space model of information retrieval [20]: $D_i = (TERM_{i1}, TERM_{i2}, ..., TERM_{in})$.
As weighting function we used binary indexing so that $TERM_{ik} = 1$ if the word k ($1 \leq k \leq n$) is present in the context of the descriptor occurrence and $TERM_{ik} = 0$ otherwise. Thus, the vectors D_i capture the context meaning as a function of the absence or presence of certain words. Figure 1 summarises the individual steps of the applied process model.

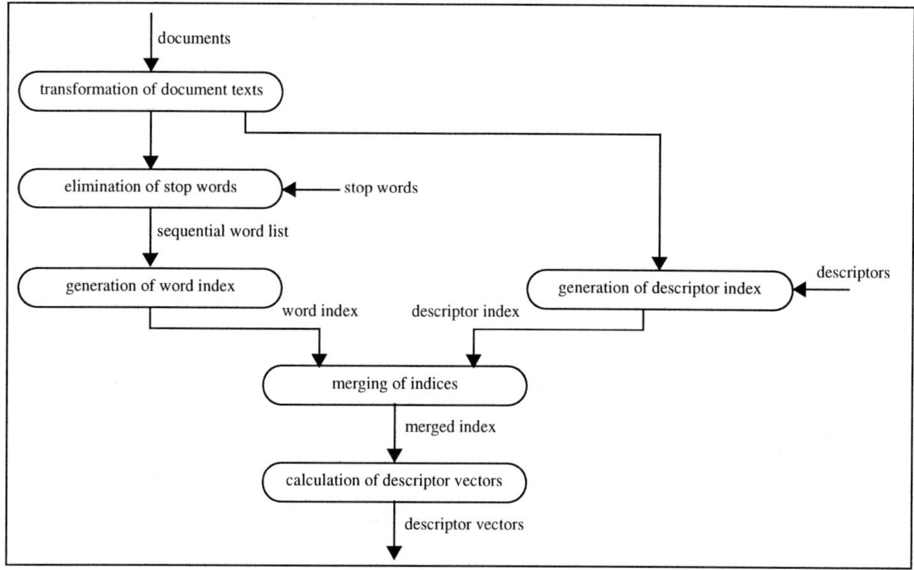

Figure 1. Process model

4 Connotation analysis of descriptors

4.1 Statistical approach

The similarity between two different occurrences of a descriptor is expressed by the number of words that are present in both contexts, that is, the number of vector components which equal 1 in both descriptor vectors. We used the symmetric *coefficient of Dice* as the similarity measure [20].

The coefficient represents exactly the percentage of words which the two contexts D_i and D_j have in common. Therefore, the value range is the interval [0, 1], the value equals 0 if the two vectors are completely different and equals 1 if they are identical.

According to the similarity values the descriptor occurrences are clustered by use of a quick partition algorithm that creates non-hierarchical disjunctive clusters [17]. The similarity value of each pair of descriptor occurrences is compared with a given threshold. If the similarity exceeds the threshold and one of the two occurrences is already a cluster member, the other one is appended to the cluster in question. Only if both participants of a similar pair are not yet included in any existing cluster, a new cluster is created.

In a second run duplicate cluster entries are removed by joining the concerned clusters. Finally, all descriptor occurrences not captured so far by the clustering process are added as single element clusters.

To simplify the interpretation of the results of clustering, the created clusters are supplemented by descriptions which represent the descriptor connotation and are created from the ten most frequent words that are part of the concerned contexts.

4.2 Connectionist approach

Artificial neural network models are specified by the network topology, i.e. the arrangement of units and connections, by the unit characteristics, i.e. the activation function and the output function, and finally by the learning rules. Learning rules specify the way in which the weighted connections have to be adapted in order to

improve the performance of the artificial neural network.
With regard to the learning process we identify at least two different paradigms. The first paradigm is commonly referred to as *supervised learning*. In this paradigm learning is performed by reducing the error between the computed output of the neural network and the desired output with respect to a given input. Thus, in this learning paradigm pairs of input and desired output data have to be specified. Learning completes when each input is mapped correctly onto its desired output.
The second paradigm is known as *unsupervised learning*. In this learning paradigm the artificial neural network constructs internal models which capture the regularities in the input domain without any additional information as, for example, a desired output. For a more detailed description of neural network basics and learning paradigms we refer to [8], [18].
Within our approach we utilise an artificial neural network adhering to the unsupervised learning paradigm, namely self-organising feature maps [9], [10], [11]. The architecture of self-organising feature maps consists of a layer of input units and a grid of output units. The output units are arranged in some topological order. In the case of our application we used a two-dimensional plane of output units. Each output unit is connected to its topological neighbours and is assigned a so-called weight vector which is of the same dimension as the input data.
The learning process of self-organising feature maps can be described as follows. Firstly, an input is randomly selected out of the set of possible inputs. This input in terms of a vector is mapped onto the input units where each input unit receives exactly one component of the input vector. The input units propagate the components as they are onto the output units. Secondly, the state of every output unit is computed. The state of an output unit is determined by the activation function which is the Euclidean distance between the unit's weight vector and the input vector currently under consideration. Thirdly, the output unit with the highest state is selected. This unit is further referred to as the best-matching unit or the winning unit. Finally, the weight vector of the winning unit as well as weight vectors of neighbouring units are adapted in such a way that the state of these units gets even higher with respect to this input vector. Thus, the learning process is a generalisation of the winner-takes-all rule. These four learning steps are performed repeatedly until no more changes to the weight vectors are observed.
More formally, the crucial steps of the learning process can be described as follows.

(1) Random selection of one input vector x.

(2) Selection of the winning unit i by using the Euclidean distance measure. In this formula w_i (w_j) denotes the weight vector assigned to output unit i (j).

$$i: \|w_i - x\| \leq \|w_j - x\|, \text{ for all output units } j$$

(3) Adaption of the weight vectors w_j in the neighbourhood of the winning unit i at learning iteration t. The strength of the adaption is determined with respect to a so-called learning rate $eps(t)$ which starts with an initial value in the range of [0, 1] and decreases gradually during the learning process to 0. The scalar function $delta_{i,j}(t)$ determines the amount of adaption dependent on the neighbourhood relation between the winning unit i and unit j which is currently under consideration. Generally, the weight vectors of units which are in close neighbourhood to the winning unit are adapted more strongly than weight vectors which are assigned to units that are far away from the winning unit. This so-called neighbourhood function has to guarantee that at the end of the learning process only the weight vector which is assigned to the winning unit is adapted. Obviously,

with these two restrictions on the learning rate and the neighbourhood function the learning process will terminate.

$$w_j(t+1)=w_j(t)+eps(t)\times delta_{i,j}(t)\times[x-w_j]$$

(4)Repeat steps (1) through (3) until no more changes to the weight vectors are observed.

The outcome of the learning process of self-organising feature maps results in a clustering of related input data in topologically near areas within the grid of output units. This is due to the fact that during the learning process the weight vectors of the winning unit as well as weight vectors of neighbouring units are moved towards the current input vector. The repetition of this adaption during the numerous presentations of input vectors makes the formation of areas possible which consist of output units specialised to regularities in the feature vectors of the various input data.
To conclude, the self-organising feature map preserves the distance between the input vectors as faithfully as possible. However, some distortion is unavoidable since a very high dimensional input space is projected onto a much lower dimensional output space. Yet, the most important neighbourhood relationships between the input data are preserved in the output space. Furthermore, these relationships are made geographically explicit in terms of the neighbourhood of the various units. This is confirmed as can be seen in the examples which are presented below.

5 Evaluation

As a test environment for our approach we used a database consisting of 41 text segments of documents from the European Community law database CELEX. The text material - terms with context windows - was produced as retrieval result from a search in the CELEX database for the term *neutrality* which is a very good example of a term with several meanings.
By intellectual separation we achieved clusters of the various context related meanings of the term *neutrality* which represented the comparison module for our automatic analysis. Due to space restrictions we can present only the various groups and the CELEX numbers of the documents.
In Figure 2 we provide the result of the intellectual document analysis. We specify each document by its CELEX number. Furthermore, each cluster is labelled by a short descriptive term which is given in parentheses in Figure 2. Note that several segments of one document are designated by using capital letters, e.g. /A, /B, etc.
In the next subsections we will compare the results which have been produced by the statistical and the connectionist approach with this very time consuming intellectual analysis.

5.1 Statistical approach

The efficient clustering algorithm of CONCAT produces good results. The clusters can be seen as types of the concept which are described automatically. A shortcoming of CONCAT is the sensitivity to the correct adjustment of the parameters (i.e., list of stop words, threshold value). However, multiple clustering with different parameters can be a useful support for the analysis of a term. More detailed evaluation results can be found in a recently published paper [22].
The outcome of the clustering algorithm is represented in Figure 3. For each cluster we give the consecutive number of the text segment as well as its corresponding CELEX number. Furthermore, we provide the cluster description which consists of the ten most frequent words that are contained in the respective contexts.

- Neutrality of States (STATE): 992E2408, 990H0306, 989H0195, 987H0184, 987H0183, 982H0240
- Fiscal neutrality:
  - Neutrality of the value-added tax system (VAT): 389L0465, 385L0361, 381Y0924(10), 367L0227/A, 367L0227/B, 690C0097, 690C0060, 690C0035
    - deduction of residial VAT (RES_VAT): 689J0159/A, 689J0119
    - import turnover tax (IMP_VAT): 689C0343
    - parent companies and subsidiaries of different member States (SUB_VAT): 390L0435
  - spirits (SPIRITS): 689C0230
  - $C0_2$/energy tax (EN_TAX): 392D0180
  - sugar sector (SUGAR): 390B0354
  - non-discrimination in matters of taxation (NON_DISC): 689J0159/B, 689J0011/A
- Neutrality of competition:
  - Neutrality of common rules for the allocation of slots at Community airports (SLOTS): 393R0095/A, 393R0095/B, 393R0095/C, 393R0095/D
  - Neutrality of the Community eco-management and audit scheme (ENVIRON): 393R1836, 392R0880
  - Neutrality of the tariff structures in the combined transport of goods (TRANSPORT): 393D0174/A, 393D0174/B, 393D0174/C
  - Neutrality of computer reservation systems for air transport services (AIR_SERV): 391R0083, 388R2672
- Neutrality of the research programmes of the Joint Research Centre (RESEARCH): 392D0274
- Neutrality of anti-dumping duties (ANTI_DUMP): 392R0738
- Chemical neutrality:
  - oil seeds (OIL): 386R2435
- Neutrality of the customs valuation system:
  - customs value of goods (CUSTOMS): 689J0011/B
- Conjunctural neutrality (CONJUNCT): 385D105.1
- Cost-neutrality (COST): 385D105.3
- Budgetary neutrality (BUDGET): 380Y1231(06)

Figure 2. Intellectual analysis of the text segments related to the term *neutrality*

5.2 Connectionist approach

During our experiments self-organising feature maps are trained with the descriptor vectors as input data. The length of these vectors is about 500 components. Obviously, the length is dependent on the stop word list. Thus, we perform a projection from a very high dimensional input space onto a two-dimensional output space by means of the self-organising map.

The most obvious difference to the statistical approach is that the neural network did not produce clusters but maps. The advantage of such maps is a better description of the relationship to the various connotations of a concept which can be described by using well-known geographical terms:

- *Hills*: Strong concentration of document segments with the same meaning,
- *Plateaux*: Loose set of document segments with similar meanings,
- *Valleys*: Document segments with meaning elements of several groups,
- *Region*: Neighbourhood relationship between hills and plateaux.

A note on the graphical representation of the final maps which are given in the figures below is in order. The graphical representation contains as many entries as there are output units in the artificial neural network. Thus, every entry corresponds to exactly one unit of the self-organising feature map. Each entry is further assigned either the CELEX number of a text segment or a dot. The appearance of a label denotes the fact that the corresponding unit exhibits the highest activation level with regard to the input vector corresponding to this CELEX number. Thus, this unit is the winning unit. Contrary to that, a dot appears in the final map when none of the input vectors is

1 41 NEUTRALITY

/1/11/ *393R1836, 392R0880*
MEMBER, STATES, COMPOSITION, COMPETENT, BODIES, INDEPENDENCE, PROVISIONS, THIS, REGULATION, CONSISTENT

/2/3/4/ *393D0174/A, 393D0174/B, 393D0174/C*
APPLICATION, TARIFF, STRUCTURE, PRINCIPLE, INCOME, RAILWAY, COMPANIES, CERTAIN, ROUTES, ADJUSTMENTS

/5/15/18/21/22/27/ *992E2408, 990H0306, 989H0195, 987H0184, 987H0183, 982H0240*
QUESTION, NO, COUNCIL, AUSTRIAN, COMMISSION, BONDE, IRISH, UNILATERAL, DECLARATIONS, WRITTEN

/6/7/8/9/ *393R0095/A, 393R0095/B, 393R0095/C, 393R0095/B*
MEMBER, STATES, AIRPORT, PRINCIPLE, NO, RESPONSIBLE, TRANSPARENCY, DISCRIMINATION, CERTAIN, REQUIREMENT

/14/20/ *391R0083, 388R2672*
PARTICULAR, NO, BASIS, CONDITIONS, ORDER, DISCRIMINATION, SUBJECT, REGARDS, SYSTEMS, CO-OPERATION

/19/30/31/33/ *389L0465, 367L0227/A, 367L0227/B, 690C0060*
TAX, VALUE, ADDED, SYSTEMS, PRODUCTION, DISTRIBUTION, MEMBER, STATES, PROVISIONS, SERVICES

/28/35/36/37/38/ *381Y0924, 689J0159/A, 689J0159/B, 689J0119, 689J0011*
MEMBER, STATES, TAX, COMPETITION, VAT, REMISSION, EXPORTATION, GOODS, COMMON, RESPECT

The other remaining clusters consist of only one single document:
392D0274, 392R0738, 392D0180, 390L0435, 390B0354, 386R2435, 385L0361, 385D0105/A, 385D0105/B, 380Y1231, 690C0097, 690C0035, 689J0011/B, 689C0343, 689C0230

Figure 3. Clusters obtained by using a statistical approach

assigned to the corresponding unit. In other words, the respective unit does not exhibit the highest activation level for any input vector. Due to the limited space in the figures the CELEX number of only one text segment is shown even in the case where more than one text segment is assigned to an output unit. The other text segments are given as footnotes. In order to ease comparison we give the short mnemonic description for each CELEX number as they are introduced in Figure 2.

Note that the topological arrangement of the labels is an indication for the similarity of the corresponding text segments. However, the distance of the labels in terms of the two-dimensional surface cannot be used as an exact metric of semantic similarity.

Figure 4 contains the final arrangement of the various text segments based on input vectors which are reduced from stop words. The neural network has produced good hills (e.g. neutrality of the common rules for the allocation of slots at Community airports, neutrality of states) but also some interesting plateaux (e.g. fiscal neutrality or neutrality of competition). An example of a valley is the combination of the meaning elements of environment and competition. A region can be seen including the meanings fiscal neutrality, cost neutrality, budgetary neutrality, and conjunctural neutrality. The results of the neural network are the same in the hard core when compared to the statistical approach, i.e. the good clusters and hills but the interpretation is more difficult. However, the self-organising feature map describes weak relationships between the various meanings better.

A necessary prerogative of the statistical method is a good adaption of the model to the problem. The choice of the stop word list and the threshold value always represents a tricky issue. The neural network overcomes this problem because both parameters are not necessary as the following examples will show. In these experiments we utilized input vectors which are not reduced from stop words.

The final map in Figure 5 is different in terms of the geographical location of the

.	367L0227/A VAT	.	689C0230 SPIRITS	.	392D0180 EN_TAX	.	390B0354 SUGAR	.	389L0465 VAT
690C0060 VAT	.	.	.	393R0095/A SLOTS	.	689J0011/B CUSTOMS	.	.	385L0361 VAT
.	.	392R0738 ANTI_DUMP	.	393R0095/C SLOTS	.	.	982H0240 STATE	987H0183[1] STATE	.
381Y0924(10) VAT	.	.	.	393R0095/D SLOTS	.	990H0306 STATE	989H0195[2] STATE	.	385D105.3 COST
.	.	689C0343 IMP_VAT	.	393R0095/B SLOTS	.	.	.	.	.
689J0011/A[3] NON_DISC	.	.	690C0035 VAT	.	392R0880 ENVIRON	393R1836 ENVIRON	386R2435 OIL	.	390L0435 SUB_VAT
.	689J0119 RES_VAT	.	.	.	.	.	.	.	.
689J0159/A RES_VAT	.	.	393D0174/B TRANSPORT	.	392D0274 RESEARCH	.	367L0227/B VAT	.	690C0097 VAT
.	.	393D0174/A TRANSPORT	.	.	.	.	.	.	.
380Y1231(06) BUDGET	.	.	393D0174/C TRANSPORT	.	391R0083 AIR_SERV	.	388R2672 AIR_SERV	.	385D105.1 CONJUNCT

1. 987H0184 (STATE)
2. 992E2408 (STATE)
3. 689J0159/B (NON_DISC)

Figure 4. Final map (with elimination of stop words)

various text segments but in the hard core the result is the same. The plateau concerning neutrality of competition has disappeared but a good new plateau has been created concerning the meaning of neutrality and environment.

392D0180 EN_TAX	.	385L0361 VAT	.	.	390L0435 SUB_VAT	.	689C0230 SPIRITS	.	385D105.3 COST
.	.	.	.	367L0227/A VAT	.	.	.	.	.
689C0343 IMP_VAT	.	392R0880 ENVIRON	393R1836 ENVIRON	.	.	398L0465 VAT	.	388R2672 AIR_SERV	391R0083 AIR_SERV
.	.	.	.	380Y1231(06) BUDGET	.	.	.	.	.
386R2435 OIL	.	982H0240 STATE	989H0195[1] STATE	.	.	392D0274 RESEARCH	.	367L0227/B VAT	.
393D0174/B TRANSPORT	.	990H0306 STATE	.	390B0354 SUGAR	.	.	.	.	689J0011/A[3] NON_DISC
393D0174/C TRANSPORT	.	987H0183[2] STATE	.	.	.	392R0738 ANTI_DUMP	.	.	689J0119 RES_VAT
393D0174/A TRANSPORT	.	689J0011/B CUSTOMS	.	385D105.1 CONJUNCT	.	.	690C0097 VAT	.	689J0159/A RES_VAT
.	.	.	.	.	.	.	.	.	.
690C0060 VAT	.	690C0035 VAT	.	393R0095/B SLOTS	393R0095/D SLOTS	393R0095/C SLOTS	393R0095/A SLOTS	.	381Y0924(10) VAT

1. 992E2408 (STATE)
2. 987H0184 (STATE)
3. 689J0159/B (NON_DISC)

Figure 5. Final map (without elimination of stop words)

In our last example we used a slightly modified version of self-organising feature maps, namely we adapted the learning rule to capture lateral inhibition of output units. Lateral inhibition may roughly be described as follows. Weight vectors which are assigned to units in close neighbourhood to the winning unit are moved towards the current input vector whereas weight vectors which are assigned to units far away from the winning unit are pushed away even farther. Such a learning function produces an earlier establishment of the final clusters as well as a better approximation to the input vectors. A more detailed description of this learning function can be found in [13]. The final map is depicted in Figure 6.

Without some emphasis on clustering the modified learning function produces not as obvious hills as they are found in the previously presented maps. Nonetheless this experiment proved to be useful because some meanings are better represented, namely the neural network detected similar patterns within the text segments. For example, in the lower left corner of the final map we find four text segments concerning the composition of bodies, i.e. 393R0095/A, 393R0095/C, 393R1836, and 392R0880. Contrary to that, in Figures 4 and 5 clustering stresses on the same meaning, i.e. the allocation of slots at Community airports and the Community eco-management and audit scheme.

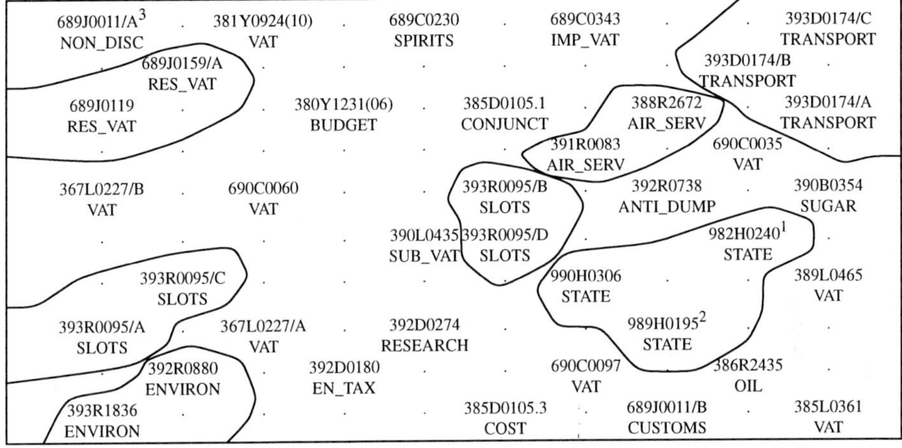

1. 987H0184 (STATE), 987H0183 (STATE)
2. 992E2408 (STATE)
3. 689J0159/B (NON_DISC)

Figure 6. Final map (lateral inhibition of output units; without elimination of stop words)

6 Conclusion and future work

The main contribution of this paper is the comparison between two approaches both aiming at data classification. The first approach adheres to statistical clustering whereas the second one applies artificial neural network technology. At first sight both approaches produced quite similar results. At a closer look, however, the neural network turned out to be paramount since it proved to be able to produce its results without the need of the time consuming tasks which are related to stop word elimination and threshold selection. Yet, the interpretation of the final maps demonstrated to be more laborious because of the different paradigm of presentation. Furthermore, the results of the neural network lack a declarative representation comparable to the cluster descriptions. The outcome of the experiments are encouraging and constitute a basis for further research using larger test data material with regard to the number of documents as well as the size of the thesaurus. The results achieved so far are useful for automatic knowledge acquisition within the legal domain.

References

1. BELEW, R.K. (1987): A Connectionist Approach to Conceptual Information Retrieval. In: Proc. Int. Conf. on Artificial Intelligence & Law. Baltimore: ACM Press.
2. BENCH-CAPON, T. (1993): Neural Networks and Open Texture. In: Proc. Int. Conf. on Artificial Intelligence & Law. Baltimore: ACM Press.
3. BING, J. (1987): Designing Text Retrieval Systems for Conceptual Searching. In: Proc. Int. Conf. on Artificial Intelligence & Law. Baltimore: ACM Press.
4. BLAIR, D.C./MARON, M.E. (1990): Full-Text Information Retrieval: Further Analysis and Clarification. In: Information Processing & Management, Vol. 26, No. 3.
5. CROSS, G.R./deBESSONET, C.G. (1985): Representation of Legal Knowledge for Conceptual Retrieval. In: Information Processing & Management, Vol. 21, No. 1.
6. DICK, J.P. (1991): Representation of Legal Text for Conceptual Retrieval. In: Proc. Int. Conf. on Artificial Intelligence & Law. Baltimore: ACM Press.
7. HAFNER, C.D. (1981): An Information Retrieval System Based on a Computer Model of Legal Knowledge. Ann Arbor: UMI Research Press.
8. HINTON, G. (1989): Connectionist Learning Procedures. In: Artificial Intelligence, Vol. 40
9. KOHONEN, T. (1982): Self-organized formation of topologically correct feature maps. In: Biological Cybernetics, Vol. 43.
10. KOHONEN, T. (1989): Self-Organization and Associative Memory. Springer: Berlin.
11. KOHONEN, T. (1990): The Self-Organizing Map. In: Proc. of the IEEE, Vol. 78, No. 9.
12. MERKL, D./TJOA, A M./VIEWEG, S. (1992): BRANT - An Approach to Knowledge Based Document Classification in the Information Retrieval Domain. Proc. Int. Conf. on Database and Expert Systems Applications. Wien: Springer.
13. MERKL, D./TJOA, A M./KAPPEL, G. (1994): Application of Self-Organizing Feature Maps with Lateral Inhibition to Structure a Library of Reusable Software Components. In: Proc. IEEE Int. Conf. on Neural Networks. Los Alamitos, CA: IEEE Comp. Soc. Press.
14. MITAL, V./STYLIANOU, A./JOHNSON, L. (1991): Conceptual Information Retrieval in Litigation Support Systems. In: Proc. Int. Conf. on Artificial Intelligence & Law. Baltimore: ACM Press.
15. OPDORP, G.J. van et al. (1991): Networks at Work - A Connectionist Approach to Non-deductive Legal Reasoning. In: Proc. Int. Conf. on Artificial Intelligence & Law. Baltimore: ACM Press.
16. PAICE, C.D. (1991): A Thesaural Model of Information Retrieval. In: Information Processing & Management, Vol. 27, No. 5.
17. PANYR, J. (1987): Vektorraum-Modell und Clusteranalyse in Information Retrieval-Systemen. In: Nachr. Dok., Vol. 38. (in German).
18. RUMELHART, D.E./McCLELLAND, J.L. (1986): Parallel Distributed Processing - Explorations in the Microstructure of Cognition. Cambridge, Mass.: MIT Press.
19. SALTON, G. (1989): Automatic Text Processing: The Transformation, Analysis, and Retrieval of Information by Computer. Reading, Mass.: Addison-Wesley.
20. SALTON, G./McGILL, M.J. (1983): Introduction to Modern Information Retrieval. New York: McGraw-Hill.
21. SCHWEIGHOFER, E./WINIWARTER, W. (1993a): Legal Expert System KONTERM - Automatic Representation of Document Structure and Contents. In: Proc. Int. Conf. on Database and Expert Systems Applications. Berlin: Springer.
22. SCHWEIGHOFER, E./WINIWARTER, W. (1993b): Refining the Selectivity of Thesauri by Means of Statistical Analysis. In: Proc. Third Int. Congress on Terminology and Knowledge Engineering. Cologne: Indeks Verlag.
23. WONG, S.K.M./ZIARKO, W./RAGHAVAN, V.V./WONG, P.C.N. (1987): On Modeling of Information Retrieval Concepts in Vector Spaces. In: ACM Trans. on Database Systems, Vol. 12, No. 2.

The Design and Implementation of a Legal Text Database

Diomidis Spinellis

SENA S.A.
Kyprou 27
GR-152 37 Filothei
Greece

Abstract. We describe the design and implementation of a legal text database. The database of provides a number of Greek Council of State decisions in the form of a computer-accessible medium (CD-ROM). A graphical front-end is provided which allows the rapid retrieval of cases based on arbitrary keywords combined using boolean operators. The database was populated by automatically converting the word-processor files into a random text retrieval data structure. The system has been designed and implemented with goals of wide availability, accessibility, extensibility, and user-friendliness.

1 Introduction

The supreme administrative court in Greece is the Council of State. It was established in 1928 after the model of the French Counceil d' Etat. Except for its advisory function with regard to delegated legislation, the Council of State is primarily (unlike perhaps its French prototype) a court of law. It is an administrative court of first and last instance with jurisdiction over applications for judicial review "petitions for annulment" of administrative acts for violation of law or abuse of discretionary power. It is also the supreme court which decides final appeals against judgments of the lower administrative courts [3]. The decisions of the Council of State carry significant weight, and are important to legislators, judges, lawyers, and civil servants. Up to 1983 each year's decisions were printed and distributed by the Council of State. The constantly increasing volume of decisions made such an endeavour impractical and currently the only official way supported for access to all decisions is through the archiving department of the Council of State. We decided to implement a text database of Council of State decisions to provide a widely accessible, practical, and user-friendly platform for their dissemination.

2 Functional Description

2.1 Retrieval Software

The database is stored on a CD-ROM. The retrieval software provides a user interface that runs under the Microsoft Windows graphical environment (Fig.

1), although front-ends for text-based operating environments such as Unix and MS-DOS are also available. The interface window contains the following items:

- the menu with the database commands,
- the *tool bar* providing rapid access to the most commonly used operations,
- the query area,
- the result selection area,
- the text viewing area, and
- the *status bar* containing query status and navigation information.

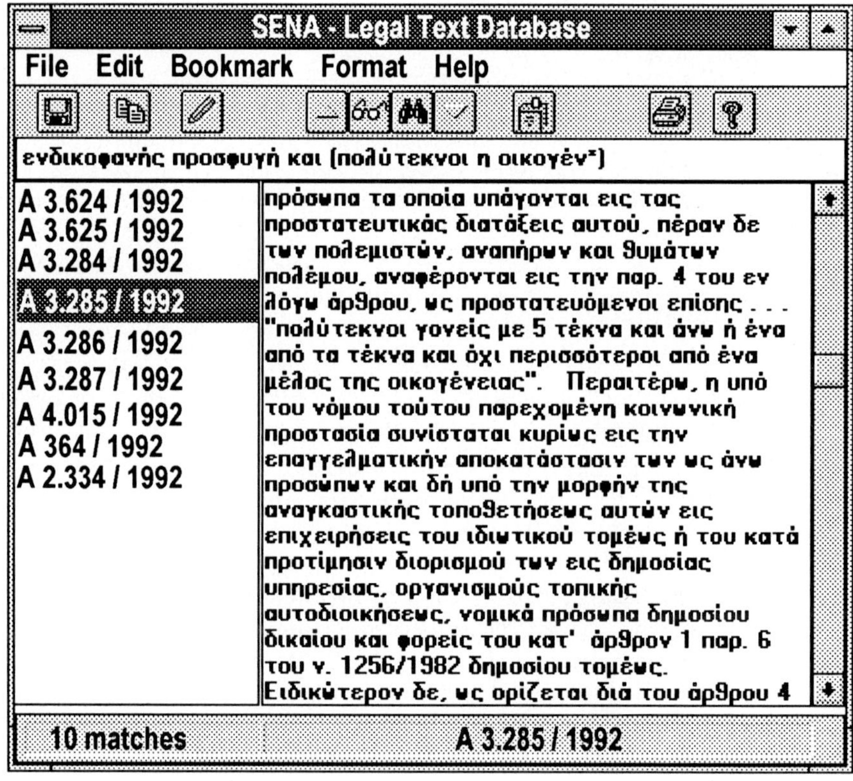

Fig. 1. Text Retrieval Interface Window

In a typical session, the user performs a search by entering a query in the query area. The query can consist of target words connected by the *and, or, not* boolean operators, and grouped using brackets. A BNF description of the query language is given in Table 1. Words can be terminated by the wildcard character $*$ to denote that any word starting with the characters specified is

query	$\rightarrow$	*orexpr*
orexpr	$\rightarrow$	*andexpr* | *orexpr* **or** *andexpr*
andexpr	$\rightarrow$	*basic* | *andexpr* [**and**] *basic*
basic	$\rightarrow$	**not** *basic* | **word** | (*query*)

Table 1. Query language BNF grammar

to be matched. In addition, the search is not sensitive to character case, and the Greek stress and diairesis character modifiers. Apart from the above no other phonetic or semantic equivalences [8] are taken into account, nor does our system ignore certain 'stop-words': we found that our users were often confused by more complicated matching schemes. The terminating wildcharacter option is a simple, yet powerful way to solve the problem of words found with multiple endings — a common phenomenon in the highly inflective Greek language.

When the query is processed the system will report the number of matching texts. A text is defined as a single Council of State decision. Typical texts are between 4K and 40K in length — a search granule convenient both for the end-user, and for searching, storing and reporting. When an excessive number of matches is found, the report list is pruned to a convenient length. The user can then select a case from the report list by double clicking on its code number, and the full text of the case appears on the text viewing area.

The user can the scroll through the text, search for a word within the text, or quickly move to previous or next matching texts using the tool-bar arrow buttons. The text found can also be saved in a file using a variety of formats, printed, or stored to the clipboard — the Windows common area for user-specified inter-process communication.

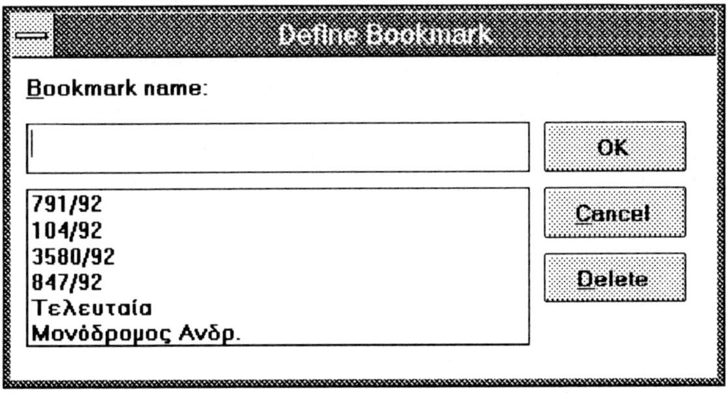

Fig. 2. Bookmark Definition Window

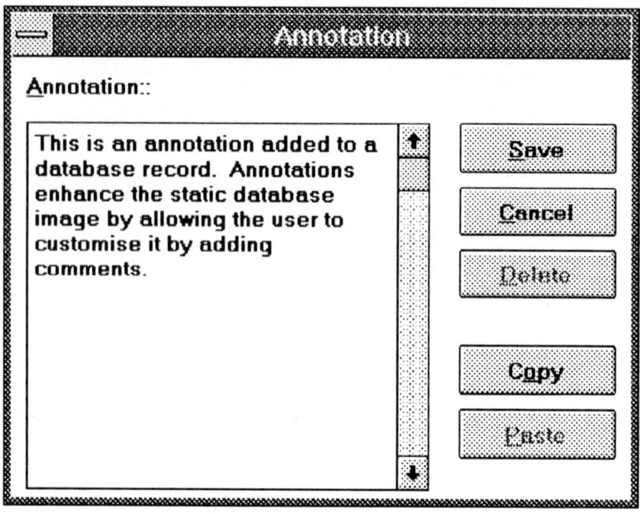

Fig. 3. Annotation Window

Although the database is stored on a read-only medium, its contents are not static. The user can define *bookmarks* throughout the database (Fig. 2) to specify specific points of interest which can then be visited by selecting their name from the bookmark menu. Furthermore, a user can add an *annotation* to a case decision. An annotation (Fig. 3) is a text entered by the user (either directly, or by pasting text from the clipboard) that corresponds to a specific case. Whenever that case is retrieved the user can also read its accompanying annotation.

The system provides a hypertext-structured, context-sensitive help system to guide the user through its operation.

2.2 Database Construction Tools

The database construction tools are used to populate the database using the case decision texts. The conversion of the case decision texts into the database is performed only once for every issue of the database by an expert operator; therefore a simple command-line-based interface guides the indexing operation. The conversion is performed in three phases:

1. Texts are converted from the word processor format used by the Council of State clean-writting department into plain ASCII format and concatenated into a single file separated by a special record separator character.
2. The text file is scanned and the following output is generated:
   - a dictionary of all words contained in the database (the *lexicon* file) together with their frequencies,

   - indices for every separate record of the file, and
   - the memory requirements for storing the data structures of the next phase.
3. The text file is scanned for a second time building the search structure that is used by the random text retrieval algorithms. The text file together with the random text retrieval search structures and a domain definition file form the released database.

3 System Design

The system consists of the database population tools which are used to create a database distribution and the database access system which is used by the end-users. The database access system is also split between the front-end user interface, and the back-end search engine.

The database population tools perform the processor and memory intensive task of creating the random text retrieval data structures. These data structures are based on an *inversion* of the text data whereby every word points to the documents that contain it. The method used for the inversion is a modified implementation of the one described in [9]. During the inversion a compressed dictionary and word index data structure is created in *main memory*, eliminating time-consuming access to disk. This is very important, as traditional techniques such as those described in [7] require large amounts of temporary space and multiple random passes over the data, resulting in slow inversion times. The amount of data generated by the Council of State is about 300MB every decade, and is constantly increasing. For this reason an efficient inversion process in both time and space was selected.

The database access system front-end is structured as a series of procedures associated with events generated by the windowing system. Each event (such as a button click, a menu command, or a text selection) triggers the appropriate procedure which handles the event and on completion returns control back to the windowing system. All low level interaction, such as the processing of scrollbar events, the scrolling of the text, and the editing of the query is automatically handled by the windowing system. The front-end also maintains the dynamic — user-defined — part of the database (bookmarks and annotations), as a parallel superimposed structure to the static part (Fig. 4).

The database access system back-end receives the queries from the front-end (Fig. 5), performs lexical analysis to split them into words and operators, and parses the query into an expression of search terms and logical connectives. The database is searched for every term and an appropriate *match vector* containing a map of the search hits is generated as a result of that search. The *match vectors* are combined and evaluated using boolean algebra rules according to the user-entered logical connectives to form the final *match vector* which is the result of the query. The result is maintained as state within the back-end, and a separate set of functions are used by the front-end to access the *match vector* as an opaque type. The words are searched by performing a binary search based on a structure

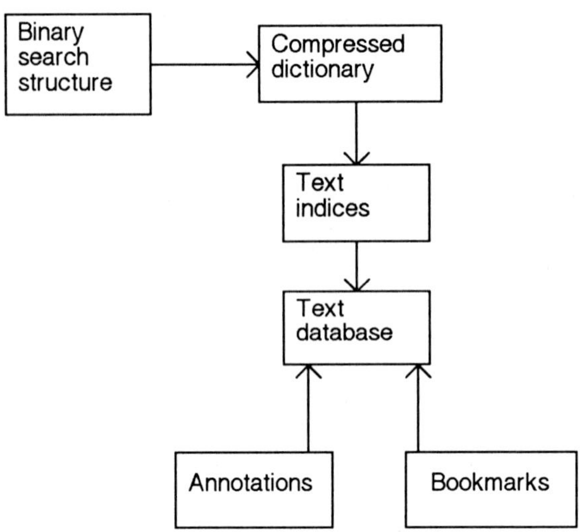

Fig. 4. Database file structure relational diagram

that points to a compressed word dictionary, which in turn is used to index the specific text records (Fig. 4). The compressed search structures (described in detail in section 4.1) are important for minimising the query response times performed using the database's CD-ROM distribution medium by clustering data together eliminating expensive (150ms) disk seek operations [10, p. 218].

4 Implementation Details

4.1 Database Population

The conversion of the texts from the word processor format into ASCII is done by a small filter program prototyped in the Perl programming language [11], and subsequently ported into C for efficiency reasons. In the test run of the system three years of data comprising 190MB of word processor data were processed to create a single 53MB file of ASCII text.

The first pass of the inversion process scans the database building a word dictionary containing the number of documents that contain each word. That number is used in the second phase to create an efficient prefix encoding method [5, 4] based on a maximum guaranteed *gap* measure between successive word occurrences. Specifically, according to [9], given that the database contains N documents and a word appears in p of them, we can encode the word gaps using a b-block code in the most efficient way if we use as b_w (the code's prefix constant) the following:

$$b_w = 2^{\lfloor \log_2 \frac{N-p}{p} \rfloor}$$

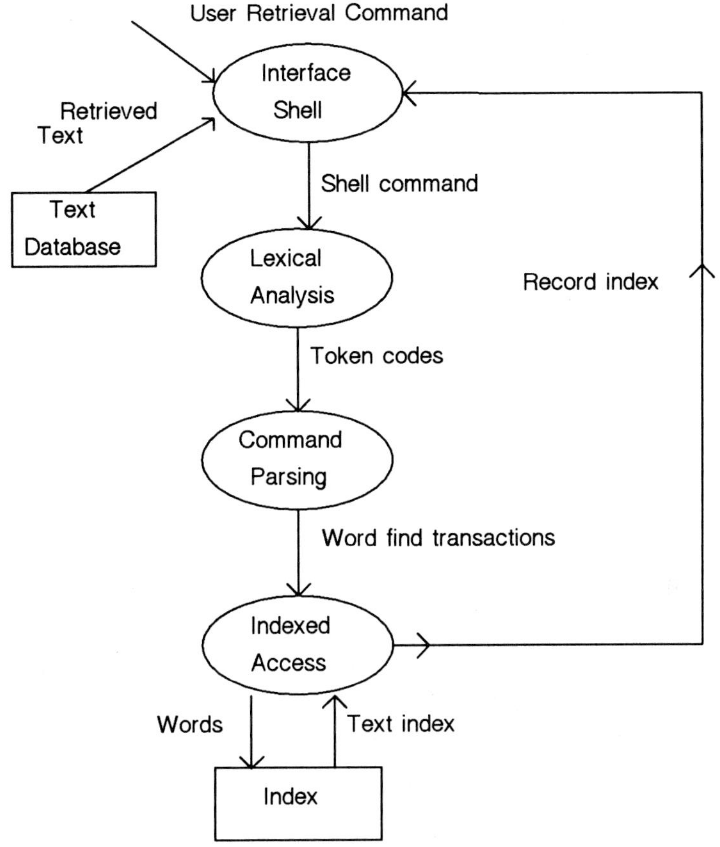

Fig. 5. System data flow diagram

In addition, the number of bits B_w needed to encode all the word gaps for a given word using a block code b (the word's B_w) is then:

$$B_w(b) \leq p \cdot (1 + \log_2 b) + \frac{N-p}{b}$$

The first phase creates the dictionary containing the B_w for every word, so that in the second phase this data structure can be filled by the gaps between the word occurrences. The main memory required by the second phase is thus given by $\sum_{i=1}^{N} B_{w_i}$. The results of the first pass on the trial data appear in Table 2. It is apparent that the main memory requirements (which are the only additional storage requirements apart from the text data) are quite modest.

The second phase of the inversion process reads the dictionary file and scans the data text building a search structure which contains:

Number	Description
6,250	documents
51,143,208	number of characters
6,853,722	number of words
100,510	number of different words
835,054	bytes size of all distinct words
32	bytes size of largest word
483,660	bytes in compressed word dictionary
14,614,289	bits upper limit on memory usage

Table 2. Results of the first inversion phase

- number of words,
- size of the compressed word dictionary,
- size of the compressed gap bitvector (in bytes),
- number of documents,
- offsets into the compressed word dictionary,
- $(p_{w_i}, \sum_{j=1}^{i} B_{w_j})$ pairs for every word,
- byte array containing $\log_2 b$ for every word,
- "1 in K" compressed word dictionary,
- document gap bit encodings, and
- document indices.

The "1 in K" compressed dictionary is used to spare memory by only storing words in groups of K words as prefix/suffix differences from the first word in the group. In our exemplar data this encoding achieved a 44% decrease in dictionary storage space with $K = 4$. The second phase works by maintaining for every word a bit pointer r into the document gap bit encoding bit vector. For every word i in the document, its gap from the previous document is encoded and appended to the bit vector at the position $r + \sum_{j=1}^{i} B_{w_j}$.

4.2 Query Processing

Queries are first translated into tokens by a simple hand-crafted lexical analyser based on a state machine. The query is then processed by a recursive descent parser [1, p. 181] which simultaneously evaluates the query by performing word searches and combining the *match vectors* described in section 3 using logical operators on bit vectors. The result of the query is then stored in a single bit vector and can be accessed by two functions: one returning the number of matches, and the other the document index for a given match.

Words are searched by performing a uniform binary search [6, p. 411] in the compressed dictionary. The search comparison function is modified to scan forward K words to deal with the dictionary's compression. Furthermore, the string comparison function is modified to treat strings ending with the wildcard character as equal to strings with the same prefix. After a matching word is found in the dictionary the ordinal numbers of the documents in which the word occurs can be easily calculated by successively adding the word's gap measures decoded from the word gap bit vector structure.

4.3 Implementation Metrics

The implementation effort of the system was relatively modest at about 5000 lines of code. The relative size of each part of the system is summarised in Table 3.

System Part	Lines of Code
Document conversion	124
Inversion first pass	452
Inversion second pass	915
Query processing engine	1001
User interface shell	2570

Table 3. Implementation of system parts

For the text data described in Table 2 the first pass of the inversion process (lexicon construction and word frequency counting) took 8 minutes, while the second pass (search structure creation) took 27 minutes. It is apparent that our process will still terminate in manageable execution times even for an order of magnitude more data (both passes use $O(\log_2 n)$ algorithms where n is the number of distinct words in the text).

5 Related Work

Legal professionals depend on accurate and complete access to legislative and case texts. Their needs are targeted by a number of commercial data providers at the national and international level. Most databases are accessed via public switched networks, although some are now distributed in CD-ROM format [2]. In Greece two companies, Databank and HellasLex, sell legal database services — including court decisions — accessible via dial-in modems. Our implementation differs in scale and approach: it can be considered as a CD-ROM publication of recent Council of State decisions.

6 Conclusions and Further Work

We have presented the design and implementation of a Legal Text Database. Using a small set of well researched data structures and algorithms together with an industry-standard windowing interface we were able to construct an efficient, user-friendly and responsive system that satisfies the needs of many legal professionals.

We are currently expanding the system adding more cases, and examining other sources of legal texts that can be incorporated into our system. The generality of our approach based on random text retrieval allows the modular and effortless addition of arbitrary texts while still providing the professional with a reasonably structured interface for retrieving the information he or she requires.

Acknowledgements

We would like to thank the President of the Council of State Mr. B. Botopoulos, the Associate Judge Mr. B. Aravantinos for their invaluable support of this project, and the EDP operator Mr. B. Koliopoulos for the technical assistance he provided.

References

1. Alfred V. Aho, Ravi Sethi, and Jeffrey D. Ullman. *Compilers, Principles, Techniques, and Tools.* Addison-Wesley, 1985.
2. Chadwyck-Healey Ltd. New CD-ROM: EUROCAT. *Eur-OP News*, 3(2):3, October 1993.
3. Prodromos D. Dagtoglou. Constitutional and administrative law. In Konstantinos D. Kerameus and Phaedon J. Kozyris, editors, *Introduction to Greek Law*, chapter 3, pages 21–91. Kluwer, second edition, 1993.
4. R. C. Gallager and D. C. Van Voorhis. Optimal source codes for geometrically distributed alphabets. *IEEE Transactions on Information Theory*, 21(2):228–230, March 1975.
5. S. W. Golomb. Run-length encodings. *IEEE Transactions on Information Theory*, 12(3):399–401, July 1966.
6. Donald E. Knuth. *The Art of Computer Programming*, volume 3 / Sorting and Searching. Addison-Wesley, 1973.
7. Michael Lesk. Some applications of inverted indexes on the Unix system. In *Unix Programmer's Manual*, chapter Volume 2A. Bell Laboratories, 1988.
8. Michael Lesk. Word manipulation in online catalog searching: Using the UNIX system for library experiments. In *Proceedings of the EUUG Spring 88 Conference*, pages 135–147, London, April 1988. European UNIX User Group.
9. Alistair Moffat. Economical inversion of large text files. *Computing Systems*, 5(2):125–139, Spring 1992.
10. Ken C. Pohlman. *The Compact Disc Handbook.* Oxford University Press, 1992.
11. Larry Wall and Randal L. Schwartz. *Programming Perl.* O'Reilly and Associates, Sebastopol, CA, USA, 1990.

MAINTENANCE OF JURICAS LEGAL COMPUTER ADVICE SYSTEMS

J.G.L. van der Wees
Centre for Computers and Law
Erasmus University Rotterdam
The Netherlands

Abstract

Maintenance of legal knowled has not had much attention so far. Most papers have been concentrated on feasibility, knowledge representation and knowledge acquisition. The fact that legal computer systems are gradually more accepted and used in the legal practice, causes a growing need for maintenance strategies and policies. Isomorphism is often mentioned if maintenance is an issue. The rules in the knowledge base should remain as close as possible to the rule in law.

Rules in the JURICAS advisory packages which are being used in legal practice in the Netherlands can remain quite close to the source. Next to that, the fact that the representation in JURICAS files is easy to read and easy to understand, can make JURICAS packages quite easy to maintain. However, there is an important role to play for the programmer of a package.

Nevertheless, JURICAS has some maintenance problems: the structure of JURICAS knowledge files can be confusing; JURICAS packages are often built by the legal experts themselves, which has benefits but certainly has disadvantages as well, as our Centre for Computers and Law has experienced; the JURICAS facility to save cases causes exchange problems, because new cases cannot be processed by old versions of packages and vice versa.

Maintenance problems can be reduced to a minimum by developing a JURICAS Development Methodology. However, some problems require an organizational or a technical solution. For some of the problems the Centre for Computers and Law has found a solution, for others, research is still to be done.

Introduction

Research into the application of legal knowledge based systems has confirmed at least one important premise; such systems are feasible. The introduction of these systems into legal practice has, however, not been really successful so far.[13] The appearance of these systems seems to reflect a technology push rather than a demand pull.[see also 1, p.5] Nevertheless, some legal knowledge based systems are currently being used in legal practice, or in fields closely related to the legal one, in the Netherlands.[note 1]

The introduction of these systems into legal practice has led to an increasing need to maintain the systems. Until now not much attention has been paid to this very crucial aspect in the development, the introduction and the acceptance of legal knowledge based systems. As Bratley a.o. wrote in their paper for the AI and Law conference in Oxford: "Our conclusion is that although most published work on legal expert systems pays lip service to the idea that they must be designed to cope with change, the problem is still entirely open". This paper supports their assertion that: ".. bringing this problem to the forefront of designers' minds is a necessary step if we are to have real, working systems."[6]

It is rather strange that the necessity of maintaining legal knowledge based systems has not been given much attention. It is particularly odd given that law in general is not a stable domain[see also 16], but is subject to change. The development of computer technologies alone has caused a flood of alterations to rules and regulations in the last decade. This lack of attention may, however, be a normal stage in the development of (legal) computer systems; first of all the feasibility is investigated, then knowledge representation and knowledge acquisition are examined and as soon as it seems that people are willing to use the systems it is about time to start thinking of management and control.[2, p.415]

The JURICAS project has had such a development cycle. The basis of the research has been defined in the 1980s.[3] So far our research has lead to the development of a legal advice system shell which can be filled with legal knowledge to produce a legal advisory package. These JURICAS packages and the JURICAS system shell are being used in legal practice in the Netherlands.[4][note 2] Although maintenance has been taken into account from the beginning, it is now becoming even more important.

The fact that the shell and packages are already being used in legal practice[4], does not mean that there will be no further development of the JURICAS system. Where possible, we will comply with users wishes regarding the system while still undertaking research to improve the JURICAS system and make it completer. We are, for example, carrying out research to improve legal information retrieval techniques[14] and to predict verdicts[15]. This research might lead to techniques which can later be integrated into the JURICAS system. First of all, however, it is the maintenance problem we have to face.

Maintenance - Development Methodology

According to Bench-Capon, one reason for the limited use of legal knowledge based systems is the fact that the systems are hard to maintain due to a lack of good software engineering techniques.[2, p.415] Whether maintenance plays such an important role as far as the use is concerned is open to query. A research in progress on the use of information technology in legal practice in the Netherlands might give some interesting answers to the usability aspect.[13] Maintenance carried out as soon as systems are up and running might show that the maintainability of a system is poor. This might be due to the engineering technique being used but that does not necessarily have to be the case.

Quite a few JURICAS advisory packages have been sold in the Netherlands but no user has ever asked questions about a maintenance programme. This is rather peculiar seeing as most users work in legal practice. They are aware, however, that the domain of law is regularly subject to change. The reason for not asking about the maintenance programme is probably strongly related to the fact that lawyers can be considered to be late adopters of information technology[17], which in the opinion of this paper is also an important argument for not using legal computer systems. On the other hand, some legal practitioners pay annually for package updates, so they know the it will be maintained and updated. The way in which the advisory package will be maintained and the problems which may arise in trying to do so is in fact not their concern: it is, however, ours. So it seems people do invest in JURICAS legal computer software without knowing exactly how it can be updated. The price of JURICAS advisory packages may play an important role in this complaisant attitude. The cheapest package is 200 Dutch guilders while the most expensive one is 1500 guilders. Users do not, therefore, take an enormous financial risk when buying a JURICAS advisory package even if it should later prove difficult to maintain.

Change is a problem which is characteristic of all software systems, certainly not only the legal ones. This might, however, be more the case in a legal knowledge based system than in, for example, an administrative system. The chance of change within the law is much greater.[6, p.69] Nevertheless, an examination of a traditional software development cycle gives an idea of how to cope with change. For this type of software system, many development techniques and methodologies already exist which are considered to provide fundamental principles for building maintainable software systems.[2, p.416] Examples are SDM (System Development Methodology)[7] or JSP (Jackson Structured Programming)[8]. The use of such a methodology means that a software engineer who is familiar with this particular methodology can work on a system at any time in any place.[2, p.416] Development environments have also been developed for knowledge based systems: ADS, CRYSTAL, NEXPERT, KADS. The latter is probably the best known.[10] and [11]. These environments do not pay specific attention to maintainability but, as the development of a system is carried out according to the rules of the specific method, it has been argued that this will facilitate maintenance.[2, p.417] As for the lip service paid in current literature to the idea that expert systems must be designed to cope with change, see Bratley a.o. who give a summary of several proposals for handling change.[6]

To avoid JURICAS maintenance problems there is the need to stress a definition of a JURICAS development methodology. JURICAS has its own characteristics and therefore probably requires a specific development methodology. However, aspects of other methodologies will be useful for JURICAS as well. This paper does not describe the outline for this development methodology but pictures the problems our Centre for Computers and Law faced and is still facing without the support of such a methodology..

Maintenance - Isomorphism

Bench-Capon and Coenen write that the intention of isomorphism in knowledge based systems is that the rule base should reflect the sources from which it has been developed. This does not only result in a disciplined and teachable development methodology, it also improves the user friendliness of a system, supports validation and facilitates maintenance.[12] If this is true for isomorphism, then one would tend to think that it is easy to build a good legal knowledge based system because the law is, like knowledge systems, rule based. Unlike other areas which are not usually expressed in a rule-based form, the law is really just a collection of rules. By taking these and putting them into a knowledge base, it would seem that an isomorph legal computer system can easily be built. This was probably the idea a senior figure in the UK government had in mind when he said the following words to encourage the building of legal expert systems: "It's just a matter of getting a group of lawyers off for a weekend together".[9] We know that this expectation turned out to be overly optimistic. The building of legal systems has proven not to be easy. Quite a few legal computer systems in the Netherlands never left the laboratories. A rule in law can often not be simply translated to a rule in a knowledge system which in turn makes it difficult to build a system which is isomorph. As Bratley a.o. explain, many conventions are necessary to transform law into a computer program. In addition, heuristic knowledge and general legal knowledge has to be implemented into the system as well, which makes the system less transparent, less isomorph.[6] Nevertheless, isomorphism seems a good goal to strive for when developing legal knowledge based systems because its advantages can be noticed during the whole development cycle. For more details on isomorphism, see the paper of Bench-Capon and Coenen.[12] The only part of the cycle which will be discussed here is, of course, maintenance.

In an isomorph knowledge base it will be easy to find exactly that part of the knowledge which is related to the legal source which is about to change, for a rule in the knowledge base is similar to, for example, a section of an act which has to be changed. After tracing the relevant rule in the knowledge base this rule can be worked on in isolation as Bench-Capon describes.[12] For some so-called "stand alone" changes isolation might be possible. All too often, however, a change in one section of an act has a knock on effect for another section of the same act or maybe even for a section in another act, which makes updating in isolation a risky enterprise. This danger was perceived by Bench-Capon. A change in law may also cause a change in heuristic and general legal knowledge in the knowledge base. Knowledge which might be harder to trace because of a lack of isomorphism. This being said, one might conclude isomorphism must be a base when developing a knowledge base system although one must be aware of the fact that complete isomorphism cannot always be attained.[6]

Maintenance - JURICAS Advisory Packages

JURICAS packages are not isomorph in the most optimum form. Conventions are necessary to translate the legal knowledge into a JURICAS text, while heuristics and general legal knowledge are often added to a JURICAS knowledge file as well. However, in JURICAS it is possible to stay quite close to the source material. Apart from that does the JURICAS programming language also result in what could be termed an intermediate representation of the legal knowledge, which is easy to read, easy to understand and easy to trace for people maintaining a JURICAS advisory package.[see also 20]

Suppose in a JURICAS advisory package on copyright law a change has to be implemented as a result of the EU directive on the protection of computer software. In section 3 of the Dutch Copyright Act there is a summary of what works of literature, science or art are deemed to be according to this law. Computer programs have been added to this summary. The part of the JURICAS copyright advisory package can be defined as follows:

```
/* Paragraph 3 Copyright, section 10 part 1.

#110#
21,1@
@
e1#

1. All other writings means ....

2. An example of a musical drama work is..

3. A recital is .............

e2#

4. pantomime is ...

etc.
@
/P008/
Section 10, part 1. According to this act works of literature,
science or art are:
1.      books, brochures, news magazines and all other writings
2.      theatre plays and musical drama works
3.      recitals
4.      pantomimes
5.      musical works with or without lyrics
6.      paintings, lithography
7.      geographical maps
8.      designs, sketches in relation to construction, geography or
        other sciences
9.      photographic works
10.     film
11.     industrial drawings and models.
---------------------------------------------
Is the work at issue here a work of literature, science or art according
to this law?  Use F4 for more explanation and/or examples.
```

```
        Yes
        No
@
110,0,120,800#
```

This is a very simple example, but it is clear that a section of an act is very easy to trace. Just start the program editor and search for the part of the act you want to see. If the programmer has forgotten to use a header which indicates which part of which act will be dealt with next in the knowledge base, it will be more difficult. However, then searching for a word which would be included in the section may give almost the same result. Needless to say, adjusting the section is easy. It must, however, be kept in mind that in the explanation screens information and/or examples are given on the section. It might be necessary to add some explanation on computer programs as well. After changing this part of the knowledge file, it is important to add a line to the header which says when and why the change has been made.

By looking at this small section of the JURICAS copyright package one has no overview of the complete Copyright Act. Complete acts are often part of JURICAS packages as well. They are not usually part of the knowledge base but are stored in a separate file we call the information file. The advantage of storing acts in this separate file is, of course, that there is only one place in the package where the act can be found and therefore only one place where the act needs to be amended. It is not necessary to store parts of an act in the knowledge file as well because JURICAS has a hypertext like facility which shows the screen containing the act which is relevant to a specific question or conclusion. This facility has to be defined by the programmer because every information file contains another act and sometimes does not even contain a complete act, which makes it impossible to know on which page of the information file a certain part of an act will be defined. After developing the information file the programmer would know which part is on which page, and then these page numbers can be added to the knowledge file. In the above example, the text of section 10 of the Dutch Copyright Act will apparently be on page 8 of the information file because what we call the page switch (P-switch) is followed by 008.

Despite what has been described above, of course, a programmer is still able to develop a JURICAS advisory package which lacks any structure and which is not isomorph at all. Therefore, a JURICAS development methodology has to be made which stresses these important requirements for maintainable packages.

Although, in general, it seems quite easy to maintain JURICAS advisory packages, because of the simple representation and because of the fact that redundancy is avoided as much as possible by including acts only once, this does not mean that we do not face any maintenance problems. Before discussing these problems, it should be pointed out that in general there are two types of JURICAS packages: ready made packages and tailor made packages. The latter are made by organisations which have bought the empty JURICAS shell in order to fill a knowledge file with their own organizational knowledge. The Dutch central police investigation and information service (CRI), for example, has built an international legal aid package using the JURICAS system shell. These organizations maintain their own packages themselves, so the maintenance of these advisory packages is not the concern of our Centre for Computers and Law. That is not the case with respect to the ready made packages which are not made or adjusted for a particular user. Quite a few of these advisory packages (Dismissal law, Inheritance law, Tracking Social Security Fraud) have been made according to the principle knowledge engineer equals expert. This means we have taught the (legal) expert how to develop the JURICAS advisory package. Since the JURICAS language is very simple and no interaction with a knowledge engineer is necessary if the expert knows the programming language, a JURICAS package development life cycle is very short. Maintenance is no problem as long as the knowledge engineer/expert wants to take care of that part of the work as well. Problems do arise though as soon as the expert quits. Experience has shown that it is hard to find another expert who is prepared to maintain the package. Sometimes we do find a person willing to assess the contents of an advisory package, but most of them do not want to learn the (simple) JURICAS language. As a result we often have to do the programming ourselves while the legal expert just says what has to be amended. This is far from being an ideal situation. This could be avoided by always taking two legal experts for one project, but we have found that it is hard enough to find just one expert who is prepared to learn JURICAS and to develop an advisory package. This is the weak spot of the theory that the knowledge engineer and the expert should be one and the same person, which we especially experience maintaining the ready made systems. However, organizations using the JURICAS system shell to develop packages themselves have to be aware of this drawback as well.

A company or a department consisting of people (knowledge engineers) with a legal background who have learned to work with the JURICAS language as a programming base may be a solution for this problem. These people can consult experts for building legal knowledge based systems. An advantage is that a programmer can easily be replaced by another programmer, particularly if the company or department has worked with a certain knowledge system development methodology which all programmers have to use. If an expert leaves, it will probably be easier to find another one who is willing to cooperate because no programming language has to be learned. The company or department would be in essence a software house or a software development department.

Another problem we face is related to the case base which every JURICAS package has. Every case processed with a JURICAS package can be stored in a case base. Users can continue processing a case over a period of time or and, therefore, a JURICAS package has to change, it is likely that the rules in the package change in such a way that an old case cannot be dealt with any more in the new version of the package. This means that every new version of a package together with a new case base has to be stored in a separate directory. If a user wants to consult an old case he or she has to go to an old directory and start an old version connected to an old case base in that directory. One advantage of the separation of versions and cases of a package is that it is easy to process a case according to the rules ex tunc.[18] Problems arise, however, if users want to see how a new case would have been dealt with according to the old regulations or how an old case would be dealt with according to the new/temporary regulations, because cases are not compatible. A new case cannot be processed by an old version of the package and vice versa. Unfortunately users often think upgrading or downgrading is just as easy as it is in, for example, Wordperfect and are unaware of the difficulty regarding old cases and new versions. One possible solution to this problem could be to connect tables to every package, which contain the item numbers (JURICAS knowledge files consist of items which all have a number, the item in the example above has number 110, see also [5]) and the answers belonging to the item numbers. The programmer then has to indicate which numbers have been changed in the new knowledge file after which the old item numbers with the answers can be transformed into the new item numbers. New cases have to be completed if large new sections of an act have been introduced. New answers have to be given.

In our maintenance of JURICAS advisory packages we have realized that the structure of JURICAS knowledge files can be a bit confusing, because they consist of one huge top-down string of items.[19] It is not easy to discover when a certain part stops and another one begins. This has been improved, however, by introducing the possibility of adding comment to the knowledge file, as can be seen in the example above. Another feature which has been developed to make the structure clearer is the possibility to divide a JURICAS knowledge file into modules. A JURICAS patent advisory package, for example, could consist of six modules: PATENT01, PATENT02, PATENT03, PATENT04, PATENT05, PATENT06. The first module can be a general module, the second the patent decision module, the sixth a print module, etc. If the programmer needs to adjust a standard letter to the patent office, only the sixth module has to be edited. The knowledge file can still be tested as a whole, because it switches automatically from one module to the other. We call this automatic file chaining.

We have also developed a preventive maintenance strategy. Every JURICAS package is examined by (legal) experts and laymen before it is marketed and sold. Much future maintenance can be avoided in this manner.[2, p.418]

Conclusion

JURICAS packages sometimes lack a lucid structure and the link with the source material (acts, case law, etc.) can be unclear as well which makes the packages not isomorph. These packages are, of course, not easy to maintain. For improving maintainability, a JURICAS development methodology needs to be defined stressing, amongst others, isomorphism and importance of the structure.

Apart from that, new features have been developed which improve maintainability. Automatic file chaining, for example, gives the programmer the possibility to divide the knowledge file in coherent pieces. Comment lines in the knowledge file can also be a useful instrument to make the structure clear.

Other maintenance problems concern the strategy knowledge engineer equals legal expert which has important drawbacks. Organizational measurements can probably avoid these drawbacks from coming to the fore. For example, at least two knowledge engineers/experts should be working on a project. The difficulties our Centre for Computers and Law has with the exchange of cases in case bases of old and new versions of the same package are harder to solve. Although we have thought of a solution, the design of it is still premature.

Notes

1. TESSEC; Twente Expert System for Social Security
   MrWBO; an expert system which calculates the amount of money the elderly have to pay from their own pockets if they go to a rest home
   JURICAS Working Conditions; a system which helps to evaluate the working conditions in companies and organisations according to the Working Conditions Act.
2. A JURICAS advisory package consists of a JURICAS shell program and a knowledge file. The first has been developed by the Centre for Computers and Law, the latter will be made by a knowledge engineer after consulting a legal expert or by a knowledge engineer/legal expert.

References

[1] Bench-Capon, Trevor J.M. and Frans Coenen, Practical application of KBS to law: the crucial role of maintenance, in: Legal knowledge based systems, Aims for research and development, eds. C.van Noortwijk, A.H.J.Schmidt, R.G.F.Winkels, Vermande, Lelystad, The Netherlands, 1991, pp.5-17.

[2] Bench-Capon, Trevor, Frans Coenen, Building knowledge based systems for maintainability, in: Database and Expert Systems Applications (DEXA 92), proceedings DEXA conference, Valencia 1992, eds. A.M. Tjoa and I. Ramos, Springer-Verlag, Vienna, New York, pp.415-420.

[3] Mulder, R.V. De, C. van Noortwijk, H.O. Kerkmeester and J.G.L. van der Wees, Knowledge systems and law - The JURICAS project in: Database and Expert Systems Applications (DEXA 90), proceedings DEXA conference, Vienna 1990, eds. A.M. Tjoa and R. Wagner, Springer-Verlag, Vienna, New York, pp.112-115.

[4] Van Noortwijk C., Piepers P.A.W., Van der Wees J.G.L. , The JURICAS System in a Social Security Environment, in: Database and Expert Systems Applications (DEXA 92), proceedings DEXA conference, Valencia 1992, eds. A.M. Tjoa and I. Ramos, Springer-Verlag, Vienna, New York, pp.127-132.

[5] Wees, J.G.L.van der, JURICAS; Legal Computer Advice Systems, Artificial Intelligence and Law, Volume 2, No.1, 1993.

[6] Bratley, P., Femont, J., MacKaay, E. and Poulin, D., Coping With Change, Proceedings of the 3rd International Conference on AI and Law, Oxford, ACM Press, 1991, pp.53-61.

[7] Snoo, H.C.R. de, Projectmanagement met SDM, Academic Service, Schoonhoven, The Netherlands, 1990.

[8] Jansen, Henk, JSP, Academic Service, Den Haag, 1984.

[9] Leith, Philip, The Computerised Lawyer, A Guide to the Use of Computers in the Legal Profession, Springer-Verlag, London, 1991.

[10] 'KADS wordt de standaard voor het bouwen van kennissystemen' (KADS (Knowledge Application Development System) is going to be the standard for developing knowledge systems), Automatisering Gids 15/10/93.

[11] Hickman, F., Knowledge Based Systems Analysis: A Pragmatic Introduction to the KADS Methodology, Ellis Horwood, 1989.

[12] Bench-Capon, T.J.M., and Coenen, F.P., Exploiting Isomorphism: Development of a KBS to Support British Coal Insurance Claims, in: Proceedings of the 3rd International Conference on AI and Law, Oxford, ACM Press, 1991, pp.62-68.

[13] Wees, L. van der, and M.Huysman, It in Legal Practice, in: Proceedings SIGCPR (Special Interest Group on Computer Personnel Research) '94, Alexandria, Virginia, USA.

[14] Wildemast, C.A.M., and R.V.De Mulder, Some design for a conceptual legal information retrieval system, in: Legal Knowledge Based Systems, Information Technology and Law, eds. C.A.F.M.Grütters, J.A.P.J.Breuker, H.J.van den Herik, A.H.J.Schmidt, C.N.J.de Vey Mestdagh, Vermande, 1992, pp.81-92.

[15] Combrink-Kuiters, C.J.M., and P.A.W. Piepers, The Implementation of Predictive Capabilities into Legal Computer Advice Systems, in: Pre-proceeding of the 8th BILETA conference, Liverpool, 1993, pp.63-72.

[16] Oskamp, Anja, Het ontwikkelen van juridische expert systemen, Kluwer, Deventer, 1990.

[17] Rogers, E.M., Diffusion of Innovations, 3rd edition, The Free Press, New York, 1983.

[18] Mazel, Mr R.G., NJB 16 januari 1992 afl.3, pp.103-106.

[19] Kralingen, R.W. van, Visser, P.R.S., Een generiek taakmodel voor het redeneren met wetteksten, in: proceedings NAIC '92, pp.53-63.

[20] Brown LLB, Graham, CHINATAX: Exploring Isomorphism with Chinese Law, in: Proceedings of the 4th International Conference on AI and Law, Amsterdam, ACM Press, 1993, pp.175-179.

Keynote Speech

Expert Systems for Industrial Process Control: A Study in Technology Transfer

J. Mylopoulos
Department of Computer Science
University of Toronto
Canada

Many research projects are building expert systems for industrial applications. A common problem faced by researchers working on such projects is: How can the results of one project be generalized so that they are easily adoptable to other development projects.

The presentation is based on results of a 5-year project whose aim is to build expert systems that help a plant operator during an emergency. The systems developed so far monitor incoming data from the plant, detect abnormal situations, propose diagnoses and verify them using advanced simulation techniques. The presentation covers the scope of the project, results obtained so far and the approach that has been adopted in order to generalize these results to a generic technology, applicable to other process control applications.

From a Passive to an Active Database Supporting Exceptions

Bruno Defude[1] and Hervé Martin[2]

[1] Institut National des Télécommunications, 9, Rue Charles Fourrier, 91011 Evry Cedex, France
Bruno.Defude@int-evry.fr
[2] Laboratoire de Génie Informatique, IMAG-Campus, BP 53X 38041 Grenoble Cedex, France
Herve.Martin@imag.fr

Abstract. This paper presents a mechanism to enforce consistency in object oriented DBMS using pre-conditions and post-conditions on methods. This mechanism is coupled with an exception mechanism to allow deferred controls and semantic tolerance. Conditions are defined using SQL-like expressions and methods composition. Exceptions are defined at the class level. We consider that an exception has a signature (the context of the exception) and an implementation (the process associated with the exception). We define the semantics of inheritance related to exceptions. The process control of this exception mechanism is also presented. This model can be considered at an execution level and we show how some general integrity rules (e.g referential integrity) can be compiled into pre(post)-conditions and exceptions.

Keywords: Integrity constraints, Object-Oriented DBMS, Pre(post)-conditions, Exceptions, Inheritance

1 Introduction

Applications such as those found in engineering require the development of large software programs (containing millions of statements) to manage large volume of persistent and shared data. Thus, complex data and their behavior have to be modeled. Many proposals meet these needs. Some of them extend existing models and others define new models (these include the semantic, functional, and object data models [3]). The object oriented approach is beginning to significantly influence software development through the use of object programming languages such as Smalltalk [8], C++ or Eiffel; and through the emergence of object oriented design methodologies such as OOA/OOD [4, 5], or OMT [12]. Several commercial object-oriented DBMS are currently on the marketplace (ObjectStore, Versant, Gemstone, O2, Ontos, Matisse [1, 3] are good examples).

The object-oriented approach is based on object behavior modeling through messages and encapsulation properties. Nevertheless, declarative tools are missing in current object DBMS generation for expressing data integrity controls. In these systems, such controls are written into the methods and so, become the user's responsibility.

We claim that integrity controls can be performed more efficiently using an object framework than using a relational framework. Indeed, RDBMS do not modelize object behavior and consequently are not able to control integrity at the right time on the right data (we mean exactly when a constraint is potentially transgressed by a relevant data).

We propose to adopt a behavioral approach to express database integrity rather than adapt a relational approach to OODBMS [2]. Our approach is close to those of programming languages where properties of programs are expressed using assertions on variable states [9]. Our contribution is to adapt these approaches to database concepts such as persistence and transactions. Integrity constraints are expressed on methods using pre and post-conditions [9] that are bound with an exception mechanism. This proposal extends [11] so that to our mechanism is integrated into the object framework.

This paper is organized in the following manner: Section 2 presents our behavioral approach. Section 3 details our proposal using examples. In section 4 we show how some general integrity rules (e.g referential integrity) can be compiled into pre or post-conditions and exceptions. Finally, we make some concluding remarks and some perspectives on this work are presented.

2 The Behavioral Approach

Our approach is based on the concept of using behavior to ensure database consistency. Instead of constraining object states, we constrain their behavior. We consider that, if the behavior of objects is consistent during a transaction, then the transaction will keep the database in a consistent state. On the other hand, if the object behavior is detected as an inconsistent one, it is possible to eliminate this inconsistency or to signal it to the user.

Our approach is based on the assumption that a sequential composition of locally consistent behavior, yields a globally consistent behavior. To check consistency using the behavioral approach, we allow the user to specify controls at two levels: at the method execution level (local level) and at the transaction level (global level).

Controls at the local level can be performed upon the reception of the message (before the beginning of the execution) or after the execution. Checks before the execution are used to verify the consistency of the execution context for the method. These checks are mainly based on the value of the parameters and/or on the state of the object that has received the message. Controls after method execution are used to check the validity of the behavior and are mainly based on the result of the method and/or the state of the object(s) after method execution.

This definition of consistency is very strong and must be relaxed to take into account two problems. First, some behaviors cannot be characterized locally at the end of the transaction. These kinds of behaviors must be considered as suspicious at the local level and then be evaluated globally at the end of the transaction when all the required information is available. According to the context, we make the decision of accepting or refusing the behavior at the global level. If one of the suspicious behaviors is judged inconsistent, the transaction will be aborted.

Second, as stated above, a consistency mechanism must be flexible enough to take into account exceptions to the general rules [7]. So before refusing a behavior, we need to check whether the present case refers to an exceptional case. Exceptional cases must be considered as correct and not as inconsistent.

3 Towards an Integrity Model with Objects

3.1 Conditions and Exceptions

Two mechanisms are proposed to define checks at local and global levels. The first one is based on the activation context of a method (in_context), and the second one is based on the validation context of a method (out_context). The out_context is used to specify controls after the method execution and controls at the end of the transaction. In_context and out_context are associated with an exception mechanism allowing to support exceptional cases and global controls.

Each time we detect either a suspicious or an abnormal behavior, an exception is raised. Each exception has a name and can have some parameters associated with it. A routine is associated with a given exception. There are two kinds of exceptions: *immediate* or *deferred*. If the exception type is *immediate*, then the exception manager calls the special routine associated with the exception. This routine either allows transaction execution to resume or triggers an abort.

If the type of the exception is *deferred*, then the exception manager stores the exception in a set of "pending exceptions" together with its parameters (global check). These parameters represent the exception context and will be used at the end of the transaction when executing the corresponding routine. Afterwards, a message *continue* is sent to the transaction.

At the end of the transaction, a message *end-of-transaction* is sent to the transaction manager. At this time, the transaction manager calls every exception routine that is pending. If all routines return a *continue* message, then the transaction commits, otherwise it aborts.

To avoid side effects and multiple exception triggering, only two actions associated with exceptions are allowed: *refuse* or *accept*.

Concepts that we propose are in the object framework. So it is necessary that general properties of the object paradigm (inheritance, overloading, encapsulation) can be applied:

- Inheritance of pre-conditions and post-conditions: we have chosen a specialization semantic, that is, if we consider a method m which is defined in class A with a pre-condition $p1$ and which is overloaded in class B sub-class of A with a pre-condition $p2$ then the real pre-condition of m in class B is p1 and p2 (the conjunction of the pre-conditions).

- Exception binding: Exception definitions are bound to class definitions, allowing us to define an inheritance mechanism and an overloading mechanism for exceptions. This approach has the additional benefit of structuring the exception set.

We detail now our behavioral approach.

3.2 Pre-condition and Post-condition Definition

Pre-conditions and post-conditions are defined into method signatures. A pre-condition is defined as a boolean expression (constructing of method calls) associated with an exception raise. If the boolean expression evaluates to true then the associated exception is raised. The general syntax is the following:

method Method_name (param_list): type_of_result **in class** class_name
in_context
{**when** condition **signal** exception(param_list)}*
out_context
{**when** condition **signal** exception(param_list)}*

- The in_context allows control of:
  1. The state of the receiver object
  2. method call parameters
  3. objects referentially linked to the receiver,
  4. the state of an object state using aggregate functions as minimum, count, ...or SQL/like expressions following the *select, from, where* syntax.

  When a pre-condition is not satisfied, the corresponding exception is immediately raised. The procedure associated with the exception is able to either detect a mistake (and then abort the transaction) or to consider the situation as exceptional and therefore acceptable (so, the transaction can continued). We do not consider suspicious behaviors that cannot be judged immediately. Indeed, judgements could not be reliable.
- The out_context allows control of:
  1. The same properties as in_context
  2. The state of the object resulting from method application.

  The out_context can raise either immediate or deferred exceptions. Deferred exceptions correspond to suspicious behaviors that can not be judged immediately (it misses information). These kinds of behavior will be judge just at the end of the transaction (before committing the transaction).

We now present an example modules for implementing a student registration system using our approach. The *Module-registration* method is defined into the class *Module* with a pre-condition to specify the maximum number of students allowed to register to each module. The method *Retrieve-Student(num:integer):Student*, applied to a set of students returns the student object with its registration number equal to the parameter *num*.

Example 1: Module-Registration

method *Module-Registration(stud:Student)* **in class** *Module*
in_context
{**when** *Count(RECEIVER)* > *Capacity(RECEIVER)*
signal *pb_of_capacity(stud)*}

This pre-condition checks that the number of registered students is less than or equal to the capacity. The condition part expresses the negation of the real pre-condition. When the method is invoked, if the condition is satisfied, the exception *pb_of_capacity* is raised. Note that the keyword RECEIVER represents the object on which the method is applied.

Example 2: Retrieve-Student
method *Retrieve-Student(num:number):Student* **in class** *Students*
out_context
{**when** *RESULT* = *nil* **signal** *not_found*}

The RESULT keyword represents the object returned by the method. If there is no student corresponding to the number *num*, an exception is raised.

3.3 Pre and Post-condition Inheritance

We have chosen a semantic of union for exception definition. Indeed, if we define a pre-condition (similarly a post-condition) in a method m of a class B (that is a subclass of A) it seems to be natural to add the new condition to the ones defined in A.

Example 3: Phd-Registration
We define the method *Phd_Registration* in the class *Student*. The registration is possible if the student possesses the required diploma. Suppose, we have a class *Foreign_Students* subclass of the class *Student*. We want to model the fact that registration is allowed only for students speaking English fluently.

method *Phd_Registration* **in class** *Student*
in_context
{**when** *not equivalent(diploma(master))* **signal** *Pb_of_Equivalence*}

method *Phd_Registration* **in class** *Foreign_Students*
in_context
{**when** *Not_fluently* **signal** *Pb_of_English*}

We do not check the consistency of the in_context (out_context) specialization (the programmer will be in charge of that). So a method may have a pre(post)-condition that is always false.

3.4 Exception Definition

Exceptions will be defined at the class level with a syntax similar to the method definition. The main advantage of this choice is that is well-suited for object context. An exception can be inherited, specialized (its signature is increased), overloaded (the same signature for different bodies).

The definition of an exception as part of a class implies that this exception is raised by an object belonging to that class (or eventually to a subclass), and therefore by a method belonging to that class. We assume the following constraint: a method can only raise exceptions defined in its own class or in its superclasses. This allows us to impose a structure on the exception set.

Definition Part As a method, an exception is composed of two parts: exception signature and exception body. The signature part describes the context of the exception and its type.

exception *Exception_name(param_list)* **of type** *type_name*
in class *class_name*

where *param_list* represents the object set that may be addressed in the exception body (by addressable we mean objects on which a method can be applied). This list contains at least one object which is the one that has raised the exception.

Exception type is either *immediate*, or *deferred*. It indicates when the exception must be evaluated (immediately, i.e. on the current state of the database, or at the end of the transaction just before commit, i.e. on the final state of the database).

One can notice that the raising of a deferred exception is based on local checks but its body evaluation is based on global checks.

The body part of the exception describes the handler associated with the exception. The normal process associated with an exception is error. The body allows us to refine this norm by defining exceptional cases (the condition parts) and associated actions (the action parts):

body exception *Exception_name(param_list)* **of type** *type_name*
in class *class_name*
{ $cond_1$:$action_1$,
...
$cond_n$:$action_n$
}

where $cond_i$ is a condition on either the object that has raised the exception (the signaler), or on some others parameters (belonging to addressable objects set). This condition is a boolean expression composed of elementary conditions that are method calls. We consider that condition evaluation has not side effects on database (only read operations are allowed). Conditions are expressions of exceptions to the general rule. We assume that an exception corresponds to an error and that the expressed conditions in the body are resumption conditions.

$Action_i$ is an action on the database. The action choice is dependent on the database transaction model. In the case of powerful mechanisms such as nested or cooperative transaction models, this choice can be efficient. At the moment, we just consider a classical (flat) transaction model and so an action can be a continuation request or a stop request (in order to abort the transaction). This limitation allows us to avoid cascading effects and so to ensure termination.

Example 4: Registration Validation

Assume we want to define exception *pb_of_capacity* that has been used in the first example. We want to relax the rule in order to accept registrations of mandatory modules.

exception *Pb_of_capacity(stud:Student)* **of type** *immediate* **in class** *Module*

body exception *Pb_of_capacity(stud:Student)* **in class** *Module*
{ *RECEIVER* **in** *Obligatory_Modules(stud):ACCEPT*}

This exception allows to accept registrations to mandatory modules. Assume that, after registration each student must have at least six modules but he might already possess one module. A module is either mandatory or optional but a student must choose every mandatory module.

Example 5: Student Registration

method *Student_Registration* **in class** *Student*
out_context
{**when** *Count_Modules(RECEIVER)< 6* **signal** *Not_enough* }

exception *Not_enough* **of type** *deferred* **in class** *Student*

body exception *Not_enough* **in class** *Student*
{ *Count_Modules(RECEIVER)≥ 6:ACCEPT*}
{ *Count_Modules(RECEIVER)= 5 and Possess(RECEIVER)=1:ACCEPT*}

Because its type is deferred, the exception handler will be executed at the end of the transaction. The exception is deferred because in order to accept the registration, we must know every module chosen by the student. We assume that this method is called in a transaction which globally registers a student. This transaction asks a student the modules he (she) wants to register and calls for each module *Student_Registration*. Until the student has chosen his (her) six modules, for each call of *Student_Registration* a *not_enough* exception is raised and deferred. At the end of the transaction the body of the exception is processed and checks if the final state of the transaction is correct, that is if the student is registered in six modules (or five plus one he already possesses).

Exception inheritance If we assume that the class B is a subclass of the class A, then B inherits of the all exceptions from A (and recursively from all superclasses of A). This implies that is possible to raise an exception, defined in class A into a method defined in class B.
It is also possible to redefine the body of an inherited exception in order to change the process associated with the exception.
In the same way, an exception can be specialized by signature refinement (in the sense of method specialization, that is by adding new parameters, or by specializing an inherited parameter).

It should also be stated that in case of exception redefinition, the new definition is applied to each use of this exception in all methods of the class (and recursively to all methods of subclasses if there is no redefinition).
Method overloading, in_context and out_context overloading and exception overloading are orthogonal and consequently all combinations of overloading are allowed.

Remark: Because exceptions are bound to classes, the exception set is structured. Exception specification must follow the same principle as the methods. More general exceptions, as *overflow*, must be defined at the highest level and are inherited by every classes (although they may be redefined).

3.5 Exception Manager

The exception manager manages the exception set during a transaction. Consistency checking, ending and efficiency are under exception manager responsibility. In the current state of our work, termination is ensured since there is no possibility of cascading raises of exceptions (the action part of an exception is limited to continuation and stop).
Several optimization techniques can be used (for example we can group together exceptions on the same object in order to optimize access time).

4 Integrity Rules Compilation

Our approach has two main drawbacks. First, it lacks of declarativity compared to RDBMS integrity rules (generally expressed in a first order logic language). Secondly, integrity rules may be fragmented among several classes using numerous pre(post)-conditions and exceptions.

We propose to consider our approach at an execution level and not at a declarative level. We are studying the way general integrity rules (expressed in a high-level language) can be compiled in conditions and exceptions. At this time, we can not give general results but only show how it works on some examples (referential integrity, symmetric links).

Example 6: Checking the Symmetry of an Association
We want to check the symmetry of an association between a car and its motor (a car can have one and only one motor and a motor is associated with one and only one car). We can express this association in class definitions:

```
class Car                          class Motor
{ number : integer,                { number : integer,
...                                ...
comp : Motor reverse car,          car : Car reverse comp,
... }                              ... }
```

In our behavioral approach, this property has to be defined in each method able to update the *comp* (or *car*) attribute of the class *Car* (or *Motor*). These methods can be statically detected at compile time and consequently we can add new pre(post)-conditions and exceptions to their definition. For example, assume that the method *m1* in class *Car* updates the *comp* attribute. We have to generate the following code to check the symmetry of the association:

method *m1* **in class** *Car*
out_context
{**when** *true* **signal** *Reverse_Motor(receiver.comp)* }

exception *Reverse_Motor(m : Motor)* **of type** *deferred* **in class** *Car*

body exception *Reverse_Motor(m : Motor)* **in class** *Car*
{ *identical(m.car,receiver) : ACCEPT*}
where *identical* corresponds to *oid* (object identifier) equality.

This type of integrity constraint is supported by post-conditions and deferred exceptions.

5 Conclusion

This paper presents an extension of the integrity model based on object behavior that has been defined in [11]. We define pre-conditions and post-conditions on methods and we use an exception mechanism in order to take into account exceptional cases and to allow deferred controls at the end of the transaction (one of the major requirement of database area).

Furthermore, we propose the consideration of exceptions as a class property. This allows a better integration of exceptions to the object paradigm (it is now possible to inherit or to overload an exception). We also give the semantic of pre-conditions and post-conditions inheritance.

An implementation of this behavioral approach has been realized on top of the O2 DBMS[11]. The goal of this implementation was to add consistency controls to method signatures. Our approach is based on code generation (a pre-processor). From in_context and out_context specification, we generate O2C code (O2C is one of the languages used in O2 DBMS [6, 10]). Then the code is executed in O2 environment. For the programmer, this means that he can extract the code related to integrity and express consistency properties in term of pre and post-conditions.

A problem with this approach is that integrity rules may be fragmented among different (and numerous) classes resulting in a lack of declarativity and a lack of a global view. To overcome this problem we propose to consider our behavioral approach at an execution level and to compile general integrity rules to this execution level.

We claim that our approach is general and can be used to support different functionalities (integrity, authorization, ...). We are studying its integration with more sophisticated transaction models such as nested transactions.

References

1. M. Atkinson, F. Bancilhon, D. De Witt, K. Dittrich, D. Maier, S. Zdonick: The Object Oriented Database System Manifesto. Proc. Deductive and Object Oriented Databases Conf. Kyoto, December 1989
2. V. Benzaken, A. Doucet: Enforcement Tests Generation for Integrity Constraint Checking Based on Simplification Methods in Object-Oriented Database Systems. Proc. 8eme Journée Bases de Données, Trégastel, September 92.
3. Communications of the ACM: Special Issue: Next Generation DBMS. Communications of the ACM, Vol. 34, No. 10, October 1991
4. P. Coad, E. Yourdon: Object-Oriented Analysis. Prentice-Hall, Englewood Cliffs, 1990
5. P. Coad, E. Yourdon: Object-Oriented Design. Prentice-Hall, Englewood Cliffs, 1991
6. O. Deux & al.: The story of O2. IEEE Trans. Knowl. Data Eng., Vol. 2, No. 1, March 1990
7. C. Esculier: Non monotonic knowledge evolution in VLKDBS. Proc. Very Large Data Bases Conf., Brisbane, August 1990
8. A. Goldberg, D. Robson: Smalltalk-80: The Language and its Implementation. Addison- Wesley, Reading, MA 1983
9. C.A.R. Hoare: An Axiomatic Approach to computer programming. Communications of the ACM pp 576-580 October 1969
10. C. Lecluse, P. Richard, F. Velez: O2, an object-oriented data model. Proc. of the ACM SIGMOD Conf., Chicago, 1988
11. H. Martin, M. Adiba, B. Defude: Consistency Checking in Object-Oriented Databases: A Behavioral Approach. Selected Papers Conf. on Information and Knowledge Management, Baltimore, Maryland, November 1992, Lecture Notes in Computer Science 752
12. J. Rumbaugh, M. Blaha, W. Premerlani, F. Eddy, W. Lorensen: Object-Oriented Modelling and Design. Prentice-Hall, Englewood Cliffs, 1991

How Does Knowledge Discovery Cooperate with Active Database Techniques in Controlling Dynamic Environment? *

Hiroyuki Kawano[1], Shojiro Nishio[2], Jiawei Han[3] and Toshiharu Hasegawa[1]

[1] Department of Applied Math. and Physics, Kyoto University, Kyoto 606-01, Japan ({kawano,hasegawa}@kuamp.kyoto-u.ac.jp)
[2] Department of Information Systems Engineering, Osaka University, Suita, Osaka 565, Japan (nishio@ise.eng.osaka-u.ac.jp)
[3] School of Computing Science, Simon Fraser University, Burnaby, BC, Canada V5A 1S6 (han@cs.sfu.ca)

Abstract. A dynamic environment, such as a production process, a communication network, highway traffic, etc., may contain a huge amount of information, changing with time, which is a valuable resource for understanding the general behavior of the environment, discovering the regularities and anomalies currently happening in the environment, controlling an evolution process, and intelligent modeling or managing the environment. Unfortunately, the data generated in a dynamic environment are often expressed in low level primitives and in huge volumes. Because of the dynamic, continuous and rapid changes of the information flow, it is difficult to catch the regularities and anomalies in a dynamic environment and react promptly for real-time applications. In this study, a knowledge discovery technique is integrated with data sampling and active database techniques to discover interesting behaviors of a dynamic environment and react intelligently to the environment changes. The discovery of the dynamics in a computer communication network and the application of the discovered knowledge for network management are taken as an example in our study. The study shows (1) data sampling is necessary in the collection of information for regularity analysis and anomaly detection; (2) knowledge discovery is important for generalizing low level data to high-level information and detecting interesting patterns; (3) active database technology is essential for real-time reaction to the changes in a dynamic environment; and (4) an integration of the three technologies forms a powerful tool for control and management of large dynamic environments in many applications.

* The research of the first author was supported in part by a scholarship from the Ministry of Education, Science and Culture of Japan, that of the second author was supported in part by the Ministry of Education, Science and Culture of Japan under Scientific Research Grant-in-Aid, and that of the third author was supported in part by grants from the Natural Sciences and Engineering Research Council of Canada and the Centre for Systems Science of Simon Fraser University. The work by the first author was done during his visit to Simon Fraser University in 1993.

1 Introduction

Natural or human-controlled processes generate huge amount of information in various kinds of large, dynamic environments. It is challenging but truly necessary to analyze the general behavior of the information flow in such dynamic environments in order to understand and/or control the environments in scientific, business and industry applications.

First, in such a dynamic environment, data are generated rapidly, continuously, dynamically and in huge volumes. It is often unrealistic to store a *complete* set of raw data in the limited amount of memory of a database system and dynamically analyze and manage the data. This forces people to dump the generated data to tapes without timely analysis. Huge data can be handled by a **data sampling** technique which samples interesting pieces of information dynamically and systematically[13].

Second, most of the data/information in a dynamic environment are presented at low, primitive levels. There may not exist clear and concise relationships or regularities expressible by low level primitives. *The discovery of clear and concise relationships or regularities among the collected data*, can be handled by a **knowledge discovery** technique which performs efficient and effective data generalization to discover useful knowledge or regularity from the collected information [11, 12].

Third, process control and system management in a dynamic environment often require *prompt, real-time*, and *intelligent* reactions in response to situation changes in the environment. These reactions can be dealt with by application of **active database** technology[1] for automatic and prompt reaction and control of the environment.

In this paper, a technique is developed for knowledge discovery in dynamic environment by extension of the attribute-oriented induction technique from relational databases[3]. In order to discover the dynamic status of those systems, the cluster of actual data with dynamics is collected during the observation time using data sampling technique, and knowledge rules regarding to the status of dynamic environment are derived effectively at real time. Those discovered rules are stored in the rule base. Our proposed technique also makes new rules from the rules in the rule base during several sampling periods. The derived rules can be stored in the active database. The condition evaluator evaluates the current condition, compares it with that of the stored rules, discovers irregularities of the current status, if there exist, and executes actions to control the system.

This paper is organized as follows. In Section 2, the ideas for knowledge discovery in dynamic environment are introduced, including a data sampling technique and the primitives for specification of generalization/learning tasks. In Section 3, an attribute-oriented induction algorithm with sampling is presented for learning several kinds of rules from a huge amount of data in a dynamic environment. The integration of knowledge discovery with active database technology is also discussed in this section. The application of knowledge discovery and active database techniques in network management is examined, and the study is summarized in Section 4.

2 Knowledge Discovery in Dynamic Environment

Generally, *data for scientific discovery* are objective and show the characteristics of natural phenomena; whereas *discovery in business database* reflect the real world and show the behaviors of human-artifacts[7]. The latter one is well known as challenging and difficult problems. The volume of data in a dynamic environment could be created by artificial systems, which is similar to other business information systems. However, the huge volume of data are generated rapidly, continuously and possibly redundantly without a break in a dynamic environment. Such features are also similar to those in scientific discovery. Therefore, in order to develop the knowledge discovery in dynamic environment, it is necessary to fuse the two discovery domains. The technique of data sampling is based on the former one; whereas the technique of induction algorithm is based on the latter one.

To simplify our discussion, we consider several assumptions regarding to the data and learning tasks for knowledge discovery.

Assumption 1. *A set of data for a learning task is collected by random sampling from a dynamic information system or a dynamic environment.*

For the attribute-oriented induction algorithm, our previous study in [13] convinced us the accuracy of the discovered rules, including both *characteristic rules* and *classification rules*, using data sampling technique based on a statistical estimation theory. It shows the validity and credibility of knowledge discovery in database by the small number of sampled tuples. Therefore, meaningful rules satisfying the conditions can be derived within a short sampling period.

It is often desirable for large databases to have rules expressed at concept levels higher than the primitive ones. Therefore, we have,

Assumption 2. *Generalized rules are expressed in terms of high level concepts.*

Using a concept hierarchy, the rules learned can be represented in terms of generalized concepts and stated in a simple and explicit form, which is desirable to most users.

Assumption 3. *Background knowledge is generally available for knowledge discovery process.*

Following these assumptions, our mechanism for knowledge discovery in dynamic environment can be outlined as follows. First, a knowledge discovery process is initiated by a learning request, which is usually in relevance to only a subset of generating data. A data retrieval process is initiated to collect the set of relevant data using a data sampling technique. Second, generalization is performed on the set of retrieved data using the background knowledge and a set of generalization operators. Third, the generalized data is simplified and transformed into one of the following kinds of generalized rules, which may facilitate query answering and other applications.

1. **current status rules.** A *current status rule* summarizes the general characteristics of a set of sampled data at the present time which satisfies certain criteria, such as, the characteristics of the traffic flow on a network at the present time.
2. **stable rules.** A *stable rule* describes the general characteristics which remain stable over a period of time, such as, the rule that helps find out the heavy traffic on a network constantly or periodically.
3. **evolution rules.** An *evolution rule* describes the general characteristic of a set of patterns which evolve over several periods of sampling time, such as, how a network flow changes drastically over the past several sampling times.

3 Attribute-Oriented Induction in Dynamic Environment

3.1 Attribute-oriented induction algorithm with data sampling

A knowledge discovery process applies generalization operators to a large volume of sampling data and generates a set of generalized rules. In general, we have the following five basic techniques, *(1) Data focusing, (2) Attribute removal, (3) Attribute generalization, (4) Vote propagation, (5) Attribute generalization control,* for attribute-oriented induction [3, 7],

A stable rule shows the constant and periodical stable pattern of characteristic rules derived from different sampled data. The vote counts in characteristic rules can be used to find the stable pattern among a set of rules. Let $r_k(t)$ be the k-th characteristic rules in the rule set derived from the sampling data at time t, and $v_k(t)$ be the vote count of $r_k(t)$, normalized by the total number of sampling tuples. The numerical sequence of $v_k(t)$ is examined in a way similar to a scientific discovery process. Since the volume of rules is also accumulated as the sampling period becomes large, it is usually assumed that the vote count is similar to the natural phenomena. Therefore, attribute-oriented induction with data sampling will be effective for rule acquisition in a dynamic environment.

Discovery of functional relationships in numerical data has been studied in the programs such as Bacon[8]. Generalization (or *abstraction*) is also an essential technique in such programs to grasp the knowledge about the status of a complex system. For numerical values, aggregation of variables is based on the eigenvalues of the system matrix [5]. On the other hand, in our proposed induction algorithm, aggregation of variables is done by climbing up the conceptual hierarchy. The vote counts in the derived rule describe the characteristics of a dynamic system. Based on such values, one can derive various functional relationships depending on the abstraction level of hierarchical concepts.

To derive the functions which describe the stability or variance of a dynamic system, it is important to examine the set $\mathcal{V}_k = \{v_k(t_i) | t_i = t + L \cdot i, (i \geq 0)\}$, where v_k is the vote count regarding to the k-th rule, t_i is the starting time of the i-th sampling operation, and L is the sampling period.

Generally, scientific discovery applies heuristic search in an infinite space of potential relations or, equivalently, the combination of possible functional forms, in order to find an appropriate functional property of $\mathcal{V}_k$. This strategy of infinite searching causes difficulties for function finding in the real time. However, in the most cases of finding characteristics of information flow in a dynamic environment, search is limited to several typical functions. In order to keep the system stable, the system with the characteristics of the stable functions in the long range of time must be constructed. Therefore, constant values or periodical functions play an important role in those stable systems. Such periodic properties will be stored as stable rules in a rule base. Moreover, if the same rules are discovered during different periods, the weight of those stable rules will increase. On the other hand, if anomalous values are observed in short/long periods, evolution rules in short/long periods can be extracted based on quantitative measurements of such anomaly.

Further, several vote counts can be examined in order to derive the complex stable/evolution rules in short/long periods. A sequence of vote counts of several rules may satisfy the following equation, $y = f(v_1(t), v_2(t), \ldots, v_i(t), \ldots, v_M(t))$, the way to derive rules is similar to the above method. However, the search space will become huge depending on the abstraction level when the number of rules increases. Such mathematical functions can be considered as another kind of generalization operators.

Therefore, we have two techniques. *(5) Stability Criterion:* , if the sequence of vote counts $v_k(t)$ satisfy the stable condition, the rule $r_k(t)$ should be stored into the set of stable rules. And *(6) Variant Criterion:* , if the sequence of vote counts $v_k(t)$ satisfy the evolutional condition, the rule $r_k(t)$ should be stored into the set of evolution rules.

The six basic learning strategies can be summarized into the following generalization algorithm which extracts generalized characteristic, stable and evolution rules from a large volume of data using sampling technique. The algorithm is an extension of the basic attribute-oriented induction algorithm [3, 4, 10] for learning rules in dynamic environment.

Algorithm: Attribute-oriented induction with random sampling in a dynamic environment
Discovery of a set of generalized characteristic, stable and evolution rules in a dynamic environment based on a user's learning request.

Input: (i) A large volume of data in dynamic environment $\mathcal{D}$, (ii) a set of concept hierarchies or generalization operators on attributes a_i, and (iii) T, a *relation threshold*, and T_i, a set of *attribute thresholds* for attributes a_i.

Output: A characteristic rule, stable rule and evolution rule based on the learning request.

Method: Attribute-oriented induction with random sampled data with density d from the time t to $(t + \ell)$ consists of the following steps:

Step 1. *Collect a set of task-relevant sampling data $\mathcal{T}$ into an initial relation r_0 (possibly by a relational query).*

Step 2. *Perform basic attribute-oriented induction on r_0 as shown below.*

begin

for each attribute a_i $(1 \leq i \leq n)$ in r_0 **do** % n: the number of attributes.
    if a_i has not reached the desired concept level T_i **then**
                                        % attribute threshold control
    begin
        if a_i cannot be further generalized
        then remove a_i % attribute removal
        else generalize a_i to the (minimal) desired level;
                                        % concept tree ascension
        merge identical tuples   % vote propagation
    end
end. (*Basic attribute-oriented induction*)

Output characteristic rules and store them into the rule base.

Step 3. *Based on the stability criterion, derive the stable rules by the evaluation of stored v_k regarding to characteristic rules.*

Step 4. *Based on the variant criterion, derive the evolution rules by the evaluation of stored v_k regarding to characteristic rules.*

Step 5. *Repeat the induction algorithm periodically based on the new set of sampling data in the new period.* □

3.2 Intelligent reactions to dynamic environments

Active database [1, 2, 9, 14] is one of the interesting subfields in database research. Since a dynamic environment requires prompt, real-time reaction to the changes of the environment, it is important to explore the integration of active database technology with machine learning techniques[7].

Fig. 1 illustrates an architecture of *active database* in a dynamic environment, which is conceptually divided into rule base, knowledge base and conditional evaluator. Our proposed algorithm derives characteristic rules, stable rules and evolution rules. Those derived rules should be stored in the active database selectively and be applied in the control of the environment.

To react intelligently to dynamic environments, the active database techniques and knowledge discovery processes can be integrated in the following five aspects, *regularity extraction, regularity updates, knowledge-assisted active rule specification, dedicated knowledge discovery, generalized triggering.* These aspects are further analyzed below.

First, regularity extraction needs the integration of both techniques. A large number of rules which summarize the current status or the stable and evolving regularities of a system can be extracted by a knowledge discovery process. However, some of these discovered regularities could be less interesting or redundant to the system. An active database method may act as knowledge discovery initiator which triggers a knowledge discovery process based on the *importance* or *freshness* of the knowledge to the system. The importance is related to some critical or sensitive aspects of an environment, such as the potential crisis of a production process, the critical condition of a chemical reaction, etc.; whereas the freshness is related to whether similar knowledge is already in the system.

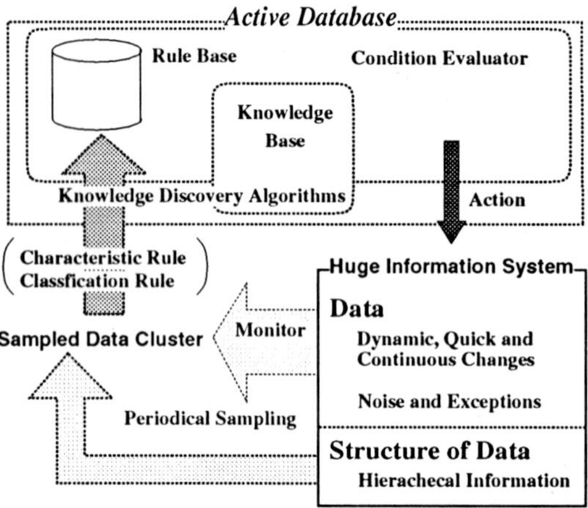

Fig. 1. Architecture of active knowledge database in dynamic environment

Furthermore, if the dynamic data is too large to be stored in a database but constantly monitoring is more preferable than data sampling, the database may store data summaries (extracted by knowledge discovery) at a level slightly higher (thus less voluminous) than the primitive data.

Second, it is important to verify, modify or invalidate the existing generalized rules stored in the rule base in a dynamic environment. Such a **regularity updating** task can also be performed by integration of knowledge discovery and active database technology. When a rule is discovered by a knowledge discovery process, the rule could be in one of the following cases: (1) it may enrich an existing rule by consolidating it in an extended period, or extending its condition or conclusion, (2) it may invalidate an existing rule because of the changed condition or conclusion, (3) it may not be interesting or fresh enough for inclusion in the rule base, or (4) it may violate certain integrity constraints, thus need to invoke some warning messages or perform appropriate actions. Knowledge rule verification, modification, invalidation or other appropriate actions can be specified as actions of triggers in an active database, which can be invoked when certain conditions are detected in the knowledge discovery process.

Third, the integration of the both techniques may facilitate **knowledge-assisted active rule specification**. It is often necessary to express active rules at the concept level higher than the primitive data in dynamic environments for comprehension and debugging by human programmers/operators. Such specification needs the help of knowledge discovery process. Moreover, the specification of appropriate conditions and actions should be based on the analysis of general characteristics in the current system, the stable and evolving regularities, and the execution history of the active rules. Obviously, such specification, refinement, and assessment of the appropriate conditions and actions of active rules need the application of knowledge discovery tools.

Fourth, **dedicated knowledge discovery** need the use of both knowledge discovery and active database mechanisms. In general, data sampling and knowledge discovery can be classified into *general* and *dedicated* processes. The former is adopted for *regular* environment checking and knowledge discovery; whereas the latter need to be invoked for a dedicated, detailed, frequent, and specialized data sampling knowledge discovery when certain condition happens. For example, when a production environment reaches a critical condition, an emergency data collection and knowledge discovery process should be invoked for close observation. Such an invocation of a dedicated sampling and discovery process can be performed by specifying conditions and actions for a dedicated process using the active database technology. When some unusual situation was detected by a knowledge discovery process, more focused and refined knowledge discovery can be initiated, and such a process can be refined progressively based on the discovered results. Such progressively refined processes can be specified by active database rules.

Finally, the integration may facilitate **generalized triggering**. Since the general status and evolution regularities of a system can be discovered by a knowledge discovery process and summarized at a high concept level, the conditions and appropriate actions of an active rule can be specified at a high level to communicate with both human and the system. Moreover, the actions of an active rule can also be specified at a high concept level. Appropriate mappings can be performed to transform high level actions into low level primitives to trigger the detailed actions and update the environment.

3.3 Management of Communication Networks by KDD

As an example to our study, the management of interconnecting communication network using data sampling[6], knowledge discovery[3], and active database techniques[14] is analyzed. The status of the network changes over time, and the difficulty of effective and stable operating of the complex system is evident. In order to operate the communication network, it is essential to find the real time characteristics for *load balancing* or the *connecting status* between several network resources[7].

Example. Let the learning task be to discover a stable rule in relevance to *Source, Destination, Size, Type* and *Port.* The learning task can be represented in a pseudo query language in Fig. 2.

```
LEARN Stable rule
FROM  Sampling period from 1 to 100
WHERE P.SrcAddress in Domain(''kuamp.kyoto-u.ac.jp'') and
      P.DestAddress not in Domain(''kuamp.kyoto-u.ac.jp'')
      and P.Size <= 300
IN RELEVANCE TO P.SrcAddress, P.DestAddress, P.Size, P.Type, P.Port
```

Fig. 2. Query for stable rule

Active database techniques can be applied to the system management based on the rules discovered in the above example. Suppose that the following definition of actions by pseudo description language, as shown in Fig. 3, is in the active database. The rule states that if the periodical length between different domains is less than 5 minutes, the system displays an alert message on the console, initiates the termination of connection-less packets, and checks the processes in the both domains. The descriptions of actions for evolution rules can be defined in a similar way.

```
Event: Update Stable Rules in Rule Base
Condition: Period(P.Vote) < 5
  Query:
  SELECT P.Vote
  FROM   P Stable Rules
  WHERE  P.SrcAddress != P.DestAddress and P.Type=CO
Action:
  Operation: begin
               Display_Console(''code red'',Stable Rules P)
               Activate(Kill_CL in Code_Red_Rules)
               Signal(Check_Processes_in (P.SrcAddress, P.DestAddress)
             end
```

Fig. 3. Pseudo definition in active database

This example shows that by integration of a knowledge discovery method with an active database technology, the interconnecting network can be managed intelligently and dynamically at a high level, which may effectively control the information network across remote distance.

4 Conclusion

In this paper, we studied knowledge discovery in dynamic environments. First, a cluster of data is collected by a data sampling technique. An attribute-oriented induction technique is then applied which integrates the learning-from-examples methodology with set-oriented database operations and extracts generalized data from actual data in databases. Attribute-oriented induction and data sampling substantially reduce the computational complexity of a database learning process. The attribute-oriented induction algorithm with data sampling discovers three kinds of rules: characteristic rule, stable rule and evolution rule. Moreover, using the technology of active database, generalized conditions can be evaluated and compared with the generalized rules for the control of the dynamic environment. Our study shows that the integration of attribute-oriented induction algorithm with data sampling technique and active database technology will substantially enhance the power and increase the flexibility of data and knowledge discovery and utilization in dynamic environments.

There are many issues which should be studied further. Both data sampling and knowledge discovery processes can be triggered by active database rules. It is not clear how close interactions should be maintained between active database rules and knowledge discovery algorithms with data sampling. A tight control by active rules may restrict the possibilities of discovery of some unexpected events; however, a loose interaction may results in the discovery of a large number of uninteresting rules. The balance of different mechanisms needs much study and experiment work. We plan to examine the effectiveness of the techniques developed in this paper and implement such mechanisms in a dynamic production control environment. The experimental results will be reported in the near future.

References

1. C. Beeri and T. Milo, "A Model for Active Object Oriented Database", Proc. of the 17th Int'l Conf. on Very Large Data Bases, Barcelona, Spain, pp.337-349, Sept. 1991.
2. U. Dayal, B. Blaustein, A. Buchmann, U .Chakravarthy, M. Hsu, R. Ladin, D. McCarthy, A. Rosenthal, S. Sarin, M. J. Carey, M. Livny and R. Jauhari, "The HiPAC Project: Combining Active Databases and Timing Constrains," ACM-SIGMOD Record 17, pp.51-70, March 1988.
3. J. Han, Y. Cai, and N. Cercone, "Knowledge Discovery in Databases: An Attribute-Oriented Approach," In *Proc. 18th Int'l Conf. on Very Large Data Bases*, Vancouver, Canada, pp.547–559, August 1992.
4. J. Han, S. Nishio, and H. Kawano, "Knowledge Discovery in Object-Oriented and Active Databases", *Proc. of International Conference on Building and Sharing of Very Large-Scale Knowldge Bases'93*, pp.205-214, Dec. 1993.
5. Y. Iwasaki and I. Bhandari, "Formal Basis for Commonsense Abstraction of Dynamic Systems," AAAI-88, pp.307-312, August 1988.
6. H. Kawano, S. Nishio and T. Hasegawa, "Knowledge Acquisition in Communication Networks," IEEE Region 10 Conference, Tencon 92, pp.881-885, Australia, Nov. 1992.
7. H. Kawano, S. Nishio, J. Han and T. Hasegawa, "Control of Dynamic Environment by Knowledge Discovery and Active Database Techniques," Dept. of Applied. Math & Physics Technical Report 94008, Kyoto University, 1994.
8. P. Langley, H.A. Simon, G.L. Bradshaw and J.M. Żytkow, "Scientific Discovery: Computational Explorations of the Creative Processes. MIT Press, 1987.
9. J. Michael, M. J. Carey, R. Jauhari and M. Livny, "On Transaction Boundaries in Active Databases: a Performance Perspective," IEEE Trans. Knowl. Data Eng., vol.3, no.3, pp.320-36, Sept. 1991.
10. S. Nishio, H. Kawano, and J. Han, "Knowledge Discovery in Object-Oriented Databases: The First Step", *Proc. of AAAI-93 Workshop on Knowledge Discovery in Databases*, pp.186-198, July 1993.
11. G. Piatetsky-Shapiro and W.J. Frawley, *Knowledge Discovery in Databases*, AAAI/MIT Press, 1991.
12. A. Silberschatz, M. Stonebraker, and J. D. Ullman, "Database Systems: Achievements and Opportunities," *Comm. ACM*, vol. 34, pp.94–109, 1991.
13. K. Sonoo, H. Kawano, S. Nishio and T. Hasegawa, "Accuracy Evaluation of Rules Derived from Sample Data in VLKD" (In Japanese), Proc. of the 5th Annual Conference of JSAI, pp.181–184, 1991.
14. J. Widom, "Active Database Rule Systems," 3rd Intn'l Conf. on Extending Database Technology, Tutorial 7, Vienna, Austria, March 1992.

EECA: An Active Knowledge Model

Waseem Naqvi and Mohamed T. Ibrahim

Database Systems Research Laboratory
University of Greenwich, London, SE18 6PF, U.K.
{w.naqvi, m.ibrahim}@greenwich.ac.uk

Abstract

General purpose triggers are central to active database management systems, along with knowledge in the form of production rules. The predominant knowledge model is based on Event-Condition-Action (ECA) triples. Our research has found this model to be limiting and inefficient in both operation and declaration clarity as it causes unnecessary replication of rules. An extension is proposed to the ECA knowledge model to permit a semantically concise and precise declaration of the knowledge. This extension (EECA) has been integrated into the REFLEX active database prototype.

This paper reports on the EECA model and gives an overview of the REFLEX model, its architecture and novel features.

Keywords: knowledge model, active database, event specification, object-orientated, EECA

1. Introduction

Conventional databases are *passive* repositories of data where actions are preformed by either user or explicit program requests. In these databases, data is separated from its meaning or semantics. However, this situation is changing and nowadays commercial database management systems provide support for integrity constraints. This support is provided by a simple collection of triggers which are usually associated with specific data objects and are not held in one place. However, there is much more domain knowledge that an application designer would like to support.

Additionally, in traditional database systems, data management is separated from the application's processing logic. The domain knowledge is hidden in and distributed across the application's code. In an active database system, data, knowledge and parts of the processing logic relating to events and conditions that require action are under the control of an *active* Database Management System (ADBMS).

What distinguishes an active database from a conventional database is that the former is enhanced with *active* behaviour. It automatically responds to internal or external events (or changes in the environment). The domain knowledge is usually captured in the form of Event-Condition-Action (ECA) triples as reported in [MD89]. When an event occurs which causes a change in the environment provided that the specified conditions are satisfied then the stated action(s) of one or more rules are automatically performed by the system without user intervention.

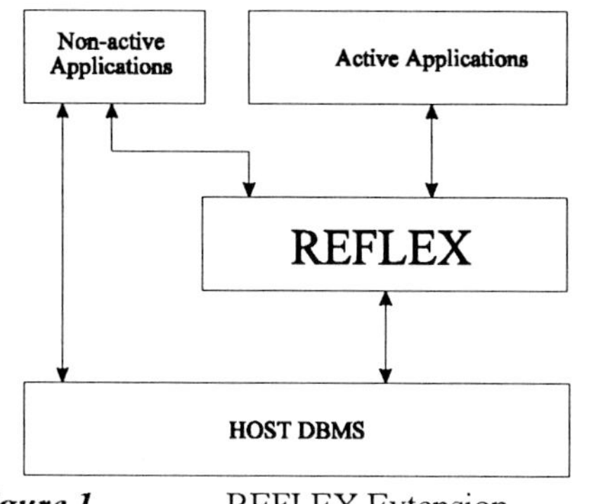

Figure 1 REFLEX Extension

The main aim of this research is to provide a flexible, portable *active database facility* for existing systems. A research prototype, known as REFLEX, has been developed which allows the host database to respond immediately to changes in the internal state of the database or its environment. It must respond within a specific time-constraint i.e. reflexively.

This paper reports on extensions to the ECA model, provided by the REFLEX active database prototype. The paper is organised as follows. An overview of REFLEX is presented in section two, including its architecture, knowledge model and some efficiency measures. Section three discusses related research efforts. Section four introduces the EECA model and finally section five concludes the paper.

2. REFLEX Overview

The work in this paper builds on the active database extension, to existing object-oriented databases, embodied in the REFLEX model. REFLEX is an active database prototype that is *loosely-coupled* to the underlying database management system. It has been designed to allow the *'bolting-on'* of the REFLEX extension to an existing object-oriented database system. Thus providing active facilities to an organisation's existing database. This has a number of advantages, firstly it makes active databases available today. Secondly, and perhaps more importantly, it allows an organisation to protect its investment in technology, resources and legacy systems. Active functionality by means of augmenting an existing and proven DBMS provides security and a migration path to the user community. Using REFLEX, new applications can utilise active functionality, whilst existing non-active applications can continue to use the host DBMS as normal. This option is available for applications that do not perceive a requirement for active functionality currently, but allows for the provision if the functionality is required at a later date, see figure 1. A brief summary of REFLEX will be given here but for further details refer to [NI93a, NI93b].

2.1. Architecture

As an active database system, REFLEX has to manage knowledge as well as data. To facilitate this, REFLEX has a Knowledge Management Kernel (KMK) which is central to its architecture. The KMKs major task is that it acts (a) as a command dispatcher to other constituent modules, and (b) as a rule evaluation scheduler. The other major modules of REFLEX are the Transparent Interface Manager (TIM), the Event Manager (EM), the Knowledge Selection Module (KSM), the Condition Evaluation Module (CEM) and the Execution Supervisor (ES), see figure 2. The adaptive and loose-coupling features are afforded by TIM, which accomplishes most of this task since it allows the monitoring of *internal* events, and flags them to the EM.

In REFLEX, it is possible to specify simple or composite events. Unlike a simple or primitive event which is regarded as being instantaneous, a complex event is composed over an interval of time (the interval being the duration from the occurrence of the first valid event to that of the final event in the specification). However, a complex event is said to occur at the point of occurrence of the final event in the specification. Hence complex events have chronologies or histories. These chronologies are realized by the EM time-stamping each occurrence of an event, before it informs the KMK of their occurrence, see section 4 for further details covering the semantics of the knowledge model.

When an event occurs, KMK instantiates a copy of the KSM (currently a uni-processor reentrant module), in order to evaluate if the event specification clause of any one or more of the rules has been satisfied and the rule has attained a state of '*in-context*'. If the event specification clauses are simple or primitive, then they are returned immediately to the KMK with the state of *in-context* set. If, however, the specification is complex, the KSM checks the *temporal log* to test if any relevant events have occurred previously. If so and the event occurred within a valid interval, the specification is again tested. If it succeeds, the KMK is informed as described earlier. Otherwise, the rule's part-satisfied event clause, is written to the *pending log* and kept for a given period of time, until its event clause is either satisfied or discharged on becoming invalid. The log maintains a copy of the state of rule evaluation ready for further events.

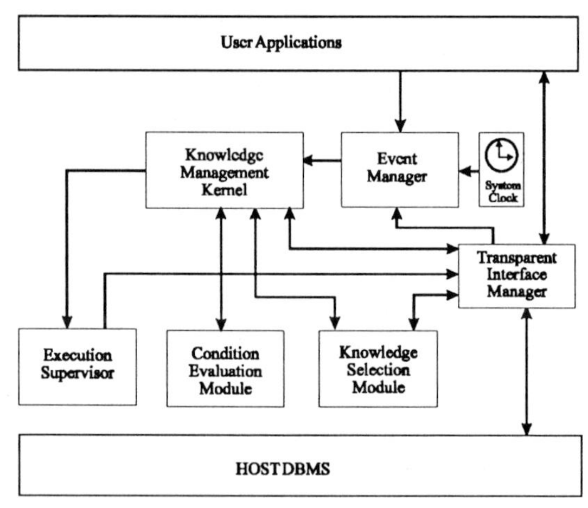

Figure 2 **REFLEX Architecture**

If a rule is in-context, it is passed to the CEM by KMK, to test its condition predicate. A condition can be declared in one of four ways: i) REFLEX's high level Object SQL dialect, ii) the proprietary language of the host database, iii) by *calling* an external module or iv) by having a NULL condition, i.e. it is always TRUE. If the condition clause is satisfied then the action clauses are executed subject to the condition-action (CA) coupling modes.

2.2. Knowledge Model

Rules are modelled as *first-class* objects, as in HiPAC [CBB*89] and ADAM [DP91, DPG91]. This is so rules to be handled in the same homogenous manner as the other objects in the database. Hence maintenance is simpler since the underlying DBMS maintains the rules as well as the data.

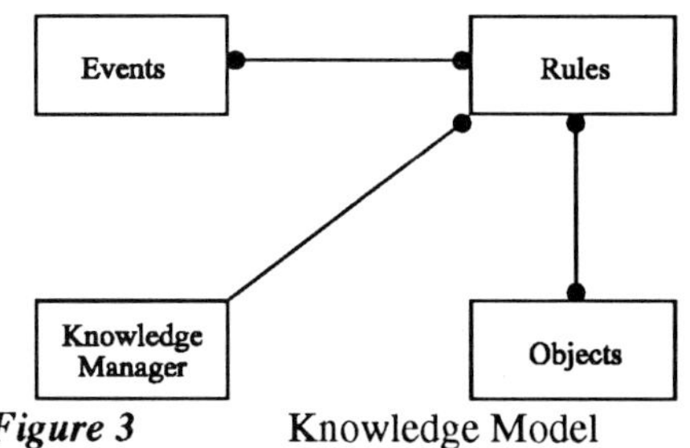

Figure 3 Knowledge Model

An object may have many rules applicable to it. Rules can be assigned to classes or to individual instances of objects. The object instances can also hold *exemptions* from certain rules as required. For each active database system, there must be one and only one Knowledge Manager. The Knowledge Manager is also modelled as an object. There may be many active database systems running against any one host DBMS. The relationships between the entities is illustrated in figure 3.

2.2.1. Event Objects

Most other active prototype systems, e.g. HiPAC and O_2 [MP90], model events as attributes. This provides fast execution and interpretation of events but is an inflexible approach. What can a user or developer do once a new event is to be added? Can the new event be added? If so, how? The answer is it can but with great difficulty and certainly not cheaply. To add the new event, the underlying active database system code must be modified, and recompiled by an active database system programmer. These modifications are costly in both monetary and system time dimensions. It may be infeasible to recompile a live database management system.

REFLEX models *events* as *first-class* objects. This provides a flexible approach, as the developer may add events at will. On first analysis, it may seem that having events as first-class objects, may cause severe degradation of service. This is because, on an event being raised, the event object must first be retrieved from the database, before its raise method can be called. Inherently, it seems to be plagued with intolerable overheads (seek, retrieve, call etc), on the other hand if events were treated as attributes, the knowledge base would have to be searched to determine those rules that are in context. This overhead can be countered by the utilization of the event object. As an object, the event has access to standard object modelling techniques. The most important being the complex object facility. Each event can maintain a list of rules to which it may apply. On the raising of any event, the KSM has immediate access to the rules which are brought into context by the particular event. Hence, the system is much faster at searching through its knowledge base, on an occurrence of an event. This feature becomes much more evident as the size of the knowledge base grows and can be aided by frequently occurring events being held permenantly in fast memory.

3. Related Research

Intensive research into active databases is being undertaken by many research centres. The widely known of these active databases are HiPAC [CBB*89], POSTGRES [SK91, SHP89], StarBurst [LLP*91], Ode [AG89] and ADAM [Pat89, DPG91].

REFLEX is, unlike many other ADBMS research prototypes, *loosely-coupled* to its underlying database. It is implemented upon commercially available DBMSs. It is designed to be portable and adaptive to many host DBMSs. Other research prototypes have not been afforded this flexibility as their active features are built into the database.

Most of the active database research prototypes use the Event-Condition-Action (ECA) model reported in McCarthy and Dayal [MD89] during their work on the HiPAC project. This ECA model is now a dominant and almost exclusive knowledge model used within the active database community.

Gehani et al [GJS92a], have proposed a new Event-Action (EA) model which folds the condition part into the event specification. The main reason given was that with the ECA model, there were simply too many coupling modes for the active database to deal with. The attraction of the EA model is that it does indeed do away with the many coupling modes. It does however, limit the functionality of the overall system for a number of reasons. The first and most obvious disadvantage is that in order to test the event clause, which includes the condition statement (including any required mask), the evaluation of the clause is sought with undue inefficiency. This is caused, we understand, by the evaluation of conditional statements even if they were not brought into context by the triggering event i.e. the event specification alone was not satisfied. The result of the event clause is not known until the conditional part of the specification was also tested. The second disadvantage is more subtle and is not handled by any other active models, since they do not handle external conditions. If the condition part of the clause is based on the state of the external environment, rather than that of the internal environment of the database, this cannot be extracted from the integrated event and condition clause that Ode proposes. For Ode or other current active databases to handle the condition based on the external environment, dummy updates are required to the database in order for the internal condition evaluation to take place.

The REFLEX model addresses this scenario, see section 4.1 on the scope of condition clause.

4. The Extended Knowledge Model

The REFLEX prototype has allowed the investigation of real data use in an active database system, using live applications. These investigations have highlighted several omissions of the standard ECA model, for example the replication of rules, and the creation of negative rules. This section examines some extensions to the ECA model, provided by REFLEX. The temporal algebraic event specification language is also described.

4.1. Scope of the Condition Clause

Most of the current active database prototypes, as far as we are aware, allow the condition clause to be declared using some sort of Data Manipulation Language (DML) query. We recognise that this form of condition declaration is useful, as it allows the user or designer to use a familiar interaction protocol. However, it is also limiting as it forces the designer to initiate unnecessary access to the database, thus adversely affecting the performance of the overall system.

Since an active database responds to changes in its environment, the above form of the condition clause addresses *only one* aspect of the total environment, that is the internal state of the database. REFLEX however, allows the *calling* of user defined condition modules. This provides support for changes in the environment which require a complex condition statement which cannot be handled by the DML language. Or the condition requires access to external or application specific parameters, possibly user initiation, which have no bearing onto the internal state of the database. The external condition module simply returns a boolean of TRUE if the condition statement is satisfied or FALSE otherwise.

This extension allows all the sections of the EECA tuple to independently access either internal or external states of the environment.

4.2. Situation Redundancy

There may be situations (both events and conditions) common to many rules, but each with alternate actions i.e. the same situation in the environment triggers these rules.

If events are raised which bring into context many rules, the event specification clauses of these rules must be evaluated. After the event specification clause has been evaluated, the condition clause must also be evaluated. If the situation of the rules, are the same, then there has been multiple or redundant evaluation of many rules event and condition clauses. Causing the overall system to be inefficient.

The proposed EECA model alleviates the problems associated with redundant situation declaration by allowing a rule to have multiple actions. This also implies that a rule must have multiple Condition-Action coupling modes.

There are occasions where it is easier to state a negative condition rather than a normal condition, as it may be far more efficient to evaluate. The EECA model accommodates this situation by using a construct that is similar to an *else* statement in conventional block structured programming languages. For this case the EECA model proposes *Fail Actions*. These are actions that may be executed if the condition clause of the rule fails (or does not hold). Multiple fail action clauses are also permitted within the EECA model, along with their respective Condition-Fail-Action coupling modes.

A rule in the REFLEX Knowledge Model is represented as:

ON	event specification
IF	condition holds i) internal: NULL, OSQL, or prop. language ii) external
THEN	execute action 1
	...
	execute action n
ELSE	execute fail action 1
	...
	execute fail action n

The Action and Fail-Action clauses are mutually exclusive, just as with the THEN-ELSE structure. The clauses may contain requests to abort the parent transaction, undertake some DML query or call some external module.

4.3. EECA Coupling Modes

Coupling modes couple one part of the ECA triple to its subsequent neighbour. The three common coupling modes are:

i) immediate, where the parent transaction is suspended while the child transaction is being executed.
ii) deferred, where the child transaction is deferred until the parent transaction is completed, at which point the child is executed
iii) decoupled or separate, where the child transaction is processed concurrently with the parent transaction.

To these coupling modes, the complex issues of dependence need to be addressed. Is the committal of the child process dependent on that of its parent? The reverse is more serious. Is the committal of the parent dependent on that of its child? What would be the outcome where in the simplest case of an immediate coupling mode, the parent is ready to commit but the child aborts, will the parent commit or abort? A more interesting problem is posed if the same question were raised but for a decoupled coupling mode. Is the committal of the parent dependent on that of a decoupled child?

The EECA model requires that all the action statements (including fail actions) for each of the rules have a flag that signifies whether the action is dependent or independent with respect to its initiating transaction. The onus for dependence has been passed to the designer of the system. Hence the action clause is effectively an object or tuple (with arity 3), as is demonstrated below:

Action clause	(execute action 1, coupling mode, dependency flag)
	...
	(execute action n, coupling mode, dependency flag)
Fail Action clause	(execute fail action 1, coupling mode, dependency flag)
	...
	(execute fail action n, coupling mode, dependency flag)

This then leads to the semantics of the coupling modes. The reader may note that for the condition clause the available EC coupling modes are unchanged i.e. the condition clause can have one of the following coupling modes: immediate, deferred or decoupled. All three modes are offered the option to be dependent or independent of the parent transaction. If, for a given situation, where there are many actions, the declaration above of using multiple actions clauses, may only be used if the EC coupling modes are the same. If the EC coupling modes are different, then different rules need be declared. This design decision was taken so that the rule declaration was not over complicated with many excess coupling modes for situations which would hardly arise.

4.4. Event Specification Language

REFLEX supports the notions of complex (composite) events, as do other active systems such as HiPAC and Ode. Simple or primitive events are relatively easy to understand. They are said to occur at a specific point in time, unlike conditions which *hold* over certain intervals or periods of time. Complex events blur this distinction. A complex event is said to occur at the point at which the last valid component (primitive) event occurred. The component events have the property of validity. An event is only valid for a given interval, after which it is no longer valid for a certain event specification. The occurrence of the event may still be valid for a different rule's event specification. Events can be internal to the database (DML commands e.g. updates, reads and transaction points), temporal (at specific points in time, relative or periodic) or the events may be abstract i.e. externally defined by user applications. All non-temporal events have an interval of occurrence i.e. **BEFORE** or **AFTER** an event point.

The temporal event algebra used by REFLEX is very powerful. Even so, ease of use has not been compromised as standard English statements are used to declare the powerful clauses. The algebra contains several logical and temporal keywords. The logical keywords are **AND** (unordered conjunction of $E_1 \wedge E_2$), **OR** (inclusive disjunction of $E_1 \vee E_2$), **XOR** (exclusive disjunction of $E_1 \veebar E_2$), **NOT** (negation $\neg E$), **PRECEDES** (sequenced conjunction of $E_1 \triangleright E_2$) and **SUCCEEDS** (sequenced conjunction of $E_1 \triangleleft E_2$). The temporal keywords are **BEFORE, AFTER, AT, BETWEEN, ON, WITHIN HOUR/MIN/SEC, EVERY HOUR/MIN/SEC, MIN, MAX, DATE, TIME**. The **EVENT** keyword precedes abstract or user-defined (external) events. The negation operator may not reference temporal events e.g. NOT 5:00pm, as this would cause the event to be raised every millisecond (or machine clock granularity) that was not 5:00pm. Parenthesis are used to override operator precedence.

Examples of the english event specification language (ESL) are:

read student	simple internal event - read
before update account **or after** update employee	$\vee$ - internal events
$Event_1$ **precedes** $Event_2$ **within hour** 24	$E_1 \triangleright E_2 \wedge ((t_{E2} - t_{E1}) < 24$ hour$)$

at 5:00pm **every** friday	periodic
event radar	user-defined or abstract

The rule may reference the object that raised the event by referencing the position in the event specification clause, and by using the **OBJECT** keyword. For example, in the above *read student* example, if the condition clause wanted to reference the raising object it would use OBJECT1 as the student class is the first mentioned class (it is the only class in this example). Similarly to reference employee in the second example, OBJECT2 would be used.

Example EECA rules could be:

E	AFTER UPDATE aircraft	AFTER UPDATE item
C	SELECT a.Name() FROM aircraft a, aircraft b WHERE a.Name() = OBJECT1 AND (a.CurX - b.CurX) BETWEEN -5 AND 5 AND (a.CurY- b.CurY) BETWEEN -5 AND 5 AND (a.CurZ - b.CurZ) BETWEEN -5 AND 5;	SELECT a.Name FROM item a WHERE a.Name = OBJECT1 AND a.QtyOnHand < a.MinQty;
EC	immediate	deferred
A	(AlertOperator OBJECT1; immediate; independent) (INSERT ON log a.itemID, XYZ; decoupled; independent)	(INSERT ON reorderItem a.itemID, a.ReorderQty; decoupled; independent) NULL
FA	NULL	NULL

5. Conclusions and Future Work

We have introduced the EECA model, with its multiple action and fail-action clauses, and its associated extension of coupling modes. This paper has highlighted several problems of application semantics caused by the EECA polyform, mainly the dependency issue. This has been resolved by introducing the action clause tuple that includes a dependency flag for each individual action or fail-action clause. The designer of the system is given the choice as to what level of transaction dependency is required for a given application.

We believe that the EECA knowledge model proposed does in fact allow the declaration of the knowledge within the active database system to be both semantically concise and obvious as to its intention. The model also allows for a more efficient evaluation and operation of the overall active database system.

REFLEX introduces a number of novel features such as its loose coupling model, its powerful knowledge model, its self-activity and its short-circuit evaluation mechanism. REFLEX also promotes a critical concurrency approach, the concept of non-destructive knowledge, a powerful and user-friendly graphical user-interface (Vis), see [NI93c] for further details.

The REFLEX prototype system has been implemented in C++ on the ONTOS

ODBMS [ONT91]. It *has been demonstrated* at various venues using a graphical simulation of an Air Traffic Control System. The prototype is currently being used to generate data on how *real active applications behave*.

We intend to make REFLEX available on the public-domain, via ftp. It will initially be released for the ONTOS DBMS system. Please contact the authors for further details.

References

[AG89] Agrawal R. and Gehani N.H., "Rationale for the Design of Persistence and Query Processing Facilities in the Database Programming Language O++", 2nd Int. Workshop on Database Programming Languages, Portland, OR, June 1989

[CBB*89] Chakravarthy S., Blaustein B., Buchmann A. et al, "HiPAC: A Research Project in Active, Time-Constrained Database Management", Final Technical Report, Xerox Advanced Information Technology Division, July 1989

[Day89] Dayal U., "Active Database Management Systems", Sigmod Record, Vol. 18, No. 3, 1989

[DP91] Diaz O. and Paton N.W., "Sharing behaviour in an object-oriented database using a rule-based mechanism", Proc. 9th British National Conference On Databases, 1991

[DPG91] Diaz O., Paton N. and Gray P., "A Rule Management in Object Oriented Databases: A Uniform Approach", Proc. of the 17th Int. Conf. on Very Large Data Bases, Barcelona, Spain 1991

[GJ91] Gehani N.H. and Jagadish H.V., "Ode as an Active Database: Constraints and Triggers", Proc. of the 17th Int. Conf. on Very Large Data Bases, Barcelona, Spain 1991

[GJS92a] Gehani N.H., Jagadish H.V. and Shmueli O., "Event Specification in an Active Object-Oriented Database", Proc. 1992 ACM SIGMOD Intl. Conf. on Management of Data

[GJS92b] Gehani N.H., Jagadish H.V. and Shmueli O., "Composite Event Specification in Active Databases: Model & Implementation", Proceedings of the 18th Int. Conf. on Very Large Data Bases, Vancouver, Canada, 1992

[LLP*91] Lohman G. M., Lindsay B., Pirahesh H. and Schiefer K. B., "Extensions To STARBURST: Objects, Types, Functions, and Rules", CACM October 1991, Vol 34, No 10

[MD89] McCarthy D.R. and Dayal U.,"The Architecture of an Active Data Base Management System", Proc. ACM SIGMOD Intl. Conf. on Management of Data, Portland, June 1989

[MP90] Medeiros C.B. and Pfeffer P., "A Mechanism for Managing Rules in an Object-oriented Database", Altair Technical Report, 1990

[NHI94] Naqvi W., Hughes C., and Ibrahim M.T., "Towards a Dynamic Schema Integration Model", Tech Report CIT-DSRL029401, University of Greenwich, December 1993, submitted for pubication

[NI93a] Naqvi W. and Ibrahim M.T., "REFLEX Active Database Model: Application of Petri-Nets", Proc. of the 4th Int. Conf. on Database and Expert Systems Applications, Prague, September 1993

[NI93b] Naqvi W. and Ibrahim M.T., "Rule and Knowledge Management in an Active Database System", Proc. of 1st Int. Workshop. on Rules in Database Systems, Edinburgh, September 1993

[NI93c] Naqvi W. and Ibrahim M.T., "The REFLEX Knowledge Acquistion User Interface", Tech Report CIT-DSRL12932, University of Greenwich, December 1993

[ONT91] "ONTOS Reference Manual", ONTOS Inc, 1991

[Pat89] Paton N.W., "ADAM: An Object-Oriented Database System Implemented In Prolog", Proc. 7th British National Conference On Databases, 1989

[SHP89] Stonebraker M., Hearst M. and Potamianos S., "A Commentary on the POSTGRES Rules System", Sigmod Record, Vol. 18, No. 3, September 1989

[SK91] Stonebraker M. and Kemnitz G., "The POSTGRES Next-Generation Database Management System", CACM October 1991, Vol 34, No 10

Active and Passive Rules for Complex Object Databases

Luigi Palopoli[1] and Riccardo Torlone[2]

[1] DEIS, Università della Calabria, 87036 Rende, Italy
[2] IASI–CNR, Viale Manzoni 30, 00185 Roma, Italy

Abstract. The problem of adding language facilities to express production rule in the framework of a complex object database with active behavior is considered. The issue of the definition of a suitable interaction between production rules and transactions is crucial in this context and is addressed in this paper: this involves questions regarding triggering and activation modes of production rules with respect to transaction execution, the management of multiple rules activation, and the definition of the related execution environment. We propose a rule-based language on complex objects that allows the definition of both (active) production rules and (passive) ordinary transactions in a unified framework.

1 Introduction

Recently, the database community has demonstrated a great interest in extending traditional relational systems with production rule definition facilities (e.g., [8, 9]). A production rule allows to specify the triggering of particular actions whenever certain events occur and some conditions are met. It generally consists of three parts: the event part, which specifies the event triggering the rule, the condition part, which states the conditions under which the rule has to be activated, and the action part, which contains the manipulations that dictate the effect of rule execution. Since such actions are taken automatically, without user intervention, the database management systems allowing the definition of this kind of rules are called *active*, to distinguish them from the conventional database systems that are *passive*, in the sense that they only manipulate data in response to explicit requests from users or applications.

It is widely accepted that production rules enhance the capability of database systems as they provide a very natural mechanism for the management of activities like, for instance, integrity constraint enforcement and derived data maintenance [2, 3]. Thus, the problem of how adding active behavior to commercial relational database systems has been largely studied in the last years [4, 5, 9, 10]. On the other hand, it is well known that the relational data model does not offer an adequate support for all the database applications (e.g., CAD, CASE, multimedia and expert systems). So, a number of new data models have been studied which allow entailing more semantics in data, and query and update languages have also been designed for these data models based on various programming paradigms (see for instance [6]). Therefore, in this paper we are concerned with the problem of adding active specification facilities to a complex object database, that is, a database organized in a hierarchy of classes of objects with object identity and complex structure.

The language we present here, called $\mathcal{RCO}$ (Rules for Complex Objects), is an extension of the update language defined in [7], and allows to uniformly define both ordinary (passive) transactions[3] and production rules. Indeed, in $\mathcal{RCO}$ an ordinary transaction differs from a production rule simply in the activation mechanism: once activated, there is no observable difference in our framework between them. This uniformity allows us to provide a unique and clean definition of the semantics of both active and passive sublanguages of $\mathcal{RCO}$. More specifically, the language allows the specification of rather general triggering events and execution conditions. The former are essentially metapredicates defined on the classes included in a database schema, which state whether some object in a particular class has undergone some specific *transition* (e.g., a modification). The latter are conjunctions of logical literals which serve the two purposes of controlling rule execution and retrieving data to be used within the rule action part. The action part of a rule may contain both sequences of basic update operations and calls to transaction rules.

In presenting our rule language, we will address several important design questions: How transaction executions and production rule activations relate? Which are the similitudes and the differences between mutual and recursive calls of the transaction component and cascading triggering in the production rule component? When rules are to be considered for execution? What happens if more that one rule is triggered?

The plan of the paper is as follows. In the next section we introduce the data model of reference. The syntax and the formal semantics of the language are presented in Sect. 3 and in Sect. 4, respectively. An execution model for such a language is proposed in Sect. 5, and in Sect. 6 an interpreter is illustrated. In Sect. 7 we discuss some adopted design decisions and finally, in Sect. 8, we summarize our conclusions.

2 A Model for Complex Objects with Identity

A $\mathcal{CO}$ database is composed by a collection of classes. A $\mathcal{CO}$ class is a set of objects with complex structure for which value equality does not imply identity – this is implemented by means of unique object identifiers, which are not visible to the user. Generalization hierarchies among classes can be defined using *is-a* relationships that allow to inherit attributes.

Formally, fixed a finite set of *base types* $\mathcal{B}$ (integers, strings, and so on), each of which has associated a set of *base values*, we call a $\mathcal{CO}$ *scheme* a triple $\mathbf{S} = (\mathbf{C}, \textsc{typ}, \textsc{isa})$ where $\mathbf{C}$ is a set of *class names*, TYP is a function that associates with each symbol in $\mathbf{C}$ a tuple type of $\mathbf{S}$ (see below), and ISA is a partial order over $\mathbf{C}$, with the condition that if $C_1 \textsc{isa} C_2$, then $\textsc{typ}(C_1)$ is a *refinement* of

[3] In this paper for transaction we mean a collection of data manipulation operations with selection conditions viewed as an atomic unit.

TYP(C_2). (The definition of refinement is not given here; informally, we can say that a tuple type τ is a refinement of another tuple type τ' if τ has *at least* the components of τ', and possibly some more [7]). The *types* of $\mathbf{S}$ are built from the base types $B \in \mathcal{B}$ and the class names $C \in \mathbf{C}$, by applying repeatedly the *tuple*, the *set* and the *sequence* constructors. Note that a class name can be used in constructing another type, which refers to the objects in that class. This allows us to express explicit references between elements of the classes.

Let $\mathcal{O}$ be a countable set of oid's and let $\perp$ be a special symbol, called the *null value*, denoting an undefined value regardless of its type. It is possible to associate with each type τ of $\mathbf{S}$ the set DOM(τ) of its possible values, called the *domain* of τ, built as usual from base values, oid's and the null value, using the set and the tuple constructs. Then, a $\mathcal{CO}$ *instance* $\mathbf{s}$ of a scheme $\mathbf{S} = (\mathbf{C}, \text{TYP}, \text{ISA})$, is a pair of functions $\mathbf{s} = (\mathbf{c}, \mathbf{o})$, where: *(i)* $\mathbf{c}$ associates with each $C \in \mathbf{C}$ a finite set of oid's ($\mathbf{c}(C) \subseteq \mathcal{O}$), *(ii)* $\mathbf{o}$ is a partial function from $\mathcal{O}$ to the union of all the domains of the types of $\mathbf{S}$, such that, that for every $C \in \mathbf{C}$ and for every $o \in \mathbf{c}(C)$, $\mathbf{o}(o) \in \text{DOM}(\tau)$, where τ is a refinement of the TYP(C) (that is, $\mathbf{o}(o)$ does not necessarily belong to the domain of TYP(C), as it can belong to DOM(TYP(C')), where C'ISAC, and therefore having associated more attributes than those of TYP(C)). An example of $\mathcal{CO}$ instance is reported in Figure 1.

person

	name	birthdate dd	mm	yy	sons
#p2	Tom	[1	6	58]	∅
#p4	Tom	[1	6	58]	∅
#p5	Tom	[4	10	43]	{#p6}
#p6	John	[12	3	70]	⊥
#p7	Jane	[15	7	47]	{#p9}
#p9	Jim	[12	2	69]	∅

student (isa person)

	st-code	follows
#p6	11056	{#c1,#c3}
#p9	23974	{#c3}

worker (isa person)

	salary	seniority
#p5	60000	4
#p7	50000	4

course

	duration	name
#c1	140	oper. syst.
#c3	160	databases

professor (isa worker)

	position	teaches	advises
#p7	associate	{#c1}	{#p9}
#p5	full	∅	{#p6}

Fig. 1. An $\mathcal{CO}$ database instance

3 Syntax of the Rule Language

Let $\mathbf{F}$ be a predefined set of interpreted *built-in functions* $\mathbf{P}$ be a predefined set of *built-in predicates*, $\mathbf{S} = (\mathbf{C}, \text{TYP}, \text{ISA})$ be an $\mathcal{CO}$ scheme and $\mathbf{U}$ be a set of symbols called *transaction names*.

The $\mathcal{RCO}$ language includes the following components.

- *Constants*: they are values from the union of the base values of $\mathbf{S}$, and *variables*, which have always associated a fixed type of $\mathbf{S}$.

- *(External) terms*: they are built from variables and constants by using functions $f \in \mathbf{F}$, and the set ($\{\ \}$) and tuple ($[\,]$) delimiters.
- *Atoms*: they can be *object* atoms of the form $C(X, t)$, where X denotes the oid of an object of the class C and t its associated values, and *built-in* atoms.
- *Literals*: they can be static or dynamic. A *static* literal can be an atom, an atom preceded by the symbol $\neg$, or a conjunction of static literals delimited by brackets and preceded by the symbol $\neg$. A *dynamic* literal can be basic, transaction or transition. A *basic* dynamic literals is one of INS(O), DEL(O), MOD($\hat{O}$), and SKIP() (it denotes the null-effect operator and is useful for technical reasons), where O is an object atom, and $\hat{O} = C(X, t \mid [A_j : t'])$. A *transaction* dynamic literal has the form $u(t_1, \ldots, t_l)$ where $u \in \mathbf{U}$. Finally, INSERTED(O), DELETED(O) and MODIFIED($\hat{O}$) are *transition* dynamic literals.

As usual, a term is *ground* if no variable occurs in it, whereas it is *closed* if all the function terms occurring in it are ground. Similarly for atoms and literals. A $\mathcal{RCO}$ *rule* is an expression of the form: $H \Rightarrow C_1, \ldots, C_m : U_1, \ldots, U_n$ where in the left hand side (the *head* of the rule) H is a non-basic dynamic literal, whereas in the right hand side (the *body* of the rule) $C_1, \ldots, C_m$ is a conjunction of static literals and is optional, and $U_1, \ldots, U_n$ is a sequence of basic or transaction dynamic literals. If the head contains a transition literal then we have a *production* rule, whereas if it contains a transaction literal the rule is called a *transaction*. A $\mathcal{RCO}$ *program* is a finite set of rules.

Example 1. The following are production rules.

```
INSERTED(worker(X)) ⇒ ¬person(X) : INS(person(X)).
INSERTED(professor(X)) ⇒ ¬worker(X) : INS(worker(X)).
DELETED(person(X)) ⇒ student(X) : DEL(student(X)).
```

Intuitively, The first rule specifies that when a new object is inserted in the class `worker` then it has to be inserted also in `person` if it does not belong to this class already. As an example of transaction specification, the following expression assigns a non-deterministically chosen professor as adviser of a student with a certain student code `C`, provided that such a student attends one of the courses taught by that professor.

```
ASSIGN-NEW-ADVISER(C) ⇒
        student(X,[st-code:C,follows:Z]),professor(P,[teaches:T]),
        Z∩T≠ ∅ : MOD(professor(P,[advises:W]|[advises:W∪{X}]).
```

4 $\mathcal{RCO}$ Semantics

Let us start with some preliminary definitions. A *substitution* θ is a function from the variables of $\mathbf{S}$ to the union of the variables and the domains of $\mathbf{S}$. If t is a term, then $t\theta$ denotes the term obtained by replacing each variable X in

t with $\theta(X)$. Similarly for literals and rules. If $t\theta$ is ground, then θ is a *ground substitution* for t.

Let $O = C(\hat{t}, t)$ and $O' = C(\hat{t}', t')$ two object atoms over the same class C; we say that O *matches* with O' if there is a substitution θ such that: $\hat{t}\theta = \hat{t}'\theta$, and $\bar{t}\theta = \bar{t'}\theta$, where $\bar{t}$ and $\bar{t'}$ are the *extensions* of t and t' to $\text{TYP}(C)$ obtained by adding new variables when needed.

A pair of dynamic literals L and L' are *compatible* if there exists a substitution θ (called a *unifier*) such that: either L and L' are both transaction literals and $L\theta = L'\theta$; or $L = B(O)$ is a basic literal, $L' = T(O')$ is a *related* transition literal (e.g., $B = \text{INS}$ and $T = \text{INSERTED}$) and O matches with O' using θ.

Let $O = C(\hat{t}, t)$ be a closed object atom; we can associate a truth value to O with respect to an instance $\mathbf{s}$ of $\mathbf{S}$ as follows: O $(\neg O)$ is true in $\mathbf{s}$ if there exists (does not exist) an element $o \in \mathbf{c}(C)$ such that the corresponding object atom $(C(o, \mathbf{o}(o)))$ matches with O using a (ground) substitution θ, which we call a *valuation* of O in $\mathbf{s}$. Note that in general there can be several valuation of the same object atom.

Let $\mathbf{s}$ be a $\mathcal{CO}$ instance of a scheme $\mathbf{S}$. The semantics of the $\mathcal{RCO}$ language is given by: (1) introducing the notion of *effect* of the application of a basic dynamic literal to $\mathbf{s}$, (2) extending this notion to a sequence of basic dynamic literals, (3) associating a truth value to a conjunction of static literals, (4) giving the semantics of a combination of static and dynamic literals, and finally, on the basis of the notion of extension of a rule with respect to a program (5), presenting the semantics for the application of a $\mathcal{RCO}$ rule to the instance $\mathbf{s}$.

1. The effect of the basic dynamic literal $B = \text{INS}(C(\hat{t}, t))$, consists in adding to $\mathbf{c}(C)$ the oid $\hat{t}$ if it is ground, or a new oid of $\mathcal{O}$ not already appearing in $\mathbf{s}$ otherwise, and by associating to this oid the extension of t to $\text{TYP}(C)$, in which all variables are replaced with the null value. The effect of $B = \text{DEL}(C(\hat{t}, t))$ consists in deleting from $\mathbf{c}(C)$ one oid o such that $C(o, \mathbf{o}(o))$ matches with $C(\hat{t}, t)$ (if any). The effect of $B = \text{MOD}(C(\hat{t}, t \mid [A_j : t']))$, consists in replacing $[A_j : t]$ with $[A_j : t']\theta$ in $\mathbf{o}(o)$, for one $o \in \mathbf{c}(C)$ such that $C(o, \mathbf{o}(o))$ matches with $C(\hat{t}, t)$ using the valuation θ (if any). Finally, $B = \text{SKIP}()$ has a null effect on $\mathbf{s}$.
2. The effect of a sequence of closed basic dynamic literals $\alpha = B_1, \ldots, B_n$ to $\mathbf{s}$ simply coincides with $B_1 \circ \ldots \circ B_n(\mathbf{s})$.
3. A conjunction of closed static literals β $(\neg(\beta))$ is true in $\mathbf{s}$ if there exists (there does not exist) a composition θ of valuations of the object atoms in β such that $\beta\theta$ is true with respect to definitions of the built-in literals, and it is false otherwise. If β is true, then θ is called a *valuation* of β in $\mathbf{s}$.
4. Let $\mu = \beta_1 : \alpha_1 : \ldots : \beta_n : \alpha_n$, be a sequence of literals such that β_i is a sequence of static literals and α_j a sequence of basic dynamic literals, for $1 \leq i, j \leq n$. Then, the effect of μ is computed as follows. For each set of basic dynamic literals α_j in μ, the conjunction of static literals β_j preceding them are evaluated in the current state that initially is $\mathbf{s}$; if β_j is true the corresponding bindings are applied to α_j, and the effect of its application becomes the current state.

5. Let P be a $\mathcal{RCO}$ program for $\mathbf{S}$ and R be a rule in P; an *expansion* R^* of R with respect to P is the last element of a sequence of rules $R = R_0, R_1, \ldots, R_k = R^*$ such that: if U_j is a transaction literal occurring in the body of R_{i-1} $(i > 0)$ and there is a transaction rule Q in P such that U_j is compatible with the head of Q using the unifier θ, then R_i is obtained from R_{i-1} by replacing the literal U_j with the body of Q, and by applying θ to the obtained rule. If no transaction literal occurs in the body of R^*, then we say that R^* is a *full* expansion of R with respect to P. Note that a body of full expansion has the form of the sequence of literals in item 4.

Now, let P a $\mathcal{RCO}$ program and R a rule in P. If there exists a full expansion R^* of R with respect to P whose effect on $\mathbf{s}$ is different from $\mathbf{s}$ itself, then we say that R *succeeds* in $\mathbf{s}$ and that a *result* for the application of R is the effect of the application of the body of R^* to $\mathbf{s}$. Otherwise, we say that R *fails*.

Hence, the execution of a ground instance $T\theta$ of a transaction literal T defined by a rule R *commits* if $R\theta$ succeeds in $\mathbf{s}$ and its execution corresponds to the effect of $R\theta$ to $\mathbf{s}$. Otherwise ($R\theta$ fails) T *aborts* and its execution is null.

Moreover, if B is a ground basic dynamic literal and there is a production rule R whose head is compatible with B with θ as unifier then, whenever B is successfully applied to an instance, R is *triggered* by B using θ, and is *activated* if $R\theta$ succeeds in $\mathbf{s}$.

Example 2. Assume that when a full professor is deleted from the database, then a new adviser must be provided for his advised students. Then, the following program can be used.

```
DELETED(professor(X,[position:full,advises:Y])) ⇒
                                      Y≠ ∅:ASSIGN-NEW-ADVISERS(Y).
ASSIGN-NEW-ADVISERS(X) ⇒ Y∈X : ASSIGN-NEW-ADVISER(Y),
                             ASSIGN-NEW-ADVISERS(X-{Y}).
ASSIGN-NEW-ADVISERS(X) ⇒ X=∅ : SKIP().
```

The first rule is triggered by a basic dynamic literal which deletes a full professor from the database. If such a professor has some advised student, the rule is activated and calls for the transaction `ASSIGN-NEW-ADVISERS` which is recursively defined: it takes as input (the oid's of) a set of students, picks one of this students, and then calls in turn the transaction defined in Example 1, which finally assigns to the selected student a new adviser. A full expansion of the transaction `ASSIGN-NEW-ADVISERS` is composed by a sequence of calls to the inner rule for all the student advised by the deleted professor.

5 An Execution Model

The execution of a transaction is simply obtained by calling the proper transaction literal. A transaction call can be specified directly by a user, by an external application program or within another transaction. So, in the case of a transaction, the activation is by explicit naming. This is formalized next.

For a basic dynamic predicate $b \in \{\text{INS}, \text{DEL}, \text{MOD}\}$, let $\bar{b}$ denote its *complementary* operator, that is, $\overline{\text{INS}} = \text{DEL}$, $\overline{\text{DEL}} = \text{INS}$, $\overline{\text{MOD}} = \text{MOD}$ (the rationale for $\overline{\text{MOD}} = \text{MOD}$ is that a modification is invalidated by a successive modification involving the same attribute). Then, we say that a triggered rule $R\theta$ is *invalidated* by $B = b(O)$ if it is triggered by $\bar{b}(O')$, and O and O' match. The family Π_T of the *valid* rules triggered by T is defined as follows: initially (before T execution), Π_T is set to $\emptyset$; then, for each ground basic dynamic literal B that is successfully executed while T is processed, the rules in Π_T invalidated by B are removed from Π_T, whereas (the instances of) those triggered by B are added to it. If T aborts then Π_T is set to $\emptyset$. Thus, at the end of the execution of T, the set Π_T contains (in its elements) all the instances of production rules triggered by the "net" result of the execution of T if T commits, and is empty otherwise.

In general, the global activation mechanism proceeds as follows. A set Π containing all the triggered rules at a specific time is used. Initially, $\Pi = \emptyset$. Assume that a transaction T is called and successfully executed yielding a result instance $\mathbf{s}$. The set Π_T is correspondently computed. If T halts successfully, the set Π is updated by removing all the rules invalidated by T and augmenting it with the rules in Π_T. When T halts (either with a commit or an abort), a rule is picked from Π according to some selection criterion, which, for the sake of generality, we consider generic here. Assume that the chosen rule is R. If R is activated in $\mathbf{s}$, then it is executed to obtain a new resulting state $\mathbf{s}'$. Otherwise, another rule is chosen from Π. The execution of a selected rule R updates the family Π of triggered rule sets in an absolutely identical manner as an ordinary transaction. Note that, in our model, a rule activated after a transaction corresponds to a new transaction independent on the activating one. The rule activation process terminates when a state is reached in which Π is empty. When this happens, further user or application program requested transactions can be processed.

6 The $\mathcal{RCO}$ Interpreter

The semantics of the $\mathcal{RCO}$ language and it execution model are implemented by the interpreter given in Fig. 2. In the interpreter, SoP denote a structure storing sets of pairs of the form (B, R), where B is a triggering basic dynamic literal and R is an instance of a rule triggered by B. The main program consists of a loop that takes as input a user or application specified transaction call, constructs the corresponding set of invoked rules and then starts an inner loop. The inner loop selects a pair from SoP according to some selection criterion, and calls the procedure EXECUTE. This procedure is in charge of executing the rule (thus, possibly modify the current database instance) and returning a set activated rules stored in SoP', or a failure, if the rule does not succeeds. If the execution of the rule is successful, then the set SoP is updated by the rules returned in the set SoP' as discussed in Sect. 5 (see procedure MERGE). The procedure EXECUTE first calls the procedure EVAL that evaluates the rule condition and returns a substitution θ. If $\theta = \emptyset$, the condition is not satisfiable, and then a failure is reported. Otherwise, the rule action instantiated by this

```
RCO INTERPRETER
Let P be a RCO program and s the current database state;
var: SoP: an initially empty set of pairs; fail: boolean;
begin {MAIN}
    repeat
        INPUT(T); {T is the invoked transaction literal}
        SoP := {(T, Rθ) | R ∈ P is triggered by T using θ};
        while SoP ≠ ∅ do
            extract (T', R') from SoP; EXECUTE(R', SoP', fail);
            if not fail then MERGE(SoP, SoP');
        endwhile;
    forever;
end {MAIN}
Procedure EXECUTE(R = H ⇒ C : U: a rule;
                  var SoP_R: an initially empty set of pairs;
                  var fail: boolean);
var: θ: a substitution;
begin {EXECUTE}
    EVAL(C, θ); if θ ≠ ∅ then PERFORM(Uθ, SoP_R,fail) else fail:=true;
end {EXECUTE}
Procedure PERFORM(U = U_1, ..., U_k: a sequence of dynamic literals;
                  var SoP_R: an initially empty set of pairs;
                  var fail: boolean);
var i: an integer initially set to 1;
begin {PERFORM}
    while i ≤ k and not fail do
        case U_i of
            basic: BASIC(U_i, SoP_{U_i}); MERGE(SoP_R, SoP_{U_i});
            transaction: EXECUTE(U_i, SoP_{U_i}, fail); MERGE(SoP_R, SoP_{U_i});
        endcase; i := i+1;
    endwhile
end {PERFORM}
Procedure BASIC(U: a basic dynamic literal;
                var SoP_U: an initially empty set of pairs);
begin {BASIC}
    case U of
        INS(O): INSERT(O); DEL(O): DELETE(O); MOD(O): MODIFY(Ô)
    endcase;
    SoP_U := {(U, Rθ) | R ∈ P is triggered by T using θ};
end {BASIC}
Procedure MERGE(var SoP_1, SoP_2: sets of pairs);
begin {MERGE}
    for each (B, R) ∈ SoP_2 do
        delete from SoP_1 all the pairs (B', R') such that R' is invalidated by B
    endfor;
    SoP_1 := SoP_1 ∪ SoP_2;
end {MERGE}
```

Fig. 2. An interpreter of the $\mathcal{RCO}$ language.

substitution is executed by a call to the procedure PERFORM. Since the action of a rule may contain other transaction literals, also the PERFORM procedure can result in a failure, that is in this case reported. Otherwise, the PERFORM procedure constructs the corresponding set of invoked rules. The procedure PERFORM simply consider all the dynamic literals occurring in the input update sequence, one by one, in the order in which they appear. For basic dynamic literals, it calls the corresponding procedure BASIC that is in charge of executing them. Transaction dynamic literals are executed by a recursive call to the EXECUTE procedure. In any case, the returned set of invoked rules are then properly put together, as explained in Sect. 5, using the procedure MERGE. The implementation of the other procedures is pretty obvious, and has not been reported here. A prototypical implementation of the interpreter is currently under development at IASI.

7 Discussions

We discuss now some of the issues mentioned in the introduction.

Query driven rule triggering. In this paper, only updates have been considered as triggering events for production rules. However, it might be useful to define rules which are triggered by querying (e.g., for authorization checking on retrievals). However, this schema can be embedded in $\mathcal{RCO}$, by using atoms like QUERIED(O) in the event part.

Activation mechanism. The $\mathcal{RCO}$ activation mechanism of production rules and that of transactions is inherently different (explicit naming vs. implicit invokation via triggering). This difference marks well, we would argue, the distinction between passive entities (transactions) and active ones (production rules).

Production rule execution point. As stated in Sect. 5, we have adopted here a decoupling activation mode, consisting in executing rule actions after the end of the triggering transaction. Alternative approaches studied in the literature are to execute rules immediately after the triggering update has occurred (immediate mode) or just before the commit point of the current transaction (deferred mode). However, they can be implemented quite easily in our framework by considering the triggered rule as a sub-transaction of the triggering one.

Activation of multiple triggered rules. Our model accounts for the possibility that more than one production rule is activated at a certain time: this rules are precisely those belonging to sets in the family Π. However, only one rule, say R, is effectively activated at a time. The non activated rules remain triggered as long as at least one of their triggering events remain valid in the state the database reaches after executing R's action. This is because a rule is activated only if the event which it is meant to handle is currently still valid.

Rule selection criteria. Non-determinism in production rule execution does not seem to be equally justified as for non-determinism in transformation languages [1], since production rule are meant to make a database move from a (somehow) undesirable state to a desirable one. In this context, it seems interesting to have the possibility of attaching priorities to rules to form a total or partial ordering to be used in determining the selection order in the case of multiple activations.

Tuple-oriented vs. set-oriented manipulation primitives. We have shown in [7] that in a complex object data model, it is not possible to rule out tuple-oriented primitives without loose a certain amount of expressive power. The same result also hold for $\mathcal{RCO}$, even if only its active component is considered. Interestingly, to adopt tuple-oriented data manipulation primitives has a beneficent impact on the definition of the execution model since the management of the set of triggered rules is simplified.

8 Conclusions

In this paper the problem of how adding production rule facilities to a complex object database has been discussed. We have proposed a framework in which production rules as well as ordinary transactions can be expressed in a similar fashion. This naturally correspond to the behaviour of an active system, where transactions trigger production rules that in turn execute transactions.

Interesting developments of this research include the design of a modified production rule execution model to fit possibly parallel execution environments, as well as the definition of static analysis techniques to detect potential non terminating loops and conflicts among rules. The formal nature of the presented language will be useful in approaching those problems.

References

1. S. Abiteboul and V. Vianu. Datalog extensions for database queries and updates. *Journal of Comp. and System Sc.*, 43(1):62–124, August 1991.
2. S. Ceri and J. Widom. Deriving production rules for constraint maintenance. In *16th VLDB, Brisbane*, 566–577, 1990.
3. S. Ceri and J. Widom. Deriving production rules for incremental view maintenance. In *17th VLDB, Barcelona*, 577–589, 1991.
4. S. Chakravarthy and S. Nesson. Making an object-oriented DBMS active: design, implementation, and evaluation of a prototype. In *EDBT'90*, LNCS 416, 1990.
5. E.N. Hanson. An initial report on the design of Ariel: a DBMS with an integrated production rule system. *ACM SIGMOD Record*, 18(3):12–19, 1989.
6. R. Hull. A survey of theoretical research on typed complex database objects. In J. Paredaens, editor, *Databases*, 193–256, Academic Press, 1988.
7. L. Palopoli and R. Torlone. Specifying the dynamics of complex object databases. In *Modelling Database Dynamic, Volkse*, 143–160, Springer-Verlag, 1992.
8. T. Sellis, C.C. Lin, and Raschid L. Implementing large production systems in a DBMS environment: concepts and algorithms. In *SIGMOD Conf.*, 404–412, 1988.
9. M. Stonebraker. The integration of rule systems and database systems. *IEEE Trans. on Knowledge and Data Eng.*, 4(5):415–423, October 1992.
10. J. Widom, Cochrane R.J., and Lindsay B.G. Implementing set-Oriented production rules as an extension of Starbust. In *17th VLDB, Barcelona*, 275–286, 1991.

Managing Entity Versions within their Contexts: A Formal Approach

Stéphane Gançarski and Geneviève Jomier

LAMSADE - Université Paris Dauphine
Place du M^{al} de Lattre de Tassigny, 75775 Paris cedex 16, France
e-mail : gancarski@lamsade.dauphine.fr, jomier@lamsade.dauphine.fr

Abstract. A formal model (concepts and operations) for multiversion databases is presented. It is based on the DBV approach [CJ90], which allows the management of entity versions within their context. The problem of reading and comparing complex object versions is presented. The model allows to better understand the potential of the DBV approach, and will be used as a framework for new multiversion functionalities.

Keywords : database, versions, context of versions, formal model.

1 Introduction

From years people work on integration of version management into design applications, using file managers first, and then other kinds of repository (DBMS, configurations management systems). However, multiversion systems may not be easily used if they are not able to show versions of entities in their contexts. In *monoversion database* (i.e., without versions), the value of an entity has no meaning if it is isolated from other entities of the database. The current state of the database models a state of the universe: it is a *context* for user's work. However, it may no more be used as a context *when objects have versions*, since all the versions of all the entities cannot belong to the same context.

Let a database contain two entities: the text and the figure of an article written in French and in English. Two contexts exist: the French one contains the French version of the text and the figure, the English one contains the English version of the text and the figure. The whole database doesn't represent any context; neither does the english version of the text alone. One always creates a new entity version *from an existing context* (here, the *french* context), creating implicitly a new context containing updated entities versions (here, the english version of the text) and existing versions of other entities (here, the figure).

Four principles for the design of a multiversion system may be deduced:
- ***principle 1:*** Entity versions should always be manipulated within an identifiable context, representing a version of the modelled universe.
- ***principle 2:*** Creation of new entity versions does not occur out of a context.
- ***principle 3:*** Several contexts may share the same entity version, but updating one entity version in a context has no side effect on other contexts.
- ***principle 4:*** Several contexts may be manipulated simultaneously.

The DataBase Versions approach [CJ90], fulfills these principles. This paper gives a formalism of this approach, enabling a precise understanding of its potential and offering a rigourous framework for the development of new multiversion functionalities. The concept of version seen by the users (logical version within its context) and the concept of version managed by the system (physical version) are clearly distinct; the model is general and may be adapted to any data model which identifies entities independently from their values.

A lot of papers related to version management have been published during the last ten years, for specific applications (CASE, CAD ...) as well as for general domains (DBMS, Hypertexts ...). As far as we know, there is no presentation of a formal version model like the one presented here, probably because those works don't distinguish between physical and logical versions. They may be grouped in three families, according to how versions and contexts are represented.

The largest number of papers is related to the first family, often called *version server approach*, which mainly concern databases. Among the most recent works [Fau92], [AN91], [KS92], [SG91], [TOC93] may be cited, as [Kat90] presents a synthesis of former works. The database is seen as a collection of *generic objects*, each one composed of a structured versions set. A new version is created from an existing one, versions with no successors may be updated. Some query languages are extended to manipulate the versions of a specific object [BH91]. The main problem is context management. To associate consistent object versions in a *configuration*, it is necessary to explicitly link versions: object version may be referenced by other object version to build complex object versions. This link is used once as a reference of an entity to another and once to associate two entity versions in a same context. This duality generates problems to manage contexts: creation of object versions implies creation of new configurations, mainly achieved manually or by automatic generation of many, often useless configurations (percolation) [Atw86]. Thus, those works are limited both in the number of contexts managed simultaneously and in the functionalities to manipulate them.

In the second family, temporal databases [AF92], [Bla91], the notion of context is implicitely established: by associating a validity time interval to entity values, the state of the modelled universe at any given date may be retrieved. The semantics of time implies a total order over object versions, thus over contexts. To allow alternatives, [LF91] proposes to disconnect timestamps from the real clock, and to organize them in a non linear way, by adding an indirection. As far as we know, no formal model has been proposed for systems based on timestamps, allowing to manage of a non linear structure between contexts.

A third family of works appears in applications area, like CASE, where context management has been for a long time under consideration. Development of source code managers, like RCS [Tic82] or SCCS [Roc75], has led to development of configuration managers based on the version server approach [Log90], [LC84]. Then software configuration managers including both file versions and context management were designed. In [Rei89], orthogonality between versioning and object grouping is established. [MSK89] presents a similar approach: project revisions are organized into a tree of *development paths*. [KA91] proposes to access data via an historical tree of contexts, where consistency may be enforced. [KRW92] presents a *top-down* approach: project versions where states of objects are consistent, are introduced. As far as we know, none of those works has led to a general formalism, comparable to the one presented here.

This paper is organized as follows. Section 2 intuitively presents the DBV approach. Section 3 presents the concepts of the formalism, while Section 4 describes functions to handle them. In Section 5, shallow-value and deep-value of complex objects are extended in the multiversion case. Section 6 concludes.

2 The DataBase Versions (DBV) Model

The DBV model makes a clear distinction between the database logical level (*seen by users*), and its physical level (*managed by the system*). It is well adapted when entities are identified independently from their values (using Oids), particularly when Oids are used into entity values to reference other entities. From now on in this paper, words "entity" and "object" are equally used.

Logical Point of View: From the user's point of view, the database is seen as a set of *DataBase Versions (DBV)*. Each DBV, identified by a DBVid, represents a "version" of the modelled universe and is composed of *Logical Versions of Object (LV)*. Each LV represents the state of one object in one DBV, and is therefore identified by a pair (Oid, DBVid). Users only manipulate DBV and LV. Thus, object versions are always manipulated within their context: the DBV they belong to. Two kinds of transactions are defined: transactions *on LV*, which update logical object versions in one or several database versions, and transactions *on DBVs*, which create or delete database versions.

This is illustrated by Figure 1. Black headed arrows indicate partial order between design steps, each one modelled by a DBV. The database contains three objects, *Text, Figure* and *Legend.* Values are represented by an acronym : e.g., in DBV *d2*, version *fv2* represents the second "french" version of the text.

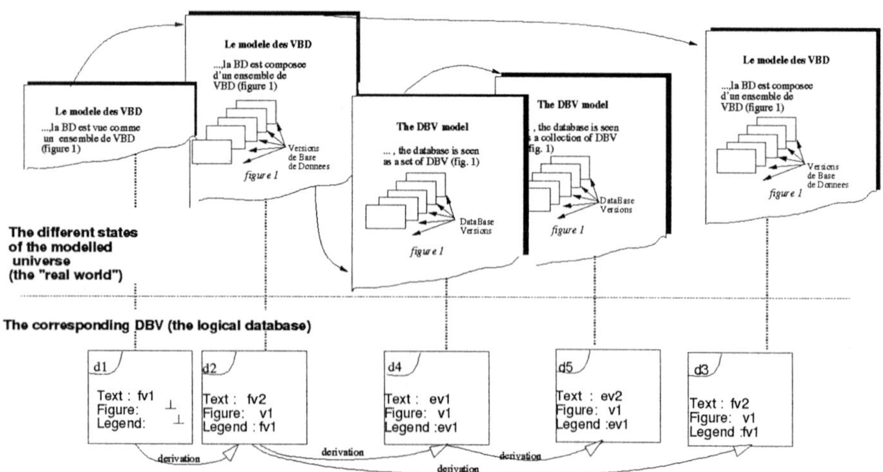

Fig. 1. Multiversion database as seen by the user

User works in a DBV like in a monoversion DB: he may *identify, update, create, delete logical object versions.* He may work simultaneously on many DBV. To create a new version of an object o and preserve his current context, he may use the *DBV derivation* (white headed arrows in figure 1), which creates a logical copy of a DBV . Users may *delete a DBV*, deleting all its logical object versions. The *creation of a multiversion object* makes it reachable in every DBV, where it may be updated later. A particular value, $\perp$, means that the object *doesn't exist in the DBV.* The *deletion of a multiversion object* removes all its versions.
Physical Point of View: [CJ90] and [CKW90] present efficient data structures and algorithms to implement version management. To avoid redundancy, values are stored in ***physical object versions*** identified by a *(PVid).* Logical versions of an object having the same value share the same physical version. For each object a table is used to map logical versions to physical versions. When a DBV is derived from another, both share the physical versions of all the objects. Thus, the physical version *implicitly* associated with a given logical version (o, d) is the physical version *explicitly* associated in the association table of o with (o, d'), d' being the nearest ascendant of d, relatively to the derivation link.
Need of a Formal Model: A formal model is necessary to clearly show how DBVs may be used. Indeed, new functionalities must be defined: language, integrity constraints and views on multiversion database. They are grouped in two families: [1] The first one is devoted to the potential of DBV, without taking semantics of applications into account. New multiversion tools may be defined: comparison of any two DBVs, merging of two DBVs to build a third one, and so on. [2] The second one helps to add application semantics to the model. A multigraph whose nodes are DBVs, with different links between DBV (temporal, equivalence,...) may be managed on top of the DBV model, enabling synthetic views of the multiversion database. The following formalism is thought as sound foundations for those tools. It only expresses semantics of the model and is without schema, since DBV approach is orthogonal to the data model.

3 Formal Model

Figure 2 shows the conceptual schema of the DBV model. Ovals represent atomic granules: identifiers and values. Arrows represent relations between granules in order to build the entities of the model, which are represented by rectangles:
- Each physical version identifier (`pvid`) is associated (*pv2val*) with a value (`val`), to form a physical object version (hidden from users, the rectangle is thus dashed) Values may contain object identifiers (`oid`).
- Each couple *(object identifier, database version identifier)*, (`oid, dbvid`), is associated with one physical object version to form a logical object version. Thus, one value is associated (*lv2val*) with each logical object version.
- A multiversion object is defined by an identifier (`oid`), associated with (*Cont*) the content of the object: its set of logical versions.
-A database version is defined by an identifier (`vbid`), associated with (*Cont*) the content of the database version: its set of logical versions.

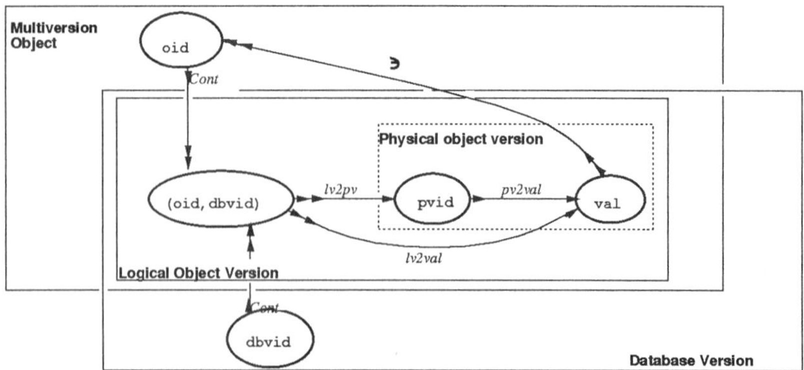

Fig. 2. Conceptual schema of the DBV model

Figure 2 illustrates the orthogonality between objects and contexts. This section continues with a definition of a *multiversion universe*. Primitives granules are presented as sets relations as functions. Then, concepts are formally defined.

3.1 Multiversion Universe (without schema)

Definition of a *Multiversion Universe* $\mathcal{M} = \{\mathcal{O}, \mathcal{D}, \mathcal{V}er, \mathcal{V}al, \mathcal{F}_{lv2pv}, \mathcal{F}_{pv2val}\}$:

- $\mathcal{O}$ is the *object identifiers* domain of $\mathcal{M}$: $\mathcal{O} = \{oid\}$,
- $\mathcal{D}$ is the *DBV identifiers* domain of $\mathcal{M}$: $\mathcal{D} = \{dbvid\}$,
- $\mathcal{V}er$ is the *physical object version* identifiers domain of $\mathcal{M}$: $\mathcal{V}er = \{pvid\}$,
- $\mathcal{V}al$ is the values domain. Values are built like object values in monoversion OODB. $\downarrow$ means : attribute has no value. $\perp$ means: object "does not exist" in a given DBV. $\mathcal{V}al$ can be built in the following way:
  - every atomic value (included $\perp$) is a value of $\mathcal{V}al$,
  - every value constructed (list, set, tuple) with Oid, $\downarrow$ and/or other values of $\mathcal{V}al$ (excepted $\perp$) is a value of $\mathcal{V}al$.
- $\mathcal{F}_{lv2pv}$ is the set of *version association functions* of $\mathcal{M}$, i.e. the set of $lv2pv$ functions such that:
  $$lv2pv : \mathcal{O} \times \mathcal{D} \rightarrow \mathcal{V}er \qquad (oid, dbvid) \mapsto pvid$$

  The following property expresses that different objects cannot share versions:
  $\forall lv2pv, \forall(o, o'), o \neq o', \forall(d, d'), (lv2pv(o, d) = lv2pv(o', d')) \Rightarrow (o = o')$
- $\mathcal{F}_{pv2val}$ is the set of *physical versions valuation functions* of $\mathcal{M}$, i.e. the set of $pv2val$ functions such that:
  $$pv2val : \mathcal{V}er \rightarrow \mathcal{V}al \qquad pvid \mapsto val$$

$\mathcal{L} = \mathcal{O} \times \mathcal{D}$ is the *logical object version identifiers* domain of $\mathcal{M}$. $\mathcal{L} = \{(oid, dbvid)\}$
$\mathcal{F}_{lv2val}$, called *logical versions valuation functions set* of $\mathcal{M}$, is the set of $lv2val$ functions such that $\exists pv2val \in \mathcal{F}_{pv2val}$ and $\exists lv2pv \in \mathcal{F}_{lv2pv}$ and:
$$lv2val : \mathcal{O} \times \mathcal{D} \rightarrow \mathcal{V}al \qquad (o, d) \mapsto val = pv2val \circ lv2pv(o, d))$$
Below, $lv2pv$, $pv2val$ and then $lv2val$ are considered as fixed elements.

3.2 Main Concepts

- **Physical Object Versions:** A *Physical Version of an object o* is a pair ***(pvid,val)***: $pvid \in \mathcal{V}er$ is the identifier, val the value. It is associated with o in at least one DBV: $(\exists d \in \mathcal{D}, pvid = lv2pv(o,d)) \wedge (val = pv2val\,(pvid))$
- **Logical Object Version:**A *Logical Version of object o* is a pair $((o,d),pv)$: $(o,d) \in \mathcal{L}$ is the identifier, and pv, identified by $lv2pv((o,d))$ is the associated physical version.
- **Multiversion Object:** A *Multiversion Object* is a pair: $o = (\boldsymbol{oid}, \boldsymbol{Cont})$:
  - oid is the object identifier of o: $oid \in \mathcal{O}$
  - $Cont = \{((oid,d),p)/d \in \mathcal{D}, p = (lv2pv(oid,d), lv2val\,(oid,d))\}$ is the *content* of o: its set of logical versions.
- **Database Version:** A *Database Version* is a pair: $d = (\boldsymbol{dbvid}, \boldsymbol{Cont})$ where:
  - $dbvid$ is the identifier of d: $dbvid \in \mathcal{D}$
  - $Cont = \{((o,dbvid),p)/o \in \mathcal{O}, p = (lv2pv(o,dbvid), lv2val\,(o,dbvid))\}$ is the *content* of d: its set of logical versions.
- **Multiversion Database:** A Multiversion Database is an instance of $\mathcal{M}$. It is represented by the sextuple: $m = \{\mathcal{O}_m, \mathcal{D}_m, \mathcal{V}er_m, \mathcal{V}al_m, lv2pv_m, pv2val_{\,m}\}$ s.t. $\mathcal{O}_m \subset \mathcal{O}$, $\mathcal{D}_m \subset \mathcal{D}$, $\mathcal{V}er_m \subset \mathcal{V}er$, $\mathcal{V}al_m \subset \mathcal{V}al$, and s.t. $lv2pv_m$ (resp. $pv2val$) is the restriction of $lv2pv$ to $O_m \times D_m$ (resp. of $pv2val$ to $\mathcal{V}er_m$). The state $m[t]$, at time t, of a multiversion database is defined by the state of its components: $m[t] = \{\mathcal{O}_m[t], \mathcal{D}_m[t], \mathcal{V}er_m[t], \mathcal{V}al_m[t], lv2pv_m[t], pv2val_{\,m}[t]\}$

Below, in unambiguous cases, a concept and its identifier may be confused.

4 Basic Functionalities

As function $lv2val$ allows reading a logical object version, only basic writing operations are defined in this section. Only modified parameters are considered. P(X) denotes the set of all the subsets of X, m and m' denotes $m[t]$ and $m[t']$.

Creation of a Multiversion Object: *creobj*

When a multiversion object is created, a physical version with $\perp$ value is created by the system and associated with every existing database version.

$$\begin{aligned} \boldsymbol{creobj} : &\rightarrow \mathrm{P}(\mathcal{O}) \times P(\mathcal{V}er) \times \mathcal{F}_{lv2pv} \\ &\mapsto (\mathcal{O}_{m'}, \mathcal{V}er_{m'}, lv2pv_{m'}, pv2val_{\,m'}), \end{aligned}$$

such that $\mathcal{O}_{m'} = \mathcal{O}_m \cup \{o\}$ and $\mathcal{V}er_{m'} = \mathcal{V}er_m \cup \{pv\}$ and $pv2val_{\,m'}(pv) = \perp$ and $lv2pv_{m'}(o, \mathcal{D}_{m'}) = pv$, i.e. $\forall d \in \mathcal{D}_{m'}, lv2pv_{m'}(o,d) = pv$

Updating a Logical Object Version: *upd_value* and *upd_assoc*

A logical object version may be updated in two different ways:
[1] affectation of a new physical version containing a new user-defined value.

$$\begin{aligned} \boldsymbol{upd\_value} : \mathcal{O}_m \times \mathcal{D}_m \times \mathcal{V}al &\rightarrow \mathrm{P}(\mathcal{V}er) \times \mathcal{F}_{lv2pv} \times \mathcal{F}_{pv2val} \\ (o,\ d,\ val) &\mapsto (\mathcal{V}er_{m'},\ lv2pv_{m'},\ pv2val_{\,m'}), \end{aligned}$$

such that $Ver_{m'} = Ver_m \cup \{pv\}$ and $lv2pv_{m'}(o,d) = pv$ and $pv2val_{\,m'}(pv) = val$

[2] by associating it with a physical version already associated with another logical version of the same object (in another DBV).

$$\begin{array}{llll} \textit{upd\_assoc} : & \mathcal{O}_m \times \mathcal{D}_m \times \mathcal{D}_m & \rightarrow & \mathcal{F}_{lv2pv} \\ & (o,\ d,\ d') & \mapsto & lv2pv_{m'} \text{ such that } lv2pv_{m'}(o,d) = lv2pv_m(o,d) \end{array}$$

Derivation of a DBV: ***derive***

After d' has been derived from d, they share physical versions for all objects:

$$\begin{array}{lll} \textit{derive} : \mathcal{D}_m & \rightarrow & \mathsf{P}(\mathcal{D}) \times \mathcal{F}_{lv2pv} \\ \qquad d & \mapsto & (\mathcal{D}_{m'}, lv2pv_{m'}) \end{array}$$

such that $\mathcal{D}_{m'} = \mathcal{D}_m \cup \{d'\}$ and $lv2pv_{m'}(\mathcal{O}_{m'}, d') = lv2pv_m(\mathcal{O}_m, d')$

Deletion of a Logical Object Version: ***del_lv***

The deletion of a logical object version is its updating with $\perp$ value. If no logical object version shares $lv2val_{\,m}(o,d)$, it has to be removed from $\mathcal{V}er_m$.

$$\begin{array}{llll} \textit{del\_lv} : & \mathcal{O}_m \times \mathcal{D}_m & \rightarrow & \mathsf{P}\,(\mathcal{V}er) \times \mathcal{F}_{lv2pv} \\ & (o,\ d) & \mapsto & (\mathcal{V}er_{m'}, lv2pv_{m'}, pv2val_{\,m'}), \end{array}$$

$$\begin{array}{ll} \text{such that} & \mathcal{V}er_{m'} = \Big(\mathcal{V}er_m \cup \{pv\}\Big) \setminus \Big(\{lv2pv_m(o,d)\} \setminus lv2pv_m(o,\mathcal{D}_m)\Big) \\ \text{and} & lv2pv_{m'}(o,d) = pv \text{ and } pv2val_{\,m'}(pv) = \perp \end{array}$$

Deletion of a Multiversion Object: ***del_mo***

Deletion of a multiversion object deletes its identifier and all its versions.

$$\begin{array}{lll} \textit{del\_mo} : \mathcal{O}_m & \rightarrow & \mathsf{P}(\mathcal{O}) \times \mathsf{P}(\mathcal{V}er) \\ \qquad o & \mapsto & (\mathcal{O}_{m'}, \mathcal{V}er_{m'}), \end{array}$$

such that $\mathcal{O}_{m'} = \mathcal{O}_m \setminus \{o\}$ and $\mathcal{V}er_{m'} = \mathcal{V}er_m \setminus lv2pv_m(o,\mathcal{D}_m)$

Deletion of a DBV: ***del_dbv***

Deletion of a database version deletes its identifier and all its versions. Physical versions not shared with logical object versions of other DBV are removed.

$$\begin{array}{lll} \textit{del\_dbv} : \mathcal{D}_m & \rightarrow & \mathsf{P}(\mathcal{D}) \times \mathsf{P}(\mathcal{V}er) \\ \qquad d & \mapsto & (\mathcal{D}_{m'}, \mathcal{V}er_{m'}), \end{array}$$

s.t. $\mathcal{D}_{m'} = \mathcal{D}_m \setminus \{d\}, \mathcal{V}er_{m'} = \mathcal{V}er_m \setminus \Big(\{lv2pv_m(\mathcal{O}_m, d)\} \setminus lv2pv_m\big(\mathcal{O}_m, \mathcal{D}_m \setminus \{d\}\big)\Big)$

5 Reading and Comparing Complex Object Versions

In data model using identification of objects and complex objects, identity, shallow-value and deep-value [KC86] are used to compare and to copy objects:
- *o1 = (oid1, val1)* and *o2 = (oid2, val2)* are *identical* iff *oid1 = oid2*,
- *o1* and *o2* are *shallow-equal* iff *val1 = val2*,
- *o1* and *o2* are *deep-equal* iff their respective deep values are equal. Deep-value is obtained by recursively replacing references to sub-objects by their value.
Following, for monoversion objects: *identity* $\Rightarrow$ *shallow equality* $\Rightarrow$ *deep-equality*. Shallow-equality is a strong-equality: two shallow-equal objects share their composition graph, except the root. Deep-equality is a weak-equality: it takes only

the structure of the composition graph and the values of its leaves into account.

Multiversion Object	Associated value in d1	Associated value in d2
O1	(O2,3,O3)	(O2,3,O3)
O2	(O4,O5)	(O4,2)
O3	5	3
O4	1	(1,5)
O5	3	⊥

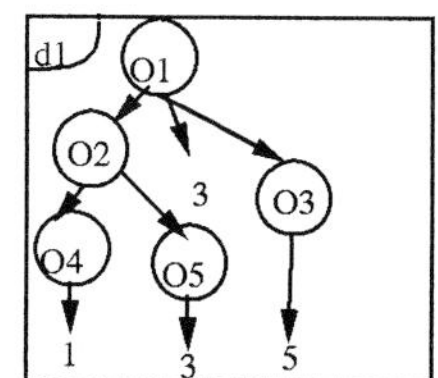

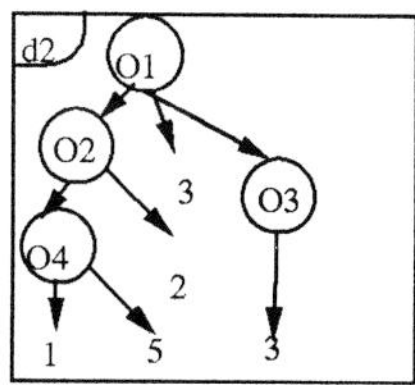

Fig. 3. Composition graphs of logical object versions *(o1,d1)* and *(o1,d2)*

Comparison of versions of complex objects in DBV approach is more complicated. Indeed, the value of a logical version (o, d) may contain reference to object o', which determines its logical version (o', d). Figure 3, presents the composition graphs of logical versions of complex object *o1* belonging to DBV *d1* and *d2*. The table shows the value of the logical version of each component object in *d1* and *d2*. To compare (o, d) and (o', d'), $d \neq d'$, new concepts must be introduced. Indeed, as shown on Figure 3, since a sub-object o_i may have different values in two different DBV, shallow-equality does not imply deep-equality *((o1,d1)* is not deep-equal to *(o1,d2))*. As shown on Figure 4 identifiers of component objects are only considered for strong-values, and they disappear for weak-values which only preserve structure. Thus, strong and weak-values, and shallow and deep-values are considered independently. Four functions define values of logical object versions: $lv2val\_d_{+}(o, d)$ strong-deep-value, $lv2val\_d(o, d)$ weak-deep-value, $lv2val\_s_{+}(o, d)$ strong-shallow-value and $lv2val\_s(o, d)$ weak-shallow-value. Four types of equality between $l = (o,d)$ and $l' = (o',d')$ may be deduced:
- *l* and *l'* are *weakly shallow equal*, denoted $l =_s l'$ if: $lv2val\_s(l) = lv2val\_s(l')$
- *l* and *l'* are *strongly shallow equal*, denoted $l =_{s+} l'$ if: $lv2val\_s_{+}(l) = lv2val\_s_{+}(l')$
- *l* and *l'* are *weakly deep equal*, denoted $l =_d l'$ if: $lv2val\_d(l) = lv2val\_d(l')$
- *l* and *l'* are *strongly deep equal*, denoted $l =_{d+} l'$ if: $lv2val\_d_{+}(l) = lv2val\_d_{+}(l')$

Following: $(l = l') \Rightarrow (l =_{d+} l') \Rightarrow (l =_d l')$ and $(l =_{d+} l') \Rightarrow (l =_{s+} l') \Rightarrow (l =_s l')$

Figure 4 shows the six different cases of comparison of *(o1,d1)* and *(o'1,d2)*.

6 Conclusion

In this paper, a formal model of the DBV approach has been presented. It is based on the orthogonality version/data model and on the possibility to manage versions of entities as well as contexts offered by this approach. It allows a better understanding of multiversion databases and of the potential of DBVs and shows how to extend database systems to implement this potential. Definition of basic operations as functions gives a framework, a fundamental language, for these extensions. These concern different parts of the DBMS: [1] Extensions of the object manager operate on logical versions and on DBV: comparison or merging of two DBV, simultaneous updatings of an object in a set of DBV, and so on. [2] In [CJK91] it was shown that the DBV approach could be extended to maintain consistency between versions of schema and versions of objects. Other works are

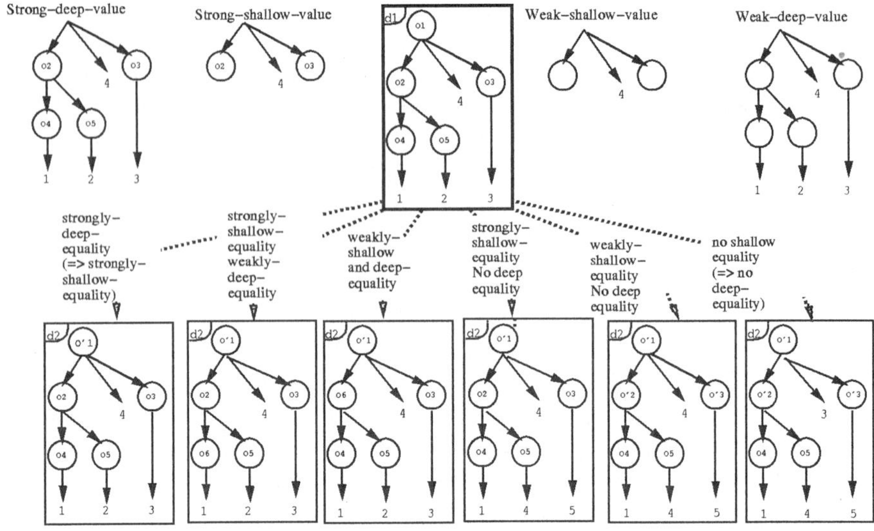

Fig. 4. Values of *(o1,d1)* - Comparison of *(o1, d1)* and *(o'1, d2)*

in progress to extend integrity constraints to multiversions databases (internal to a DBV or across DBV) [BMCJ93]. [3] Manipulation language must be extended as well as the user interface to allow users to browse the multiversion DB, taking the dimension added by versioning into account. [4] Work is also in progress to study the interest of DBV in the management of configurations in CASE [BCJ92], and on spatio-temporal evolution of data in Geographic Information Systems [BMJ93].

A prototype, implemented by the research group of Professor W. Cellary [CKW90] in Poznań (Poland), validates the DBV approach. A second one, implemented above O_2 at Lamsade Lab., simulates the management of versions, offers a graphical interface and is used to implement new DBV functionalities.

Acknowledgements : The authors are grateful to Claudia Bauzer-Medeiros, Marie-Jo Bellosta, Wojciech Cellary and Anne Doucet for helpful comments.

References

[AF92] P. G. Anick and R. A. Flynn. Versionning a full-text information retrieval system. *Proc. 15th SIGIR*, pp. 98–111, Copenhagen, Denmark, June 92.

[AN91] R. Ahmed and S. B. Navathe. Version management of composite objects in CAD databases. *Proc. SIGMOD*, pp. 218–227, Denver, Colorado, June 91.

[Atw86] T.M. Atwood. An object-oriented DBMS for design support applications. In *Proc. COMPINT*, pages 299–307, Montréal, September 1986.

[BCJ92] M.J. Blin, W. Cellary, and G. Jomier. A model of configurations for hardware/software system deliveries. *Proc. 5th Int. Conf, on Software Engineering and its Applications*, pp 338–347, Toulouse, France, December 1992.

[BH91] A. Björnerstedt and C. Hultén. Version control in an Object-Oriented architecture. *OO Concepts, Databases, and Applications*, chap. 18. ACM 91.

[Bla91] H. Blanken. Implementing version support for complex objects. *Data and Knowledge Engineering*, 6:1–25, 1991.

[BMCJ93] C.M. Bauzer-Medeiros, W. Cellary, and G. Jomier. Maintaining integrity constraints across versions in a database. In *Proc. 8th Brazilian Database Conference*, pages 83–97, Campina Grande, 1993.

[BMJ93] C.M. Bauzer-Medeiros and G. Jomier. Managing alternatives and data evolution in GIS. *Proc. ACM Workshop on Advances in GIS*, Arlington 93.

[CJ90] W. Cellary and G. Jomier. Consistency of versions in object-oriented databases. In *Proc. 16th VLDB*, Brisbane (Australia), 1990.

[CJK91] W. Cellary, G. Jomier, and T. Koszlajda. Formal model of an object-oriented database with versioned objects and schema. *Proc. DEXA 91.*

[CKW90] W. Cellary, T. Koszlajda, and W. Wieczerzycki. Database version manager: Prototype. Technical report, Technical University of Poznań, July 1990.

[Fau92] M. C. Fauvet. Versions and histories in object-oriented applications. *Proc. 7th International Symp. on Databases*, Porto-Allegre (Brasil), May 1992.

[KA91] J. Kimball and L. Aaron. Epochs, configuration schema, and version cursors in the KBSA framework CCM model. In *Proceedings of the Third International Workshop on Software Configuration Management*, pp 33–42, 1991.

[Kat90] R. H. Katz. Toward a unified framework for version modeling in engineering databases. *ACM Computing Surveys*, 22(4):375–408, December 1990.

[KC86] S. N. Khoshafian and G. P. Copeland. Object identity. In *Proc. OOPSLA*, pages 406–416, September 1986.

[KRW92] M. H. Kay, P. J. Rivett, and T. J. Walters. The Raleigh activity model : Integrating versions, concurrency, and access control. *Proc. BNCOD*, 92.

[KS92] W. Käfer and H. Schöning. Mapping a version model to a complex-object data model. In *Proc. Data Engineering*, Tempe (Arizona), 1992.

[LC84] D.B. Leblang and P.C. Chase. Computer-aided software engineering in a distributed workstation environment. *Proc. ACM Symposium on Practical Software Development Environments*, pp. 104–112, Pittsburgh 1984.

[LF91] E. Lippe and G. Florijn. Implementation techniques for integral version management. In *Proc. ECOOP*, Genève, July 1991.

[Log90] SYSECA Logiciel. SPMS+ : Manuel utilisateur. Saint-Cloud, France, 90.

[MSK89] D. B. Miller, R. G. Stockton, and C. W. Krueger. An inverted approach to configuration management. In *Proc. of the Third International Workshop on Software Configuration Management*, pp. 1–4, October 1989.

[Rei89] C. Reichenberger. Orthogonal version management. *Proc. of the Third Int'l Workshop on Software Configuration Management*, pp. 137–140, 1989.

[Roc75] M.J. Rochkind. The Source Code Control System. *IEEE, Transaction on Software Engineering*, 1(4):364–370, December 1975.

[SG91] S. Simmel and I. Godard. The kala basket : A semantic primitive unifying object transactions, access control, versions and configurations. *OOPSLA '91*

[Tic82] W.F. Tichy. Design, implementation and evaluation of a Revision Control System. *Proc. Int'l Conference on Software Engineering*,1982.

[TOC93] G. Talens, C. Oussalah, and M.F. Colinas. Versions of simple and composite objects. In *Proc. 19th VLDB*, Dublin, 1993.

Tracking the Evolution of Concepts in Dynamic Worlds

Udo Hahn & Manfred Klenner

Albert-Ludwigs-Universität Freiburg
CLIF Linguistische Informatik / Computerlinguistik
Werthmannplatz
D-79085 Freiburg i. Brsg., Germany
e-mail: {hahn, klenner}@coling.uni-freiburg.de

Abstract. Technical domains are affected by continuous change as a reflection of technological progress. Correspondingly, concept descriptions of terminological knowledge bases for such domains must be adjusted to these dynamics. In this paper we propose a concept versioning methodology which accounts for the evolutionary adaptation of already established concepts according to the gradual shaping of new standards. The approach is based on the provision of a qualitative progress model for the given domain, measures for the prediction and evaluation of the significance of progress, and a representation and update scheme for concept version management.

1 Introduction

Technical domains, such as information, hi-fi, or automobile technology, share a common feature, namely that their underlying concept systems undergo continuous change. These dynamics are exhibited either by the substantial augmentation of concept systems in terms of *concept innovations* (mirroring the introduction of new products, technologies, etc.) or by the evolutionary adaptation of already established concepts according to the gradual shaping of new standards that evidence continuous technological progress in the field. This latter type of change is illustrated, e.g., by growing main memory capacities for personal computers (with ranges from 64 to 256 KB in the early 80's to today's 1 to 4 MB of internal storage). The learning problem with respect to these time-varying concepts is usually referred to as *concept change* ([1], [2]) or *concept drift* ([3], [4]).

Why bother at all about concept drift phenomena? The problem becomes acute for the long-term engineering of non-toy knowledge bases covering rapidly changing domains. Usually, technical standards are frozen in terms of static value restrictions or integrity constraints in order to assure valid reasoning, e.g., as a basis for up-to-date recommendations (what's good?) and evaluations (what's dated or overpriced?). However, when technical standards continuously evolve in the lifetime of a knowledge base these dynamics must be directly incorporated at the knowledge representation level in order to preserve its inferential adequacy. As an alternative to manual updates of integrity constraints by some human knowledge engineer we propose an automatic procedure for dealing with these concept drift phenomena. It produces a generational stratification of the underlying level of generic concepts in terms of *concept versions* -- each stage of technical development is represented in terms of a version-specific constraint expression which defines a particular "standard" holding at that stage of development; single instances are then related to their associated concept version.

The version tracker introduced in this paper forms part of the concept learning component of a natural language text understanding system that processes product announcements and reviews from various information technology magazines. Given this application context we may factor out the following general requirements for an appropriate concept versioning methodology:

- Texts from information technology magazines usually contain *only positive examples* of the (goal) concept to be learned. This precludes a learning strategy which is exclusively based on a similarity-based approach, since the continuous *generalization* of a goal concept is not sufficient. As concept drift phenomena affect the entire value range of attributes -- new permitted values must be added, while obsolete ones have to be removed (e.g., consider the drift from 64-256 KB to 1-4 MB of internal storage for PCs) -- facilities for *discrimination learning* must supplement generalization-driven procedures in order to generate different, non-overlapping value ranges for each concept version. This requirement contrasts with previous work (e.g., [3], [4]), where preclassified positive and negative examples are available for the determination of concept drift.
- Due to on-line processing requirements (texts are continuously fed into the system as they become available), we are committed to an *incremental learning* mode. Thus, versioning decisions in our approach are tentative, since they always rely upon *incomplete* data sets. The capability of performing *revisions* of once-established version boundaries thus constitutes an integral part of our concept drift model. This contrasts with the assumptions underlying the experiments in [5] and [6], where the complete training sets are given once and for all and learning proceeds under closed data sets.
- In accordance with previous approaches, we maintain the most recent concept description which specifies the currently valid standards in the domain. Additionally, we need to *preserve the developmental stages* of a concept in order to prevent prior and obsolete instances from being abandoned in the course of concept drifts. As a consequence, we require that concept versioning must not affect the concept class of an instance as a whole, but that a history-preserving, generational stratification has to be imposed on it, yielding a tri-partite description in terms of a common generic concept, its partition into several concept versions, each covering a set of associated instances. This contrasts with work as described in [7], where destructive updates are performed, thus overwriting prior information, as well as in [1] and [2], where only the most recent concept description is maintained.

Based on these considerations our concept drift model requires positive examples, allows incremental processing and adaptive revisions of once-established versions, while it preserves exhaustive classification of instances under the covering generic concept.

2 Concept Versioning: an Overview

As the most recent texts are entered into the natural language processor, evolutionary changes in a dynamic concept system are signalled when the text parser [8] tries to assign values to some attribute of an instance that are inconsistent with the value range constraints set up by the concept intended to classify that instance. Consider Fig. 1 which depicts numerical value restrictions for the attributes weight and hard disk size of the concept notebook_1 (the "worst" and "best" values allowed are enclosed in square brackets). Although the parser has strong linguistic evidences to consider LTE lite/25 as a special kind of notebook, the assignment of 5 lbs. to the weight attribute contradicts the associated value restriction of the notebook_1 concept.

The system may react either by adapting the description of the already given concept class (generalizing the violated conditions), or by creating a new, versioned concept class (with appropriately updated constraints) as a successor to the currently valid one. But care must be taken to balance both alternatives. Generalization, on the one hand, must be constrained so as not to produce timeless concepts, in order to assure that no overgeneralized concepts be created. Versioning, on the other hand, must be constrained so as not to apply too many times, in too short intervals, since otherwise a large amount of only slightly differing concept versions would result, with representation structures suffering to discriminate between really significant developmental steps.

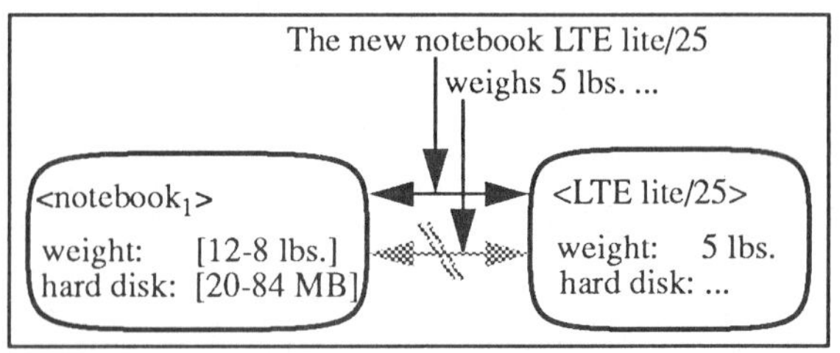

Figure 1. A new instance occurring with inconsistent attribute values relative to the value range constraints set up by the classifying concept

In order to cope with these requirements three major constructs will be introduced in this paper: a predictive *progress model* of the domain, which specifies in qualitative terms the foreseeable developmental directions of change in the underlying domain, an empirical *progress measure* which is sensitive to the actual development of attribute values, and a *significance criterion* which actuates the aforementioned balance between generalization and versioning. As long as the significance criterion is not fulfilled only generalization is allowed to occur. This process leads to the successive refinement of the diagnostic data indicative of the domain's continuing progress. Once the significance criterion is satisfied by a new instance, a versioning process is triggered and the results of quantitative developmental analysis are used to estimate a significance threshold for the new concept version, thus starting the diagnostic cycle again.

3 Knowledge Representation Background of Concept Versioning

We assume the underlying terminological layer of the knowledge base to consist of frame representations for concept definitions. These concepts fall into three main categories: *generic concepts* carry the description of an entire concept class (e.g., notebook, printer, operating system), *concept versions* represent different generations of such a single concept class in terms of technical standards holding at a certain stage of development (i.e., the result of the methodology described in this paper), and *instances* characterize the outer fringe of the concept hierarchy in terms of concrete subclasses (in our domain, products such as LTE lite/25, Unix) classified by generic concept classes. (Note that the level of instances in this intensional reading is strictly distinguished from the extensional level of *individuals* as direct representations of countable, uniquely identifiable entities in the domain.) Each concept description of an instance (cf. Fig. 2) consists of a distinguished name and a list of associated attributes, to each of which so-called *attribute facets* are attached, which are particularly relevant for the versioning procedure. We distinguish between an attribute's *value*, indicating the actual value for that attribute, and its *g-space*, describing the most specific generalization space which is spanned by a bottom and a top value; *g-space* is successively built from the first up to the most recent one (relative to a quality ranking discussed below) and locally maintained by each instance. Finally, the attribute facet *diff-vals* specifies the number of different values encountered so far for that attribute with respect to the current version.

Structure of an Instance		Sample Instance
<name>		*<LTE lite/25>*
attributes$_i$:		*clock frequency*:
value$_i$:	InstVal$_i$	value: *25 MHz*
g-space$_i$:	[Bottom$_i$-Top$_i$]	g-space: *[20-25]*
diff-vals$_i$:	DiffVals$_i$	diff-vals: *3*
facets	*values*	

Figure 2. Concept description of instances

As far as the family of frame-style, classification-based concept languages [9] is concerned, the subsumption relation establishes a specialization hierarchy which relates concept classes among each other and to their associated instances, but usually no relation holds among the instances of the same generic concept. As it turns out to become crucial for efficient version management to locate the proper position of any incoming instance relative to the previously analyzed ones (cf. section 8 for an in-depth discussion of these update mechanisms), we define a complementary partial ordering among these instances. It is based on a measure that scores each instance's quality (see Def.-1) and thus establishes a predecessor-successor ordering among all those instances which are classified by the same generic concept, according to their fitting into the global quality scale.

Let *inst** denote the new, currently analyzed instance and *att* be one of its relevant attributes (relevance information (see section 4) is accessible via its classifying generic concept, *genc*, using the function *RelAtts*). Let *Val(inst*, att)* be an access function returning the value for attribute *att* of instance *inst**. We then define a simple quality metric that expresses the distance of *inst** to the unique *root* instance whose attribute values are taken to be the least favorable ones for the corresponding generic concept (*root* has to be carefully determined by a human knowledge engineer on the basis of empirical data; it can be considered a kind of bottom-line instance all whose values are unlikely to be undercut by yet another instance, thus serving as a reference point from which improvements can be reasonably assessed):

Global_Quality(inst)* :=

$$\sum_{att \in RelAtts(genc)} \frac{|Val(inst^*, att) - Val(root, att)|}{Val(root, att)}$$

This measure is global in scope, since the more distant an instance is from *root* the "better" it is on a qualitative scale.

Definition-1. Global quality measure

4 Progress Model

The progress model - similar to a domain theory in EBL approaches [10] - captures in qualitative terms the regularities of foreseeable developments in a technical domain. It is currently restricted to scalar quantitative attribute dimensions and estimates, if possible, innovation directions for technical features. The human domain expert in charge of its acquisition must specify two Boolean variables, viz. whether an attribute of a generic concept is *relevant* for versioning or not and whether future attribute values will *increase* or *decrease* compared with its current top value (cf. Fig. 3). The consideration of relevance accounts for the obvious fact that various conceptual attributes differ in their potential to contribute to versioning processes (e.g., the speed of a processor is a relevant attribute, while its size is not relevant). In order to ease the knowledge acquisi-

scope:	*computer* (also for all subclasses, e.g., *portable*)		
predictions:	(1) *clock frequency*:	increasing	[relevant]
	(2) *main memory size*:	increasing	[relevant]
	(3) *weight*:	nil	[irrelevant]

Figure 3. Fragment of the progress model

tion process the predictions of the progress model are each associated with the most general concept to which they apply. Their scope is thus determined by the classifier mechanisms underlying terminological reasoning [9]: each statement related to some concept class also holds for its subclasses unless its constraints are overwritten by more specialized ones. This is the case, e.g., for portable, a subclass of computer, where the inherited entry for weight is modified (*decreasing* replaces *nil*).

5 Measuring Progress: the Mean Developmental Step

Two types of knowledge, predictive and empirical, come into play when progress actually occurs in a technical domain. The first one relates to the domain's progress model which captures in qualitative terms the main direction of changes to come. Knowledge relating to the actual dynamics of change is only available from empirical data continuously flowing into the system. The determination of real progress in our approach then consists of combining the predictive qualitative estimates as expressed in the progress model with the actual development as indicated by empirical data in terms of quantitative attribute values.

First, consider Def.-2 for the abstraction from increasing or decreasing change modes of attribute values.

Let *att* denote an attribute shared by two concept descriptions, *con1* and *con2*. Let *genc* be the generic concept that classifies both, *con1* and *con2*. The relation ***exceeds*** ($>_{ex}$) is then defined by:

$$Val(con1, att) >_{ex} Val(con2, att) :\Leftrightarrow$$

$$\begin{cases} Val(con1, att) > Val(con2, att), \text{ if } incr(genc, att) \\ Val(con1, att) < Val(con2, att), \text{ if } decr(genc, att) \end{cases}$$

The predicate *incr* (*decr*) is true iff the progress model contains an entry for *att* in *genc* such that it predicts "increasing" ("decreasing") values for future instances; otherwise it is false.

Definition-2. Ordering of values in terms of the *exceeds* relation

Given predictive knowledge about the developmental direction of an attribute's value domain in the progress model and given two concrete attribute values, the exceeding one represents an explicit technical developmental step compared with the exceeded one. We may rephrase this simple observation in more general terms as follows. Let the values for some attribute of instances, all classified by the same concept (version), be ordered according to the *exceeds* relation. (In particular, this ordering yields the *top value*, exceeding all other values of this set, and the *bottom value* which is exceeded by all others; cf. the *g-space* facet in Fig. 2.) We may now call any difference between two successive values in that value list a single developmental step. The *mean developmental step* of a value collection can then be determined as stated in Def.-3. The computation of the mean developmental step yields a factor which, on the one hand, describes the observable behavior of a distribution of attribute values (its mean growth rate). On the other hand, it can also be used to predict future value developments by way of heuristic projection, as will be discussed in the next section.

MeanDevStep(inst, att) :=

$$\begin{cases} \dfrac{|Top\,(inst,\,att) - Bottom\,(inst,\,att)|}{DiVa\,(inst,\,att) - 1} & \text{if } DiVa(inst,\,att) > 1 \\ \text{undefined} & \text{else} \end{cases}$$

The function *DiVa* yields the number of different values for an attribute *att* maintained under the *diff-vals* facet by the selected instance *inst*, while *Top* and *Bottom*, respectively, access the top and bottom values specified in the attribute's *g-space* facet.

Definition-3. Mean developmental step

6 Predicting Progress: the Predicted Top Value

The processing of any new instance causes the mean developmental step, the model's major construct for the prediction of progress, to be updated subsequently. This update even takes into consideration the values of the version-triggering instance (that particular instance whose values fulfil the significance criterion (cf. Def.-5), thus causing a versioning process actually to be started). That decision is crucial for the quality of predictions, since taking into account new trends as derivable from the most recent top instances improves the predictions to be made for the next version generation. Additionally, as a projection heuristic, we incorporate the number of developmental steps of the current version into the estimate of the minimal upper bound for any new version, hence the slightly modified expression for the mean developmental step in Def.-4. The underlying assumption is that new versions with non-linear growth rates should differ from previous ones through proportionally lower/higher value ranges, while the number of developmental steps should be approximately the same for each version (a strong first-shot assumption, that may, nevertheless, be overridden by subsequent computations to account for unexpected or biased growth rates).

Let *inst* be an immediate predecessor (according to the quality metric as defined in Def.-1) of *inst**, a version-triggering instance. The function *Best* yields the most favorable of two values w.r.t. the *exceeds* relation; we may then determine *BestVal* := *Best(Val(inst*, att), Top(inst, att))*. The computation of the *predicted top value, PTV,* w.r.t. some (increasing) attribute *att* for a newly formed concept version, *succV,* is based on the following criterion:

***PTV**(succV, att)* :=

$$Top(\,inst,\,att) + \frac{|BestVal - Bottom\,(inst,\,att)|}{DiVa\,(inst,\,att)}\,(DiVa\,(inst,\,att) - 1)$$

Definition-4. Predicted top value (PTV)

The basic construct for guiding the predictions of any value development is the *predicted top value, PTV* (see Def.-4), whose definition reflects the considerations from above. A *PTV* is maintained for every relevant attribute of some concept underlying the versioning mechanism; it fixes a minimum value expansion that must be reached by (at least) one instance before versioning is allowed to occur. Unless this condition is fulfilled for every relevant attribute of the concept version, or if a value for a relevant attribute of a new instance is below the *PTV*, only generalization may occur.

At the very beginning of the learning cycle (i.e., for the initial knowledge base), *PTVs* are usually set equal to the top values of the available concept class description; later on they are managed by the version tracker, once a versioning process has occurred.

7 Evaluating Progress: the Significance Criterion

In the previous two sections we have specified the major building blocks for evaluating real progress in a dynamic domain. They can now be assembled in terms of a significance criterion on the basis of which version-triggering instances will be recognized.

> In order to determine the version significance of any new instance, *inst**, one must assess the deviation between the predicted top values of the currently valid concept version, *currV*, and *inst** for any attribute value of *inst** exceeding the corresponding *PTV*. Relating each relevant attributes' deviation with the mean developmental steps holding for *currV* and summing up the values for these ratios gives a useful measure for the significance of the violations. Let (according to the quality metric) *inst* be the predecessor of *inst**, *currV* be the concept version classifying *inst*, and *genc* be the generic concept classifying *currV*. The function *PredTopVal* accesses the value of *PTV* of version *currV* for its attribute *att*.
>
> **IF** $\forall att \in RelAtts(genc)$:
> $Val(inst^*, att) \geq_{ex} PredTopVal(currV, att)$
>
> **THEN** ***Significance** (inst*)* :=
>
> $$\sum_{att \in RelAtts(genc)} \frac{|PredTopVal(currV, att) - Val(inst^*, att)|}{MeanDevStep(inst, att)}$$
>
> **ELSE** ***Significance** (inst*)* := 0

Definition-5. Version significance

Since the estimates of the value ranges of any new version rely upon few data items only, the concept system faces the danger of possible *"version oscillation"*, i.e., it may be affected by instances that only "slightly" violate the newly established *PTV*, but nevertheless continuously trigger new versioning processes. We thus specify the significance criterion as a kind of delay mechanism. It requires that the values of a version-triggering instance, *inst**, must exceed the *PTVs* of the most recent version for <u>all</u> relevant attributes, on average, by the mean developmental step. This is implied by the additional requirement that a violation of relevant attributes is *version-significant* iff $Significance(inst^*) \geq |\ RelAtts(genc)\ |$ (cf. Def.-5). One might also conceive less rigid criteria for larger numbers of relevant attributes, e.g., subsets of relevant attributes whose values float into the same direction. Anyhow, this criterion yields an adaptive threshold, since the values of the mean developmental steps will be successively refined as new instances become available.

8 Managing Progress

It is crucial for our approach that the most recent version needs <u>not necessarily</u> classify the currently considered instance. If the most recent version turns out to be inadequate other versions are tried for that instance, moving backwards in the direction of the predecessors of the currently considered version. The classification of instances is based solely on the fulfillment of criteria specified by the integrity constraints of the versions. Therefore, our learning and classification scheme is not a temporal, but predominantly a *qualitative* one (usually, but not always, top scores in the attribute dimension and temporal recency nevertheless coincide). In order to guarantee proper, i.e., almost non-overlapping value partitions based on the quality of instances, the following constraints have been set up:

- For the most recent version, generalization of relevant attributes is allowed only if the deviations are in conformity with the predicted direction of progress in the domain (i.e., only "exceeding" values are allowed);
- For the remaining versions, generalization of relevant attributes is not allowed at all.

As a consequence, when two or more relevant attributes have to be considered for versioning and the violating values of a new instance refer to at least two relevant attributes of at least two different versions, so-called *transition instances* are formed and grouped under their generic concept without further relating them to any concept version. In general, these restrictions were chosen to avoid large overlapping value ranges resulting from an exclusively temporal classification and learning criterion (however, minor overlaps may result from the versioning process, cf. section 9).

The instances sorted back to a prior version directly influence the values for the mean developmental steps of that version's attributes (the value of *diff-vals* increases). Consequently, the value for the mean developmental step decreases (see Def.-3) while the significance value increases accordingly (see Def.-5). This way, formerly version-insignificant instances might then become version-significant (cf. [11] for an illustration of such a propagation effect). Therefore, we need mechanisms for the re-evaluation of instances. Two questions then arise: Which instances need to be re-evaluated and what is the correct evaluation space? At this point, the benefits of the ordering of instances according to global quality become evident. The proper location of an instance in the global quality ranking simultaneously discloses its corresponding set of predecessor and successor instances on the quality scale. Thus, the correct generalization space for evaluating any new instance is accessible via that instance's immediate predecessor, considering its *g-space* facet (it contains the generalization space successively built from all predecessor instances). At the same time, the instances yet to be re-evaluated are supplied by all the successor instances. If a newly integrated instance itself is not version-significant then only one of its successor instances may possibly become version-significant, but none of its predecessors (the successor instances are, by definition (see Def.-1), of a "better" quality, which is a prerequisite to be of "higher" version significance).

9 Experimental Results

We tested the version tracker on training sets for personal computers, portables, printers, hard disks and monitors (altogether about 600 instances). The test sets were taken from information technology magazines covering the time period from 1987 to 1993. The instances were entered into the system in chronological order by year, while an arbitrary (we chose an alphabetical) ordering was effective for each annual set. The chronological ordering by year (or any other comparable large-scale ordering) is justified by the on-line character of the system and its incremental learning mode.

We here concentrate on the sample set for portables comprising 141 instances. Table 1 shows the resulting concept versions w.r.t. the set's relevant attributes. The versioning system generated 3 versions, classified 124 instances properly and encountered 17 transition instances. Trying to escape from subjective face validity judgments, we performed a preliminary statistical evaluation of the concept drift model. The discriminance analysis we chose from the SPSS package measures the fit of instances classified by concept versions. The difference between both approaches lies in the fact that the version tracker determines version boundaries incrementally, with the classifier actually relating instances to concept versions, while discriminance analysis computes the validity of some *a priori* assignment of instances to concept versions and thus judges the discriminative power of the assignment decisions. The overlap of the membership assignments between the version tracker (VT) and discriminance analysis (DA) is stated in the bottom line of Table 1. These data indicate that reasonable version boundaries were determined by the incremental procedure underlying our concept drift model.

	version 1	version 2	version 3	generic concept
clock frequency main memory size	[4.7 - 10] [128 - 768]	[10 - 20] [640 - 2048]	[20 - 33] [2048 - 8000]	[4.7 - 33] [128 - 8000]
covered instances	34	76	14	124
overlap (VT vs. DA)	100 %	89.4 %	95.9 %	-

Table 1. Final partitions for portable and results of the statistical evaluation

10 Conclusions and Outlook

Concept versioning as a machine learning methodology can be considered a kind of instance-based empirical learning that is located between two well-known paradigms, viz. learning from examples and learning by observation, especially incremental conceptual clustering. As in learning from examples, the system is provided with preclassified instances of some goal concept. The preclassification of the instances results from natural language text analysis (as in *"the new notebook LTE lite/25"*) and usually yields positive instances only. As in the standard approach to learning from examples, a single goal concept has to be learned, but unlike that approach an additional intermediary concept layer must be acquired, viz. the different versions of a goal concept. This extended concept formation task shares a somewhat superficial similarity with the problem of determining classes in conceptual clustering.The problem of whether to generalize a given class (version) or to bring up a new one is common to both learning techniques. Usually, this is achieved in conceptual clustering by means of a quality measure which maximizes intra-class similarity and inter-class dissimilarity. As far as concept versioning is concerned, maximizing inter-class dissimilarity seems inappropriate, since versions represent successive developmental stages of a common concept, not completely distinct concept classes. As a consequence, entirely different quality measures had to be supplied for concept versioning and conceptual clustering. Note also that our data are characterized by only slight differences between successive instances. This poses a serious problem for standard incremental conceptual clustering systems, such as UNIMEM [12] or COBWEB [13], as those systems perform optimally only when their data either are randomly distributed or exhibit large differences of values between successive instances. Furthermore, in the area of conceptual clustering instances never come preclassified and usually more than one (intermediary) layer has to learned. It thus turns out that concept versioning is neither a complicated form of learning from examples nor a simplified case of (incremental) conceptual clustering, but constitutes a special concept learning task with its own requirements (see also section 1).

These requirements have led us to results which can be summarized from two perspectives. From a concept learning point of view, we have introduced a model of concept versioning that only requires positive examples, allows incremental processing and adaptive revisions of once-established version generations, while it preserves exhaustive classification of instances under the covering generic concept. Since many of these criteria were motivated by applicational constraints of real-world knowledge base maintenance, we may also consider the results worked out as a contribution to knowledge acquisition methodology. Actually, we propose to automate the knowledge engineering process as far as the on-going evolution of a concept system in a dynamic domain is concerned. The proposed methodology only requires a human knowledge engineer to supply a progress model that contains the foreseeable developmental directions of changes in the domain -- this includes the distinction of relevant from irrelevant attributes for technological progress. Any other criteria (global quality, measures for predicting and evaluating the significance of progress, the representation and management of progress) are domain-independent and constitute our contribution to automated concept drift tracking methodology (for a more elaborated treatment, cf. [14])

Besides broadening the empirical basis of our model, we are currently planning to incorporate qualitative attributes into the model. This is an obvious extension which not only must account for the principles and versioning criteria for qualitative attribute dimensions, but also for combinations of qualitative and quantitative ones. Note, however, that "quality" in technical domains usually boils down to numerically-valued attributes. Future work will also concentrate on the validation of the concept version descriptions (e.g., by comparing the results from the version tracker to those of appropriately tuned non-incremental clustering procedures or relating machine-generated versions to those provided by human domain experts) and the application of that methodology to other dynamic domains (e.g., automobile or hi-fi technology).

The versioning model has been implemented in Quintus Prolog and runs on SUN SPARCStations. An implementation in LOOM [15] is under way.

Acknowledgments. This research is funded by a grant from DFG (grant no. Ha 2097/2-1).

References

[1] S. Carey, *Conceptual Change in Childhood*, MIT Press, Cambridge/MA, 1985.

[2] P. Thagard, 'Concepts and conceptual change', *Synthese, 82*, 255-274, (1990).

[3] J.C. Schlimmer and R.H. Granger, 'Beyond incremental processing: tracking concept drift', *AAAI-86: Proc. 5th National Conf. on Artificial Intelligence*, 502-507, Morgan Kaufmann, Los Altos/CA,1986.

[4] P. Langley, 'A general theory of discrimination learning', In D. Klahr; P. Langley and R. Neches (Eds.), *Production System Models of Learning and Development*, 99-161, MIT Press, Cambridge/MA, 1987.

[5] P.L. Bartlett, 'Learning with a slowly changing distribution', *COLT'92: Proc. 5th Workshop on Computational Learning Theory*, 243-252, 1992.

[6] D.P. Helmbold and P.M. Long, 'Tracking drifting concepts by minimizing disagreements', *Machine Learning, 14* (1), 27-45, (1994).

[7] L. DeRaedt and M. Bruynooghe, 'Belief updating from integrity constraints and queries', *Artificial Intelligence, 53*, 192-307, (1992).

[8] U. Hahn, 'Making understanders out of parsers: semantically driven parsing as a key concept for realistic text understanding applications', *International Journal of Intelligent Systems, 4* (3), 345-393, (1989).

[9] R. MacGregor, 'The evolving technology of classification-based knowledge representation systems', In J. Sowa (Ed.), *Principles of Semantic Networks*, 385-400, Morgan Kaufmann, San Mateo/CA, 1991.

[10] T.M. Mitchell; R.M. Keller and S.T. Kedar-Cabelli, 'Explanation-based generalization: a unifying view', *Machine Learning, 1* (1), 47-80, (1986).

[11] U. Hahn and M. Klenner, 'A version tracker for dynamic technical domains as a tool for automated knowledge base evolution', *FLAIRS-94: Proc. 7th Florida Art. Intell. Research Symp.*, 131-136, 1994.

[12] M. Lebowitz, 'Experiments with incremental concept formation: UNIMEM'. *Machine Learning, 2*, 103-138 (1987).

[13] J.H. Gennari; P. Langley and D. Fisher, 'Models of incremental concept formation', *Artificial Intelligence, 40*, 11-63 (1989).

[14] U. Hahn and M. Klenner, *Concept Versioning*. CLIF-Report 8/94, AG Linguistische Informatik/Computerlinguistik (CLIF), Universität Freiburg, 1994.

[15] R. MacGregor and R. Bates, *The LOOM Knowledge Representation Language*. ISI/RS-87-188, ISI, University of Southern California, 1987.

TRACING THE EVOLUTION OF ARTIFACTS[1]

Colette Rolland
Université de Paris Sorbonne
17, rue de la Sorbonne
75231 Paris Cedex 5
France

Naveen Prakash
Delhi Institute of Technology
Kashmere Gate, Old IG Block
Delhi 110006
India

ABSTRACT: *A model called the Evolutionary Object Model is proposed as a means of keeping track of the Requirements Engineering(RE) decisions, their rationales and their effects on the RE product. Under this model an RE artifact is looked upon as an object that can evolve in three ways, by transformation, mutation, and expansion. The history of object evolution under these different evolutionary forms is kept track of in the inner, spatial and temporal histories of evolutionary objects respectively. In addition, the context in which an evolution occurs as well as the history of the decision making process which has led to it is maintained in the trace.*

1. INTRODUCTION

It is traditional to consider an Information System (IS) as representing a slice of real world history. As a result, the emphasis in IS development has been on the *product* aspects of information systems [Che76], [Gus82], [Rol82], [Bro82], [Gre86], [Pra92] with a view to improving the quality of IS products. This has indeed resulted in better quality products but it is now becoming clear that the limits of this improvement are being reached. Consequently, attention has been shifting to the way in which an IS product is produced, that is, to the information system *development process* itself (see for example the special issue of the IEEE Transactions on Software Engineering on "Knowledge Representation and Reasoning on Software", Vol.18, No.6, June 1992). This process has been viewed as a collection of steps for the creation, maintenance, and evolution of information system products.

The SEI [Hum89] has developed a framework known as the "capability maturity model" which can be used to assess a development process. Under this model the development process being followed in an organisation is rated on a scale of five points. The lowest point characterises the process as "chaotic", the next higher level as "repeatable", and so on. The highest rating characterises the process as "optimised". These ratings are arrived at with a view to building an action plan for process improvement.

---

[1]This work was supported in part by the ESPRIT project 6612 entitled F3 (From Fuzzy to Formal).

Assessment studies have shown that the number of processes that can be rated as "chaotic" is very large. Such processes are incoherent and implicit [Dow93]. This leads to lack of predictability and repeatability, both of which, pre-empt improvement.

The principal reason for incoherent, implicit processes is that the knowledge which forms the basis of a process decision is lost because it is not kept track of in the process itself [Bal92], [Cur88]. For example, the reason to transform a given product to a different form may be that the product does not meet a requirement constraint. Such a transformation is indeed caused by most processes but it is usual that the reason for the transformation, the non-satisfaction of a requirement constraint, is not recorded anywhere. Consequently, the process is not explicit because the rationale for the process decision is not available subsequently.

Additionally, it is not usual to keep track of the process decisions themselves. Thus, the decision taken at a given stage in the process is also lost. Consequently, if it is desired to repeat the process again then enough information does not exist to do so.

From the foregoing, it is clear that loss of process knowledge is one of the reasons for "chaotic" processes. In order to move to the next higher process rating, that of "repeatable" processes, it is necessary to provide means to the information system developer by which this knowledge is retained and made available for subsequent use.

The need to capture and store process knowledge is considered to be a key issue in requirements engineering today. The need for tracing the Requirements Engineering (RE) process is advocated in a number of research works (see for example the proceedings of the First IEEE International Conference on Requirements Engineering 1993, the seven International Software Process Workshops and the two International Conferences on Software Process). This view is also reinforced by empirical evidence as reported, for instance, in [Cur88]. Additionally, Gotel and Finkelstein [Got93], Potts and Bruns [Pot88], and Ramesh and Edwards [Ram93] consider the issues involved in the requirements traceability problem.

We adopt the view that an RE process is [Poh93] a movement from an initial input to the desired output. The initial input is characterized as opaque and personal views of the system represented using informal languages, whereas the desired output is a complete specification of the system, formally described, on which agreement has been gained.

Using this view, we propose a trace model called the Evolutionary Object Model(EOM) as a means of keeping track of the RE decisions, their rationales and their effects on the RE product. Under the EOM, an RE artifact is looked upon as an object that can evolve in three ways, by transformation, mutation, and expansion. The history of object evolution under these different evolutionary forms is kept track of in the inner, spatial and temporal histories of evolutionary objects respectively. In addition, the context in which an evolution occurs as well as the history of the decision making process which has led to it is maintained.

This paper is organized as follows. The Evolutionary Object and the typology of evolutionary forms is introduced in section II. In section III, the notion of the history of the evolutionary object based on this typology is considered. The RE process model which is the cause of object evolution is presented in the next section. Finally, the

Evolutionary Object Model which relates evolutionary histories to the process contexts causing them is presented.

2. EVOLUTIONARY OBJECT AND EVOLUTIONARY FORMS

We propose to look upon any RE artifact as an object. An artifact is an element of a product under development, say for instance an Entity-Relationship schema. Such an element is an instance of one of the concepts (Entity-Type, Atttribute, Domain, Role, and Relationship-Type of E/R model) or constraints (Key and Cardinality of the E/R model) used to build the product.

2.1. The evolutionay object

It is usually considered that a model is composed of concepts and constraints together with some definitional properties attached to them. For instance Entity-Type, Atttribute, Domain, Role, and Relationship-Type are examples of concepts of the E/R model. Key and Cardinality are examples of E/R constraints. Valuation is called a definitional property of the Attribute concept (attributes can be mono/multi-valued).

We refer to each instance of a concept or a constraint of a particular model belonging to a given product under development as an *object* . For instance the entity-type 'client' with the attributes 'client-number' and client-address' of the E/R schema of a customer application will be referred to as objects. Similarly, the two attributes 'client-number' and 'client-address' are objects. But the multi-valuation of the 'client-address' attribute is considered as a property of the object 'client-address'.

Objects evolve as the RE process proceeds. For instance the entity-type 'client' is first created, then refined by adding the two attributes 'client-number' and 'client-address' and finally the mono and multi valuation properties are respectively added to the definition of the two attributes. For this reason we will refer to objects as evolutionary objects.

2.2. Types of Object Evolution

Object evolution takes three different forms
- transformation
- expansion
- mutation.

We consider each of these in turn.

A *transformation* is a change which affects the *inner environment* of an object. The inner environment results from the definitional properties of an object. For example, the name of an object is a property which is generic (every object has a name) and belongs to its inner environment. Thus the change of name of an object from 'customer' to 'client' is an example of a transformation.

Expansion is a change in the object *spatial environment.* The spatial environment of an object results from the relationships existing among the concepts of the model in use. For instance, due to the definition of the relationship-type concept within the E/R model, the role 'client-order' and the role 'order-product' belong to the environment of the relationship-type 'orders'. Conversely, these roles will participate, respectively, to the environments of the entity-types 'client' and 'product'. The attachment of attributes to entity-types implies that the 'client-number' attribute is part of the environment of the entity-type 'client' and vice-versa. A constraint associated to a concept instance belongs to its environment. Defining the 'client-number' as key of the entity-type 'client' is part of the 'client' environment.

An object *mutates* when its type changes i.e when it becomes an instance of the concept *x* whereas it was an instance of the concept *y*. This can occur within the same model; for instance the attribute 'client-address' could be mutated into the entity-type 'department' if it happens that the various departments of the same client can order goods autonomously and pay themselves the corresponding invoices. It can also happen between objects which are instances of concepts belonging to different models; for example, the entity-type 'client' could be further mapped into a relational table 'client-table'. These mutations will occur quite often in current system developments. Indeed, most of the time, the IS development is viewed as a process of mutation which abstracts the conceptual specification of the system from users requirements and then converts it into a technical specification and finally into an implemented system.

The relationship between an object and other objects into which or from which it mutates is contained in the *temporal environment* . We will say, for example, that the entity-type 'client' belongs to the temporal environment of the relational table 'client-table' and vice-versa.

3. TRACKING OBJECT EVOLUTION

The notion of environment is intensively used to structure the object history which can be seen as composed of three parts : the *inner part* which keeps track of the object transformations i.e changes in its definitional properties, the *spatial environment* which explains how the object definition has been progressively expanded, and the *temporal environment* which describes the object mutations. This structured history of an object is embedded in the object itself. As a result, the full history of the transformations, expansions, and mutations undergone by an object are kept track of.

Figure 1 illustratres with a simple example, our view of object evolution and its tracking. The evolutionary process is represented through a sequence of planes, each corresponding to one object transformation, mutation or expansion. The ordering of planes in the sequence reflects the chronological evolution of the product under development.

In plane 1 for instance, the requirement *x:* ' information about customers has to be maintained in the information system' is captured in the evolutionary object eo1. Plane 2 shows that eo1 has mutated into the entity-type 'customer' which is itself an evolutionary object eo2. The mutation links will be kept in both objects in order to know where the entity-type 'customer' is coming from as well as to record that the requirement *x* has motivated the creation of the entity-type 'customer' into the IS specification. Plane 3 states a transformation of eo2 due to the change of its name (the entity is now called 'client'). Finally in planes 4 and 5, eo2 is expanded; the eo3(

attribute 'client-number') and eo4 (attribute 'client-address') evolutionary objects are created in the spatial environment of eo2. Finally, plane 6 introduces a mutation of the eo2 'client' into the relational table 'client-table' (eo5).

This illustrates the three dimensional approach that we propose to deal with object evolution : the current definition of an object results from transformations, mutations and expansions that occurred in its life span. These are actions which are performed as the RE process proceeds.

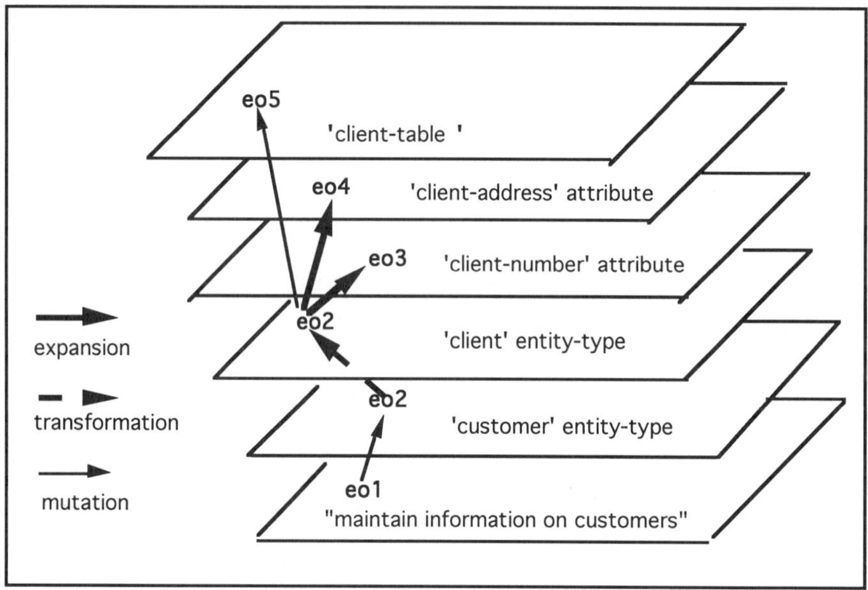

Fig. 1: Illustration of an evolutionary process

As mentioned in section I, it is not enough to just keep track of the evolutions that occur in the life of an object. Additionally, we need to keep track of the rationale behind these evolutions. This rationale is available in the development process which causes an object to evolve. Therefore, it is necessary to consider the process model underlying object evolution and to keep track of the process flow which causes this evolution.

4. THE PROCESS MODEL

We have developed a process model [Rol93], [Rol & Pra93a], [Rol & Pra93b] which is *decision-oriented.* This means that in our view, objects evolve as consequences of RE decisions. Decision-oriented models are the more recent process models and correspond to one of the three process model categories introduced by Dowson [Dow87] namely :

- Activity-oriented models
- Product-oriented models
- Decision-oriented models

The central aspect of our process model, shown in Figure 2, is that it makes the notion of the situation explicit and relates it to the broader question of context handling. The four basic concepts on which our process model rests [Rol93], [Rol & Pra93a], [Rol & Pra93b], [Sch93] are the ones of situation, decision, action and argument :

- *situation* to explain the decision context,
- *decision* to guide the RE process,
- *action* to perform the product transformations,
- *argument* to support decision-making.

A *situation* is most often a part of the product under development it makes sense to take a decision on. It can be a statement about the application domain or a requirement. It can also refer to part of existing products resulting from previous developments or a piece of generic domain knowledge.

A *decision* reflects a choice that a requirements engineer makes at a given point in time of the RE process. A decision can be looked upon as the intention of product transformations. It explicitly represents the resolution of an issue.

An *action* performs a transformation on the product. It is a materialisation of the decision. Performing it changes the product and may generate new situations which, in turn, are subjects of new decisions.

Arguments are statements which support or object to decisions within a given context.

The contextual approach is introduced by the notion of a *context* which is a couple <situation,decision>. Contexts can be of two kinds, macro contexts and micro contexts. Macro contexts are built out of other simpler macro or micro contexts. However, micro contexts are primitive contexts, they cannot be decomposed into other simpler contexts. Macro contexts differ from micro contexts in that they present the developer with alternatives in decision making but do not directly modify the product under development. A micro context, on the other hand, presents no decision making alternatives but causes product modifications. The development process is a decision making activity during which the developer chooses alternatives offerred by macro contexts till finally micro contexts are reached. These micro contexts invoke actions which cause changes in the product leading to new situations. These situations participate in new contexts and the process continues.

As an example consider a situation in the ER schema in which there are entities, E1, E2, and relationships R(E1,E2), R(E2,E1) respectively. It is possible to take the decision to structure this situation. Then, the macro context is

< E1, E2, R(E1,E2), R(E2,E1), STRUCTURE>

It is possible to STRUCTURE in different ways: one can partition, embed, historise, and so on. Thus, the context above can be decomposed into other contexts, for example,

< E1, R(E1,E2), PARTITION> and
< E1, R(E1,E2), E2, EMBED>

Assuming PARTITION to be a micro context, it results in a a partitioned E1 which gives rise to a new situation and, consequently, to new contexts.

A more detailed view of the process model is given in the proceedings of DEXA93 [Rol &Pra93].

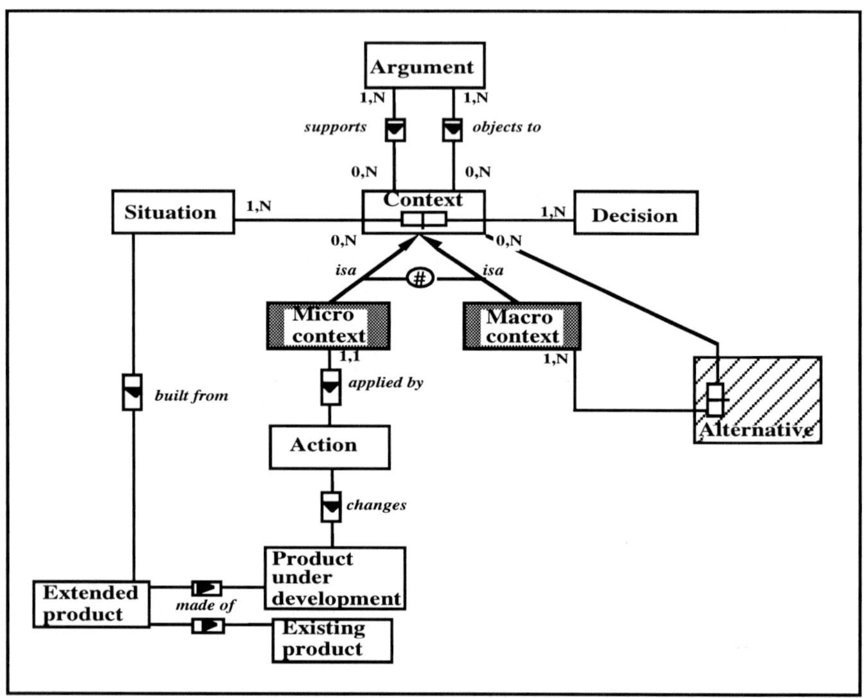

Fig. 2: The Process Model

5. THE EVOLUTIONARY OBJECT MODEL

The Evolutionary Object Model (EOM) allows us to keep track of both, the *object history* (the transformations, expansions and mutations) and the corresponding *process history* (the decisions, their contexts, arguments and related actions leading to object evolution). The EOM is generic i.e independent of a specific product model. It provides the notion of an Evolutionary Object (EO) which is itself generic : one that can be adapted to various methodologies and tool environments. An EO is an instance of the Evolutionary Object Class (EOC). The EOC definition is the intentional definition of the potential set of evolutionary objects.

The EOC has two aspects to it, its environmental aspects and its process aspects. The former is graphically presented in Figure 3 and is concerned with object history. The latter is depicted in Figure 5. It emphasises the process history behind object evolution. When both these aspects are taken together then it can be seen that the EOC is capable of providing the full history of what happened, when it happened, and why it happened.

As shown in Figure 3, the object history is composed of three parts : the *Inner_History* which keeps track of the object transformations, the *Spatial_History* describing how the object has been expanded and the *Temporal_History* which tells us about object mutations. In terms of the process model of Figure 2, every transformation, expansion, or mutation is an *action* executed as a consequence of a micro-decision which is itself, part of a micro context. This fact is represented in Figure 3 by the links from *Property_History, Expansion_link_History,* and *Mutation_Link__History* to *Micro_Context_Taken* respectively. We can thus say that Figure 3 shows the manner in which the historical view of object evolution is recorded within its inner, spatial, and temporal environments.

The process aspect view of the EOC contained in Figure 5 explains how the evolutionary process, which provides the rationale of these evolutions, is recorded. The *Micro_Context_Taken* represented in Figure 3 could be the result of a decision making process which has required several decomposition steps of an initial macro-decision. This macro-decision is itself a part of the initial macro-context. This fact is represented in Figure 5 by the *Macro_Context_Taken.* All the aspects of decision making in the evolutionary process, namely, the contexts explored, those accepted or rejected, and the alternatives taken are modelled according to our process view and structured as presented in Figure 5. In this way, Figure 5 shows the entire deliberation process underlying object evolution.

We now consider the environment and process aspects of an EOC in turn. Consider Figure 3.
Every EO is an instance of a concept of a given model which corresponds to a certain abstraction level. These are the three aspects of the object *description.* For example the eo2 'client' in Figure 1 is an instance of the Entity-type concept which is part of the E/R model allowing conceptual abstraction.

The *Inner_History* describes the history of transformation links, that is, of object properties. Each property has a *Property_Name* , a *Value* and an *Active_status* telling if the property is still alive or not, in the current object state. 'Customer' and 'client' are two property names successively given in Figure 1 to the entity-type under definition. The name 'customer' is currently non-active whereas the name 'client' is. The property history is expressed in terms of transformations that occurred on the object properties. This is modelled by the link to the set of *Micro_Context _Taken* which have performed these transformations.

The *Spatial_History* and the *Temporal_History* respectively describe the history of expansion and mutation links i.e they tell us how the object has been progressively involved in its spatial environment and in its temporal environment. The link has a *Link_name* and refers to an *EO.* This conforms to our definitions of the expansion and mutation links which relate one evolutionary object to another belonging, respectively, in its spatial environment or in its temporal environment. For example, the eo3 'client-number' and the eo4 'client-address' introduced in Figure 1 belong to the spatial environment of the eo2 'client' and will be referred to in the *Expansion_Link_History* of eo2. The *Expansion_Link_History* and the *Mutation_Link_History* is expressed through a set of Micro_Context_Taken which have motivated the respective expansions and mutations of the evolutionary object.

Figure 4 shows in a simplified way, the contents of the eo2 'client' memory conforming to the sketch presented in Figure 1.

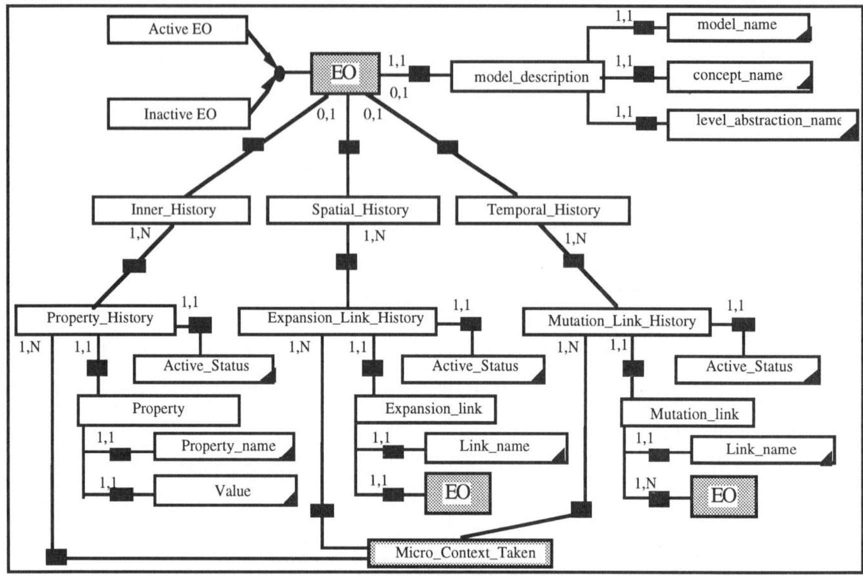

Fig. 3 : Evolutionary object class : the environment aspects

The eo2 history tells us that the creation of the entity-type at time t2 by action 2, with the entity-type name 'customer' (inner history) and an empty spatial environment (spatial history) results of the mutation of eo1 (temporal environment). At time t3 its name has been transformed into 'client' through action a3 (inner history). Further on its spatial environment has been expanded by adding the two attributes 'client-number' (a4 at t4) and 'client-address' (a5 at t5).

The context in which these actions have been performed as well as the decision making process history which has led to these actions is detailed in the Evolutionary Object Class part shown in Figure 5.

Every expansion, mutation or transformation performing an object's evolution is an *Action* which implements a *Decision* taken within a *Micro_Context._Taken*. For instance, adding the attribute 'client-address' in the environment of the eo2 'client' is an action a5 (according to Figure 4) resulting from the decision "Attributise Entity-type" taken in the context composed of the entity-type 'client'. One can notice through this example, the difference between a decision and an action. The decision is the intention to "Attributise Entity-type", whereas the action creates the expansion link between the eo2 'client' and the eo4 'client-address'.

eo2

inner history :	< t2, [entity-type-name = 'customer'], a2 >
	< t3, [entity-type-name = 'client'], a3 >
spatial history :	< t2, [ ], a2 >
	< t4, [eo3], a4 >
	< t5, [eo3, eo4], a5>
temporal history :	< t2, [eo1], a2 >
	< t6, [eo5], a6 >

Fig. 4 : Example of evolutionary object history

According to our process view, a micro context can itself result from the exploration of various alternatives related to a macro context. We believe it is worthwhile to record the deliberation process which is behind the decision making process leading to an action making the object evolve. Thus, the evolutionary object keeps track of the *Macro_Context_Taken* from which the *Micro_Context_Taken* is issued, as well as the *Alternative_Taken* and the *Alternative_Rejected.* which reflect the deliberation process. For instance, the different alternatives considered by the requirements engineer to "Define the key" of the entity-type 'client' will be recorded in the eo2 history. The *Macro_Context_Taken* <eo2, "Define key"> could be associated to the *Alternative_Rejected* <eo2, "Define Weak-Entity-Type"> ('client' is not a weak-entity type) and with the *Aternative_Taken* <eo2, "Define Attribute 'client-number'as key"> which is the Micro_Context_Taken resulting in the creation of the expansion link between eo2 and eo6 (key constraint object).

As suggested by our process model, there is a choice among the various alternatives of a given macro-context. This choice is based upon *Arguments* which *support* or *object* to decisions within a given *Context_Explored.* The fact that the 'client-number' is unique wihin the set of clients is an argument which supports the macro context <eo2, "Define 'client-number' as key">. The selection of an alternative results from *Decision Criteria* which are conditions based upon a combination of arguments.

Finally, Figure 5 shows that a *Situation* is constructed upon *Evolutionary Objects.* For instance, the situation mentioned in the macro context <eo2, "Define 'client-number' as key"> is composed of the evolutionary object 'client' i.e eo2.

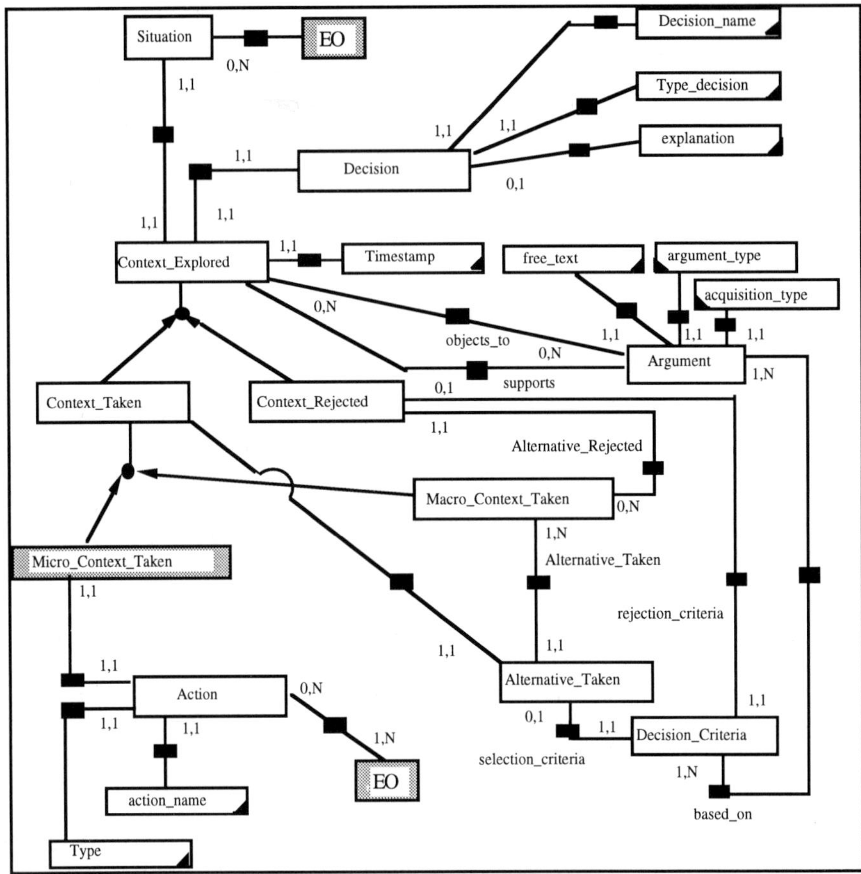

Fig. 5 : Evolutionary Object Class : the process aspects

6. CONCLUSION

A search for better quality products can be partially successful if the processes supporting development become at least repeatable. For this, it is necessary to keep track of process knowledge. This knowledge concerns both, the evolution of the product as well as the process which causes this evolution. This is because the one cannot act without the other: product evolution occurs because of development decisions. Thus, not only the knowledge of evolutions but also that concerning the motivations behind evolutions is necessary to make the entire development process repeatable.

The proposals contained in this paper achieve this by maintaining object history. as well as process history. These notions are integrated together through the notion of an Evolutionary Object Class.

Further work involves the development of a tracing environment which includes modules for the capture of the trace, its documentation and exploitation. Particular attention will be paid to the exploitation part of the trace to provide effective feedback for process improvement and guidance.

7. REFERENCES

[Bal92] : Balasubramanian R., Vasant D., "Supporting systems development by capturing deliberations during software engineering, IEEETSE 18, 6, 1992

[Bro82] : Brodie M.L.; "Active and Passive Component Modelling : ACM/PCM"; in Olle82.

[Bru91] : J. Brunet; "Modelling the World with Semantic Objects", Int. IFIP Conf. on "Object Oriented Approach in Information Systems", F.Van Assche, B.Moulin, C.Rolland (eds), North Holland (pub), 1991.

[Che76] : Chen P.P.; "The Entity-Relationship model : Towards a Unified View of Data"; ACM Trans. on Databases Systems, Vol 1, n° 1, 1976.

[Cur88] : Curtis. B, Krasner.H, Iscoe.N; "A field of study of the software design process for large systems", ACM Trans. on IS, 31(11), 1988.

[Dow87] : M. Dowson; "Iteration in the Software Process", Proc.9th Int. Conf. on Software Engineering, Monterey, USA, 1987.

[Dow93] : M. Dowson; "Software process themes and issues"; Proc. 2nd Int. Conference on the Software Process, Berlin, Germany, 1993

[Got93] : Gotel O., Finkelstein A.C.W. ; An Analysis of the Requirements Engineering Traceability Problem, Tech. Rep., Imperial College, Department of Computing, TR-93-41, 1993

[Gre86] : Greenspan S.J., Borgida A., Mylopoulos J.; "A Requirement Model Language and its logic"; Information Systems 11(1), 1986.

[Gus82] : Gustafsson M.R., Karlsson T., Bubenko J.A.; "A declarative Approach to Conceptual Information Modeling"; in Oll82.

[Hum89] : Humphrey W.S.; "Software Process Management"; Addison-Wesley, reading, MA, 1989.

[Oll82] : Olle T.W.,Sol H.G.(eds.), Verrijn-Stuart A.A.; Information System Design Methodologies:A Comparative Review, North Holland, 1982

[Poh93] : Pohl K.; "The three dimensions of requirements engineering", Proc. CAISE'93 Conference, C. Rolland, F. Bodart, B. Pernici (eds), Sringer-Verlag (pub), 1993.

[Pot93] : Potts C., Bruns G.; Recording the Reasons for Design Decisions, IEEETSE, 17(3), 226-240, 1991

[Pra92] : Prakash N, An object oriented methodology for information systems design, in Information systems concepts:improving the understanding, Falkenberg et al(eds.), 53-86, North Holland

[Ram93] : Ramesh B., Edwards M ; Issues in the Development of a Requirements Traceability Model, in IEEE Int. Symp.On Requirements Engineering, San Diego, Calif. 1993

[Rol82] : Rolland C., Richard C.; "The Remora Methodology for Information System Design and Management"; in Oll82.

[Rol93] : C. Rolland, "Modelling the Requirements Engineering Process", European-Japanese Workshop, Budapest, 1993.

[Rol & Pra93a] : C. Rolland, N. Prakash; "Reusable Process Chunks", DEXA'93, Int. Conference on Databases and Expert Systems Applications, Prague, 1993.

[Rol & Pra93b] : C. Rolland, N. Prakash; "Modelling Decisions in the Requirements Engineering Process", CISMOD'93 Conference, Int. Conference on Information Systems and Management of Data, Delhi, 1993.

[Sch93] J R Schmitt; Product Modelling in the Requirements Engineering Process, Proc. IFIP TC8 Intl. Conf. on "Information System Development Process", N Prakash, C Rolland, B pernici (eds) North Holland(Pub)

Supporting Information Disclosure in an Evolving Environment

A.H.M. ter Hofstede and H.A. Proper and Th.P. van der Weide

Department of Information Systems, University of Nijmegen
Toernooiveld, NL-6525 ED Nijmegen, The Netherlands
{arthur,erikp,tvdw}@cs.kun.nl

Abstract. Even if high-level query languages are used, query formulation may cause problems. This is notably so in case of large and complex application domains. Typical examples of these kinds of application domains are evolving application domains. In an evolving application domain not only populations may change, but also the conceptual schema. Even more, the history of the application domain should be recorded, and be retrievable.
This paper focuses on support for query formulation in the context of large conceptual schemata. The solution presented uses the idea of query-by-navigation in conjunction with query-by-construction. First this idea is illustrated by means of some examples, then it is formally defined.

1 Introduction

Nowadays a large number of organisations use automated information systems. A large body of vital corporate information is stored in these information systems. As important decisions are to be based on this information, a primary function of information systems is the retrieval of stored information. Adequate support for information disclosure is far from a trivial problem, as conceptual schemata of real-life applications tend to be quite large and complicated. This problem becomes even more complicated in the context of *evolving information systems*.

In rapidly changing organisations, the flexibility offered by evolving information systems is indispensable. Evolving information systems support the evolution of *all* aspects of applications models [MS90, BKKK87, KBC+89, PW93]. Traditional information systems only allow the evolution of populations. Application models not only contain populations, but also structural aspects of the Universe of Discourse involved, such as constraints and action specifications (see [PW93]). For information disclosure in evolving information systems, not only the current application model, but also past application models may be of interest. Evidently, this yields extra complications for information disclosure. Traditional query languages such as SQL are inadequate for information disclosure in evolving information systems, as they do not accommodate for changes in the *structure* of the involved information. In some approaches to evolving information systems, manipulation languages for relational schemata are extended with historical operations, both on the instance (population) and the schema level [MS90, BKKK87, KBC+89]. However, as a result of their strong connection with the Relational Model, these languages are not on a conceptual level and consequently, not suited for information disclosure.

The approach followed in this paper is inspired by [Big88, GS90, Hag92, Pro93], in which hypertext browsers for (evolving) information systems are described. A further refinement of the idea of a hypertext browser is a *query-by-navigation* interface, allowing users to formulate queries interactively [BPW93]. This approach is based on an identical approach followed in information retrieval systems [BW92]. Query-by-navigation, described in [BPW93], allows for the formulation of rather simple queries only. In this paper the formulation of more complex queries is supported also. This is achieved by extending *query-by-navigation* with *query-by-construction*.

The idea outlined in this paper is presented in terms of the stratified hypermedia architecture described in [BW92]. This architecture consists of two layers, a descriptive layer, referred to as the *hyperindex*, and an instantiation layer, referred to as the *hyperbase*. The hyperindex can be seen as a hypertext of characterisations. The hyperbase contains the actual information. In this paper the hyperindex corresponds to an information structure, while the hyperbase corresponds to a population of that structure. During the query formulation process, users are guided through the descriptive layer.

The structure of this paper is as follows. In section 2 the notion of evolving information system is illustrated. This section also addresses the concept of disclosure schema. A disclosure schema covers all retrievable information of an evolving information system. The necessity of a query-by-navigation system in the context of evolving information systems is stressed. In section 3 the ideas behind a query-by-navigation/query-by-construction system are discussed by a sample session. Section 4 presents the main ingredients of a formal foundation of such a system. Finally, it should be stressed that the approach described in this paper is a generic one, in the sense that the results can be applied to any object-role based data modelling technique. Examples of object-role based data modelling techniques are ER or EER, NIAM ([NH89]), and PSM ([HW93]).

2 Evolving Information Systems

For evolving information systems, an application model is not restricted to instantiations (populations) of the schema involved. Application models then also describe the object types, constraints, and action specifications involved. A collective noun for these modelling concepts is *application model element*. In an evolving information system each application model element is allowed to change in the course of time.

In this section the concept of evolving information system is illustrated by means of a simple example. Next, the disclosure schema of an evolving information system is discussed.

2.1 Example evolving domain

As an illustration of an evolving Universe of Discourse, consider an insurance company for cars. For each policy sold, the insured car and owner are recorded. For each insured car the registration number and type are recorded. Clients are identified by their name and address. In figure 1 an ER schema of this simple Universe of Discourse is presented. The following conventions are used. Names of attributes are preceded by a hash (#). A name above a line, connecting an entity type with a relationship type, verbalizes how that entity type participates in that relationship type (e.g. Car insured by Policy). A name below such a line verbalizes the reverse connection (e.g. Policy insuring Car).

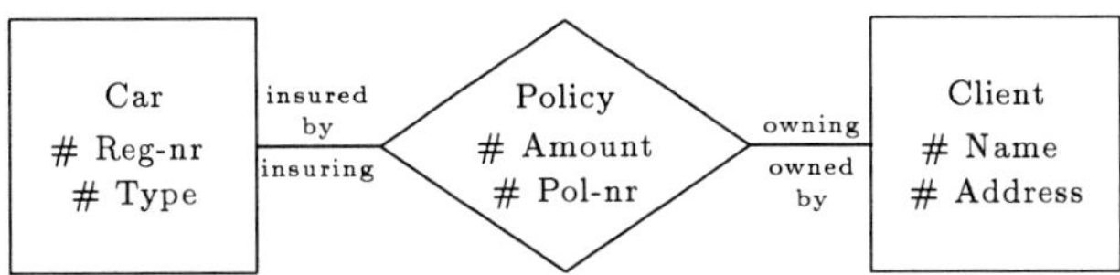

Fig. 1. The information structure of a car insurance company

Suppose that after some time the insurance company notices a substantial difference between damage claims for private cars and those for company cars. Rather than raising the overall policy prices, they effectuate a price differentiation. Policy prices for company cars are raised by some fixed percentage. Policy prices for private cars become dependent on the usage of the car, i.e. the number of kilometers per year. The new ER schema is depicted in figure 2. Entity type Car now has two subtypes, Private car and Company car. Only for Private car the number of kilometers per year is recorded.

After some time a number of small companies, not using their cars very intensively, start to protest against the introduced price differentiation. The insurance company then decides to abolish the price differentiation. Instead, a no-claims reduction is introduced. This leads to the attribute Reduction for relationship type Policy. The resulting ER schema is shown in figure 3.

2.2 Disclosure schema

In our approach, the history of an application domain is captured by the history of its elements. For example, the object type history for policies starts as a relationship type with two attributes, and then evolves to a relationship type with three attributes.

In an evolving information system, not only queries about the current application model can be formulated, but also about past application models. The disclosure schema of an evolving information system is defined as the conceptual schema capturing all information in the evolving information system that can be retrieved. A disclosure schema therefore contains the following components:

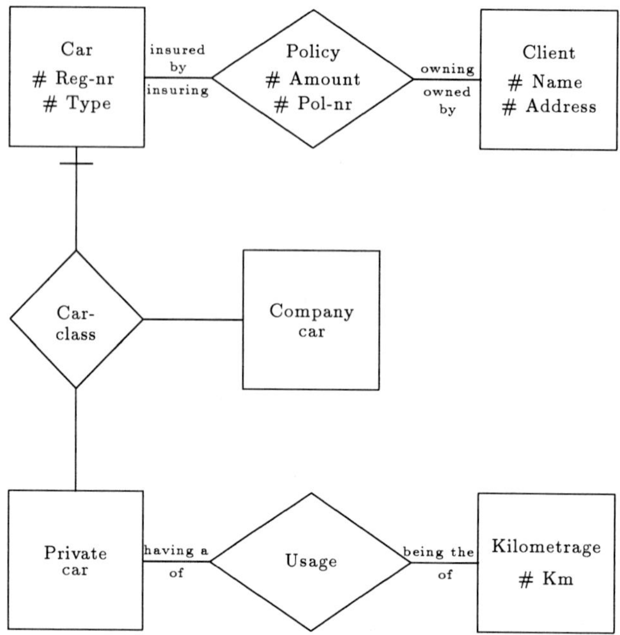

Fig. 2. Car insurance with price differentiation

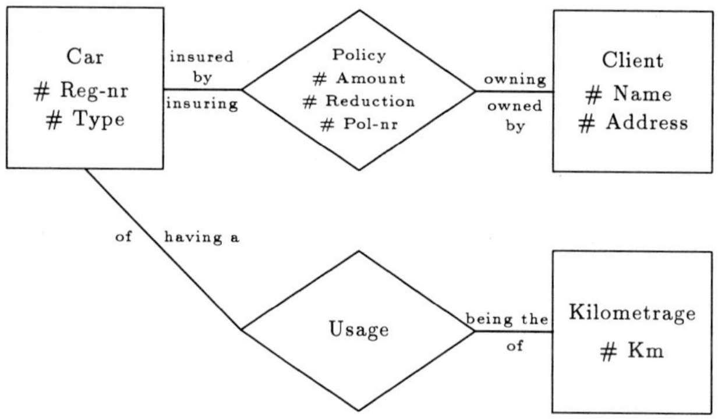

Fig. 3. Car insurance with reduction rates

Extra-temporal schema The *extra-temporal schema* of an evolving application domain is the union of past and present information structures. In case of the car insurance company, the extra-temporal schema at least comprises the schemata represented in figures 1, 2 and 3.

Meta-schema The meta-schema(ta) of the modelling techniques used for the application model should also be present in the disclosure schema involved, enabling the formulation of queries about structural aspects of evolving information systems. Further, the notion of time, used to describe versions of application models, has to be available in the disclosure schema.

Integration In the disclosure schema, the meta and application level are integrated. Concepts in the application level are linked to their corresponding concepts in the meta level. To this end, the meta-schema and extra-temporal schema are integrated in the disclosure schema via **instance of** relationships. The meta-schema(ta) of the modelling techniques used for the application model should also be present in the disclosure schema involved.

Evidently, a disclosure schema can easily become very large. Adequate information disclosure support is therefore imperative. In the following section the idea of guided query construction is introduced by a sample session.

3 Guided Query Construction

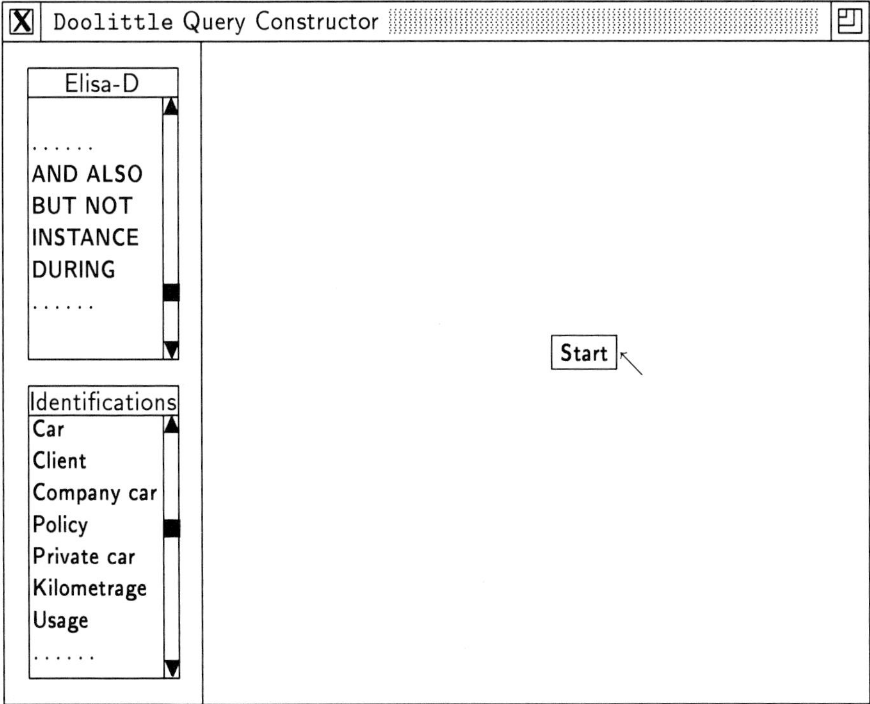

Fig. 4. Opening screen of the query constructor

In this section, we give an idea of the look and feel of the query constructor by a sample session. As sample query language the language LISA-D ([HPW93]) is employed. LISA-D can be seen as a general query language for object-role based data modelling techniques.

Suppose a searcher is interested in insured cars with a usage less than 1000 kilometers per year. In figure 4 the starting screen of the query constructor is depicted. In the middle of the query screen, the current query is depicted. Since the searcher has not yet started, the current focus is **Start**. After selecting the **Start** box, a navigation session is initiated, leading to the screen in figure 5,which is referred to as the *starting node* of the navigator.

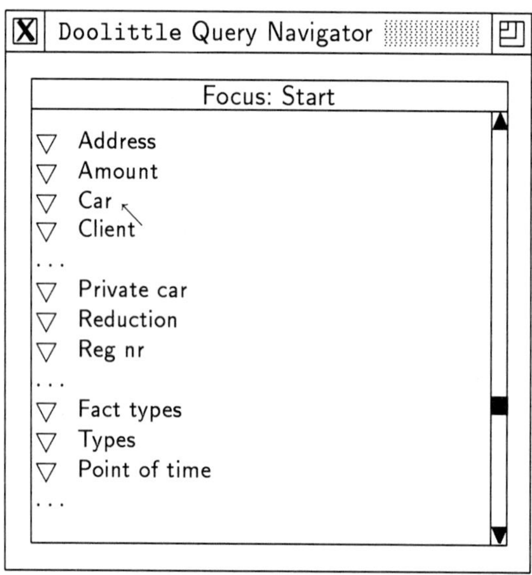

Fig. 5. Selecting a start object type

This screen contains the names of all object types of the disclosure schema under consideration (both object types from the application, and the meta level). The searcher can now proceed by selecting one of the presented items. This selection is the first refinement of the searcher's information need. A selection of an item in a node is denoted by the symbol ↖ in the figures. The symbol ▽ represents a button for a refinement step, while the symbol △ is used for enlargement. Finally, ▷ represents a button used for related formulations.

Since the searcher is mainly interested in cars, the item **Car** is selected. This choice leads to the screen of figure 6. The focus has changed from **Start** to **Car**, and the screen depicts all possible continuations for queries starting from **Car**. Further, **Company car** and **Private car** are offered to the searcher as alternative formulations, since they are subtypes of **Car**. Mostly, alternative formulations originate from subtyping and generalisation. The searcher is interested in insured cars, and

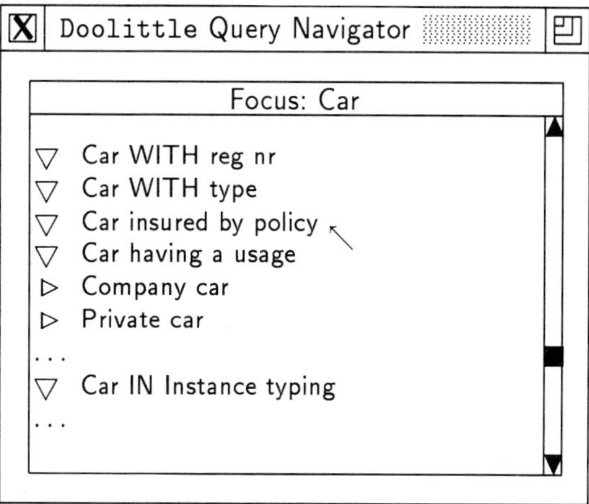

Fig. 6. Starting point: cars

consequently selects the item **Car insured by policy**. This brings the searcher to a next screen, in which the item **Car insured by policy owned by client** is selected. In the mean time, the query builder screen has changed its focus accordingly.

As the searcher is not interested in all insured cars, but rather those with a usage of less than 1000 kilometers, the searcher continues with selecting the **AND ALSO** operator from the **Elisa-D** menu, a binary operator on LISA-D queries. This is an example of *query by construction.* The searcher can now start another navigation session to specify the interest in cars with a usage less than 1000km.

Now suppose that the searcher realises that only cars insured in 1993 are of interest. Therefore, a restriction of the original query is necessary. This can be achieved by a selection of the **DURING** operation from the **Elisa-D** menu. A during clause can be put anywhere in a query. As only the policies of 1993 are of interest, the **DURING** clause is inserted after **policy**. The resulting screen is shown in figure 7.

4 The Underlying Architecture

In this section a more formal background of the query-by-navigation/query-by-construction system is provided. For the underlying stratified hypermedia architecture, we refer to [BW92]. This architecture offers the possibility to make a separation between several information abstraction levels. In the two level approach, one level (the hyperbase) is concerned with concrete information, the second level (the hyperindex) addresses the structural aspects of the information. In the previous section, it was demonstrated how the hyperindex is used to describe and access information from the hyperbase. We saw how queries can be constructed via a guided tour, using the mechanisms of query-by-construction and query-by-navigation. We restrict ourselves in the rest of this paper to the description of the latter mechanism.

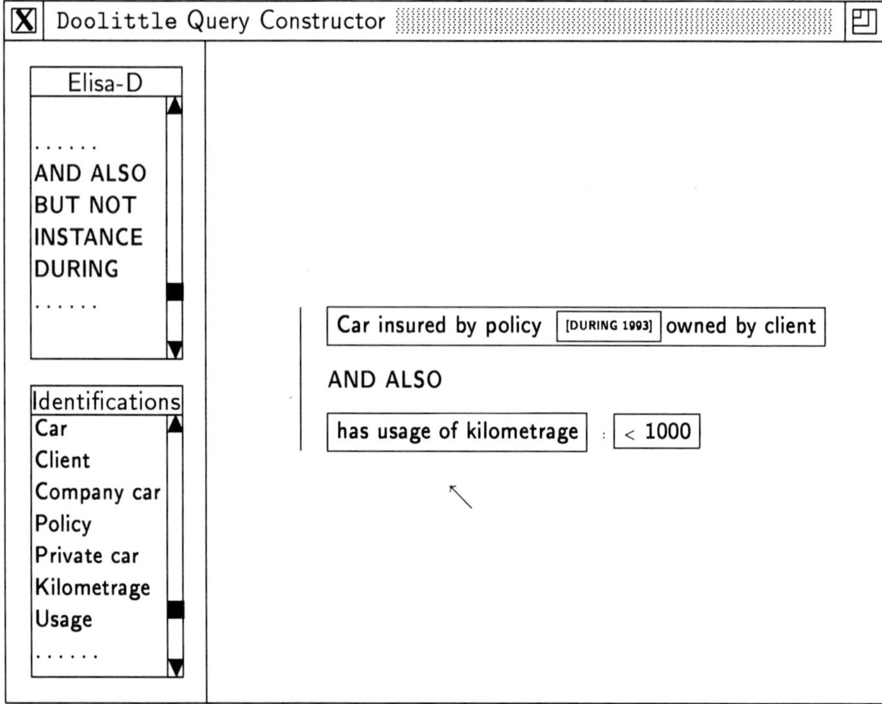

Fig. 7. Query extended with a temporal selection

4.1 The Hyperindex

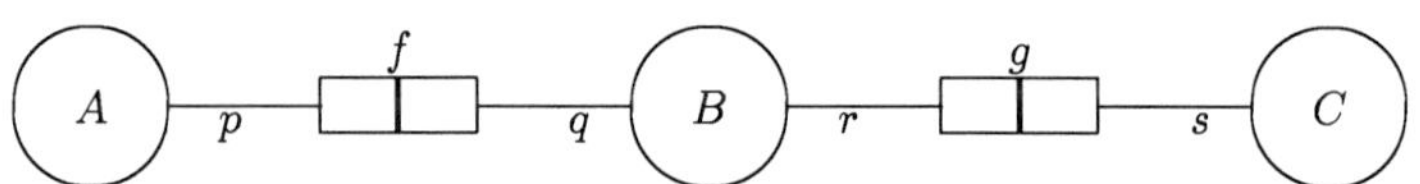

Fig. 8. A small schema with identified predicators

Object role models (such as NIAM, ER, EER, PSM), allow for the verbalization of queries by so-called linear path expressions. A linear path expression describes a (linear) path through the information structure, via object types and predicators (we prefer the term predicator above the term role, see [BHW91]). In figure 8, A is a path expression which describes a path from A to A. Predicator p is also a valid path expression, representing the path from A (its base) to f (its fact type) via this predicator. The reverse path (from f to A) is denoted as $p^{\leftarrow}$. A more complex example is path expression: $A \circ p \circ f \circ q^{\leftarrow} \circ B \circ r \circ g \circ s^{\leftarrow} \circ C$.

This expression corresponds to the path from A to C via f, B and g. Later, we will see how linear path expressions can be verbalized as almost natural language sentences. For more details on (linear) path expressions, refer to: [HPW93].

Linear path expressions will be the molecules for the hyperindex to be constructed. The associated nodes will contain, amongst others, the verbalization of linear path expressions. The components of this hyperindex will be introduced successively.

Fragment base The fragment base ($\mathbb{F}_{\text{ind}}$) of the hyperindex consists of the names for elementary path expressions: object types, predicators and reverse predicators.

Node base Nodes are used to visualize (abstract) molecules, or, linear path expressions. Besides verbalizing the path expression, they present the searcher some context sensitive information, that may help during the process of query formulation.

The structure of a node is as follows. The node heading contains the verbalized path expression $\rho(c)$. The node body consists of three components, a set of less specific path expressions $(u_1, \ldots, u_l)$, a set of more specific path expressions $(d_1, \ldots, d_m)$, and a set of associated path expressions $(a_1, \ldots, a_n)$. The verbalization function ρ will be introduced at the end of this section.

Schema The simple structure of linear path expressions can be described using a single syntactic category $\langle P \rangle$. The context-free production rules define the way in which linear path expressions can be extended. For any predicator $p \in \mathcal{P}$ and abstract object type $x \in \mathcal{N}$, we have the following rules:

$$
\begin{aligned}
\langle P \rangle &\rightarrow x \\
\langle P \rangle &\rightarrow \langle P \rangle \circ p \circ \mathsf{Fact}(p) \\
\langle P \rangle &\rightarrow \langle P \rangle \circ p^{\leftarrow} \circ \mathsf{Base}(p)
\end{aligned}
$$

Views The hyperindex for a disclosure schema, contains only one single view. The start symbol of this view is obviously $\langle P \rangle$. The molecules $\mathbb{M}_{\text{ind}}$ are formed by the set of linear path expressions. The parse trees ω_{ind} describe the construction of these expressions. The presentation of molecules by π_{ind} is covered in the next subsection.

In this view, two associative link schemata are introduced. The first link schema is used to handle specialisation and generalisation occurring in the disclosure schema. If object type x is a supertype of object type y, then with a reference to x may be associated a reference to y. For example, figure 6 contains the link from Car to Company car. This association is, however, only recorded in $\mathbb{L}_{\text{ind}}$ for linear path expressions ending in object type x. The second link schema is used for reversal of the current focus. Normally, a focus is enlarged or refined by operating on the tail of this expression. It may, however, be convenient to be able to operate on the head of the focus also. For this purpose, reversal of the currently focussed path expression can be employed, and is added as an associative link.

Presentation of molecules Molecules (linear path expressions) are presented by nodes that provide a verbalization of the path expression, and an overview of the immediate context of the expression. This presentation is described by the function π_{ind}.

What remains to be done with respect to the presentation of the molecules, is a proper definition of the verbalization function ρ. This is achieved by means of a set of derivation rules, which also derive an associated preference for verbalizations (using penalty points). The predicate $\rho(P, n, x)$ is employed to denote that path expression P is verbalised as n, with penalty x.

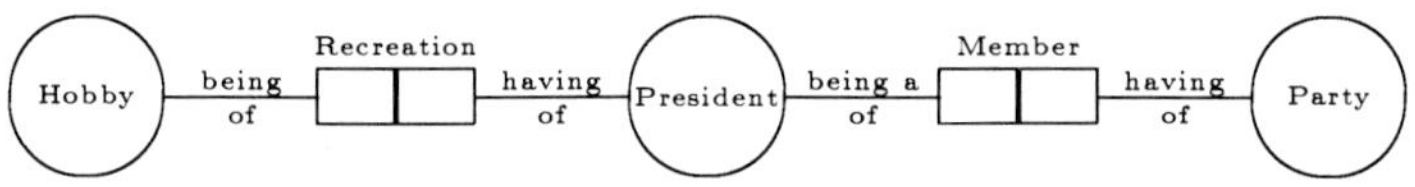

Fig. 9. A naming of figure 8

The name of the empty path expression is defined by the following rule:

[Verb1] (*empty path expression*) $\vdash$ $\rho(\epsilon, \textsf{Start}, 0)$

Object types and predicators are abstract objects, which are verbalized by associating meaningful names. Object types get a unique name, recorded by the naming function ONm. Predicators have associated a name, which identifies the predicator within its fact type. This predicator name (PNm) also verbalizes the linear path from its base to its associated fact type. Besides, predicators have a reverse name (RNm), which verbalizes the reversed path, from fact type to base. A possible naming for the schema in figure 8 is provided in figure 9:

$$\begin{array}{lll}
\textsf{ONm}(A) = \textsf{Hobby} & \textsf{PNm}(p) = \textsf{being} & \textsf{RNm}(p) = \textsf{of} \\
\textsf{ONm}(B) = \textsf{President} & \textsf{PNm}(q) = \textsf{having} & \textsf{RNm}\, q = \textsf{of} \\
\textsf{ONm}(C) = \textsf{Party} & \textsf{PNm}(r) = \textsf{being a} & \textsf{RNm}\, r = \textsf{of} \\
\textsf{ONm}(f) = \textsf{Recreation} & \textsf{PNm}(s) = \textsf{having} & \textsf{RNm}\, s = \textsf{of} \\
\textsf{ONm}(g) = \textsf{Member} & &
\end{array}$$

As another example, the name 'insuring' in figure 1 refers to the association between the relationship type named 'Policy', and the object type named 'Car'. Predicator names are always placed above lines connecting entity types and relationship types, while reverse predicator names are placed below those lines.

In the derivation of a verbalization for linear path expressions, names provided by the user are exploited as much as possible. This leads to the following derivation rules, assigning no penalties to these names:

[Verb2] (*predicator naming*) $\mathsf{PNm}(p) = n \vdash \rho(p, n, 0)$

[Verb3] (*reverse predicator naming*) $\mathsf{RNm}(p) = n \vdash \rho(p^{\leftarrow}, n, 0)$

[Verb4] (*object type naming*) $\mathsf{ONm}(x) = n \vdash \rho(x, n, 0)$

Verbalization of concatenated path expressions is easily derived via juxtaposition. In order to favour user names assigned to path expressions, the derivation assigns a penalty for each such derivation step.

[Verb5] (*concatenation*) $\rho(P_1, n_1, \alpha_1) \wedge \rho(P_2, n_2, \alpha_2) \vdash \rho(P_1 \circ P_2, n_1\ n_2, \alpha_1 + \alpha_2 + 1)$

This leads, for the schema in figure 8 with namings as provided by figure 9, to the following verbalizations:

$$\rho(A \circ p \circ f \circ q^{\leftarrow} \circ B, \textsf{Hobby being Recreation of President}, 4)$$
$$\rho(B \circ r \circ g \circ s^{\leftarrow} \circ C, \textsf{President being a Member of Party}, 4)$$

The verbalization rules using predicator names and reverse predicator names, sometimes lead to clumsy sentences. Therefore, extra names for transitions via fact types of the form $(p \circ f \circ q^{\leftarrow})$ are usually introduced (by the analyst) in a schema. Such a transition is referred to as a *connector*, and denoted as $\langle p, q \rangle$. In the example of figure 8 we introduce the following connector names:

$\mathsf{Connector}(\textsf{of}) = \langle p, q \rangle$ $\qquad$ $\mathsf{Connector}(\textsf{being member of }) = \langle r, s \rangle$

Connector names are used for verbalizations as follows:

[Verb6] (*connector naming*) $\mathsf{Connector}(n) = \langle p, q \rangle \vdash \rho(p \circ \mathsf{Fact}(p) \circ q^{\leftarrow}, n, 0)$

The verbalizations of the previous example can now be extended with:

$$\rho(A \circ p \circ f \circ q^{\leftarrow} \circ B, \textsf{Hobby of President}, 2)$$
$$\rho(B \circ r \circ g \circ s^{\leftarrow} \circ C, \textsf{President being member of Party}, 2)$$

Note the lower penalty value for these verbalizations.

The derivation rules for verbalizations are used to derive a verbalization with highest preference (lowest penalty), as follows.

$$\mathsf{Cost}(P) \triangleq \mathsf{min}\left\{\alpha \mid \exists_n\left[\rho(P, n, \alpha)\right]\right\}$$
$$\rho(P) \triangleq n \text{ such that } \rho(P, n, \mathsf{Cost}(P))$$

In our example, we have: $\mathsf{Cost}(A \circ p \circ f \circ q^{\leftarrow} \circ C) = 2$, leading to the following verbalization:

$$\rho(A \circ p \circ f \circ q^{\leftarrow} \circ C) = \textsf{Hobby of President}$$

References

[BHW91] P. van Bommel, A.H.M. ter Hofstede, and Th.P. van der Weide. Semantics and verification of object-role models. *Information Systems*, 16(5):471–495, October 1991.

[Big88] J. Bigelow. Hypertext and CASE. *IEEE Software*, 5(2):23–27, 1988.

[BKKK87] J. Banerjee, W. Kim, H.J. Kim, and H.F. Korth. Semantics and Implementation of Schema Evolution in Object-Oriented Databases. *SIGMOD Record*, 16(3):311–322, December 1987.

[BPW93] C.A.J. Burgers, H.A. Proper, and Th.P. van der Weide. Organising an Information System as Stratified Hypermedia. In H.A. Wijshoff, editor, *Proceedings of the Computing Science in the Netherlands Conference*, pages 109–120, Utrecht, The Netherlands, November 1993.

[BW92] P.D. Bruza and Th.P. van der Weide. Stratified Hypermedia Structures for Information Disclosure. *The Computer Journal*, 35(3):208–220, 1992.

[GS90] P.K. Garg and W. Scacchi. A Hypertext System to Manage Software Life-Cycle Documents. *IEEE Software*, 7(3):90–98, 1990.

[Hag92] T.M. Hagensen. Hyperstructure CASE Tools. In B. Theodoulidis and A. Sutcliffe, editors, *Proceedings of the Third Workshop on the Next Generation of CASE Tools*, pages 291–297, Manchester, United Kingdom, May 1992.

[HPW93] A.H.M. ter Hofstede, H.A. Proper, and Th.P. van der Weide. Formal definition of a conceptual language for the description and manipulation of information models. *Information Systems*, 18(7):489–523, 1993.

[HW93] A.H.M. ter Hofstede and Th.P. van der Weide. Expressiveness in conceptual data modelling. *Data & Knowledge Engineering*, 10(1):65–100, February 1993.

[KBC+89] W. Kim, N. Ballou, H.-T. Chou, J.F. Garza, and D. Woelk. Features of the ORION Object-Oriented Database. In W. Kim and F.H. Lochovsky, editors, *Object-Oriented Concepts, Databases, and Applications*, ACM Press, Frontier Series, pages 251–282. Addison-Wesley, Reading, Massachusetts, 1989.

[MS90] E. McKenzie and R. Snodgrass. Schema evolution and the relational algebra. *Information Systems*, 15(2):207–232, 1990.

[NH89] G.M. Nijssen and T.A. Halpin. *Conceptual Schema and Relational Database Design: a fact oriented approach.* Prentice-Hall, Sydney, Australia, 1989.

[Pro93] H.A. Proper. Towards an Integration of Evolving Information Systems and CASE-Tools. In S. Brinkkemper and F. Harmsen, editors, *Proceedings of the Fourth Workshop on the Next Generation of CASE Tools*, pages 23–33, Paris, France, June 1993.

[PW93] H.A. Proper and Th.P. van der Weide. EVORM: A Conceptual Modelling Technique for Evolving Application Domains. Technical Report 93-16, Information Systems Group, Computing Science Institute, University of Nijmegen, Nijmegen, The Netherlands, 1993. To appear in: Data & Knowledge Engineering.

Geographic Data Handling in a Deductive Object-Oriented Database

Alia I. Abdelmoty, Norman W. Paton, M. Howard Williams,
Alvaro A.A. Fernandes, Maria L. Barja, Andrew Dinn

Department of Computing and Electrical Engineering,
Heriot-Watt University
Riccarton, Edinburgh EH14 4AS, Scotland, UK
e-mail: <alia,norm,howard,alvaro,marisa,andrew>@cee.hw.ac.uk
phone: +44-31-449-5111 ; fax: +44-31-451-3431

Abstract.
This paper describes how a deductive object-oriented database (DOOD) can be used to support the storage and management of data which is typical of that found in geographic information systems (GIS). This is done with two aims in mind: to illustrate how a combination of deductive and object-oriented facilities can be applied effectively in an advanced application, thereby motivating the development of DOOD systems; and to show how geographic database systems stand to gain from the utilisation of advanced data modelling and inference facilities as supported by a DOOD. The paper describes the DOOD system which has been used for prototyping a range of geographic concepts, presents a framework for the structural organisation of GIS data using an object-oriented data model, and shows how a logic query language can be used within this structural framework to perform a range of analyses.

1 Introduction

Geographic information systems (GISs) present a major challenge to the developers of advanced databases. The complexity of the data to be modelled – which may be richly structured, spatially distributed, time-variant and subject to complex operations – strains the relational model, which has been shown to be inadequate for many geographic applications [WHM90, Ege92]. Systems have been proposed for managing geographic data which add explicit support for spatial data types into the relational model [Gut88, AS91], but such systems retain the widely recognised weaknesses of relational systems for handling the aspatial aspects of geographic applications, thereby diluting the gains achieved as a result of incorporating spatial data types and operations.

This paper presents an approach to the combined use of deductive and object-oriented facilities for managing geographic data. It is shown how object-oriented modelling constructs can be used to capture the structural semantics of a range of geographic concepts, and how deductive rules can be used to infer the existence of complex relationships within a geographic database.

The paper is structured as follows. Section 2 outlines the principal facilities of the DOOD system which is being used with geographic applications. Section 3 indicates how the modelling facilities of the DOOD can be used to describe a range of geographic concepts. Section 4 shows how deduction can be used in this context to infer the existence of additional relationships between geographic concepts. Conclusions are presented in section 5.

2 ROCK & ROLL - A Deductive Object Oriented Database

This section presents an informal overview of the ROCK (Rule Object Computation Kernel) & ROLL (Rule Object Logic Language) DOOD system. ROCK & ROLL has three principal components – an object-oriented data model (OM), a logic query language (ROLL), and an imperative manipulation language (ROCK). In ROCK & ROLL, the object-oriented data model has been used as the basis for the design of the other components. The data model describes the structural characteristics of the data which can be processed by both the logic and imperative languages, and thus the two programming languages can be integrated in a way which avoids the introduction of the impedance mismatch [BPF+94]. Support for the two languages enables the user to select the programming paradigm which is most suitable for particular tasks within a complex application, and thus allows the benefits of both a deductive database and an imperative programming language in a single system.

2.1 Data Model

This section gives an informal overview of the constructs used to model an application domain both structurally and behaviourally.

Atomic values and compound data items are called *primary objects* and *secondary objects* respectively. Each object is assigned an *object type*, and must conform to the structure associated with that type. Every secondary object has a unique object identifier.

A type definition can describe references of two kinds. The first kind of (optional) reference definition is used to model the *properties* of the type. This results, for each type, in a possibly empty set of type names which are the attributes of the type. For example, the definition in figure 1 indicates that a `road` has a single property of type `roadName`.

```
type road
    properties:
        roadName;
    { roadSegment };
    ...
end-type
```

Figure 1: Definition of type road.

The second kind of (optional) reference definition, which is referred to as the *construction* of the type, is used to distinguish the fundamental structural characteristic of a type from its other stored properties. A type can be structured by *association, sequentiation* or *aggregation*, which support the modelling of sets, lists and tuples, respectively. For example, the definition in figure 1 indicates that a **road**, is constructed as an association of **roadSegment** objects (represented by curly brackets).

Schema diagrams for the data model can be constructed using the following notation. Secondary object types are represented using rectangles, primary object types using ellipses, and operations as round-cornered rectangles. Labelled directed edges represent modelling features thus: ○ – attribution, ◬ – specialisation, ⊗ – aggregation, ⊛ – association, and ◎ – sequentiation. Unlabelled directed edges represent the aliasing of type names. This notation is used to describe part of a geographic database in figure 2. Shaded types in this figure are discussed later.

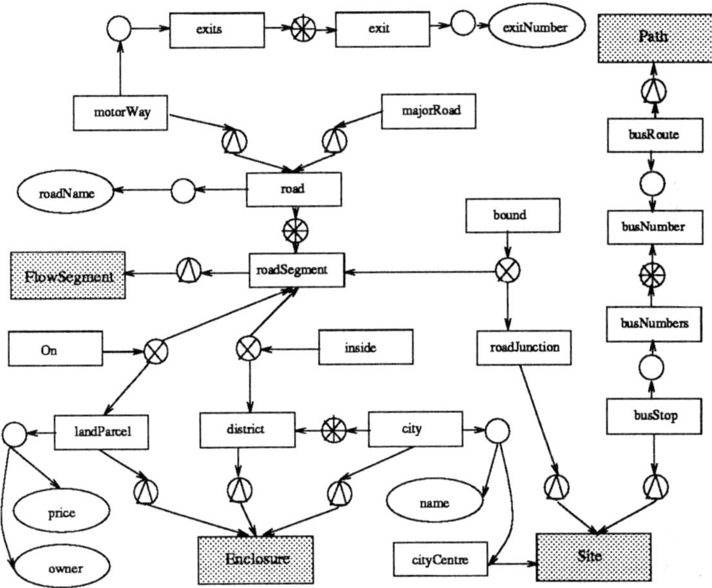

Figure 2: Application schema showing the structure of some of the involved objects.

The behavioural properties of objects are defined using methods. The signatures of public methods are included as part of the definition of a type. Every type is associated with a class of the same name as the type. The class specifies the private properties of the type and gives the code which implements the methods. The intention is that the type specifies all that a user of the type needs to know in order to use the type, while method code and other implementation details are specified in the class. Methods can be implemented using either the imperative language ROCK or the logic language ROLL.

2.2 Logic Language

ROLL is a Horn clause language. Familiarity with the latter subclass of first-order languages is assumed at the level of [CGT90].

The *ROLL alphabet* consists of logic variables, constant symbols and predicate symbols, but not function symbols. The set of *constant symbols* is the set of names of values (e.g. `5`, `"Edinburgh"`, `true`). There is no need for object identifiers to appear as constant symbols in ROLL expressions, as specific objects are either passed into a ROLL expression from ROCK, or are retrieved from the extensional database.

The set of *predicate symbols* is the set of operation names declared by operation interfaces. It follows that ROLL queries abide by strict encapsulation.

A ROLL *term* τ is either a ROLL *constant* or a *(logical) variable*. A ROLL *atom* has the form $\beta(\tau_1, \ldots, \tau_{n-1})@\alpha == \tau_n$, which is read as "send the *message* β with the arguments $\tau_1, \ldots, \tau_{n-1}$ and the result τ_n to the object α". An operation interface $\beta(T_1, \ldots, T_{n-1})@\alpha == T_n$, is assumed to be defined, such that each τ_i denotes an instance of T_i', where $T_i' \leq T_i$. If the operation β has no distinguished result (as is the case with ROLL methods), then the term has the form $\beta(\tau_1, \ldots, \tau_n)@\alpha$. If $n = 0$ then $\beta@\alpha =_{def} \beta()@\alpha$.

A *ROLL clause* is a Horn clause, and the usual convention is followed of rewriting a clause as a reverse implication, i.e. *head* '`:-`' *body*.

The following query over the schema presented graphically in figure 2 retrieves as bindings for `LP` the `landParcel` objects which are associated with the `owner "Acme Products"`, and which have a `price` greater than 1000.

```
get_owner@LP == "Acme Products", get_price@LP == P, P > 1000.
```

This example uses a number of facilities which bear explanation: methods with the prefix `get_` are generated automatically by the system to allow access to the structural characteristics of an object; the results of the messages `get_owner` and `get_price`, each of which are sent to `landParcel` objects bound to the logic variable `LP`, are unified with the constant `"Acme Products"` and the variable `P` respectively; ROLL queries and methods are strongly typed, and a type inference system is used to infer types for logic variables – for example, that the logic variable `LP` is associated with the type `landParcel` is inferred from the fact that the methods `get_owner` and `get_price` are applicable to objects of type `landParcel`; in this example there is no explicit iteration over the instances of `landParcel` – the ROLL query evaluator optimises a query, and plants iterators within the evaluation graph wherever there is no other way of obtaining a binding for a logic variable associated with an object type.

The following method definition introduces a method called `roads` attached to the class `district`, which retrieves as bindings for `Road` the `road` objects which pass through the `district` which is the recipient of the message, namely `District`.

```
class district
    ...
    roads(Road)@District :-
        get_roadSegment@Inside == Segment,
        get_district@Inside == District,
        get_member@Road == Segment.
end-class
```

In this example, it can be seen that rules are associated with object classes, thereby allowing the rule base to be organised in an object-oriented manner. That the variable **District** is of type **district** is established from the fact that it fulfills the role of message recipient in the method definition which is specified within the class **district**. The system generated method **get_member** is used to retrieve the objects which are stored within an object constructed by association, in this case the association **Road**.

3 Object-Oriented Modelling of the Geographic Domain

In defining a geographic entity, two kinds of property can be distinguished: descriptive properties and spatial properties. The former refers to textual and numeric information (e.g. the name and rate of flow of a river, the density of population of a region), while the latter specify spatial characteristics of that entity, i.e. its shape and location. The current generation of GISs [Mor86] is characterised by the presence of:

- Distinct underlying representations: a dichotomy exists between the systems used for the representation and manipulation of the spatial and aspatial aspects of an application (e.g. a relational DBMS for managing aspatial data and specialised systems for managing the spatial data) with an integration layer to link them.

- Data source dependence: two categories of geographic data source can be recognised, which yield vector data and raster data. The spatial representations of geographic objects in these two forms are different, both in terms of structure and in the geometric operations which can be efficiently supported. Current GISs are restricted to only one of these categories due to the strong link between the representation of the application level concepts and the geometric data structures.

With a view to overcoming the above problems a three level conceptual model for the geographic domain is proposed, in which a level of geographic abstract data types acts as a buffer between the geometric level of representation, where only the graphical aspects of the data are modelled, and the level where application concepts are modelled. Figure 3 illustrates the mapping between the three levels, which is discussed in more detail later.

In what follows a brief overview is given of the three levels and their representation using the ROCK & ROLL data model.

3.1 Application Level Concepts

Figure 2 shows a sample schema of part of a geographic application. The shaded object types in the figure are sample GADTs which are discussed in the next subsection. Application objects are modelled as specializations of GADTs, from which structure and behaviour are inherited.

Spatial hierarchies of geographic concepts are represented using the modelling constructs aggregation, association and sequentiation. For example, a

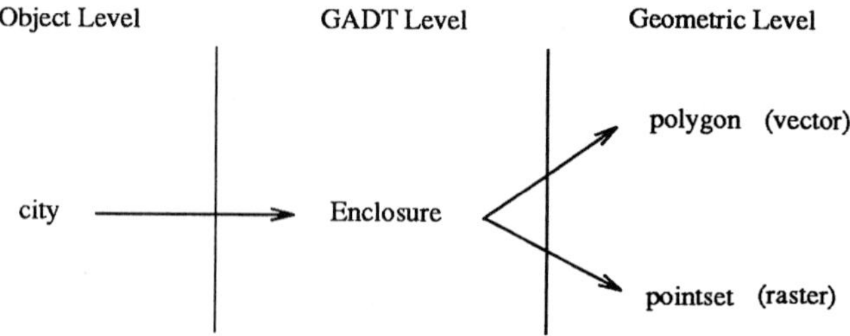

Figure 3: Example types from the three levels of representation showing the indirect mapping between the object and the geometric levels.

city is a set of **districts**. Objects can have complex object types as attributes, for example, the type **motorWay** has an attribute **exits** which is a set of **exit** objects.

The example schema shows both the flexibility and directness of representation of the geographic domain concepts using the semantic constructs provided by the data model. Furthermore, lower level details are hidden from the application level using the GADTs introduced in the next subsection.

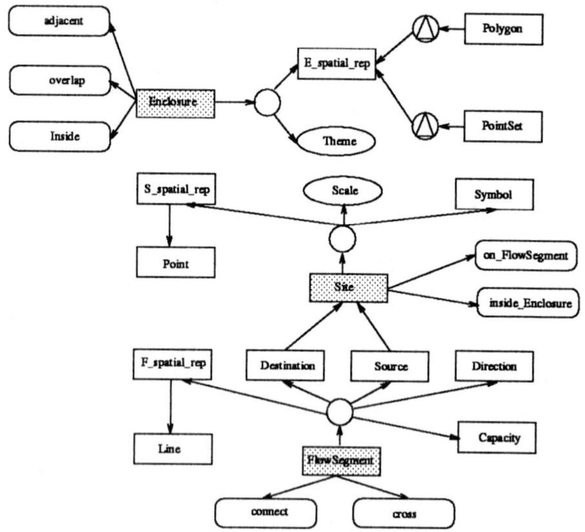

Figure 4: Examples of structure of some GADTs.

3.2 Geographic Abstract Data Types

Figure 4 presents the structure of some of the GADTs used in figure 2. For example, an **Enclosure** is a representation of a real world object enclosing a property or an activity which has an areal spatial representation. Examples include *house*, *district*, *city*, etc. The spatial representation of the enclosure is hidden as one of its attributes, and is chosen in this case to generalize both the polygon (vector) and the pointset (raster) representations, thus allowing objects from different data sources to be homogeneously modelled. Spatial operations such as *overlap*, *inside* and *adjacent* are defined on the class `Enclosure`, and implemented on both its spatial representations.

More complex objects can be built using the above GADTs, such as the `Path` in figure 2, which represents a list of `FlowSegments`, where a `busRoute` is a specialisation of `Path` representing an ordered set of `roadSegments`.

3.3 The Geometric Level of Representation

Types from the geometric level of representation represent concepts such as points, lines and polygons. Spatial operations on the application level objects map to operations on the geometric level through the GADTs. For example, the *overlay* operation between two thematic maps, e.g. soil types and rain-fall maps, is interpreted as an overlap operation between their component regions, represented as `Enclosures`. Such an operation is implemented as an intersection operation over the spatial representation of the `Enclosure` objects, where the method of implementation may be different for the two spatial representations. Spatial indexes can be used at this level to enhance spatial search.

4 Deductive Inference in a Geographic Database

Section 3 has shown that the rich semantic modelling constructs offered by the object data model have allowed the realisation of a three level conceptual model for the geographic domain. This model also provides an effective framework within which operations representing spatial relationships can be developed.

By virtue of possessing a location in space, geographic objects exhibit spatial relationships with all other objects in this space. Ad-hoc spatial relationships between objects in a GDB, which are a consequence of their relative positions, are very common in GIS queries. For example, the following are typical: find the dwellings which are adjacent to a post office; find the dwellings which are down-stream of a given chemical factory on a river and south-of a given city; find the dwellings which are within 1/2 hour driving distance from a given shopping centre.

It is generally accepted that it is not feasible to store all the relationships required to answer such queries explicitly. Considerations such as storage overheads, frequency of usage and cost of derivation are used in assessing which spatial relationships to store and which to derive. In most GISs, such as ARC/INFO [Mor86], some topological relationships are stored at the geometric level, and computational geometry is used for the dynamic evaluation of others. More recently, qualitative spatial reasoning over some of the above relationships has been proposed [Ege91, AWP93] as a complementary mechanism to computational geometry for the derivation of spatial relationships. This section illustrates how deduction can be used to support the inference of spatial relationships.

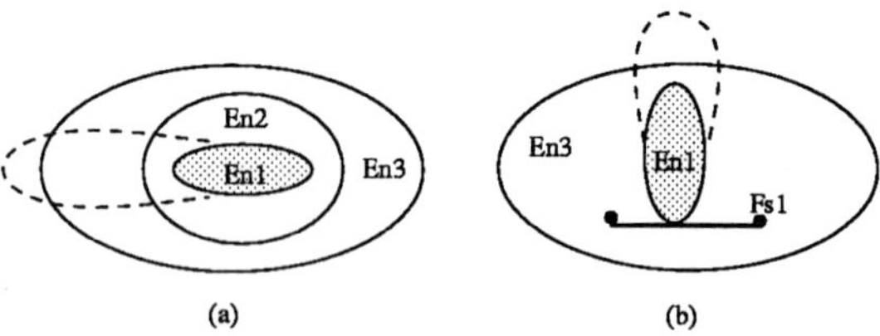

Figure 5: Defining the overlap operation on two Enclosures using a third Enclosure in (a) and a FlowSegment in (b).

4.1 Inference of Spatial Relationships

Spatial relationship composition, i.e. the deduction of a relationship between two objects given their relationship with a common intermediate object, is used below to illustrate spatial reasoning in a GDB.

For example, figure 5 shows different situations where an enclosure **En1** can be said to overlap the enclosure **En3**. In 5(a) **En1** is held to overlap **En3** because it overlaps **En2** and **En2** is inside **En3**. In figure 5(b) **En1** is held to overlap **En3** because **En1** is on the **flowSegment Fs1** and **Fs1** is inside **En3**. These observations can be incorporated into a definition of **overlap** as shown below:

```
class enclosure
    ...
    overlap(En3)@En1 :-
       inside(En1)@En2, inside(En2)@En3:enclosure.
    overlap(En3)@En1 :-
       on_flowSegment(En1)@Fs1, inside(Fs1)@En3:enclosure.
end-class
```

In the above example, the suffix **:<typename>** associated with some of the variables is used to give hints to the type inference system, which is otherwise unable to infer an unambiguous type for each variable in this case.

An example of the use of recursive rules in method definitions is illustrated in the **path** relationship between two **flowSegments** as follows:

```
class flowSegment
    ...
    path(Fs2)@Fs1 :-
       get_Destination@Fs1 == Connection, get_Source@Fs2 == Connection.
    path(Fs2)@Fs1 :-
       path(Fs3)@Fs1, path(Fs2)@Fs3.
end-class
```

4.2 Using Rules on Application Level Concepts

Methods over application level classes in figure 2 can also be defined using rules. For example, **motorWaysInCity** is an operation defined on the object class **city** to determine which instances of the class **motorWay** pass through a particular **city** object.

```
class city
    ...
    motorWaysInCity(M)@City :-
       get_member@M:motorWay == RS, get_roadSegment@In:inside == RS,
       get_district@In == District, get_member@City  == District.
end-class
```

In the above example, the class **inside** is used to represent a relationship between **roadSegments** and **districts**. As ROLL queries and methods are optimised, the order in which the subgoals within a query or rule are entered does not determine how it is evaluated. In practice, ROLL queries are evaluated bottom-up after being optimised using a technique based upon Static Filtering [CGT90].

A query which calls this method to retrieve the **motorWays** passing through the city of **Athens** can be written as follows:

```
var mset := [{M} | get_name@City == "Athens", motorWaysInCity(M)@City]
```

This example shows how the result of a ROLL query can be assigned to a variable in the imperative programming language ROCK [BPF+94]. The embedded query is enclosed in square brackets, the result being the set of objects `M` which satisfy the goal expressed to the right of the `|`. It is possible to process the set assigned to **mset** using the normal facilities of ROCK. For example, the following program would print out the **roadName** of every **motorWay** in **mset**:

```
foreach o in mset do
    write get_roadName@o, nl;
```

Note that as ROLL is a logic language, it is possible to run the method **motorWaysInCity** with different variable bindings, i.e. to find the **motorWay** objects associated with a given **city**, to find the **city** objects through which a given **motorWay** passes, to find out if a given **motorWay** passes through a given **city**, or to find out which **motorWays** pass though which cities.

5 Conclusions

This paper has presented a new approach to the modelling and management of geographic data in a GIS, using a deductive object-oriented database system. The approach has two main features:

- A three level conceptual model for structuring geographic data, with the underlying geometric layer accessed through a collection of geographic abstract data types, which are in turn referenced by application level concepts. The model facilitates the effective modelling of complex geographic phenomena with possibly different underlying spatial representations.

- Spatial reasoning rules for the derivation of implicit spatial relationships which are too numerous to store in the database. Rules for the derivation of such relationships are complementary to computational geometry algorithms which are usually associated with large computation costs.

This approach to geographic data modelling is being prototyped using the deductive object-oriented database system ROCK & ROLL, where the following features have been exploited: an expressive object-oriented data model which can directly capture the structural characteristics of a range of geographic concepts at different levels of abstraction; a fully integrated logic language, which can be used to infer the existence of spatial or aspatial relationships between geographic concepts, which are typically too numerous to store; and a fully integrated imperative database programming language, which can be used for manipulating the database, but which also complements the logic language for retrieval tasks in this domain, where the execution of complex geometric algorithms is central to the efficiency of the overall system.

Acknowledgements The work that resulted in this paper has been funded by the Science and Engineering Research Council through the IEATP programme. We are also grateful to Dr. Keith G. Jeffery of RAL for useful discussions on the subject of this paper, and Dr. J.M.P. Quinn representing ICL and Mr Neil Smith of Ordnance Survey as the industrial partners in the project.

References

[AS91] W.G. Aref and H. Samet. Extending a DBMS with Spatial Operations. In O. Gunther and H.J. Scheck, editors, *Advances in Spatial Databases, SSD'91*, LNCS 525, pages 299–318, ., 1991. Springer-Verlag.

[AWP93] Alia I. Abdelmoty, M.Howard Williams, and Norman W. Paton. Deduction and Deductive Databases for Geographic Data Handling. In *Design and Implementation of Large Spatial Databases, Third International Symposium, SSD '93*, LNCS 692, pages 443–464. Springer Verlag, June 1993.

[BPF+94] M.L. Barja, N.W. Paton, A.A.A. Fernandes, M.H. Williams, and A. Dinn. An Effective Deductive Object-Oriented Database Through Language Integration. In *Proc. 20th VLDB*, 1994.

[CGT90] S. Ceri, G. Gottlob, and L. Tanca. *Logic Programming and Databases.* Springer-Verlag, Berlin, 1990.

[Ege91] M.J. Egenhofer. Reasoning About Binary Topological Relations. In O. Gunther and H.J. Scheck, editors, *Advances in Spatial Databases, 2nd Symposium, SSD'91*, Lecture Notes in Computer Science, 525, pages 143–161, Zurich, Switzerland., 1991. Springer-Verlag.

[Ege92] M.J. Egenhofer. Why not SQL! *Int. J. Geographic Information Systems*, 6(2):71–85, 1992.

[Gut88] R.H. Guting. Geo-Relational Algebra: A Model and Query Language for Geometric Database Systems. In J.W. Schmidt and M. Missikoff, editors, *Advances in Database Technology- EDBT'88*, Lecture Notes in Computer Science, pages 506–527, Venice, Italy, 1988. Spriger Verlag.

[Mor86] S. Morehouse. ARC/INFO: A Geo-Relational Model for Spatial Information. In *Proceedings of 7th Int. Symposium on Computer Assisted Cartography*, pages 388–398, Washington, DC, 1986.

[WHM90] M.F. Worboys, H.M. Hearnshaw, and D.J. Maguire. Object-Oriented Data Modelling for Spatial Databases. *Int. J. Geographic Information Systems*, 4(4):369–383, 1990.

Expert Spatial Knowledge: an Expert Geographical Information System in Diffusion of Water

El-Yamine KETTAL
Laboratoire d'Ingénierie des Sytèmes d'Information
Institut National des Sciences Appliquées.
20, Avenue Albert Einstein, F-69621 Villeurbanne, France

Keywords: GIS, Expert System, Hydrology, TIN.

Abstract. The modeling of expert spatial knowledge is obtained by the combining of two different domains: GIS and Expert System. This system, the combining of each domain, enables both expert system and GIS to perform new tasks. An overview of the system in the hydrologic/hydraulic domain is presented. Our object is to provide tools for spatial reasoning in an expert system, for which a prototype is being realized. It will drive the simulation, by choosing differential equations corresponding to a situation in a zone of land, and will ensure the continuity of values of variables near boundaries and the evolving of parameters of equations in zones. Once the parameters are chosen, we can change scenarios (e.g. add a wall or dam, ...) to see the changes in water diffusion. This modeling applied to differential equations of water diffusion in case of natural or artificial rivers enables the risk of flooding to be limited.

1 Introduction

To create a computer tool allowing simulations of diffusion phenomena using logic rules and spatial data analysis in varied scenarios, will allow users to simulate the diffusion phenomena and help them to take decisions.

The system makes it possible to connect three very important components to the expert system: hydraulic methods, hydrologic methods and the spatial data base. The hydrologic methods are performed first, and so the system simulates river flows using hydraulic methods. The system can simulate water flowing without having evalued hydrologic methods but it acquires an up-river hydrogram by the user, or it evaluates the hydrogram of a watershed using hydrologic methods according to the features of the land.

The Expert System must backtrack in case of an invalid choice made by the execution of an equation or in case of a parameter which temporarily changes due to ground conditions.

The modeling of spatial-temporal knowledge, applied to the diffusion of water has to pass through two steps; firstly, by the modeling of the land surface with adequate models, like the irregular triangulated network model (TIN), and, secondly, by the information which can evolve in time or which may consist of constants: they are driven by differential equations following spatial and hydrological data located on the watershed. Once the system is implemented, it can simulate only the diffusions defined above. So the system is very specific for the diffusion models used.

For this reason, a model is suggested for a system, which combines artificial intelligence and spatial data modeling, and can treat all kinds of diffusion models for all kinds of terrains. In this way, the system is composed of:

. the land topographical base,
. the data base of land zones,
. the inference engine which can drive the system,
. the programs to resolve differential equations,
. and the man/machine interface which can return the results and acquire data.

After the system has integrated expert system specifics, like modularity, it may become very flexible and rich by adding other models of diffusion of water in hydrology or in hydraulics.

2 Hydro-Geographic Information

The water diffusion simulation system must consider two aspects of modeling: lands geometry and mathematical models of water diffusion.

2.1 Hydrologic/Hydraulic Data

Hydrology allows the using of hydrograms in outlet of watershed and hydraulics, using performed hydrogram and land information, allow us to simulate water flow all along the river.

Hydraulics models used modeling which uses more or fewer parameters and a simplified geometry of the river, varying according to integration hypothesis [Farissier 93].

Hydrologic models can provide rising hydrograms (curves flow in terms of time in a point of the river) corresponding to return periods (annual, decennial, ...). Resolving theses models requires hydraulics or hydrologics constraints checking and knowing land data. For example: slope, wet area, hydraulic radius, ... for hydraulics and watershed area, rain intensity, ... for hydrology. Method data are required by these models, but cannot be checked in the land model. This information may be variables or parameters which can change in time, and can be specific to one or more models and land type. Example of this information: rain data, water elevation, Euler coefficient ...

2.2 Geographic Data

They regroup spatial information (DTM) and information needed by diffusion models (grid attributes). Attributes are defined [Delclaux 93] for every grid: physiography, minimal altitude, drainage direction, production function kind and nature of grid (a grid is considered "river" if it contains a hydrometric post or a hydraulic layout, or if it is located between a two "rivers" grid otherwise it is considered a watershed "bassin". Diffusion models also require other information like slopes, kinds of land for each zone (vegetation, gravels, ...) ...

Figure 1 presents land in two different situations: the case of normal flow and the case of flooding.

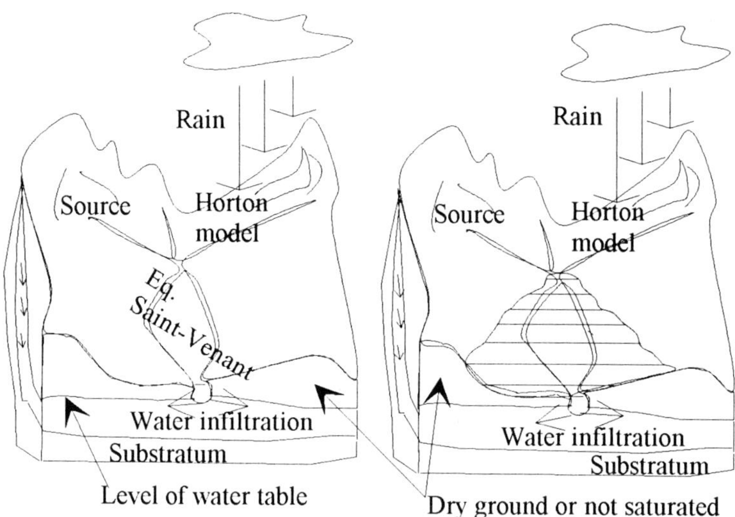

Fig. 1. Representation of a flood

2.3 Land Model

Hydrologic and hydraulic models use a lot of spatial models for flow simulation modeling. To develop a system which can integrate the functionalities of these models, it needs for land topography, a powerful and precise model land. The irregular triangulated network model (TIN) seems to be the adequate model:

The TIN model is, compared to others models, economical in data size and allows calculation of [Rouet 91]:

. slope and direction of face,

. flow (the highest slope),

. contour maps, the nodes of which are located in the intersection of the face edges with a horizontal plan at a given altitude.

Also a TIN model allows to recognise holes and hills on the terrain [Silfer 87]. The TIN model belongs to the vector family, and can be generated from many sources: digital terrain model (DTM), digitized contour maps ... It works by deleting altimetric points which do not bring any information. It stores triangle vertices. Big triangles for flat terrain and small triangles in the contrary case. In other case, the TIN model can be transformed into other terrain models (necessary to apply diffusion methods for example grid models). [Bork and al. 86] present a variety of parameters derived from grid terrain representation and digital mapping and relate them to hydrological applications. Grid algorithms are best applied to large rural watersheds not having abrupt changes in terrain elevation at any location. TINs are better suited for urban terrain because they permit arbitrary placement of elevation points and better capture changes in terrain such as those associated with constructed surfaces. Also TINs are the standard form of terrain representation produced by land surveyors [Djokic and al 91]. For our system and considering our means, triangles are generated from digitized contour maps on which the Delaunay triangulation is applied. The next example shows a terrain in TIN model with its nodes, faces and an alphanumeric attribute: type of terrain.

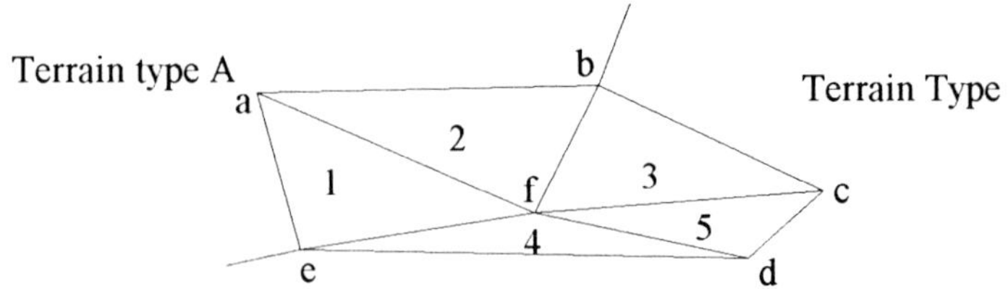

Fig. 2. Example of Triangulated Irregular Network (TIN)

2.4 Example of Diffusion Model

Flow models studied terrain, are water flow simulation model in rivers and flow rate calculation model in watersheds [Thibault 82]. For water flow modeling in ground, the Darcy model is used.

One of the aspects of water is its fluidity and deformation relative to its environment. In case of flows gradually varying, transitory or permanent, and on ground, the Barre de Saint Venant model is used. Flows on ground and underground are very different but can communicate together. For example the rain produces water ground flow and water underground flow. And flow infiltrates water in the underground.

a) the Barre de Saint Venant model makes it possible to calculate speed and flow rate knowing the boundary conditions.

This model can be used under the following constraints:

. necessity to have gradually varying flows;

. necessity of simplification, especially when analytic resolution is impossible.

These models are complex and difficult to validate. Their precision and physical relevance of results are connected directly to the quality (and quantity) of used data, geometric and hydraulic [Farissier 93].

b) An example of a hydrologic model is the Caquot model [Bourrier 85]: this method which is a version of rational method, calculates the flow rate of a watershed.

c) A Flow model example in underground is Darcy law [Laréal 75]. Darcy's law (used only in saturated underground) serves to evaluate the water height variation or the quantity of water infiltrated. It calculates the velocity of discharge considering the permeability of the terrain. This method may be valid if we have :

. a water saturated environment,

. a permanent flow,

. a laminar flow, (low flow velocity).

3 System Architecture

The system architecture is defined in a manner to provide modularity for the system, so possible modifications in any part of the system have no effects over other parts of the system. Figure 3 represents the system and its components:

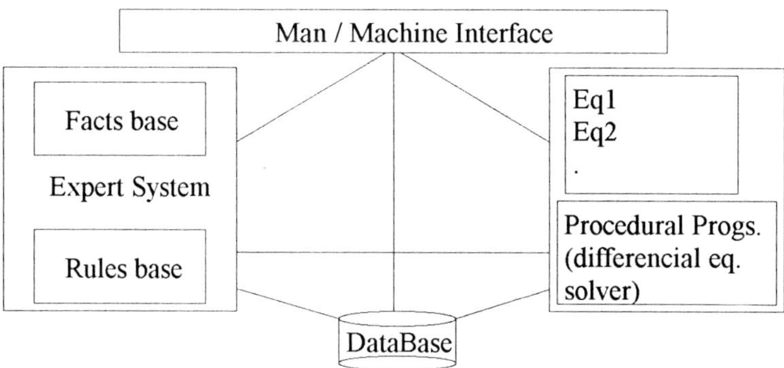

Fig. 3. System Architecture

The system is composed of :

. A Man/Machine interface which makes it possible to acquire such different data like : nodes of triangles, hydraulic stations, rains ...

. Expert system which infers facts for choosing hydraulic/hydrologic equations,

. Set of independent equations,

. Data base of hydro-geographic data,

. Module which evaluates results of diffusion methods.

3.1 Data Base and Knowledge Base

The data base includes all the terrain data and hydrologic/hydraulic data (Figure 4). The knowledge data represents the rules and facts for which the inference engine needs to choose a water diffusion method.

But hydrologic/hydraulic methods depend on spatial data and on other hydrologic attributes in the data base (example: area of zones or watersheds, type of watershed soil,...). So to execute these methods, the system expert must communicate with the data base, to acquire, for example, the spatial data or kind of soil...

In a watershed, there exist some small rivers or channels which drive water to the watershed outlet and are considered watershed ramifications. These ramifications are represented by a list of lines, and a watershed outlet is represented by a point. Flow rate watershed is calculated into outlet point.

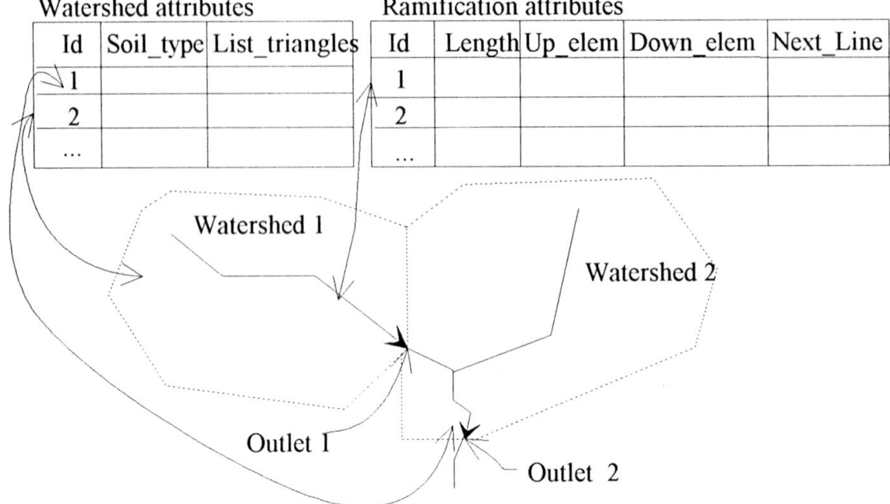

Fig. 4. A part of the data base

In the "Ramification attribute table" given in Figure 4, all ramification elements are described by means of an identifier together with an up ward and down ward element and its next ramification line.

The watershed or zone which has common characteristics, is represented by one or more triangles as represented in Figure 5.

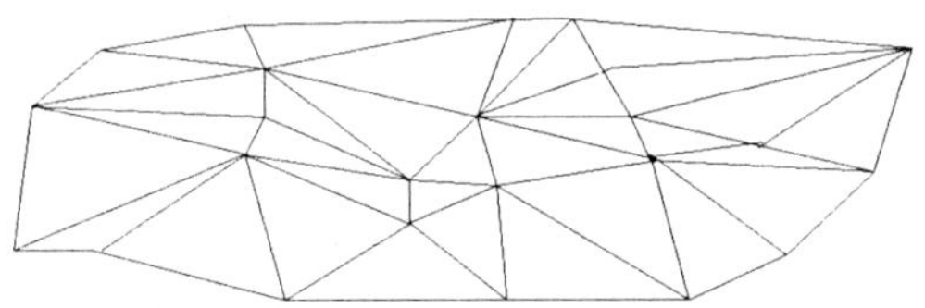

Fig. 5. A set of zone triangles

3.2 Expert System

Linking an expert system with a GIS enables both the expert system and the GIS to perform new tasks, and opens the way for more complex spatial analyses and more flexible querying of GIS data bases than has been possible previously [Thomas 93]. An Expert GIS can serve as a development base for applications which provides spatial data and decision aid tools.

The expert system is the nucleus of our system, because its objective is to choose and execute flow equations and recover results.

This expert system is composed of:

- a fact base,
- a rule base,
- an inference engine (or system nucleus).

The facts are defined by the user to launch the system. The rules can be of two types: generic and specific. The generic rules will compose the future metarule base and the specifics rules will compose the future environment of the development of an expert system called CIA.

3.3 Man/Machine Interface

The Man/Machine interface of the system consists of independent shutters:

. Expert system, data models and differential equations;

. Hydrologic / hydraulics models.

The holding data regroup:

. Rule base and fact base: an editor which allows creation, modification, and consultation of knowledge base;

. topographic data: a set of points are triangulated to generate triangles;

. terrain and hydrologic data are selected in a list of data: the user selects one or more triangles, and clicks on eventual characteristics defined on a palette;

. differential equations are added to the system by adding a new solution program and affecting a new equation identifier.

Each new equation leads us to hold or to modify one or more rules.

4 System Functionalities

Minimal fonctionalities, are presented here, that a system, devoted to simulation of water diffusion with "intelligent" choices, requires.

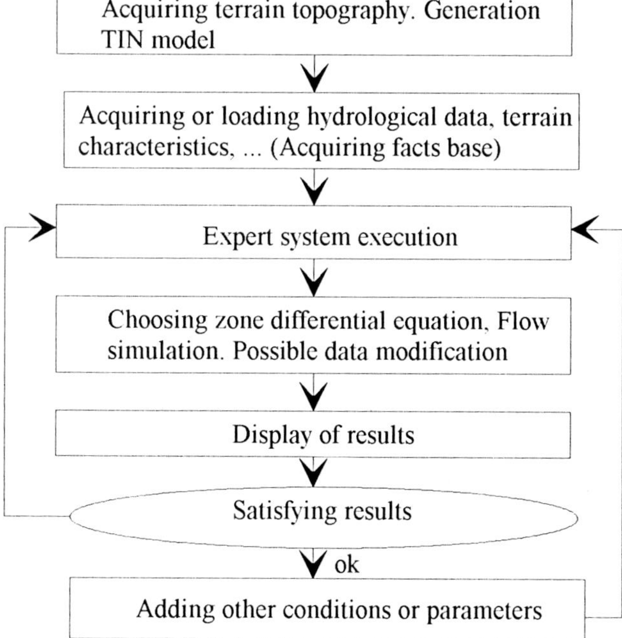

Fig. 6. System Functionalities

4.1 Symbolic and Procedural Information Processing

In the system, there is a mixing of two information processing methods: symbolic and procedural. These methods are implemented in the expert system and in the solver of differential equations. These processings are generally represented in Figure 6.

Expert System

The facts must refer to precise terrain zones, and for this reason, facts have also spatial and temporal indexation to specify where equations have to be executed. It is also the same for rules which have to allow spatial temporal indexations, for two following reasons:

. to pass zones to equations (retrieved in a data base),

. to compare results of two rules at the boundary.

An example of some rules:

1- If Slope(#zone) And TransversalSection(#zone) And WaterSpeed(#zone) = constant Then WaterMovement(#zone) = uniform.
2- If TimeMovement(#zone) = constant
Then WaterMovement(#zone) = permanent.
3- If Environment = urban And Area(#zone) < 200 And 2% <= Slope(#zone) And Slope(#zone) <= 5% Then Eq_Caquot.
4- If NoParallel(FreeArea(#zone), Bottom(#zone))
Then WaterMovement(#zone) = varying.

These rules show some predicates which require interaction with the geographic data base, so predicates in the expert system are called functions in others domains like hydrology and spatial reasoning. For example: Slope(#zone) is a function which calculates the slope of a zone. There are two kinds of functions: functions which calculate values and functions which retrieve data from the data base.

The system expert has two passes :

. in the first pass, the inference engine chooses equations for each zone according to their areas and characteristics,

. in the second pass, the inference engine chooses parameters for each equation according also to their areas and characteristics.

So after choosing equations and parameters, the engine can start equation execution at time t and can stop simulation after any change in facts. It does the same task, seen above, for each zone, for the choice of equations and parameters. And moreover the system works in two steps :

. First step : execution of equations at time t.

. Second step : comparison of value variables at the boundaries. If values variables are too different then it executes the equations several times to have less different values at these boundaries; else the system executes the first step for the time $t + \Delta t$.

Differential Equations

Two different kinds of equations must be distinguished: numerical equation methods and finite difference methods. The first are resolved by an arithmetic expression compiler which translates arithmetic expressions and evaluates them; a compiler allows the solving of equations without writing a program corresponding to each equation. The second type of programs for each equation will have to been written, according to different equation solutions.

4.2 Boundary Continuity

The variables for diffusion methods will indicate, in case of no boundary continuity, (Figure 7) to the expert system the necessity to change parameter values for ensuring their continuity. Example:

If velocity *U1* in *zone 1* is different than velocity *U2* in *zone 2* neighbour of *zone 1*, then the system must change values or introduce another intermediate model. These variables can be modified at each resolving program execution.

Due to a library for variables, associed variables to each existent method in the system can be known whether they need to be calculated or given as constants. If they need to be calculated, the values of boundary variables are compared and normalized in case of inequality.

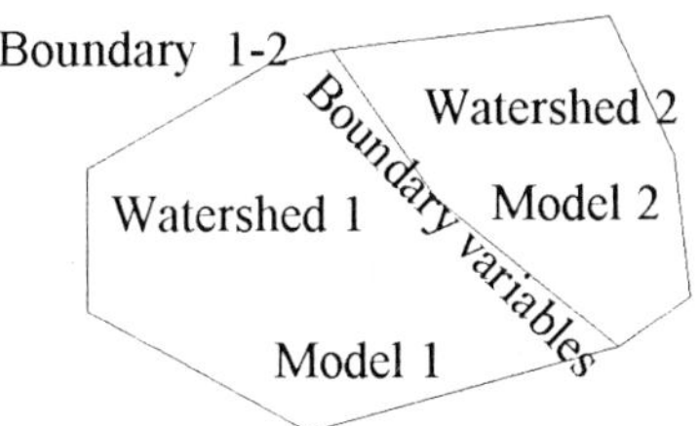

Fig. 7. Zones boundary values

4.3 Results Restoration

System results can be graphic or alphanumeric:

. In graphic cases, curves like hyetogram of a watershed are drawn by graphic programs, the possible use of interpolations.

. In alphanumeric cases, variables values are displayed in answering to queries like velocity value, flow rate ...

5 Conclusion

The system described in this article treats a few equations, well known, of water diffusion, and this to show that it is possible to mix different domains (Hydraulics/Hydrology, Expert system, Spatial data base), and for facilitating this implementation approch without geographic information systems.

The main reason for developing a system which integrates GIS fonctionalities and an expert system is to develop a prototype of spatial reasoning and analysis. So this prototype can serve as the basis for development of a spatial decision support system by providing both the spatial data and decision making tools.

The future prospects are numerous, in development of systems, like expert system development, binding between spatial reasoning and spatial analysis, the introduction of new fonctionalities as GIS fonctionalities, ... and systems developing in easier integration of new water diffusion methods.

References

[Bork and al. 86]: H. R. Bork and H. Rohdenburg 1986. *Transferable Parametrization Methods for Distributed Hydrological and Agroecological Catchment models.* Catena, 13, pp. 99-117.

[Bourrier 85]: R. Bourrier. *Les Réseaux d'Assainissement. Calculs Applications Perspectives.* 2 eme Ed. Technique et Documentation Lavoisier 1985.

[Delclaux 93]: F. Delclaux, G. Boyer. *Exemple d'utilisation d'un SIG pour la gestion des données d'un modèle hydrologique à mailles carrées.* IAHS n° 211 Avril 1993, pp. 475-484.

[Djokic 93]: Dean Djokic. *An Expert GIS for Support of Hydrological Modeling.* University of Texas at Austin, 1993, 10 p.

[Djokic and al.]: Dean Djokic and David R. Maidment. *Terrain Analysis for Urban Stormwater Modelling.* Hydrogical Processes, Vol. 5, pp. 115-124(1991).

[Farissier 93]: P. Farissier. *Etude d'un modèle cartographique adapté à la simulation des écoulements en rivières.* Thèse de doctorat Université de Claude Bernard 1993.

[Laréal 75]: P. Laréal. INSA Lyon. *Mécanique des sols. L'eau dans les sols.* Département Génie Civil et Urbanisme. Service Géothechnique. 1975.

[Rouet 91]: P. Rouet. *Les données dans les systèmes d'information géographique.* Ed. Hermes 1991.

[Silfer 87]: Andrew T. Silfer, Gerald J. Kinn and James M. Hassett. *A Geographic Information System Utilizing The Triangulated Irregular Network as a basis for Hydrologic Modeling.* Auto-carto 8 Baltimore, Maryland, 1987, pp. 129-136.

[Thibault 82]: B. Chocat, D. Seguin et S. Thibault. *Hydrologie Urbaine et Assainissement Urbain.* INSA de LYON, Département Génie Civil et Urbanisme 1982.

[Thomas 93]: Thomas A. Evans, Dean Djokic, David R. Maidment. *Development and Application of an Expert Geographic Information System.* University of Texas at Austin 1993, 25 p.

Using Versions in GIS

Claudia Bauzer Medeiros[1], Geneviève Jomier[2]

[1] DCC – UNICAMP, 13081-970 Campinas – SP – Brazil
cmbm@dcc.unicamp.br
[2] LAMSADE –Université Paris IX Dauphine, 75015 Paris - France
jomier@lamsade.dauphine.fr

Abstract. GIS have become important tools in public planning activities (e.g, in environmental or utility management). This type of activity requires the creation and management of alternative scenarios, as well as analysis of temporal data evolution. Existing systems provide limited support for these operations, and appropriate tools are yet to be developed. This paper presents a solution to this problem. This solution is based on managing temporal data and alternatives using the DBV version mechanism.
Keywords: versions, GIS, georeferenced data evolution.

1 Introduction

Geographic Information Systems (GIS) are automated systems that manipulate *georeferenced data* – data about geographic phenomena associated with their spatial relationships and location on the terrestrial surface. The term *georeferenced entity*, in this paper, refers to any type of entity whose components are georeferenced (be it a house, a residential plot or a geographic region).

GIS data contains *spatial* and *thematic* components. Thematic components are alphanumeric values related to georeferenced entities, e.g., the name of a mountain, or the type of vegetation cover. Texts or images are considered to be unconventional thematic data. Spatial data has two different properties: *geometric properties* such as size and shape of spatial objects; and *topological properties* such as adjacency and containment. Data are stored in *thematic layers*, which are combined in different ways in order to process a query.

GIS queries involve one or more of the following issues [Flo91, Peu93]:

1. *What* kind of phenomenon is this? (describe non-spatial characteristics)
2. *Where* is this phenomenon located? (describe the spatial characteristics of a given georeferenced entity, which comprises its location, topological and geometrical characteristics, and often its relationships with other entities).
3. *When* was this data collected? (determine data validity period).
4. What did this entity look like at some *past* period? What will happen to it in some *future* period? (examine previous states of an entity and predict its future evolution, given its recorded behavior).
5. *What* would happen to an entity *if* certain events were to take place? (simulation and comparison of alternative scenarios by changing existing data).

Database research for GIS support has been centered on *spatial databases*, especially in what concerns algorithms for storing and accessing spatial data (e.g., [Sam89]). Database researchers are concerned with providing users with fast access to georeferenced data by means of spatial indices. They are, furthermore, developing different types of query languages and mechanisms in order to allow processing the first two kinds of queries (i.e., *what, where*). Existing systems also provide different facilities for handling these two questions.

The remaining kinds of queries, however, involve other types of knowledge and distinct storage and indexing facilities. *When* processing (queries 3 and 4) requires temporal database management, itself a matter of intensive research (see, for instance, the discussion of open issues in [Sno92]).

The simulation of scenarios (query 5) is supported by some systems for specific situations, in a limited scale, using controlled parametrization of data values (e.g., [HQGW93]). The combination of simulation results is, however, not allowed, especially when the user wants to compare alternatives. Users have to store the different scenarios in separate files, and have to handle themselves the management of these files, by embedding appropriate code into their applications.

This paper extends the work of [MJ93], presenting and detailing a framework which allows processing queries 1 through 5. This solution is based on the notion of database versions, and adopts the DBV version model of [CVJ94], now being simulated on the O2 database system.

The DBV model enables the simultaneous management of distinct alternative scenarios, as well as handling georeferenced feature evolution through time with considerable savings in space. The DBV model can be embedded in any database system and does not require that the end-user control the different data configurations.

This paper's main contributions are:

- analysis of the problem of georeferenced data evolution from a database point of view, rephrasing this problem in a versioning framework;
- description of how the DBV version model can support the management of this evolution, using concrete examples. So far, GIS have not considered version mechanisms, given the complexity of the factors involved.

The research discussed in this paper is part of the DOMUS[PMB93] environmental planning project, which uses real-life data from non-settled areas in the state of São Paulo, Brazil.

The rest of this paper is organized as follows. Section 2 characterizes GIS applications. Section 3 gives an overview of the DBV mechanism. Section 4 presents a detailed example of how this mechanism can support management of scenarios and data evolution. Section 5 shows how other version mechanisms are unable to perform this task satisfactorily. Section 6 presents conclusions and directions for future research.

2 GIS application requirements

GIS demand that DBMS keep track of massive amounts of georeferenced data, of different natures, collected using heterogeneous devices, and at different time periods.

The rapid growth in GIS has resulted in a large number of systems, each of which with its own data storage and handling characteristics. Present systems are based on relational database management systems (DBMS). However, several of the requirements of GIS applications are not provided by standard relational DBMS. Thus, special data handlers have been developed to interact with the stored relations and allow the management and display of georeferenced data.

Relational databases do not provide an adequate underlying model to support most types of geographic data [Ege92]: the use of tables with fixed number of attributes does not allow flexibility in the management of georeferenced data, nor the incremental development of applications. Thus, researchers have directed their attention to new architectures: extensible relational, object-oriented or rule-based systems [MP94].

In all of these, there is no consideration for temporal queries or comparison of scenarios (such as queries 3 through 5 of section 1). The difficulties posed to answering these queries involve factors that cannot be handled adequately by present GIS. The first factor is due to the nature of GIS data, which requires special indexing and buffering techniques. This is aggravated by the introduction of the time element, not supported in commercial databases. Thus, users are forced to manage time values themselves, if they want to analyze data evolution.

Another issue concerns data integration over time. Georeferenced data may be collected at different time periods. This creates another type of value inconsistency, which is due to the temporal evolution of georeferenced entities. Thus, if the mapping of a region takes several months (or sometimes years), differences will occur which must be taken into consideration. As pointed out by [Flo91], another related problem is the difference in time scales. Some phenomena (e.g., vegetation) fluctuate according to a seasonal cycle, whereas others (e.g, temperature) may vary on a daily basis. These factors must be considered for queries on the evolution of georeferenced phenomena for a given region.

3 The DBV Version Mechanism

As seen above, present GIS still lack facilities for providing the following services:

- automatic representation and management of data evolution in time;
- management of alternative scenarios for planning purposes.

These are the same type of problems that are faced by version mechanisms (even though the latter have not yet considered georeferenced data). Thus, it is only natural to examine the feasibility of adopting versions to allow such services.

3.1 Versions in databases

Versions are a means of storing different states of a given entity, thereby allowing the control of alternatives and of temporal data evolution. The management of versions in databases has centered on different ways for keeping files. Research has appeared mostly in the context of CASE systems and CAD/CAM projects (e.g., [KSW86, Kat90, BBA91, TG92, KS92, LST93]). The subjects discussed cover the creation and manipulation of entity versions, their identification, the handling of time, status, authorization, and concurrency mechanisms. Versions are also commonly proposed for dealing with concurrency control, especially for long transactions. In this last context, different users are granted access to copies (i.e., versions) of the same set of data, thus allowing them to work in parallel.

3.2 An overview of the DBV mechanism

Version mechanisms must put together entity versions to reflect a given state of the modelled universe. Existing approaches support this by means of chains of pointers, which keep track of connections among versions of a given entity, as well as among entities that belong to a given version state. Thus, the database is perceived as a set of entities connected by several linked chains. There is often confusion between version management and the underlying data model.

The DBV mechanism [CJ90, CVJ94] has a different approach. The main principles of this model are the following:

- The user should always be able to manage entity versions within a specific, identifiable, context. This context is called *database version – Dv* for short. *Dv* represents a "version", or identifiable state, of the modelled universe.
- Each *Dv* contains a logical version of each (identified) entity of the database. The value of this version may be *nil*, meaning that it does not exist in a given *Dv*.
- If several logical versions of an entity have the same value, there is no physical replication. Rather, these logical versions share the same physical version. The mechanism of mapping logical/physical versions of entities is transparent to the user.

Thus, rather than keeping track of versions of individual entities, the problem is treated from a point of view where the unit of versioning is the *Dv* context, which corresponds to a state of the universe modelled by the database, regardless of the underlying data model. The notion of version as seen by the user (the *logical database versions*) is independent of what is actually stored (*physical versioning*), and there is no replication of data.

From a logical point of view, the database is perceived as a set of consistent database versions *Dv*, which can evolve independently of each other. The user works in this augmented database by selecting the *Dv* context(s) of interest. Once the desired *Dv* is selected, the user can treat it as a database on its own, querying and updating it. Logical operations on *Dv* are translated into actual physical versioning operations by the version management system. Temporal and alternative data are naturally managed by this model.

The versioning of an entity is logically performed by versioning the entire logical database to which it belongs. The logical independence of Dv allows defining two types of update transactions: those that manipulate some Dv; and those that derive a new Dv. The latter can be described in two steps. Let $\mathcal{E}$ be an entity of a given Dv, for which the user wants to create a new version $\mathcal{E}_1$:

- first, a (logical) copy of Dv is created, corresponding to a new Dv_1 database version, identical to Dv;
- second, Dv_1 is updated (i.e., $\mathcal{E}_1$ is created from $\mathcal{E}$, and additional updates are performed in order to maintain the consistency inside Dv_1).

Thus, a multiversion database is a set of logical *consistent* states, each of which corresponds to a different version of the world, created by the user. Each Dv is, therefore, a unit of consistency and can evolve independently.

Physically, in order to properly associate an entity with its versions, the DBV mechanism relies on the notion of *identity*: each Dv has an associated identifier which is used for managing purposes. The identifier mechanism associates every logical entity version $\mathcal{E}_i$ to its proper context Dv_i.

The retrieval of each Dv is automatically ensured by the version manager by examining tables of identifiers. Implementation details appear in [CJ90].

In this context, time may be supported by mapping timestamps into the DBV identifiers. Thus, temporal queries do not require handling of special attributes; rather, they are processed by the versioning mechanism, which puts together data that belongs to the same identifiable temporal state.

4 Applying the DBV model to GIS

This section shows an extended example of how the DBV approach allows handling GIS queries for evolution of data and comparison of alternatives.

Consider the following sequence of queries:

- Analysis of temporal data evolution: "What has been the observed modifications of the forest cover in a given area for a specific time period $\mathcal{P}$?"
- Prevision of future based on recorded past: " What is the probability of this forest cover decreasing in area, given information collected along $\mathcal{P}$? What are the possible damages – extent and intensity?"
- Comparative analysis between actual data and simulated scenarios: "Given the actual state of the forest cover in the area, how accurate were simulations performed along $\mathcal{P}$ to determine its evolution during the same period?

All these queries concern the same type of theme – vegetation – for the same geographical area. They require searching through different (historical) scenarios, first identifying the area and then its forest cover.

The first query requires doing a statistical analysis of a historical sequence of vegetation data. The second query requires using the previous analysis to perform prediction of phenomena. The third query assumes that the two other queries were periodically posed in the past, and that their results were stored. Thus, it demands comparison of predicted behavior and actual observed behavior for several periods in the database's history.

In the DBV approach, the user is provided with an integrated view of the world: it is perceived as a set of database states (*Dv*), each corresponding to an independent consistent version of the user's universe. The evolution of georeferenced entities is accompanied by the corresponding evolution of *Dv* states. For the user, there is no predefined link between different *Dv*, which allows working either on one context or navigating across contexts. This corresponds to what the user manipulates in reality, since no georeferenced phenomenon can be treated in isolation.

There is no difference in treatment for actual (measured) data values or (alternative) predicted values. Thus, several *Dv* may exist for the same time period, each describing a state of the world – either an actual recorded state or some alternative artificial state generated for planning purposes. Therefore, for any time period, the database may contain a set of logical databases: the modelled real world and different simulated scenarios. For vegetation cover, for instance, one can keep track of several parallel scenarios by modifying distinct parameters, e.g,, rainfall or evolution of human settlements.

Thus, for any of the three queries, the processing is performed as:

- (i) Select all *Dv* within the specified time period;
  (The version manager performs this operation by accessing the identifier of each *Dv*, which in this case will contain a timestamp identification)
- (ii) For each such *Dv*, select the area and its cover, by performing standard GIS (nontemporal) database queries;
  (Each *Dv* selected in the previous step is seen by the user as an independent consistent database. Thus, it can be queried independently of the rest of the DBV database, regardless of other existing versions.)
- (iii) Perform the simulation operations on the set of areas and covers obtained from the execution of the two previous steps.

Physically, the creation of a logical database does not require physical duplication of entities, just creation of identifiers and recording of data changes (differential information). These changes and the corresponding identifiers are used to build the complete (logical) database states *Dv*.

The *Dv* are built by gathering together all entities present at a given database state, by means of special index structures. This means retrieving all entities that have compatible identifier values.

Query processing may be speeded up by using the notion of configuration. In fact, configurations characterize units of work inside a context (and thus of consistency). Thus, users may decide to specify a configuration containing the area and its cover (requested in the three queries). This will speed up version processing for this type of query (in a way similar to precomputed views).

5 Other version mechanisms and GIS

A good introduction to the problems of handling spatio-temporal data in GIS are the set of papers in [FCF92], which cover different issues. They range from problems in database support of time [Sno92] to discussing the concept of a region in creating study scenarios [Gut92]. The need for flexible mechanisms to allow managing of these scenarios is stressed in several papers.

Database research on versions has not dealt with problems related to GIS, and there are very few reports of GIS using version mechanisms (e.g., [Bat92, NTE92]). The main reasons for this are:

- Most version management mechanisms available in database systems become cumbersome when it comes to managing the evolution of instances. They require maintaining complex data structures to follow data evolution.
- GIS data is complex and occupies considerable space. Thus, its management already presents so many challenges to a DBMS that there is no question of coupling it to the usual version mechanisms.
- In many cases, it is impossible to follow the evolution of phenomena across time periods, since entities may disappear or suffer unexpected modifications.

Thus, even though versioning solves users' problems, it has not, so far, been seriously considered in the GIS context, and is used at most to support parallel access to data. Their use as a means to manage temporal data evolution is not considered. Rather, researchers consider (historical) versions of entire files – e.g., the sequence of file versions for a given thematic layer. Finally, when versions are associated with georeferenced entities, there is no concern with how to manage them from a database point of view.

The GFIS [Bat92] system uses a standard relational DBMS coupled to a geographic data manager. Version management is left to the database system, and is geared towards controlling parallel access. There is no possibility of selecting versions for queries, or of handling sequences of past states.

[NTE92] discuss different data structures for implementing versions on top of tables using an object-oriented language. The paper provides a comparative analysis of these structures, but does not apply them to real data.

We now briefly review how traditional version schemes would cope with the queries of section 4. In such schemes, two types of approach are possible:

• **Snapshot view** The complete data files (layers, with spatial and thematic information) have to be stored, together with time stamp indication. (I.e., the database is in fact a set of database snapshots, where each snapshot contains several thematic layers.) Thus, in order to answer the first two queries, the system has to:

- (i) retrieve the entire layer files for the time period;
- (ii) for each layer, select the desired area and determine its forest cover;
- (iii) produce the time series analysis desired.

In order to answer the third query, the database must contain not only the entire layers for every period of interest, but also files with simulation results.

The snapshot view, though relatively simple to process, entails massive storage occupation, and is therefore not feasible for practical purposes. Furthermore, it requires the actual recording of the entire database, and thus the variety and periodicity of stored phenomena is limited, due to size constraints.

• **Historical chain view** The history of entities is maintained through a linked list of data values and timestamps: only differential values are kept. (The database is seen as a conglomerate of linked chains in all directions.)

In this case, queries can only be answered for entities whose history has been maintained through chains. This requires that the database designer has previous knowledge of all possible queries that will involve version manipulation. Alternatively, these chains can be maintained for every entity and value in the database. Whereas the first alternative limits user exploratory activity, the second alternative requires a heavy overhead of pointers.

Supposing the historical chain of the designated area is available, then the queries are processed by the following procedure:

- (i) find the area and its vegetation cover in the present;
- (ii) follow back pointers of this area and cover, retrieving past information and rebuilding past states;
- (iii) produce the time series analysis desired.

Finally, the third query requires that not only actual historical chains be maintained, but also prevision chains for the same entity. This, again, complicates the housekeeping algorithms.

Pointer version mechanisms soon become too cumbersome to manage when each time period contains many entities that vary in different ways, as is typically the case in geographical applications.

It is interesting to compare these approaches to the DBV solution. The snapshot approach favors users who need to access entire contexts. However, it does not automatically support navigation through these contexts, since there is no sharing of entities across the snapshots. For instance, any update to an entity in a snapshot must be manually performed by the user in the other snapshots. The historical chain approach is geared towards management of versions of individual entities, through manipulation of their chains. However, it does not automatically support the building of contexts, which must be performed by the user.

The DBV model, on the other hand, automatically supports both working within a context and comparing entity versions across contexts. This is achieved thanks to the fact that it separates the logical versioning from the physical versioning level. It thus combines the advantages of the other approaches, without the inconvenients: it does not imply the waste of space of the snapshot approach, and neither does it demand the complex computation procedures of the historical chain approach.

6 Conclusions

This paper presented a solution for the management of evolution of georeferenced data in GIS which consists in using the DBV version mechanism. This solution allows the development of automated tools to keep track of different versions of the same georeferenced entity through time. This facility enables users to create and manage alternative scenarios, as well as to keep track of temporal data evolution. This type of support has so far been unavailable in commercial GIS, though required by different kinds of planning applications.

The use of a version mechanism, as pointed out in this paper, seems to be an obvious choice to cope with GIS users' demands. However, GIS databases do not consider this type of facility, since the handling of georeferenced data presents in itself many problems. Furthermore, available version management systems are complex and cannot readily satisfy GIS requirements.

The DBV mechanism, on the other hand, allows efficiently keeping track of data and schema versions in a database, with considerable savings in space and computation time, as compared to other database version mechanisms. It allows dissociating the issues of context and configuration consistency from version maintenance, which is not possible in other version models.

Its main advantage, from a GIS point of view, is that it allows users to access entire consistent database states for any given georeferenced entity. Thus users can create different scenarios by just modifying individual entities, and need not worry about keeping them within their appropriate context. This is achieved without additional overhead, by the appropriate management of version identifiers (as opposed to traditional mechanisms that require handling pointer chains). Finally, the DBV model is orthogonal to the underlying data model and to concurrency control, which are complicating factors in other version models.

Acknowledgements

The research described in this paper was partially financed by grants FAPESP 91/2117-1, CNPq 453176/91, and CNPq 452357/93-4.

References

[Bat92] P. Batty. Exploiting relational database technology in a GIS. *Computers and Geosciences: An international journal*, 18(4):453–462, 1992.

[BBA91] M. Borhani, J-P Barthès, and P. Anota. Versions in Object-Oriented Databases. Technical Report UTC/GI/DI/N 83, Universite de Technologie de Compiegne, 1991.

[CJ90] W. Cellary and G. Jomier. Consistency of Versions in Object-Oriented Databases. In *Proc. 16th VLDB*, pages 432–441, 1990.

[CVJ94] W. Cellary, G. Vossen, and G. Jomier. Multiversion Object Constellations: a new Approach to Support a Designer's Database Work. *To appear, Engineering with Computers*, 1994.

[Ege92] M. Egenhofer. Why not SQL! *International Journal of Geographical Information Systems*, 6(2):71–86, 1992.

[FCF92] A. Frank, I. Campari, and U. Formentini, editors. *Theories and Methods of Spatio-Temporal Reasoning in Geographic Space.* Lecture Notes in Computer Science 639. Springer-Verlag, 1992.

[Flo91] R. Flowerdew. *Geographical Information Systems - volume I,* chapter Spatial Data Integration, pages 375–387. John Wiley and Sons, 1991.

[Gut92] J. Guttenberg. Towards a Behavioral Theory of Regionalization. In *Proc International Conference on GIS - From Space to Territory: Theories and Methods of Spatial Reasoning,* Springer Verlag Lecture Notes in Computer Science 639, pages 110–121, 1992.

[HQGW93] N. Hachem, K. Qiu, M. Gennert, and M. Ward. Managing Derived Data in the GAEA Scientific DBMS. In *Proc 19th VLDB,* pages 1–12, 1993.

[Kat90] R. H. Katz. Toward a Unified Framework for Version Modelling in Engineering Databases. *ACM Computing Surveys,* 22(4):375–408, 1990.

[KS92] W. Kafer and H. Schoning. Mapping a Version Model to a Complex-Object Data Model . In *Proc IEEE Data Engineering Conference,* pages 348–357, 1992.

[KSW86] P. Klahold, G. Schlageter, and W. Wilkes. A General Model for Version Management in Databases. In *Proc XII VLDB,* pages 319–327, 1986.

[LST93] G. Landau, J. Schmidt, and V. Tsotras. Efficient Support of Historical Queries for Multiple Lines of Evolution. In *Proc. IEEE Data Engineering Conference,* pages 319–326, 1993.

[MJ93] C. B. Medeiros and G. Jomier. Managing Alternatives and Data Evolution in GIS. In *Proc. ACM/ISCA Workshop on Advances in Geographic Information Systems,* pages 34–37, 1993.

[MP94] C. B. Medeiros and F. Pires. Databases for GIS. *ACM Sigmod Record,* 23(1):107–115, 1994.

[NTE92] R. Newell, D. Theriault, and M. Easterfieldy. Temporal GIS - modeling the evolution of spatial data in time. *Computers and Geosciences: An international journal,* 18(4):427–434, 1992.

[Peu93] D. Peuquet. What, Where and When - a Conceptual Basis for Design of Spatiotemporal GIS Databases. In *Proc. ACM/ISCA Workshop on Advances in Geographic Information Systems,* pages 117–122, 1993.

[PMB93] F. Pires, C. B. Medeiros, and A. Barros. Modelling Geographic Information Systems using an Object Oriented Framework. In *Proc XIII International Conference of the Chilean Computer Science Society,* pages 217–232, 1993.

[Sam89] H. Samet. *The Design and Analysis of Spatial Data Structures.* Addison-Wesley, 1989.

[Sno92] R. Snodgrass. Temporal Databases. In *Proc International Conference on GIS - From Space to Territory: Theories and Methods of Spatial Reasoning,* Springer Verlag Lecture Notes in Computer Science 639, pages 22–63, 1992.

[TG92] V. Tsotras and B. Gopinath. Optimal Versioning of Objects . In *Proc IEEE Data Engineering Conference,* pages 358–365, 1992.

Keynote Speech

The Strategic Role of Information Technology towards the Information Society

G. Metakides
Director DG II/F
European Commission
Brussels, Belgium

We are in the midst of a major transformation in society, industry and economy and the transition to the information society. It is a transformation that has been compared in its effects to the industrial revolution.

The "engine" of the information society is the information infrastructure – the set of services and technologies providing easy access to usable information for any citizen or enterprise, at any time, in any place. The return to a strong economy and fuller employment will be heavily influenced by the speed and success with which the transition to the information society is be completed and the new information infrastructure put into place.

But this depends upon a massive research and development effort. R&D in information and communication technologies must be oriented so as to optimise its impact on the growth and development of the information infrastructure, an orientation which implies an increased emphasis on user and market pull, and on access to technologies and their use and usability.

Keynote Speech

Federating Object-Oriented and Relational Databases

G. Gardarin
Université de Versailles
Laboratoire PRiSM
France

Semantically heterogenous federated databases require rich data models to represent heterogenous distributed entities with relationships and to integrate them in consistent views accessed through high level query languages. We first survey a few heterogeneous database projects, focusing on those based on a rich pivot modell, such as Multibase and Pegasus. Then, we point out technical issues to address when designing an object-oriented federated database. Finally, we present the IRO-DB project, which proposes three layers of software to make object-oriented and relational databases interoperate around a common object model.

Bridging the gap between knowledge engineering and efficient implementation in an intelligent tutoring system[1]

Randy M. Kaplan
Educational Testing Service
Division of Cognitive and Instructional Science
Princeton, New Jersey

0. Abstract

Symbolic manipulation languages, such as LISP and Prolog, are advantageous in that they can describe a problem space symbolically. However, they are inefficient when handling large rule-based systems. In order to create practical and usable implementations, two systems are often implemented. One system is the knowledge engineering prototype in which rules are formulated symbolically and manipulated as such. The other is a production version that guarantees realistic response time and execution profile to an end user. To create the second version it is usually necessary to recode the system in a traditional non-symbolic language like C or C++. This paper describes an automatic approach to transforming a symbolic knowledge base into an efficient non-symbolic representation resulting in an extremely efficient and practical implementation.

Keywords: expert systems, knowledge engineering, implementation, intelligent tutors.

1. Introduction

HYDRIVE (Kaplan, Trenholm, 1993) is an intelligent tutoring system created to instruct flight line mechanics in problem solving and troubleshooting strategies for the hydraulic systems of fighter aircraft. The system consists of several large knowledge bases containing a description of approximately 500 aircraft components, and 200 rules that control the instructional aspects of the system. Among the largest of these are knowledge bases that describe the operation of the systems in the aircraft. Others include knowledge bases that direct instruction and student modeling. The knowledge base for a single aircraft system may require as much as 600 Kbytes of symbolic information accounting for the description of the operation of approximately 200 components of the aircraft.

HYDRIVE is constructed such that users can see results of manipulations they perform on the aircraft. While sitting at a computer, users can perform actions such as moving the control stick, setting switches, and configuring power systems in the aircraft. When the user completes one of these actions, the system model is

---

[1] I would like to thank Larry Frase, Drew Gitomer, Irv Katz, Iris Tabak, and Harriet Trenholm for their careful review and useful suggestions during the writing of this paper.

altered. The system model reconfigures itself as would the actual aircraft and the user can then see the results of the action. For example, if the user moves the aircraft control stick from left to right, he or she will be able to see the left and right ailerons (control surfaces) of the aircraft move (if there are no faults in that part of the aircraft). Visual feedback is given by displaying graphic and video sequences.

A key feature of the system model knowledge base is that it describes both the operating and failed states of the aircraft system being modeled. An instructor can cause any component to fail. The task for the user of the system is to locate and repair the failed component.

One of the characteristics of usability of any computer system is response time. If users have to wait a long time for a response from the system, chances are that they will become frustrated and eventually consider the system unusable. In the context of an instructional system, a long delay in response may result in a user losing context which, in turn, hampers learning. The response time for the system model is correlated with the number of knowledge base entries that describe its operations. Since any one action taken by the user might result in hundreds of components being manipulated, the time required to propagate an action through the model can become significant. In fact, the Prolog implementation of **HYDRIVE**'s model required 5 to 6 minutes[2] to perform a typical action. Typical problems require the performance of 30 or 40 actions. The problem we faced was how to re-design the system implemented in Prolog to increase efficiency with minimal re-implementation of any of the components of the system.

2. Representation and Re-Representation

To understand how we achieved our performance improvement, it is instructive to observe how the knowledge which describes the operation of an aircraft system is represented[3]. A sample rule for a single component of the system model is given in Figure 1.

```
[[[f_xor(f_or(reng_ep(power),leng_ep(power)),
    external_ep(power))],ep_t1(power),ep_t2(power),
    ep_t3(power),ep_t4(power),ep_t5(power),ep_t7(power),
    ep_t8(power),ep_t9(power),ep_t10(power),ep_t11(power),
    ep_t12(power),ep_t13(power),ep_t14(power),ep_w1(power),
    ep_w2(power),ep_w3(power),ep_w4(power),ep_w5(power),
    ep_w6(power),ep_w7(power),ep_w8(power),ep_p3(power),
    ep_p4(power),ep_cb1(power),ep_cb2(power),ep_mule(power)]]
```

Figure 1 - Sample rule for the operation of a system model component

---

[2] These times are based on the current **HYDRIVE** hardware platform, an IBM PC clone with an Intel 80486 chip running at 33 Mhz.

[3] In order to distinguish between the models, we will refer to the original model (the symbolic version) as the **Prolog-based** or **original model**. The new model will be referred to as the **C-based** model.

Figure 1's rule describes the operation of a component named **ep**. Each rule is encoded as a series of conditions possibly connected with a logical operator, and a series of assertions representing actions. In the rules above, two logical operators are used - f_xor[4] and f_or. The notation **ep_xx** is used to denote an edge in the system between device **ep** and another arbitrary device **xx**. Thus, **ep_t4** represents the connection between device **ep** and device **t4**. The notation **ep_xx(y)** means that the connection from **ep** to **xx** will be set to **y**. The assertion, created using these combined facts represents the state of the system model. A component in this model can be diagramatically represented as shown in figure 2.

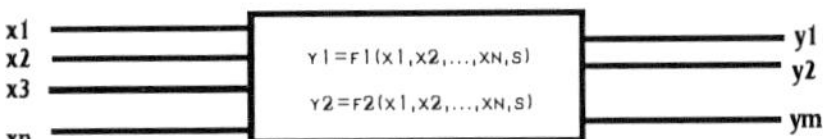

Figure 2 - Diagrammatic representation of a component in the system model

A component is a series of inputs and outputs. The rules are the functions inside of the component box shown in Figure 2. The description of a component is the sum of all of functions that define it. A series of these components are logically connected as shown in Figure 3.

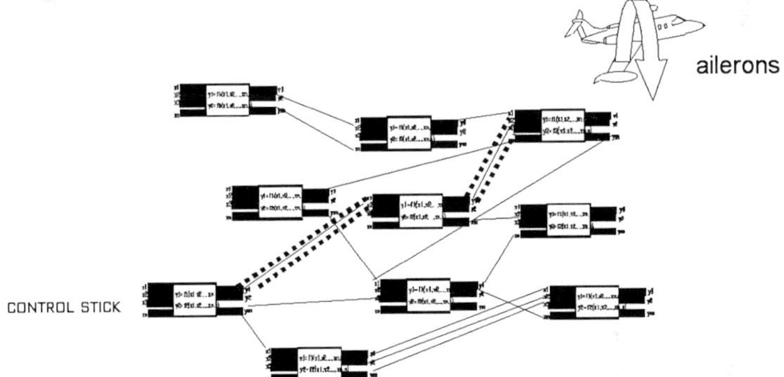

Figure 3 - System of components

When a rule fires, assertions are made that effect the system state. These assertions may satisfy conditions of other rules, and subsequently may cause these other rules to be fired. An action is propagated through the system in this manner. The determination of what rule(s) is/are potential candidates to be fired can be very time consuming. By transforming rules into a simpler form, greater efficiency can be achieved.

In the first part of the simplification process, rules like the one shown in Figure 1 are simplified using Boolean algebra. Figure 4 is a partial listing based on the example in Figure 1.

---

[4] The names f_or, f_and, and f_xor were used to denote logical or, and, and exclusive or respectively. This was necessary because of the keyword status of the logical operation names in Prolog.

```
rule(epR1,[edgeOp(not(reng_ep(power))),edgeOp(not(leng_ep(power))),
        edgeOp(external_ep(power)),asserta(edge(ep_t1(power)))]).
rule(epR1,[edgeOp(reng_ep(power)),edgeOp(not(external_ep(power))),
        asserta(edge(ep_t1(power)))]).
rule(epR1,[edgeOp(leng_ep(power)),edgeOp(not(external_ep(power))),
        asserta(edge(ep_t1(power)))]).
rule(epR1,[edgeOp(not(reng_ep(power))),edgeOp(not(leng_ep(power))),
        edgeOp(external_ep(power)),asserta(edge(ep_t2(power)))]).
rule(epR1,[edgeOp(reng_ep(power)),edgeOp(not(external_ep(power))),
        asserta(edge(ep_t2(power)))]).
rule(epR1,[edgeOp(leng_ep(power)),edgeOp(not(external_ep(power))),
        asserta(edge(ep_t2(power)))]).
.
.
```

Figure 4 - "Simplification" of ep operation rule (partial listing)

Each original **ep** rule is transformed into one or more simplified rules. Each assertion in an original **ep** rule will have a corresponding simplified rule.

2.1 Re-Representation

The result of the Boolean manipulation described above gives us rules of the form:

```
if a and b and c and ... then x
if a and b and c and ... then y
.
.
if d and e and f and ... then z
```

A decision tree is created to represent the rules. An example of a simple decision tree is shown in Figure 5.

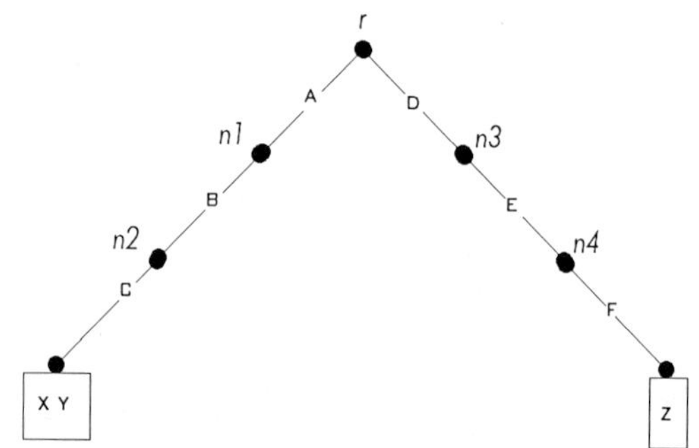

Figure 5 - Decision tree (T_1) representation of rules

In this decision tree there are three possible assertions that can be made. They are **x**, **y**, and **z**. In order that **x** and **y** be asserted, **a**, **b**, and **c** must be present in the database i.e., they must have been previously asserted. When an edge label in the decision tree corresponds to an assertion in the database, traversal between the nodes connected with the edge is allowed. In other words, if we assume **a** is asserted, beginning at node **r** of decision tree $\mathbf{T_1}$ we can move from node **r** to node $\mathbf{n_1}$.

Likewise, if **b** is asserted then a traversal from node $\mathbf{n_1}$ to node $\mathbf{n_2}$ can be made. If **c** is asserted, then the traversal ends at the **xy** leaf node from node $\mathbf{n_2}$. **x** and **y** can be asserted upon arriving at this leaf node.

In the decision tree, the conditions of a model rule label the edges between nodes of the decision tree. The decision tree edge labels name edges in the model that name connections between components in the model. The relationship is depicted in the next figure.

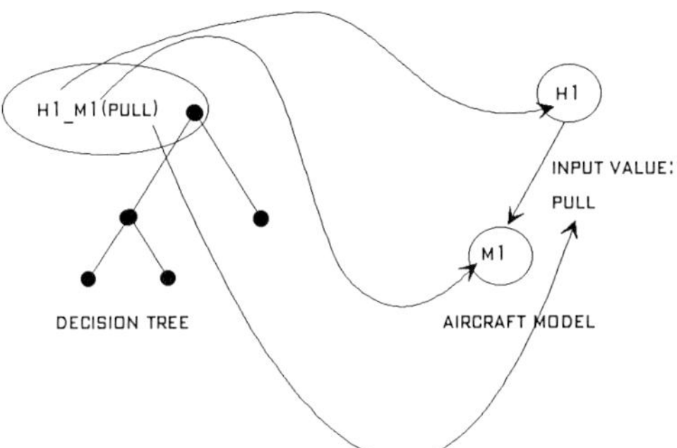

Figure 6 - Relationship of decision tree "edges" to aircraft model "edges"

Prior to the construction of the decision tree, each model edge and value combination, called an **aircraft model edge** is assigned a unique integer value. The assignment is made by processing each model rule to extract each unique aircraft model edge. Once all unique aircraft model edges are extracted from the simplified rules of the model, they are assigned a unique integer value. Instead of using the symbolic version of the aircraft model edges to label decision tree edges, the integers assigned to the aircraft model edges are used. This simplifies the edge labeling process in the decision tree and also simplifies comparisons that will be made while traversing the decision tree.

The Prolog model uses the symbolic aircraft model edges in its operation. The existing Prolog code will use the C-based model. This means that there must be a bridge between the symbolic aircraft model edges and the unique integer assigned to each aircraft model edge. The bridge is a Boolean vector whose length is equal to the number of aircraft model edges. The integer value assigned to each aircraft model edge is an index into the Boolean vector. Suppose you have the following aircraft model edges.

```
1 h1_m1(pull)
2 h1_m2(push)
3 h1_m3(static)
```

The numbers to the left of each aircraft model edge are the unique integers assigned to each edge. The Boolean edge vector associated with this sequence of edges would have three elements, the first associated with aircraft model edge h1_m1(pull), the second with h1_m2(push), and the third with h1_m3(static). An edge vector 101 would mean that aircraft model edges h1_m1(pull) and h1_m3(static) are asserted.

The decision tree that results from this encoding consists of a series of nodes that contain integer values. An example of a decision tree that encodes several model rules is shown in the next figure.

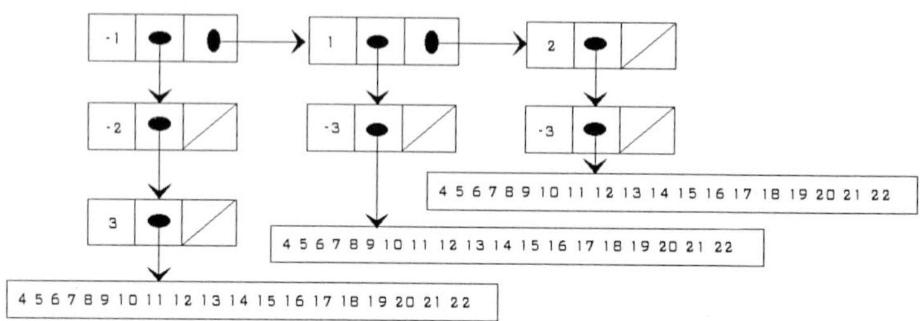

Figure 7 - ep rules in tree representation

The structure shown in Figure 7 consists of two kinds of nodes. One of these is an edge node. Edge nodes are depicted as -1 . The node contains three fields. The first field is an integer value corresponding to an aircraft model edge. This field may be positive or negative. A positive integer means that the aircraft model edge at that position in the Boolean edge vector is true (meaning that the corresponding aircraft model edge is asserted). A negative integer means that the aircraft model edge is not true in the Boolean edge vector (meaning that the model edge is not asserted). The second field of the node is a pointer to the child node (the next edge required for the rule), and the third field points to a sibling node. The sibling is explored when the integer of the edge field of the current node is not set (or reset) as required in the field.

When the Prolog model runs, it asserts symbolic aircraft model edges. The analog to this in the C-based model is the setting of an element in the edge vector to true. In the C-based model, the second type of node is a leaf node. It consists of a list of elements to set in the edge vector. Reaching a leaf node in a traversal will cause all of the Boolean edge vector elements listed in the leaf node, to be set in the Boolean edge vector. When a leaf node is reached, a traversal of the decision tree is complete.

To ensure that the system state is accurate, the rule tree is traversed as many times as necessary. If a traversal results in an aircraft model edge being asserted (an element of the edge vector changing), then another iteration of the traversal process will be executed. If no new edge is set, then the traversal process is terminated and the system state now represents an accurate representation of the state based on the original settings of the edge vector.

3.0 Time and space considerations

The largest Prolog knowledge base consisting of descriptions of 200 components required approximately 600 Kbytes. The decision tree representation of the same knowledge base requires less than 100 Kbytes. A total of 1932 rules were represented in the decision tree. The tree required a total of 1420 edge nodes and 1932 leaf nodes. (One leaf node required for each rule.) Table 1 compares the execution times and steps required in two different runs of the model. Both run 1 and run 2 involved a movement of the aircraft's control stick. When this particular component of the aircraft is manipulated, many other components respond to the manipulation. The first run involved a movement of the control stick to the left. The second involved a movement forward.

As you can see in Table 1 on the next page, a user must wait 13 minutes for run 1 and 12 minutes for run 2 to see the result of the manipulation. This is not an acceptable waiting time for the user. These processing times are derived using a computer with an Intel 80386 processor running at 20 megahertz. The running times can be reduced by running the system model on a computer with a faster processor.

Observe the contrast in time between the Prolog and C-based models, with the running times produced for the recoded C model. In both cases, roughly the same number of processing steps were used. Also, the running time for the C-based model was 1/1000 second which translates into a 300,000 fold increase in processing efficiency.

	Run 1		**Run 2**	
	Time	Steps	Time	Steps
Prolog Model	13m 18s	341	11m55s	327
C-based model	.001s	332	.001s	322

Table 1 - Comparison of Run Times[5] and Processing Steps between Prolog and C-based System Model Engines

4.0 Re-engineering the Tutor to use the C-based model

A goal of this work was to not have to re-engineer the complete system, but rather, use presently existing components which meet system performance and functionality requirements. Many of the components of the system did meet these requirements. For this reason, the Prolog model was treated as a module that could be removed and replaced with a new implementation of the system model, specifically the C-based model.

[5] The running times shown in this table are the result of running the system model independent of the full **HYDRIVE** tutoring system.

To accomplish this change, the existing Prolog code must supply the C-based model with the input it expects (the Boolean edge vector), and the C-based model must produce output that the Prolog expects, a sequence of symbolic aircraft model edges. A table is maintained that contains the correspondence between integer values and symbolic edges. On input to the C-based model, this table is used to set elements in the Boolean edge vector. On the output side, the Boolean edge vector is translated into a series of symbolic aircraft model edges using the same table. By creating these incoming and outgoing translations, all existing Prolog code remains intact without change. The only re-written code was the C-based system model. This constitutes a small portion of the code of the system. Table 2 shows the total number of code lines written for the tutor broken down by code function.

Function	Lines
Interface (C and IL code)	160,523
System model, student model, instructional model (Prolog code)	4,722
Control module (C code)	9,762
Total	175,007

Table 2 - Code lines written for the HYDRIVE tutor implementation

The C-based system model was written in 1280 lines of C code, representing 0.7% of all of the code written for the system.

4.1 Automatically generating the encoded knowledge base

The time consuming task when re-implementing any knowledge-based system is the recoding of the rules in the knowledge base. In a cost-conscious or schedule bound software development environment, any re-implementation would have to be done automatically. The knowledge base used by the C-based model is re-implemented by a utility program written in Prolog that transforms the symbolic representation of the rules into an encoded form, and then into a decision tree.

The knowledge base of Prolog rules is recoded in two passes. In the first pass, all of the possible edges are collected from the rules of the knowledge base. Each aircraft model edge is assigned a unique integer value. The second pass recodes each of the rules into a record consisting of the name of the rule (for identification and reference during debugging and model verification), and a sequence of integers. The number of integers in the sequence can vary depending on the number of edges that are part of the condition of the rule. The last integer of each record is always the integer value representing the aircraft model edge that is asserted if the other edges have been set. So the encoding

```
a1R1 1 2 3
```

can be interpreted as,

```
Rule a1R1: If a9_a1(pressure(eq(higha))) and  13_a1(push(eq(1))) then
              assert a1_p2(pull(eq(1))).
```

Each encoded rule is processed one at a time and may result in the following:

```
1)  a new path in the decision tree
2)  an addition to a path in the decision tree (nodes are added
    to a path before a new leaf is added)
3)  a new leaf element being added to an existing path
```

To add any rule to the tree, the existing tree is traversed. Nodes, as described earlier, consist of sibling/child pointers. Each element of an encoded rule is matched against the current index field of a node. A match permits movement to a child. A failure to match permits movement to the sibling. No match along a sibling list results in the addition of a new sibling and path from the sibling. This is best explained in the following examples. Consider first, the empty tree. The encoded rule we will process will be:

```
a1R1 1 2 3
```

Since there are no nodes in the tree, processing this record will result in a tree with a single path as shown in the next figure.

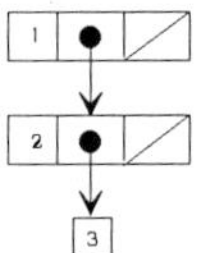

Figure 8 - Processing an encoded rule (decision tree is empty)

The next rule to be processed is:

```
a1R1 1 2 9
```

Traversing the decision tree, the encoded record permits a traversal from node 1 to node 2. The last field of the record is the assertion, so this index will be added to the leaf node of the tree. The result is shown in Figure 9.

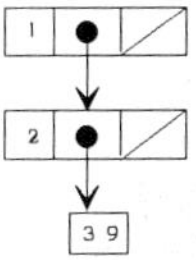

Figure 9 - Processing a second encoded rule - duplicate path

If an encoded rule matches part of a path, but not the complete path during the traversal, a new subpath is added at the point of divergence. The next rule processed is:

```
a1R1 1 11 14
```

and the result of processing this encoded rule is shown in Figure 10.

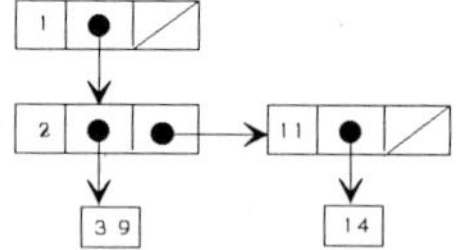

Figure 10 - Processing a third encoded rule - duplicate subpath

Finally, the rule may constitute a completely new path in the tree. When this occurs a new sibling is added to the list the begins at the root node of the tree. A rule that would result in an addition like this would be:

```
a1R1 4 2 3
```

and the result of processing this rule is shown in Figure 11.

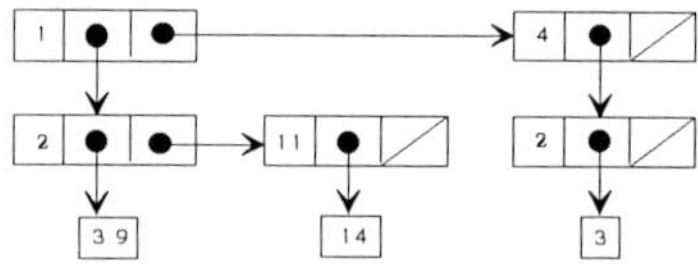

Figure 11 - Processing an encoded rule resulting in a new root node sibling path

5.0 Comparing Our Approach to the RETE Algorithm

The RETE algorithm (Forgy, 1982) is a procedure developed for improving the efficiency of rule-based systems. RETE was developed to work in conjunction with OPS5-type (Brownston, Farrell, Kant, Martin, 1985) rules to improve the efficiency of creating the conflict set. This conflict set are those rules that could be potentially fired in an iteration of the expert system. The RETE algorithm avoids the need to make many comparisons at each iteration of the expert system. The key to RETE is the compilation of rules into a network representing the conditions of the rules. In the RETE algorithm, constant and variable elements of rules can be tested.

In our representation, efficiency is achieved by encoding the rules and their associated edges into an integer representation. The operations necessary to process the decision tree that results are integer comparisons, Boolean tests, and integer subscripting. In RETE, an abstract machine is defined to implement the traversal of the network and tests. OPS5 rule-based programs are compiled into instructions that are executed by a RETE abstract machine.

6.0 Conclusions

The methodology described in this paper provides a means to substantially increase the efficiency of a rule-based processing system with minimal code modification and automatic transformation of the symbolic rules into an integer encoding. Compiling symbolic rules into an alternate representation is an approach used in the well-known RETE procedure.

A major difficulty with creating any large knowledge-based system is the difficulty of making the implementation efficient. The effectiveness of using symbolic representations to create knowledge-based systems is well-known and a significant reason for using symbolic tools to create these systems. Unfortunately, as knowledge increases, these systems run less efficiently. The dilemma is how to minimize the re-implementation cost while improving efficiency. By using a decision tree representation, integer recoding, Boolean manipulation, and automatic compilation of rules, the performance of the model has been improved and at the same time, the recoding effort has been minimized.

References

Brownston, L., Farrell, R., Kant, E., & Martin, N. (1985). **Programming expert systems in ops5**. Reading: Addison-Wesley.

Forgy, C.L. (1982). Rete: a fast algorithm for the many pattern/many object pattern match problem. **Artificial Intelligence, 19**, 17 - 38.

Kaplan, R.M., & Trenholm, H. (1993). **A practical and generalizable architecture for an intelligent tutoring system**. In Applications of Artificial Intelligence 1993: Knowledge-Based Systems in Aerospace and Industry. April 1993.

Mechanisms for Structuring Knowledge-Based Systems

Dieter Landes and Rudi Studer
Institut für Angewandte Informatik und Formale Beschreibungsverfahren
Universität Karlsruhe, D-76128 Karlsruhe, Germany
e-mail: { landes | studer }@aifb.uni-karlsruhe.de

In order to reduce the complexity of large knowledge-based systems and promote reusability, means for decomposing them to smaller chunks are required. MIKE, our knowledge engineering framework, provides three basic means for structuring which are described in this paper: different kinds of knowledge are separated at different knowledge layers, knowledge layers can be structured by modules, and knowledge within modules is expressed in terms of an object-centred data model. In addition, ideas from entity relationship model clustering are adapted and extended to facilitate the understandability of domain knowledge and support the formation of modules.

1 Introduction

Two main principles for structuring programs evolved in computer science: modularization and object-orientation. While these mechanisms are commonly employed in "conventional" programs in order to exploit their well-known benefits, the situation is slightly different for knowledge-based systems (KBS). Common knowledge representation formalisms for KBS such as production rules, frames, or semantical networks impose structure on the knowledge they embody by expressing it in terms of concepts or rules, which are comparable to objects (and expressions involving such objects) in object-oriented approaches with respect to granularity. In these representation formalisms, however, usually no additional, more coarse-grained structuring primitives are available which might constitute the counterpart to modules in traditional computer science. Conversely, several proposals have been made for modularizing logic programs or logical theories (cf., e.g., [9], [10], [11]). These proposals usually use modules or contexts as the only structuring primitive, i.e. the contents of such structures are basically unstructured collections of first order logic sentences.

Due to the complexity of KBS in realistic settings, appropriate structuring mechanisms at different levels of granularity are required. For that reason, three types of structuring mechanisms are available in MIKE (Model-based Incremental Knowledge Engineering), our framework for developing KBS [1]. MIKE provides three distinct layers to separate domain knowledge, knowledge on inference steps, and knowledge on the control over these inference steps. This distinction is inspired by an analogous separation in the KADS framework (cf., e.g., [12]) for knowledge engineering. The layer containing domain-specific knowledge (i.e. the domain layer) can be structured further by means of domain modules, while portions of the two other layers (i.e. inference and task layer) can be encapsulated in so-called processing modules. Domain and inference knowledge in modules is expressed primarily in terms of object classes and objects, thus introducing an object-centred notion.

Structuring systems using these three basic mechanisms facilitates understandability since it allows to obtain global overviews as well as to go into the details of relevant parts. Such an organization also supports maintenance since parts of the system that must be adapted due to a changed context are easier to determine. Furthermore, reuse is supported since constituents of the system interact in a controlled way, e.g., via interfaces in the case of modules.

In section 2 of this paper, we will shortly address the three knowledge layers and outline the primitives of KARL ([2], [5], [3]), the formal and executable specification language used for expressing knowledge at these layers in MIKE. The main parts of the paper deal with the two types of modules (section 3) and with so-called clusters (section 4) as additional structuring mechanism which is inspired by work on clustering entity relationship models. Clusters are intended to promote understandability and facilitate the formation of domain modules. Section 5 puts the structuring mechanisms of MIKE into perspective of related work and section 6 concludes the paper. Object classes and objects are not particularly addressed here since they are discussed at length in the context of KARL. Language primitives for describing modules are part of DesignKARL, the design language of MIKE [7]. It should be noted that the structuring primitives of MIKE are not part of a particular implementation environment, but rather indicate how an appropriately structured KBS might be realized within a suitable implementation environment.

2 Knowledge Layers

Like KADS (cf., e.g., [12]), MIKE distinguishes three types of knowledge each of which is kept at a distinct knowledge layer. The domain layer contains domain-specific knowledge while the inference layer comprises knowledge about inference steps that might potentially be performed for solving a problem. Control over these inference steps is not specified at the inference layer, but at the task layer. This separation of different knowledge types allows to describe problem-solving methods (i.e. inference plus task layer) in a generic and domain-independent way, thus making it possible to reuse problem-solving methods in a different domain or, conversely, reuse (parts of) a domain model for a different application and problem-solving method. The description of the problem-solving method is accomplished at two different layers as experience showed that maintenance may become very complicated if control knowledge is intertwined with the knowledge what the inference steps actually are.

Knowledge is described in MIKE using the declarative specification language KARL [2] which is intended to be used during knowledge acquisition, i.e. focuses on conceptual issues. Therefore, KARL provides epistemological primitives which allow to model the knowledge of an expert precisely without immediately casting it into the peculiarities of a particular representation formalism. To that end, KARL uses primitives which resemble the primitives of (extended) entity relationship models, data flow diagrams, and structured program flow diagrams. Domain knowledge is expressed basically in terms of *objects* (denoting individual entities in the domain of discourse together with their properties), *classes* (denoting concepts), and *predicates* (describing relationships between entities). Additionally, sufficient conditions for properties of objects or tuples of predicates can be expressed as Horn clause expressions. Knowledge about inference steps is expressed mainly by means of (elementary or composed) *inference actions* and *roles*. Inference actions correspond to processes in data flow diagrams. Like hierarchical data flow diagrams, composed inference actions can be decomposed, resulting in a collection of roles and more elementary inference actions. The behaviour of elementary inference actions is specified declaratively with Horn clauses. Roles correspond to data stores in data flow diagrams, i.e. provide input to or collect output of inference actions. Roles are associated with class and predicate definitions establishing the terminology of the problem-solving method. Some roles (namely, views and terminators) are connected to the domain layer, thus making domain knowledge accessible to inference actions. Finally, control knowledge is expressed by means of *programs* which are calls to inference actions, assignments to boolean variables, or more complex constructs built by sequence, alternative, and iteration. Programs may be combined to *subtasks*, which constitute the analogue to composed inference actions at the inference layer and define their internal control flow. The connection between task and inference layer is established by the fact that inference actions can be called at the task layer.

3 Modules

The distinction of knowledge layers in MIKE is one step towards decomposing large software systems into manageable pieces. Additionally, MIKE collects data objects sharing the same properties in classes and encapsulates descriptions of properties (i.e. attributes) with the objects they apply to. Still, additional means for imposing structure on a KBS are required between these opposite ends of the spectrum of granularity. Modules are an appropriate additional structuring primitive since they further reduce the overall complexity by splitting a software system into meaningful and manageable pieces while bringing about the advantages of information hiding.

The separation of knowledge layers and the notion of concepts and individual entities is part of the conceptual model underlying MIKE. Therefore, these structuring mechanisms are already present in KARL (and even in a preceding semiformal representation). The definition of modules, however, is a matter of realization, to be addressed during system design, rather than a conceptual issue. Consequently, modules are introduced as a language primitive of DesignKARL [7], which extends KARL by the ability to express realization-oriented aspects. In order to facilitate maintenance, the design phase in MIKE aims at preserving the structure of the model developed in the analysis phase, in particular the distinction between domain knowledge and domain-independent knowledge about the problem-solving method. Therefore, DesignKARL provides two types of modules, namely *domain modules* and *processing modules*.

3.1 Domain Modules

Domain modules collect related domain knowledge in a single place. A module may use knowledge defined elsewhere as well as supply knowledge to other modules. Access to external knowledge, i.e. classes and predicates, is restricted by module interfaces: knowledge defined elsewhere may be used only if it is mentioned in the import interface of the module intending to use it and if another module makes the knowledge available in its export interface. Imported knowledge may be renamed. Additional classes and predicates may be defined in the declaration part. In the body, extensions of classes and predicates from the interface and declaration parts are described by means of Horn clauses or simple facts. The body comprises an additional subsection for facts that are subject to change when the system is solving another case, thus distinguishing case data from knowledge which is constant across different cases. A subset of imported and locally defined classes and predicates may be exported to other modules. Exporting classes or predicates implies that their extension will also become known to the importing module. Elements of object classes and tuples of predicates cannot be exported selectively. The rules defining the extension are not accessible, but determine the semantics that must be respected by the importing modules (cf., e.g., [10]).

Example 1: [8] report on a KARL specification of a solution to a configuration task, namely configuring elevator systems. A valid configuration of an elevator system consists of a collection of components such that none of the constraints on their compatibility is violated. Knowledge concerning such components might then be collected in domain modules. Knowledge concerning, e.g., the car might be found in the module *car-data* (cf. Fig. 1.) which exports some knowledge to the outside without using knowledge described elsewhere (i.e. the import interface is empty). ♦

```
DMODULE car-data
  INTERFACE
    EXPORT          // Class and predicate definitions to be used elsewhere ...
      CLASS car
          car_platform:  { platform };
          car_sling:     { sling };
          car_door:      { door };
          ...
      END;
      CLASS platform
          pl_base:   { base };
          pl_width:  { INTEGER };
          ...
      CLASS base
          bs_model:   { STRING };
          bs_height:  { INTEGER };
      END;
      ...
      PREDICATE base_order
          act:     { base };
          next:    { base };
      END;
      ...
  BODY
    DEFINITIONS     // Class and predicate definitions to be used only locally ...
      PREDICATE intermediate_base
          lb:      { base };
          ub:      { base };
      END;
    RULES           // Intensional descriptions of classes and predicates ...
      ∀x_B ∀y_B ∀z_B ∀x_M ∀y_M ∀z_M
        ( intermediate_base(lb: x_B, ub: y_B)
            ← x_B[base_model: x_M] ε base ∧ y_B[base_model: y_M] ε base ∧
              z_B[base_model: z_M] ε base ∧ x_M < z_M ∧ z_M < y_M ) .
      ∀x_B ∀y_B ∀x_M ∀y_M
        ( base_order(act: x_B, next: y_B)
            ← x_B[base_model: x_M] ε base ∧ y_B[base_model: y_M] ε base ∧
              x_M < y_M ∧ ¬ intermediate_base(lb: x_B, ub: y_B) ) .
    FACTS           // Extensional descriptions of classes and predicates ...
      base25B[bs_model: "2.5B", bs_height: 6.625] ε base .
      base6B[bs_model: "6B", bs_height: 6.6875] ε base .
    INPUTDATA       // Case-specific data ...
      pltf[pl_width: 70] ε platform .
END;
```

Fig. 1. A domain module

3.2 Processing Modules

The notion of composed inference actions and subtasks in KARL already constitutes a means of abstraction at the inference and task layer. *Processing modules* are based on this notion since each of them describes a composed inference action and its associated subtask, thus resembling procedures in common programming languages. Due to the close relationship of task and inference layer, processing modules collect knowledge of both layers. The body of a module details the decomposition of an inference action into more basic inference steps and roles in the interface part, while the control flow among these inference steps is described in the control part. Thus, the distinction between the two different types of knowledge is still largely retained.

Like domain modules, processing modules communicate through interfaces. Processing modules interact with modules at the same level of abstraction by exchanging data via roles, but may also call modules which are part of their decomposition. The interface signifies which data or control information the processing module exchanges with other parts of the system or external agents such as the user, but also which data are exchanged within the problem-solving method and between problem-solving method and domain knowledge base. That is, the interface lists input and output roles of the inference action described by the processing module as well as domain modules which supply domain knowledge to views and receive knowledge through terminators. Roles appearing only in the body of a module are not accessible to other processing modules at the same level of decomposition, may, however, be used as input stores or output stores by more elementary processing modules. Processing modules may be parameterized with respect to roles and associated classes and predicates and can be instantiated as needed at various places.

The functional decomposition carried out during knowledge acquisition implies an initial modularization, yet may not be the best decomposition from a realization point of view. Therefore, this initial decomposition may be subject to modifications during the design phase.

Example 2: A major step in solving the elevator configuration task of Example 1 consists in proposing a yet unknown value of a parameter of the elevator (e.g., the model of the platform base) which is computed on the basis of previously determined parameter values, thus extending the set of known parameter values in the store *KnownParameters*. Knowledge about how to actually compute a parameter is available in domain modules which are accessible through the view *Parameters*. This can be summarized in a processing module as shown in Fig. 2. ♦

4 Clusters

An initial partitioning of task and inference layer into processing modules is based on the functional abstraction brought about by composed inference actions and subtask. For the formation of domain modules, however, related portions of domain knowledge must be identified, e.g. by abstracting from unnecessary detail and thus improving understandability of large models. A similar problem arises when conceptual models in database applications grow so large that the entity relationship (ER) models describing them become unreadable. Several proposals (cf., e.g., [13], [4], [6]) tackle this problem by constructing hierarchies of ER models by means of clustering. The basic idea is to abstract from the internal structure of a portion of an ER model in a new model where

```
PMODULE propose
 INTERFACE
  PREMISES                                        CONCLUSIONS
   STORE KnownParameters                            STORE KnownParameters
    CLASS KnownParam                                 ...
       value:       { };                            END;
       depends:     SET OF { Param };
    END;
   END;
   VIEW Parameters
    CLASS Param                                   DMODULES
       value:      { };                             elevator-data, car-data, ...
       depends:    SET OF { Param };
     ...
   END;
 BODY
   CONTROL
    (STORES PossibleParameters) :=
     SelectPossibleParameters(STORES KnownParameters, VIEWS Parameters);
         // Determine set of parameters that can currently be computed
    IF ( ¬ Ø(PossibleParameters, PossibleParam) ) THEN
         // If there is a parameter that can currently be computed ...
     ...
    ELSE end := TRUE;       // Otherwise we are done
    ENDIF;
   INFERENCE
    STORE PossibleParameters
     CLASS PossibleParam ISA Param;
     END;
    END;
    ...
    INFERENCE ACTION SelectPossibleParameter
     PREMISES KnownParameters, Parameters
     CONCLUSIONS PossibleParameters
     ...
     RULES
      ∀x_p ( x_p ε PossibleParam
          ← x_p ε Param ∧ ¬ x_p ε KnownParam ∧ ¬ unknown_deps(p: x_p) ).
    END;
    ...
 END;
```

Fig. 2. A processing module

the respective sub-model is substituted by a new artificial object, a so-called *cluster*. Since the language primitives that KARL supplies for describing the ontology of an application correspond to those of an extended ER model, ideas from ER model clustering also apply to KARL descriptions of domain layers. Three basic clustering mechanisms are distinguished: *concept clustering*, *property clustering*, and *complex clustering* which largely correspond to entity clustering, simple relationship clustering, and complex relationship clustering in [6]. Notice that clustering does not pay attention to the extension of classes and predicates.

Concept clustering maps related object classes into a higher-order cluster, e.g., by clustering a "dominating" concept with its "dominated" concepts. Concepts forming the range of an attribute may be clustered with the concept forming its domain. In this case, the attribute (which is viewed as a special kind of predicate in this context) is included in the cluster. Likewise, relationships (i.e., predicates) are usually included in such a cluster if they only involve the concept forming the range of the attribute in question. Concept clusters may also be formed by abstracting several semantically similar concepts into a cluster (cf. abstraction grouping in [6]). For instance, subconcepts may be clustered with their common superconcept. Clusters that are formed using concept clustering have the character of concepts and may be used like elementary classes in predicates or when forming even more abstract clusters.

Property clustering abstracts semantically similar relationships into a cluster. Relationships in this context comprise predicates as well as attributes with non-elementary range. Attributes with elementary ranges such as, e.g., strings or integer numbers are not considered in our clustering scheme since they are assumed to be an integral part of the concept constituting their domain. Thus, such attributes may simply be neglected as a first step of abstraction. Property clusters may either collapse only predicates or only attributes into a cluster which then behaves as an abstract predicate or abstract attribute. Before applying property clustering the classes or clusters involved in the relationships or constituting the domains and ranges of the affected attributes must be clustered by concept clustering. This treatment of attributes extends the proposals in [13], [4], or [6].

Finally, complex clustering allows to collapse parts of domain ontology into a cluster which cannot be clustered according to the concept or property clustering schemes, but still bear sufficient similarities. Depending on its contents, the resulting cluster may have the character of either a class or a predicate.

Example 3: Returning to the elevator configuration problem of the previous examples, a small part of the domain ontology (which comprises a total of some 50 classes and 40 predicates) is shown in the graphical notation of KARL (which is quite similar to an ER diagram) in Fig. 3. Due to the complexity of the complete model, clustering is useful in order to abstract from some of the details.

Concept clustering can be applied to cluster the platform base with the platform of the

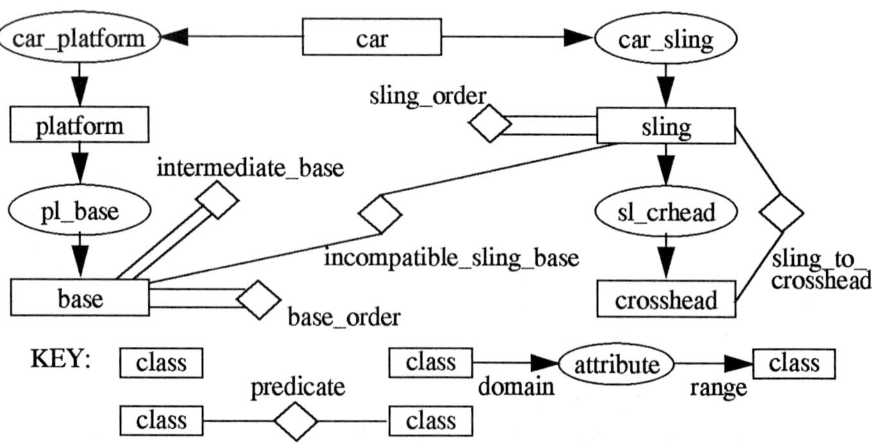

Fig. 3. Part of the domain ontology for an elevator configuration task

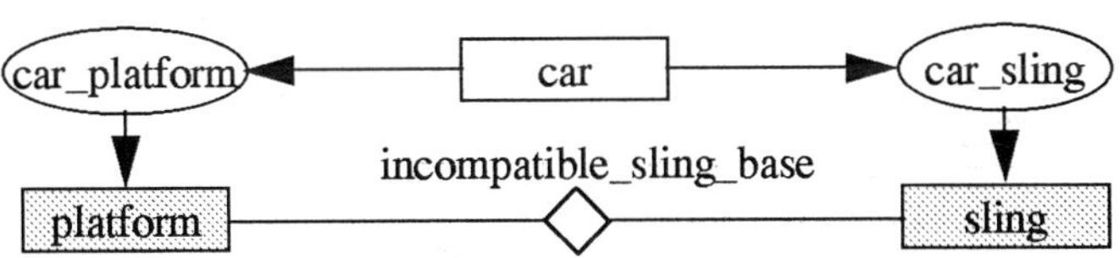

Fig. 4. Part of the domain ontology after introducing two clusters *platform* and *sling*

elevator. The predicates *base_order* and *intermediate_base* and the attribute *pl_base* are also included in the newly formed cluster. Since *platform* is the dominating class, the cluster will be called *platform* as well. Since the predicate *incompatible_sling_base* refers to the platform base as one of its arguments, this reference has to be replaced by a reference to the cluster *platform* since the class *base* is encapsulated in the respective cluster and no longer visible in the abstract representation (cf. Fig. 4.). Complex clustering is applied to form a second cluster, *sling*, comprising the classes *sling* and *crosshead*, the attribute *sl_crhead*, and the predicates *sling_order* and *sling_to_crosshead*.

Clustering might be carried even further by collapsing the clusters *platform* and *sling* (and other constituents of an elevator's car which are not shown in Fig. 4.) into a new cluster *car_components* (abstraction grouping) and by forming an attribute cluster *components* from the attributes *car_platform*, *car_sling* etc. (property clustering). ♦

Especially when forming clusters using complex clustering, links between a cluster and its environment, i.e. all classes, attributes, or predicates to which the cluster is connected, must be consistent with the links in more detailed representations. For instance, it is illegal to form a predicate-like cluster in such a way that it is linked to another predicate. Furthermore, arguments of predicates as well as domains and ranges of attributes must be adapted when forming clusters. In the previous example, the link of the predicate *incompatible_sling_base* to the class *base* must be changed into a connection to the cluster *platform*. The transformation of a cluster into its refinement and vice versa is expressed quite similar as in [4] by indicating which items in the abstract representation are replaced by which items in the refinement and vice versa.

Example 4: Taking the cluster *platform* from the previous example, the relationship between the cluster and its refined representation is specified by the transformation below:

```
CLUSTER platform
    ABS   platform, PRED(incompatible_sling_base, platform, sling);
    SPEC  platform, base,
          PRED(incompatible_sling_base, base, sling), PRED(base_order, base, base),
          PRED(intermediate_base, base, base), ATT(pl_base, platform, base);
END;
```

The classes *platform* and *base*, the predicates *base_order*, *intermediate_base*, and *incompatible_sling_base*, and the attribute *pl_base* are removed from the model while the class (cluster) *platform* and the predicate *incompatible_sling_base* (with modified first argument) are added in the abstract view. If the internals of the cluster are to be inspected the transformation is applied in the reverse direction, i.e. the items in the *SPEC* section are replaced for the constituents in the *ABS* section. ♦

In contrast to modules, which prescribe a partitioning of the implemented system (provided the implementation environment includes a possibility to define modules), clustering is a means to improve understandability during development, but has no direct counterpart in the implementation. Clustering is useful early in the design process since clusters may indicate which parts of knowledge might be candidates for encapsulation in the same module. The clusters defined in Example 3, e.g., indicate that their contents should be collected in one module (cf. Example 1).

5 Related Work

[14] present an approach to structuring knowledge bases into three knowledge layers. Layer H1 contains factual data on the basis of which layer H2 draws inferences. Pragmatic guidance of when to draw which inferences is provided by layer H3 which embodies heuristics which hold in particular applications. Layer H1 partly corresponds to the domain layer in MIKE, layer H2 is the counterpart of the inference layer, and layer H3 can be viewed as an analogue to the task layer with an additional strategic component. The layers H1 and H2 do not coincide completely with the domain and inference layers of MIKE since H1 only contains factual domain data and H2 is not generic in the sense of the MIKE inference layer, but also contains domain specific knowledge in addition to particular inferential capabilities. Therefore, layer H2 roughly corresponds to the MIKE inference layer plus the part of the domain layer comprising case-independent knowledge.

Each layer is composed of sub-structures. H1 usually consists of several autonomous data bases, whereas layer H2 contains so-called SoDs. Layer H3 may consists of several applications. Basically, an application consists of an appropriate collection of SoDs which in turn establish suitable views on the data at the bottom layer. [14] focus on SoDs which, in principle, correspond to processing modules. In contrast to processing modules which describe a complex inference step and its internal control flow and which define a method-specific ontology, SoDs are larger granules. The main problems of this decomposition scheme are the missing separation of different types of knowledge, thus making reuse of parts of the system more difficult, and the fairly large granularity of SoDs, which still leaves the need for smaller constituents which are more easily understood.

In [11], a (logic) knowledge base is viewed as a theory which is developed from a generic kernel by applying construction operators, i.e. specific theory morphisms. These theory morphisms correspond to the semantic primitives of the chosen knowledge representation approach. Thus, each application of such a theory morphism introduces an instance of the corresponding representation primitive into the knowledge base. Intermediate theories may serve as the building blocks that can be reused across applications. However, these reusable chunks are not modules in the usual sense since they do not have an explicit interface that protects some of the chunk's contents from unwanted access. Furthermore, it is not clear if this type of organization of the knowledge base can actually be exploited efficiently since the computation of the construction steps which is required for arriving at a particular stage in the development of the global development (i.e. a particular intermediate theory or "module") can be quite costly.

6 Discussion

Three different kinds of structuring mechanisms are used in MIKE already during KBS development. First, knowledge is represented at three different knowledge layers, thus separating domain knowledge from the generic problem-solving method. Second, knowledge layers can be structured further by means of domain modules and processing modules. Third, the contents of modules are expressed in terms of an object-centred data model. Through this organization, reuse of knowledge is supported at various levels of granularity. Furthermore, understandability of the overall system is improved since attention can be focused on particular, largely self-contained parts of the system. The understandability of domain knowledge is facilitated further by the possibility to abstract from details by means of clustering.

Further work is required to develop stronger guidelines which clusters should be formed and what their contexts should be, in particular when complex clustering has to be employed. Currently, a tool supporting the formation and manipulation of clusters is under development. In addition, the semantics of KARL ([5], [3]) is extended to cover the module concept outlined informally in this paper. This might also improve the efficiency of the KARL interpreter since the perfect Herbrand models constituting the semantics of inference action only need to include the relevant domain modules instead of the complete domain knowledge. The framework presented in this paper is applied quite successfully to the elevator configuration problem [8] mentioned in the examples.

References

[1] J. Angele, D. Fensel, D. Landes, S. Neubert, and R. Studer: Model-Based and Incremental Knowledge Engineering: The MIKE Approach. In *Knowledge Oriented Software Design*, J. Cuena, ed. IFIP Transactions A-27, Elsevier, Amsterdam, 1993, 139-168.

[2] J. Angele, D. Fensel, and R. Studer: The model of expertise in KARL. In *Proc. 2nd World Congress on Expert Systems* (Lisbon/Estoril, Portugal, Jan. 10-14), 1994.

[3] J. Angele: Operationalisierung des Modells der Expertise mit KARL (Operationalization of the model of expertise with KARL). infix Verlag, St. Augustin, Germany, 1993 (in german).

[4] C. Batini, G. Di Battista, and G. Santucci: Structuring primitives for a dictionary of entity relationship data schemas. In *IEEE Trans. on Software Engineering 19(4)*, 1993, 344-365.

[5] D. Fensel: The knowledge acquisition and representation language KARL. Doctoral dissertation, University of Karlsruhe, Germany, 1993.

[6] P. Jaeschke, A. Oberweis, and W. Stucky: Extending ER model clustering by relationship clustering. In *Proc. 12th Int. Conf. on the Entity-Relationship Approach ERA'93* (Arlington, Texas, Dec. 15-17), 1993, 447-459.

[7] D. Landes and R. Studer: The design process in MIKE. In *Proc. 8th Knowledge Acquisition for Knowledge-Based Systems Workshop KAW'94* (Banff, Canada, Jan. 30 - Feb. 4), 1994.

[8] K. Poeck, D. Fensel, D. Landes, and J. Angele: Combining KARL and configurable role limiting methods for configuring elevator systems. In *Proc. 8th Knowledge Acquisition for Knowledge-Based Systems Workshop KAW'94* (Banff, Canada, Jan. 30 - Feb. 4), 1994.

[9] U. Pletat: The knowledge representation language L_{LILOG}. In *Text Understanding in LILOG*, O. Herzog and C.-R. Rollinger, eds. LNAI 546, Springer, Berlin, 1991, 357-379.

[10] U. Pletat: Modularizing knowledge in L_{LILOG}. IWBS Report 173, IBM Germany, Stuttgart, 1991.

[11] C. Sernadas, J. Fiadeiro, and A. Sernadas: Modular construction of logic knowledge bases: an algebraic approach. In *Information Systems 15(1)*, 1990, 37-59.

[12] G. Schreiber, B. Wielinga, and J. Breuker, eds.: *KADS - A Principled Approach to Knowledge-Based Systems Development*. Academic Press, London, 1993.

[13] T.J. Teorey, G. Wei, D.L. Bolton, and J.A. Koenig: ER model clustering as an aid for user communication and documentation in database design. In *CACM 32(8)*, 1989, 975-987.

[14] G. Wiederhold, P. Rathmann, T. Barsalou, B.S. Lee, and D. Quass: Partitioning and composing knowledge. In *Information Systems 15(1)*, 1990, 61-72.

Distributed System Intelligent Design

M. Nikolaidou, D. Lelis, D. Mouzakis, P. Georgiadis

Department of Informatics
University of Athens
Panepistimiopolis
15771 Ilissia
Athens, Greece
tel: (+)301 - 7291885
fax: (+)301 - 7219561

Abstract

As the importance of Distributed Systems is rapidly increasing and relevant applications become more demanding, optimal design of Distributed Systems becomes a critical issue. Distributed System design is not a trivial task, since various parameters influencing the overall performance of the system have to be considered. For the successful integration of Distributed System components knowledge from different areas must be combined leading to increasing complexity. In this paper is presented the recent research work undertaken by the authors towards the development of an intelligent tool for designing Distributed Systems. Methodologies from the Artificial Intelligent domain are integrated within our research framework in order to propose alternatives solutions for the Distributed System architecture.

Key Words:

Knowledge Representation, Knowledge Exploitation, Distributed System Design, Distributed Applications, Network Design.

1. Introduction

The improvement of Distributed System (DS) performance is accomplished through the successful combination of different components, such as processing elements, storage devices and communication networks. In order to achieve maximum utilisation of available resources, distributed systems must be cautiously designed. The main reason that the design of DS is not a trivial task is the complexity of these systems, since many different concepts, such as process and data allocation as well as network design, must be explored and integrated [1].

The extensive number of different architectural solutions and the combination of knowledge from different areas impose the development of software tools facilitating experts to deal with distributed systems complexity and assisting them to design distributed systems. There is a variety of tools investigating data or resource allocation problems using mathematical models, simulation techniques or quite often a combination of both ([2],[3],[4]). In the expert systems domain one can find examples exploring the design of simple LAN and WAN architecture as in ([5],[6],[7]), but not an integrated environment supporting DS design. In this paper an *Intelligent Tool for Distributed System Design*, abbreviated to *IDIS*, is presented, having as objective the proposal of alternatives for the DS architecture according to the provided user requirements and the available technology.

2. System Description and Architecture

Distributed Systems are viewed as a combination of two discrete components: the distributed applications supported and the underlying network platform. IDIS aims at proposing solutions for :

- the placement of back-end processes operating in the distributed environment, in order to minimise network traffic and to ensure the efficient operation of the system
- the design of the network infrastructure in order to satisfy the Quality of Service parameters imposed by the distributed applications

IDIS builds a uniform environment composed by interconnected locations. Locations are defined by the user and scaled according to the described applications, e.g. they can be different floors in a building, different buildings in the same area, different areas or even a combination of the above. For each location the user specifies the front-end processes operating on it and their requirements from the network resources. Network resources consist of processing elements, terminal stations, storage devices and communication networks. Access to storage devices is possible only through system back-end processes called File Servers (FS). Back-end processes, either FS or others defined by the user, are placed by IDIS or alternatively by the user himself. Resources residing in the same location are physically connected through a network. Networks are described by protocol stacks and are interconnected via relay systems or internetworks. IDIS proposes the optimal network architecture for each location (which can be either a single or interconnected networks) and the location interconnection schema by consulting user specifications and the Knowledge Base it incorporates. The Knowledge Base maintains information concerning the supported protocols and resources along with selection and combination rules as well as rules for process and data placement. IDIS output is a detailed parametric description of the resources included in each location, the processes operating in it, and the protocol stacks used for the interconnected network environment implementation.

IDIS is based upon the ISO/ISO Reference Model for the description of the network architecture. For the description of the three upper OSI layers the RPC mechanism is used. RPCs is the most common protocol for interprocess communication in Distributed Systems, since it allows application development outside the OSI application layer, thus ensuring full extendibility and providing network transparency. For the description of the four lower layers of OSI RM, IDIS supports a variety of protocols for the implementation of LANs and WANs. All the protocols are selected because they are market and organisation standards and considered to fulfil current and future communication needs. Protocol stacks are formed with respect to user specifications and protocol compatibility rules. Network interconnection is carried out according to the OSI RM in the data link and network layer via bridges and gateways.

As shown in figure 1, IDIS consists of three different modules, exchanging information through a common Knowledge Base. Each module is responsible for the execution of operations or transformation functionally related, resulting in the construction of a portion of knowledge enriching the Knowledge Base. The added knowledge depends on the current usage of the system. It produces "intermediate" conclusions which orientates the inference engine during the exploration of the permanent knowledge. Once IDIS has completed its operation, the "intermediate" results are lost.

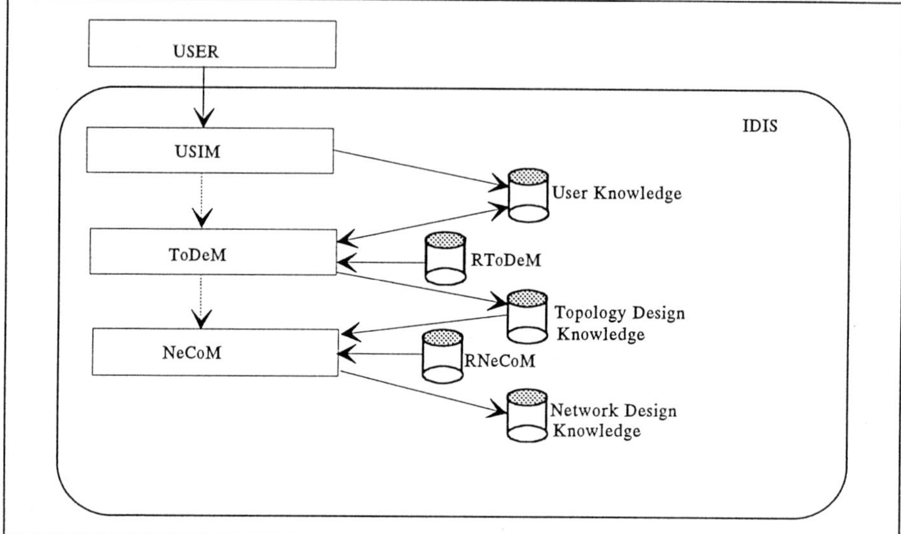

Fig. 1. IDIS Overall Architecture

The modules are invoked in the following order:

• *User Interface Module (USIM):* It facilitates the user to define the locations in which the distributed applications operate, and to describe the specific characteristics of each application and its requirements from the network resources. The user interface is fully guided by the system in order to avoid inconsistency, contradiction and incoherence. In this way the user does not provide additional information and is prevented from omitting some of the information required. The part of the Knowledge Base containing the information obtained by the user is called *User Knowledge.*

• *Topology Design Module (ToDeM):* It is responsible for the placement of back-end processes (user defined and File Servers) and the construction of the internetwork topology.

A successful back-end process placement contributes to minimising the network load, facilitating the network resources and increasing the applications performance. In parallel ToDeM creates different scenarios which constitute alternatives solutions for the interconnection of locations. It determines the internetwork type (LAN and WAN) and instantiates the values of the parameters needed for the description of network resource characteristics. These parameters describe the maximum application requirements imposed to the network resources. The scenarios are temporarily stored in the Knowledge Base and are lost when a satisfactory final solution is reached.

ToDeM explores two parts of the Knowledge Base, User Knowledge, as described above, and a set of rules, called *RToDeM* (Rules of ToDeM), which consists of formal descriptions of experimental, mathematical and empirical techniques for data and process placement, topology design and parameters instantiation. This knowledge is permanently stored in the Knowledge Base and can be subjected to update. IDIS is equipped with the mechanisms to properly update it. The exploration of knowledge by ToDeM produces the fact base *Topology Design Knowledge*, incorporated in the Knowledge Base.

• *Network Construction Module (NeCoM):* It designs the network infrastructure using User Knowledge, Topology Design Knowledge and a set of rules, called *RNeCoM (Rules of NeCoM)*. RNeCoM contains rules for protocol selection and combination and the assignment of network resources to processes. It is part of the Knowledge Base and can be updated by IDIS proper mechanisms. NeCoM builds the network infrastructure in order to satisfy the maximum user requirements. The proposed network architecture must conform with the user specifications without wasting valuable processing or communication resources. If NeCoM can not satisfy user requirements, it suggests the best acceptable solution. NeCoM is responsible for:

a. Formulating protocol stacks for all the networks and internetworks and determining the architecture of the relay nodes needed for network interconnection.

b. Determining the characteristics of each location processing nodes and storage devices. Processing and relay nodes consists of communication elements (the protocol stacks they support) and processing elements (determine their processing power).

c. Determining the set of processes, that operate on each processing node.

The exploration of knowledge performed by NeCoM results in the fact base *Network Design Knowledge*.

For the description of user requirements and the proposed network architecture "normative" or "prescriptive" mathematical models can be used. The grate disadvantage of such models is that numerical data is associated by mathematical relations. There must be a function which must be optimised ([8]). This technique should be avoided in DS design, since it is hard to provide a function which will be used by the user to describe with mathematical relations all the application requirements and it is even harder to construct a function describing the network architecture in order to optimise it. Both ToDeM and NeCoM are based upon an Expert System approach. They adopt "empirical" or "descriptive" methods based upon symbolic calculus. For the implementation purposes the Prolog programming language is used, since it offers a uniform environment for IDIS development.

3. User Interface

The User Interface Module is a fully system driven environment. The user must explicitly provide the information requested in a predefined form. He is responsible for the complete description of the applications, while USIM is responsible for testing that this description is correct. The above information is stored in the knowledge base as presented in figure 2.

```
location (LocCode)                           /* location specification by a unique name */
locdist (LocA, LocB, Distance)               /* distance between locations */

application (ApplCode, BackEndProcessList,   /* application specification by a unique name */
             FrontEndProcessList)            /* for each application the user must specify */
                                             /* back-end and front-end processes by a unique name */
parameters (FrontEndCode, Location, StartTime, EndTime, /* front-end process parameters */
            Variance, Repetition, ResponceTime, Users)
shared__data(FrontEndCodeList)               /* front-end processes using shareable data */

                                             /* information amount exchanged between processes */
network(FrontEndCode, SourceLoc, SourceProcess, DestLoc, DestProcess, Amount, Kind, Shareable)
                                 /* information amount needed to be processed by each process */
processing(FrontEndCode, Location, Process, Amount)
terminal(FrontEndCode, Location, Process, Amount)
                                 /* information amount needed to be stored by each process */
diskIO(FrontEndCode, Location, Process, Amount, Kind, Shareable)
```

Fig.2. User Knowledge Representation

In figure 2, the ResponceTime and Variance parameters are computed in seconds, the distance in kilometers and the Amount in bytes. The Repetition parameter is the statistical distribution of execution for each process. The Kind flag (appl, data) represents if the information is application code or application data and the Shareable flag(Y,N) if the information is shareable or not.

User Knowledge representation is based upon the frame formalism. It permits a convivial transformation of the elements that describe the User Knowledge, e.g. decomposition of certain attributes to others more elementary or composition of certain attributes to more general ones. During application description USIM is responsible for ensuring that the information provided by the user conforms with the predefined structure and form, as well as checking for any possible contradictions and omissions (knowledge acquisition control), e.g. there must be a *processing()* predicate for the back-end processes each time there are invoked be a *network()* predicate. USIM also extracts possible implicit knowledge from the user descriptions, e.g. for each *diskIO()* predicate, USIM also constructs a *network()* predicate indicating the information exchange between the process and a File Server, which location remains unspecified, and a *processing()* predicate for the File Server.

4. Topology Design

ToDeM deduction operation phase is divided in two parts. The first part corresponds to the back-end process placement and the design of internetwork topology. The completion of the first part triggers the second one, corresponding to the instantiation of parameters values describing network resources characteristics. For the production of conclusions the first part of ToDeM uses the User Knowledge. The whole operation is supervised by metarules belonging to RToDeM. The algorithm for the back-end process placement is based on the avoidance of unnecessary data transfer between locations. File Server placement is accomplished in order to satisfy application response time and to optimise the distribution of internetwork average load.

The topology design is based upon the following empirical assumptions (rules of thumb):

- LAN protocols are used for interconnection of resources in the same location.
- Locations are connected via LANs when the distance between them is less that 2 Km.
- Front-end processes are forced to use the same back-end proocess replicant, if they share common data. The replicant is placed within the LAN that causes the maximum load.
- Front-end processes are forced to use the same back-end process replicant, if they can be interconnected by LAN.
- There is only one back-end process replicant in each location.
- Within a LAN, the back-end process replicant is been placed in the location which causes the maximum load.

- Common File Servers are used for the locations interconnected via a LAN backbone.
- In locations interconnected with others only via WANs a File Server is placed, unless the location has no back-end processes and no interactive front-end, which require low throughput (‹9.6Kbps). In this case the location processes are using the nearest File Server.
- Within a LAN File Servers are placed according to the following criteria:
  a. FS are placed in locations with back-end process replicants. If there in more that one in the same LAN backbone, the load is divided, so that the average processing of FS will be minimised.
  b. If there are no back-end processes, an FS is placed in the location with the most interactive applications.
  c. If there aren't any, an FS is placed in the location which causes the maximum load.

The execution of the first part of ToDeM deduction operation asserts knowledge for the internetworks connecting locations and the placement of back-end processes.

The second part of ToDeM deduction operation instantiates the values of parameters necessary to determine the configuration of the network resources. This is an intermediate phase, which transforms the information given by the user to information needed by NeCoM in order to construct the protocol stacks describing all the networks, the processing elements needed in each location, and the relay systems needed for network interconnection. These parameters are related with rules RNeCoM used to construct network resources. If these rules are altered in the future in order to extent systems functionality, the parameters may alter also.

The output ToDeMs second part is incorporated in Topology Design Knowledge and consists of the predicates presented in figure 3:

```
networkReq (NetID, LocList, MaxDistance, MaxAvgMessage, MaxUsers, JobsCovert,
            MaxThroughput, KindOfThroughput)
commonNet Req(ID, CommonNetList, JobsCovert, MaxAvgMessage)
relayNodeReq (ID, Loc, InterNetworkList, MaxThroughput)
processReq (ID, Loc, Proc, MaxProcThroughput, MaxNetThroughput)
commonNodeReq (ID, Loc, ProcessesList, MaxUsers)
diskReq (ID, Loc, MaxThroughput, Amount)
```

Fig 3. Representation of Network Requirement Parameters

The facts *networkReq()* contain parameters determining the requirements for location networks and internetworks. These parameters are:

LocList — Contains the location code if the network is used to interconnect resources in a single location or the locations codes if the network is used to interconnect locations.
MaxDistance — Maximum distance between location.
MaxAvgMessage — Indicates the maximum average message size. The average message size is computed in bytes for each individual front-end process using the network.
MaxUsers — Indicates the maximum number of concurrent users
JobsCovert — Indicates if the majority of front-ends are batch or interactive.
MaxThroughput — Indicates the maximum required throughput in Mbps.
KindOfThroughput — Indicates whether the applications impose homogeneous or heterogeneous load to the network.

Applications running in different locations need a uniform network environment in order to communicate. Since IDIS builds protocol stacks containing one protocol per layer, common protocols must be used in all locations for end-to-end communication between process. These protocols correspond to OSI layers 7-4, e.g. the RPC mechanism and the transport layer protocol, and must satisfy common parameters contain in c*ommonNetReq()* facts. The *CommonNetList* parameter indicates the networks forced to use common end-to-end protocols .

The facts r*elayNodeReq()* indicate the existence of relays interconnecting networks. Each location network communicates with others via one or more internetworks. In order to ensure communication one relay node is defined per location. The *MaxThroughput* parameter indicates the maximum processing rate required from the relay node in bytes/sec.

The facts *processReq()* contain parameters indicating the user requirements for the processes running in each location. They are:

MaxThroughput — Maximum throughput needed for data processing (bytes/sec)
MaxNetThroughput — Maximum throughput needed for data transfer processing (bytes/sec)

The facts *commonNodeReq()* indicate processes that can be executed in the same processing node. Processes can be executed by the same processing node, if they are not simultaneous. Each process can participate in more that on ProcessList, since it can be executed by different kind of nodes if they are offering the necessary processing power. The main objective of the algorithm used is to minimise the number of nodes for each location without taken into account their cost. *MaxUser* parameter indicates the number of nodes needed to satisfy all the users.

The facts *diskReq()* contain the requirements imposed for data storage in each location. Parameters characterising storage devices are:

MaxThroughput — Maximum Access Rate computed in bytes/sec.
Amount — Total amount of data in bytes

Since IDIS must be able to support the design of real scale Distributed Systems that extent to multiple locations, it should facilitate the acquisition of a Knowledge Base dynamically increasing. ToDeM efficient operation depends upon its ability to group the knowledge provided by the user according to specified criteria (e.g. find the groups of simultaneous processes) and efficiently estimate the result of complex computations and combinations (e.g. compute max. required Throughput for each network). In order to increase ToDeM performance, we concentrated on an effective factorisation of the Knowledge Base in order to force the inference engine to explore the part where useful information resides and to avoid any search to the rest of it. The partition of the Knowledge Base (also called compilation) is done dynamically. Moreover, the fact that the exhaustive exploration of the compiled Knowledge Base does not guarantee the inference engine performance and can cause its saturation, leaded us to introduce control strategies forcing the inference engine to deliberately unstackings ([9]).

During back-end process placement and internetworks' construction, ToDeM needs to find location sets, interconnected via LAN. Locations belong in the same set when the distance between each pair of them is less than 2 km. In order to depict this relation graphs can be used, where locations are viewed as nodes and edges indicate that the distance between two locations is less than 2 Km, as shown in figure 4. The same question can be raised for all the locations (e.g. the whole graph) or locations specified by certain criteria, such as locations involved in the invocation of a back-end process (e.g. subgraphs).

```
location (HeadQuarters).                          /* Description of Locations */
location (BuildingA).
location (BuildingB).
location (BranchOfficeA).
location (BranchOfficeB-Buildingl).
location (BranchOfficeB-Building2).

locdist (HeadQuarters, BuildingA, 0.2).           /* Three of the locations HeadQuarters, BuildingA */
locdist (HeadQuarters, BuildingB, 0.3).           /* and BuildingB are placed in Company's Park */
locdist (BuildingA, BuildingB, 0.5).

locdist (HeadQuarters, BranchOfficeA, 13.1).  /* Brach office A is 13 Km away */
locdist (BuildingA, BranchOfficeA, 13.4).
locdist (BuildingB, BranchOfficeA, 13).

locdist(HeadQuarters, BranchOfficeB-Buildingl, 2.4).        /* Branch office B is 2 Km away */
locdist (BuildingA, BranchOfficeB-Buildingl, 2.3).          /* and occupies two buildings */
locdist (BuildingB, BranchOfficeB-Buildingl, 1.9).
locdist (BranchOfficeA, BranchOfficeB-Buildingl, 16).
locdist(HeadQuarters, BranchOfficeB-Building2, 2.6).
locdist (BuildingA, BranchOfficeB-Building2, 2.7).
locdist (BuildingB, BranchOfficeB-Building2, 2.3).
locdist (BranchOfficeA, BranchOfficeB-Building2, 16.3).
locdist (BranchOfficeB-Buildingl, BranchOfficeB-Building2, 16.3).
```

Fig. 4a. A example of Locations involved in a Distributed System

Locations can be interconnected via a LAN, when they belong in the same full subgraph. For the formulation of full subgraphs by avoiding slowing down the inference engine, graph compilation techniques are introduced ([9]).

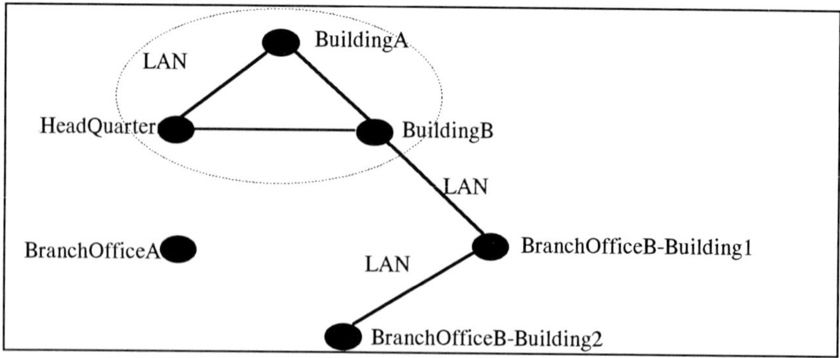

Fig. 4b. Graph Representation of Locations interconnected via LANs

The same techniques are also applied in the construction of simultaneous process sets, which are used to estimate maximum application requirements from the network resources.

5. Network Design

NeCoM builds the network infrastructure using the Topology Design Knowledge specified by ToDeM. NeCoM constructs the fact base Network Design Knowledge incorporated in Knowledge Base. It is presented in figure 5.

```
communicationElement(Instance, [LocationList], [PeerComID, RoutComID]).
relayProcessingNode(Instance, [SourceLocation, TargetNetLocationList, ProcessingPower]).
processingNode(Instance, [Location, ProcessList, ProcessingPower, Number], []).
storageDevice(Instance, [Location, Capacity, Speed], []).
```

Fig. 5. Network Design Knowledge Representation

As shown in figure 5, network resources are represented as frames, using the basic structure *network-resource-element-type(ID, ListValues, ListPointers)*. ID attribute specifies uniquely the instance of each network resource type. *ListValues* attribute contains each frame slots which represent the parameters describing network resources. *ListPointers* attribute specifies the frames invoked by the original frame. Each Communication Element invokes two frames, Peer Communication Element (corresponding to layers 7-4) and Routing Communication Element (corresponding to layers 3-1). Each one of them either is empty or invokes protocol frames corresponding to the incorporated layers. The hierarchy tree defining Communication Element structure in depicted in figure 6.

NeCoM is using RNeCoM knowledge in order to fill all the slots of the constructed frames. The structure of those rules is presented in figure 7.

```
frame_name(Instance, [Value1, Value2, ..., ValueN], [Pointer1, Pointer2, ... , PointerX]) :-
        find_frame_name_value1(Value1), .......,
        find_frame_name_valueN(ValueN),
        call_frame(Pointer1), .......,
        call_frame(PointerX).
call_frame (Pointer) :- call(Pointer), Pointer=pointer(Inst, ListValues, listPointers).
```

Fig.7. RNeCoM Selection Rules Representation

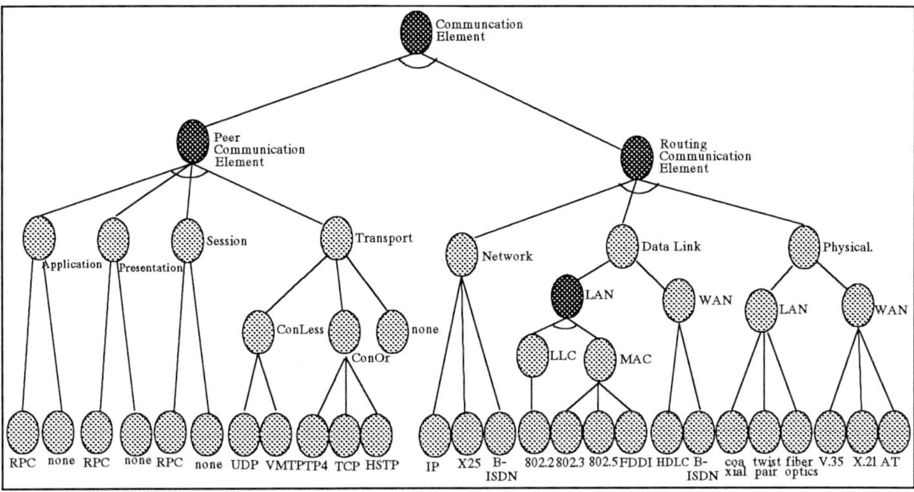

Fig. 6. Communication Element Hierarchy Tree

Frames can be called parametrically by adding rule *find_pointer(Pointer)* that selects the proper frame in rule *call_frame(Pointer)*. Parametric selection of frames allow us to choose which protocol will be used for OSI layer implementation, as shown in figure 8.

```
transport(InstTP, [], [TransProtType]):-
    findtransport1(TransProtType),      /* decides whether Connection Oriented or Connectionless */
    call(TransProtType).                /* Protocol will be used */

transConLess(InstTP, [Name, Processing, MaxTPDU, MaxOverHead], []):-
    findtransConLess1(Name),            /* decides which protocol will be used IP or VMTP */
    findtransConLess2(Processing),      /* estimates processing */
    findtransConLess3(MaxOverHead),     /* estimates max Overhead */
    findtransConLess4(MaxTPDU).         /* estimates max TPDU size according to user req. */

transConOr(InstTP, [Name, Processing, MaxTPDU, MaxOverHead, Window, Numbering,
        ErrorCorrection, ConnectionSetup, ConnectionRelease, OutOfBand, Priorities],
        []):-
    findtransConOR1(Name),              /* decides which protocol will be used TP4, TCP or HSTP */
    findtransConOR2(Processing),        /* estimates processing */
    findtransConOR3(MaxOverHead),       /* estimates max Overhead */
    findtransConOR4(MaxTPDU),           /* estimates max TPDU size according to user req. */
    findtransConOR7(RateControl),       /* decides if rate control will be supported */
    findtransConOR5(Numbering),         /* decides the numbering scheme (TPDUs or bytes) */
    findtransConOR6(ErrorDetect),       /*desides the error detection mechansim */
                                        /* (go-back-n,selective)*/
    findtransConOR7(FlowControl),       /* desides if flow control will be supported */
    findtransConOR7(RateControl),       /* desides if rate control will be supported */
    findtransConOR7(Window),            /* estimates window size according to user requirements */
    findtransConOR8(ConSetup),          /* desides the connection setup mechanism */
    findtransConOR9(ConRelease)         /* (3-way, 2-way, fast-connect) */
    findtransConOR10(OutOfBand),        /* desides whether Out of band will be enabled */
    findtransConOR11(Priorities).       /* desides on the priority levels */
```

Fig. 8. Transport protocol selection

The value of a frame slot can be determined independently or it can be influenced by another slot's value. The dependence between slots belonging in the same or different frames is indicated by the assertion of temporary knowledge specifying the parameters influencing slot's calculation. The same applies to frame selection rules also, when the selection of one frame imposes the selection of another one as well, e.g. the use of B-ISDN AMT protocol in Data Link layer imposed the use of the ATM in the physical layer.

NeCoM operation consists of the following stages:

1. Peer Communication Element design for all the networks belonging in the same commonNet.
2. Communication Element design for all the networks, which includes Peer Communication and Routing Communication element construction. If the network belongs in a commonNet the specified Peer Communication Element is used.
3. RelayProcessingNode design for each location.
4. ProcessingNode design for each location.
5. StorageDevice design for each location.

6. Concluding Remarks

The resent versions of all the modules constructing IDIS are implemented using Sepia Prolog in a SUN/SUNOS 3.1 network environment. The system is tested using scenarios of the academic and commercial community and produces results considered as quite efficient up to this current early stage.

IDIS development in based on the integration of techniques from the AI domain in order to efficiently design Distributed Systems. Future work will focus on the exploration the system performance and the integration of new protocols parametrically described by the user.

7. Bibliography

[1]: Sape Mullender (1989), Distributed Systems, ACM PressFrontier Series.

[2]: B. Gavish and H. Pirkul, "Computer and Database Locations in Distributed Computer Systems", IEEE Transactions on Computers, vol c-35, no. 7, June 1986.

[3]: P. M. Apers, "Data Allocation in Distributed Computer Systems", ACM Transaction on Database Systems, September 1988.

[4]: R. L. Bagrodia and C. Shen, "MIDAS: Integrated Design and Simulation of Distributed Systems", IEEE Transactions on Software Engineering, vol. 17, no. 10, October 1991.

[5]: K. S. Leung, M.H. Wong, "An Expert-System Shell Using Structured Knowledge - An Object-Oriented Approach", IEEE Computer, March 1990.

[6]: S. Ceri, L. Tanca, "Expert Design of Local Area Networks", IEEE Expert, October 1990.

[7]: A. Sato, R.P. Hamalainen, "Seteli: The Strategy Expert for Telecommunication Investments", IEEE Expert, October 1990.

[8]: C. Riveline, "L'enseignement du dur et l'enseignement du mou, Gerer et comprendre", pp.42-45, December 1986.

[9]: D. Lelis, "Le mecanisme d' exploitation de connaissances d' un systeme d'aide a la decision", These de doctorat, CRISS, Univ. de Grenoble, 1989

A Model for Hypermedia Based on Production Systems

Ioanis Gaviotis* and Dimitris Christodoulakis

Computer Technology Institute and
Department of Computer Science and Engineering,
University of Patras, 26500 Rion, GREECE
{ gaviotis,dxri } @ cti.gr

Abstract. The structure and semantics of hypermedia systems are described formally by theoretical models. We review state-of-the-art models that focus on capturing the synchronization during browsing, the manipulation of the hyper structure and the information retrieval capabilities. We introduce a new model for hypermedia that employs a production rule system to express the structural characteristics, the dynamics of document navigation and the preservation of constraints on the hyper document. Our model expresses naturally various hypermedia properties and allows flexible customization for each application. To demonstrate its practical use, we define views and describe version control. We compare all models on the basis of standard hypermedia features and argue that our model is suitable for general-purpose hypermedia systems.

1 Introduction

Modern hypertext technology *re*-emerged in the late 80s reflecting on the pioneering work of Engelbart and Nelson in the 60s. As hypertext moves toward maturity, we observe a deliberate and steady shift away from individual applications toward generic conceptual and architectural designs.

Usually, designers provide an architectural description for their system. However, in order to get a clear insight and assess a hypermedia system in an implementation independent way, it is necessary to express its concepts, properties and philosophy using a formal mathematical model. A formal model capitalizes on the abstract description of the system and outlines its distinguished priorities. It also suggests a generic architectural design and serves as a tool for the validation of the end product.

Until now, researchers have not reached a consensus on the formal model to be used for hypermedia. As [2] points out: "The problem [of complexity of hypermedia systems] is compounded when users must cope with a multitude of systems that have inconsistent data models. Standardizing the user interface produces, at best, a superficial similarity, but it does not truly address the problem ... We would like to see standards develop for data models." Toward this end, a major effort has been the Dexter Reference model [13].

* Partially supported by the Greek Scholarship Foundation (grant no. 1205).

The purpose of this paper is to propose a new model based on production rule systems. In the next section, we review hypermedia models and summon up related characteristics borrowed from information retrieval and layered data models. In Sect. 3, we present the form of the production rules and customize the facts that model hypermedia entities. We demonstrate the model's practicality and connote an architectural design. The last sections assess the suitability of the rules for open, active hypermedia and compare the models using a standard set of hypermedia features.

2 Models for Hypermedia

Each model places emphasis on different hypermedia aspects. We present various approaches to critical hypermedia issues and show the repercussions on the generality and usefulness of respective systems.

2.1 The Petri Net Model

The Petri Net (PN) model describes the hyper document structure, provides a non-trivial execution semantics for monitoring the sequence of visiting hyper nodes and depicts the inter-node synchronization dependencies.

Formally, a Petri Net is a triple $N = (S, T, F)$, where S is the set of states, T is the set of transitions, and F is the flow relation defined as a subset of $(S \times T) \cup (T \times S)$. The preset of any $x \in S \cup T$ is the set $\bullet x = \{y|(y,x) \in F\}$, whereas the postset of x is $x\bullet = \{y|(x,y) \in F\}$. We define a PN state as a boolean function $M : S \rightarrow \{0,1\}$ with the logical connotation that a marked state s has $M(s) = 1$; 0 otherwise. Execution begins with an initial state M_0. The **yields** relation $\vdash$ maps a state M_i to M_{i+1}, iff there is an active transition that is fired. A transition t is called active when the states of its preset are all marked. When one of the active transitions t is fired, the new state M_{i+1} has $(\forall s \in \bullet t - t\bullet : M(s) = 0)$ and $(\forall s \in t\bullet : M(s) = 1)$, while the rest of the states retain the same marking.

Mapping a PN state to a hypermedia presentation unit brings up the inconvenience of not distinguishing a logical and a presentation entity. For this reason, [23] separate hypertext contents from the link structure adopting a layered approach. At the lower level lay PN entities, viz. states and transitions. The contents C, the windows W and the buttons B comprise the logical projection $P_l = (C_l, W_l, B_l)$, which maps states to contents, states to windows and transitions to buttons. Additionally, there is a display projection P_d that maps logical entities to physical display formats. Figure 1 depicts a PN modeling a simple hypertext. The logical and display projections have been left out.

The navigation of a hypertext H starts with an initial marking M_0. Marked states represent rendered hyper nodes. Firing a transition (via the selection of a button which is its display or logical projection equivalent) causes deactivation of the contents and windows that comprise its preset and presentation of those in its postset.

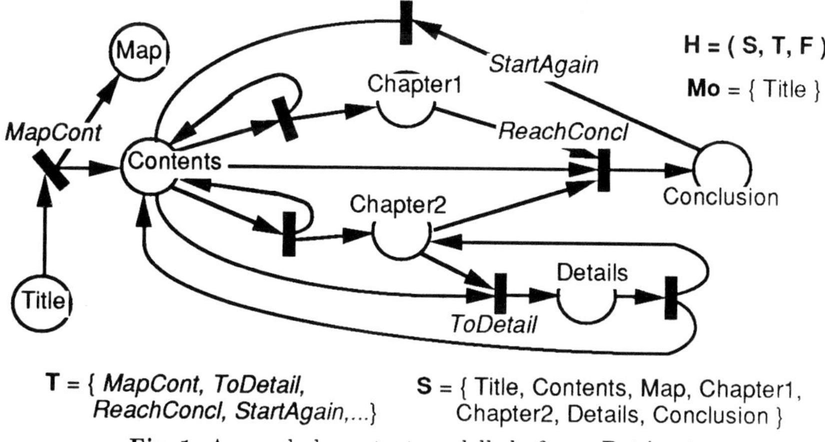

Fig. 1. A sample hypertext modelled after a Petri net

2.2 The Graph-Based Models

Labelled Directed Graphs (LDGs) are the natural choice when it comes to the modeling of hypertext, because the basic objects comprising a hypertext are nodes interconnected with links in a mesh. The usual semantics attached to such structures are that of navigation. To overcome the shortcomings of the LDG model that come from its restricted edge relation, [24] used hypergraphs as the formal structure on which hypertexts are modelled.

For a hypertext $H = (N, L, E)$ modelled by a hypergraph, the links are depicted using $E : 2^N \times 2^L \longrightarrow 2^N$. That means that a hyper link relates a set of nodes to a set of nodes using a set of labels. A state is any set of marked nodes $M \subseteq N$. The navigation semantics is that the user can choose to follow any edge whose source has at least one node in the set of marked nodes. Then all the nodes in the edge's target set will become marked.

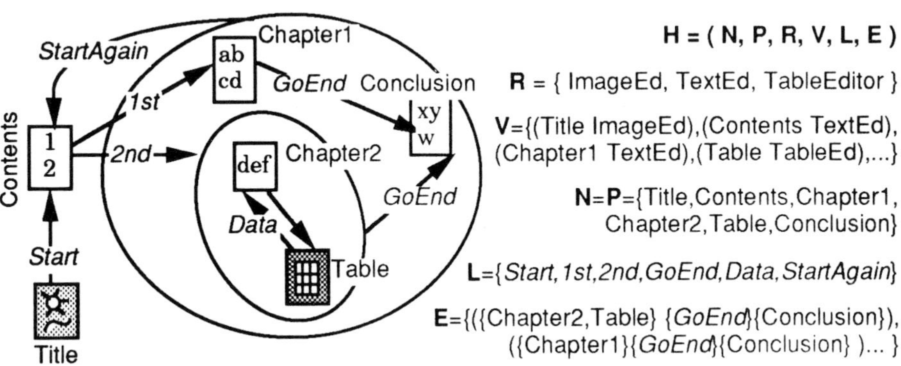

Fig. 2. A sample hypertext modelled using a hypergraph

A hypertext is modelled as a sextuple (N, P, R, V, L, E) consisting of a set of hyper nodes N, a set of pages P that hold the contents of the nodes, a set of page readers R that manipulate pages, a function $V : N \rightarrow P$ that maps nodes to pages, a set of labels L, and the set of hyper edges E (Fig. 2).

In this model, the media type of the pages is recognized by relating each page with a reader responsible for the page's manipulation (creation, rendering, editing). Essentially, the page can be thought of as a unimedia node. Many pages constitute a multimedia node.

2.3 Other Models

Hypertext organization and techniques have been effectively applied to information retrieval and serve as alternative methods for locating information when the user can not state a relevant query and searching cannot be done systematically [17]. Some recent architectures attempt to combine information retrieval methods (usually the keyword vector model) with layered hypertext (usually two-level) placing the content descriptors at the upper or hyperindex level, and the actual contents at the lower or hyperdocument level [8]. In [1], the hyperindex encapsulates a classification mechanism on index terms. Stratified Hypermedia [4] enriches this schema with views which may be either structural or arbitrary link structures (for example cross-references). Additionally, a low-level entity (content) is described by its index terms and this characterization propagates to upper level entities, so that information overlap can be estimated quantitatively, constituting an information disclosure machine based on a characterization calculus.

The neural net model has been used to identify access points and to suggest paths for guiding user navigation [3]. A neural net creates and updates the link weights inducing knowledge from example use of the hypertext (learn by example) until the network reaches a stable state. Then browsing appears as a statistical operation, since different nodes may appear as neighbors during the lifetime of the document.

HAM offers a transaction-based storage server for hypertext [5]. It deploys nodes and links decorated with attributes to build graphs and formulate partitions on them. HAM operations are similar to database operations; they are grouped in the create, delete, destroy, change, get, filter and special categories. The proposed architecture can operate in a distributed fashion on many applications. Our proposed model not only has the power of a database system, but also permits the flexible customization of the integrity constraints.

A widely accepted hypertext data model is the Dexter model [16], [13] that distinguishes three layers: (a) the *within-component* layer is concerned with the representation of atomic information pieces; (b) the *storage* layer identifies components and aggregates the base components into composite ones; and (c) the *run-time* layer is responsible for the presentation and "execution" of hypertext.

In our work with the production rule system we follow closely the Dexter conventions, because we recognize its wide dissemination and acceptance and maintain its appropriateness for general hypertext system design.

3 Production Systems Model

> "A feature which is conspicuously absent from the current generation of hypermedia systems is integrated support for inference upon the knowledge of the network." D. Carlson & S. Ram [6, pp. 315]

We define the rule form and we customize a fact base to reflect the hypermedia entities. Then we show how hypertext features and functionality are depicted with the production rule model.

3.1 The Production Rule Model

A production rule system (PRS) is a triple $S = (A, V, R)$, where A is the alphabet of atomic words, V is the set of variables and R are the rules. Patterns are phrases created by the concatenation of words and variables. A rule has the form

`IF PRESENT` {pattern}* `ABSENT` {pattern}* `WHEN` [predicate]
`THEN ADD` {pattern}* `REMOVE` {pattern}*

Its informal semantics is that the inference engine tries to find facts that match the patterns of the `IF` part, and makes sure there are *no* facts that match the `ABSENT` part. If additionally the predicate of the `WHEN` part is true, the rule may fire, thus adding the facts implied by the `THEN` patterns and deleting from the base the facts implied by the `REMOVE` part.

We define a fact base F as a set of ground phrases $F \subseteq A^*$, analogous to the tuples of a relation. A binding is a pair in $V \times A$. A matching is a set of bindings of all the variables in a pattern. In our examples, we precede variables with a ? to discriminate them from words.

The function **matches** relates a pattern with a fact under a given matching. The function **unifies** applies the matching function on two sets of patterns and facts. In order for a rule to become active (ie. candidate for execution):

1. there must exist a matching of *all* the variables participating in the `IF` part,
2. the facts that arise from the substitution of the variables of the patterns in the `ABSENT` part under the matching must not exist in the current fact base, and
3. the `WHEN` predicate must evaluate to true.

Firing a rule causes the transition to a new fact base that includes the facts of the previous state plus those in `THEN` part minus those in the `REMOVE` part.

For experimentation reasons, we developed ROGES, an environment that maintains a fact base and supports the above specified rule format for its inference engine. ROGES is data-driven (forward chaining); later, we describe its use to validate our hypermedia model.

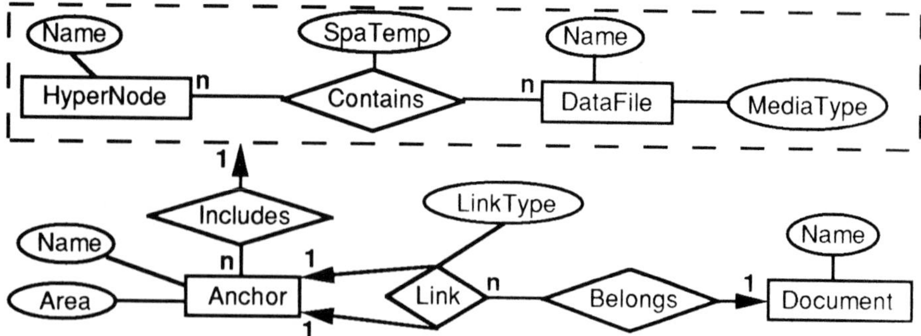

Fig. 3. Entity Relationship diagram for hypermedia

3.2 Customization of the Model for Hypermedia

Assuming we have an inference engine that accepts and executes production rules as specified above, we are going now to depict in the fact base the hypermedia information. We start by representing the hyper graph structure. The basic entities involved in a hypermedia system are structured in Fig. 3.

Let's consider the raw information data. It can be anything representable and storable in some kind of electronic form, for example text, images, audio, video, executables, graphics, etc. We call DataFiles the place holders for the raw material and all we need to about them is their type (or the media editor they are associated with). For the hypermedia system, DataFiles are just sequences of uninterpreted data.

Many DataFiles make up a HyperNode. This is a hypermedia level entity, whereas a DataFile is a storage level entity. Since a HyperNode may be regarded as an aggregation of DataFiles, it is generally multimedial. A HyperNode does not copy the contents of its constituent DataFiles; it just contains references to the actual data. Notice that a DataFile may participate in zero, one, or more HyperNodes.

A HyperNode needs to contain certain information concerning the placement and synchronization of its constituent DataFiles [18]. Such information may be dynamically computed. This is a general principle throughout the model: where ever a value can be, coded data whose evaluation returns a proper value can be. Anchor is a selectable area of a DataFile. Links are ordered pairs of anchors.

Table 1. Hypermedia entities for the PRS model

```
( DataFile  ?DFname MediaType ?MTinfo )
( HyperNode ?HNname Contains ?DFname SpatioTemp ?STinfo )
( Anchor    ?ARname IncludedIn ?HNname ?DFnm Area ?Designator )
( Link      ?LKname From ?ARname To ?ARname OfType ?LT BelongsTo ?DOC)
```

Table 1 depicts the patterns we use in the fact base for the hypermedia system. They are kept simple, so that rules are easy to follow. The patterns are not relational transformations of the ER diagram; actually, they are better accomodated in an object-oriented DBMS (hence the `?XXname` identifiers).

Navigation. We introduce facts of the form `( Active ?HNname )` that denote currently active (rendered) nodes. Using the following rule, we express the transition from node to node.

```
IF   PRESENT ( Active ?HNname )
             ( Anchor ?FromAnch IncludedIn ?HNname ... )
             ( Link   ?LKname From ?FromAnch To ?ToAnch ... )
             ( Anchor ?ToAnch IncludedIn ?AnotherHN ... )
THEN ADD     ( Active ?AnotherHN )
     REMOVE  ( Active ?HNname )
```

It is possible that many rules are candidates for firing. Our PRS model chooses non-deterministically among them. To express explicitly the action of the reader to choose a specific link, we may add `( Selected ?AnchoR )` facts and append the proper pattern to the `IF` part of the navigation rule. Collecting and timestamping the `Active, Selected` facts, one monitors the *interactions* and the path of the reader in the document (*history preservation*).

The production rule formalism has the expressive power of the relational algebra and calculus. Therefore, its appropriate for expressing selections, constraints and properties on the hyper graph structure.

Support for Views. Views are virtual hypertexts—they do not exist in stored form, they are computations based on the selection or merging of other hypertexts (or views) [15]. A view may be expressed easily using rules. For example, the following rule detects the files that contain video and creates a view that omits those nodes that contain video. Remark: the rule deletes no DataFile—it only affects the currently active hypertext.

```
IF   PRESENT ( DataFile ?AnyDFile MediaType "Video" )
THEN REMOVE  ( HyperNode ?aHypNod Contains ?AnyDFile . . . )
```

Firing such a rule may cause inconsistencies. For example, omitting a HyperNode may lead to *orphan anchors*. A rule would detect and discard those anchors:

```
IF   PRESENT ( Anchor    ?ThisAR IncludedIn ?AnyHN ... )
     ABSENT  ( HyperNode ?AnyHN ... )
THEN REMOVE  ( Anchor    ?ThisAR IncludedIn ?AnyHN ... )
```

Note that removal of anchors may lead to *dangling links*. A similar rule would deal with those, too. The chain of firings eventually leads the hypertext to a stable and consistent state. The behavior of each hyper document follows some standard rules; however, the hypertext engineer depending on the application may easily customize it using the production rule formalism.

Version Control. A versioning mechanism captures the temporal evolution of a hypertext [12]. The PRS model deals with versions as consecutive instances of HyperNodes that are connected with special `Next Edition` links. This conceptual solution gracefully integrates in the hyper space the time dimension. Particular applications are free to provide custom-tailored semantics to the creation, browsing and maintenance of versioning links. The following rule reflects the purge operation deleting all versions of a node except the most recent one.

```
IF   PRESENT ( HyperNode ?OldHN ... )
             ( Anchor    ?SomeAR IncludedIn ?OldHN ... )
             ( Link      ?LKname From ?SomeAR OfType Next-Edition )
THEN REMOVE  ( HyperNode ?OldHN ... )
```

Versions are also produced when many concurrent users manipulate the same document changing the DataFile contents and modufying the hyper structure. This is the case especially in hypermedia applications for computer-supported cooperative work [22]. Rules may be specified to coordinate access and modification to the hypertext.

3.3 Model Suitability

[7] evaluated the utility of production systems in general domains and concluded that they are especially appropriate when the following three properties hold. We argue that they are indeed well-suited for hypermedia systems.

Knowledge is diffuse and not a concise, unified theory. Generally, the structure of the graph is a mesh of nodes interconnected with links; one cannot assume without losing in generality a stricter graph topology. Some hypertexts may appear to have more regular shape, for example a tree or a sequence; such regular topologies usually emanate from a simple minded transformation of the original text to hypertext [21]. On closer and more careful inspection the hypertext engineer will recognize implicit relationships between the text parts and will depict them with an enriched graph structure.

Therefore, our knowledge about the structure and use of information is better communicated extensively and not as a small set of axioms or properties. The diffusion of knowledge stems from the very nature of hypertext: the material is structured almost freely and the user selects navigation paths from many alternatives. Contrast this to the strict sequential reading of a traditional book, or the systematic selection from catalogs and encyclopedias.

Processes are independent actions—not dependent subprocesses. The primary process in hypermedia is navigation. Yet one can recognize other activities, such as authoring (creating or altering the contents of hyper nodes), graph customization (defining user views and paths dependent on certain conditions), communicating with other users through sharing and annotation of common nodes [20], etc. All these activities may proceed independently and even concurrently, essentially exploiting the hypertext as a substrate or blackboard where all changes are reflected upon. There need not be any coupling of those processes—at least for conceptual reasons. The imposition of such unnecessary restrictions on the hypertext system is a sign of immature design and poor implementation strategy.

Knowledge and the way it is used are separate; uncoupled representation and control. The hypertext representation as exemplified in the fact base and its manipulation by the rules form a level of separation. The deletions/insetions are transparent to the fact base front-end where the document behavior and reader browsing are performed.

A model must balance precision of description with usability and naturalness. We argue that the production rule model achieves this balance and is adequate for the expression of hypermedia system functions.

4 Comparison

In [10], we state seven features that comprise a kernel for state-of-the-art hypermedia (see Table 2). In this section, we examine the degree to which the models cover those aspects of hypermedia functionality.

Table 2. Basic hypermedia features

FEATURES	**A hypermedia system should ...**
Document structure	Capture the static and dynamic aspects of the graph. Express aggregations, hierarchies on entities.
Navigation semantics	Offer browsing facilities that eliminate the 'lost-in-the-hyperspace' problem.
Multimedia support	Accomodate disparate media types. Support dynamic media requiring strong synchronization.
Document manipulation	Express modifications in the components of the hyper document.
User interaction	Capture tightly the reactions of the reader or writer to the system.
Document evolution	Follow the document life cycle and preserve the time dimension.
Active hypertext	Cater for document responsive to events. Add programmability to its behavior.

The merit of labelled directed graphs (LDGs) as models for hypertext, besides simplicity, is that one may readily exploit the existing and well-understood graph algorithms for node reachability, document traversal, etc.

One limitation of the LDG model is that a hypertext state is constrained to be a single node, so only one node can be rendered to the user at a time. This implies that the presentation objects are indistinguishable entities to the logical or stored objects. To model multimedia nodes, one's only option is to create an aggregate media type that includes many components. A unimedia storage-level object is replicated many times, if it needs to be included in many presentation level objects.

An interesting aspect of the Petri net (PN) model is that a whole hypertext may be placed as a PN state, in essence forming a hierarchy, a natural and useful modeling concept. Apparently, there are markings that may cause activations of more than one transitions. Then, it is the user's responsibility to choose the one that will eventually fire, or to fire more than one transitions essentially creating parallel trails.

The PN formalizes the synchronization constraints that exist between different nodes during user navigation. The PN model offers solutions for display complexity, concurrent browsing, node reachability, access control and versioning [23]; however, all these facilities are realized by proper arrangement of the Petri net structure. This is an indirect and rather unnatural way to achieve such results. In order to support them, generally the PN model must be extended to include attributes and predicates that test their values. This implies the incorporation of an attribute manipulation formalism and its corresponding computational substrate.

The hypergraph model supports the notion of *user views*. Unfortunately, views are not explicitly defined as dynamically computed queries executed on hypertexts; they are defined as modified sets of the entities that constitute other hypertexts. Quoting from [24, pp. 98]: "... a view can be represented by a distinct copy of a Node Table, Label Table, and Node Set Table, together with a reference to the view or database state on which it is built ...". There are dedicated view constructors (for example, linear, hierarchical, tabular) and other primitive operations that manipulate views; however, a general querying mechanism that accepts hypertexts and selects subsets of them or combines them is missing. We perceive the lack of a query formalism for hypertexts as a significant omission from a hypertext system.

The PRS model depicts the structure and the navigation in the hypertext. It also covers various entities and operations usually found in hypertext systems, for example browsers, maps, fish-eye views [26], prerecorded trails, histories, versions [25], time stamps, interactions [19].

The primary advantage of a PRS is the computational substrate offered by the inference engine. The other models depict properties as statically defined functions on attributes. The PRS model excels in capturing activeness, ie. hyper documents in computable representation. Active documents offer increased added value to the information actually contained the raw material.

Moreover, PRS are programmable and customizable both at the application and the document level. They offer a straightforward way to implement *active* or perceptive hypertext. Typically, an implementation of our model would use

Table 3. Model comparison based on the hypertext features (• denote strong support of a feature; ∘ denote weak or indirect support.)

FEATURES	MODELS			
	LDG	PN	HG	PRS
Document structure	∘	∘	•	•
Navigation	•	•	∘	•
Multimedia support	∘	•	∘	∘
Document manipulation	∘	∘	•	•
User interaction		•	∘	∘
Document evolution			∘	•
Active hypertext				•

a DBMS to store the facts of the hypermedia system and its query mechanism to simulate the inference engine. Table 3 summarizes the remarks made in this section.

4.1 Concluding Remarks

We proposed a new model for hypermedia and we compared it to other models. The PRS model is general; it does not target a specific application or hypermedia domain. It succeeds in capturing the major hypermedia features in a coherent way. We believe that the PRS model is a powerful and suitable tool for capturing hypermedia both at the conceptual and the architectural level.

In [9] and [14], we present the evolution of a distributed architecture that is based on the model presented here. It consists of a kernel module that manipulates the various hypermedia entities and executes the inference engine, and other peripheral modules that act as clients to the kernel (replication, caching, securuty, etc.). The functionality of the architecture is presented to local and remote applications and documents via the trading mechanism of the distributed system. Remote procedure calls effect communication in different address spaces. This work exemplifies the merits of open, active hypermedia for information organization and dissemination.

References

1. M. Agosti, et all: Issues of data modelling in information retrieval, *Electr. Publ.*, vol. 4, no. 4, pp. 219–237, Dec. 1991.
2. R. Akskyn, et all: KMS: A distributed hypermedia system for managing knowledge in organizations, *Comm. ACM*, vol. 31, no. 7, pp. 820–835, Jul. 1988.
3. F. Biennier, et all: Connectionist methods for accessing hyperdocuments, *Comp. in Planning*, vol. 1, pp. 77–93, Multimedia Urban Inf. Sys., 1989.

4. P. Bruza, T. van der Weide: Stratified hypermedia structures for information disclosure, *The Comp. Jour.*, vol. 35, no. 3, pp. 208–220, Mar. 92.
5. B. Campbell, J. Goodman: HAM: A general hypertext abstract machine, *Comm. ACM*, vol. 31, no. 7, pp. 856–861, Jul. 1988.
6. D. Carlson, S. Ram: Hyperintelligence: the next frontier, *Comm. ACM*, vol. 33, no. 3, pp. 311–321, Mar. 90.
7. R. Davis, J. King: An overview of production systems, in *Mach. Intell. 8*, E. Elcock, D. Michie (eds.), pp. 300–332, 1977.
8. R. Furuta: An object-based taxonomy for abstract structure in document models, *The Comp. Jour.*, vol. 32, no. 6, pp. 494–504, Jun. 1989.
9. I. Gaviotis, A. Hatzimanikatis, D. Christodoulakis: An architecture for active hypertext on distributed systems, *Proc. IEEE CompEuro '92 Conf.*, pp. 377–382, the Hague, May 4–8, 1992.
10. I. Gaviotis, et all: Requirements for open distributed hypermedia, *ESPRIT Proj. ISA*, AR/W04, 1993.
11. B. Haan, et all: IRIS hypermedia services, *Comm. ACM*, vol. 35, no. 1, pp. 36–51, Jan. 1992.
12. F. Halasz: Reflection on NoteCards: seven issues for the next generation of hypermedia systems, *Comm. ACM*, vol. 31, no. 7, pp. 836–852, Jul. 1988.
13. F. Halasz, M. Schwartz: The Dexter hypertext reference model, *NIST Hypertext Stand. Worksh.*, Jan. 1990.
14. A. Hatzimanikatis, I. Gaviotis, D. Christodoulakis: Distributed Documents: an architecture for open distributed hypertext, *Electr. Publ.*, 1993.
15. C. Kacmar, J. Leggett: PROXHY: A process-oriented extensible hypertext architecture, *ACM Trans. Inf. Sys.*, vol. 9, no. 4, pp. 399–419, Oct. 1991.
16. R. Killough, J. Leggett: *Hypertext Interchange with the Dexter model*, Hypertext Res. Lab., Texas A & M Univ., Aug. 1990.
17. G. Marchionini, B. Schneiderman: Finding facts vs. browsing knowledge in hypertext systems, *IEEE Comp.*, vol. 21, no. 1, pp. 70–80, Jan. 1988.
18. S. Newcomb, et all: The HyTime Hypermedia/Time-based document structuring language, *Comm. ACM*, vol. 34, no. 11, pp. 67–83, Nov. 1991.
19. J. Nielsen: The art of navigating through hypertext, *Comm. ACM*, vol. 33, no. 3, pp. 296–310, Mar. 1990.
20. R. Rada, et all: Collaborative hypertext and the MUCH system, *Jour. Inf. Sci.*, vol. 17, pp. 191–196, 1991.
21. G. Salton, C. Buckley: Automatic text structuring & retrieval experiments in automating encyclopedia searching, *Proc. of Conf. on R&D in Inf. Retr.*, pp. 21–34, Oct. 13–16, 1991.
22. M. Stefik, et all: Beyond the chalkboard: computer support for collaboration and problem solving in meetings, *Comm. ACM*, vol. 30, no. 1, pp. 32–47, Jan. 1987.
23. D. Stotts, R. Furuta: Petri-net-based hypertext: Document structure with browsing semantics, *ACM Trans. Inf. Sys.*, vol. 7, no. 1, pp. 3–29, Jan. 1989.
24. F. Tompa: A data model for flexible hypertext database systems, *ACM Trans. Inf. Sys.*, vol. 7, no. 1, pp. 85–100, Jan. 1989.
25. R. Trigg: Guided tours and tabletops: tools for communicating in a hypertext environment, *ACM Trans. Inf. Sys.*, vol. 6, no. 4, pp. 398–414, Oct. 1989.
26. K. Utting, N. Yankelovich: Context and orientation in hypermedia networks, *ACM Trans. Inf. Sys.*, vol. 7, no. 1, pp. 58–84, Jan. 1989.
27. N. Yankelovich, et all: Intermedia: the concept and the construction of a seamless information system, *IEEE Comp.*, vol. 21, no. 1, pp. 81–96, Jan. 1988.

Hypermedia Databases: A Specification and Formal Language

Yoshinori Hara[1] and Rodrigo A. Botafogo[2]

[1] C&C Research Labs
[2] Media Technology Research Labs
NEC Corporation, 4-1-1, Miyazaki, Miyamae-ku, Kawasaki, Kanagawa 216, Japan

Abstract. Improving authoring and browsing techniques is fundamental if large hypermedia applications are to be authored and browsed efficiently. This paper presents a new, two step approach, for the development of hypermedia systems. First data modeling is done using standard database techniques. Second, a selected part of the database is "projected" onto the "hypertext world." Using this approach, hypertext and database technologies are integrated forming a powerful symbiosis: *hypermedia databases.*

Advantages of this new approach are: (a) applications can be developed using structured design, (b) nodes and links can be automatically generated, (c) it becomes much easier to author and update the application, (d) query mechanisms are improved, (e) the same data can be reused for different applications, (f) reduction of redundancies and inconsistencies, data sharing, improved security, etc., are obtained by having the hypertext build on top of a database management system.

1 Introduction

Once upon a time, a 200 line program was considered a feat of intellectual power, but with new compiling techniques, structured and object oriented programming, a 200 line program can now be written in an afternoon. 200 nodes and a couple of hundred links, and hypertext developers start talking about medium size hypertext. Make it a thousand nodes and a couple of thousand links and we are talking very large hypertext. It is now great time to start developing hypertext with thousands of nodes and some hundred thousand links. If such hypertext sizes are ever to be reached, we need to start thinking about more automatic authoring (just think how much time it would take to add 100,000 links manually).

However, in the hypertext community, when one talks about automatic authoring, immediately the image of low quality hypertext, not properly tailored for its purpose is conveyed. This is clearly not our goal. We want high quality hypertext, well planned and clearly structured. It should be clear that only by improving authoring techniques can one move towards this goal. Instead of saying: "add a link from node 250 to node 1273," authors should say: "create an index of all french painters sorted by their date of birth and add links from this index to the appropriate painter node."

A first step for the improvement of authoring, browsing and search is the development of stronger hypermedia models that escape or extend the node and link paradigm. Only in the last European Hypertext conference, ECHT'92, three such models are presented [3, 9, 15]. Although having composite nodes, typed links, etc., is a requirement for future generations of hypertext systems, one is still at lost when having to decide which nodes to aggregate, or what type of links to use.

On the other hand, database technology has been concerned exactly with the issues stated above. Through schema organization, declarative access, views, and also aggregation and generalization or more recently with Object Oriented Database Systems, a strong theory about data structuring and retrieval has been developed. Database systems, however, lack some features that make the strength of hypertext: author's structuring, navigational access, history, browsing, etc.

This paper proposes new theoretical concepts, and practical formal language operations that provide a natural integration of both hypermedia and database technologies. Some effort has already been done in that direction [11, 12], but basically the database is used to implement the underlying hypertext data model and not for its strong data modeling capabilities. In this paper we propose a two step authoring approach: first we model our data using a standard database modeling approach such as the E-R model, the relational model, etc. On a second step we "project" the database into the hypermedia space.

2 Design Philosophy for Hypermedia Database

Hypermedia technology has now matured to the point that authors are starting to write large applications, such as engeneering manuals [8], electronic libraries [4], and large scale CSCW's [13]. However, writing a large application is still a very complex process. Authors have to manage hundreds of nodes and thousands of links manually and there is still the famous "disorientation" problem.

In order to develop large applications in a more effortless and less error-prone fashion one needs to abandon add-hoc development techniques and move to a *structured design* approach based on well defined design methodologies [14]. This approach was taken in database systems with the development of *schemas* and *schema languages*. In the hypertext field, Garzotto et al. proposed this very same idea; however claiming that, since hypertexts have different characteristics from databases new models needed to be developed. HDM–Hypertext Design Model [5]–is the result of their efforts.

We believe, however, that database models can and should be used in the development of hypertext applications. In order to address the different characteristics of hypertexts, we propose a two step development approach. First, information is modeled using standard database techniques. At this step hypertext is not considered at all. On a second step, we "project" selected parts of the database onto the *hypertext world* (see Fig. 1).

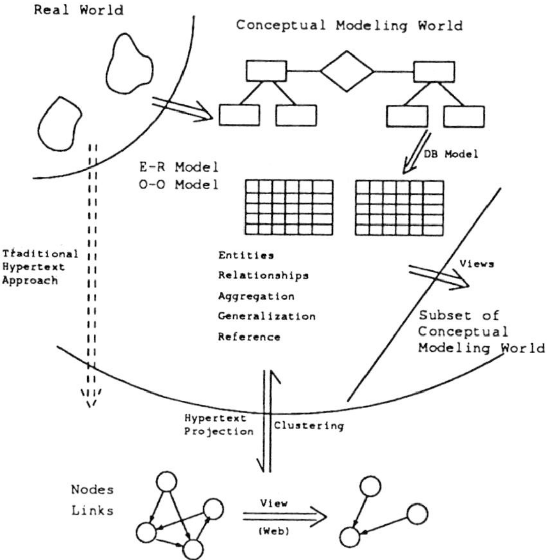

Fig. 1. Two step development process: First model the real world using standard DB techniques, then project the DB onto the hypertext world.

Reusing database models provides great advantages: first, those models are well understood and many commercial products exit that support their development. Second, there is an abundance of well trained personnel. Third, there is a large research community trying to improve those models further. Fourth, by doing so, we provide a smooth connection between two technologies, database and hypertext, and bring forth all the advantages of this integration. In particular we can use existing database applications to start generating hypertexts immediately. Also, if hypertexts are build on top of a database management system we inherit extra functionality: reduction of redundancies and inconsistencies, improved security and integrity maintenance, etc. Other advantages are:

Consistent Node Layout: Nodes are obtained from records by defining templates. The use of templates ensure that every node of a same type will have a consistent layout. Furthermore, if the database allows hierarchies of objects, layouts can also be inherited.

Automatic Link Generation: Relationships in a database are implicit, based on record content. Using *link definitions*, i.e., by making relationships explicit through some language constructs, links can be automatically generated, greatly reducing the risk of mistakes such as forgotten or dangling links.

Easy to Author/Update: Since nodes are created through the use of templates, changing them will affect whole families of nodes consistently. Also, since links are automatically generated based on link definitions, which are easily added or removed, authors can experiment at will.

Many Applications/Same Data: Two main activities need to be performed when trying to transmit information: collecting the data, and presenting it in an interesting way for the reader. Those two activities, although interelated, are quite different. When you buy a book, you are not only buying the facts, you are also buying the authors view of those facts. Dynamic hypertexts (those in which links are created on the fly) only give you the facts; static hypertexts (structured beforehand by the author) give the facts and the view, but there is no way to separate one from the other. This is very unfortunate, as having the facts stored in electronic form should also permit you to easily change its presentation.

Reconciling the Literalists and the Virtualists: For the literalists links are created and represented explicitly and navigation is done by traversing those links. The virtualists, on the other hand, say that any structure is implicit in the form or content of the nodes, and links are computed over the nodes. It is clear that each vision brings advantages and disadvantages.
We reconcile the two views in our two way authoring approach, by having an author at "compile" time create link definitions, e.g., "Add links between all 17th century painters sorted by date of birth," or "Add link between politicians and the events in which they were participants." Those author defined links are then browsed in a static way, but readers can issue their own queries in the same query language obtaining dynamic links. In short, static links are dynamic links (queries) issued by a knowledgeable author prior to the application delivery.

3 Formal Specifications for Hypermedia Database

A hypermedia database is a system that integrates database models and hypertext structures and in which it is possible to smoothly translate from one model to the other. For the bulk of this paper, we will work with the relational model and a minor extension to the node and link model. Although we concentrate our analysis to the E-R model, a similar approach could be taken for any other database model.

3.1 Value Space v.s. Object Space

Definition 1. The *value space* (V-space) is the database space, while the *object space* (O-space) is the hypertext space.

One of the advantages to consider both the V-space and the O-space is that several useful operations in these spaces can be defined: *hypertext projection* and *hypertext clustering* between the V-space and the O-space; *hypertext view* and *hypertext view update* in the O-space; *relational view* and *relational view update* in the relational model (see Fig. 2). These operations integrate effectively existing hypertext models with database technologies.

For lack of space, on this paper we will only discuss "hypertext projection." Relational view and update are the same as in relational databases. For hypertext clustering see [1, 2, 10, 6, 7].

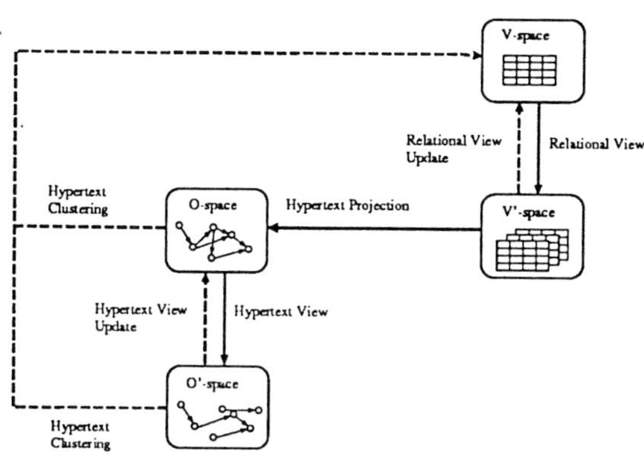

Fig. 2. Operations on V-space and O-space

In the figure as one moves from top to bottom (V-space to O'-space) there is a loss of information. However, while information is lost structure and relevance are gained.

3.2 Hypertext Projection

Hypertext projection is an operation to translate relations in the V(V')-space into a specific hypertext structure in the O-space. The basic procedure of hypertext projection consists of the following three steps:

Forming Appropriate Relations: The first step is not really part of the projection, but it consists of forming, through relational operators (cartesian product, projection, etc.), relations that are appropriate to be projected into the O-Space. Which relations are appropriate depends, of course, on the application being build. For instance, if one is constructing a hypermedia about french painter of the 19th century, records containing painters from the 20th century might not be appropriate.

Creating nodes from tuples and relations: To create a node from a tuple or a relation it is sufficient to specify a *visualization* for them. For tuples, a visualization is a description of how and where each attribute should be shown on the display. For a relation, the visualization describes a global view of all its tuples. A node is, then, an explicit visualization of a tuple or a relation. Note that the translation from an object in the V-space to a node is one-to-one.

Creating links by specifying constraints: This step creates links between related nodes. It consists of the following three sub-steps:

Specifying a set of source nodes, O_S This step specifies a set of nodes to be used as source for the links.

Specifying a set of destination nodes, O_D This step specifies a set of nodes to be used as destination for the links.

Specifying the constraint between O_S and O_D This step is necessary to produce meaningful hypertext links. Examples of such constraints are *select all*, i.e., all nodes in O_S are connected to all nodes in O_D, *select one*, i.e., a node in O_S is connected to a specific node in O_D, etc.

4 Translating Language

In the previous section we presented a method for translating from the V-space to the O-space. In this section we make things more concrete, by presenting an SQL-like language for the translation. Two steps are necessary for this translation: creating nodes from relations and tuples, and adding links between nodes.

We will show how those constructs are applied by giving some examples. All our examples will be based on a hypothetical art database, with painters from many countries, their works, etc.

The general syntax for creating nodes is:

```
CREATE NODE [<Relation>]
 [SELF:
    [NAME = <string>];
    [TEMPLATE = <template-name>];
    [ASSOCIATE <attribute-commalist>
               <field-commalist>] ];
 [CHILD:
    [NAME = {<string> | attribute}];
    [TEMPLATE = <template-name>];
    [ASSOCIATE <attribute-commalist>
               <field-commalist>] ];
```

Arguments inside square brackets ([]) are optional, those inside angle brackets (<>) are to be substituted by the appropriate arguments, and only one argument from those in braces ({}) separated by '|' is to be selected. A "Relation" is a relation of the database; "string" is any string of character; "template-name" is the name of a *template*; "attribute" and "field" are respectively attributes in the relation and fields defined in the template. The "commalist" indicates that a list of elements separated by commas can be used. In ASSOCIATE the size of the attribute-commalist and field-commalist should be the same.

The above construct creates two types of nodes: a *composite node* generated directly from the given "relation," and a set of nodes obtained from the tuples of the relation. There is an implicit ordering of those nodes, following the same ordering as the tuples in the relation. Also, nodes inherit all the attributes from the relation, even if they are not seen through the template. The SELF part gives information on how to create the composite node, while the CHILD part indicates how to create nodes from tuples. If SELF.NAME is omitted, this name will be the same as the "relation." If TEMPLATE is omitted, the node cannot be seen/browsed, but still exists. Finally, if ASSOCIATE is omitted, there is an implicit relationship between the "attributes" and the "fields" based on their names. An example will make things clear.

Assume that a painter relation has at least attributes: name, birth, death, photo and biography. The next command will create composite node "Painter" and child nodes obtained from the tuples in the relation "Painter." For example, if relation "Painter" had 10 tuples, 11 nodes would be created: 1 composite node called "Painter," and 10 nodes created from the painter's tuples. Note that each node will also receive a name coming from attribute "Painter.name."

```
// Create node from relation Painter.
CREATE NODE Painter
 SELF: // Composite node
   TEMPLATE = ''index.temp''; // will be an index.
   ASSOCIATE = (name, birth), (name, date);
 CHILD: // Nodes from tuples.
   NAME = name; TEMPLATE = ''painter.temp''
   ASSOCIATE = // Rel. -> Temp.
      (name, birth, death, photo, biography);
      (name, born, died, picture, description)
```

Assume now that for the application being created the author wants to have a composite node having only the french painters. In that case two steps are necessary: first, define a view over the database using its access language (in our example SQL). Then create the nodes:

```
// Creates a view FPainters for the database. For convenience uses
// the same names as the painter template attributes
CREATE VIEW FPainters (name, born, died, picture, description)
As SELECT Painter.name, Painter.birth, Painter.death,
          Painter.photo, Painter.biography;
   FROM Painter; WHERE Painter.country = ''France''

// Create nodes from the view
CREATE NODE FPainters
 SELF:
   TEMPLATE = ''browser.temp''; // Graphical browser.
 CHILD:
   NAME = name; TEMPLATE = ''painter.temp''
```

In the above specification a set of nodes is created. Assuming that there are 5 french painters in the database, Fig. 3-(a) shows the painters' nodes create from template "painter.temp," and Fig. 3-(b) shows the graphical browser created from template "browser.temp." There is yet no way to browse through this set. We now specify how to create links:

```
CREATE LINK [link-name]
 SOURCE:
```

```
    NAME = <node-name>;
    IN {SELF | CHILD};
    [ANCHOR <field>];
  DEST:
    NAME = <node-name>;
    IN {SELF | CHILD};
    [ANCHOR <field>];
  DIRECTION {FORWARD | BACKWARD | BIDIRECTIONAL};
  [WHERE <constraint-list>];
```

"link-name" specifies the type of the link. SOURCE and DEST are respectively the source and destination nodes of the links. If CHILD is specified in the IN clause, then links will be added to the children of the node; otherwise, the link is added to the node itself. ANCHOR indicates to what field in the template the link should be anchored. Note that DEST has also an ANCHOR. This is necessary in case the DIRECTION of the link is either BACKWARD or BIDIRECTIONAL. WHERE specifies constraints on the links. It is possible to use in WHERE all attributes of nodes, e.g., SOURCE.name.

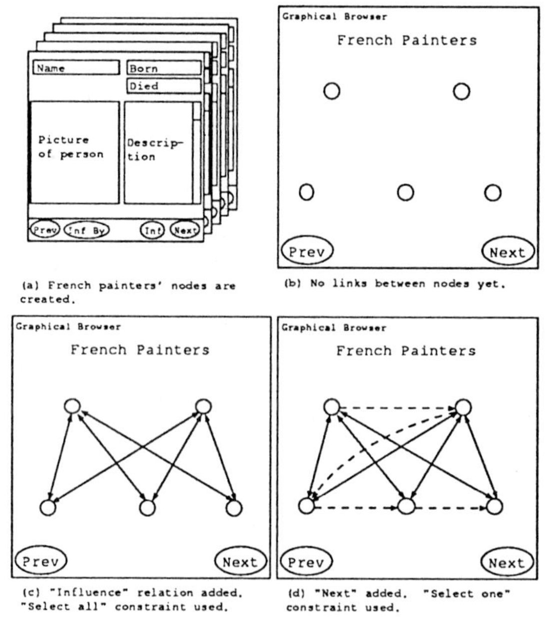

(a) French painters' nodes are created.

(b) No links between nodes yet.

(c) "Influence" relation added. "Select all" constraint used.

(d) "Next" added. "Select one" constraint used.

Fig. 3. Conversion from the V-space to the O-space.

We now specify the influence relationship form the "Impressionists" to the "Post-impressionists." Links added are BIDIRECTIONAL so that both "influenced" and "was influenced by" traversals can be performed.

```
CREATE LINK Influenced
SOURCE:
  NAME = FPainters; IN CHILD; ANCHOR ''Inf''
DEST:
  NAME = FPainters; IN CHILD; ANCHOR = ''Inf By''
DIRECTION BIDIRECTIONAL;
WHERE SOURCE.school = ''Impressionism'',
      DEST.school = ''Postimpressionism''
```

Note that links do not need to be one-to-one (see Fig. 3-(c)). In this example it is most likely that an one-to-many relationship exists. How to decide to which node to jump when button "Inf" is clicked, is part of the user interface. One possible solution, though, would be to show the list of all possible destination nodes.

It is now possible to start browsing through the FPainter node, but it is not necessarily true that all nodes are accessible. It would be interesting to have all painters sorted by their date of birth and linked using a "next" button (see dotted links in Fig. 3-(d))[3]. The sorting is done by defining a view on the database (remember that there is an implicit ordering of the nodes which is identical to the tuples' ordering), and the linking is similar as above. ANCHOR the link to the "next" button, the DIRECTION is FORWARD, and the constraint "WHERE SOURCE.next = DEST," where "next" is an implicitly defined attribute of the node. Other attributes are: first, last, and a number, e.g., DEST.5.

5 Conclusion

In this paper we proposed a novel approach for authoring hypermedia applications: first, we model our data using standard database techniques, and then, we project the database into the hypermedia space. This novel technique when provided with four operations: hypertext projection, hypertext clustering, relational view, and hypertext view, effectively and smoothly integrates hypertext and database technology creating what we call a *hypermedia database*.

With a formal framework to work with, it became possible to provide and SQL-like language for the translation between the database world and the hypermedia world. This language not only provides this translation but can also be used at run time to help retrieve information. Consequently, not only is authoring improved, as nodes and links can be created automatically, but also browsing is enhanced. We believe, that this formal specification and its declarative hypermedia access language provides a useful perspectives for the next generation of hypermedia systems.

Although for this paper we exemplified our approach using the E-R model and an SQL-like language, the approach is general and could be applied for any DB-model. What is requires is that the DB-model supports an access language

[3] Do not confuse the "next" button in template "painter.tem" and the "next" button in template "browser.temp." Specifying CHILD indicates that the links are to be added to the painters.

through which restructuring of the data is possible. In that case instead of an SQL-like language, a language similar to the DB access language should be build.

References

1. R. A. Botafogo. Cluster analysis for hypertext systems. In *16th ACM SIGIR International Conference on Research and Development in Information Retrieval*, pages 116–125, Pittsburgh, Pensylvania, June 1993.
2. R. A. Botafogo, E. Rivlin, and B. Shneiderman. Structural analysis of hypertexts: Identifying hierarchies and useful metrics. *ACM Transactions on Information Systems*, 10(2):142–180, April 1992.
3. P. De Bra, G. Houben, and Y. Kornatzky. An extensible data model for hyperdocuments. In *Proceedings of the European Conference on Hypertext*, pages 222–231, Milano, Italy, 1992.
4. D. E. Egan, M. E. Lesk, R. D. Ketchum, C. C. Lochbaum, J. R. Remde, M. Littman, and T. K. Landauer. Hypertext for the electronic library? core sample results. In *Proceedings of the Hypertext 91 Conference*, pages 299–312, San Antonio, Texas, December 1991.
5. F. Garzotto, P. Paolini, and D. Schwabe. HDM – A model based approach to hypertext application design. *ACM Transactions on Information Systems*, 11(1):1–26, January 1993.
6. Y. Hara, A. M. Keller, and G. Wiederhold. Implementing hypertext database relationships through aggregation and exceptions. In *Proceedings of the Hypertext 91 Conference*, pages 75–90, San Antonio, Texas, December 1991.
7. Y. Hara, A. M. Keller, and G. Wiederhold. Relationship abstractions for an effective hypertext design: Augmentation and globalization. In *DEXA'91*, pages 270–274, 1991.
8. K. C. Malcolm and S. E. Poltrock. Industrial strength hypermedia: Requirements for a large engineering enterprise. In *Proceedings of the Hypertext 91 Conference*, pages 13–24, San Antonio, Texas, December 1991.
9. M. Marmann and G. Schlageter. Towards a better support for hypermedia structuring: The hydesign model. In *Proceedings of the European Conference on Hypertext*, pages 232–241, Milano, Italy, 1992.
10. E. Rivlin, R. A. Botafogo, and B. Shneiderman. Navigating in hyperspace: Designing a structure-based toolbox. *Communications of the ACM.*, 37(2):87–96, February 1994.
11. J. L. Schnase, J. J. Leggett, and Szabo R. L. Semantic data modeling of hypermedia associations. *ACM Transactions on Information Systems*, 11(1):27–50, January 1993.
12. H. A. Schütt and N. A. Streitz. Hyperbase: A hypermedia engine based on a relational database management system. In *Proceedings of the European Conference on Hypertext*, pages 95–108, Paris, France, 1990.
13. K. Watabe, S. Sakata, K. Maeno, and H. Fukuoka. Distributed multiparty desktop conferencing system: MERMAID. In *Proceedings of the Conference on Computer-Supported Cooperative Work*, pages 27–38, Los Angeles, CA, October 1990.
14. G. Wiederhold. *Database Design*. McGraw-Hill, 1983.
15. Y. Zheng and M. Pong. Using statecharts to model hypertext. In *Proceedings of the European Conference on Hypertext*, pages 242–250, Milano, Italy, 1992.

Implementing Open Hypermedia Services on top of the Postgres Extended Relational Database Management System

A. Hatzimanikatis A. Papadopoulos D. Christodoulakis

Dept. of Computer Engineering and Informatics,
University of Patras
and
Computer Technology Institute, Patras

Abstract

This paper presents the design and implementation of an open hypermedia system using the Postgres extended relational database management system. Openness, extensibility and support for views and computations are among the most important requirements set for advanced hypermedia systems. We show how these requirements can be satisfied using an open architecture and the facilities of a next-generation database management system such as Postgres.

1 Introduction

Hypermedia systems have found application in many diverse areas[Nie90], and seem to offer a promising new approach to very large scale information management. The main reason is their simple model and the ability to structure and support the diversity of types and media that information is usually represented in.

Early hypertext systems were stand–alone applications organizing their data following the hypertext principle of interconnections and offering facilities for navigation and management of the hypermedia graph [Con87]. It was soon realized that as helpful as these applications could be, they suffered from a number of limitations. First, they were *closed systems*. They were using their own storage formats and user interface, and no cooperation was possible with other applications or hypertext systems. Second, these systems were designed and implemented for a single user and a single machine. It was not possible for multiple users to work on the same information and create shared structures. Most systems used the data management facilities offered by the underlying file system or a commercial database management system.

Various architectures and systems have been proposed and implemented trying to solve these problems. Among them, systems for the provision of *open linking services* [HKR+92] [Pea89], to support the cooperation and linking of information between applications that could use a common linking protocol, and *hyperbase* systems [SLH93] [WL92], offering data management facilities tailored to the needs of the hypermedia model.

The requirements set for such next generation hypermedia systems are:

- *Openness.* The system should easily integrate new media types and applications.
- Support for different *views* on the same underlying hypermedia information.
- Support for *computations* in the hypertext structure. According to the path followed, the entry point, or other conditions, different parts of the hypertext graph should be accessible.
- *Efficient storage* of huge amounts of multimedia information.
- Support for *concurrent* access to the information by multiple users.

In this paper we present the design and implementation of an open hypermedia system on top of the Postgres database management system. Postgres extends the relational data model with support for complex objects, inheritance, rules, extensibility of the set of basic data types and support for large objects [SK91] [SJGP90]. We show how the facilities offered by such an extended relational database system can satisfy the requirements set by next generation hypermedia systems.

The architecture of the system is based on our earlier work on the *Distributed Documents architecture* [HGC], an architecture that has been proposed for the provision of open hypermedia services in a distributed environment.

In the next section we present the system's architecture and data model. In section 3 we discuss how a prototype was implemented, using the facilities offered by Postgres. Finally, we draw conclusions and give directions for future work.

2 System's Architecture

The system is partitioned in three layers, namely *presentation*, *storage* and *hypermedia* (Figure 1). Each layer handles different classes of objects in order to provide a set of services to other layers. In Figure 2, the classes that constitute the architecture and their relations are presented using an Entity Relationship diagram. *Nodes*, *links*, *anchors*, *hypertext documents* and *view documents* are the basic classes in the hypermedia layer, while *contents* objects are handled at the storage layer and *viewer* objects are used by the presentation layer.

The *presentation layer* provides two services. The first is the presentation of hypermedia nodes' contents. *Viewer* objects specify the applications that can be used for the display and manipulation of a media type. These applications can be text editors, image viewers, or any other application wishing to use hypermedia functionality. The *media types* class describes the types of data that the system can deal with. For each media type object a set of viewers, either cooperative or uncooperative, are available.

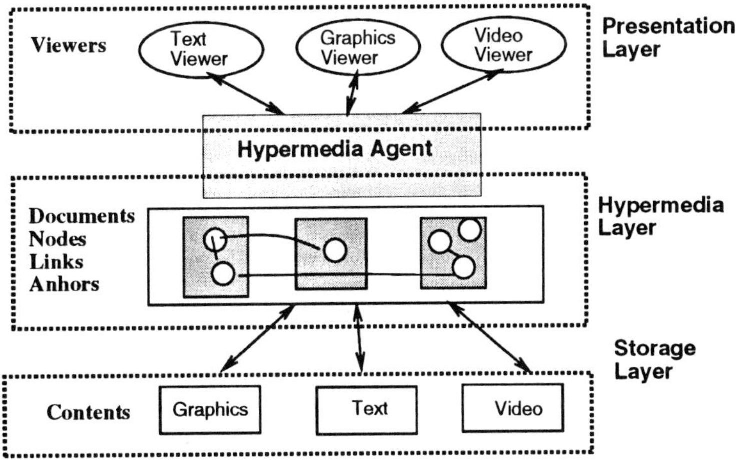

Fig. 1. The layers of the architecture.

The second service provided by the presentation layer is the support of user's navigation within the hypertext structure. This functionality is offered by special applications, called *hypermedia agents* (Figure 1). They keep track of user's position in the hypermedia graph and are responsible for the activation of the required viewers. Furthermore, each hypermedia agent is associated with a *view document* object of the hypermedia layer and acts as the intermediary between the presentation and hypermedia layers.

The *storage layer* maintains objects of the *contents* class. *Contents* objects encapsulate the actual multimedia data of the hypermedia graph together with information like the media type of the data and any special storage requirements imposed by the data.

The *hypermedia layer* handles hypermedia objects that offer the linking functionality, i.e. nodes, links, anchors, hypertext documents and view documents. The service of maintaining the hypertext structure is provided by this layer.

Nodes, Links and Anchors *Nodes*, *links* and *anchors* are the objects that constitute a hypertext graph. Nodes contain *contents* objects and they can possess a list of attributes like author, title, etc. There can exist *simple* nodes, that refer to a single contents object, or *composite* nodes, referring to more than one contents objects that should be presented as a single entity. *Display information* is associated with composite nodes. This information takes the form of a script that describes how the viewers of the referenced contents should cooperate. The same contents object can be referenced by more than one nodes, so that different hypertext structures can be imposed on the stored information.

The *anchor* abstraction plays a central role in the architecture. Anchors describe *media areas*, spatial or temporal. Such areas could be, for example, the third paragraph of a text chunk, or a time frame from the third to the fifth second in a video sequence. The description and the nature of media areas are

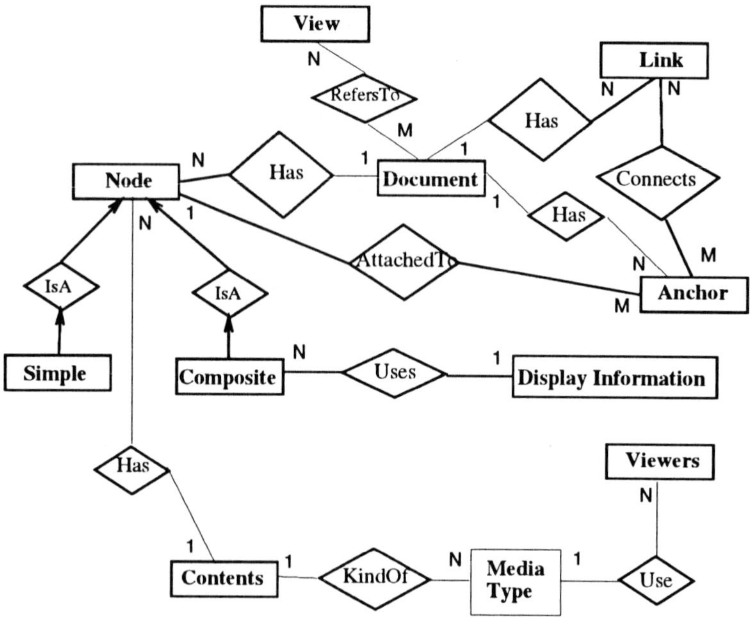

Fig. 2. The entities of the architecture.

not relevant to the rest of the system, excluding viewer applications that are responsible for displaying anchors to users. Anchor objects encapsulate this information, so that they are treated uniformly throughout the system and are accessed through a single identifier. A node contains a set of anchors and every anchor is attached to only one node.

Links connect a set of *source* and a set of *destination* anchors. They have no knowledge of the media areas encapsulated in anchors. Even when the area in an anchor is changed, e.g. the string associated with a text anchor is edited, the link still maintains the right information.

Hypertext and View Documents We define a *hypertext document* as the packaging of a set of nodes, a set of anchors and a set of links. The notion of documents is useful in order to group relevant hypermedia objects that refer, for example, to a single subject or are created by the same user. Each hypermedia object can belong to only one hypertext document. Furthermore it contains attributes, like title, author and date of creation.

View documents are *virtual* documents, in the sense that they are dynamically computed. A view document refers to at least one, but maybe more, documents, and it contains a *computation*, in the form of queries to the hypermedia objects belonging to the referenced documents. In the trivial case a view document can refer to only one document. At the presentation layer users can only access documents indirectly, through view documents.

This model allows different hypertext structures on the same information.

A hypertext document creates a hypertext graph using the information stored in contents objects, and different documents can impose different structures. Using view documents, a second level of structuring is introduced. Furthermore, computations can be introduced at different points. Wherever a reference to an object exists, this reference can be the result of a computation, e.g. a function call or a query. For example, links associate sets of source and destination anchors. The set of destination anchors can be defined as a function, that returns anchor references, according to the path the user has followed until now. Such functions can also be used wherever node and contents objects are referenced.

In the following section we discuss how these layers are implemented in our prototype using the Postgres extended relational database system.

3 System's Implementation

The prototype system has been implemented on Unix workstations using the Postgres database management system and the Tcl/Tk X windows toolkit [Ous90] [Ous91]. Postgres is used for the implementation of the storage and hypermedia layers, while Tcl/Tk has been used for the implementation of the presentation services.

Tcl stands for "tool command language", and it is a simple scripting language for controlling and extending applications. Tcl is embeddable, and its interpreter is implemented as a library of C procedures that can easily be incorporated into applications, and each application can extend the core Tcl features with additional commands specific to that application. The Tk toolkit is an extension to Tcl. It is a toolkit for the X Window System and it extends the core Tcl facilities with commands for building user interfaces. Furthermore, Tk provides an easy method for the exchange of messages between applications running on the same X Windows server. This method has been used for the communication between viewer applications and hypermedia agents at the presentation layer.

3.1 The Postgres System

Postgres is an extended relational database management system. It is based on the well known relational model but extends it in various ways in order to support new useful features.

Postgres uses a novel query language, Postquel, which introduces several new concepts. First, there are three kind of data types: base types (built-in, system, and user defined), array types (fixed and variable length) and composite types (tuple, set of tuples and class). Also functions are supported, and can be normal functions (C or Postquel), operators (binding of a symbol to a function) and aggregate functions (count, sum, etc). Finally the powerful rule system is used to support many complex operations as well as the views and versioning control.

Generally, the most important characteristics in Postgres are the following:

- User defined data types and operators. Users can define new data types with their own functions and operators.

- Inheritance. A class (relation) can inherit all fields of one or more existing classes. This enables the construction of a class hierarchy while preserving the ability to query all the classes together as if they were a single class.
- Support for complex objects. A function returning a set of objects can be used as a class attribute.
- User defined rules. Rules have the form "on condition then do action" and they are used to trigger DBMS actions. Condition refers to events (retrieve, replace, delete, append) and user defined qualifications on a class or a class attributes.
- Support of unique ids. Each instance of a class is given a unique id which can be used to identify this instance.
- Views and Versioning. Postgres supports the creation of versions of a class as well as the creation of views to one or more classes. Both of them are supported by the rule system and in addition user defined rules can be used to specialize them.
- Support for large objects. Postgres provides mechanisms for the storage and retrieval of large binary objects that are usually found in multimedia applications.

3.2 The Implementation of Hypermedia and Storage Layers

Postgres is used to implement the hypermedia and storage layer functionality. For each entity of the entity–relationship diagram of Figure 2 a corresponding Postgres class is defined. The classes *Node*, *Link*, *Anchor*, *Document* and *View-Document* are defined for the hypermedia layer, and the class *Contents* is defined to encapsulate the storage layer. Finally, the *MediaType* and *Viewer* classes are defined. Although they are not part of neither the hypermedia nor the storage layer they are a convenient way for storing and passing information to the applications of the presentation layer. All hypermedia classes are implemented as Postgres complex objects. Functions that return sets of objects are defined to access the Document's nodes, links and anchors, Node's anchors and Link's source and destination anchors.

Postgres supports *inheritance*. New classes can be defined that inherit attributes from one or more already defined classes, while they can still add their own attributes. All the objects belonging to a hierarchy of classes can be queried, using a single statement. In our prototype for each hypermedia class we have defined a minimal set of attributes that is required for the provision of a general linking service. For example, the Document class contains only a Title and Author attribute while the Link class has no attributes, apart from the functions that compute the sets of source and destination links and the Anchor class has a single attribute, the reference to the Node an Anchor is attached to. From these base classes we have defined inherited classes for TypedLinks and TypedNodes (links and nodes having a Type attribute). We expect users to add their own class definitions and extend the hierarchy, while retaining the hypermedia functionality. Using inheritance is the first step towards an open hypermedia system.

New specialized hypermedia objects can be defined to satisfy applications' requirements and enrich the semantics of the basic, simple hypermedia model.

A second step towards openness is the ability for the seamless integration, storage and manipulation of new media types. As far as hypermedia services are concerned, a media type is defined by the viewer application used to handle it and the anchor areas that can be defined on it. So, when we want to add a new media type we have to add the corresponding Viewer object and the type of the media anchor. Postgres allows the extension of the type system with new user defined base types. For each new media type added, we define a new base type for the value of anchors that can be created on it. In our first prototype we have defined a text anchor type–an array of two integers–and we have used the box base type, already provided by Postgres, for the implementation of the image anchor type. Using them we have inherited from the Anchor class the TextAnchor and ImageAnchor classes, that add a Value attribute of the corresponding anchor type.

Supporting different views has been one of the most important requirements in our design. Views on classes are implemented in Postgres using rules, and we have used the same mechanism for implementing views on hypertext documents. A ViewDocument object contains a set of rules, stored as text in the database. When the ViewDocument is activated, the corresponding rules are defined. The rules specify which hypermedia objects should be retrieved when the ViewDocument's nodes, links or anchors are accessed. The rules can be used for the specification of simple constraints like "all the nodes, links and anchors belonging to the document entitled Introduction", to complex structural constraints. After the rules have been defined, the hypermedia objects of a ViewDocument can be accessed and queried like any other Document.

Actually, the rule manager provides a powerful and efficient mechanisms for the implementation of computations on the hypermedia structure, and the enforcement of integrity constraints. A rule that removes all the anchors attached to a Node, when the Node is removed, and a rule to delete dangling Links, i.e. links that have an empty set of source or destination anchors, have been defined. The limitation is that these computations can only be performed inside the Postgres database.

In our prototype we have added a second kind of computation to support computations that are taking part outside the database. These computations are defined using the Tcl language. A special class, Computation, has been defined with a single text attribute that is used to store a Tcl script. Then ComputationNode, ComputationLink and ComputationAnchor classes have been defined, inheriting from the Computation class and the Node, Link and Anchor classes respectively. The hypermedia agent is capable of evaluating Tcl scripts when such objects containing a computation are retrieved. Such scripts can be used for integrating external sources of information, and even hypermedia data stored in other Postgres databases.

3.3 Presentation Services and the Hypermedia Agent

Information about viewer applications that constitute the presentation services are stored in objects of the viewer class. The name of the application, the type of data it can display, if it is cooperative or not, and a Tcl script that describes how the application should be activated, are stored.

There can be cooperative and uncooperative viewer applications in the user's environment. Cooperative applications are aware of hypermedia functionality and services. They are able to display the contents of the hypermedia nodes, as well as the attached anchors, and identify requests made by users for selecting an anchor and navigating a link. On the other hand, uncooperative applications can display the contents of a node, but are not able of handling anchors on the data. Special action is taken when an uncooperative application is used, and anchors attached to the node are displayed as a list in a separate window.

Hypermedia agents are the central Postgres clients. Each one is associated with a view document. On the other hand, hypermedia agents are acting as servers for the viewer applications that want to access hypermedia data and functionality. The interface that hypermedia agents provide to applications consists of operations for creating and deleting hypermedia objects, navigating a link and defining or removing a query used for the definition of the associated view document.

A hypermedia agent process is activated when the user wishes to add hypermedia services in the environment. Upon activation, the agent connects to the Postgres server and the rules stored in the associated view document object are established. Moreover, hypermedia agents identify what viewers are available in the current environment, using information found in the viewers class.

While the user is navigating, it keeps track of user's current position in the hypertext graph. The current position is defined as the set of nodes that are displayed and the viewers that are used for their display. When an anchor is selected, and link navigation is requested, the relevant hypermedia objects are retrieved from the database. As there can be computations stored in the form of Tcl scripts, the hypermedia agent is responsible for their evaluation. The corresponding destination anchor is identified and the associated node information and contents are retrieved. According to the contents type, a suitable viewer application is activated and user's current position is updated.

As the user is viewing node contents he or she can select an area of the data, e.g. some words in a text editor or a graphic component in a structure graphics editor, and issue a "start link" command. The viewer application sends a command to the hypermedia agent for the creation of a source anchor, together with a description of the selected data. Similar action will be taken for the specification of a destination anchor. The command "end link" is sent to the hypermedia agent for the creation of a link and the update of the corresponding view document.

4 Conclusions and Further Work

Although a general purpose database management system, Postgres satisfies most of the requirements set by by next–generation hypermedia systems. Inheritance and extensibility cover the openness requirement, while rules are an elegant way for supporting views and computations in the hypermedia structure. Furthermore, Postgres supports a high level language that makes it easy to express even complex queries on the hypermedia structure.

At the moment we are working in two directions, support of versions of hypermedia structures and data, and concurrency control and notification control mechanisms to better support collaboration and sharing. Postgres already supports the notion of versions but it is only applied to whole classes. It also supports the notion of *time expression*, for retrieving instances of objects valid at a specified time. We are investigating how this model can be used for the support of versioning in hypermedia systems. For concurrency control, a mechanism is required to support lengthy transactions that are needed in a hypermedia system, and no such mechanism is supported by Postgres at the moment.

References

[Con87] Jeff Conklin. Hypertext: An introduction and survey. *IEEE Computer*, 20(9):17–41, September 1987.

[HGC] A. Hatzimanikatis, I. Gaviotis, and D. Christodoulakis. Distributed documents: An architecture for open distributed hypertext. *Electronic Publishing: Origination, Dissemination and Design*. Accepted for publication.

[HKR+92] Bernard Haan, Paul Kahn, V.A. Riley, J.H. Coombs, and N.K. Meyrowitz. IRIS hypermedia services. *Communications of the ACM*, 35(1):36–51, January 1992.

[Nie90] J. Nielsen. *Hypertext and Hypermedia*. Academic Press, New York, 1990.

[Ous90] J. Ousterhout. Tcl: An embeddable command language. In *Proceedings Winter USENIX Conference*, pages 133–146, 1990.

[Ous91] J. Ousterhout. An X11 toolkit based on the Tcl language. In *Proceedings Winter USENIX Conference*, pages 105–115, 1991.

[Pea89] Amy Pearl. Sun's link service: A protocol for open linking. In *Hypertext '89 Proceedings*, pages 137–146. ACM, November 1989.

[SJGP90] M. Stonebraker, A. Jhingan, J. Goh, and S. Potamianos. On rules, procedures, caching and views in database systems. In *ACM-SIGMOD Conference on Management of Data*, Atlantic City, 1990. ACM.

[SK91] M. Stonebraker and G. Kemnitz. The POSTGRES next-generation database management system. *Communications of the ACM*, 34(2):78–92, 1991.

[SLH93] J.L. Schnase, J.J. Leggett, and D.L. Hicks. Semantic data modeling of hypermedia associations. *ACM Transactions on Information Systems*, 11(1):27–50, January 1993.

[WL92] U.K. Will and J.J. Leggett. Hyperform: Using extensibility to develop dynamic, open and distributed hypertext systems. In *Proceedings of the European Conference on Hypertext (ECHT '92)*, pages 251–261, Milan, Italy, 1992.

A SUPPORT SYSTEM FOR BUILDING HYPERMEDIA TRAINING APPLICATIONS

A. Tsalgatidou, Z. Palaskas*, C. Halatsis, M. Hatzopoulos

Dept. of Informatics, University of Athens
Panepistimiopolis, TYPA Buildings, Ilisia 157 71 Athens, Greece
email: {afrodite, halatsis, mike} @ uranus.di.uoa.ariadne-t.gr

Abstract
Current multimedia platforms are not suitable for the development of hypermedia training applications because they lack features dedicated to support the specific task of training. HTAS is an integrated and customisable support system for building and executing hypermedia training applications by adopting the Systematic Approach to Training (SAT) methodology [14] and the Hypertext Design Model HDM [9]. HTAS also provides a set of tools which support the construction of a generic application schema and a schema instance which defines a particular application. An innovative feature of HTAS is the customisation of the individual courses according to the individual trainees' profiles using appropriate knowledge based tools. Distance learning support is also provided by HTAS.

Keywords: Hypertext, Hypermedia, Computer Based Training (CBT), Hypermedia Training Applications, Hypertext/Hypermedia Design Model, Trainee Modelling

1 Introduction

Training as an activity is a methodological process that takes advantage of the pedagogical experience and expertise of human teachers. Computer based training (CBT) systems, exploiting modern multimedia technology, may prove to be much more effective, compared to current self-training techniques such as studying manuals, instruction booklets etc.

Today, there is a proliferation of multimedia platforms which can be used for developing applications for education, recreation, tourism, publishing etc. However, a common characteristic of such platforms is the lack of dedicated features to support specific tasks such as training. Developers of training packages have to use general purpose multimedia platforms and thus, they face a number of problems, such as implementing training specific features on a general purpose multimedia platform, a fact that in turn imposes an additional overhead to the overall cost of developing an application. Other problems may be related with porting the developed application to other development platforms and/or modifying it to satisfy different training requirements.

This paper presents the design of an integrated and customisable application support system for building Hypermedia Training Applications (the HTAS system). HTAS is based on existing and widely available technologies for authoring and adapts existing methodologies for structuring hypermedia information. The goals of the HTAS project are to:

* investigate and implement knowledge based techniques for hypermedia information classification
* define a methodology for developing hypermedia training applications
* develop an efficient and cost effective platform for building hypermedia training applications.
* test and evaluate the HTAS system capabilities through the development of application exemplars.

---

* 01-PLIROFORIKI S.A., 438 Aharnon str., Athens, email: zpalas@isosun.ariadne-t.gr

The following section describes the HTAS system architecture. Section 3 discusses the methodology and the design model used for developing training applications. Distance learning support is another facility offered by HTAS and is analysed in section 4. The HTAS platform is validated using an application pilot discussed in section 5. Section 6 refers to work related to HTAS and section 7 conludes this work.

2 The HTAS Architecture

Figure 1 depicts the HTAS system architecture. The first level of this architecture shows the *authoring environment,* which is divided in two parts: the *authoring-in-the-large* part, which refers to the design and specification of the global aspects of a hypermedia application, and the *authoring-in-the-small* part which refers to the development of the contents of the hypermedia nodes. This terminology is used in HDM [9], which is a Hypertext Design model that is adopted by HTAS and is briefly described in section 3.

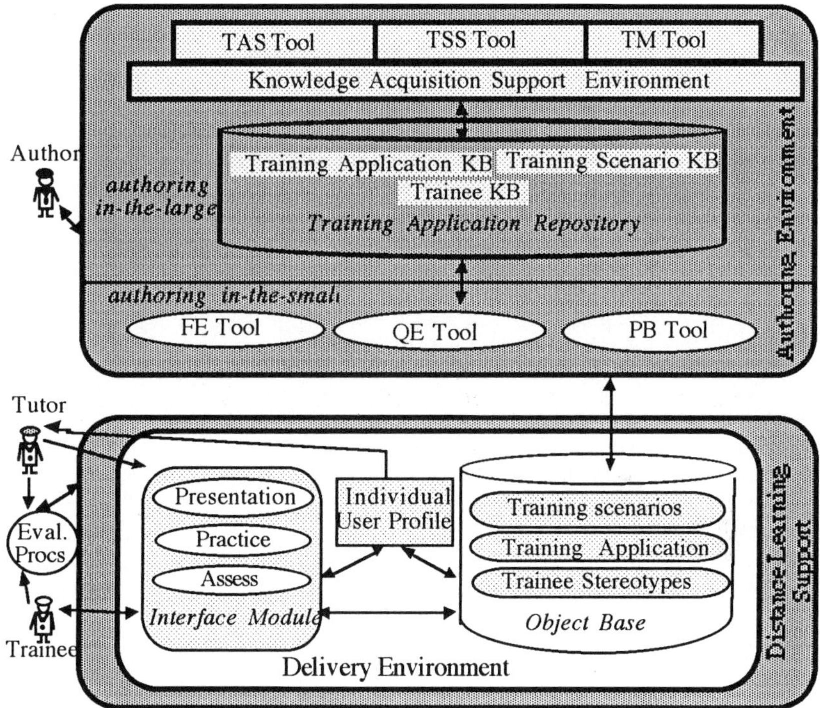

Fig. 1. The HTAS architecture

The specification of a hypermedia application consists of three parts: the specification of training application domain, the specification of the training scenarios and the modelling of the trainee, which are stored in a multi-purpose hypermedia *training application repository.* These specifications are constructed by an author using respectively the three tools of the *authoring-in-the-large* environment, i.e. the *training application specification tool (TAS tool),* the *training scenarios specification tool (TSS tool)* and the *trainee modelling tool (TM Tool).* It is worth to stress here the importance of the modelling of a trainee. Training applications are systems serving diverse groups of users which require different modes of interaction according to their roles and levels of knowledge. Most of the time, user behaviour does not only depend on the sole knowledge of an application domain but also, on integrated knowledge from many related application domains. The *TM tool* of HTAS captures behaviour of classes of users over training sessions, and adjusts the level of training according to a user's expertise on domain concepts. The relationships between the application depended training concepts and the corresponding user profiles are captured early in the application specification phase and are stored in the *training application repository.* Also, in the same repository are stored the procedures and the structures required for the production of customised courses with optional topics and emphasis levels.

A hypermedia training application is generated by an author who takes as input the generic specification of an application stored in the *training application repository* and generates the target application using a set of intelligent tools which allow him/her to specify the functionality and the user interface of the application. The tools which support this *authoring-in-the-small* process also support flow controll editing, question generation and presentation of material. The corresponding tools are the *flow editing tool (FE tool)*, the *question editing tool (QE tool)* and the *presentation builder tool (PB tool).*

The *FE tool* enables an author to create customised courses and control the flow of the information presented. Thus, this tool supports the definition of the flow of the course in a simple and interactive manner and also manages the presentation of questions and exercises. The *QE tool* supports the generation of questions as individual entities which can be used several times in different contexts. The *PB tool* supports the creation of a sequential time-based presentation. Different items coming from a media folder can be put on a time scale and the synchronisation problems are resolved by the system.

The resulting hypermedia training system consists of an *object base,* which has three parts: a *training scenarios* object base, a *training application* object base and a set of *trainee stereotypes*. It also contains a knowledge base of *individual user profiles* for customising training scenarios to individual user needs. The interaction between the user and the system is carried out through an *interface module*. This module is responsible for the *presentation* of information, the *practise* of students and their *assessment*. The user interface usually consists of a set of screens and dialogue structures. More specifically, the *training application* object base describes the application domain in terms of objects and links between objects thus, describing the domain knowledge necessary to support the training requirements. The *training scenarios* object base describes the training requirements for individual domain objects as well as the possible combinations of them to define a complete training session. The system is populated with a set of *trainee stereotypes* which model the most frequent trainee types of the system. These stereotypes are captured during application specification and they are further extended and adapted based on the knowledge captured for individual users. The latter is the responsibility of a course *tutor* who uses the *individual user profiles* knowledge base that reads in *interaction information* for a particular user and then customises the training scenarios to maximise training quality and minimise training time for each particular user.

Thus, the users in the delivery environment are the *tutors* and the *trainees* who interact with it for different reasons. The *trainee's* goal is to learn and the *tutor's* goal is to adjust the application's interface according to the profile of an individual trainee, to assist trainees and to monitor their progress. Tutors and trainees are also considered as part of the *evaluation procedure* the aim of which is to evaluate the success of the overall course and adjust it according to the evaluation results. Tutors and trainees contribute in the *evaluation procedure* by giving answers to questionnaires, by making remarks on the course, by participating in interviews, etc. In fig. 1, it can be seen that tutors and trainees interact with the delivery environment through the distance learning support provided by HTAS. This latter feature of HTAS is analysed in section 4.

3 Design Methodology and Design Model

Training is the activity which aims to increase people's performance by teaching them the rules and procedures of a knowledge domain. Computer Based Training (CBT) is a form of a self paced training, but in order to be better accepted by the trainees, the computer courses have to be well designed and the new possibilities offered by technology have to be exploited. The development of team based design for CBT courses must address the phases of the learning process, namely it should:

* arouse trainee's interest by using graphics, opening questions etc.
* present an advanced organiser including orientation screens with key concepts of the modules, window based explanations and user manual.
* identify the necessary pre-knowledge which should be implemented as introduction screens.
* present the actual learning material using advanced presentation means for holding a trainee's interest.
* practise and apply the learned material, with multiple choice questions on the theory of the modules and with cases studies.
* evaluate and test the level of trainee's proficiency with test cases
* identify and remedy the misconceptions
* perform final test cases with integration of the concepts between different modules

It is obvious that, in order to tackle the complexity of developing hypermedia CBT and produce well designed training systems, a methodological approach is required to analyse the training requirements and identify the training problems. A Systematic Approach to Training (SAT) [14] proposes a five stage activity mapping of a training process. These stages may be followed by an author using appropriate HTAS tools supporting each stage. More specifically, these stages are:

* *Application Domain Analysis*. This activity involves the definition of the application procedures and tasks, the skills and the knowledge needed to complete these tasks and the job objectives. This stage is supported by the *TAS tool* of HTAS.
* *Training Specifications*. This stage takes a pragmatic view of the required training and relates it to what it is achievable by performing a cost-benefit analysis. It specifies the training requirements of the application domain in terms of training tasks, contents of the training, performance conditions and standards. The *TSS* and *TM* tools of HTAS support an author during this stage.
* *Course Design*. Based on the training objectives, this stage decides the material of the course, the sequence of the material, the series of courses, the sections to be included, the section composition, the selection of section material and the media that this material will be presented upon (e.g. screen designs etc.). This stage is mainly supported by the *FE, QE* and *PB tools*.
* *Course Implementation*. This stage involves the actual implementation of a designed course and course execution.The HTAS tools used for the previous stage, support the actual course implementaion. Other external tools are used for capturing raw data which are then incorporated in the *object base* of the application. The *interface monitor* of HTAS supports the execution of the implemented course.
* *Course Assessment*. This phase attempts to identify the strengths and the weaknesses of a course. Thus, it establishes that the course is achieving the initial goals and it satisfies the course objectives. The results are fed back to the training application domain analysis to improve new versions of the course. The *Evaluation Procedure* is the HTAS component that supports this task.

The SAT identifies the following training concepts: (a) *objectives* which describe what has to be achieved, how well an objective is to be achieved and under which context, (b) *enabling objectives* which are items of knowledge or skills that enable a trainee to achieve higher level objectives and (c) *teaching points* which are items of information that the learner must acquire.

A number of factors, like the method of presentation, the medium of presentation, the time allocated to the training material, or the sequence of the training material, may influence the training quality of a CBT. The sequence that a material is presented to a trainee must conform to the course's objectives.

It is noted here that, when learners are free to select their own way of learning strategies, they do not always select wisely. Research has shown [12] that when learners are given control over instructional variables, they do not make the best decisions. This problem may be alleviated in systems that allow the explicit definition of the instructional strategies by the authors. Instruction is a goal-oriented teaching process that is based on pre-planning and formative evaluation [15]. Instructional systems must support argumentation and rhetorics.

The knowledge based approach to describing the training process may model user's behaviour as one's ability to navigate in the hypermedia training web. In HTAS, this behaviour may be expressed as a set of rules with pre-conditions and post-conditions in the knowledge base schema. The *enabling objectives* correspond to the pre-conditions of the rules which capture the training *objectives* of a course.

Apart from a design methodology, what is needed for the design of a hypertext application is a design model. There are a number of design models used in hypermedia development which are analysed in section 6. The conceptual model of HTAS supports a semantic-oriented description of the application components. HTAS provides an application oriented model for the capturing of the training requirements. HTAS emphasises in the methodological development of hypermedia systems and adopts the Hypertext Design Model (HDM) [9]. HDM describes the structure of the training concepts in terms of the entities populating the application, their features and their interelations. HDM assumes an *authoring-in-the large* approach. This method facilitates the design of the structural and semantic aspects of hypertext/hypermedia applications in a system independent manner, and without much concern on the node contents and the node lay-out. HDM provides a set of modelling primitives for authoring-in-the-large, which are adopted by HTAS.

The methodology of HTAS follows the HDM paradigm and allows the description of hypermedia applications in terms of a *schema*, an *instance of a schema* and the *access structures*. A *schema* is a collection of type definitions that describe an application at the global level. Thus, a schema defines the structural, the navigational, and the semantic properties of a class of applications. The *training application repository* in the authoring environment of HTAS corresponds to the *schema* notion of HDM. An *instance of a schema* defines the actual information structures of a specific application according to the schema prescriptions. The *object base* in the delivery environment of HTAS corresponds to the notion of the *instance of a schema* of HDM. The *access structures* define user-oriented entry points for directly accessing information structures in an instance of a schema and navigating the application along predefined paths. This is very useful since the definition of navigational properties of the contents of a course, i.e. how information browsing is facilitated in a hypermedia CBT, is an important issue in the development of hypermedia training applications. In HTAS, the *access structures* are incorporated in the *training application repository* of the authoring environment, as well as in the *object base* of the delivery environment.

It is clear now that, in the HTAS environment, authors develop hypermedia training applications by following the SAT methodology and constructing a HDM model. They are assisted by appropriate tools during the specification and design of a global model of a class of applications which is stored in the *training application repository*. Then, they exploit the information stored in this repository by using it in the development of various applications on a specific field, using appropriate tools. Special purpose browsers let authors to interactively select and retrieve the required information from the repository. Other platform tools enable authors to capture an application definition in terms of instantiated application frames (*schema instances*) from the information repository. These frames are derived by generic application templates (part of the global *schema*) which describe the common features of specific classes of applications. Meta-level descriptions of training sessions give the content of the information nodes and the sequences of the information presented to the trainees. The above relationships can be entered into the training system only when a thorough understanding of the application has been achieved.

According to the *authoring-in-the-large* approach, the primitives selected are totally independent from specific development/delivery environments, used for the applications, thus the same description of an application may be compiled towards different hypertext/hypermedia environments (e.g., ToolBook™, HyperCard™). The tools of HTAS allow hypermedia applications to be designed and developed at a higher level than node-link level, and in a system independent manner.

4 Distance Learning Support

Distance learning technologies enable learners to follow courses from places remotedly located from the organisations offering the training. Therefore, the conventional classroom setting is being replaced by a distributed learning environment. Distance learning allows a learner to follow up a class with a CBT program either at a workplace or in the classroom and to receive assistance, when needed by a tutor. Additionally, the communication infrastructure may let individuals communicate with other trainees and work in groups by conferencing or by using electronic mail. The principal aim of the distance learning component of the HTAS architecture [20] is to enable a training organisation to perform centralised monitoring and follow up of the training process with respect to the progress of the trainees.

The functionality of the telecommunications based distance training approach of HTAS may be described as follows:

* one way satellite communication may be used to deliver certain kinds of educational material (e.g. video) cheaper than conventional means (e.g. post)
* conventional data transmission may distribute software or text based material. The high volume training material may be available on CD-ROM and the telecommunication network will be available for updating the information and for logging the training transactions of the trainees. Narrow-band ISDN will improve the economics of this operation.
* Telecommunications may support human to human interactivity, electronic mail and simple computer conferencing. ISDN can provide extra opportunities.

The communications architecture in HTAS [20] recognises three distinct kinds of stations, namely; the *Author's* station, the *Tutor's* station and the *Trainee's* station. The progress of an individual trainee is described as changes in a central historical database which holds the profiles of the trainees. Changes in the *Trainee* database are recorded as transactions initiated by the interactions of individual trainees, in terms of topics attended, sequences of material browsed, questions visited, answers to questions, performance to given tests, etc. A *Tutor* who has been assigned to a number of trainees, may monitor the performance and the progress of the individual trainee. A knowledge based intelligent subsystem of the training architecture may function both as a tutor's and trainee's assistant. The purpose and the functionality of this intelligent subsystem is to support the optimal execution of courses by minimising human intervention.

The technical support for the communications infrastructure is foreseen to be provided directly by the PTT. However, the implementation of distance learning in HTAS is based on a pragmatic view of the current economics situation for the communications in Greece and in Europe.

5 HTAS Application Exemplar

The HTAS platform will be validated in a sample application which is a modular courseware on Object-Oriented Analysis and Design (OOAD). This courseware is targeted to undergraduate and postgraduate students as well as to professionals of different specialities (e.g. managers of EDP departments, project managers, systems analysts, programmers, etc.) who are interested in this topic for various reasons. Following the SAT methodology and the HTAS tools, we begin with the first stage of the pilot application development, which is the *application domain analysis* and involves the specification of the training levels and the respective educational goals. The pilot provides the user with such a flexibility so as to allow him/her either to study the full course, or to select certain sessions of particular interest. This stage is carried out with the use of the *TAS tool*. The second stage is the development of *training specifications* and is accomplished using the *TSS* and *TM tools*. In this stage it is decided that the training in OOAD will be carried out in two levels: basic training and advanced training. Thus, users who are not interested in the details of OOAD will be just introduced to the object-oriented philosophy (OO) and its application to systems analysis and design. Users with high interest in this topic will take the advance training on specific OOAD methodologies.

The third stage of application development, called *course design*, deals with the design of the training material which is also very important for the successful completion of the courseware. This design is accomplished with the use of the *Flow Editing*, *Question Editing* and *Presentation Builder tools* of HTAS. The basic training course includes a hyperbook with sections related to: OO philosophy, its origins and concepts, the use of OO approach to various fields of computer science (and in particular in software development), the characteristics and advantages of object-oriented systems and their comparison to function-oriented systems, the characteristics of OO programming languages and finally an introduction to OOAD. The advanced training course is a hyperbook with sections related to OOAD according to Booch [3], Coad & Yourdon [6, 7] and Rumbaugh et al [16]. *Access structures* are also defined here. At this stage, the *schema* of the application has already been constructed.

The CBT can be more effective if certain tests are given to trainees. Therefore, the design of evaluation tests for trainees is another important issue in this application pilot. At the end of each training session, there is a list of computerised questions and exercises addressed to the user. The purpose of these questions and exercises is to check, record and analyse the progress of each trainee as well as to aid him/her to assimilate the concepts used in the session. These tests are also designed during the third stage and are incorporated in the application *schema*, while their actual construction takes place during the next stage which is the *course implementation* stage.

The *course implementation* is carried out mainly with the tools of the previous stage and with other external tools which are used for the capturing of raw data and their incoroporation to the HTAS environment. Furthermore, the presentation of material is accomplished by using different kinds of media in order not only to attract and hold the trainee's interest, but also because certain material necessarily requires certain presentation media. The *access structures* defined in the previous stage are refined during course implementation. Thus, here the actual contents of the designed course are constructed and an application is generated, i.e. an *object base* is constructed. This application is *an instance of the schema* and is then executed and used by *trainees* who interact with it via the *interface module* of the HTAS delivery environment and perform the constructed tests.

The results of the various evaluation tests, the remarks of *trainees* and *tutors* and any other information related to the course progress, are used as input to the *evaluation procedures* the execution of which is carried out duting the next stage of application development which is the *course assessment*. The results of the course assessment are fed back to the previous stages and thus maximise the chances of having an acceptable and efficient multimedia application, prior to being formatted on optical media.

6 Related Work

The peculiarities of hypertext and hypermedia (e.g. the role of links, navigation, multimedia facility etc.) require the development of new models appropriate for the specific features of hypertext [9]. A number of hypertext models have appeared lately. Some of them describe specific application domains and activities, e.g. gIBIS [8] - a hypertext tool which explicitly models the semantics of the domain of exploratory policy discussion. Other models are more "system" oriented than application-oriented design models. These are attempts to capture the important abstractions found in a wide range of existing (and future) hypertext systems rather than of existing (and future) applications.

A representative example of the "system" oriented models is the Dexter Hypertext Reference Model [10] which aims to provide a principled basis for comparing systems as well as for developing interchange and interoperability standards. This model is divided into three layers: the *storage layer* (which describes the network of nodes and links), the *run-time layer* (which describes mechanisms for supporting the user's interaction with the hypertext) and the *within-component layer* (which covers the content and structures within hypertext nodes). The latter layer is purposefully not elaborated within the Dexter model and is considered to be outside the model per se. Another model is the Trellis model [18] which is mainly a "behavioural" model for hypertext. Hypertext networks are modelled as Petri nets and various browsing semantics are discussed in terms of Petri nets computations. The Trellis model completely abstracts from the contents and structure of the nodes, which can be arbitrarily complex information structures.

Ogawa et al [13] propose a four-level design model and describe a number of design strategies, based on the model, for scenario-based hypermedia applications, i.e. applications in which the basic structure is based on a written story or a detailed scenario. Each level of the design model specifies respectively the global structure, the detailed structure and the content specification and the presentation style of an application. Ogawa et al claim that since the model and the strategies are described in general terms, they can be a good framework to construct a general scenario writing method for hypermedia applications.

HDM [9] is an application oriented model for *authoring-in-the-large*. HDM is used to describe generic applications and it has been adopted by HTAS as it is more suitable than others for application generation. HDM prescribes the definition of an application *schema*, which describes overall classes of information elements in terms of their common presentation characteristics, their internal organisation structure, and the types of their mutual interconnections. A schema, therefore, captures semantic and structural regularities in the representation structures for a given class of applications. Once a schema has been specified, the model also allows it to define a particular application, by providing primitives to describe a *schema instance*, i.e., actual *instances* of information classes and of connection types. In defining a schema instance, a significant number of connections can be left implicit, since they can be automatically derived from a conceptual-design level description. Additionally, HDM can be used to generate running implementations of hypertext applications. The HCT [5] is a set of tools which translate HDM specifications of hypertext-hypermedia applications into applications implemented by the commercial hypertext system ToolBook™. HDM differs from gIBIS [8] in the fact that it does not freeze, a priori, the application domain, and therefore its representation primitives are more "general", oriented towards allowing the design of hypertext applications in most domains. HDM differs form the Dexter model [10] as it is aimed at modelling applications rather than systems. It also differs from the Trellis model [18] as it is more concerned with representational issues rather than behavioural aspects of hypertext.

Other approaches, less formal, emphasize preferred topological structures as building blocks to create the structure of hypertext networks. For example, HyperCard [2] uses linear structures to organise the constructed hyperdocuments. Guide [4] also prescribes the extensive use of linear structures while KMS [1] prescribes the extensive use of hierarchical structures for organising information.

From all the above models and approaches, it was decided that the HTAS environment adops the HDM model since it is application oriented, it has a well defined set of primitives for designing hypermedia applications and it can be used for desigining applications in a system independent way. The HTAS environment can be related to the ThyDoc [17] and SEPIA [19] hypermedia authoring environments. ThyDoc is an *authoring-in-the-large* environment, which treats authoring as a knowledge-acquisition process that captures formally (in terms of a conceptual schema) and informally (through text, graphics, etc.) all the knowledge needed by teams of authors for the analysis, design, development and maintenance of complex hypertext documents. SEPIA is built on top of a multi-user DBMS and provides persistent and shared data storage, hypermedia data model with composites, and authoring functionality and support for cooperative work. HTAS differs from these environments in the sense that it is oriented for building hypermedia *training* applications; thus it addresses the peculiarities of training and places much emphasis on the trainee modelling, the trainee scenarios modelling, the adaptation of the scenarios according to the individual trainee's profile and the support for distance learning.

7 Conclusions

The proposed HTAS platform addresses the complexity of the effort for developing interactive hypermedia training applications and at the same time it offers *distance learning* facilities. HTAS addresses the deficiencies in current hypemedia technology with respect to the production of hypermedia training systems by enabling the systematic integration of teaching strategies in the production of courseware. Furthermore, HTAS addresses the problems observed in existing multimedia and AI authoring tools [11] by providing adequate methodology support (data collection and analysis), computer managed instruction support (course planning, grading), support for customising paradigmatic training examples for new domains, and support for integrating training into workplaces as job aids.

More specifically, the advantages accruing from the innovative architecture of HTAS are:

* enhanced productivity of authors, as the tools offered to them minimize the effort for producing courses
* improved courseware production, due to the closer cooperation between hypermedia development experts and subject matter experts
* fast delivery of new courses and minimized production cost, due to the reuse of existing courses and/or due to the use of generic course templates for production specific courses
* improved quality assurance due to the evaluation procedures which contribute significanlty in the improvement of the quality of a course
* individualisation of courses by taking into account the trainee stereotypes and using the individual user's profile
* distance learning support.

The HTAS is currently at the end of the design stage, while a number of prototypes have already been implemented for visualising the various parts of the system. We believe that the HTAS environment will contribute significantly in the quality production of training hypermedia applications and will facilitate the overall hypermedia training applications production process

References

1. R.M.Akscyn, D.L. McCracken & E.A. Yoder, "KMS: A distributed hypermedia system for managing knowledge in organisations", *Communications of the ACM,* Vol 31, No 7, July 1988.
2. W. Atkinson, "HyperCard", in *Software for Macintosh Computers,* Apple Computer Co, Cupertino, 1987.
3. G. Booch, *Object-Oriented Design with Applications*, Benjamin Cummings, 1992.
4. P. J. Brown, "Turning ideas into products: The Guide System", In *Proceedings of the ACM Hypertext '87*, Chapel Hill, N.C. 1987, pp. 33-40.
5. A. Caloini, "Matching Hypertext Models to Hypertext Systems: a Compilative Approach", *Proceedings of ECHT-92,* Milano, Nov. 30 - Dec. 4, 1992, ACM Press, pp. 91-101.
6. P. Coad & E. Yourdon, *Object-Oriented Analysis*, Prentice-Hall, 1991.
7. P. Coad & E. Yourdon, *Object-Oriented Design*, Prentice-Hall, 1991.
8. J. Conklin & M. L. Begeman, "gIBIS: A Hypertext Tool for Exploratory Policy Discussion", *ACM Trans. on Information Systems* 6 (4), 1988, pp. 303-331.
9. F. Garzotto & P. Paolini, "HDM - A Model-Based Approach to Hypertext Application Design", *ACM Transactions on Information Systems,* 11 (1), Jan. 1993, pp. 1-26.
10. F. Halasz & M. Schwartz, "The Dexter Hypertext Reference Model", *Comm. of ACM,* 37 (2), pp. 30-39, Feb, 1994.
11. A. James & J.C. Spohrer, *Simulation-based Learning Systems: Prototypes and experiences,* In proceedings of CHI '92, Monteray Cal, May 3-7, 1992, ACM, NY, 1992, pp. 523-524.
12. D.H. Jonassen & R.S. Grabinger, *Problems and Issues in Designing Hypertext/Hypermedia for Learning,* in Designing Hypermedia for Learning, D.H. Jonassen, H. Mandl, Eds, NATO ASI Series, Springer Verlag 1990.
13. R. Ogawa, E. Tanaka, D. Taguchi & K. Harada, "Design Strategies for Scenario-Based Hypermedia: Description of its structure, dynamics and style", *Proceedings of ECHT-92,* Milano, Nov. 30 - Dec. 4, 1992, ACM Press, pp. 71-80.
14. R. Palmer, "Designing and Using CBT Interactive Video", NCC Publications, Manchester 1988.
15. M. Richartz & T.D. Rudebusch, *Collaboration in Hypermedia Environments,* in Designing Hypermedia for Learning, D.H.Jonassen, H. Mandl, Eds, NATO ASI Series, Springer Verlag 1990.
16. J. Rumbaugh, M. Blaha, W. Premerlani, F. Eddy, W. Lorensen, *Object-Oriented Modelling and Design*, Prentice-Hall, 1991.
17. R. Sobiesiak & J. Mylopoulos, "A Conceptual Modelling Approach to Authoring-in-the-Large for Hypertext Documents", *Proceedings of ACM Conf. on Organizational Computing Systems,* Atlanta, Georgia, *SIGOIS Bulletin,* 12 (2,3), pp. 225-239.
18. P.D. Stotts & R. Furuta, "Petri-Net-Based Hypertext: Document Structure with Browsing Semantics", *ACM Transactions on Information Systems,* 7(1), Jan. 1989, pp. 3-29.
19. N. Streitz, J. Haake, J. Hannemann, A. Lemke, W. Schuler, H. Schütt, M. Thüring, "SEPIA: a Cooperative Hypermedia Authoring Environment", *Proceedings of ECHT-92,* Milano, Nov. 30 - Dec. 4, 1992, ACM Press, pp. 11-22.
20. A. Tsalgatidou & Z. Palaskas, "An Integrated and Customisable Support System for Building Hypermedia Training Applications", Techn. Report, UoA, 1994.

OMNIS/Myriad Document Retrieval and its Database Requirements

R. Bayer[1,2], P. Vogel[1], S. Wiesener[2]

[1]Department of Computer Science,
[2]Bayerisches Forschungszentrum für Wissensbasierte Systeme (FORWISS)
Technical University of Munich

email: [vogel, wiesener]@informatik.tu-muenchen.de

Abstract: Traditional manual indexing of the literature is so expensive that only a part of the total literature, the books, can be disclosed to the library search. The information retrieval system OMNIS supported by the fulltext database system Myriad provides the archiving, disclosing and searching functions at drasticaly reduced costs by utilizing the latest achievements of data technology. These techniques like scanning, OCR, multimedia document architecture, fulltext search, and client-server architecture allow also novel and comfortable services in worldwide network environment and demand nontraditional support by the underlying database system. The system implementation is independent of the particular document structure and so it can be used for information retrieval problems also outside of the library world. The discussion of the running applications and the experience resulting from the first year of operation close the paper.

Keywords: library system, information retrieval, fulltext search, multimedia documents, client-server architecture, distributed databases, document archiving.

1 Introduction

OMNIS is a novel information retrieval system for administration of documents in libraries and office organizations [1]. It has been developed at the Computer Science Department of the Technical University of Munich and FORWISS (Bayerisches Forschungszentrum für Wissensbasierte Systeme). It is supported by Myriad, a fulltext database system [3]. OMNIS runs in a client-server environment and offers a number of economic and functional advantages by consequent utilization of latest achievements of the data technology. At the moment, implementations for Sun SPARC and HP 9000 Series 700 under Unix operating system and IBM AT under MS-Windows are available.

The start of the OMNIS-Project was motivated by the well known problems in the area of scientific literature. Nearly every scientific team is confronted with a huge amount of scientific documents. Only a small part of them, the books, are subject to the individual cataloguing and indexing procedure in scientific libraries and thus open to (mostly manual) literature search. The cataloguing and indexing is done in a so-called Library Association. The costs are about $40,- per book, (personal costs only) and consume a substantial part of the library budget. These costs are the reason why single articles in scientific magazines, conference proceedings, lecture notes, etc., are not cataloged individually and thus no subject to the existing library systems.

Beyond these "official" documents distributed by commercial channels, every scientific team works with a lot of “gray literature” like internal reports, preliminary copies, personal notes, etc. This very interesting class of scientific documents escapes completely the ordering and disclosing influence of the libraries, remaining unknown and unaccessible except for a few specialists.

An indispensable prerequisite for an efficient scientific work is a quick, easy, and well-aimed access to the most interesting documents in a given context out of the complete literature of the discipline. Neither the traditional manual administration, nor the existing electronic library administration systems can offer this service at an acceptable price. OMNIS solves this problem combining a very selective document retrieval, low response time, and simple and comfortable user interface with very modest costs. The cataloguing costs achieved by the pilot installation are lower than $1,50 per document, i.e. less then a twentieth of the traditional costs.

In contrast to the existing library systems which mostly simulate the traditional bibliographical procedures in the computer, OMNIS approaches the document administration utilizing any usable progress in the area of data technology and adjusts the way of administration to these possibilities. It can even be stated that the OMNIS solution became feasible through the latest technological innovations and would not have been possible a few years ago. These new technological resources can be characterized with the catch words multimedia, scanning, OCR (Optical Character Recognition), fulltext database systems, electronic documents, user-friendly interfaces, and client-server architecture.

OMNIS system is suitable for WAN operating. On account of the latest developments in network infrastructure, OMNIS document archiving and retrieval has to be seen in the context of worldwide use: specialized libraries now may be accessible for a wide range of different uses with the full OMNIS retrieval power.

Lately, it has become clear that the originally targeted library world is just a special case of the general document archiving and retrieval problem. This generalization has been accomplished in the OMNIS software components by making them adaptable to the applications document structure.

A crucial problem for applications like OMNIS is the adequate support by the underlying database system. Throughout this paper a lot of attention is devoted to the interrelation between OMNIS and the database management system Myriad used for the implementation. This interrelation has many facets and so it is discussed on the level of document architecture, data compression, client-server architecture and data distribution, multimedia ability, support of the novel optical and magneto-optical disk devices and full text search.

2 System Architecture

OMNIS has primarily been developed as an administration tool for scientific libraries and other collections of scientific documents in paper form and consists of the archiving [6], searching [5] and lending components [7]. This partition is predefined by the three classes of systems users: people archiving the documents, users performing the literature search, and professional library personnel, responsible for the library operation. The system structure is given in figure 1. The archiving and searching components, however, are also designed for document archiving and retrieval in general form, without any parallel keeping and administration of material paper documents. They can be used separately. The lending component supports the usual library services and can be added to the general document retrieval system.

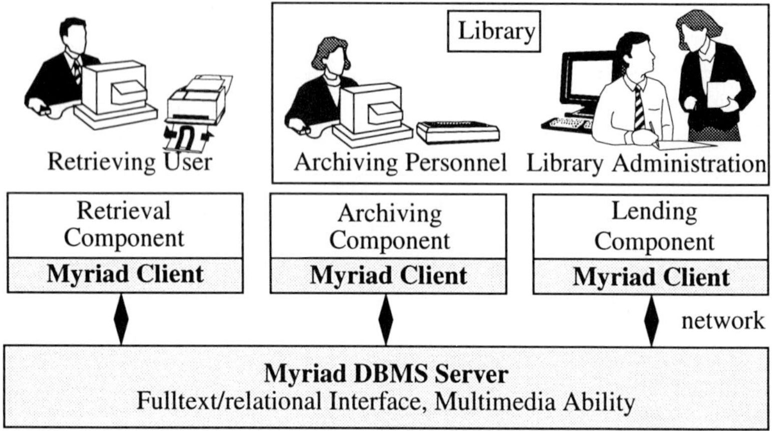

Fig. 1. OMNIS system components and user groups

2.1 OMNIS Documents

The basic parts of an OMNIS document are some structure fields describing the document (like author, title, publisher, edition, etc.) and a piece of ASCII text. Optionally, picture information (scanned in document pages) and/or full length document in postscript format may be attached. The document structure is shown in figure 2. For documents existing in electronic form the postscript format has been chosen because it preserves the layout of the document, is easy to print and very frequently used for document distribution. It is a common standard to all practically used text systems: any text system can produce a postscript file [9].

The preservation of information in the original layout (picture and/or postscript) proved to be essential to OMNIS users because it offers much more information (formulas, graphics, headings, italics, etc.) and is much more convenient to read than a plain ASCII text.

The structure fields are formatted, have values and constitute the attributes of the document relation in a relational database. The text as well as the picture and postscript are called medial data. Such data cannot be included as attributes in a relation: they have no supported type. It is characteristic for medial data that the value of an instance is composed of a long sequence of small elements (medium) like pixels or characters. They may have a complex internal structure usually not known to the database system.

2.2 Multimedia and Fulltext Ability

For the medial data constituting an OMNIS document, some sort of multimedia ability [8] is necessary in the underlying database system. The basic function of a database system is to store entities and to retrieve them selectively when its internal properties match those described in the query. A lot of standardization work has to be done till such multimedia database systems can be constructed. And even then, the interpretation and update of medial data might overload the database management system. At this point some pragmatical solution is required.

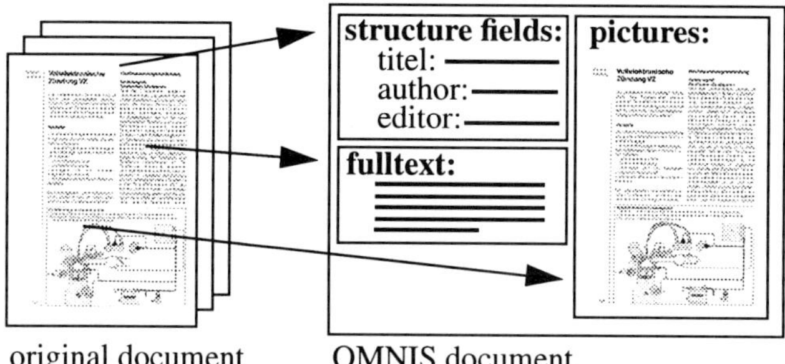

Fig. 2. OMNIS document structure

A simple solution, available also in the Myriad database system, is the BLOB (Binary Large OBject) - a data entity of any size and structure. A BLOB is a "black box" to the database system and any interpretation of the medial data can be located in the application program. BLOBs, however, can only be linked to a relational document item and are stored separately. To retrieve such a medial entity selectively due to some of its internal properties, as much information as possible about this entity has to be extracted and held as values in the database.

Due to its full text ability, Myriad is able to interpret an ASCII text and answer queries to the existence of word parts, words, phrases, and boolean expressions of them. Internally, Myriad uses a special text access method with a separate index structure designed for fast analysis of an existing text. Thus, the ASCII text is the basis of the full text interface of the database. The structure fields, on the other hand, use the relational part of the interface. Both interfaces can be used in combination for document retrieval. In contrast to text, picture and the postscript data are "black boxes" for the database system, and OMNIS can only display and print them as a whole.

3 Archiving Component

3.1 Archiving Procedures

Depending on the available form of data to be archived, three different archiving approaches have been realized in OMNIS.

Paper Documents

Nearly all human knowledge has been printed on paper and so the archiving of paper documents is the basic approach in OMNIS. In order to disclose a document to the electronic search the related characteristic phrases and expressions are needed. Instead of using highly trained people like librarians to extract these expressions by hand, OMNIS utilizes the fact that these expressions have to be in the document text itself, especially in parts like abstract, table of contents, summary, etc. Of course, these parts also contain some general words, but the space to store them is no substantial cost factor. The cheapest way to read this data into a computer is to scan it in and transform the text from the picture format to ASCII with an OCR (Optical Character Recognition) program. Most of the structure fields can be served from the text by the cut and paste facility. The structure fields, the text, and the picture constitute an OMNIS document.

Editorial publications like journals and conference proceedings can be archived on the level of volume with table of contents as the characteristic text or on the level of single contributions and their abstracts. Whether the more precise and more expensive level of individual contributions is affordable is an economic question.

The used scan and OCR software PIXEL!FX is a stand-alone commercial product. Unfortunately it does not offer an API (Application Program Interface) and so the pictures and the text have to be passed to OMNIS in a clumsy way as disk files with some name conventions.

Electronic Documents

A great number of current scientific documents are available in some computer-readable form and can easily be converted to postscript. It is a natural requirement to archive them directly without printing them to paper and to make the whole document accessible to the user [9]. Since storing the whole electronic documents as characterizing text might overload the fulltext database, the characterizing part of the document is converted to TIFF as produced by the scanner and the ASCII text is produced by the OCR program. Thus, the archiving procedure is similar to that of the foregoing case and the document structure is just enlarged with the postscript BLOB. It is interesting that the picture representation of the text produced from postscript has a very good quality and OCR works virtually without errors.

For the retrieval, the picture format is shown to the user for a first quick information about the document since the display time is under two seconds in Ethernet LAN operation. Showing the first postscript page takes about 10 - 20 seconds (the following pages come immediately), which can be demanded for a deeper study of a document.

Library Catalog Data

German professional libraries exchange their electronic version of the catalog information in MAB format (Maschinenlesbares Austauschformat für Bibliotheken) [10]. It contains the bibliographic data about the available titles and book instances, sometimes extended by a few keywords. Pictures and additional text information like abstracts are not available. This information is also provided for the literature search by storing it as structure fields and fulltext in an OMNIS archive.

MAB files of a university library may contain several hundreds of thousands of items. The MAB format is rather complicated: the data cannot be sequentially read and downloaded into an OMNIS archive. Multiple sorts of links between single scattered MAB records have to be resolved to obtain record groups which finally form one OMNIS document. It proved to be very useful to transfer first the MAB data into a temporary database, where consistency checks and link resolving are performed, using optimized database operations. Afterwards, Myriad spool files are generated and performed out of this processed data.

A general problem in library data is the sometimes insufficient data acquisition. Therefore, the data often is not totally consistent. Type violations (i.e. mixing of numbers and strings like "between 1676 and 1680" in the structure field "year") are common. Many conventional library database systems allow such "features" for lack of type control. Unfortunately the MAB exchange format is "flexible" enough to cope with this. The OMNIS MAB archiving tool offers means to check consistency and adapt values.

3.2 Archiving Tools

Spelling Check

The recognition rate of the OCR software strongly depends on the print quality of the paper document, but even with good quality and recognition rates over 99%, errors in the resulting text are disturbing. When stored in the database, the misspelled words cannot be recognized by the searching component: therefore the errors have to be corrected.

One way to do this is the proofreading of the text - an expensive and error prone method (an A4 page text takes at least three minutes). The method implemented in OMNIS is based on the fact that nearly all OCR errors lead to spelling errors in the text [11]. In default of better methods, the spelling check implemented compares the words of the OCR-text with words in a dictionary containing correct words in all used natural languages with all flections. A missing match is indicated to the user with the possibility to correct the text or to include the missing correct word into the dictionary. Such check of an A4 page of correct text takes between two and three seconds and it is much faster than a usual spelling check of a text system. A useful starting version of the dictionary may be obtained by collecting all words from available electronic documents.

Data Compression

The pictures and the full length postscript documents represent large amounts of data. An uncompressed A4 page in black & white TIFF and 300 dpi takes about 1 MB (i.e. 1000 pictures take 1 GB), one compressed page in OMNIS about 33 KByte. These numbers illustrate how important compression techniques are.

The pictures are compressed in two steps. The first step is the compression with information loss from 300 dpi necessary for OCR to 150 dpi adequate for the usual screen size and quality. This reduces the storage demand to 250 KByte. For the second step, a classical picture compression without information loss, several compression tools have been tested. The result is that all the tools yield nearly the same compression rate between 70% for very densely and 97% for very sparsely filled pages, but there are great performance differences between implementations.

While most modern scientific literature may be archived in black & white without information loss, some OMNIS applications demand color or at least grey pictures. An example is the project "Oettingen-Wallerstein", as described in chapter 7.1. An uncompressed A4 300 dpi image with 256 colors or grey levels takes about 8 MB! Here, lossy compression is the only way to archive more than a handful of documents. Above all, it is important to choose the lowest archiving quality limit for every single document, which preserves enough information for the retrieval.

4 Retrieval Component

The interface of the literature search is intended for a broad range of users. Therefore it must be so simple that no learning process is required and that the system is intuitively and immediately mastered. A very simple and powerful tool is the fulltext query but also queries aimed at individual structure fields are possible. The first one is related to the whole text body of the document including the contents of the structure fields and can contain just the words, word fragments or phrases of interest without any further formal specification about to which structure field it has to be related. The queries are part of an intuitive and self-explaining interactive interface, see figure 3.

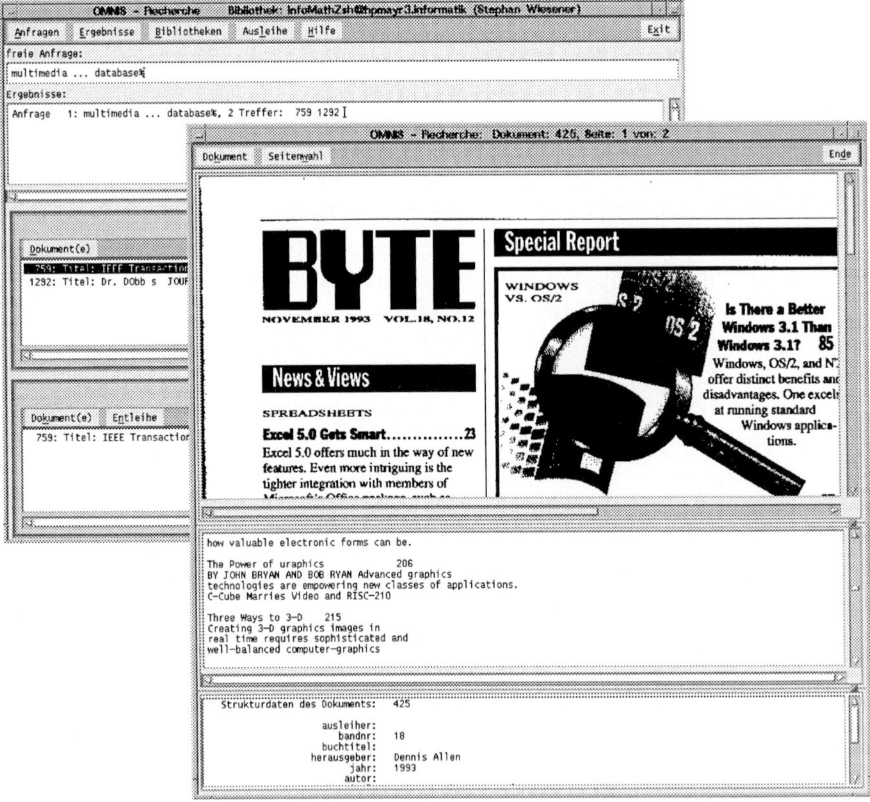

Fig. 3. OMNIS user retrieval interface

4.1 Fulltext vs. Structure Search

In the total fulltext body of the database each document is represented by its ASCII text extended by the contents of the structure fields. This means that both, structural information and text can be subject to a fulltext query. The fulltext body of a database is stored in a special data structure, where the existence of all words and their occurrences in a document including actual position are recorded. This data structure is designed for fast retrieval to a set of documents when phrases, single words or word parts are given. Though all information to reconstruct the original document text is available, this would be a time consuming activity, as the data structure is not feasible for this task. The document texts in their original form are therefore stored separately as BLOBs.

Retrieval of the documents is achieved by a fulltext search over the total text body of the complete set of documents. If the text pattern of the associative query is found in the text of a document, this document is a hit. It is a good help for the user to highlight the words which caused the document to be a hit. If the number of hits seems too large, the query has to be refined interactively, until an acceptable number of hits result.

The structure fields and the links to the existing BLOBs are stored in the relational part of the database. So a structure query has to be a selection of a document set based on a value or a value range of some attribute(s). Though the structural query is supported by a screen form, and some simple wildcards are available a fulltext search within a field is planned in a future version. Then a question like "Give me all documents containing the word 'black' in the author field" will be efficiently possible.

To handle interrelations between documents (which is in fact not possible in OMNIS today) OMNIS could easily be enlarged into a full hypermedia system [4]. This would not only allow document acces by declarative queries but also by hypertext-like link resolving. Such a HyperOMNIS system is planned for the future.

4.2 Fulltext Query Language

Further background and motivation to the fulltext query language can be found in [1,2]. At this point we want to illustrate the language just by a few query examples:

```
1. multimedia ... database% & ?Year > 1993
2. #1 & ?Author = 'K. Meyer-Wegener'
```

Hits are those documents containing the above search patterns somewhere in the text. These patterns may be composed of elementary queries like single words, phrases and distance search ("...", one period is standing for at most one arbitrary word). The wildcards "_" for one and "%" for an arbitrary number of characters are allowed. Elementary queries are then logically composed to Boolean search expressions of arbitrary depth. "#1" represents the result of the query 1. This language feature allows successive refinement of queries.

It is often doubted, particularly by librarians, that desired documents can be specified in this way with sufficient precision. Our experience is that the precision of the retrieval is very good. Especially the expressive power of the phrase compared to a Boolean expression cannot be overestimated: e.g. "`database language`" is much more powerful then "`database & language`". The extensive practical use of the OMNIS retrieval component showed that query refinement is fast and simple, though it is not necessary in most cases.

5 Lending Component

The lending component supports the operation of a public library with professional personnel, sensitive data, readers, reader identity cards, reader classes, reader accounts, books, book reservations, barcodes, demand-notes, etc. Though it is just a classical application of a relational database, it is very extensive and more complicated then a usual library user can imagine.

The subject to lending is a book copy. There are some connections between the data of the search and the lending. The searching user is allowed to see the number of available document copies and their status. He is also allowed, in some limits, to make book reservations and prolongation of the lending period.

6 Implementation Aspects

6.1 Functional Distribution

OMNIS/Myriad is designed as a distributed system in client-server architecture. Each server may contain multiple independent OMNIS databases of documents. A client system offers the OMNIS retrieval and/or archiving functionality to the users. In contrast to some other popular information systems, the process of archiving documents is fully concurrent and does not block worldwide retrieval.

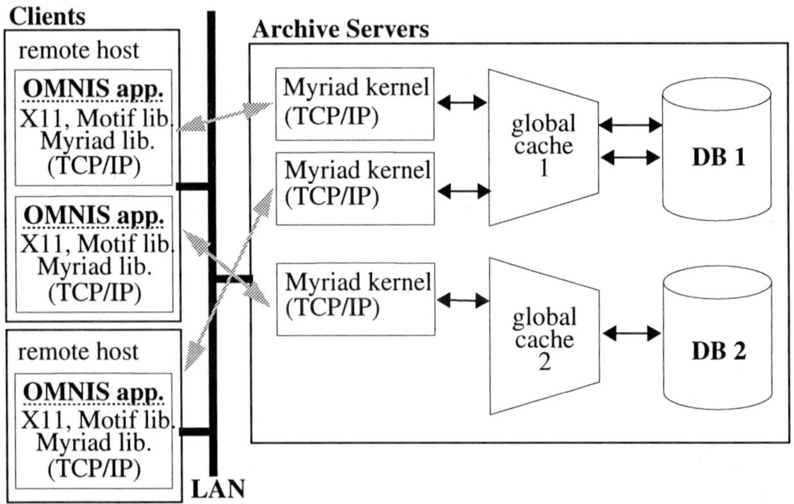

Fig. 4. Functional distribution

Time consuming functions, e.g. decompression of image data or query preprocessing are located in the client software to guarantee short server reaction times. Only compressed document images go via network, which meets the requirements for WAN use. As client computers, Unix workstations (Hewlett Packard 9000 Series 700, SUN SPARC) as well as personal computers (MS-DOS/MS-Windows with TCP/IP) are suitable [12]. As archive server a Unix system is indispensable, see figure 4.

For each activation of an OMNIS program, a connection to the archive on the user specified server is established. The database requests are transformed on the level of TCP/IP and transferred to the server via network. Due to the underlaying database system Myriad, all operations are safe guarded by transactions. This allows network-based archiving, where retrieval will not be restricted by inconsistent temporary database states. The number of concurrent connections can be individually specified for each OMNIS database.

7 Applications and Experiences

7.1 Types of OMNIS applications

TUM (Technical University oif Munich) Libraries

At the computer science and mathematics department, about 2,500 students and 300 scientists on more than 400 clients use OMNIS for retrieval in the following libraries:

TUM Central Library: consists of several hundreds of thousands titles downloaded from MAB format.

Library of the Computer Science Department: data up to August 93 were downloaded from MAB format, after that point the documents are available with scanned picture, OCR fulltext and structural informations.

Chair Libraries: 13 chairs have created their own specialized OMNIS archives.

Germany Wide Historical Archives

In two running projects, the research center FORWISS developes an OMNIS based archive for historical documents. A medieval library as well as the whole stock of German prints of the 17th century shall be archived as pictures in a central database.

Several hundreds of thousends of documents, partly in color, will be stored on CD-ROM jukeboxes managed by the OMNIS server. OMNIS therefore was extended to deal with color bitmaps. The only difference for the user is a slightly slower reaction time.

The Munich Metropolitan Area high-speed Libraries Network [2]

Several leading Bavarian libraries will share their catalogs and subscribed journals in a high-speed network.

7.2 First Experience with OMNIS

After its first year of operation, OMNIS became an integral part of the research activity at the department and the interest from outside exceeded by far the expectations. However, also the amount of data is growing day by day. In the library of the department 2,860 documents (books, journals, technical reports) with at least one picture each have been archived in the first half year, occupying 168 MByte of storage. These numbers illustrate how important it is that the database has no predefined maximum size, that it is extensible beyond one disk volume and integration of CD jukebox devices is possible.

Simple measurements proved the OMNIS Internet suitability. In a long distance 2 Mbit/s Internet access (a Berlin client retrieved pictures in a Munich library), the time to show seven black & white pictures in sequence did not exceed 35 seconds. Even in a connection with 64 KBit/s at client side and 2 MBit/s at server side, a single black & white picture appeared on the client screen in less than 25 seconds. Of course, simple text retrieval is much faster. For practical use these access times are sufficient.

8 Acknowledgments

Many people have invested a lot of effort to design and implement the OMNIS system components. We thank our master students W. Bauer, S. Breutel, P. Essler, M. Kurzmann, A. Oppitz, A. Meyer, J. Mödl, J. Pichel, J. Porada, M. Rupprecht, V. Vöcking, B. Wiserner and S. Zimmermann for their enthusiastic cooperation. Special thanks go to H. Göttsch for his thorough system administration and maintenance.

References

[1] Bayer, R.: OMNIS/Myriad: Electronic Administration und Publication of Multimedia Dokuments. In: Informatik, Wirtschaft und Gesellschaft. 23. GI-Jahrestagung, Dresden 1993, Springer Verlag, pp. 482 - 487 (in German)

[2] Bayer, R., Vogel, P., Göttsch, H.: The Munich Metropolitan Area high Speed Network of digital Libraries, ftp-server: ftp.informatik.tu-muenchen.de, path: /local/lehrstuhl/bayer/papers/mmanetwork.ps.gz, 1994

[3] TransAction Software: Myriad System and Administration Guide, Myriad Fulltext Database system Version 3.0. TransAction Software GmbH München, 1992

[4] W. Kowarschick, Ch. Roth, P. Vogel, S. Wiesener, R. Bayer: OMNIS/Myriad on its Way to a Full Hypermedia Information System, 1st European Workshop on Human Comfort and Security, EITC, Brussels 1994

[5] Meyer, A.: Design and Implementation of the Lending and Searching Components of the Library System OMNIS/Myriad. Master Thesis TU München, 1992 (in German)

[6] Essler, P.: Design and Implementation of the Archiving Component of the Library System OMNIS/Myriad. Master Thesis TU München, 1992 (in German)

[7] Pichel, J.: Design and Implementation of the Lending Component of the Library System OMNIS/Myriad. Master Thesis TU München, 1993 (in German)

[8] Meyer-Wegener, K.: Multimedia Databases. B. G. Teubner Stuttgart, 1991 (in German)

[9] Rupprecht, M.: Documents of Elektronic Origin in the Library System OMNIS/Myriad. Master Thesis TU München, 1993 (in German)

[10] Die Deutsche Bibliothek: MAB - Maschinelles Austauschformat für Bibliotheken. Die Deutsche Bibliothek, Frankfurt, 1992 (in German)

[11] Mödl, J.: Design and Implementation of the Spelling Check for the Library System OMNIS/Myriad. Master Thesis TU München, 1993 (in German)

[12] Vöcking, V.: Realisation of the Searching Function of OMNIS/Myriad under Microsoft-Windows. Master Thesis TU München, 1993 (in German)Bayer, R.: OMNIS/Myriad: Electronic Administration und Publication of Multimedia

Constructing an Information Retrieval System with Neural Networks

R. LAYAIDA[1], M. BOUGHANEM[1][2], A.CARON[3]
(1) MSI, Université des Sciences de Limoges,123, Avenue Albert THOMAS 87060 Limoges France, Tel : 55.45.72.34 Fax : 55.45.73.15 e_mail : layaida@unilim.fr
(2) IRIT/SIG Université Paul SABATIER- 118, Route de Narbonne 31062 Toulouse Cedex France, Tel : 61.55.63.22 Fax : 61.55.62.58 e_mail : bougha@irit.fr
(3) LERIA IUT/CGI Université de Bretagne Occidentale, 10 Rue Jean Zay 56100 Lorient France, Tel : 97. 87 28 34 Fax : 97. 87.28.08 e_mail : caron@moorea.univ-brest.fr

Abstract

This paper describes an Information Retrieval System (IRS) based on the neural approach. Our goal is to construct an IRS able to evolve. We propose a network containing document, term and author nodes and a set of links between these different nodes. A set of activation/propagation rules on which is based the information retrieval and the queries expansion are presented. At last, we propose a learning strategy inspired by the backpropagation algorithm for dynamically organizing the information base.

Keywords : Information Retrieval, Neural Network, Learning, Dynamic Organization.

1 Introduction

The goal of an Information Retrieval System(IRS) is to bring relevant documents to users according to their information need. However, it has been recognized that even the best of the IRS has a limited recall ; users may retrieve a few relevant documents in response to their queries but almost never all of them. Thus, it becomes necessary to modify or expand the initial query. Two kinds of methods have been proposed to achieve it automatically. The first one is the relevance feedback, it consists in adding new terms on the basis of a first research on the user's original query. The second one, is based on the use of the semantic relationships established manually or automatically between terms. Unfortunately, whenever we use the vector space model, the probabilistic model or the extended boolean model, these improvements are limited by many aspects as follows :

- whenever the associative relationships between terms are fixed definitively, in most of the cases by statistical methods, they do not guarantee the validity neither the identification of all the relationships that may exist between the terms. Raghavan showed the limits of this approach on the vector space model [1].
- whenever the semantic weight relationship, that is the degree of a term in the specification of a document content, is fixed by statistical laws, then, it probably will not identify the real importance of each indexing term in the corresponding document. Thus, whenever this term is used to retrieve the relevant documents and to expand the queries [2] [3], it may retrieve some irrelevant documents,
- the documents are written by authors, they, generally, are neither linguists nor experts in indexing. Thus after the automatic indexing, the descriptor of these documents may ignore some essential terms.

A possible solution for these problems is to construct an IRS where the different relationships are fixed automatically, and then to find a way to modify them according to the relevance of the documents they retrieve. The IRS built in this way is *dynamic* and able to *learn*.

Moreover, an important and a possible advantage of our IRS is that it organizes the documents by their set of common references in addition to the indexing terms. This kind of organization has rarely been used in the information retrieval systems. However, whenever it is used with the research based on the indexing terms, it allows to improve appreciably the retrieval effectiveness[2].

In order to realize the IRS dynamic, the neural approach seems to be the most appropriated. Indeed, according to its learning property, a neural network can change its behavior in respect to the previous experiences results [4]. Interesting works based on this approach have been realized [5] [6] [7].

The network is built on the basis of a set of nodes and a set of links. The nodes represent the terms, the authors and the documents. The links represent the different relationships which may exist between these nodes. According to the users' judgements on the IRS responses, the network will carry out a kind of *relevance feedback* in order to adjust the weights. We think that the *backpropagation* algorithm seems to be adaptable. In the first part of our paper, we expose the back propagation algorithm. In the second part, we present the model retained for representing the documentary base and the methods used to weight the different links. The third part is dedicated to the information retrieval where we suggest an activation/propagation process and present the automatic query expansion process. In the last part, we present the learning process.

2 Backpropagation Algorithm

Basically, a neural network is made up of various layers of basic nodes(neurons). Generally, the network has one input layer, one output layer and some hidden layers. The set of the synaptic weights w_{ij} (that is the connexion from a node i to a node j) defines the architecture of the network. According to the synaptic weights, and to the updating rules, the neural network associates a set of input patterns to a set of output patterns in a strongly non-linear way. A very important property of the neural networks is their learning ability. The synaptic weights are progressively computed during the training phase, so that the network performs some specified task. In order that the backpropagation can work, the backward path from the network output to an internal node must be differentiable. This means that the nodes must use a continous and differentiable function in computing their activation signal, such as the sigmoid function. Each network node, computes its input signal from the output signals it receives from the preceding layer nodes and then by using its activation rule (sigmoid function of the weighted sum of the incoming signals), computes the output signal and then sends it to the neurons of the following layer. The same process is applied till the output layer. The error is, then, computed between the desired and the obtained outputs by measuring the quadratric mean difference. This error is backpropagated in the network from the output layer to the preceding layer in order to adjust the weights so that the obtained ouput matches the desired ouput. This process is then applied from each layer to its preceding one, till the input layer. The learning process is stopped when the network gives satisfacory outputs for a set of test input patterns [8] [9].

3 Neural Model

3.1 Architecture of the Model

The documents we use are bibliographic references. A document is described by a title, an abstract, authors and a set of bibliographic references (authors). The network is constructed on the basis of four layers (see Figure 1).

The D layer represents the documents of the documentary base. Each node d_i represents a document descriptor.

The T layer represents the indexing terms. Each term retained by the *indexing procedure* 3.2 below is represented by a node t_i. A semantic link p_{ij} is then, established between the term node t_i and a document node d_j. Associative links w_{ih} are also established between two nodes t_i and t_h whenever t_i and t_h are present jointly in at least one document. These links express the cooccurrence relationship between two terms.

The Layer A represents all the documents authors of the documentary base where each node a_i represents an author. A reference link r_{ij} is established between an author a_i and a document d_j he writes. Then, association links s_{hk} are created between two authors a_h and a_k. These links groups the authors who work in the same research field.

The Q layer represents the users' queries. Each node t'_i represents an indexing term. These nodes are activated whenever they are present in a user's query. The links q_{ii}^k are created between the nodes t'_i of Q and t_i of T on the kth retrieval operation(q_{ii}^k=1). The documents and the queries are represented by the vector space model [2] :

$$d_j = (p_{1j},\ p_{2j},\ \dots p_{ij},\ \dots p_{mj}) \text{ and } Q^k = (q_{11}^k,\ q_{22}^k,\ \dots q_{ii}^k,\ \dots q_{mm}^k)$$

where m is the number of terms in the documentary base,

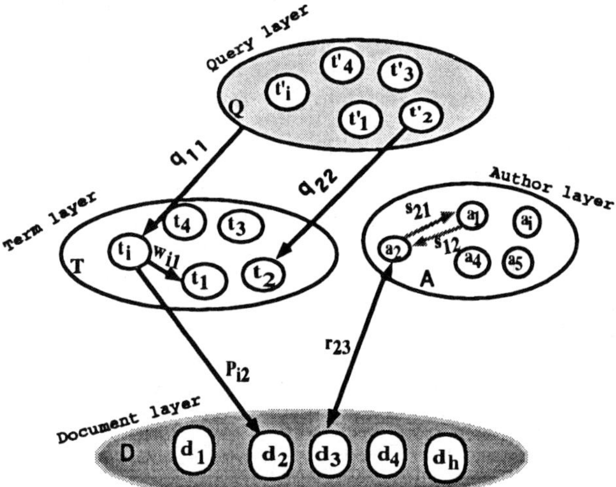

Figure 1. Architecture of the information retrieval system

We will describe next the indexing procedure, the establishment of the links and the initial values given to these different links before any retrieval operation.

3.2 The Indexing Process

The indexing process is applied to the title and to the abstract of the documents. It leads to a reduced representation of their informational content. Before any document indexing operation, we constructed a stop list containing the different insignificant terms like articles, conjunctions etc. The lexical units of the title and

the abstract are extracted according to their order of appearance in the text. For each retained form(that is not contained in the stop list), we apply a special treatment in order to bring back each lexical unit to its basis form known in a dictionary containing the indexing terms.
This treatment is inspired by the MMI2 model applied in the Esprit project (on the French Language Analysis) where the goal is to reach from a text statement written in the natural language its logical representation [10]. However, we realize some limitations, because our goal is different, that is to extract a roll of the most significant terms of the document content.

3.3 Link Weighting

3.3.1 The p_{ij} Initialisation

For each term retained for the description of the document, we measure its relative frequency FreqRel and its total frequency FreqTot, the weight is [11]:

$$p_{ij} = FreqRel(t_i, d_j)\left[\log_2\left(\frac{n}{FreqTot(t_i)}\right) + 1\right] \qquad (1)$$

FreqTot(t_i) : number of documents containing the term t_i,
FreqRel(t_i,d_j): the relative frequency of t_i in d_j.
n : the number of documents in the documentary base,

The weight p_{ij} is so high whenever it appears with a high relative frequency and a low total frequency according to the documentary base dimension.

3.3.2 The r_{ij} Initialisation

The link r_{ij} is established between an author node a_i and a document node d_j that he writes. We give to this link a value equal to 1 (r_{ij}=1). This link allows to retrieve from the document d_j its authors and from the author a_i the documents he writes.

3.3.3 The w_{ij} Initialisation

The T layer nodes are entirely connected. Their weights are automatically computed by measuring their cooccurrence degree. This association allows to alleviate the problems of the different representations given by the automatic indexing and the users. The link creation and weighting are based on the principle that the associative relationship between two terms is more important whenever they appear frequently in the same documents. It's decreased whenever these terms appear separately in the documents [12] [13]. Each factor expresses the ability of the term t_i to recall a term t_j whenever the term t_i is extracted from a query and a query expansion process is requested by the user. This weight is defined as :

$$w_{ij} = \frac{\sum_{k=1}^{n} p_{ik} * p_{jk}}{\sum_{k=1}^{n} p_{ik}^2 + \sum_{k=1}^{n} p_{jk}^2 - \sum_{k=1}^{n} p_{ik} * p_{jk}} \quad \text{where } 0 \le w_{ij} \le 1 \qquad (2)$$

n: is the number of documents in the base,

The different values w_{ij} are gathered in a symetric matrix W where the diagonal terms are equal to 1. We remember that this method does not guarantee neither the identification of all the possible relationships (that are the synonymy, the specificity and generality) nor their validity. During the learning process, the weights w_{ij} and w_{ji} will be adjusted independently allowing the expression of the *"right"* relationships.

3.3.4 The s_{ij} Initialisation

The documents organization by using the bibliographic references as we introduced it previously, has been rarely used in the information retrieval systems. Nevertheless whenever it's used with the research based on the indexing terms, it increases the retrieval effectiveness [2]. It allows to gather the authors who work in the same field.

After studying different possible strategies, we have choosen to organize the links between two authors a_i and a_j by using their number of common references in the documents they have written. The use of this strategy is justified by the fact that all the documents treated exist in the documentary base. We use the following formula :

$$s_{ij} = \frac{Card(N_{ai} \cap N_{aj})}{Card(N_{ai} \cup N_{aj})} \quad (3)$$

Card(N) : The cardinal of the set N and N_{ai} : the set of authors held by the author a_i. s_{ij} is more important whenever two authors a_i and a_j refer to an important number of common authors. These weights will be adjusted during the learning phase because some authors working in the same field may have no common reference.

4 The Information Retrieval and the Learning Process

The user submits his query to the system which retrieve the documents they may satisfy his query and presents them as an ordered list. The user selects then the documents that he judges as relevant. By considering these judgements, the system realize the base arrangements. We can distinguish two main functions in the system.

- the information retrieval function,
- the learning function.

4.1 The Information Retrieval Function

The user's query may have different forms, it can be constructed on the basis of the database authors, on the terms or on both of them Actually, we developed the retrieval function based on the terms. The user system presents as an input a query written in natural language. This query is analyzed like the document indexing in order to construct the network k^{th} input Q^kon the query layer Q. After, the insignificant query terms elimination , the nodes corresponding to the retained terms are activated ($I_T(t'_j)=1$). The activation rule of each node of this layer is the identical function (that is $O_Q(t'_j)=I_Q(t'_j)$). Then the activated nodes t'_i are related to their similar on the T layer by the links q^k_{ii} which the value is 1. Each T node computes an input value according to :

$$I_T(t_j) = \begin{cases} 1 & if \ t_j = t'_i (the \ same \ indexing \ term) \\ 0 & else \end{cases} \quad (4)$$

Each activated node computes its output function according to the input signals it receives by using the sigmoid function below :

$$O_T(t_j) = \frac{e^{I_T(t_j)} - 1}{e^{I_T(t_j)} + 1} \quad (5)$$

This function is frequently used in the neural networks because it is a continuous and derivative function whom the values are included in [0..1]. It presents a polished version of the threshold function.

Our model proposes to the user, an immediate research from the terms extracted from the query or a research after the query expansion. In this last case, the output signals of the term activated nodes are directly sent to the nodes of the document layer [14]. Otherwise, the user expects a query expansion in order to increase the retrieval effectiveness. Two types of query expansion are possible :

•an explicit query expansion where the process is applied after a first retrieval operation on the user's query. According to the users judgements. It consists in increasing the weights of the terms they allow to retrieve the relevant documents and in decreasing the ones they allow to retrieve the irrelevant documents. Different query expansion methods were established in the retrieval information systems, for more information we advise the reader to consult [2] [15] [16].

• an implicit query expansion before any retrieval operation. In this case, the nodes of the term layer activated by the user's query propagate their signals through the links w_{ij}. It 's also possible to transmit directly the signals to the document layer and realize the propagation on this layer [17] [18].

In our model, we establish an implicit query expansion. Whenever the user asks for an expansion of his query, a propagation of the signals on the T layer is realized . Thus, every activated node t_i sends its output signal through the w_{ij} links to the other inactivated t_j nodes. The latters compute their input as :

$$I_T(t_i) = \sum_{\substack{j=1 \\ j \neq i}}^{n} O_T(t_j) * w_{ji} \qquad (6)$$

The propagation is realized in several passes, considering the fact that whenever some nodes are newly activated, they may induce the activation of other inactivated nodes. The propagation process is in principle, stopped when there is no more new term nodes recently activated. We construct in this manner, some sublayers on the T layer where the nodes of each sublayer are activated at the same pass. In practise, two passes are enough for recalling all the strongly bound terms. We construct, thus on the T layer three sublayers T1, T2 and T3 (see figure 2) :

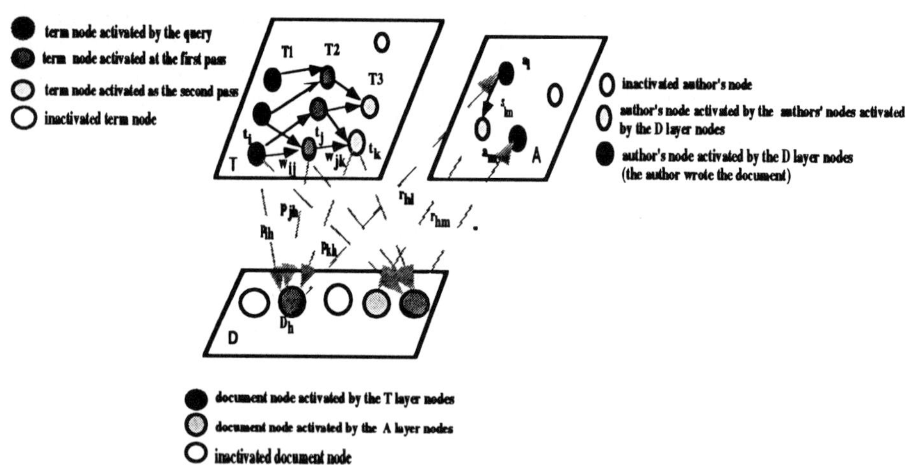

Figure 2. the network functionning.

Next, each activated node, computes its output function following the formula (5) and transmits its output signal through the links p_{ij} of the layer D. In the same way, each node d_j computes its input function as following :

$$I_D(d_j)=\sum_{j=1}^{m} O_T(t_i)*p_{ij} \qquad (7)$$

Its output signal according to the sigmoid function : $O_D(d_j)=\dfrac{e^{I_D(d_j)}-1}{e^{I_D(d_j)}+1}$ *(8)*

We construct then, a set EE_T of the document nodes activated by the T layer nodes. From this set, the output signals are sent to the corresponding authors nodes on the layer A through the links r_{ij}. Only the authors of the documents already selected are activated. Each author node, computes its input signal by :

$$I_A(a_i)=\sum_{j/\ d_j\in EE_T} O_D(d_j).r_{ij} \text{ where } \begin{cases} r_{ij}=1 \ \ if \ \ a_i \ \ wrote \ \ d_j \\ r_{ij}=0 \ \ else \end{cases} \qquad (9)$$

and then computes its output signal : $O_A(a_i)=\dfrac{e^{\beta I_A(a_i)}-1}{e^{\beta I_A(a_i)}+1}$ where β is a constant *(10)*

A propagation is effected at this A layer level to activate the strongly jointed author's nodes :

$$I_A(a_i)=\sum_{\substack{j=1\\ j\neq i}}^{l} O_A(a_j)*s_{ji} \qquad (11)$$

l : the authors number on the A layer,

From these input signals, each node measures its output signal using the formula *(10)*. The nodes recently activated send their nodes to the D layer. Each node d_i which is not belonging to EE_T computes its input function like :

$$I_D(d_i)=\sum_{\substack{j=1\\ j\neq i}}^{l} O_A(a_j)*r_{ji} \qquad (12)$$

and its output signal by the formula *(8)*. Then, we constitute a second set EE_A of the documents nodes activated by the propagation on A. The list of the nodes sufficiently activated are sorted by a decreasing order of their activating value. The user selects, then, the documents they agree to his interests. Hence, the backpropagation of the retrieval results is effected in the system in order to adjust the links weights in respect to the user's choices. The system is then in its learning phase.

4.2. The Learning Process

The learning process is performed in respect with a desired functioning for the network. The learning mechanism begins when the user establishes his choices from the retrieved documents. A score is associated to each retrieved document, a value of 1 whenever the document is judged relevant, -1 if it is irrelevant and 0 if he has no opinion. We obtain two sets respectively for the relevant documents E_r and the irrelevant documentsE_{irr}.

We construct a virtual document vector Y_k representing the desired output to associate to the user's query (we retrieve here an analogy with the term reweighting used in the relevance feedback strategies [15]).

$Y_k=(y_{1k},y_{2k},\dots,y_{ik},\dots y_{mk})$ where k is the kth learning phase and m : number of indexing terms in the base.

Each y_{ik} is expressed by [11]: $$y_{ik} = \gamma \sum_{d_j \in E_r} \frac{p_{ij}(k)}{Card(E_r^i)} p_{ij}(k) - \lambda \sum_{d_j \in E_{irr}} \frac{p_{ij}(k)}{Card(E_{irr}^i)} \qquad (13)$$

card(E) : cardinal of the set E^i of documents containing t_i,

whenever $y_{ik}<0$, then $y_{ik}=0$

γ,λ : are appropriated constants in [0..1] and $\gamma+\lambda=1$.

if $\gamma > \lambda$, we further the recall (that is the ratio of the number the relevant documents retrieved on the number of relevant documents on the documentary base). If $\gamma<\lambda$, we further the precision (that is the the ratio of the number of the relevant documents retrieved on the number of the retrieved documents). From (13), the input signal and its corresponding output are computed for each retrieved document. It constitutes the correct output to associate to the user's query.

$$I_D((Y_k)_j) = \sum_{i=1}^{m} (y_{ik})_j * O_T(t_i) \text{ where } (y_{ik})_j = \begin{cases} y_{ik} \text{ if } p_{ik} \neq 0 \\ y_{ik} = 0 \text{ else} \end{cases} \quad (14)$$ and the output $$O_D((Y_k)_j) = \frac{e^{I_D((Y_k)_j)} - 1}{e^{I_D((Y_k)_j)} + 1} \qquad (15)$$

The learning process consists minimises the quadratic error collected on the entire examples presented to the system by an approximate gradient descent given by :

$$\Delta(k) = \sum_{j/d_j \in EE_T} (O_D((Y_k)_j) - O_D(d_j))^2 \qquad (16)$$

This error is backpropagated towards the network nodes through p_{ij} , s_{ij} and w_{ij} links.

4.2.1. The Modification of the Weights p_{ij}

The modification of the links p_{ij} is established between the nodes t_i and d_j whenever t_i and d_j are activated. The rule is given by :

$$p_{ij}(k+1) = p_{ij}(k) - \Delta 1_{ij}(k).\alpha(k) \qquad (17)$$

$\alpha(k)$: the learning rate decreasing at each retrieving phase k,

$\Delta 1_{ij}(k)$ is given by the following formula where only the output $O_D(d_j)$ depends on p_{ij} [18].

$$\Delta 1_{ij}(k) = \frac{\partial \Delta(k)}{\partial p_{ij}} = -2.(O_D((Y_k)_j) - O_D(d_j)).f'(I_D(d_j))O_T(t_i) \qquad (18)$$

$O_D(d_j)$: the d_j output at k^{th} phse and $(O_D(Y_k))_j$: the desired output for d_j.

The modifications are established till the network becomes stable in a state reflecting a global tendency of the system users. There is a reinforcement if ($\Delta 1_{ij}(k) <0$), in the other case, there is an attenuation($\Delta 1_{ij}(k) >0$).

4.2.2 Modification of the Weights w_{ij}

After the learning realized on the links p_{ij}, the error is backpropagated towards the T layer links. Only the links that permit the original query expansion will be modified. If we refer to the figure 3, these corrections are backpropagated from the sublayer T3 towards the sublayer T2 and from T2 towards T1.

The learning process is : *if t_i participates in the activation of the term t_j after the query expansion, then the error is backpropagated from t_j towards t_i .*

$$w_{ij}(k+1) = w_{ij}(k) - \alpha(k)\ \Delta 2_{ij}(k) \qquad (19)$$

$\alpha(k)$: is a decreasing gain function after each learning step and converge towards 0.

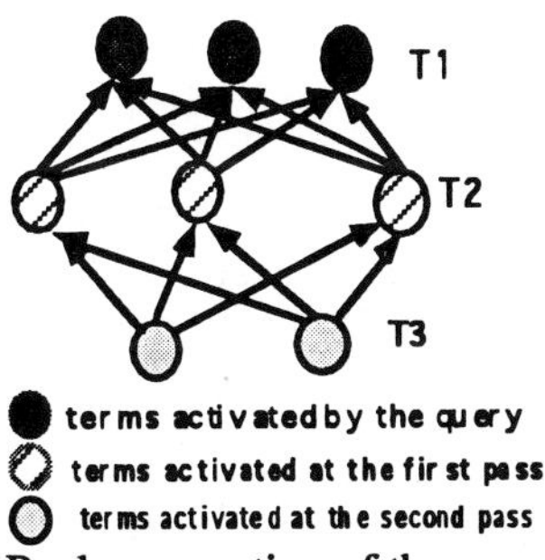

Figure 3. Backpropagation of the error to layer T.

The modification rule of the links w_{ij} depends on which pass a term node was activated. Here, two kinds of modifications are considered :

The backpropagation of the error collected on the p_{jh} links :

The error clerked on the w_{jk} between a node t_j of T2 and a node t_k of T3 (resectively of T1 and T2) belong to the links p_{kh} where d_h is an activated document node and t_k an activated term node of T3 or T2. The error is given by :

$$\Delta 2_{ij}(k) = \sum_{h \in EE_T} \Delta 1_{jh}(k) p_{jh} f'(I_T(t_j))\ O_T(t_i) \qquad (20)$$

The backpropagation of the error collected on the w_{jh} links from T2 to T1 :

The error on w_{ij}, where t_i is a node of T1 and t_j a node of T2, depends on the links w_{jh}. This error is measured by :

$$\Delta 2_{ij}(k) = \sum_{t_h \in T2} \Delta 2_{jh}(k)\ w_{jh}\ f'(I_T(t_j))\ O_T(t_i) \qquad (21)$$

h : go over all the activated nodes of T3.

4.2.3 Modification of Weights s_{ij}

We apply the Hebb's rule on the layer A because there is no error on the reference links r_{ij}. Indeed, these links represent objective information, consequently, their weights can not be modified. From the list of the relevant and the irrelevant documents, a link s_{ij} is modified as follows. The learning law applied is then :

$$s_{ij}(k+1) = s_{ij}(k) \pm \mu\ \ \alpha'(k)\ \ O_A(a_i)\ \ O_A(a_j) \qquad (22)$$

μ :ratio of the relevant documents on the irrelevant documents.

$\alpha'(k)$: decreasing gain function .

5 Conclusion

The Information retrieval system we have developed, is totaly based on the neural approach, that is we use many formulas well-known like the input, the activation and propagation rules. Hence, we obtained first results using these different functions. In comparison with the functions used in the classical information retrieval systems, the performances of the two sytems remain the same in the case of the query expansion and the learning.

However, the advantage in the use of this neural approach resides in the feasibility of the integration of the learning process. Moreover, we demonstrated in this paper the analogy between the gradient backpropagation algorithm used in our documentary base and the relevance feedback. Thus, we have used this algorithm in

order to resolve the problems of the automatic determination of the association weights (w_{ij}, s_{ij})and of the semantic weights (p_{ij}).
Very interesting results were obtained in our prototype concerning the cooccurrence and the author links, we have also noticed important improvements in the recall ratio. Actually, we carry out many experiences in order to fix the different parameters supervising the learning process like the learning gain functions. We are also measuring the effectiveness of the system for different values of γ and λ.

References

[1] V.RAGHAVAN , S.WONG,"*A Critical Analysis of Vector Space Model in Information Retrieval*", Jour. of the American Society for Information Science, 1986

[2] G. SALTON " *Automatic Text Processing: the Tranformation, Analysis and Retrieval of Information by Computer*", (Edition McGraw Hill 1989).

[3] J.J.ROCCHIO JR, "*Relevance FeedBack in Information Retrieval in the Smart System, Experiments in Automatic Document Processing*", in [2] pp 313-323.

[4] R.HECHT-NIELSEN, "*Neurocomputing*" (Edition Addison Wesley 1990).

[5] K. L. KWORK, "*Query Modification and Expansion in a Network with Adaptative Architecture*",Proceedings of the 14th ACM/SIGIR Conference on Research and Development in Information Retrieval, Chicago, USA, Octobre 1991.

[6] X.LIN, D.SOERGEL & G.MARCHIONINI "*A Self Organizing Map of Information Retrieval*" Proceedings of the 14th ACM/SIGIR Conference on Research and Development in Information Retrieval, Chicago, USA, Octobre 1991.

[7] S.K.M. WONG & Y.J.CAI, " *Computation of Term Association by a Neural Network*", ACM'Press SIGIR'93 (Pittsburg, USA 1993).

[8] D.RUMELHART, G.E.NINTON & R.WILLIAMS, "*Learning Internal Representation by Error Propagation* " MIT'Press 1986 (Vol 1).

[9] Y. LECUN, "*Modèles Connexionnistes pour l'Apprentissage*" PhD Thesis (Paris VI, France 1987).

[10] G.LALLICH "*Analyse du Français: Achèvement et Implantation de l'Analyseur Morpho-syntaxique*", Les cahiers du CRISS, (Grenoble 1990).

[11] G. SALTON & M.J McGILL, " *Introduction to Modern Information Retrieval*", (Edition McGraw Hill 1983).

[12] J.SPARCK, K.BARBER, " *What makes an Automatic Keyword Classification Effective?*" , Journal of the ASIS 1971.

[13] PEAT H.J, WILETT P. " *The Limitations of Term Co-occurrence data for Query Expansion in Documental Retrieval Systems*" Journal of the AIS, 1991

[14] R. LAYAIDA& A. CARON "*Un Modèle Connexionniste pour la Recherche Bibliographique*", Journées Volcan-IAA* Clermont-Ferrand 1993.

[15] D.HARMAN, "*Relevance feedback revisited in a Network with Adaptative Architecture*",Proceedings of the 15th ACM/SIGIR Conference on Research and Development in Information Retrieval, Copenhagen, Denmark, 1992

[16] W.B.CROFT & H.R TURTLE , "*Efficient Probabilistic Inference for Text Retrieval*" Proceedings RIAO'91 (Barcelona, Spain 1991),

[17] M.BOUGHANEM, " *Les Systèmes de Recherche d'Information: d'un Modèle Classique à un Modèle Connexionniste*", PhD Thesis, (Toulouse, France 1992).

[18] R. LAYAIDA, M. BOUGHANEM & A. CARON "*A Neural Network Model Documentary Base Self-Organising and Querying*", IEEE'Press ICCI'93 (Sudbury, Canada).

The *HS* File : A New Dynamic Signature File Method for Efficient Information Retrieval

Jae Soo Yoo[1], Yoon-Joon Lee[1], Jae Woo Chang[2] and Myoung Ho Kim[1]

[1] Dept. of Computer Science
Korea Advanced Institute of Science and Technology
373-1, Kusung-dong, Yusung-gu, Taejon, 305-701, Korea
[2] Dept. of Computer Engineering, Chonbuk National University Chonju,
Chonbuk 560-756, Korea

Abstract. Many works on the signature file methods have been made in the past, but they are mainly for static environments. However, many recent applications in practice require a dynamic information storage structure that effectively supports insertions, deletions and updates. Though there are a few signature file techiniques for dynamic environments, they suffer from serious performance degradation when query signature weights are light. In this paper, we propose a new dynamic signature file organization, called the hierarchical signature(*HS*) file, that solves the problem of light query signature weights. We perform simulation experiments by using wide range of parameter values. We show through performance comparison based on experiments that the *HS* file improves performance significantly in both the retrieval time and the storage overhead over the other dynamic signature file methods proposed earlier.

Keywords : information retrieval, signature file, performance evaluation, dynamic environment

1 Introduction

Information retrieval and management have been a major field of computing for a long time. This is evident from the rapid development and widespread use of database management systems, which are well suited for a variety of business applications. These applications typically deal with formatted data. However, there are many recent applications in which a large amount of data are unformatted, such as office information systems, geographical information systems, library systems, CAD/CAM systems and multimedia database systems[2]. An approach widely advocated for efficient retrieval of unformatted data is to use the signature file method, which has been shown to be effective for textual data processing[5].

The signature file is an abstraction of documents, which has been extensively studied as a storage structure for unformatted data such as texts or documents[5]. Since the size of the signature file is much smaller than that of a data file, the signature file can effectively work as a filter that immediately discards most non-qualifying documents for a given query. Although many extraction methods for creating the signature from a document have been proposed, most of the signature file methods typically use superimposed coding. Superimposed coding can result in a false match because a document signature can qualify a query signature, though the document itself does not satisfy the query. A signature extraction method that reduces the number of false matches is also important, but is not main concern of this paper.

Many works on the storage structure of the signature file have been made in the past, but they are mainly for static environments[7, 8, 1, 9]. Though there are certain applications having archival nature, i. e., insertions are less frequent and updates/deletions are seldom necessary, many applications in practice require a dynamic information storage structure[10].

There are a few signature file techniques for dynamic environments. The *S-tree* proposed in [3] groups similar document signatures in its terminal nodes and then builds a B-tree-like index structure on top of them. Since, however, the filtering capability of *S-tree* heavily depends on the query signature weight, which is the number of bits set to '1' in the query signature, its performance degradation is quite significant for light query signature weights[10]. It also has much space overhead. The *Quick Filter* proposed in [10] uses partitioning principles based on linear hashing, which tends to cluster the signatures having the same suffixes(or prefixes) in the same page. The *Quick Filter* has the advantage that the more the number of bits set to '1' is, the less the number of blocks accessed is. However, it has the same problem of serious performance degradation for light query signature weights as that in the *S-tree*.

In this paper, we propose a new dynamic signature file organization, called the hierarchical signature(*HS*) file. The proposed *HS* file overcomes the problem of light query signature weights. The *HS* file is a height balanced multiway tree that is a hierarchy of nodes containing signatures. It uses frame sliced approach[6] to leaf node construction to improve a filtering effect of the signature file. In order to verify the efficiency of the proposed *HS* file, we perform experiments for the *HS* file, *S-tree* and *Quick Filter*. The 10,000 and 100,000 documents with various types of parameters and queries are used. The results show that the *HS* file improves retrieval performance significantly over the *Quick Filter* and *S-tree*.

The remainder of this paper is organized as follows. In section 2, we presents a new dynamic signature file method and its characteristics. In section 3, we performs simulation experiments and shows that the proposed method achieves good performances over other dynamic signature file methods. Finally, conclusions are described in section 4.

2 The Hierarchical Signature(*HS*) File

In this section we describe a new dynamic signature file organization called the hierarchical signature(*HS*) file. It solves the problem of light query signature weights that is the major obstacle in the other methods proposed earlier. The *HS* file is also space-efficient.

The *HS* file is a height balanced multiway tree that is a hierarchy of nodes containing signatures. The *HS* file has two types of nodes, namely a leaf node and a nonleaf node. It uses frame sliced approach[6] to leaf node construction to improve a filtering effect of the signature file.

2.1 The Structure of the *HS* File

Frame-based Document Signature Construction Rule. A word-signature is a bit string of length k generated by a hash function that chooses, among k bit positions, m bit positions set to '1'. Then, each word-signature is divided into c substrings, each of which has the size $\frac{k}{c}$ that is equal to the frame size. These c substrings are allocated into c frames, among f frames, that are chosen by another hash function. The frame-signature is constructed by superimposing the parts of the word-signatures mapped into that frame. If some frames are not chosen by words in the document, all bits in those frame-signatures are set to '0'. Finally, the document-signature is a concatenation of all the frame-signatures.

For example, suppose that a document is represented by four words, say "Text", "Database", "Information" and "Retrieval". Fig.1 illustrates the construction of a document-signature when the length of document-signature is twelve and the number of frames is three. We assume that the number of bits which are set to '1' in a word-signature is two and the number of frames chosen by a hash function to construct a word-signature, c, is two.

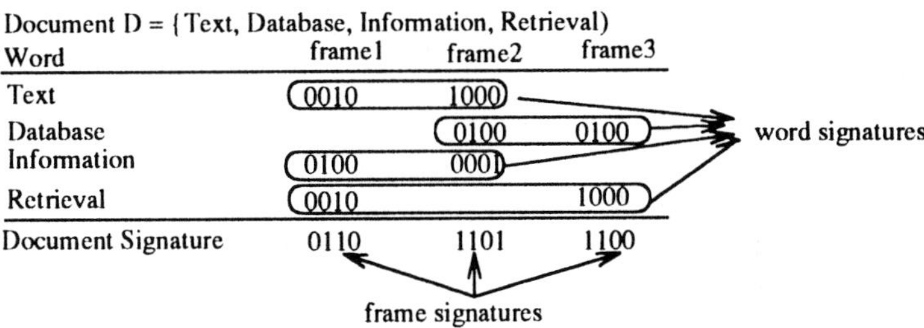

Fig. 1. Construction example of a document signature

Node Construction Rule. As mentioned before, the *HS* file has two types of nodes, namely a leaf node and a nonleaf node. A leaf node consists of as many blocks as the predetermined number of frames and one pointer block, while a nonleaf node consists of a single block. The index record in the nonleaf node, which consists of a signature and a pointer, is used to branch to the subtree that potentially contain the document satisfying the given query signature. The index record in the leaf node, which consists of f frame-signatures and a pointer, points to the real document. Node configurations of the leaf nodes and nonleaf nodes are defined as follows:

- The leaf node $\{F_1, F_2, ..., F_f, P\}$ is a set of f frame blocks and a pointer block such that
  - $F_i :< fs_{i1}, fs_{i2}, ..., fs_{ik} >$, where fs_{ik} is the k-th frame-signature in the i-th frame.
  - $P :< p_1, p_2, ..., p_k >$, where p_k is the pointer to a real document.
  - A signature $< fs_{1j}, fs_{2j}, ..., fs_{fj} >$ with a pointer p_j constitutes an index record in the leaf node.
- The nonleaf node $\{S_1, S_2, ..., S_j\}$ is a set of index records, where S_j consists of a signature and a pointer. The signature in S_j is a concatenation of f frame-signatures, each of which is constructed by superimposing all the corresponding frame-signatures in the son node of S_j and the pointer in S_j points to its son node.

Fig.2 shows an example of the *HS* file, where the number of frames is two and the size of the frame-signature is four bits. In this example, document-signatures consist of two frame-signatures and are stored into the leaf node in such a way that each frame-signature is allocated into the corresponding frame. As shown in Fig.2, the leaf node is composed of two frame blocks and one pointer block. The pointers in the pointer block point to the real documents corresponding to document-signatures. A nonleaf node includes two index records, each of which consists of a signature and a pointer. The signatures in the nonleaf node are constructed by superimposing all the signatures in the son node. For example, the signature $< 0111, 1110 >$ in N6 comes from superimposing all the signatures in N4. The signature $< 1110, 0011 >$ in N5 comes from superimposing all the signatures in the frames F_{31} and F_{32} of N3.

Now we define the *HS* file of type (b_1, b_2, f) with the following properties, where b_1 and b_2 are the blocking factors of a leaf node and a nonleaf node respectively, and f is the number of frames in the leaf node:

1. Each path from the root to any leaf node has the same length.
2. A leaf node consists of f blocks and one pointer block. Each leaf node has at most b_1 document signatures that are stored into f frames, and b_1 pointers to the corresponding documents.
3. A nonleaf node is composed of only one block. Each nonleaf node has at most b_2 sons and signatures.
4. The signatures in the nonleaf nodes are constructed by superimposing the signatures contained in their son node.

According to this definition, the *HS* file of Fig.2 is of type (8,2,2).

2.2 Operations on the *HS* File

Retrieval. To demonstrate the retrieval process in the *HS* file, we consider a light weight query signature S(Q) $= < 1000, 0000 >$ for the *HS* file in Fig.2. The

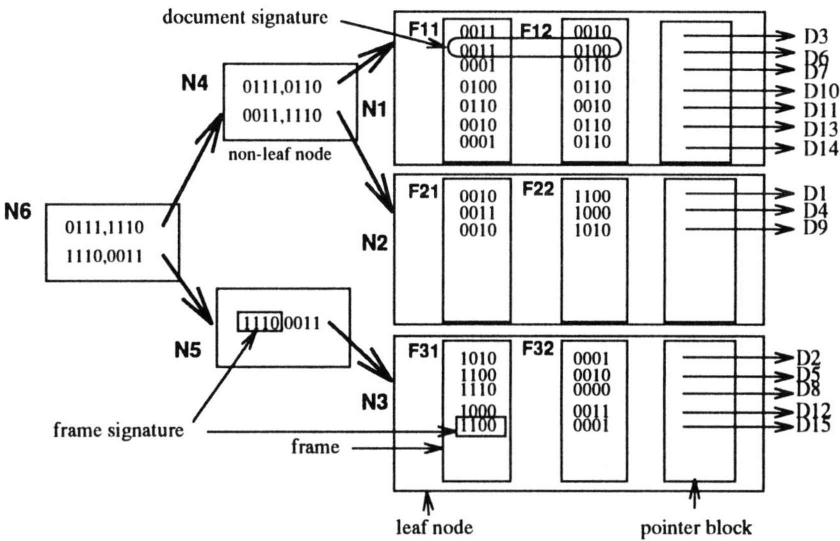

Fig. 2. Example of The *HS* file

second signature of the root node leads us to node N5, since the first bit position of its first frame signature contains '1'. Since the signature in N5 satisfies the query signature, the leaf node N3 is accessed.

If we arrive at the leaf node, in order to determine the access order of frames we first divide the query signature into the number of frames, f, with the same size as the frame-signature. After obtaining the f query frame-signatures, we access the corresponding frames in such a order that the weight of the query frame-signatures are high. Therefore, the first frame F_{31} in N3 is accessed first since the first query frame-signature $< 1000 >$ has more '1's than the second one.

The reason is that if we first access the frame corresponding to the heaviest query frame-signature, the filtering effect is greatly improved. If a frame has only one frame-signature that satisfy the query frame-signature, we can avoid accessing the remaining frames. As a result, the number of block accesses is reduced. We need not access the second frame in node N3 since the second frame-signature of S(Q) does not contain '1' at all. This is because the query frame-signature does not filter non-qualifying documents.

Maintenance of the *HS* File. To insert the first document signature, the *HS* file first creates a root node with a single block and a leaf node. The leaf node consists of as many blocks as the number of frames and one pointer block. The document signature is stored into the leaf node in such a way that each frame signature is allocated into the corresponding frame. Finally, the entry (fs_1, fs_2,

..., fs_f, ptr) is inserted into the root node. Here the frame signature fs_f is obtained by superimposing f-th frame signatures in the leaf node and ptr points to the leaf node.

When inserting new document signatures, we first find an appropriate leaf node to store the document signatures. For example, when we insert the document signature S16=$< 0100, 1010 >$ of document D16 into the *HS* file of Fig.2, we access root node N6 and compare the first bit of first frame-signature of S16 with those of first frame-signatures in N6. Since the first signature $< 0111, 1110 >$ is qualified, we access its son node N4. We again compare the first bit of the first frame-signature of S16 with those of first frame-signatures in N4. Because the first bits of two signatures in N4 satisfy the first bit of the first frame-signature of S16, we compare the first bit of the second frame-signature of S16 with those of second frame-signatures in N4 and find the matched second signature $< 0011, 1110 >$. As a result, the first frame-signature $< 0100 >$ and second frame-signature $< 1010 >$ of S16 are inserted into F_{21} and F_{22} in the leaf node N2 respectively and the pointer to the document D16 is inserted into the pointer block. The signature $< 0011, 1110 >$ of N4 is changed into $< 0111, 1110 >$ by superimposing S16 to itself. We repeat this process until the root node is reached. If an overflow occurs, it is solved by splitting algorithm. We call it frame bitwise bipartition strategy.

Fig.3 illustrates on the domain space how the overflow is solved in the leaf node, when we construct the *HS* file of Fig.2. In the *HS* file, the number of frames determines the dimension on the domain space and one leaf node corresponds to one region of the domain space. In this example, since the number of frames is two, we consider two dimensional domain space, where x-axis and y-axis represent first frame and second one respectively. Since the blocking factor of the leaf node is eight, the overflow occurs when inserting ninth document-signature.

In order to solve the overflow, the *HS* file first bipartitions the domain space based on x-axis and obtains Fig.3(b). As shown in Fig.3(b), the left region contains the document-signatures that the first bit of frame signatures in the first frame is '0' and the right region includes the document signatures that the first bit of frame signatures in the first frame is '1'. We call this splitting strategy frame bitwise bipartition one. Fig.3(c) shows the situation that twelve documents have been inserted without overflow since nine document signatures were stored. The overflow occurs again when D13 is inserted into the left region that already contains eight document signatures. We split the left region based on y-axis to overcome the overflow and then get Fig.3(d). Finally, after inserting fifteen documents, we can obtain Fig.3(e) that shows the situation of leaf node level in Fig.3. The overflow in the nonleaf node is also processed by the frame bitwise bipartition strategy.

2.3 Advantages of the *HS* File

The *HS* file reduces the number of block accesses for a document retrieval through the unique signature extraction method and retrieval process described

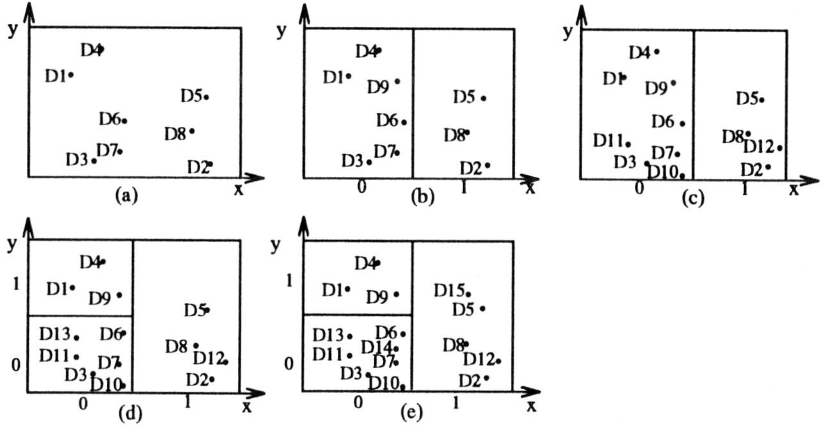

Fig. 3. Leaf node construction on the domain space

in 3.1.1 and 3.2.1. That is, when the *HS* file processes light weight query signatures that significantly degrade the performance of the *S-tree* and the *Quick Filter*, it accesses only a few blocks by the unique signature extraction method and retrieval process over them. For example, if the number of frames chosen by a word in extreme case is one, in the leaf node level only one random disk access is required for a single word query and thus at most n frames are scanned for n word queries. Since light weight query signatures also have many query frame-signatures with all bits set to '0', we need not access the corresponding frame blocks in the leaf nodes.

When the leaf node is constructed based on the node construction rule , the *HS* file can reduce the number of splits and save the storage space. This is because the leaf node of the *HS* file includes much more document signatures than the leaf node of the *S-tree* and the page of the *Quick Filter*. We can see through operations on the *HS* file that the *HS* file is relevant to applications which require a dynamic information storage structure.

3 Performance Evaluation

In this section, to estimate the performance of dynamic signature file methods, we actually implement them and perform simulation experiments. Table 1 shows the notations and descriptions of the input and design parameters used for performance evaluation. The values of each input and design parameter are presented in Table 2. The simulation experiments are performed for various sizes of databases and various performance parameters. We use 100 sample queries to evaluate the characteristics of the *HS* file and the performances of the dynamic signature file methods. To save the space, we discuss the performance comparison of the dynamic signature file methods only when 100,000 documents with various numbers of frames and with various types of queries are used and the page size is 1 kbytes. This is because experimental results of remaining cases are very similar to those of this case.

Parameters	Description
N	Total number of documents
P	Size of disk page(block) in bits
D	Number of words per one document
Q	Query signature
s	Document signature size in bits
k	Average document signature weight
f	Number of frames in the *HS* file
m	Number of bits set to '1' by one word
w	Number of words in the query
t	Size of pointer in bytes
l	Hashing level of *Quick Filter*
b_1	Blocking factor of a leaf node in the *HS* file
b_2	Blocking factor of a non-leaf node in the *HS* file, a node in the S-tree and a page in the query signature
W(Q)	Query weight, i.e., the number of ones in the query signature

Table 1. Input/Design Parameters

First, we investigate whether frame-based document signature construction affects the retrieval performance or not. When the number of frames chosen for word signature is sixteen, we found that the retrieval performance of frame-based document signature construction is about 20% better than conventional document signature extraction method. Second, we investigate the retrieval performance of the *HS* file according to the number of frames in the leaf node when the number of documents is 100,000. We can see through the experiments that the more the number of frames is, the better the retrieval performance is. In this environment, the maximum number of frames that the leaf node of the *HS* file can have is sixteen since it depends on the size of document signature and the size of pointer. As a result, the retrieval performance of the *HS* file using sixteen frames is about 3.3 times better than that of the *HS* file using two frames.

Fig.4 shows an experimental result on retrieval when the number of documents is 100,000 and the number of frames in the leaf node of the *HS* file is 16. It is shown that the *HS* file is much more efficient than the other dynamic signature file methods independently of the number of words in the query. From the experimental result, we showed that the *HS* file achieved about 180 ~ 360% and about 200 ~ 400% performance gains on retrieval over *Quick Filter* and *S-tree* on the average. This is because the *HS* file uses frame-based signature extraction method and an unique retrieval process.

When the number of documents is 100,000 and the number of frames is 16,

(NA:Not Applicable)

Methods / Parameters	HS File	Quick Filter	S-tree
N	10,000 100,000	10,000 100,000	10,000 100,000
P	1 Kbytes 2 Kbytes	1 Kbytes 2 Kbytes	1 Kbytes 2 Kbytes
D	20	20	20
f	2, 4, 8, 16	NA	NA
m	16	16	16
w	2 ~ 10	2 ~ 10	2 ~ 10
t	4	4	4
s	512 bits	512 bits	512 bits
k	240 bits	240 bits	240 bits
b1	256	NA	NA
b2	16	16	16
W(Q)	32-160	32-160	32-160

Table 2. The values for parameters

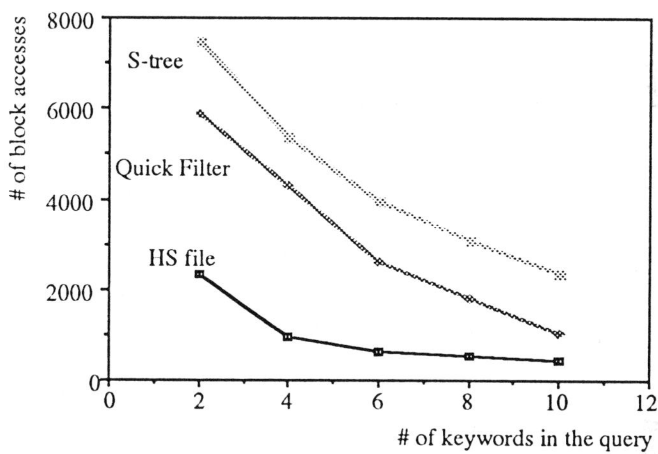

Fig. 4. Retrieval performance of dynamic signature file methods

the storage overheads of the *HS* file, *Quick Filter*, and *S-tree* are about 9.8%, 10.3% and 21.2% respectively. As a result, the storage overhead of the *HS* file is much less than that of *S-tree*, while it is similar to that of *Quick Filter*. We also found that the *Quick Filter* achieves the best insertion performance, while *HS* file is the worst. The reason is that the *Quick Filter* is constructed based on the linear hashing and *HS* file uses the frame-sliced approach to the leaf node. However, the difference of insertion performance among them is not important since it is much smaller than the difference of retrieval performance, and insertion operation occurs much less frequently than retrieval operation in the field of information retrieval.

4 Conclusions

We have proposed a new dynamic signature file method for efficient information retrieval, called the *HS* file. The *HS* file is a height balanced multiway tree that is a hierarchy of nodes containing signatures. It uses frame sliced approach to leaf node construction to improve a filtering effect of the signature file. To solve the overflow of nodes, the *HS* file utilizes a special splitting algorithm, called the frame bitwise bipartition strategy. The *HS* file has solved problems of light query signature weights that were major obstacles in the other methods proposed earlier.

We have compared the performance of the *HS* file with the *Quick Filter* and the *S-tree* in terms of retrieval time, storage overhead and insertion time. For this, we have carried out extensive performance experiments with wide range of parameter values and evaluated the space-time performance of these methods. Through the experiments, we have shown that the *HS* file has improved performance significantly in both the retrieval time and the storage overhead over the methods proposed earlier.

References

1. J. W. Chang, J. H. Lee and Y. J. Lee, "Multikey Access Methods Based on Term Discrimination and Signature Clustering," *ACM SIGIR*, 1989, pp. 176-185.
2. S. Christodoulakis and C. Faloutsos, "Design Considerations for a Message File Server," *IEEE Trans. on Soft. Eng.*, Vol. SE-10, No. 2, Mar. 1984, pp. 201-210.
3. U. Deppisch, "S-tree: A Dynamic Balanced Signature Index for Office Retrieval," *ACM SIGIR*, 1986, pp. 77-87.
4. C. Faloutsos and S. Christodoulakis, "Description and Performance File Method for Office Filing," *ACM TOIS*, Vol. 5, No. 3, 1987, pp. 237-257.
5. C. Faloutsos, "Signature-based Text Retrieval Methods : A Survey," *IEEE Computer Society Technical Committee on Data Engineering*, Vol. 13, No. 1, Mar. 1990, pp. 25-32.
6. Z. Lin and C. Faloutsos, "Frame-Sliced Signature Files," *IEEE Trans. on Knowledge and Data Engineering*, Vol. 4, No. 3, Jun. 1992, pp. 281-289.
7. C. S. Roberts, "Partial Match Retrieval via the Method of the Superimposed Codes," *Proc. IEEE 67*, Dec. 1979, pp. 1624-1642.
8. R. Sacks-Davis and K. Ramamohanarao, "Multikey Access Methods based on Superimposed Coding Techniques," *ACM TODS*, Vol. 12, No. 4, Dec. 1987, pp. 655-696.
9. J. S. Yoo, J. W. Chang, Y-J Lee and M. H. Kim, "Performance Evaluation of Signature-Based Access Mechanisms for Efficient Information Retrieval," *IEICE Trans. on Information and Systems*, Vol. E76-D, No. 2, Feb. 1993, pp. 179-183.
10. P. Zezula, F. Rabitti and P. Tiberio, "Dynamic Partitioning of Signature Files," *ACM TOIS*, Vol. 9, No. 4, Oct. 1991, pp. 336-369.

A Multi-Agent Architecture for an Evolving Expert System Module

Sophie Billet-Coat
Danièle Hérin-Aime

LIRMM,UMR 9928 CNRS-Montpellier II
161, rue ADA
34395 Montpellier Cedex 5 France
tel: 67 41 85 83 / fax: 67 41 85 00
e-mail: billet@lirmm.fr / dh@lirmm.fr

Abstract. This paper presents the multi-agent architecture of the expert system module included in the acquisition system *Amon-Re* dedicated to an application in egyptology. The main point of our approach is that this architecture has to support the evolution of the module. Indeed, the architecture is built so that the whole agent society configuration doesn't have to change when the module is evolving. Therefore, the architecture is based on data structuring and fits a natural decomposition of domain objects. Another characteristic of our architecture is dynamism. Dynamic aspect appears through the variation of the number of agents during the solving process. The agents are responsible for the part of the solving process they are in charge of. In order to get the best result as possible, they exchange their views and constraints, are able to negotiate and self-evaluate.

1 Introduction

Evolving knowledge is difficult to handle in an expert system. A multi-agent architecture provides the knowledge engineer with a simplified management of the knowledge, in the modelling process as well as in the processing of the knowledge evolution itself. Indeed, it provides a modular framework that makes easier knowledge representation and consistency maintenance process. Moreover, since multi-agent programming is a quite new paradigm, very few works focus on evolution. The originality of our work is that it takes advantage of a multi-agent architecture to handle task evolution. The specification of a multi-agent architecture is quite difficult to undertake when the problem is not naturally distributed [DEC93]. So we try in this paper to show that there is a way to design a multi-agent architecture particularly suitable for an evolving expert system.

Our claim is that an architecture based on *data* structuring is more suitable for an evolving module than an architecture based upon *task* structuring, as in CARAMEL [SAB90] or TALISMAN [STE92]. In this last case indeed, the structure of agent society has to be re-shaped if tasks are modified. This won't be the case if the society is based on data structuring. In our architecture, the structure of the society is based on data structuring, with planning distributed over the agents: each data structure has a goal, tasks to perform this goal, and integrated planning.

An important feature of multi-agent systems is to be dynamic, i.e. new agents are created during the solving process. In our application, dynamic aspect appears with variation of complexity during the solving process.

The presented expert system module corresponds to the problem solving module of the knowledge acquisition system *Amon-Re*, still under development in the actor-like language ACTALK [BRI89]. The main characteristics of the acquisition methodology are direct interaction with the expert with an interaction-based acquisition and so incremental acquisition [BIL94b]. The interaction reproduces a *human apprenticeship by doing*, i.e. in a problem solving situation. In this situation, the teacher is the human expert, and the student the acquisition system [BIL94a]. Mainly, the acquisition is driven by the interaction, unlike in KADS methodology where acquisition is guided by the knowledge models [WIE92]. Thus, the problem solving module integrated in such an acquisition system needs to be able to evaluate results, explain results - i.e. justifications which permit the teacher to control student knowledge - and support evolution.

In this paper, we propose an overview of the multi-agent architecture of the problem solving module of the system *Amon-Re* on which these abilities will be added. We emphase here that there is a way to handle the organization of a multi-agent architecture which is suitable for supporting these abilities. The architecture of the module is presented through an original application domain: the transliteration of Egyptians hieroglyphic texts.

In the first part of the paper, we briefly present the application domain. Then, we describe the multi-agent architecture of the problem solving module based on data structuring. A simple example is then presented to sum up the solving process. We conclude with some pragmatic considerations about this architecture and introduce new perspectives.

2 Presentation of the application domain

The ancient Egyptian writing consists in sequences of figurative signs, without any caesura between words. The signs may have three functions to characterize a word: phonograms describe a sound; determinatives represent or precise an idea; ideograms describe the whole word and so correspond to a word with its corresponding sound.

This kind of writing had been elaborated little by little at the end of the fourth millennium B.C. First ideograms appeared, since the simplest way of writing was to draw what had to be meant. But very soon, it became important to render such things as feeling, abstractions, etc. There was no way to represent these with just one sign. As ideograms were pronounced, they could as well become phonograms in a system where the sign was to be read and not understood. The signs could be arranged in group to render complicated sounds and complete words. Nevertheless, egyptians didn't solve all problems with phonograms and ideograms: there were quite a lot of homophonic words. So they chose to add one or two signs at the end of the word to classify the sound in a class of meaning. For instance, the name of a man is followed by a sign showing a little man, the words meaning an action of strength is followed by the sign of the striking arm... But these signs must not be pronounced as they just express a kind of semantics. Finally, they also used what we call phonetic complements to help the reading of a complicated sign. They are just phonograms which must not be pronounced. Phonetic complement were also used to organize the writing so that it appears well balanced.

It is understandable now that a same sign can represent in different words, either a phonogram, either an ideogram, either a determinative. This way of writing implies a very flexible vocabulary. The grammar is quite strict but contains a great lot of exceptions.

Transliteration is a necessary step during the translation process. It acts as literal translation where words are separated and grammatical marks are visible. Transliteration is the transposition of the text into our alphabetic letters. Transliteration needs to identify all words and grammatical marks, so the interpretation of each sign has to be identified too.

The methodology of text analysis *doesn't use a linguistic approach* like most part of natural language processing system.

So, the transliteration process doesn't use a dictionary to store the words and their different writings. It is based on two main points noticed from experts interviews : the use of *contextual knowledge* and a *simplified theory*. Context may have a lot of meanings [BRE93]. We mean here a set of descriptors of the text and the document it is attached to. The context is used in the evaluation of the results. Some of the descriptors can be noticed by the user and transmitted together with the text to the solving process. For instance, the iconography is described with signs that we will probably find in the text as ideograms or determinatives. Other descriptors result from the solving process. This is the case for instance of tense descriptor: if we have found this tense once, it will probably be found further in the text. Simplified theory means that we won't try to acquire encyclopaedic grammatical rules, but simple rules based on empirical experience. Experts noticed that sentences are bipartites. So couples of words are gathered into a clause. A clause may contain a couple of clauses, or a mixed couple of a word and a clause, thus having a recursive definition.

In the next section, we present the specification of the multi-agent problem solving module that corresponds to a compound society devoted to transliteration process. The structure of the compound society is based on the natural structure of hieroglyphic texts.

3 Description of the architecture of the solving process

The architecture is based upon data structuring. First, data are broken up into *structural units*. In our application, data are hieroglyphic texts. A text is a set of hieroglyphics *signs*, making up *words* and then making up *clauses*. The solving process consists in identifying the signs, words and clauses forming the text. Besides this decomposition, the text has to be split into intermediate *working units*: *sign groups* and *windows*. Sign groups constitute a contextual information which will be taken in account when making up words. Windows are created in order to decompose the problem into subproblems: windows are just small independent parts of the text. The decomposition of the data into structural and working units is shown on fig.1. Basing the solving process upon these units means that the task structure is organized according to these units and not the other way round. The general working principle is that the problem is transmitted to the lowest level unit *via* the working units, and goes up through the structural units. Each structural or working unit is represented by a society with a non-fixed number of agents. We consider here a society as a net of autonomous agents [BER92], and autonomous agents as defined in [DEM90]. Each society has the same structure, and so do the agents making up these societies. First, we present what is common to all the societies, then we describe their role and study their working.

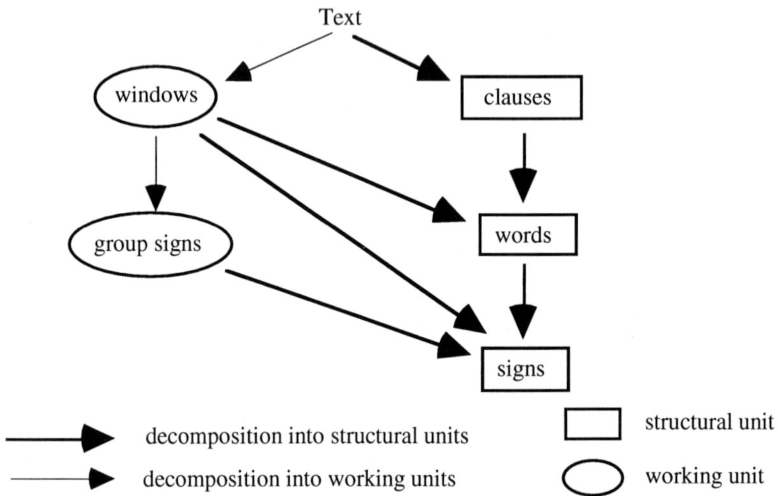

fig. 1 data decomposition into structural and working units

A society S is made of :
- a coordinator agent (C) which manages its society
- basic agents (A) which perform the solving. Basic agents need to communicate with agents from another society in order to transmit the problem and get necessary informations. The general structure of a society is shown on fig.1.

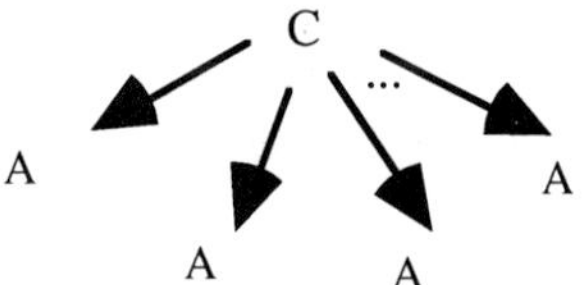

fig.1 structure of a society

The function of the coordinator agents (C) is to create and manage the work of the basic agents of their society. Coordinator agents store domain knowledge [COU93] when a solving is not in process. When a solving is about to be performed, they become active and create the basic agents.

Basic agents (A) are in charge of the solving process of a particular problem corresponding to their society. Their knowledge is transmitted by their coordinator agent. Basic agents stay alive until the result is correct and justified. Indeed, building the explanation needs all the basic agents. For instance, basic agents whose part of result is not accepted are used to build a negative explanation. So, if the result is not correct, other basic agents have to be investigated any further.

In the next part, we describe the different societies of the problem solving module corresponding to each unit of the data structure. Each society is described according to the following steps:
- aim of the society
- description and work of the agents of the society

The organization of the society represented on fig.1 is always the same. Only the sign society has a more complex organization which will be described.

3.1 TEXT Society

Aims: - triggering the solving process
- making the communication between problem solving module and other modules of the system

Description and Work of the agents: First the coordinator agent (Ct) receives a problem to solve with its associate context - i.e. a hieroglyphic text to transliterate and some description of it. (Ct) creates a basic agent (At) and distributes part of context to the coordinator agent of the appropiate society. (At) sends the text to the coordinator agent of the window society (Cwi). When the processing is completed, (At) assembles the results and transmits it outside the problem solving module. The basic agents (At) never die, since they constitute the set of solved problems which is used by the learning module [BIL94b].

3.2 WINDOW Society

Aim: - splitting the text into independent working units, the windows
- triggering the solving process of each window

Description and Work of the agents: the coordinator agent (Cwi) splits the text into independent working units, the *windows*. It creates one basic agent (Awi) per window and gives it its part of context. Each basic agents (Awi) transmits its portion of the problem simultaneously to the group sign society, in order to detect group signs inside the window, and to the sign society.

3.3 GROUP SIGNS society

Aim: - detecting groups of complex signs, either new or already stored in memory

Description and work of the agents: the coordinator agent (Cgs) receives from all (Awi) the windows of the text. Depending on the free memory, it groups some windows and creates a basic agent (Ags) for each group. (Ags)s have to detect groups of signs. Each group detected is sent to (Cgs) and then directly to the Sign society as a kind of context.

3.4 SIGNS Society

Aim: - determining the interpretation of the signs forming the text.

Organization: This society is more complex than the others. It is organized in a hierarchic way, according an object-oriented model with multiple inheritance. This view agrees with [SHO93] who sees Agent-oriented programming as a specialization of object-oriented programming. The hierarchy is made according to the classification of the signs. Each class has a coordinator agent which stores the knowledge corresponding to its class. But basic agents (As) are found only as leaves inside the tree: only leaf classes are able to create basic agents. So, basic agents (As) are linked to instances of signs and not instances of a class of signs. The root of the hierarchy is an abstract coordinator agent named (CS) and the coordinator agents of the leaf classes are named (Cs).

Description and work of the agents: The root coordinator agent (CS) orders the coordinator agent (Cs) of each sign of the text the creation of one basic agent (As) per sign of the text. Basic agents try to identify themselves according to the context and their localization in the text. Then, they send their first result to (Cwo). When several interpretations are possible, they are all sent to (Cwo), ordered by an evaluation reflecting the probability of each one. Later, (Cwo) may also give them some more contextual information and they have to compute again their interpretations with this new information.

3.5 WORD Society

Aim: - creating words and evaluating them

Description and work of the agents: The coordinator agent (Cwo) receives from all (As) of the text one or several interpretations. Using this information and the context, it tries to assemble the signs and make up words. Then, it creates one basic agent word (Awo) per word found and gives it its own specification. Then, each (Awo) tries to extend itself by finding out lexical or grammatical extensions. To do this, it asks (Cwo) for corresponding signs. During this process ambiguity may appear, so (Awo) eventually duplicates itself and each one has its own extension. The grammatical extension helps (Awo) to find its grammatical function. Then (Awo) can evaluate itself, using the context and the evaluation of the signs interpretation. For instance, if tense context is preterit, the words having the corresponding grammatical extension will get points for the evaluation. In the case of (Awo)s sharing signs, the evaluation is computed after they have negociated. After this negociation, some (Awo)s may disappear. At the end, each (Awo) sends their word and associated evaluation to the clause society. In some cases, the clause society asks (Cwo) for a particular grammatical word. Thus, (Cwo) may create words which wouldn't be created at the first step.

3.6 CLAUSE Society

Aim: - gathering words inside bipartite clauses
- participating to words evaluation

Description and work of the agents: The coordinator agent (Cc) receives words from the (Awo)s. (Cc) knows the gathering principle of words according to their grammatical function. The integration of a word in a clause can be made in two ways: either it constitutes the first element of a clause which is so just created by (Cc); either it is absorbed by an existing basic agent (Ac) which already contains at least one word. When an (Ac) is able to make some prediction about the grammatical function of the next word, it asks directly (Cwo) for it. If this word can be created, (Cwo) does it. Eventually, (Cwo) has to ask the sign society for re-interpreration of some signs. The resulting word is directly sent back to the (Ac) by the corresponding (Awo). When clauses are completed, (Cc) tries to assemble the clauses. The final result is sent to (At). (Cc) and (Ac) take into account the evaluation of the words to compute their own one. At the end, several solutions can be transmitted to the user.

4 Application Example

Here is the portion of text of a Window basic agent (Awi):

(Awi) passes on the problem and its associated context to (CS) then transmitted to each (Cs) corresponding to the signs of the text:
- average number of signs per cadrat : 2.3
- number of cadrat : 3

(Cs) creates a basic agent (As). Each one has the following knowledge:
- Domain knowledge (coming from the hierarchy of the sign society): different interpretations of the sign; spatial shape of the sign.
- Problem knowledge: position of the sign inside the window and the cadrat; context;
- Accointances: previous and next (As) in the text; coordinator agent of the word society (Cwo)

Here is the first (As) corresponding to the exemple:

(As1)

- Domain knowledge:	ideogram -> phonetic value: *irt* phoneme -> phonetic value: *ir* shape horizontal
- Problem knowledge:	1st sign inside the window and the cadrat; 2nd signs in the cadrat
- Accointances:	next sign (As2); (Cwo)

Each (Asi) computes its interpretation and tells it to (Cwo):

(As1): phoneme ***ir*** (As3): phoneme ***n*** (As5): phoneme ***r***

(As2): phoneme ***r*** (As4): phoneme ***f*** (As6): phoneme ***n***

(As7): phoneme **f**

Here, (Cwo) is just able to create one basic agent (Awo) because the text just contains one complex phoneme (As1)

(Awo1) -> ***ir*** (As1)

(Cwo) has the following knowledge:
- Domain knowledge: method of writing words, dictionary of grammatical words
- Problem knowledge: grammatical, iconographic and semantic context; interpretations of the different signs received from the sign society
- Accointances: the (As)s with which it is in charge to create words; the coordinator agent of the clause society (Cc).

(Awo) has the following knowledge:
- Domain knowledge: how to find lexical and grammatical extensions; how to characterize the grammatical function; how to evaluate itself
- Problem knowledge: spatial context (for instance average number of signs per cadrat), grammatical context (tense...); position of the first and last sign in the text
- Accointances: (Cwo); (Awo)s with which it shares signs for negociation;

In the exemple, (Awo1) extends itself with:
- lexical extension: (As2) as a phonetic complement
- two grammatical extensions: ***.[n]*** (As3) and ***.[f]*** (As4)

So (Awo1) becomes: ***ir.[n].[f]*** (As1 to As4)

Now, (Awo1) can predict its grammatical value is a verb because of its position in the text and its possible extensions.

This result is sent to the coordinator agent of the clause society (Cc). (Cc) has the following knowledge:
- Domain knowledge: grammatical conditions for creating a clause (first grammatical function of a word in a clause); method of assembling clauses
- Problem knowledge: grammatical context
- Accointances: (Ac)s it has created; (At)

(Ac) has the following knowledge:
- Domain knowledge: order of the words in a clause
- Problem knowledge: grammatical context
- Accointances: (Cwo) (in order to ask it a word with particular function)

In the exemple, (Cc) creates two new clauses and their corresponding agent (Ac1) and (Ac2):
- (Ac1) with the root of (Awo1): ***ir*** (As1 + As2)
- (Ac2) with the whole (Awo1): ***ir.[n].[f]*** (As1 to As4)

(Ac1) asks (Cwo) for a preposition beginning at (As3) because it often follows a verb while (Ac2) asks (Cwo) for the same word beginning at (As5).

(Cwo) creates the new word (Awo2): ***n*** (As3)

(Awo2) tries to extend itself. One grammatical extension is found: ***.[f]*** (As4)

So, (Awo2) becomes: ***n.[f]*** (As3 + As4)

This result is sent back directly to (Ac1) which becomes: ***ir n.[f]*** (As1 to As4).

Then, (Ac1) ask (Cwo) for any word beginning at (As5) (like (Ac2) as we may notice)

(Cwo) answer to (Ac2) that there is no preposition beginning at (As5). So (Ac2) asks to (Cwo) for any word beginning at (As5).

Then, (Cwo) tries to create words beginning at (As5). It creates two words:

(Awo3): ***rn*** (As5 + As6)

(Awo4): ***rnf*** (As5 to As7).

(Awo3) and (Awo4) have to negociate because they share the signs (As5) and (As6). Only (Awo3) stays alive because it has found a grammatical extension ***.[f]*** while (Awo2) didn't find any lexical or grammatical extension.

(Awo3) sends to (Cc) the word ***rn.[f]*** which can be integrated in (Ac1) as well as in (Ac2).

As (Ac1) and (Ac2) share words, they have to negociate themselves, but their evaluation is equal. So, the two final results are sent to (At):

ir.n.f rn.f

and ***ir n.f rn.f***

5 Conclusion and perspectives

In this paper, we presented the multi-agent architecture of the problem solving module included in the acquisition system *Amon-Re*. We saw how is built an architecture based upon data structuring. Such an architecture is more suitable to knowledge evolution than an architecture based on task structuring because the whole society doesn't have to be re-shaped when the solving process is evolving. Indeed, the knowledge revision process only affect the method of building the solution of each structure independently. When the task structure is built independently from the natural data structure, one cannot be sure it is definitively correct.

This architecture mainly relies on six components viewed as societies which perform the processing. Each society is made of coordinator agents and basic agents. Each society participates to a particular processing according to the kind of structure it represents. To find out a correct result, these societies have to communicate their constraints and build the result by holding constraints of others. Though the problem is naturally sequential, parts of the process can be run simultaneously, as the solving of independent parts of the problem and the development of different solutions

One may question about a too important number of agents, since it is non-planned. If this situation occurs, it can be handled by reducing the size of the sub-problems which are processed independently without needing external communications outside the expert system module. In order to minimize the number of agents simultaneously alive, the results have to be exported more frequently. So the agents retained only for explanation or for result revision can die as soon as the part of the text there are concerned by is processed.

The revision process is over the subject of this paper. Knowledge revision process occurs when the user desagrees with the system. It begins with a dialogue including justifications from the system and critique from the user [BIL94b]. The justification process is managed by an outer society which communicates with all agents of the problem solving module. The revision process is also managed by an outer society which has to check the consistency of the knowledge before modifying the domain knowledge of an agent. We are currently working on the justification process which is necessary to the diagnostic of erroneous knowledge, carried out in a solution computed by the system, before the knowledge revision module manages its updating.

Bibliography

[BER92]Berthet S., Demazeau Y., Boissier O., Knowing each other better, in Proc. of the 11th International workshop on Decentralized AI, Glen Arbor MI, Feb. 92

[BIL94a] Billet-Coat S., Processus interactif d'acquisition de connaissances basé sur un apprentissage humain, Actes du 9° congrès Reconnaissance des formes et Intelligence Artificielle, Jan.94

[BIL94b] Billet-Coat S., Interaction between a human teacher and an artificial learner, Proc. of the 3rd International Conference "Interface to real & virtual worlds", Feb. 94

[BRE93] Brezillon P., Proc. of the IJCAI-93 Workshop on "Using Knowledge in its Context", LAFORIA 93/13, April 93

[BRI89] Briot J.P., ACTALK: a testbed for classifying and designing actor languages in the Smalltalk-80 environment, Proc. ECOOP'89

[COU93] Courdier R., Hérin-Aime D., Galéra R., An Object and Semantic Networks based Design Model and Methodology, Techniques et Sciences Informatiques vol.12 n°3, 1993

[DEC93] Decker K., Lesser V., An approach to analyzingthe Need for Meta-Level Communication. Proc. of IJCAI'93 (vol.1), Chambery (France) 1993

[DEM90] Demazeau Y., J.P. Müller, Decentralized Artificial Intelligence, in Decentralized AI, Demazeau & Müller eds, North Holland / Elsevier, 1990

[DEM91] Demazeau Y., J.P. Müller, From reactive to intentional agents, in Decentralized AI, Demazeau & Müller eds, North Holland / Elsevier, 1991

[SAB90] Sabah G., CARAMEL: A Computational Model of Natural Language Understanding using Parallel Implementation. Proc. of ECAI'90, Stockholm Aug. 90

[STE92] Stefanini M.H., TALISMAN: un système de traitement de la langue fondée sur une approche multi-agents. Research Report, CRISS, France Feb. 92

[SHO93] Shoham Y., Agent-Oriented Programming. Artificial Intelligence 60, 1993

[WIE92] Wielinga B.J., Schreiber A.T., Breuker J.A., KADS : a modelling approach to knowledge engineering, Knowledge Acquisition 4(1)

Improving Integrity Constraint Checking for Stratified Deductive Databases

Sin Yeung LEE & Tok Wang LING
Department of Information Systems and Computer Science
National University of Singapore
Lower Kent Ridge, Singapore 0511, Singapore.
email : jlee@iscs.nus.sg, lingtw@iscs.nus.sg

Abstract Integrity checking for stratifiable deductive databases has been studied by many authors. In order to handle recursive relations, most of these methods adopt update driven approach to validate each given constraint. These methods start their algorithm from the given update and perform some operations (refutations) until it reaches the constraint formula. However, when the update is irrelevant to the constraint, these methods still perform their operations only to find that the constraint formula cannot be violated. In this case considerable effort is wasted. In this paper, we shall explore this problem and propose a set called relevant-set which can be incorporated with most of these existing constraint checking methods, to detect some of these unnecessary checkings. The relevant-set needs only to be calculated once for each integrity constraint. Furthermore, the set can also take advantage of some evaluable functions in the constraint and rules so that more unnecessary checkings can be detected.

1 INTRODUCTION

Integrity constraint checking for stratifiable deductive databases has been under study by many authors. After [1] first proposed to make use of the assumption that the integrity was satisfied before update, several different methods were proposed for integrity validation for deductive databases. [4] proposed to compute a set of possibly-inserted tuples and a set of possibly-deleted tuples based on the given update. The method then evaluates the set of given constraints after restricting to only those possibly-inserted and possibly-deleted tuples. [2] adopts another approach, which actually evaluates the exact inserted and deleted tuples, and applies each of them to a simplified version of integrity constraint. The consistency method introduced by [3] uses an extension of the SLDNF proof procedure which construct a refutation tree from each of the updates as a top clause. If all refutations fail then the integrity is preserved. [6] proposed another method which constructs a path from each update literal to the head of an integrity constraint. If such a path can be constructed, then the integrity constraint is violated.

However, since all these methods are working from the update literal, they all suffer one important inadequacy: they may redundantly compute some facts, refutation paths or partially instantiated predicates which are irrelevant to the constraint. For example, given the rule

$p(X,Y) \leftarrow a(X,U), b(U,V), c(V,Y)$

and if all constraints does not involve the predicates b, as well as p, then insertion of tuples into relation b will not violate any constraint. However, existing methods [2,3,4,6,7] still requires to perform the evaluation of p only to find that it is redundant. This is very inefficient.

In view of this problem, [5] improved on [2] by defining a set of relevant updates which can give some early detections whether an update is relevant to the constraint. However, [5] does not totally eliminate this type of redundant checking. For example, given the following deductive rule,

$p(X,Y) \leftarrow a(X,U), b(U,V), c(V,Y)$

and a constraint

$\neg p(X,5) \vee (X>0)$

inserting $b(1,2)$ is not relevant to this constraint if $c(2,5)$ is not in the database. However, [5] cannot detect this unnecessary checking because its simplification process is separated from the constraint verification, and therefore cannot use any database-dependent information such as "$c(2,5)$ is not in the database". In this paper, we shall discuss how our method can detect this type of redundant checking before the given constraint is fully computed.

Furthermore, it is easy to show why inserting $b(1,2)$ cannot violate the constraint if $c(2,5)$ is not in the database: for the relational occurrence of p in the constraint, the second parameter is bounded to be 5, which implies that the second attribute of relation c must also be 5. Note that equality function is not the only evaluable function which restricts value, consider the following example, given the rule :

$p(X,Y) \leftarrow a(X,Z), b(Z,Y)$

and an integrity constraint,

$\neg p(X,Y) \vee \neg(X \neq 5) \vee s(Y)$

Insertion of $a(5,2)$ cannot violate this constraint because such insertion can only induce updates of the form $p(5,Y)$. However, when $p(5,Y)$ participates in the constraint evaluation, $(\neg(X \neq 5))\{X/5\}$ in the constraint is always true, and hence the constraint is not violated. Most existing methods [2,3,4,5,6,7] fail to see that insertion of $a(5,2)$ is irrelevant to this constraint until the entire constraint is evaluated. This unnecessary checking can be quite a high cost, especially when there is a lot of tuples in relation b with their first attribute equal to 2.

Hence, to eliminate this type of redundant checking, it requires to have the knowledge of those evaluable functions which restrict the selection of tuples during constraint evaluation. With this, we propose a new method which can be incorporated with many existing bottom-up constraint evaluation methods to improve their performances.

2 POSSIBLE FALSIFIER AND RELEVANT SET

Definition 2.1 An *extended literal* is a duple either of the form $[\![p,C]\!]$ or $[\![\neg p,C]\!]$ where p is an atom and is called the *associated atom.* C is a conjunction of evaluable functions which use only variables appeared in p and is called the *associated condition.* If the number of evaluable functions in C is zero, then it is replaced by TRUE. □

Example 2.1 $[\![a(X,5),(X{\neq}5)]\!]$ and $[\![\neg a(X,Y),(X{\neq}Y)]\!]$ are extended predicates. However, $[\![a(X,5),(X{\neq}Y)]\!]$ is not because itş associated condition uses the variable Y which is not found in its associated atom. □

Definition 2.2 A positive atom t is *extended unified* with an extended literal $[\![p,C]\!]$ if t is unifiable with p with a most general unifier (mgu) σ, and $C\sigma$ is evaluated to be *true*. A negative atom $\neg t$ is extended unified with an extended literal $[\![\neg p,C]\!]$ if t is unifiable with p with a mgu σ, and $C\sigma$ is evaluated to be *true.* □

Example 2.2 The positive atom $a(1,2)$ can be extended unified with $[\![a(X,Y),(X{\neq}Y)]\!]$. However, the positive atoms $a(1,1)$ and $b(1,2)$ cannot be extended unified with the same extended literal. □

Definition 2.3 An extended literal P is called a *possible falsifier* with respect to a given integrity constraint IC if

1. for any insertion of tuple t, which is extended unifiable with P, there is a database DB such that IC is satisfiable, but is violated after the insertion, and
2. for any deletion of tuple t, if $\neg t$ is extended unifiable with P, then there is a database DB such that IC is satisfiable in DB, but is violated after the deletion. □

Example 2.3 Given a constraint

$$\neg p(X,Y) \vee \neg(X>1) \vee \neg(Y{\neq}2) \vee q(X,Y)$$

$[\![p(2,5),\text{TRUE}]\!]$, $[\![p(2,Y),(Y{\neq}2)]\!]$, $[\![p(X,Y),(Y{\neq}2)\wedge(X>5)]\!]$, $[\![\neg q(X,Y),\text{TRUE}]\!]$ are some possible falsifiers with respect to the above constraint. On the other hand, $[\![p(1,5),\text{TRUE}]\!]$ is not a possible falsifier as inserting $p(1,5)$ cannot falsify the constraint. Its first attribute is 1, and will not be satisfied by the evaluable function $(X>1)$. $[\![p(2,2),\text{TRUE}]\!]$ is also not a possible falsifier as inserting $p(2,2)$ cannot falsify the constraint. Its second attribute is 2, and will not be satisfied by $(Y{\neq}2)$. Similarly, $[\![q(X,Y),\text{TRUE}]\!]$ is not a possible falsifier. □

Definition 2.4 A possible falsifier $[\![P_1,C_1]\!]$ (or $[\![\neg P_1,C_1]\!]$) is said to *subsume* another possible falsifier $[\![P_2,C_2]\!]$ (or $[\![\neg P_2,C_2]\!]$ respectively) if there is a mgu σ such that

i) $P_2 = P_1\sigma$,
ii) $C_2 \rightarrow C_1\sigma$. □

Example 2.4 $[\![p(X,Y),\text{TRUE}]\!]$ subsumes $[\![p(X,2),(X>5)]\!]$; and $[\![p(X,Y),(X{\neq}2)]\!]$ subsumes $[\![p(Z,X),(Z>5)]\!]$. However, $[\![p(X,Y),(X{\neq}2)]\!]$ does not subsume $[\![p(X,Y),(Y>5)]\!]$.

Theorem 2.1 Given any integrity constraint *IC*, if the possible falsifier *P* wrt *IC* subsumes another possible falsifier *Q* wrt *IC*, then for any updates *U* which violates *IC*, *U* is extended unifiable with *Q* implies it is also extended unifiable with *P*. □

Definition 2.5 A *relevant set* with respect to an integrity constraint is a complete collection of possible falsifiers such that any possible update which violates the constraint can be extended unified with some of the possible falsifiers in the set. □

2.1 Computation of relevant set

The computation of a relevant set with respect to a given constraint is essentially top-down. As we do not require the set to be fully instantiated, we do not need to access the database to generate the set and the process can always terminate. Moreover, this computation needs only to do once for each constraint until some database rules or constraints are changed. Hence, it can be classified as compile approach. The following algorithm describes how we construct a relevant set with respect to a given constraint,

Algorithm 2.1 Given a stratifiable deductive database *DB* and a constraint *IC*, we do the following:

1. Temporary add the deductive rule
   $violated \leftarrow \neg IC$
   into *DB* where the predicate *violated* is not an existing predicate in *DB*. Convert $\neg IC$ to a closed first-order formula if necessary.
2. Initialize *S* to contain only a single possible falsifier $[\![violated, \text{TRUE}]\!]$
3. If $[\![p(y_1, \ldots, y_n), C]\!]$ is in *S*, and if there is a deductive rule in *DB*,
   $p(x_1, \ldots, x_n) \leftarrow W(x_1, \ldots, x_n)$
   such that $p(y_1, \ldots, y_n)$ can unify with $p(x_1, \ldots, x_n)$ with a mgu θ, then
   i) for each positive literal $p'(z_1, \ldots, z_{n'})$ in the body of *W*,
      include $[\![p'(z_1, \ldots, z_{n'})\theta, C' \wedge C'']\!]$ into *S* if it is not just a renaming of any existing element in *S*, and where C' is same as C except that all evaluable functions in C which do not use the variable $z_1, \ldots, z_{n'}$ are removed, and C'' is the conjunction of evaluable functions in *W* conjuncted with $p'(z_1, \ldots, z_{n'})$ such that they only use the variable $z_1, \ldots, z_{n'}$.
   ii) for each negative literal $\neg p'(z_1, \ldots, z_{n'})$ in the body of *W*,
      include $[\![\neg p'(z_1, \ldots, z_{n'})\theta, C' \wedge C'']\!]$ into *S* if it is not just a renaming of any existing element in *S*, and where C' is same as C except that all evaluable functions in C which do not use the variable $z_1, \ldots, z_{n'}$ are removed, and C'' is the conjunction of evaluable functions in *W* conjuncted with $p'(z_1, \ldots, z_{n'})$ such that they only use the variable $z_1, \ldots, z_{n'}$.
4. If $[\![\neg p(y_1, \ldots, y_n), C]\!]$ is in *S*, and if there is a deductive rule in *DB*,
   $p(x_1, \ldots, x_n) \leftarrow W(x_1, \ldots, x_n)$
   such that $p(y_1, \ldots, y_n)$ can unify with $p(x_1, \ldots, x_n)$ with an unifier θ, then

i) for each positive literal $p'(z_1, \ldots, z_{n'})$ in the body of W, include $[\![\neg p'(z_1, \ldots, z_{n'})\theta, C' \wedge C'']\!]$ into S if it is not just a renaming of any existing element in S, and where C' is same as C except that all evaluable functions in C which do not use the variable $z_1, \ldots, z_{n'}$ are removed, and C'' is the conjunction of evaluable functions in W conjuncted with $p'(z_1, \ldots, z_{n'})$ such that they only use the variable $z_1, \ldots, z_{n'}$.

ii) for each negative literal $\neg p'(z_1, \ldots, z_{n'})$ in the body of W, include $[\![p'(z_1, \ldots, z_{n'})\theta, C' \wedge C'']\!]$ into S if it is not just a renaming of any existing element in S, and where C' is same as C except that all evaluable functions in C which do not use the variable $z_1, \ldots, z_{n'}$ are removed, and C'' is the conjunction of evaluable functions in W conjuncted with $p'(z_1, \ldots, z_{n'})$ such that they only use the variable $z_1, \ldots, z_{n'}$.

5. [Optional simplification step] For any pair of possible falsifier $P1$ and $P2$ in S, if $P1$ subsumes $P2$, then remove $P2$ from S.
6. Repeat step 3 until no more new possible falsifier is included in S.
7. Remove the possible falsifier $[\![$*violated*, TRUE$]\!]$ from S and remove the temporary deductive rule,

   violated$\leftarrow \neg IC$

   from the deductive database.
8. Return S as relevant set with respect to IC. □

Theorem 2.2 Algorithm 2.1 will always terminate, and correctly generated a relevant set. In another word, any update which is not extended unifiable with the elements of the set generated from Algorithm 2.1 cannot falsify the constraint.

PROOF First, we prove that Algorithm 2.1 will always terminate. The algorithm will terminate once there is no new extended literal being generated. Hence, if the algorithm is not terminated, then it will generate an infinite number of extended literals in the relevant set. However, a relevant set is a finite set. It is because for any extended literal in a relevant set, its associated atom must be a predicate symbol used in the database, and if the extended literal is (partially) instantiated with constants, then these constants must be those which appear in the deductive rules or in the constraint. There are only finite number of these predicate symbols and constants. Similarly, the number of possible conjunctions of evaluable predicates is also finite. Hence, the relevant set is a finite set and Algorithm 2.1 will always terminate.

To prove its correctness, we will first show that if an update u induces another v which can unify with some possible falsifier in the generated set, then u can also unify some possible falsifier in the generated set. Given an update (insertion or deletion) on the deductive database, it can induce some insertions (at least the predicate *violated* as defined in Algorithm 2.1 if the constraint is violated.) or deletions. If an (induced) insertion $q(c_1, \ldots, c_{n_q})$ induces an insertion $r(d_1, \ldots, d_{n_r})$ via the following deductive rule:

$r(x_1,\ldots,x_{n_r}) \leftarrow \cdots ,q(t_1,\ldots,t_{n_q}),\cdots$

where $q(t_1,\ldots,t_{n_q})$ can unify $q(c_1,\ldots,c_{n_q})$ with a mgu θ. Obviously,

$r(d_1,\ldots,d_{n_r}) = r(x_1,\ldots,x_{n_r})\theta$

Now assume $r(d_1,\ldots,d_{n_r})$ can extended unify with $[\![r(y_1,\ldots,y_{n_r}),C]\!]$ with a mgu α, then

$\theta = \sigma\alpha$, where $\sigma = \{x_1/y_1,\ldots,x_{n_r}/y_{n_r}\}$, and

$C\alpha$ is true.

Now, according to the step 3(i) in Algorithm 2.1, $[\![q(t_1,\ldots,t_{n_r})\sigma, C' \wedge C'']\!]$ will be generated where C' and C'' are defined as in Algorithm 2.1. In another word, $q(t_1,\ldots,t_{n_r})\sigma$ can be unified with $q(c_1,\ldots,c_{n_r})$ with the mgu α. It is obvious that both $C'\alpha$ and $C''\alpha$ are true. Hence, $q(c_1,\ldots,c_{n_q})$ can extended unify with some elements in the generated set, whenever $r(d_1,\ldots,d_{n_r})$ can. The other three cases such as insertion induced by a deletion can be considered in a similar way.
Hence, if an update u induces another update v, which is extended unifiable with some elements in the set generated from Algorithm 2.1, then u can also be unifiable with some elements in the generated set. By induction, if an update induces *violated* and violates the constraint, then this update must be extended unify with some elements in the relevant set. In another word, if an update cannot extended unify with any element in the relevant set with respect to IC, then the update cannot falsify IC. □

Example 2.5 Given the following deductive rules,

$p(X,Y) \leftarrow a(X,Y)$ (Rule 1)

$p(X,Y) \leftarrow a(X,Z),(Z>5),p(Z,Y)$ (Rule 2)

and the constraint

$\neg p(X,2) \vee b(X)$

To generate a relevant set S of the constraint, we first temporary add the following rule in the deductive database,

$violated \leftarrow p(X,2),\neg b(X)$

We apply the above algorithm and construct S after the following iterations,

1. S is initialized to contain only $[\![violated, \text{TRUE}]\!]$.
2. Only the newly addition rule of which the rule head can unify with *violated*, and there is no evaluable function in the rule, we add the following into S:
   $[\![p(X,2), \text{TRUE}]\!]$ and $[\![\neg b(X), \text{TRUE}]\!]$.
3. Since $b(X)$ is a base relation, no further generation can be done through it.
4. $p(X,2)$ can unify with the heads of both rule 1 and rule 2. For rule 1, we generate the new possible falsifier $[\![a(X,2), \text{TRUE}]\!]$ and include it into S.
5. For rule 2, we include $[\![a(X,Z),(Z>5)]\!]$ and $[\![p(Z,2),(Z>5)]\!]$ into S. The associated conditions are constructed from the conjunctive evaluable function $(Z>5)$ conjuncted with both $a(X,Z)$ and $p(Z,Y)$. S now is,
   $\{ [\![violated, \text{TRUE}]\!], [\![p(X,2), \text{TRUE}]\!], [\![\neg b(X), \text{TRUE}]\!],$
   $[\![a(X,2), \text{TRUE}]\!], [\![a(X,Z),(Z>5)]\!], [\![p(Z,2),(Z>5)]\!] \}$
6. However, as the possible falsifier $[\![p(Z,2),(Z>5)]\!]$ is subsumed by

$[\![p(X,2), \text{TRUE}]\!]$, hence it is discarded.

7. No new possible falsifier is generated. The algorithm terminates after removing the possible falsifier $[\![\mathit{violated}, \text{TRUE}]\!]$. The final relevant set S is

$$\{ [\![p(X,2), \text{TRUE}]\!], [\![\neg b(X), \text{TRUE}]\!], [\![a(X,2), \text{TRUE}]\!], [\![a(X,Z), (Z>5)]\!] \}$$

Hence, if database updates are only done on base relations, then only deletions from relation b, or insertions into relation a with their first attribute value either greater than 5 or equal to 2, may violate the constraint. Other update such as "insert a(1,4)" cannot violate the constraint. Note that other methods [2,4,5,7] fail to draw the same conclusion until the entire constraint is evaluated. □

3 APPLICATION OF THE RELEVANT SET

In this section, we shall discuss how relevant sets can be used in various steps of constraint validation process. Furthermore, we will show that the additional overhead cost is negligible as compared with the expected saving we should achieve.

3.1 Eliminate irrelevant updates

A relevant set provides the information if a partially instantiated update can violate a given constraint. Hence, the direct application of this method is to eliminate irrelevant updates in a transaction. We shall now show how our method can improve the method in [4] by eliminating more unnecessary checkings.

[4] computes the possibly-inserted and possibly-deleted partially instantiated instances iteratively without first consulting the database. To apply the relevant set, we only need to check if the update literal can be extended unified with any of the possible falsifier of the relevant set. If none is found, then no further computation is necessary. Otherwise, we shall apply [4] to verify the constraint.

Example 3.1 Given the rules,

$$p(X,Y) \leftarrow a(X,Z), b(Z,Y)$$
$$q(X,Y) \leftarrow p(X,Z), c(Z,Y)$$

and a constraint

$$\neg p(X,X) \vee (q(1,X) \wedge r(X))$$

A relevant set for this constraint will be

$$\{ [\![p(X,X), \text{TRUE}]\!], [\![\neg q(1,X), \text{TRUE}]\!], [\![\neg r(X), \text{TRUE}]\!], [\![a(X,Z), \text{TRUE}]\!], [\![b(Z,X), \text{TRUE}]\!], [\![\neg p(1,X), \text{TRUE}]\!], [\![\neg c(Z,Y), \text{TRUE}]\!], [\![\neg a(1,Z), \text{TRUE}]\!], [\![\neg b(Z,Y), \text{TRUE}]\!] \}$$

Since $\neg a(2,2)$ cannot extended unify with any element in the relevant set, hence no checking is required for this constraint for deleting $a(2,2)$. Note that without the relevant set, [4] needs to redundantly compute both the positive and negative sets only to discover that no checking is necessary.

When evaluable functions appear in the constraint, our method can improve even more. For example, given the same deductive rules in Example 3.1 and the constraint

$$\neg(p(X,Y) \wedge (X>5)) \vee c(X,Y)$$

our method can conclude that inserting $a(1,2)$ is irrelevant without any database access, and thus eliminate the checking altogether. However, [4] still needs to evaluate the entire constraint only to find that the constraint can never be violated. This is very costly. This problem also exists in [2, Bas87, 5, 7]. □

3.2 Using the relevant set during the SLDNF refutation

While our method can be applied to eliminate irrelevant updates in a transaction, it can also be used during the computation process of constraint evaluation. In particular, given a bottom-up constraint checking method, we can inspect if the intermediate computed instances are unifiable with some possible falsifier in the relevant set. If it is not, then further computation from that instance is irrelevant to the validation. For example, during [2] is computing exact induced updates, we can check if each computed update is relevant to the constraint. If it is not, then further computations based on it can be eliminated. This idea can be applied to other bottom-up constraint evaluation process such as in [6]. We shall illustrate how the relevant set can be used to improve [6].

[6] uses a refutation procedure to construct a refutation path to reach to the given constraint. If such path exists, then the constraint is violated. Now, given the following deductive database with the rules,

$$p(X,Y) \leftarrow q(X,Y) \qquad \text{(R1)}$$
$$p(X,Y) \leftarrow q(X,U), p(U,V), q(V,Y) \qquad \text{(R2)}$$
$$q(X,Y) \leftarrow a(X,U), b(U,Y) \qquad \text{(R3)}$$
$$r(X,Y) \leftarrow c(X,Y), \neg q(X,Y) \qquad \text{(R4)}$$

and the facts

$$a(2,0),\ a(3,0), \ldots, a(99,0),\ \ c(2,1),\ c(3,1), \ldots, c(99,1),\ \ d(1)$$

To verify the constraint,

$$\neg d(X) \vee r(1,X)$$

after an insertion of $b(0,1)$, [6] will try to construct a path which leads to the constraint as shown in *figure 1*.

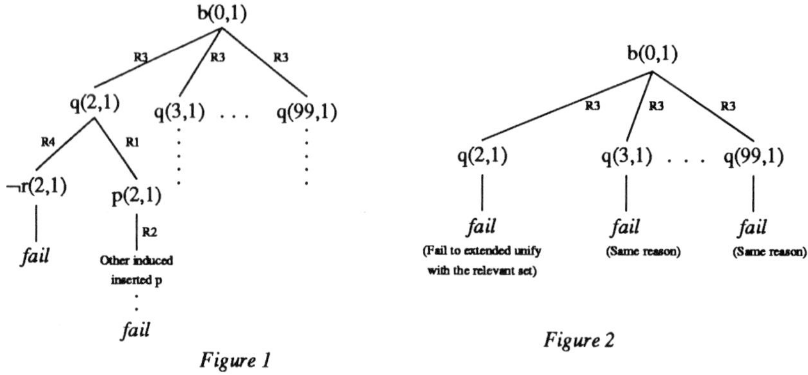

Figure 1

Figure 2

The search space involves many unnecessary computations, such as $\neg r(2,1)$ and all the induced insertions of predicate p. However, knowing that the relevant set with respect to this constraint is

$$\{ [\![d(X), \text{TRUE}]\!], [\![\neg r(1,X), \text{TRUE}]\!], [\![\neg c(1,X), \text{TRUE}]\!],$$

$[\![q(1,X), \text{TRUE}]\!], [\![a(1,X), \text{TRUE}]\!], [\![b(X,Y), \text{TRUE}]\!]$

We can actually reduce the search space by aborting further computation from the branch of $q(X,1)$ whenever X is not 1. This gives a much smaller search space as in figure 2. Without the relevant set, [Das87] needs to explore much larger search space to prove that there is no successful path to the constraint formula, and thus the constraint is not violated. Hence, using the relevant set in this case proves to gain a great saving, especially when the relation p and q are considerably large.

Note that methods which clearly separate constraint simplification from constraint evaluation such as [2, 5] cannot eliminate this type of irrelevant evaluation as no database facts are known to these methods during the simplification step.

3.3 Overall Performance of relevant set method

We now further discuss the extra costs incurred by the method and show that these extra costs are insignificant. There are three extra costs incurred in our method:

1. Computation of a relevant set,
2. extra cost of extended unification as compared with conventional unification,
3. extra cost to access the relevant set before each step of the refutation process.

The computation of the relevant set needs only to do once for each constraint until some deductive rules are changed. Furthermore, this one-time computation does not need to access database and is done in the main memory. Hence, the cost is insignificant for normal database applications.

As compare with the conventional unification, our extended unification does just one extra thing, which is to check for its associated condition. However, as the condition is only conjunctions of evaluable functions, which are fully instantiated once its associated predicate is instantiated, the evaluation of the condition does not involve any database access nor searching. It is therefore insignificant compare to the possible reduction of the number of database accesses by our method.

Lastly, as the size of a relevant set is usually small, it can be stored in the main memory and hence, searching possible falsifiers in the relevant set to test for extended unification does not require any extra database accesses.

The savings gained from the relevant set can vary a lot. While the relevant set can eliminate the entire integrity checking process which other methods fail to do, or reduce the search space during refutation by a significant proportion, it is also possible that no saving is achieved. Recall that unnecessary checkings are detected based on those constants, evaluable functions as well as predicate symbols which are relevant to the constraints. Hence, if there is no constant and evaluable function in the constraint and all the deductive rules, as well as all the deductive predicate symbols need to be re-calculated in order to evaluate the constraint, (i.e. no irrelevant predicate) then there will be no saving gained from using the relevant set. However, when this situation happens, it can be easily identified by the following,

i) The associated atom for each extended literal is not instantiated with any constant, and

ii) The associated condition for each extended literal is TRUE, and

iii) Every deductive relation is included in the set.

In this case, such relevant set cannot reduce the search space. However, we can implement an extra flag to disable the relevancy checking if necessary. So even in this worst case, our method, as compared as the existing methods, only requires an additional pre-computation of the relevant set once for each integrity constraint, and to check the flag in O(1) time for each transaction. The extra cost is insignificant as no database access is involved. With this flexibility, our method can give much better overall performance then other existing methods in most of the time.

4 CONCLUSION

We have presented the relevant set method and how it can be used to improve other methods by eliminating some unnecessary checkings. Our method also makes use of existing evaluable functions in the deductive rules and constraints to further detect irrelevant updates. For further research, we can explore the possibility to use not only evaluable functions, but also deductive predicates in the deductive rules and the given constraint for eliminating more unnecessary checking.

REFERENCE

[1] J.M. Nicolas, "Logic for improving integrity checking in relational databases", *Acta Informatica* 18,(3), 1982, 227-253.

[2] H. Decker, "Integrity enforcements on deductive databases", in L.Kerschberg (ed.) *Proceedings of the First International Conference on Expert Database Systems*, Charleston, South Carolina (April 1986) 271-285.

[3] R.A. Kowalski, F. Sadri and P. Soper, "Integrity constraint in deductive databases", *Proceedings of the 13th VLDB Conference*, Brighton (1987) 61-69.

[4] J.W. Lloyd, E.A. Sonenberg and R.W. Topor, "Integrity Constraint Checking in Stratified Databases", Journal of Logic Programming, Vol 4, No 4, 1987.

[5] F. Bry, H. Decker and R. Manthey, "A uniform approach to constraint satisfaction and constraint satisfiability in deductive databases", *Proceedings of Extending Database Technology*, Venice, 1988, 488-505.

[6] S.K. Das and M.H. Williams, "A path finding method for constraint checking in deductive databases", *Data and Knowledge Engineering 3* (1989) 223-244.

[7] M. Celma, J.C. Casamayor and H. Decker, "Improving Integrity Checking by Compiling Derivation Paths", *Proccedings of the Fourth Australian Database Conference*, Australia, 1993.

RTSORAC: A Real-Time Object-Oriented Database Model *

J. J. Prichard, Lisa Cingiser DiPippo, Joan Peckham, Victor Fay Wolfe

Department of Computer Science and Statistics
The University of Rhode Island, Kingston, RI, 02881 USA
lastname@cs.uri.edu

Abstract. A *real-time database* is a database in which both the data and the operations upon the data may have timing constraints. We have integrated real-time, object-oriented, semantic and active database approaches to develop a formal model called RTSORAC for real-time databases. This paper describes the components of the RTSORAC model including objects, relationships, constraints, updates, and transactions.

1 Introduction

A *real-time database* is a database in which both the data and the transactions may have timing constraints. Typically, a real-time database manages data from the environment, processes environmental information in the context of previously acquired information and provides a timely response to transactions that use the data [7]. Much of the current research has been directed towards developing relational real-time databases [7, 8]. Although the relational model is useful for many applications, we believe that it is not as well-suited as an *object-oriented database model* (OODM) for applications that require complex data, complex relationships among data, first-class support for timing constraints, and more scheduling flexibility than serializability can provide. RTSORAC (**R**eal-**T**ime **S**emantic **O**bjects **R**elationships **A**nd **C**onstraints) is a real-time object-oriented database model that incorporates these concepts.

The RTSORAC model is based upon an earlier model called SORAC [5]. The SORAC data model combines features of the object-oriented [13] and semantic data models [6]. The prototype implementation of the SORAC model translates object and relationship definitions into code that executes on a commercial object-oriented database system. In SORAC, enforcement rules specifying the explicit means for maintaining interobject constraints are directly specifiable by the database designer.

This paper represents an extension of the SORAC model for real-time applications. We have drawn from our experience in the design and implementation of the *RTC* real-time programming language constructs [11] and SORAC to identify the basic research issues involved in the design of real-time object-oriented

* This material is based upon work supported by the U.S. National Science Foundation under grant No. IRI-9308517 and the U.S. Naval Undersea Warfare Center

databases (RTOODBs). The next section of the paper provides background information on real-time databases, and summarizes the properties that are unique to real-time databases. The third section describes the RTSORAC model, and the last section describes the ongoing implementation of the RTSORAC model. Issues for future investigation are also briefly mentioned.

2 Real-Time Databases

A real-time database system has two distinguishing features: the notion of temporally consistent data, and the ability to place real-time constraints on transactions. These features are useful to time critical applications that need to collect, modify, and retrieve shared data. Since the data used by these applications must closely reflect the current state of the application environment, we need mechanisms for measuring this closeness. These measures are based upon time intervals that specify the temporal consistency of the data. Temporal consistency can be measured in two ways: absolute consistency and relative consistency [7]. A piece of data is considered absolutely consistent with respect to time as long as the age of a data value is within a given interval. For example, in a radar system, the data corresponding to a contact, such as its speed, should be updated often, (e.g. every five seconds). Hence, the value of the speed is temporally consistent as long as it is no more than five seconds old. Relative consistency is of interest when multiple values are used in computations. It provides a mechanism for checking the ages of the multiple data values with respect to each other. For example, if the radar system computes the new location of a contact using the speed and bearing, it would be important that the ages of the speed and bearing be relatively close to one another (e.g. within two seconds).

Timing constraints on transactions come from one of two sources. First, temporal consistency requirements of the data impose timing constraints on a transaction. For instance, the period of a sensor transaction is dictated by the valid time of the sensor data that it writes. The second source of timing constraints on transactions is system or user requirements on reaction time. There are typically two types timing constraints on transactions: absolute timing constraints (i.e. earliest start time, latest finish time) and periodic timing constraints. Given the added dimension of time on transactions, one of the interesting areas of study in real-time databases is that of transaction scheduling [2, 12]. Not only must the schedules meet timing constraints, they must also maintain the logical consistency of the data in the database. An additional challenge is to provide a strategy for recovery that adheres to the temporal and logical consistency requirements of the system.

Hence, a real-time database system should provide support for specifying:

- the absolute validity interval of a data value
- relative temporal consistency among a set of data values
- absolute timing constraints on transactions
- periodic timing constraints on transactions
- recovery from violations of timing constraints

$$
\begin{aligned}
\textbf{Object} &= \langle N, A, M, C, CF \rangle \\
N &= UniqueID \\
A &= \{a_1, a_2, ..., a_m\} \text{ where attribute } a_i = \langle N_a, V, T, I \rangle \\
M &= \{m_1, m_2, ..., m_n\} \text{ where method } m_i = \langle N_m, Arg, Exc, Op, OC \rangle \\
C &= \{c_1, c_2, ..., c_s\} \text{ where constraint } c_i = \langle N_c, AttrSet, Pred, ER \rangle \\
CF &= \text{compatibility function}
\end{aligned}
$$

Fig. 1. Object characteristics in RTSORAC

3 The RTSORAC Model

RTSORAC has three components that model the properties of a real-time object-oriented database: *objects*, *relationships* and *transactions*. *Objects* represent database entities. *Relationships* represent associations among the database objects. *Transactions* are executable entities that access the objects and relationships in the database.

3.1 Objects

An *object* (Figure 1) consists of five components, $\langle N, A, M, C, CF \rangle$, where N is a unique name or identifier, A is a set of attributes, M is a set of methods, C is a set of constraints, and CF is a compatibility function. Attributes, methods, constraints, and the compatibility function are described below. Figure 2 illustrates an example of a **Train** object (adapted from [1]) for storing information about a railroad engine in a database.

Attributes. A is set of attributes for the object, where each attribute is characterized by $\langle N_a, V, T, I \rangle$. N_a is the name of the attribute. The second field, V, is used to store the value of the attribute, and may be of some complex data type. The next field, T is used to store the timestamp of the attribute, and is of some data type capable of expressing a time. Access to the timestamp of an attribute is necessary for determining temporal consistency of the attribute. For example, in the **Train** object, there is an attribute for storing the oil pressure called `OilPressure` to which a sensor regularly provides readings. This update is expected every thirty seconds, thus the `OilPressure` attribute is considered temporally inconsistent if the update does not occur within that time frame. The timestamp value of the `OilPressure` attribute must be utilized by the system to determine that the update did not occur as expected.

The last field I is used to store the amount of imprecision associated with the attribute, and is of the same type as the value field V. In order to meet real-time constraints it may not be possible to maintain precise data values. Furthermore, many real-time control applications allow a certain amount of imprecision. For instance, within the **Train** object, the value of `OilPressure` attribute may not have to be precise.

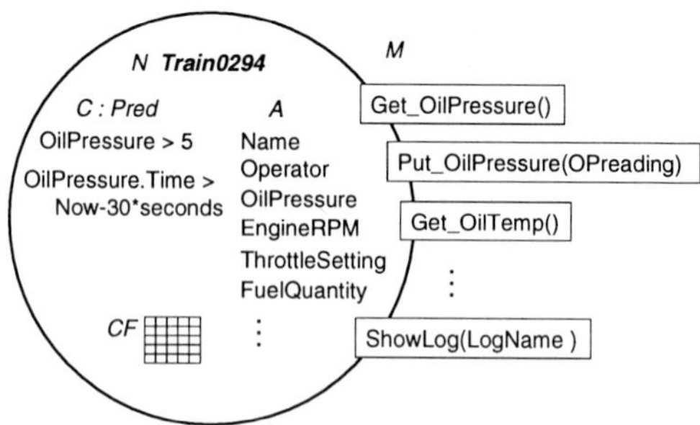

Fig. 2. Example of **Train** object

Methods. The third component of an object, M, is a set of methods, where each method is of the form $\langle N_m, Arg, Exc, Op, OC \rangle$. N_m is the name of the method. Arg is a set of arguments for the method, where each argument has the same components as an attribute, and is used to pass information in and/or out of the method. Exc is a set of exceptions that may be raised by the method to signal that the method has terminated abnormally. Op is a set of operations which represent the implementation of the method. These operations include statements for conditional branching, looping, I/O, and reads and writes to an attribute's value, time, and imprecision fields.

The last characteristic of a method, OC, is a set of operation constraints. An operation constraint is of the form $\langle N_{oc}, OpSet, Pred, ER \rangle$ where N_{oc} is the name of the operation constraint, $OpSet$ is a subset of the operations in Op, $Pred$ is a Boolean expression, and ER is an enforcement rule. The predicate is specified over $OpSet$ to express precedence constraints, execution constraints, and timing constraints [11]. The enforcement rule is used to express the action to take if the predicate evaluates to false. A more complete description of an enforcement rule can be found in the next section on constraints.

Here is an example of an operation constraint predicate in the **Train** object:

Pred : `complete(Put_OilPressure) < NOW + 5*seconds`

A deadline of `NOW + 5*seconds` has been specified for the completion of the `Put_OilPressure` method. Note the use of a special atom `complete(e)`, which represents the completion time of the executable entity `e`. Other atoms that are useful in the expression of timing constraints include `start(e)`, `wcet(e)`, and `request(e)` which represent the execution start time, worst case execution time, and the execution request time of entity `e` respectively.

Constraints. The fourth component of an object is a set of constraints, C, which permits the the specification of correct object state. Each constraint is of the form $\langle N_c, AttrSet, Pred, ER \rangle$. N_c is the name of the constraint. $AttrSet$ is a subset of attributes of the object. $Pred$ is a Boolean expression that is specified using attributes from the $AttrSet$. The predicate can be used to express the logical and temporal consistency requirements of the data stored in the object by referring to the value, time, and imprecision fields of the attributes in the set.

The enforcement rule (ER) is executed when the predicate evaluates to false, and is of the form $\langle Exc, Op, OC \rangle$. As with methods, Exc is a set of exceptions that the enforcement rule may signal, Op is a set of operations that represent the implementation of the enforcement rule, and OC is a set of operation constraints on the execution of the enforcement rule.

Logical and temporal consistency constraints on data require two distinct methodologies for evaluation. Predicates based upon logical consistency requirements are evaluated when write operations are performed on the attributes in *AttrSet*. All writes in the database are the result of a transaction which may be either user initiated or system initiated. Hence an enforcement rule associated with such a predicate will always be executed in the context of a transaction. This execution may be synchronous or asynchronous and may involve signaling an exception that is propagated back to the transaction. Predicates based upon temporal consistency requirements may be violated simply due to the passage of time and the semantics of predicate evaluation can vary. Once a constraint violation has been detected, the corresponding enforcement rule is executed. It is possible that there is no context (such as a transaction) for the execution of the enforcement rule. In this case the implementation must provide a means of handling exceptions raised outside of the context of a transaction, perhaps through the use of a monitor that can detect and act upon signaled exceptions.

For example, as mentioned earlier, the **Train** object has an oil pressure attribute that is updated with the latest sensor reading every thirty seconds. To maintain the temporal consistency of this attribute, the following constraint is defined:

```
N :       OilPressure_avi
AttrSet : {OilPressure}
Pred :    OilPressure.time <= Now - 30*seconds
ER :      if Missed <= 2 then
            OilPressure.time = Now
            Missed = Missed + 1
            signal OilPressure_Warning
          else signal OilPressure_Alert
```

The enforcement rule specifies that if only one or two of the readings have been missed, a counter is incremented indicating that a reading has been missed and a warning is signaled using the exception `OilPressure_Warning`. If more than two readings have been missed, then an exception `OilPressure_Alert` is signaled, which might lead to a message being sent to the train operator. The counter `Missed` is reset to zero whenever a new sensor reading is written to attribute `OilPressure`.

Compatibility Function. The last component of an object, CF, is a compatibility function that expresses the semantics of simultaneous execution of each ordered pair of methods in the object. For each ordered pair of methods, (m_i, m_j),

$$
\begin{array}{ll}
\textbf{Relationship} & = \langle N, A, M, C, CF, P, IC\rangle \\
N & = UniqueID \\
A & = \{a_1, a_2, ..., a_m\} \text{ where attribute } a_i = \langle N_a, V, T, I\rangle \\
M & = \{m_1, m_2, ..., m_n\} \text{ where method } m_i = \langle N_m, Arg, Exc, Op, OC\rangle \\
C & = \{c_1, c_2, ..., c_r\} \text{ where constraint } c_i = \langle N_c, AttrSet, Pred, ER\rangle \\
CF & = \text{compatibility function} \\
P & = \{p_1, p_2, ..., p_s\} \text{ where participant } p_i = \langle N_p, OT, Card\rangle \\
IC & = \{ic_1, ic_2, ..., ic_t\} \text{ where interobject constraint} \\
 & \quad ic_i = \langle N_{ic}, PartSet, Pred, ER\rangle
\end{array}
$$

Fig. 3. Relationship characteristics in RTSORAC

a Boolean expression ($BE_{i,j}$) is defined. $BE_{i,j}$ is evaluated to determine whether or not m_i and m_j can execute concurrently. In many object-oriented systems, the execution of a single method of an object prevents any other methods of the object from being executed, i.e. the entire object is locked upon invocation of a single method. Through the use of the compatibility function, the designer of an object can allow more flexibility by defining the semantics of the compatibility of each pair of methods. By allowing a higher degree of concurrent access to the object through its methods, perhaps even relaxing serializability, the affected data may become imprecise. An in depth discussion of the semantic locking technique that utilizes the compatibility function to provide concurrency control to an object in RTSORAC can be found in [4].

Consider the following examples of compatibility function specifications:

```
CF(Get_OilPressure(), Get_OilTemp()) = TRUE
CF(Put_OilPressure(OP_reading), ShowLog(Log)) = (Log <> "OilPressure")
```

In the first example, the compatibility function is used to specify that the methods `Get_OilPressure` and `Get_OilTemp` of the **Train** object can always run concurrently (always `TRUE`). This is appropriate since these two methods operate on different attributes, `OilPressure` and `OilTemp`. The second example specifies that `Put_OilPressure` and `ShowLog` can run concurrently as long as the log to be displayed is not "OilPressure". If the requested log is "OilPressure", then the execution of the `ShowLog` method may be delayed or aborted.

3.2 Relationships

Relationships represent aggregations of two or more objects. In the RTSORAC model, a *relationship* (Figure 3) consists of $\langle N, A, M, C, CF, P, IC\rangle$. The first five components of a relationship are identical to the same components in the definition of an object. In addition, objects that can participate in the relationship are specified in the participant set P, and a set of interobject constraints is specified in IC.

Figure 4 illustrates an example of a **Energy Management** relationship for relating a **Train** object with a **Track** object. The **Track** object stores information such as track profile and grade, speed limits, maximum load, and power

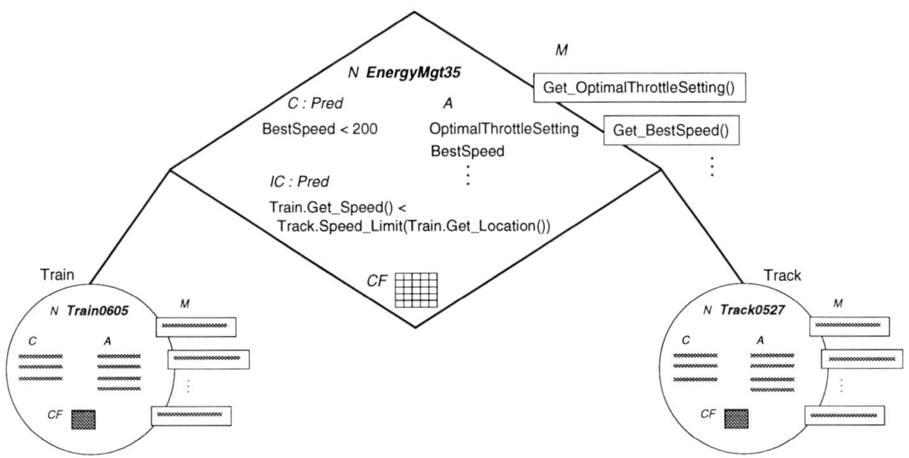

Fig. 4. Example of **Energy Management** relationship

available. The energy management relationship uses both train and track information to determine fuel efficient throttle and brake settings.

Participants. P is a set of participants in the relationship, each participant is of the form $\langle N_p, OT, Card \rangle$. N_p is the name of the participant. OT is the type of the object participating in the relationship. $Card$ is the cardinality of the participant, which is either *single* or *multi* [3]. Constraints can be used to express cardinality requirements of the relationship, such as minimum and maximum cardinality of the participants. In Figure 4, `Train` and `Track` are single cardinality participants.

Interobject Constraints. IC is a set of interobject constraints placed on objects in the participant set, and is of the form $\langle N_{ic}, PartSet, Pred, ER \rangle$. N_{ic}, $Pred$, and ER are as in object constraints, and $PartSet$ is a subset of the relationship's participant set P. The predicate is expressed using objects from the $PartSet$, allowing the constraint to be specified over multiple objects participating in the relationship. Enforcement rules are defined as before by $\langle Exc, Op, OC \rangle$, however the operations Op can now include invocations of methods of the objects participating in the relationship.

As an example of an interobject constraint, consider the **Energy Management** relationship in Figure 4. A **Train** object will be on one specific segment of track, represented by the **Track** object participating in the relationship. The train should obey the speed limits set on the track, so the following interobject constraint predicate could be specified:

$Pred:$ `Train.Get_Speed() < Track.Speed_Limit(Train.Get_Location())`

If the speed of the train exceeds the speed limit posted at the train's location on the track, then the corresponding enforcement rule signals `SpeedLimitExceeded`.

3.3 Transactions

A *transaction* has six components, $\langle N_t, O, OC, PreCond, PostCond, Result\rangle$, where N_t is a unique name or identifier, O is a set of operations, OC is a set of operation constraints, $PreCond$ is a precondition, $PostCond$ is a postcondition, and $Result$ is the result of the transaction. Each of these components is briefly described below.

Operations. O is set of operations that represent the implementation of the transaction. These operations may include method invocations (MI), initiations of subtransactions, *commit* or *abort* statements, and statements for conditional branching, looping, and reads/writes on local variables. A subtransaction initiation allows for transactions to appear within the scope of other transactions. Method invocations (MI) are of the form $\langle MN, ArgInfo\rangle$, where MN is the method name (prepended with the appropriate object id) and $ArgInfo$ is a set of tuples containing argument information. Each tuple is of the form $\langle aa, maximp, tcr\rangle$ where aa is the actual argument to the method, $maximp$ is the maximum allowable imprecision of the argument, and tcr is the temporal consistency requirement of the argument. The fields $maximp$ and tcr are specified only for arguments that are used to return information to the transaction. These fields allow the transaction to specify requirements that differ from those defined on the data in the objects. For example, the transaction might be willing to accept a value whose temporal consistency requirements have been violated so as to meet other timing constraints. The data may still be useful to the transaction because of other available information (for example, it may be able to do some extrapolation). A transaction may also specify that data returned by a method invocation must be precise ($maximp$ is zero).

Operation Constraints. OC is a set of constraints on operations of the transaction. These constraints are of the same form as the operation constraints specified for methods, $\langle N_c, OpSet, Pred, ER\rangle$. As with methods, these constraints can be used to express precedence constraints, execution constraints, and timing constraints. For example, a transaction may require that a sensor reading which has been stored in the database be returned within two seconds.

Precondition, Postcondition, Result. $PreCond$ represents preconditions that must be satisfied before a transaction is made ready for execution. For example, it may be appropriate for a transaction to execute only if some specified event has occurred. The event may be the successful termination of another transaction, or a given clock time. $PostCond$ represents postconditions that must be satisfied upon completion of the operations of the transaction. The postconditions can be used to specify the semantics of what constitutes a *commit* of a transaction containing subtransactions. $Result$ represents information that is returned by the transaction. This may include values read from objects as well as values computed by the transaction.

Fig. 5. Mapping of the models to database systems

4 Implementation

As mentioned in the introduction of this paper, RTSORAC is based upon an earlier model called SORAC. Figure 5 illustrates the prototype implementation of the SORAC model, and shows the parallel implementation of RTSORAC. The implementation of SORAC provides a data definition language called OIL (Object Interaction Language), which allows the specification of objects and relationships, as well as interobject constraints [5]. These specifications are compiled into standard C++ object definitions with calls to the underlying ONTOS object-oriented database system.

A similar approach is proposed for implementation of RTSORAC. There are two main efforts involved with this implementation. First is the extension of Open OODB [9] to support objects and transactions that have real-time characteristics. Thus, the real-time version of Open OODB will replace ONTOS as the underlying database system. Second is the real-time extension of OIL (RTOIL) to support characteristics of the RTSORAC model that do not appear in SORAC. These characteristics include the compatibility function for concurrency control, extended data types to support time, and the incorporation of time into the specification of constraints upon objects and relationships. RTOIL must automate the mapping of each component of an object or relationship to the attributes and methods of standard C++ objects with library calls to real-time version of Open OODB.

The effort to extend Open OODB for real-time will involve modification or replacement of many of the components of Open OODB. As an alpha site for Open OODB, we have had an opportunity to gain a full understanding of its modular implementation structure. Open OODB is organized as a series of replaceable policy managers such as the Transaction Policy Manager, and the Persistence Policy Manager. We have recently implemented a prototype Object Policy Manager capable of supporting a RTSORAC object. Details on the design of our real-time extensions to Open OODB can be found in [10].

5 Conclusions

This paper has provided a general model for real-time object-oriented databases. The model combines features of object-oriented databases, semantic data models, real-time databases, and active databases. Our current implementation experiences using Open OODB indicate the applicability of the RTSORAC model.

As the design and implementation of the RTSORAC model progresses, a number of issues related to the RTSORAC model will be investigated. These have been identified and include inheritance, query language support, recovery techniques, and necessary operating system support. While these represent a diverse set of database issues, we have discovered that none can be investigated in isolation. Thus, of particular interest will be the unique interaction among these constructs that arise in the real-time environment.

Acknowledgements. We thank Paul Fortier, Gary Hyslop, and John Black for their helpful comments and suggestions.

References

1. Grady Booch. *Object-Oriented Design.* The Benjamin/Cummings Publishing Company, Redwood City, CA, 1991.
2. A.P. Buchmann, D.R. McCarthy, M. Hsu, and U. Dayal. Time-critical database scheduling: A framework for integrating real-time scheduling and concurrency control. In *The Fifth International Conference on Data Engineering*, February 1989.
3. Oscar Diaz and Peter M.D. Gray. Semantic-rich user-defined relationship as a main constructor in object-oriented databases. In R.A. Meersman, W. Dent, and S. Khosla, editors, *Object-Oriented Databases: Analysis,Design & Construction (DS4).* Elsevier Science Publishers, B.V. (North-Holland), 1991.
4. L. Cingiser DiPippo and V. Fay Wolfe. Object-based semantic real-time concurrency control. *Proceedings of the 14th Real-time Systems Symposium*, Dec. 1993.
5. Michael Doherty, Joan Peckham, and Victor Fay Wolfe. Implementing relationships and constraints in an object-oriented database using monitors. In *Rules in Database Systems, Proceedings of the 1st International Workshop on Rules in Database Systems.* Springer-Verlag, August 1993.
6. Joan Peckham and Fred Maryanski. Semantic data models. *ACM Computing Surveys*, 20(3):153–189, September 1988.
7. Krithi Ramamritham. Real-time databases. *International Journal of Distributed and Paralled Databases*, 1(2), 1993.
8. Sang Son, editor. *ACM SIGMOD Record (Special Issue on Real-Time Database Systems).* ACM Press, March 1988.
9. David Wells, Jose Blakely, and Craig Thompson. Architecture of an open object-oriented database management system. *IEEE Computer*, 25(10), Oct. 1992.
10. V. F. Wolfe, L. C. DiPippo, J. J. Prichard, J. M. Peckham, and P. J. Fortier. The design of real-time extensions to the open object-oriented database system. Technical Report URI-TR94-236, University of Rhode Island, Department of Computer Science, May 1994.
11. Victor Wolfe, Susan Davidson, and Insup Lee. *RTC*: Language support for real-time concurrency. *Real-Time Systems*, 5(1):63–87, March 1993.
12. P. Yu, K. Wu, K. Lin, and S. Son. On real-time databases: Concurrency control and scheduling. *Proceedings of the IEEE*, 82, January 1994.
13. Stanley Zdonik and David Maier. *Readings in Object Oriented Database Systems.* Morgan Kauffman, San Mateo, CA, 1990.

Applying Database Technology to Real-Time Systems

Özgür Ulusoy

Department of Computer Engineering and Information Science
Bilkent University
Bilkent, Ankara 06533, TURKEY
e-mail: oulusoy@bilkent.edu.tr, fax: (90)(312)266-4126

Abstract. Real-time systems is becoming one of many application areas whose development requires the involvement of database system concepts. Due to ever increasing volume of information being handled by data-intensive real-time applications, a need has arisen for applying database technology to real-time systems. Management of real-time information through a database system requires the integration of concepts from database systems and real-time systems, which is not a trivial task. Some new criteria have to be developed to involve timing constraints of real-time applications in many database system design issues, such as the structure and organization of the underlying data, transaction scheduling, query processing, data buffering, CPU and IO scheduling. In this paper, we mention about benefits and potential problems of applying database technology to real-time systems, provide the current status of the research in this field, and summarize our work on scheduling database transactions with timing constraints.

1 Introduction

In a real-time system, each transaction is associated with a timing constraint, typically in the form of a deadline, and it needs to be scheduled to terminate before its deadline expires. Some real-time systems, characterized to be data-intensive, require to handle large volumes of information. Examples of data-intensive real-time applications include stock market, computer-integrated manufacturing, telephone switching systems, network management, and command and control systems. It is crucial to apply database technology to those systems for efficient storage and manipulation of information.

A database system which is designed to provide timely response to transactions of data-intensive real-time systems is usually called a real-time database system (RTDBS). Similar to a conventional real-time system, transactions processed in a RTDBS have associated deadlines. What makes a RTDBS different from a conventional real-time system is the requirement of preserving the consistency of underlying data besides considering the deadlines of transactions. This makes it difficult to schedule RTDB transactions so as to satisfy the deadlines of all transactions processed in the system.

Traditional database systems are designed to provide functionally correct information. The correctness of a database operation is not affected by the speed of executing a transaction. Maintaining data consistency is the primary consideration in scheduling transactions. On the other hand, the basic issue considered in traditional real-time systems is the satisfaction of timing constraints associated with transactions. The problem of maintaining the consistency of shared data is usually not addressed. Real-time systems are typically categorized into two groups as *hard* and *soft* real-time systems [22]. Hard real-time systems are characterized by the fact that severe consequences will result if timing constraints of transactions are not satisfied. In soft real-time systems, satisfaction of timing constraints is still a key issue in scheduling transactions, however, in this case there is no guarantee that all transaction deadlines will be met.

Design of a RTDBS requires the integration of concepts from both real-time systems and database systems to handle the timing and consistency requirements together. However, this integration is not a trivial task. With the current database technology it is extremely difficult to provide schedules guaranteeing the deadlines of RTDB transactions. This difficulty comes from the unpredictability of transaction response times. Each transaction operation accessing a data item takes a variable amount of time due to concurrency control and disk IO [22].

The following section summarizes the current status of the research conducted so far on RTDBSs. The RTDBS research is categorized into two groups based on the type of timing constraints (i.e., hard or soft) issued by the underlying application. Section 3 presents our work on transaction scheduling in RTDBSs. Finally, Section 4 concludes the paper.

2 Recent Research on Real-Time Database Systems

Implementation of RTDBSs is difficult due to the conflicting requirements of meeting deadlines and maintaining data consistency. In many applications, it is not possible to satisfy both requirements [15]. For some applications the deadline requirement cannot be relaxed (i.e., timing constraints are hard); thus, the data consistency requirement has to be modified. In those systems getting timely but partially incorrect information is preferable to getting correct but late information [20]. On the other hand, in some RTDBS applications maintaining data consistency can be more crucial than satisfying deadlines. Schedulers should not violate the data consistency requirement while observing the timing constraints of transactions. The following subsections discuss a variety of studies performed so far on both types of RTDBSs.

2.1 RTDBSs with Hard Timing Constraints

A database system preserves the consistency of data by employing a concurrency control protocol which orders conflicting operations of transactions based on a correctness criterion. Serializability is a widely accepted correctness criterion which ensures that transactions provide correct results and leave the database consistent. However, serializability is not a suitable technique to implement in hard real-time systems because of the limitation of concurrency allowed by serializable executions. Existing concurrency control protocols ensuring serializability are based on either one of two techniques: blocking transactions or restarting transactions. Both techniques are inappropriate for time-critical scheduling. Blocking can cause priority inversion; i.e., a high priority transaction (e.g., with an urgent deadline) can be blocked by a lower priority transaction [17]. Restarting a transaction, on the other hand, causes a waste of processing time and other system resources already used by that transaction.

Although a general purpose consistency criterion that is less stringent than serializability has not yet been proposed, some possible solutions to the data consistency problem in hard RTDBSs have been provided. The consistency model proposed in [15] is an attempt for the relaxation of strict serializability rules. The model satisfies timing constraints by sacrificing database consistency temporarily to some degree. *External* data consistency is defined in contrast to *internal* data consistency as maintained by traditional database systems. The external consistency constraint requires that the data used by a transaction reflect the physical environment at the time; this is in contrast to internal consistency which requires that all data must meet some predefined constraints in the database. The model is based on the assumption that for most RTDBS applications a timely and externally consistent result is more desirable than an out-of-date though internally consistent response. For instance, the trace of an unidentified object detected by an on-board system is externally consistent but may not be internally consistent before it is interpreted and filtered by the system.

Another approach to designing a RTDBS with extremely fast response requirements is to redesign conventional database systems or their components. Main memory database systems are capable of providing fast response for RTDBS applications. As we mentioned above, one of the factors leading to unpredictable transaction response times is disk IO. Main memory database systems can eliminate disk access delays from database access. However, main memory databases introduce some problems and design issues of their own [20].

2.2 RTDBSs with Soft Timing Constraints

RTDBS concept is largely limited to soft real-time systems due to the difficulty of providing schedules guaranteeing all transaction deadlines. In many RTDBS applications consistency of data is as important as the timeliness of transaction response. Banking, stock market, and airline reservation systems are several examples of such application areas where the data consistency requirement cannot be relaxed. While maintaining the consistency of underlying database, the management and scheduling of system resources should also take the timing constraints into account; i.e., CPU, main memory, IO devices and access to shared data all should be managed to make a best effort to satisfy transaction deadlines [3].

The general approach to the scheduling problem in soft RTDBSs is using existing techniques in CPU scheduling, buffer management, IO scheduling, and concurrency control, and to apply time-critical scheduling methods to observe the timing requirements of transactions. The performance goal in satisfying timing constraints can change depending on the application environment. If the only real-time parameter associated with each transaction is the assigned deadline, the goal is to minimize the number of transactions that miss their deadlines. A priority order is established among transactions based on their deadlines. There are RTDB applications where transactions may be assigned different values, where the value of a transaction reflects the return the application expects to receive if the transaction commits within its deadline [4, 12, 9]. For such applications, the performance goal is to maximize the value realized by the in-time transactions. Transactions are assigned priorities which are functions of both their values and deadlines.

The scheduling problem in soft RTDBSs has been addressed by a number of recent studies. The first attempt to evaluate the performance of scheduling algorithms in soft RTDBSs was provided in [1, 2]. Abbott and Garcia-Molina described and evaluated through simulation a group of real-time scheduling policies based on enforcing data consistency by using a two-phase locking concurrency control mechanism. In [3], they provided a study of various algorithms for scheduling IO requests with deadlines. Carey et al. [5] and Chen et al. [6] also discussed some new approaches to priority-based IO scheduling. In [17] and [18], Sha et al. presented a new priority-based concurrency control protocol and the performance of this protocol was examined in [19] by using simulations. In [12], Huang et al. developed and evaluated several real-time policies for handling CPU scheduling, concurrency control, deadlock resolution, transaction wakeup, and transaction restart in RTDBSs. Later, their work was extended to the optimistic concurrency control method [13]. Haritsa et al. studied, by simulation, the relative performance of two well known classes of concurrency control algorithms (locking protocols and optimistic techniques) in a RTDBS environment [7, 10]. They presented and evaluated a new real-time optimistic concurrency control protocol through simulations in [8]. In [21], Son et al. examined a priority-driven locking protocol which decomposes the problem of concurrency control into two subproblems, namely read-write synchronization and write-write synchronization, and integrates the solutions to two subproblems considering transaction priorities. Kim and Srivastava [14] proposed new multiversion concurrency control algorithms to increase concurrency in RTDBSs. Özsoyoğlu et al. [16] introduced new techniques to process database queries within fixed time quotas. Different degrees of accuracy of the responses to the queries can be achieved by using those techniques. In [11], Hong et al. proposed a cost conscious real-time scheduling algorithm which assigns transaction priorities dynamically to adapt to the dynamic changes in the system load.

Our research in soft RTDBSs has basicly concentrated on development and evaluation of concurrency control protocols and investigating the performance impact of various aspects of data distribution. A summary of our findings are provided in the next section.

3 Concurrency Control in Soft Real-Time Database Systems

In [24], we studied the relative performance of existing concurrency control approaches in RTDBSs. We also proposed a new locking-based concurrency control protocol which prevents the priority inversion problem by scheduling data lock requests based on prioritizing data items. The protocol, called Data-Priority-Based Locking, is described in the next subsection.

Two of the most popular locking protocols chosen for evaluation were the Priority Inheritance protocol (PI) which allows a low priority transaction to execute at the highest priority of all the higher priority transactions it blocks [17], and the Priority-Based conflict resolution protocol (PB) which aborts a low priority transaction when one of its locks is requested by a higher priority transaction [1]. In protocol PI, when a transaction blocks higher priority transactions, it is executed with the highest priority of blocked transactions; in other words, it inherits the highest priority. The idea is to reduce the blocking times of high priority transactions. In protocol PB, the winner in the case of a conflict is always the higher priority transaction. In resolving a lock conflict, if the transaction requesting the lock has higher priority than the transaction that holds the lock, the latter transaction is aborted and the lock is granted to the former one. Otherwise, the lock-requesting transaction is blocked by the higher priority lock-holding transaction.

Another interesting concurrency control protocol we evaluated was the optimistic protocol (OP) described in [8]. In this protocol, the validation check for a committing transaction is performed against the other active transactions and the transactions that are in conflict with the committing transaction are aborted. The proposed protocol uses a '50 percent' rule as follows: If half or more of the transactions conflicting with a committing transaction are of higher priority, the transaction is made to wait for the high priority transactions to complete; otherwise, it is allowed to commit while the conflicting transactions are aborted. While the transaction is waiting, it is possible that it will be restarted due to the commit of one of the conflicting transactions with higher priority.

3.1 Data-Priority-Based Locking Protocol (DP)

In protocol DP, each data item carries a priority which is equal to the highest priority of all transactions currently in the system that include the data item in their access lists. When a new transaction arrives at the system, the priority of each data item to be accessed is updated if the item has a priority lower than that of the transaction. The protocol assumes that a list of data items that are going to be accessed is submitted to the scheduler by the arriving transaction. When a transaction terminates, each data item that carries the priority of that transaction has its priority adjusted to that of the highest priority active transaction that is going to access that data item. The DP protocol assumes that there is a unique priority for each transaction.

A transaction list is maintained for each individual data item. The list contains the id and priority of the active transactions requiring access to the item. The list is sorted based on the transaction priorities, and the highest priority transaction determines the priority of the data item. The list is updated by the scheduler during the initialization and the commit/abort of relevant transactions.

Suppose that a transaction T requests a lock on data item D. In order to obtain the lock, the priority of transaction T must be equal to the priority of D; in other words, it should be the transaction responsible for the current priority of D. Otherwise (if the priority of T is less than that of D), transaction T is blocked.

A data item D may have been locked by a transaction T' when a new transaction T, containing the item D in its access list and carrying a priority higher than the priority of D, arrives at the system and updates the priority of D. If D is still locked by T' at the time T needs to access it, the lower priority transaction T' is aborted and T obtains its lock on D. The assumption that each transaction has a unique priority makes DP deadlock-free, since a high priority transaction is never blocked by lower priority transactions.

The DP protocol can be augmented with read/write lock semantics. For this augmentation, each data item is associated with two priority values, one for read accesses and one for write accesses. To obtain a read lock on a data item D, the priority of a transaction T must be larger than or equal to the write priority of D. A write lock request of transaction T on data item D is honored if T has a priority equal to the write priority of D, and larger than or equal to the read priority of D.

3.2 Performance Considerations in a Single-Site RTDBS

A simulation model based on an open queuing model of a single site database system was used to evaluate the performance of the concurrency control protocols. In the model, each transaction submitted to the system is associated with a deadline and assigned a unique real-time priority based on its deadline. The *Earliest Deadline First* policy is used in assigning priorities; i.e., a transaction with an earlier deadline has higher priority than a transaction with a later deadline. If any two of the transactions have the same deadline, the one that has arrived at the system earlier is assigned a higher priority. The transaction deadlines are *soft*; i.e., each transaction is executed to completion even if it misses its deadline. Concurrent data accesses of transactions are ordered based on the concurrency control protocol executed. Both CPU and IO queues are organized on the basis of the transaction priorities. Other details of the simulation model, such as the deadline assignment procedure for each new transaction, can be found in [24].

A Sample Performance Experiment: In this subsection, we present the results of one of the performance experiments conducted. In all experiments, the set of parameters presented in Table 1 was used to specify the system configuration and workload. Since the concurrency control protocols are different in handling data access conflicts among the transactions, the best way to compare the performance characteristics of the protocols is to conduct experiments under high data conflict conditions. The small *db_size* value is to create a data contention environment which produces the desired high level of data conflicts among the transactions. This small database can be considered as the most frequently accessed fraction of a larger database. *slack_rate* is the parameter used in assigning deadlines to new transactions. The slack time of a transaction[1] is chosen randomly from an exponential distribution with a mean of *slack_rate* times the estimated processing time of the transaction.

Table 1. Performance Model Parameter Values

Parameter	Meaning	Value
db_size	Database size	200 items
mem_size	Main memory size	50 items
cpu_time	CPU time to process an item	12 msec
io_time	IO time to access a disk-resident item	12 msec
iat	Mean transaction interarrival time	100 msec
tr_type_prob	Fraction of update-type transactions	0.5
access_mean	Mean number of items accessed by a transaction	6
data_update_prob	Fraction of updated items by an update transaction	0.5
slack_rate	Average slack-time/processing-time for a transaction	5

The basic performance metric used in the evaluation of protocols is *success_ratio*; i.e., the fraction of transactions that satisfy their deadline constraints.

In this sample experiment, the real-time performance characteristics of concurrency control protocols were investigated for varying transaction loads in the system. The parameter *iat* was varied from 75 msec to 135 msec in steps of 10. The performance results are displayed in Figure 1.

We found that PI's performance cannot reach the level achieved by protocol PB. Remember that PB never blocks higher priority transactions, but instead aborts low priority transactions when necessary. PB also eliminates the possibility and cost of deadlocks. We can conclude that aborting a low priority transaction is preferable in RTDBSs to blocking a high priority one, even though aborts lead to a waste of resources. The performance of our protocol DP is better than that of protocol PB, especially at high transaction load. Some of the transaction aborts, and the resulting resource waste, experienced with protocol PB can be prevented by protocol DP, which employs prior knowledge of data requirements

[1] The slack time of a transaction specifies the maximum length of time the transaction can be delayed and still satisfy its deadline.

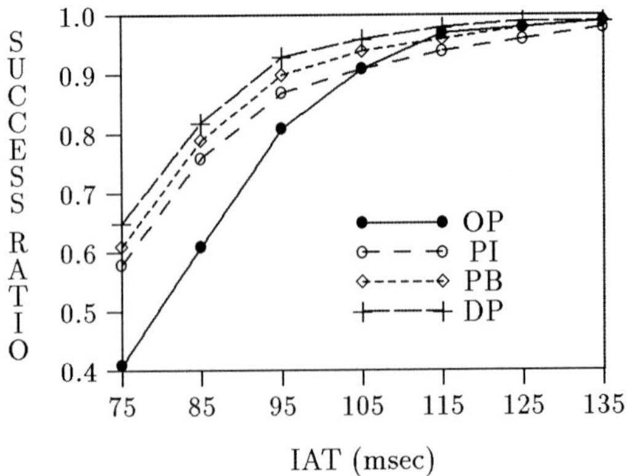

Fig. 1. Real-time performance of the protocols in terms of *success_ratio* as a function of the mean interarrival time of transactions.

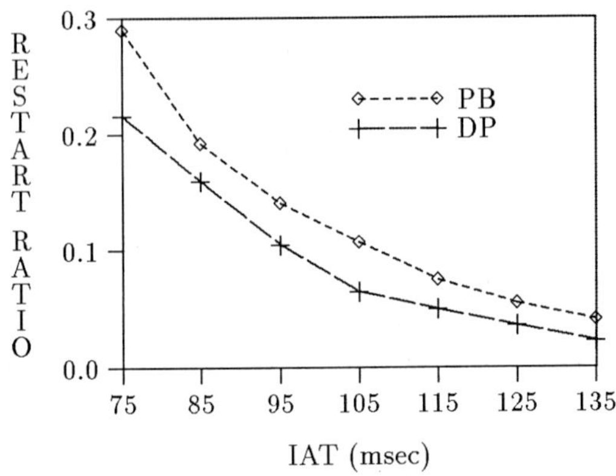

Fig. 2. Restart ratio obtained with protocols PB and DP.

in access scheduling. Protocol DP restricts the possibility of aborts to only the situation that between any two conflicting transactions, the low priority transaction accesses the data item before the high priority transaction is submitted to the system (before the priority of the data item is adjusted by the entry of the high priority transaction). For this special case the lower priority transaction is aborted when and if the higher priority transaction accesses the data item before the commitment of the low priority transaction. Figure 2 shows the restart ratio (i.e., the total number of restarts observed over the total number of transactions processed) obtained by executing these two protocols under varying levels of transaction load. The optimistic protocol (OP) performs very well for large values of interarrival time; i.e., when the system is lightly loaded. There is no overhead of checking for conflicts at each data access. Since the number of conflicts is small under low load levels, only a few transactions fail to be validated at commit time. However, under high load levels the performance of protocol OP is worse than other protocols. This can be explained by the increased number of restarts due to increased conflicts among transactions. The transactions that are in conflict with a committing transaction are aborted and restarted from the beginning. The wasted execution time due to the large number of restarts substantially increases the number of missed deadlines.

The results of some other experiments (e.g., performance impact of different priority assignment policies, fraction of update type transactions, database size, locality of references, the value of *slack_rate* parameter, etc.) are provided in [24].

In [23], we described the distributed versions of the concurrency control protocols presented in this paper, and studied the relative performance of the protocols in a nonreplicated database environment. In [25], we focused our attention on the *data replication* aspect of distributed RTDBSs.

4 Conclusions

A database system that processes transactions with timing constraints is usually called a real-time database system (RTDBS). A RTDBS attempts to satisfy the properties of both traditional database systems and real-time systems. Traditional database systems focus on maintaining database consistency in scheduling transactions. The users are not allowed to specify timing constraints. In real-time system scheduling, on the other hand, the emphasis is on satisfying transaction deadlines and the problem of maintaining the consistency of shared data is usually not addressed. Implementation of RTDBSs is rather difficult due to the conflicting requirements of meeting deadlines and maintaining data consistency. In many applications, it is not possible to satisfy both requirements. In this paper, we have discussed the main problems and the basic approaches taken in designing a RTDBS. We have also provided a summary of our current research that has focused on development and evaluation of concurrency control protocols.

References

1. Abbott, R., Garcia-Molina, H.: Scheduling Real-Time Transactions: A Performance Evaluation. 14th International Conference on Very Large Data Bases. (1988) 1–12
2. Abbott, R., Garcia-Molina, H.: Scheduling Real-Time Transactions with Disk Resident Data. 15th International Conference on Very Large Data Bases. (1989) 385–396
3. Abbott, R., Garcia-Molina, H.: Scheduling I/O Requests with Deadlines: A Performance Evaluation. 11th Real-Time Systems Symposium. (1990) 113–124
4. Biyabani, S., Stankovic, J., Ramamritham, K.: The Integration of Deadline and Criticalness in Hard Real-Time Scheduling. 9th Real-Time Systems Symposium. (1988) 152–160
5. Carey, M., Jauhari, R., Livny, M.: Priority in DBMS Resource Scheduling. 15th International Conference on Very Large Data Bases. (1989) 397–410

6. Chen, S., Stankovic, J., Kurose, J., Townley, D.: Performance Evaluation of Two New Disk Scheduling Algorithms for Real-Time Systems. Real-Time Systems Journal. **3** (1991) 307–336
7. Haritsa, J., Carey, M., Livny, M.: On Being Optimistic About Real-Time Constraints. ACM SIGACT-SIGMOD-SIGART. (1990) 331–343
8. Haritsa, J., Carey, M., Livny, M.: Dynamic Real-Time Optimistic Concurrency Control. 11th Real-Time Systems Symposium. (1990) 94–103
9. Haritsa, J., Carey, M., Livny, M.: Value-Based Scheduling in Real-Time Database Systems. Technical Report No.1024, Dept. of Computer Science, University of Wisconsin-Madison. (1991)
10. Haritsa, J., Carey, M., Livny, M.: Data Access Scheduling in Firm Real-Time Database Systems. Real-Time Systems Journal. **4** (1992) 203–241
11. Homg, D., Johnson, T., Chakravarthy, S.: Real-Time Transaction Scheduling: A Cost Conscious Approach. ACM SIGMOD Conference. (1993) 197–206
12. Huang, J., Stankovic, J., Towsley, D., Ramamritham, K.: Experimental Evaluation of Real-Time Transaction Processing. 10th Real-Time Systems Symposium. (1989) 144–153
13. Huang, J., Stankovic, J., Ramamritham, K., Towsley, D.: Experimental Evaluation of Real-Time Optimistic Concurrency Control Schemes. 17th International Conference on Very Large Data Bases. (1991) 35–46
14. Kim, W., Srivastava, J.: Enhancing Real-Time DBMS Performance with Multiversion Data and Priority Based Disk Scheduling. 12th Real-Time Systems Symposium. (1991) 222–231
15. Lin, K.J.: Consistency Issues in Real-Time Database Systems. 22nd Hawaii International Conference on Systems Sciences. (1989) 654–661
16. Özsoyoğlu, G., Özsoyoğlu, Z.M., Hou, W.C.: Research in Time and Error-Constrained Database Query Processing. 7th IEEE Workshop on Real-Time Operating Systems and Software. (1990) 32–38
17. Sha, L., Rajkumar, R., Lehoczky, J.: Concurrency Control for Distributed Real-Time Databases. ACM SIGMOD Record. **17** (1988) 82–98
18. Sha, L., Rajkumar, R., Lehoczky, J.: Priority Inheritance Protocols: An Approach to Real-Time Synchronization. IEEE Transaction on Computers. **39** (1990) 1175–1185
19. Sha, L., Rajkumar, R., Son, S.H., Chang, C.H.: A Real-Time Locking Protocol. IEEE Transactions on Computers. **40** (1991) 793–800
20. Singhal, M.: Issues and Approaches to Design of Real-time Database Systems. ACM SIGMOD Record. **17** (1988) 19–33
21. Son, S.H., Park, S., Lin, Y.: An Integrated Real-Time Locking Protocol. 8th International Conference on Data Engineering. (1992) 527–534
22. Stankovic, J., Zhao, W.: On Real-Time Transactions. ACM SIGMOD Record. **17** (1988) 4–18
23. Ulusoy, Ö., Belford, G.G.: Real-Time Lock Based Concurrency Control in a Distributed Database System. 12th International Conference on Distributed Computing Systems. (1992) 136–143
24. Ulusoy, Ö., Belford, G.G.: Real-Time Transaction Scheduling in Database Systems. Information Systems. **18** (1993) 559–580
25. Ulusoy, Ö.: Processing Real-Time Transactions in a Replicated Database System. International Journal of Distributed and Parallel Databases (to appear)

Database Exploration with Dynamic Abstractions

Sudhir Aggarwal, Inje Kim, Weiyi Meng
Department of Computer Science
State University of New York
Binghamton, NY 13902-6000

Abstract

For the efficient management of a large database we need a more friendly user-interface, more powerful abstraction capabilities, and more flexible data structures than is usually provided. A new database system called SCOPE was developed with the following three objectives: (1) unsophisticated end-users should be able to explore and navigate in a database system fairly intuitively, (2) the structures and the operations related to representing the data should be easily and efficiently modifiable, and (3) there should be abstraction techniques that allow the same data to be viewed in multiple ways. In the navigation for finding the desired data, views (or scopes) of the data are automatically generated with different levels of "coarseness" to facilitate the user's exploration of the database. Each scope is automatically and efficiently generated using certain dynamic abstractions of the data. Furthermore, an attribute-oriented tree structure is used in SCOPE to handle its data (including token data and metadata) uniformly and flexibly. An operational prototype of SCOPE has also been implemented to test the design.

Keywords: database systems, meta data, structural flexibility, database exploration, data abstraction, abstract view, user-interface

1 Introduction

Most conventional database systems deal with data that are rather rigidly structured in accordance with their database definitions. In these systems, the structures or schemas relating to the data must be defined with a great deal of information about how the data and the structures can be manipulated. Once defined, such schemas are often difficult to modify. In practice, however, real world applications typically require frequent changes of schemas [Rodd92, Monk93], such as those necessitated by the discovery of a mistake in an earlier schema design. Structural flexibility is a desirable feature of a database system, especially when the system is used to manage dynamically changing data. For such data that is "raw" with its type unknown, it is hard to define the logical structures fully in a database system at the time when the data is collected. Clearly, a database system that allows easy and efficient modification of its data structures would be more suitable for dealing with data that is evolving continuously.

When a database has a large number of entity sets and each entity set contains a large number of instances, it is very difficult, if not impossible, for an unsophisticated user to find the desired data from the database. Lately, this data "mining" is one of the popular topics among database researchers, because the end user has difficulty in formulating an appropriate query in a database with a large number of entity sets and the huge amount of data returned from the database may be overwhelming [Ston93, Barb93]. The problem with such a database system is that the user is provided with only one level of data, i.e., the raw data. This problem can be alleviated if the contents of the database can be somehow summarized and presented at different levels of coarseness. It suggests that the ability to generate multiple views with different levels of coarseness of the raw data in the database could allow a user to find the desired data more quickly since a more detailed view is examined only when it is of enough interest.

The SCOPE system is designed to address the above challenges. All data in the SCOPE database, including token data and metadata, is uniformly represented using tree structures. As such, modifying a schema and modifying raw data can be handled uniformly. Also, in the SCOPE system, minimum semantic constraints are traded for conceptual simplicity. These features make it easier for an unsophisticated user to modify the data structures in the SCOPE system, as compared to traditional database systems. Note that the tree structure itself also provides a convenient conceptual model to use when browsing in the database [Came88]. In the SCOPE system, at any point in the current search (at a specific node in the tree), a user is allowed to change the current scope to a coarser scope (rough but outlined view) or a finer scope (detailed but limited view). The new scope will be generated dynamically and automatically by the system. Several abstraction techniques (discussed later) such as *pruning*, *pulling-up*, and *aggregate function computation* are used to manipulate the scoping.

Among the existing data models, the one closest to our tree structure based data model is the hierarchical data model used in IMS [IMS]. SCOPE differs from the hierarchical model by storing attribute-oriented data on the edges rather than record-oriented data at the nodes. SCOPE also has a tying method to connect one node to another resulting in an arbitrary directed graph, rather than a strict tree. Many browsing approaches have been suggested to access database contents easily and efficiently. For a browser, basic operations such as structuring, filtering, navigating, and zooming are generally used [Lars86]. These operations are performed based on the target database structure that already exists, but the SCOPE system builds its own database structure for efficient browsing and it also has the more general features of a database system. In [Rafa91a, Rafa91b], several data models (SUBJECT, SAM, STORM, Mefisto, etc.) involving abstraction processes in databases are introduced. In contrast, abstractions in SCOPE are generated automatically and dynamically. The SCOPE system generates a new abstract view for a user based on the user's current view point in the tree with its own abstraction techniques which are not used in other systems. In recent years, system support for schema modification has been recognized as an important feature of the next-generation database systems. The proposed techniques include version control of schema [Kim88], schema evolution [Anda91, Rodd92], and schema transformation [Tres93]. These techniques all try to minimize database reorganization after a modification of the schema, but they generally have to maintain different versions of schema and transform one to the other. The SCOPE system offers an alternative approach to this problem. It uses parallel trees with data attributes on the edges for presenting both schema and data uniformly and allows flexible mapping between them to make a modification of the schema relatively easy.

2 Data Structures of SCOPE

2.1 Tree Data Structures

To express information relating to the raw data, SCOPE uses three characteristics of data: *token*, *interpretation*, and *representation*. A token is an individual instance of data such as "John", "45", "123 Vestal", etc., and can be viewed as uninterpreted raw data. An interpretation is an (arbitrary) meaning assigned to a set of data tokens. For example, token "John", "45" and "123 Vestal" might be interpreted as "Name", "Age" and "Address", respectively. Also, it is possible to have multiple interpretations for the same set of data tokens ("Address" or "Residence"). A representation is a storage/representational property common to a set of data tokens with the same interpretation and it determines the physical operations available on that data set. The data appears as labels on edges of the trees. Some commonly used primitive representation types are *character, string, integer*, etc. An example of an artificial representation may be *index*, which represents unique identification of tokens implicitly generated by the system. The three characteristics of data are combined together to express structured information. SCOPE uses parallel tree-structures to express this structured information, since a tree provides a natural and flexible way of organizing information. A tree-structure has the ability to organize data with more and more details as needed following the hierarchical order in which data are linked, and it also allows many opportunities to derive abstracted data from the raw data (i.e., the base data).

In SCOPE, data is organized as three types of parallel trees with the possibility of defining equivalences through tying nodes together that turn the tree into a directed graph. Three different types of trees in the SCOPE system are: *representation tree* (R-Tree), *interpretation tree* (I-tree), and *tokens trees* (T-trees). The R-tree has representation edges, the I-tree has interpretation edges, and each T-tree has token edges. These data trees (R-tree, I-tree, and T-trees) are used to express data in a uniform structure and they are always traversed in parallel by the system. By maintaining parallel tree (or graph) structures and synchronizing the user's location on each tree during exploration, multiple data tokens can be accessed with their corresponding interpretations and representations and sometimes with their multiple interpretations. Due to space limitations more details regarding this "tying" concept will not be discussed in this paper, so interested readers are refered to [Agga93]. Through the directed connection of nodes in a tree, relationships such as the IS_A relationships, the many-to-many relationships, and the recursive relationships can be efficiently implemented.

Most conventional database systems represent data in a record-oriented form, which inevitably causes a loss of flexibility in structuring their data [Stam93]. In SCOPE there are no such restrictions when defining entities and relationships. SCOPE only requires that attributive characteristic of data be a label on the edge in a tree. In other words, an attribute name (usually called an attribute) is implemented by a labeled edge in the I-tree, its domain type by a labeled edge in the R-tree, and its values by labeled edges in T-trees (Fig. 1). A major benefit of this attribute-oriented database system is to allow the maximum flexibility in defining data, which can be refined or modified easily after the creation of an entity. Edges in one tree may have any possible correspondence to those in other trees for its structural flexibility. For instance, an interpretation may be mapped to a set of tokens (or null tokens), and a set of tokens may be mapped to multiple interpretations, which has not been considered in other database models. In SCOPE, the addition of an attribute becomes the addition of an edge and the addition of a relationship is a connection of related edges in the tree. Deletion of an attribute or a relationship is a deletion of an edge or a disconnection of edges. A modification of schema information in the R-tree and I-tree does not require immediate physical reorganization of T-trees since the SCOPE system assumes the schema to be the right structure and ignores the difference from schema to data trees.

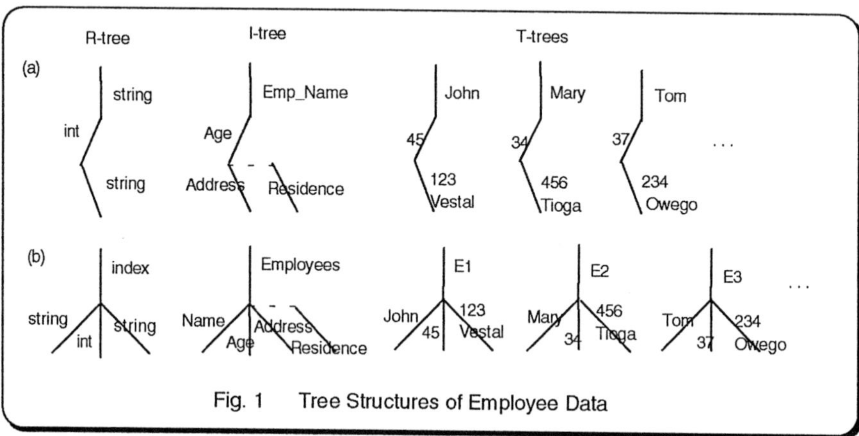

Fig. 1 Tree Structures of Employee Data

2.2 Planes and Mappings

The tree structure for the representation, interpretations, and tokens in each plane enables us to map one to the other as if they are geometrically superimposed on one another. Conceptually, different trees can be assumed to be in different *data planes*: An R-tree is in the *representation plane*, I-trees are in the *interpretation planes*, and T-trees are in the *tokens planes*. When a tree structure is placed in a plane, we define that each edge be located at a specific *angle*. If the corresponding edges in each plane maintain the same angle, trees in the three different types of data planes can be mapped correctly. A basic assumption of this angle assignment is that every edge under a parent edge have a unique angle value for its identification in a data plane. If there are parallel edges with the same angle, they should be located in different data planes. As there are multiple token edges that map to a single interpretation edge in general, token edges with the same angle are connected to their parent edge such that the token subtrees are located in their own tokens planes. The same is true for multiple interpretation edges with the same angle. SCOPE maintains the parallel access for the three different types of data planes and does the mapping of trees between data planes automatically. In Fig. 2, if we overlap the I-trees in the interpretation plane with the corresponding T-trees in the tokens planes, we can obtain a correct (sometimes multiple) interpretation about each data token.

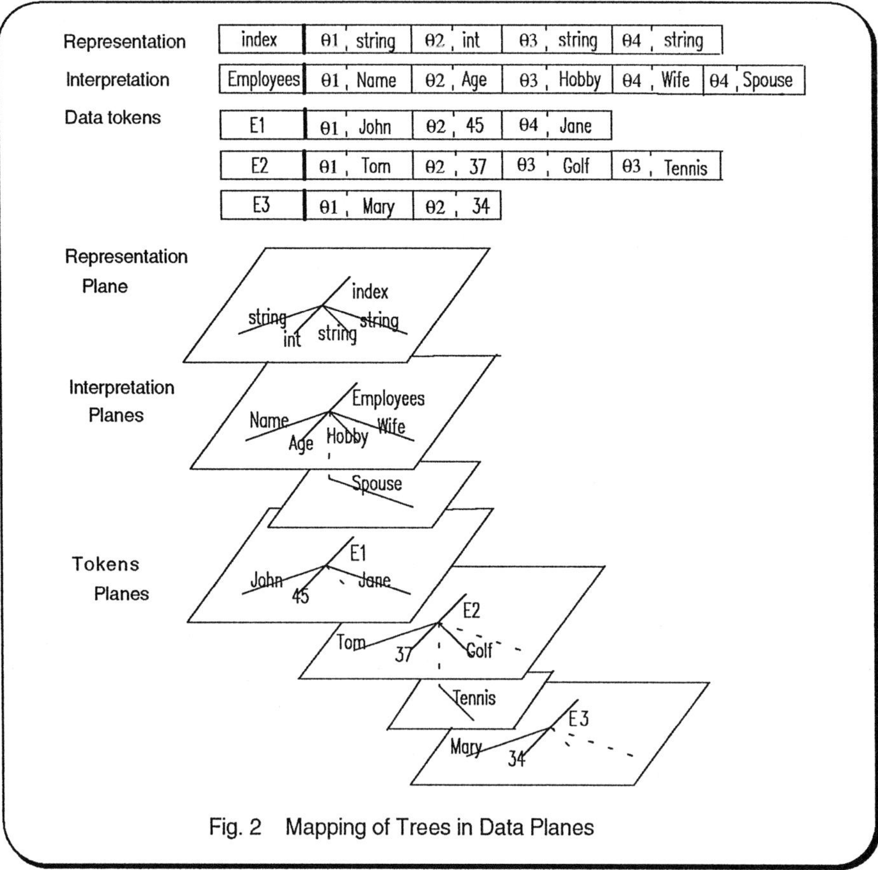

Fig. 2 Mapping of Trees in Data Planes

3 Dynamic Abstractions

A major use of a database system can be to provide varying descriptions of the real world by applying different levels of abstractions on existing data. Abstraction enables us to obtain summaries of data, to hide detail, and to concentrate on general, common properties of a set of objects. In this era when computer use is widespread and the expertise of the user is consequently less, a database with conceptually simple abstraction capabilities is needed [Kort91]. The SCOPE data model gives a user a flexible view of the data by dynamically changing the abstractions as the user navigates in the database and as the user voluntarily changes the "scope" at any point in this navigation.

3.1 Pruning

The first step in building a higher-level view from a complex tree is to reduce the scope of an entity at a particular location when it has multiple child edges. For this reduction process, a *pruning abstraction* can be applied to a tree. The pruning abstraction cuts down the number of child edges at a tree node by eliminating less important edges, and thus provides an abbreviated view. For the selection of which edges in a tree to retain, we assign a priority value *Rp* for each edge and let the pruning parameter *pr_num* controls the amount of pruning. The pruning process eliminates edges with lower priorities in each step of its reduction. Fig. 3a is a simple example of pruning for a single level of child edges in a tree. If the same concept of pruning is applied to multiple levels of edges in a tree, less important edges in the whole tree will be eliminated for the pruned overview of it. Now, to compare the priority between edges at different levels in a tree, a location dependent absolute priority is required for each edge. This absolute priority can be computed based on the current node location of the user and the relative edge priority already assigned. It is desirable for the absolute priority values to be controlled by parameters provided by the user so that the pruning may result in different scopes, from a deeper view to a wider view of a tree. For this purpose, a weighting factor is applied to yield more of a depth-first or a breadth-first selection of edges in a tree according to the user request. Our suggested formula for calculating the absolute priority of an edge is;

$$Ap = Pp + Rp * Dw^{L} \qquad (3.1)$$

where Ap is the absolute priority of an edge, Pp is the absolute priority of the parent edge, Rp is the relative priority of the edge, Dw is the depth weight for pruning, L is the level number of the edge relative to the current top edge of the tree.

Our observation from formula (3.1) is: (1) assuming Dw is always greater than zero (Dw > 0), a child edge's absolute priority is always lower than its parent's (Ap > Pp); (2) pruning with a smaller value of Dw makes deeper edge selections in a tree and pruning with larger values of Dw makes wider edge selection in a tree, hence this

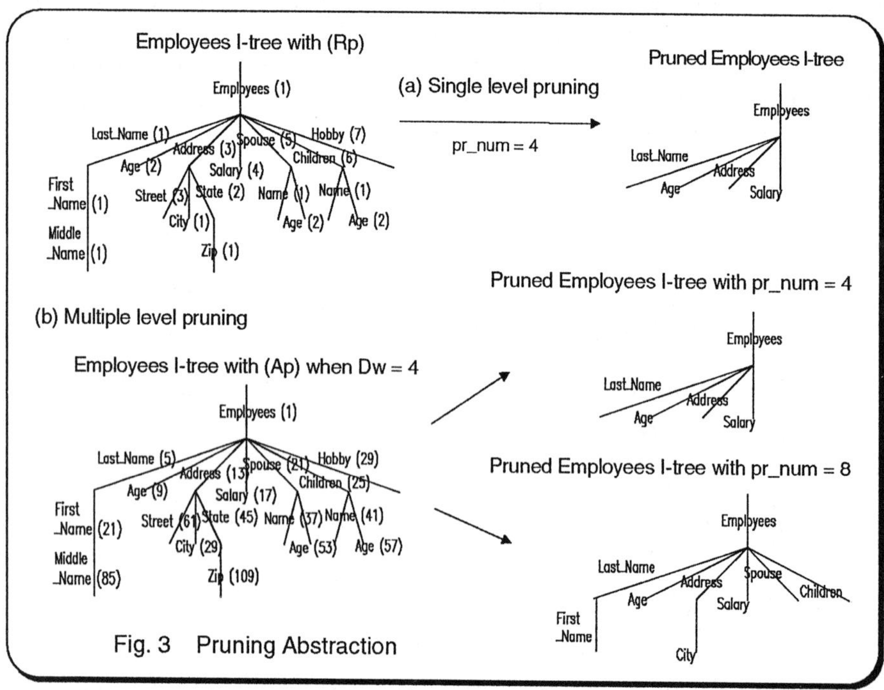

Fig. 3 Pruning Abstraction

builds deeper or wider abstraction trees respectively; (3) pruning with a value of Dw equal to pr_num leaves only the first level of child edges and pruning with a value of Dw smaller than pr_num leaves multiple levels of child edges in a tree. If the default value of Dw is set equal to pr_num, it will produce the same result as in single level pruning (Fig. 3a). With the parameter settings in the figure, each pruned abstraction tree in multiple levels (Fig. 3b) can be produced according to the Ap's calculated by formula (3.1) as follows: For example, with Dw = 4,

$$Ap(Employee) = Pp(Employee) + Rp(Employee) * Dw^{L} = 0 + 1 * 4^{0} = 1$$

$$Ap(Address) = Pp(Address) + Rp(Address) * Dw^{L}$$

$$= Ap(Employee) + Rp(Address) * Dw^{L} = 1 + 3 * 4^{1} = 13$$

$$Ap(State) = Pp(State) + Rp(State) * Dw^{L} = 13 + 2 * 4^{2} = 45$$

$$Ap(Zip) = Pp(Zip) + Rp(Zip) * Dw^{L} = 45 + 1 * 4^{3} = 109$$

3.2 Pulling-up

After the pruning abstraction certain edge labels might not provide much information. For example, when the parent edge is an index edge, the token value of an index edge may not mean much for the user since it only shows the index value. The *pulling-up abstraction* pulls up the most important data attributes from the lower level descendant edges in a tree structure to show more meaningful information than that of the current edge. The difference between pruning and pulling-up is that the pruning abstraction just prunes away lower priority edges in a tree and does not change the value of an edge, but the pulling-up abstraction pulls up identifying data attributes from the descendant edges and substitutes the current parent edge with them. Hence, after the pulling-up, the user has the illusion that multiple level edges deeper in the tree have been transformed to single level edges higher in the tree. When we represent a set of related data items by a pair S = (I, D), where "I" is a set of identifying data items and "D" is a set of detailed data items as suggested in the *form* concepts for a data modeling mechanism [Shu82, Laen84], the pulling-up abstraction pulls out identifying data items for "I" according to the priorities of the edges.

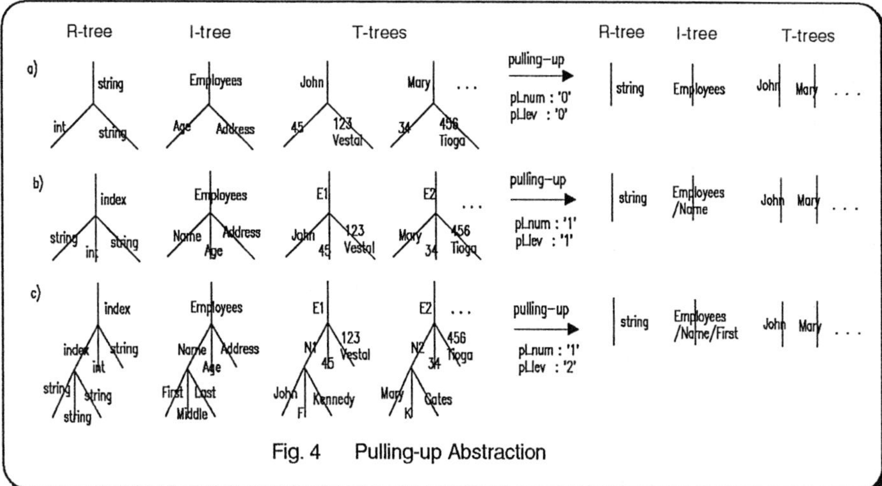

Fig. 4 Pulling-up Abstraction

The number of identifying data items is controlled by the parameter *pl_num*. For index edges it is necessary to pull up attributes from its children edges, but for non-index edges the edge itself can be an identifying data item. There could be a case that a pulling-up should be applied recursively because a pulling-up of an edge may require another pulling-up. To control unnecessary deep pulling-up, the parameter *pl_lev* limits the number of levels to be examined in the pulling-up process. To represent the pulled-up edge in the I-tree, the parent interpretation is combined with the selected child edge interpretation with a "/" (slash) between the two. This is used as the new label on the parent edge in the SCOPE tree structure. The representation of the new edge is the same as that of the child edge that is pulled up. For example, suppose Employees = (I, D), where I = {Name} and D = {Age, Address}. Fig. 4 shows three different pulling-up abstractions, based on different control parameters.

3.3 Aggregation

Another abstraction process is applied to a set of token edges corresponding to an interpretation edge. The *aggregation abstraction* yields a single aggregate value computed from the values on the token edges. There are many operations to aggregate multiple tokens into one statistic such as count, sum, average, maximum, minimum, etc. These aggregate functions can be system-defined statistical functions or user-defined functions depending on the characteristics of the edge. Some edges may require more than one aggregate function. The aggregate operations to be applied should be associated with the interpretation edge. This can be set by the user manually, or by the system automatically. For automatically determining the correct aggregation operation to use, we need some intelligent process that can derive possible aggregations from the properties of data. For instance, a reasonable aggregation for a set of nonnumeric tokens may be the count of the number of child edge tokens, and for a set of numeric data tokens it may be a sum or average of the tokens. After the aggregation, the user has an illusion that the multiple data tokens are aggregated to a single token edge for each aggregate operation. The interpretation and representation of the aggregated edge are determined according to the aggregation operations (Fig. 5).

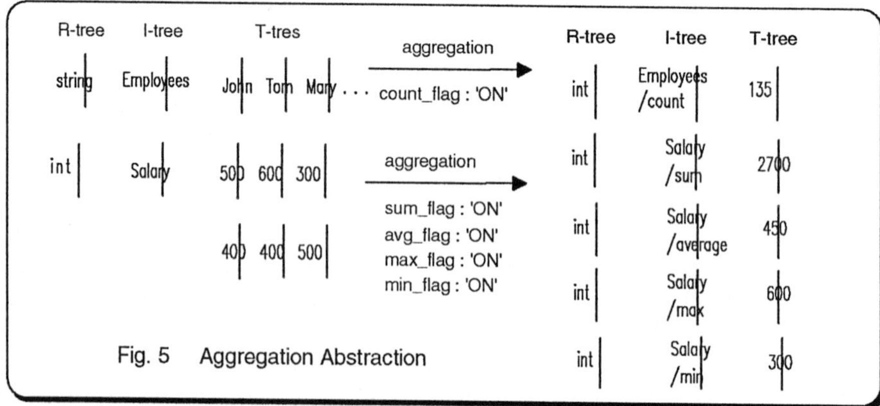

Fig. 5 Aggregation Abstraction

3.4 Applications

By applying the abstraction processes to tree structured data we provide the user a more flexible view of the database with varying levels of abstraction. When we create a university database with the university's name, address, employee, department, and student information, SCOPE builds various abstract views as in Fig. 6 by applying the abstraction processes that have been proposed previously. As we can see, each different abstraction level provides different depths of view that would match a user's interest. SCOPE applies the dynamic abstractions starting with the base data and produces multiple levels of hierarchical views automatically.

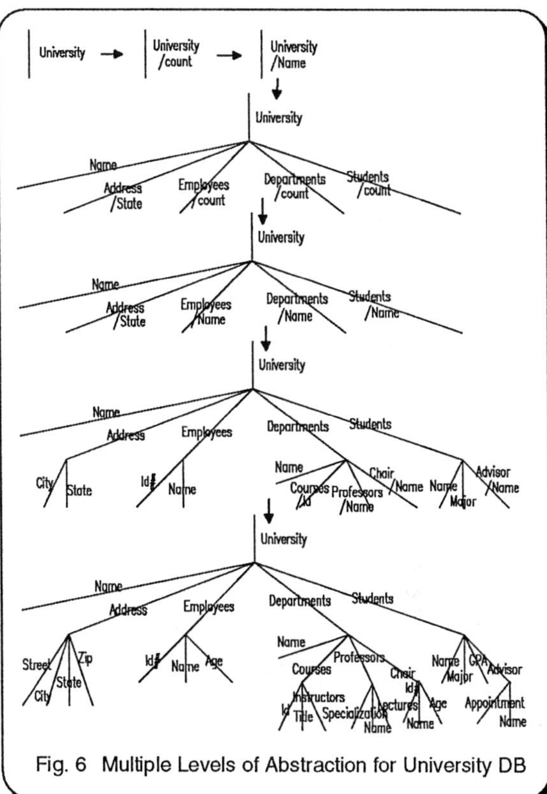

Fig. 6 Multiple Levels of Abstraction for University DB

4 Conclusions

In this paper, we described a new prototype database system SCOPE that allows naive users to explore a large database by simply following intuition. To achieve this, we proposed to use the tree structure to uniformly represent all data in the database, including metadata such as interpretation and representation of token data. Such a representation provides not only better structural flexibility but also an excellent framework for natural data exploring. We also developed and/or applied different techniques such as pruning, pulling-up and aggregation to allow views with different coarsenesses be generated to facilitate users' exploration in the database. The techniques described in this paper have been implemented in a prototype system and the details of the user interface for the system is discussed in [Agga93].

We are also investigating several issues for the expansion of the SCOPE system. One is to provide a query capability that may help users find desired data faster. Due to the SCOPE system's graphical user interface, a combination of exploring capabilities and query capabilities may be the best solution. Another issue is performance evaluation. Investigation will be conducted to see whether naive users can indeed find desired data from a very large database easily and efficiently. A third issue will be to explore tools to add large amounts of data quickly to the database. Such tools will be necessary when incorporating large volumes of data coming automatically from real-time sensors. Finally, we intend to extend SCOPE to a distributed environment, as we expect multiple users to be exploring the database simultaneously with updates being performed at several locations in the database. We feel that our initial design will allow this, as our data manipulation, exploration, and abstraction operations are all based on localized information and never depend on anything but a fairly local scope around the current location.

References

[Agga93] S.Aggarwal, I.Kim, and W.Meng, *SCOPE: A Database System for Managing Massive and Dynamically Changing Data.* SUNY/Binghamton CS-TR-93-17, 1993

[Anda91] J.Andandy, M.Leonard, and C.Palisser, *Management of Schema Evolution in Database.* VLDB Conference, 1991.

[Barb93] D.Barbara, *Extending the Scope of Database Services.* SIGMOD RECORD, Vol.22, No.1, March 1993

[Came88] E.Cameron, D.Cohen, B.Gopinath, W.Keese, L.Ness, P Uppaluru and J.Vollaro, *The IC* Model of Parallel Computation and Programming Environment.* IEEE TSE., Vol.14-3, March 1988.

[IMS] IBM Corporation. *Information Management System/Virtual Storage General Information manual.* IBM Form No. GH20--1260.

[Kim88] W.Kim and H.Chou, *Versions of Schema for Object-Oriented Databases.* VLDB Conference, 1988.

[Kort91] H.F.Korth and A.Silberschatz, *Database System Concepts.* McGraw-Hill, 1991.

[Laen84] A.H.F.Laender, *An Approach to Interactive Definition of Database Views.* Proc. 3rd BNCOD (British National Conference On Database), 1984.

[Lars86] J.A.Larson, *A Visual Approach to Browsing in a Database Environment.* IEEE Computer, Dec. 1986.

[Monk93] S.Monk and I.Sommerville, *Schema Evolution in OODB Using Class Versioning.* SIGMOD RECORD, Vol.22, No.3, Sep.1993.

[Rafa91a] M.Rafanelli, *Data Models'.* Statistical and Scientific Databases, Ellis Horwood Ltd., 1991.

[Rafa91b] M.Rafanelli and F.L.Ricci, *A Functional Model for Macro-databases.* SIGMOD RECORD, Vol.20, No.1, Mar. 1991.

[Rodd92] J.F.Roddick, *Schema Evolution in Database Systems - An Annotated Bibliography.* SIGMOD RECORD, Vol.21, No.4, Dec. 1992.

[Shu82] N.C.Shu, V.Y.Lum, F.C.Tung, and C.L.Chang, *Specification of Forms Processing and Business Procedures for Office Automation.* IEEE TSE, Vol.SE-8, No.5, Sep. 1982

[Stam93] J.P.Stamen, *Structuring Databases for Analysis.* IEEE Spectrum, Oct. 1993.

[Ston93] M.Stonebraker, R.Agrawal, U.Dayal, E.Neuhold, and A.Reuter, *DBMS Research at a Crossroads: The Vienna Update.* VLDB Conference, 1993

[Tres93] M.Tresch and M.H.Scholl, *Schema Transformation without Database Reorganization.* SIGMOD RECORD, Vol.22, No.1, March 1993.

Soft Querying, a New Feature for Database Management Systems

Patrick BOSC, Ludovic LIETARD and Olivier PIVERT

IRISA/ENSSAT
BP 447 22305 LANNION Cédex
FRANCE

Abstract. This paper deals with imprecise querying of regular relational databases which is intended to make database management systems more powerful. A special emphasis is put on flexible queries addressed to regular databases. We first show that when comparing various attempts made to deal with such queries, the fuzzy set approach turns out to generalize the other solutions. Secondly, we present some key features of SQLf, an extension of the SQL query language. SQLf allows the expression of a wide range of flexible queries whose interpretation is based on fuzzy set theory.

Key-words: Relational databases, Fuzzy sets, Flexible queries, SQL query language.

1 Introduction

In order to extend data base querying capabilities, some efforts have been made in the last few years to propose alternatives to the use of Boolean logic, which remains the only way to characterize the information required in the existing DBMSs. Boolean queries occasionally reveal themselves to be too rigid in the specification of the authorized values and limited in the choice and semantics of the available operators. Several research works have been dedicated to the definition of more or less "flexible" systems [9, 14]. In this paper, we consider usual relational databases where data are exactly known and we use the terms "flexible" or "soft" or "imprecise" to characterize the systems which allow for the expression of preferences in the queries. In such a system, the objective no longer consists in finding the elements which satisfy a criterion, but rather in determining the extent to which an element satisfies it, which induces a ranking over the elements.

Two main approaches have been investigated in order to express flexible queries. The first one is based on ad'hoc extensions of the Boolean framework where the notion of preference is introduced. More precisely, the idea is to select elements with a Boolean condition and then to use the preferences to order the previously selected elements. The second approach advocates the use of fuzzy conditions. One important difference between (extended) Boolean and fuzzy systems resides in the fact that the former uses two sequential mechanisms - selection then ordering - whereas the latter relies on a single mechanism: all the elements are, a priori, concerned with a process aimed at the determination of a satisfaction degree which provides a canonical ordering. We will see in the course of the paper that the fuzzy set based approach has several interests (such as the use of linguistic terms inside queries, wide range of queries) and can be considered a general setting for the expression of flexible queries delivering discriminated answers. Another important aspect for database flexible querying is to provide users with appropriate query languages and it is necessary to define languages supporting flexible querying capabilities.

Since no usual relational language offers a sufficient framework to authorize flexible interrogation, we have extended the functions of an existing language in order to allow the formulation of imprecise criteria, with a fuzzy set interpretation. A first fuzzy set based extension of the language SEQUEL [8] has been proposed [2], which only allowed the expression of simple fuzzy queries (mainly projection-selection-join queries). Now based on SQL, we have defined a more complete extension, called SQLf, by studying some aspects not yet dealt with, particularly those which concern the extension of nesting operators and also selection operators applying to sets of tuples, e.g. quantifiers. We have attempted to make SQLf as much like SQL as possible, particularly with regard to query equivalences [4]. For each type of query, we have therefore been induced to examine whether the equivalences between several formulations which are valid in a Boolean context remained when the relations resulted from fuzzy restrictions and when the used connectors themselves became imprecise.

This paper is organized as follows. In section 2, we present the essential elements of the framework offered by fuzzy sets. Section 3 concerns a comparison between several attempts to flexible querying of regular databases. The originality of our work is the expression of queries in a single framework (fuzzy sets), which makes the comparaison straightforward possible. In section 4, the main features of SQLf, an extension of the relational query language SQL, allowing imprecise queries are briefly outlined.

2 Fuzzy Sets and Vague Predicates

2.1 Fuzzy Sets

The concept of fuzzy sets, introduced by L.A. Zadeh [19], involves extending the notion of a regular set in order to express classes with ill-defined boundaries (corresponding in particular to linguistic values, e.g. tall, young, well-paid, important, etc). Within this framework there is a gradual transition between non-membership and total membership. A degree of membership is associated to every element x of a referential X. It takes its values in the interval [0,1] instead of the pair {0,1}. When F is a finite and discrete fuzzy set, it is denoted: $F = \Sigma\mu_F(x_i) / x_i = d_1/x_1 + ... + d_n/x_n$, where d_i/x_i stands for an element x_i with the degree d_i ($\mu_F(x_i) = d_i$) and + is the union operation. It is important to clarify that beyond these degrees themselves, the idea above all is to order the elements of the universe. We will see in section 2.2 that this notion is used to define imprecise predicates. The combination of such predicates will rely in particular on the set operations : intersection, union, complement and difference which are applicable to fuzzy sets according to the following definitions (A and B represent two fuzzy sets defined in the universe X):

$$\forall x \in X, \mu_{A \cap B}(x) = \min(\mu_A(x), \mu_B(x)), \quad \mu_{A \cup B}(x) = \max(\mu_A(x), \mu_B(x)),$$
$$\mu_{\bar{A}}(x) = 1 - \mu_A(x), \quad \mu_{A - B}(x) = \mu_{A \cap \bar{B}}(x) = \min(\mu_A(x), 1 - \mu_B(x)).$$

Other operations specific to fuzzy sets (i.e. having no counterpart in usual sets) have been defined, such as averaging operators [10, 18].

2.2 Fuzzy Relations and Fuzzy Predicates

In this paper, a fuzzy relation R is built over a set of domains $D_1, ..., D_n$ as a fuzzy subset of the Cartesian product and each element r of the relation R is provided with a membership degree $\mu_R(r)$ which expresses the extent to which r belongs to R. It is obvious that a regular relation is just a special case of a fuzzy relation where $\mu_R(r)$ equals 1. In the context of this paper, fuzzy relation will be derived from regular relations belonging to a database with the aid of fuzzy predicates. A fuzzy predicate is similar to a fuzzy set as it expresses the extent to which the arguments fit the predicate. An elementary predicate (single or multi-variable) allows for the comparison between variables and constants or between variables and they can be combined by means of connectors such as conjunction, disjunction and mean operators. Hereafter, is an example of fuzzy predicate (age = "young").

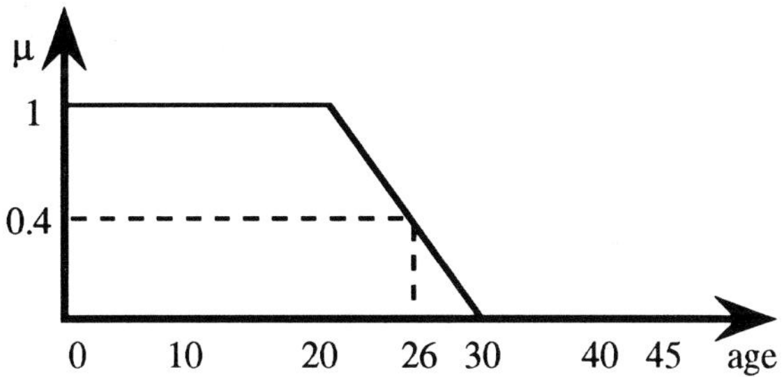

Fig. 1. The fuzzy predicate: "age = young"

3 Comparing Approaches to Flexible Querying

In the next subsections, we will show how the queries allowed in ad'hoc extensions of relational systems can be expressed in terms of fuzzy sets. Basically, any such query involves two aspects: a selection part (S) and an ordering part (O) and can be seen as : "select the tuples satisfying S, then rank them according to O". In the framework of fuzzy sets, we will have one component for S (S') valued over {0,1} (generally S itself) and one for O (O') expressing the ordering behaviour of the system as a membership degree over [0,1].

These two parts cannot be connected by a conjunction since we have to translate the "then" operation which is not symmetric. Let us consider an element which matches the selection part (S) but receives a null grade with respect to O. A usual conjunction would result in discarding this element since its overall grade would be null, as well as for an element which does not satisfy S and should really be eliminated. To distinguish between these two very different situations, a specific combination operator similar to those presented in [18], denoted *THEN*, is introduced: $A \; THEN \; B = A \cap (B \cup \beta)$ where $0 < \beta < \inf_{x \in B} \{\mu_B(x) > 0\}$ (1). According to this definition, any element matching the selection part obtains an overall membership degree which is strictly positive, whereas it is null for any element which does not satisfy the selection part. Finally, the expression of any query in the framework of fuzzy sets will be: S' *THEN* O'. It is of course of importance that the effect of O' is exactly the same as that of the initial mechanism expressed by O. One major problem is then to find out an appropriate fuzzy set expression in each case, which will be pointed out in the following subsections.

3.1 Complementary Ordering Criterion

In the PREFERENCES system [12], a question is composed of a principal condition C and a complementary part P that is relative to the description of preferences, both of which are based on Boolean expressions. The meaning of this type of question is : "find the tuples which satisfy C and rank them according to their satisfaction of P." This system allows for the combination of preference clauses (P) by means of two constructors : nesting (hierarchy of conditions) and juxtaposition (conditions of equal importance). Following on from R_C, subset of the tuples of a relation R satisfying condition C, the nesting (resp. juxtaposition) of preference clauses $P_1, \ldots, P_n$ leads to the sets : S_1 the subset of R_C satisfying P_1 and not P_2 (resp.

one single clause); S_2 the subset of R_C satisfying P_1 and P_2 but not P_3 (resp. exactly two clauses); ... ; S_n the subset of R_C satisfying P_1 and ... and P_n. The user receives as an initial response the set S_i not empty and with the highest index, and he can go back to the previous sets, all of which corresponds to a weakening of the preference condition. One of the significant advantages of this system is the avoidance of successive formulations in reaching a desired set of responses. However, the discrimination capacity remains limited to the number of preference predicates given by the user. It is possible to show that the initial queries written: C, nest(P_1, ... , P_n) (resp. C, juxt(P_1, ... , P_n)) can be equivalently expressed as: C *THEN* $AG_1(P_1, \ldots, P_n)$ (resp. C *THEN* $AG_2(P_1, \ldots, P_n)$) where AG_1 and AG_2 are defined by the characteristic functions: $\mu_{AG_1}(P_1,\ldots, P_n)(x) = \sum_{i=1}^{n} \mu'_{P_i}(x)/n$ and $\mu_{AG_2}(P_1,\ldots, P_n)(x) = \sum_{i=1}^{n} \mu_{P_i}(x)/n$ where $\mu'_{P_i}(x) = \min_{j \leq i} \mu_{P_j}(x)$ and $\mu_{P_i}(x) = 1$ if $P_i(x)$ is true, 0 otherwise.

3.2 Distance to an Ideal Object

A second idea relies upon questions which include conditions resting on the notion of resemblance (≈) rather than strict equality. Here conditions of the type "X ≈ v" are used where "v" represents an ideal value, but where other values are nevertheless acceptable (for instance salary ≈ $2000 means that $2000 is excellent but values around (the interval [1950-2050] for instance) can also be accepted). The evaluation of such a condition on an element t is aimed at defining a distance d(t) and obeys the following principle : if X(t) is somewhat close to the value "v", then the value for d(t) is the fixed distance between X(t) and v, otherwise d(t) is infinite. In the presence of connectors such as conjunction and disjunction, an overall distance must then be calculated, thus allowing the elements concerned to be ordered. The systems ARES [11] and VAGUE [13] use this approach and we point out the correspondence of ARES queries in the context of fuzzy sets.

|age1 - age2|	distage
0	0
1	1
2	1
3	2
4	2
5	2
6	3

job1	job2	distjob
engineer	engineer	0
engineer	professor	1
engineer	ass-prof.	2
engineer	technician	4
engineer	analyst	3
analyst	analyst	0
.	.	.

Fig. 2. Two examples of distance relations in ARES

In ARES, elementary distances are attached to a given domain and a relation describes the distance between any two values (see figure 2 for an example). In a given query (containing both Boolean (B_i) and predicates involving resemblance (S_i) that can only be ANDed), the user chooses a threshold (t_i) for each predicate S_i. The global distance is the sum of the elementary distances tied to the resemblance predicates involved in the query (Euclidian distance in VAGUE). It is possible to show that the initial query (2) and the expression (3) in the context of fuzzy sets are equivalent:

B_1 *and* ... *and* B_p *and* S_1 *and* ... *and* S_n (2)

(B_1 *and* ... *and* B_p *and* S'_1 *and* ... *and* S'_n) *THEN* $AG_3(S_1, \ldots, S_n)$ (3)

where S'_i represents the constraint over all more or less acceptable values with respect to S_i and the chosen threshold t_i. For instance, the query:

"find the employees whose age is around 25 and job is close to engineer" (4)

involves two resemblance predicates and, in reference to figure 2, age ≈ 25 (S_i) with a threshold 2 leads to S'_i: age ∈ [20,30], whereas job ≈ 'engineer' (S_j) with a threshold 1 leads to S'_j : job = 'engineer' or 'professor'. $AG_3(S_1, \ldots, S_n)$ computes a rank according to: $\mu_{AG_3}(S_1,\ldots, S_n)(x) = (\sum_{i=1}^{n} \mu_{S_i}(x) * t_i) / (\sum_{i=1}^{n} t_i)$ with $\mu_{S_i}(x) = (t_i - dist_{S_i}(x)) / t_i$ if $dist_{S_i}(x) \leq t_i$, 0 otherwise (t_i being the threshold for S_i).

In ARES (as well as in VAGUE), only elements which satisfy more or less any term of a conjunction are ordered. It is clear that this behaviour may cause some discontinuity since an element which is satisfying very poorly each term will be retained whereas one satisfying very well all terms but one, will be definitely rejected.

3.3 Criteria with Preferences and Weighting

In the framework of information retrieval, the flexible retrieval system called MULTOS [16] has been proposed. Its principle consists in replacing a traditional criterion with a set of criteria to which an explicit preference (value between 0 and 1, or linguistic term) is attached. Thus, if we are interested in the year of publication, we might write : {year ∈ [1978, 1982] *preferred*, year [1983, 1988] *accepted*}. Furthermore, we can weight each set of criteria (e.g. the subject matter is more important (*high*) than the price of the document (*medium*) which in turn is more important than the year of publication (*low*)). The connectors, conjunction and disjunction, allow the combination of several criteria of querying. In particular, the semantics of the conjunction is expressed by the weighted sum (the aforementioned linguistic values *high*, *medium* and *low* or values between 0 and 1 expressing a normalized weight) of the results associated with the different criteria according to the preference attached to them (*accepted*, *preferred*). In this system, a query is expressed as:

$$(X_1 = v_{1,1}\ p_{1,1}\ X_1 = v_{1,2}\ p_{1,2}\ \ldots\ X_1 = v_{1,n_1}\ p_{1,n_1})\ w_1\ \textit{and} \ldots \textit{and}$$
$$(X_k = v_{k,1}\ p_{k,1}\ X_k = v_{k,2}\ p_{k,2}\ \ldots\ X_k = v_{k,n_k}\ p_{k,n_k})\ w_k$$

where $v_{i,j}$ represents one or several possible values for X_i with the associated preference $p_{i,j}$ and w_i is the weight tied to the condition applied to variable X_i. The corresponding expression in the context of fuzzy sets is :

$$((X_1 = v_{1,1}\ \textit{or}\ X_1 = v_{1,2}\ \textit{or} \ldots \textit{or}\ X_1 = v_{1,n_1})\ \textit{and}\ \ldots\ \textit{and}$$
$$(X_k = v_{k,1} \text{ or } X_k = v_{k,2} \text{ or } \ldots X_k = v_{k,n_k}))\ \textit{THEN}\ AG_5(C_1, \ldots, C_n).$$

The aggregation is: $\mu_{AG_5}(C_1,\ldots, C_k)(x) = (\sum_{i=1}^{k} \mu_{C_i}(x) * w_i(x) / (\sum_{i=1}^{k} w_i)$ and each term C_i is a fuzzy set obtained from the preferences attached to the variable X_i: $C_i = v_{i,1}/p_{i,1} + v_{i,2}/p_{i,2} + \ldots + v_{i,n_i}/p_{i,n_i}$. For instance, if we consider the expression : year ∈ [1978, 1982] *preferred*, year [1983, 1988] *accepted*, a possible corresponding fuzzy set could be: 1/1978 + 1/1979 + ... + 1/1982 + .6/1983 + .6/1984 + ... + .6/1988.

3.4 Conclusion

This overview of non fuzzy set based approaches aiming at discriminated answers shows that in any case: i) queries are expressible in the context of fuzzy sets, ii) the ordering mechanism is basically a mean, iii) the discrimination scale remains limited. Moreover, the allowed queries have a very special typology (a selection followed by an ordering) and each system proposes only one or two aggregation mechanisms for the ordering. Lastly we can notice that these queries are restricted to the selection of tuples, the qualification of sets of tuples being impossible.

4 An Overview of SQLf

The SQLf language aims at extending the relational querying language SQL, in order to accept flexible queries. The interpretation of queries is based on fuzzy sets and a wide range of queries is allowed. For the sake of simplicity, we will only consider queries addressed to usual relations although it would be possible to deal with temporary fuzzy relations produced by previous queries. The forthcoming examples will apply to the schema comprising the relations:

EMPLOYEE(#emp, name, #dep, age, job, salary, city) where #emp is the key,
DEPARTMENT(#dep, budget, speciality, town) where #dep is the key.

4.1 Syntax of SQLf

In SQL, a possible way of expressing queries of type Projection-Selection-Join consists of using a multi-relation block, without nesting. Such a block is written as :

select <attributes> *from* <relations> *where* <condition> (5)

Its role is to select the tuples belonging to the Cartesian product of the specific relations which satisfy the requirement and to project them onto the specified attributes (duplicates are kept except otherwise specified: keyword *distinct*).

In our extension, the select block remains fundamentally the same. The differences concern essentially two points. The first one is a necessity for a parameter intended for the result calibration (either a number of desired responses denoted n, or a qualitative threshold denoted t, or both). The second difference is related to the nature of the permitted conditions which are no longer solely Boolean ones. In SQLf, the new formulation of the select block is similar to (5):

select [n | t | n,t] <attributes> *from* <relations> *where* <fuzzy condition> (6)

where <fuzzy condition> can involve fuzzy and Boolean basic conditions at the same time, linked by some connectors. We have no room here to detail the <fuzzy condition> component and the interested reader can refer to [2, 6, 10, 18]. Let us illustrate the expression in SQLf of query (4) originally addressed to the ARES system: age ≈ 25 and job ≈ 'engineer'. We will have:

select * *from* EMPLOYEE *where THEN* (age *between* 20 *and* 30 *and*
job *in* ('engineer', 'professor'), AG_3(age ≈ 25, job ≈ 'engineer'))

where "*THEN*" is a predefined operator, "≈" is a closeness operation defined on each domain and "AG_3" is a user-defined connector.

4.2 Fuzzy Restriction and Fuzzy join

Expression (6) can be interpreted as a fuzzy restriction of the Cartesian product of the relations concerned, followed by a projection onto the attributes mentioned in the select clause and the calibration of the result (not be explicited in the forthcoming examples). The extended select block can return duplicates if several tuples have the same value on <attributes> and different degrees of membership. We will assume that only the tuple with the highest degree is kept if *distinct* is used. The query: "*select distinct* A *from* R *where* fc", (fc is a fuzzy condition), delivers a fuzzy relation Rf where: $\mu_{Rf}(a) = \sup_{x \in R \text{ and } x.A = a} \mu_{fc}(x)$, x.A being the projection of the tuple x on A.

In SQLf, a multi-relation block allows the expression of fuzzy selections as well as of fuzzy joins and fuzzy semi-joins, which are generalizations of the usual relational operations of selection, join and semi-join (the semi-join of a relation R by a relation S is the join of R and S projected on attributes of R [1]). A fuzzy join is expressed by :

select distinct R.A, S.B *from* R, S *where* fc_1(R) *and* fc_2(S) *and* R.C θ S.D

where θ is a fuzzy join operator (resemblance, etc). A pair (a,b) belonging to the result Rf will receive the degree :

$$\mu_{Rf}(a, b) = \sup_{x \in R \text{ and } x.A = a,\ y \in S \text{ and } y.B = b} \min(\mu_{fc_1}(x), \mu_{fc_2}(y), \mu_\theta(x.C, y.D))).$$

4.3 Extending the Membership Operator ("in")

In SQL, the operator "*in*" is used for the membership operation. For instance, the query: "find any employee working in a department whose budget is 1000 times his own salary" may be expressed:

select #emp, nom *from* EMPLOYEE *where* #dep *in* (*select* #dep
from DEPARTMENT *where* budget = (EMPLOYEE.salary * 1000)) (7)
or: *select* #emp, nom *from* EMPLOYEE *where* (salary*1000) *in*
(*select* budget *from* DEPARTMENT *where* #dep = EMPLOYEE.#dep) (8).

If this query is changed into: "find any employee working in a department whose budget is about 1000 times his own salary", expressions (9) and (10) (counterparts of queries (7) and (8)) will be equivalent:

select #emp, nom *from* EMPLOYEE *where* #dep *in* (*select* #dep
from DEPARTMENT *where* budget ≈ (EMPLOYEE.salary * 1000)) (9)

select #emp, nom *from* EMPLOYEE *where* (salary*1000) in_f
(*select* budget *from* DEPARTMENT *where* #dep = EMPLOYEE.#dep) (10)

where ≈ is a closeness operator (about), as far as "*in*" (which stands for the fuzzy relation membership) and "in_f" (which represents the fuzzy membership) are defined as:

$$\mu_{in}(a,E) = \sup_{b \in Domain(B)} \min(\mu_=(a,b), \mu_E(b)) \quad (11)$$
$$\mu_{in_f}(a, E) = \sup_{b \in Domain(B)} \min(\mu_\approx(a, b), \mu_E(b)) \quad (12)$$

B being the attribute selected by the inner block. These definitions have the advantage of preserving some equivalences which are valid in SQL and it has been shown [4, 6], that according to (11), expressions (13) and (14) are equivalent:

select distinct R.* *from* R, S *where* fc_1(R) *and* fc_2(S) *and* R.A = S.B (13)
select * *from* R *where* fc_1 *and* A *in* (*select* B *from* S *where* fc_2) (14)

as well as expressions (15) and (16) according to (12):

select distinct R.* *from* R S *where* fc_1(R) *and* fc_2(S) *and* R.A ≈ S.B (15)
select * *from* R *where* fc_1(R) *and* A in_f (*select* B *from* S *where* fc_2) (16)

fc_i(R) (resp. S) denoting a fuzzy condition applying to relation R (resp. S).

4.4 Other Nestings and Set Operations

The constructs "*exists*", "θ *any*|*all*" (where θ is a relational operator such as =, < , >), scalar comparisons (between a numeric value and the result of an aggregate function applied in a nesting block) have also been extended. The equivalences valid in SQL have been maintained such as between (9) and (10) on the one hand and:

select #emp, nom *from* EMPLOYEE *where exists*
(*select* * *from* DEPARTMENT *where* #dep = EMPLOYEE.#dep
and budget ≈ (EMPLOYEE.salary * 1000))

select #emp, nom *from* EMPLOYEE *where* #dep = *any*
(*select* #dep *from* DEPARTMENT
where budget ≈ (EMPLOYEE.salary * 1000))

select #emp, nom *from* EMPLOYEE *where* (salary * 1000) ≈ *any*
(*select* budget *from* DEPARTMENT
where #dep = EMPLOYEE.#dep)

on the other hand.

It is even possible to define nestings where the quantifiers are themselves fuzzy [17, 20] ("about one half", "almost all", "a dozen") , thus enlarging "θ *any*|*all*". Lastly, it is ob-viously possible to use "*not in*" and "*not in*$_f$" (and "*not exists*") whose definitions are obtained from (11) and (12) by taking the complement of the degree.

In SQLf, the union operator is available to combine two base blocks:

(*select* A *from* R *where* fc_1) *union* (*select* A *from* S *where* fc_2)

and the resulting relation RES is defined by:

$$\mu_{RES}(a) = \max (\sup_{x \in R \text{ and } x.A=a} \mu_{fc_1}(x), \sup_{y \in S \text{ and } y.A=a} \mu_{fc_2}(y))$$

which corresponds to the set definition of the union. The intersection and the difference have no specific operator and we have shown [4, 6] that they can be expressed using "*in*" and "*exists*," similarly to twhat is done in SQL.

4.5 Partitioning

The notion of grouping is kept in SQLf where conditions aiming at the selection of sets of tuples are extended to imprecise ones belonging to one of the following kinds: fuzzy criterion applied to the result of an aggregate and fuzzy quantified proposition. In SQLf, aggregate functions can be used in fuzzy predicates. Let us point out that we consider only usual aggregate functions (i.e. applied to regular sets). For example the query "find the departments where the average value of the engineer salaries is about 3000$" may be written:

select #dep *from* EMPLOYEE *where* job = "engineer"
group by #dep *having* avg (salary) ≈ 3000.

This example complies with the requirement that the "*where*" clause must not involve fuzzy predicates. As in SQL, this query may also be expressed using a nesting as:

select #dep *from* EMPLOYEE E *where* job = "engineer" *and* 3000 ≈
(*select* avg(salary) *from* EMPLOYEE *where* job = "engineer" *and* #dep = E.#dep).

More generally it is possible to show that the expressions (17) and (18) are equivalent in SQLf:

select A *from* R *where* bc *group by* A
having $fc_1(agg_1(B_1))$ *and/or* ... *and/or* $fc_p(agg_p(B_p))$ (17)

select distinct A *from* R R_1 *where* bc *and*
(fc_1(*select* $agg_1(B_1)$ *from* R *where* A = R_1.A *and* bc)) *and/or* ... *and/or*
(fc_p(*select* $agg_p(B_p)$ *from* R *where* A = R_1.A *and* bc)) (18)

where agg_i is an aggregate function, bc (resp. fc_i) is a Boolean (resp. fuzzy) condition.

It is also possible to introduce fuzzy conditions which have no counterpart in SQL, namely fuzzy quantified propositions of the type "Q X *are* A" or "Q X B *are* A" where Q is a fuzzy quantifier ("about 3"), A and B are fuzzy predicates and X stands for a regular set of elements. An example of query calling on this mechanism is: "find the departments where most of the engineers are middle-aged" expressed as:

select #dep *from* EMPLOYEE *where* job = "engineer"
group by #dep *having* most *are* well-paid (19).

In this query, "most *are* well-paid" corresponds to "Q X *are* A" where Q is "most", A is "well-paid" and X is a set of engineers working in a given department (all departments will be successively examined). The result of query (19) depends strongly on the interpretation adopted for "Q X *are* A". The interested reader can refer to [7, 15, 17, 20].

5. Conclusion

In this paper, we have considered the expression of imprecise queries addressed to ordinary relational databases. By imprecise queries, we mean queries able to produce discriminated answers (depending on their adequacy) with the aid of preferences (implicit or explicit) involved in the conditions appearing inside queries. We have devoted a first part to the comparison of ad'hoc extensions of Boolean systems and fuzzy set oriented approaches. The expression of extended Boolean systems queries in terms of fuzzy predicates was the basis to show that fuzzy set theory provides a general setting for database flexible querying since i) any query can be translated and ii) fuzzy predicates are capable to represent a wider range of imprecise queries.

A syntactic framework, SQLf, for the expression of fuzzy queries has been chosen, which is inspired from the SQL language. Some of the capabilities offered by SQLf have been presented: i) the multi-relation block aims at the extension of the selection, join (semi-join) and projection by means of fuzzy conditions where new kinds of connectors (with respect to the usual "*and/or*") may appear, ii) nesting predicates using the keywords "*in*" (membership to a fuzzy set), "in_f" (fuzzy membership to a set), "*exists*"(set emptiness), etc and iii) partitioning of relations and selection of sets using fuzzy predicates such as fuzzy quantified propositions.

An important aspect which is not dealt with in this paper concerns the processing of fuzzy queries. This problem is similar to that appearing in any relational language where the DBMS is in charge of translating a query (what) into an algorithm (how). Some initial works [3, 5] have investigated this topic for fuzzy queries and this is of course a key point for efficiency. The main idea is to reduce the data to be examinated by deriving Boolean conditions and heuristics from the fuzzy query. Once this problem solved reasonably it will be possible to imagine the development of commercial DBMSs supporting imprecise querying capabilities.

References

[1] Bernstein P. & Chiu D., "Using semi-joins to solve relational queries", *Journal of the ACM*, 28(1), 25-40, (1981).

[2] Bosc P., Galibourg M. & Hamon G., "Fuzzy querying with SQL : extensions and implementation aspects", *Fuzzy Sets and Systems*, 28, 333-349, (1988); also in *Readings in Fuzzy Sets for Intelligent Systems*, D. Dubois, H. Prade, R.R. Yager eds, Morgan-Kaufmann publishers, 686-694, (1993).

[3] Bosc P. & Pivert O., "Algorithms for flexible selections in relational databases", *Proc. ASLIB Conference*, York (GB), 211-225, (1989).

[4] Bosc P. & Pivert O., "About equivalences in SQLf, a relational language supporting imprecise querying", *Proc. Int. Fuzzy Engineering Symposium*, Yokohama (Japan), 309-320, (1991).

[5] Bosc P.& Pivert O., "On the evaluation of simple fuzzy relational queries : principles and measures", in *Fuzzy Logic : State of the Art* (R. Lowen ed.), Kluwer Academic Publishers, 355-364, (1993).

[6] Bosc P. & Pivert O., "SQLf: A relational database language for fuzzy querying", to appear in *IEEE Transactions on Fuzzy Systems*.

[7] Bosc P., Lietard L. & Pivert O., "Quantifications and database fuzzy querying", to appear in *Fuzzy Sets and Possibility Theory in Database Management Systems* (Bosc P. and Kacprzyk J. eds.), Physica-Verlag, Heidelberg.

[8] Chamberlin et al., "SEQUEL2 : a unified approach to data definition, manipulation and control", *IBM Journal of Research and Development*, 20(6), 560-575, (1976).

[9] Cuppens F. & Demolombe R., "How to regognize interesting topics to provide cooperative answering", *Information Systems*, 14(2), 163-173, (1989).

[10] Dubois D. & Prade H.,, "A review of Fuzzy Set Aggregation Connectives", *Information Sciences*, 36, 85-121, (1985).

[11] Ichikawa T. & Hirakawa M., "ARES : a relational database with the capability of performing flexible interpretation of queries", *IEEE Trans. on Software Engineering*, 12(5), 624-634, (1986).

[12] Lacroix M. & Lavency P., "Preferences : putting more knowledge into queries", *Proc. 13th VLDB Conference* , Brighton (GB), 217-225, (1987).

[13] Motro A., "VAGUE : a user interface to relational databases that permits vague queries", *ACM Trans. on Office Information Systems*, 6(3), 187-214, (1988) .

[14] Motro A., "A trio of database user interfaces for handling vague retrieval requests", *Data Engineering Bulletin*, 12(2), 54-63, (1989).

[15] Prade H., "A two-layer fuzzy pattern matching procedure for the evaluation of conditions involving vague quantifiers ", *Journal of Intelligent and Robotic Systems*, 3, 93-101, (1990).

[16] Rabitti F., "Retrieval of multimedia documents by imprecise query specification", *Lecture Notes on Computer Science*, 416, (1990).

[17] Yager R.R., "On ordered weighted averaging aggregation operators in multicriteria decisionmaking", *IEEE Transactions on Systems, Man and Cybernetics*, 8, 183-190, (1988).

[18] Yager R.R., "Non-monotonic set theoretic operations", *Fuzzy Sets and Systems*, 42, 173-190, (1991).

[19] Zadeh L.A., " Fuzzy sets", in *Information and Control*, 8, (Academic Press, New York), 338-353, (1965).

[20] Zadeh L.A., "A computational approach to fuzzy quantifiers in natural languages", *Computer Mathematics with Applications*, 9, 149-183, (1983).

OR-SML: A Functional Database Programming Language for Disjunctive Information and Its Applications

Elsa Gunter and **Leonid Libkin***

AT&T Bell Laboratories
600 Mountain Ave., Murray Hill, NJ 07974, USA
email: {elsa,libkin}@research.att.com

Abstract. We describe a functional database language OR-SML for handling disjunctive information in database queries, and its implementation on top of Standard ML [12]. The core language has the power of the nested relational algebra, augmented by or-sets which are used to deal with disjunctive information. Sets, or-sets and tuples can be freely combined to create objects, which gives the language a greater flexibility. It is configurable by user-defined base types, and can be used independently or interfaced to other systems built in ML. We give examples of queries which require disjunctive information (such as querying incomplete or independent databases) and show how to use the language to answer these queries.

1 Introduction

Disjunctive information in databases. There are many reasons why disjunctive information may be present in databases. One arises in the areas of design, planning, and scheduling, as was shown in [8]. For example, consider a design template used by an engineer, see figure 1. The template may indicate that the whole part being built consists of two subparts, A and B, but the component A can be built by either module $A1$ or module $A2$. Such a template is structurally a complex object whose component A is the collection containing $A1$ and $A2$; however, its meaning is not $A1$ *and* $A2$ as in the usual database interpretation of sets, but rather $A1$ *or* $A2$. Moreover, B, $A1$ and $A2$ can in turn have a similar structure. In figure 1, vertical lines indicate subparts that must be included, and the slopping lines indicate possible choices. For example, B consists of $B1$ and $B2$. Further down the tree, $B1$ is either w or k and $B2$ is either l or m. Each smallest subpart (a leaf of the tree) may have some parameters like cost and reliability, which affect the properties of a completed design.

A designer employing such a template should be allowed to query the structure of the template, for example, by asking what are the choices for component A, or what is the most reliable choice for component $B2$. We call such queries *structural*. They ask about the structure of the object, and they can be easily answered in most of the languages for complex objects.

On the other hand, the designer should also be allowed to query about possible completed designs. Such queries are called *conceptual*, as they ask questions about objects which are not stored in the database, but only represented by those that are. A query that asks to compute the number of completed designs is an example of a conceptual query. For each particular incomplete design this

---

* Partial support was provided by NSF Grant IRI-90-04137 and AT&T Doctoral Fellowship, while this author was a graduate student at the University of Pennsylvania.

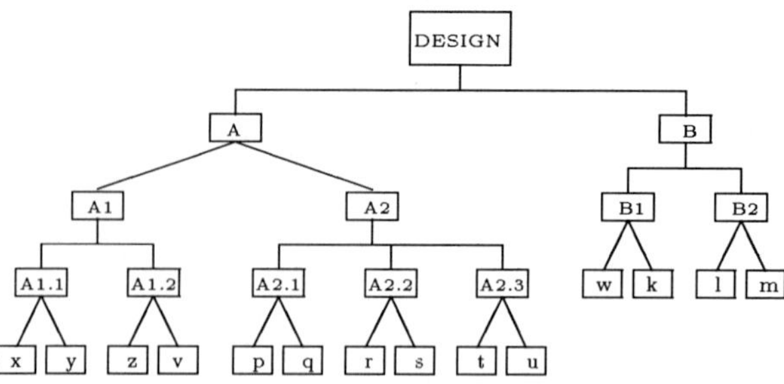

Fig. 1. An incomplete design

number can be calculated just by looking at the structure and multiplying the numbers of possibilities each disjunctive set contributes.

However, there are problems with this approach. In particular, it is not robust. In existing languages for complex objects a modest change to the structure of the incomplete design will require creating a new query to answer the same question. This query is relatively simple, but it is conceivable that a designer would want to ask if it is possible to complete design using $\$n$ and achieving reliability of at least $r\%$. Writing such a query seems to be a formidable problem that may take hours of programming, and it is even less robust: if the design object is changed slightly, there is no way to reuse the old query to answer the new questions.

Disjunctive information may also show up in the form of *interpretation* of already existing objects with respect to queries being asked. Assume that we have two relations in a university databases. One is the relation of employees, and the other is the relation of teachers of a basic course CS1, that can be taught only by teaching assistants (TAs). Suppose we want to find the set of TAs (or an approximation thereof) assuming that all TAs are employees. In this case we know that *all* teachers of CS1 are TAs, and each TA is *one of* the employees. Interpreting the relation of employees as a disjunctive set helps answer queries about various groups of employees, like TAs, as will be demonstrated later.

There are various other forms in which disjunctive information appears in database applications. For example, when combining a number of databases, there may be two records from different databases with the same values of the keys (like SS#) and conflicting values of other attributes (like Age). In this case in the combined database we must store the fact that the value of the Age attribute is one of the values from the different databases. Another kind of examples arises in the problem of proof planning in automated theorem provers. We refer the reader to the full paper [7] in which we discuss these problems.

Goals of the paper. We describe a functional language, OR-SML, for querying databases with incomplete and disjunctive information. It is capable of solving a number of problems that typically accompany disjunctive information; in particular, the problems we discussed above. To handle disjunctive information, we allow a new type constructor of *or-sets* (hence the name – OR-SML). Or-sets have been studied in [8, 10, 14]. Or-sets are in essence disjunctive information, but they are distinguished from the latter by having two distinct interpretations. The *structural* level concerns the precise way in which an or-set is constructed.

The *conceptual* level sees an or-set as representing an object which is equal to some member of the or-set. For example, the or-set $\langle 1, 2, 3\rangle$ is structurally a collection of numbers; however, conceptually it is either 1, 2, or 3. (Angle brackets $\langle\rangle$ are used for or-sets and $\{\}$ for the usual sets.) The language OR-SML supports both views of or-sets and therefore can answer conceptual queries.

The language design. Our language is based on the functional paradigm. Design of functional database query languages has been studied extensively in the past few years and proved very useful. (See, for example [1, 2, 10, 11, 13, 16].) Functional languages have certain advantages over logical languages for complex objects. They have clear syntax, they can be typechecked, their semantics is generally easy to define and they allow a limited form of polymorphism.

Since entries in databases are allowed to be or-sets possibly containing other sets, the databases are no longer in the first normal form. Therefore, we have to deal with nested relations, or complex objects. The language we describe contains the nested relational algebra as a sublanguage. The standard presentations of the nested relational algebra (cf. [15]) have a cumbersome syntax. Therefore, we have decided to follow the approach of [2], which gives a very clean and simple language that has precisely the expressive power of the nested relational algebra. The language obtained from the nested relational algebra by adding appropriate primitives dealing with or-sets was called *or-$\mathcal{NRA}$* in [10].

One of the problems that should be addressed during the language design is a mechanism for incorporating both structural and conceptual queries into the same language. It was shown in [10] that conceptually equivalent objects can be reduced to the same object by repeated applications of just three *or-$\mathcal{NRA}$* operators which will be described later. The induced normal form is *independent* of the sequence of applications of these operators. Therefore, one can take the conceptual meaning of any object to be its normal form under the rewriting induced by the those operators. Consequently, a conceptual query language can be built by extending a structural language with a single operator `normal` which takes the input object to its normal form. A query at the conceptual level is then simply a query performed on normal forms.

The system OR-SML includes much more than just *or-$\mathcal{NRA}$*. Normalization is present as a primitive. Some arithmetic is added to elevate the language to the expressive power of the *bag* language $\mathcal{BQL}$ of [11]. This allows correct evaluation of aggregate functions. OR-SML is extensible with user-defined base types. It provides a mechanism for converting any user-defined functions on base types into functions that fit into the type system of OR-SML. It also gives a way "out of complex objects" into SML values. This is necessary, for example, if OR-SML is a part of a larger system and the OR-SML query is part of a larger computation that needs to analyze the result of the query to proceed. OR-SML comes equipped with libraries of derived functions that are helpful in writing programs or advanced applications such as querying independent databases.

We chose Standard ML (SML) as the basis for our implementation in order to combine the simplicity of *or-$\mathcal{NRA}$* queries with features of a functional programming language [12]. OR-SML benefits from it in a number of ways:

1. OR-SML queries may involve and become involved in arbitrary SML procedures. The presence of higher-order functions in SML allows SML functions to be arguments to queries and queries to be arguments to SML functions.

2. OR-SML is implemented as a library of modules in SML. This allows the user to build just the database language as an independent system, or to interface it to other systems built in SML. Using this feature, we were able to connect OR-SML to an existing interactive theorem prover.
3. One interacts with OR-SML by entering declarations and expressions to be evaluated into the top-level read-evaluate-print loop of SML. The results are then bound to SML identifiers for future use.
4. The SML module system makes the implementation of different parts of the language virtually independent and easily modifiable.

In the next section we give a quick overview of OR-SML. In section 3 we show how OR-SML can be used to answer some of the problems we mentioned above. All examples in this paper are obtained from a working version of OR-SML.

2 An overview of OR-SML

The core language. The theoretical language upon which OR-SML is based was developed by Libkin and Wong in [10]. We describe this core language, called *or-$\mathcal{NRA}$*, and show how it is built on top of Standard ML. We have changed the names of all constructs of *or-$\mathcal{NRA}$* to the names that are used in OR-SML.

The *object types* are given by the following grammar:

$$t ::= b \mid unit \mid bool \mid t \times t \mid \{t\} \mid \langle t \rangle$$

Here b is one of base types (which in OR-SML include `int`, `string`, and a user-supplied SML type), $unit$ is a special type whose domain has a unique element denoted by $()$, $bool$ is the type of booleans, $t \times s$ is the product type, whose objects are pairs of objects of types t and s. The set type $\{t\}$ denotes finite sets of elements of t and the or-set type $\langle t \rangle$ denotes finite or-sets of elements of t.

The specific types of the *or-$\mathcal{NRA}$* operators are given by the rules in the table in Fig. 1. All occurrences of s, t and u in that table are object types. Let us briefly recall the semantics of these operators. **comp**(f,g) is composition of functions f and g. First and second projections are called **p1** and **p2**. **pair**(f,g) is pair formation: **pair**$(f,g)(x) = (f(x), g(x))$. **id** is the identity function. **bang** always returns the unique element of type $unit$. **cond**$(c,f,g)(x)$ evaluates to $f(x)$ if condition c is satisfied and to $g(x)$ otherwise.

The semantics of the set constructs is the following. **emptyset**$()$ is the empty set. This constant also has name **empty**. **sng**(x) returns the singleton set $\{x\}$. **union**(x,y) is $x \cup y$. **smap**(f) maps f over a set, that is, **smap**$(f)\{x_1,\ldots,x_n\} = \{f(x_1),\ldots,f(x_n)\}$. **pairwith** pairs the first component of its argument with every item in the second component: **pairwith**$(y,\{x_1,\ldots,x_n\}) = \{(y,x_1),\ldots,(y,x_n)\}$. Finally, **flat** is flattenning: **flat**$\{X_1,\ldots,X_n\} = X_1 \cup \ldots \cup X_n$. The semantics of the or-set constructs is similar.

The operator **alpha** provides interaction between sets and or-sets. Given a set $\mathcal{A} = \{A_1,\ldots,A_n\}$, where each A_i is an or-set $A_i = \langle a_1^i,\ldots,a_{n_i}^i \rangle$, let $\mathcal{F}$ denote the set of all functions $f : \{1,\ldots,n\} \to \mathbb{N}$ such that $f(i) \leq n_i$ for all i. Then **alpha**$(\mathcal{A}) = \langle \{a_{f(i)}^i \mid i = 1,\ldots,n\} \mid f \in \mathcal{F} \rangle$.

We shall need some of the SML syntax. In SML, **val** binds an identifier and `-` is the prompt, so `- val x = 2;` binds `x` to 2 and `val x = 2 : int` is the SML response saying that `x` is now bound to 2 of type `int`. **fun** is for function

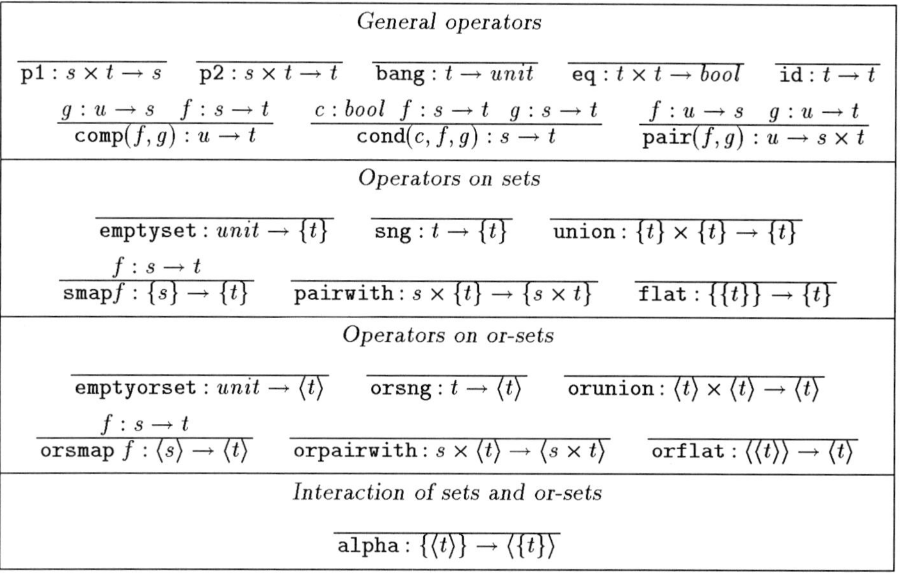

Fig. 2. *or-$\mathcal{NRA}$* Type Inference of OR-SML Terms

declaration. Functions can also be created without being named by using the construct `(fn x =>` *body*`(x))`. If a function is applied to its argument and the result is not bound to any variable, then SML assigns it a special identifier `it` which lives until it is overridden by the next such application. For example, the SML response to `- factorial 4;` is `val it = 24 : int`. `let` ... `in` ... `end` is used for local binding. The `[...]` brackets denote lists; `""` is used for strings.

Let us now describe how OR-SML constructs are represented over SML. Every complex object has type `co`. We refer to the type of an object or a function in *or-$\mathcal{NRA}$* as its *true type*. True types of objects can be inferred using the function `typeof`. They are SML values having type `co_type`. When OR-SML prints a complex objects together with its type, it uses `::` for the true type, as `: co` is used to show that the SML type of the object is `co`. Values can be input by functions `create : string -> co` (or `make : unit -> co` for interactive creation, if the input needs to be broken over several lines). For example:

```
- val a = create "{ <1,2,3>, <4,5,6>, <7,8> }";
val a = {<1, 2, 3>, <7, 8>, <4, 5, 6>} :: {<int>} : co
```

The order in which elements appear in a set (or-set) is irrelevant. The order of elements of `a` was changed as the result of the duplicate elimination algorithm.

Typechecking is done in two steps. Static typechecking is simply SML typechecking; for example, `union(a,a,a)` causes an SML type error. However, since all objects have type `co`, the SML typechecking algorithm can not detect all type errors statically. For example, SML will see nothing wrong with `union(a,(create "5"))` even though the true types of its arguments are $\{\langle int\rangle\}$ and *int*. Hence, this kind of type errors is detected dynamically by OR-SML and an appropriate exception is raised. In our example, OR-SML responds by `uncaught exception Badtypeunion`.

The language can express many functions commonly found in query languages. Among them are boolean connectives, membership and subset tests, difference, selection, cartesian product and their counterparts for or-sets, see [2, 10]. These functions are included in OR-SML in the form of a structure called `Set`. Some examples are given below.

```
- alpha (create "{<1,2>,<2,3>}");
val it = <{2}, {1, 2}, {1, 3}, {2, 3}> :: <{int}> : co
- val x1 = create "{1,2}";
val x1 = {1, 2} :: {int} : co
- smap (pair(id,id)) x1;
val it = {(1, 1), (2, 2)} :: {int * int} : co
- Set.cartprod(x1,x1);
val it = {(1, 1), (1, 2), (2, 1), (2, 2)} :: {int * int} : co
```

OR-SML allows a limited access to user-defined base types. Values of these types have type `base` in OR-SML. The user is required to supply a structure containing basic information about the base type when a particular version of OR-SML is built. Objects of base type are printed in parentheses and preceded by the symbol `@`. They also must be input accordingly, so that the parser would recognize them.

There are a number of functions that make complex objects out of SML objects. For example, `mkintco: int -> co` and `mksetco : co list -> co` make an integer complex object, or a set whose elements come from a list of complex objects. These functions can be used as an alternative to `create` and `make`. OR-SML has a variety of printing styles which can be changed at will.

Normalization. Assume that an object x of type t contains some or-sets. What is x conceptually? Since we want to list all possibilities explicitly, it must be an object $x' : \langle t' \rangle$ where t' does *not* contain any or-set brackets. Intuitively, for any given object x we can find the corresponding x' but the question is whether we can do it in a coherent manner.

Such a way was found in [10]. Define the following rewrite system on types:

$$t \times \langle s \rangle \to \langle s \times t \rangle \quad \langle s \rangle \times t \to \langle s \times t \rangle \quad \langle\langle s \rangle\rangle \to \langle s \rangle \quad \{\langle s \rangle\} \to \langle\{s\}\rangle$$

Intuitively, we are trying to push the or-set brackets outside and then cancel them. With each rewrite rule we associate a basic OR-SML function as follows:

$$\texttt{orpairwith} : t \times \langle s \rangle \to \langle s \times t \rangle \qquad \texttt{orpairwith1} : \langle s \rangle \times t \to \langle s \times t \rangle$$
$$\texttt{orflat} : \langle\langle s \rangle\rangle \to \langle s \rangle \qquad \texttt{alpha} : \{\langle s \rangle\} \to \langle\{s\}\rangle$$

where `orpairwith1` is "pair-with" with changed arguments. This function is definable in OR-SML.

If $s_1 \to \ldots \to s_n$, $n \geq 1$ by rewrites in the above rewrite system, then we write $s_1 \twoheadrightarrow s_n$. We associate with each sequence $s_1 \to \ldots \to s_n$ a *rewrite strategy* $r = [r_1, \ldots, r_{n-1}] : s_1 \twoheadrightarrow s_n$, where each r_i is the basic OR-SML function associated with $s_i \to s_{i+1}$. It is possible to "apply" a rewrite strategy $r : s_1 \twoheadrightarrow s_n$ to any object $x : s_1$, getting an object of type s_n which is denoted by $\mathsf{app}(r)(x)$. It can be obtained by using functions from the core language, see [10]. Moreover, the following result was proved in [10]:

Theorem (Coherence) *The rewrite system above is Church-Rosser and terminating. In particular, every type t has a unique normal form denoted $nf(t)$. Moreover, for any two rewrite strategies $r_1, r_2 : t \twoheadrightarrow nf(t)$ and any $x : t$,* $\mathsf{app}(r_1)(x) = \mathsf{app}(r_2)(x)$. □

This theorem tell us that a new primitive **normal : co -> co** can be added to OR-SML to give it adequate power to work with conceptual representations of objects. The true type of **normal** is $t \rightarrow nf(t)$ and its semantics is $\mathsf{app}(r)$ where $r : t \twoheadrightarrow nf(t)$. Normalization of types is represented by the function **normalize** of type **co_type -> co_type**. For example:

```
- val x = create "{(1,<2,3>),(4,<5,6>)}";
val x = {(1, <2, 3>), (4, <5, 6>)} :: {int * <int>} : co
- normalize (typeof x);
val it = <{int * int}> : co_type
- val y = normal x;
val y = <{(1,2),(4,5)}, {(1,3),(4,5)}, {(1,2),(4,6)}, {(1,3),(4,6)}> : co
```

Additional features. OR-SML has integers as a base type with a number of supported operations. Among them are two summation constructs. **sum** takes a function f of true type $s \rightarrow int$ and a set $\{x_1, \ldots, x_n\}$ of true type $\{s\}$ and returns $f(x_1) + \ldots + f(x_n)$. **orsum** acts similarly on or-sets. These operations endow a set language with the power of languages for nested *bags* as in [5, 11]. Equivalently, they allow us to define and correctly evaluate a number of aggregate functions. For example, **sum p2** is "add up all elements in the second column".

The system provides a way of making functions on user-defined base types into functions that fit into its type system. For example, if the user-defined base type is **real**, the function **apply_unary** will take a function **fn x => x + 1.0** of SML type **real -> real** and return the function **addone_co** of type **co -> co** whose semantics is $\lambda x.x + 1.0$. OR-SML also provides a way of converting binary functions and functions with arbitrary number of arguments into functions on complex objects. Predicates on base types can also be converted by means of **apply_test** to be used later with **cond** or **select**.

Structural recursion [1] is a very powerful programming tool for query languages. Even though it is not guaranteed to be well-defined, it is often helpful in writing programs or changing types of big databases (rather than reinputting them). It is available in OR-SML as two constructs **SR.sr** and **SR.orsr** that take an object e of type t and a function f of type $s \times t \rightarrow t$ and return a function **SR.sr**(e, f) of type $\{s\} \rightarrow t$ (or **SR.orsr**(e, f) of type $\langle s \rangle \rightarrow t$.) Their semantics is as follows: **SR.sr**$(e, f)\{x_1, \ldots, x_n\} = f(x_1, f(x_2, f(x_3, \ldots f(x_n, e) \ldots)))$ and similarly for **SR.orsr**. For example, to find the product of elements of a set, one may use structural recursion by first producing a function **set_mult: co -> co** as **val set_mult = SR.sr((create "1"),mult)** and then applying it to a set, say **{1,2,3,4,5}**, obtaining 120.

To support a form of persistence for databases, OR-SML provides means for writing lists of complex objects to files and reading them back in later. There are two modules for file I/O: one for binary files and one for ASCII files.

To enable the user to write programs to deal with the results of queries, OR-SML provides a way out of complex objects to the usual SML types. See the system manual [7] for details.

3 Applications of OR-SML

Querying incomplete design databases. Recall the example of an incomplete design from figure 1. Assuming that each smallest subpart has two parameters – its cost (of type *int*) and its reliability (of type *real*) – we can use or-sets to represent the incomplete design as an object in OR-SML as follows:

```
val design =
  (<{<('z', (13, @(0.95))), ('v', (14, @(0.955)))>,
     <('y', (20, @(0.98))), ('x', (21, @(0.999)))>},
    {<('p', (12, @(0.95))), ('q', (13, @(0.96)))>,
     <('s', (17, @(0.96))), ('r', (18, @(0.97)))>,
     <('t', (19, @(0.98))), ('l', (20, @(0.99)))>}>,
   (<('k', (11, @(0.93))), ('w', (17, @(0.96)))>,
    <('l', (12, @(0.94))), ('m', (14, @(0.95)))>)) : co
```

Assume that we want to answer the following conceptual queries. How many completed designs are there? Is it possible to complete the design using \$62? What is the most reliable design that costs under \$$n$?

To answer these queries, we first infer the type of the normalized database.

```
val ndt = <({(string * (int * real))} *
    ((string * (int * real)) * (string * (int * real))))> : co_type
```

Guided by this type, we can write the cost and reliability functions for the completed designs. The function `cost` adds up all occurrences of integers in `ndt`. The function `reliability` can also be written straightforwardly in OR-SML for any type of connection of subparts. Assume parallel connection of $B1$ and $B2$ and series connection of A and B. Now to answer the first query, we write

```
- val nd = normal design; (* output omitted *)
- val num_choices = orsum (fn z => mkintco(1)) nd;
val num_choices = 48 : co
- orsmap (fn x => mkprodco ((cost x), (reliability x))) nd; (* output omitted *)
```

Thus, we have 48 completed designs. Notice that the query for `num_choices` is independent of the internal structure of the incomplete design. The output of the last query shows that the price range is from \$56 to \$82. Hence, the design can be completed with \$62.

To find the design that has the best reliability for a given cost, we first write a query `is_best` that selects the design with the best reliability from a given collection (this can be done using just the structural component of the language.) Then `bestunder` selects the most reliable design with a given cost limit.

```
- fun bestunder n = let val des_under_n = (Set.orselect
     (fn y => eq(mkintco(0), monus(cost(y),mkintco(n)))) nd)
in Set.orselect (fn y => is_best(y,des_under_n)) des_under_n end;
val bestunder = fn : int -> co
```

Applying this function yields some intersting results. The most reliable design (obtained by writing `bestunder 82`) costs only \$66. The most reliable design that costs less than \$62 has an actual cost of \$60. So, as it often happens, one does not have to buy the most expensive thing to get the best quality.

Summing up, we see that normalization is a very powerful tool for answering conceptual queries. Many queries that would be practically impossible to answer in just the structural language, now can be programmed in a matter of minutes in OR-SML.

Querying independent databases. Let us see how OR-SML can be used to solve a simple problem of querying independent databases. Consider the problem described in the introduction. The university database has two relations, Employees and CS1 (for teaching the course CS1) and we would like to compute the set of TAs. We know that only TAs can teach CS1 and every TA is a university employee. In this paper, we also assume that the Name field is a key.

Employees :

Name	Salary
John	15K
Mary	12K
Sally	17K

CS1 :

Name	Room
John	076
Jim	320
Sally	120

Note that the databases are inconsistent: Jim teaches CS1 and hence he is a TA and an employee, but there is no record for Jim in Employees. If we believe the Employees relation, then, to get rid of this anomaly, we must remove Jim from CS1. After that, we find an approximation of the set of TAs; that is, we find people who certainly are TAs and those who could be.

We always assume that all records have the same fields. It can be achieved by putting $\bot$ (null) into the missing fields or, in OR-SML representation, by using empty sets to represent nulls. This also allows us to take joins and meets of records. For example, $\boxed{\text{John}|\text{15K}|\bot} \vee \boxed{\text{John}|\bot|\text{076}} = \boxed{\text{John}|\text{15K}|\text{076}}$ and $\boxed{\text{John}|\text{15K}|\bot} \wedge \boxed{\text{John}|\bot|\text{076}} = \boxed{\text{John}|\bot|\bot}$. Notice that the join of two records is not necessarily defined.

In our solution we rely on the theory of partial information conveyed by means of partial orders which was worked out in [3, 4, 9, 10]. In particular, we use the fact that orders can be defined at arbitrary types, and consequently we have an OR-SML library of orderings and functions `meet`, `join` : $s \times s \to \langle s \rangle$ (the empty or-set indicates a non-existent join or meet; otherwise a singleton or-set is produced). Using these functions, it is easy to write a function (called `compatible`) to test whether two records have a join.

We treat Employees as a relation of possible upper bounds for TAs, so we make it an or-set. All entries in CS1 are TAs, so CS1 is a set. We represent the data as below, and remove the anomaly (Jim) using the test for a join `compat` as a parameter:

```
val emp = <('Mary', ({@(12.0)}, {})), ('John', ({@(15.0)}, {})),
   ('Sally', ({@(17.0)}, {}))> : co
val cs1 = {('John', ({},{76})), ('Sally', ({},{120})), ('Jim', ({},{320}))} : co
- fun remove_anomaly compat (R,S) = let fun compat_to_X (X,x) =
        Set.ormember(mkboolco(true),(orsmap (fn z => compat(z,x)) X));
   in Set.select (fn z => compat_to_X (R,z)) S end;
- val new_cs1 = remove_anomaly compatible (emp,cs1);
val new_cs1 = {('John', ({}, {76})), ('Sally', ({}, {120}))} : co
```

Now consider the solution proposed in [3] (see also [6]). Given an element $x \in$ CS1, let $y_1, \ldots, y_n$ be those elements in Employees that can be joined with x. Then $x' = \bigwedge_i (x \vee y_i)$ is called a *promotion* of x. (Intuitively, it adds all information about x from Employees.) The solution to the TA query is to take all promotions of elements in CS1 as "sure TAs" and elements of Employees not consistent with those promotions as "possible TAs". (We use the function `big_meet` that calculates the meet of a family.)

```
- fun promote compat (R,S) =
   let fun compat_to_x (X,x) = Set.orselect (fn z => compat(z,x)) X
   in alpha (smap (fn z => big_meet (orflat(orsmap (fn v => join(z,v))
  (compat_to_x (R,z))))) S) end;
- val promoted_cs1 = promote compatible (emp,new_cs1);
val promoted_cs1 = <{('John', ({@(15.0)}, {76})),
   ('Sally', ({@(17.0)}, {120}))}> : co
```

Thus, John from office 76 and Sally from office 120 are certainly TAs (and we know their salaries) and Mary could be a TA.

If the name field is not a key, this solution will not work: if there are several Johns in Employees, all will be joined with John from CS1, and when the meet is taken, the salary field is lost. But this is not what the information in the database tells us. We know that one John from Employees teaches CS1, but we do not know which John. Since either could be, the solution is to use an *or-set* to represent this situation. See [7] for details.

Acknowledgements: We would like to thank Peter Buneman and Limsoon Wong for many helpful discussions.

References

1. V. Breazu-Tannen, P. Buneman, and S. Naqvi. Structural recursion as a query language. In *Proc. of DBPL-91*, pages 9–19.
2. V. Breazu-Tannen, P. Buneman, and L. Wong. Naturally embedded query languages. In *LNCS 646: Proc. ICDT-92*, pages 140–154. Springer, October 92.
3. P. Buneman, S. Davidson, A. Watters, A semantics for complex objects and approximate answers, *JCSS* 43:170–218, 1991.
4. P. Buneman, A. Jung, A. Ohori, Using powerdomains to generalize relational databases, *Theoret. Comp. Sci.* 91:23–55, 1991.
5. S. Grumbach, T. Milo, Towards tractable algebras for bags, *Proceedings of the 12th PODS*, Washington DC, 1993, pages 49–58.
6. C. Gunter, The mixed powerdomain, *Theoret. Comp. Sci.* 103:311–334, 1992.
7. E. Gunter and L. Libkin. A functional database programming language with support for disjunctive information, AT&T Technical Memo, 1993.
8. T. Imielinski, S. Naqvi, and K. Vadaparty. Incomplete objects — a data model for design and planning applications. In *Proc. of SIGMOD, Denver CO, May 1991.*
9. L. Libkin, A relational algebra for complex objects based on partial information, In *LNCS 495: Proc. of MFDBS-91*, Springer-Verlag, 1991, pages 36–41.
10. L. Libkin and L. Wong, Semantic representations and query languages for or-sets, *Proceedings of the 12th PODS*, Washington DC, 1993, pages 37–48.
11. L. Libkin and L. Wong, Some properties of query languages for bags, In *Proc. of DBPL-93*, Springer Verlag, 1994, pages 97–114.
12. R. Milner, M. Tofte, R. Harper, *"The Definition of Standard ML"*, The MIT Press, Cambridge, Mass, 1990.
13. A. Ohori, V. Breazu-Tannen and P. Buneman, Database programming in Machiavelli: a polymorphic language with static type inference, In *SIGMOD 89.*
14. B. Rounds, Situation-theoretic aspects of databases, In *Proc. Conf. on Situation Theory and Applications*, CSLI vol. 26, 1991, pages 229–256.
15. H.-J. Schek and M. Scholl, The relational model with relation-valued attributes, *Inform. Systems* 11 (1986), 137–147.
16. P.W. Trinder and P.L. Wadler, List comprehensions and the relational calculus, In *Proceedings of the Glasgow Workshop on Functional Programming*, pages 187–202.

Semantic Query Optimization in OODB Systems

Young-Whun Lee and Suk I. Yoo

Department of Computer Science
Seoul National University
Shilim-dong, Kwanak-ku, Seoul, KOREA

Abstract. Semantic query optimization becomes more important in OODB systems where object queries are complex due to presence of the object-oriented concepts such as subclassing relationship, is-part-of relationship, and object-identifier. However, there are few research works on them. In this paper we investigate the representation and maintenance of semantic constraints and present a semantic query optimization technique in OODB systems. Our semantic query optimizer deals semantic transformations of the object query graph. We also develop new transformation heuristics which guide useful semantic transformations.

1 Introduction

Recently, object-oriented database(OODB) systems are rapidly gaining popularity, and show a promise of supplanting relational database systems. Thus, object query optimization has become an increasingly important issue and many studies have been conducted in recent years. These researches have extended the conventional query optimization techniques into OODB systems. However, since these conventional query optimizers lack the entire body of semantic knowledge assured to be satisfied by all the instances of a particular database, in many cases they produce suboptimal forms of the query for execution. Since more semantics are captured in OODB systems, moreover, it is desirable that available semantic knowledge is used to optimize the query. Semantic query optimization utilizing semantic knowledges becomes more important in OODB systems where object queries are much complex due to presence of the object-oriented concepts such as *subclassing relationship*, *is-part-of relationship*, and *object-identifier*.

The object-oriented paradigm in OODB system is sufficient to guarantee a high degree of integrity and consistency. However, many situations demand complex, application specific semantic constraint control which is beyond the capabilities of the object-oriented paradigm. Thus, a few OODB systems, such as ODE system[2], provide the capability to associate explicit semantic constraints with a class definition. Jagadish [2] describes an approach for integrating inter-object constraint maintenance into an OODB system and a constraint compilation scheme. Many studies on semantic query optimization in relational/deductive database systems have been conducted[5,7,8,9,11]. There have, to our knowledge, been no studies on semantic query optimization in OODB systems except for [10]. Sung [10] attempted to apply the semantic information for the efficient processing of the queries in an OODB system. But, he did not investigate semantic constraints in OODB systems and presented the transformations focused on only nested structure of complex objects.

In this paper, we investigate the representation of semantic constraints in OODB systems and present a semantic query optimization technique for object queries. we considers in our semantic query optimizer basic object-oriented concepts, such as subclassing relationship, is-part-of relationship, and object identifier, in order to obtain performance improvements through semantic reduction using these concepts. Our semantic query optimizer deals semantic transformations of the *object query graph* which is a global query representation and is also used to factorize common sub path expressions among path expressions in an object query. We also develop new transformation heuristics which guide useful semantic transformations.

The rest of paper is organized as follows. In the next section we describe the basic concepts of object model and object query representation. In Section 3 we investigate the classification and representation of semantic constraints. In Section 4 we present a semantic query optimization technique in OODB systems. Finally, concluding remarks are presented and future researches are discussed in Section 5.

2 Preliminaries

We assume that the reader is responsibly familiar with most of the concepts found in object models and OODB systems.

Each object is associated with an unique *object identifier*(called an OID) that makes the object distinguishable from other objects. The *is-part-of relationship* among classes organizes them in a directed graph, sometimes called a *class composition hierarchy*. The *subclassing relationship* among classes organizes them in a directed acyclic graph, sometimes called a *class inheritance hierarchy*, which is orthogonal to the class composition hierarchy. We denote by `Subclass(`C`)` all subclasses of class C and by `Ext(`C`)` heterogeneous collection of all objects of C and all objects of subclasses of C.

Path expressions are the most common forms of referring to objects and represent the is-part-of relationships among objects. The definition of a path expression is as follows.

Definition 2.1 Path expression: $o.a_1.a_2. \ldots a_n$ is a path expression traversing classes $C_0 - C_1 - \ldots C_n$ if the following conditions hold for all i, $1 \leq i \leq n$:

1. o is an object of class C_0 and
2. a_i is an attribute of class C_{i-1} of which domain type is either C_i or set type of domain type C_i.

We say that the *path length* of a path expression is the number of attributes in the path expression. The attribute a_n is called the *target attribute* and the class of the object o, C_0 is called the *starting class*. The domain type of a target attribute, C_n is called the *reference type* of the path expression. The path expression with one or more set attributes is called a *set path expression*; otherwise, a *scalar path expression*. We define the *extension* of a path expression to be collection of tails of all object paths satisfying the path expression. We denote by $\mathtt{Ext}(P)$ the extension of a path expression P. Given a class C, a path expression $C.a_1.a_2. \ldots a_n$ is a set path expression of which extension are as follows: $\mathtt{Ext}(C.a_1.a_2. \ldots a_n) = \cup_{o \in Ext(C)} \mathtt{Ext}(o.a_1.a_2. \ldots a_n)$.

A query expression which represents the object query has the following structure:

SELECT *target clause* FROM *range clause* WHERE *qualification clause*;

1) Target clause: It specifies what must be retrieved by the object query. It is composed of one or more object expressions. In this paper, we denote by $oe(o)$ an object variable o or a path expression starting from o.

2) Range clause: It defines the binding of an object variable. It is composed of one or more range expressions. The range expression has one of the following forms: o in C; o in $C.a_1.a_2....a_n$, where o is an object variable. The object variable in the range expression binds an object in $\mathtt{Ext}(C)$ (or $\mathtt{Ext}(C.a_1.a_2. \ldots a_n)$).

3) Qualification clause: It is a boolean combination of unit query predicates by using logical connectives: and, or, and not. We distinguish three kinds of unit query predicates: *domain predicates*, *One-Variable-Join(OVJ) predicates*, and *Two-Variable-Join(TVJ) predicates*. Let c be a constant, o and o' be object variables, and θ be comparison operator. Then the forms of query predicates are as follows:

- domain predicate: $c \; \theta \; o.a_1.a_2. \ldots a_n$
- OVJ predicate: $o.a_1.a_2. \ldots a_n \; \theta \; o.b_1.b_2. \ldots b_m$
- TVJ predicate: $o.a_1.a_2. \ldots a_n \; \theta \; o'.b_1.b_2. \ldots b_m$.

We assume that the qualification clause is limited to a conjunctive predicate.

The subclassing relationship between a pair of classes has impacts on the semantics of object queries. The access scope of a class(or path expression) in a query encompasses the objects of the class and those of all subclasses of the class.

Definition 2.2 Access scope: The access scope of a class C, denoted by Ascope(C), is a set of which elements are C and its subclasses; $\mathtt{Ascope}(C) = \{C\} \cup \mathtt{Subclass}(C)$. The access scope of a path expression $o.a_1.a_2....a_n$ traversing classes $C_0 - C_1 - C_2 - \ldots C_n$ is defined as the following: $\mathtt{Ascope}(o.a_1.a_2. \ldots a_n) = \cup_{0 \leq i \leq n} \mathtt{Ascope}(C_i)$.

3 Semantic Constraints

3.1 Classification of Semantic Constraints

By virtue of object-orientation, some semantic constraints are represented naturally and maintained for free in an object-oriented database, in that they are directly captured by the database schema. Semantic constraints of this sort are called the *implicit semantic constraints.* Typical examples of the implicit semantic constraints are subclassing relationship and is-part-of relationship, which are two inherent relationships in OODB systems. Semantic constraints that are explicitly specified in the class definition by users are called the *explicit semantic constraints.* The explicit semantic constraints are divided into two kinds according to whether they are associated with set values of objects or not: *scalar constraints* and *set constraints.* We distinguish four classifications of scalar constraints: *domain constraints*, *attribute-join constraints*, *dependency constraints*, and *production constraints.* We denote by $dc(o)$ a domain predicate or an OVJ predicate with the object variable o. Then the semantic constraints have the following forms:

- domain constraint:
  $(\forall o/C)(oe(o)\ \theta\ c)$
- attribute-join constraint:
  $(\forall o/C)(oe_1(o)\ \theta\ oe_2(o))$
- dependency constraint:
  $(\forall o/C)(dc_1(o)$ and $dc_2(o)$ and ... $dc_n(o) \rightarrow dc_{n+1}(o)),\ n \geq 1$
- production constraint:
  $(\forall o_1/C_1)(\forall o_2/C_2)(dc_1(o_1)$ and ... $dc_n(o_1)$ and $oe_1(o_1)\ \theta\ oe_2(o_2)$ and $dc_{n+1}(o_2)$ and ... $dc_{n+m}(o_2) \rightarrow dc_{n+m+1}(o_2)),\ m, n \geq 1$,

where θ is one comparison operator of $\{ =, \neq, >, \geq, <, \leq \}$ and c is a constant.

There are special cases of the above semantic constraints, which are of particular importance in semantic query optimization. The first special case is *semantic equality* of objects. A semantic equality can be specified in a class definition by a class designer or an user[6]. It has the following form: $(\forall o_1/C)(\forall o_2/C)(sep(o_1, o_2) \rightarrow o_1 = o_2)$, where *sep* is a two variable predicate which represents the semantic equality of two objects in class C. Two objects o_1 and o_2 is said to be *semantically equal* if they satisfy the predicate *sep*. The semantic equality may be considered as a special kind of a production constraint. As an example, a semantic constraint, say $(\forall o_1/C)(\forall o_2/C)(o_1.a = o_2.a \rightarrow o_1 = o_2)$, represents semantic equality for objects of class C. That is, two objects of class C are semantically equal if they have the same value to the attribute a.

The second special case is to specify constraints by the *inverse relationship* represented in the database schema[2,6]. Whenever an object is modified on one side of an inverse relationship, it is automatically modified on the other side. By virtue of the inverse relationship among classes, many useful semantic constraints can be deduced. As an example, assume that two attributes a_1 of class C_1 and a_2 of class C_2 being inverses(denoted by $C_1.a_1 = C_2.a_2^{-1}$), then the following semantic constraints hold[2]:

- $(\forall o_1/C_1)(o_1.a_1.a_2 = o_1)$
- $(\forall o_2/C_2)(o_2.a_2.a_1 = o_2)$
- $(\forall o_1/C_1)(\forall o_2/C_2)(o_1.a_1 = o_2 \rightarrow o_2.a_2 = o_1)$
- $(\forall o_1/C_1)(\forall o_2/C_2)(o_2.a_2 = o_1 \rightarrow o_1.a_1 = o_2)$.

3.2 Maintenance of Semantic Constraints

We define a *semantic knowledge base*(SKB) to be collection of all semantic constraints in the database. We assume that our semantic knowledge base is always consistent. There are two kinds of the restriction propagation that can be deduced due to two inherent relationships in OODB systems. Assume that given a path expression $o.a_1.a_2. \ldots a_n$ traversing classes $C - C_1 - \ldots C_n$, a semantic constraint $(\forall o/C)(o.a_1.a_2. \ldots a_n\ \theta\ c)$ is defined or deduced. The first case is the propagation of semantic constraints under the subclassing relationship. That is, for any subclass of C, say C'', $(\forall o/C'')(o.a_1.a_2. \ldots a_n\ \theta\ c)$ holds. The second case is the propagation of semantic constraints under the is-part-of relationship. That is, for all i, $1 \leq i \leq n$, $(\forall o/C.a_1.a_2. \ldots a_i)(o.a_{i+1}.a_{i+2}. \ldots a_n\ \theta\ c)$ is deduced. These propagation can be viewed as special cases of propagation due to set inclusion relationship. Given a class C and its subclass C'', $\texttt{Ext}(C) \supseteq \texttt{Ext}(C'')$ holds by virtue of the subclassing relationship. Also, $\texttt{Ext}(C.a) \subseteq \texttt{Ext}(C'')$ holds by virtue of the is-part-of relationship, if the reference type of $C.a$ is class C''.

We present a constraint typing scheme and a typed grouping scheme to effectively handle large number of semantic constraints. If a semantic constraint SC has only one bound class C then the *type* of SC is C. If SC has two bound classes, say C_1 and C_2, then its type is the most specific common superclass of C_1 and C_2. The *relevant type* of a semantic constraint SC is a class C if SC is either a domain constraint or an attribute-join constraint which has an object expression of which the reference type is class C. In our approach, semantic constraints are grouped according to their relevant types. To retrieve relevant semantic constraints for a query, all semantic constraints of which relevant types are classes involved in the query are retrieved. Such a typed grouping of semantic constraints reduces the overhead of retrieving semantic constraints and checking whether each constraint is relevant to the current query.

4 Semantic Query Optimization

4.1 Object Query Graph

An *object query graph*(OQG) is a quadruple <Ctree, Rset, Jset, Tseq>. Ctree is a hyper-graph which is defined as a tuple <V, E>, where V is the collection of object nodes that denote classes involved in the query and E is the collection of directed arcs which are labeled by attribute names. Ctree represents the is-part-of relationship between classes in the query. Rset and Jset are the collection of domain predicates and collection of join predicates respectively. Jset is separated into OVJset and TVJset. Tseq is the sequence of object nodes that compose the query result. Rset, Jset, and Tseq are used to annotate the Ctree.

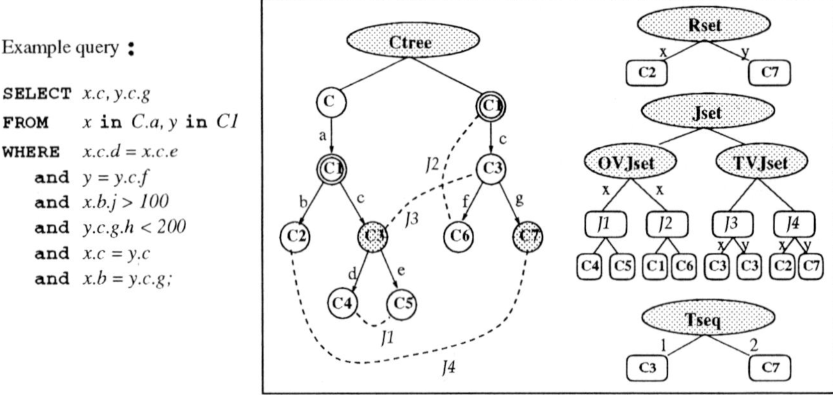

Fig. 1. Object query graph

Fig. 1 depicts an example query and its *OQG*. We assume that the reference type of $C.a$ in the example query is C_1. The double circles in Ctree correspond to the *range object nodes* which denote the object variables specified in the range clause of the query. The shadowed circles in Ctree correspond to the *target object nodes* which denote the query result represented in the target clause. Our *OQG* can have multiple target object nodes if the object query specify the explicit join. Moreover, Each target object node is not necessarily root node. The dashed lines depict join predicates, OVJ predicates and TVJ predicates, in the qualification clause. The transformation from an object query to the corresponding object query graph is straight-forward. We do not discriminate two terms, (object) query and object query graph, throughout the remainder of this paper if there is no ambiguity.

Our object query graph is a global representation of the query itself and is used to factorize common sub path expressions. And our semantic query optimizer will deal the semantic transformation of the object query graph.

4.2 Semantic Transformations

Two queries are *semantically equivalent* if their answers are the same for all the instances of the database that satisfy the specified set of semantic constraints. Semantic query optimization is the process of determining the set of semantic transformations that results in a semantically equivalent query with lower execution cost. There are three ways in which semantic transformations can be done.

- Insertion transformation: If the qualification clause p_1 **and** p_2 **and** ... p_n and *SKB* imply a new predicate p', then p' can be added to the qualification clause.
- Deletion transformation: If the qualification clause p_1 **and** p_2 **and** ... p_{i-1} **and** p_{i+1} **and** ... p_n and *SKB* imply a predicate p_i, then p_i may be removed from the qualification clause.

- Modification transformation: If the object expression oe in the query has an equivalent object expression oe' with respect to SKB, then oe can be replaced by oe'.

The semantic transformations are performed through modification of the object query graph. The insertion transformation inserts a new query predicate to the Rset/Jset and the deletion transformation removes a query predicate from the Rset/Jset. The modification transformation adapts the path structure in the Ctree. As described in [3], the classes in a query graph representation of a query are reduced through decomposition into *clusters*, and there are two graph traversal methods for evaluating a cluster: *forward traversal method* and *backward traversal method*. We believe that our semantic transformations of the object query graph can be combined with the graph clustering methods and graph traversal methods in conventional query optimization.

4.3 Transformation Heuristics

King [5] suggested useful transformation heuristics in relational database systems. In this subsection, we extend King's heuristics and suggest new transformation heuristics which are specific to the basic object-oriented concepts and semantic constraints discussed in Section 3. Our transformation heuristics limit the size of the applicable transformations and guide the whole process in a meaningful way without a combinational explosion.

1) *Access Scope Reduction Heuristic*: Evaluation of object queries requires logical access scopes of classes(or path expressions) involved in the query. This reduction of the access scope can be obtained because semantic constraints of the class can be redefined in its subclasses. Given a query predicate $o.a_1.a_2. \ldots a_n \ \theta \ c$, classes in $\texttt{Ascope}(o.a_1.a_2. \ldots a_n)$ should be evaluated. However, if there exists a semantic constraint which is contradictory with a query predicate, then the class which is type of the semantic constraint may be removed from the corresponding access scope. After access scope reduction, if there exists a query predicate which has empty access scope, then the query is resolved without accessing the database and has NULL answer. Using this type of heuristic, the scope of database accesses can be reduced and the evaluation of the query can be more efficiently performed.

2) *Object Reduction Heuristic*: Replace a path expression of large path length by semantically equivalent path expression of small path length according to the attribute-join constraints with $=$ comparison operators. In case that the semantic constraints are specified according to the inverse relationship, this heuristic is very useful. For example, we assume that an inverse relationship $C_1.a_1 = C_2.a_2^{-1}$ is specified in the database schema. Then the semantic constraint $(\forall o_1/C_1)(o_1.a_1.a_2 = o_1)$ holds in SKB and the path expression $o_1.a_1.a_2$ in the query can be replaced by the object variable o_1.

Application of object reduction heuristic results in decrease the number of object accesses. Note that if there may exist an object path with null value for the path expression, then this heuristic should not be applied to the path expression.

3) *Scan Reduction Heuristic*: Insert the new restriction with the constraint type C_i into the qualification clause. Given a path expression $o.a_1.a_2. \ldots a_n$ traversing classes $C_0 - C_1 - C_2 - \ldots C_n$, adding a new restriction of class $C_i(0 \leq i \leq n)$ can decrease the number of the intermediate object accesses in evaluation of the path expression. The following guidance can lead to more improvements. If the foreward traversal method for evaluating a path expression is used, then add a restriction of class close to the starting class of the path expression. If the backward traversal method is used, then add a restriction of class close to the target attribute of the path expression.

Scan reduction heuristic can be applied to the explicit join operation as well as above the implicit join operation. The application to the explicit join operation results in decrease in the number of the objects participating in the join operation.

4) *Join Reduction Heuristic*: Replace a query predicate $oe_1(o_1) = oe_2(o_2)$ by a query predicate $oe_3(o_1) = oe_4(o_2)$ in the query qualification clause if the following conditions hold:

1. $oe_1(o_1) = oe_2(o_2) \rightarrow oe_3(o_1) = oe_4(o_2)$ holds with respect to SKB,
2. oe_1 is left-duplicated to oe_3 and oe_2 is left-duplicated to oe_4,
3. the path length of oe_1 is larger than that of oe_3 and the path length of oe_2 is larger than that of oe_4.

This replacement is possible because from the first condition, a new query predicate $oe_3(o_1) = oe_4(o_2)$ is deduced and from the second condition and the third condition, $oe_3(o_1) = oe_4(o_2) \rightarrow oe_1(o_1) = oe_4(o_2)$ holds. For example, assume that a semantic constraint $(\forall o_1/C)(\forall o_2/C)(o_1.a = o_2.a \rightarrow o_1 = o_2)$ is derived for the semantic equality of the class C. Then the query predicate $x.a = y.a$ can be replaced by a new query predicate $x = y$. This heuristic reduces accesses of object bodies into accesses of object identifiers.

5) *Dangling Class Elimination Heuristic*: A class C involved in the query is a dangling class if it satisfies all of the following conditions:

1. C is a leaf object node in OQG,
2. No query predicates are specified in C,
3. C is not target object node.

During semantic transformations, a dangling class can be occurred in the object query graph. Such a dangling class can be always removed because the dangling class do not affect the query result

6) *Target Class Movement Heuristic*: Change a target object node from the object node of deep depth to the object node of shallow depth, if there exists an equi-OVJ predicate or an equi-OVJ predicate connecting these nodes in SKB and the query predicates. Application of this heuristic may lead to effective accesses of objects required to the query result.

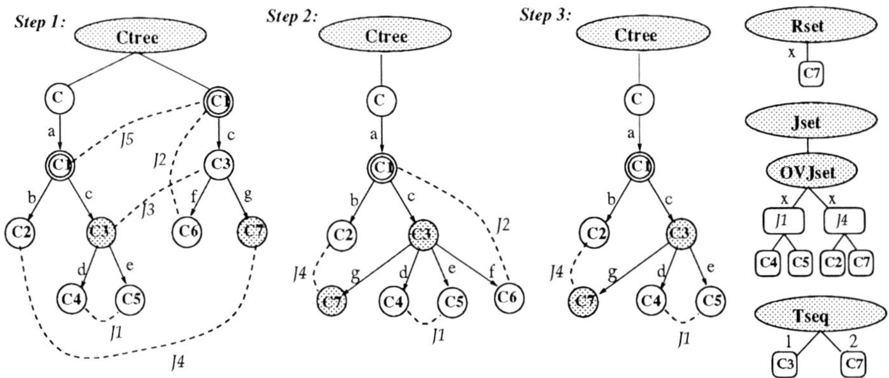

Fig. 2. Transformation of object query graph

Example 4.1 We will explain semantic transformations for the object query in Fig. 1. The sequence of applications of semantic transformations of the object query graph for the example query is illustrated in Fig. 2. This example is not necessarily typical but does help demonstrate what our semantic query optimizer does. We assume that the following semantic constraints hold in *SKB*:

SC1: $(\forall o_1/C1)(\forall o_2/C1)(o_1.c = o_2.c \rightarrow o_1 = o_2)$,

SC2: $(\forall o_1/C1)(o_1.c.f = o_1)$,

SC3: $(\forall o_2/C2)(o_2.j > 1000)$.

Step 1: According to the join reduction heuristic, a new query predicate $x{=}y$(denoted as *J5*) is deduced from the semantic constraint *SC1* and the query predicate $x.c{=}y.c$.

Step 2: According to the set-inclusion relationship, $\texttt{Ext}(C.a) \subseteq \texttt{Ext}(C1)$ holds. Thus two subpaths in *OQG* are merged and the TVJ predicate *J5* and *J3* are removed. And then the object variable y is replaced by the object variable x.

Step 3: According to the object reduction heuristic and the semantic constraint *SC2*, the OVJ predicate *J2* is removed. Since object node *C6* is a dangling class, *C6* is removed. Next, according to the restriction elimination heuristic, because the semantic constraint *SC3* implies the query predicate $x.b.j > 100$, this query predicate is removed. ∎

5 Conclusions

In this paper, we have investigated the representation of semantic constraints and the semantic query optimization technique in OODB systems. We have discussed the propagation of semantic constraints due to two relationships, subclassing relationship and is-part-of relationship. Also for efficient semantic optimization process, the constraint type and the typed grouping of relevant constraints were presented. We have presented a semantic query optimization technique which deals the semantic transformation of an object query graph. New transformation heuristics which guide useful semantic transformations are also developed in order to limit the size of the search space.

We would like to point out that our investigations are preliminary. The research presented in this paper can be improved, generalized, and extended in several directions. Especially, our semantic transformations of the object query graph can be tightly combined with query evaluation schemes such as graph clustering strategies and graph traversal strategies.

Acknowledgements

This research has been supported by Hyundai Electronics Industries Co. in Korea. Specially, the authors appreciate Mr. M. H. Chung, the chairman of Hyundai Electronics Industries Co., for his financial support and encouragement.

References

1. Avron Barr and Edward A. Feigenbaum, *The Handbook of Artificial Intelligence*, William Kaufmann, 1981.
2. H.V. Jagadish and Xiaolei Qian, "Integrity Maintenance in an Object-Oriented Database," *Int'l Conf. on Very Large Data Bases*, August 1992.
3. B. Paul Jenq, Darrell Woelk, Won Kim, and Wan-Lik Lee, "Query Processing in Distributed ORION," *Proc. Int'l Conf. on Extending Database Technology*, March 1990.
4. Setrag N. Khoshafian and George P. Copeland, "Object Identity," *Proc. Int'l Conf. on Object-Oriented Programming Systems, Languages, and Applications*, October 1986.
5. Jonathan J. King, "QUIST: A System for Semantic Query Optimization in Relational Databases," *Proc. ACM SIGMOD Conf. on Management of Data*, 1981.
6. Young-Whun Lee, et. al., "Design and Implementation of Obase OODBMS," *Technical Report, Dept. of Computer Science, Seoul National University*, September 1993.
7. Hwee Hwa Pang, HongJun Lu, and Beng Chin Ooi, "An Efficient Semantic Query Optimization Algorithm," *Proc. IEEE Int'l Conf. on Data Engineering*, April 1991.
8. Shashi Shekhar, Jaideep Srivastava, and Soumitra Dutta, "A Formal Model of Trade-off between Optimization and Execution Costs in Semantic Query Optimization," *Proc. Int'l Conf. on Very Large Data Bases*, August 1988.
9. Sreekumar T. Shenoy and Zehra Meral Ozsoyoglu, "Design and Implementation of a Semantic Query Optimizer," *IEEE Trans. on Knowledge and Data Engineering*, Vol. 1, No. 3, September 1989.
10. Jong-Jin Sung and Jong-Tae Park, "Semantic Query Processing in Object-Oriented Database Systems," *Proc. Int'l Database Symposium on Database Systems for Advanced Applications*, April 1991.
11. Michael Siegel, Edward Sciore, and Sharon Salverter, "A Method for Automatic Rule Derivation to Support Semantic Query Optimization," *ACM Trans. of Database Systems*, Vol. 17, No. 4, December 1992.

A Medical Terminology Server

Carole Goble, Peter Crowther and Danny Solomon

Medical Informatics Group, Department of Computer Science,
University of Manchester, Oxford Road, Manchester, M13 9PL, UK
tel: +44 61 275 6133; fax: +44 61 275 6932;
internet: <cag/pjc/wds>@cs.man.ac.uk

Abstract. GRAIL is a semantically constrained, generative compositional descriptive logic with subsumption and multiple inheritance designed to cope with the scale, complexity and variable granularity of medical concepts. It effectively represents a medical vocabulary for any application such as decision support systems, hospital record systems, clinical workstations and bibliographic systems. The EU-funded GALEN project aims to create a multilingual Terminology Server capable of being used as a resource by any medical application. The Terminology Server relates descriptive medical concepts represented in GRAIL to their natural language terms in a number of European languages and to corresponding (or best match) codes in conventional clinical coding schemes. In this paper we present GRAIL, the GALEN Terminology Server and make some remarks on the coupling of the classification-based clinical knowledge base (implemented in Smalltalk) with a relational database (Sybase).

1 Introduction

Scientific disciplines generally develop precise terminology or notation that is accepted and standardised. Medicine has surprisingly failed to develop a standardised vocabulary and nomenclature. Data retrieval and analysis is difficult with discrepancies between the meanings intended by the observers and recorders. What is an 'upper respiratory infection'? Does it include infections of the trachea? Is an 'ache' a pain? Such imprecision is problematic when we aggregrate data recorded by a number of professionals for trends and we must especially identify synonyms if we are not to get misrepresentations.

Free text is flexible, but is slow and unpopular with clinicians as well as being insufficiently structured and often ambiguous. The alternative is to use a coding or classification scheme to structure entries (the first classification of diseases was undertaken by Carl von Linne in 1749). Unfortunately, existing schemes were often developed for purposes with very different requirements, such as data aggregation for population statistics, rather than for the representation and manipulation of detailed clinical concepts which is required today.

Coding and classification schemes can either be enumerative or generative. Enumerative systems (e.g. ICD-9 [1]) rely on being able to define *pre-hoc* all that can be said clinically; this becomes explosive if sufficient detail for everyday patient care is included, and unmanageably large and complex especially if cross-referencing or multiple axes are incorporated.

Multi-axial generative systems, such as SNOMED [3] can be acceptably expressive, but most insufficiently restrict what can be generated—permitting medically nonsensical constructs such as 'orange headaches' or 'broken eyelashes'. The claim that these would be rejected by doctors is irrelevant, for the need for manual intervention prevents the system validating or actively supporting data input by clinicians (or other clinical systems)[4], or the reliable exchange of information. The lack of constraints also limits consistency of structure; the semantics of the classification hierarchies are often heterogeneous and implicit, which severely limits the inferences that can be drawn.

A representation of the semantics of medicine and medical terminology and its active enforcement is essential for the integrity of the patient record. The medical terminologies required are moving away from the paper-based coding systems to computer-based representations of medical concepts with their semantic relationships. Such terminologies, especially if they are multi-lingual, not only support the Electronic Patient Record (EPR) but also faciliate information exchange and transfer.

Research into the exploitation of the knowledge inherent in medical terminology, coding systems and classifications for the EPR has progressed along seven main streams [5]; the three most relevant to us are:

1) developing controlled vocabularies of medical information systems;

2) finding methods for computer-supported automatic translation between different external representations; for example from medical text to one coding system, or in pairs between coding systems;

3) combining existing coding systems and controlled vocabularies within a common framework to support mapping between these systems for information retrieval.

1.1 A Descriptive Logic for Medicine

Rector and Nowlan [6] suggest that in order to deal with the scale, complexity and variable granularity of the clinical record requires a knowledge representation which is generative but is sure to only generate statements that are medically semantically correct. A descriptive model seems to be more promising than a traditional prescriptive one since the description of what was actually observed cannot be constrained to fit within a predefined view of what ought to have happened. The consequence of this is the ability to control what can be sensibly said about the observations of a patient—the schema of a patient's record. A patient can have a fractured bone, but not a fractured eyebrow; a fracture can only occur in one place at a time; there is no such thing as an orange headache; drugs can be prescribed for patients, diseases cannot.

GRAIL (GALEN Representation and Integration Language) [12] is a descriptive logic with subsumption and multiple inheritance based on semantic networks. It belongs to the KL-ONE [8] family of knowledge representation schemes, and is generative by being recursively compositional, defining complex entities in terms of composite descriptions composed of a limited set of elementary concepts. Such descriptive entities are classified and placed in the correct place in the lattice. In addition, there is a semantic constraint mechanism which constrains the composition of the complex entities by the use of layers of sanctions. It also controls redundancy, tautologies and equivalent concepts (a process called canonisation). It is the sanctioning mechanism which separates GRAIL from such systems as CLASSIC [9] and BACK [10]. The sanctions ensure that only *semantically sensible* concepts are created, eg. a *Fracture which hasLocation Bone* and not *Fracture which hasLocation Tongue*. Without such sanctioning mechanisms it is easy to create nonsensical concepts. These particularization concepts are often implicit, unstored (un-reified) and must be generated during the classification process—they do not represent permanent data.

The medical concepts modelled are not confined to terminology but include assertions, such as *Cancer necessarily hasSeverity severe*. The 'severity' is not strictly terminology but clinical fact, making it impossible to record information about 'mild cancers'. GRAIL not only models the clinical concepts, eg. *Fracture which hasLocation Femur*, but also models the information model *Patient which has Condition*. The GRAIL classifier has a functional approach like Krypton, though the medical concepts are an enhanced form of the T-Box [2]. Transitive relationships across part-whole compositions are also controlled. GRAIL and its classifier is described in detail in [7,12].

2 A Medical Terminology Server

GRAIL effectively models the medical concepts required for any application such as decision support systems, hospital record systems, clinical workstations and bibliographic systems. It is a controlled vocabulary for medical information systems.

The GALEN [11] (Generalised Architecture for Languages Encyclopaedias and Nomenclatures in Medicine) project aims to create a multilingual Terminology Server (TeS) capable of being used as a resource by any medical application. The Terminology Server relates descriptive medical concepts represented in GRAIL to their natural language terms in a number of European languages and to corresponding (or best match) codes in conventional clinical coding schemes.

An example application for the TeS is that of supporting the accurate collection of data for the EPR. Doctors cite the time and effort required to enter data as the single biggest barrier to using computers. PEN&PAD [6] is a prototype clinical workstation that uses a early version of GRAIL to represent the intensional concept and information mode. PEN&PAD uses predictive data entry as a particularly effective way of entering highly structured data quickly and easily. Given a complaint, the system generates a data entry form from the terminological knowledge base held in the TeS which contains all the likely options for modifiers and additional statements. The process of predictive data entry can be thought of as a clinician asserting or refuting belief in potential concepts generated by the knowledge base.

PEN&PAD not only used GRAIL to represent the intensional conceptual model but also the extensional asserted patient-related instances of the concepts, such as *Mrs Smith which <has (Fracture which hasLocation Femur) on 23/12/92>*. This unified model (described in detail in [13]) ensures that the data in the clinical record is accurate and semantically correct, as well as using the same classification mechanisms for data as for concepts.

2.1 Architecture

The TeS is a networked resource; it responds to requests from applications, and is intended as a service for any clinical application that needs to have an understanding of medical knowledge and medical terms. The TeS could be asked to ratify the description of a concept as being sound, or respond with known information about that concept.

Internally, the TeS is divided into three modules, illustrated in Figure 1:

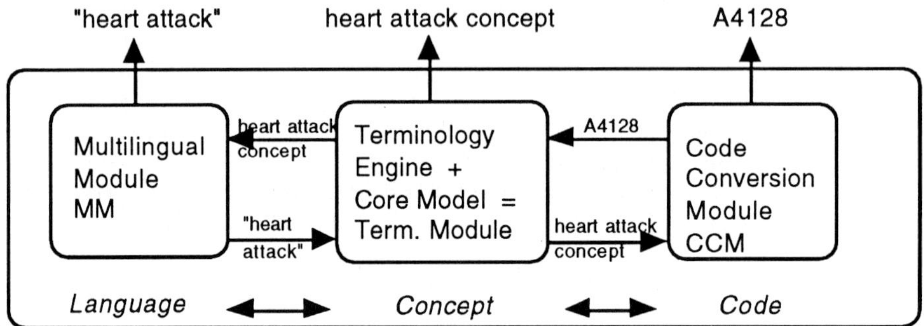

Fig 1: The GALEN Terminology Server

The **Terminology Module** (TM) deals with clinical concepts as abstract concepts. The Core Model is the representation of medicine (the Universe of Discourse data model). The Terminology Engine is the data model used to express the Core Model (the schema model). Together these form the *concept* model of medicine. The concept model is used as an 'interlingua' in translating between different external representations: natural languages or elements of existing coding schemes.

The **Multi-lingual Module** (MM) translates these clinical concepts to and from natural languages. It must also be able to take a name and map this to a clinical concept in the TM, and it maps concepts back to strings or names. Names are unique and are usually in the language of the modeller, and can therefore be thought of keys with cognitive semantics. The names might be used to infer strings—strings are the rendering in any language of the names.

The **Code Conversion Module** (CCM) takes a clinical concept and does a best fit mapping to a standard medical coding scheme such as SNOMED. Any number of coding schemes are supported. It can also take a code and map this to a clinical concept in the TM.

Thus the **Terminology Server** provides a framework for computer-supported automatic translation between pairs of coding systems and combines existing coding systems and controlled vocabularies within a common framework. It encapsulates the three modules; handles all the inter-module communication and all the external communication to users, applications and databases. In addition, it provides a model of reference by which external applications can refer to concepts.

An internal representation language, TesLa, is used as the integration medium for modules in the TeS. External communication with the TeS is via the API; client bindings are available for Smalltalk and C.

The TeS has been implemented in Objectworks/Smalltalk. The data requirements are substantial—the estimate for the number of reified medical concepts in the Core Model is around 1 million with up to 5 million edges. Hence the TeS is integrated with a database, or rather with several databases, implemented in Sybase.

2.2 Functionality

The TeS has two support roles:

1. A read-only role to support an application such as PEN&PAD. An application is likely to have predictable behaviour and hits, and a database could be clustered and optimised to suit (however this presumes that the TeS is only supporting one application area). Different applications will have different emphasis on the Core model, and different levels of specifity applicable. Eg. *Fracture which haslocation Humerus* could be the most specific description required for an epidemiology system but is not sufficient for a osteopathology application.

2. A read-write role to support a co-operative incremental distributed development environment for the Core Model of medicine. The Core Model is experimental and evolutionary with many versions requiring evaluation and possible reconciliation. In addition is is intended that users of applications will be able to extend a read-only common core with their own models, perhaps later seeing these incorporated in the common core. This role has unpredictable behaviour and hits.

Consequences of these two roles on the functionality of the TeS include:

- multiple Core models or sub-models, represented by multiple semantic networks or sub-networks;
- each sub-model must have authoring/versioning information;
- each user/application can be related to a specific Core Model/sub-model.

3 The TeS in detail

A more detailed representation of the TeS architecture is given in Figure 2. Note that different solutions may be appropriate for each module. Superficially the MM and CCM have a good deal in common and have a similar data and execution model, (though different databases). The support of the TE requires a different solution.

Entities are the categorial elementary or composite (particularised) entities and are only dealt with in the TM. *Rodents* are encapsulations of an entity in the Terminology Engine.and are the currency of concepts within the Terminology Server. Rodents could encapsulate a name or a description (a particularization) which can be thought of as a specification. Entities can be generated by lazy evaluation from their specifications (particularizations can be thought of as views for those readers familiar with databases). The fact that particularization concepts are often implicit, unstored (un-reified) and must be generated during the classification process causes some difficulties when the TM is interfaced with a database (see Section 3.3). The rodent also provides the *interface* to the TM for the other internal modules. The CCM and MM communicate with the TM via the rodents. The TM puts the wrapper on entities as they are sent out of it.

The TeS has a four level model of reference for concepts which external applications can use, and which take into account the fact that a TeS is accessible on network:

• **Handles.** An object id whose lifetime is restricted to a particular session (single connection with the TeS).

• **Local Name.** Linguistically relevant strings for concepts, valid across connections but restricted to one TeS running a particular version of the model; generated by applications.

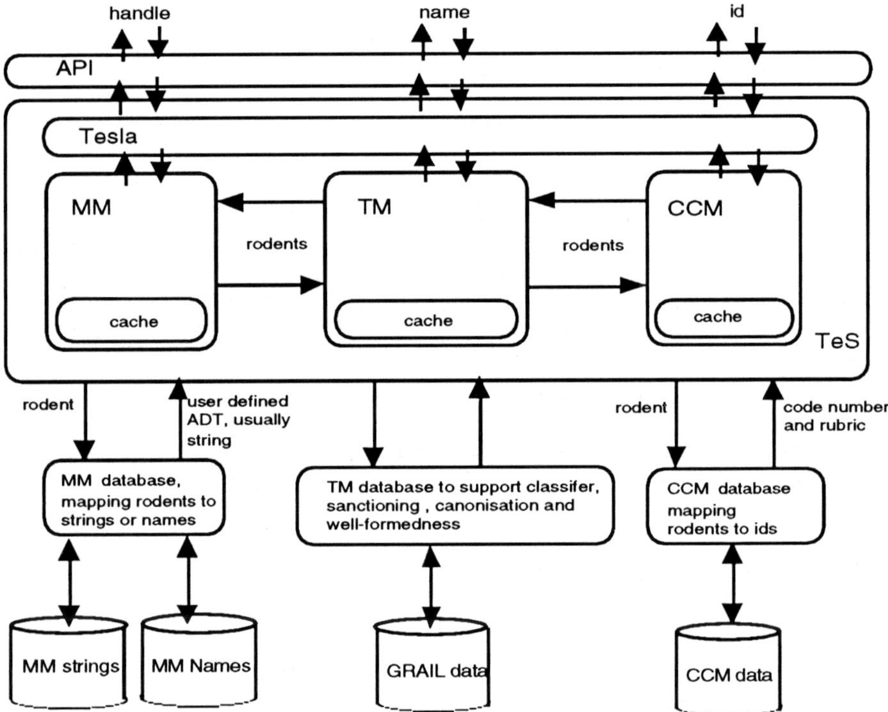

Fig 2. Architecture of the TeS

• **Local Id.** These have the same persistence and visiblity as local names, but are generated from within the TeS. They are an easily storable (linguistically meaningless) identifier for an entity—valid across time, but only to the originating TeS. These can be used to generate 'application-specific local coding schemes'.

• **Global Id.** A persistent object id. Valid across versions of the TeS—the global id is the only way of connecting across servers, and hence it is generated by the TM, but managed by the TeS.

The TeS maintains a set of mappings: between rodents and handles; between rodents and application-specific names and between rodents and application-specific local coding schemes which persist between connections with those applications. The database is needed to populate the data types in those implementations.

3.1 Multilingual Module (MM)

The MM is concerned with maintaining the relationship between the language-independent concept model and natural languages. The mapping between the concepts and their names is completely separate and independent of the Terminology Module. The MM passes a rodent to a database, which can returns any type, but usually returns a string. This doesn't necessarily mean that the database stores rodents—they don't need to exist as objects outside the TeS. The MM has a cache for each session and we are considering whether it is better to have multiple caches, one for each language or whether a language should have a cache used by multiple sessions. Languages are completely pluggable with an unlimited number running concurrently in different sessions and within a session.

3.2 Code Conversion Module (CCM) and the Code Store

The Code Store is capable of storing any (known) coding scheme in a flexible but consistent way. In particular, it can handle different versions of the same coding scheme; subdivisions of coding schemes, such as SNOMED's modules and chapters; no, single and multiple inheritance within a coding scheme; different languages for rubrics; cross-references between coding schemes and boolean properties of codes. The CCM stores typed linked between these codes and concepts in the CORE model.

3.3 The Terminology Module

The problem here is the support of large models expressed in GRAIL. Various degrees of coupling have been proposed for the GRAIL databases and terminology. Three are considered below:

1. A loosely coupled approach where the database and Terminology Engine are independent and the entities and their relationships are stored atomically;

2. A layered approach with the database layer trying to anticipate what goes on in higher layers. The data concepts are stored in an optimised way where possible, but make it all appear atomic to higher levels of code.

3. A tightly coupled approach, with the database highly integrated with the terminology engine. This accommodates advanced schemes like pre-fetching and cacheing, but is the most complex to implement.

In an early version the loose coupling approach was used; however there were major problems with performance. The latest version adopts the tightly coupled approach. The majority of the classification, sanctioning, well-formedness etc activities of the classifier are undertaken by the classifier with little active support by the database—the database is really just an extension of the virtual memory. CLASSIC couples with an SQL database and attempts to do some of the classification work within the database [14]. The next version of the TeS moves to a more active role for the database. For example, if the question is 'does this entity exist' that might be done by the database without having to page in the network for the test. Although [14] has interfaced a descriptive logic representation with a relational database it supports classification only—not sanctioning or canonisation. In addition, the GRAIL classifier must support two kinds of query:

1. Given concept X, is it legal and what is its position it in the classification lattice?

2. Given concept X, how can I further specialise it?,

[14] deals with the first, but not the (expensive) second use, essential in the support of predictive data entry applications.

The high latency involved in any database request means that we need to minimise the number of requests made; we also need to maximise the parallelism between the TeS and the RDBMS. This can be done by requesting entities as far in advance as possible—one reason for tight coupling. The database can also help by performing closures on entities to find eg. parents, and passing those back as well. However, a balance needs to be found: in our experience the DBMS is slower at finding paths than the TeS, and the TeS frequently has parent entities cached anyway. The retrieval operations running inside the SQL server need to know what the TeS has in its caches, so that the minimum of extra querying is done at the server and the minimum is transferred across the TeS/DBMS link. There are two kernel page sets for every session that must be in memory permanently, assuming that the network can be semantically partitioned into pages : 1) application independent part of the network (e.g 'TopObject') and 2) application dependent part. The semantic partitioning is part of future work.

There is a spectrum of approaches to storing entities and relationships, two fundamental approaches originate from the *generative* nature of particularisations possible in GRAIL:

1. Store a definition of the entity or the relationship, and derive the interrelationships between entities when they are paged in.

2. Store the inter-relationships with the entity, and update them as concepts are added to the knowledge base Core Model.

The spectrum is produced by combining portions of these approaches—what information is stored versus what is derived each time. Definitions are faster to create, as less is stored, and may not need to be altered if additions to the network cause them to be reclassified. However, the approach relies on canonisation of all input entities and appropriate indexing (to ensure that the definition is retrieved if it exists) and is critically dependent on the speed of classification in memory.

Storing a network places less reliance on the classifier, as retrieval of an entity does not require it to be (re)classified. However, it is dependent on the speed of the database. The problem is presumed NP-hard—classification is probably exponential on some property of the network. As networks get larger, the time to classify an entity is likely to grow relatively quickly.

A major problem is the latency of the database (Sybase) coupled with the Smalltalk implementation of the classifier. It appears that (somewhat unsurprisingly):

1. storing a definition is better for applications with relatively small knowledge bases and high creation-to-retrieval rates.
2. storing a classified network is better for applications with large knowledge bases and low creation-to-retrieval rates.

An entity is retrieved even if it is only required for the classification of another entity, or for an investigation of another entity's properties; depending on the cache, this will tend to decrease the creation-to-retrieval rate. We have adopted the stored classified network approach.

Core model network names are integrated with the name of the database opened by the DBMS. In this way we can use the DBMS security mechanisms to prevent unauthorised changes to a model stored using that DBMS, as the user of the database is now the user of the network.

4 Summary

In this paper we have presented the GALEN Medical Terminology server. Version 1 of the server has been implemented and is being used within the GALEN project consortium to support the distributed building of a large medical concept model, and to support demonstrator clinical applications. The main difficulty is the co-ordination of the classification process of the GRAIL model with a database, especially as many of the GRAIL concepts are 'virtual' and merely specifications. Sophisticated caching and pre-fetching requires a tightly coupled system with semantic partitioning of the concept (GRAIL network) space integrated with the application the server is supporting. Eventually we envisage electronically-linked distributed communities of users extending a common concepts model held on Terminology Servers as part of the common infrastructure for developing coherent clinical systems which can interwork and be integrated.

Acknowledgements

The authors would like to acknowledge the other members of the Medical Informatics Group and GALEN consortium. This research is supported by the European Union under the Advanced Informatics in Medicine (AIM) GALEN project 2012.

References

1. World Health Organization. International Classification of Diseases: Ninth Revision. Geneva, 1977.
2. Brachman RJ, Fikes RE and Levesque HJ (1983) “KRYPTON: A functional approach to knowledge representation” in: IEEE Computer **16**(10) pp. 73-76
3. College of American Pathologists. Systematized Nomenclature Of Medicine. (Versions 1-3) Skokie, Illinois, USA: College of American Pathologists, 1977-1992.

4. Rector AL, Horan B, Fitter M, Kay S, Newton PD, Nowlan WA, Robinson D and Wilson A (1991) "User Centred Design Development of a General Practice Medical Workstation: The PEN&PAD Experience" in: Bauersfeld P, Bennett J, Lynch G (eds) Proceedings of Computer Human Interaction CHI '92, ACM, Monterey, Addison Wesley pp.447-453

5. Linnarson, R: Methods, design and components for a computer-based patient record to promote quality care in general practice. Linkoping University Medical Dissertations No 378, 1993

6. Rector AL, Nowlan WA and Kay S (1992) "Conceptual Knowledge: The Core of Medical Information Systems" in: Lun KC, Degoulet P, Pierre TE, Rienhoff (eds) MEDINFO 92, Proceedings of the Seventh World Congress on Medical Informatics, Geneva, North-Holland pp.1420-1426

7. Goble CA, Glowinski AJ , Jeffrey KG (1993). ''Semantic Constraints in a Medical Information System'' in: (Eds) Worboys M, Grundy F, Proceedings of BNCOD11, Lecture Notes in Computer Science 696 Advances in Databases, Springer-Verlag, pp. 40-57

8. Brachman RJ and Schmoize JG (1985) ''An overview of the KL-ONE knowledge representation system'' in: Cognitive Science **9**, pp. 171-216

9. Borgida A, Brachman RJ, McGuiness DL, Resnick LA, CLASSIC: A structural data model for objects, Proc 1989 ACM SIGMOD Conference on Management of Data, SIGMOD Record 18(2) Portland OR, June 1989,pp. 58-67

10. Nebel B, (1988): Computational complexity of terminological reasoning in BACK Artificial Intelligence, **34**(3) pp. 371-383

11. Rector A.L., Nowlan W.A., Glowinski A.J: Goals for Concept Representation in the GALEN project. in the 17th annual Symposium on Computer Applications in Medical Care, Washington, USA, SCAMC '93, 1993, .pp. 414-418

12. Goble CA, Glowinski AJ, Nowlan WA, Rector AL (1992) ''A Descriptive Semantic Formalism for Medicine'' in: Proceedings of the Ninth International Conference on Data Engineering, IEEE Computer Society Press, pp. 624-632

13. Goble C.A., Crowther P.J: Schemas for telling stories in medical records, in M.Jarke, J.Bubenko K.Jeffery (eds) Proceedings of the 4th International Conference on Extending Database Technology (EDBT94), Cambridge, UK March 1994, Lecture Notes in Computer Science 779 Springer Verleg 1994 pp 393- 406

14. Borgida A, Brachman RJ, Loading Data into Description Reasoners, Proc 1993 ACM SIGMOD Conference on Management of Data, 1993, pp. 217-226

BIND: A Biomedical INteroperable Database System*

Catherine Houstis[1], Theodore S. Papatheodorou[2], Vassilios Verykios[3], Aris Floratos[3], Ahmed Elmagarmid[4]

[1] Department of Computer Sciences, University of Crete, Heraklion, Greece
[2] Department of Computer Engineering and Informatics, University of Patras, Patras, Greece
[3] First Informatics S.A., Patras, Greece
[4] Department of Computer Sciences, Purdue University, West Lafayette, IN 47907, USA

Abstract. We describe a Biomedical INteroperable Database System (BIND), which is part of a larger research project, the Biomedical Equipment Assessment and Management (BEAM) system. BEAM is an AIM (Advanced Informatics in Medicine) awarded project and it is funded by the European Community. It integrates a number of heterogeneous database systems which store Biomedical information, over public communications networks. The databases are located in various European countries. Users access the information via a common user interface and are able to run transactions over the multidatabase system.

1 Introduction

There are a growing number of medical computer applications in which the health care provider interacts directly with the computer. These applications are referred to generally as medical, biomedical or clinical information systems. Such systems usually involve computer stored databases containing appropriate information. Most hospitals own computer systems where such information is stored for patient care.

In the BEAM project [1], an ambitious objective has been set forward. It is the interconnection of hospital stored databases containing biomedical equipment information for the purpose of their assesment and management at the European level. This involves clinical applications which utilize an underlined computer system for its implementation. The BIND system [2], [3], [4], is the underlined computer software system, which integrates heterogeneous databases found in various countries, with the objective of providing interoperations between them. These databases reside on various hardware platforms and utilize

* This work was partially supported by AIM grant, Project Number: $A2001$ and First Informatics S.A.

their own database management system, query language and data model. By data model we mean data structures and associated data semantics. The BIND system integrates the differences of the various member database systems and provides an interface which can be used for the implementation of the clinical applications. This interface contains a high level language into which the applications are expressed. The clients (users) of the BIND system consist of two kinds. They are clinical or hospital related personnel which interact with the system through the BIND system interface in order to access data in member database systems. They can also be member database systems interacting for data exchange. The interaction between member databases can use the BIND system interface to satisfy transfer of information. The information exchanged can be concerning biomedical equipment or medical devices specifications, their quality assurance requirements and management functions associated with them. This information is stored in these databases which for the present constitute the BIND system databases. They are (a) the European Community DataBase (ECDB), which contains information on medical devices, (b) the MEdical Devices Quality ASsurance database (MEDQAS), which contains quality assurance procedures and data for medical devices and (c) the Medical Equipment Management System (MEMS) which contains management functions for medical devices. The three databases are located in the Netherlands, Denmark and Italy respectively. These were originally local databases which have been extended and supplemented to include information of interest to the European user. All databases are connected to the Internet communications network, which is the public communication access network used in BIND.

In section 2, we give a detailed overview of the BIND system and we discuss the integration problem. In section 3, we outline a solution to the data integration problem pursued by the project consortium. In section 4, we present the system integration solution which is our work in the project. In section 5, we give an account of the current status of the project.

2 Overview of the BIND System

In the BIND system one of the objective was to provide an easy access for European users to a number of existing databases containing biomedical information. Three such databases were selected, the ECDB [6], MEDQAS [7], and MEMS [8], for their diverse information and thus the immediate interest they create for biomedical users. By biomedical users we mean clinical personnel in hospitals or hospital related institutions. We refer to all of these users as global users or European users. They can access the above mentioned databases via the BIND system. We distinguish them from the local users which can only access their local database, for instance the ECDB, independently of the global users. If local users wish to have access to the rest of the databases in BIND, then they have to connect to the BIND system. In that case they become global users.

In BIND, each database has its own management system and runs on its own hardware/software platform. The ECDB and MEMS databases use different versions of the Oracle database system and run on Sun/Unix and HP/Unix platforms respectively. The MEDQAS uses its own database and an PC/OS2 platform. The databases run autonomously. They use a considerable ammount of common data which need to be exchanged between them. Initially these common data were incompatible, since they used different semantics and data structures. Thus in BIND, we deal with heterogeneous and autonomous database systems which need to be integrated. Moreover, present the user with a transparent access to them and capability of transaction processing over them. The integration clearly involved two different efforts. One which addresses the data integration problem and the other the database systems integration problem. The data integration was pursued by the clinical engineers in the project since it involved clinical issues while the system integration was pursued by the computer engineers. The results of the data integration are necessary for the system integration to complete. Next, we describe the data integration problem and the solution followed in the project.

3 Data Integration

Data integration was among the first problems we had to resolve. A simplified way of describing it is, the same medical device had different names and data structures in different databases. Thus, common data which consisted mostly of data about medical devices could not be exchanged because they were incompatible. The solution to this problem guided efforts in two different directions. One direction was towards work in classification and codification standards of medical devices. This is an going activity put forward by the biomedical and clinical engineering community standard organizations and have been in progress independent of the project. In the project, there has been an investigation regarding this issue and some participation towards its resolution. Nevertheless, the standards organization work on this problem has not yet been completed. This lead to the second direction which was followed in the project. This direction involved two steps.

First, the semantic differencies in the data (we refer to naming semantics) were resolved within the project members by agreeing upon a common terminology on medical devices. This has taken into account the effort that is put forward by the standard organizations and a commonly accepted terminology established by the ECRI organization (Emergency Care Research Institute). This commonly agreed terminology is documented in [9]. It was felt that it is very close to the standard organizations directions.

Second, for each database a data dictionary would be built based on the common terminology agreement. An entry into the dictionary would point for instance at the name of a medical device as stored in the database once the corresponding common name was supplied of the same medical device. Thus databases would keep their own data structures for medical devices and had only to translate (via the dictionary) the name they had used to the common name (term) adopted for each one of them. Therefore, the common terminology

or the naming semantics agreement within the project would be instrumental in solving the data integration problem, since the dictionary implements the results of the semantics agreement.
In the project a simpler solution was followed. The common data that needed to be exchanged were not enough to justify the creation of a dictionary for each database. Thus, the only data that followed the common terminology were the common data and thus they were manually changed to conform to it. Next, we present the system integration which is our contribution in this project.

4 Heterogeneous Database System Integration

BIND is a multidatabase system. In [2] we give a review of multidatabase systems. For the BIND system we have utilized a prototype system, the InterBase system, [10], [11], [12] which we have developed and adopted to the project needs [4].

4.1 The InterBase System Architecture

The InterBase system is a general system that integrates heterogeneous database and non-database systems. In BIND we only dealt with database systems. Here we present an overview of the InterBase system, and more detailed information is presented in [10]. The InterBase system architecture is shown in Figure 4.1 and consists of two main components:

1. The Distributed Flexible Transaction Manager (DFTM). The DFTM is responsible for managing global transaction executions. Global transactions are specified using the InterBase Parallel Language (IPL) [11].
2. The Remote System Interface (RSI). RSIs act as an interface between DFTM and Local database systems integrated into InterBase.

The DFTM functions are to ensure the reliable execution of global transactions. A global transaction accesses multiple databases, it consists of subtransactions each of which is executed as a local transaction of a single local database system. A local transaction accesses only a single local database system. In addition, the DFTM manages the data flow within global transactions, provides global concurrency control and recovers InterBase from errors. It consists of DFTM images, with one DFTM image per global transaction.

The DFTM is distributed over all the machines from which IPL programs are executed; that is, each global transaction G_i is associated with a single DFTM image D_i. G_i usually consists of subtransactions, each of which must be executed on a local system through its associated RSI. In order to provide the correct concurrent execution of global transaction, D_i must first communicate with relevant RSIs to arrange the relative execution order of G_i's subtransactions on corresponding RSIs. The corresponding RSIs then execute G_i's subtransactions in the specified order. Remote System Interfaces provide a uniform system-level

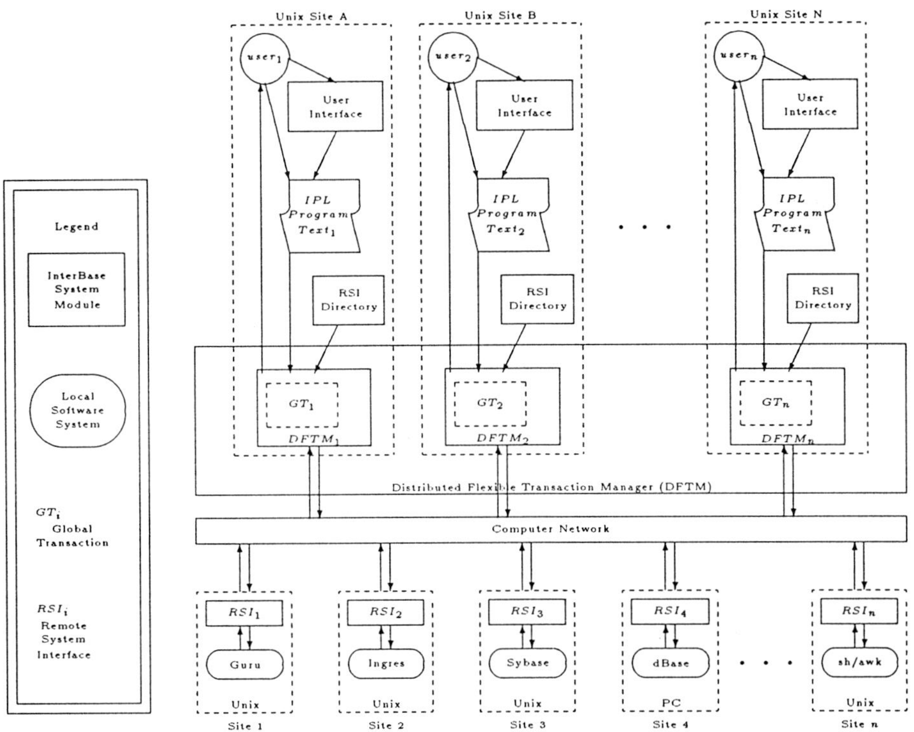

Fig. 1. The logical architecture of InterBase

interface between the DFTM and local systems and deal with the heterogeneity of the local systems, including commands and data format transformation, thus relieving the DFTM from dealing with each local system directly. The RSI Directory stores information such as location and communication protocols and allowable data transfer methods for different RSIs, thus supporting location and distribution transparency for the system.

An RSI consists of an RSI server and RSI services. The RSI server is designed to accept the execution requests of concurrent DFTM images for their associated global transactions and negotiate with the DFTM images to arrange for the execution order of the subtransactions of these global transactions on its associated local systems. It then creates RSI services for these subtransactions according to the specified order. In this way, InterBase allows several DFTM images to be executed concurrently as long as their execution is serializable, thus increasing the throughput of InterBase. An RSI service is responsible for the consistent and reliable execution of the subtransaction and is coincident with its life cycle. The RSI server needs also to trace the status of running and completed RSI services, so as to decide when to schedule the execution of the upcoming and queued subtransactions.

While RSI *servers* are local-system-independent since they do not interact directly with local systems, RSI *services* are local-system-specific, since they communicate directly with local systems, and therefore must have knowledge of the language and data formats used by the local system. This allows the RSI server code to be shared by different RSI servers, whereas, the code for RSI services needs to be modified for new local systems. This versatility is an advantage of dividing the RSI function between RSI servers and RSI services. A second advantage of this division is that concurrent execution of subtransactions in InterBase is allowed. Another advantage is that all RSI servers can always run on the same platform as DFTM images no matter where their corresponding RSI services run. This type of RSI structure not only makes communication among DFTM images and RSI servers easy to handle, but also makes it easy for InterBase component crash detection and recovery.

4.2 The InterBase Parallel Language

The InterBase Parallel Language (IPL) is the transaction specification language of InterBase. IPL allows users to specify all actions associated with a global transaction, such as the control flow and data flow among subtransactions. And, InterBase will automatically execute subtransactions in parallel when it can do so without violating the specified control flow or data flow constraints.

An IPL program contains three parts that respectively are used to specify: definitions of data types, definition of subtransactions, and dependency relations among subtransactions.

Definitions of Data Types: In IPL programs, a subtransaction is associated with a data type which specifies the data structure of the result if the subtransaction is successfully executed (i.e., reaching its ready-to-commit state). The predefined data types provided are **int, real, boolean**, and **charString**, and users can define complex types through the aggregation.

Definition of Subtransactions: This part provides mechanisms for specifying subtransactions within an IPL program. Its execution step, optional confirm step, and optional undo step are defined between IPL keyword pairs **beginexec** and **endexec**, **beginconfirm** and **endconfirm**, and **beginundo** and **endundo**, respectively. These steps, consisting of uninterpreted blocks of statements, are passed through the IPL interpreter to the appropriate RSI. The RSI will translate these statements to statements compatible with its associated local system, if necessary, before their execution. These statements can be in SQL, the native query language of the local system, or a mixture of the two. If these statements are in SQL, a syntax check will be performed before the execution of the IPL program.

IPL variables are quoted by $$. Before the execution of a subtransaction, the IPL variables must be replaced by corresponding values. The keyword **output** is used to produce the output of the IPL program.

Dependency Description: The dependency description provides users with a mechanism for specifying the execution order among the subtransactions of a global transaction.

The major advantage of using IPL is its semantic power and suitability. Through dependency description, programmers in IPL can specify control flow among subtransactions, which gives IPL the flexibility to support parallel execution and synchronization among subtransactions. IPL provides a method for specifying data flow within a global transaction. IPL permits the construction of mixed global transactions by allowing the extent of compensatability to be specified in the declarations of subtransactions. Commit and abort operations of subtransactions are deferred until their global transactions commit or abort, if they are defined, and thus support atomic transactions. IPL also allows the specification of transactions that may include subtransactions that access non-database systems, and database systems with complex data models, because statements in the native language can be incorporated into IPL programs. A detailed account of the IPL is found in [11].

4.3 The InterBaseView Graphical User Interface

The InterBase View graphical [12] consists of two parts: an *execution interface* and an *IPL program editor*. The execution interface can load an IPL program and invoke it as a global transaction. The execution history of the transaction is displayed to track its execution status. The execution interface supports Flex transactions by graphically displaying the dependence relations among subtransactions and providing intermediate results, allowing users to select among acceptable alternative subtransactions in committing the transaction. If the user decides to commit the transaction, the final result will be displayed. The IPL program editor allows a user to conveniently construct IPL programs. After a keyword button is clicked, the keyword is automatically inserted into the edited IPL program at the appropriate position, and help information is simultaneously displayed in the help area leading the user through the process with pop-up menus and dialog windows. Users can always easily undo their last action. The RSI directory is referenced to provide users with the available software system names and the corresponding machine names. All user defined record types and subtransactions names are kept for use in the program. A window displays a sample IPL program, providing an example as an aid to learning. To assist in the writing of applications that presuppose a structural knowledge of the component database systems, InterBaseView provides facilities for users to access these database schemas. After editing an IPL program, a user can check its syntax in the working area execution. InterBaseView was implemented using OSF/MOTIF widgets on top of the X window system.

5 Current Status of the BIND System

The configuration of the BIND system is shown in Figure 2. Currently it runs on a SUN LX platform running SUN OS 4.1.3C and is capable of integrating two of the three databases as described in section 2. The RSI for Oracle version #6 and version #7 corresponding to the ECDB and MEMS database is built and connected into the system. The MEDQAS database is not yet connected since its platform change is pending from OS2 to Unix. A working prototype of the BIND system [5], was demonstrated in the project's review. Several applications programs have been written for the BIND users in IPL. The common user interface activates several of these in an effective and simple way using the facilities of the InterBaseView graphical interface. At this point we are conducting experiments over a local network configuration. Perfomance studies are also under way. Perfomance experiments are designed and will be carried out. The BIND system perfomance will depend on the availability and reliability of the Internet communications network. We are not very concerned about this though, since Internet is a reliable network and the information accessed in BIND can be easily regarded as common Internet traffic.

Nevertheless, we plan to conduct experiment of the BIND system perfomance to verify our intuition. Future plans about BIND's availability to all European users who wish to connect to it are being discussed. The project has one more year to complete from the writing of this paper. Interested users have to have a Unix platform available to install a BIND host and an Internet connection. Simple users can access a BIND host system using simple dial-up service.

References

1. Biomedical Equipment Assessment and Management – BEAM, Technical Annex
2. C. Houstis, T. Papatheodorou, A. Floratos, K. Pantazopoulos, "A comparative evaluation of existing Heterogeneous Database Management Systems – State of the Art", BEAM project, deliverable #2, March 1992
3. C. Houstis, T. Papatheodorou, A. Floratos, K. Pantazopoulos, "User and Technical Requirements for the BIND system", BEAM project, deliverable #5, June 1992
4. C. Houstis, T. Papatheodorou, A. Floratos, K. Pantazopoulos, "Design of the BIND system, Potential Modifications of a selected system", BEAM project, deliverable #11, September 1992
5. C. Houstis, T. Papatheodorou, V. Verykios, K. Pantazopoulos, "Demonstrator of the BIND Subsystem", BEAM project, deliverable #18, September 1993
6. J. Boter, C. V. Nimwegen, W. Cavens, "Status of the Medical Devices Databases", BEAM project, deliverable #19, September 1993
7. S. S. Nielsen, A. Månsson, J. Seest, H. Wistreich, A. Talbot, "Quality Control DB Design and Requirements for European QA Databases", BEAM project, deliverable #17, June 1993
8. C. Lamberti, "Demonstrator of the MEMS Documentation and Support", BEAM project, deliverable #20, September 1993
9. L. Rystrom, G. Kronborg, "Updated Integration Architecture", BEAM project, deliverable #15, April 1993

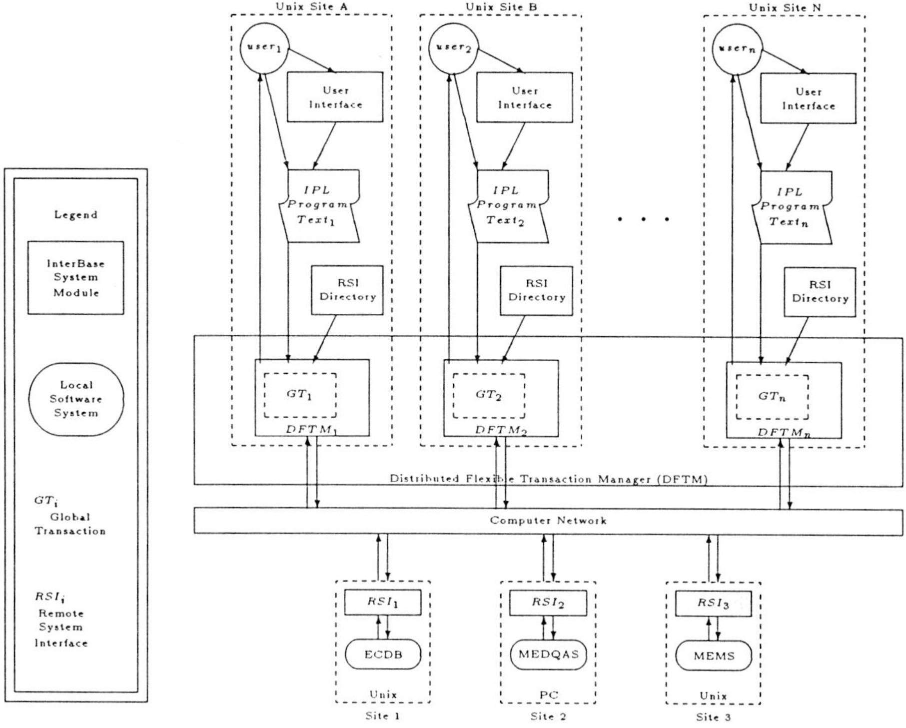

Fig. 2. The logical architecture of the BIND system

10. A. Elmagarmid, J. Chen, W. Du, O. Bukhres, and R. Pezzoli. InterBase: An Execution Environment for Global Applications over Distributed, Autonomous, and Heterogeneous Software Systems. Technical Report CSD–TR–92 – 016, Department of Computer Sciences, Purdue University, March 1992.
11. J. Chen, O. A. Bukhres, and A. K. Elmagarmid. IPL: A Multidatabase Transaction Specification Language. *In Proc. of the* 13*th International Conference on Distributed Computing Systems*, 1993.
12. X. Liu, J. Chen, and R. Pezolli. The InterBaseView Graphical User Interface. Technical Report SERC–TR–126–P, Department of Computer Sciences, Purdue University, Nov. 1992.

DEVELOPMENT OF SECURE MEDICAL DATABASE SYSTEMS

Pangalos G. (1), Pomportsis A. (3), Bozios L. (2), Khair M.(1).

(1) Computers Division, Faculty of Technology, General Department, Aristotelian University, Thessaloniki 540 06, Greece
(2) Information Systems Department, AHEPA University Hospital, Thessaloniki 54636, Greece
(3) Department of Informatics, Aristotelian University, Thessaloniki 540 06, Greece

Abstract
Security is an important issue directly related to the quality and effectiveness of medical care. Database security in particular plays a significant role in the overall security of medical information systems and networks. The general framework and requirements for medical database security and the major secure database development methodologies are discussed briefly. An experimental implementation which aims to improve medical database security is then presented and discussed. An important characteristic of this development is that mandatory security controls are used additionally to the discretional ones in order to enhance database security.

Keywords: Medical database security, Information system security, database security policies, database security

1. Introduction
Security is a basic requirement for the appropriate introduction and use of information and communication technologies in health care. These technologies contribute to improving the efficiency and quality of health care services and they are valuable tools for their management. They create however new situations regarding security that should be dealt with in a thorough and convincing manner. The patient should never doubt for example that information given in confidence to a health professional is collected and stored in medical databases correctly, disclosed only to authorised persons, and used lawfully (41,42).

Current thinking in information systems security is that the issues centre on confidentiality (information is only disclosed to those users who are authorised to have access to it), integrity (information is modified only by those users who have the right to do so), and availability (information and other IT resources can be accessed by authorised users when needed). Medical systems are 'risky' systems with respect to at least these goals. The level of security that should be included in a medical information system involves however some judgement about the dangers associated with the system and the resource implications of various means of avoiding or minimising those dangers.

In the context of medical information systems and networks, the issue of medical database security appears as a crucial point. This is both because of the role and the nature of the database technology (handles stores of valuable and sensitive data), and its widespread use (over 90% of computer systems in use today contain some kind of database system (10)). In addition to the more common security concerns of integrity, access control, audit etc., database systems add concerns for granularity, inference, aggregation, filtering, journaling etc. (1,41,50). Database systems also provide new tools for enforcing and control security. They also make it possible to increase granularity by enforcing security at a record or even at a data item level. Databases have also introduced a centralised means of storage and retrieval of structured data. From this starting point, they developed as a general tool for communication among individuals within an organisation. Thus "storing of data" is now essentially "communication".

2. Database Systems Security

Database security is concerned with the ability of the system to enforce a security policy governing the disclosure, modification or destruction of information. Within health care organisations humans typically use a database as a technical tool for storing, processing and communicating information. At any time an amount of data has been stored in it, a large amount of messages has already been sent and the corresponding data can be called for duplication and further transmission on demand from potential receivers. The database relays the messages by persistently memorising the corresponding data following the three phase procedure (2): "*accept messages ==> store / process data ==> assemble, duplicate and communicate data on demand*". The quality of mediation is dependably assured by special protocols enforcing completion of transactions and integrity constraints on stored data. Mediation is shared among many users and is required to be efficient in time and space (2).

The following general principles related to database security have been widely accepted today (10,11,14):

a. The database system security considerations must take into account all system S/W and H/W that touches information flowing into, and out of, the database. For example, an easily penetrated operating system would render a superbly protected *DBMS* useless.
b. Data integrity is a key requirement. The database system must preserve the integrity of the data stored in it. The user must be able to trust the system to give back the same data that is put in the system and to permit data to be modified only by authorised users. The data should not be destroyed or altered either accidentally, as in a system crash, or maliciously, as in some unauthorised person modifying the data. At the very least, the user should know if the data was corrupted.
c. Data should be available when needed. This implies system fault tolerance and redundancy in data, software and hardware. Inference and aggregation must be studied and controlled.
d. Audit should be detailed enough to be useful and sufficient enough so as not to severely burden system performance.
e. The aim should be at providing adequate level of secrecy (prevent disclosure) and yet preserving integrity by using appropriate concurrence and integrity controls (e.g. referential integrity).
f. The prototypes should be of general purpose, commercial quality and, according to most proposers, relational systems. The relational system has been chosen because it is (10) currently the model of preference in the commercial world.

Given the above definition and general framework of medical database security, if more technically, we can regard a database as a channel in the sense of communication theory. Then a database security policy states (2): (i) which type of sub-channels between (groups of) users can be established, (ii) the requirements of the availability of certain facilities of the sub channels, and (iii) the requirements on the (partial) separation and non-interference of sub channels. Seen from this point of view, we can identify two prominent proposals for database security policies (1,2,41,45):

a. The Mandatory (or Multilevel or Military) Security Approach.

The need for such a policy arises when a database system contains information with a variety of classifications and has some users which are not cleared for the highest classification of the information contained in the system. The Mandatory Access Control (MAC) is based on the following assumption (constructs) : there are users, data items, and a lattice of security levels. The sensitivity label that describes the data security level is formed of two parts: the category and the sensitivity level of the information. The category of the information is depending on the belonging of the data to a certain party. For example the medical record of a patient can be defined as belonging to a specified ward, so the access of a doctor working at another ward must be prohibited. The responsible doctor of a ward is thus permitted to have access to the whole medical record of the patients hospitalised at the rooms of that specified ward. The sensitivity level of the information is depending only on the data without consideration of the management procedures. For example, the sensitivity levels of the diseases are defined according to the nature of the illness and the possible social impact of an unauthorised disclosure.

b. The Discretional (or Commercial) Security Approach.
It is designed to enforce a specific access control policy and is based on the following assumption (constructs) : there are users, (well informed) transactions, and (constraint) data items. The concept of the 'user role' has special importance in this policy. A role is a set of actions and responsibilities associated with a particular organisational function. People in an organisation can play various roles which are functions that they carry out in the organisation. Every individual person can play one or more roles. The separation of roles and people playing them provides flexibility in binding people to roles and allows the people that play a role to change without affecting other activities that depend on their roles. The specification of access rights to data can thus be implemented independently of the specific individuals that may be associated within an organisation.

3. Medical Database Security

There are several reasons why a discussion on database security especially focused on the health care environment is necessary. Medical database security aims primarily at high availability, accuracy and consistency of stored data, the medical professional secrecy and confidentiality and the protection of the privacy of the patient. These properties, though of technical nature, basically require that the system is actually *helpful* for medical care and *not harmful* to patients. These later properties require in turn not only that fundamental ethical principles are not violated by employing database systems, but instead, are effectively enforced by technical means.

Beyond their potential administrative, financial, etc. value, health related data have a serious impact on clinical decision making and on patient treatment. Incorrect or unavailable information could for example, in certain circumstances, mislead a health care practitioner or cause a delay in treatment which could result in extended patient suffering, or in the worst case, in premature death. The more dependent the medical user becomes on computer-held data, the more stringent becomes the need for integrity and availability. Untimely, biased, or inaccessible information might prevent adequate care. Health care information systems also contain many data related directly to identifiable persons, their illness and their treatment, sometimes their social habits, where these data are considered highly confidential. Disclosure of information may affect the patients social standing as well as their health or even their life.

The lack of a generally accepted model of medicine, or of patient treatment, or of the information needed for this treatment, is another characteristic problem in the health care field. Lacking such a universal (and yet practical) model, it is almost impossible to construct an information system which caters for the wishes of the health care community and its security needs. The organisational structure of the health care profession is also somehow "flat", less hierarchical than in any administrative or industrial concern, which allows risks of having differing standards of information security procedures (42). Further than that, there is an inherent duality in the management of the health care establishments (HCEs) with a strong influence of some professional groups (e.g. medical doctors and, to a lesser extent, nurses). Although the general rules in HCEs are set up and guarded by the management, quite often in practical situations the professional judgement may take precedence since doctors are the prime responsible persons for the patient's health. This underlying difference influences attitudes concerning HCEs information systems and their security measures (scope, communication needs etc.). The multiple users of health care (physicians, nurses, administrators etc.) may have a valuable "need to know" for the benefit of the patient that might easily overlap with the needs of other users. For health professional this "need to know" might lead however to an absence of conformity with security procedures, although awareness of the need for security increases as familiarity with computer systems develops, and becomes acute once health care personnel becomes dependent on the system.

In this context, the development of medical information systems *becomes a safety related issue* requiring a high degree of integrity during every aspect of system development and implementation. The development of appropriate secure medical database design and implementation methodologies is an important problem in this area and a necessary prerequisite for the successful development of such systems (2,4,8,29).

4 Secure Medical Database Development Methodologies

From the perspective of a user who needs a secure medical database system, there are three possible basic approaches for its development, depending on the scope of the target database system and on the expected degree of trust: exploiting the security functions of a DBMS, enhancing the security functions of a DBMS, and the use of a "secured" DBMS.

4.1 Exploiting the Security Functions of a A DBMS

The first approach is to use a general purpose DBMS that optionally provides some security functions, such as user authentication, access control, auditing etc.. These functions can be *exploited* by including them into the applications that perform security-crucial functions (29). In these cases the design and implementation problem becomes that of introducing the appropriate security checks in the applications and of designing the data schemas according to security requirements. Some examples of general purpose DBMSs that provide security mechanisms are: INGRES (17), where security and integrity constraints can be specified in the system query language QUEL; QBE (18), that supports field-level access control by means of rules stored in access tables; System R (19), where access rules and integrity constraints are stored in access tables; IMS (20), that provides control of transaction access to data on a value-independent basis and control of end-user access to transactions; etc..

4.2 Enchanting the Security Functions of a A DBMS

Security of general purpose systems can also be *enhanced* by retrofitting security features, that is, by adding new security functions through the introduction of add-on security packages or security special-purpose hardware (21). For example, a number of software packages exist that can be added to the DBMS for access control purposes, these include: ACF2 (22), which was designed as an extension to the IBM OS/VS_MVS operating system; SECURE (23), which authorises access to data in the TSO environment by replacing the OS, VS, or MVS password facilities with its own modules etc.. A promising approach to security retrofitting seems to be the so-called integrity-lock one (24) that combines cryptography and front-end architecture issues, thus exhibiting high security qualities without requiring dramatic changes to an existing system.

4.3 Use of "Secured" DBMSs

Exploiting or enhancing the security functions of a general purpose DBMS is, however, an appropriate approach only in cases when security is not the most crucial concern for the database. In fact, the degree of trust that can be achieved in data handling is limited in that security checks are optional and in that the DBMS software that performs the security-related functions does not undergo a certification process according to some evaluation criteria (11,14). When security of the database system is a prominent feature, for example in cases where the target database system is demanded to operate in a critical environment (as for example a hospital information system), a "secured" DBMS is needed.

"Secured" means that some security mechanisms are automatically invoked upon each data access operation. These mechanisms are often required to perform quite complex checks, depending on the kinds of threats the system is required to face, and must have been *formally proved* to work correctly. Formal proves need a security policy for the database to have been stated and modelled through a database security model. Formal models of the security policies have guided the design and implementation of several secured databases (25). The benefits of this approach have been widely recognised (25,26). The availability of such a model directly focused onto one (or more) security problems (e.g. information flow, access control, integrity, statistical inference etc.) allows to execute design checks and to prove correctness properties of the future systems. For example, models of revocation control for database authorisation mechanisms (such as (27,28)) prove the correctness of the privileges revocation strategies in the system.

In general a formal database security model identifies the set of entities and operations which are security relevant for the future system and has an associated set of axioms expressing the security policies. Then some algorithms are run against the model structures for proving the correct behaviour of the system that will interpret the model. Security models for databases are still an open subject of thorough research. Multilevel military systems are for example the systems where many attempts have been made in the past for solving the certification problem and for tackling a number of sophisticated security problems. Often their design and implementation has been based on a formal model of the so-called multilevel security policy and on an architectural approach based on security kernels, or, on trusted computer base concepts, etc. (1,2).

5. An Experimental Development to Enhance Database Security

Work is currently under way in the university hospital of AHEPA in Thessaloniki in studying the security problem of the hospital and provide and evaluate various techniques for improving hospital database security. The security database development methodologies described earlier [4.1, 4.2] have been followed for this purpose. The 'CRAMM' risk analysis software developed in UK (41) has been used for risk analysis. The domain of the external patients has been chosen for the pilot implementation. Implementation is based both on the concept of the physical separation of subsystems and the use of software tools. The later is attempted mainly by exploiting existing features of the already installed commercial DBMS systems (INGRES and ORACLE) and enhancing their capabilities.

An important characteristic of the system is that mandatory security controls are used additionally to the discretional security ones in order to enhance database security (the ORACLE database management system is used for this purpose). Mandatory security controls have been based on the concepts of data sensitivity and levels of clearness of the users, while discretional security controls have been based on a set of "user roles" (37), each one of which corresponds to one (or more) types of medical users. The definition of the "user roles" has been based on the "need to know" principle, which is widely accepted today in health care environments (41). The use of discretionary controls has made it possible to control the access to objects based on the identity of the subjects and/or the groups to which they belong and to control various operations (select, update etc.) related to individual tables, views or 4GL applications. The use of the concept of "user roles" in particular, which has been implemented through database subschemas, has made it possible for every user to have access just to that part of the application he needs to use in order to satisfy his "need to know" requirements. The use of multilevel security on the other hand has made it possible to provide additional security to sensitive medical records and to provide possible explanations (cover stories) for unavoidable observable information that would otherwise lead to partial or complete inference of sensitive information (41).

5.1 The Hospital.

AHEPA University Hospital is a general hospital which is part of the Aristotelian University of Thessaloniki. The following figures describe the hospital: 16 clinics including the reference and hospitalisation centre for Aid's patient from all Northern Greece; 40 laboratories; a radiological department including M.R.I., C.T., U.S., D.S.A, X-rays, e.t.c.; a nuclear medicine department (SPECT, Gamma-Camera); 705 beds; 520 medical doctors including consultants; 762 nursing personnel; 466 personnel for financial and general support; 28,000 inpatients per year; 2,500 surgical procedures per year; 107,000 outpatients per year; 23,450,000 laboratory tests per year.

An integrated information system is available that covers the patient administration system (inpatient-outpatient), billing, financial, personal management and payroll. The system was developed in-house. This system, which has been running since 1990, operates on an inter network with distributed databases based on the client-server model. Users login through their terminals (or workstations) to 'clients' (process servers) where application programs are executed. The location or stored data (two database servers connected to the backbone) is transparent to the end users. For research and e-mail purposes uses login to the University's network through the hospital's network.

5.2 The Hospital's Security Features.

The current security subsystem for the hospital information system has the following characteristics:

1) System features are localised. On every node (application server) reside only the required application programs and views. None of the users is permitted to run any application on another node other than that the one he is physically or logically connected to.

2) A centralised authorisation system maintains all objects (users, groups, activities) covered by security and the links between them.

3) On every node (depending on the local O.S.) a login management system controls system access and verification of users.
4) A dialogue management system permits users to use only those objects allowed by their specific authorisation level.
5) An audit trail (at O.S. level) makes it possible to review all user's login activity.
6) A discretionary security policy is implemented which has been based on the following constructs : There are users (subjects), data items (objects) , and transactions between them which are represented in the form of access control lists.

5.3 Current Security Problems.

The risk and requirements analysis of the hospital information system has shown a number of serious security deficiencies of the current system. For example:

1- Both the Greek legislation and the internal hospital regulations lack a framework which would facilitate the use of the medical information system (MIS) and at the same time would provide sufficient guarantees against the unauthorised use of private medical information.
2- Medical security problems were found to be more intensive in the cases of diseases with higher confidentiality requirements. For example, in the existing system the permission to access a certain view of data by a group of users, performing the same task was the same for all the members of that group. There is however a necessity to have different levels of information security to be able to deal with the different levels of diseases and the hierarchical levels of working parties.
3- Although the medical, paramedical and nursing personnel generally meet the confidentiality and privacy requirements of information, as derived from ethical and deontological principles, this is not always the case in the managerial work flow lines. To be more specific, it has be found that there is an increased flow of information (printouts or/and electronic media) from administrative departments to external organisations or individuals. These might be insurance bodies (public or private), statistical organisations, research institutes, governmental bureaux, or any third party. This flow of information that may include critical information (diagnosis, laboratory examination and treatment,) may cause an extensive harm, direct or indirect, to the privacy and confidentiality rights of a patient.
4- From a purely technical point of view, defining a view for every user or role is a costly procedure (in time and computer resources) in the given topology of our environment.

5.4 The Implementation

Because of technical difficulties it has not been possible yet to implement our system on a trusted version of the DBMS, which would support directly the use of both mandatory (MAC) and discretional (DAC) database security policies. For this reason and in order to simulate (for research purposes) the way our model works, we implemented temporarily the sensitivity label concept indirectly, as a special field in the record, using the ORACLE DBMS. In what concerns the details of the implementation, we have used the features of ORACLE DBMS version 7 along with the existing data schema and system architecture (client-server application). This have been done according to the following steps:

1. A special, additional column has been used for the internal representation of the sensitivity label of the data (since our DBMS does not support directly MAC).
2. Separated tables have been used for the representation of the users and the corresponding sensitivity labels. This was based on the decision by the security officer, according to the hospital and departmental regulations.
3. Several interface applications (views) were constructed, depending on the node in which these applications would run. Each node serves one or several user types according to the user definition role. There are different kinds of interfaces in correspondence with the services provided by each individual node. The interface applications required by the ward staff are for example completely different from those required by the administrative support staff or the paramedical staff.

In the runtime environment, the interface between a user and the application depends on: (i) the physical access to the terminal, (ii) the node, and (iii) the identification and authorisation procedures supported by the O.S.. During execution the sensitivity labels (level, category) are passed as dynamic parameters to transparently reduce the user view based on his task in the application or on his need-to-know.

5.5 Classification of Users

Users have been classified into two major categories, according to the nature and security requirements of the tasks they perform: the administrative users, and the general, or non-administrative users. The administrative users, in which we include the developers and the maintenance support staff of the applications (DBA, programmers etc.), do not have to pass through discretionary security controls but they have access directly to the database, depending on their clearance level (multilevel security controls). The general users are divided again in two categories: the ward staff (doctors, nurses, etc.) and the administration support staff (financial, managers, etc.). Because of the nature of their work, the medical ward staff should have access only to the information related to the patients that are hospitalised in the wards, or in certain rooms that they are responsible for. This is assured during the login procedure by the introduction of the location control in the sensitivity label of the data. On the other hand, the administration support users, due to the nature of their work, which is not restricted to a part of patients, it is not necessary to pass through the location control layer. Their access is based on the view they are authorised to access and on their sensitivity level.

The major advantage of using this method for representing of the users, is the fact that the granting and revoking rights are only given to the administrative users. Using the multilevel security policy for the representation of these users, the problem of revocation of authorities (cascading, or normal) that is found in the discretionary security policy is eliminated. Another advantage of the this methodology is that the definition of the views is spread among administrative users. For example an administrative user with a sensitivity level 3 is responsible for the definition and granting of views for all the financial staff, because all the information that this staff can access is of security level 3 or less.

5.6 An Example

We will use the following simplified model, which consists of just a part of the entities and roles of a real life medical organisation, in order to illustrate the way the implemented system works. The records that we will use in our example are shown in figure 1.

Example procedures:

i. After a successful identification procedure, a doctor (a typical example of a ward staff type of user) will have access to a view containing all the information that he might need as a doctor (based on the need to know principle, (41)). The category and sensitivity levels are assigned automatically depending on the given identification attributes (user id, password, network node). Only information that satisfies the specific category and sensitivity level will be returned. The doctor will thus be able to have access only to the records of the patients that he needs to perform his task. These controls are implemented by 'pre' or 'on-query' triggers in which the category and sensitivity level are treated as dynamic parameters (doctor (d-ward, d-sensitivity level)), (41). From the user's point of view an example query may look as follows :

```
select p-name, disease, examinations
from A,B,C,D,
where B.patient-code = A.patient-code
and C.in-charge-code = B.in-charge-code
and D.in-charge-code = B.in-charge-code
and p-name = 'smith'
```

the query actually executed by the system will be however the following:

```
select p-name, disease, examinations
from A,B,C,D,
where B.patient-code = A.patient-code
and C.in-charge-code = B.in-charge-code
and D.in-charge-code = B.in-charge-code
and p-name = 'smith'
and B.ward = d-ward
and C.sensitivity level <= d-sensitivity-level
and D.sensitivity level <= d-sensitivity-level
```

ii. Similar procedures, like the ones executed by a doctor above, are performed by the non-ward type of users. The only difference is that, since their work is not restricted to a special location (e.g. ward), this type of users are not assigned to a specified category. Thus only the security level is required, which is used to permit the user access just to the records available according to his clearance (a-sensitivity-level, above). From the user's point of view an example query executed for this type of user may look as follows:

```
select p-name, examinations,
from A,B,D,
where B.patient-code = A.patient-code
and D.in-charge-code = B.in-charge-code
and p-name = 'smith'
```

the query actually executed by the system however will be the following:

```
select p-name, examinations,
from A,B,D,
where B.patient-code = A.patient-code
and D.in-charge-code = B.in-charge-code
and p-name = 'smith'
and C.sensitivity level <= a-sensitivity-level
```

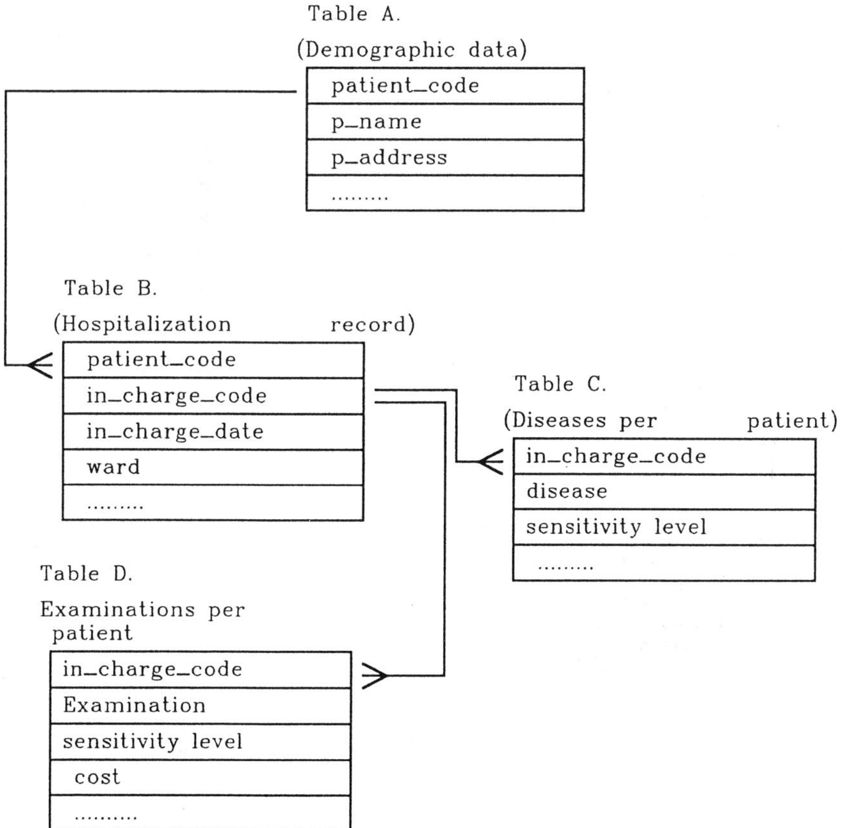

Figure 1

5.7 Discussion

Based on the experience from using the above system in the hospital, the following remarks can be made:

Some management overheads have been observed, due mainly to the complexity and the multiplicity of login tasks. This was however expected because of the distributed systems environment. The storage overheads are minimal when compared to the large volume of stored objects. The processing overheads are also neglectable, provided that indexes and clustering are build properly. We have noticed however a reduced effectiveness of the system, especially during night shifts. This has been mainly due to the absence of the security officer, the mall-structured hospital organisation and the existing paper hard copies organisation.

6. Conclusions

Security is an important issue when dealing with medical information systems which is directly related to the quality and effectiveness of medical care. Database security in particular plays a significant role in the overall security of medical information systems. The general framework and requirements for medical database security and a number of parameters of the secure medical database development problem have been presented and discussed. An experimental development in a major Greek hospital has also been presented which aims to improve medical database security. An important characteristic of this development is that mandatory security controls are used additionally to the discretional security ones. In this way it has been possible to enhance further medical database security.

7. References

1. Lunt T., Security in database systems, Computers and security journal, Vol. 11,No.1, March 1992, pp. 41-56
2. Biskup J., Medical database security, in data protection and confidentiality in health informatics, EEC/DGXII ed.,IOS press, 1991.
3. Landwehr C., ed., Database security II: Status and prospects, North-Holland, 1989.
4. Spooner D., Landwehr C., eds., Database security III, North-Holland, 1990.
5. Proceedings ESORICS (European Symposium on Research in Computer Security), Toulouse, France, 1990.
6. Jajodia S., Landwehr C., eds., Database security IV, North-Holland, 1991.
7. EEC/DGXII, ed., Data protection and confidentiality in health informatics, IOS press, 1991.
8. Biscup J., Analysis of the privacy model for the information system DORIS, in (3).
9. Cannataci A., Data protection issues in database management and expert systems, in (7).
10. Campbell J, A research and development program for trusted distribute DBMSs, in Database security IV, Jaodia (ed), North Holland, 1991.
11. DoD, Department of Defence Trusted computer system evaluation criteria, DoD 5200.28-STD, 1985
12. National Computer Security Centre, Draft trusted DBMS interpretation of the DoD trusted computer system evaluation criteria, USA, 1989
13. National Computer Security Centre, Trusted network interpretation of the trusted computer system evaluation criteria, NCSC-TG-005, USA, 1987.
14. Information Technology Evaluation Criteria (ITSEC), Version 1.2, EEC Document, Brussels, June 1991.
15. Information Technology Security Evaluation Manual (ITSEM), Draft V0.2, EEC Draft Document, April 1992.
16. Landwehr C. E., Minutes of IFIP-TC11 1986 meeting, Montecarlo, December 1986.
17. Stonabraker M., The design and implementation of INGRES, ACM TODS, Vol. 1, No. 3, 1976.
18. Zloof M., Query by example: a database language, IBM systems Journal, Vol. 16, No. 4, 1977.
19. Astrahan M., System R: Relational approach to database management, ACM TODS, Vol. 1, No. 2, June 1976.
20. McGee W., The information Management System IMS/VS. Part V: Transaction processing facilities, IBM systems journal, Vol. 16, No. 2, 1977.
21. Landwehr C., The best available technologies for computer security, IEEE Computer, Vol. 16, No. 7, 1983.
22. ACF2: The access control facility - General information manual, 1983.
23. Secure product description, Bull and Babbage publ., 1979.

24. Duffy K. and Sullivan J., Integrity lock prototype, in the Proceedings 4th IFIP international security conference, Montecarlo, 1986.
25. Cerniglia C. and Millen J., Computer security models, MTR project, Report No. 9531, 1984.
26. Landwehr C., Formal models for computer security, ACM computer surveys, Vol. 13, No. 3, 1981.
27. Griffiths P. and Wade B., An authorisation mechanism for a relational database system, ACM TODS, Vol. 1, No. 3, 1976.
28. Fagin R., On an authorisation mechanism, ACN TODS, Vol. 3, No. 3, 1976.
29. Fugini M., Secure database development methodologies, in (3)
30. Dwyer P., Multilevel security in database management systems, Computers and security, Vol. 6, No. 3, 1987.
31. Akl S., Views for multilevel database database security, IEEE Trans. on S/W Eng., Vol. 13, No. 2, 1987.
32. Hartson H., Database security - system architectures, Information systems, Vol. 6, NO.1, 1981.
33. Leveson J., Safety analysis using Petri nets, IEEE Trans. on S/W Eng., Vol. 13, No. 3, 1987.
34. Bussolati U., A database approach to modelling and managing of security information, Proc. 7th Int. Conf. on VLDB, Cannes, 1981.
35. Bussolati U., Data security management in distributed databases, Information systems, Vol. 7, No. 3, 1982.
36. Date C., An introduction to database systems, Vol. 2, second ed., Addison-Wesley, 1986.
37. Ting T., Application information security semantics: A case of mental health delivery, in (4).
38. Hinke T., DBMS trusted computing base taxonomy, in (4).
39. Graubart R., A comparison of three secure DBMS architectures, in (4).
40. Hosmer H., Designing multilevel secure distributed databases, in (3).
41. Pangalos G., Security in medical database systems, EEC, SEISMED project report, No. INT/S.3/92, 1992.
42. J.V. Marel, A.B. Bakker, User accessrights in an intergrated hospital information system, IFIP-IMIA, North-Holland, 1988.
43. J. BisKup, A general framework for database security, Proc. EROSICS, Toulouse, France, 1990, pp. 35-41.
44. J. Biskup, Medical database security, Proc. GI-20, Jahrestagung II, Stutgart, October 1990, Springer-Verlag, 1990, pp. 212-221.
45. T.C. Ting, S.A. Demurjian, M.Y. Hu, A specification methodology for user-role based security in an object-oriented design model, Proc. 6th IFIP WG11.3 on database security, 1993.
46. Pfleeger, C., Security in computing, Prentice hall, 1991.
47. S. Katsikas, D. Gritzalis, High level security policies, SEISMED report, June 1993.
48. Russel, D., Computer security basics, O'Reilly & Associates, inc, 1991.
49. Denning, D., Views for multilevel database security, IEEE transactions on S.E., vSE-13, no2, 1987.
50. Groubert, R., Design overview for retrofitting integrity lock architecture onto a commercial DBMS, proc. 1985 symp. Security and privacy, IEEE comput Soc 1985, pp. 147-159.
51. G. Pangalos, Security guidelines for database system developments, 8th Annual IFIP conference on database security, Germany, 23-26 August, 1994.

Using Inductive Machine Learning, Expert Systems and Case Based Reasoning to Predict Preterm Delivery in Pregnant Women

M. Van Dyne
Department of Electrical Engineering and Computer Science
University of Kansas, Lawrence, KS 66045 USA
(816) 444-8063
vandyne@eecs.ukans.edu

C. Tsatsoulis
Center for Excellence in Computer-Aided Systems Engineering
Department of Electrical Engineering and Computer Science
University of Kansas, Lawrence, KS 66045, USA
(913) 864-7749
tsatsoul@eecs.ukans.edu

J. Thorp, MD
St. Luke's Perinatal Center
4401 Wornall Rd., Kansas City, MO 64111, USA
(816) 932-3586

Abstract

A previously constructed prototype expert system was extended to include case-based reasoning and learning, in order to improve the system's predictive accuracy in assessing preterm delivery risk. The initial expert system was developed by using an inductive machine learning technique on 9,445 data records of pregnant women, providing production rules to predict preterm delivery. Its predictive accuracy was tested on a separate set of 9,445 data records. Next, the capability to reason from both production rules and input test cases was added to the system, in addition to the capability to internally modify its confidence in each piece of knowledge (rule or case) and the relative importance of patient attributes which appear to be predictive of preterm delivery. The system was structured such that the accuracy of either type of reasoning could be measured individually to determine how rule-based and case-based reasoning perform alone, and to determine how they perform together. Results show that the predictive accuracy of the system was improved, with different trends emerging, dependent on the bias of the learning data, with the hybrid system providing the best predictive accuracy.

1. Introduction

1.1. Problem Domain

Pregnancy is considered fullterm at 40 weeks gestation, however, 37 weeks is generally used as the criterion to determine whether a delivery is preterm or not. Accurate identification of pregnant women who are high-risk for preterm birth is important in determining which women will benefit from interventions designed to prolong gestation. Prolonging gestation can result in significant improvements in infant survival and reduced costs of neonatal intensive care (McLean, Walters, & Smith, 1993).

The problem domain is complex because it is not clear what symptoms may be predictive of preterm delivery, and consequently, during the course of prenatal care, hundreds of data items may be collected. Furthermore, different data is collected at different facilities. From all this data, the healthcare provider must make decisions concerning preterm birth risk, and any plans for intervention (NIH Guide, 1992). Currently used manual screening tools have been estimated to be between 17 - 38 % predictive in determining preterm risk (McLean, Walters, & Smith, 1993).

1.2. Previous Work

A prototype expert system was built in a previous effort (Woolery, et.al., 1994; Van Dyne, et.al., 1994) which used production rules generated by an inductive machine learning technique, LERS (Grzymala-Busse, 1988; 1989; 1991), in order to generate a knowledge base. A retrospective sample of high risk pregnant women was obtained from three databases containing 18,890 subjects from one local and two national sources. The databases were split into two equal halves, and one half of each database was used to generate production rules while the other half was used to test the accuracy of the prototype expert system. Accuracy was measured as the percentage of times the prototype's predicted outcome matched the actual patient outcome.

Once rules were generated from the inductive machine learning program, LERS, they were translated into Kappa PC rule format via a translation program. Additionally, the attributes from each database were combined into a single patient object so that rules generated from any of the learning databases could be run on examples from any of the test databases, even though each database contains a different (albeit overlapping) set of attributes for each patient. Because of poor predictive performance of rules generated from the third database, only rules generated from the first two databases were included in the prototype expert system. This resulted in 520 rules included in the prototype system.

Using measurements of rule and rule base effectiveness generated by LERS, in addition to information on how many examples were used to learn the rule, a prioritization scheme, or confidence rating, was developed for rules in the prototype expert system. The formula used was:

*(overall rule base accuracy rate) * (rule confidence)*
*+ (10 * number of cases used to generate the rule)*
*- (10 * number of cases misclassified by the rule)*

Because the system works from a large amount of data about an individual patient, forward chaining was chosen as the inference technique. False positive predictions occur when the prototype system predicts preterm delivery and the patient actually delivered fullterm. False negative predictions occur when the prototype system predicts fullterm delivery and the patient actually delivered preterm.

2. Motivation for Including Case Based Reasoning

The prototype expert system is static; that is, whenever a new case is entered, the outcome prediction process will always follow the same reasoning, even if it has seen that particular case before and knows that its prediction was incorrect. No learning takes place in the system. If the predictive accuracy of the rule base was perfect, this would not be a concern, but the accuracy of the expert system ranges only from 51 - 88% correct. This is certainly an improvement over manual risk assessment techniques currently used, but the question arises, can the system learn from its mistakes, and improve upon its predictive accuracy.

In using a case based approach in this situation, the existing knowledge base can be viewed as domain knowledge, albeit, faulty domain knowledge. Each rule can also be thought of as a generalized case because it was generated from a set of actual examples, and contains those attributes which the inductive system determined to be important across several cases. Since each piece of knowledge, or rule, in the system already has a confidence associated with it, and the system will use the rule with the highest confidence that applies in a given situation, the confidence in that rule can be modified according to its success or failure on a case. Furthermore, cases can be added to the system to begin to fill in areas where the rule base is lacking. Each case can be thought of as a specific rule with values provided for each attribute in the antecedent.

Unlike a rule, however, the attribute/value pairs in the input case do not have to exactly match the attribute/value pairs in the case. In a rule, all antecedent attribute value pairs must match before the rule becomes eligible to fire. The same confidence scheme used for the rule base can also be used for the case base, and additionally, as attributes tend to become associated more with the success or failure of a prediction, the strength or importance of these attributes/features can be modified so that future case to case matches pay more attention to features that have been shown to be more predictive of the outcome (indices).

The intention, then, behind using case based reasoning in addition to the rule based reasoning is to enhance the predictive accuracy of the preterm risk assessment system. For medical verification of the system, it is also important that the system be able to explain why it chose to use a particular rule or case to make its prediction, and what attributes or features it believes are important in making that prediction.

3. Hybrid System Architecture

3.1. System Functionality

Depending on the database specified by the user, a database record is read into the system from one of three databases. Each one of these databases has a different record structure, and sometimes different ways of representing the same attribute/value pair, although there is overlap between all three of them. Since the structure is different, the first thing the system must do is map the attributes and their values into a composite or standardized record structure. The attribute/value pairs in this record structure are then used to compare past cases in the system (if any) and to determine the rule with the highest confidence associated with it.

When the system first starts out, it has no cases in its case base, and must therefore rely on rules to make predictions. As cases are entered, however, they are added to the case base with a confidence level just below that of the average rule confidence (in this system, that value is 80). The system makes an outcome prediction using the best match case and the highest confidence rule. The piece of knowledge (rule or case) that has the highest confidence level is chosen for the single system prediction. This prediction is compared to the actual outcome of the patient, and is used to update the overall system accuracy. Each of the two possible predictions are then also compared to the actual patient outcome, and the confidence in each piece of knowledge (case and rule) is modified according to the success or failure of that piece of knowledge, regardless of which one was chosen for the system prediction. If the piece of knowledge failed to predict correctly, its confidence is decremented by 10, and if successful, its confidence is incremented by 10. This is consistent with the initial prioritization coding of the rules. When the confidence level of either a case or a rule decreases below 0, that case or rule is deleted from the system. Because of this, rules that had a negative confidence level in the initial expert system prototype are not included in the current system, reducing the number of rules in the system from 520 to 510 rules.

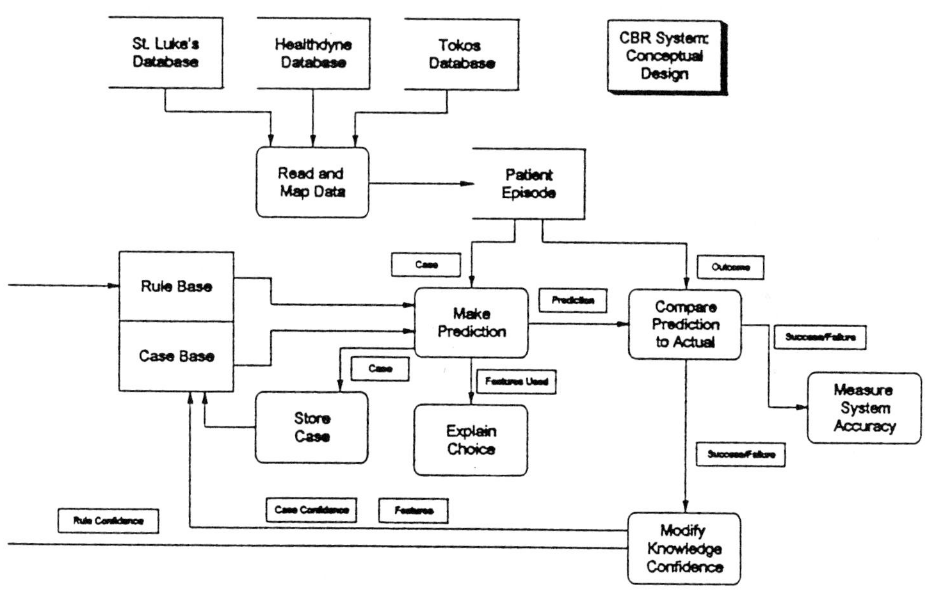

Figure 1: Conceptual design of the system

Furthermore, the attributes or features used in making the prediction are also considered. Each time a feature is used in successfully predicting an outcome, its weight is incremented by 1, and each time it is used unsuccessfully, its weight is decremented by 1. Features used by both rules and cases are treated in the same manner. The intention behind this scheme is to begin to weight each attribute according to its predictive value of the outcome, and thus allow the system to build an indexing scheme as its experience increases. The case matching is done by determining which features of the input case have the same value as features of cases in the case base, and producing a match score according to the weight of each matching feature. Presumably, future case matches will be more appropriate when features / indices with more weight are considered than if a feature count match is used.

Whether successful or unsuccessful, the system explains its choice of using a rule or a case for prediction according to the features used so that medical verification of the system's reasoning can be done. Furthermore, methods are used to report when a particular feature's weight passes certain numeric thresholds in order to report whether the feature is considered "Unimportant" (0 - 9), "Somewhat Important" (10 - 49), "Important" (50 - 99), or "Very Important" (100 or higher). This provides a method of tracking which features tend to be associated more with successful prediction of outcome, and can be used as an additional tool in medical verification of the system. A diagram of the conceptual design of the system can be found in Figure 1.

3.2. Case Based Reasoning Concepts

Case Base

The structure of the case base in this system is flat; that is, no generalization or abstraction of cases is performed. Presumably, if abstraction of cases were included, it would improve system efficiency in case retrieval because it could serve as a discrimination net in choosing which features to compare first. However, because the weight of the features is dynamic, the abstraction hierarchy would also be very dynamic, particularly when the system first starts, and the restructuring of the case knowledge could hinder system performance.

Case Retrieval

Cases are chosen according to the best match score between the input case and cases in the case base. Each case in the case base is considered every time a new case is entered, slowing system performance as the number of cases increases. The best match score is determined by the number of feature values in a case that match the input case feature values, and the weight of those features. Therefore, if a few "important" features match, it will be considered to be a better match than if many "unimportant" features match.

Indexing

The variable weighting of features depending on their track record in being associated with successful predictions can be considered a method of building indices over time. Those features with more importance tend to be used more to determine case matches as time goes on. However, all features are still considered, rather than restricting the number of features according to their strength. Again, this may impede system performance, but because the feature strength is so volatile, particularly at first, restricting which features are considered could adversely affect predictive accuracy.

Explanation
The system explains its success or failure only in terms of the features used to make that prediction. The explanation provided if a rule is chosen is static because if a rule is chosen, it is the same features that apply each time it is chosen. The explanation for using a case is dependent on the strength of the features used in choosing that case, and may vary at different times. Whether the case or rule is successful or not does not influence what explanation is given; that is, the explanation applies only to the choice of a piece of knowledge, and does not try to explain why the prediction was successful or failed.

Learning
There are three areas in which the system learns to improve its own performance. The first of these is modification of rule confidence depending on the success or failure of a rule in a given case. The second is the modification of case confidence, again depending on it predictive success. These two types of learning occur whenever a rule or case is chosen to be considered, not just when the actual prediction from that rule or case is used as the system prediction. The third area of learning is discriminating the more important features from the less important features so that more appropriate case matches can be made as the system's experience level increases. Note that the learning occurs for both success and failure, rather than simply using failure driven learning, as is proposed by dynamic memory theorists.

4. Implementation

The system was implemented using the Kappa PC expert system development environment from IntelliCorp, Inc. The shell runs under Microsoft Windows and provides rule-based and object-oriented capabilities, both of which were used in this program. Kappa PC also provides an internal functional language which was used rather than using a standard programming language. User interface capability is provided through the predefinition of object classes representing different interface components, and these were used to build the user interface of the system.

The system starts out with 510 rules generated from two of the databases, and the potential for deletion of rules exists as there confidence goes below 0. In practice, however, as the confidence in a rule or case is decreased, it is not considered for use, which means it has no chance of further lowering its confidence; therefore the confidence does not decrease below 0 and no knowledge is deleted.

Forward chaining was chosen as the inference technique in the original expert system because of the structure of the problem. The rules used in that system, however, had no side effects, and as such, were suitable for use in backward chaining if one wanted to run the system in that mode. In the hybrid system, however, the consequents of the rules are used to produce side effects influencing the weighting of features, the confidence in the rule, and an explanation of the reason for choosing the rule. Because of this, the rules are no longer suitable for use in a backward chaining system.

The user is not allowed to interactively enter new cases in the hybrid system, a capability that was present in the original expert system prototype, because each case influences the system's performance, and inaccurate information entered would have an adverse effect on predictive accuracy. Since the original expert system was static, the entry of inaccurate cases had no adverse effect, and was therefore allowed. In the hybrid system, cases are read in only from the databases.

5. Results

Tests were run on the original expert system prototype and the current case based reasoning system to determine the differences in predictive accuracy between the two systems. Results shown below are all from a run of 300 test cases from each of the three databases. In each pair of runs, the case based system outperformed the original expert system. Note that each run was stopped at 300 cases for comparison purposes, although at this number, the system accuracy has not yet completely stabilized.

Table 1: Prototype Expert System; Database 1

	Number of Cases	Correct	Mis-classified	Un-classified
Overall	300	279 (91%)	25 (8%)	1 (0%)
Fullterm	255	242 (94%)	12 (4%)	1 (0%)
Preterm	45	32 (71%)	13 (28%)	0 (0%)

Table 2: Rule-Only vs. Case-Only Performance; Database 1

	Correct	Fullterm Misclassified	Preterm Misclassified
Rules Only	274 (91%)	4 (2%)	22 (49%)
Cases Only	240 (80%)	35 (14%)	25 (56%)

Table 3: Hybrid Reasoning System; Database 1

	Number of Cases	Correct	Mis-classified	Un-classified
Overall	300	275 (91%)	25 (8%)	0 (0%)
Fullterm	255	251 (94%)	4 (1%)	0 (0%)
Preterm	45	24 (53%)	21 (46%)	0 (0%)

The first database is the one that originally provided the best predictive accuracy, and from which about 2/3 of the rules originate. It represents a population at higher risk for preterm delivery than the population at large because it is a referral center for patients experiencing problems in pregnancy (not always preterm delivery problems, however). The percentage of women who deliver preterm in this population is approximately 25%.

The expert system required about 20 minutes to process these 300 cases, while the case based system required 2 hours and 20 minutes. The efficiency issues discussed previously greatly affect the case based reasoning system's performance.

The case based reasoning system was only able to increase its predictive accuracy in this database by one additional correct prediction over the expert system. Note that the original expert system was unable to classify one input case (meaning there was no rule available that matched the criteria for that case), whereas the case based system produced no "NULL" classifications. This single case cannot be used to explain the accuracy difference of one case though. It is apparent that the hybrid system accuracy on full term cases was much better than the expert system's performance in that category, while accuracy on preterm prediction was better in the expert system. Rules in the system are split almost equally in number between full term and preterm predictions, while cases reflect the bias of the population. Since only 25% of this population delivers preterm, one might expect that the case based system would learn better in areas where it has more experience, that is, on full term cases. This conclusion is supported from results of the second database, shown below.

The second portion of the table on the case based system performance shows predictive accuracy if only the chosen rules were used, and if only the chosen cases were used. It is apparent that using a combination of the two increases system accuracy over using either one individually.

The second database came from a home uterine monitoring company. The data represents a nationwide sample of very high risk women, as only very high risk patients (all for preterm delivery) are referred for this expensive service. The population represented in this data delivers preterm approximately 73% of the time.

Table 4: Prototype Expert System; Database 2

	Number of Cases	Correct	Mis-classified	Un-classified
Overall	300	180 (60%)	107 (35%)	13 (4%)
Fullterm	87	48 (55%)	37 (42%)	2 (2%)
Preterm	213	132 (61%)	70 (32%)	11 (5%)

Table 5: Rule-Only vs. Case-Only Performance; Database 2

	Correct	Fullterm Misclassified	Preterm Misclassified
Rules Only	192 (64%)	52 (60%)	56 (26%)
Cases Only	199 (66%)	70 (80%)	31 (15%)

Table 6: Hybrid Reasoning System; Database 2

	Number of Cases	Correct	Mis-classified	Un-classified
Overall	300	212 (70%)	88 (29%)	0 (0%)
Fullterm	87	35 (40%)	52 (59%)	0 (0%)
Preterm	213	177 (83%)	36 (16%)	0 (0%)

The hybrid system performed at 10 percentage points better predictive accuracy than did the expert system in this database, providing correct outcome predictions in an additional 32 cases. Furthermore, while in both runs, the predictive performance was better on preterm deliveries, it is much better in the case based system, supporting the idea that the amount of experience the system gains in an area or on a concept, the better its performance will be in that area. As before, the case based system produced no "NULL" outcome predictions, and also, as before, the performance of the combined rule and case base is superior to either one considered alone.

The final database was provided by another home uterine monitoring company. Again, the population is considered very high risk for preterm delivery, although the preterm delivery rate is lower than the previous database; approximately 66% of the patients deliver preterm in this database. Recall that the rules generated from this data had poor predictive performance and were not included in the original expert system. The data from this database was encoded as insurance reimbursement codes rather than as a true indication of all the symptoms that the patient may be experiencing. As such, a good deal of information about the patient was lost in the encoding, contributing to the poor performance of the rules generated from the data (about 35% predictive accuracy). Nonetheless, when these records were run through the original expert system, using rules generated from the other two databases, predictive performance was still adequate, indicating that the rules are tapping underlying constructs of factors contributing to preterm delivery. This was an encouraging result in the original prototype expert system, and the predictive accuracy obtained on this database from the case based reasoning system is even more encouraging.

Table 7: Prototype Expert System; Database 3

	Number of Cases	Correct	Mis-classified	Un-classified
Overall	300	149 (49%)	91 (30%)	60 (20%)
Fullterm	191	102 (53%)	45 (23%)	44 (23%)
Preterm	109	47 (43%)	46 (42%)	16 (14%)

Table 8: Rule-Only vs. Case-Only Performance; Database 3

	Correct	Fullterm Misclassified	Preterm Misclassified
Rules Only	183 (61%)	63 (33%)	54 (50%)
Cases Only	197 (66%)	40 (21%)	63 (58%)

Table 9: Hybrid Reasoning System; Database 3

	Number of Cases	Correct	Mis-classified	Un-classified
Overall	300	215 (71%)	85 (28%)	0 (0%)
Fullterm	191	167 (87%)	24 (12%)	0 (0%)
Preterm	109	48 (44%)	61 (55%)	0 (0%)

As with the other two databases, the hybrid system outperformed the expert system, this time by 22 percentage points, or by 85 cases. Note that the sample of data used for testing in this case contained more full term examples than preterm, although the overall population in this database has a reverse bias. Because of this, it appears, the case based system had better predictive accuracy on full term cases than on preterm. Interestingly enough, the case based reasoning system had an overall accuracy rate on this database that was higher than the accuracy rate on the second database, although the predictive accuracy rates were reversed in the expert system. The performance of the case based reasoning system on this run may be explained by the fact that the rules used on the data were not generated from the data, therefore, the cases provided a better source of prediction than did the rules. In fact, looking at the Case vs. Rule Accuracy, the cases, if run alone, would have performed better than the rules, although, again, the combination of the two produced better accuracy than if either one were run alone. Note that this phenomenon occurs in the second database run also.

Overall, then, the hybrid system performed better than the expert system alone, although this increase in predictive accuracy was more notable on the databases that had lower accuracy rates from the expert system to begin with.

6. Conclusions and Future Directions

The results of the case based reasoning system versus the expert system create many different questions, and ideas that could be tested in future work. Several areas that could benefit from additional investigation include:

Atrophy: It was mentioned earlier that once a case or rule reached a negative confidence level, that case or rule would be deleted from the system. Because of the nature of the system, however, once a piece of knowledge reached a certain low level of confidence, it was never considered again, therefore its confidence never decreased below 0 and it was never removed from the knowledge base. Keeping unused knowledge in the system hinders overall system performance. For this reason, it might be interesting to implement a concept of atrophy which would decrement confidence in a piece of knowledge that was seldom used. The concept of atrophy could also be used in weighting features such that those features that are very unimportant in matching cases would eventually be eliminated from the matching process, thereby creating a true indexing system. The actual deletion of a piece of knowledge would implement the concept of "forgetting".

Outcome Driven Learning: The system as implemented learns equally from both its successes and failures. Dynamic memory theory postulates that people learn better from failures than from successes, though, and it would be an interesting extension to test this in the system (Schank, 1982; Riesbeck & Schank, 1989). The system could be only punished for wrong predictions (which might alleviate the need for an atrophy consideration), or it could be punished more severely for failures than it is rewarded for successes.

Database Combinations: The data runs reported in this document discuss only single database results. It would be interesting to test various combinations of databases to determine the overall accuracy. Determining whether concepts learned from one database carry over to another would be one aspect of interest. Another aspect would be if equalizing the number of preterm and fullterm cases in a test set would improve performance in both areas or not. Also, the order of presentation of cases could be varied to determine the effect on the system.

Confidence Levels: Presently, when choosing between a case or a rule to use for the system prediction, the system uses the confidence level in that piece of knowledge. A variation of this is to use some combination of the confidence and the strength of the match between the knowledge and the input case, and then determine the effect this has on predictive accuracy.

Iterative Training: In some types of machine learning systems (most notably, neural networks), the same learning set of data is presented to the system until an acceptable level of performance is reached. The learning capability is then turned off and the system tested. It would be interesting to determine how overall system accuracy could be increased as a result of "overtraining" on a subset of the data, but the appropriate mix of cases for the learning database would need to be determined.

Clinical Guidance: The most important future direction is to work with healthcare professionals in system verification. At present, the system uses database attributes that may not be clinically significant, although correlated, with preterm delivery, and it does not include attributes that have been shown in the literature to be predictive. This comes primarily because the data used was a retrospective sample of data that was available, and what is needed is a prospective data collection effort where information collected is targeted toward predicting prematurity. While the system may not be clinically significant at present, clinical review has revealed that the methodology has great potential, and should be used in conjunction with clinical guidance to produce a system that could have significant impact on risk assessment.

7. Acknowledgments

The authors of this paper would like to thank St. Luke's Perinatal Center, Healthdyne, and Tokos for providing data for the study. The initial prototype expert system development was funded by a Small Business Innovation Research (SBIR) grant to IntelliDyne, Inc., through the National Institutes of Health (NIH), National Center for Nursing Research, grant number 1 R43 NR02899-01A1. The case based learning extension was completed through the University of Kansas, Department of Electrical Engineering and Computer Science. This work was supported in part through a KTEC grant to the Center for Excellence in Computer-Aided Systems Engineering.

8. References

Grzymala-Busse, J. (1988). Knowledge acquisition under uncertainty - a rough set approach. *Journal of Intelligent and Robotic Systems.* 3-16.

Grzymala-Busse, J. (1989). An overview of the LERS1 learning system. in *Proceedings of the Second International Conference on Industrial and Engineering Applications of Artificial Intelligence and Expert Systems.* Volume 2, 838-844.

Grzymala-Busse, J. (1991). *Managing Uncertainty in Expert Systems.* Boston. Kluwer Academic Publishing.

McLean, M., Walters, W., & Smith, R. (1993). Prediction and early diagnosis of preterm labor: a critical review. *Obstetrical and Gynecological Survey.* 48 (4), 209-225.

NIH (National Institutes of Health) (1992). *Guide to Grants and Contracts.* July.

Riesbeck, C. & Schank, R. (1989). *Inside Case-Based Reasoning.* Hillsdale, N.J. Lawrence Erlbaum Associates Publishers.

Schank, R. (1982). *Dynamic Memory: A Theory of Learning in Computers and People.* Cambridge University Press.

Van Dyne, M., Woolery, L., Grzymala-Busse, J. & Tsatsoulis, C. (1994). Using machine learning and expert systems to predict preterm delivery in pregnant women. in *Proceedings of the Tenth IEEE Conference on Artificial Intelligence Applications '94*. 344-350.

Woolery, L., Van Dyne, M., Grzymala-Busse, J. & Tsatsoulis, C. (in press). Machine learning for development of an expert system to support assessment of preterm labor risk. *Nursing Informatics '94*.

Integrating Frames, Rules and Uncertainty in a Database-Coupled Knowledge-Representation System

Petra Drescher, Martin Holeňa, Rainer Kruschinski, Gernod Laufkötter

Cadlab – Joint Research & Development Institute
University of Paderborn and Siemens Nixdorf Informationssysteme
Bahnhofstraße 32, 33102 Paderborn, Germany *

Abstract. This paper describes a knowledge-representation system IFS (Intelligent Framework Services) being developed as a part of the JESSI Common Frame project. The system is based on a combination of frames and rules, which are integrated through the object-oriented view with multiple approaches to uncertainty processing, and coupled to an object-oriented database.
Keywords: knowledge representation, object-oriented paradigm, frames, rules, uncertain knowledge, uncertainty processing, KBS – DB coupling

1 Introduction

Knowledge-based and knowledge-representation systems belong to the most intensively developing areas of computer science. Their development is a crossroad of many different approaches and paradigms – logic, theory of probability, semantic networks, frames and scripts, production systems and artificial neural networks being only several important among them. On the other hand, their development is at the same time a supply of real problems, such as the mappings between knowledge and data and between knowledge and information, evolution of knowledge, uncertainty, vagueness of concepts, imprecise, incomplete or missing information, unreliable knowledge etc.

Our paper describes principles of a knowledge-representation *system IFS* (Intelligent Framework Services) being developed as a part of the JCF project (JESSI Common Frame). Similar to the goal of the whole JCF project, the goal of developing IFS is mainly a practical one – to build a real-world applicable knowledge-representation system, powerful and flexible enough to cope with a broad spectrum of user problems, mainly in the industrial area. Therefore, we did not seek any new knowledge processing approach, but instead we based our system on two of the concepts which have already proven as an expressive means of dealing with knowledge, namely on *frames* and *rules.*

On the other hand, the IFS system has three new important features distinguishing it from all hybrid knowledge-representation systems known to us (e.g. [3], [6], [16]):

* Research reported in this paper was supported by ESPRIT Project 7364

- it supports multiple approaches to *handling uncertain knowledge,*
- frames, rules and uncertainty processing are *integrated* using the object-oriented paradigm,
- the knowledge representation is consistently *mapped to an object-oriented database.*

In the following section, the architecture and the metaschema of the system are described. The section focuses on the object-oriented approach to integration and on the uncertainty processing. In section 3, the specification language HyKl is briefly presented, and in the final section 4, the technical concepts of coupling the knowledge representation to an OODBMS are outlined. The problems of production rules representation and schema evolution are dealt with.

2 Architecture of the system IFS

2.1 General characteristics

The IFS system is a hybrid system enabling a frame-based knowledge representation relying on the IMKA standard proposal for frames ([14]), and a rule-based knowledge deduction in a setting inspired by the OPS5 system. Frames and rules are extended to enable dealing with uncertain knowledge.

Three approaches to uncertainty processing are supported in the system: the algebraic approach ([7],[8]), the approach based on the theory of evidence ([7], [9]), and the fuzzy set approach ([21]). The possibility to include two other important approaches, namely the probabilistic approach ([20]) and the neural network paradigm ([5]) in some later version is still a matter of research ([10]).

Incorporating different approaches makes the system very flexible with respect to handling uncertain knowledge. Such a flexibility is in our opinion necessary to arrive to a practically applicable uncertainty processing, mainly for the following reasons:

- to compensate for the subjectivity inherent especially in the algebraic approach and the fuzzy set approach,
- to cope with uncertainty of different origin and character (e.g. vague concepts, incomplete information, unreliable knowledge, random influences).

2.2 An object-oriented view of frames, rules and inference control

The integration of the factual knowledge, rule base and inference mechanism is in the IFS system performed in the *object-oriented way.* Consequently, all frames, slots and relations, as well as rules, sets of rules and all aspects of the inference process are viewed as particular instances of a generic class of objects forming the system, called *IFS objects.* This class has a number of various subclasses, which all can be derived from it through a hierarchy of subclass-of relationships. In addition, those subclasses are sometimes connected also through other types of relationships. All subclasses of IFS objects, together with relationships connecting them, form the *metaschema of the IFS system* (see figures 1–5).

At the top level, the class of IFS objects partitions into the following classes:

- *frames,* representing the factual part of the knowledge base,
- *rules,* representing its deductive part,
- *rulesets,* representing the grouping of rules according to the reasoning strategy used,
- *control objects,* representing methods and operators through which the inference engine of the system is realized,
- *uncertainty processing,* representing the decision whether to consider facts and rules as absolutely certain and true, or to allow them being assigned some uncertainty, along with the choice of an uncertainty processing approach.

2.3 Uncertainty Processing

Various aspects of uncertainty processing pertain to many classes at several levels of the IFS metaschema. Basically, these aspects include:

(i) the uncertainty processing approach used during the inference,

(ii) uncertainty factors, which can be attached both to facts and to rules,

(iii) uncertainty operators to propagate uncertainty through the knowledge base.

The system requires at most one *uncertainty processing approach* to be used with each specified set of rules. However, different approaches may be used with different rulesets, whereas those rulesets may still share common rules, and access the same factual knowledge.

If uncertainty processing is performed with a set of rules, *uncertainty factors* must be attached to rules from the set, as well as to facts represented by relation and attribute slots accessed within that ruleset. The form of the uncertainty factor depends on the considered approach: in the *algebraic approach,* it is a weight $w \in \mathbb{R}$, in the *theory of evidence,* it is a weight-pair $(w_1, w_2) \in \langle 0,1\rangle \otimes \langle 0,1\rangle$, and in the *fuzzy set approach,* it is a particular fuzzy set. Besides the usual fuzzy sets, the IFS system supports also *type 2 fuzzy sets* and *intuitionistic fuzzy sets* ([10], [21]).

Each approach to uncertainty processing requires specific kinds of operators to compute the uncertainty of the knowledge derived during the inference. Though the class of uncertainty operators may have arbitrary user-defined subclasses, a hierarchy of system subclasses of that class has a crucial importance (see figure 5). If an uncertainty operator from a particular class is to be used during the inference, then either the operator must be a particular instance of that class, or a *method* must exist which belongs to that class and *yields a parametrized family of operators* including the desired one. It is actually *not necessary to specify* particular uncertainty operators or methods producing them. In that case the *default operator* from the respective class is used.

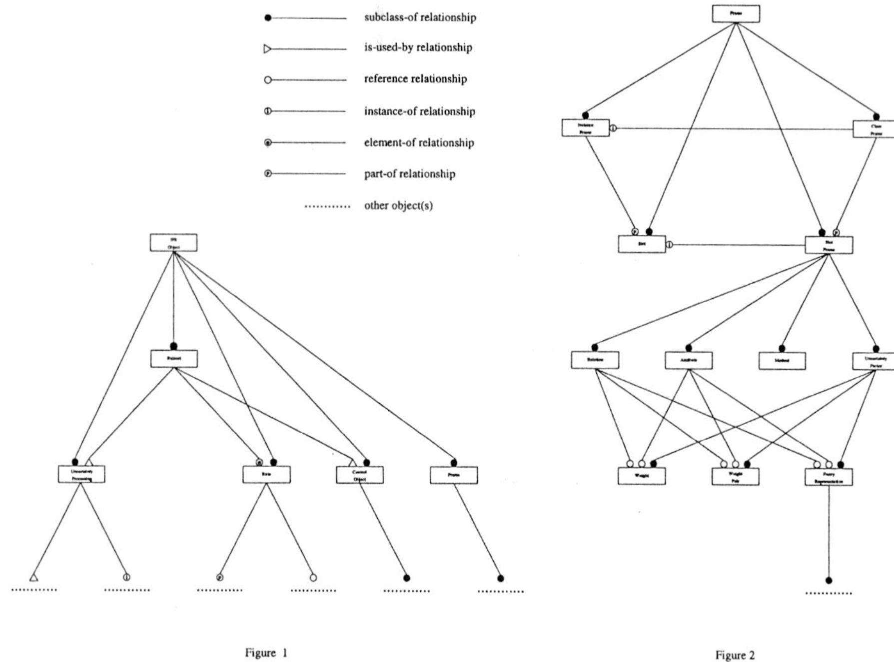

Fig. 1. Top classes of the IFS metaschema

Fig. 2. Frames

3 HyKL – a specification language for the IFS system

To describe the knowledge base of an application and the desired inference control, the user of a knowledge-representation system needs a specification formalism. In the IFS system, the *specification language HyKL* (hybrid knowledge description language) is used to this end. A HyKL specification is a collection of definitions, by means of which the user describes the classes, relationships between them, and their permanent instances, forming together the *schema of the application.* In addition, connections between the application schema and the metaschema of the system are also described in a HyKL specification.

Each class and instance of the application schema is described in a separate definition, except for system classes and instances, and for slot frames with default properties, which need not to be explicitly specified. Relationships between

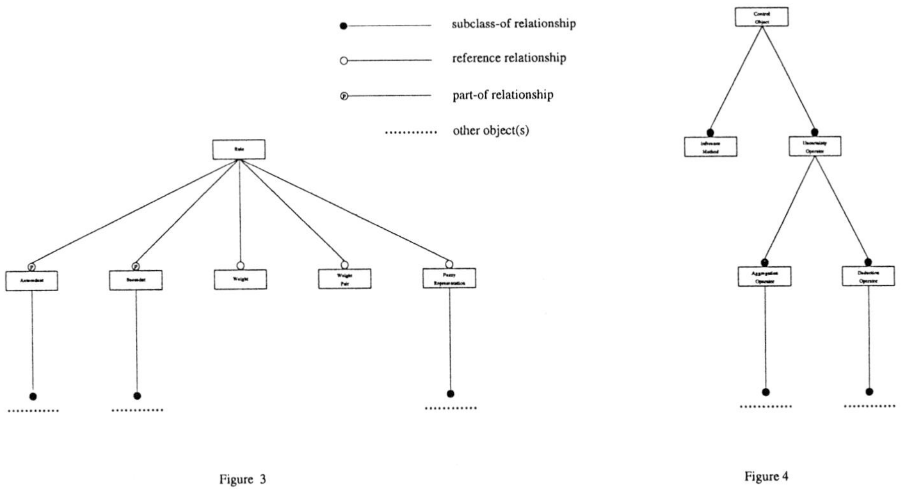

Fig. 3. Rules

Fig. 4. Control objects

classes or between their instances are specified in definitions of those classes, respectively instances, unless defaults are to be accepted. HyKL differentiates 2 kinds of definitions of classes, namely

–general class definitions,
–slot control class definitions,

and 3 kinds of instance definitions,

–general instance definitions,
–rule definitions,
–ruleset definitions.

The grammar and a detailed description of the language HyKL can be found in [11].

4 Database coupling

The IFS System captures the view of knowledge modelling for industrial problem solving. Frames and rules have proven as expressive paradigms for modelling knowledge. With the TREAT algorithm [15], a powerful evaluation scheme for

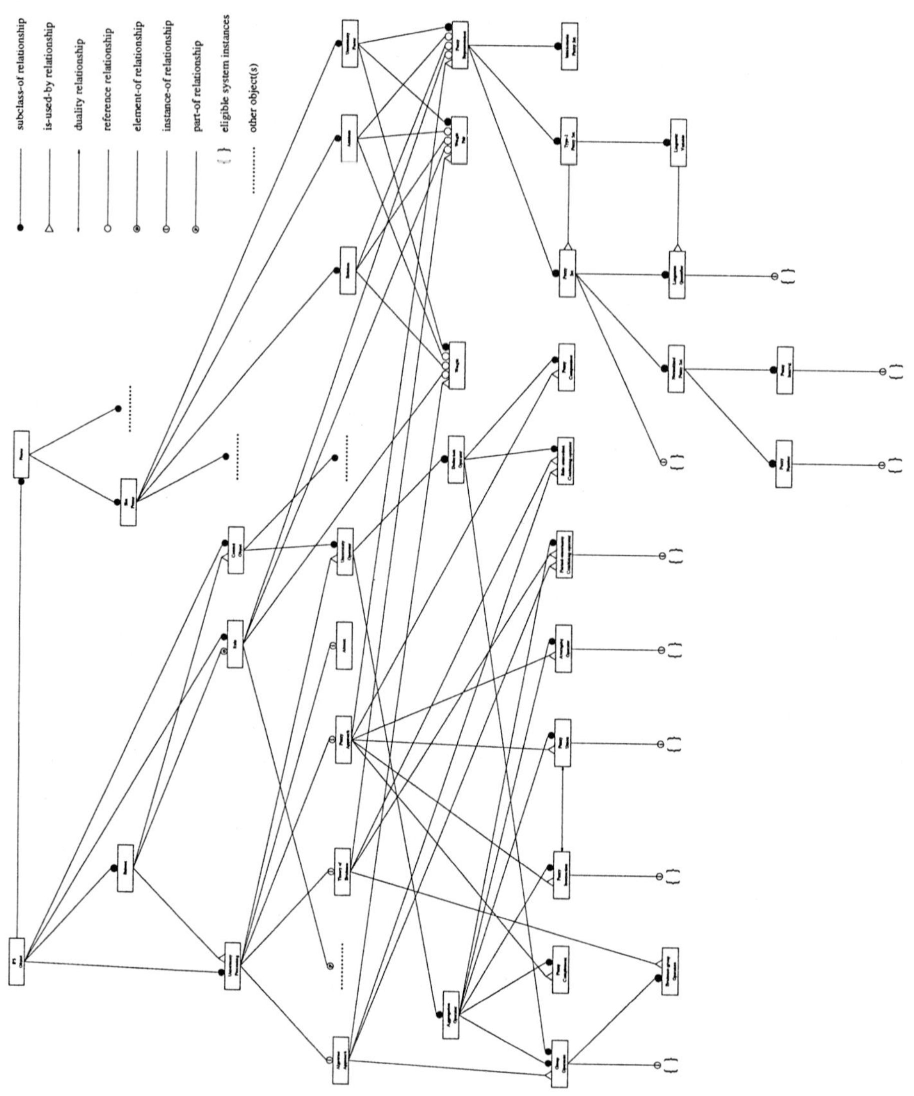

Fig. 5. Uncertainty processing in the IFS metaschema

production rules exists. Since real world problem solving sometimes involves large amounts of data and a needs for multi user access, efficient database systems are required to be used together with knowledge-representation systems. Hence we decide to couple the HyKL development and runtime system tightly to an object oriented database system (OODBS). In this section we describe the principles of the coupling and treat the related problems with respect to rules in subsection 4.2.

4.1 Principles of mapping a HyKL-specification to an OODBS

Recall from subsection section 3 that the basis of the HyKL specification of an application schema is formed by definitions of *classes* connected through *relations* and equipped with *attributes* and *methods*. Each class definition serves as a template for the creation of *instances*. Similarly, an *OODBS* consists of a schema and a database where the latter is meant as a set of persistent instances of classes, each with a unique identity [1][13]. An OODBS to be employed should allow adding, deleting and renaming attributes of instances. Class definitions themselves are represented in the database as persistent instances of so called metaclasses. Together with the base functionality mentioned above, this allows for schema access and manipulation at runtime. In a first implementation, we employ the Object Management System (OMS) by Cadlab and SNI [17], that provides the needed base functionality.

To map a HyKL-specification to the OMS, the concepts of the IFS metaschema (see subsection 2.2) are modelled with OMS metaclasses. The abstract metaclass *frame* in the IFS system is modelled with a collection class derived from the OMS metaclass SCO (Structured Container Object). With its ability to maintain a collection of objects, it allows to build the main classes of the IFS metaschema: Objects from the classes *slot-frame* and *slot* are modelled as OMS Primitive Objects (POs). POs are simple objects which usually contain attributes of primitive data types. These primitive attributes of a PO suffice to represent all necessary properties of a slot frame, such as demons, slot cardinality, default value, and the actual value. The different kinds of *uncertainty factors* are also modelled as such properties. Objects from the class *class-frame* are then modelled as a collection of slot frames. Objects from the class *instance-frame* for the representation of individual entities are modelled as a collection of slots. With this model, we obtain the ability for application schema evolution by the manipulation of instances in the OMS database. The task of transferring a HyKL script into the OODBS is done by a compiler, which also generates parts of the runtime system, e.g. for method and demon dispatching. A complete description of the functions of the HyKL Knowledge Access Interface can be found in [11] where it is referred to as HyKL-API.

4.2 Representation and evaluation of rules viewed as production rules

Beyond method and demon execution, rules acting on persistent frames are the main dynamic component of the IFS system. The concern of this subsection is restricted to the treatment of rules as production rules. The Evaluation of complex sets of production rules by naive query processing of a rule antecedent each time a particular rule is considered for execution is a computationally intractable task [15]. A compilation of rules into an effective runtime structure like that of the TREAT algorithm [15] is required.

The basic entity of interest to describe a TREAT-like structure for production rules in our system is a *single condition, SC* in a rule antecedent which can match a set of frames in the database (see [11] for details). The antecedent must be viewed as a conjunction of SCs.

The principle of applying the TREAT algorithm is to maintain a structure, which refers for each SC to *the complete set of frames matching the SC.* Recall, that the term *frame* comprises even class frames and slots frames. For each SC, this structure is called the *alpha-memory* of an SC. For each rule, subsets of the union of the alpha-memories satisfying the entire antecedent have to be selected and kept in the so called *conflict set.* Such a subset is also called an *instantiation* of a rule. The conflict set thus contains a complete set of rule instantiations once the TREAT structure is initially built. With the alpha- memories and the conflict set, the process of determining applicable rules together with the appropriate frames is just an access to the conflict set and no search is necessary at all. The structure needs updating when ever changes to the database occur. Updating roughly works by applying the SCs as tests to newly created frames to determine new content of the alpha-memories. With new frames in the alpha-memories, new possible rule instantiations for the conflict set have to be calculated then. Deleted frames have to be removed from the alpha memory and from the conflict set, together with their corresponding rule instantiations. Updating in the case of negated SCs or OCs is slightly more complicated and will not be explained here. Details of the TREAT algorithm can be found in [15].

The TREAT structure of a ruleset is then mapped to the OODBS as follows: All SCs of a ruleset are compiled into a collection of tests, the *SC-collection.* These tests, the *SC-tests*, must be able to be efficiently evaluated to examine changes to the set of frames in the database. Note, that these SC-tests resp. the SCs reflect parts of the frame schema in the database and may be affected by schema evolution. Each entry of the SC-collection is linked to a further collection, that represents the alpha-memory. Again, SC-tests belonging to an OC refer to the same alpha-memory collection (see above). For each rule, another Collection structure serves as the conflict set. These *Conflict-Set-Collection* must be able to represent *multiple lists of references to frames.* Each of these lists represents a possible instantiation of the particular rule. Finally, the rule entity itself is represented by a container object which refers to its conflict-set-collection and to its set of actions. The latter are at least calls to the HyKL Knowledge Access Interface, while the conflict-set-collection delivers possible arguments to these calls. This coupling of rules to a frame/database-environment yields two main kinds of problems:

Transaction Management. Since frames are represented as objects in an OODBS, they may be accessed asychronously, regardless of whether they belong to the same rule instantiation. To handle such situations consistently, the HyKL runtime environment must apply an adequate transaction management, in which rule evaluation has to be embedded. The approaches already discussed in literature ([12],[2]) must be taken into consideration. The current idea is to allow updating the TREAT structure triggered by frame manipulations from outside of the current ruleset during its evaluation, rather than naively locking all frames involved in an inference process. To improve efficiency of rule evaluation, a cache mechanism for frames and TREAT structures also has to be discussed.

Schema Evolution. As hinted above, the conditions of rule antecedents may be directly affected by schema evolution. This applies also to Knowledge Access Interface calls in the action part of a rule. To have a chance to handle rulesets which are running out of schema adequacy as the frame schema evolves, we need the possibility to alter the structure of rules within the TREAT structure. This means, that the SC-tests, which perform the check for particular rule conditions, must be open for modifications: They have to be compiled into an interpretative intermediate representation, which can be both evaluated and modified efficiently. The same is required for the actions of a rule. Frames for which schema changes are expected, should be only accessable via an interpretative interface, which generates exceptions for schema violating access. Conditions and actions of a rule, which access dynamic frames, need to be interpreted. This allows the dynamic modification of rules with respect to corresponding schema evolution. A formal scheme to adapt schema changes to affected production rules though is an aim of current and future work and will not be contained in early versions of the IFS system.

5 Conclusion

This paper presents a hybrid knowledge-representation IFS system being developed as a part of the JESSI Common Frame project. The paper reflects predominantly the conceptual view of the system since its implementation is only in an early stage. A prototype of a HyKL compiler currently works for the frame representation part of the language. It will be extended to rule representation and evaluation until the end of 1994. Many open problems are still connected with efficient evaluation of rules when uncertainty processing is performed, and with dynamic adaptation of schema evolution to rules. Seeking theoretically founded solutions to those problems will be the main direction of our research in the future.

References

1. Stewart M. Clamen. Schema evolution and integration. *International Journal of Parallel and Distributed Databases*, 2(1):101–126, 1994.

2. Umeshwar Dayal, Alejandro P. Buchmann, and Dennis R. McCarthy. Rules are objects too: A knowledge model for an active object-oriented database system. In *Proceedings of (AOODB88)*, pages 129–143, 1988.
3. F. di Primio and K.H. Wittur. Babylon: A meta interpretation modell for handling mixed knowledge representations. In *Proceedings of 7th International Workshop on Expert Systems and their Applications*, pages 821–833, 1987.
4. P. Drescher, R. Kruschinski, and G. Laufkötter. Report on hybrid knowledge representation, Deliverable IDKM-7 Nr. 064. Technical report, JCF – ESPRIT Project 7364, Cadlab, 1993.
5. P. Frasconi, M. Gori, M. Maggini, and G. Soda. Unified integration of explicit knowledge and learning by example in recurrent networks. *IEEE TDKE*, 8, 1993.
6. H.W. Güsgen, U. Junker, and A. Voß. Constraints in a hybrid knowledge representation system. In *Proceedings of the IJCAI*, pages 30–33, 1987.
7. P. Hájek, T. Havránek, and R. Jiroušek. *Uncertain Information Processing in Expert Systems.* Kluwer Academic Publishers, Dordrecht, 1992.
8. P. Hájek and J.J. Valdes. Algebraic foundations of uncertainty processing in rule-based expert systems (group-theoretical approach). *CAI*, 9:325–347, 1990.
9. P. Hájek and J.J. Valdes. Generalized algebraic foundations of uncertainty processing in rule-based expert systems (dempsteroids). *CAI*, 10:29–56, 1991.
10. M. Holeňa. Theoretical principles of uncertainty processing in expert systems. Technical report, JCF – ESPRIT Project 7364, Cadlab, 1993, 57 pages.
11. M. Holeňa and R. Kruschinski. Specification of HyKL 1.0 description language for hybrid knowledge representation and management. Technical report, JCF – ESPRIT Project 7364, Cadlab, 1993, 62 pages.
12. Meichun Hsu and Thomas E. Cheatham Jr. Rule execution in cplex: A persistent objectbase. In *Proceedings of (AOODB88)*, pages 150–161, 1988.
13. Setrag N. Koshafian and George P. Copeland. Object identity. In *Proceedings of (OOPSLA86)*, pages 406–416, 1986.
14. S. Laufman, editor. *Standard for a Frame-Based Knowledge Representation*, volume Draft 2.1b. P1252 Working Group, 1993.
15. Daniel P. Miranker. *TREAT: A New and Efficient Match Algorithm for AI Production Systems.* Morgan Kaufmann Publishers, Inc., San Mateo, California, 1990.
16. B. Nebel and K. von Luck. Issues of integration and balancing in hybrid knowledge representation systems. In K. Morik, editor, *Proceedings of the GWAI*, pages 115–123, 1987.
17. Siemens Nixdorf Informationssyteme AG 1993, Universität Paderborn, Delft University of Technology. *JCF V3.0 - Development System: Object Management System, Administrators Guide*, preliminiary edition, 1993.
18. Andrea H. Skarra and Stanley B. Zdonik. The management of changing types in an object-oriented database. In *Proceedings of the (OOPSLA86)*, pages 483–495, 1986.
19. J.D. Ullman. *Principles of Database Systems.* Computer Science Press, 1982.
20. J. Whittaker. *Graphical Models in Applied Multivariate Statistics.* John Wiley and Sons, New York, 1990.
21. H.J. Zimmermann. *Fuzzy Set Theory and its Applications.* Kluwer Academic Publishers, Dordrecht, 2. edition, 1991.

A Prototype Rule-Based Front End System for Integrity Enforcement in Relational Databases: An Application to the Naval Aircraft Flight Records Database

Magdi N. Kamel

Information Systems Group, Naval Postgraduate School
Monterey, CA 93943 USA
kamel@nps.navy.mil

Abstract. An important goal of any database system is to model the real world accurately in a manner consistent with the user's perception of the data. One way to accomplish the accuracy of information in relational databases is through the enforcement of integrity constraints that represent rules pertaining to the organization. Unfortunately most DBMS today do not provide adequate integrity features to ensure the accuracy of data in their databases. This paper discusses the design and implementation of a prototype rule-based front end system for integrity enforcement for the Naval Aircraft Flight Record relational database. The system includes a set of rules that define 1) the update operation that triggers the testing of an integrity rule, 2) a specification of the condition to be tested, and 3) the action to be taken in case of attempted violation. These rules are stored in a knowledge base, which the inference engine of the system uses to enforce database integrity.

1 Introduction

Relational databases are widely being used in organizations to store, organize, and retrieve data to manage its activities. Since an important goal of any database system is to accurately model an organization and its activities, it is extremely important for the organization to maintain the accuracy of information in their databases. One way to accomplish the accuracy of information in relational databases is the enforcement of integrity constraints that represent rules pertaining to the organization. By enforcing these constraints, the data in the database is guaranteed to be continually in compliance with these rules.

Ideally the enforcement of integrity constraints should be the responsibility of the Database Management System (DBMS) managing the database [10]. An integrity subsystem would continually monitor updates to the database detecting those updates that would lead to an inconsistent database state and taking appropriate actions. Unfortunately and for various reasons, DBMS vendors have failed to include adequate integrity features in their products. This situation has shifted the responsibility of enforcing integrity constraints from the DBMS to the application programs that access the database. This approach, however, has a number of severe drawbacks:

1. Specification of integrity constraints could be quite elaborate, placing a significant burden on application programmers
2. Enforcing same integrity constraints could occur in any number of applications, leading to duplication of effort and introduction of inconsistencies
3. Integrity rules are buried in procedures and are, therefore, hard to understand and maintain
4. Integrity constraints could be easily bypassed by excluding them from application programs

In absence of a centrally implemented integrity constraint enforcement by the DBMS, any approach to enforcing integrity should satisfy the following objectives:

1. Constraints should be specified in a form that are easily understood and maintained
2. Constraints should be centrally created and maintained
3. All access to the database, whether by an interactive user or application program, should be subject to integrity checking

In this paper we propose the use of a rule-based front end system to accomplish the above objectives. The rule-based system includes a set of rules that define 1) the update operation that trigger the testing of an integrity rule, 2) a specification of the condition to be tested, and 3) the action to be taken in case of attempted violation. As such, it is a special purpose rule based system that follow the same paradigm as alerters [1] and triggers [5]. These rules are stored in a knowledge base, which the inference engine of the system uses to enforce database integrity. The system continually monitors updates—insertions, modifications, and deletions—to the database. Once it identifies a violation, an appropriate action would be taken to prevent the update from corrupting the database. This action usually results in rejecting the update operation and notifying the user of the violation.

The organization of the paper is as follows. Section 2 describes a relational database, the Naval Aircraft Record Database, that serves as the case study for implementing the prototype rule-based system. It also describes the integrity constraints that need to be enforced for this application. Section 3 describes the design and construction of the front end system. Finally Section 4 concludes the paper by discussing the benefits and limitations of the proposed approach and suggesting directions for future work.

2 Naval Aircraft Flight Record Database

2.1 Background

The relational database of this application is based on the Naval Aircraft Flight Record. This record serves as the sole source of all naval aircraft flight data and is also applicable in specific areas to aircraft simulators [6]. This record is prepared for each attempt at flight of naval aircraft or training evaluation for simulators. The type of data collected on this form include aircraft and aircrew data related to the flight, a record of all logistic actions performed during the flight, a record of weapons proficiency, a record of training areas utilized and other miscellaneous data.

The Operations Department within the aircraft squadron is responsible for verifying the accuracy and completeness of the naval flight records submitted for data processing as well as verifying the daily audit reports, and coordinating the correction of errors with a maintenance analyst. Data from completed records is subsequently used to produce a variety of reports on pilot flight activities and to provide valuable information for flight safety analysis, budget justification, past and future program evaluation, and pilot compliance with established minimum standards. The accuracy of data entered in the database is, therefore, of paramount and critical importance. A semantically rich integrity enforcer would greatly enhance the Operations Department ability to accomplish its mission and ensure the accuracy of data, thus improving the quality of decisions based on this data.

2.2 Database Schema

The relational schema for the database consists of 20 relations, 82 distinct attributes, and 19 relationships. Due to space limitations we shall focus our discussion on a subset of the overall schema that contains the principal relations, attributes, and relationships. This subset schema is shown in Figure 1 and described below.

A tuple of the ORGANIZATION relation represents a naval aircraft squadron. It is identified by an organization code and includes attributes related to the organization such as data processing code, organization short name, support code, departure time zone, etc. This relation is associated in a one to many optional relationship with the AIRCRAFT relation.

A tuple of the AIRCRAFT relation represents a naval aircraft. It is identified by the aircraft side number and includes attributes that describe the aircraft such as type, equipment code, and number of engines. This relation is associated in a one to many optional relationship with the FLIGHT relation.

A tuple of the FLIGHT relation represents a naval aircraft flight. It is identified by a document number and includes properties such as aircraft side number, exception code, mission code *n*, mission hours *n* (for *n*=1,2,3), total flights, ship/field operations code, catapult/jato launches, airlift mission number, number of hoists, and remarks. This relation is associated in a one to many optional relationship with the ENGINE relation.

A tuple of the ENGINE relation represents an engine information during a flight. It is identified by the composite attribute of document number and engine number and includes an engine hours attribute.

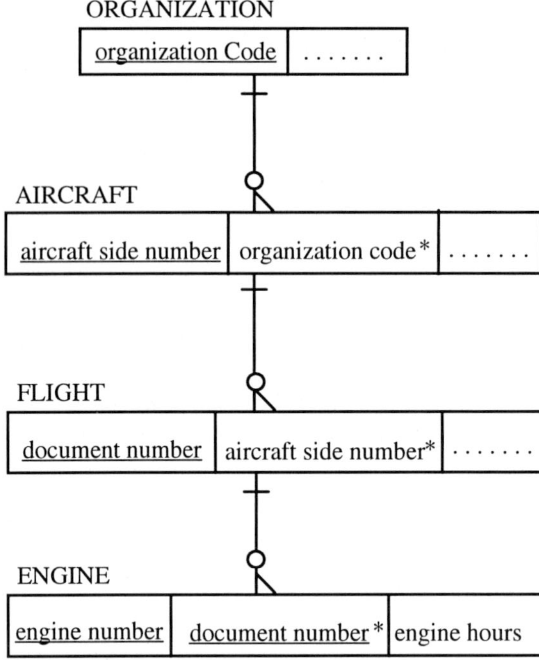

Fig. 1. Subset of Naval Flight Record Database Schema

2.3 Integrity Constraints

We adopt a classification of integrity constraints as proposed by Codd [2]. Integrity constraints are of five types: 1) domain integrity constraints, 2) column integrity constraints, 3) entity integrity constraints, 4) referential integrity constraints, and 5) user-defined integrity constraints. Based on the above classification, we present in this section the semantic integrity rules that need to be enforced in the Naval Aircraft Flight Record database. Due to the sheer size of rules for the database, we shall focus our discussion on the integrity constraints pertaining to the relations described in the previous section.

2.3.1 Domain Integrity Constraint

A domain is the set of all possible values an attribute can draw from. A domain integrity constraint consists of those integrity constraints that are shared by all attributes that draw that value from that domain. It includes a physical description like 1) the data type, 2) ranges of values permitted, and 3) allowable comparison operators. The definition of domain integrity constraint also includes a description of the semantics or meaning for that domain.

While the concept of domain is central to relational databases, it is not supported by today's DBMS's. Instead, most DBMS's provide integrity support at the attribute (column) level as described in the following section.

Domain constraints to be enforced for the Naval Record Application include the data type and range of values permitted for that domain. Most range constraints, however, are enforced at the attribute (column) level.

2.3.2 Column Integrity Constraint

Column integrity constraints are an extension of domain constraints. They provide additional constraints that are specific to the column in addition to the constraints inherited from the associated domain. A column integrity constraint may include 1) an added range constraint that provides a more confined range than in the domain declaration, 2) whether values in a column must be distinct (definition of primary keys), and 3) whether missing values are allowed within a column. Most modern DBMS provide some support for this type of constraint. The following are some column integrity constraints that need to be enforced for the Naval Flight Record database:

- Exception code must be C, D, X, or Blank
- Position 1 of mission code *n* where *n*=1 must be in the range of 1 – 6 or Blank
- Mission hours *n* where *n*=1 must be in the range of 0.1 – 72.0 or Blank

2.3.3 Entity Integrity Constraint

Entity integrity implies that the primary key or any component thereof of the any relation is not allowed to have null values. It also implies that duplicates of the primary key are not allowed. For example, the attribute document number, the primary key to the FLIGHT relation, is not allowed to be null or duplicate. Similarly, the composite attribute of engine number and document number, which is the primary key of the ENGINE relation, is not allowed to be wholly or partly null and duplicate values are not allowed.

2.3.4 Referential Integrity Constraint

For every value of a foreign key in a relation there must exist a matching value of a primary key in some tuple of another relation or the value of the foreign key be wholly null. For example, the foreign key aircraft side number in the FLIGHT relation must have a matching primary key value in the AIRCRAFT relation. Few commercial relational DBMS provide this type of support.

2.3.5 User Defined Integrity Constraint

In addition to domain, column, entity, and referential integrity constraints, user defined constraints that are particular to an end-user or organization are needed. They allow organization practices, policy, or governmental legislation to be reflected in the database. While this type of support is extremely desirable and useful, most commercial DBMS provide no support at all for this important type of constraints. The user defined constraints for the Naval Aircraft Flight Record database include intra-attribute constraints, intra-relation constraints, and inter-relation constraints.

a. *Intra-Attribute Constraints.* An intra-attribute constraint is a constraint on the relationship between components of an attribute. Intra-attribute constraints that need to be enforced include:

- If position 1 of attribute mission code n for n=1 or n>1 is 1, then position 2 of the attribute must be R or in the range of A – I or N – P
- If position 1 of attribute mission code n for n=1 or n>1 is 2, then position 2 of the attribute must be in the range of J – R

b. *Intra-Relation Constraints.* An intra-relation constraint is a constraint placed on data within a relation. The intra-relation constraint to be enforced include:

- If exception code is X, then position 2 of attribute mission code n for n=1 must be O or N
- If exception code is X, then attribute mission code n for n>1 must be Blank

c. *Inter-Relation Constraints.* An inter-relationship constraint is a constraint on the relationship of data value between or among relations. Examples of inter-relation constraints enforced by the system include:

- If exception code in the FLIGHT relation is X, the associated values in the attributes engine hours in the ENGINE relation must be Blank
- If exception code in the FLIGHT relation is not X, the sum of the corresponding engine hours in the ENGINE relation must be in the range of 0.1 to sum of mission hours n, (n=*1,2,3*), in the FLIGHT relation

3. Design and Implementation of the Front End System

The design of the front end system is based on the use of production rules to specify and enforce the integrity constraints. These rules define 1) the update operation that trigger the testing of an integrity rule, 2) a specification of the condition to be tested, and 3) the action to be taken in case of attempted violation. The system continually monitors updates —insertions, modifications, and deletions—to the database to detect violations and take appropriate actions to prevent the data from being corrupted.

A rapid prototyping methodology was used to develop the system. Using the integrity constraints classification described in Section 2, an initial prototype was developed and tested using the rule based system shell VP-Expert. New rules, variables, values, choices, were continually added until all types of operations and constraints were included. Currently, the prototype system has a knowledge base of approximately 150 rules.

Rules stored in the knowledge base are grouped by update operations. Update operations that trigger the testing of an integrity rule include append, modify, and delete. In the following sections we briefly describe each group of the rule base with sample rules of each group.

3.1 Append Records

In its interactive mode, the system initiates a two-way dialogue with the user to generate a new record. Each value of attribute entered by a user triggers the firing of one or more rules. These rules determine whether a value of an attribute is valid. If the value of an attribute does not satisfy the integrity constraint of that attribute, the system rejects the value and offers assistance as to a valid value that would be accepted. At the end of the append operation, if all values assigned to the attributes satisfy the integrity constraints, they are committed to the database, otherwise the append operation is rolled back and the database is not affected.

In the following sections we present sample rules used to enforce column, entity, referential, and user defined rules.

3.1.1 Column Integrity

RULE Column_Integrity_Exception_Code

```
IF      Excd = C OR
        Excd = D OR
        Excd = X OR
        Excd = UNKNOWN OR
        Excd = (Blank)
THEN
        Excd_Valid = True
ELSE
        Display "You Need to Enter a Valid Exception Code to Continue."
        RESET Excd
        FIND Excd;
```

This rule checks that the Exception Code is C, D, X, or Blank. If not, it prompts the user to enter a valid code before he/she can continue.

3.1.2 Entity Integrity

RULE Entity_Integrity_Docnum_Missing

```
IF      Docnum_New = UNKNOWN OR
        Docnum_New = (Blank)
THEN
        WHILETRUE Docnum_New = UNKNOWN OR Docnum_New = (Blank)
        THEN
                DISPLAY "You will not be able to Proceed unless you enter a
                Document Number."
                RESET Docnum_New
                FIND Docnum_New
        END
```

```
        Docnum_Not_Missing = True
ELSE
        Docnum_Not_Missing = True
```

This rule checks that the key of the FLIGHT relation, the attribute document number, is neither blank or unknown. Thc rule will not allow the user to proceed unless a valid value is specified.

3.1.3 Referential Integrity

RULE Referential_Integrity_Sidenum_Exists

```
    IF  Sidenum_New <> UNKNOWN OR
        Sidenum_New <> (Blank)
THEN
        GET Sidenum_New = Side, Aircraft, Side
        WHILETRUE Side = UNKNOWN
        THEN
                CLOSE Aircraft
                DISPLAY "No Aircraft Exists in the Organization with the side
                        number {Sidenum_New}."
                RESET Sidenum_New
                FIND Sidenum_New
        END
        Sidenum_Exists = True
        Sidenum = (Side);
```

This rule checks that a value of the foreign key aircraft side number in the FLIGHT relation has a matching primary key value in the AIRCRAFT relation. The GET statement attempts to find a record of the AIRCRAFT relation whose side number attribute matches the value of the side number of the FLIGHT relation. If a matching value is not found, the user is requested to enter another value for the side number attribute until a match is found.

3.1.4 User Defined Integrity

RULE User_Defined_Mission12A_Code

```
IF      Msn1_1 <> 1 OR
        Msn1_2 = A OR
        Msn1_2 = B OR
        Msn1_2 = C OR
        Msn1_2 = D OR
        Msn1_2 = E OR
        Msn1_2 = F OR
        Msn1_2 = G OR
        Msn1_2 = H OR
        Msn1_2 = I OR
```

```
        Msn1_2 = N OR
        Msn1_2 = O OR
        Msn1_2 = P OR
        Msn1_2 = R
THEN
        Msn12_Valid = True
ELSE
        WHILETRUE Msn12_Valid <> True
        THEN
                DISPLAY "Position 2 must be R, A – I, or N – P.  Press Enter to
                Continue."
                RESET Msn1_2
                FIND Msn1_2;
```

This rule is an example of an Intra-Attribute User Defined Integrity Constraint. It ensures that if position 1 of attribute mission code n for n=1 or n>1 is 1, then position 2 of the attribute must be R or in the range of A – I or N – P, where Msn1_1 and Msn1_2 are position 1 and 2 of mission code 1, respectively.

3.2 Modify Records

Similar to the append operation, the system prompts the user to select the relations and attributes to modify. Modifying the value of an attribute would normally fire multiple rules for attributes that are affected by the modification of that attribute. For example, if a canceled flight, indicated by a record with the attribute exception code equal to X and no flight data, is later flown, i.e., the exception code is changed to a value other than X, a number of rules will be fired to ensure that other attributes of the flight record contain valid values. No attribute values are committed to the database unless they satisfy all relevant integrity rules. The following sample rule is fired when the exception code is changed to X (canceled flight). It ensures that a valid mission code 1 is accepted and sets all other flight attributes to null.

RULE Exception_Code_Update_1

```
IF      Field_to_Update = Exception_Code AND
        Excd_New = X
THEN
        GET Docnum_Update = Docnum, Flight, Excd
        RESET Excd
        Excd = (Excd_New)
        RESET Msn1
        FIND Msn1
        RESET Msn1_Valid
        FIND Msn1_Valid
        Hrs1 = (Blank)
        Msn2 = (Blank)
```

```
        PUT Flight
        CLOSE Flight;
```

3.3 Delete Records

The last operation that triggers the checking of integrity rules is the delete operation. A delete operation could lead to a referential integrity violation, if, for example, an attempt is made to delete a flight for which there exist matching engine records. In general there are three possible actions to a referential integrity violation [3,4]: 1) the delete operation "cascades" to delete matching tuples in the child relation, 2) the delete operation is rejected, and 3) in some cases, the foreign key in the child relation could be set to null. The following sample rule deletes all associated engine records for a deleted flight.

RULE Delete_Flight

```
IF      Delete_Flight = Yes
THEN
        GET Docnum_Delete = Docnum, Flteng, All
        WHILETRUE Engnum <> UNKNOWN THEN
                {Delete Flteng Record}
                PUT Flteng
                GET Docnum_Delete = Docnum, Flteng, All
        END
        CLOSE Flteng;
```

4 Summary and Future Work

This paper addressed the issue of dynamic enforcement of integrity constraints in relational databases through the use of a rule-based front end system. A comprehensive classification of integrity constraints is used as a framework for designing and building the system. The Navy's Naval Aircraft Flight Record Database served as vehicle for demonstrating the feasibility of this concept in a well-defined, structured area.

The initial use of the front end system was very successful. The use of an expert system shell with production rules proved to be a viable method for testing and enforcing integrity constraints by providing modularity and standardization of representation. The ability to store the rules in one central repository (knowledge base) and in a format that is easy to understand and maintain is the most significant benefit of using this approach. The "Why" capability of the expert system shell allowed users to ask why a particular response was obtained allowing them to examine and thus better understand the semantics of the data.

The initial prototype of the system was developed using VP-Expert/SQL, an expert system shell with integrated SQL database server. This approach, though very appealing in that it provides the power of a non procedural language to access SQL databases, was not successful due to the instability and error of the software. A less elegant approach was used in the final prototype through the use of VP-Expert, an expert system shell with primitive capabilities to interact with database files. We believe that a robust expert system shell with built-in non procedural database access language, like SQL, is easier to use and would result in a more powerful, efficient, and readable system.

As new rules are added or old ones modified, redundancy and inconsistencies could be easily introduced. Techniques and tools should be developed to validate the system after making changes to the knowledge base.

Finally, this approach for using a rule based system for enforcing integrity constraints could be extended to include other database services such as access control and view processing [8,9,10]. Rather than having an independent module for each type of service, a single rule system could provide all these database services, thus resulting in a more compact and efficient database code.

References

[1] Buneman, P. and Clemons, E., "Efficiently Monitoring Relational Databases," *ACM Transactions on Database Systems*, Vol. 4, No. 3, Sept. 1979, pp. 368–382.

[2] Codd, E. F., *The Relational Model for Database Management, Version 2,* Addison-Wesley Publishing Co., Inc., 1990.

[3] Date, C. J., *An Introduction to Database Systems,* Vol. 1, Fourth Edition, Addison-Wesley Publishing Co., Inc., 1986.

[4] Date, C. J., "Referential Integrity," *Proc. 7th International Conference on Very Large Data Bases,* September 1981.

[5] Eswaren, K. P., "Specifications, Implementations and Interactions of a Trigger Subsystem in an Integrated Database System," *IBM Research Report RJ1820*, San Jose, CA, November 1976.

[6] Department of the Navy, Office of the Chief of Naval Operation, "OPNAVINST 3710.7N," *Natops General Flight and Operating Instructions,* April 1990.

[7] Fernandez, E. B., Summers, R. C., and Wood, C., *Database Security and Integrity,* Addison-Wesley Publishing Co., Inc., 1986.

[8] Stonebraker, M., "The Integration of Rule Systems and Database Systems," *IEEE Transactions on Knowledge and Data Engineering*, Vol. 4, No. 5, October 1992, pp. 415–423.

[9] Stonebraker, M., "Adding Semantic Knowledge to a Relational Database System," In *On Conceptual Modeling,* Brodie, M. L., Mylopoulos, J., and Schmidt, J. W. (Eds.), New York, NY: Springer-Verlag, 1984. pp. 334–353.

[10] Stonebraker, M., "Implementation of Integrity Constraints and Views by Query Modification," *Proc. 1975 ACM SIGMOD International Conference on the Management of Data*. San Jose, CA, 1975, pp. 65–68.

MODELING UNCERTAINTY IN DEDUCTIVE DATABASES

Laks V. S. Lakshmanan Fereidoon Sadri

Concordia University, Montreal, Canada
{laks,sadri}@cs.concordia.ca

Abstract. Information Source Tracking (IST) method has been developed recently for the modeling and manipulation of uncertain and inaccurate data in relational databases. In this paper we extend the IST method to deductive databases. We show that *positive uncertain databases*, i.e. IST-based deductive databases with only positive literals in the heads and the bodies of the rules, enjoy a least model/least fixpoint semantics. Query processing in this model is studied next. We extend the top-down and bottom-up evaluation techniques of logic programming and deductive databases to our model. Finally, we study negation for uncertain databases, concentrating on *stratified uncertain databases.*

1 Introduction

Database systems are evolving into *knowledge-base* systems, and are increasingly used in applications where handling inaccurate data is essential. In a recent study, uncertainty management was listed as one of the important future challenges in database research. "Further research [*in uncertainty*] is essential, as we must learn not only to cope with data of limited reliability, but to do so efficiently, with massive amounts of data" [18].

Information Source Tracking (IST) method has been developed recently for the modeling and manipulation of uncertain and inaccurate data in relational databases [14, 15, 16, 17]. In this paper we extend the IST method to deductive databases. First we concentrate on *positive uncertain databases*, i.e. IST-based deductive databases with only positive literals in the heads and the bodies of the rules, and show that they enjoy a least model semantics, which coincides with the least fixpoint of an immediate consequence operator. Query processing is studied next. We show that top-down (e.g. SLD-resolution) and bottom-up (e.g. magic sets) query processing can be extended to uncertain databases. Finally, we study negation for uncertain databases, concentrating on *stratified uncertain databases.*

The rest of this paper is organized as follows. A short summary of recent research in modeling and handling uncertainty in databases is presented in Section 2. In Section 3 we present the Information Source Tracking (IST) method, and its extension to deductive databases, which we will call *uncertain databases.* Section 4 is devoted to the semantics of uncertain databases. The minimal model/fixpoint semantics of regular deductive databases is extended to uncertain databases.

Top-down and bottom-up query processing techniques for uncertain databases are studied in Section 5. In Section 6 we study negation in the context of uncertain databases, and concluding remarks are presented in Section 7.

2 A Brief Review

Earlier works on uncertainty in database systems dealt with incomplete data and null values. More recently there has been a significant interest in more general treatment of uncertain and inaccurate data. The model proposed by Liu and Sunderraman [8, 9] partitions relations into definite, indefinite, and maybe segments. Relational algebra operations are extended to operate on this extended model. Lee [7] studies uncertainty in databases based on the Dempster-Shafer theory of evidence. He makes a distinction between imprecise information, where the value of an attribute is one out of a set of values, and uncertainty, where a probability distribution function is associated with the value(s). Processing of simple and compound queries on one relation is also discussed. The model studied by Barbara, Garcia-Molina and Porter [4] captures uncertainties at the level of attributes, and is based on an implicit independence assumption regarding values of different attributes in a relation. Special attention is paid to the question of missing probabilities, combining the issues of inaccuracy and incompleteness. Lakshmanan [6] formalizes definite and indefinite answers in a database containing null values using intuitionistic logic, and studies the complexity of query processing in this paradigm.

Van Emden's work [21] was one of the early studies in uncertainty in logic programming and deductive databases. He extends the classical results of logic programming [22] to a model that captures uncertainty. Nilsson's work [12] is in the more general framework of mathematical logic. Using a "possible worlds" model, he shows how probabilistic assertions on logic formulas translate into inequalities on the probability distribution of possible worlds. Kifer and Li [5] study a more general model in which different functions can be used for combining uncertainties. They show that if these functions satisfy certain properties, then the least model/least fixpoint semantics holds. Query processing in this model is also discussed. Ng and Subrahmanian [11] extend the previous works in several directions. They use intervals of probabilities, as opposed to point probabilities, and apply mathematical programming (linear programming) to handle the inequalities arising in the system.

Our approach in Information Source Tracking (IST) differs from the other works in that we do not directly associate certainties with information [14, 16]. We assume that information is supplied, or confirmed, by information sources, and the reliability of the contributing source determines the certainty of information. For each "piece" of data in the database, e.g. for each tuple in a relation, we also record the contributing information source(s). Query processing algorithms handle data as well as sources information. An answer to a query also identifies sources contributing to the answer and their nature of contribution. The calculation of certainties are left as the (optional) last step of query processing.

3 Uncertain Databases

In this section we will focus on the application of the Information Source Tracking (IST) method to deductive databases. We use a first order language for IST-based deductive databases. A deductive database in our model consists of a set of annotated rules. The annotation of a rule identifies the information sources contributing to the rule and their nature of contribution. The facts, i.e. raw database information, are special cases of the rules. We will make these notions precise in the following definitions.

The alphabet of our language consists of the usual classes of symbols, namely, *variables*, *constants*, and *predicate symbols*, as well as the set of *information source constants*, $\{\bot, -1, +1, \top\}$. The purpose and meaning of these special constants are explained in the next subsection. *Terms* and *literals* are defined as in the classical case. A term is a variable or a (ordinary) constant. A literal is of the form $p(x_1, \ldots, x_n)$ or $\neg p(x_1, \ldots, x_n)$ where p is an n-ary predicate symbol and $x_1, \ldots, x_n$ are terms. The information source constants are used to form vectors to annotate logical rules. An *information source vector* (*source vector*, for short) is a vector $v = (a_1 \cdots a_k)$, $a_i \in \{\bot, -1, +1, \top\}$, $i = 1, \ldots, k$, where k is the number of information sources.

A *rule* r is a statement of the form $(p \leftarrow q_1, \ldots, q_n)@x$, where p is a positive literal, $q_1, \ldots, q_n$ are literals, and x is a set of information source vectors. We call p the *head* and $q_1, \ldots, q_n$ the *body* of the rule r. As usual, we require the rules to be *range restricted*, that is, all the variables appearing in the head of the rule must also appear in the body of the rule. A *fact* is a rule with an empty body, and no variables in the head. We usually write a fact $(p\leftarrow)@x$ as $p@x$. Facts play the same role played by base relations in the relational database model. An *uncertain IST-based deductive database* (*uncertain database*, for short) is a finite set of rules.

3.1 Information Source Vectors

A set of information source vectors is used to annotate a rule or a fact. In a source vector $v = (a_1 \cdots a_k)$, corresponding to the rule (or fact) r, the value of a_i specifies the role of the information source S_i as follows:

$$a_i = \begin{cases} \bot & S_i \text{ is inconsistent with respect to } r \\ -1 & S_i \text{ denies } r \\ +1 & S_i \text{ confirms } r \\ \top & S_i \text{ neither confirms nor denies } r \end{cases}$$

More precisely, the role of information sources is captured by the *expression* corresponding to a set of source vectors defined as follows. We associate a Boolean variable s_i with each information source S_i, $i = 1, \ldots, k$. Let $v = (a_1 \cdots a_k)$ be a source vector, then the set of information sources $S^+ = \{S_i \mid a_i = +1 \text{ or } a_i = \bot\}$ are contributing positively to the rule (or fact) associated with v, while the set of information sources $S^- = \{S_i \mid a_i = -1 \text{ or } a_i = \bot\}$ are contributing negatively. Note that the case of inconsistent information source, $a_i = \bot$, is treated as the source s_i is contributing positively as well as negatively to the corresponding information. The expression $e(v)$ corresponding to the source vector $v = (a_1 \cdots a_k)$, is defined as: $e(v) = \bigwedge_{S_i \in S^+} s_i \bigwedge_{S_j \in S^-} \neg s_j$. The expression $e(x)$ corresponding to a set x of source vectors is $e(x) = \bigvee_{v \in x} e(v)$.

3.2 Source vector operations

Our aim is to answer queries in a deductive database where data (facts) and rules are uncertain. The uncertainty of facts and rules are modeled by the reliability of the information sources, and captured by their corresponding information source vectors. The answer to a query also reflects its uncertainty by accompanying appropriate information source vectors. In the IST approach the answers to a query also include their respective source vectors. Query processing in IST-based uncertain databases uses the information source vector operations *s-conjunction*, *s-disjunction*, and *s-negation*. Given two source vectors $v = (a_1 \cdots a_k)$ and $w = (b_1 \cdots b_k)$, their s-conjunction $u = v \overset{s}{\wedge} w$ is a source vector $u = (c_1 \cdots c_k)$, obtained as follows:

a_i	b_i	c_i
$\bot$	$\bot$	$\bot$
$\bot$	-1	$\bot$
$\bot$	$+1$	$\bot$
$\bot$	$\top$	$\bot$

a_i	b_i	c_i
-1	$\bot$	$\bot$
-1	-1	-1
-1	$+1$	$\bot$
-1	$\top$	-1

a_i	b_i	c_i
$+1$	$\bot$	$\bot$
$+1$	-1	$\bot$
$+1$	$+1$	$+1$
$+1$	$\top$	$+1$

a_i	b_i	c_i
$\top$	$\bot$	$\bot$
$\top$	-1	-1
$\top$	$+1$	$+1$
$\top$	$\top$	$\top$

The s-conjunction of two sets of source vectors x and y is performed componentwise: $x \overset{s}{\wedge} y = \{v \overset{s}{\wedge} w \mid v \in x \text{ and } w \in y\}$.
The s-disjunction of two sets of source vectors x and y, written $x \overset{s}{\vee} y$, is their union: $x \overset{s}{\vee} y = x \cup y$.

Observation 1 *The s-conjunction and s-disjunction operators are* monotone *with respect to the subset ordering of sets of source vectors. That is, if $x \subseteq x'$ and $y \subseteq y'$, then, $(x \overset{s}{\wedge} y) \subseteq (x' \overset{s}{\wedge} y')$, and $(x \overset{s}{\vee} y) \subseteq (x' \overset{s}{\vee} y')$.*

The s-negation of a source vector $v = (a_1 \cdots a_k)$, written $\overset{s}{\neg} v$, is defined as follows: let u_i denote the source vector $(b_1 \cdots b_k)$ where $b_i = +1$ and $b_j = \top$, for $j \neq i$, and similarly let w_i denote the source vector $(b_1 \cdots b_k)$ where $b_i = -1$ and $b_j = \top$, for $j \neq i$, then $\overset{s}{\neg} v = \{u_i \mid a_i = -1 \text{ or } a_i = \top\} \cup \{w_i \mid a_i = +1 \text{ or } a_i = \top\}$.
The s-negation of a set $x = v_1, \ldots, v_m$ of source vectors is calculated as follows: $\overset{s}{\neg} x = (\overset{s}{\neg} v_1) \overset{s}{\wedge} (\overset{s}{\neg} v_2) \overset{s}{\wedge} \ldots \overset{s}{\wedge} (\overset{s}{\neg} v_m)$.

The following results were proven in [14]. In the following x, y, and z are sets of source vectors, and $e(x)$, $e(y)$, and $e(z)$ are their corresponding expressions, respectively.

Theorem 1. *Let $z = x \overset{s}{\wedge} y$, then $e(z) = e(x) \wedge e(y)$. Similarly, if $z = x \overset{s}{\vee} y$, then $e(z) = e(x) \vee e(y)$, and if $z = \overset{s}{\neg} x$, then $e(z) = \neg e(x)$.*

4 Minimal Model and Fixpoint Semantics

In this section we restrict our attention to uncertain IST-based deductive databases with no negation, that is, only positive literals are permitted in the body of the rules, which we will call *positive uncertain databases* henceforth. We will show the existence of a unique minimal model for positive uncertain databases, which characterizes the information content of the database. First, we need some definitions.

The *pure Herbrand base* H_D of an uncertain database D is the set of ground atoms that can be obtained using the symbols of D. A *Herbrand interpretation* I of D is a function that maps each atom in the Herbrand base H_D to a set of source vectors. That is, $I : H_D \longrightarrow 2^{\mathcal{V}}$, where $\mathcal{V}$ is the set of all source vectors.

We define a partial order $\leq$ on the set of Herbrand interpretations $\mathcal{I}_D$ of an uncertain database D as follows: For $I, J \in \mathcal{I}_D$, $I \leq J$ if and only if $I(A) \subseteq J(A)$ for all atoms $A \in H_D$. The set of interpretations $\mathcal{I}_D$ together with the partial order $\leq$ form a lattice $\mathcal{L}$, with the following meet and join operations: Let $I_1, I_2 \in \mathcal{L}$, then $I_1 \otimes I_2 = I$, where $I(A) = I_1(A) \cap I_2(A)$, for all $A \in H_D$. Similarly $I_1 \oplus I_2 = I$, where $I(A) = I_1(A) \cup I_2(A)$, for all $A \in H_D$.

An interpretation I of an uncertain database D satisfies a ground instance of a rule $(p \leftarrow q_1, \ldots, q_n)@x$ if $I(p) \supseteq x \overset{s}{\wedge} I(q_1) \overset{s}{\wedge} \ldots \overset{s}{\wedge} I(q_n)$. An interpretation I of an uncertain database D satisfies a rule r if it satisfies all ground instances of r. An interpretation I of an uncertain database D is a *model* of D if it satisfies all the rules in D.

Now we can show the "model intersection" property for positive uncertain databases. That is, the meet of two Herbrand models of a positive uncertain database D is also a Herbrand model of D. The proofs have not been included here to save space. Interested readers are referred to the full paper for proofs.

Lemma 2. *Let $\mathcal{L}$ be the lattice of Herbrand interpretations of an uncertain database D, and $M_1, M_2 \in \mathcal{L}$ be Herbrand models of D. Then $M = M_1 \otimes M_2$ is also a Herbrand model of D.*

The *least* model of an uncertain database D is defined as a Herbrand model M_D of D such that for every Herbrand model M of D we have $M_D \subseteq M$. It follows from the above lemma that the meet (intuitively, intersection) of all Herbrand models of a positive uncertain database D is also a model of D, and it is the least model of D.

Theorem 3. *Let D be a positive uncertain database. Then D has a least model M_D that is equal to the intersection of all models of D.*

The least model of an uncertain database D characterizes the information content of D. In fact, we can regard the least model of an uncertain database as a collection of relations (instances), as in the relational model, and evaluate queries against this relational interpretation. The characterization of the least model as the intersection of the models does not provide an effective algorithm to obtain the least model. In what follows we will introduce the *immediate consequence operator*, T_D, and show that its least fixpoint coincides with the least model for positive uncertain databases. This provides an effective algorithm for the computation of the least model.

4.1 The Immediate Consequence Operator T_D and its Fixpoint

Given a positive uncertain database, the operator T_D maps interpretations of D into interpretations of D. That is $T_D : \mathcal{I} \rightarrow \mathcal{I}$, where $\mathcal{I}$ is the set of all interpretations of D. Let $I \in \mathcal{I}$, $T_D(I)$ is defined as follows. Let $(p \leftarrow q_{i1}, \dots q_{in_i})@x_i$, $i = 1, \dots, m$, be all the ground instances of rules in D that have p in the head, then,

$$T_D(I)(p) = \overset{s}{\vee}_{i=1}^{m} V_i \tag{1}$$

where $V_i = x_i \overset{s}{\wedge} I(q_{i1}) \overset{s}{\wedge} \dots \overset{s}{\wedge} I(q_{in_i})$. The following example shows how T_D works.

Example 1. The uncertain database D is the following set of facts and rules:
road(a,b) @ 1 ⊤ ⊤ ⊤ ⊤
road(b,c) @ ⊤ 1 ⊤ ⊤ ⊤
road(c,d) @ ⊤ ⊤ 1 ⊤ ⊤
(reach(X,Y) ← road(X,Y)) @ ⊤ ⊤ ⊤ 1 ⊤
(reach(X,Y) ← road(X,Z), reach(Z,Y)) @ ⊤ ⊤ ⊤ ⊤ 1
Starting from the interpretation $I = \phi$, the result of applying T_D repeatedly is shown below (only the new facts are shown for each iteration):

First iteration	*Second iteration*
road(a,b) @ 1 ⊤ ⊤ ⊤ ⊤	reach(a,b) @ 1 ⊤ ⊤ 1 ⊤
road(b,c) @ ⊤ 1 ⊤ ⊤ ⊤	reach(b,c) @ ⊤ 1 ⊤ 1 ⊤
road(c,d) @ ⊤ ⊤ 1 ⊤ ⊤	reach(c,d) @ ⊤ ⊤ 1 1 ⊤
Third iteration	*Fourth iteration*
reach(a,c) @ 1 1 ⊤ 1 1	reach(a,d) @ 1 1 1 1 1
reach(b,d) @ ⊤ 1 1 1 1	

Nothing new is generated during the fifth iteration.

The result is actually the *least fixpoint* of T_D for this example, which is equal to the least model of D. We will discuss these issues below. □

Definitions. The *pre-fixpoint* of T_D is an interpretation $I \in \mathcal{L}$ such that $T_D(I) \leq I$. If $T_D(I) = I$ then I is a *fixpoint* of T_D. The *least fixpoint* of T_D is an interpretation $I \in \mathcal{L}$ that is a fixpoint of T_D such that for all fixpoints $I' \in \mathcal{L}$ of T_D we have $I \leq I'$. An operator T_D is *monotonic* if for all $I, J \in \mathcal{L}$, if $I \leq J$ then $T_D(I) \leq T_D(J)$.

Proofs of the following results can be found in the full paper.

Lemma 4. *An interpretation I of a positive uncertain database D is a model of D if and only if it is a pre-fixpoint of T_D, that is, if and only if $T_D(I) \leq I$, where $\leq$ is the partial order of the lattice $\mathcal{L}$ of the interpretations of D.*

Lemma 5. *The operator T_D is monotone.*

Theorem 6. *Let D be a positive uncertain database, then the least fixpoint of T_D is the least model of D.*

5 Top-Down and Bottom-Up Evaluation

Materializing the minimal model of an uncertain database D by repeated applications of the T_D operator, and evaluating a query against it will be inefficient in general. Two classes of methods have been extensively explored for logic programming and query processing in deductive databases. The first class, often referred to as top-down (or goal-directed) methods, are based on theorem proving techniques (e.g. the SLD-resolution technique). They benefit from the structure of the goal to be proven to reduce the search space. These techniques are more suitable for logic programming applications. Their record-at-a-time behaviour makes it difficult to integrate them into database systems, where a rich repertoire of query optimization techniques is available.

The second class, bottom-up methods, can be readily combined with database query processing and optimization techniques. There has been a substantial interest in these methods in recent years, resulting in optimization techniques that can also benefit from the structure, e.g. the constant values, of the query to reduce further the search space.

In this section we will briefly study the application of these techniques to the IST-based uncertain deductive databases.

5.1 SLD-Resolution for Uncertain Databases

The top-down computation process in logic programming, known as the *SLD-resolution*, can be extended to our model. In the following discussion we assume the reader is familiar with SLD-resolution [1, 10]. Because of space limitations we will only include a brief discussion here. Deatils can be found in the full paper. We need to add the manipulation of source vectors to classical SLD-resolution. The idea is to "combine" the sets of source vectors of the rules and facts used in the resolution process, by source vector conjunction. If the resolution succeeds, then the combined set of source vectors is the annotation for the goal clause.

It is well known that SLD-resolution method produces one answer at a time, while in database applications we are usually interested in all answers. In our model even for a single ground instance of an IDB predicate there may be several derivations in the SLD-resolution, which might produce different sets of source vectors. To produce an accurate answer to a query, we need to produce all answers, i.e. all ground instances, and for each instance, all corresponding source vectors. However, producing fewer source vectors sacrifices completeness, but not correctness. The reliability calculation algorithm is monotonic with respect to sets of source vectors, hence we are protected against concluding a higher degree of validity for an answer that is implied by the database. In other words, the results will be "conservative" if some of the source vectors are eliminated.

5.2 Bottom-Up Query Processing

The advantage of top-down evaluation over straightforward bottom-up techniques is in using the structure of the goal, e.g. constants appearing in the goal clause, to reduce the search space. A straightforward bottom-up evaluation will generally generate a large number of facts which are not relevant to the query. Rule rewriting techniques have been introduced to "mimic" the goal-oriented evaluation. Magic sets and templates method [3, 13] adds certain predicates and rules to the database, which eliminate the generation of irrelevant facts during a bottom-up evaluation. The same techniques can be used for uncertain databases. The only difference is that the true source vector $(\top, \ldots, \top)$ is associated with the new rules, while the source vectors of the modified rules remain unchanged. We will demonstrate the process using an example adapted from [19].

Example 2. Consider the following rules in an uncertain database (we are not showing the facts for brevity).

(sg(X,X) ← person(X)) @ u
(sg(X,Y) ← par(X,Xp), sg(Xp,Yp), par(Y,Yp)) @ v

Assume the query to be answered is sg(a,W), where "a" is a constant. The Magic sets algorithm generates the fact m_s(a) @ $(\top, \ldots, \top)$, and the following rules:

(m_s(Xp) ← $\text{sup}_{2.1}$(X,Xp)) @ $(\top, \ldots, \top)$
($\text{sup}_{1.0}$(X) ← m_s(X)) @ $(\top, \ldots, \top)$
($\text{sup}_{2.0}$(X) ← m_s(X)) @ $(\top, \ldots, \top)$
($\text{sup}_{2.1}$(X,Xp) ← $\text{sup}_{2.0}$(X), par(X,Xp)) @ $(\top, \ldots, \top)$
($\text{sup}_{2.2}$(X,Yp) ← $\text{sup}_{2.1}$(X,Xp), sg(Xp,Yp)) @ $(\top, \ldots, \top)$
(sg(X,X) ← $\text{sup}_{1.0}$(X), person(X)) @ u
(sg(X,Y) ← $\text{sup}_{2.2}$(X,Yp), par(Y,Yp)) @ v

The idea then is to evaluate the modified program above using the bottom-up evaluation strategy for uncertain databases.

6 Incorporating Negation

Up to now we had restricted our attention to positive uncertain databases. In this section we will see how rules with negative literals in their bodies can be handled in the IST-based uncertain databases. Because of space restriction we will only give a brief discussion. Details can be found in the full paper.

A subclass of general logic programs and deductive databases, that of *stratified* programs and databases, have received considerable attention. Intuitively, a stratified program or database allows negation in rule bodies, but the query processing can be carried out in such a manner that a negative literal in the body of a rule is completely evaluated before the rule is ever needed. More precisely, a deductive database D, with negative literals in the body of its rules, is *stratified* if the predicates of D can be partitioned into sets $P_1, \ldots, P_k$ such that, for all rules r of D, if $p \in P_i$ is the head predicate of r and q $(\neg q)$ appears in the body of r, then $q \in P_j$ for some $j \leq i$ $(j < i)$. The P_i's are called the *strata* of D. Stratified databases can have more than one minimal model, but there is a unique minimal model among them, called the *perfect model*, that coincides with the following procedural semantics [2]: To materialize the derived predicates of a stratified deductive database, compute the predicates in the order of the strata, starting with the lowest stratum, P_1.

It should be obvious that the same approach can be applied to *stratified uncertain databases*. A stratified uncertain database is defined as an IST-based deductive database where the rules, without source vectors, form a stratified program. The source vector negation operation described in Section 3 is needed for the manipulation of source vectors for negative literals. For example, for a rule of the form $(p \leftarrow q_1, \ldots, q_n, \neg r_1, \ldots, \neg r_m)@x$ in the stratified uncertain database D, if $q_i@U_i$, $i = 1, \ldots, n$ and $r_j@V_j$, $j = 1, \ldots, m$ are already obtained, then, we can derive:

$$p@(U_1 \overset{s}{\wedge} \ldots \overset{s}{\wedge} U_n \overset{s}{\wedge} (\overset{s}{\neg} V_1) \overset{s}{\wedge} \ldots \overset{s}{\wedge} (\overset{s}{\neg} V_m) \overset{s}{\wedge} x)$$

7 Conclusions

In the Information Source Tracking (IST) method accuracy (certainty) of data is modeled by the reliability of information source(s) contributing to the data. In this paper we extended the IST method to deductive databases, and studied query processing techniques for this model. We showed how SLD-resolution, a top-down (or goal-directed) query processing technique used in logic programming, can be extended to our model. Similarly, the magic sets method, a rule-rewriting technique used in conjunction with bottom-up query evaluation in deductive databases, was also extended to our model. Finally, we studied negation for IST deductive databases, and demonstrated that stratified negation can be handled in a similar manner to regular deductive databases.

In the IST method, the calculation of numerical measures of certainty (validity) of answers to queries is done as the last (optional) step of the query processing process. The query processing manipulates data as well as contributing source information, identifying for answers to a query, the contributing sources and their nature of contribution. From this information the certainty measures can be calculated. Consequently, IST method is capable of modeling (probabilistic) data interdependencies, an issue which causes substantial difficulties in other systems. Algorithms for certainty calculations in IST were not given in this paper due to space limitations, and can be found in [14, 16].

References

1. K. R. Apt, "Introduction to Logic Programming." Technical Report CS-R8741, September 1987, Centre for Mathematics and Computer Science, Computer Science/Department of Software Technology, The Netherlands.
2. K. R. Apt, H. A. Blair, and A. Walker, "Towards a Theory of Declarative Knowledge." in Foundations of Deductive Databases and Logic Programming, J. Minker Ed., Morgan Kaufmann, 1988, pp 89-148.

3. F. Bancilhon, D. Maier, Y. Sagiv, and J.D. Ullman, "Magic Sets and Other Strange Ways to Implement Logic Programs." Proceedings of the 1986 ACM Symposium on Principles of Database Systems, pp 1-15.
4. D. Barbara, H. Garcia-Molina, and D. Porter, "The Management of Probabilistic Data." IEEE Transactions on Knowledge and Data Engineering, Vol. 4, No. 5, October 1992, pp 487-502.
5. M. Kifer, and A. Li, "On the Semantics of Rule-Based Expert Systems with Uncertainty." Proceedings of the 2nd International Conference on Database Theory, Springer Verlag LNCS 326, M. Gyssens, J. Paredaens, and D. Van Gucht, eds., 1988, pp 102-117.
6. V. S. Lakshmanan, "Query Processing with Null Values: How Complex is Completeness?" Proc. Int'l Conf. Foundations of Software Technology and Theoretical Computer Science, Bangalore, December 1989, Lecture Notes in Computer Science, Vol. 405, pp 204-222, Springer, 1989.
7. Suk Kyoon Lee, "Imprecise and Uncertain Information in Databases: An Evidential Approach." Proceedings of the 1992 IEEE International Conference on Data Engineering, pp 614-621.
8. K-C. Liu, and R. Sunderraman, "Indefinite and Maybe Information in Relational Databases." ACM TODS, Vol. 15, No. 1, March 1990, pp 1-39.
9. K-C. Liu, and R. Sunderraman, "A Generalized Relational Model for Indefinite and Maybe Information." IEEE Transactions on Knowledge and Data Engineering, Vol. 3, No. 1, March 1991, pp 65-77.
10. J. W. Lloyd, *Foundations of Logic Programming*, Springer-Verlag, 1984.
11. R. Ng, and V. S. Subrahmanian, "A Semantical Framework for Supporting Subjective and Conditional Probabilities in Deductive Databases." Tech. Rep. No. CS-TR-2563, Dept. of Computer Science, University of Maryland, November 1990.
12. N. J. Nilsson, "Probabilistic Logic." Artificial Intelligence, Vol. 28, 1986, pp 71-87.
13. R. Ramakrishnan, "Magic Templates: A Spellbinding Approach to Logic Programs." Proc. Fifth Int'l Symp. on Logic Programming, 1988, pp 140-159.
14. F. Sadri "Reliability of Answers to queries in Relational Databases." IEEE Transactions on Knowledge and Data Engineering, Vol. 3, No. 2, June 91, pp 245-251.
15. F. Sadri "Modeling Uncertainty in Databases." Proceedings of the 1991 IEEE International Conference on Data Engineering, pp 122-131.
16. F. Sadri, "Information Source Tracking Method: Efficiency Issues." Manuscript. December 1992. Submitted for publication.
17. F. Sadri "Integrity Constraints in the Information Source Tracking Method." To appear in IEEE Transactions on Knowledge and Data Engineering.
18. A. Silberschatz, M. Stonebraker, and J. D. Ullman, "Database Systems: Achievements and Opportunities." Comm. ACM, Vol. 34, No. 10, October 1991, pp 110-120.
19. J. D. Ullman, *Principles of Database and Knowledge-Base Systems, Volume II,* Computer Science Press, 1989.
20. J. D. Ullman, "Bottom-up Beats Top-down for Datalog." Proceedings of the 1989 ACM Symposium on Principles of Database Systems, pp 140-149.
21. M. H. Van Emden, "Quantitative Deduction and its Fixpoint Theory." Journal of Logic Programming, Vol. 4, No. 1, 1986, pp 37-53.
22. M. H. Van Emden, and R. A. Kowalski, "The Semantics of Predicate Logic as a Programming Language." Journal of the ACM, Vol. 23, No. 4, October 1976, pp 733-742.

Dependency-Directed Binding of Variables For Constraint Logic Programming

G. Papakonstantinou C. Voliotis, N. M. Sgouros

National Technical University of Athens
Department of Electrical and Computer Engineering
Zografou Campus, GR-15773, Athens, Greece
E-mail: papakon@theseas.ntua.gr

Abstract: Constraint Logic Programming (CLP) environments should be able to delay, if necessary, the evaluation of variables in a constraint (e.g. equation) until they become bound at some later point in processing. This paper presents a general method for supporting the automatic creation of delayed bindings in CLP environments that is applicable not only in the case of constraints but for any predicate in a logic rule as well. Consequently this method supports rule representations in CLP languages with no restrictions on the ordering of subgoals.

Keywords: *Knowledge Engineering, Expert Systems Architecture, Deductive Databases.*

1. Introduction

The creation and support of large and complex databases and expert systems is greatly facilitated with the development of CLP languages that support complex types (e.g. constraints) [1,2]. The introduction of these types poses new requirements on the processing of subgoals in these environments. As the following example indicates, delayed evaluation of variables for logic rules becomes necessary in CLP environments.

Let us assume that we have the system of equations:

$$D = C \times 2,\ K = B \times 3$$
$$C = A + 1,\ B = D + -3$$

which we want to solve for B and K given that A is known (e.g. A=2). A rule for solving this system in a CLP language can be written as:

$$s(A,B,K) :- D = C \times 2,\ K = B \times 3,\ C = A + 1,\ B = D + -3.$$

where $\times$ and $+$ correspond to constraints for integer multiplication and addition respectively. These constraints produce a value for the third variable whenever the other two are bound. For example if Y and Z are known, then $X=Y\times Z$ binds X to their product, while if X and Z are known, then Y binds to the value for X/Z and so on. A Prolog interpreter is unable to answer the query ?s(2,B,K), because the subgoal $D=C\times 2$ (or more precisely *D is C*2* in Prolog) fails since both D and C are unbound at the time of evaluation. However, this should not be the case because when the subgoal $C=A+1$ is executed later in the rule C gets bound to 2 and the whole rule execution produces values for both K and B.

Until recently Logic Programming (LP) systems tried to deal with this problem either with the explicit introduction of a *freeze(X,P)* predicate in the program which postpones the interpretation of P until X is bound, or with multiple definitions of predicates that take into consideration all possible cases for determining the values of variables [1]. Both solutions are inadequate because in the case of the *freeze* predicate it requires from the programmer to explicitly identify the cases for which delayed binding should be used in the program, while in the second case the user is required to supply all possible binding scenarios for a predicate.

In this paper we describe a general solution to this problem based on attribute grammars (AGs) [3]. AGs were proposed by Knuth [4] as a formalism for the definition of semantics of context-free languages (CFLs). Our group has studied AGs extensively during the last years and we have described several AG parsers [5,6]. The relation of AGs with LP has also been examined [5]. It has been shown that using AGs it is possible to develop logic systems with full theorem proving as well as inexact reasoning capabilities [7,8].

This paper describes a novel method that extends the applicability of AGs from logic programming to the implementation of CLP environments. The method creates automatically a dependency network between the variables of a rule. For each variable in a rule we indicate the rightmost predicate in the rule on which the binding of the variable depends and delay the binding of the variable until this predicate is evaluated. This method is based on a technique known as 'semantically driven parsing of CFLs' (SDP) [6] and used for multipass parsing of AGs. This research extends this technique by describing semantic rules that allow SDP to support the implementation of CLP languages.

The paper is organised as follows. Section 2 briefly describes AGs and gives an overview of the SDP technique. Section 3 explains how we use AGs and SDP in logic programming. Section 4 describes how we extend the SDP method to support the construction of CLP languages. Section 5 gives an example for the application of this new method. Section 6 presents the conclusions and some future work for extending this research. Finally there are two appendices that analyze in more detail the example of section 5.3.

2. Attribute Grammars and Semantically-Driven Parsing of CFLs.

An AG is based on a Context-Free Grammar (CFG) G=(N,T,P,Z), where N is the set of non-terminal symbols, T is the set of terminal symbols, P is the set of syntactic rules and Z (which is an element of N) is the start symbol. Each symbol X in the vocabulary V ($V=N\cup T$) has an associated set of attributes A(X), which is partitioned in two disjoint sets; the set of inherited attributes *IA(X)* and the set of synthesised attributes *SA(X)*. Each syntax rule (production) is augmented with semantic rules and conditions which give and test the values of the attributes in each application of the syntax rule.

An AG parser creates the parse trees which correspond to a derivation of a string of terminals. An AG evaluator gives values and tests the values of the attribute instances of every node of the parse tree according to the predefined semantics. The compound dependency graph D(t) of a parse tree t is constructed in such a way that its arcs go from (X_i,a_j) to (X_k,a_l) if the value of a_l depends directly on the value of a_j. (Note that X_i,X_k are nodes of the parse tree, and a_j, a_l are attributes of these nodes).

while there are semantically correct parse trees of the input string **do**
find a semantically correct parse tree using Floyd's parser modified to call the algorithm of Fig. 2 for each new node; evaluate synthesised attributes of root of the parse tree;

Fig. 1. General description of the parsing algorithm.

```
i = 1;
 repeat
   flag := true;
   evaluate all semantic rules (that can be evaluated) of alternative i of the
   nonterminal which is the label of node Y;
   for each node X of the already constructed parse tree do
      if right__end(X) = node__number(Y) then
         evaluate conditions of node X;
         if condition = false then
           flag := false; break;
   i := i + 1;
 until flag=true or alternative i does not exist;
```
(The algorithm returns control to the parser, which analyses the nonterminal which is the label of node Y, according to the ith alternative. If the ith alternative does not exist, the parser backtracks.

Fig. 2. Algorithm executed by the parser for each node under construction.

The parsing algorithm for semantically-driven parsing [6] is generally described in Fig. 1. It is a multipass AG evaluator based on the parser of Floyd [9]. Each time a new node of the parse tree is constructed, the algorithm of Fig. 2 is executed. The conditions are evaluated by an algorithm based on the incremental evaluator for AGs of Jalili [10].

SDP defines a function *node__number* that assigns a unique natural number to each node X of a parse tree t, in a top-down, left-to-right order. For each attribute instance n SDP defines the set *NW(X,n)* of node numbers of nodes X which have at least one attribute instance m which affects the value of n. The set of such m consists of those m for which there is an oriented path from m to n in D(t). For each n of a node X, SDP defines *right_end(X,n) = max{Y}*, where Y is an element of NW(X,n). For each X we also define *right_end(X) = max{right_end(X,n)}*.

Consequently, the function *right_end(X)* defines the remotest node whose attributes must be computed first, before the conditions of node X are evaluated. While parsing continues, only some attribute instances take values (from those semantic rules that can be evaluated). For every new node Y, all the conditions of the nodes X that have node Y as their right_end are evaluated. If the conditions of X do not pass the test, the next alternatives of Y are tried. If all the alternatives of Y fail, the algorithm backtracks to the predecessor of Y.

3. Logic Programming with Attribute Grammars

Floyd's parsing algorithm [9] has also been extended by our group towards a direction that enables us to use AGs for the implementation of CLP environments [5,7,8]. The basic idea is to transform a logic program into an equivalent AG, in the sense that when the AG is processed by an AG evaluator it will produce the same results as the logic program when processed by the inference mechanism. One pass AG evaluators (from left to right) are adequate for this purpose.

The transformation is simple: From each logic rule we extract a syntax rule (production) and the corresponding semantic rules and conditions. For each argument of each predicate symbol we define two attributes, one inherited (ia) and one synthesised (sa). The semantics are defined in such a way so that the values of the attribute instances in the parse tree correspond to the values of the arguments of the predicate symbols in the proof tree.

The input string is defined as the empty string, therefore the parser always succeeds, generating all the possible derivations. However, the parser calls the AG evaluator in predefined positions, and if the semantic conditions fail, then the parser backtracks. The parser fails to recognise the input string only when all the semantic conditions have failed. The constructed AG is the 'structure' that stores the knowledge (knowledge representation), while the parser with the semantics evaluator correspond to the inference mechanism (knowledge processing).

4. Constraint Logic Programming with AGs

We assume that the knowledge base can be written in the form of logic rules in a PROLOG-like notation as:

$$
\begin{array}{l}
R_0^{e}(t_{01}^{e}, ..., t_{0k_0}^{e}) \text{ is true if} \\
\quad R_1^{e}(t_{11}^{e}, ..., t_{1k_1}^{e}) \text{ is true and} \\
\quad \cdot \\
\quad \cdot \qquad\qquad\qquad\qquad (1) \\
\quad R_{me}^{e}(t_{me1}^{e}, ..., t_{mek_{me}}^{e}) \text{ is true}
\end{array}
$$

where t_{ij}^{e}, $0 \le i \le me$, $1 \le j \le k_i$, $1 \le e \le n$ is a constant or a variable, and e is the rule number, assuming that the rules are numbered from 1 to n. If me=0 then the rule is a fact. For each logic rule a corresponding syntax rule and corresponding semantic rules can be written for an 'equivalent' attribute grammar. An equivalent attribute grammar is one which when processed by an attribute grammar evaluator will give the same results with the corresponding logic program consisting of rules as in (1).

The corresponding syntax rule for the logic rule (1) is written as:

$$\langle R_0{}^e\rangle = \langle R_1{}^e\rangle ... \langle R_{me}{}^e\rangle \mid \blacklozenge$$

where the combination of the last two characters signifies the end of the syntax rule.

For each logic rule (1) the corresponding semantic rules of the equivalent AG can be written in a mechanical way. With each $R_g{}^e$ symbol we associate k_g synthesized attributes $sa_j(R_g{}^e)$, $1 \le j \le k_g$ and k_g inherited attributes $ia_j(R_g{}^e)$, $1 \le j \le k_g$. Each pair of these attributes corresponds to each of the k_g arguments of $R_g{}^e$, e.g. $sa_j(R_g{}^e)$ means the synthesized attribute of $R_g{}^e$ corresponding to its jth parameter.

In order to support the automatic generation of delayed bindings in a CLP environment we extend SDP with a set of eight tranformation rules. Table 1 describes this set of rules. Each column in the table represents a transformation rule. The second row in the table describes the conditions under which each rule is applicable, while the third row describes the actions taken by each rule. Table 1 summarizes all possible cases for the term $R_g{}^e$, $1 \le e \le n$, $1 \le g \le me$ of a logic rule and for the parameter $t_{gi}{}^e$, $1 \le i \le k_g$, of $R_g{}^e$.

We note here that the organisation of the AG parser in our method allows the user to supply additional semantic rules. These rules have to be written in the language in which the AG evaluator is developed and they can be used in conjunction with the produced semantics to enhance the capabilities of the system with procedural knowledge such as simplex or approximate methods for solving systems of constraints based on the attributes for each node in the parse tree.

5. An illustrative example

This example indicates how the extended AG parser handles rules in CLP environments. Let us assume again that we have the logic rule (2):

s(A,B,K) :- D = C × 2, K = B × 3, C = A + 1, B = D + -3. (2)

and we pose the query ?s(2,B,K). Rule (2) is transformed by the system into the following AG syntax rule shown with the corresponding variables for each symbol in the rule:

‹S› ::=	‹Mult›$_1$	‹Mult›$_2$	‹Add›$_1$	‹Add›$_2$ |♦	*Rule2*
(A,B,K)	(D,C,2)	(K,B,3)	(C,A,1)	(B,D,-3)	

Based on this rule and using our dependency-directed binding method the AG interpreter creates the dependency graph for rule 2 (see Figure 3) and evaluates the attributes. No matter what the query is, the system finally evaluates the

	0	1	2	3	4	5	6	7
CONDITION	t_{gi}^e is a constant c and g=0	$t_{gi}^e$is a variable and there is no other occurence of this variable to the left and e=1 (query)	$t_{gi}^e$is a constant and g#0	$t_{gi}^e$is a variable and g=0	$t_{gi}^e$is a variable and t_{qj}^e is the nearest textual occurence of same variable to the left of t^e_{gi}, q=0 and g#0	$t_{gi}^e$is the first occurence of a variable from the left and t^e_{qj} is the last occurence of this variable to the right and g#0	$t^e_{gi}$is a variable and t^e_{qj} is the nearest textual occurence of the same variable to the left of t^e_{gi}, also q#g and g#0 and q#0	there are many occurences of the same variable in a relation $R^e{}_g{}^e$
ACTIONS	if $ia_i(R_g{}^e)$ # c and $ia_i(R_g{}^e)$ # nil then flag := FALSE else $sa_i(R_g{}^e)$:= c	$ia_i(R_g{}^e)$:= $sa_i(Rg^e)$	$ia_i(R_g{}^e)$:= c	if t_{gi} is the only occurence of the variable inthe rule then $sa_i(R_g{}^e)$:= $ia_i(R_q{}^e)$ else if t_{qj} is the last textual occurence of the same variable in the production e $sa_i(R_g{}^e)$:= $sa_j(R_q{}^e)$	$ia_i(R_g{}^e)$:= $ia_j(R_q{}^e)$	$ia_i(R_g{}^e)$:= $sa_j(R_q{}^e)$	$ia_i(R_g{}^e)$:= $sa_j(R_q{}^e)$	if all the variables have not the same value or those which are different are not nil then flag := FALSE else make those which are nil take the value of the others.

Table 1. Semantics for parameter $t_{gi}{}^e$ of $R_g{}^e$.

synthesised attributes of the parameters for the example, given of course that at least one of the query's inherited attributes is instantiated. The query ?s(2,B,K) is evaluated correctly according to the dependency graph of Figure 3 resulting in B=3, K=9. In Appendix I the automatically generated semantic rules are given, based on Table 1. In Appendix II the semantics evaluation tracing is given, based on the semantic rules of Appendix I.

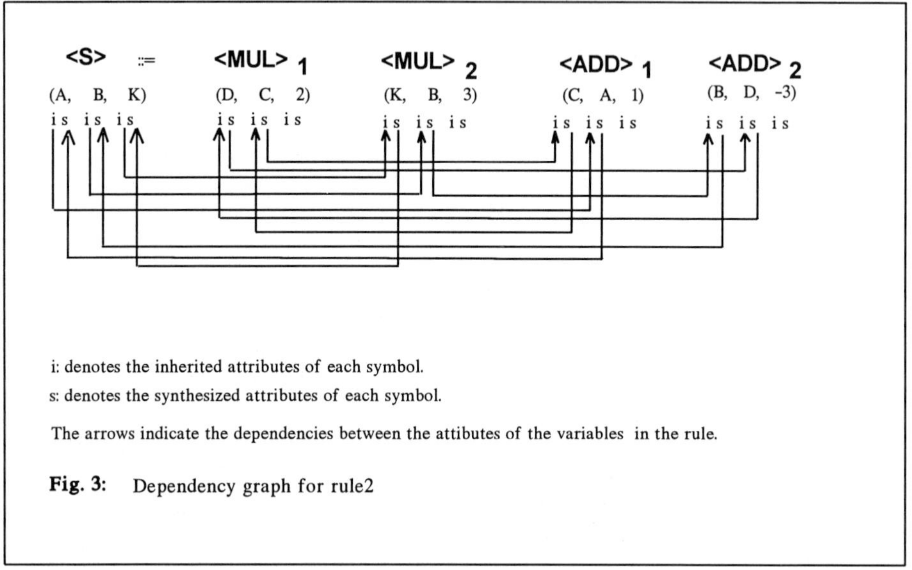

i: denotes the inherited attributes of each symbol.

s: denotes the synthesized attributes of each symbol.

The arrows indicate the dependencies between the attibutes of the variables in the rule.

Fig. 3: Dependency graph for rule2

6. Conclusions and Future Work

We described a method that automatically creates delayed bindings in CLP environments. The method generates a dependency network between the variables of the rule in compile time that guides the binding of variables of a logic rule during execution. We showed how dependency-directed binding of variables facilitates the implementation of CLP languages by allowing representations for rules without any restrictions on the ordering of subgoals. The method is general enough and applies not only to constraints but to any predicate in a logic rule as well.

We have identified three areas in which this work can be extended. The first one concerns the development of intelligent backtracking facilities for CLP languages. In particular we are exploring the use of the dependencies created by our method in conjunction with *dependency-directed backtracing* techniques from pure constraint languages [11] to increase the efficiency of backtracking in CLP systems.

The second one is the creation of explanations for the behaviour of a logic program. Again we are exploring the use of the dependencies between the variables of a logic

rule along with representations of causal relations between the predicates of logic rules [12] to create more intuitive explanations for the program behaviour.
Finally we are exploring the parallel execution of the method in a transputer-based environment.

References

[1] Jacques Cohen, *Constraint Logic Programming Languages*, Communications of the ACM,vol. 33,no. 7,pp.52-68,July 1990.

[2] Pascal van Hentenryck, *Constraint Satisfaction in Logic Programming*, MIT Press, 1989.

[3] P. Deransart et al., *Attribute Grammars*, Goos G., Hartmanis J., (eds.), Springer-Verlag, 1988.

[4] D.E. Knuth, *Semantics of context free languages*,Mathematical Systems Theory, vol.2, no.2, pp.127-145, 1968 and vol.5, no.1, pp95-96, 1971.

[5] G. Papakonstantinou, C. Moraitis, T. Panayiotopoulos, *An Attribute Grammar Interpreter as a Knowledge Engineering Tool*, Angewandte Informatik, 9/86, pp.382-388, 1986.

[6] M. Sideri, S. Efremidis, G. Papakonstantinou, *Semantically Driven Parsing of Conext-free Languages*,The Computer Journal, vol.32, no.1, pp.91-93, 1989.

[7] T. Panayiotopoulos, G. Papakonstantinou, G. Stamatopoulos, *An Attribute Grammar Based Theorem Prover*, Information and Software Technology, vol.30, no.9, pp.553-560, November 1988.

[8] T. Panayiotopoulos, G. Papakonstantinou, N.M. Sgouros, *An Attribute Grammar Interpreter for Inexact Reasoning*, Information and Software Technology, vol.32, no.5, pp.347-356, June 1988.

[9] R. Floyd, *The syntax of programming languages-a survey,* IEEE Transactions on Electronic Computers, vol.EG-13, no.4, pp.346-353, 1964.

[10] F. Jalili, *A general incremental evaluator for attribute grammars*, Science of Computer Programming, vol.5, pp.83-96, 1985.

[11] K. Forbus, J. de Kleer, *Building Problem Solvers*,MIT Press, 1993.

[12] D. Weld, J. de Kleer (eds), *Readings in Qualitative Reasoning about Physical Systems*, Morgan Kaufmann, 1990.

APPENDIX I : Generated semantic rules

e=1.					
g=0		g=1			
Z	:-	S(A, B, K)	*;; Rule 1*		
e=2					
g=0		g=1	g=2	g=3	g=4
S(A, B, K)	:-	Mult1(D, C, 2)	Mult2(K, B, 3)	Add1(C, A, 1)	Add2(B, D, -3) *;; Rule 2*

#	Semantic Rule	Corresp. column of table1.	#	Semantic Rule	Corresp. column of table1.
	e=1, g=1			e=2, g=2	
1	$ia_1(S) := 2$	2	10	$ia_1(Mult2) := ia_3(S)$	4
2	$ia_2(S) := sa_2(S)$	1	11	$ia_2(Mult2) := ia_2(S)$	4
3	$ia_3(S) := sa_3(S)$	1	12	$ia_3(Mult2) := 3$	2
	e=2, g=0			e=2, g=3	
4	$sa_1(S) := sa_2(Add1)$	3	13	$ia_1(Add1) := sa_2(Mult1)$	6
5	$sa_2(S) := sa_1(Add2)$	3	14	$ia_2(Add1) := ia_1(S)$	4
6	$sa_3(S) := sa_1(Mult2)$	3	15	$ia_3(Add1) := 1$	2
	e=2, g=1			e=2, g=4	
7	$ia_1(Mult1) := sa_2(Add2)$	5	16	$ia_1(Add2) := sa_2(Mult2)$	6
8	$ia_2(Mult1) := sa_1(Add1)$	5	17	$ia_2(Add2) := sa_1(Mult1)$	6
9	$ia_3(Mult1) := 2$	2	18	$ia_3(Add2) := -3$	2

Note: Rule 1 is generated automatically by the system for each user query. Z is the start symbol of the AG while the body of the rule corresponds to the user query. Rule 2 is the rule in the knowledge base. The *e* symbol indicates the rule number and the *g* symbol indicates the sequence number of each predicate in a rule. The *#* symbol in the table indicates the serial number of each generated semantic rule. The symbolism $ia_1(Mult2)$ indicates the inherited attribute corresponding to the first argument of the predicate Mult2. The rest of the ia and sa attributes in the table. should be interpreted in an analogous way.

APPENDIX II : Semantics evaluation tracing.

S(A, B, K) Multl(D, C, 2) Mult2(K, B, 3) Addl(C, A, 1) Add2(B, D, -3)

		A	B	K	D	C	2	K	B	3	C	A	1	B	D	-3
stepl		1			9			12			15			18		
	ia	2	-	-	-	-	2	-	-	3	-	-	1	-	-	-3
	sa	-	-	-	-	-	-	-	-	-	-	-	-	-	-	-
step2		4						12			17, Add					
	ia	2	-	-	-	-	2	-	-	3	-	2	1	-	-	-3
	sa	2	-	-	-	-	-	-	-	-	3	2	1	-	-	-
step3					8, Multiply											
	ia	2	-	-	-	3	2	-	-	3	-	2	1	-	-	-3
	sa	2	-	-	6	3	2	-	-	-	3	2	1	-	-	-
step4											13			17, Add		
	ia	2	-	-	-	3	2	-	-	3	3	2	1	-	6	-3
	sa	2	-	-	6	3	2	-	-	-	3	2	1	3	6	-3
step5		5, 2			7			11, Multiply						16		
	ia	2	3	-	6	3	2	-	3	3	3	2	1	3	6	-3
	sa	2	3	-	6	3	2	9	3	3	3	2	1	3	6	-3
step6		6														
	ia	2	3	-	6	3	2	-	3	3	3	2	1	3	6	-3
	sa	2	3	9	6	3	2	9	3	3	3	2	1	3	6	-3

Note : The numbers at each 'stepi' line indicate the serial number of each semantic rule applied (Appendix I). The numbers at the lines 'ia', 'sa', indicate the values of the corresponding attributes. The symbol '-' indicates that an attribute has not yet received a value .

Flexible and Dynamic Integration of Multiple Information Bases

Hamideh Afsarmanesh, Michiel Wiedijk, L. O. Hertzberger

Computer Systems Department, University of Amsterdam,
email: hamideh@fwi.uva.nl, wiedijk@fwi.uva.nl, bob@fwi.uva.nl

Abstract. To support the information sharing in a high performance distributed network of cooperative nodes, a flexible and dynamic *integration facility* must be developed. A node in the network is typically one user behind his workstation. On one hand, the nodes in the network are developed and evolved independent of each other, primarily to support their local needs, and thus their independence and autonomy must be supported. On the other hand, some nodes tightly and some nodes loosely cooperate, therefore every node wishes to have access to a part of the information available in some other nodes. Since the nodes and their cooperation are intrinsically dynamic, the integration facility must support the systematic and incremental derivation/integration of the imported information from other nodes with the local information. The integration facility must also provide user-friendly interface tools to ease the burden of information integration and the consistency checking for complex interrelationships established among the nodes. These requirements of multiple information base integration, that we claim to be fundamental in supporting the inter-operability of cooperating autonomous nodes are addressed in this paper by a novel approach. In specific, the paper presents the definition and manipulation of object clusters and two interface tools, the Schema Manipulation Tool and the Database Browsing Tool to assist users with their integration of nodes' information. The concepts described in this paper are developed and prototypically implemented as a part of the PEER object-oriented federated information management system [1].

keywords: object-oriented databases, federated databases, cooperation network, distributed schema management, schema integration

1 Introduction

A high performance distributed and inter-operable platform consists of a network of teams of heterogeneous and autonomous systems (nodes). Every node in the network has a distinct information management system that properly supports the local needs of the node. Many of the todays' large existing applications, such as the banking and reservation systems and the public and private chain-organizations as well as the recently growing applications of engineering design and manufacturing and the medical and biological studies fall in this category of inter-operable systems. These systems require strong support for their information sharing and integration of their multiple information systems. To support the information sharing and exchange of knowledge/data in such

[1] The work described here has been partially supported by the ESPRIT II project P2256 - ARCHON.

network, two kinds of cooperation must be supported. A tight-cooperation that may exist among the nodes within a specific cooperation team, and a loose-cooperation that can be established among the nodes that belong to different cooperation teams.

The main focus of this paper is to address two important requirements of high performance inter-operable platforms. First, a modeling construct and a set of functions are defined to support the creation, access and transformation of *object-clusters* among different representation environments in different nodes. The transformation of object clusters from the information base environment (e.g abstract data type representation), to the application development environment (e.g. concrete data structures) are addressed. Second, an *integration facility* is described that introduces two user-friendly interface tools for data and meta-data manipulation in the cooperative environment. An interface tool SMT (Schema Manipulation Tool) is introduced to support the manipulation of the schema-definitions, schema-derivations, and schema-integrations within the network of nodes. This is a necessary tool to support complex interrelated schemas defined among different nodes since it automatically performs many syntactic and semantic consistency checks when the definition of one schema is modified in the node. Another user-friendly tool DBT (Database Browsing Tool) is introduced to support the user of the node with browsing through both data and meta-data (schemas) accessible through the node. The browsing tool replaces the need for an interface language by which the user of a node can access both local and remote information, while hiding the physical distribution of the information. Both the integration mechanism and the modeling concepts described in this paper are implemented within the framework of the PEER federated object management system [5]. PEER aims at providing a common information-representation, -access, -retrieval, and -management environment, where all nodes in the cooperation network are equal (i.e. peers) in their powers and in maintaining their interest in the network.

More details on the federated database architecture of PEER and its distributed schema management language can be found in [4]. Detailed description of the distributed query evaluation; namely, the conversion algorithms for derived types and derived mappings, kernel-storage of the converted information, query decomposition, and query rewriting are presented in [5]. Other topics, outside the scope of this paper are versions, data update problems regarding the shared schemas, optimization of distributed query processing, transaction management and distributed concurrency control that are subjects of forthcoming papers.

The remainder of the paper is organized as follows. Section 2 provides a brief overview of the PEER system, describing its architecture and the object model and object retrieval and update language. Section 3 presents the object-cluster handling and its linearization mechanism. Section 4 discusses the integration facility and presents two user-friendly interface tools, SMT and DBT. Finally, Section 5 presents the conclusion of the paper. All examples presented in this paper are chosen from the hospital application domain. The examples address the integration of distributed information stored in a chain of hospitals with many branches located in different cities.

2 Overview of PEER

PEER is a federated object-oriented information management system developed to support the sharing and exchange of information among cooperating autonomous and heterogeneous nodes [5]. The PEER federated architecture consists of a network of tightly/loosely interrelated nodes. Both the *information* and the *control* is distributed within the network. Namely, PEER can be characterized by: (1) There is no single global schema defined on the shared information, unlike many other distributed object-oriented database systems (such as in [8], to support the entire network of database systems. (2) The interdependencies between two nodes' information is established through the schemas defined on their information; thus there is no need to store the data redundantly in different nodes. (3) There is no central (global) control within the network. The functionality of the PEER federated system is supported by the specific architecture of each PEER node and its PEER-*kernel*, and by the existence of the *community dictionary* in the network. A prototype implementation of PEER federated system is developed in the C language that runs on a network of SUN workstations. The main applications where the PEER system has been or is being applied are within the two ESPRIT projects ARCHON and CIM-PLATO, and within the RACE project DESSERT.

2.1 Architecture

Every PEER node in the cooperation network contains several interrelated schemas (i.e. LOC, IMPs, EXPs and INT schemas described in Section 4). The PEER-*kernel* is itself a predefined schema that acts as a unifying superstructure to support the investigation of data, meta-data, and meta-meta-data of the PEER [5]. It primarily supports the representation of multiple schemas, the information on the node's involvement in the cooperation network and provides an environment to model the schema integration/derivation relationships. The meta-meta-data is the information that describes the meta-data (schema elements) of the database. Therefore, any component of a typical schema, such as types and maps, as well as the schema definitions themselves (being derived such as INT,or defined such as LOC), and their interrelationships are all systematically represented in the PEER-kernel.

The *community dictionary* is the 'source of information' within the network and can be consulted at any time by other nodes. Its function is to provide up-to-date information on all nodes in the network. It contains the network addresses of the active nodes and their current state. For every node, it also stores its export schemas and the specific access rights and schema modification rights that the node supports. The dictionary can also be used as the general store for other static information that concerns the entire community such as objects' name-tables. Although, in the architectural design of PEER the community dictionary is represented as a separate node to be accessed when needed, any other node in the community can keep local copies of all or parts of its information.

2.2 Information model and Language

The PEER information base model and the PEER language has roots in the 3DIS [2] database model and the 3DIS/ISL language [3]. The PEER data model is a binary-based object-oriented database model. Any identifiable piece of information is uniformly represented as objects. It represents atomic, composite, and type objects. A type object is a structural specification of a group of atomic or composite objects. It denotes a collection of database objects called its members (instances). The PEER supports multiple inheritance; the subtype/supertype relationships defined among types form a Directed Acyclic Graph (DAG). The information retrieval/manipulation language designed for

PEER supports both the local access and modification of nodes' information, and the remote access and sharing of information among nodes. The retrieval of information is based on queries on binary relations among objects [5].

3 Manipulation of Object-clusters

In PEER all information is uniformly modeled by inter-related objects. A collection of inter-related objects can be defined and viewed as a single *object-cluster*. An example object-cluster (see Figure 1) defines a patient-record that contains the patient's name, and several cases of illnesses; where every case of illness is defined by the doctor who treated it, and the examination-record; where the doctor is defined by the name; and where an examination-record is described by the tests-results and the status report While some other works, choose a specific attribute 'PART-OF' as the only attribute inter-connecting objects in an object-cluster definition [9, 11], in PEER object-clusters are defined as instances of cluster-templates. This approach regulates the definition of object-clusters uniformly to the type/member definition, and it further supports the definition and manipulation of object-clusters that are distributed over several nodes in the network, as addressed in [13]. In this paper however, we describe a specific implementation approach to object-clusters and cluster templates in a PEER node in the network.

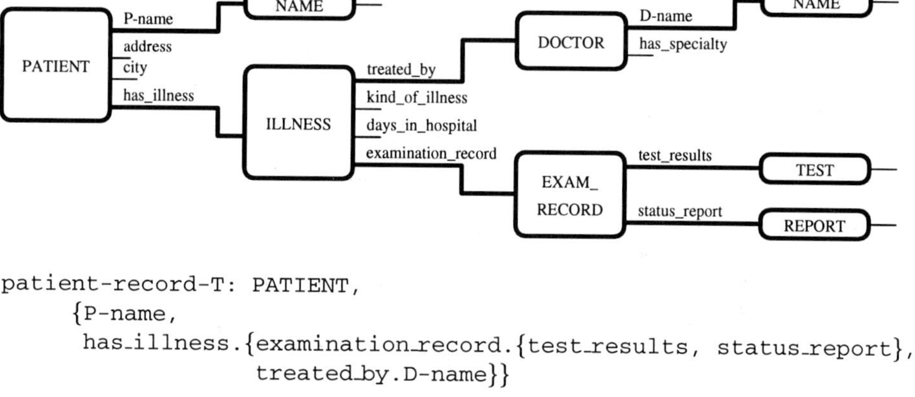


```
patient-record-T: PATIENT,
     {P-name,
      has_illness.{examination_record.{test_results, status_report},
                   treated_by.D-name}}
```

Fig. 1. The template defined for the object-cluster patient-record-T

Both interactive users and the application programs need support for retrieving and updating large object-clusters as single entities. The impedance mismatch between the information base environment and the application development environment is most severely felt when object-clusters are retrieved. Here, we resolve this problem by retrieving an object-cluster as a single entity in the *linear format* of a list of lists, that we refer to as *A-list* in this paper. A set of operations (functions) are also developed that support the creation, retrieval and transfer of object-clusters in form of A-lists that are described in Section 3.3. As such an object-cluster can be transferred to a C program as a list of lists. Similarly, an object-cluster defined in a C program as an A-list can be converted into objects in a PEER node. This linear representation can then be converted into other data structures in the application program. Standard procedures can be defined that carry out this conversion automatically. Linear representations of object-clusters are also needed for transporting them as messages between different PEER objectbases.

3.1 Cluster-Template

An object-cluster's boundary is defined by a 'template', that specifies its collection of relevant objects. A template for object-clusters is defined by a type (that is the 'root' of the template) and a 'derivation expression'. The derivation expression is defined as an ordered set of mappings defined among the types, starting at the root and continued on to the next type using a mapping on the path. For instance, for the patient-record example of Figure 1, we can define the patient-record-T template to include all the types in that figure, but for every type only some of its mappings (represented by dark solid lines). Thus, the instances of patient-record-T template are defined only by those mappings. Now an object-cluster can be defined as an instance of this template by a tuple, with the object-id of its root object as the first element, and the name of its template as the second element. For instance, for a patient-record, pr-112/G7, we can define its patient-record-T object-cluster by (pr-112/G7 , patient-record-T) tuple.

3.2 The A-list data structure specification

The concrete data structure of A-list and its semantics carefully map into the abstract definition of a group of interrelated objects in PEER. For every object in the cluster, its type and mappings (attributes) are encoded within the A-list. In Figure 2, a BNF specification of an A-list is provided.

```
a_list ::=                ( <object> ) | ( <object> <object_list> )
object ::=                ( <object_cluster_name>~<type_name> <pair_list> )
object_list ::=           <object> | <object> <object_list>
pair_list ::=             ( <list_of_pairs> )
list_of_pairs ::=         <pair> | <pair> <list_of_pairs>
pair ::=                  ( <map_name> <value> ) | ( <map_name> ( <list_of_values> )
list_of_values ::=        <value> | <value> <list_of_values>
value ::=                 <string> | <number> | <object>
<object_cluster_name> ::= a user defined object-name for this object-cluster
<type_name> ::=           the type-name of the object
<map_name> ::=            a map defined on the type of the object
<string> ::=              a string delimited by double quotes (")
<number> ::=              an integer or float number, e.g. 1 or 1.5
```

Fig. 2. A BNF specification of the A-list data format

For each (*object_cluster_name~type_name pair_list*) in an A-list definition, a corresponding object-cluster will be created in PEER. The root object of this cluster is defined as a member of the type specified by the type_name, and the object_cluster_name will be assigned to this root object. The pair_list defines the mappings for that object and their related values, and itself contains a set of pairs of (*map_name value*). The map_name in this pair corresponds to a mapping defined on the type of the object in PEER. A value can be from the domain of integers, floats, strings, or another object. When objects appear as values, they specify the other objects of which this object-cluster is composed. Thus, an object-cluster specification may include the specification of several other objects. A typical A-list is defined by the following specification: (object_cluster_name~type_name ((map_name value) (map_name value) ...))

3.3 The Application Interface to PEER

A set of interface functions are defined to manipulate object-clusters as A-lists and interface the application programs to PEER [5]. These functions include store-A-list, retrieve-A-list, and retrieve-objects (see Figure 3).

- `char *store_A_list( a_list, template_name )`
  `char *a_list, template_name;`
  This function stores an A-list as an object-cluster in PEER and returns the object_id of the root object in the object-cluster. For example:
  store_A_list("(illness-65~ILLNESS ((treated_by doctor-463)(days_in_hospitals 12)))", "illness_treatment_T")
- `char *retrieve_A_list( object_cluster_name, template_name )`
  `char *object_cluster_name, template_name;`
  This function retrieves an object-cluster from PEER as an A-list, where the object-cluster is identified by its object_cluster_name. For example:
  retrieve_a_list("illness_65", "illness_treatment_T")
  returns
  "(illness-65~ILLNESS ((treated_by doctor-463)(days_in_hospitals 12)))"
- `char *retrieve_objects( object_id, template_name )`
  `char *object_ids, template_name;`
  This function retrieves an object-cluster from PEER as an A-list, where the object-cluster is identified by its object-id. For example:
  retrieve_objects("doctor_398", "doctor_record_T")
  The argument passed to this function can itself be a query-update PEER command that returns an object-id.

Fig. 3. The Application Interface Functions of PEER

4 Integration Facility

The main principle behind the design of the integration facility is to preserve the node's autonomy. Cooperating nodes wish to share with other nodes as much as possible a part of their information that they want to *release*, while there is always a part of the information that is *underdevelopment*, and the nodes wish to keep it private. Another principle, is to decouple as much as possible the design decisions made by individual nodes concerning their object organizations and object representations private to the node. Typically, nodes are developed and evolved independently of each other, but preexisting nodes may decide to merge together in a bigger cooperation network. An example situation is the merging of preexisting hospitals into one chain of hospitals.

The integration facility presented in PEER is supported by a sophisticated schema integration mechanism and two user-friendly and powerful interface tools. The schema integration mechanism supports the re-classification of objects by a different organization (than their origin) through a specific set of type derivation operations, and the re-interpretation of relationships defined between objects through some map derivation operations [4]. Some methodologies for distributed database integration is also addressed in [6, 10, 12, 1, 7]. But PEER's approach is principally different, since it provides an environment for cooperation and information integration where the main emphasis is on node's autonomy.

4.1 Schema Integration

For each PEER node there is one schema that specifies the type structure of all objects stored locally. This schema is called the *local* schema (LOC). Derived from the local schema are one, or more, *export* schemas (EXPs) that each define a particular view on the local objects. Usually, an export schema contains only a part of the concepts (types and mappings) defined in the local schema. An export schema can be imported by other PEERs; that will be called *import* schema (IMP). Each PEER node has one *integrated* schema (INT), which is derived from the local schema and the various imported schemas. The integrated schema provides a single uniform type structure defining all the objects that are accessible by this PEER, both locally and remote. Since the integrated schema is defined local to a node, different PEERs may establish different correspondences between their schema and other nodes' schemas, and thus there is no single global schema for the network.

The Schema Definition/Derivation Language (SDDL) of PEER [4] offers both a set of 'schema definition environments' and a number of 'type-derivation' and 'map-derivation' primitives that support the integration/derivation of different schemas within a node. The type and map derivation primitives are defined formally by their operational semantics [4]. The operational semantics is given in terms of rewriting rules that specify how a query in the context of a derived schema should be rewritten into queries that can be evaluated in the context of the defined schemas.

4.2 User Interface Tools

To better support users of the integration facility and for high level access to data and meta-data, two powerful and user-friendly interface tools are developed. The Schema Manipulation Tool and the Database Browsing Tool are both window-oriented and implemented using X-windows on SUN workstations. These interface tools support users with their access, retrieval and modification of both data and meta-data in PEER nodes. More details and examples on the two tools are presented in [14].

The Schema Manipulation Tool (SMT) This tool supports the definition, derivation and modification of the schema elements, namely the meta-data describing a PEER database. In specific, it supports the following: (1) the definition and update of types and maps (mappings) in all defined schemas, (2) the derivation of types and maps for all derived schemas, (3) checking the syntax, correctness, semantic completeness, and consistency of the schemas definitions, and (4) notifying the user in case of any errors. The Schema Manipulation Tool helps the developer of a node to define his / her schemas in a simple and systematic way. Namely, it supports the definition of defined schemas (local and imports) and derived schemas (exports and integrated) and facilitates the formulation of the derivation specification through its many debugging tests and helpful error and warning messages.

Figure 4 shows an example session where the INT schema for hospital database H1 is being defined. The three windows on the right side of this figure contain the LOC, IMP3, and the INT schemas respectively. On the left, the top window contains the status information on the schemas of H1, and the bottom left window contains system messages on the syntax, semantic, and other consistency checks of every schema individually, as well as of the derivation checks among the schemas.

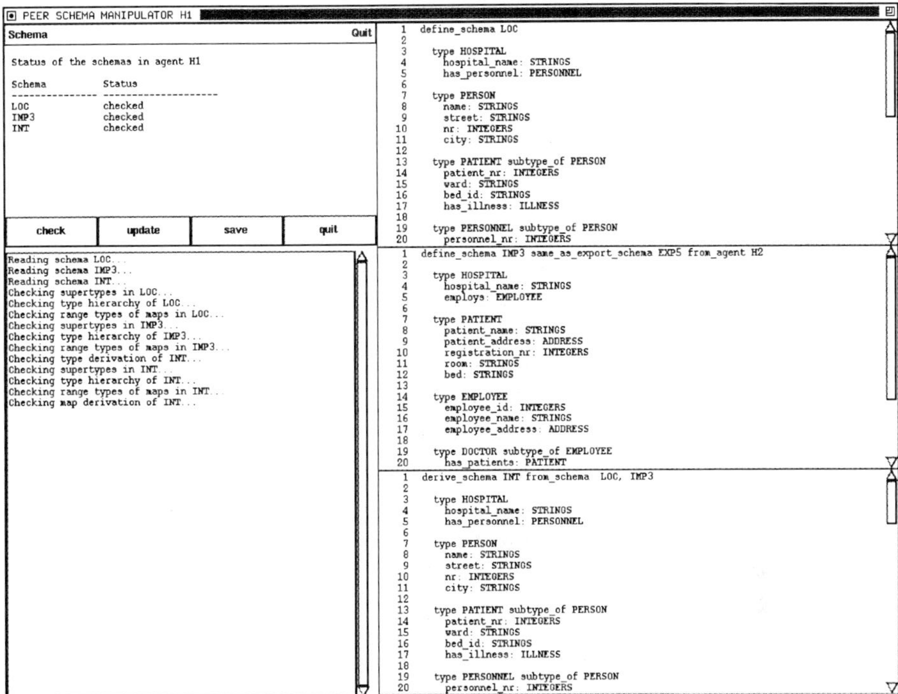

Fig. 4. The Schema Manipulation Tool

The Database Browsing Tool (DBT) This tool supports the browsing of both data and meta-data stored in nodes' databases. Users can select an object and browse through any and all objects related to that object. The browsing supported by this tools can replace the use of a database query language. Namely, DBT can support an unstructured retrieval of all information stored in a node. Three kinds of browsing operations are supported by the Database Browser:

Schema Browsing This browser enables the user to access and browse through the type definitions and their inheritance relationships in any schema.

Type Browsing This browser displays the definition of a particular type with its mappings (attributes). Users can display the members of a type and browse through their detailed description; the displayed information can be restricted by the user, by specifying conditions on certain mappings, and/or choosing specific mappings to be displayed.

Navigational Browsing This browser supports the navigation of one selected object together with all other objects related to it. The navigation process is done one step at a time, therefore there is no loop in the navigation, even in the case of a recursive definition of an objects.

Figure 5 shows an example of a DBT browsing session for the hospital example database. A Type Browser window shows the members of type PATIENT. Only the values (or objects) of the selected mappings (object_id, name, street, nr and has_illness) are displayed for members. The Navigational Browser displays the result of a navigation from illness instance IL-21132 selected in the Type Browser.

```
PEER Type Browser
Display Hide Expand Navigate                                  Quit
agent H1
schema LOC
type PATIENT
■ object-id:
■ name: STRINGS
■ street: STRINGS
■ nr: INTEGERS
□ city: STRINGS
□ patient_nr: INTEGERS
□ ward: STRINGS
□ bed_id: STRINGS
■ has_illness: ILLNESS

patient_24024(name="Fourie M."
              street="Donora"
              nr='40'
              has_illness=IL-39292(treated_by=doctor_982(name="Russ J."
                                                         street="Main"
                                                         nr='28'
                                                         personnel_nr='130958')
                                   kind_of_illness=DIS-3282
                                   days_in_hospital='0'
                                   examination_record=ER-3848439(test_results=T-28191
                                                                 status_report=RP-562)))
patient_18004(name="Shiu W."
              street="Ivy"
              nr='14'
              has_illness=IL-2383)
patient_10995(name="Lista M."
              street="Olsen"
              nr='58'
              has_illness=IL-21132)
patient_38702(name="Neal R."
              street="Halsey"
              nr='65'
              )
patient_39217(name="Birze H."
```

```
PEER Navigational Browser
Display Navigate Expand Hide                                  Quit
agent H1
schema LOC
object   IL-21132

(
(IL-21132 is_member_of ILLNESS)
(IL-21132 is_member_of LOC_TYPES)
(IL-21132 is_member_of LOC_SCHEMA_ROOT)
(IL-21132 is_member_of SCHEMA_ROOT)
(IL-21132 is_member_of ROOT)
(IL-21132 is_member_of TYPES)
(IL-21132 treated_by doctor_522)
(IL-21132 kind_of_illness DIS-7892)
(IL-21132 days_in_hospital '15')
(IL-21132 examination_record ER-28383 is_member_of EXAM_RECORD)
                             ER-28383 is_member_of LOC_TYPES)
                             ER-28383 is_member_of LOC_SCHEMA_ROOT)
                             ER-28383 is_member_of SCHEMA_ROOT)
                             ER-28383 is_member_of ROOT)
                             ER-28383 is_member_of TYPES)
                             ER-28383 test_results T-18329)
                             ER-28383 status_report RP-234)
                             ER-28383 inv(examination_record) IL-21132
                             ER-28383 inv(examination_record) IL-21132)
(IL-21132 inv(has_illness) patient_10995)
)
```

Fig. 5. The Database Browsing Tool

5 Conclusion

This paper presents an integration facility to support the systematic creation and the evolution of the information interdependencies among the autonomous nodes in an inter-operable environment. The application environment discussed here is a chain of hospitals, where different branches need to interrelate and integrate a part of their information. At any time, an existing hospital may decide to merge with a chain and become their branch. Now, on one hand this hospital has a preexisting information base that contains the information on its staff, patients, etc. and on the other hand, because of the merge the hospital needs to access the information bases of other hospitals in the chain and vice versa. In General, the interdependencies created among the nodes in the cooperating network are complex and require flexible and dynamic tools to help the user with their incremental definition and modification. The integration facility presented here consists of an schema integration mechanism that is supported by two powerful and user-friendly interface tools.

The paper also presents an approach to handle the representation and transformation of a collection of interrelated objects as single entities. The concepts of object-clusters and cluster-templates are described. A specific data structure A-list is defined to represent object-clusters in a linear format while preserving the semantics of their interrelations. A-lists provides an interface to transmit the object-clusters among the nodes, and between the nodes and the application development programming environment.

References

1. S. Abiteboul and A. Bonner. Objects and Views. In *Proceedings ACM SIGMOD91*, pages 238–247, May 1991.
2. H. Afsarmanesh and D. McLeod. The 3DIS: An Extensible Object-Oriented Information Management Environment. *ACM Transaction on Information Systems*, 7:339–377, October 1989.
3. H. Afsarmanesh, F. Tuijnman, P. Trenning, and G. Wiedijk. The 3DIS/ISL User Manual. Technical Report CS-92-08, Dept. of Computer Systems, University of Amsterdam, June 1992.
4. H. Afsarmanesh, F. Tuijnman, M. Wiedijk, and L.O. Hertzberger. Distributed Schema Management in a Cooperation Network of Autonomous Agents. In *Proceedings of the 4th IEEE International Conference on "Database and Expert Systems Applications (DEXA)"*, Lecture Notes in Computer Science (LNCS) 720. Springer Verlag, September 1993.
5. H. Afsarmanesh, F. Tuijnman, M. Wiedijk, and L.O. Hertzberger. The Implementation Architecture of PEER Federated Object Management System. Technical report, Dept. of Computer Systems, University of Amsterdam, January 1994.
6. R. Elmasri, J. Larson, and S.B Navathe. Integration algorithms for federated databases and logical database design. Technical report, Honeywell Corparate Research Center, 1987.
7. S. Heiler and S. Zdonik. Object Views: Extending the Vision. In *Proceedings Sixth Int. Conf. on Data Engineering*, pages 86–93. IEEE, February 1990.
8. W. Kim, N. Ballou, J.F. Garza, and D. Woelk. A Distributed Object-Oriented Database System Supporting Shared and Private Databases. *ACM Transaction on Information Systems*, 9(1):31–51, January 1991.
9. W. Kim, E. Bertino, and J.F. Garza. Composite Objects Revisted. In *Proceedings of ACM SIGMOD International Conference on the Management of Data, Portland, Oregon*, June 89.
10. W. Litwin. From database systems to multidatabase systems: Why and how. In *Proc. The 6th British National Conference on Databases*, pages 161–188, July 1988.
11. R. Lorie and W. Plouffe. Complex Objects and Their Use in Design Transactions. In *Proc. Databases for Engineering Applications, Database week 1983, ACM, New York*, pages 115–121, 1983.
12. A. Motro and P. Buneman. Constructing Superviews. In *Proceedings of ACM SIGMOD International Conference on the Management of Data*, April 1981.
13. F. Tuijnman and H. Afsarmanesh. Management of shared data in federated cooperative PEER environment. *International Journal of Intelligent and Cooperative Information Systems (IJICIS)*, 2(4), December 93.
14. M. Wiedijk and H. Afsarmanesh. The PEER User Interface Tools Manual. Technical report, Dept. of Computer Systems, University of Amsterdam, February 1994.

PPOST: A Parallel Database in Main Memory

László Böszörményi, Johann Eder, Carsten Weich

Institut für Informatik, Universität Klagenfurt
Universitätsstr. 65, A-9020 Klagenfurt, Austria
e-mail: {laszlo,eder,carsten}@ifi.uni-klu.ac.at

Abstract We present the PPOST-architecture (Persistent Parallel Object Store) for main-memory database systems on parallel computers, that is suited for applications with challenging performance requirements. The architecture takes full advantage of parallelism, large main memories and fast switching networks. An important property of this architecture is its excellent scaling behavior.

Keywords parallel database system, main-memory database system, object oriented database system, object store, database architecture.

1 Introduction

New advances in hardware and systems software demand to revisit design criteria for database management systems. Some well known obstacles against main memory databases (main memory is too small, too expensive and does not scale up) are no longer valid. With (highly) parallel systems made of powerful commodity processors and fast switching networks main memory database systems managing Gigabytes to Terabytes of data can easily be envisioned. While most database vendors take advantage of these developments by extending their (disc-oriented) DBMS with better management of large buffer areas or porting their DBMS to parallel hardware, we take the other approach. Data should reside primarily in main memory (where it can be retrieved and processed very efficiently) and is brought to secondary storage only for the sake of safety and recoverability. Furthermore, the trend to object oriented databases (or extended relational databases) requires that database systems have not only to deal with storing and retrieving data but also with processing user defined data manipulation methods on that data. Of course, this processing is performed much more effective, if data resides in main memory.

In the PPOST architecture parallelism is employed in two ways. With vertical parallelism we delegate processes for logging, checkpointing and archiving to own processors such they do not influence the performance of user operations. With horizontal parallelism we can spread the objects managed by the database across several (maybe many) processors for speeding up the processing of queries or methods and for increasing the size of the databases.

2 The Architecture of PPOST

PPOST's main components are (figure 1): *object store* (consisting of a number of object storage machines), *log machine*, *checkpoint machine*, *archive machine*

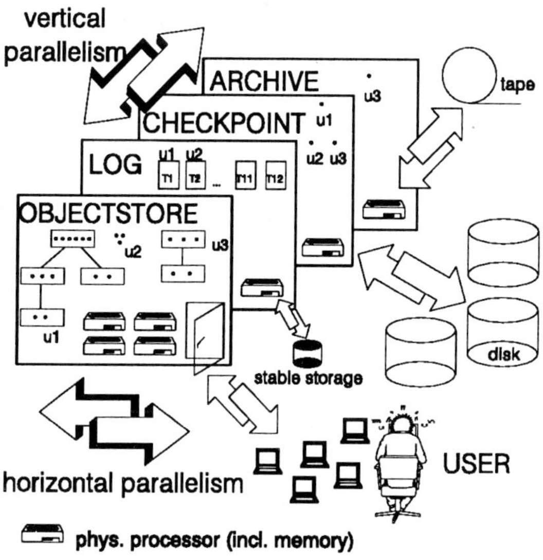

Fig. 1. The components of PPOST

and *users* (consisting of a number of user machines). All the data of the stored objects (i. e. their attributes and methods) lie in the memory of the storage machines. Every transaction that reads or changes the data is executed on those machines. PPOST is transaction-oriented. Transactions are initiated by the user machines and processed by the object store. Changes of the data in the object store are reported to the log machine which saves the information onto a logfile in nonvolatile memory.

The checkpoint machine reads the log produced by the log machine and saves all commited changes to the disc-based database. Only the checkpoint and the log machine is involved in producing the disc image. The user transaction can go on as soon as the information about the changes is transmitted to the log machine.

The archive machine saves the disc-database to a secondary storage, like a magnetic tape. This is considered as a normal activity of the data-store and again is done in background without interrupting the user-transactions.

We call this pipeline-like way to decouple user-transactions from issues of persistence *vertical parallelism.*

3 Transactions

When data is changed in the object store, log information is produced and sent to the log machine. The log machine would ideally store the log-tail in stable main memory. In this case, transactions whose log information arrived in the log machine can be committed immediately. We do not insist, however, on the existence of a stable main memory. In the lack of this, we precommit [5, 7] the corresponding transactions and let run other transactions (locks are released). In the meantime, the log information is stored on disc in the form of simple sequential files (this can be done at full disc-speed). After that, precommitted transactions may be committed. In case of a system crash precommitted transactions are handled as not-yet-committed.

3.1 Parallel checkpointing and archiving

The task of the checkpoint machine is to apply the logs on the last valid disc image [6]. After processing a certain amount of log information, a new image is created, and the corresponding log files are deleted. Checkpointing is done by a separate machine, therefore its speed has no influence on the response time of the transactions. If the database is more or less quiescent, the disc image may come very close to the primary copy. During heavy load the backup might become relatively "old" and the log files become long. This is unlikely, however, because a database rarely has a constant heavy load over a long period of time (i. e. days). The newest image generated by the checkpointer can be archived on additional nonvolatile storage (such as tapes).

3.2 Transaction undo

For transaction undo we use before-images or shadow copies in volatile storage. In the case of a system crash, the primary copy of the database in memory is lost anyway. All not-yet-committed transactions are trivially "undone". Therefore, transaction undo is in accordance with the concept of a memory-resident database.

3.3 Recovery

In the case of a system crash, a recovery must be executed. The image of the disc based database is loaded in main memory and the log is applied on it. Note that in this case the actual memory image is generated with "memory speed" (instead of "disc-speed", as in the case of checkpointing).

4 Scalability

If we have more than one physical storage machine, we can use *horizontal parallelism* either to speed up operations or to scale up the size of the database without loosing performance: When we spread the objects that are processed by an operation over several nodes of the object store (we call this *data distribution*) then each node can process its part of the set independently of the others. Operations like selecting certain objects or starting a method of a certain set of objects can be done in parallel: The only condition is that the set of objects to be distributed has to be large enough, such that the enhanced speed gained by parallelism can make up for the time needed for communication – otherwise we would lose performance.

When the databases increases in size, we add nodes to the object store. This means, we not only add storage capacity but also computational power. We can show that in many cases it is possible to scale up the size of an object set without degrading the performance of a certain operation on that set by adding nodes [1].

On the other hand we can add nodes to a data distribution to enhance performance. It is possible to calculate the optimal number of nodes with which an operation runs fastest. It is not possible though to keep this optimized speed when the size of the distributed object set grows. Then a new optimal distribution has to be calculated which will be slower in most cases.

Example Our prototype installation consists of very fast processors but comparatively long network latency times (12 DEC/ALPHA OSF1 workstations connected by a FDDI net). For a simple selection-operation distributed among 2 nodes we need 2,000 objects in the set to equal the performance of the same operation with all objects on one node. If the set is smaller than 2,000 objects the parallel operation will become slower than the sequential. If the set is much larger than that we can achieve nearly linear speedup when we add nodes to the distribution. With a setsize of 500,000 objects we reach a speedup of factor 7 with 8 nodes for the selection operation. If we add even more nodes, the additional speedup gets poorer: 10 with 14 nodes for instance. It reaches a maximum of 11.2 with 22 nodes – adding more than 22 nodes will lead to a less than optimal performance [1].

5 Conclusions

We have presented the architecture of PPOST and demonstrated that parallelism can overcome the limitations of memory resident database systems. The horizontal extendability together with little performance penalties are very desired features. PPOST will be the implementation platform for an object oriented database system supporting views [2]. In particular object oriented databases can take advantage of the proposed architecture because it facilitates the integration of databases and programming languages. Major design issues like pointer swizzling strategies become less crucial since the disc is accessed only in the background and all conversions between internal and external format do not slow down user processes. This promises a great performance gain.

The application areas of PPOST are those with high performance requirements. Currently we analyze how PPOST can be integrated with disc-based DBMS such that PPOST will be responsible for the *hot* data while the disc based DBMS manages *cold* data. One of the approaches we investigate is to use a standard DBMS as backup database which contains a (probably through the logging process delayed) image of the main memory database in form of a replication.

References

1. L. Böszörményi, K. H. Eder, C. Weich, *PPost – A Persistent Parallel Object Store*, to appear in the Proceedings of the International Conference Massively Parallel Processing Applications and Development, Delft 1994.
2. M. Dobrovnik, J. Eder, *A Concept of Type Derivation for Object-Oriented Database Systems*, Proceedings of the Eight International Symposium on Computer and Information Sciences (ISCIS VIII), Istanbul 1993.
3. P. Apers, C. van den Berg et. al., *PRISMA/DB: A Parallel, Main Memory Relational DBMS*, IEEE Transactions On Knowledge And Data Engineering, Vol. 4, No. 6, December 1992.
4. H. Garcia-Molina, K. Salem, *Main Memory Database Systems: An Overview*, IEEE Transactions On Knowledge And Data Engineering, Vol. 4, No. 6, December 1992.
5. H. Garcia-Molina, K. Salem, *System M: A Transaction Processing Testbed for Memory Resident Databases*, IEEE Transactions On Knowledge And Data Engineering, Vol. 1, No. 2, March 1990.
6. H. Garcia-Molina, K. Salem, *Checkpointing Memory Resident Databases*, International Conference On Data Engineering, Los Angeles 1989.
7. J. Gray, A. Reuter, *Transaction Processing - Concepts and Techniques*, Morgan Kaufmann Publishers Inc, 1993

Exploiting Inter-Operation Parallelism for SQL Query Optimization

A. Hameurlain, F. Morvan

Université Paul Sabatier, Lab. IRIT
118 Route de Narbonne -31062 Toulouse - France
Tél. 61 55 82 48; Fax: 61 55 62 58; E-mail: hameur@irit.fr

Abstract. In this paper, we describe an approach to determine parallel scheduling for extended SQL query operations [12]. The parallelization strategy generate a parallel program which includes the pipeline and partition parallelism taking into account resource contention. Performance evaluation shows the efficiency of each type of parallelism as a function of number of processors. The main contributions of this work is the consideration of all search spaces (left-deep trees, right-deep trees and bushy trees).

1. Introduction

Usually, the optimization process for SQL query proceeds through the following three steps: logical optimization, physical optimization and parallelization. The parallelization phase (intra-operation and inter-operation) [6, 7, 23, 18, 19, 22, 26] is the most critical step, notably the establishment of an inter-operation parallelization method in a database program. In this paper, we will only consider *inter-operation parallelism.*

In previous work [22], several execution strategies derived from different formats representing multi-way join queries are proposed and analyzed. Such strategies, associated with *left-deep trees, right-deep trees and bushy trees*, are based on the use of hash-join algorithms [21]. The work demonstrates that strategies associated with right-deep trees are well suited to exploit the parallelism. However, there is no analytical cost expression which can be used by an optimizer to decide whether and when to switch from a left-deep tree to a right-deep tree. In [6], an innovative approach is proposed to determine the query execution plan based on segmented right-deep trees, which are bushy trees of right-deep subtrees. A similar approach [26], called zig-zag tree, enlarges the search space to include an intermediate format lying between left-deep trees and right-deep trees. The zig-zag tree improves response time compared to the right-deep tree in case of memory limitation. [18, 19] have proposed an optimization strategy of parallel query execution plans in a shared-memory environment XPRS [24]. [18] has only considered intra-operation parallelism and left-deep tree plans. Recently this work has been continued [19] to complete this approach by exploiting both intra-operation parallelism and inter-operation parallelism and bushy tree plans. [19] has proposed a scheduling algorithm, which achieves maximum resource utilizations by running *two carefully selected tasks* in parallel at their IO-CPU balance point.

In this paper we continue our study on parallel query processing which has been previously described in [16] and present a more complete approach that exploits both pipelined parallelism and partitioned parallelism. We propose a parallelization method for *SQL query containing relational operators* and the *Fixpoint operator* [1, 20, 25]. The parallelization process respects *posteriority constraints* between operations as well as *limitations in resources* (processors, memory).

This paper is organized as follows: section 2 presents the basic concepts. Section 3 describes the parallelization method. In section 4 performance evaluation shows the efficiency of each type of parallelism as a function of the number of processors. Section 5 compares our work with related work. Finally conclusions are given in section 6.

2. Dependency Graph

Several efficient join algorithms have been developed in the literature. Experiments have shown that hash-based algorithms (Simple hash-join, Hybrid hash-join and Grace hash-join) achieve the best performance [21]. The operation dependency graphs (Fig. 1b) presented in this paper are based on the use of one of the hash-join algorithms (Simple or Hybrid) [22]. With hash-join algorithms, the computation of the join operation can be viewed as consisting of *two phases*. The first phase *builds* a hash table with the smallest of the two relations (R). The second phase uses the tuples of the second relation (S) to *probe* the hash table and find the pertinent tuples for the join computation.

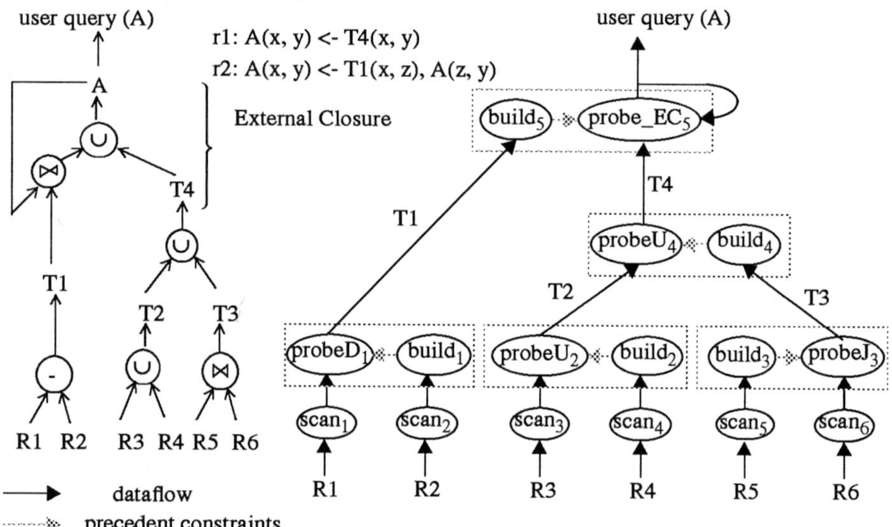

Fig. 1a. Resolution Graph

Fig. 1b. Dependency Graph

In order to exploit the *pipeline* parallelism of the difference (R - S) and union (R ∪ S) operators, the second operand must be completely computed before its execution may begin. *Consequently, we use the relation S to build the hash table*. The *scan*$_i$ of relation Ri produces a relational data stream as output. A scan$_i$ operation and its successor must not be completely dissociated so that the successor may consume in pipeline the tuples produced by a scan$_i$. In the dependency graph (Fig. 1b) associated to resolution graph (Fig. 1a) [13], each binary relational operation, noted X_i (Join, Union,...) will be represented by the operations: $\{build_i; probeX_i\}$. A specialized operation i (External / Transitive Closure) will be represented by two operations $\{build_i; probeX_i\}$ where the $probeX_i$ operator is extended by integration of an *iterative process* based on semi-naive or magic sets methods [1, 2].

3. Parallelization Strategy

Our approach to determine parallel scheduling relies on *serial methods* [9, 8]. To use these methods, we associate with each operation i (dependency graph) *a local response time LRT (i) and an optimal (economical) number of processors* [5, 15]. The determination of the number of processors and the local response time is carried out *before* inter-operation parallelization in order to favour intra-operation parallelism. In previous work [15] we have presented an analytical method to allocate processors for relational and fixpoint operators taking account of the main-memory constraints.

3.1 Scheduling Algorithm

The basis of our method is to schedule the operations with time increments beginning at time tp=0. At any time tp, resources are affected to the operations with the highest priority amongst the ones ready. The operations which verify the following conditions are considered as *ready*:
(1) All the direct predecessors of the operation are either terminated or being executed.
(2) The operation does not require more resources than the amount available at time tp.
(3) If the operation is a $probeX_i$ then the corresponding operation $build_i$ is terminated.

The priority rule we apply, orders the operations according to increasing *deadline*. If two operations have the same deadline, we take into account their *late*. Our parallelization method consists in two steps:

E1: Compute the deadline for each operation,

E2: Schedule operations according to the priority rules and constraints defined above.

E1: In the first step, to compute *deadline*, we are led to compute the late start times Late defined in a recursive way, as follows:

$$\text{Late (i)} = \begin{cases} \text{RT(i)-LRT (i)} & \text{if succ (i)}=\emptyset \text{ (* succ (i) = direct successors for i*)} \\ \text{Late (succ(i))- LRT (i)} & \text{else} \end{cases}$$

A first run through the resolution graph (figure 1a), from the scan operations to the user query node, gives the response time RT. RT is computed as follows:

$$\text{RT (i)} = \begin{cases} \text{LRT(i)} & \text{if pred (i)}=\emptyset \text{ (* pred (i) = direct predecessors for i*)} \\ \text{LRT(i)+max (RT(j))} & \text{else with } j \in \text{pred (i)} \end{cases}$$

A second run, from the user query node to the scan operations, gives Late(i) for each operation i and the deadline (Late (i) + LRT (i)) defined as follows:

$$\text{Dl (i)} = \begin{cases} \text{RT (i)} & \text{if succ (i)}=\emptyset \\ \text{Late (succ (i))} & \text{else} \end{cases}$$

E2: Prior to the development of the scheduling algorithm (below), we give the notations used:

- I : the operations of the dependency graph,
- List_E: the set of ordering operations,
- S_N : the set of not-processed operations,
- O_E : selected operation,
- tp : triggering time,
- E_O_E : the set of operations being processed at time tp,
- Dmax : number of processors not used at time tp,
- Proc_nb : total number of processors,
- Di : number of economical processors allocated to the operation i.

Our objective is to assign a *triggering time* for each operation of the dependency graph and to take into account *the number of processors*. The algorithm's principle (Fig. 2) is to determine the set of operations P ready at any time tp as a function of the number of processors not allocated (Dmax) and of the operations not treated (S_N). If P is not empty, then processors are allocated to the operation with highest priority, and the *triggering time* tp is assigned to this operation. In case P is empty (the number of remaining processors is insufficient or one or more probeX_i operations are waiting for the termination of their corresponding $build_i$), then the smaller instant tp is determines such as at least one operation E_O_E is terminated. The scheduling process is repeated until all the operations of the dependency graph have all been treated.

```
Procedure scheduling (I: operation)
begin
  tp := 0; Dmax := Pro_nb; S_N := I;
  While S_N <> ∅ do
  begin
    ready_operation (S_N, P, Dmax);
    if P <> ∅ then
    begin
      selected_operation (P, O_E);
      starting (O_E) := tp;
      add (List_E, O_E);
      S_N := S_N - {O_E};
      E_O_E := E_O_E ∪ {O_E};
      Dmax := Dmax - proc_nb(O_E);
    end
    else
      term_op (E_O_E, Dmax, tp);
  end
end.
```

```
Procedure ready_operation (S_N, P: operation,
Dmax: processors_nb);
This procedure determines the ready operations
set from the set of not treated operations S_N and
the number of processors Dmax.
```

```
Procedure selected_operation (P: operation,
O_E: selected_operation)
begin
  minima (P, S_P); % this function determines
  the operation set S_P such as
  Deadline(i)) / i ∈ P be minimum%
  if card(S_P) > 1 then
    minima2 (S_P, O_E); % this function
    determines the selected operation O_E such
    as Late(i) / i ∈ S_P be minimum%
  else O_E := S_P;
end.
```

```
Procedure term_op (E_O_E: operation, Dmax:
processors_nb, tp: times);
This procedure determines the smaller instant tp
such as at least one operation E_O_E is terminat-
ed. It updates the variables E_O_E, and Dmax.
```

Fig. 2. Scheduling Algorithm for SQL Query Operations

Applying the algorithm schedule to the data of the dependency graph (Table 1) yields a schedule represented by the Gantt diagram (Fig. 3).

Table 1: Data of the Operation dependency Graphs

	$scan_1$ $probeD_1$	$scan_2$ $build_1$	$scan_3$ $probeU_2$	$scan_4$ $build_2$	$scan_5$ $build_3$	$scan_6$ $probeJ_3$	$build_4$	$probeU_4$	$build_5$	probe $\_EC_5$
Di	4 5	3 5	3 5	2 5	2 3	4 3	5	5	5	5
LRT(i)	5 5	4 3	4 7	3 2	2 3	4 6	4	9	3	12
RT(i)	17	7	16	5	5	15	19	28	20	40
Late(i)	15	8	8	3	0	5	15	19	25	28
Dl(i)	25	15	19	8	5	15	19	28	28	40

Pro_nb=20 processors.

The number of processors allocated to a $scan_i$ operation of a relation Ri is its degree of partitioning. The number of processors allocated to $build_i$ /$probeX_i$ is the number of processors allocated to operation X_i.

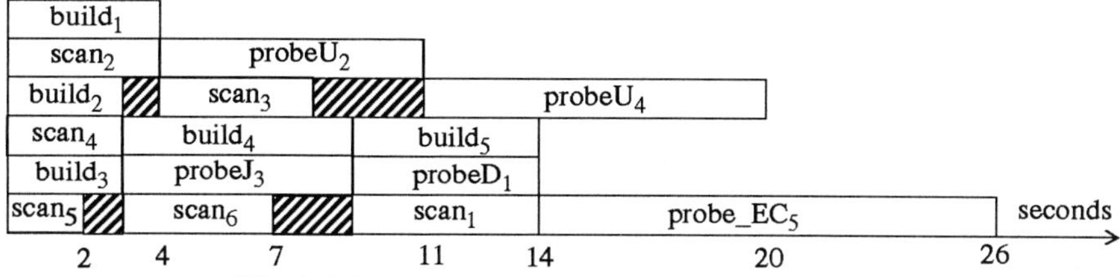

Fig. 3. Scheduling representation with Gantt diagram

3.2 Parallel Program Generation

This sub-section shows how we can integrate the constructors *seq, par and pipe* in order to generate a parallel program. The scheduling algorithm sorts the ready operations according to increasing deadline. Hence, we obtain a set of operations, named List_E, sorted according to increasing tp. The generation process of a parallel program constits of two steps:

E3: Integration of *Pipeline* parallelism pipe. This step transforms the List_E into List_E_P by locating all the pipeline chains.

E4: Integration of *partition* parallelism par. This step determines the set of operations, which must be executed in parallel by integrating the constructor par.

```
seq
 par
  seq
   pipe scan5, build3 epipe;
   pipe scan6, probeJ3, build4 epipe; send_m1;
rec_m3; pipe scan1, probeD1, build5 epipe;
   probe_EC5
  eseq

  seq
   pipe scan4, build2 epipe; send_m2
  eseq

  seq
   pipe scan2, build1 epipe; send_m3;
rec_m2; pipe scan3, probeU2 epipe;
rec_m1; probeU4
  eseq
 epar
eseq
```

Fig. 4a. Parallel Program according the first approach.

```
seq
 par
  seq
   pipe scan5, build3 epipe;
   pipe scan6, probeJ3, build4 epipe; send_m2;
rec_m3; probeU4
  eseq

  seq
   pipe scan4, build2 epipe;
rec_m1; pipe scan3, probeU2 epipe; send_m3;
  eseq

  seq
   pipe scan2, build1 epipe; send_m1;
rec_m2; pipe scan1, probeD1, build5 epipe;
   probe_EC5
  eseq
 epar
eseq
```

Fig. 4b. Parallel Program according the second approach.

The parallel program generation process must verify the following 2 constraints:

(i) respect the triggering (tp) of operations determined in step E2,

(ii) sequence the operations {build$_i$; probeX$_i$} where X$_i$ denotes a relational operation or a fixpoint operator.

The control mechanisms which enforce a sequential (seq), partition parallelism (par) and pipeline (pipe) execution are not sufficient to guarantee that execution will conform to the result of the parallelization strategy. This arises from the logical operation {build$_i$; probeX$_i$} dissociation. From the parallelization strategy viewpoint, these two operations are considered as independent but to be sequentially executed.

For this, we have proposed two approaches: the first one (Fig. 4a) consists in respecting the triggering of the operations by use of control mecanisms seq and par, and ensuring the operations sequencing {build$_i$; probeX$_i$} with the control messages : *send_mi, receive_mi*. The second approach (Fig. 4b) consists in respecting the triggering of operations by the control messages and ensuring operations sequencing {build$_i$; probeX$_i$} with the control mechanisms seq and par.

A parallel program generation method based on the first approach was implemented and restricted to the constructors seq and par. Communication and control operations associated with seq, eseq, par and epar are already implanted using the communication primitives of UNIX system, in particular *sockets*. In order to facilitate the parallel program generation process, we have *integrated* the control messages in the build$_i$ and probeX$_i$ operations (Fig. 5).

```
Procedure build_ni
begin
  pi := receive_data (Ri);
  While not Termination do
  begin
    build (Bi, pi);
    pi := receive_data (Ri)
  end;
  send_ctrl_build
end.
                    pi : set of pages
```

```
Procedure probeX_ni
%where X = Difference / Union / Join %
begin
  receive_ctrl_build;
  pj := receive_data (Sj);
  While not Termination do
  begin
    pk := probeX (Bi, pj);
    send_data (pk); pj := receive_data (Sj)
  end
end.
```

Fig. 5. Control Integration of {build$_i$; probeX$_i$}.

The pipelining External Closure algorithm [14] is described in figure 6.

```
Procedure probe_EC_ni( r1, r2, d)
% r1 and r2 define the EC; see page 3
d: number of processors allocated to the EC %
begin
  receive_ctrl_build;
  pi := receive_data (T4); copy (pi, res);
  send_data (res); % result initialization %
  While not Termination do
  begin
    Δpk := probe_EC (Bi, pi, d);
    pi := receive_data (T4);
    pi := pi ∪ Δpk; copy (pi, res);
    send_data (res) % partial result %
  end
end.
```

```
Function probe_EC (Bi, pi, d)
begin
% i: represent the ith processor %
  for j := 1 to d do
  begin
    RTi[j] := probeJ (Bi[j], pi);
    if i ≠ j then send (RTi[j], CAj)
  % communication between the
  EC processors %
  end;
  compute (CAi, Δpk);
  return (Δpk)
end.
```

Fig. 6. Pipelining External Closure Algorithm

4. Performance Analysis

We have evaluated the response time (RT) of the dependency graph of figure 1b, in order to analyse performance in the following cases:

(i) *full desclustering*: an operation is executed over all the available nodes. Each node of the machine is composed of a processor, a local memory, and a disk. The execution plan, noted P1 uses intra-operation parallelism only.

(ii) *partial desclutering*: an operation is executed over a subset of nodes.

We consider:

- the execution plan P2 which uses intra-operation parallelism and the partition parallelism.
- the execution plan P3 which uses intra-operation, partition parallelism and pipeline.

For performance evaluation we rely on the benchmarks described by [3]. The database is composed of six relations of 1, 000, 000 tuples. Each relation consists of thirteen 4-bytes integer and three 52-byte string attributes. For flexibility and efficiency reasons, the architecture proposed for our Parallel Inference System *PARIS* [14] is a distributed-memory architecture. This type of architecture has been validated by many database machines *Bubba* [4] *Gamma* [10, 11]. To measure the contribution of parallelism, the simulation parameters used are [25, 22]:

The number of instructions per seconds for a processor = 4, 000, 000
The reading time of a 18 K disk page = 32 800 instructions
The writing time of a 18 K disk page = 61 500 instructions
The tuple transfer time = 5 μs
The time to send a message = 1 ms.

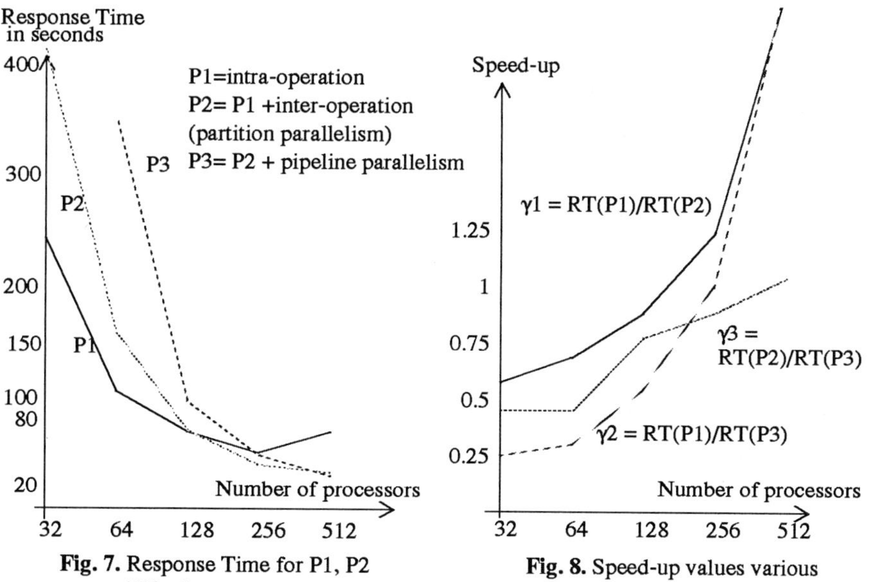

Fig. 7. Response Time for P1, P2 and P3 of execution plans

Fig. 8. Speed-up values various parallelism types

In figure 7 the response time for different execution plans are presented as a function of the number of processors. Figure 8 shows speed-up values γ1 = RT(P1)/RT(P2),

$\gamma 2$ = RT(P1)/RT(P3) and $\gamma 3$ = RT(P2)/RT(P3), as a function of the number of processors. Four statements can be made by observing the curves in figures 7 and 8:

1- The execution plan P1, which only uses intra-operation parallelism is more efficient for small number of processors such as 32 to 130 processors.

2- The execution plan P1 suffers an increase in response time beyond 256 processors, due to larger data message communication times.

3- The execution plan P2 using intra-operation and partition parallelism has the best response time between 130 and 512 processors.

4- The execution plan P3 using all parallelization forms is best for very large number of processors, over 512 processors.

The results obtained show pipeline to be of limited value. Indeed, the pipeline chains are *seldom very long* (the largest in our example is 3) either because of resources limitations or because aggregate functions (Max, Min, Average,...) or sort operators must wait for complete consumption of the operands before they can produce a result. Furthermore, if the response time for an operation at the start of the chain in a pipeline is much larger than the others, then the following operations immobilize resources for a longer time. Thus the system's throughput and speed-up factor are limited. For example in the pipeline chain *pipe* $scan_1$, $probeD_1$, $build_5$ *epipe*, the processors allocated to the $build_5$ operator remain inactive 80% of the time while waiting for the tuples produced by the $probeD_1$ operator. The pipeline parallelism improves speed-up only if the target machine contains a large number of processors.

5. Related Work

In the sliced right-deep, segmented right-deep, and zig-zag strategies, the operations of a subtree cannot begin execution as long as the operations of the preceeding subtree are not terminated. For example in figure 9, if the joins *j1, j2, j3* are computed, then the liberated resources remain inactive as long as *jp* is not terminated. On the other hand, with our strategy, the available resources are affected to the operations as early as possible. Indeed, for the example depicted in figure 9, if the joins *j1, j2 , j3* are computed, then their resources are immediately affected, for example to the joins *jp+1, jp+2*.Therefore, this decreases response time and maximizes the use of processors (throughput maximization).

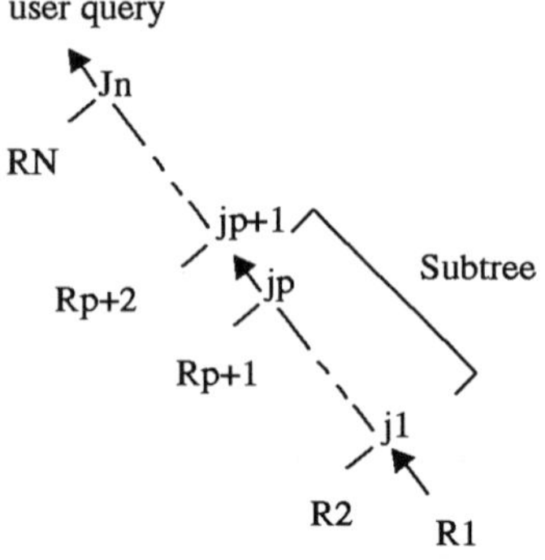

Fig. 9. Sliced right-deep tree

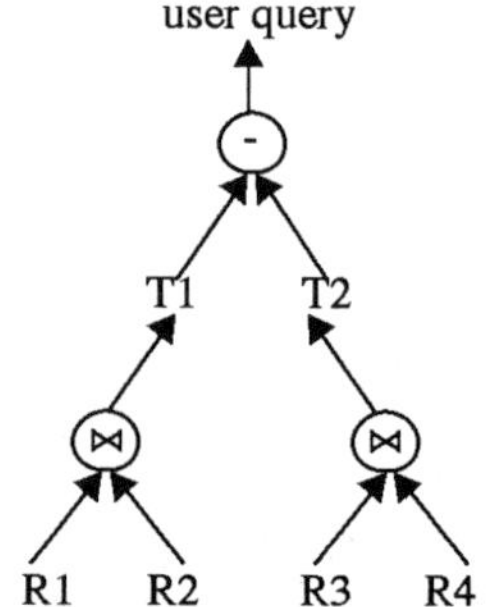

Fig. 10. Bushy tree

Our method applies to all search space, which allows us to consider relational operations and the fixpoint operation. Indeed such fixpoint or relational operations may generate bushy trees (Fig. 10), which cannot be transformed into left-deep trees or right-deep trees. Furthermore, our method bears close similarity to the scheduling method proposed by [19] in as much as both allow number of processors for each operation and apply to all search space. However, our approach differs from that of XPRS mainly in that several tasks can be executed in parallel fashion whereas only two are possible with the XPRS system. In addition, the number of processors are allocated with due consideration of minimization, when possible, of data communication [17].

6. Conclusion

In this paper, we have presented an inter-operation parallelization method. This method determines a parallel execution plan which includes intra-operation parallelism, inter-operation partition parallelism, and pipeline parallelism.

From performance evaluation two consequences stand out concerning the use of parallelism for the processing of SQL queries:

(i) The pipeline parallelism is efficient for cases where the target machine comprises a very large number of processors (massively parallel machine).

(ii) In case the number of processors of the parallel machine is approximately 20 or less, intra-operation parallelism is the only efficient one.

The originalities of our approach lie in the integration, in a homogeneous way, in the conception process of an Optimizer-Parallelizer and in the consideration of bushy trees which allow to take account of the fixpoint operator and all relational operators. Furthermore, our method provides a good trade-off between response time minimization and throughput maximization.

The parallelization strategy presented in this paper generates, at compile time, a parallel execution plan. This strategy can be easily integrated into a *run-time environment*. Indeed, instead of assigning a triggering time for each operation, it is possible to execute immediately each selected operation. Thus, the parallelization method becomes more *flexible* in as much as the *degree of parallelism* of an operation may be *dynamically adjusted* either in case of errors in cost estimation models, or in the case of *failure* of one or more processors. Furthermore, the run-time environment allows for convenient *inter-query parallelism* consideration, by handling the set of not-processed operations in queue. We therefore plan to extend our parallelization method to inter-query parallelism in a run-time environment.

References

1. F. Bancilhon, R. Ramakrishnan, "An Amateur's Introduction to Recursive Query Processing Strategies", Proc. of ACM-SIGMOD, W.D.C., May 1986, pp. 16-52.
2. C. Beeri, R. Ramakrishnan, “On the Power of Magic”, Proc of the ACM SIGMOD Symposium on Principles of Database Systems, 1987, pp.269-283.
3. D. Bitton et al., "Benchmarking Database Systems - a Systematic Approach", Proc. of the 1983 VLDB conf., Oct. 1983, pp. 8-19.
4. H. Boral et al., "Prototyping Bubba, a Highly Parallel Database System", IEEE TKDE. Vol. 1, No. 1, March 1990, pp. 4-24.

5. M.S. Chen et al., "Scheduling and Processor Allocation for Parallel Execution of Multi-Join Queries", 8th Int. Conf. on Data Eng., Tempe, Feb. 1992, pp. 58-67.
6. M.S. Chen et al., "Using Segmented Right-Deep Trees for the Execution of Pipelined Hash Joins", 18th Int. Conf. VLDB, Vancouver, Aug. 1992, pp. 15-26.
7. M.S. Chen et al., "Applying Hash Filters to Improving the Execution of Bushy Trees", Proceedings of the 19th VLDB Conf., Dublin, August 1993, pp. 505-516.
8. E.G. Coffman, et al., "Operating Systems Theory", Prentice-Hall, 1973.
9. R.W. Conway, et al., "The Theory of Scheduling", Addition-wesley, 1967.
10. D.J. Dewitt et al., "The Gamma Database Machine Project" , IEEE TKDE. Vol. 2, No. 1, March 1990, pp. 44-61.
11. D.J. Dewitt, J. Gray, "Parallel Database Systems: The Future of High Performance Database Systems", Com. of the ACM, Vol. 35, No. 6, June 1992, pp. 85-98.
12. G. Gardarin, P. Valduriez, “ESQL2: An Object-Oriented SQL with F-Logic Semantcis”, IEEE Int. conf. on Data Eng., Phoenix, Feb. 1992, pp. 320-327.
13. A. Hameurlain, F. Morvan, "An Algorithm For Selection Operator Propagation in Resolution Graph”, Intl. Conf. DEXA’90, Vienna, Aug. 1990, pp. 550-553.
14. A. Hameurlain, F. Morvan, "Parallel Deductive Databases: Design and Implementation of a Parallel Algorithm for Computing Recursive Queries", 9th Conf. Distributed Appli. and Multiprocessor Technology, CA, Dec. 1991, pp. 181-189.
15. A. Hameurlain et al., "An Analytical Method to Allocate Processors in High Performance Parallel Execution of Recursive Queries", Intl. Conf. DEXA’92, Valencia, Sept. 1992, Spring Verlag, pp. 44-47.
16. A. Hameurlain, F. Morvan, "A Parallel Scheduling Method for Efficient Query Processing", 22nd Intl. Conf. on Parallel Processing, St. Charles IL., Aug. 1993, Vol. 3, pp. 258-261.
17. A. Hameurlain, F. Morvan, "An Optimization Method of Data Communication and Control for Parallel Execution of SQL Queries", Intl. Conf. DEXA’93, LNCS 720 , Prague, Sept. 1993, pp. 301-312
18. W. Hong, M. Stonebraker, "Optimization of Parallel Query Execution Plans in XPRS", First Intl. Conf. on Parallel Distributed Information Systems, Dec. 91 Florida, pp. 218-225.
19. W. Hong, "Exploiting Inter-Operation Parallelism in XPRS", ACM SIGMOD Intl. Conf. on Management of Data, USA, June 1992, pp. 19-28.
20. M. A. W. Houtsma, et al., "Implementation and Performance Evaluation of a Parallel Transitive Closure Algorithm on PRISMA/DB", Proc. of the 19th VLDB Conf., Dublin 1993, pp. 206-217.
21. D. Schneider, D. Dewitt, "A Performance Evaluation of Four Parallel Join Algorithms in a Shared-Nothing Multiprocessor Environment", Proc. of the ACM SIGMOD Conf., 1989, pp. 110-121.
22. D. Schneider, D. Dewitt, "Tradeoffs in Processing Complex Join Queries via Hashing in Multiprocessor Database Machines", Proc. of the16th VLDB Conf., Brisbane, Australia 1990, pp. 469-480.
23. E. J. Shekita et al., "Multi-Join Optimization for Symmetric Multiprocessors", Proceedings of the 19th VLDB Conf., Dublin, Aug. 1993, pp. 479-492.
24. M. Stonebraker, et. al, "The Design of XPRS", 14th Intl. Conf. VLDB, 1988.
25. P. Valduriez, S. Khoshafian, "Parallel Evaluation of the Transitive Closure of a Database Relation", Intl. Jo. of Parallel Programming, Vol. 17, No. 1, Feb. 1988.
26. M. Ziane et al., "Parallel Query Processing in DBS3", 2nd Int. Conf. on Parallel and Distribued Information Systems, San Diego, Jan. 1993.

Reactive Object-Oriented Databases and CIM

Mikael Berndtsson
University of Skövde, Sweden
spiff@ida.his.se

ABSTRACT

This paper proposes a simple and powerful approach to associating rules with events in reactive object-oriented database systems. In it we propose a new run time subscription mechanism, which associates rules with specific event definitions. This brings optimization considerations - when to fire a rule - to the language level. The proposed subscription mechanism reduces rule checking to a minimum. It can be applied to both primitive events and composite events. Both rules and events are represented as first class objects. This architecture has been adopted in the ACOOD2 prototype on top of ONTOS™.

Keywords: (re)active databases, CIM, object-oriented databases.

1 Introduction

There are several applications within manufacturing management such as computer integrated manufacturing (CIM) and shop floor control (SFC), that require automatic situation monitoring of the production environment. Several attempts have been made to build applications that require automatic monitoring with conventional DBMS. Conventional database systems are passive in their behaviour, which means that they only do things when you actually require them to do so. Previous approaches to support automatic situation monitoring can be broadly classified into: i) periodically poll the database, ii) embed or encode event detection and related action execution in the application code.

The major disadvantage with first approach is that the queries must be run exactly when the event occurs. The frequency of polling can be increased in order to detect the event, but if the polling is too frequent, then the database is overloaded with queries that most of the time will fail. On the other hand if the frequency is too low, the event will be missed. The second approach has several drawbacks. Firstly, rules are embedded in application code, which means that modification of rules and events implies making changes in every method supporting the rule. Secondly, the programmer has to understand all the rules, so that interaction between rules can be handled properly.

Neither of the two above approaches can efficiently support automatic situation monitoring. Reactive[1] databases have been proposed as an approach to efficiently support automatic situation monitoring. Reactive database technology opens up a new paradigm within database research, where the database is not seen as a slave to an application but as a peer. That is, a reactive database system can react to events, both primitive and composite events, which might have occurred within the system or external to it. The cooperation between a DBMS and an application can then be viewed as a two way

---

1. We adopt the use of the term *reactive* instead of the previously used term *active*, since the term reactive describes the semantics of such a database system better than the previous used term active[AMC93].

communication, where the DBMS can support and control the application's activities.

Early research on reactive databases was largely within the context of relational database systems ([Han89], [WF90]), where rules are treated as global constraints. More recently, there have been a number of proposals for introducing reactive behaviour, expressed by event-condition-action (ECA) rules, in the context of object-oriented database systems ([AMC93], [BL92], [Ber94], [DPG91], [MP91], [GD93], [GJS92]). Several important design issues for introducing ECA-rules in object-oriented database systems have been identified in [AMC93].

In section 2 of this paper, we focus on event and rule management for reactive object-oriented databases, highlighting the architecture of one such system, ACOOD2. We adopt the ECA paradigm [CB+89] with both event and rule definitions represented as first class objects. In section 3 we introduce a subscription mechanism between rules and *specific* events, which reduces rule checking further than previous solutions such as centralized rule checking or rules indexed by classes (Sentinel [AMC93], ADAM [DPG91]). The proposed subscription mechanism can easily be applied to both primitive and composite events, since rules are indexed by event object identifiers. In section 4 we discuss how CIM applications can make use of the proposed subscription mechanism. Conclusions are presented in section 5.

2 Event and Rule Management

2.1 Event Generators

In object-oriented database systems, all communication between different objects is made via methods. By sending a message to an object we invoke a method, which can raise an event. The invocation of a method generates two events: i) before the execution of a method, and ii) after the execution of a method. It is important that the user can specify which methods will generate events, since every method invocation might potentially generate a primitive event. A method that is allowed to generate a primitive event is called an *event generator (EG)*. The concept of event generators can be extended to capture any system that produces events which may need a special response. Thus, both a system clock and an application that produces events can be viewed as event generators. In this paper we will concentrate on methods as event generators.

Object-oriented database systems provide the user with mechanisms such as inheritance. This means that we cannot assume that a method name alone will identify a triggering event. Therefore, we must also know in which class the triggering event has occurred, since a method may have different meaning according to which class it was invoked in. Given the previous paragraphs, we follow the ADAM project [DPG91] and define a triggering method event in our reactive object oriented model as:
MethodEvent = Mode + Class + Method.

When a method has been invoked in ACOOD2 a primitive event is generated as follows:

Generated primitive event = [EventOid + Oid + Parameters + Time]
EventOid - event object identifier, (event type).
Oid - object identity of the object that generated the event.

Parameters - the parameters that were involved when the method was invoked.
Time - the time when the event occurred.

Information about whether the event was generated before or after the method execution is captured by the event definition.

2.2 Events

We propose that the term event should be clearly separated into two terms: *event definition* and *event occurrence*. It is sometimes confusing when we just talk about events. Do we mean the definition of an event or do we mean the actual occurrence of an event? An *event occurrence* is a signal that indicates that a specific situation has occurred and certain actions may have to be performed due to the event occurrence. Furthermore, the task of an *event definition* is to specify the moment when rules might be triggered. Current approaches to representing event definitions can be broadly classified into: i) event definitions as expressions within class definitions (Ode [GJS92]), ii) event definitions as rule attributes (O2 [MP91]) and iii) event definitions as first class objects (Sentinel [AMC93], SAMOS [GD93], ADAM [DPG91]).

In this paper we follow the approach of representing event definitions as first class objects. This approach has several advantages. Event definitions can have attributes and methods of their own, that describes their state and behaviour. This means that they are not dependent upon the existence of other objects, e.g. rules, in contrast to the two other approaches. They can easily be added, deleted and modified. Furthermore, we can use the parameters computed when the event is raised.

Briefly, events can be decomposed into i) primitive events such as method events and temporal events and ii) composite events, where a composite event consists of a set of primitive events or composite events related by defined operators. In this paper we will concentrate on method events, which is a specialization of primitive events. Method events in ACOOD2 are defined as follows:

DEFINE EVENT <event_object_identifier>

ON <[BEFORE | AFTER] <class> <method>

A method event in ACOOD2 is identified by its *event object identifier* (event name), which is specified when the event definition is created. In order to specify an event generator, we need to know both the *class* and the name of the *method* to which the event definition is related. Furthermore, event generators can signal an event occurrence either *before* or *after* the execution of a method.

2.3 Rules

Several approaches have been taken to representing rules within object-oriented databases. Representation of rules in object oriented databases can be broadly classified into: i) rules declared within the class definition Ode[GJS92], ii) rules as data members, iii) rules as first-class objects ([DBM88], Sentinel [AMC93], SAMOS [GD93], ADAM [DPG91], O_2 [MP91]).

In ACOOD2 we represent rules as first class objects. This means that rules are subject to normal database operations like any other system defined object. The transaction model can be used for locking of rule objects. We can thereby lock a rule for updates, not allowing it to be fired during the update operation (a write lock is set on the rule). When a rule is subject to be fired we must obtain a read lock in order to execute the rule. Following HiPAC [CB+89], rules in ACOOD2 are in the form of ECA rules and are defined as follow:

DEFINE RULE <rule_object_identifier>

ON EVENT <event_object_identifier> {AND instance_object_identifier}

IF <condition> DO <action>

A rule in ACOOD2 is identified by its *rule object identifier*, which is specified when the rule is created. When new rules are added to the database, they subscribe to (are associated with) a previously defined *event object identifier*. Rules that want to subscribe to an event definition can subscribe to either: i) all instances of a particular class that generates a specific event (class level rules) or ii) only identified instances of a class that generates a specific event (instance level rules). The condition part of a rule in ACOOD2 is an *ONTOS*™ *SQL* statement, which is satisfied if the return value of the SQL statement is not empty. Finally, the *action* is an identifier of the method/program that should be executed.

3 Association Between Rules and Events

Rules are defined to react in response to situations. Thus if rules are associated with an object, then rules can be introduced to enhance the behavioural characteristics of that object. Applications that heavily depend upon a large number of rules will affect the system's overall performance. It is pointed out in [DPG91] that introducing rules into database systems usually means that programs becomes twice as slow as without rules. Thereby, it becomes important to optimize rule checking as much as possible in order to achieve better performance. Previous approaches to rule checking can be broadly classified into: i) centralized rule checking and ii) rules indexed by classes.

We propose a third approach - rules associated with *specific* events - which reduces rule checking further than previous approaches. Furthermore, formulae for estimating the costs of rule checking are presented.

3.1 Centralized Rule Checking

Centralized rule checking is the most straightforward and has the following semantics:

> When an event has been generated, check all rules in order to determine which rules are to be triggered.

This approach is clearly inefficient, since most of the rules involved in this form of rule checking will not be triggered. Assume that the total number of ECA-rules for a CIM application is 250. The triggering event for those rules can be either a primitive event or a composite event. Among these rules we have 25 rules which are interested in event *E12*, e.g. *machine break down*. This can also be described as follows:

$$COST_{E12} = \frac{R}{R} = \frac{250}{250} = 1$$

$$URC_{E12} = 1 - \frac{RE_{E12}}{R} = 1 - \frac{25}{250} = 1 - 0,1 = 0,9$$

where

$COST_{Ei}$: The share of rules which are involved in rule checking when event E_i is generated.

R : Total number of rules.

URC_{Ei} : Unnecessary rule checks which are performed when event E_i is generated.

RE_i : Set of rules that are interested in event E_i.

Given the previous formulae, we can easily see that when event *machine break down* occurs all rules will be checked in order to find RE_i, i.e. *E12*. Thus, several rules are checked which have no interest in event *E12*. As much as 90 percent of the rule checking performed in this example is unnecessary, since only 10 percent of the rules are interested in event *E12*.

3.2 Rules Indexed by Classes

A more efficient approach to rule checking can be achieved by enlarging objects with a special rule list attribute, such as the *list-of-notifiable-subscribers* in Sentinel [AMC93] and *class-rules* in ADAM [DPG91]. A *subscription* mechanism is introduced to associate rules with reactive objects, i.e. objects which can generate primitive events. This means that rules can subscribe to a reactive object that generates a primitive event. Rules indexed by classes have the following semantics:

> When a reactive object generates a primitive event, check those rules which have subscribed to the reactive object.

Before we apply the previous example from a CIM application, we make an assumption that 60 rules of the 250 rules have subscribed to a reactive class, e.g. CIMstation. Among these 60 we will find those which are interested in occurrences of event *E12* (25 ECA-rules).

$$COST_{E12} = \frac{RC_m}{R} = \frac{60}{250} = 0,24$$

$$URC_{E12} = 1 - \frac{RE_{E12}}{RC_m} = 1 - \frac{25}{60} = 1 - 0,42 = 0,58$$

where

RC_m : Rules that have subscribed to a reactive class m which generates primitive events.

Thus, the cost for finding rules interested in $E12$ has dropped from 1 to 0,24. Furthermore, unnecessary rule checks have been reduced from 0,9 to 0,58. In both calculations it is obvious that both the number of rules and unnecessary rule checks have been significantly reduced. Adopting rules indexed by classes reduces rule checking significantly in contrast to a centralized approach. Despite this, we have not reached the optimal solution were we only check those rules which are interested in the generated event, i.e URC_{Ei}=0.

We argue that the approach of indexing rules by classes cannot reach the optimal solution. The reason why indexing rules by classes still implies unnecessary rule checks, is a consequence of the architecture. By design each reactive object can have several different event generators attached to it, that will generate different types of events. Furthermore, each reactive object has a *special rule list attribute*, which is a set of rules that want to be notified when a reactive object generates a primitive event. This means that when an event generator generates a primitive event E_1, it will notify all rules in the *special rule list attribute* about event E_1. The event field value of those rules can be E_{1+n}, i.e. $E_1, E_2, ..., E_n$.

In [AMC93] it is identified that the subscription between rules and reactive objects can take place at two different levels of granularity. The rule can either subscribe to *all* events that are generated by a reactive object (rules indexed by classes, i.e. RC_m) or it can subscribe to *specific* events generated by a reactive object (RE_i). The first approach implies that rules are checked whenever each event generator within the reactive object generates an event. The second approach is more efficient since only rules that have subscribed to the generated event are notified. The major problem in adopting the second approach is that the reactive object needs to maintain one special rule list for each of its event generators, whereas only one special rule list needs to be maintained with the first approach.

3.3 Rules Associated with Specific Events

We propose a third approach to rule checking which supports subscription between rules and *specific* events generated by a reactive object. The semantics for associating rules with *specific* events generated by a reactive object are:

> When an event has been generated by an object check only those rules which have subscribed to the generated event.

The major advantage with this approach is that, run-time rule checking is reduced further than previous approaches, since only those rules that have subscribed to the generated event are notified. Furthermore, the subscription between rules and events can be established at run-time.

In [AMC93] it is identified that subscription between rules and specific events generated by a reactive object is more efficient than rules indexed by classes. However, the major problem in adopting subscription between rules and specific events is that the reactive object needs to maintain one special rule list for each of its event generators. This is in contrast to adopting rules indexed by classes, where only one special rule list needs to be maintained. Our claim is that this approach is too restrictive and implies that rules are notified about event occurrences that they are not interested in. The problems in adopting a subscription between rules and specific events generated by a reactive object arise from the underlying architecture. Thus, to accommodate subscription between rules and specific events generated by a reactive object we propose that the underlying architecture needs to be changed.

First of all we argue that the *special rule list* that every reactive object has should be removed. Thus only event generators that generate event occurrences need to be supported by a reactive object, e.g. methods as event generators. Secondly, we propose that the architecture should reflect the semantics of reactive behaviour. To accommodate this we propose that the event definition object should be extended to capture those rules that are to be notified about a specific event, i.e. the special rule list. To accommodate rule subscription we need to maintain at least two rule lists in the event definition object: one for class level rules; one for instance level rules. The lists of rules can be split into enabled and disabled rules to achieve better performance.

Adopting the previous formulae for rules associated with specific events:

$$COST_{E12} = \frac{RE_{E12}}{R} = \frac{25}{250} = 0,1$$

$$URC_{E12} = 1 - \frac{RE_{E12}}{RE_{E12}} = 1 - \frac{25}{25} = 1 - 1 = 0$$

In the example above, we have reduced the cost for finding rules interested in *E12* to a minimum. The cost have dropped from 0,24 to 0,1, which means that only those rules which have specifically subscribed to *E12* are involved in rule checking. This is also reflected in that no unnecessary rule checks are performed, i.e. URC_{E12}=0.

4 CIM Applications Based on Reactive Database Technology

Computer Integrated Manufacturing (CIM) and Shop Floor Control (SFC) are two of the areas where traditional databases have tried to manage problems such as monitoring quality, material resource and work in progress. In the following sections we will briefly describe an application for CIM/SFC which make use of the proposed architecture for ACOOD2.

4.1 Order Release Control

Order release control [HH+92] ensures that an order is not released to the shop floor until it is certain that all resources are available. With a good strategy for order release control it is possible to reduce order waiting times, work in progress and cycle times. For example, before an order is released to the shop floor, we must know that resources such as material, machine and operators are available. In order to meet due dates, we need to consider earliest feasible date for start of manufacturing and last feasible deadline for start of manufacturing. This can be expressed by the following primitive events:

DEFINE EVENT E12 ON AFTER Production::materialReady
DEFINE EVENT E13 ON AFTER Production::operatorReady
DEFINE EVENT E14 ON AFTER CIMstation::machineReady

Each of the event definitions are associated with an event generator. The previously defined primitive events can be combined to a composite event, which describes the situation when all resources are available.

DEFINE EVENT E15 AS (E12 AND E13 AND E14)

Rules can then be defined, which can react upon the occurrence of event *E15*, i.e. all resources are available. For example, we can define a rule *R1*, which handles order release control.

DEFINE RULE R1 ON EVENT E15
IF IsWithin(CurrentTime, EarliestFeasibleDeadline, LastFeasibleDeadline)
DO Scheduler.releaseOrderToShopFloor(int orderNo)

This means that the reactive database system can react to signals which indicate weather that resources are available. In this example, signals are sent from two different classes, i.e. Production and CIMstation. As soon as event occurrences for *E12*, *E13* and *E14* have been detected, then this will also mean that the composite event *E15* has occurred. When an event has been detected, we need to notify those rules which are interested in the detected event. In previous sections we have introduced a subscription mechanism which establishes an association between rules and specific events. Here, this mechanism would be used to notify all subscribers of occurrences of the above event. The notify mechanism notifies all rules that have subscribed to the detected event. It is important to notice that only those rules which have specifically subscribed to the detected event will be notified, i.e. URC_{Ei}=0.

This means that rule *R1* will be triggered as soon as the composite event *E15* has been completed.

4.2 Reactive Shop Floor Scheduling

The shop floor is a dynamic and sometimes also a unpredictable environment, where breakdowns and missing tools appear randomly. For example, when a machine breakdown occurs, reactions must be taken to update available capacity, re-route lots, change priority of affected lots, reschedule orders, and notify production manager.

There are several applications in Artificial Intelligence (AI) that are working with reactive shop floor scheduling [Ker90]. However these systems assume a small number of objects, that is rules and facts, which are stored in main memory and not in databases on secondary storage. Thus they do not support sharing, consistency, and concurrent execution of transactions.

Assume that an object-oriented application for CIM-machines is provided (Figure 1). Two event generators are provided, i.e. *E20* and *E12*. Event generator *E20* is associated with the invocation of method *updateStatus* in class *CIMstation* and *E12* is associated with the invocation of method *updateCapacity* in class *CIMstation*. Assume that the following event and rule definitions take place (only definitions related to *E20* are explicitly shown):

DEFINE EVENT E20 ON AFTER CIMstation::updateStatus(char* Status)

DEFINE RULE R2 ON EVENT E20
IF Status = 'break-down' DO Reschedule Orders

DEFINE RULE R3 ON EVENT E20 AND CIMstation100
IF Status = 'break-down' DO Notify Production Manager

When instance *CIMstation100* generates event *E20*, a signal will be sent to event definition *E20*, indicating an event occurrence of *E20*. It is important to notice that no unnecessary search for event definitions are done, since the event generator provide us with the event object identifier, i.e. *E20*. The event definition object of *E20* will then send a notification *only* to those rules that have subscribed to *E20*. In our example, both rule *R2* and *R3* will be notified.

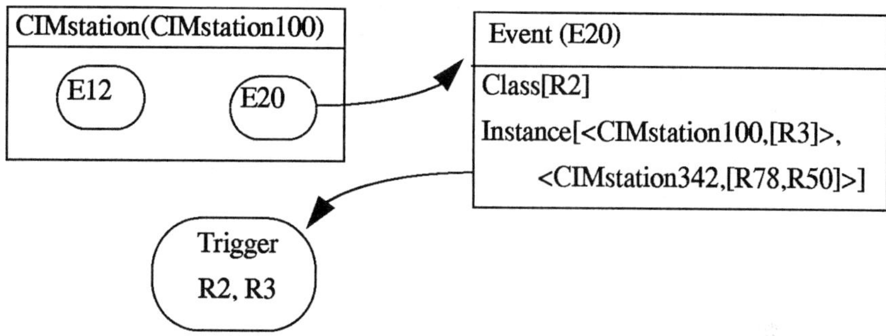

Fig. 1. Rules indexed by event object identifiers

Note that, although rule *R78* and *R50* are interested in event *E20*, they are not notified about the occurrence of event *E20*, since they have subscribed to event occurrences of *E20* generated by instance *CIMstation342*.

This example shows that it is possible to react upon specific situations such as a machine break-down for a specific instance. Thus, rules can be associated with events at two different levels of granularity: class level or instance level. That is, a rule can react to events generated by all instances of a particular class or it can react to events generated by a specific instance of a class.

5 Conclusion

In this paper we have explored a number of issues in providing powerful, systematic and efficient facilities for event and rule management in an object-oriented database management system.

Our approach allows a rule to subscribe to *specific events* that are generated by a reactive object. This means that only rules that have subscribed to the generated event are notified. This is in contrast to previous solutions where a rule subscribe to *all* events that are generated by a reactive object. Thus, rules are checked whenever each event generator within the reactive object generates an event. Furthermore, we have enhanced the concept of treating event definitions as first class objects, by extending them with *special rule lists*, instead of extending application classes. Thus only event generators need to be implemented in application classes.

Finally, we have introduced formulae for estimating the costs of rule checking.

References

[AMC93] E. Anwar, L. Maugis and S. Chakravarthy. Design and Implementation of Active Capability for an Object-Oriented Database. *UF-CIS Technical Report TR-93-001*, University of Florida, 1993.

[Ber94] M. Berndtsson. Management of Rules in Object-Oriented Databases. In *Proceedings of the Baltic Workshop on National Infrastructure Databases,* vol 1, pages 78-85, Vilnius, Lithuania, May 1994.

[BL92] M. Berndtsson and B. Lings. On Developing Reactive Object-Oriented Databases. *IEEE Data Engineering, Special issue on active databases*, vol 15 (1-4), pages 31-34, December 1992.

[CB+89] S. Chakravarthy, B. Blaustein, et al.. *HIPAC: A research project in active, time-constrained database management*, Final Technical report. Technical Report XAIT-89-02, Xerox Advanced Information Technology, August 1989.

[DBM88] U. Dayal, A. Buchmann, and D. McCarthy. Rules are Objects Too: A Knowledge Model for an Active, Object-Oriented Database Management System. In *Proceedings of the 2nd International Workshop on Object-Oriented Database Systems*, Sept. 1988.

[DPG91] O. Diaz, N. Paton and P. Gray. Rule Management in Object Oriented Databases: A Uniform Approach. In *Proc. of the 17th International Conference on VLDB*, pages 317-326, Barcelona, Spain, Sept. 1991.

[GD93] S. Gatziu and K. R. Dittrich. Events in an Active Object-Oriented Database System. In *Proceedings of the 1st Workshop on Rules in Database Systems,* Edinburg, pages 23-39, Edinburg, August 1993.

[GJS92] N. Gehani, H. V. Jagadish and O. Smueli. Event Specification in an Active Object-Oriented Database. In *Proc. of the ACM SIGMOD International Conference on Management of Data*, pages 81-90, San Diego, June 1992.

[Han89] E. Hanson. An Initial Report on the Design of Ariel: A DBMS With an Integrated Production Rule System. *SIGMOD Record, Special Issue on Rule Management and Processing in Expert Database Systems*, vol 18 (3), pages 12-19, Sept. 1989.

[HH+92] K. Hadavi, W-L. Hsu, et al. An Architecture for Real-Time Distributed Scheduling. In *Artificial Intelligence Applications for Manufacturing*, pages 215-234, AAAI Press/MIT Press, 1992.

[Ker90] Kerr, R. Knowledge-Based Manufacturing Management. Addison-Wesley, Sydney, 1990.

[MP91] C. B. Medeiros and P. Pfeffer. A Mechanism for Managing Rules in an Object-Oriented Database.*Technical Report Altair 65-91*, 1991.

[WF90] J. Widom and S.J. Finkelstein. Set-Oriented Production Rules in Relational Database Systems, In *Proc. of the ACM SIGMOD Inter national Conference on Management of Data*, pages 259-270, Atlantic City, New Jersey, May 1990.

Advanced Computer Integrated Technology for Furniture Manufacturing

Martin Eberl

Forschungszentrum Informatik, Haid-und-Neu-Str. 10-14
76131 Karlsruhe, Germany

Abstract. In this paper a system for integrated furniture manufacturing is described. The upcoming international standard STEP was adopted to specify the product models. As an integration platform an object-oriented database system is used. The client/server architecture allows simultaneous access to the product data by different CIM tools. Various data access methods are provided by the system. Tools for design, process planning, shop floor control etc. were developed or adopted and communicate with the help of the information system. In this way a continuous information flow is realized which may link together the different sections of a furniture enterprise.

1 Introduction

The reason for the work presented in this paper is the lack of flexibility and efficiency in the European furniture industry. The competition in this market sector often requires in particular the small and medium sized enterprises to react immediately on changing customer demands and to specialize on batch production. This however necessitates a well organized information flow throughout the whole enterprise, which often is not available. In other domains this could be attained by introducing computer integrated manufacturing (CIM) concepts. The particular requirements in the manufacturing of furniture and the special properties of the material wood, have so far often prevented the installation of advanced CIM technology within the furniture industry. It is therefore the objective of this paper to show how existing and newly developed CIM components can be introduced to furniture factories, and particularly in small and medium sized enterprises.

The system described here is based on an object-oriented database, which is the platform for integrating the different CIM tools. Data modelling and the specification of the interfaces of the system are achieved by using the upcoming international standard STEP. Information exchange can be done in several ways with the help of the product database. The client/server architecture provides simultaneous access by multiple users.

2 Information System

The information system is based on a distributed multi-user object-oriented database (see also [1]). Different tools (also called applications in this text) are implemented which access the database through various interfaces, as shown in Fig. 1. Examples are a design tool and a process planning tool.

The information system allows the specification and management of the product model, with its partial models. It also provides mechanisms to ensure a safe data access by the different tools. A tool can operate on a reserved part of the model or share information with other tools. In the second case, the manipulation of the data is monitored by special application programs called data managers. These resolve conflicts occurring when different processes try to manipulate information used by other processes.

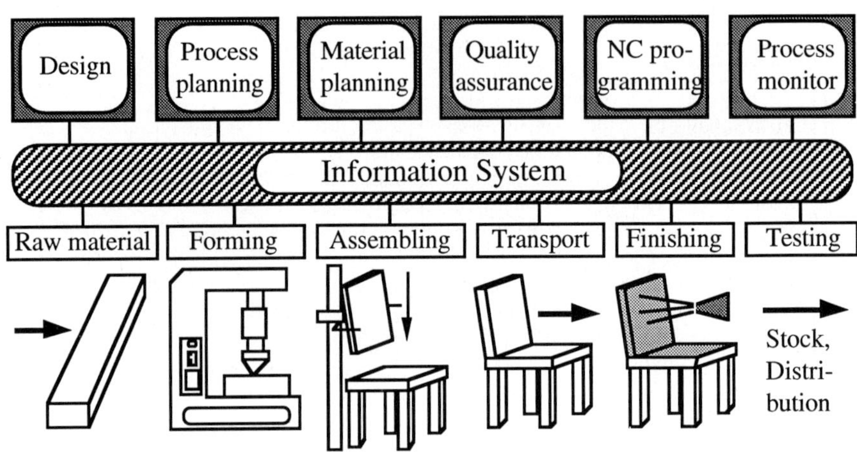

Fig. 1. Integration by the information system

Communication between the different tools is achieved with the help of a common product model for furniture. To solve the data exchange problem between different tools, the approach of the international standard ISO 10303, *Industrial automation systems and integration - Product data representation and exchange*, commonly known as STEP (Standard for the Exchange of Product Model Data), was followed. The goal of STEP is to effectively integrate computer-aided systems (see also [2]). Unlike approved standards such as IGES, for the exchange of drawing data and VDA-FS, for the exchange of freeform surfaces, STEP makes possible an implementation independent description of products throughout their whole life cycle. This is achieved with the help of the formal description language EXPRESS [3], which is used to describe the product data. A graphical representation of the models can be given with the help of EXPRESS-G. For each model specified by the use of EXPRESS a corresponding physical file format is defined.

Different models are defined in EXPRESS by using the SCHEMA construct. It declares the objects (named ENTITIES in EXPRESS) of a specific domain. Declarations of a SCHEMA can be made visible to other SCHEMAS. This allows references between objects of different models, which are necessary for example if objects for process planning have to deal with geometry data.

All SCHEMAS are processed by a compiler, generating for the corresponding EXPRESS ENTITIES a set of C++ classes. The definitions of these classes are used to generate the meta-information of the product database. The applications can then manipulate the instances of these classes by functions generated by the compiler or additional functions implemented in the scope of the application. The processing of the SCHEMAS and the access by the applications is shown in Fig. 2. The specification with the help of EXPRESS is a condition for correct data manipulation and transfer. Syntactical correctness is verified by the compiler, semantic aspects are under the responsibilty of the developer.

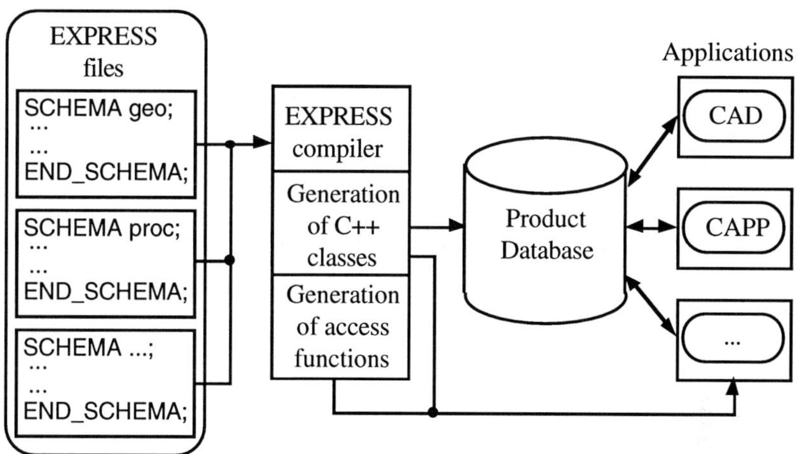

Fig. 2. Generating a product database

The definitions of the C++ classes are used both for the meta schema of the product database as well as in the application programs to specify the interface to the database. Being connected to the database, an application can now manipultate the corresponding objects.

3 Product Model for Furniture

The product model has to fulfill the requirements that occur when dealing with furniture and wood (see [4]). Solid wood is a heterogeneous, porous raw material and its quality is influenced by many circumstances such as the wood species, climatic conditions and the preparation of the raw part. In the case of sheet materials, quality is determined by fabrication and the raw materials. Another important aspect is the quality of each wooden part including e.g. the texture of a solid wood shelf.

The product model comprises the different types of solid wood and sheet materials with their special properties, which are part of the workpieces used for furniture manufacturing. Other workpieces used are fittings such as hinges, graspings and closings or connection means like screws, dowels and nails. Workpieces as sub-assemblies or furniture products are represented by a topology which describes the components of the part.

Further sub-models exist which describe woodwork and furniture manufacturing under the aspects of drawings and geometry, process planning, production planning, stock management of production components and shop floor control. Using another model, functional aspects of furniture and furniture components can then be modelled. This allows the design of furniture, for example, to be considered ergonomically.

Information of the different models is then stored and managed in the product database. A group of data managers is responsible for ensuring the integrity of the data.

4 Applications

Some applications were developed which access the product database. In Fig. 3 the communication between the furniture modeler and the product database is shown.

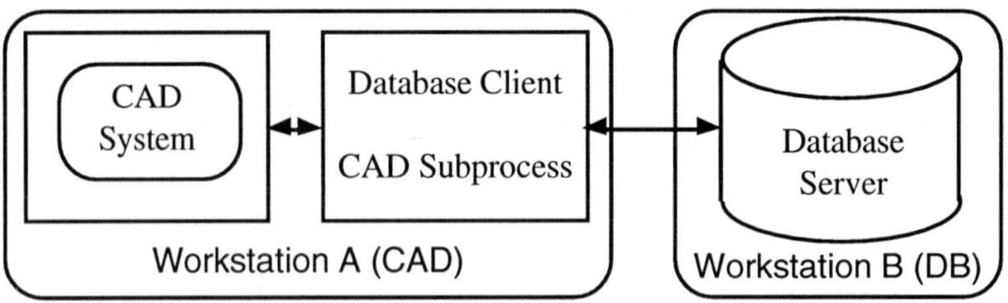

Fig. 3. Integration of the furniture modeler

The modeler is based on a commercial CAD system with an application programming interface. After starting the CAD system, at least one application process is started by this system. This may also be database client processes. These processes add new functions to the existing geometric modelling facilities of the system, including functions for information transfer to and from the product database. The modeler is described in detail in [5].

Besides defining the geometry of the product, the modeler also helps to add further information about furniture products. This enables the designer to act with more than just the simple geometric data. He can also make use of information related to process planning and manufacturing of the products. The new facilities are then added to the CAD system, with the help of an advanced user interface containing menu support. Fig. 4 shows the furniture modeler, WoodCAD, and an example of furniture modelled with the system.

Various functions serve to select materials and parts necessary for the furniture manufacturing process. Apart from solid wood and sheet materials, veneers are used for covering and surface finishing. The furniture modeler takes this into account by offering menus used for selecting the different materials. Since solid wood parts are limited to certain sizes, jointed parts are often used in furniture production. The modeler offers jointing methods such as overfolded joints, tongued or doweled joints, which are commonly used in furniture manufacturing. Standard parts such as fittings, may also be selected and inserted into the drawing.

A second set of functions offers the manufacturing operations most commonly used when working with furniture. Since the designers modelling the furniture parts often think in terms relating to the manufacturing process, including this information at an early stage of the product development process is hereby made possible. This information is important for further stages of the development process, e.g. for planning the process steps or for choosing the corresponding machine tools of the shop floor.

The manufacturing of grooves and tongues, normally done by a sawing or moulding process, is one of these operations. The system also helps to specify the position of the grooves and tongues, relative to the part, for example perpendicular to the surface. Drilling processes are often used to manufacture joints by using dowels or screws. Different types of holes, e.g. sink, step or tenon holes are available for this process. Profile moulding is carried out by a moulding machine with specially shaped moulding cutters or heads. It is useful for the designer to have a choice of moulding cutters at his disposal. The system can represent the shape of available cutters in a graphical manner. The profile moulding along the edge of a part is supported particularly by the system. It also offers assembling methods such as gluing, nailing, screwing or doweling and in addition supports the specification of the corresponding glue type, screws etc.

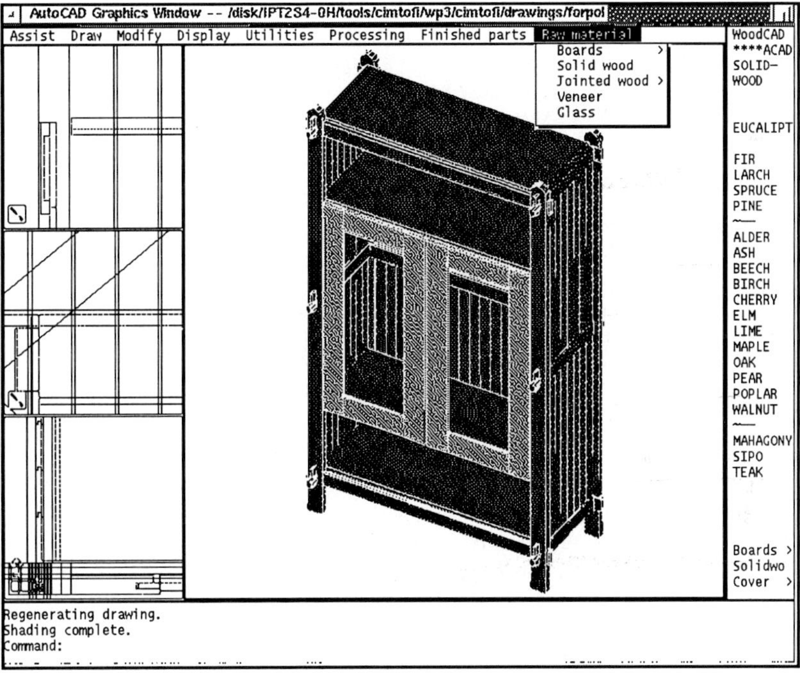

Fig. 4. The furniture modeler WoodCAD

These operations, together with other functions, are implemented with the application programming interface of the CAD system and can be applied to the design process. All the information relating to process steps, materials etc. is automatically stored together with the geometry in the product database. Another application, for instance the process planning tool, can then use this information.

The geometry browser is another tool accessing information stored in the product database. It can display the geometry data graphically together with the additional information of materials, manufacturing data etc. This is helpful in getting an overview of the product and to discover similarities with other products.

5 Conclusions

The system described in this paper uses commercially available software products as well as newly developed extensions for the use in furniture factories. Existing components can be used but have to be adopted because of the special requirements of the material and the manufacturing of furniture.

A specification of the models used for wood and furniture products as well as the interfaces of the system, is achieved with the help of the formal language EXPRESS of the international standard STEP. The product information is stored in an object-oriented database, serving as an integration platform for the different applications.

Applications can access the product database directly over a network or may communicate by file transfer. The information system provides simultaneous access by multiple users and concurrent work is supported by the use of different tools.

Following the strategies described in this paper, CIM technology can be applied in the domain of furniture manufacturing. This will increase the flexibility and efficiency of product development and in addition lead to reduced costs and an improved product quality.

Acknowledgements

This research was partly funded by the European Community under the scope of the Brite/Euram project CIMTOFI (CIM System with Improved Capabilities for Furniture Industry). The author wishes to thank Prof. Dr.-Ing. R. Dillmann for his appreciated support of this research.

References

1. Andleigh, P. K., Gretzinger, M. R.: Distributed Object-Oriented Data-Systems Design. PTR Prentice Hall, Englewood Cliffs, New Jersey (1992)
2. Mason, H., ed., ISO 10303: Industrial Automation Systems - Product Data Representation and Exchange, Part 1: Overview and fundamental principles. ISO committee draft (1992)
3. Spiby, P., ed., ISO 10303: Industrial Automation Systems - Product Data Representation and Exchange, Part 11: Description Methods: The EXPRESS Language Reference Manual. ISO release draft (1991)
4. Erdmann, Th.; Entwurf und Implementierung eines objektorientierten Produktmodells zur Möbelfertigung. Diploma thesis, University of Karlsruhe (1992)
5. Willhauck, C.; Ein objektorientiertes Konstruktionssystem für Möbel. Diploma thesis, University of Karlsruhe (1992)

A Distributed System for CIM

Vladimír Mařík, Jiří Lažanský, Jiří Koutník, Tomáš Hazdra

Czech Technical University, Faculty of Electrical Engineering
Technická 2, CZ 16627 Praha 6, Czech Republic
e-mail: marik@lab.felk.cvut.cz

Abstract

This paper describes some basic issues and requirements for software structure of distributed CIM systems. Such systems have a wide applicability, especially in the context of geographically distributed manufacturing and business facilities. The paper describes also some introductory experiments on coupling and communication between the autonomous agents that act as stand-alone systems and can cooperate*.

1. Introduction

The idea of CIM (Computer Integrated Manufacturing) emphasizes its global strategic goal: to integrate all company activities into a unified management structure exploring a large scale hierarchy of computers. It is expected to embrace corporate product design, manufacturing, marketing, sales management, planning, scheduling, real-time machine control, material handling, assembling, quality control and product dispatching.

The up-to-date CIM software development methodology is based on the idea of a global Product Life Cycle Model (PLCM). The PLCM prescribes which sequence of steps should be taken to develop a final product and its *product model* (PM). PM contains all the data and processes connected (manipulated or generated) within all phases of the product life cycle from its creation to maintenance phases. The complex task of CIM includes many complicated phases, like CAD, CAP (Process Planning), PPS (Production Planning and Scheduling), CAM (Manufacturing Control), CAQ (Quality Assurance), and CAB (Computer Aided Business Administration). Each of these subtasks requires specific algorithmic solutions exploring huge amount of data and problem-oriented knowledge.

It has been recognized that iterative cycles among different phases of the PLCM are necessary. For instance, the design phase can be significantly influenced by the knowledge/data concerning planning and manufacturing phases. Very large savings of the total costs are possible if right decisions are done taking the information about the "neighboring" stages.

As shown in [Mar93], there is a good analogy between the up-to-date CIM-software life cycle methodologies and the PLCM. These methodologies utilize the idea of the performance-based specification and take into account such features like fast prototyping and iterative development cycles. They represent a good theoretical background of concurrent engineering in both CIM-software and product model engineering.

---

* This research has been done as a preparatory phase of the EU–PECO Project No. 9645 *Eurosat - CIM via Satellite* and the Austrian government project No. GZ 45.339/2-IV/6a/94 *The Open Architecture of Knowledge-Based Systems*.

The CIM task becomes much more complicated in the case of a company with geographically distributed units (e.g. when the technology development department, administration headquarters, and production facilities are located in different towns/countries). Efficient cooperation among the geographically distributed CIM subsystems requires new approaches. It is expected that these will be based on present techniques of *distributed artificial intelligence* (DAI) [Dor92].

Most CIM tasks are very *data-intensive*. The need for flexibility in manufacturing implies fast prototyping according to the PLCM. It involves *cycles* in the product development that must manipulate huge amounts of data. Considering now the geographical distribution of all these activities we arrive at extremely high demands on communication channels in the system.

Some aspects of complex CIM tasks in a geographically distributed environment are discussed in this paper. Results of initial experiments with the first prototype of distributed knowledge-based system are presented.

2. Methods of Distributed AI and CIM Tasks

The methods of DAI may be explored for the top-level control strategy of loosely coupled CIM subsystems. The DAI is usually split into two primary areas [Bon88]:

- *Distributed problem solving:* The subsystems are viewed as modules that cooperate at the level of dividing and sharing data/knowledge about the current Product Model.
- *Multi-agent systems:* The subsystems are considered as active autonomous intelligent agents coordinating their behavior by negotiations or protocols to achieve their joint goal. A unified system of communication channels is usually applied. The more autonomous subsystems, the less global data and strategic knowledge must be stored and explored on the top control level.

The control and cooperation among the subsystems may be performed either by the method of *shared global memory* or by *message passing*. The former method is usually implemented in the form of a *blackboard* control structure, whereas the latter is implemented in *actor models* [He77].

The trials to organize an analogy of the global shared memory for CIM tasks in the form a centralized database have failed. Obviously, the centralized database becomes even more unrealistic in the case of geographically distributed CIM systems. The technique of multi-agent systems and actor models fits much better the real-life demands of distributed CIM systems.

An actor is an autonomous unit that communicates by messages with the other actors. The actor contains a set of operations determining the actor's reactions to messages received. These reactions may be: sending messages, changing its internal state, creating new actors, etc. The messages of an actor have defined destination and may be sent only to those actors that are known to the sending actor.

The philosophy of actors leads to the possibility of considering actors as structures that combine both procedures and data into a single entity - *object*. That is why the *object-oriented methodology* may be regarded as one of favorable schemes applicable in development of distributed CIM systems. The object-oriented (OO) approach is a good paradigm for organizing and facilitating the communication among the CIM subsystems. The subsystems may be not only linked but really *integrated* through the object entities that can reflect various aspects of the PLCM at the same time. As shown in [Za86], the notion of object plays an important unifying role in organizing both the databases and knowledge bases as well as in establishing an efficient information transfer between them. The mutual communication between knowledge-based systems and data retrieval systems can be organized in a natural and straightforward way.

3. Architecture of Multi-Agent Systems for CIM

There are four fundamental questions associated with each multi-agent systems design, namely:

a) How to decompose the task into subtasks?
b) How to allocate the tasks to the problem solving units?
c) How and what to communicate?
d) How to control the system globally?

3.1. Task decomposition and allocation

Let's expect that the CIM task should be solved at various geographically distributed sites (network nodes). The decomposition of the entire CIM task is usually already given by the physical location of the facilities (workshops, design departments, marketing units, etc.) and relatively very specific, well-defined functions of these facilities. According to the functionality, many typical units can be found. Let's mention some of the most important units that should be involved in the overall system design:

- *Selling agencies*. There are multiple geographically distributed selling agencies offering the assortment of products. Their task is also to accept orders and maintain the entire negotiation with the customers. This includes the following tasks:
  - The customer is provided with detailed information on available goods, on production conditions, on typical pilot case-studies, etc.
  - The customer orders the goods.
  - Before the contract confirmation, the agency has to send the order to a business coordination unit that can determine the delivery conditions (due-date, pricing, etc.)
  - The agency keeps track of each order having been accepted.
- *Business coordination unit*. This unit is central for every group of goods. The desired activities are:
  - Negotiation with selling agencies about their requirements.
  - Negotiation with the manufacturing units on their ability to deliver particular products at a given price in the desired time.
  - Keeping track of manufacturing units' capacities and long-term planning
  - Assignment of orders to particular manufacturing units.
- *Manufacturing units* carry out the appropriate manufacturing. Their activities (from the information point of view) among others include:
  - Determination of production constraints for the capacity planning
  - Short-term (operative) production scheduling. This task can be provided by separate scheduling centers, each of them serving several manufacturing units.

The scheduling task is computationally expensive. This approach can be efficient if costly computers are involved but it requires additional communications.

- Material requirement planning and material supply.

- *Technology development unit.* These units are responsible for product design and development, and manufacturing documentation. These units interact with:
  - sales agencies providing them with technical information on new products and collecting innovative customers' demands,
  - manufacturing units supplying them with technical documentation and receiving feedback on design modifications (*concurrent engineering*),
  - business coordination unit consulting strategic decisions.

This concise description takes into account the main technical information flows, only. In the real-world tasks also accounting, maintenance of resources, legal affairs, and marketing activities has to be supported.

From the facts presented in this paragraph it follows immediately that both the CIM task decomposition and the allocation of subtasks are usually predefined and do not represent a substantial problem.

3.2. Inter-agent communication and control strategy

Every functional unit (agent) of a multi-agent system may be considered as a computational process that consists of two parts:

- domain-dependent problem solving part which does not contain knowledge about the other agents or about the overall control strategy,
- domain-independent coordination part responsible for communication and coordination activities. The coordination parts contain all the knowledge about the rest of the multi-agent system.

The coordination parts of agents represent elementary control units inside the multi-agent system as there is no central control unit. The only way how to accomplish the global control strategy is to do it through knowledge owned by the individual agents. This part of knowledge usually has the form of explicit rules describing the behaviour of each agent itself as well as the behaviour of other agents. There are general rules (valid for all agents) and very specific rules used to express the control knowledge owned by a single agent. The agent-specific knowledge is extensive in CIM tasks where it plays the dominant role because of strong functional specialization of the CIM-subsystems.

One of the main problems of practical applications of multi-agent CIM systems is the design of agents and their communication channels. A detailed analysis of many interdependencies, mutual requirements on coordination, and on data and knowledge flow should be carried out. This work is tedious, time consuming, and expensive. The necessary analysis represents a real bottleneck and is usually done "by hand" in the current systems. There are only a few systems (like, e.g. HITOP-A [Gas93]) which already contain some modules supporting this analytical process.

Recently, much effort has be aimed to the development of environments supporting the efficient and rapid prototyping and subsequent maintenance of multi-agent systems. These environments provide a set of tools and the associated corresponding design methodologies are usually called *agent factories* (e.g. AFACT [O'Ha93]).

Another approach, called *agent-oriented programming* [Sho90] can be viewed as a specialization of the object-oriented programming. An agent is considered as an object with a particular structure that includes some pre-defined elements. The inter-agent communication in the form of message passing is considerably more stylized than the object-oriented approach.

Both these approaches seem to be very promising, but still very far from commercial availability. Nearly all the CIM solutions, even based on DAI philosophy, are implemented ad hoc. Even the well-theory-based multi-agent systems are usually implemented from scratch and the software engineers have to tailor both the agent structures and communication methods. Well-developed methodologies and suitable tools are still missing.

Our long-term goal is to explore the advantages of both the agent factory and agent-oriented approaches and to develop a user-friendly environment. This environment should enable to explore a library of CIM prototype agents as well as to implement the inter-agent communication in a very transparent and efficient style.

The multi-agent system needs a good communication support. Designing of the communication support is extremely influenced by

- the platform where the global communication should run,
- the language chosen for the implementation of the control algorithms,
- the type of communication chosen.

The platform should provide the network support and communication support, control and synchronization resources (tools for controlling and arbitrating among several communicating parallel processes) as well as data encapsulation and protection possibilities. Typical platforms that satisfy these conditions are, for instance, UNIX-based workstations.

The language for multi-agent information processing should also satisfy several basic conditions: It should be an object-oriented, supported by tools for distributed development, transparent and easily understandable, equipped with a sufficient library. The comparative analysis of the common object oriented languages discovered that each of these languages (C++, SMALLTALK, OPAL, EIFFEL) provides some advantages and some drawbacks. None of them has a complete distributed development support. None of them could be unambiguously preferred as the best one.

In principle, there are two basic concepts of inter-agent connection: (1) *client-server* and (2) *peer-to-peer*.

The CIM tasks require that the communication is organized by peer-to-peer links. The current platforms usually support the client-server connections, only. Communication possibilities include facility of *interprocess communication* (IPC), *Berkeley socket specification*, and higher-level *remote procedure calls* (RPC).

The designer usually faces the problem how to ensure the mutual peer-to-peer communication by the client-server supporting means. This problem can be solved in the following two ways:

One possibility is to use directly some low level network communication protocol that allows the peer-to-peer connections (e.g. UDP). The main disadvantage of these low level protocols is the unsafe communication. The message in this protocol could be lost or duplicated and the time ordering of the messages could be changed.

Additional specific algorithms avoiding these unwanted features make the multi-agent system implementation more complicated.

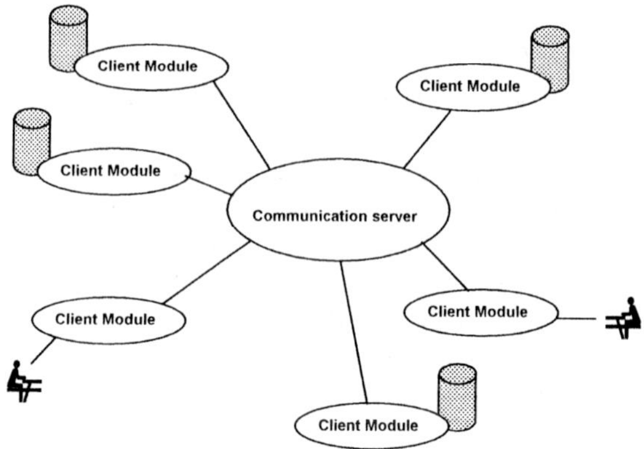

Fig. 1: Client-server star-like scheme

An alternative approach is to organize the communication so that the peer-to-peer behavior is emulated by the client-server connections where a star-like structure is used (Fig. 1). It consists of a central server that provides the connection service among the clients. The behavioral level looks like a set of peer-to-peer connections (Fig. 2). This structure has several advantages. It enables to add new agents during the multi-agent system operation, to control the communications states, to broadcast messages in a simple way, etc. The main shortcoming of this topology it is that when the central node fails, the entire multi-agent system fails, too.

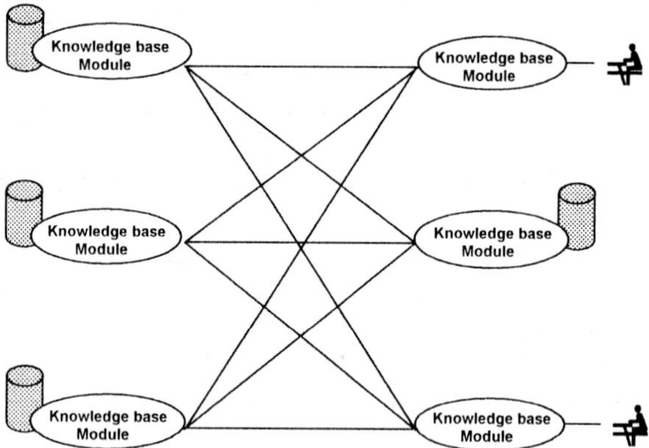

Fig. 2: Application look: peer-to-peer

4. Experiments

4.1. The task specification

According to our discussions above, an experimental version of a multi-agent system has been developed and implemented. As the team has had some experience in design and application of rule-based expert systems [Mar92], it was decided to implement a distributed rule-based expert system as the first prototype of a distributed CIM system.

The developed system, as a whole, looks like a set of agents communicating to each other through the INTERNET. Each agent is represented by an individual expert system and the communication is accomplished by sending messages among the individual systems.

The individual expert system is classical rule-based expert system whose inference engine works with Bayesian model of uncertainty. The knowledge base has the form of an inference net that is used to permanently update the actual model of the case.

The knowledge base or the actual model of an individual expert system can be incomplete - some information could be missing. In this case, the coordination part of this agent generates a message containing a query for the required information. The message is broadcasted to the other agents (expert systems). If any of them contains the required piece of information, the acknowledge message is generated and sent back to the requesting agent. This message indicates to the system-requester that it is worth waiting for the required piece of information. In the meantime, the agent having the required piece of information interrupts its activity and tries to answer the received query. The answer message is sent to the waiting agent-requester. If the agent-requester does not receive any response to its query, it has to keep satisfied with the local (maybe default) values. The solution is less accurate in this case but the best possible.

Each of the expert systems can be explored as standalone. The domain-dependent knowledge base (which solves the local tasks) contains only some little additions for the problem-independent coordination parts of the agents. The information that is not locally available is flagged "*remote*" in the inference net. This flag means that there might be some other agent that can provide the required information.

4.2. Implementation aspects

Communication support has been divided into two parts. The first part was the implementation of client-server connection in INTERNET. We have used TCP/IP communication protocol and the socket mechanism. The second part was the message passing between agents that emulates peer-to-peer connections.

There were two experimental implementations for achieving the peer-to-peer communication model. The first experiment exploited the standard socket mechanism and built the peer-to-peer model by direct emulation.

The second attempt to implement the peer-to-peer structure was based on the support of *parallel virtual machine* (PVM) mechanism [Ge91]. The PVM supports the peer-to-peer connection model on the network level. It also enables to start remote processes that can run as autonomous agents. Unfortunately, the system requires a precise and complete list of workstations used in the built network. However, this disadvantage could be removed by including the original socket based system as one component of the PVM system implementation.

The system has been developed according to the object-oriented software paradigm in the EIFFEL language. A class hierarchy was designed. The implementation continued by the design of the communication subsystem and stand-alone expert system shells that represent individual agents. The communication layering and the main classes of our multi-agent system are shown in Fig. 3.

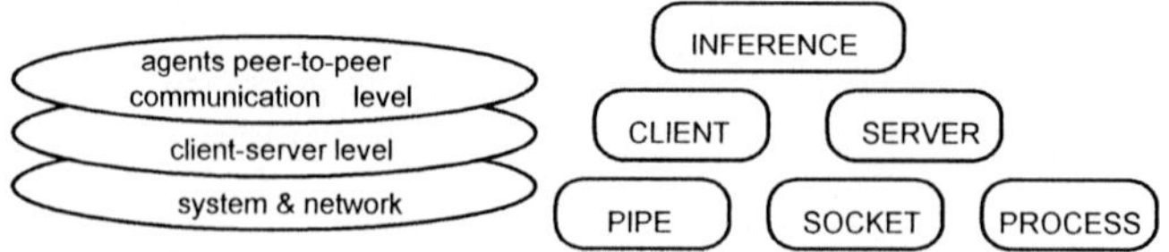

Fig. 3: Communication layering and classes

The basic level represents the system, the network distributed environment, and the resources. The classes PIPE, SOCKET, and PROCESS are the object representations of resources. The basic system level is covered by the client-server level, where two types of processes are implemented. The first is *server system* (Fig. 4) which forks into two slave processes: *transmitter* and *receiver* to accomplish the communication among clients. The second is the *client system* (Fig. 5) which represents an individual agent. The corresponding classes were created according to this idea (SERVER, CLIENT, RECV, TRANSMT).

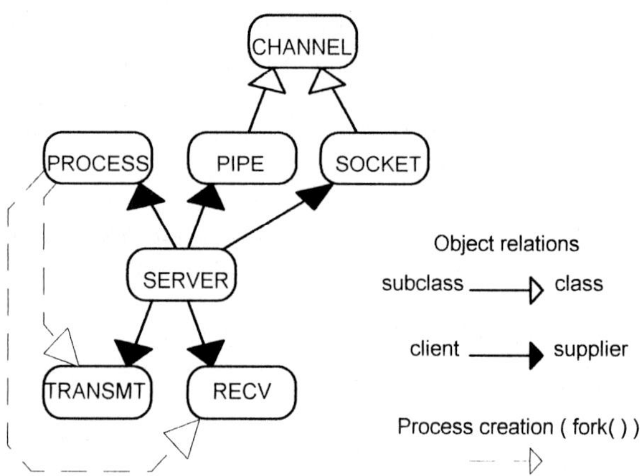

Fig. 4: Server system

At the end, the agents - experts were implemented. The classes INFERENCE, NODE, RULE and ACTUAL_MODEL were developed and used to join both parts of the system (Fig. 5). This solution ensures easy modification of the systems' functionality.

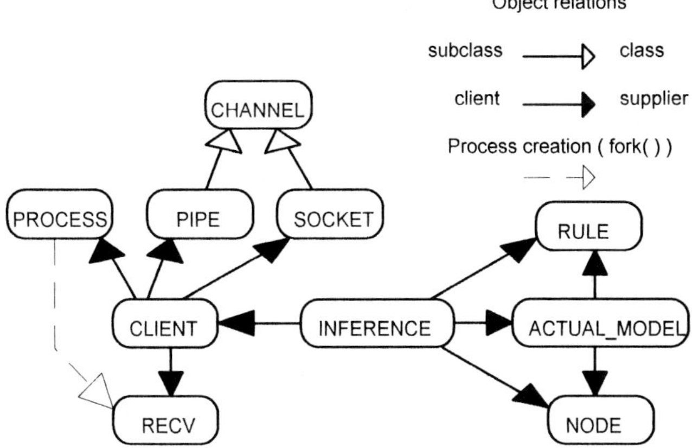

Fig. 5: Client system joined with expert (agent)

4.3. Higher-level control

The actual model of each consultation is represented as a set of nodes in the inference net. Relationships among them are represented by weighted links. When probability of some node is changed, all its descendants are updated recursively. The inference engine works as follows [Mar92]:

- At each step, one of the goal assertions is investigated. This assertion is chosen by the system when it is not completely resolved. During the consultation, three phases of the system activity alternate:
  1. *Selection of a question*: According to the actual probabilities in the model, the system selects such a question, the answer to which will contribute to the model accuracy most strongly.
  2. *Updating of the actual model*: The new information obtained from the reply is propagated along the links in the inference net from the current node to the goal nodes.
  3. *Message processing*: The messages obtained during one inference cycle are processed.
- The solution is absolved if all goal nodes are resolved, i.e. if all possible questions were asked.

The missing information concerning an assertion is represented by marking the assertion by the flag *remote*. It informs the inference engine that there could be some other system in the network which knowledge base contains the same assertion. If such a system exists it should respond to the query broadcasted through the network.

4.4. Evaluation of experiments and future plans

The first experiment had been aimed to verify the communication capabilities of the proposed system. Three nodes (2 of them at CTU in Prague, the third located at FAW Linz, Austria) were involved into the topology. Real life knowledge bases (from the area of diagnostics) were used in the first experiments. It was verified that the entire distributed system behaves better than expected even though the INTERNET connections from Prague are very slow.

In the near future, the fourth node (in U.K.) is planned to be added and other types of agents will be included. One of the planned agents should include data retrieval subsystem based on POSTGRESS database. Another agent will include a qualitative reasoning tool, and still another is supposed to search for optimal solutions using genetic algorithms.

References:

[Bon88] Bond, A. H., Gasser, L. (editors): *Readings in Distributed Artificial Intelligence*. Morgan Kaufmann, 1988

[Dor92] Doran, J.: *Distributed AI and its Applications*. In: Advanced Topics in AI, Springer Verlag, Heidelberg, LNAI No. 617, 1992, pp. 368-372

[Gas93] Gasser, L.: *DAI Approaches to Coordination*. In: Distributed AI: Theory and Praxis (Avouris, M.N., Gasser, L. eds.), Kluwer Academic Publ., Dordrecht, 1993, pp. 31-52.

[Ge91] Geist, A., Sunderam, V.: *Network Based Concurrent Computing on the PVM System*. Available by FTP from the University of Atlanta from 1991

[He77] Hewitt, C.: *Control Structures as Patterns for Passing Messages*. Artificial Intelligence, vol. 8 (1977), pp. 323-363

[Mar92] Mařík, V., Lažanský, J., Vlček, T., Retschitzegger, W.: *Experiments on Coupling Expert and Database Systems*. In: Proc. of DEXA'92 (Tjoa, A.M., Ramos, I. editors), Springer Verlag, Vienna, 1992, pp. 525-530

[Mar93] Mařík, V., Lažanský, J., Štěpánková, O.: The AI Impacts on CIM-Concepts. In: Proc. of 4th Annual Int. Conf. AIS'93, Tucson, IEEE Computer Society Press, 1993, pp. 288-294.

[O'Ha93] O'Hare, G.M.P., Wooldridge, M.J.: A Software Engineering Perspective on Multi-Agent System Design. In: Distributed AI: Theory and Praxis (Avouris, M.N., Gasser, L. eds.), Kluwer Academic Publ., Dordrecht, 1993, pp. 109-128.

[Sho90] Shoham, Y.: Agent Oriented Programming. Tech. Rep. Stan-CS-90-1335, Stanford University, Palo Alto, CA, 1990.

[Za86] Zaniolo, C. and others: *Object-Oriented Database Systems and Knowledge Systems*. In: Expert Database Systems (Kerschberg, L. ed.), Benjamin/Cummings Publ., Menlo Park, 1986, pp. 49-651

Integrated-Company-Software (INCOSOFT) - a special solution for small- and medium-sized companies

Peter Starzacher, Wolfram Wöß

Research Institute for Applied Knowledge Processing (FAW), Johannes Kepler University Linz, Hauptstraße 99, A-4232 Hagenberg, Austria, Net: wolfram@faw.uni-linz.ac.at, Tel: (+43-732) 2468/9589, Fax: (+43-732) 2468/9308

Abstract. The goal of this paper is to systematize CIM-laboratories with a detailed description of a real CIM-factory which realises the solving proposals of model factories.

In the first half of the paper we explain the importance of CIM for small- and medium-sized companies. In order to support these kinds of companies in the development of CIM-systems research institutes and universities have built model factories and simulation models to present their theoretical knowledge in a practical way. Because these model factories do not provide on appropriate CIM-solutions for small- and medium-sized companies we developed INCOSOFT (Integrated Company Software), which is a special solution for small sized companies.

The second half of the paper is devoted to the description of the components of INCOSOFT, the hard- and software-requirements, some implementation aspects and the differences between the software systems of small- and medium-sized companies and and those of large scale industry. Programming was done in a 4th generation language, data administration is handled by a relational database. The CIM-software runs on a PC-LAN with a central file server and a database server. INCOSOFT fulfils the special requirements of small- and medium-sized companies and integrates standard software with non-standard-software. Therefore INCOSOFT pays attention to the low financial power of small- and medium-sized companies.

Key Words. CIM, leitstand, INCOSOFT, database application, small- and medium-sized companies, CIM-laboratory, CIM-factory, model factory.

1. CIM in Order to Gain the Competitiveness

The transformation of the market from a selling market into a buyers' market leads to major changes in a substantial number of companies. Nowadays companies are forced to produce products of a high technical standard in small quantities and in numerous variants. One strategy to meet these requirements is to implement a CIM-system in the company.

Recent research of the VDMA (Verband Deutscher Maschinen- und Anlagenbau) about the use and potential of CIM-systems of small- and medium-sized companies show that these companies compared to large scale industry have an enormous backlog demand in the use of such computer supported factory automation.

Two aspects must be taken into consideration in order not to decrease the competitiveness of small- and medium-sized companies compared to large scale industry in the next few years.

- Only solutions which are built up step-by-step under consideration of the whole operational area and a future expansion lead to positive results and economic success. Especially a limited capital investment is of importance for small companies. Therefore the economical and well-aimed use of the available limited financial resources is of first priority [Schossig 1992].

- Small- and medium-sized companies must be supported in the training of their employees and in the consultance of these companies. This is important all the more as in these companies only little experience exists with computer supported automation and the realisation of such computer supported systems is bound up with high costs [Schulz 1990].

1.1. Training and Consulting of Companies

In small- and medium-sized companies a bottleneck often exists in the capital intensive research and development. In order to help these companies out of this dilemma some universities offer company specific and producer neutral consultance as well as objective information about the field possibilities, state of the art and consequent effects of computer supported systems.

In order to present this theoretical knowledge more and more universities make use of CIM-laboratories.

1.2. Systematisation of CIM Laboratories from a Technical Point of View

Simulation models which can be used to reproduce CIM-systems can be subdivided into two categories:

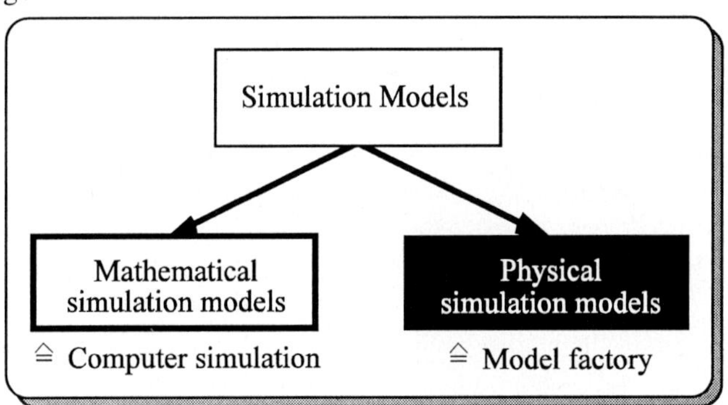

Fig. 1. Systematisation of simulation models.

- mathematical simulation models = computer simulation programs

  These are programs which mainly represent parts respectively special machines of a CIM-factory and which run interactively with the user of the program. It is possible to simulate different operating runs by changing the parameters.

  Computer simulations make the instruction of technical facts feasible, but demand abstract intellectual power and do not enable, for reasons of their model character, a production oriented training. This is the reason why they remain limited to the level of a symbolic representation. Accordingly, a real production as a product and production oriented activity, which also stimulates the practical knowledge, is not possible. In addition staff members are often overcharged with this symbolic representation of a system and therefore they cannot identify themselves with this kind of simulation.

Furthermore, it is impossible to demonstrate with computer simulations in which different ways systems are co-operating with each other. But to link different systems by interfaces are one of the most important problems within a CIM-system from a technical point of view.

- physical simulation models = model factories

  They are characterised by an extensive objective correspondence. In order to limit the modelling effort, simplifications during the development of the model are a prerequisite. Like computer simulations, this kind of model is often used for planning and checking systems if the direct examination of the real system is too expensive or too dangerous, and for demonstration and training purposes. Recently, more and more miniature or conventional industrial machines and robots, which are integrated by information and communication technologies, are used for these CIM-teaching and demonstration purposes.

Model factories can be divided into two categories:

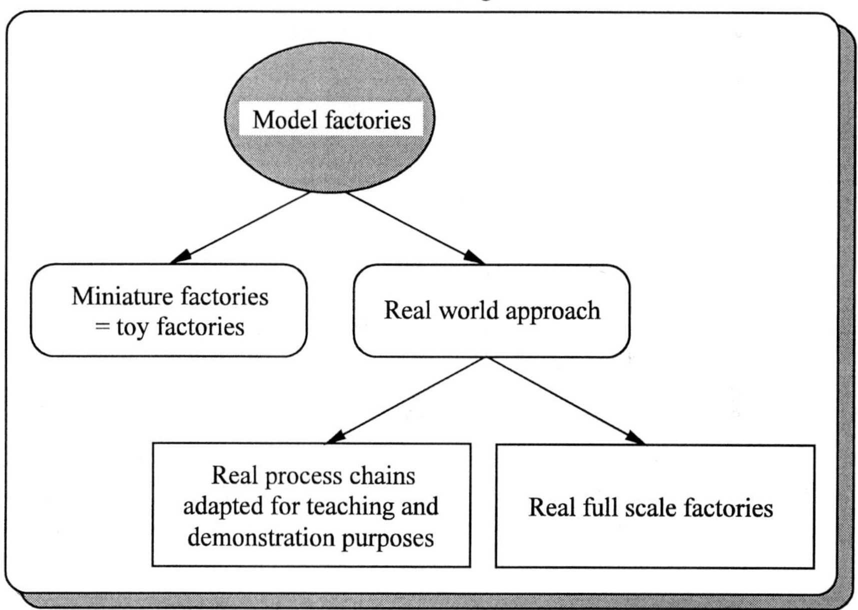

Fig. 2. Systematisation of model factories.

Miniature or Toy Factories

Miniature or toy factories are CIM-factories on a small scale. These factories are made of a construction set from Festo, Lego or similar firms.

On the basis of the use of miniature machines the limited space consumption is one of the fundamental characteristics. This limited space consumption does also result in an excellent clearness over the system and therefore represents the essential difference to the real world systems. Another characteristic of these factories is that they focus on the integration of as many CIM-components as possible. On the other hand employees often find it difficult to accept these miniature factories because they view them as a toy.

Real World Approach

Unlike miniature factories the local requirements for real world factories is much higher. Conventional industrial NC, CNC, DNC machines are used to build such factories. Real world factories can be divided into two categories,

- real process chains adapted for teaching and demonstration purposes
- real full scale factories

which we describe now.

Real Process Chains Adapted for Teaching and Demonstration Purposes

Not the integrated order processing from order reception to dispatch is in the centre of interest, but the realisation of single CAD/CAM process chains. Flexibility is probably the most important advantage of these solutions. With such a model factory it is possible to solve different problems and to remove or assemble process chains without influencing other parts of the model factory.

Real Full Scale Factories

Real full scale factories focus their attention on the entire integration of conventional industrial systems and machines.

On the one hand this kind of a model factory has the advantage of a realistic demonstration object by the use of real machines and therefore a high acceptance of employees. But on the other hand the costs for the implementation, operation and maintenance of the factory are extremely high and as a consequence these factories can hardly be financed.

So we have put the emphasis of our analysis on finding out whether CIM-model factories represent good demonstration objects for CIM-applications of small- and medium-sized companies.

1.3. Special Characteristics of Small- and Medium-sized Companies Compared to Large Scale Industry

The major result of our analysis was that the structure of the workflow in both categories is quite similar, but the production capacity is different. Furthermore, an important attribute of small companies is the flexibility, which means that customer orders have to be treated very flexibly and therefore the organisation is not restrictive.

In comparison to Scheers "Y" [Scheer 1987], information systems for small- and medium-sized companies (see fig. 3.) require nearly the same operational tasks, but several technical tasks are given up. This has its origins in producing most products manually or in small series or in customer production. In large scale industry it is important to produce great series in a short time at low cost. Therefore the production is often done by machines and robots. In some cases small- and medium-sized companies also use CAM-components, but as already mentioned, these components of a typical CIM-factory are rather rare.

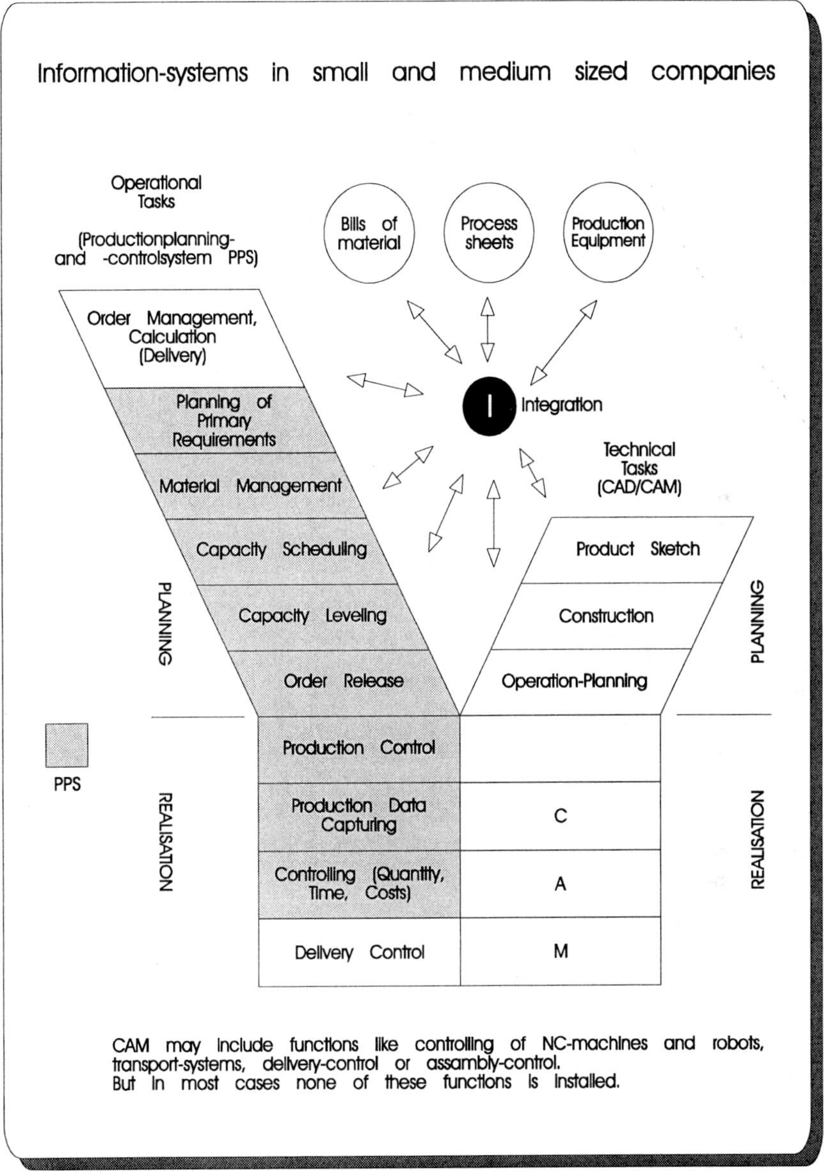

Fig. 3. Computer Integrated Manufacturing (CIM) in small- and medium-sized companies.

Therefore integration aspects between CAD, CAP and PPS are mainly important for small- and medium-sized companies, whereas at every kind of model factory the full integration or the integration between CAD- and CAM-components are in the centre of interest. For that reason our project partner, the saddlery company Niedersüß in

Rohrbach, proposed to build a CIM-factory which can be designated as a special one for small- and medium-sized companies and attached to the real full scale factories, an approach which is described in detail on the following pages.

2. Introduction to INCOSOFT

INCOSOFT (Integrated-Company-Software) is the name of a product, which is the result of a co-operation between a saddlery and the Research Institute for Applied Knowledge Processing at the Johannes Kepler University in Linz (FAW Linz).

First of all we tried to find an integrated software system appropriate for small- and medium-sized companies, which should be a standard software product with the following requirements:

- a relational database is the basis of the whole system
- a client-server architecture for data transfer
- a server-PC-network (LAN) is supported
- a graphic user interface with mouse-support

Unfortunately, we have not found any software product which fulfils these requirements. There are some systems for large companies, but the installation and adaptation of these systems in small and medium companies is impossible. The reasons are that in small- and medium-sized companies:

- Normally no electronic data processing department (EDP) exists and the budget for hardware and software is rather small.
- The organisation of the company is unstructured and often managed with practical knowledge.
- Data for controlling is not available due to the structureless organisation. Therefore an exact calculation of the products is impossible.
- The orders of the clients must be treated very flexibly because small- and medium-sized companies in most cases do not produce in series.
- The employees are not skilled in handling a computer environment and therefore the requirement to the system is a user-friendly interface.

Due to the lack of an adaptable existing system we had to start the development of our own software-system INCOSOFT.

3. SPECIFICATION of INCOSOFT

3.1. Hardware

The basis of the hardware structure of INCOSOFT is a local area network (LAN) including a file server, a database server and several workstations. The additional hardware consists of a streamer and an electronic control clock. Electricity is provided by an uninterruptible power supply. As a result of this hardware equipment INCOSOFT has become a very safe system.

The electronic control clock is connected to a workstation. This makes it possible to read the information of every production step from the production-order-sheets by a barcode-reader and to transmit data from the control clock to the workstation and from the workstation to the database.

3.2. Software

INCOSOFT is based on MS-DOS [Microsoft Corporation 1991] in combination with the graphic user interface MS-Windows [Microsoft Corporation 1992]. This environment makes the system compatible with most hardware platforms and software systems, thereby meeting one of our main requirements.

In the last two years we have made the experience that only graphic user interfaces meet the special demands of end-users. In many cases such users have no or only little experience with computers.

3.3. Integration aspects

One important aim of CIM is the integration of all necessary components to a global system which is required to achieve computer integrated manufacturing in a company. The operating system extension Microsoft Windows of the CIM-software, as the basis of the whole system, makes it possible to integrate standard software with non-standard software. The outcome is a high level standard and a high compatibility with many hardware systems.

The use of standard software is very important for a small- and medium-sized company, because these well-tested products are components of the global system with a high functionality and in many cases with a low price in relation to the functionality. Under the operating-system-extension Microsoft Windows our saddlery uses four standard-software products:

- Microsoft *Excel* (spreadsheet),
- Microsoft *WinWord* (word processing),
- Corel Systems *CorelDraw* (drawing program)
- *MaxonCAD* (CAD-System).

This standard software is fully compatible in the outfit and handling with INCOSOFT. A special interface makes database access possible.

3.4. User Interface

The user interface of INCOSOFT meets the IBM-CUA/SAA standard and was developed not only for skilled users but also for unskilled ones. Our demand was to design a user interface so that the handling with the CIM-software makes less expenditure for the employees of the firm. This seems to be important, because a small- or medium-sized company is not big enough for the employment of a specialist for handling the CIM-software.

4. Components of the System

INCOSOFT consists of all well-known parts of a CIM-architecture (see fig. 4). Most of these components are already implemented. For the additional components financial accounting, word-processing, spreadsheet and computer aided design (CAD) we use appropriate standard software.

A result of modelling the real workflow of a company is the fact that many activities have to run in parallel. In order to fulfil this requirement and to integrate standard software with non-standard software INCOSOFT supports multi-user access in a local area network (LAN).

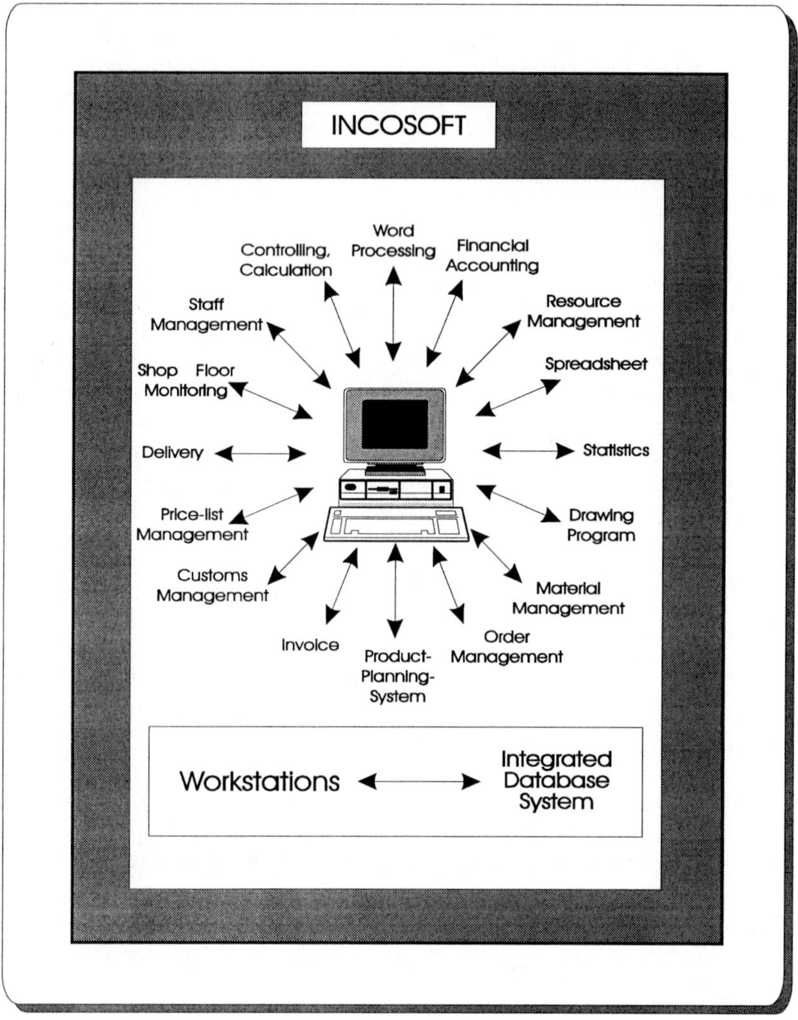

Fig. 4. The components of INCOSOFT.

5. Implementation Aspects

After the analysis of the requirements was completed we used the Entity Relationship Model [Chen 1976] to develop the data model for the entire company. For the dynamic representation of the universe of discourse we used the Structured Analysis and Design Technique. The entire data model was transferred into a relational database and the functions of the SA-Method are implemented in a 4th generation language.

As already mentioned, a relational database is the basis of the whole system and a client-server architecture is the underlying concept of the database. Furthermore, a server-PC-network (Local Area Network) is supported.

As most parts of the CIM-software are implemented in a 4th generation language, the underlying object-oriented design of the software-system makes it easy to adapt the sourcecode to special demands of other companies.

A few smaller parts of the system are implemented in C. For instance the functions for the data-transmission to and from the electronic control clock. These and other functions are collected in special dynamic link libraries, so that they can be used by many other client applications.

The concept of shop floor monitoring has been developed especially for the demands of small- and medium-sized companies. The difficulty was to find out which functions are necessary and which are not needed for a company of this size.

We have also established a barcode system, so that it is very easy for the employees to use the electronic control clock. The customer-orders are collected to production-orders. For every production-order the steps of the production are printed on a special sheet. At the beginning and at the end of every production-step the employee has to transmit special data (begin and end time of the step, flow time etc.) to the database. For a correct transmission of this data to the database we use the electronic control clock in combination with the barcode system. Entering data in this way is very easy for the employees.

6. Conclusions and directions for future research

We have tried to systematize different model factories which are realised at several research institutes and universities. As we have developed a special CIM-system for small- and medium-sized companies in co-operation with a saddlery, we have given special attention to the real full scale CIM-factories.

In the second part of the paper we have introduced our system INCOSOFT. We have discussed the specification of the system INCOSOFT especially the hardware and software specification and the components of INCOSOFT. We have sketched the differences between the installation of software-systems in large scale industry and small or medium sized companies.

After the realisation, INCOSOFT should be used for both exemplary operation as well as training and demonstration purposes for other innovative small- and medium-sized companies.

7. References

Chen P. P. (1976). The Entity Relationship Model: Towards a unified view of data. ACM TODS, 1st edition, Volume 1, 9-36, 1976.

Microsoft Corporation (1991). Microsoft MS-DOS Benutzerhandbuch und Referenz für das Betriebssystem MS-DOS Version 5.0. Microsoft Corporation, Irland, 1991.

Microsoft Corporation (1992). Microsoft Windows Benutzerhandbuch Version 3.1. Microsoft Corporation, Irland, 1992.

Scheer A.-W. (1987). "CIM, Der Computergesteuerte Industriebetrieb", Springer Verlag Heidelberg-Berlin-New York-Paris-Tokyo, 2. Auflage, BRD 1987.

Schossig H.-P. (02/1992) "Rechnergeführte Produktion in mittelständischen Betrieben", CIM-Management 02/1992.

Schulz H. (1990): "CIM-Planung und -Einführung: Ein Leitfaden für die Praxis", CIM-Fachmann, Berlin / Heidelberg / New York: Springer, Köln: Verlag TÜV Rheinland 1990.

Wöß Wolfram (1992). "CIM-KM Computer Integrated Manufacturing für Klein- und Mittelbetriebe, Betriebsdatenverwaltung und Produktionsleitstand", Diplomarbeit, Forschungsinstitut für Anwendungsorientierte Wissensverarbeitung, Abteilung für Datenbank- und Expertensysteme, Johannes Kepler Universität Linz, 1992.

Author Index